© Alexander Chernyakov/Getty Images

MANAGEMENT

LEADING & COLLABORATING IN A COMPETITIVE WORLD

Thomas S. Bateman
McIntire School of Commerce
University of Virginia

Scott A. Snell
Darden Graduate School of Business
University of Virginia

Robert Konopaske
McCoy College of Business
Texas State University

Mc
Graw
Hill
Education

MANAGEMENT: LEADING & COLLABORATING IN A COMPETITIVE WORLD,
TWELFTH EDITION

Published by McGraw-Hill Education, 2 Penn Plaza, New York, NY 10121. Copyright © 2017 by
McGraw-Hill Education. All rights reserved. Printed in the United States of America. Previous editions
2015, 2013, 2011, and 2009. No part of this publication may be reproduced or distributed in any form or by
any means, or stored in a database or retrieval system, without the prior written consent of McGraw-Hill
Education, including, but not limited to, in any network or other electronic storage or transmission, or
broadcast for distance learning.

Some ancillaries, including electronic and print components, may not be available to customers outside the
United States.

This book is printed on acid-free paper.

1 2 3 4 5 6 7 8 9 0 DOW/DOW 1 0 9 8 7 6

ISBN 978-1-259-54694-5
MHID 1-259-54694-2

Senior Vice President, Products & Markets: *Kurt L. Strand*
Vice President, General Manager, Products & Markets: *Michael Ryan*
Vice President, Content Design & Delivery: *Kimberly Meriwether David*
Managing Director: *Susan Gouijnstook*
Director: *Michael Ablassmeir*
Director, Product Development: *Meghan Campbell*
Lead Product Developer: *Kelly Delso*
Product Developer: *Kaitlyn Eddy*
Marketing Manager: *Casey Keske*
Director, Content Design & Delivery: *Terri Schiesl*
Program Manager: *Mary Conzachi*
Content Project Managers: *Christine Vaughan; Keri Johnson*
Buyer: *Laura M. Fuller*
Design: *Srdjan Savanovic*
Content Licensing Specialists: *Lori Hancock; DeAnna Dausener*
Cover Image: *© Alexander Chernyakov/Getty Images*
Marginal Icons: *© Vinko93/Shutterstock*
Compositor: *SPi Global*
Typeface: *10/12 STIX Mathjax*
Printer: *R.R. Donnelley*

All credits appearing on page or at the end of the book are considered to be an extension of the copyright page.

Library of Congress Cataloging-in-Publication Data

Names: Bateman, Thomas S., author. | Snell, Scott, 1958- author. | Konopaske,
  Robert, author.
Title: Management: leading & collaborating in a competitive world / Thomas
  S. Bateman, McIntire School of Commerce, University of Virginia, Scott A.
  Snell, Darden Graduate School of Business, University of Virginia, Robert
  Konopaske, McCoy College of Business, Texas State University.
Description: Twelfth Edition. | McGraw-Hill Education: Dubuque, 2016. |
  Revised edition of Management, 2015.
Identifiers: LCCN 2015045634 | ISBN 9781259546945 (alk. paper)
Subjects: LCSH: Management.
Classification: LCC HD31 .B369485 2016 | DDC 658—dc23 LC record available at http://lccn.loc.
gov/2015045634

The Internet addresses listed in the text were accurate at the time of publication. The inclusion of a website does
not indicate an endorsement by the authors or McGraw-Hill Education, and McGraw-Hill Education does not
guarantee the accuracy of the information presented at these sites.

mheducation.com/highered

For my parents, Tom and Jeanine Bateman,
and Mary Jo, Lauren, T.J., and James

and

My parents, John and Clara Snell,
and Marybeth, Sara, Jack, and Emily

and

My parents, Art and Rose Konopaske
and Vania, Nick, and Isabella

About the Authors

THOMAS S. BATEMAN

Thomas S. Bateman is Bank of America professor and management area coordinator in the McIntire School of Commerce at the University of Virginia. He teaches leadership courses and is director of a new leadership minor open to undergraduate students of all majors. Prior to joining the University of Virginia, he taught organizational behavior at the Kenan-Flagler Business School of the University of North Carolina to undergraduates, MBA students, PhD students, and practicing managers. He also taught for two years in Europe as a visiting professor at the Institute for Management Development (IMD), one of the world's leaders in the design and delivery of executive education. Professor Bateman completed his doctoral program in business administration in 1980 at Indiana University. Prior to receiving his doctorate, Dr. Bateman received his BA from Miami University. In addition to Virginia, UNC–Chapel Hill, and IMD, Dr. Bateman has taught at Texas A&M, Tulane, and Indiana universities.

Professor Bateman is an active management researcher, writer, and consultant. He serves on the editorial boards of the *Academy of Management Review,* the *Academy of Management Journal,* and the *Asia Pacific Journal of Business and Management.* His articles have appeared in professional journals such as the *Academy of Management Journal, Academy of Management Review, Journal of Applied Psychology, Organizational Behavior and Human Decision Processes, Journal of Management, Business Horizons, Journal of Organizational Behavior,* and *Decision Sciences.*

Tom's current consulting and research center on practical wisdom in business executives, leadership in the form of problem solving at all organizational levels, various types of proactive behavior by employees at all levels, and the successful pursuit of long-term work goals. He works with organizations including Singapore Airlines, the Brookings Institution, the U.S. Chamber of Commerce, the Nature Conservancy, and LexisNexis.

SCOTT A. SNELL

Scott Snell is professor of business administration at the University of Virginia's Darden Graduate School of Business. He teaches courses in leadership, organizational capability development, and human capital consulting. His research focuses on human resources and the mechanisms by which organizations generate, transfer, and integrate new knowledge for competitive advantage. He is co-author of four books: *Managing People and Knowledge in Professional Service Firms, Management: Leading & Collaborating in a Competitive World, M: Management,* and *Managing Human Resources.* His work has been published in a number of journals such as the *Academy of Management Journal, Academy of Management Review, Strategic Management Journal, Journal of Management, Journal of Management Studies,* and *Human Resource Management,* and he was recently listed among the top 100 most-cited authors in scholarly journals of management. He has served on the boards of the Strategic Management Society's human capital group, the Society for Human Resource Management Foundation, the Academy of Management's human resource division, the *Human Resource Management Journal,* the *Academy of Management Journal,* and the *Academy of Management Review.* Professor Snell has worked with companies such as AstraZeneca, Deutsche Telekom, Shell, and United Technologies to align strategy, capability, and investments in talent. Prior to joining the Darden faculty in 2007, he was professor and director of executive education at Cornell University's Center for Advanced Human Resource Studies and a professor of management in the Smeal College of Business at Pennsylvania State University. He received a BA in psychology from Miami University, as well as MBA and PhD degrees in business administration from Michigan State University.

ROBERT KONOPASKE

Rob Konopaske is an associate professor of management and principles of management course coordinator in the McCoy College of Business at Texas State University. A passionate educator who cares deeply about providing students with an exceptional learning experience, Rob has taught numerous undergraduate, graduate, and executive management courses, including Introduction to Management, Organizational Behavior, Human Resource Management, International Human Resources Management, and International Business. He has received numerous teaching honors over the years, most recently the 2014 Gregg Master Teacher Award and 2012–2013 Namesake for the PAWS Preview new student socialization program at Texas State University (an honor bestowed annually upon eight out of approximately 2,000 faculty and staff throughout the university). Rob earned his doctoral degree in business administration (management) at the University of Houston, a master in international business studies (MIBS) degree from the University of South Carolina, and a Bachelor of Arts degree (Phi Beta Kappa) from Rutgers University. He has taught at the University of Houston, the University of North Carolina at Wilmington, and Florida Atlantic University.

Rob is co-author of several recent editions of six books: *Management: Leading & Collaborating in a Competitive World, M: Management, Organizational Behavior and Management, Human Resource Management, Global Management and Organizational Behavior,* and *Organizations: Behavior, Structure, Processes.* The eleventh edition of *Organizations* won a McGuffey Award (for longevity of textbooks and learning materials whose excellence has been demonstrated over time) from the national Text and Academic Authors' Association.

Rob's research has been published in such outlets as the *Journal of Applied Psychology, Academy of Management Executive, Management International Review, Business Horizons, Human Resource Management, Journal of Business Research, Journal of Management Education, Nonprofit Management and Leadership, Journal of Managerial Psychology,* and *Human Resource Management Review.* Dr. Konopaske currently serves on the editorial board of the *International Journal of Human Resource Management.*

Rob has lived and worked internationally, speaks three languages, and has held management positions with a large nonprofit organization and a Fortune 500 multinational firm. He consults, trains, and conducts research projects for a wide range of companies and industries. Current or former clients include PricewaterhouseCoopers, Credit Suisse, KPMG, New Braunfels Utilities, and Johnson & Johnson.

Preface

Welcome to our 12th edition! Thank you to everyone who has used and learned from previous editions. We are proud to present to you our newest and most exciting edition.

Our Goals

Our mission with this text hasn't changed from that of our previous editions: to inform, instruct, and inspire. We hope to inform by providing descriptions of the important concepts and practices of modern management. We hope to instruct by describing how you can take action on the ideas discussed. We hope to inspire not only by writing in an interesting and optimistic way but also by providing a real sense of the opportunities ahead of you. Whether your goal is starting your own company, leading a team to greatness, building a strong organization, delighting your customers, or generally forging a positive, and sustainable future, we want to inspire you to take constructive actions.

We hope to inspire you to be both a thinker and a doer. We want you to think about the issues, think about the impact of your actions, think before you act. But being a good thinker is not enough; you also must be a doer. Management is a world of action. It is a world that requires timely and appropriate action. It is a world not for the passive but for those who commit to positive accomplishments.

Keep applying the ideas you learn in this course, read about management online outside of this course, and keep learning about management after you leave school and continue your career. Make no mistake about it: Learning about management is a personal voyage that will last years, an entire career.

Competitive Advantage

Today's world is competitive. Never before has the world of work been so challenging. Never before has it been so imperative to your career that you learn the skills of management. Never before have people had so many opportunities and challenges with so many potential risks and rewards.

You will compete with other people for jobs, resources, and promotions. Your organization will compete with other firms for contracts, clients, and customers. To survive the competition, and to thrive, you must perform in ways that give you an edge over your competitors, that make the other party want to hire you, buy from you, and do repeat business with you. You will want them to choose you, not your competitor.

To survive and thrive, today's managers have to think and act strategically. Today's customers are well educated, aware of their options, and demanding of excellence. For this reason, managers today must think constantly about how to build a capable workforce and manage in a way that delivers the goods and services that provide the best possible value to the customer.

By this standard, managers and organizations must perform. Six essential types of performance, on which the organization beats, equals, or loses to the competition, are *cost, quality, speed, innovation, service,* and *sustainability.* These six performance dimensions, when managed well, deliver value to the customer and competitive advantage to you and your organization. We will elaborate on all of these topics throughout the book.

The idea is to keep you focused on a type of bottom line to make sure you think continually about delivering the goods that make both you and your organization a competitive success. This results-oriented approach is unique among management products.

Leading & Collaborating

Yes, business is competitive. But it's not that simple. In fact, to think strictly in terms of competition is overly cynical, and such cynicism can sabotage your performance. The other fundamental elements in the success equation are collaboration and leadership. People working with, rather than against, one another are essential to competitive advantage. Put another way, you can't do it alone—the world is too complex, and business is too challenging.

You need to work with your teammates. Leaders and followers need to work as collaborators more than as adversaries. Work groups throughout your organization need to cooperate with one another. Business and government, often viewed as antagonists, can work productively together. And today more than ever, companies that traditionally were competitors engage in joint ventures and find other ways to collaborate on some things even as they compete in others. Leadership is needed to make these collaborations happen.

How does an organization create competitive advantage through collaboration? It's all about the people, and it derives from good leadership. Three stereotypes of leadership are that it comes from the top of the company, that it comes from one's immediate boss, and that it means being decisive and issuing commands. These stereotypes may contain grains of truth, but the reality is much more complex. First, the person at the top may or may not provide effective leadership—in fact, many observers believe that good leadership is far too rare. Second, organizations need leaders at all levels, in every team and work unit. This includes you, beginning early in your career, and this is why leadership is an important theme in this book. Third, leaders should be capable of decisiveness and of giving commands, but relying too much on this traditional approach isn't enough. Great leadership is far more inspirational than this and helps people both to think differently and to work differently—including working collaboratively with a focus on results.

Leadership—from your boss as well as from you—generates collaboration, which in turn creates results that are good for the company and good for the people involved.

As Always, Currency and Variety in the 12th Edition

It goes without saying that this textbook, in its 12th edition, remains on the cutting edge of topical coverage, updated via both current business examples and recent management research. Chapters have been thoroughly updated, and students are exposed to a broad array of important current topics. Moreover, we have expanded and strengthened our coverage of sustainability and social enterprise, topics on which we were early leaders and that we continue to care about as much as today's students.

We have done our very best to draw from a wide variety of subject matter, sources, and personal experiences. We continue to emphasize throughout the book themes such as real results, ethics, cultural considerations, and leadership and collaboration. Here is just a sampling of new highlights in the 12th edition—enough to convey the wide variety of people, organizations, issues, and contexts represented throughout the text.

Chapter 1

- New Social Enterprise about Richard Branson and the "B-Team" encouraging governments to act more quickly to limit greenhouse gas emissions.

- New Multiple Generations at Work about Boomer retirements creating career opportunities for Gen Xers and Millennials.

- New or revised high-impact exhibits: 1.1, 1.2, 1.3, and 1.4.

- New text example about the Internet, mobile applications, Big Data analytics, and cloud computing.

- New example of Singapore Airlines being named the most admired airline.

- New text example about Yum! Brands receiving most of its revenue from international markets.

- New example of Netflix using technology to disrupt Blockbuster in the movie rental space.

- New quote by W. Edwards Deming about the impact of long-term relationships on quality.

Chapter 2

- New Social Enterprise about Terracycle eliminating waste through "upcycling."

- New Multiple Generations at Work about CVS Caremark turning to older workers to address staffing shortages.

- New or revised high-impact exhibits: 2.1, 2.3, 2.4, 2.5, 2.6, and 2.10.

- New text discussing post-recession employment and participation rates.

- New example about Google's Project Loon delivering high-speed Internet to people out of range of cell towers.

- New example of how companies use LinkedIn Pages, Google+ Communities to connect directly with customers.

- New text example of Affordable Care Act impacting the health care industry.

- New Concluding Case: "Tata Motors: From Cheap to Awesome?"

Chapter 3

- New Social Enterprise about Saul Garlick creating a self-sustaining organization to reduce poverty.

- New Multiple Generations at Work about PepsiCo and Intel crowdsourcing to generate ideas and buzz about new products.

- New or revised high-impact exhibits: 3.2, 3.4, 3.5, 3.6, 3.7, 3.8, 3.9, 3.10, and 3.11.

- New text example of PillPack changing how customers interact with pharmacies.

- New passage about social loafing influencing team cohesiveness and performance.

- New exhibit highlighting the successes of college student entrepreneurs.

Chapter 4

- New Social Enterprise about Novo Nordisk monitoring progress toward achieving its Triple Bottom Line.
- New Multiple Generations at Work about employees and managers perceiving workers from other generational cohorts.
- New or revised high-impact exhibits: 4.2, 4.3, and 4.10.
- New example of Starbucks planning to open 3,400 stores in China.
- New text example of Walmart creating emergency plans to offer water, food, and pharmaceutical supplies in the wake of a natural disaster.
- New example about Ocean Renewable Power Company producing electric power from ocean and river currents.
- New example of AT&T acquiring DirecTV.
- New Bottom Line about how low-cost strategy impacts competitors' prices.

Chapter 5

- New Social Enterprise about a former yoga instructor trying to clean up the trucking industry.
- New Multiple Generations at Work about which generation is the least trusting of people.
- New or revised high-impact exhibits: 5.1, 5.2, 5.3, 5.5, and 5.6.
- New example of officials of Petroleo Brasilieiro acting in an unethical manner.
- New text example describing why some companies post fake reviews on Yelp and Google Places.
- New example of Kickboard empowering teachers to use data to improve student performance in high-poverty areas.
- New example of Coca-Cola's goal to be "water-neutral" by 2020.

Chapter 6

- New Social Enterprise about student social entrepreneurs competing for a $1 million Hultz Prize Foundation award.
- New Multiple Generations at Work about Millennials' need for international work experience to further their careers.
- New or revised high-impact exhibits: 6.1, 6.3, 6.5, and 6.8.
- New example about trade and foreign direct investment contributing to a flat world.

- New text example of New York Delhi, a small spice business in London, becoming a global exporter of spiced nuts and snacks.
- New example about the growing trend known as *inshoring*.
- New example of European Union regulators deciding to fine Google for alleged antitrust activities.
- New text example of Western and Chinese universities forming joint ventures in China.

Chapter 7

- New Social Enterprise about Nely Galan's Adelante movement to empower Latina entrepreneurs.
- New Multiple Generations at Work about how the Millennial founder of Attend.com believes three generations are better than one.
- New or revised high-impact exhibits: 7.1, 7.2, and 7.4.
- New example about Elon Musk's journey from birth in South Africa to entrepreneurial success in the United States.
- New text example of Johnson & Johnson collaborating with Google to develop advanced robots to aid in surgeries.
- New example of the Panera Bread chain of bakery-cafés expanding rapidly in recent years.
- New example of Houston Technology Center, an incubator for start-ups, specializing in energy and nanotechnology solutions.
- New example of peer-to-peer loans from Prosper and Lending Club helping entrepreneurs launch or expand their businesses.

Chapter 8

- New Social Enterprise about Kiva, a micro lender to entrepreneurs in 86 countries, using a functional organizational structure.
- New Multiple Generations at Work about why Millennials prefer collaborative, network-driven workplaces.
- New or revised high-impact exhibits: 8.2, 8.5, and 8.8.
- New example about how Steve Jobs viewed delegation.
- New example of global food giant Nestlé following a decentralized approach to decision making.
- New text example of IT firm EMC helping customers transition to cloud computing.
- New example of Avon Products restructuring of its sales force to focus more on the fast-growing Hispanic women market.

Chapter 9

- New Social Enterprise about organizations like Network for Good scaling their operations to increase reach and impact.
- New Multiple Generations at Work about companies creating internal structures that attract and retain early career employees.
- New or revised high-impact exhibits: 9.1, 9.2, 9.4, 9.7, and 9.9.
- New example of Tag Heurer, Google, and Intel collaborating to develop a smartwatch.
- New example of QuickenLoans expanding into the online banking market.
- New example of Netflix using insights mined from voluminous subscriber data ("Big Data") to create its hit show *House of Cards*.
- New text examples of Baldrige National Quality Award winners, including PricewaterhouseCoopers Public Sector Practice and St. David's Healthcare of Texas.
- New example about Wipro using lean methods to develop high-quality software projects.

Chapter 10

- New Social Enterprise about business school graduates' willingness to work for social enterprises.
- New Multiple Generations at Work about ways that college students can develop the skills desired by employers.
- New or revised high-impact exhibits: 10.1, 10.5, 10.6, and 10.8.
- New example of Target, Valero Energy, and Verizon establishing internships to address the shortage of IT workers.
- New example of a former CEO of Yahoo being removed after listing a nonexistent computer science degree on his résumé.
- New text example describing AutoZone's fine for gender and pregnancy discrimination.
- New example applying performance standards to a decision about pay.
- New section about organizations reducing health care benefits due to costs associated with the Patient Protection and Affordable Care Act.

Chapter 11

- New Social Enterprise about Change.org embracing diversity and inclusion.
- New Multiple Generations at Work about tips for individuals who want jobs that offer work–life balance.
- New or revised high-impact exhibits: 11.1, 11.2, 11.3, 11.4, 11.6, and 11.7.
- New example of Microsoft sponsoring undergraduate college minority students pursuing computer science or software engineering degrees.
- New example of industries most at risk of skill shortages, including health care (hospitals and nursing facilities), transportation, and social assistance.
- New text example about Zappos posting entertaining videos on YouTube to attract job applicants.
- New example of Procter & Gamble valuing diversity as an important part of fulfilling its strategy.
- New example of Lincoln Electric using ambicultural management practices.

Chapter 12

- New Social Enterprise about Richard Murphy using his leadership to serve the needs of tens of thousands of disadvantaged youth.
- New Multiple Generations at Work about some key attributes that Millennials desire in their leaders.
- New or revised high-impact exhibits: 12.1, 12.2, 12.3, 12.4, 12.5, and 12.12.
- New example of Howard Schultz, CEO of Starbucks, sharing his vision.
- New example of Steve Jobs having inspired extraordinary performance from employees.
- New text examples of transformational leaders, including Indra Nooyi (CEO of PepsiCo), Richard Branson (founder and CEO of Virgin Group), and Brad Smith (CEO of Intuit).

Chapter 13

- New Social Enterprise about Team Rubicon giving veterans a renewed sense of purpose.
- New Multiple Generations at Work about Ultra Mobile helping Millennial employees fulfill higher-order needs.
- New or revised high-impact exhibits: 13.1, 13.2, 13.3, 13.5, and 13.9.
- New example of the FBI setting goals to prevent terrorist attacks.
- New text example of Whole Foods wanting to improve people's health and well-being.
- New example of YouEarnedIt creating a mobile app to increase employee engagement at work.
- New example about W.L. Gore encouraging associates to reach their full potential by directing their own work activities.

Chapter 14

- New Social Enterprise about individuals paying for coworking space with social capital.
- New Multiple Generations at Work about universities training students to work effectively in global virtual teams.
- New or revised high-impact exhibits: 14.1, 14.2, 14.4, and 14.5.
- New example of U.S. senators forming a task force to investigate how insurance companies assessed damage after Hurricane Sandy.
- New example of measuring team effectiveness and productivity.
- New text example of Geonetric giving employees responsibility for budgets and revenues.
- New example of Amazon using a two-pizza rule to determine optimal team size.

Chapter 15

- New Social Enterprise about key differences between social enterprises and other organizational forms.
- New Multiple Generations at Work about the advantages and disadvantages of employees bringing their own devices to work.
- New or revised high-impact exhibit: 15.2.
- New example of Groupon, IBM, and Blue Cross/Blue Shield using an online platform to generate anonymous ideas for problem solving.
- New text example of Microsoft's SharePoint enabling employees to collaborate on Web pages, documents, lists, calendars, and data.
- New example about Unisys and Sprint providing training programs to help employees use social media in a productive manner.
- New example of JPMorgan dropping voicemail service for its retail banking employees.
- New example of Automattic being a global virtual organization where employees stay connected through video chat and instant messaging.
- New example of Google Cafés encouraging employee interaction.

Chapter 16

- New Social Enterprise about measuring organizational impact.
- New Multiple Generations at Work about Adobe dropping traditional performance appraisals.

- New or revised high-impact exhibit: 16.10.
- New example of Accurid Pest Solutions installing GPS tracking software on company-issued smartphones to monitor employee movement.
- New example of Coca-Cola dealing with suppliers' violations related to employee overtime and rest days.
- New example of employees at the U.S. Department of Veteran Affairs falsifying the number of days it took veterans to receive medical help.
- New example of the National Marrow Donor Program using a balanced scorecard to achieve its mission.

Chapter 17

- New Social Enterprise about Bibak's inexpensive device to detect landmines buried near villages.
- New Multiple Generations at Work about companies using gamification to engage their customers and employees.
- New or revised high-impact exhibits: 17.1 and 17.5.
- New example of deploying robots in human–machine contexts.
- New text example of Apple adding "force of touch" to its next iPhone.
- New example about IBM developing a powerful new million-neuron chip.
- New example of General Motors launching InnovationXchange to tap employees' creative ideas.
- New example of Nestlé Health Sciences and Chi-Med establishing a joint venture.
- New text section about IDEO applying design thinking to help companies solve problems.

Chapter 18

- New Social Enterprise about co-creation between diverse stakeholders amplifying the impact of organizations.
- New Multiple Generations at Work about ways to align skills with the future of work.
- New or revised high-impact exhibits: 18.3, 18.4, 18.5, 18.7, and 18.11.
- New Management in Action about Shell Oil and its position on climate change.
- New example of futurists Fred Rogers and Richard Lalich predicting smart machines and processes will transform how we live.
- New text examples about how Airbnb, Uber, and PayPal disrupted the travel, taxi, and credit industries.

A Team Effort

This book is the product of a fantastic McGraw-Hill team. Moreover, we wrote this book believing that we are part of a team with the course instructor and with students. The entire team is responsible for the learning process.

Our goal, and that of your instructor, is to create a positive learning environment in which you can excel. But in the end, the raw material of this course is just words. It is up to you to use them as a basis for further reflection, deep learning, and constructive action.

What you do with the things you learn from this course, and with the opportunities the future holds, *counts*. As a manager, you can make a dramatic difference for yourself and for other people. What managers do matters *tremendously*.

Acknowledgments

This book could not have been written and published without the valuable contributions of many individuals.

Special thanks to Lily Bowles, Taylor Gray, and Meg Nexsen for contributing their knowledge, insights, and research to Appendix B: Managing in Our Natural Environment.

Our reviewers over the last 11 editions contributed time, expertise, and terrific ideas that significantly enhanced the quality of the text. The reviewers of the 12th edition are

Maria Aria
Camden County College

Charles Beem
Bucks County Community College

Patricia Crisp
University of Texas-Arlington

Randall Fletcher
Sinclair Community College

John Gironda
Nova Southeastern University

Frank Harber
Indian River State College

Nathan Himelstein
Essex County College

Carrie Hurst
Tennessee State University

Michael Marzano
Lindenwood University

Erin McLaughlin
Nova Southeastern University

Thomas Norman
California State University

Martha Robinson
University of Memphis

Mansour Sharifzadeh
California State Polytechnic

Christy Shell
Houston Community College

Many individuals contributed directly to our development as textbook authors. Dennis Organ provided one of the authors with an initial opportunity and guidance in textbook writing. Jack Ivancevich did the same for one of the other authors. John Weimeister has been a friend and adviser from the very beginning. The entire McGraw-Hill Education team, starting with director Mike Ablassmeir (who spontaneously and impressively knew *Rolling Stone*'s top three drummers of all time), provided great support and expertise to this new edition. Many thanks to managing development editor Christine Scheid for so much good work on previous editions and for continued friendship. And to our superb product developer, Katie Eddy, and Sam Deffenbaugh, marketing coordinator, thank you for your skills, professionalism, collegiality, good fun, and for making the new edition *rock!* What a team!

Finally, we thank our families. Our parents, Jeanine and Tom Bateman and Clara and John Snell, provided us with the foundation on which we have built our careers. They continue to be a source of great support. Our wives, Mary Jo, Marybeth, and Vania, demonstrated great encouragement, insight, and understanding throughout the process. Our children, Lauren, T.J., and James Bateman, Sara, Jack, and Emily Snell, and Nick and Isabella Konopaske,

Thomas S. Bateman
Charlottesville, VA

Scott A. Snell
Charlottesville, VA

Robert Konopaske
San Marcos, TX

In this ever more competitive environment, there are six essential types of performance on which the organization beats, equals, or loses to the competition: cost, quality, speed, innovation, service, and sustainability. These six performance dimensions, when done well, deliver value to the customer and competitive advantage to you and your organization.

Throughout the text, Bateman, Snell, and Konopaske remind students of these six dimensions and their impact on the bottom line with marginal icons. This results-oriented approach is a unique hallmark of this textbook.

Questions have also now been added to this edition to emphasize the bottom line further. Answers to these questions can be found in the Instructor's Manual.

Bottom Line

Bottom Line
In all businesses—services as well as manufacturing—strategies that emphasize good customer service provide a critical competitive advantage.
Name a company that has delivered good customer service to you.

Bottom Line
In all businesses—services as well as manufacturing—strategies that emphasize good customer service provide a critical competitive advantage.
Name a company that has delivered good customer service to you.

Bottom Line
In all businesses—services as well as manufacturing—strategies that emphasize good customer service provide a critical competitive advantage.
Name a company that has delivered good customer service to you.

Bottom Line
In all businesses—services as well as manufacturing—strategies that emphasize good customer service provide a critical competitive advantage.
Name a company that has delivered good customer service to you.

Bottom Line
In all businesses—services as well as manufacturing—strategies that emphasize good customer service provide a critical competitive advantage.
Name a company that has delivered good customer service to you.

Bottom Line
In all businesses—services as well as manufacturing—strategies that emphasize good customer service provide a critical competitive advantage.
Name a company that has delivered good customer service to you.

In CASE You Haven't Noticed . . .

Bateman, Snell, and Konopaske (new co-author) have put together an outstanding selection of case studies of various lengths that highlight companies' ups and downs, stimulate learning and understanding, and challenge students to respond.

Instructors will find a wealth of relevant and updated cases in every chapter, using companies—big and small—that students will enjoy learning about.

CHAPTER UNFOLDING CASES

Each chapter begins with a "Management in Action: Manager's Brief" section that describes an actual organizational situation, leader, or company. The Manager's Brief is referred to again within the chapter in the "Progress Report" section, showing the student how the chapter material relates back to the company, situation, or leader highlighted in the chapter opener. At the end of the chapter, the "Onward" section ties up loose ends and brings the material full circle for the student. Answers to Management in Action: section questions can be found in the Instructor's Manual.

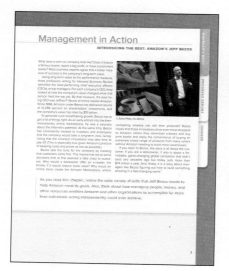

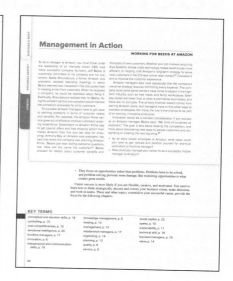

SOCIAL ENTERPRISE (NEW)

Social Enterprise boxes have been added to each chapter to familiarize students with this fast-growing sector. Answers to Social Enterprise questions are included in the Instructor's Manual.

MULTIPLE GENERATIONS AT WORK (NEW)

In each chapter, a Multiple Generations at Work box is added to highlight some of the intergenerational challenges faced by managers and employees today.

CONCLUDING CASES

Each chapter ends with a case based on disguised but real companies and people that reinforces key chapter elements and themes.

SUPPLEMENTARY CASES

At the end of each part, an additional case is provided for professors who want students to delve further into part topics.

Assurance of Learning

① This 12th edition contains revised learning objectives for each chapter, and ② learning objectives are called out within the chapter where the content begins. ③ The Retaining What You Learned for each chapter ties the learning objectives back together as well. And, finally, our test bank provides tagging for the learning objective that the question covers, so instructors will be able to test material covering all learning objectives, thus ensuring that students have mastered the important topics.

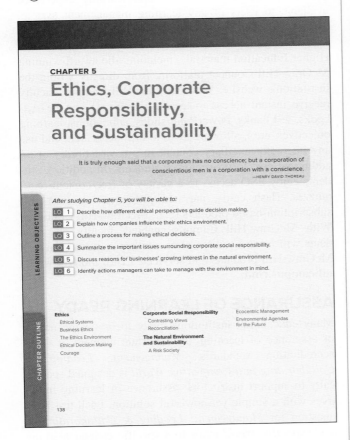

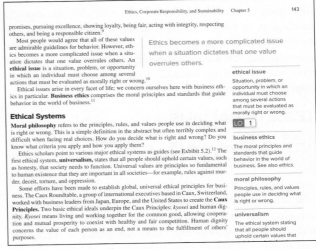

CREATE

 Instructors can now tailor their teaching resources to match the way they teach! With McGraw-Hill Create, **www.mcgrawhillcreate.com**, instructors can easily rearrange chapters, combine material from other content sources, and quickly upload and integrate their own content, such as course syllabi or teaching notes. Find the right content in Create by searching through thousands of leading McGraw-Hill textbooks. Arrange the material to fit your teaching style. Order a Create book and receive a complimentary print review copy in three to five business days or a complimentary electronic review copy via e-mail within one hour. Go to **www.mcgrawhillcreate.com** today and register.

TEGRITY CAMPUS

 Tegrity makes class time available 24/7 by automatically capturing every lecture in a searchable format for students to review when they study and complete assignments. With a simple one-click start-and-stop process, you capture all computer screens and corresponding audio. Students can replay any part of any class with easy-to-use browser-based viewing on a PC or Mac. Educators know that the more students can see, hear, and experience class resources, the better they learn. In fact, studies prove it. With patented Tegrity "search anything" technology, students instantly recall key class moments for replay online or on iPods and mobile devices. Instructors can help turn all their students' study time into learning moments immediately supported by their lecture. To learn more about Tegrity, watch a two-minute Flash demo at **http://tegritycampus.mhhe.com**.

BLACKBOARD® PARTNERSHIP

McGraw-Hill Education and Blackboard have teamed up to simplify your life. Now you and your students can access Connect and Create right from within your Blackboard course—all with one single sign-on. The grade books are seamless, so when a student completes an integrated Connect assignment, the grade for that assignment automatically (and instantly) feeds your Blackboard grade center. Learn more at **www.domorenow.com**.

McGRAW-HILL CAMPUS™

 McGraw-Hill Campus is a new one-stop teaching and learning experience available to users of any learning management system. This institutional service allows faculty and students to enjoy single sign-on (SSO) access to all McGraw-Hill Higher Education materials, including the award-winning McGraw-Hill Connect platform, from directly within the institution's website. With McGraw-Hill Campus, faculty receive instant access to teaching materials (e.g., eTextbooks, test banks, PowerPoint slides, animations, learning objectives, etc.), allowing them to browse, search, and use any instructor ancillary content in our vast library at no additional cost to instructor or students. In addition, students enjoy SSO access to a variety of free content (e.g., quizzes, flash cards, narrated presentations, etc.) and subscription-based products (e.g., McGraw-Hill Connect). With McGraw-Hill Campus enabled, faculty and students will never need to create another account to access McGraw-Hill products and services. Learn more at **www.mhcampus.com**.

ASSURANCE OF LEARNING READY

Many educational institutions today focus on the notion of assurance of learning, an important element of some accreditation standards. *Management: Leading & Collaborating in a Competitive World* is designed specifically to support instructors' assurance of learning initiatives with a simple yet powerful solution. Each test bank question for *Management: Leading & Collaborating in a Competitive World* maps to a specific chapter learning objective listed in the text. Instructors can use our test bank software, EZ Test, to easily query for learning objectives that directly relate to the learning outcomes for their course. Instructors can then use the reporting features of EZ Test to aggregate student results in similar fashion, making the collection and presentation of assurance of learning data simple and easy.

AACSB TAGGING

 McGraw-Hill Education is a proud corporate member of AACSB International. Understanding the importance and value of AACSB accreditation, *Management: Leading & Collaborating in a Competitive World* recognizes the curricula guidelines detailed in the AACSB standards for business accreditation by connecting selected questions in the text and the

test bank to the eight general knowledge and skill guidelines in the AACSB standards. The statements contained in *Management: Leading & Collaborating in a Competitive World* are provided only as a guide for the users of this product. The AACSB leaves content coverage and assessment within the purview of individual schools, the mission of the school, and the faculty. While the *Management: Leading & Collaborating in a Competitive World* teaching package makes no claim of any specific AACSB qualification or evaluation, we have within *Management: Leading & Collaborating in a Competitive World* labeled selected questions according to the eight general knowledge and skills areas.

McGRAW-HILL CUSTOMER EXPERIENCE GROUP CONTACT INFORMATION

At McGraw-Hill Education, we understand that getting the most from new technology can be challenging. That's why our services don't stop after you purchase our products. You can e-mail our Product Specialists 24 hours a day to get product training online. Or you can search our knowledge bank of Frequently Asked Questions on our support website. For Customer Support, call **800-331-5094** or visit **www.mhhe.com/support**. One of our Technical Support Analysts will be able to assist you in a timely fashion.

Outstanding Pedagogy

Management: Leading & Collaborating in a Competitive World is pedagogically stimulating and is intended to maximize student learning. With this in mind, we used a wide array of pedagogical features—some tried and true, others new and novel:

END-OF-CHAPTER ELEMENTS

- **Key terms** are page-referenced to the text and are part of the vocabulary-building emphasis. These terms are defined again in the glossary at the end of the book.

- **Retaining What You Learned** provides clear, concise responses to the learning objectives, giving students a quick reference for reviewing the important concepts in the chapter.

- **Discussion Questions,** which follow, are thought-provoking questions on concepts covered in the chapter and ask for opinions on controversial issues.

- **Experiential Exercises** in each chapter bring key concepts to life so students can experience them firsthand.

KEY TERMS

affective conflict, p. 90	devil's advocate, p. 91	maximizing, p. 82
bounded rationality, p. 94	dialectic, p. 91	nonprogrammed decisions, p. 77
brainstorming, p. 92	discounting the future, p. 86	optimizing, p. 82
certainty, p. 77	framing effects, p. 85	programmed decisions, p. 77
coalitional model, p. 94	garbage can model, p. 95	ready-made solutions, p. 79
cognitive conflict, p. 90	goal displacement, p. 89	risk. p. 78
conflict, p. 78	groupthink, p. 89	satisficing, p. 82
contingency plans, p. 81	illusion of control, p. 85	uncertainty, p. 77
custom-made solutions, p. 79	incremental model, p. 94	vigilance, p. 84

RETAINING WHAT YOU LEARNED

In Chapter 3, you learned that most managers make less than perfectly rational decisions because they lack the necessary information, time, or structure. The ideal decision-making process includes six steps (see Exhibit 3.3 below) and requires managers to ask themselves questions at each stage. The best decision hinges on the manager's ability to be vigilant at all stages of the decision-making process. Barriers can diminish the effectiveness of the decision-making process. While there are advantages and disadvantages of making decisions in groups, a good leader can manage the challenges by using the right leadership style, allowing constructive conflict, encouraging creativity, and brainstorming.

Decision making in organizations is complex and individuals are often bounded by multiple constraints. Decisions

- a discrepancy between the current state and a desired state and then delving below surface symptoms to uncover the underlying causes of the problem.
- The second phase, generating alternative solutions, requires adopting ready-made or designing custom-made solutions.
- The third, evaluating alternatives, means predicting the consequences of different alternatives, sometimes through building scenarios of the future.
- Fourth, a solution is chosen; the solution might maximize, satisfice, or optimize.
- Fifth, people implement the decision; this phase requires more careful planning than it often receives.

DISCUSSION QUESTIONS

1. Discuss Boeing's Dreamliner in terms of risk, uncertainty, and how its managers handled the company's challenges. What is the current news on this company?
2. Identify some risky decisions you have made. Why did you take the risks? How did they work out? Looking back, what did you learn?
3. Identify a decision you made that had important unexpected consequences. Were the consequences good, bad, or both? Should you, and could you, have done anything differently in making the decision?
4. What effects does time pressure have on your decision making? In what ways do you handle it well and not so well?
6. What do you think are some advantages and disadvantages to using computer technology in decision making?
7. Do you think that when managers make decisions they follow the decision-making steps as presented in this chapter? Which steps are apt to be overlooked or given inadequate attention? What can people do to make sure they do a more thorough job?
8. Discuss the potential advantages and disadvantages of using a group to make decisions. Give examples from your experience.
9. Suppose you are the CEO of a major corporation and one of your company's oil tanks has ruptured, spilling thousands of gallons of oil into a river that empties into

---

EXPERIENTIAL EXERCISES

3.1   DECISION MAKING IN ACTION

OBJECTIVE
Learn how to improve your ability to make good decisions.

INSTRUCTIONS
Refer back to Exhibit 3.3 in the chapter. Think back to a recent expensive purchase you made. It could have been a bike, mobile device, suit for interviews, and so forth. In order to evaluate the quality of your decision, please think about your purchase when answering each of the questions below.

Decision Making Worksheet
1. What problem did you hope to solve by making this purchase?

2. What alternative (or competing) products did you consider?

Comprehensive Supplements

INSTRUCTOR'S MANUAL

The Instructor's Manual was revised and updated to include thorough coverage of each chapter as well as time-saving features such as an outline, key student questions, class prep work assignments, guidance for using the unfolding cases, video supplements, and, finally, PowerPoint slides.

TEST BANK

The Test Bank includes more than 100 questions per chapter in a variety of formats. It has been revised for accuracy and expanded to include a greater variety of comprehension and application (scenario-based) questions as well as tagged with Bloom's Taxonomy levels and AACSB requirements.

POWERPOINT PRESENTATION SLIDES

The PowerPoint presentation collection contains an easy-to-follow outline including figures downloaded from the text. In addition to providing lecture notes, the slides also include questions for class discussion as well as company examples not found in the textbook. This versatility allows you to create a custom presentation suitable for your own classroom experience.

MANAGER'S HOT SEAT

This interactive, video-based application puts students in the manager's hot seat, building critical thinking and decision-making skills and allowing students to apply concepts to real managerial challenges. Students watch as 21 real managers apply their years of experience when confronting unscripted issues such as bullying in the workplace, cyber loafing, globalization, intergenerational work conflicts, workplace violence, and leadership versus management. In addition, Manager's Hot Seat interactive applications, featuring video cases and accompanying quizzes, can be found in Connect.

Required=Results

McGraw-Hill Connect®
Learn Without Limits

Connect is a digital teaching and learning environment that improves student performance over a variety of critical outcomes; it is easy to use; and it is proven effective.

Connect empowers students by continually adapting to deliver precisely what they need, when they need it, and how they need it, so your class time is more engaging and effective.

88% of instructors who use **Connect** require it; instructor satisfaction **increases** by 38% when **Connect** is required.

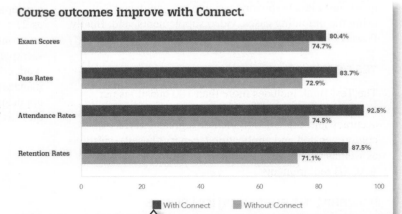

Course outcomes improve with Connect.

	With Connect	Without Connect
Exam Scores	80.4%	74.7%
Pass Rates	83.7%	72.9%
Attendance Rates	92.5%	74.5%
Retention Rates	87.5%	71.1%

Using **Connect** improves passing rates by **10.8%** and retention by **16.4%**.

Analytics

Connect Insight®

Connect Insight is Connect's new one-of-a-kind visual analytics dashboard—now available for both instructors and students—that provides at-a-glance information regarding student performance, which is immediately actionable. By presenting assignment, assessment, and topical performance results together with a time metric that is easily visible for aggregate or individual results, Connect Insight gives the user the ability to take a just-in-time approach to teaching and learning, which was never before available. Connect Insight presents data that empowers students and helps instructors improve class performance in a way that is efficient and effective.

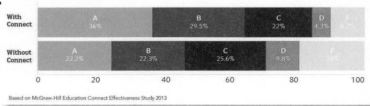

Connect helps students achieve better grades

	A	B	C	D	F
With Connect	36%	29.5%	22%	4.3%	8.2%
Without Connect	22.2%	22.3%	25.6%	9.8%	20%

Based on McGraw-Hill Education Connect Effectiveness Study 2013

Students can view their results for any **Connect** course.

Mobile

Connect's new, intuitive mobile interface gives students and instructors flexible and convenient, anytime–anywhere access to all components of the Connect platform.

Adaptive

THE FIRST AND ONLY **ADAPTIVE READING EXPERIENCE** DESIGNED TO TRANSFORM THE WAY STUDENTS READ

More students earn **A's** and **B's** when they use McGraw-Hill Education **Adaptive** products.

SmartBook®

Proven to help students improve grades and study more efficiently, SmartBook contains the same content within the print book, but actively tailors that content to the needs of the individual. SmartBook's adaptive technology provides precise, personalized instruction on what the student should do next, guiding the student to master and remember key concepts, targeting gaps in knowledge and offering customized feedback, driving the student toward comprehension and retention of the subject matter. Available on smartphones and tablets, and fully accessible offline, SmartBook puts learning at the student's fingertips—anywhere, anytime.

Over **4 billion questions** have been answered, making McGraw-Hill Education products more intelligent, reliable, & precise.

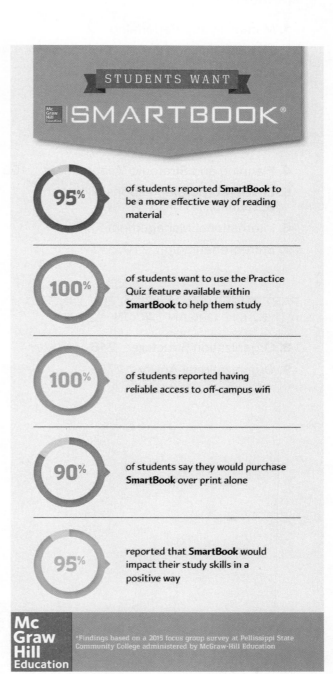

STUDENTS WANT

Mc Graw Hill Education **SMARTBOOK®**

95% of students reported **SmartBook** to be a more effective way of reading material

100% of students want to use the Practice Quiz feature available within **SmartBook** to help them study

100% of students reported having reliable access to off-campus wifi

90% of students say they would purchase **SmartBook** over print alone

95% reported that **SmartBook** would impact their study skills in a positive way

Mc Graw Hill Education

*Findings based on a 2015 focus group survey at Pellissippi State Community College administered by McGraw-Hill Education

Brief Contents

Contents

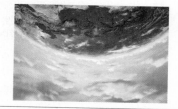

PART TWO   PLANNING: DELIVERING STRATEGIC VALUE

PART THREE ORGANIZING: BUILDING A DYNAMIC ORGANIZATION

CHAPTER 11

Managing the Diverse Workforce   346

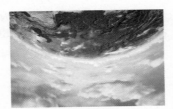

PART FOUR   LEADING: MOBILIZING PEOPLE

CHAPTER 12

Leadership   380

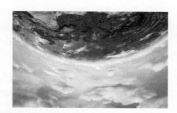

PART FIVE CONTROLLING: LEARNING AND CHANGING

TOC image: © *Alexander Chernyakov/Getty Images*

The Management Process

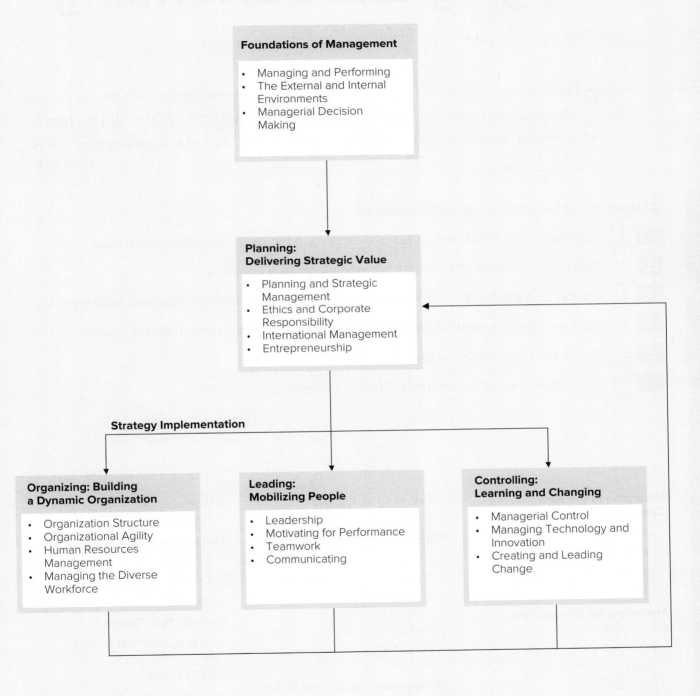

Foundations of Management

- Managing and Performing
- The External and Internal Environments
- Managerial Decision Making

Planning:
Delivering Strategic Value

- Planning and Strategic Management
- Ethics and Corporate Responsibility
- International Management
- Entrepreneurship

Strategy Implementation

Organizing: Building a Dynamic Organization

- Organization Structure
- Organizational Agility
- Human Resources Management
- Managing the Diverse Workforce

Leading:
Mobilizing People

- Leadership
- Motivating for Performance
- Teamwork
- Communicating

Controlling:
Learning and Changing

- Managerial Control
- Managing Technology and Innovation
- Creating and Leading Change

CHAPTER 1

Managing and Performing

> Management means, in the last analysis, the substitution of thought for brawn and muscle, of knowledge for folklore and tradition, and of cooperation for force.
>
> —PETER DRUCKER

Management in Action

INTRODUCING THE BEST: AMAZON'S JEFF BEZOS

What does a well-run company look like? Does it feature a famous brand, report a big profit, or have a prominent leader? Most business experts agree that a better measure of success is the company's long-term value.

Using *long-term value* as the performance measure, three professors writing for *Harvard Business Review* identified the best-performing chief executive officers (CEOs), or top managers. For each company's CEO, they looked at how the company's value changed while that person held the top job. By that measure, the best living CEO was Jeffrey P. Bezos of online retailer Amazon. Since 1996, Amazon under Bezos has delivered returns of 12,266 percent on shareholders' investments, and the company's value has risen by $111 billion.

To generate such breathtaking growth, Bezos has to get a lot of things right. As an early entrant into the then-revolutionary online marketplace, he was a visionary about the Internet's potential. At the same time, Bezos has consistently insisted to investors and employees that the company would take a long-term view, recognizing that the smartest innovations may take time to pay off. (This is especially true given Amazon's practice of keeping costs and prices as low as possible.)

Bezos sets the tone for the company by insisting that customers come first. This mantra has led to some decisions that at first seemed a little crazy to outsiders. Why would a bookseller offer an e-reader, the Kindle, if it would reduce book sales? Why would an online store create the Amazon Marketplace, where

© Zuma Press, Inc./Alamy

competing retailers can sell their products? Bezos insists that those innovations drive ever more shoppers to Amazon, where they download e-books and buy print books and enjoy the convenience of buying an extremely broad range of products from many sellers without Amazon needing to build more warehouses.

If you listen to Bezos, this story is all about the customer. If you are a storeowner, it also is about a formidable, game-changing global competitor that didn't exist two decades ago but today sells more than $74 billion a year. And, finally, it is a story about managers like Bezos figuring out how to build something amazing in a fast-changing world.[1]

As you read this chapter, notice the wide variety of skills that Jeff Bezos needs to help Amazon meet its goals. Also, think about how managing people, money, and other resources enables Amazon and other organizations to accomplish far more than individuals acting independently could ever achieve.

Amazon's CEO, Jeff Bezos, is one of the most interesting leaders in business today. He is an innovator who combines financial know-how with a vision for the future of technology and an unswerving drive to serve customers. Together, those qualities have helped him build a business idea into a major corporation that continues to transform industry.

Bezos and the other top business leaders identified by *Harvard Business Review* are chief executives who have been far more than a flashy presence in the media; they have delivered strong performance over years at the helm. In the 2014 rankings, Bezos garnered the top spot. After Bezos, other top CEOs on the list were Cisco Systems' John Chambers (number 3), Novo Nordisk's Lars Rebien Sorensen (number 6), and Yum! Brands' David Novak (number 12).[2]

Consider Groupon as a contrasting example. You might have been one of its many fans if you like low prices for local goods and services. The new company was booming as it strived to become the Amazon.com of local commerce, but then its performance collapsed, and the board in 2013 fired CEO and cofounder Andrew Mason. Groupon's great deals brought businesses new one-time customers wanting rock-bottom prices, angering customers who paid full price. Not enough customers returned. The jury is still out regarding the ability of Eric Lefkofsky, who replaced Mason as CEO, to transform Groupon into a successful company by diversifying into the sale of physical goods and offering longer lasting discounts via mobile phones.[3]

In business, there is no alternative to managing well. Companies may fly high for a while, but they cannot do well for very long without good management. It's the same for individuals: the best managers succeed by focusing on fundamentals, knowing what's important, and managing well. The aim of this book is to help you succeed in those pursuits.

Managing in the New Competitive Landscape

LO 1

When the economy is soaring, business seems easy. Starting an Internet company looked easy in the 1990s, and ventures related to the real estate boom looked like a sure thing just a few years ago. But investors grew wary of dot-com start-ups, and the demand for new homes dropped off the table when the economy crashed in late 2008. At such times, it becomes evident that management is a challenge requiring knowledge and skills to adapt to new circumstances.

> Management is a challenge requiring knowledge and skills to adapt to new circumstances.

What defines the competitive landscape of today's business? You will be reading about many relevant issues in the coming chapters, but we begin here by highlighting four ongoing challenges that characterize the current business landscape: globalization, technological change, the importance of knowledge and ideas, and collaboration across organizational boundaries.

Globalization

Far more than in the past, today's enterprises are global, with offices and production facilities in countries all over the world. Corporations operate worldwide, transcending national borders. Companies that want to grow often need to tap international markets, where incomes are rising and demand is increasing. The change from a local to a global marketplace is gaining momentum and is irreversible.[4]

Fortune magazine annually publishes a list of the world's most admired companies. Whereas U.S. companies used to dominate, Switzerland-based Nestlé was the most admired maker of consumer food products in 2014, Germany's BMW was the most admired producer of motor vehicles, and Singapore Airlines was the most admired airlines company.[5]

According to *Fortune*'s 2014 Global 500 list, the top five largest firms are Royal Dutch Shell (Netherlands), Sinopec Group (China), China National Petroleum (China), Walmart (U.S.), and ExxonMobil (U.S.).[6]

Globalization also means that a company's talent and competition can come from anywhere. As with its sales, more than half of GE's 307,000 employees live outside the United States.[7] Kentucky-based Yum! Brands (KFC, Pizza Hut, and Taco Bell) has over 40,000 restaurants in more than 125 countries. In 2013, almost 70 percent of its profits came from outside the United States. On average, Yum! Brands opens 5 stores per day in international locations.[8]

PepsiCo's chief executive, Indra Nooyi, brings a much-needed global viewpoint to a company whose international business has been growing three times faster than sales in the United States. Nooyi, who was raised in India and educated there and in the United States, has steered the company toward more "better for you" and "good for you" snacks such as Chudo Drinkable Yoghurt in Russia, Quaker Stila Cereal in Mexico, and Sabra Roasted Garlic Hummus in the United States.[9]

Globalization affects small companies as well as large. Many small companies export their goods. Many domestic firms assemble their products in other countries. And companies are under pressure to improve their products in the face of intense competition from foreign manufacturers. Firms today must ask themselves, "How can we be the best in the world?"

Globalization has changed the face of the workforce. Management in this new competitive landscape will need to attract and effectively manage a talent pool from all over the globe.

© *Paper Boat Creative/Getty Images*

For students, it's not too early to think about the personal ramifications. In the words of CEO Jim Goodnight of SAS, the largest privately held software company in the world, "The best thing business schools can do to prepare their students is to encourage them to look beyond their own backyards. Globalization has opened the world for many opportunities, and schools should encourage their students to take advantage of them."[10]

Technological Change

The Internet, mobile applications, Big Data analytics, and cloud computing are only some of the ways that technology is vitally important in the business world. Technology both complicates things and creates new opportunities. The challenges come from the rapid rate at which communication, transportation, information, and other technologies change.[11] For example, after just a couple of decades of widespread desktop use, customers switched to laptop models, which require different accessories. More recently, users are turning to mini-laptops, tablets, and smartphones to meet their mobility technology needs.[12] Any company that served desktop users had to rethink its customers' wants and needs, not to mention the possibility that these customers are now working at the airport or a local Starbucks outlet rather than in an office.

Later chapters discuss technology further, but here we highlight the rise of the Internet and its effects. Why is the Internet so important to business?[13] It is a marketplace, a means for manufacturing goods and services, a distribution channel, an information service, and more. It drives down costs and speeds up globalization. It improves efficiency of decision making. Managers can watch and learn what other companies are doing—on the other side of the world. Although these advantages create business opportunities, they also create threats as competitors sometimes capitalize on new developments more than you do.

Things continue to change at breakneck speed. In 2003, tech guru Tim O'Reilly coined the term "Web 2.0" to describe the exciting new wave of social networking start-ups that allow users to publish and share information. But most failed or are stalled; very few, other than Facebook, make a profit.[14] Nevertheless, Web 2.0 not only is a continuing reality, it is redefining the ways that customers and sellers, employees and employers are sharing knowledge. (And the saying is true: knowledge really is power.) Looking forward, the managers of the future will take Web 2.0 for granted and must be ready for Web 3.0, which has been described as a "read-write-execute" web where applications, search findings, and online services are more tailored, integrated, and relevant to users.[15]

Knowledge Management

Companies and managers need good new ideas. Because companies in advanced economies have become so efficient at producing physical goods, most workers have been freed up to provide services or "abstract goods" such as software, entertainment, data, and advertising. These workers, whose primary contributions are ideas and problem-solving expertise, are often referred to as *knowledge workers*. Managing these workers poses some particular challenges, which we examine throughout this book. For example, determining whether they are doing a good job can be difficult because the manager cannot simply count or measure a knowledge worker's output. Also, these workers often are most motivated to do their best when the work is interesting, not because of a carrot or stick dangled by the manager.[16]

Because the success of modern businesses so often depends on the knowledge used for innovation and the delivery of services, organizations need to manage that knowledge. **Knowledge management** is the set of practices aimed at discovering and harnessing an organization's intellectual resources—fully using the intellects of the organization's people. Knowledge management is about finding, unlocking, sharing, and capitalizing on the most precious resources of an organization: people's expertise, skills, wisdom, and relationships. The nearby "Multiple Generations at Work" box explores how important knowledge transfer is to organizational survival.

Knowledge managers find these human assets, help people collaborate and learn, generate new ideas, and harness those ideas into successful innovations.

In hospitals, important knowledge includes patients' histories, doctors' orders, billing information, dietary requirements, prescriptions administered, and much more. With lives at stake, many hospitals have embraced knowledge management. For example, at Virginia Commonwealth University (VCU) Health System, a single information system lets doctors write prescriptions, look up patient information and lab results, and consult with one another. Billing also is automated as part of VCU's knowledge management system, making the process more efficient and connecting with patient data so that it can remind the physician of all the conditions being treated—and billed for.[17] Hospitals can also give patients access to the knowledge management system so that they can schedule appointments, request prescription refills, and send questions to their doctors.

Collaboration across Boundaries

One of the most important processes of knowledge management is to ensure that people in different parts of the organization collaborate effectively with one another. This requires productive communications among different departments, divisions, or other subunits of the organization. For example, "T-shaped" managers break out of the traditional corporate hierarchy to share knowledge freely across the organization (the horizontal part of the T) while remaining committed to the bottom-line performance of their individual business units (the vertical part). This emphasis on dual responsibilities for performance and knowledge sharing occurs at pharmaceutical giant GlaxoSmithKline, large German industrial company Siemens, and London-based steelmaker Ispat International.[18]

For example, Toyota keeps its product development process efficient by bringing together design engineers and manufacturing employees from the very beginning. Often, manufacturing employees can see ways to simplify a design so that it is easier to make without defects or unnecessary costs. Toyota expects its employees to listen to input from all areas of the organization, so this type of collaboration is a natural part of the organization's culture. Employees use software to share their knowledge—best practices they have developed for design and manufacturing.[19] Thus, at Toyota, knowledge management supports collaboration and vice versa.

knowledge management

Practices aimed at discovering and harnessing an organization's intellectual resources.

Multiple Generations at Work

Boomer Retirements = Opportunities for Gen Xers and Millennials

The workforce is changing rapidly. A large number of Baby Boomers (born 1946–1964) will be exiting the workforce over the next 20 years. Approximately 10,000 Boomers are turning 65 years old each day in the United States. Though some Boomers will work into their later years, others will step out of the workforce to engage in hobbies, travel opportunities, and family time.

Senior talent exodus of top-level executives, managers, and leaders will translate into significant career opportunities for younger generations in the workplace. Gen Xers (born 1965–1979) currently occupy many of the middle-level managerial roles in organizations. There are not enough of them to fill all of the soon-to-be-vacant positions. Enter the Millennial generation (born 1980–2000), who make up the largest demographic cohort on record.[20] Not only are these early 30- and 20-somethings flooding into the job market, but they're also moving up into team leader and frontline managerial positions.

An important consideration is that before Gen Xers and Millennials can assume higher-level positions in businesses, schools, government agencies, and nonprofits, organizational knowledge must be transferred from senior management to the less experienced Gen Xers and Millennial employees. Senior managers and leaders

© Andrey Popov/Getty Images/RF

possess a great deal of "know how" and "know who" that are critical to the long-term success and survival of their respective organizations. Prior to retirement, senior talent will look to transfer their knowledge to younger employees.

Complicating this organizational need is the fact that generations, like individuals, differ in their attitudes, personalities, and behaviors. These differences can affect everything from communication, customer service, teamwork, job satisfaction, morale, and retention to overall organizational performance.

Collaboration across boundaries occurs even beyond the boundaries of the organization itself. Companies today must motivate and capitalize on the ideas of people outside the organization. Customers, for instance, can be collaborators. Companies must realize that the need to serve the customer drives everything else.

In the Web 3.0 era, customers *expect* to share their ideas and be heard. Companies collaborate with their customers by actively and continuously listening and responding. L.L.Bean, for example, tracks customer comments and reviews on its website; if any product averages fewer than three stars out of five, the company removes it and directs the product manager to resolve the problem.[21] Businesses also pay attention to customer comments on Amazon, Zappos, Yelp, TripAdvisor, Facebook, Twitter, and many more. Customer feedback management software can search these and other sites and generate statistics and reports. Also, companies can respond to negative online reviews with the goal of winning over their critics.[22]

Managing for Competitive Advantage

 LO 2

The turbulent dot-com era turned careers (and lives) upside down. Students dropped out of school to join Internet start-ups or start their own. Managers in big corporations quit their jobs to do the same. Investors salivated, and invested heavily. The risks were often ignored or downplayed—sometimes tragically as the boom went bust. Or consider an earlier industry with similar transforming power: automobiles. There have been at least 2,000 carmakers—how many remain?

---

innovation

The introduction of new goods and services; a change in method or technology; a positive, useful departure from previous ways of doing things.

---

quality

The excellence of your product (goods or services).

What is the lesson to be learned from the failures in these important transformational industries? A key to understanding the success of a company—whether traditional, Internet-based, or a combination of both—is not just how much the industry in which it operates will affect society or how much it will grow. The key is the competitive advantage a particular company holds and how well it can sustain that advantage.

To survive and win over time, you have to gain and sustain advantages over your competitors. You gain competitive advantage by being better than your competitors at doing valuable things for your customers. But what does this mean, specifically? To succeed, managers must deliver performance. The fundamental success drivers of performance are innovation, quality, service, speed, cost competitiveness, and sustainability.

Innovation

Companies must continually innovate. **Innovation** is the introduction of new goods and services. Your firm must adapt to changes in consumer demands and to new competitors. Products don't sell forever; in fact, they don't sell for nearly as long as they used to because competitors are continuously introducing new products. Your firm must innovate, or it will die. In 2000, Blockbuster was the market leader of the video rental industry. It didn't see the need to offer customers an alternative to driving to their retail stores to rent a movie, nor did the company feel it wise to eliminate late charges as they were a major source of revenue. Reed Hastings, founder of Netflix, eventually displaced market leader Blockbuster by allowing customers to order a video which would be delivered by mail. Customers could watch the video for as long as they wanted, then mail it back to Netflix. In 2010, Blockbuster filed for bankruptcy. Netflix has become a successful $28 billion company.[23]

The need for innovation is driven in part by globalization. One obvious reason is that facilities in other countries can manufacture appliances or write software code at a lower cost than facilities in the United States; U.S. facilities thus operate at a disadvantage. Therefore, they must provide something their foreign competitors can't—and often that requires delivering something new. This is a challenge as developing nations such as China increase their engineering prowess. Philips, which started out making light bulbs in the Netherlands in the 1890s, has set up research as well as manufacturing operations in China because that country is becoming a key source of technical know-how, not just cheap labor.[24] Nevertheless, as labor and other costs rise overseas, and as U.S. companies find ways to improve efficiency at home, the future for North American facilities is brightening. Nissan, for example, has expanded production in Smyrna, Tennessee, including assembly of its Infiniti JX luxury car and Leaf electric car. Other companies that have announced plans to expand in the United States, especially in the South, include Toyota, General Motors, Ford, and Honda.[25]

Innovation is today's holy grail (2014's number one most admired company in *Fortune*'s innovativeness category was Apple, and number two was Amazon).[26] Like the other sources of competitive advantage, innovation comes from people, it must be a strategic goal, and it must be managed properly. Later chapters show you how great companies innovate.

Quality

When Spectrum Health, a hospital chain based in Grand Rapids, Michigan, asked patients how well they were served, patients rated staff low on helpfulness and their attitude toward visitors and said they didn't get good information about procedures or how to take care of themselves after being released to go home. Spectrum set up an advisory council of patients and family members, making visiting hours more flexible, getting patient input into who was allowed to hear medical information and make decisions about treatment, and calling discharged patients at home to make sure they understood the directions they had received. Satisfaction scores of Spectrum patients improved dramatically.[27]

Spectrum Health's efforts reflect a commitment to quality. In general, **quality** is the excellence of your product. The importance of quality and the standards for acceptable quality have increased dramatically in recent years. Customers now demand high-quality goods and services, and often they will accept nothing less.

Historically, quality pertained primarily to the physical goods that customers bought, and it referred to attractiveness, lack of defects, reliability, and long-term dependability. The traditional approach to quality was to check work after it was completed and then eliminate defects, using inspection and statistical data to determine whether products were up to standards. But then W. Edwards Deming, J. M. Juran, and other quality gurus convinced managers to take a more complete approach to achieving *total* quality. This includes *preventing* defects before they occur, *achieving zero defects* in manufacturing, and *designing* products for quality. The goal is to solve and eradicate from the beginning all quality-related problems and to live a philosophy of *continuous improvement* in the way the company operates.[28]

© Purestock/SuperStock

Quality is further provided when companies customize goods and services to the wishes of the individual consumer. Choices at Starbucks give consumers thousands of variations on the drinks they can order, whether it's half-caff or all caffeine, skim milk or soy milk, or shots of espresso and any of a variety of flavored syrups. For a premium price, candy lovers can select M&M's candies bearing the message of their own creation.[29]

Providing world-class quality requires a thorough understanding of what quality really is.[30] Quality can be measured in terms of product performance, customer service, reliability (avoidance of failure or breakdowns), conformance to standards, durability, and aesthetics. Only when you move beyond broad, generic concepts such as "quality" and identify specific quality requirements can you identify problems, target needs, set performance standards more precisely, and deliver world-class value.

By the way, *Fortune* magazine's 2014 number one company for quality of products and services was Apple; Starbucks' was number two.

> The result of long-term relationships is better and better quality, and lower and lower costs.
>
> —W. Edwards Deming

Service

As noted, important quality measures often pertain to the service customers receive. This dimension of quality is particularly important because the service sector has come to dominate the U.S. economy. In recent years, the fastest-growing job categories have been almost entirely services and retailing jobs, and the jobs with the greatest declines are primarily in manufacturing (although some manufacturing is returning to the United States).[31] Services include intangible products such as insurance, hotel accommodations, medical care, and haircuts.

Service means giving customers what they want or need, when they want it. So service is focused on continually meeting the needs of customers to establish mutually beneficial long-term relationships. Thus cloud computing companies, in addition to providing the online access to software, applications, and other computer services, may help their customers store and analyze large amounts of customer and employee data.

An important dimension of service quality is making it easy and enjoyable for customers to experience a service or to buy and use products. The Detroit Institute of Arts recently hired a manager formerly with the Ritz-Carlton hotel chain, noted for its exceptional level of service, to be vice president of museum operations. As the art museum prepared for a grand reopening following a major renovation, the manager analyzed the types of customer interactions that occur in a museum, identifying ways to make the experience more pleasant. He also worked with his staff to identify ways to customize services, such as offering tours tailored to the interests of particular groups.[32]

service

The speed and dependability with which an organization delivers what customers want.

Speed

Google constantly improves its search product at a rapid rate. In fact, its entire culture is based on rapid innovation. Sheryl Sandberg, a Google vice president, once made a mistake because she was moving too fast to plan carefully. Although the mistake cost the company a few million dollars, Google cofounder Larry Page responded to her explanation and apology by saying he was actually glad she had made the mistake. It showed that she appreciated the company's values. Page told Sandberg, "I want to run a company where we are moving too quickly and doing too much, not being too cautious and doing too little. If we don't have any of these mistakes, we're just not taking enough risks."[33]

speed

Fast and timely execution, response, and delivery of results.

Although it's unlikely that Google actually favors mistakes over moneymaking ideas, Page's statement expressed an appreciation that in the modern business environment, **speed**—rapid execution, response, and delivery—often separates the winners from the losers. How fast can you develop and get a new product to market? How quickly can you respond to customer requests? You are far better off if you are faster than the competition—and if you can respond quickly to your competitors' actions.

Speed isn't everything—you can't get sloppy in your quest to be first. But other things being equal, faster companies are more likely to be the winners, slow ones the losers. Even pre-Internet, companies were getting products to market and in the hands of customers faster than ever. Now the speed requirement has increased exponentially. Everything, it seems, is on fast-forward.

Speed is no longer just a goal of some companies; it is a strategic imperative. In the auto industry, getting faster is essential just for keeping up with the competition. A recent study found that employees at Ford's assembly plant in Atlanta needed just 15.4 hours to assemble a vehicle. Compare that with the 1980s, when GM employees needed 40 hours to assemble a vehicle.[34] Another important measure of speed in the auto industry is the time the company takes to go from product concept to availability of the vehicle in the showroom. During the 1980s, that time was about 30 or 40 months. Today, Toyota has cut the process to an average of 24 months.[35]

Walmart's goal is to provide products at low costs to retain its large customer base. To remain successful and cost competitive, it has devised and followed through with many plans to lower its operational costs.

© Joe Raedle/Getty Images

Cost Competitiveness

Walmart keeps driving hard to find new ways to cut billions of dollars from its already very low distribution costs. It leads the industry in efficient distribution, but competitors are copying Walmart's methods, so the efficiency no longer gives it as much of an advantage.[36] Walmart has sought to keep costs down by scheduling store employees more efficiently. It introduced a computerized system that schedules employees based on each store's sales, transactions, units sold, and customer traffic. The system is intended to schedule just enough workers, with full staffing only at the busiest times of day and days of the week, so it requires more flexibility from Walmart's employees.[37]

cost competitiveness

Keeping costs low to achieve profits and be able to offer prices that are attractive to consumers.

Walmart's efforts are aimed at **cost competitiveness,** which means keeping costs low enough so that the company can realize profits and price its products (goods or services) at levels that are attractive to consumers. Needless to say, if you can offer a desirable product at a lower price, it is more likely to sell.

Singapore Airlines, one of the world's most admired companies, kept profiting during the economic recession while the global airline industry lost money. It did so by cutting costs more strategically than the competition. While competitors cut prices and still didn't fill their planes (and risked a backlash to later price hikes), SA slashed flights, parked planes, and reduced salaries, including the CEO's.[38]

In contrast to the high-quality, even luxurious flying experience offered by Singapore Airlines, Ryanair is a European low-cost airline. *Bloomberg Businessweek* reported that CEO Michael O'Leary was "remaking commercial air travel in his image: shabby, crabby, and cheap, cheap, cheap." O'Leary thought that short flights need only one toilet, and every flight needs only one pilot because the computer or a trained member of the cabin crew can fly if necessary. Less frighteningly, he believed that commercial air passengers do not need free pillows, blankets, and snacks; they just want to arrive at their destination cheaply and with their luggage. His vision is for profits to come from inflight sales, high luggage fees, low-cost secondary airports, and commissions on travel products sold through the airline's website.[39] O'Leary's no-frills business model appears to be working. In 2014, Ryanair experienced significant increases in both profits and passenger traffic.[40]

One reason every company must worry about cost is that consumers can easily compare prices on the Internet from thousands of competitors. Consumers looking to buy popular items, such as cameras, printers, and plane fares, can go online to research the best models and the best deals. If you can't cut costs and offer attractive prices, you can't compete.

Sustainability

Avoiding wasteful use of energy can bolster a company's financial performance while being kind to the environment. Efforts to cut energy waste are just one way to achieve an important form of competitive advantage: **sustainability,** which at its most basic is the effort to minimize the use and loss of resources, especially those that are polluting and nonrenewable.

sustainability

The effort to minimize the use of resources, especially those that are polluting and nonrenewable.

Although sustainability means different things to different people,[41] in this text, we emphasize a long-term perspective on sustaining the natural environment and building tomorrow's business opportunities while managing today's business.[42] The nearby "Social Enterprise" box discusses how Richard Branson, CEO of Virgin, and other global business leaders are encouraging governments to act more quickly to limit greenhouse gas emissions. In the United States, corporate efforts aimed at sustainability have fluctuated somewhat as environmental laws are strengthened or loosened; overall, the worldwide trend has been in the direction of greater concern for sustainability. The clashes among the rising demand for resources, limited supplies, and changing social attitudes toward environmental protection mean that the coming decade is likely to have greater focus on resource productivity, the emergence of clean-tech industries, and regulation.[43]

As many companies have discovered, addressing that concern often produces bottom-line benefits. Companies with strong sustainability performance that have also become financial winners include athletic-shoe maker Adidas, Spanish fashion group Inditex, French luxury-goods maker Hermès International, and Eaton, a power management company.[44]

Patagonia Sur is a for-profit company that has created the first private land trust in Patagonia to protect the company's land permanently; it plans to create up to 10 profitable, environmentally sustained businesses on that land.[45] The goals are to apply free-market forces to develop the land for profit, do no harm, and spread this radically different land management model to developing nations around the world.

Sustainability is about protecting our options.[46] Done properly, sustainability allows people to live and work in ways that can be maintained over the long term (generations) without depleting or harming our environmental, social, and economic resources. In 2014, Westpac Banking of Australia won accolades for being the first bank to join that country's Greenhouse Challenge Plus and to more effectively manage the bank's energy, carbon, water and waste.[47]

Social Enterprise

Global Business Leaders Push for Zero CO$_2$ Emissions by 2050

Sir Richard Branson, CEO of Virgin, has joined forces with other powerful leaders of multinational companies to encourage world government officials to set the ambitious goal of reaching net zero CO$_2$ or greenhouse gas (GHG) emissions by 2050. Net zero emissions refer to the elimination of GHGs by "replacing fossil fuels and ensuring that any remaining emissions are balanced out by carbon-saving projects such as tree-planting and carbon capture and storage."

While Branson has long been an outspoken advocate for preventing climate change, it is notable that the B-Team (as they call themselves) includes a diverse set of business leaders: Paul Polman, the CEO of Unilever, Ratan Tata, the chair of Tata Group, Arianna Huffington, a media entrepreneur, Guilherme Leal, a Brazilian billionaire, and Mo Ibrahim, a telecommunications billionaire, among others.

Reaching net zero GHG emissions by midcentury is a more aggressive goal than the one adopted currently by many governments, which is to reach an 80 percent reduction in emissions by 2050. After reaching the 80 percent goal, government officials will then attempt to reduce emissions to net zero by the end of the 21st century. A concern voiced by the B-Team is that if achieved, the current goal of 80 percent by midcentury will be too little, too late to keep the average world temperature from rising by 2 degrees Celsius (3.6 Fahrenheit). A recent Organisation for Economic Co-operation and Development (OECD) report agrees: "global average temperature is likely to exceed this goal [2-degree increase in global average temperature] by 2050, and by 3 degrees C to 6 degrees C higher than pre-industrial levels by the end of the century." Similar to environmental researchers, members of the B-Team are concerned that this projected increase in global warming will lead to catastrophic climate change.

The B-Team, like most business leaders, tries to manage risk. In this case, the team is attempting to influence government officials who have the power to set GHG emission goals. The timing could not be better. World government leaders are currently preparing for a historic round of climate negotiations at the United Nations–sponsored Conference of Parties in December 2015 in Paris. Armed with a combination of the latest scientific climate change research, and analyses of business and economic risks of failing to stay within the 2-degree C increase threshold, the B-Team will be encouraging conference attendees to adopt their ambitious goal of net zero GHG emissions by 2050.

By setting such an ambitious climate change prevention goal, governments can send a strong, clear message to the market that it needs to take climate change seriously. Also, it makes good business sense: "A net zero position allows business leaders to take short-term action and make long-term plans to develop profitable ways to be competitive, even as they limit emissions, increase efficiency and find strategies to offset the remaining emissions that can't be avoided." Adoption of the B-Team's goal will likely have the added effect of boosting innovation and development of cost-effective renewable energies so world economies can rely less on environmentally damaging fossil fuels.[48]

- To what degree do you agree or disagree with the B-Team's goal for world governments to reach net zero CO$_2$ or greenhouse gas (GHG) emissions by 2050?

- Should governments of developing economies like China and Brazil be held to the same goals for the reduction of CO$_2$ or greenhouse gas (GHG) emissions as the governments of developed nations?

Delivering All Types of Performance

Don't assume that you can settle for delivering just one of the six competitive advantages: low cost alone, or quality alone, for example. As illustrated in Exhibit 1.1, the best managers and companies perform on all of these types of performance.

Virginia Mason Medical Center, like many hospitals, felt challenged in delivering low costs along with high quality and superior services. Virginia Mason has a reputation for high-quality care, but it was losing money treating certain patients. So Virginia Mason collaborated with Aetna, an insurer that pays for 10 percent of the medical center's business, and found ways to treat some of the most expensive conditions so that they became more economical to insure but were paid for at higher rates that would be profitable for Virginia Mason. The medical center has also improved quality through measures that enhance speed—in this case, cutting waiting times for patients, such as a reduction in the four-hour wait for chemotherapy to 90 minutes.[49]

Trade-offs may occur among the six sources of competitive advantage, but this doesn't need to be a zero-sum game in which one has to suffer at the expense of another.

EXHIBIT 1.1
Staying Ahead of the Competition

The Functions of Management

Management is the process of working with people and resources to accomplish organizational goals. Good managers do those things both effectively and efficiently. To be *effective* is to achieve organizational goals. To be *efficient* is to achieve goals with minimal waste of resources—that is, to make the best possible use of money, time, materials, and people. Some managers fail on both criteria, or focus on one at the expense of another. The best managers achieve high performance by focusing on both effectiveness *and* efficiency. These definitions have been around for a long time. But as you know, business is changing radically. The real issue is how to *do* these things.[50]

Although the context of business and the specifics of doing business are changing, there are still plenty of timeless principles that make great managers, and great companies, great. While fresh thinking and new approaches are required now more than ever, much of what has already been learned about successful management practices remains relevant, useful, and adaptable, with fresh thinking, to the 21st-century business environment.

In the business world today, great executives not only adapt to changing conditions but also apply—fanatically, rigorously, consistently, and with discipline—the fundamental management principles.

These fundamentals include the four traditional functions of management: *planning, organizing, leading,* and *controlling.* They remain as relevant as ever, and they still provide the fundamentals that are needed in start-ups as much as in established corporations. But their form has evolved.

Planning: Delivering Strategic Value

Planning is specifying the goals to be achieved and deciding in advance the appropriate actions needed to achieve those goals. Planning activities include analyzing current situations, anticipating the future, determining objectives, deciding in what types of activities the company will engage, choosing corporate and business strategies, and determining the resources needed to achieve the organization's goals. Plans set the stage for action and for major achievements.

 LO 3

management

The process of working with people and resources to accomplish organizational goals.

planning

The management function of systematically making decisions about the goals and activities that an individual, a group, a work unit, or the overall organization will pursue; see also *strategic planning.*

value

The monetary amount associated with how well a job, task, good, or service meets users' needs.

The planning function for the new business environment, discussed in Part 2 of this book, is more dynamically described as *delivering strategic value*. **Value** is a complex concept.[51] Fundamentally, it describes the monetary amount associated with how well a job, task, good, or service meets users' needs. Those users might be business owners, customers, employees, society, and even nations. The better you meet those needs (in terms of quality, speed, efficiency, and so on), the more value you deliver. That value is strategic when it contributes to meeting the organization's goals. On a personal level, you will do well when you periodically ask yourself and your boss, "How can I add value?" Answering that question will enhance your contributions, your job performance, and your career.

> You will do well when you periodically ask yourself and your boss, "How can I add value?"

Delivering strategic value is a continual process in which people throughout the organization use their brains and the brains of customers, suppliers, and other stakeholders to identify opportunities to create, seize, strengthen, and sustain competitive advantage. This dynamic process contributes to the objective of creating more and more value for the customer. Effectively creating value requires fully considering a new and changing set of stakeholders and issues, including the government, the natural environment, globalization, and the dynamic economy in which ideas are king and entrepreneurs are both formidable competitors and potential collaborators. You learn about these and related topics in Chapter 4 (planning and strategic management), Chapter 5 (ethics, corporate responsibility, and sustainability), Chapter 6 (international management), and Chapter 7 (entrepreneurship).

organizing

The management function of assembling and coordinating human, financial, physical, informational, and other resources needed to achieve goals.

Organizing: Building a Dynamic Organization

Organizing is assembling and coordinating the human, financial, physical, informational, and other resources needed to achieve goals. Organizing activities include attracting people to the organization, specifying job responsibilities, grouping jobs into work units, marshaling and allocating resources, and creating conditions so that people and things work together to achieve maximum success.

Part 3 of the book describes the organizing function as *building a dynamic organization*. Historically, organizing involved creating an organization chart by identifying business functions, establishing reporting relationships, and having a human resources department that administered plans, programs, and paperwork. Now and in the future, effective managers will be using new forms of organizing and viewing their people as perhaps their most valuable resources. They will build organizations that are flexible and adaptive, particularly in response to competitive threats and customer needs. Progressive human resource practices that attract and retain the very best of a highly diverse population will be essential aspects of the successful company. You learn about these topics in Chapter 8 (organization structure), Chapter 9 (organizational agility), Chapter 10 (human resources management), and Chapter 11 (managing the diverse workforce).

leading

The management function that involves the manager's efforts to stimulate high performance by employees.

Leading: Mobilizing People

Leading is stimulating people to be high performers. It includes motivating and communicating with employees, individually and in groups. Leading involves close day-to-day contact with people, helping to guide and inspire them toward achieving team and organizational goals. Leading takes place in teams, departments, and divisions as well as at the tops of large organizations.

In earlier textbooks, the leading function described how managers motivate workers to come to work and execute top management's plans by doing their jobs. Today and in the future, managers must be good at mobilizing people to contribute their ideas—to use their brains in ways never needed or dreamed of in the past.

As described in Part 4, manager's must rely on a very different kind of leadership (Chapter 12) that empowers and motivates people (Chapter 13). Far more than in the past, great work must be done via great teamwork (Chapter 14), both within work groups and across group boundaries. Ideally, underlying these processes will be effective interpersonal and organizational communication (Chapter 15).

Controlling: Learning and Changing

Planning, organizing, and leading do not guarantee success. The fourth function, **controlling,** monitors performance and implements necessary changes. By controlling, managers make sure the organization's resources are being used as planned and that the organization is meeting its goals such as quality and safety.

When managers implement their plans, they often find that things are not working out as planned. The controlling function makes sure that goals are met. It asks and answers the question, "Are our actual outcomes consistent with our goals?" It then makes adjustments as needed.

Successful organizations, large and small, pay close attention to the controlling function. But Part 5 of the book makes it clear that today and for the future, the key managerial challenges are far more dynamic than in the past; they involve continually *learning and changing.* Controls must still be in place, as described in Chapter 16. But new technologies and other innovations (Chapter 17) make it possible to achieve controls in more effective ways and to help all the people throughout the company, and across company boundaries (including customers and suppliers), to use their brains, learn, make a variety of new contributions, and help the organization change in ways that forge a successful future (Chapter 18).

The four management functions apply to you personally as well. You must find ways to create value; organize for your own personal effectiveness; mobilize your own talents and skills as well as those of others; monitor performance; and constantly learn, develop, and change for the future. As you proceed through this book and this course, we encourage you not merely to do your textbook learning of an impersonal course subject but to think about these issues from a personal perspective as well, using the ideas for your own personal development.

Performing All Four Management Functions

As a manager, your typical day will not be neatly divided into the four functions. You will be doing many things more or less simultaneously.[52] Your days will be busy and fractionated, spent dealing with interruptions, meetings, and firefighting. There will be plenty to do that you wish you could be doing but can't seem to get to. These activities will include all four management functions.

Some managers are particularly interested in, devoted to, or skilled in one or two of the four functions but not in the others. But you should devote adequate attention and resources to *all four* functions. You can be a skilled planner and controller, but if you organize your people improperly or fail to inspire them to perform at high levels, you will not be realizing your potential as a manager. Likewise, it does no good to be the kind of manager who loves to organize and lead, but who doesn't really understand where to go or how to determine whether you are on the right track. Good managers don't neglect any of the four management functions. Knowing what they are, you can periodically ask yourself whether you are devoting adequate attention to *all* of them.

controlling

The management function of monitoring performance and making needed changes.

Management Levels and Skills

Organizations—particularly large organizations—have many levels. In this section, you learn about the types of managers found at three broad organizational levels: top level, middle level, and frontline.

 LO 4

Management in Action

HOW BEZOS BUILT A BUSINESS

Amazon CEO Jeff Bezos has quantitative skills, computer expertise, and formal training in management. After earning a bachelor's degree in computer science and a master's in business administration, he worked as a hedge fund manager. As he pursued that career during the 1990s, he observed some of the early changes the Internet was making in the way people did business.

Bezos decided that this new technology offered an opportunity to sell books in a new way, offering a far bigger selection than any bricks-and-mortar store could hold. In 1994, he wrote a business plan for a company he wanted to launch. He would call it Amazon, and it would be the world's largest bookstore, serving U.S. customers from its website. In his plan, he estimated that the company could achieve sales of $100 million a year within a decade. As it turned out, Bezos was wrong. He started Amazon and was selling that much in just a few years. In 1997, he took the company public, raising funds by selling shares to investors. And his idea for a U.S. bookstore

became a global enterprise employing 70,000 people and selling music, games, tools, electronics, clothing, and almost any other product that is available on the retail market.

Bezos sets clear priorities. He insists on excellent services but at a low cost. That requires seeking efficiency and avoiding frills in the company's operations. He seizes new opportunities when they offer a chance to meet customer needs. For example, when hardware makers began to create e-readers, Bezos saw a way for readers to have access to even more titles. Initially, consumers were reluctant to try the new technology, so Amazon got involved in developing a more enticing model. From the start, the Kindle was priced so low it just covered the cost. The goal wasn't to make money on the hardware but to make it available to consumers so they could buy electronic books, magazines, and more. Incidentally, the low-price strategy also makes it harder for computer companies to beat Amazon at the e-reader game.[53]

- What are Amazon's areas of competitive advantage? How does Jeff Bezos help the company compete in those areas?
- Give an example of something Bezos does or would need to do to carry out each of the four functions of management.

Top-Level Managers

top-level managers

Senior executives responsible for the overall management and effectiveness of the organization.

Top-level managers are the senior executives of an organization and are responsible for its overall management. Top-level managers, often referred to as *strategic managers,* are supposed to focus on long-term issues and emphasize the survival, growth, and overall effectiveness of the organization.

Top managers are concerned not only with the organization as a whole but also with the interaction between the organization and its external environment. This interaction often requires managers to work extensively with outside individuals and organizations.

The chief executive officer (CEO) is one type of top-level manager found in large corporations. This individual is the primary strategic manager of the firm and has authority over everyone else. Others include the chief operating officer (COO), company presidents, and other members of the top management team (TMT). In the 1970s, finance was by far the most common single function represented in the TMT. The top team now typically includes the CEO, COO, chief information (or technology, or knowledge) officer, and other chiefs in the C-suite, including ethics, strategy (or corporate development), and marketing (or branding). Functional chiefs sometimes have the title of senior vice president (SVP).[54] A role for the C-suite of the future could well be chief sustainability officer or even climate change officer.[55]

Traditionally, the role of top-level managers has been to set overall direction by formulating strategy and controlling resources. But now top managers are more commonly called

Top managers are more commonly called on to be not only strategic architects but also true organizational leaders.

on to be not only strategic architects but also true organizational leaders. As leaders, they must create and articulate a broader corporate purpose with which people can identify—and one to which people will enthusiastically commit.

Middle-Level Managers

As the name implies, **middle-level managers** are located in the organization's hierarchy below top-level management and above the frontline managers. Sometimes called *tactical managers,* they are responsible for translating the general goals and plans developed by strategic managers into more specific objectives and activities.

Traditionally, the role of the middle manager is to be an administrator who bridges the gap between higher and lower levels. Middle-level managers break down corporate objectives into business unit targets; put together separate business unit plans from the units below them for higher-level corporate review; and serve as translators of internal communication, interpreting and broadcasting top management's priorities downward and channeling and translating information from the front lines upward.

As a stereotype, the term *middle manager* connotes mediocrity: unimaginative people behaving like bureaucrats and defending the status quo. But middle managers are closer than top managers to day-to-day operations, customers, frontline managers, and employees—so they know the problems and opportunities. They also have many creative ideas—often better than their bosses'. Middle managers play crucial roles in determining which entrepreneurial ideas are blocked and which are supported,[56] and how well they integrate with top management is crucial to formulating and implementing strategy.[57] Good middle managers provide the operating skills and practical problem solving that keep the company working.[58]

Frontline Managers

Frontline managers, or *operational managers,* are lower-level managers who supervise the operations of the organization. These managers often have titles such as *supervisor, team leader,* or *assistant manager.* They are directly involved with nonmanagement employees, implementing the specific plans developed with middle managers. This role is critical in the organization because operational managers are the link between management and non-management personnel. Your first management position probably will fit into this category.

Traditionally, frontline managers have been directed and controlled from above to make sure that they successfully implement operations in support of company strategy. But in leading companies, the role has expanded. Whereas the operational execution aspect of the role remains vital, in leading companies frontline managers are increasingly called on to be innovative and entrepreneurial, managing for growth and new business development.

Managers on the front line are crucial to creating and sustaining quality, innovation, and other drivers of financial performance.[59] In outstanding organizations, talented frontline managers are not only *allowed* to initiate new activities but are *expected* to by their top- and middle-level managers. And they are given freedom, incentives, and support to find ways to do so.[60]

Exhibit 1.2 elaborates on the changing aspects of different management levels. You learn about these aspects of management throughout this course.

Working Leaders with Broad Responsibilities

In small firms—and in those large companies that have adapted to the times—managers have strategic, tactical, *and* operational responsibilities. They are *complete* business-people; they have knowledge of all business functions, are accountable for results, and focus on serving customers both inside and outside their firms. All of this requires the ability to think strategically, translate strategies into specific objectives, coordinate resources, and do real work with lower-level people.

In short, today's best managers can do it all; they are working leaders.[61] They focus on relationships with other people and on achieving results. They don't just make decisions, give orders, wait for others to produce, and then evaluate results. They get dirty, do hard work themselves, solve problems, and produce value.

What does all of this mean in practice? How do managers spend their time—what do they actually do? A classic study of top executives found that they spend their time engaging

middle-level managers

Managers located in the middle layers of the organizational hierarchy, reporting to top-level executives.

frontline managers

Lower-level managers who supervise the operational activities of the organization.

EXHIBIT 1.2

Transformation of
Management Roles
and Activities

	Frontline Managers	Middle-Level Managers	Top-Level Managers
Changing Roles	From: Operational implementers To: Aggressive entrepreneurs	From: Administrative controllers To: Supportive coaches and mentors	From: Resource allocators To: Institutional leaders and strategic thinkers
Key Activities	1. Creating and pursuing new growth opportunities for the business.	1. Developing individuals and supporting their activities.	1. Establishing high performance standards.
	2. Attracting and developing resources.	2. Linking dispersed knowledge and skills across units.	2. Institutionalizing a set of norms and values to support cooperation and trust.
	3. Managing continuous improvement within the unit.	3. Managing the tension between short-term purpose and long-term ambition.	3. Creating an overarching corporate purpose and ambition.

SOURCE: Adapted from C. Bartlett and S. Goshall, "The Myth of the Generic Manager: New Personal Competencies for New Management Roles," *California Management Review* 40, no. 1, Fall 1997, pp. 92–116.

in 10 key activities or roles, falling into three categories: interpersonal, informational, and decisional.[62] Exhibit 1.3 summarizes these roles. Even though the study was done decades ago, it remains highly relevant as a description of what executives do. And even though the study focused on top executives, managers at all levels engage in all these activities. As you study the table, you might ask yourself, "Which of these activities do I enjoy most (and least)? Where do I excel (and not excel)? Which would I like to improve?" Whatever your answers, you will be learning more about these activities throughout this course.

Must-Have Management Skills

Performing management functions and roles, and achieving competitive advantage, are the cornerstones of a manager's job. However, understanding this fact does not ensure success. Managers need a variety of skills to do these things well. Skills are specific abilities that result from knowledge, information, practice, and aptitude. Although managers need many individual skills, which you will learn about throughout this textbook, there are three essential categories: technical skills, conceptual and decision skills, and interpersonal and communication skills.[63]

First-timers can underestimate the challenges of the many technical, human, and conceptual competencies required.[64] But when the key management functions are performed by managers who have these critical management skills, the result is high performance.

Technical

technical skill

The ability to perform a specialized task involving a particular method or process.

A **technical skill** is the ability to perform a specialized task that involves a certain method or process. Most people develop a set of technical skills to complete the activities that are part of their daily work lives. The technical skills you learn in school will provide you with the opportunity to get an entry-level position; they will also help you as a manager. For example, your accounting and finance courses will develop the technical skills you need to understand and manage the financial resources of an organization.

Decisional Roles	Informational Roles	Interpersonal Roles
Entrepreneur: Searching for new business opportunities and initiating new projects to create change.	*Monitor:* Seeking information to understand the organization and its environment; serving as the center of communication.	*Leader:* Staffing, developing, and motivating people.
Disturbance handler: Taking corrective action during crises and other conflicts.	*Disseminator:* Transmitting information from source to source, sometimes interpreting and integrating diverse perspectives.	*Liaison:* Maintaining a network of outside contacts that provide information and favors.
Resource allocator: Providing funding and other resources to units or people; includes making significant organizational decisions.	*Spokesperson:* Speaking on behalf of the organization about plans, policies, actions, and results.	*Figurehead:* Performing symbolic duties (for example, ceremonies) and serving other social and legal demands.
Negotiator: Engaging in negotiations with parties outside the organization as well as inside (for example, resource exchanges).	n/a	n/a

EXHIBIT 1.3
Managerial Roles: What Managers Do

SOURCE: Adapted from H. Mintzberg, *The Nature of Managerial Work* (New York: Harper & Row, 1973), pp. 92–93.

Conceptual and Decision

Conceptual and decision skills involve the ability to identify and resolve problems for the benefit of the organization and everyone concerned. Managers use these skills when they consider the overall objectives and strategy of the firm, the interactions among different parts of the organization, and the role of the business in its external environment. As you acquire greater responsibility, you must exercise your conceptual and decision skills with increasing frequency. Much of this book is devoted to enhancing your conceptual and decision skills, but experience also plays an important part in their development.

conceptual and decision skills

Skills pertaining to the ability to identify and resolve problems for the benefit of the organization and its members.

Interpersonal and Communication

Interpersonal and communication skills influence the manager's ability to work well with people. These skills are often called *people skills*. Managers spend the great majority of their time interacting with people,[65] and they must develop their abilities to lead, motivate, and communicate effectively with those around them.

The importance of these skills varies by managerial level. Technical skills are most important early in your career. Conceptual and decision skills become more important than technical skills as you rise higher in the company. But interpersonal skills such as communicating effectively with customers and being a good team player are important throughout your career, at every level of management.

An example of a manager with these skills is Mark Bertolini, chief executive of Aetna, which provides health insurance and related services. As a young man doing assembly work for Ford Motor Company, Bertolini acquired an interest in union management, so he decided to study business and earned a degree in accounting and then a master's degree in finance. Those two specialties involve valuable technical skills, but Bertolini rose through the management ranks at a series of insurance companies because he also has a passion for people. He recently told an interviewer that he is constantly engaged in learning about people and forging networks with them. He sees tapping into those networks and figuring out how to lead people as the kinds of skills that allow managers to get results.

interpersonal and communication skills

People skills; the ability to lead, motivate, and communicate effectively with others.

At Aetna, Bertolini is not only an expert at insurance matters, but also a promoter of employee diversity. Furthermore, challenges in his personal life—he survived a spinal cord injury and donated a kidney to his son—have placed him in a position to empathize with others, including clients who use his company's services.[66]

You and Your Career

LO 6

At the beginning of your career, your contribution to your employer depends on your own performance; that's all you're responsible for. But on becoming a manager, you are responsible for a whole group. To use an orchestra analogy, instead of playing an instrument, you're a conductor, coordinating others' efforts.[67] The challenge is much greater than most first-time managers expect it to be.

Throughout your career, you'll need to lead teams effectively as well as influence people over whom you have no authority; thus the human skills are especially important. Businesspeople often talk about **emotional intelligence,**[68] or EQ—the skills of understanding yourself (including strengths and limitations), managing yourself (dealing with emotions, making good decisions, seeking and using feedback, exercising self-control), and dealing effectively with others (listening, showing empathy, motivating, leading, and so on). The common phrase "emotional intelligence" is controversial.[69] For instance, you should *not* consider it as a type of intelligence but as a set of skills that you can learn and develop—but these skills do matter in many ways, as you will learn in future chapters.

© Dmytro Sidelnikov/Alamy

emotional intelligence

The skills of understanding yourself, managing yourself, and dealing effectively with others.

A common complaint about leaders, especially newly promoted ones who had been outstanding individual performers, is that they lack what is perhaps the most fundamental of EQ skills: empathy. The issue is not lack of ability to change (you can), but the lack of motivation to change.[70] William George, former chair and CEO of Medtronic, says some people can go a long way in their careers based on sheer determination and aggressiveness, but personal development—including EQ—ultimately becomes essential.[71] Executives who score low on EQ are less likely to be rated as excellent on their performance reviews, and their divisions tend not to perform as well.[72] A vice president at an aerospace company underwent a program to improve her EQ after colleagues kept complaining that she was overly demanding and inclined to put people down. An assessment found that she lacked social awareness. The vice president eventually learned to respond after calming herself as well as to explore colleagues' ideas rather than demeaning them. Before long, her colleagues began to appreciate the change, and her career took a more successful path.[73]

What should you do to forge a successful, gratifying career? You are well advised to be both a specialist and a generalist, to be self-reliant and connected, to actively manage your relationship with your organization, and to know what is required not only to survive but also to thrive in today's world.

Be Both a Specialist and a Generalist

If you think your career will be as a specialist, think again. Chances are, you will not want to stay forever in strictly technical jobs with no managerial responsibilities. Accountants are promoted to accounting department heads and team leaders, sales representatives become sales managers, writers become editors, and nurses become nursing directors. As your responsibilities increase, you must deal with more people, understand more about other aspects of the organization, and make bigger and more complex decisions. Beginning to learn now about these managerial challenges will yield benefits sooner than you think.

EXHIBIT 1.4
Career Advice from the Experts

Escape the industry-specific silo.	*Develop a skill set that transcends a single function, industry, or career path.*
Know what you know.	*And find ways to apply it.*
Keep learning throughout your life.	*No one can rest on what they already know.*
Pay attention.	*Seriously evaluate where you are and where you want to be.*
Never compromise your integrity.	*Succumbing to temptations can destroy a career.*
Take a long view.	*Look at your career as a whole, and stay true to yourself.*
Prevent obsolescence.	*Job security comes from transportable skills.*
Zig-zag strategically.	*Job changing can be high-risk but not if you have measurable accomplishments.*
Be willing to take on tough jobs.	*Continually challenge yourself.*

SOURCE: Joyce Lain Kennedy, "Best Career Advice for 2013," *Chicago Tribune*, December 23, 2012, http://www.chicagotribune.com; Lorraine Sanders, "Hilary Novelle Hahn's Zig-Zag Career Guide," *Fast Company*, November 13, 2012, http://www.fastcompany.com; Dan Kadlec, "Graduation Day Advice: 5 Steps to a Great Career," *Time*, May 9, 2012, http://business.time.com.

So it will help if you can become both a specialist and a generalist.[74] Seek to become a *specialist:* you should be an expert in something useful. This will give you specific skills that help you provide concrete, identifiable value to your organization and to customers. And over time, you should learn to be a *generalist,* knowing enough about a variety of disciplines so that you can think strategically and work with different perspectives. Exhibit 1.4 gives you career advice from experts.

Be Self-Reliant

To be self-reliant means to take full responsibility for yourself and your actions. You cannot count on your boss or your company to take care of you. A useful metaphor is to think of yourself as a business, with you as president and sole employee.

To be self-reliant, find new ways to make your overall performance better. Take responsibility for change; be an innovator.[75] Don't just do your work and wait for orders; look for opportunities to contribute in new ways, to develop new products and processes, and to generate constructive change that strengthens the company and benefits customers and colleagues. Success requires more than talent; you also have to be willing to work hard. The elite, world-class performers in many fields (including managers and leaders) reach the top tier only after 10 years or more of hard work and skillful coaching.[76] The key is to engage in consistent practice, looking at the results and identifying where to improve.

> Don't just do your work and wait for orders; look for opportunities to contribute in new ways.

It's easy to see how this works for violinists or basketball players, but what about business managers? The answer is to focus on getting better results each time you try any business task, whether it's writing a report, chairing a meeting, or interpreting a financial statement. To know whether you're getting better, make a point of asking for feedback from customers, colleagues, and bosses.

To develop your full potential, assess yourself, including your interests, aptitudes, and personal character strengths. Think about it, ask others who know you well, conduct a formal exercise in which you learn what others consider to be your "best self,"[77] and use the resources of recent advances in psychology to identify your signature strengths.[78] Consider the professional image and reputation you would like to develop,[79] and continue building your capabilities. Consider the suggestions found throughout this book, and your courses, as you pursue these objectives.

Bottom Line

If you want people who see your LinkedIn profile to think of you as a future manager, what should *not* be on the profile?

social capital

Goodwill stemming from your social relationships; a competitive advantage in the form of relationships with other people and the image other people have of you.

Connect with People

Being connected means having many good working relationships and interpersonal contacts and being a team player with strong interpersonal skills. For example, those who want to become partners in professional service organizations such as social media marketing, accounting, advertising, and consulting firms strive constantly to build a network of contacts. Their connectedness goal is to work not only with multiple clients but also with a half dozen or more senior partners, including several from outside their home offices and some from outside their country. A study of new auditors showed that social relationships improved newcomers' knowledge of the organization and their jobs, their social integration into the firm, and their commitment to the organization.[80] Networks of diverse individuals can make huge contributions to your professional development no matter what your career—including if you hope to be inducted into the Major League Baseball Hall of Fame on the first ballot.[81]

Social capital is the goodwill stemming from your social relationships, and you can mobilize it on your behalf. It aids career success, compensation, employment, team effectiveness, successful entrepreneurship, and relationships with suppliers and other outsiders.[82] Today much of that social capital can be tapped online at social networking websites. Besides the purely social sites such as Facebook, some of these sites are aimed at helping people tap business networks. For example, LinkedIn has more than 300 million registered users worldwide, with revenue from premium subscriptions of $95.5 million.[83]

States *Fortune,* "Facebook is for fun. . . . If you're serious about managing your career, the only social site that really matters is LinkedIn."[84]

All business is a function of human relationships.[85] Building competitive advantage depends not only on you but on other people. Management is personal. Commercial dealings are personal. Purchase decisions, repurchase decisions, and contracts all hinge on relationships. Even the biggest business deals—takeovers—are intensely personal and emotional. Without good work relationships, you are an outsider, not an effective manager and leader.

Actively Manage Your Relationship with Your Organization

Many of the previous comments suggest the importance of taking responsibility for your own actions and your own career. Unless you are self-employed and your own boss, one way to do this is to think about the nature of the relationship between you and your employer. Exhibit 1.5 shows two possible relationships—and you have some control over which relationship you will be in.

Relationship #1 is one in which you view yourself as an employee and passively expect your employer to tell you what to do and give you pay and benefits. Your employer is in charge, and you are a passive recipient of its actions. Your contributions are likely to be adequate but minimal—you won't make the added contributions that strengthen your organization, and if all organizational members take this perspective, the organization is not likely to be strong for the long run. Personally, you may lose your job, or keep your job in a declining organization, or receive few positive benefits from working there and either quit or become cynical and unhappy in your work.

In contrast, relationship #2 is a two-way relationship in which you and your organization both benefit from one another. The mind-set is different: Instead of doing what you are

EXHIBIT 1.5
Two Relationships: Which Will You Choose?

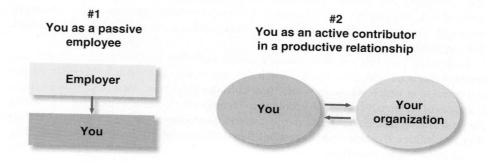

told, you think about how you can contribute—and you act accordingly. To the extent that your organization values your contributions, you are likely to benefit in return by receiving full and fair rewards, support for further personal development, and a more gratifying work environment. If you think in broad terms about how you can help your company, and if others think like this as well, there is likely to be continuous improvement in the company's ability to innovate, cut costs, and deliver quality products quickly to an expanding customer base. As the company's bottom line strengthens, benefits accrue to shareholders as well as to you and other employees.

What contributions can you make? You can do your basic work. But you can, and should, go further. You can also figure out new ways to add value—by thinking of and implementing new ideas that improve processes and results. You can do this using your technical knowledge and skills, as in developing a better information system, accounting technique, or sales strategy.

You also can contribute with your conceptual and human skills and your managerial actions (see Exhibit 1.6). You can execute the essential management functions and deliver competitive advantage. You can deliver strategic value (Part 2 of this book). You can take actions that help build a more dynamic organization (Part 3). You can mobilize people to contribute to their fullest potential (Part 4). And you can learn and change—and help your colleagues and company learn and change—to adapt to changing realities and forge a successful future (Part 5).

Survive and Thrive

Now more than ever, you will be accountable for your actions and for results. In the past, people at many companies could show up, do an OK job, get a decent evaluation, and get a raise equal to the cost of living and maybe higher. Today, managers must do more, better. Eminent management scholar Peter Drucker, in considering what makes managers effective, noted that some are charismatic whereas some are not, and some are visionary whereas others are more numbers-oriented.[86] But successful executives do share some common practices:

- They ask "What needs to be done?" not just "What do I want to do?"
- They write an action plan. They don't just think, they do, based on a sound, ethical plan.
- They take responsibility for decisions. This requires checking up, revisiting, and changing if necessary.

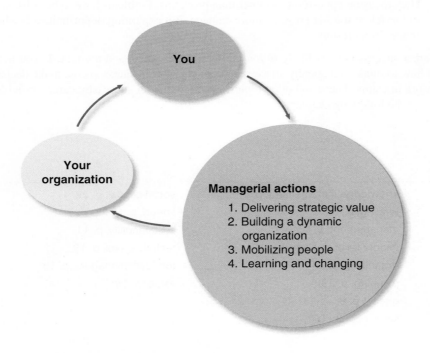

EXHIBIT 1.6
Managerial Action Is Your
Opportunity to Contribute

Management in Action

WORKING FOR BEZOS AT AMAZON

To be a manager at Amazon, you must thrive under the leadership of an intensely driven CEO. Like many successful company founders, Jeff Bezos is supremely committed to his company and his customers. Nadia Shouraboura, a former Amazon vice president, recalled attending meetings in which Bezos seemed less interested in the discussion than in reading e-mail from customers. When he received a complaint, he could be relentless about fixing it. Eventually, Shouraboura realized that, for Bezos, fixing the problem behind one complaint would improve the company's processes for all its customers.

To succeed, Amazon managers have to get used to defining problems in terms of customer needs and benefits. For example, the Amazon Prime service grew out of efforts to improve customers' ordering experience. Subscribers to Amazon Prime pay to get special offers and free shipping (which then makes Amazon their first and last stop for shopping). Anthony Bay, an Amazon vice president, has said that when the company was planning Amazon Prime, "Bezos just kept asking everyone questions like: 'How will this serve the customer?'" Bezos pressed for details about customer benefits and forecasts of new customers. Whether your job involves acquiring Kiva Systems, whose robot technology makes warehouses more efficient, or helping craft Amazon's long-term strategy to serve new customers in the Chinese online retail market,[87] innovations aim to improve the customer experience.

Amazon managers also must appreciate that the company's low-price strategy requires minimizing every expense. The company lacks some perks workers have come to expect in the high-tech industry, such as free meals and fancy workspaces. Even pay scales are lower than at other e-commerce businesses, and there are no bonuses. The primary financial reward comes from owning Amazon stock, and managers have to find other ways to motivate employees. For many, the lure is the chance to be part of an exciting, innovative enterprise.

Innovation would be a constant consideration if you worked as an Amazon manager. Bezos says, "We think of ourselves as explorers." The goal is less about beating the competition, and more about discovering new ways to please customers and recognizing or creating the next big thing.[88]

- As an early career employee at Amazon, what steps could you take to get noticed and position yourself for eventual promotion to frontline manager?
- How could you manage your career to be a successful middle manager at Amazon?

- They focus on opportunities rather than problems. Problems have to be solved, and problem solving prevents more damage. But exploiting opportunities is what creates great results.

Career success is most likely if you are flexible, creative, and motivated. You need to learn how to think strategically, discern and convey your business vision, make decisions, and work in teams. These and other topics, essential to your successful career, provide the focus for the following chapters.

KEY TERMS

RETAINING WHAT YOU LEARNED

You learned that change is the only constant for managers in today's business world. You also learned the concept that high-performance managers seek to deliver superior value to customers by providing high-quality, innovative services or products in a timely, cost-effective, and sustainable manner. The fundamental functions and activities of management are just as important as they were "back in the day." Depending on your organizational level, you'll be expected to engage in certain roles and master different skills. Your career, and the degree to which you succeed, is primarily in your hands.

LO 1 Summarize the major challenges of managing in the new competitive landscape.

- In business, there is no alternative to managing well. The best managers succeed by focusing on the fundamentals and knowing what's important.
- The goal of this book is to help you become an effective, high-performance manager.
- Managers today must deal with dynamic forces that create greater change than ever before, including: globalization, technological change (including the development and applications of the Internet), knowledge management, and collaboration across organizational boundaries.

LO 2 Describe the sources of competitive advantage for a company.

- Because business is a competitive arena, you need to deliver value to customers in ways that are superior to what your competitors do.
- Competitive advantages result from innovation, quality, service, speed, cost competitiveness, and sustainability.

LO 3 Explain how the functions of management are evolving in today's business environment.

- Despite massive change, management retains certain foundations that will not disappear.
- The primary functions of management are planning, organizing, leading, and controlling.
- Planning is analyzing a situation, determining the goals that will be pursued, and deciding in advance the actions needed to pursue these goals.
- Organizing is assembling the resources needed to complete the job and coordinating employees and tasks for maximum success.
- Leading is motivating people and stimulating high performance. Controlling is monitoring the progress of the organization or the work unit toward goals and then taking corrective action, as necessary.
- In today's business environment, these functions more broadly require creating strategic value, building a dynamic organization, mobilizing people, and learning and changing.

LO 4 Compare how the nature of management varies at different organizational levels.

- Top-level, strategic managers are the senior executives responsible for the organization's overall management.
- Middle-level, tactical managers translate general goals and plans into more specific objectives and activities.
- Frontline, operational managers are lower-level managers who supervise operations.
- Today, managers at all levels must perform a variety of interpersonal, informational, and decisional roles.
- Even at the operational level, the best managers think strategically and operate like complete businesspeople.

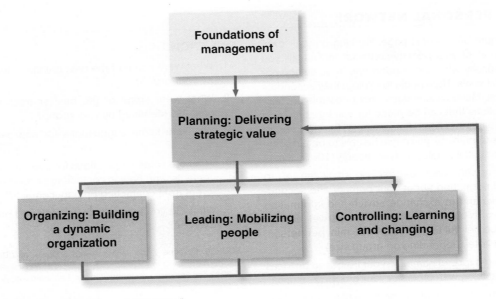

The Management Process (see page 1)

LO 5   Define the skills you need to be an effective manager.

- To execute management functions successfully, managers need technical skills, conceptual and decision skills, and interpersonal and communication skills.
- A technical skill is the ability to perform a specialized task involving certain methods or processes.
- Conceptual and decision skills help the manager recognize complex and dynamic issues, analyze the factors that influence those issues or problems, and make appropriate decisions.
- Interpersonal and communication skills enable the manager to interact and work well with people.
- As you rise to higher organizational levels, technical skills tend to become less important and conceptual skills become more important, whereas interpersonal and communication skills remain extremely important at every level.

LO 6   Understand the principles that will help you manage your career.

- You are more likely to succeed in your career if you become both a specialist and a generalist. You should be self-reliant but also connected.
- You should actively manage your relationship with your organization and continuously improve your skills so you can perform in the ways demanded in the changing work environment.

DISCUSSION QUESTIONS

1. Identify and describe a great manager. What makes him or her stand out from the crowd?
2. Have you ever seen or worked for an ineffective manager? Describe the causes and the consequences of the ineffectiveness.
3. Describe in as much detail as possible how the Internet and globalization affect your daily life.
4. Identify some examples of how different organizations collaborate across boundaries.
5. Name a great organization. How do you think management contributes to making it great?
6. Name an ineffective organization. What can management do to improve it?
7. Give examples you have seen of firms that are outstanding and weak on each of the six pillars of competitive advantage. Why do you choose the firms you do?
8. Describe your use of the four management functions in the management of your daily life.
9. Discuss the importance of technical, conceptual, and interpersonal skills at school and in jobs you have held.
10. What are your strengths and weaknesses as you contemplate your career? How do they correlate with the skills and behaviors identified in the chapter?
11. Devise a plan for developing yourself and making yourself attractive to potential employers. How would you go about improving your managerial skills?
12. Consider the managers and companies discussed in the chapter. Have they been in the news lately, and what is the latest? If their image, performance, or fortunes have gone up or down, what has changed to affect how they have fared?

EXPERIENTIAL EXERCISES

1.1   YOUR PERSONAL NETWORK

1. See the figure on the next page. Working on your own, write down all of your primary contacts—individuals you know personally who can support you in attaining your professional goals. Then begin to explore their secondary connections. Make assumptions about possible secondary connections that can be made for you by contacting your primary connections. For example, through one of your teachers (primary), you might be able to obtain some names of potential employers (secondary). (10–15 min.)
2. Then meet with your partner or small group to exchange information about your primary and secondary networks and to exchange advice and information on how best to use these connections as well as how you could be helpful to them. (about 5 min. per person; 10–30 min. total, depending on group size)
3. Add names or types of names to your list based on ideas you get by talking with others in your group. (2–5 min.)
4. Discuss with your large group or class, using the following discussion questions. (10 min.)

QUESTIONS

1. What were some of the best primary sources identified by your group?
2. What were some of the best sources for secondary contacts identified by your group?
3. What are some suggestions for approaching primary contacts?
4. What are some suggestions for approaching secondary contacts, and how is contacting secondary sources different from contacting primary contacts?
5. What did you learn about yourself and others from this exercise?

SOURCE: Suzanne C. de Janasz, Karen O'Dowd, and Beth Z. Schneider, *Interpersonal Skills in Organizations* (New York: McGraw-Hill, 2002), p. 211. © 2002 The McGraw-Hill Companies, Inc. Reprinted with permission.

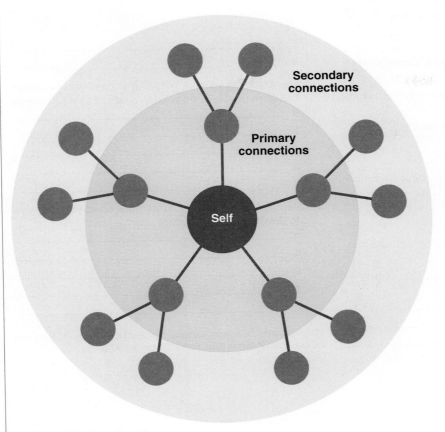

Primary and Secondary Connections

SOURCE: Excerpted from Lawrence R. Jauch, Arthur G. Bedeian, Sally A. Coltrin, and William F. Glueck, *The Managerial Experience: Cases, Exercises, and Readings,* 5th ed. © 1989 South-Western, a part of Cengage Learning, Inc.

1.2   ARE YOU AN EFFECTIVE MANAGER?

OBJECTIVES

1. To recognize what behaviors *contribute* to being a successful manager.
2. To develop a ranking of critical behaviors that you personally believe are important for becoming an effective manager.

INSTRUCTIONS

1. Following is a partial list of behaviors in which managers may engage. Rank these items in terms of their importance for effective performance as a manager. Put a 1 next to the item that you think is most important, 2 for the next most important, down to 10 for the least important.

2. Bring your rankings to class. Be prepared to justify your results and rationale. If you can add any behaviors to this list that might lead to success or greater management effectiveness, write them in.

Managerial Behaviors Worksheet

_____ Collaborates with people from different parts of the organization.

_____ Looks for ways to incorporate technology into the operation.

_____ Ensures that services/products are of a high quality and delivered on time.

_____ Keeps costs down and looks for ways to be more efficient.

_____ Makes decisions to help achieve the goals of the organization.

_____ Is organized and effectively allocates resources.

_____ Motivates others to perform at a high level.

_____ Makes sure goals are met and implements changes when necessary.

_____ Exhibits good interpersonal and communication skills.

_____ Is skilled at identifying and resolving problems.

SOURCE: Adapted from Lawrence R. Jauch, Arthur G. Bedeian, Sally A. Coltrin, and William F. Glueck, *The Managerial Experience: Cases, Exercises, and Readings,* 5th ed. © 1989 South-Western, a part of Cengage Learning, Inc.

1.3 CAREER SKILLS DEVELOPMENT

OBJECTIVES

1. To develop an understanding of your career-related strengths.

2. To identify career-related skills and behaviors requiring development.

3. To increase confidence in your marketability.

INSTRUCTIONS

Read the instructions for each activity, think about them, and then provide your response.

Career Development Worksheet

Think about a part- or full-time job, or a volunteer role that you've held.

1. Describe activities and skills at which you excelled and which helped you succeed:

   a. _____

   b. _____

   c. _____

   d. _____

   e. _____

2. Identify activities and skills that you wanted to master but were unable to do so due to lack of training or time:

   a. _____

   b. _____

   c. _____

   d. _____

   e. _____

3. Referring to your list in #2, what steps could you take now to develop these important activities and skills:

   a. _____

   b. _____

   c. _____

   d. _____

   e. _____

SOURCE: Adapted from Judith R. Gordon, *Diagnostic Approach to Organizational Behavior* (Upper Saddle River: Person Education; 1983).

CONCLUDING CASE

A NEW MANAGER AT USA HOSPITAL SUPPLY

As Charlie Greer drove to work, he smiled, recalling the meeting at the end of the previous day. Inez Rodriguez, the owner of the company where he worked, USA Hospital Supply, had summoned him to her office, where she warmly shook his hand and exclaimed, "Congratulations!" As they settled into chairs, Inez reviewed the conversation she'd had with the company's board of directors that morning: USA Hospital had been growing steadily for the past 10 years despite the economy's ups and downs. As the company's founder, Inez had always been an insightful and enthusiastic leader of the five-person sales team, but the level of activity was becoming too much of a distraction. Inez needed to think about the long-range vision of the company, so she needed a leader who could focus on sales. She had interviewed several candidates outside the firm as well as Charlie and two of the other sales representatives. In the end, Inez told Charlie, the choice was obvious: Charlie was far and away the best sales rep on the team, he had extensive knowledge of the company's product mix, and if anyone could help the sales team achieve its goals, it was Charlie. She offered him the job as the company's first sales manager. He eagerly accepted. When he left work that evening, his head was full of ideas, and his heart was full of confidence.

Now Charlie pulled into the office park where USA Hospital Supply was located and easily found a parking space in the lot outside the one-story office and warehouse facility. As usual, he was one of the first employees to arrive. By habit, he strode toward his cubicle, but after a second, he recalled that Inez had arranged for the small firm's accountant and computer systems manager to share an office so he could have an office of his own. Charlie entered his new domain and settled into the swivel chair behind his desk.

At that instant, the eagerness to enjoy his new status and responsibility began to give way to nervousness. Charlie realized that although he knew a lot about selling supplies to hospitals and doctor's offices, he had never given much thought to managing. Obviously, he mused, his job was to see that his department met or exceeded its sales targets. But how?

Charlie started his computer and then opened his e-mail and his word-processing software, intending to get some ideas into writing. He typed out a list of the four sales reps: Cindy, Paula, John, and Doreen. Cindy handled the large corporate accounts, Paula covered the East Coast, John called on accounts in the South, and Doreen handled the Midwest. Until today, Charlie had been building a fast-growing territory west of the Mississippi. Now who was going to do that? Charlie was tempted to keep that work for himself; he knew he could build a base of loyal clients better than anyone else. Still, he wondered whether he could excel as a manager and as a sales rep at the same time.

While he was pondering that challenge, Cindy walked past the office door and, without stopping, politely called,

"Congratulations!" through the doorway. Charlie's heart sank as he realized that Cindy had also wanted this job. They had always enjoyed a friendly rivalry as talented sales-people; now what would happen to the fun of being team members? It was easier to think about the other representa-tives at the moment. Charlie scanned his e-mail inbox and saw status reports from John and Doreen, both of them out of the office to call on clients. What about Paula? Charlie wasn't quite sure he remembered her plans for this week. Obviously he needed to catch up on what everyone was doing, and that gave him a new idea. He could build on his strengths by traveling with each of the sales reps and coach-ing them. That way, he could show them all his proven meth-ods for closing a sale, and they could learn to sell as well as he did. Charlie thought, "That's what a good manager does: shows employees how to do the job right." He was starting to feel less nervous as he began to compose an e-mail to Paula.

DISCUSSION QUESTIONS

1. How will Charlie's approach to quality and service affect his company's performance?

2. Which of the basic functions of management has Charlie considered? How well is he preparing to carry out these functions?

3. Which management skills does Charlie have? In what areas do you think he has the greatest need to develop skills? How can he actively manage his development as a manager?

The Evolution of Management

For thousands of years, managers have wrestled with the same issues and problems confronting executives today. Around 1100 BC, the Chinese practiced the four management functions—planning, organizing, leading, and controlling—discussed in Chapter 1. Between 400 BC and 350 BC, the Greeks recognized management as a separate art and advocated a scientific approach to work. The Romans decentralized the management of their vast empire before the birth of Christ. During medieval times, the Venetians standardized production through the use of an assembly line, building warehouses and using an inventory system to monitor the contents.[1]

But throughout history, most managers operated strictly on a trial-and-error basis. The challenges of the Industrial Revolution changed that. Management emerged as a formal discipline at the turn of the century. The first university programs to offer management and business education, the Wharton School at the University of Pennsylvania and the Amos Tuck School at Dartmouth, were founded in the late 19th century. By 1914, 25 business schools existed.[2]

Thus, the management profession as we know it today is relatively new. This appendix explores the roots of modern management theory. Understanding the origins of management thought will help you grasp the underlying contexts of the ideas and concepts presented in the chapters ahead.

Although this appendix is titled "The Evolution of Management," it might be more appropriately called "The Revolutions of Management" because it documents the wide swings in management approaches over the past 100 years. Out of the great variety of ideas about how to improve management, parts of each approach have survived and been incorporated into modern perspectives on management. Thus, the legacy of past efforts, triumphs, and failures has become our guide to future management practice.

EARLY MANAGEMENT CONCEPTS AND INFLUENCES

Communication and transportation constraints hindered the growth of earlier businesses. Therefore, improvements in management techniques did not substantially improve performance. However, the Industrial Revolution changed that. As companies grew and became more complex, minor improvements in management tactics produced impressive increases in production quantity and quality.[3]

The emergence of **economies of scale**—reductions in the average cost of a unit of production as the total volume produced increases—drove managers to strive for further growth. The opportunities for mass production created by the Industrial Revolution spawned intense and systematic thought about management problems and issues—particularly efficiency, production processes, and cost savings.[4]

Exhibit A.1 provides a time line depicting the evolution of management thought through the decades. This historical perspective is divided into two major sections: classical approaches and contemporary approaches. Many of these approaches overlapped as they developed, and they often had a significant impact on one another. Some approaches were a direct reaction to the perceived deficiencies of previous approaches. Others developed as the needs and issues confronting managers changed over the years. All the approaches attempted to explain the real issues facing managers and provide them with tools to solve future problems.

Exhibit A.1 will reinforce your understanding of the key relationships among the approaches and place each perspective in its historical context.

CLASSICAL APPROACHES

The classical period extended from the mid-19th century through the early 1950s. The major approaches that emerged during this period were systematic management,

EXHIBIT A.1
The Evolution of Management Thought

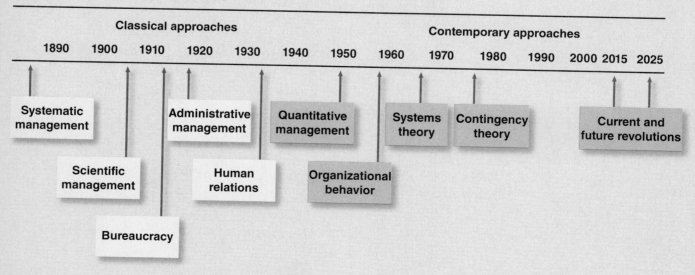

scientific management, administrative management, human relations, and bureaucracy.

Systematic Management

During the 19th century, growth in U.S. business centered on manufacturing.[5] Early writers such as Adam Smith believed the management of these firms was chaotic, and their ideas helped to systematize it. Most organizational tasks were subdivided and performed by specialized labor. However, poor coordination caused frequent problems and breakdowns of the manufacturing process.

The **systematic management** approach attempted to build specific procedures and processes into operations to ensure coordination of effort. Systematic management emphasized economical operations, adequate staffing, maintenance of inventories to meet consumer demand, and organizational control. These goals were achieved through

- Careful definition of duties and responsibilities.
- Standardized techniques for performing these duties.
- Specific means of gathering, handling, transmitting, and analyzing information.
- Cost accounting, wage, and production control systems to facilitate internal coordination and communications.

An Early Labor Contract

The following rules, taken from the records of Cocheco Company, were typical of labor contract provisions in the 1850s.

1. The hours of work shall be from sunrise to sunset, from the 21st of March to the 20th of September inclusively; and from sunrise until eight o'clock, p.m., during the remainder of the year. One hour shall be allowed for dinner, and half an hour for breakfast during the first mentioned six months; and one hour for dinner during the other half of the year; on Saturdays, the mill shall be stopped one hour before sunset, for the purpose of cleaning the machinery.

2. Every hand coming to work a quarter of an hour after the mill has been started shall be docked a quarter of a day; and every hand absenting him or herself, without absolute necessity, shall be docked in a sum double the amount of the wages such hand shall have earned during the time of such absence. No more than one hand is allowed to leave any one of the rooms at the same time—a quarter of a day shall be deducted for every breach of this rule.

3. No smoking or spiritous liquors shall be allowed in the factory under any pretense whatsoever. It is also forbidden to carry into the factory, nuts, fruits, etc. books, or papers during the hours of work.

SOURCE: W. Sullivan, "The Industrial Revolution and the Factory Operative in Pennsylvania," *The Pennsylvania Magazine of History and Biography* 78 (1954), pp. 478–79.

Systematic management emphasized internal operations because managers were concerned primarily with meeting the explosive growth in demand brought about by the Industrial Revolution. In addition, managers were free to focus on internal issues of efficiency, in part because the government did not constrain business practices significantly. Finally, labor was poorly organized. As a result, many managers were oriented more toward things than toward people.

Systematic management did not address all the issues 19th-century managers faced, but it tried to raise managers' awareness about the most pressing concerns of their job.

Scientific Management

Systematic management failed to lead to widespread production efficiency. This shortcoming became apparent to a young engineer named Frederick Taylor, who was hired by Midvale Steel Company in 1878. Taylor discovered that production and pay were poor, inefficiency and waste were prevalent, and most companies had tremendous unused potential. He concluded that management decisions were unsystematic and that no research to determine the best means of production existed.

In response, Taylor introduced a second approach to management, known as **scientific management**.[6] This approach advocated the application of scientific methods to analyze work and to determine how to complete production tasks efficiently. For example, U.S. Steel's contract with the United Steel Workers of America specified that sand shovelers should move 12.5 shovelfuls per minute; shovelfuls should average 15 pounds of river sand composed of 5.5 percent moisture.[7]

Taylor identified four principles of scientific management:

1. Management should develop a precise, scientific approach for each element of one's work to replace general guidelines.

2. Management should scientifically select, train, teach, and develop each worker so that the right person has the right job.

3. Management should cooperate with workers to ensure that jobs match plans and principles.

4. Management should ensure an appropriate division of work and responsibility between managers and workers.

To implement this approach, Taylor used techniques such as time-and-motion studies. With this technique, a task was divided into its basic movements, and different motions were timed to determine the most efficient way to complete the task.

After the "one best way" to perform the job was identified, Taylor stressed the importance of hiring and training the proper worker to do that job. Taylor advocated the standardization of tools, the use of instruction cards to help workers, and breaks to eliminate fatigue.

Another key element of Taylor's approach was the use of the differential piecerate system. Taylor assumed workers were motivated by receiving money. Therefore, he implemented a pay system in which workers were paid additional

Frederick Taylor (left) and Dr. Lillian Gilbreth (right) were early experts in management efficiency.

© Corbis

© Underwood/Corbis

Scientific Management and the Model T

At the turn of the century, automobiles were a luxury that only the wealthy could afford. They were assembled by craftspeople who put an entire car together at one spot on the factory floor. These workers were not specialized, and Henry Ford believed they wasted time and energy bringing the needed parts to the car. Ford took a revolutionary approach to automobile manufacturing by using scientific management principles.

After much study, machines and workers in Ford's new factory were placed in sequence so that an automobile could be assembled without interruption along a moving production line. Mechanical energy and a conveyor belt were used to take the work to the workers.

The manufacture of parts likewise was revolutionized. For example, formerly it had taken one worker 20 minutes to assemble a flywheel magneto. By splitting the job into 29 operations, putting the product on a mechanical conveyor, and changing the height of the conveyor, Ford cut production time to 5 minutes.

By 1914, chassis assembly time had been trimmed from almost 13 hours to 1½ hours. The new methods of production required complete standardization, new machines, and an adaptable labor force. Costs dropped significantly, the Model T became the first car accessible to the majority of Americans, and Ford dominated the industry for many years.

SOURCE: H. Kroos and C. Gilbert, *The Principles of Scientific Management* (New York: Harper & Row, 1911).

wages when they exceeded a standard level of output for each job. Taylor concluded that both workers and management would benefit from such an approach.

Scientific management principles were widely embraced. Other proponents, including Henry Gantt and Frank and Lillian Gilbreth, introduced many refinements and techniques for applying scientific management on the factory floor. One of the most famous examples of the application of scientific management is the factory Henry Ford built to produce the Model T.[8]

The legacy of Taylor's scientific management approach is broad and pervasive. Most important, productivity and efficiency in manufacturing improved dramatically. The concepts of scientific methods and research were introduced to manufacturing. The piecerate system gained wide acceptance because it more closely aligned effort and reward. Taylor also emphasized the need for cooperation between management and workers. And the concept of a management specialist gained prominence.

Despite these gains, not everyone was convinced that scientific management was the best solution to all business problems. First, critics claimed that Taylor ignored many job-related social and psychological factors by emphasizing only money as a worker incentive. Second, production tasks were reduced to a set of routine, machinelike procedures that led to boredom, apathy, and quality control problems. Third, unions strongly opposed scientific management techniques because they believed management might abuse its power to set the standards and the piecerates, thus exploiting workers and diminishing their importance. Finally, although scientific management resulted in intense scrutiny of the internal efficiency of organizations, it did not help managers deal with broader external issues such as competitors and government regulations, especially at the senior management level.

Administrative Management

The **administrative management** approach emphasized the perspective of senior managers within the organization and argued that management was a profession and could be taught.

An explicit and broad framework for administrative management emerged in 1916, when Henri Fayol, a French mining engineer and executive, published a book summarizing his management experiences. Fayol identified five functions and 14 principles of management. The five functions, which are very similar to the four functions discussed in Chapter 1, are planning, organizing, commanding, coordinating, and controlling. Exhibit A.2 lists and defines the 14 principles. Although some critics claim Fayol treated the principles as universal truths for management, he actually wanted them applied flexibly.[9]

A host of other executives contributed to the administrative management literature. These writers discussed a broad spectrum of management topics, including the social responsibilities of management, the philosophy of management, clarification of business terms and concepts, and organizational principles. Chester Barnard's and Mary Parker Follet's contributions have become classic works in this area.[10]

Barnard, former president of New Jersey Bell Telephone Company, published his landmark book *The Functions of the Executive* in 1938. He outlined the role of the senior executive: formulating the purpose of the organization, hiring key individuals, and maintaining organizational communications.[11] Mary Parker Follet's 1942 book *Dynamic Organization* extended Barnard's work by emphasizing the continually changing situations that managers face.[12] Two of her key contributions—the notion that managers desire flexibility and the differences between motivating groups and individuals—laid the groundwork for the modern contingency approach discussed later in the chapter.

All the writings in the administrative management area emphasize management as a profession along with fields such as law and medicine. In addition, these authors offered many recommendations based on their personal experiences, which often included managing large corporations. Although these perspectives and recommendations were considered sound, critics noted that they might not work in all settings. Different types of personnel, industry conditions, and technologies may affect the appropriateness of these principles.

EXHIBIT A.2
Fayol's 14 Principles of Management

1. *Division of work*—divide work into specialized tasks and assign responsibilities to specific individuals.

2. *Authority*—delegate authority along with responsibility.

3. *Discipline*—make expectations clear and punish violations.

4. *Unity of command*—each employee should be assigned to only one supervisor.

5. *Unity of direction*—employees' efforts should be focused on achieving organizational objectives.

6. *Subordination of individual interest to the general interest*—the general interest must predominate.

7. *Remuneration*—systematically reward efforts that support the organization's direction.

8. *Centralization*—determine the relative importance of superior and subordinate roles.

9. *Scalar chain*—keep communications within the chain of command.

10. *Order*—order jobs and material so they support the organization's direction.

11. *Equity*—fair discipline and order enhance employee commitment.

12. *Stability and tenure of personnel*—promote employee loyalty and longevity.

13. *Initiative*—encourage employees to act on their own in support of the organization's direction.

14. *Esprit de corps*—promote a unity of interests between employees and management.

Human Relations

A fourth approach to management, **human relations,** developed during the 1930s. This approach aimed at understanding how psychological and social processes interact with the work situation to influence performance. Human relations was the first major approach to emphasize informal work relationships and worker satisfaction.

This approach owes much to other major schools of thought. For example, many of the ideas of the Gilbreths (scientific management) and Barnard and Follet (administrative management) influenced the development of human relations from 1930 to 1955. In fact, human relations emerged from a research project that began as a scientific management study.

Western Electric Company, a manufacturer of communications equipment, hired a team of Harvard researchers led by Elton Mayo and Fritz Roethlisberger. They were to investigate the influence of physical working conditions on workers' productivity and efficiency in one of the company's factories outside Chicago. This research project, known as the *Hawthorne Studies,* provided some of the most interesting and controversial results in the history of management.[13]

The Hawthorne Studies were a series of experiments conducted from 1924 to 1932. During the first stage of the project (the illumination experiments), various working conditions, particularly the lighting in the factory, were altered to determine the effects of those changes on productivity. The researchers found no systematic relationship between the factory lighting and production levels. In some cases, productivity continued to increase even when the illumination was reduced to the level of moonlight. The researchers concluded that the workers performed and reacted differently because the researchers were observing them. This reaction is known as the **Hawthorne Effect.**

This conclusion led the researchers to believe productivity may be affected more by psychological and social factors than by physical or objective influences. With this thought in mind, they initiated the other four stages of the project. During these stages, the researchers performed various work group experiments and had extensive interviews with employees. Mayo and his team eventually concluded that productivity and employee behavior were influenced by the informal work group.

Human relations proponents argued that managers should stress primarily employee welfare, motivation, and communication. They believed social needs had precedence over economic needs. Therefore, management must gain the cooperation of the group and promote job satisfaction and group norms consistent with the goals of the organization.

Another noted contributor to the field of human relations was Abraham Maslow.[14] In 1943, Maslow suggested that humans have five levels of needs. The most basic needs are the physical needs for food, water, and shelter; the most advanced need is for self-actualization, or personal fulfillment. Maslow argued that people try to satisfy their lower-level needs and then progress upward to the higher-level needs. Managers can facilitate this process and achieve organizational goals by removing obstacles and encouraging behaviors that satisfy people's needs and organizational goals simultaneously.

Although the human relations approach generated research into leadership, job attitudes, and group dynamics, it drew heavy criticism.[15] Critics believed that one result of human relations—a belief that a happy worker was a productive worker—was too simplistic. Whereas scientific management overemphasized the economic and formal aspects of the workplace, human relations ignored the more rational side of the worker and the important characteristics of the formal organization. However, human relations was a significant step in the development of management thought because it prompted managers and researchers to consider the psychological and social factors that influence performance.

Bureaucracy

Max Weber, a German sociologist, lawyer, and social historian, showed how management itself could be more efficient and consistent in his book, *The Theory of Social and Economic Organizations.*[16] The ideal model for management, according to Weber, is the **bureaucracy** approach.

Weber believed bureaucratic structures can eliminate the variability that results when managers in the same organization have different skills, experiences, and goals. Weber advocated that the jobs themselves be standardized so that personnel changes would not disrupt the organization. He emphasized a structured, formal network of relationships among specialized positions in an organization. Rules and regulations standardize behavior, and authority resides in positions rather than in individuals. As a result, the organization need not rely on a particular individual but will realize efficiency and success by following the rules in a routine and unbiased manner.

A Human Relations Pioneer

In 1837, William Procter, a ruined English retailer, and James Gamble, son of a Methodist minister, formed a partnership in Cincinnati to make soap and candles. Both were known for their integrity, and soon their business was thriving.

By 1883, the business had grown substantially. When William Cooper Procter, grandson of the founder, left Princeton University to work for the firm, he wanted to learn the business from the ground up. He started working on the factory floor. "He did every menial job from shoveling rosin and soap to pouring fatty mixtures into crutchers. He brought his lunch in a paper bag . . . and sat on the floor [with the other workers] and ate with them, learning their feelings about work."

By 1884, Cooper Procter believed, from his own experience, that increasing workers' psychological commitment to the company would lead to higher productivity. His passion to increase employee commitment to the firm led him to propose a scandalous plan: share profits with workers to increase their sense of responsibility and job satisfaction. The surprise was audible on the first dividend day, when workers held checks equivalent to seven weeks' pay.

Still, the plan was not complete. Workers saw the profit sharing as extra pay rather than as an incentive to improve. In addition, Cooper Procter recognized that a fundamental issue for the workers, some of whom continued to be his good friends, was the insecurity of old age. Public incorporation in 1890 gave Procter a new idea. After trying several versions, by 1903 he had discovered a way to meet all his goals for labor: a stock purchase plan. For every dollar a worker invested in P&G stock, the company would contribute four dollars' worth of stock.

Finally, Cooper Procter had resolved some key issues for labor that paid off in worker loyalty, improved productivity, and an increasing corporate reputation for caring and integrity. He went on to become CEO of the firm, and P&G today remains one of the most admired corporations in the United States.

SOURCES: O. Schisgall, *Eyes on Tomorrow* (Chicago: J. G. Ferguson, 1981); T. Welsh, "Best and Worst Corporate Reputations," *Fortune,* February 7, 1994, pp. 58–66.

According to Weber, bureaucracies are especially important because they allow large organizations to perform the many routine activities necessary for their survival. Also, bureaucratic positions foster specialized skills, eliminating many subjective judgments by managers. In addition, if the rules and controls are established properly, bureaucracies should be unbiased in their treatment of people—both customers and employees.

Many organizations today are bureaucratic. Bureaucracy can be efficient and productive. However, bureaucracy is not the appropriate model for every organization. Organizations or departments that need rapid decision making and flexibility may suffer under a bureaucratic approach. Some people may not perform their best with excessive bureaucratic rules and procedures.

Other shortcomings stem from a faulty execution of bureaucratic principles rather than from the approach itself. Too much authority may be vested in too few people; the procedures may become the ends rather than the means; or managers may ignore appropriate rules and regulations. Finally, one advantage of a bureaucracy—its permanence—can also be a problem. Once a bureaucracy is established, dismantling it is difficult.

CONTEMPORARY APPROACHES

The contemporary approaches to management include quantitative management, organizational behavior, systems theory, and the contingency perspective. The contemporary approaches have developed at various times since World War II, and they continue to represent the cornerstones of modern management thought.

Quantitative Management

Although Taylor introduced the use of science as a management tool early in the 20th century, most organizations did not adopt the use of quantitative techniques for management problems until the 1940s and 1950s.[17] During World War II, military planners began to apply mathematical techniques to defense and logistics problems. After the war, private corporations began assembling teams of quantitative experts to tackle many of the complex issues confronting large organizations. This approach, referred to as **quantitative management,** emphasizes the application of quantitative analysis to management decisions and problems.

Quantitative management helps a manager make a decision by developing formal mathematical models of the problem. Computers facilitated the development of specific quantitative methods. These include such techniques as statistical decision theory, linear programming, queuing theory, simulation, forecasting, inventory modeling, network modeling, and break-even analysis. Organizations apply these techniques in many areas, including production, quality control, marketing, human resources, finance, distribution, planning, and research and development.

Despite the promise quantitative management holds, managers do not rely on these methods as the primary approach to decision making. Typically, they use these techniques as a supplement or tool in the decision process. Many managers will use results that are consistent with their experience, intuition, and judgment, but they often reject results that contradict their beliefs. Also, managers may use the process to compare alternatives and eliminate weaker options.

Several explanations account for the limited use of quantitative management. Many managers have not been trained in using these techniques. Also, many aspects of a management decision cannot be expressed through mathematical symbols and formulas. Finally, many of the decisions managers face are nonroutine and unpredictable.

Organizational Behavior

During the 1950s, a transition took place in the human relations approach. Scholars began to recognize that worker productivity and organizational success are based on more than the satisfaction of economic or social needs. The revised perspective, known as **organizational behavior,** studies and identifies management activities that promote employee effectiveness through an understanding of the complex nature of individual, group, and organizational processes. Organizational behavior draws from a variety of disciplines, including psychology and sociology, to explain the behavior of people on the job.

During the 1960s, organizational behaviorists heavily influenced the field of management. Douglas McGregor's Theory X and Theory Y marked the transition from human relations.[18] According to McGregor, Theory X managers assume workers are lazy and irresponsible and require constant supervision and external motivation to achieve organizational goals. Theory Y managers assume employees *want* to work and can direct and control themselves. McGregor advocated a Theory Y perspective, suggesting that managers who encourage participation and allow opportunities for individual challenge and initiative would achieve superior performance.

Other major organizational behaviorists include Chris Argyris, who recommended greater autonomy and better jobs for workers,[19] and Rensis Likert, who stressed the value of participative management.[20] Through the years, organizational behavior has consistently emphasized development of the organization's human resources to achieve individual and organizational goals. Like other approaches, it has been criticized for its limited perspective, although more recent contributions have a broader and more situational viewpoint. In the past few years, many of the primary issues addressed by organizational behavior have experienced a rebirth with a greater interest in leadership, employee involvement, and self-management.

Systems Theory

The classical approaches as a whole were criticized because they (1) ignored the relationship between the organization and its external environment, and (2) usually stressed one aspect of the organization or its employees at the expense of other considerations. In response to these criticisms, management scholars during the 1950s stepped back from the details of the organization to attempt to understand it as a whole system. These efforts were based on a general scientific approach called **systems theory.**[21] Organizations are open systems, dependent on inputs from the outside world, such as raw materials, human resources, and capital. They transform these inputs into outputs that (ideally) meet the market's needs for goods and services. The environment reacts to the outputs through a feedback loop; this feedback provides input for the next cycle of the system. The process repeats itself for the life of the system and is illustrated in Exhibit A.3.

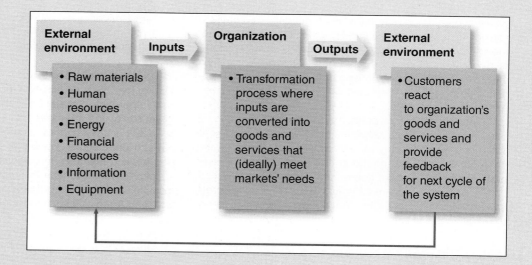

EXHIBIT A.3
Open-System
Perspective of an
Organization

Systems theory also emphasizes that an organization is one system in a series of subsystems. For instance, Southwest Airlines is a subsystem of the airline industry, and the flight crews are a subsystem of Southwest. Systems theory points out that each subsystem is a component of the whole and is interdependent with other subsystems.

Contingency Perspective

Building on systems theory ideas, the **contingency perspective** refutes universal principles of management by stating that a variety of factors, both internal and external to the firm, may affect the organization's performance.[22] Therefore, there is no one best way to manage and organize because circumstances vary.

Situational characteristics are called **contingencies.** Understanding contingencies helps a manager know which sets of circumstances dictate which management actions. You will learn recommendations for the major contingencies throughout this text. The contingencies include

1. Circumstances in the organization's external environment.

2. The internal strengths and weaknesses of the organization.

3. The values, goals, skills, and attitudes of managers and workers in the organization.

4. The types of tasks, resources, and technologies the organization uses.

With an eye to these contingencies, a manager may categorize the situation and then choose the proper competitive strategy, organization structure, or management process for the circumstances.

Researchers continue to identify key contingency variables and their effects on management issues. As you read the topics covered in each chapter, you will notice similarities and differences among management situations and the appropriate responses. This perspective should represent a cornerstone of your own approach to management. Many of the things you will learn about throughout this course apply a contingency perspective.

2008–2009 U.S. auto industry collapses
2010–2012 Gulf Oil Spill
    Troubled Asset Relief Program
    General Motors comeback
    Occupy Wall Street
    U.S. and European debt crisis
    Facebook IPO
2013 – Manufacturing comeback?
    Economic recovery, U.S. and global?

AN EYE ON THE FUTURE

This appendix has summarized the major schools of management thought. Some schools offer more general courses in business history, and the subject is well worth knowing. What goes on today derives from what went on yesterday, which stemmed from what began years, decades, even centuries ago. It is reasonable to believe that if decision makers paid more attention to history, the subprime mortgage crisis of 2007 and the more general financial panic of 2008 could have been avoided.[23] It helps to examine the past for help in making good decisions today and in the future.

Knowledge of history could help with the economic recovery and mitigate or prevent future fiascos. Knowing history *could*—if used properly—have a positive effect on the future.[24]

KEY TERMS

administrative management A classical management approach that attempted to identify major principles and functions that managers could use to achieve superior organizational performance, p 33.

bureaucracy A classical management approach emphasizing a structured, formal network of relationships among specialized positions in the organization, p 34.

contingencies Factors that determine the appropriateness of managerial actions, p 36.

contingency perspective An approach to the study of management proposing that the managerial strategies, structures, and processes that result in high performance depend on the characteristics, or important contingencies, of the situation in which they are applied, p 36.

economies of scale Reductions in the average cost of a unit of production as the total volume produced increases, p 30.

Hawthorne Effect People's reactions to being observed or studied resulting in superficial rather than meaningful changes in behavior, p 34.

human relations A classical management approach that attempted to understand and explain how human psychological and social processes interact with the formal aspects of the work situation to influence performance, p 33.

organizational behavior A contemporary management approach that studies and identifies management activities that promote employee effectiveness by examining the complex and dynamic nature of individual, group, and organizational processes, p 35.

quantitative management A contemporary management approach that emphasizes the application of quantitative analysis to managerial decisions and problems, p 35.

scientific management A classical management approach that applied scientific methods to analyze and determine the one best way to complete production tasks, p 31.

systematic management A classical management approach that attempted to build into operations the specific procedures and processes that would ensure coordination of effort to achieve established goals and plans, p 31.

systems theory A theory stating that an organization is a managed system that changes inputs into outputs, p 35.

DISCUSSION QUESTIONS

1. How does today's business world compare with the one of 40 years ago? What is different about today, and what is not so different?

2. What is scientific management? How might today's organizations use it?

3. Exhibit A.2 lists Fayol's 14 principles of management, first published in 1916. Are they as useful today as they were then? Why or why not? *When* are they most, and least, useful?

4. What are the advantages and disadvantages of a bureaucratic organization?

5. In what situations are quantitative management concepts and tools applicable?

6. Choose any organization and describe its system of inputs and outputs.

7. Why did the contingency perspective become such an important approach to management? Generate a list of contingencies that might affect the decisions you make in your life or as a manager.

8. For each of the management approaches discussed in the appendix, give examples you have seen. How effective or ineffective were they?

Experiential Exercises
A.1 APPROACHES TO MANAGEMENT

OBJECTIVES

1. To help you conceive a wide variety of management approaches.

2. To clarify the appropriateness of different management approaches in different situations.

INSTRUCTIONS

Your instructor will divide your class randomly into groups of four to six people. Acting as a team, with everyone offering ideas and one person serving as official recorder, each group will be responsible for writing a one-page memo to your present class. The subject matter of your group's memo will be "My advice for managing people today is . . ." The fun part of this exercise (and its creative element) involves writing the memo from the viewpoint of the person assigned to your group by your instructor.

Among the memo viewpoints your instructor may assign are

- An ancient Egyptian slave master (building the great pyramids).
- Henri Fayol.
- Frederick Taylor.
- Mary Parker Follet.
- Douglas McGregor.
- A contingency management theorist.
- A Japanese auto company executive.
- The chief executive officer of IBM in the year 2030.
- Commander of the Starship *Enterprise* II in the year 3001.
- Others as assigned by your instructor.

Use your imagination, make sure everyone participates, and try to be true to any historical facts you've encountered. Attempt to be as specific and realistic as possible. Remember, the idea is to provide advice about managing people from another point in time (or from a particular point of view at the present time).

Make sure you manage your 20-minute time limit carefully. A recommended approach is to spend 2 to 3 minutes putting the exercise into proper perspective. Next, take about 10 to 12 minutes brainstorming ideas for your memo, with your recorder jotting down key ideas and phrases. Have your recorder use the remaining time to write your group's one-page memo, with constructive comments and help from the others. Pick a spokesperson to read your group's memo to the class.

SOURCE: R. Krietner and A. Kinicki, *Organization Behavior*, 3rd ed. (New York: Richard D. Irwin, 1994), pp. 30–31.

A.2 THE UNIVERSITY AS AN OPEN SYSTEM

OBJECTIVES

1. To learn to identify the components of a complex system.
2. To understand better how organizations function as systems.

INSTRUCTIONS

1. Think about your university from the perspective of being an open system.
2. Answer the questions on the University System Analysis Worksheet individually, or in small groups, as directed by your instructor.

University System Analysis Worksheet

1. Referring back to Exhibit A.3, what subsystems compose your university system? Diagram the system.

   _____

   _____

   _____

2. Identify the following in your university system: inputs, transformations, outputs, and goods or services.

   _____

   _____

   _____

3. What are the strengths of the current system? What are the weaknesses? (Is it a system failure when a student fails to graduate?)

   _____

   _____

   _____

4. What changes (if any) would you make to the transformation process?

   _____

   _____

   _____

SOURCE: Adapted from J. Gordon, *A Diagnostic Approach to Organizational Behavior* (Englewood Cliffs, NJ: Prentice Hall, 1983), p. 38.

CHAPTER 2

The External and Internal Environments

> The essence of a business is outside itself.
>
> —PETER DRUCKER

After studying Chapter 2, you will be able to:

LO 1 Describe how environmental forces influence organizations and how organizations can influence their environments.

LO 2 Distinguish between the macroenvironment and the competitive environment.

LO 3 Explain why managers and organizations should attend to economic and social developments.

LO 4 Identify elements of the competitive environment.

LO 5 Summarize how organizations respond to environmental uncertainty.

LO 6 Define elements of an organization's culture.

LO 7 Discuss how an organization's culture and climate affect its response to its external environment.

The Macroenvironment

The Economy

Technology

Laws and Regulations

Demographics

Social Issues

Sustainability and the Natural Environment

The Competitive Environment

Competitors

New Entrants

Substitutes and Complements

Suppliers

Customers

Environmental Analysis

Environmental Scanning

Scenario Development

Forecasting

Benchmarking

Responding to the Environment

Changing the Environment You Are In

Influencing Your Environment

Adapting to the Environment: Changing Yourself

Choosing a Response Approach

The Internal Environment of Organizations: Culture and Climate

Organization Culture

Organizational Climate

Management in Action

CAN MARK ZUCKERBERG HELP FACEBOOK REACH THE NEXT LEVEL BY OUTMANEUVERING THE COMPETITION AND REFOCUSING ON ITS DEVELOPERS?

Some managers transform an industry; many others are swept up by change. Some do both. In the unprecedented pace of the Internet era, a few managers do both within a mere decade. One of those is Facebook founder Mark Zuckerberg.

Zuckerberg started Facebook in 2004, when as a Harvard student, he developed a way for his classmates to connect online. Today, Facebook, with 1.2 billion active users a month, is the largest online social network.

To carry out its mission to "make the world more open and connected," Facebook added capabilities making it easier to post photos, video clips, and links to websites. The ever-present Like button encourages users to signal their opinions to all their friends—and to Facebook's database. Facebook's user database thus becomes its most precious resource. For users, Facebook can deliver more relevant links, ads, and services. It also can sell highly targeted advertising.

Driven by Zuckerberg's vision to connect individuals more and more, Facebook became part of everyday life. The only thing holding back even more enormous growth seemed to be cash from eager investors. So Facebook made an initial public offering of stock.

Yet technology almost left Facebook behind. The Internet underwent a mobile revolution. Spurred by the launch of the powerful iPhone and iPad tablet computer, people began wanting to be online always, everywhere. While Facebook continued adding features and advertising to its main website, people were switching to mobile devices; in 2013, for the first time, the number of mobile devices in use exceeded the number of personal computers (desktops and laptops). Almost

© David Paul Morris/Bloomberg via Getty Images

as many people now access Facebook via its mobile app—the most-downloaded app for the iPhone—than at computers. Unfortunately for Facebook, most of its ads were displaying on the computer website—and what mobile advertising it sold went for a lower rate. Therefore, just as the company began selling stock, investors were seeing trouble.

In the initial days of trading, Facebook's stock price fell. However, Facebook's managers scrambled to catch up to the mobile Internet. They improved their mobile site and began pushing up ad rates; in less than three years, mobile ad revenues went from 0 percent to over 60 percent. Stock prices have begun to trend upward. Does this mean the uncertainty is over for Facebook's managers? Far from it. Technology will continue advancing, and computer users will keep looking for the next big thing.[1]

Technology and social behavior are just two of the forces shaping the environment in which Facebook operates. As you study this chapter, consider what other forces Facebook's managers should be monitoring and engaging with.

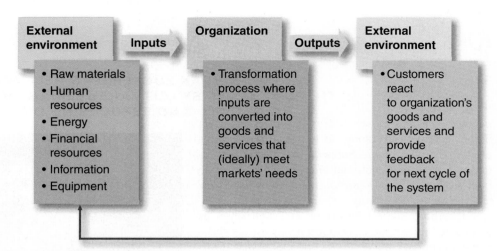

EXHIBIT 2.1
Open-System Perspective of an Organization

---

open systems

Organizations that are affected by, and that affect, their environment.

---

inputs

Goods and services organizations take in and use to create products or services.

---

outputs

The products and services organizations create.

---

external environment

All relevant forces outside a firm's boundaries, such as competitors, customers, the government, and the economy.

---

competitive environment

The immediate environment surrounding a firm; includes suppliers, customers, rivals, and the like.

As a technology leader, Facebook is affecting how people play, shop, and communicate today, as well as preparing for how they might want to do so in the future. Its management must therefore keep a sharp watch on a broad spectrum of influences and events that can affect its operations. In this chapter, we discuss in detail how pressures from outside the organization help create the context in which managers and their companies must operate.

As we suggested in the first chapter, organizations are **open systems**—that is, they are affected by and in turn affect their external environments. For example, they take in **inputs** such as goods or services from their environment and use them to create products and services that are **outputs** to their environment, as shown in Exhibit 2.1. But when we use the term **external environment** here, we mean more than an organization's clients or customers; the external environment includes *all* relevant forces outside the organization's boundaries.

Many of these factors are uncontrollable. Companies large and small are buffeted or battered by recession, government regulations, competitors' actions, and other factors. But their lack of control does not mean that managers can ignore such forces, use them as excuses for poor performance, and try to just get by. Managers must stay abreast of external developments and react effectively. Moreover, as we will discuss later in this chapter, sometimes managers can influence components of the external environment. We will examine ways in which organizations can do just that.

Exhibit 2.2 shows the external and internal environments of a business organization. The organization exists in its **competitive environment,** which is composed of the firm

EXHIBIT 2.2
The External and Internal Environments of Organizations

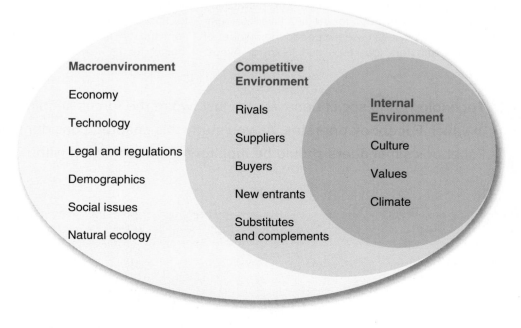

and its rivals, suppliers, customers (buyers), new entrants, and substitute or complementary products. At the more general level is the **macroenvironment,** which includes legal, political, economic, technological, demographic, and social and natural factors that generally affect all organizations.

This chapter discusses the basic characteristics of an organization's environment and the importance of that environment for strategic management. We also examine the *internal environment,* or *culture,* of the organization and the way that culture may influence the organization's response to its environment. Later chapters elaborate on many of the basic environmental forces introduced here. For example, technology will be discussed again in Chapter 17. The global environment gets a thorough treatment in Chapter 6, which is devoted to international management. Other chapters focus on ethics, social responsibility, and the natural environment. Chapter 18 reiterates the theme that recurs throughout this text: Organizations must change continually because environments change continually.

macroenvironment

The general environment; includes governments, economic conditions, and other fundamental factors that generally affect all organizations.

The Macroenvironment

All organizations operate in a macroenvironment, which is defined by the most general elements in the external environment that potentially can influence strategic decisions. Although a top executive team may have unique internal strengths and ideas about its goals, it must consider external factors before taking action.

The Economy

Although most Americans think in terms of the U.S. economy, the economic environment for organizations is much larger—created by complex interconnections among the economies of different countries. Wall Street investment analysts begin their workday thinking not just about what the New York Stock Exchange did yesterday but also about how the London and Tokyo exchanges did overnight. Growth and recessions occur worldwide as well as domestically.

The economic environment dramatically affects managers' ability to function effectively and influences their strategic choices. Interest and inflation rates affect the availability and cost of capital, growth opportunities, prices, costs, and consumer demand for products. Steeply rising energy and health care costs have had a great effect on companies' ability to hire and their cost of doing business. Changes in the value of the dollar on world exchanges may make American products cheaper or more expensive than their foreign competitors. Unemployment rates affect labor availability and the wages the firm must pay as well as product demand.

During boom times, hiring accelerates, and unemployment rates fall. Generally, unemployment rises as workers are laid off in a recession (a period of falling economic output). During the Great Recession of 2007–2009, the drop-off in employment was especially severe. Exhibit 2.3 shows how long it has taken the United States to recover jobs lost during each of the past four recessions. Six and one-half years after the start of the Great Recession, employment levels returned to the pre-recession level. That is two and one-half years longer than with previous recessions. Long periods of slow hiring pose difficult challenges for societies and their governments. In contrast, the participation rate or percent of eligible individuals who could be working has not returned to pre-recession levels; it dropped from 66 percent in 2008 to just below 63 percent in 2015.

An important economic influence is the government where a business is operating. In the United States, the federal government is a major employer and customer for business and military goods and services. When it spends more money than it is receiving, it also is a major borrower in the financial markets (adding to the national debt). These government activities can increase or decrease a nation's economic activity. To be effective, managers educate themselves about the impact of the government on the societies in which they work.

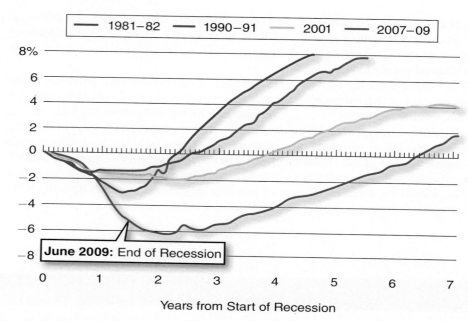

SOURCE: Center on Budget and Policy Priorities, "Chart Book: The Legacy of the Great Recession," Special Series: Economic Recovery Watch, updated February 15, 2015, http://www.cbpp.org.

Another important economic influence is the stock market. When investors bid up stock prices, they are paying more to own shares in companies, which means the companies have more capital to fuel their strategies. Observers of the stock market watch trends in major indexes such as the Dow Jones Industrial Average, Standard and Poor's 500, and NASDAQ Composite, which combine many companies' performance into a single measurement. Stock indexes tell managers about overall expectations for business value. Of course, managers also follow trends in stocks for their industry and their own company.

The stock market may have a profound effect on the behavior of individual managers. In publicly held companies, managers throughout the organization may feel required to meet Wall Street's earnings expectations. Such external pressures usually have a positive effect—they help make many firms more efficient and profitable. But failure to meet those expectations can cause a company's stock price to drop, making it more difficult for the firm to raise additional capital for investment. The compensation of managers may also be affected, particularly if they have been issued stock options. The net effect of these pressures may sometimes be that managers focus on short-term results at the expense of the long-term success of their organizations. Even worse, a few managers may be tempted to engage in unethical or unlawful behavior that misleads investors.[2] We will discuss managerial ethics in Chapter 5 and stock options in Chapter 10.

Economic conditions change over time and are difficult to predict. Bull and bear markets come and go. Periods of dramatic growth may be followed by a recession. Every trend undoubtedly will end—but when? Even when times seem good, budget deficits or other considerations create concern about the future.

Bottom Line

With increased competition from foreign and domestic companies, managers must pay particular attention to cost. *Does low cost mean low quality? Why or why not?*

Economic conditions change over time and are difficult to predict.

Technology

Today a company cannot succeed without incorporating into its strategy the astonishing technologies that exist and continue to evolve. Technological advances create new products, advanced production techniques, and better ways of managing and communicating. In addition, as technology evolves, new industries, markets, and competitive niches develop. For example, early entrants in nano technology or 3D printing are trying to establish dominant positions, whereas later entrants work on technological advances that will give them a competitive niche. Advances in technology also permit companies to enter markets that would otherwise be unavailable to them, such as Google's *Project Loon* that aims to deliver high-speed Internet access to many of the 4.3 billion people in the world who are currently out of range of cell towers. Internet service will be delivered via specially equipped helium balloons that will float in the stratosphere.[3]

New technologies also provide new production techniques. In manufacturing, sophisticated robots perform jobs without suffering fatigue, requiring vacations or weekends off, or demanding wage increases. New methods, such as injecting steam into oil fields at high pressure (popularly known as fracking), are enabling Shell, ExxonMobil, and other oil companies to extract that valuable resource from locations that had once been considered depleted. In this case, technological and economic forces overlap: the rising price of oil has made it worthwhile for companies to develop and try the new technology.[4]

© Marty Melville/AFP/Getty Images

In addition, new technologies provide new ways to manage and communicate. Computerized management information systems (MISs) make information available when needed, and networking via the Internet makes that information available where it is needed. Computers monitor productivity and note performance deficiencies. Telecommunications allow conferences to take place without requiring people to travel to the same location. Such technological advances create innovations in business. Strategies developed around the cutting edge of technological advances create a competitive advantage; strategies that ignore or lag behind competitors' technology lead to obsolescence and extinction. This issue is so important that we devote an entire chapter (Chapter 17) to the topic.

Laws and Regulations

U.S. government policies impose strategic constraints on organizations but may also provide opportunities.[5] In the United States, the Affordable Care Act of 2010 is a relevant example because it contains such a variety of provisions that some managers have identified mainly costs of compliance whereas others have identified opportunities for their companies.[6] Some provisions of this law impose requirements for insurance coverage (for example, covering dependent children up to age 26 and covering preventive services without charging the patient a copay or deductible). Giving employees more generous benefits could add to the cost of compensating them. Other provisions, such as insurance exchanges and tax credits for small businesses, may help smaller firms compete in the market for talent. Some consequences of the law will differ by industry: a retailer that needs to add an insurance benefit would see a new expense, whereas hospitals are hoping that broader insurance coverage will lower their expense of providing services to patients who cannot pay. As businesspeople, managers also need to sort through the details, plan how to limit any harm, and build on any opportunities.

The government can affect business opportunities through tax laws, economic policies, and international trade rulings. An example of restraint on business action is the U.S. government's standards regarding bribery. In some countries, bribes and kickbacks are common and expected ways of doing business, but for U.S. firms, they are illegal practices. Some U.S. businesses have, in fact, been fined for using bribery when competing internationally. But laws can also assist organizations. Because U.S. federal and state governments protect property rights, including copyrights, trademarks, and patents, it is economically more attractive to start businesses in the United States than in countries where laws and law enforcement offer less protection.

As described in Exhibit 2.4, *regulators* are specific government organizations in a firm's macroenvironment. These agencies have the power to investigate company practices and take legal action to ensure compliance with laws.

EXHIBIT 2.4
Governmental Agencies
That Regulate Businesses

Agency Name	Purpose
Securities & Exchange Commission (SEC)	Protects investors and maintains fair, honest, and efficient markets.
Food & Drug Administration (FDA)	Protects the public health by ensuring the safety and efficacy of drugs, products, and food.
Environmental Protection Agency (EPA)	Protects human health and the environment.
Occupational Safety & Health Administration (OSHA)	Enforces workplace safety and health standards.
Federal Aviation Administration (FAA)	Regulates civil aviation to promote safety.
Equal Employment Opportunity Commission (EEOC)	Enforces federal laws that prohibit discrimination in the workplace.
National Labor Relations Board (NLRB)	Safeguards employees' rights to organize and to determine whether to have unions as their bargaining representative.
Office of Federal Contract Compliance Programs (OFCCP)	Monitors federal contractors to make sure they take affirmative action to ensure equal employment opportunities.

demographics

Measures of various characteristics of the people who make up groups or other social units.

As the number of people in the workforce with a college education increases, managers must consider how this affects their work.

© Photodisc/Getty Images

Often, the corporate community sees government as an adversary. However, many organizations realize that government can be a source of competitive advantages for an individual company or an entire industry. Public policy may prevent or limit new foreign or domestic competitors from entering an industry. Government may subsidize failing companies or provide tax breaks to some. Federal patents protect innovative products or production process technologies. Legislation may be passed to support industry prices, thereby guaranteeing profits or survival. The government may even intervene to ensure the survival of certain key industries or companies, as it has done to help auto companies, airlines, and agricultural businesses.

Demographics

Demographics are measures of various characteristics of the people who make up groups or other social units. Work groups, organizations, countries, markets, and societies can be described statistically by referring to demographic measures such as their members' age, gender, family size, income, education, occupation, and so forth.

Managers must consider workforce demographics in formulating their human resource strategies. Population growth influences the size and composition of the labor force. In the decade from 2012 to 2022, the U.S. civilian labor force is expected to grow at a rate of 10.8 percent, reaching 163.5 million.[7] This growth is slower than during the previous decade, partly because young workers—those between the ages of 16 and 24—are declining in numbers. The fastest-growing age group will be workers who are 55 and older, who are expected to represent over one-fourth of the labor force in 2022. The nearby "Multiple Generations at Work" box discusses what this may mean for older workers and their employers.

The education and skill levels of the workforce are another demographic factor managers must consider. The share of the U.S. labor force with at least some college education has been increasing steadily over the past several decades, from less than one-fourth of the workforce in 1970 to two-thirds today.[8] Even so, many companies find that they must invest heavily in training their entry-level workers, who may not have been adequately

Multiple Generations at Work

Using Older Workers to Fill the Gap

In order to address pending labor shortages over the next decade, organizations will need to find ways to retain and fully use the talents of their experienced, older employees while competing for qualified entry-level workers. There are many reasons why organizations will want to hire or retain seasoned employees. Experienced employees can coach younger employees, maintain relationships with key customers, or fill in during busy seasons. Research suggests that many of older employees are willing to work past the traditional retirement age 65, one reason being a lack of pensions and adequate savings will make retirement unaffordable for many of today's Baby Boomers.

What are companies doing to court seasoned employees? CVS Caremark has a *Talent is Ageless* program to recruit, hire, and train employees between 50 and 99 years of age. Since the program's inception over 15 years ago, the percentage of its 50 and over workforce has tripled from 6 to 18 percent. New Jersey–based Atlantic Health System rehires retirees on a part-time or per diem basis. These skilled part-timers are invited to work up to 999 hours each year so as not to interfere with their ability to collect retirement benefits.

Once hired (or rehired), organizations are taking steps to motivate and retain seasoned workers, including:

1. ***Offering flexible work arrangements.*** Shorter work shifts, more control over when breaks are taken, and project-based work that allows older workers time for quality of life activities while in between assignments.
2. ***Encouraging phased retirement.*** Some workers are given the opportunity to reduce gradually their job responsibilities with employers prior to full retirement. During this transitional phase, older workers can earn necessary income while transferring their knowledge to younger employees and managers.
3. ***Providing health care benefits.*** A primary reason why some older individuals are working past traditional retirement age is to pay for rising health care costs for themselves and people who depend on them. At Cianbro, a construction company based in Maine, employees who work 20 hours per week are eligible for individual and family medical, dental, prescription, and vision coverage and short- and long-term disability insurance.[9]

prepared for some of the more complex tasks the modern workplace requires. (We discuss training in greater detail in Chapter 10.) Also, as college has become a more popular option, employers are finding it difficult to recruit employees for jobs that require knowledge of a skilled trade, such as machinists, electricians, and toolmakers, especially in areas where the cost of living is so high that most residents are professionals.[10] However, as education levels improve around the globe, more managers find they are able to send even technical tasks to lower-priced but highly trained workers overseas, which we discuss further in Chapter 6.

Another factor that significantly influences the U.S. population and labor force is immigration. Immigrants represent over 16 percent of the U.S. workforce, although they are a stronger presence in the West (almost 24 percent of the workforce) than in the Midwest (less than 8 percent).[11] Immigrants are frequently of working age but have different educational and occupational backgrounds from the rest of the labor force. Immigration is one reason the labor force in the future will be more ethnically diverse than it is today. The biggest percentage employment increases will be by Hispanics and Asian Americans, followed by African Americans.

> Immigration is one reason the labor force in the future will be more ethnically diverse than it is today.

Since the last quarter of the 20th century, women have joined the U.S. labor force in record numbers. Throughout the 1970s and 1980s, they became much more likely to take paying jobs. In the 1970s, only about one-third of women were in the labor force, but 60 percent had jobs in 1999. Since then, women's labor force participation rate has declined slightly to about 58 percent in 2012. Women's participation contrasts with a participation rate of 70 percent for men, also declining gradually as the workforce ages and more adults retire.[12] Women are attaining higher levels of education than in the past. The proportion of working women with a college degree more than tripled from 1970 to 2012.[13]

A more diverse workforce has many advantages, but managers have to make certain they provide equality for women and minorities with respect to employment, advancement opportunities, and compensation. They must make strategic plans to recruit, retain, train, motivate, and effectively use people of diverse demographic backgrounds who have the skills to achieve the company's mission. We discuss the issue of managing the diverse workforce in detail in Chapter 11.

Social Issues

Societal trends regarding how people think and behave have major implications for management of the labor force, corporate social actions, and strategic decisions about products and markets. For example, during the 1980s and 1990s, women in the workforce often chose to delay having children as they focused on their careers, but today more women are having children and then returning to the workforce. As a result, companies have introduced more supportive policies, including family leave, flexible working hours, and child care assistance. Deloitte LLP has earned numerous awards for assisting working parents balance life and work demands.[14] Many firms also extend these benefits to all employees or allow them to design their own benefits packages, where they can choose from a menu of available benefits that suit their individual situations. Domestic partners, whether they are in a marital relationship or not, also are covered by many employee benefit programs. Firms provide these benefits as a way of increasing a source of competitive advantage: an experienced workforce.

How companies respond to these and other social issues may also affect their reputation in the marketplace, which in turn may help or hinder their competitiveness. For companies in the soft-drink industry, one of the issues demanding a response is the epidemic of obesity and associated health problems such as diabetes. The New York City Board of Health has gone as far as banning sales of sweetened drinks in containers larger than 16 ounces at restaurants and other establishments inspected by the agency. In this social environment, Coke has run ads pointing out that soft drinks aren't the only source of the problem and encouraging consumers to engage in calorie-burning exercise. PepsiCo has been exploring ways to make its soft drinks and snacks "better for you," including research into tastier low-calorie and natural sweeteners. All the major soft-drink makers have introduced reduced-calorie sodas, including Coca-Cola's Life and PepsiCo's Pepsi True, which they hope will appeal to consumers who dislike diet drinks.[15]

Sustainability and the Natural Environment

Directly or indirectly, organizations depend on the natural environment to provide them with resources. Depending on their processes, they may need trees for paper, steel for manufacturing goods, petroleum to fuel transportation or make plastics, and adequate air and water quality to maintain a healthy workforce. In addition, the ways in which organizations operate will have some impact on the quantity and quality of natural resources available. When the quantity is depleted or the quality is damaged, costs for resources skyrocket. Furthermore, the impact on natural resources—whether negatively by poisoning wells or positively by restoring forests—affects the quality of life for citizens in the areas where companies operate. Decisions that affect the natural environment therefore shape the climate of social issues and the political and legal environment in which organizations operate.

A dramatic example was the explosion of BP's Deepwater Horizon drilling rig in the Gulf of Mexico, which killed 11 workers and caused millions of barrels of oil to gush into the gulf and spread toward the coastlands of Mississippi and Louisiana. During the weeks that followed, fisheries closed, and tourists vacationed elsewhere. BP was forced to set

Social Enterprise

Terracycle Wants to Eliminate All Waste

Tom Szaky, founder and CEO of Terracycle, is on a mission to "find waste and turn it into something useful, at a profit." His firm collects hard-to-recycle waste like juice containers, chip bags, cigarette butts, and so forth and converts them into high-quality products like backpacks and totes, school supplies, plastic bins and benches, packing material and office supplies. Szaky forsees a future planet with zero waste. The 33-year-old social entrepreneur admits that this is a lofty goal, but his green message and social enterprise are making a notable impact on the environment. Since its founding in 2001 in a college dormitory, Terracycle has prevented 2.5 billion pieces of waste from entering landfills, engaged multiple large organizations to partner with Terracycle, and inspired individuals (known as Brigades) from 26 countries to collect and mail him bags of hard-to-recycle waste.

As an immigrant from then-communist Hungary, Szaky and his family were impressed at the amount of waste they saw. After arriving to study at Princeton University, Szaky and his roommate learned that liquefied warm poop was an effective, natural fertilizer for plants. Lacking the resources to purchase new packaging materials, they collected used soda bottles from garbage bins and recycled them to help sell their organic fertilizer. Walmart and Home Depot were early customers of Terracycle's.

Since then, the company has expanded its waste collection efforts. The company makes charitable donations on behalf of the Brigades that collect and mail the waste to its recycling operations. Terracycle enters into contracts with companies like Johnson & Johnson and Kenco to pick up their waste; which is later converted to products that are sold by Walmart and other large retailers.

Is Szaky building Terracycle only for the feel-good reward of doing something good for the environment and society? No. He believes that social enterprises should be profitable. Szaky walks the talk. Recently, Terracycle reported sales of over $20 million. According to Szaky: "Many young entrepreneurs think you can either do good

© Renee Bonnafon/Sacramento Bee/MCT via Getty Images

for the world and earn nothing, or you can do something negative and earn loads of money." Terracycle rejects these two extreme positions by pursuing a triple bottom line strategy whereby the company makes impact on environmental and social challenges while being profitable.[16]

Questions

- To what extent do you agree with Szaky that organizations can be profitable while making a positive impact on the environment and society?

- Can you envision a world that doesn't produce waste? If so, what changes would need to be made before that could happen?

aside tens of billions of dollars to cover all costs of the spill and its cleanup. In addition, the U.S. government assessed billions of dollars in fines against the company; and to prevent similar accidents in the future, it imposed additional regulations on any oil companies that want to drill in the Gulf.[17]

Protecting the natural environment has become so important to managerial decisions that we devote Appendix B following Chapter 5 to that subject.

The Competitive Environment

LO 4

All managers are affected by the components of the macroenvironment we just discussed. But each organization also functions in a closer, more immediate competitive environment. The competitive environment includes the organizations with which the organization directly interacts. As shown in Exhibit 2.5, the competitive environment includes rivalry among current competitors and the impact of new entrants, substitute and complementary products, suppliers, and customers. This model was originally developed by Michael Porter, a Harvard professor and a noted authority on strategic management. According to Porter, successful managers do more than simply react to the environment; they act in ways that actually shape or change the organization's environment. In strategic decision making, Porter's model is an excellent method to help managers analyze the competitive environment and adapt to or influence the nature of their competition.

Competitors

Among the various components of the competitive environment, competitors within the industry must first deal with one another. When organizations compete for the same customers and try to win market share at the others' expense, all must react to and anticipate their competitors' actions.

The first question to consider is this: Who is the competition? Sometimes the answer is obvious. The major competitors in the market for soft drinks are Coca-Cola and PepsiCo. But consumer tastes have shifted away from soda to bottled water and other beverages. Young people, who in the past were the main consumers of soft drinks, increasingly prefer to buy water, coffee, or energy drinks, so for years, sales of soda have been declining. Therefore, Coca-Cola and PepsiCo have had to compete in introducing new products, not just in winning consumers over to their brand of cola.[18]

Thus, as a first step in understanding their competitive environment, organizations must identify their competitors. Competitors may include (1) small domestic firms, especially their entry into tiny, premium markets; (2) strong regional competitors; (3) big new domestic companies exploring new markets; (4) overseas firms, especially those that either try to solidify their position in small niches (a traditional Japanese tactic) or are able to draw on an inexpensive labor force on a large scale (as in China); and (5) newer entries, such as firms offering their products on the web. The growth in competition from other countries has been especially significant in recent years with the worldwide reduction in international trade barriers. For example, the North American Free Trade Agreement (NAFTA) sharply reduced tariffs on trade between the United States, Canada, and Mexico. Managers today confront a particular challenge from low-cost producers abroad (see Chapter 6).

Bottom Line

Companies often compete through innovation, quality, service, and cost. We will discuss the issue of competitors and strategy in further detail in Chapter 4. *In which of these areas would you say PepsiCo tried to create a competitive advantage? (If you aren't sure, come back to this question after you've studied this section.)*

EXHIBIT 2.5
The Competitive Environment

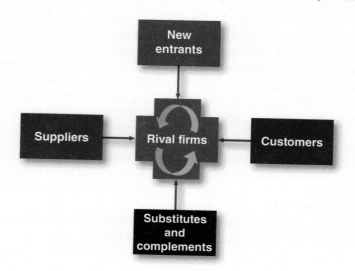

Once competitors have been identified, the next step is to analyze how they compete. Competitors use tactics such as price reductions, new-product introductions, and advertising campaigns to gain advantage over their rivals. In its competition against PepsiCo, Coca-Cola outdoes its rival with much heavier spending on advertising. The emphasis on promotion helps the company win a larger share of not only the cola market but also juices (its Minute Maid outsells PepsiCo's Tropicana) and sports drinks (its Powerade is beating PepsiCo's Gatorade). PepsiCo has tried to catch up by spending more on advertising, but this is a difficult game to win.[19]

The competition between Coke and Pepsi products is intense. Often, the products are found side by side, as is the case with these vending machines.

© Alpha and Omega Collection/ Alamy

It's essential to understand what competitors are doing when you are honing your own strategy. If soft-drink consumption continues to fall, Coke will have to be careful not to be complacent about its leadership role versus Pepsi. Most of Coke's sales are beverages. PepsiCo, in contrast, has expanded into a broader range of products, hoping to grow sales whether consumers are looking for a fun treat or a healthful snack. And besides reducing salt and sugar in traditional snacks such as chips, the company is expanding healthful options under its Quaker brand (for example, Real Medleys multigrain cereal) and in a joint venture called Müller Quaker Dairy, which produces the popular line of Greek yogurt in a new manufacturing facility in New York.[20] These are areas in which Coke lacks a presence—but also are less profitable than soft drinks.[21]

> It's essential to understand what competitors are doing when you are honing your own strategy.

Competition is most intense when there are many direct competitors (including foreign contenders), when industry growth is slow, and when the product or service cannot be differentiated in some way. New, high-growth industries offer enormous opportunities for profits. When an industry matures and growth slows, profits drop. Then intense competition causes an industry shakeout: weaker companies are eliminated, and the strong companies survive.[22] We will discuss the issue of competitors and strategy in further detail in Chapter 4.

New Entrants

New entrants into an industry compete with established companies. New entrants in the market for entertainment have come from unexpected quarters as increasing broadband speeds and more powerful microprocessors have enabled a whole host of ways to enjoy videos and games online. Cable and satellite television saw viewers flock to Hulu, Blockbuster lost movie sales to Netflix, and the makers of game consoles have watched sales dry up as consumers switched to playing Farmville via Facebook and downloading the Candy Crush Saga app for their smartphones.

If many factors prevent new companies from entering an industry, the threat to established firms is less serious. If there are few such **barriers to entry,** the threat of new entrants is more serious. Some major barriers to entry are government policy, capital requirements, brand identification, cost disadvantages, and distribution channels. The government can limit or prevent entry, as occurs when the FDA forbids a new drug entrant. When a patent expires, other companies can then enter the market and threaten once-dominant pharmaceutical companies. For example, Novartis'~ hypertension drug Diovan lost patent protection in 2012 and in anticipation of lost sales to generic drug makers, laid off nearly 2,000 workers and closed three plants in the United States. Similarly, Pfizer cut 4,200 employees after losing its patent protection over its top-selling cholesterol-lowering drug, Lipitor. The company is currently bracing for the expiration of its anti-impotence drug Viagra in 2019.[23]

Other barriers are less formal but can have the same effect. Capital requirements may be so high that companies won't risk or try to raise such large amounts of money. Brand identification forces new entrants to spend heavily to overcome customer loyalty. Imagine,

barriers to entry

Conditions that prevent new companies from entering an industry.

Bottom Line

Cost is often a major barrier to entry.
Would cost be a bigger barrier for someone who opens a new bicycle shop or a developer of mobile game apps? Why?

for example, the costs involved in trying to launch a new cola against Coke or Pepsi. The cost advantages established companies hold—due to large size, favorable locations, existing assets, and so forth—can also be formidable entry barriers.

Finally, existing competitors may have such tight distribution channels that new entrants have difficulty getting their goods or services to customers. For example, established food products already have supermarket shelf space. New entrants must displace existing products with promotions, price breaks, intensive selling, and other tactics.

Substitutes and Complements

Besides products that directly compete, other products can affect a company's performance by being substitutes for or complements of the company's offerings. A *substitute* is a potential threat; customers use it as an alternative, buying less of one kind of product but more of another. A *complement* is a potential opportunity because customers buy more of a given product if they also demand more of the complementary product. Exhibit 2.6 lists a dozen products and their potential substitutes and complements.

Technological advances and economic efficiencies are among the ways that firms can develop substitutes for existing products. After Amazon introduced the Kindle e-reader and Barnes & Noble introduced the competing Nook—and even more so as the companies were able to lower the price of these devices—consumers began treating e-books as an attractive substitute for printed books. But even as consumers were still gravitating toward e-readers, Apple launched the iPad tablet computer. Because it is lightweight and versatile, consumers are treating it as a substitute not only for e-readers but also in some cases as a substitute for a basic laptop computer.

Companies don't have to be at the mercy of customers switching to a substitute. To avoid losing out when others create a new supplement, some companies try to create their own supplementary products. PepsiCo's investment in development of new sweeteners and more healthful snacks is a way to offer substitutes for consumers avoiding the calories, fat, and sugar of its "fun for you" products. Anticipating that a growing share of consumers will care about healthful snacking, PepsiCo CEO Nooyi believes the company's products should include many choices that are "better for you" or "good for you."[24]

Besides identifying and planning for substitutes, companies must consider complements for their products. When people are buying new homes, they are also buying appliances and landscaping products. When customers purchase new smartphones, they may also buy new cases, screen protectors, selfie sticks, car jacks, extra batteries, and insurance. And when consumers munch on Lays, Doritos, or Cheetos snacks, they are bound to get thirsty and need a complementary product—say, an ice-cold Pepsi or Sierra Mist. PepsiCo owns all these food and drink brands; the company sells products that are complements as well as supplements. If PepsiCo meets its goal to shift more of its product line to healthier fare, it may become known for

> Organizations are at a disadvantage if they become overly dependent on any powerful supplier.

EXHIBIT 2.6
Potential Substitutes for and Complements of Products

If the Product Is . . .	The Substitute Might Be . . .
Chipotle burrito bowl	Subway sandwich
Dell laptop computer	iPad tablet computer
Face-to-face course	Online course
SanDisk USB flash drive	CrashPlan online backup service

If the Product Is . . .	The Complement Might Be . . .
Starbucks coffee	Starbucks Coffee Cake
Netflix streaming video	Orville Redenbacher's popcorn
Evernote app	Evernote scanner
Apartment rental	IKEA furniture

complementary products there, too—say, some Tropicana juice with your Quaker oatmeal or some Aquafina water with your Müller by Quaker yogurt.[25]

As with substitutes, a company needs to watch for new complements that can change the competitive landscape. Publishers that originally saw e-readers and tablet computers as a threat—as substitutes for their print publications—have tried to develop profitable ways of providing complements for the devices: electronic books and magazines as well as apps for reading content online. Textbook and cookbook publishers have teamed up with a software company called Inkling to prepare e-book versions of titles that support the use of multimedia and interactive features. In this case, the books offer capabilities that would be impossible in the print version of the book and therefore sell at a higher price.[26]

Suppliers

Recall from our earlier mention of open systems that organizations must acquire resources (inputs) from their environment and convert those resources into products or services (outputs) to sell. Suppliers provide the resources needed for production, and those resources may come in the form of people (supplied by trade schools and universities), raw materials (from producers, wholesalers, and distributors), information (supplied by researchers and consulting firms), and financial capital (from banks and other sources). But suppliers are important to an organization for reasons that go beyond the resources they provide. Suppliers can raise their prices or provide poor-quality goods and services. Workers may produce either outstanding or defective work. Powerful suppliers, then, can reduce an organization's profits, particularly if the organization cannot pass on price increases to its customers.

Organizations are at a disadvantage if they become overly dependent on any powerful supplier. A supplier is powerful if the buyer has few other sources of supply or if the supplier has many other buyers. Dependence also results from high **switching costs**—the fixed costs buyers face if they change suppliers. For example, once a buyer learns how to operate a supplier's equipment, such as computer software, the buyer faces both economic and psychological costs in changing to a new supplier. Of course, close supplier relationships can also be a source of advantages. Food and beverage companies work closely with the makers of the flavorings and additives that make their products appealing to consumers. With companies such as PepsiCo and Coca-Cola looking to offer more healthful and natural versions of their soft drinks, suppliers such as Archer Daniels Midland and Wild Flavors are coming up with blends of vitamins and minerals, sweeteners based on the stevia plant, energy boosters extracted from coffee beans, and new flavors such as ginger and chili.[27]

In recent years, supply chain management has become an increasingly important contributor to a company's competitiveness and profitability. By **supply chain management,** also known as the extended enterprise, we mean the managing of the entire network of facilities and people that obtain raw materials from outside the organization, transform them into products, and distribute them to customers.[28] In recent years, increased competition has required managers to pay very close attention to their costs. For example, they can no longer afford to hold large and costly inventories, waiting for orders to come in. Also, once orders do come in, some products still sitting in inventory might well be out of date.

With the emergence of the Internet, customers look for products built to their specific needs and preferences—and they want them delivered quickly at the lowest available price. This requires the supply chain to be not only efficient but also *flexible,* so that the organization's output can quickly respond to changes in demand.

Today, the goal of effective supply chain management is to have the right product in the right quantity available at the right place at the right cost. When Atlanta-based medical device maker EndoChoice wanted to expand into global health care markets, it called on United Parcel Service (UPS) to help manage its international supply chain. UPS has partnered with multiple health care companies to manage and deliver medical equipment, pharmaceuticals, and surgical supplies from factories in the United States to hospitals and patients' homes throughout the world.[29]

In sum, choosing the right supplier is an important strategic decision. Suppliers can affect manufacturing time, product quality, and inventory levels. The relationship between suppliers and the organization is changing in many companies. The close supplier

switching costs

Fixed costs buyers face when they change suppliers.

supply chain management

The managing of the network of facilities and people that obtain materials from outside the organization, transform them into products, and distribute them to customers.

Bottom Line

The ability to manufacture even customized products quickly has become a competitive requirement. *To meet this requirement, what qualities would a company need in its employees?*

UPS partners with many health care companies to provide logistics of all types from factory floor to a patient's front door.

© *The McGraw-Hill Companies, Inc./Andrew Resek, photographer*

final consumer

A customer who purchases products in their finished form.

intermediate consumer

A customer who purchases raw materials or wholesale products before selling them to final customers.

Bottom Line

In all businesses—services as well as manufacturing— strategies that emphasize good customer service provide a critical competitive advantage.
Name a company that has delivered good customer service to you.

relationship has become a new model for many organizations that are using a just-in-time manufacturing approach (discussed further in Chapters 16 and 17). And in some companies, innovative managers are forming strategic partnerships with their key suppliers in developing new products or new production techniques. We describe this kind of strategic partnership in more detail in Chapter 9.

Customers

Customers purchase the goods or services an organization offers. Without customers, a company won't survive. Customers can be intermediate (wholesalers and retailers) or final (end users), depending on where they are in the value chain. You are a **final consumer** when you buy a pair of Nike running shoes or lunch at Panera Bread. **Intermediate consumers** buy raw materials or wholesale products and then sell to final consumers, as when Lenovo, Dell, and Hewlett Packard buy processors from Intel to use in their laptop computers. Intermediate customers actually make more purchases than individual final consumers do. Types of intermediate customers include retailers, who buy clothes from wholesalers and manufacturers' representatives before selling them to their customers, and industrial buyers, who buy raw materials (such as chemicals) before converting them into final products. Selling to intermediate customers is often called *business-to-business* (B2B) selling. Notice in these B2B examples that the intermediate customer eventually goes on to become a seller.

Like suppliers, customers are important to organizations for reasons other than the money they provide for goods and services. Customers can demand lower prices, higher quality, unique product specifications, or better service. They also can play competitors against one another, as occurs when a car buyer (or a purchasing agent) collects different offers and negotiates for the best price. Many companies are finding that today's customers want to be actively involved with their products, as when the buyer of an iPhone customizes it with ring tones, wallpaper, and a variety of apps. Dell Inc. took customer input a step further by asking customers what they want the company to develop next. At Dell's IdeaStorm website (www.ideastorm.com), visitors can post ideas and comments about products. One of IdeaStorm's most enthusiastic customer-users became so involved with the resulting community that he was eventually hired as the project's manager and helped expand the site's customer interactions.[30]

The Internet has further empowered customers. It provides an easy source of information—both about product features and about pricing. In addition, today's Internet users informally create and share messages about a product, which provides flattering free "advertising" at best or embarrassing and even erroneous bad publicity at worst. Companies try to use this to their advantage by creating opportunities for consumers and the brand to interact. Another way companies are connecting with customers is through social media sites like LinkedIn *Company Pages,* which allows companies to invite individuals to join up to three company-related groups. Online retailer Zappos uses LinkedIn to answer questions about its products and the company's culture. Similarly, Google+ *Communities* offers companies a way to interact with individuals who might be interested in their products or services while increasing its visibility and brand awareness.[31]

As we discussed in Chapter 1, customer service means giving customers what they want or need, the way they want it, the first time. This usually depends on the speed and dependability with which an organization can deliver its products. As illustrated in Exhibit 2.7, there are several actions and attitudes that contribute to excellent customer service.

An organization is at a disadvantage if it depends too heavily on powerful customers. Customers are powerful if they make large purchases or if they can easily find alternative places to buy. If you are the largest customer of a firm and you can buy from others, you have power over that firm, and you most likely can negotiate with it successfully. Your firm's biggest customers—especially if they can buy from other sources—will have the greatest negotiating power over you. Customer relationship management is discussed more

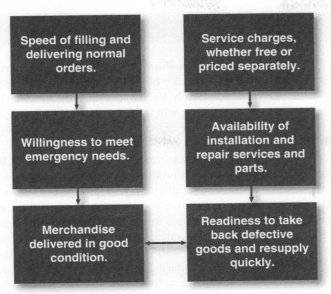

EXHIBIT 2.7
Actions and Attitudes =
Excellent Customer Service

SOURCE: Adapted from P. Kotler, *Marketing Management: Analysis, Planning, Implementation and Control,* 9th ed. (Englewood Cliffs, NJ: Prentice Hall, 1990).

fully in Chapter 9. As you read "Management in Action: Progress Report," consider how Facebook distinguishes itself with customers by seeking advantages in its relationships with other parties in the competitive environment.

Management in Action

FACEBOOK'S FIERCELY COMPETITIVE ENVIRONMENT

Even as technology transformed the macroenvironment for Facebook, its competitive environment is shifting almost as rapidly. Four Internet-era giants—Facebook, Amazon, Apple, and Google—once ruled separate domains but now are increasingly fighting for the same territory. Amazon started as a bookstore but now sells information for its Kindle Fire, making it a competitor with Apple. Google created a social-networking service (Google+), and Facebook launched a search tool for its site. Some observers predict Google and Facebook will be players in the market for mobile devices, to drive more usage of their services.

As they seek ever-larger shares of online activity, Facebook and these competitors rely on their customer data. As you saw at the beginning of this chapter, details about consumers and their behavior make advertising on Facebook valuable. Facebook has commissioned studies of the value of social marketing. In one case, it found that if Facebook users were fans of Starbucks (by "liking" the brand's page and therefore getting messages from the brand), they and their friends bought from Starbucks more often. Promoting such results helps Facebook charge more for promotions on its site. The other Internet giants gather different kinds of data. Amazon has information about product searches and purchases. Google knows what a person is searching for but not necessarily the person's opinions about the content. Until it launched

Google+, Google would not have known personal details such as age, interests, and relationships; adding a social network delivers a powerful combination of information sources.

No wonder, then, that Facebook launched its own search tool. But can a social search engine compete with Google? It's handy for discovering what restaurants your friends like. But it won't give you a weather forecast or directions to your job interview; for that, Facebook's search engine has partnered with Microsoft's Bing. Facebook's hope is that the tools will be helpful enough to keep people from leaving Facebook. If it can do so, it will have succeeded against a formidable competitor. So far, Google is taking in three-quarters of the ad spending on search ads (the links that show up beside users' search results). Some people see Facebook at a disadvantage because it waited until recently to offer a search function; others see Google+ as far behind Facebook in the social-networking arena.[32]

- Are Amazon, Apple, and Google competitors in Facebook's competitive environment or sellers of complements? Explain.
- Facebook has two major kinds of customers: the users of its site and the advertisers on its site. What challenges does Facebook face from Google in serving each customer group?

ONWARD

PROGRESS REPORT

MANAGER'S BRIEF

Environmental Analysis

If managers do not understand how the environment affects their organizations or cannot identify opportunities and threats that are likely to be important, their ability to make decisions and execute plans will be severely limited. For example, if little is known about customer likes and dislikes, organizations will have a difficult time designing new products, scheduling production, or developing marketing plans. In short, timely and accurate environmental information is critical for running a business.

But information about the environment is not always readily available. Managers find it difficult to forecast how well their own products will sell, let alone how a competitor might respond. In other words, managers often operate under conditions of uncertainty. **Environmental uncertainty** means that managers do not have enough information about the environment to understand or predict the future. Uncertainty arises from two related factors: complexity and dynamism. Environmental *complexity* refers to the number of issues to which a manager must attend as well as their interconnectedness. For example, industries that have many firms that compete in vastly different ways tend to be more complex—and uncertain—than industries with only a few key competitors. Similarly, environmental dynamism refers to the degree of discontinuous change that occurs within the industry. High-growth industries with products and technologies that change rapidly tend to be more uncertain than stable industries where change is less dramatic and more predictable.[33]

As environmental uncertainty increases, managers must develop techniques and methods for collecting, sorting through, and interpreting information about the environment. We discuss some of these approaches in this section of the chapter. (In the next chapter, we will also discuss how managers make decisions under conditions of uncertainty.) By analyzing environmental forces—in both the macroenvironment and the competitive environment—managers can identify opportunities and threats that might affect the organization.

environmental uncertainty

When managers do not have enough information about the environment to understand or predict the future.

> Managers often operate under conditions of uncertainty.

Environmental Scanning

Perhaps the first step in coping with uncertainty in the environment is pinning down what might be important. Frequently, organizations and individuals act out of ignorance, only to regret those actions in the future. IBM, for example, had the opportunity to purchase the technology behind xerography but turned it down. Xerox saw the potential, and the rest is history. However, Xerox researchers later developed the technology for the original computer mouse, but not seeing the potential, the company missed an important market opportunity.

environmental scanning

Searching for and sorting through information about the environment.

To understand and predict changes, opportunities, and threats, organizations such as Monsanto, Weyerhaeuser, and Union Carbide spend a good deal of time and money monitoring events in the environment. **Environmental scanning** means both searching out information that is unavailable to most people and sorting through that information to interpret what is important and what is not. Managers can ask questions such as these:

Who are our current competitors?
Are there few or many entry barriers to our industry?
What substitutes exist for our product or service?
Is the company too dependent on powerful suppliers?
Is the company too dependent on powerful customers?[34]

competitive intelligence

Information that helps managers determine how to compete better.

Answers to these questions help managers develop **competitive intelligence,** the information necessary to decide how best to manage in the competitive environment they have identified. Porter's competitive analysis, discussed earlier, can guide environmental scanning and help managers evaluate the competitive potential of different environments.

EXHIBIT 2.8
Attractive and Unattractive Environments

Environmental Factor	Unattractive	Attractive
Competitors	Many; low industry growth; equal size; commodity	Few; high industry growth; unequal size; differentiated
Threat of entry	High threat; few entry barriers	Low threat; many entry barriers
Substitutes	Many	Few
Suppliers	Few; high bargaining power	Many; low bargaining power
Customers	Few; high bargaining power	Many; low bargaining power

Exhibit 2.8 describes two extreme environments: an attractive environment, which gives a firm a competitive advantage, and an unattractive environment, which puts a firm at a competitive disadvantage.[35]

Scenario Development

As managers attempt to determine the effect of environmental forces on their organizations, they frequently develop **scenarios** of the future. Scenarios create alternative combinations of different factors into a total picture of the environment and the firm. For example, when Congress and the president must forecast the size of the federal budget deficit, they develop several scenarios about what the economy is likely to do over the next decade or so. Frequently, organizations develop a *best-case scenario* (the occurrence of events that are favorable to the firm), a *worst-case scenario* (the occurrence of unfavorable events), and some middle-ground alternatives. The formal practice of scenario development was pioneered by Royal/Dutch Shell.

The value of scenario development is that it helps managers develop contingency plans for what they might do given different outcomes.[36] For example, as a manager, you will quite likely be involved in budgeting for your area. You will almost certainly be asked to list initiatives that you would eliminate in case of an economic downturn and new investments you would make if your firm does better than expected.

Effective managers regard the scenarios they develop as living documents, not merely prepared once and put aside. Instead they constantly update the scenarios to take into account relevant new factors that emerge, such as significant changes in the economy or actions by competitors.

Forecasting

Whereas environmental scanning is used to identify important factors, and scenario development is used to develop alternative pictures of the future, **forecasting** is used to predict exactly how some variable or variables will change in the future. For example, in making capital investments, firms may try to forecast how interest rates will change. In deciding to expand or downsize a business, firms may try to forecast the demand for goods and services or forecast the supply and demand of labor they probably would use. Publications such as PricewaterhouseCoopers's *Trendsetter Barometer Business Outlook,* Kiplinger's *Economic Outlook,* and The Conference Board's economic reports provide forecasts to businesses.

Although forecasts are designed to help executives make predictions about the future, their accuracy varies from application to application. Because they extrapolate from the past to project the future, forecasts tend to be most accurate when the future ends up looking a lot like the past. Of course, we don't need sophisticated forecasts in those instances. Forecasts are most useful when the future will look radically different from the past. Unfortunately, that is when forecasts tend to be less accurate. The more things change, the less confidence we tend to have in our forecasts. The best advice for using forecasts might include the following ideas:

Use multiple forecasts, and perhaps average their predictions.
Remember that accuracy decreases the further into the future you are trying to predict.

As a manager, you will likely be involved in budgeting. Using what you have learned in this chapter, how would you approach this task?

© Purestock/Superstock

scenario

A narrative that describes a particular set of future conditions.

forecasting

Method for predicting how variables will change the future.

Forecasts are no better than the data used to construct them.

Use simple forecasts (rather than complicated ones) when possible.

Keep in mind that important events often are surprises and represent a departure from predictions.[37]

Benchmarking

benchmarking

The process of comparing an organization's practices and technologies with those of other companies.

In addition to trying to predict changes in the environment, firms can undertake intensive study of the best practices of various firms to understand their sources of competitive advantage. **Benchmarking** means identifying the best-in-class performance by a company in a given area, say, product development or customer service, and then comparing your processes to theirs. To accomplish this, a benchmarking team would collect information on its own company's operations and those of the other firm to determine gaps. These gaps serve as a point of entry to learn the underlying causes of performance differences. Ultimately, the team would map out a set of best practices that lead to world-class performance. We will discuss benchmarking further in Chapter 4.

Responding to the Environment

For managers and organizations, responding effectively to their environments is almost always essential. Clothing retailers who pay no attention to changes in the public's style preferences, or manufacturers who don't make sure they have steady sources of supply, are soon out of business. To respond to their environment, managers and companies have a number of options, which can be grouped into three categories: (1) selecting a new environment, (2) influencing the environment, and (3) adapting to the environment. This section describes the options briefly; we will elaborate on them in Chapter 4.

Changing the Environment You Are In

strategic maneuvering

An organization's conscious efforts to change the boundaries of its task environment.

Organizations need not be stuck within some given environment; they have options for defining where they operate. We refer to this category of responses as **strategic maneuvering.** By making a conscious effort to change the boundaries of its competitive environment, a firm can maneuver around potential threats and capitalize on arising opportunities.[38] Managers can use several strategic maneuvers, including domain selection, diversification, merger and acquisition, and divestiture.[39]

domain selection

Entering a new market or industry with an existing expertise.

Domain selection is the entrance by a company into another suitable market or industry. For example, the market may have limited competition or regulation, ample suppliers and customers, or high growth. PepsiCo's decision to begin selling yogurt was based on the company's goal of selling more healthful snacks coupled with the recent growing popularity of yogurt in the United States. The company also saw an opportunity to do more with its Quaker brand by offering varieties with granola and other tidbits to mix in.[40]

diversification

A firm's investment in a different product, business, or geographic area.

Diversification occurs when a firm invests in different types of businesses or products or when it expands geographically to reduce its dependence on a single market or technology. Apple successfully diversified its product line when it added the iPod, iTouch, iPad, and iPhone to its offerings of personal computers. As the popularity of the devices has spread, Apple has identified an opportunity to further diversify its product offerings to tap the fast growing mobile app market. In 2014, Apple's App Store offered 1.2 million apps and reported 75 billion downloads. This part of Apple's business empire generated over $10 billion for app developers of which Apple retained 30 percent of the revenues.[41]

merger

One or more companies combining with another.

acquisition

One firm buying another.

A **merger** or **acquisition** takes place when two or more firms combine, or one firm buys another, to form a single company. Mergers and acquisitions can offer greater efficiency from combined operations or can give companies relatively quick access to new markets or industries. Acquisitions can also give a company quick expertise in an area where it wants to grow. In 2014, the health care industry experienced nearly $319 billion in M&A activity, due in large part to the rollout of the Affordable Care Act. The telecommunications industry witnessed several M&A deals, including Comcast's acquistion of Time Warner Cable and AT&T's purchase of DirecTV.[42]

Divestiture occurs when a company sells one or more businesses. At Ford Motor Company, recent operating losses and the costs of restructuring its workforce have brought about a cash shortage. To address anti-monopoly concerns that the proposed merger between Sysco and U.S. Foods will not reduce the competitiveness of the food services market, Sysco agreed to sell 11 distribution centers worth $4.6 billion in revenue to a competitor, Performance Food Group.[43]

Organizations engage in strategic maneuvering when they move into different environments. Some companies, called **prospectors,** are more likely than others to engage in strategic maneuvering.[44] Aggressive companies continuously change the boundaries of their competitive environments by seeking new products and markets, diversifying, and merging or acquiring new enterprises. In these and other ways, corporations put their competitors on the defensive and force them to react. **Defenders,** in contrast, stay within a more limited, stable product domain.

Influencing Your Environment

In addition to redefining the boundaries of their environment, managers and organizations can develop proactive responses aimed at changing the environment. Two general types of proactive responses are independent action and cooperative action.

Independent Action   A company uses **independent strategies** when it acts on its own to change some aspect of its current environment.[45] Exhibit 2.9 shows the definitions and uses of these strategies. For example, Southwest Airlines demonstrates competitive aggression by cutting fares when it enters a new market, and Apple uses competitive aggression whenever it launches a new product such as the iPhone or iTunes with great fanfare to establish its dominance as a technological leader. In contrast, when Kellogg Company promotes the cereal industry as a whole, it demonstrates competitive pacification. Weyerhaeuser Company advertises its reforestation efforts (public relations). Starbucks, SAP, Bank of America, Apple, and Bed Bath & Beyond, and other companies

divestiture

A firm selling one or more businesses.

prospectors

Companies that continuously change the boundaries for their task environments by seeking new products and markets, diversifying and merging, or acquiring new enterprises.

defenders

Companies that stay within a stable product domain as a strategic maneuver.

independent strategies

Strategies that an organization acting on its own uses to change some aspect of its current environment.

EXHIBIT 2.9   Independent Action

Strategy	Definition	Examples
Competitive aggression	Exploiting a distinctive competence or improving internal efficiency for competitive advantage	Aggressive pricing, comparative advertising (e.g., Walmart)
Competitive pacification	Independent action to improve relations with competitors	Helping competitors find raw materials
Public relations	Establishing and maintaining favorable images in the minds of those making up the environment	Sponsoring sporting events
Voluntary action	Voluntary commitment to various interest groups, causes, and social problems	Johnson & Johnson donating supplies to tsunami victims
Legal action	Engaging company in private legal battle	Warner Music lawsuits against illegal music copying
Political action	Efforts to influence elected representatives to create a more favorable business environment or limit competition	Issue advertising; lobbying at state and national levels

SOURCE: Adapted from *Journal of Marketing,* published by the American Marketing Association. C. Zeithaml and V. Zeithaml, "Environmental Management: Revising the Marketing Perspective," Spring 1984.

have signed on to Product Red, a program in which they market special Red-themed products and donate a percentage of the profits to the Global Fund, a project to help end AIDS in Africa (voluntary action).[46] Viacom sued Google for allowing users to post copyrighted video clips on the Google-owned YouTube website (legal action). In 2013, pharmaceutical companies spent $225 billion to lobby members of Congress (political action).[47] Each of these examples shows how organizations—on their own—can have an impact on the environment.

Cooperative Action   In some situations, two or more organizations work together using **cooperative strategies** to influence the environment.[48] Exhibit 2.10 shows several examples of cooperative strategies. An example of contracting occurs when suppliers and customers, or managers and labor unions, sign formal agreements about the terms and conditions of their future relationships. These contracts are explicit attempts to make their future relationship predictable. An example of cooptation might occur when universities invite wealthy alumni to join their boards of directors.

Finally, an example of coalition formation might be when local businesses band together to curb the rise of employee health care costs and when organizations in the same industry form industry associations and special interest groups. You may have seen cooperative advertising strategies, such as when dairy producers, beef producers, orange growers, and the like jointly pay for television commercials. Life Is Good, a New England–based T-shirt company, used the latest economic downturn as an opportunity to strengthen cooperative action with the retailers that stock its products. According to cofounder Bert Jacobs, employees at Life Is Good began calling retailers to ask how they could help them through the slow times. Based on the feedback, Jacobs identified a need to establish online networks that retailers—his company's customers—could use for sharing ideas.[49]

At the organizational level, firms establish strategic alliances, partnerships, joint ventures, and mergers with competitors to deal with environmental uncertainties. Cooperative strategies such as these make most sense when (1) taking joint action will reduce the organizations' costs and risks and (2) cooperation will increase their power—that is, their ability to accomplish the changes they desire successfully.

cooperative strategies

Strategies used by two or more organizations working together to manage the external environment.

How did T-shirt company Life Is Good use the economic downturn as an opportunity?

© Zuma Press, Inc./Alamy

EXHIBIT 2.10
Cooperative Action

Strategy	Definition	Examples
Contraction	Negotiation of an agreement between the organization and another group to exchange goods, services, information, patents, and so on	Contractual marketing systems
Cooptation	Absorbing new elements into the organization's leadership structure to avert threats to its stability or existence	Consumer and labor representatives and bankers on boards of directors
Coalition	Two or more groups that coalesce and act jointly with respect to some set of issues for some period of time	Industry associations; political initiatives of the Business Roundtable and the U.S. Chamber of Commerce

SOURCE: Reprinted from *Journal of Marketing,* published by the American Marketing Association. C. Zeithaml and V. Zeithaml, "Environmental Management: Revising the Marketing Perspective," Spring 1984.

Adapting to the Environment: Changing Yourself

To cope with environmental uncertainty, organizations frequently make adjustments in their structures and work processes. When uncertainty arises from environmental complexity, organizations tend to adapt by decentralizing decision making. For example, if a company faces a growing number of competitors in various markets, if different customers want different things, and if production facilities are being built in different regions of the world, it may be impossible for the chief executive (or a small group of top executives) to keep abreast of all activities and understand all the operational details of a business. In these cases, the top management team is likely to give authority to lower-level managers to make decisions that benefit the firm. The term **empowerment** is used frequently today to talk about this type of decentralized authority. We will address empowerment and decision making in more detail in Chapters 3 and 9.

In response to uncertainty caused by change (dynamism) in the environment, organizations tend to establish more flexible structures. In today's business world, the term *bureaucracy* generally has a bad connotation. Most of us recognize that bureaucratic organizations tend to be formal and very stable; frequently they are unable to adjust to change or exceptional circumstances that "don't fit the rules." And although bureaucratic organizations may be efficient and controlled if the environment is stable, they tend to be slow-moving and plodding when products, technologies, customers, or competitors are changing over time. In these cases, more *organic* structures give organizations the flexibility to adjust to change. We will discuss organic structures in more detail in Chapter 9, but we can simply say here that they are less formal than bureaucratic organizations—making decisions through interaction and mutual adjustment among individuals rather than from a set of predefined rules. Exhibit 2.11 shows four approaches that organizations can take in adapting to environmental uncertainty.

Adapting at the Boundaries   Because they are open systems, organizations are exposed to uncertainties from both their inputs and outputs. To help them compete, they can create buffers on both the input and output boundaries with the environment. **Buffering** creates supplies of excess resources to meet unpredictable needs. On the input side, organizations establish relationships with employment agencies to hire part-time and temporary help during rush periods when labor demand is difficult to predict. In the U.S. labor force, these workers, known as *contingent workers,* include 2.5 million on-call workers, 1.2 million temporary help agency workers, and more than 800,000 workers provided by contract firms, suggesting widespread use of this approach to buffering labor input uncertainties.[50] Contingency work opportunities are growing. According to Adecco, a firm that places workers in temporary assignments, the number of positions for contingent workers will grow at least three times as fast as the number of traditional (full-time, permanent) jobs. The demand for temporary workers in finance, administrative support, health care, engineering, and information technology is especially strong. A significant reason is that companies still in shock from the Great Recession are cautious about expanding payrolls. This is good news for people who do contingent work because they may prefer a variety of assignments, enjoyment of independence, or the ability to design work arrangements that fit with personal needs.[51] On the output side of the system, most organizations use some type of ending inventories that allow them to keep merchandise on hand in case a rush of customers decide to buy their products. Auto dealers are a common example of this use of buffers, but we can see

empowerment

The process of sharing power with employees, thereby enhancing their confidence in their ability to perform their jobs and their belief that they are influential contributors to the organization.

buffering

Creating supplies of excess resources in case of unpredictable needs.

In today's business world, the term *bureaucracy* generally has a bad connotation.

EXHIBIT 2.11
Four Approaches for Managing Uncertainty

	Stable	Dynamic
Complex	Decentralized	Decentralized
	Bureaucratic (standardized skills)	Organic (mutual adjustment)
Simple	Centralized	Centralized
	Bureaucratic (standardized work processes)	Organic (direct supervision)

smoothing

Leveling normal fluctuations at the boundaries of the environment.

similar use of buffer inventories in fast-food restaurants, bookstores, clothing stores, and even real estate agencies.[52]

In addition to buffering, organizations may try **smoothing**, or leveling normal fluctuations at the boundaries of the environment. For example, during winter months in the north, when automobile sales drop off, it is not uncommon for dealers to cut the price of their in-stock vehicles to increase demand. At the end of each clothing season, retailers discount their merchandise to clear it out to make room for incoming inventories. These are examples of smoothing environmental cycles to level off fluctuations in demand.

Adapting at the Core   Although buffering and smoothing manage uncertainties at the boundaries of the organization, firms also can establish **flexible processes** that allow for adaptation in their technical core. For example, firms increasingly try to customize their goods and services to meet the varied and changing demands of customers. Even in manufacturing, where it is difficult to change basic core processes, firms are adopting techniques of mass customization that help them create flexible factories. Instead of mass-producing large quantities of a "one-size-fits-all" product, organizations can use mass customization to produce individually customized products at an equally low cost. Whereas Henry Ford used to claim that "you could have a Model T in any color you wanted, as long as it was black," auto companies now offer a wide array of colors and trim lines, with different options and accessories. The process of mass customization involves the use of a network of independent operating units in which each performs a specific process or task such as making a dashboard assembly on an automobile. When an order comes in, different modules join forces to deliver the product or service as specified by the customer.[53] We will discuss mass customization and flexible factories in more depth in Chapter 9.

flexible processes

Methods for adapting the technical core to changes in the environment.

Bottom Line

The Internet lets customers quickly find products with the cost and quality features they want.

What might "flexible processes" mean for a fast-food restaurant? For an auto company?

Choosing a Response Approach

Three general considerations help guide management's response to the environment. First, organizations should attempt to change appropriate elements of the environment. Environmental responses are most useful when aimed at elements of the environment that (1) cause the company problems, (2) provide it with opportunities, and (3) allow the company to change successfully. Thus, PepsiCo recognized that public concern about the obesity epidemic and its impact on health could be a problem for the sales and reputation of a company that makes snacks and soft drinks. CEO Nooyi believed it would be irresponsible to try to change that concern, so she focused on what the company could do: change its product mix to include more healthful alternatives without abandoning the idea that an occasional fun snack is fine to enjoy. In terms of success, the company has been able to develop alternative products; the jury is still out on whether this approach will be profitable.

Second, organizations should choose responses that focus on pertinent elements of the environment. If a company wants to manage its competitive environment better, competitive aggression and pacification are viable options. Political action influences the legal environment, and contracting helps manage customers and suppliers.

Third, companies should choose responses that offer the most benefit at the lowest cost. Return-on-investment calculations should incorporate short-term financial considerations as well as long-term impact. Strategic managers who consider these factors carefully will guide their organizations to competitive advantage more effectively.

The Internal Environment of Organizations: Culture and Climate

LO 6

Of course an organization is more than a collection of responses to the external environment. The ways people in an organization behave, including the goals they set and the manner in which they treat their customers, are also shaped by forces within the organization. These forces, which include an organization's culture and its climate, are sets of conditions that influence the decisions and behavior of employees at all levels of the organization.

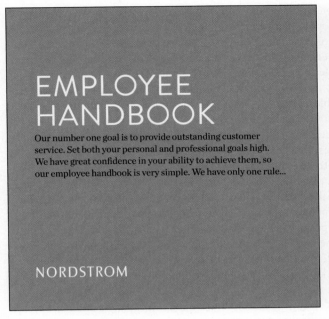

At Nordstrom, the fashion retailer, new employees are given a five-by-eight-inch card with one rule on it, along with a full handbook containing policies and legal regulations.

© *Nordstrom, Inc.*

On a day-to-day basis, an employee's experience of an organization's culture and climate may feel hard to sort out, much as your experience of a hot summer day may result from a combination of your region's climate and the day's weather or your experience of happiness from a combination of your general personality and your mood in response to recent events.

Organization Culture

One of the most important factors that influence an organization's response to its external environment is its culture. **Organization culture** is the set of important assumptions about the organization and its goals and practices that members of the company share. It is a system of shared values about what is important and beliefs about how the world works. In this way, a company's culture provides a framework that organizes and directs people's behavior on the job.[54] The culture of an organization may be difficult for an observer to define easily, yet like an individual's personality, it can often be sensed almost immediately. For example, the way people dress and behave, the way they interact with each other and with customers, and the qualities that are likely to be valued by their managers are usually quite different at a bank than they are at a rock music company, and different again at a law firm or an advertising agency.

Cultures can be strong or weak; strong cultures can have great influence on how people think and behave. A strong culture is one in which everyone understands and believes in the firm's goals, priorities, and practices. A strong culture can be a real advantage to the organization if the behaviors it encourages and facilitates are appropriate ones. For example, the Walt Disney Company's culture encourages extraordinary devotion to customer service; the culture at design firm IDEO encourages innovation. Employees in these companies don't need rule books to dictate how they act because these behaviors are conveyed as "the way we do things around here"; they are rooted in their companies' cultures.

In contrast, a strong culture that encourages inappropriate behaviors can severely hinder an organization's ability to deal effectively with its external environment—particularly if the environment is undergoing change, as is almost always the case today. For instance, a small start-up may have an informal culture that becomes less suitable when the company

organization culture

The set of important assumptions about the organization and its goals and practices that members of the company share.

grows, faces more competition, and requires decision making by a wide range of specialized employees spread out over many locations.

Similarly, when a merger or acquisition brings together organizations with strong cultures, cultural differences can encourage behaviors that are harmful to the combined organization. After Procter & Gamble acquired Gillette, integration of the two cultures took much longer than expected. One key difference was that Gillette preferred to make decisions rapidly whereas Procter & Gamble took a more deliberative approach.[55] Such differences in style can be unsettling to employees on both sides and may help to explain why research has found much higher turnover rates among managers at companies that have been acquired.[56]

In contrast to strong cultures, weak cultures have the following characteristics: different people hold different values, there is confusion about corporate goals, and it is not clear from one day to the next what principles should guide decisions. Some managers may pay lip service to some aspects of the culture ("we would never cheat a customer") but behave very differently ("don't tell him about the flaw"). As you can guess, such a culture fosters confusion, conflict, and poor performance. Most managers would agree that they want to create a strong culture that encourages and supports goals and useful behaviors that will make the company more effective. In other words, they want to create a culture that is appropriately aligned with the organization's competitive environment.[57]

Diagnosing Culture   Let's say you want to understand a company's culture. Perhaps you are thinking about working there and you want a good fit, or perhaps you are working there right now and want to deepen your understanding of the organization and determine whether its culture matches the challenges it faces. How would you go about making the diagnosis? A variety of things will give you useful clues about culture:

Corporate mission statements and official goals are a starting point because they will tell you the firm's desired public image. Most companies have a mission statement—even the CIA, as shown in Exhibit 2.12. Your school has one, and you can probably find it online. But are these statements a true expression of culture? A Gallup research study of nearly 50,000 business units across 192 organizations

EXHIBIT 2.12
CIA Vision, Mission, and Values

Vision	We will provide knowledge and take action to ensure the national security of the United States and the preservation of American life and ideals.
Mission	We are the eyes and ears of the nation and at times its hidden hand. We accomplish this mission by: • Collecting intelligence that matters. • Providing relevant, timely, and objective all-source analysis. • Conducting covert action at the direction of the president to preempt threats or achieve United States policy objectives.
Values	In pursuit of our country's interests, we put Nation before Agency, Agency before unit, and all before self. What we do matters. • Our success depends on our ability to act with total discretion and an ability to protect sources and methods. • We provide objective, unbiased information and analysis. • Our mission requires complete personal integrity and personal courage, physical and intellectual. • We accomplish things others cannot, often at great risk. When the stakes are highest and the dangers greatest, we are there and there first. • We stand by one another and behind one another. Service, sacrifice, flexibility, teamwork, and quiet patriotism are our hallmarks.

SOURCE: CIA website at www.cia.gov/information/mission.html.

found that 41 percent of employees are not aware of their companies' mission.[58] So, even after reading statements of mission and goals, you still need to figure out whether the statements truly reflect how the firm conducts business.

Business practices can be observed. How a company responds to problems, makes strategic decisions, and treats employees and customers tells a lot about what top management really values. The Tribune Company's repeated efforts to cut costs at the *Los Angeles Times* and consolidate its Washington bureau with that of the chain's other newspapers told the acquired company's employees about the parent company's priorities.

Symbols, rites, and ceremonies give further clues about culture. For instance, status symbols can give you a feel for how rigid the hierarchy is and for the nature of relationships between lower and higher levels. Who is hired and fired—and why— and the activities that are rewarded indicate the firm's real values.

The stories people tell carry a lot of information about the company's culture. Every company has its myths, legends, and true stories about important past decisions and actions that convey the company's main values. The stories often feature the company's heroes: people once or still active who possessed the qualities and characteristics that the culture especially values and who act as models for others about how to behave. A famous company hero, Sam Walton, expressed his frugality by driving an old pick-up truck when visiting his stores.

A strong culture combines these measures in a consistent way. The Ritz-Carlton hotel chain gives each employee a laminated card listing its 12 service values. Each day it carries out a type of ceremony: a 15-minute meeting during which employees from every department resolve problems and discuss areas of potential improvement. At these meetings, the focus is on the day's "wow story," which details an extraordinary way that a Ritz-Carlton employee lived up to one of the service values. For example, a family arrived at the Bali Ritz-Carlton with special eggs and milk because of their son's allergies, but the food had spoiled. The manager and dining staff couldn't find replacements in town, so the executive chef called his mother-in-law in Singapore and asked her to buy the necessary products and fly with them to Bali.[59]

In general, cultures can be categorized according to whether they emphasize flexibility or control and whether their focus is internal or external to the organization. By juxtaposing these two dimensions, we can describe four types of organization cultures, depicted in Exhibit 2.13:

Group culture. A group culture is internally oriented and flexible. It tends to be based on the values and norms associated with affiliation. An organizational member's compliance with organizational directives flows from trust, tradition, and long-term commitment. It tends to emphasize member development and values participation in decision making. The strategic orientation associated with this cultural type is one of implementation through consensus building. Leaders tend to act as mentors and facilitators.

Hierarchical culture. The hierarchical culture is internally oriented by more focus on control and stability. It has the values and norms associated with a bureaucracy. It values stability and assumes that individuals will comply with organizational mandates when roles are stated formally and enforced through rules and procedures.

Rational culture. The rational culture is externally oriented and focused on control. Its primary objectives are productivity, planning, and efficiency. Organizational members are motivated by the belief that performance that leads to the desired organizational objectives will be rewarded.

Adhocracy. The adhocracy is externally oriented and flexible. This culture type emphasizes change in which growth, resource acquisition, and innovation are stressed. Organizational members are motivated by the importance or ideological appeal of the task. Leaders tend to be entrepreneurial and risk takers. Other members tend to have these characteristics as well.[60]

EXHIBIT 2.13
Competing Values Model
of Culture

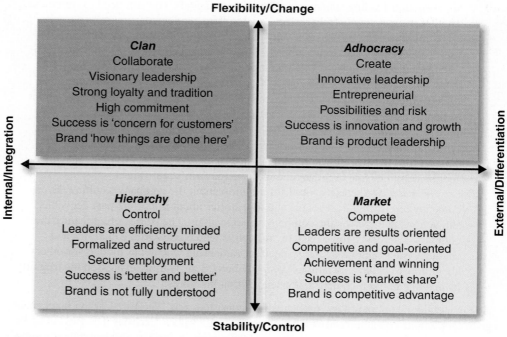

SOURCE: Adapted from Kim S. Cameron and Robert E. Quinn, *Diagnosing and Changing Organizational Culture,* 3rd ed. (San Francisco: Jossey-Bass, 2011).

This type of diagnosis is important when two companies are considering combining operations, as in a merger, acquisition, or joint venture, because as we noted, cultural differences can sink these arrangements. In some cases, organizations investigating this type of change can benefit from setting up a clean team of third-party experts who investigate the details of each company's culture.[61]

Managing Culture   We mentioned earlier in this chapter that one important way organizations have of responding to the environment is to *adapt* to it by changing the organization itself. One of the most important tools managers have for implementing such a change lies in their management of their organization's culture. A culture that is inwardly instead of customer focused, for example, will resist a manager's efforts to make it more market driven. Simple directives alone are often ineffective; the underlying values of the organization also have to be shifted in the desired direction. Most companies today know that adopting a customer orientation, improving quality, and making other moves necessary to remain competitive are so essential that they require deep-rooted cultural changes. When that kind of change occurs, organization members may then begin to internalize the new values and display the appropriate behaviors on their own.

Top managers can take several approaches to managing culture. First, they should espouse lofty ideals and visions for the company that will inspire organization members. (We will discuss vision more fully in Chapter 4, on strategy, and in Chapter 12, on leadership.) That vision—whether it concerns quality, integrity, innovation, or whatever—should be articulated over and over until it becomes a tangible presence throughout the organization.

Second, executives must give constant attention to the mundane details of daily affairs such as communicating regularly, being visible and active throughout the company, and setting examples. Not only should the CEO talk about the vision, but he or she should also embody it day in and day out. This makes the CEO's pronouncements credible, creates a personal example others can emulate, and builds trust that the organization's progress toward the vision will continue over the long run.

Important here are the moments of truth when hard choices must be made. Imagine top management trumpeting a culture that emphasizes quality and then discovering that a

Bottom Line

A culture aligned with its environment helps the organization succeed. *To be aligned with its environment, what values should an organic grocery store chain company have?*

Management in Action

FACEBOOK'S WAY FORWARD

During the recent Facebook-sponsored F8 conference for developers, Mark Zuckerberg made it clear that Facebook will be developing tools for developers to grow and make more revenue from their apps on the social-networking site. In turn, this goal will "make users happier and marketers smarter, so business owners will be able to more easily reach large audiences."

Some of the initiatives announced by Zuckerberg and his management team at the F8 conference include:[63]

1. *User anonymity when trying apps.* When users try an app for the first time, they can remain anonymous and exert more control over how the app interacts with their personal information. Facebook hopes this feature will encourage more users to sample and sign up for apps.

2. *FbStart program.* For companies that want tools and services to get their early-stage apps developed and online as quickly as possible, they can purchase the Bootstrap program for $5,000. If a company has pre-existing apps that need to get to the next level of success, there's the Accelerate program that costs $30,000.

3. *Stable mobile platform.* Developers are promised that their apps will function properly for a minimum of two years even as newer versions of the programming

interface emerge. The platform is expected to reduce the risk and increase the revenue associated with app development.

4. *Mobile.* An overarching emphasis of the conference was on making the mobile experience for users more seamless and enjoyable. App Links will enable developers to create apps that allow users to move between apps while staying in one app.

5. *More targeted ad placement.* Facebook's Audience Network will allow marketers "to tap into rich personal data" to better monetize apps with targeted ads. For example, online jewelry business Joseph Nogucci targets ads to its main audience of women ages 18–54.[64]

Facebook has renewed its focus on developers and entrepreneurs. It is betting its growth and reputation that these contributors will fuel the company's growth well into the future.

- How well do you think Facebook has been responding to its fast-changing environment? Identify risks it is taking that could negatively impact its future growth.
- How can Mark Zuckerberg strengthen Facebook's culture to help the company fulfill its mission?

---

part used in a batch of assembled products is defective. Whether to replace the part at great expense in the interest of quality or to ship the defective part just to save time and money is a decision that will go a long way toward reinforcing or destroying a quality-oriented culture.

To reinforce the organization's culture, the CEO and other executives should routinely celebrate and reward those who exemplify the new values. Another key to managing culture involves hiring, socializing newcomers, and promoting employees on the basis of the new corporate values. In this way, the new culture will begin to permeate the organization. Although this may seem a time-consuming approach to building a new culture, effective managers recognize that replacing a long-term culture of traditional values with one that embodies the competitive values needed in the future can take years. But the rewards of that effort will be an organization much more effective and responsive to its environmental challenges and opportunities.

Organizational Climate

In contrast to a culture's deeply held beliefs, values, and so on, an organization's climate can be measured more readily. **Organizational climate** consists of the patterns of attitudes and behavior that shape people's experience of an organization.[62] For example, an organization's climate might include clear performance standards, frequent conflict, great trust in leaders, and open communication between supervisors and their employees. Researchers have developed and tested surveys for measuring organizational climate in terms of factors such as morale, employees' relationships with managers and co-workers,

organizational climate

The patterns of attitudes and behavior that shape people's experience of an organization.

handling of conflicts, openness and effectiveness of communication, methods for measuring and rewarding performance, and the clarity of one's role in the organization. An organization's climate and its culture both shape the experience of working there and the organization's effectiveness. However, because organizational climate is easier to measure, managers often find that dimensions of organizational climate are more manageable. Later chapters explore a variety of management responsibilities that shape organizational climate, including maintaining ethical conduct (Chapter 5), creating a structure for the organization (Chapter 8), appraising and rewarding performance (Chapter 10), valuing diversity (Chapter 11), leading (Chapter 12), motivating employees (Chapter 13), fostering teamwork (Chapter 14), communicating (Chapter 15), and leading change (Chapter 18). An organization is most effective when it has a climate that motivates and enables workers to achieve the organization's strategy. As you read "Management Connection: Onward," consider how a healthy organizational climate would strengthen Facebook under the leadership of Mark Zuckerberg.

KEY TERMS

acquisition, p. 58

barriers to entry, p. 51

benchmarking, p. 58

buffering, p. 61

competitive environment, p. 42

competitive intelligence, p. 56

cooperative strategies, p. 60

defenders, p. 59

demographics, p. 46

diversification, p. 58

divestiture, p. 59

domain selection, p. 58

empowerment, p. 61

environmental scanning, p. 56

environmental uncertainty, p. 56

external environment, p. 42

final consumer, p. 54

flexible processes, p. 62

forecasting, p. 57

independent strategies, p. 59

inputs, p. 42

intermediate consumer, p. 54

macroenvironment, p. 43

merger, p. 58

open systems, p. 42

organization culture, p. 63

organizational climate, p. 67

outputs, p. 42

prospectors, p. 59

scenario, p. 57

smoothing, p. 62

strategic maneuvering, p. 58

supply chain management, p. 53

switching costs, p. 53

RETAINING WHAT YOU LEARNED

You learned how pressures from outside the organization create the context in which managers must function. The macroenvironment includes broad forces like the economy, laws, and technology. In contrast, the competitive environment is closer to the organization and includes forces like competitors, suppliers, and customers. Effective managers need to stay aware of labor force and related trends that can impact their businesses. An organization's competitive environment can range from favorable to unfavorable. Proactive managers attempt to manage environmental uncertainty through a variety of strategies. Organization culture provides an internal framework that organizes and directs people's behavior at work. Cultures are strong or weak and may be one of four types: group, hierarchical, rational, or adhocracy.

 1   Describe how environmental forces influence organizations and how organizations can influence their environments.

- Organizations are open systems that are affected by, and in turn affect, their external environments.

- Organizations receive financial, human, material, and information resources from the environment; transform those resources into finished goods and services; and then send those outputs back into the environment to meet market needs.

LO 2   Distinguish between the macroenviroment and the competitive environment.

- The macroenvironment is composed of economic, legal and political, technological, demographic, social, and natural environment forces that influence strategic decisions.

- The competitive environment is composed of forces closer to the organization, such as current competitors, new entrants, substitute and complementary products, suppliers, and customers.

- The simplest distinction between the macroenvironment and the competitive environment is in the amount of control a firm can exert on external forces.

- Macroenvironmental forces such as the economy and social trends are much less controllable than are forces in the competitive environment such as suppliers and customers.

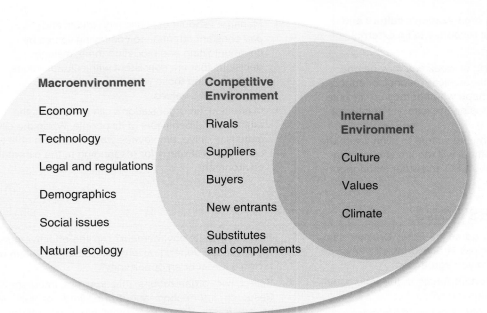

EXHIBIT 2.2
The External and Internal
Environments
of Organizations

LO 3 **Explain why managers and organizations should attend to economic and social developments.**

- Developments outside the organization can have a profound effect on the way managers and their companies operate. For example, higher energy costs or increased spending on security may make it harder for managers to keep their prices low.
- The growing diversity of the labor force gives managers access to a much broader range of talent but also requires them to make sure different types of employees are treated equally.
- Effective managers stay aware of trends like these and respond to them appropriately.

LO 4 **Identify elements of the competitive environment.**

- Elements in the environment can range from favorable to unfavorable. To determine how favorable a competitive environment is, managers should consider the nature of the competitors, potential new entrants, threat of substitutes, opportunities from complements, and relationships with suppliers and customers.
- Analyzing how these forces influence the organization provides an indication of potential threats and opportunities.
- Effective management of the firm's supply chain is one way to achieve a competitive advantage.
- Attractive environments tend to be those with high industry growth, few competitors, products that can be differentiated, few potential entrants, many barriers to entry, few substitutes, many suppliers (none with much power), and many customers.
- After identifying and analyzing competitive forces, managers must formulate a strategy that minimizes the power external forces have over the organization.

LO 5 **Summarize how organizations respond to environmental uncertainty.**

- Responding effectively to the environment often requires devising proactive strategies to change the environment.
- Strategic maneuvering involves changing the boundaries of the competitive environment through domain selection, diversification, mergers, and the like.
- Independent strategies require not moving into a new environment but rather changing some aspect of the current environment through competitive aggression, public relations, legal action, and so on.
- Cooperative strategies, such as contracting, cooptation, and coalition building, involve the working together of two or more organizations.
- Organizations also may make themselves better able to handle environmental change by decentralizing authority, buffering or smoothing, and establishing flexible processes.

LO 6 **Define elements of an organization's culture.**

- An organization's culture is its set of shared values and practices related to what is important and how the world works.
- The culture provides a framework that organizes and directs people's behavior at work.
- Elements of the culture may be expressed in corporate mission statements and official goals, assuming these reflect how the organization actually operates.
- Business practices are a basic measure of culture. Symbols, rites, ceremonies, and the stories people tell express and reinforce their cultural values.

LO 7 **Discuss how an organization's culture and climate affect its response to its external environment.**

- A culture may be strong or weak and may be one of four types: group, hierarchical, rational, or adhocracy. These cultures shape whether they are flexible and whether the focus is on the external or internal environment.
- Managing and changing the culture to align it with the organization's environment will require strong, long-term commitment by the CEO and other managers.

- Managers should espouse high ideals and pay constant attention to conveying values by communicating and modeling them, making decisions that are consistent with cultural values, and rewarding those who demonstrate the organization's values.
- In addition, an organization's climate shapes the attitudes and behaviors of its people. When the climate is positive, employees want to and are able to carry out its strategy for responding to the external environment.

DISCUSSION QUESTIONS

1. This chapter's opening quote by Peter Drucker said, "The essence of a business is outside itself." What do you think this means? Do you agree?
2. What are the most important forces in the macroenvironment facing companies today?
3. What are the main differences between the macroenvironment and the competitive environment?
4. What kinds of changes do companies make in response to environmental uncertainty?
5. We outlined several proactive responses that organizations can make to the environment. What examples have you seen recently of an organization's responding

effectively to its environment? Did the effectiveness of the response depend on whether the organization was facing a threat or an opportunity?

6. Select two organizations that you are interested in. Research information about the firms or talk with an employee, if possible. What types of cultures do they have? Write a paragraph that describes each culture.
7. When you visited colleges to select one to attend, were there cultural differences in the campuses that made a difference in your choice? Did these differences help you decide which college to attend?

EXPERIENTIAL EXERCISES

2.1   EXTERNAL ENVIRONMENT ANALYSIS

OBJECTIVE
To give you the experience of performing an analysis of a company's external environment

INSTRUCTIONS
Select a company you want to learn more about. Using online and/or library resources, including websites on the company's industry and its website and annual report, fill out the following External Environment Worksheet for that company:

External Environment Worksheet

Laws and regulations
What are some key laws and regulations under which this company and industry must operate?

_____

_____

The economy
How does the state of the economy influence the sales of this company's products?

_____

_____

Technology
What new technologies strongly affect the company you have selected?

_____

_____

Demographics

What changes in the population might affect the company's customer base?

_____

_____

Social issues

What changes in society affect the market for your company's products?

_____

_____

Suppliers

How does your company's relationship with suppliers affect its profitability?

_____

_____

Competitors

What companies compete with the firm you have selected? Do they compete on price, on quality, or on other factors?

_____

_____

New entrants

Are new competitors to the company likely? Possible?

_____

_____

Substitutes and complements

Is there a threat of substitutes for the industry's existing products? Are there complementary products that suggest an opportunity for collaboration?

_____

_____

Customers

What characteristics of the company's customer base influence the company's competitiveness?

_____

_____

DISCUSSION QUESTIONS

1. What has the company done to adapt to its environment?

2. How does the company attempt to influence its environment?

SOURCE: From Steven L. McShane and Mary Ann Von Glinow, _Organizational Behavior_ 3rd edition, 2005, p. 499. Reprinted with permission of The McGraw-Hill Companies.

2.2 CORPORATE CULTURE PREFERENCE SCALE

OBJECTIVE

This self-assessment is designed to help you identify a corporate culture that fits most closely with your personal values and assumptions.

INSTRUCTIONS

Read each pair of the statements in the Corporate Culture Preference Scale and circle the statement that describes the organization you would prefer to work in. This exercise is completed alone so students assess themselves honestly without concerns of social comparison. However, class discussion will focus on the importance of matching job applicants to the organization's dominant values.

Corporate Culture Preference Scale

I would prefer to work in an organization:

1a.	Where employees work well together in teams.	**OR**	1b. That produces highly respected products or services.
2a.	Where top management maintains a sense of order in the workplace.	**OR**	2b. Where the organization listens to customers and responds quickly to their needs.
3a.	Where employees are treated fairly.	**OR**	3b. Where employees continuously search for ways to work more efficiently.
4a.	Where employees adapt quickly to new work requirements.	**OR**	4b. Where corporate leaders work hard to keep employees happy.
5a.	Where senior executives receive special benefits not available to other employees.	**OR**	5b. Where employees are proud when the organization achieves its performance goals.
6a.	Where employees who perform the best get paid the most.	**OR**	6b. Where senior executives are respected.
7a.	Where everyone gets his or her job done like clockwork.	**OR**	7b. That is on top of new innovations in the industry.
8a.	Where employees receive assistance to overcome any personal problems.	**OR**	8b. Where employees abide by company rules.
9a.	That is always experimenting with new ideas in the marketplace.	**OR**	9b. That expects everyone to put in 110 percent for peak performance.
10a.	That quickly benefits from market opportunities.	**OR**	10b. Where employees are always kept informed of what's happening in the organization.
11a.	That can quickly respond to competitive threats.	**OR**	11b. Where most decisions are made by the top executives.
12a.	Where management keeps everything under control.	**OR**	12b. Where employees care for each other.

SOURCE: Steven L. McShane and Mary Ann Von Glinow, *Organizational Behavior*, 3rd ed., McGraw-Hill, 2005, p. 499. Copyright © 2005 The McGraw-Hill Companies, Inc. Reprinted with permission.

Scoring Key for the Corporate Culture Preference Scale

Scoring instructions: In each space, write in a "I" if you circled the statement and "O" if you did not. Then add up the scores for each subscale.

Control culture
$$\frac{}{(2a)} + \frac{}{(5a)} + \frac{}{(6b)} + \frac{}{(8b)} + \frac{}{(11b)} + \frac{}{(12a)} = \underline{\quad}$$

Performance culture
$$\frac{}{(1b)} + \frac{}{(3b)} + \frac{}{(5b)} + \frac{}{(6a)} + \frac{}{(7a)} + \frac{}{(9a)} = \underline{\quad}$$

Relationship culture
$$\frac{}{(1a)} + \frac{}{(3a)} + \frac{}{(4b)} + \frac{}{(8a)} + \frac{}{(10b)} + \frac{}{(12b)} = \underline{\quad}$$

Responsive culture
$$\frac{}{(2b)} + \frac{}{(4a)} + \frac{}{(7b)} + \frac{}{(9a)} + \frac{}{(10a)} + \frac{}{(11a)} = \underline{\quad}$$

Interpreting your score: These corporate cultures may be found in many organizations, but they represent only four of many possible organization cultures. Also, keep in mind none of these subscales is inherently good or bad. Each is effective in different situations. The four corporate cultures are defined here, along with the range of scores for high, medium, and low levels of each dimension based on a sample of MBA students:

Corporate Culture Dimension and Definition

Control culture: This culture values the role of senior executives to lead the organization. Its goal is to keep everyone aligned and under control.

Score Interpretation

High: 3 to 6

Medium: 1 to 2

Low: 0

Performance culture: This culture values individual and organizational performance and strives for effectiveness and efficiency.	High: 5 to 6 Medium: 3 to 4 Low: 0 to 2
Relationship culture: This culture values nurturing and well-being. It considers open communication, fairness, teamwork, and sharing a vital part of organizational life.	High: 6 Medium: 4 to 5 Low: 0 to 3
Responsive culture: This culture values its ability to keep in tune with the external environment, including being competitive and realizing new opportunities.	High: 6 Medium: 4 to 5 Low: 0 to 3

CONCLUDING CASE

TATA MOTORS: FROM CHEAP TO AWESOME?

The barriers to entry are so high in the automotive industry that it is rare to see a new entrant. A notable exception has been India's Tata Motors, the country's largest maker of commercial vehicles, which about five years ago promised to become a leading carmaker in the fast-growing economies of the developing world. Comparing its ambitious plan to the iconic Volkswagen Beetle and Ford Model T, Tata launched the Nano in 2009. Branded a "people's car," the Nano was priced at $2,000 to $2,500 (or 1 lakh in Indian currency). Tata Motors marketed the stripped-down minicar to first-time automobile customers in rural areas. The goal was to make the Nano the standard transportation for Indian families working their way up to the middle class.

The promised launch was so ambitious that Tata could not realistically meet expectations. Production was postponed for about a year and a half, and then the company determined it couldn't afford to sell the Nano profitably at the promised price. The first Nanos to roll off assembly lines were priced just $800 below Suzuki's competing Alto, which offered more storage space and a more powerful engine. The Nano's safety performance also ran into embarrassing problems; some reportedly caught fire.

Sales of the Nano have been disappointing. After reaching its maximum sales of 10,000 in April 2012, recent reports of the "people's car" indicate 2,500 units are sold each month. It has been suggested that the low sales were a result of the unacceptably low level of quality and features built into the vehicle, including an underpowered and noisy motor, no stereo or air conditioning, and wires visible in the driver's compartment. Another reason for the Nano's demise was a missed target market, namely young urban drivers. The cheap and unsafe image associated with the Nano turned off many of these would-be buyers.

The Nano's failure was frustrating to Tata Motors that had invested $400 million to develop the Nano and "hundreds of millions more building a factory capable of manufacturing 15,000 to 20,000 of the tiny cars a month." If it were to be successful in the long run, Tata Motors would need to adjust its strategy to overcome the myriad barriers to success in the Indian automotive industry.

Tata Motors has changed both its marketing and manufacturing strategies. Shifting its focus from first-time rural buyers to young urban customers, the company recently launched the Nano Twist and Nano LX. It is trying to rebrand the Nano from "cheapest car in the world" to an "awesome" car that is also affordable. Priced as high as $3,578, these improved Nano models can include several upgrades like power steering, music system with Blue-tooth connectivity, and enhanced interior and exterior features.

Also, Tata has responded with maintenance contracts, test drives, and safety improvements. It has revenues from its commercial vehicles and its Jaguar Land Rover operations to stay afloat. Perhaps the Nano will still become the people's car. Start-ups often make mistakes, and some of them recover brilliantly. What made Tata's stumble remarkable was its grand scale.

DISCUSSION QUESTIONS

1. Which barriers to entry contributed most to Tata Motors' lack of success with the original Nano?

2. Which macroenvironmental factors did Tata Motors consider when adjusting the marketing and manufacturing strategies to achieve success with the more recent Twist and LX models?

3. To what degree do you believe Tata Motors will succeed in delivering a successful low-cost vehicle to consumers in India and other developing economies?

SOURCES: A. Mahendra, "Tata Nano Twist Review," *Auto Tech Review* (online), http://www.automotechreview.com, accessed February 26, 2015; V. Able, "Tata Nano: The Car That Was Just Too Cheap," *The Guardian* (online), February 3, 2014, http://www.theguardian.com; S. McClain, "Why the World's Cheapest Car Flopped," *The Wall Street Journal* (online), October 14, 2013; M. Eyring, "Learning from Tata Motors' Nano Mistakes," *Bloomberg Businessweek*, January 11, 2011, http://www.businessweek.com; and S. Philip, "Tata Motors Profit Rises 100-Fold on Jaguar Land Rover Sales," *Bloomberg Businessweek*, November 10, 2010, http://www.businessweek.com.

CHAPTER 3

Managerial Decision Making

> The business executive is by profession a decision maker. Uncertainty is his opponent. Overcoming it is his mission.
>
> —JOHN MCDONALD

After studying Chapter 3, you will be able to:

LO 1 Describe the kinds of decisions you will face as a manager.

LO 2 Summarize the steps in making "rational" decisions.

LO 3 Recognize the pitfalls you should avoid when making decisions.

LO 4 Evaluate the pros and cons of using a group to make decisions.

LO 5 Identify procedures to use in leading a decision-making group.

LO 6 Explain how to encourage creative decisions.

LO 7 Discuss the processes by which decisions are made in organizations.

LO 8 Describe how to make decisions in a crisis.

Management in Action

HOW HIGH-STAKES DECISIONS MAKE BOEING AN INDUSTRY LEADER

When the first Boeing 787 Dreamliners soared into the sky, they looked like the greatest advance in passenger aircraft in decades. Lightweight materials and efficient engine technology meant they would fly farther on less fuel. Besides being less expensive to operate, the planes had interiors offering passengers greater comfort. Airlines eagerly placed orders, and Boeing's major competitor, Airbus, hastened to improve its own product designs.

Within months, however, Boeing acknowledged problems with the aircraft's performance. Particularly troubling, fires started in power distribution panels and in batteries installed to provide auxiliary power. Boeing grounded the 787s until the battery problem could be resolved, and some people wondered whether the Dreamliner was actually a nightmare.

Why did Boeing have so much trouble with implementing its decision to produce the 787? Was the decision a mistake? For answers, we must look at Boeing's history as an innovator. Under the forceful leadership of engineer George Schairer, the company after World War II studied a German idea to increase speed by angling the wings toward the back of the plane. It was a risky, difficult change to the earlier designs of propeller aircraft, but Boeing created first the B-47 bomber and then the 707 jet airliner. The 707 put Boeing far ahead of its competitors, Douglas and Lockheed. A few decades later, the company again offered an impressive development, the first jumbo jet—its 747, introduced in 1970.

Based on its commitment to technology, Boeing dominated the commercial aircraft market until the 1980s, when a European consortium called Airbus launched its A320 with a highly automated cockpit and began stealing market share from Boeing. Under

© Paul Thomas/Bloomberg via Getty Images

the leadership of Alan Mulally, who headed the commercial-aircraft division until 2006, the company decided to make its next daring move into the future. The complex undertaking that became the Dreamliner was approved unanimously by Boeing's board of directors in 2003.

Today, Boeing's management insists that the decision was sound. Although the plane was completed behind schedule and over budget, customers have been placing orders at a record pace. By early 2015, Boeing delivered 228 Dreamliners to 29 airlines around the world. And observers note that innovative planes often have problems that must be fixed as they are identified. Airbus has had problems with its own innovative superjumbo jet, the A380. Launched over a decade ago, recent sales of the Airbus have been so low that its future is in question. According to Airbus Group CEO Tom Enders: "The group will face a decision over the near to midterm on the future of the A380."[1]

Developing the 787 Dreamliner was a complex decision for Boeing, but it seemed worthwhile because of the potential to remain at the forefront of aircraft technology. As you read this chapter, consider what makes managers' decisions difficult and what skills and resources can help managers overcome those difficulties and make the right choices.

Bottom Line

You'll be making decisions constantly. It may seem obvious, but it's worth stating: If you know how to make good decisions, you'll deliver good results.

What qualities or results of a management decision make it a "good" decision?

The best managers make decisions constantly. Some are difficult and strategic, while others are smaller decisions that affect day-to-day operations and procedures. Marie Robinson, the former chief logistics officer at Toys "R" Us, tapped into her experience with army logistics to make sure toys arrived to the retailer's 600 U.S. stores and to online customers' homes efficiently and on schedule. Robinson used stores as a tool for making logistics more efficient and speedier than an Internet-only retailer can. For routine decisions, she set up a decision-making system in which toys were shipped from either warehouses or stores based on which locations are most economical and have enough of the item in stock. Other decisions must be made in crisis mode. When superstorm Sandy shut down transportation systems in the New York City region in October 2012, Robinson learned that a ship loaded with merchandise for the holidays was being rerouted from New Jersey to the Bahamas. She worked with the shipper, so that the toys could still reach stores in time for Black Friday.[2] Robinson's managerial talent led to fashion retailer Michael Kors hiring her (without any experience in the fashion industry) in 2014 as its new senior vice president of global operations.[3]

The typical organization has the potential to more than double its decision effectiveness in terms of impact on financial results.[4] If you can't make decisions, you won't be an effective manager. This chapter discusses what kinds of decisions managers face, how they are made, and how they *should* be made.

Characteristics of Managerial Decisions

 Managers face problems and opportunities constantly. Some situations that require a decision are relatively simple; others seem overwhelming. Some demand immediate action; others take months or even years to unfold.

Actually, managers often ignore challenges.[5] For several reasons, they avoid taking action.[6] First, managers can't be sure how much time, energy, or trouble lies ahead once they start working on a challenge. Second, getting involved is risky; tackling a problem but failing to solve it successfully can hurt a manager's track record. Third, because problems can be so perplexing, it is easier to procrastinate or to get busy with less demanding activities. For these reasons, managers may lack the insight, courage, or will to decide.

It is important to understand why decision making can be so challenging. Exhibit 3.1 illustrates several characteristics of managerial decisions that contribute to their difficulty and pressure. Most managerial decisions lack structure and entail risk, uncertainty, and conflict.

EXHIBIT 3.1
Characteristics of Managerial Decisions

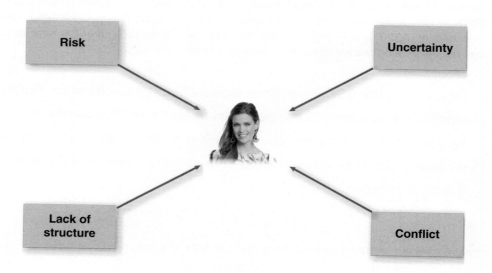

Lack of Structure

Lack of structure is the usual state of affairs in managerial decision making.[7] Although some decisions are routine and clear-cut, for most there is no automatic procedure to follow. Problems are novel and unstructured, leaving the decision maker uncertain about how to proceed.

An important distinction illustrating this point is between programmed and nonprogrammed decisions. **Programmed decisions** have been encountered and made before. They have objectively correct answers and can be solved by using simple rules, policies, or numerical computations. If you face a programmed decision, a clear procedure or structure exists for arriving at the right decision. For example, if you are a small-business owner and must decide the amounts for your employees' paychecks, you can use a formula—and if the amounts are wrong, your employees will prove it to you. Exhibit 3.2 gives some other examples.

If most important decisions were programmed, managerial life would be much easier. But managers typically face **nonprogrammed decisions:** new, novel, complex decisions having no certain outcomes. They have a variety of possible solutions, all of which have merits and drawbacks. The decision maker must create or impose a method for making the decision; there is no predetermined structure on which to rely. As Exhibit 3.1 suggests, important, difficult decisions tend to be nonprogrammed, and they demand creative approaches.

Uncertainty and Risk

If you have all the information you need and can predict precisely the consequences of your actions, you are operating under a condition of **certainty.**[8] Managers are expressing their preference for certainty when they are not satisfied hearing about what might have happened or may happen and insist on hearing what did or will happen.[9] But perfect certainty is rare. For important, nonprogrammed managerial decisions, uncertainty is the rule.

Uncertainty means the manager has insufficient information to know the consequences of different actions. Businesspeople do not like uncertainty; it can hold them back

programmed decisions

Decisions encountered and made before, having objectively correct answers, and solvable by using simple rules, policies, or numerical computations.

nonprogrammed decisions

New, novel, complex decisions having no proven answers.

certainty

The state that exists when decision makers have accurate and comprehensive information.

uncertainty

The state that exists when decision makers have insufficient information.

EXHIBIT 3.2

Comparison of Types of Decisions

	Programmed Decisions	Nonprogrammed Decisions
Problem	Frequent, repetitive, routine. Much certainty regarding cause-and-effect relationships.	Novel, unstructured. Much uncertainty regarding cause-and-effect relationships.
Procedure	Dependence on policies, rules, and definite procedures.	Necessity for creativity, intuition, tolerance for ambiguity, creative problem solving.
Examples		
Business firm	Telephone scripts for customer service employees to follow.	Diversification into new products and markets.
University	Necessary grade point average for good academic standing.	Raising funds to build new student housing and classrooms.
Health care	Procedure for admitting patients.	Purchase of experimental equipment.
Government	Merit system for promotion of state employees.	Reorganization of state government agencies.

SOURCE: J. Gibson, J. Ivancevich, and J. Donnelly Jr., *Organizations: Behavior, Structure, Processes,* 10th ed. 2000. Copyright © 2000 by The McGraw-Hill Companies, Inc. Reprinted with permission.

from taking action. For example, uncertainty about the strength and timing of the economic recovery made businesses slow to start hiring.[10] But economies don't strengthen until consumer demand picks up, which doesn't happen until employment rises.

When you can estimate the likelihood of various consequences but still do not know with certainty what will happen, you are facing **risk.** Risk exists when the probability of an action being successful is less than 100 percent and losses may occur. If the decision is the wrong one, you may lose money, time, reputation, or other important assets.

risk

The state that exists when the probability of success is less than 100 percent and losses may occur.

Risk, like uncertainty, is a fact of life in managerial decision making. But this is not the same as taking a risk. Although it sometimes seems as though risk takers are admired and entrepreneurs and investors thrive on taking risks, the reality is that good decision makers prefer to manage risk. They accept the fact that decisions have consequences entailing risk, but they do everything they can to anticipate the risk, minimize it, and control it.

The stories detailed in *The Greatest Business Decisions of All Time* are creative approaches to managing risk. A classic example is how Henry Ford, when facing high levels of employee turnover and discontent, doubled workers' pay and switched from two 9-hour shifts to three 8-hour shifts per day. These improvements cost Ford $10 million but his gamble paid off with higher retention rates and productivity levels.[11] Ford could not have known with certainty that his changes would work but he assessed his options and took a calculated risk.

A more recent example is a T-shirt company called Threadless, which reduces uncertainty and manages risk by basing its whole marketing model on collaboration with customers. Professional and amateur graphic designers submit their ideas for T-shirt designs at the Threadless website, where customers vote on the designs they like. From hundreds of submissions, the company selects four to six of the top vote getters each week and pays their designers $1,000. But it makes and sells them only after a minimum number of customers have already ordered the shirt design.[12]

T-shirt designers have a chance to get their designs printed through the Threadless website, but only after enough customers have given them high ratings and ordered a shirt.

© Threadless.com/Jérémie Royer

Conflict

Important decisions are even more difficult because of the conflict managers face. **Conflict,** which exists when a manager must consider opposing pressures from different sources, occurs at two levels.

conflict

Opposing pressures from different sources, occurring on the level of psychological conflict or conflict between individuals or groups.

First, individual decision makers experience psychological conflict when several options are attractive or when none of the options is attractive. For instance, a manager may have to decide whom to lay off when she doesn't want to lay off anyone. Or she may have three promising job applicants for one position—but choosing one means she has to reject the other two.

Second, conflict arises between people. A chief financial officer argues in favor of increasing long-term debt to finance an acquisition. The chief executive officer, however, prefers to minimize such debt and find the funds elsewhere. A marketing department wants more product lines to sell, and the engineers want higher-quality products. But the production people want to lower costs by having longer production runs of fewer products with no changes. Few decisions are without conflict.

The Phases of Decision Making

Faced with these challenges, how can you make good decisions? The ideal decision-making process includes six phases. As Exhibit 3.3 illustrates, decision makers should (1) identify and diagnose the problem, (2) generate alternative solutions, (3) evaluate alternatives, (4) make the choice, (5) implement the decision, and (6) evaluate the decision.

Identifying and Diagnosing the Problem

The first phase in the decision-making process is to recognize that a problem exists and must be solved. Typically, a manager realizes some discrepancy between the current state (the way things are) and a desired state (the way things ought to be). Such discrepancies—say, in organizational or unit performance—may be detected by comparing current performance against (1) *past* performance, (2) the *current* performance of other organizations or units, or (3) *future* expected performance as determined by plans and forecasts.[13] Michael Ortner and Rakesh Chilakapati cofounded a company called Capterra, which created an online directory of companies that sell business software. Their problem was that they wanted to bring more traffic to their website; more listings would make the site more valuable to buyers, and more buyers would make the site more attractive to vendors.[14] We will refer to this example throughout this section.

The problem may be an opportunity that needs to be exploited: a gap between what the organization is doing now and what it can do to create a more positive future. In that case, decisions involve choosing how to seize the opportunity. To recognize important opportunities as a manager, you will need to understand your company's macro- and competitive environments (described in Chapter 2).

Recognizing that a problem or opportunity exists is only the beginning of this phase. The decision maker must dig in deeper and attempt to diagnose the situation. For example, a sales manager knows that sales have dropped drastically. If he is leaving the company soon or believes the decreased sales volume is due to the economy (which he can't do anything about), he won't take action. But if he does try to solve the problem, he should not automatically reprimand his sales staff, add new people, or increase the advertising budget. He must analyze *why* sales are down and then develop a solution appropriate to his analysis. Asking why, of yourself and others, is essential to understanding the real problem. In the case of Capterra, the company had asked *why* traffic was low by conducting surveys of the directory's users. The results showed that buyers wanted to find reviews of the vendors—a feature that the directory was not offering. To Capterra's founders, it seemed plausible that the underlying problem was that their website lacked a key feature that would make it helpful.[15]

Exhibit 3.4 lists some useful questions to ask and answer in this phase.[16]

Generating Alternative Solutions

The second phase of decision making links problem diagnosis to the development of alternative courses of action aimed at solving the problem. Managers generate at least some alternative solutions based on past experiences.[17]

Solutions range from ready-made to custom-made.[18] Decision makers who search for **ready-made solutions** use ideas they have tried before or follow the advice of others who have faced similar problems. **Custom-made solutions,** by contrast, must be designed for specific problems. This technique often combines ideas into new, creative solutions. For example, IDEO, a

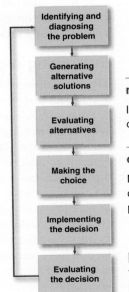

ready-made solutions

Ideas that have been seen or tried before.

custom-made solutions

New, creative solutions designed specifically for the problem.

EXHIBIT 3.3

The Phases of Decision Making

EXHIBIT 3.4

Questions to Ask in the
Problem Identification
and Diagnosis Stage

What specific short- and long-term goals should be met?
What is/are the cause(s) of the deviation?
How can you describe the deviation as specifically as possible?
Which of these goals are absolutely critical to the success of the decision?
Is there a difference between what is actually happening and what should be happening?

design and innovation firm, is helping its start-up-in-residence, PillPack, to change how customers of advanced age, limited mobility, or with serious illnesses interact with their pharmacy. PillPack has launched a simple, fast home-delivery service that sorts patients' prescriptions and over-the-counter medicines into packets that are organized by the date and time they should be taken. Pills arrive in an organized, recyclable dispenser with a label that includes an image of the pill. Customers can coordinate refills with or ask questions of PillPack's pharmacists via phone or e-mail on a 24/7 basis. The service costs $20 per month.[19] Potentially, custom-made solutions can be devised for any challenge. Later in the chapter, we will discuss how to generate creative ideas.

Often, many more alternatives are available than managers may realize. For example, what would you do if one of your competitors reduced prices? Managers sometimes assume that cutting prices in response to a competitor's price cuts is their only option, but it is not. Alternatives include emphasizing consumer risks to low-priced products, building awareness of your products' features and overall quality, and communicating your cost advantage to your competitors so they realize that they can't win a price war. If you do decide to cut your price as a last resort, do it fast—if you do it slowly, your competitors will gain sales in the meantime, which may embolden them to employ the same tactic again in the future.[20]

> *Often, many more alternatives are available than managers may realize.*

Returning to the example of Capterra, Michael Ortner, whose background was in sales, was eager to launch the product reviews, but his colleague, Rakesh Chilakapati, the company's technology manager, wanted to proceed cautiously because of the time and expense required to add the feature, along with fear that some vendors would get bad reviews and leave the directory. So to generate alternatives, the two partners studied existing websites with product reviews (for example, Amazon, eBay, and Edmunds.com). They identified a variety of ways to offer some kind of reviewing feature. They could simply post testimonials from satisfied customers. They could allow or forbid anonymous comments. They could require reviewers to list both positive and negative points. The big question that remained was whether the features attractive to buyers would repel sellers.[21]

Evaluating Alternatives

The third phase of decision making involves determining the value or adequacy of the alternatives that were generated. In other words, which solution will be the best?

Especially when decisions are important, alternatives should be evaluated with careful thought and logic. Fundamental to this process is to predict the consequences that will occur if the various options are put into effect. Managers should consider several types of consequences, including quantifiable measures of success such as lower costs, higher sales, lower employee turnover, and higher profits. The evaluation of alternatives at Capterra weighed the expected impact of reviews on buyers against the expected impact on vendors. Posting testimonials instead of inviting reviews seemed likely to protect the goodwill of vendors, but this one-sided approach seemed unlikely to satisfy buyers, so the founders doubted it would have much impact on traffic to the website. Anonymous reviews seemed risky because vendors' competitors could abuse the system, so that alternative was easily abandoned. Requiring both pros and cons in the reviews would encourage balanced information about vendors, an apparent plus. One issue that remained was that any review feature opened the possibility that vendors would be upset by negative comments. Ortner

Which goals does each alternative meet and fail to meet?
Which alternatives are most acceptable to you and to other important stakeholders?
If several alternatives may solve the problem, which can be implemented at the lowest cost or greatest profit?
If no alternative achieves all your goals, can two or more of the best ones be combined?

EXHIBIT 3.5
Questions That Help Managers Evaluate Alternatives

investigated further by sending a survey to the site's vendors, and he learned that many, in fact, did worry about that risk.[22]

An important technological change affecting the analysis of alternatives is the ability to collect and analyze Big Data. The term refers to massive amounts of structured and unstructured data that exceed the capabilities of a traditional computer database. Businesses today can gather details about Internet usage, consumer behavior, and employee skills and activities, among many other things. Computer technology enables organizations of all sizes to store the data, search it for patterns or trends, and analyze the information to identify alternatives that previously would have gone unnoticed. Evaluation that would have relied heavily on intuition or experience now can be data-driven. For example, companies are using big data to make more effective decisions about pay. PricewaterhouseCoopers assumed that pay raises would help it keep consultants from leaving early in their careers, but evaluating Big Data showed a larger effect from helping employees balance their work and personal commitments.[23]

To evaluate alternatives, refer to your original goals, defined in the first phase. Next, you should consider the questions in Exhibit 3.5.

Several additional questions help:[24]

> Is our information about alternatives complete and current? If not,
>   can we get more and better information?
> Does the alternative meet our primary objectives?
> What problems could we have if we implement the alternative?

Of course, results cannot be forecast with perfect accuracy. But sometimes decision makers can build in safeguards against an uncertain future by considering the potential consequences of several scenarios. Then they generate **contingency plans**—alternative courses of action that can be implemented depending on how the future unfolds.

For example, during an economic crisis when it is unclear when a recovery might begin and how strong it will be or what shape it will take, the range of potential outcomes is very large, and many companies will not survive. Firms could consider at least four scenarios:[25]

1. A most optimistic scenario in which trade and capital flows resume, further recession is averted, globalization stays on course, and developed and emerging economies continue to integrate as confidence rebounds quickly.
2. A battered-but-resilient scenario in which the recession continues for a long period, recovery is slow, confidence is shaken but does rebound, and globalization slowly gets back on course.
3. Stalled globalization, in which the global recession is significant, the intensity varies greatly from nation to nation (for example, with China and the United States proving resilient), but the integration of the world's economies stalls and growth is slow.
4. A long freeze, in which the recession lasts more than five years, economies everywhere stagnate, and globalization goes into reverse.

As you read this, what economic scenario is unfolding? What are the important current events and trends? What scenarios could evolve six or eight years from now? How will *you* prepare?

contingency plans

Alternative courses of action that can be implemented based on how the future unfolds.

Some decisions do not work out. Although it can be surprising and frustrating, you will need to create alternative courses of action, or contingency plans, that will allow you to achieve your desired goals.

© *Yuri Arcurs/Alamy/RF*

Making the Choice

Once you have considered the possible consequences of your options, it is time to make your decision. Quantitatively inclined people can easily tweak the assumptions behind every scenario in countless ways. But the temptation can lead to paralysis by analysis— that is, indecisiveness caused by too much analysis rather than the assertive decision making that can help an organization seize new opportunities or thwart challenges. This kind of indecisiveness became a risk at Capterra because Ortner and Chilakapati had conflicting worries. Ortner continued to see the lack of reviews as a missed opportunity, whereas Chilakapati remained focused on the risks of adding this feature. Ortner further researched the situation by calling vendors who had expressed concerns about reviews; he became convinced that they, too, were simply failing to see the opportunities of this additional feature and would come around when experience showed them the value of reviews. Finally, after three months of debate, Ortner was enjoying his regular five-mile run when he concluded that the analysis had to end, and a decision must be made. As president, he made the final call, respecting Chilakapati's concerns but announcing that it was time to try the reviews.[26]

> The process of considering multiple scenarios raises important "what if" questions for decision makers and highlights the need for preparedness and contingency plans.

As you make your decision, important concepts include maximizing, satisficing, and optimizing.[27]

maximizing

A decision realizing the best possible outcome.

Maximizing is achieving the best possible outcome. The maximizing decision realizes the greatest positive consequences and the fewest negative consequences. In other words, maximizing results in the greatest benefit at the lowest cost, with the largest expected total return. Maximizing requires searching thoroughly for a complete range of alternatives, carefully assessing each alternative, comparing one to another, and then choosing or creating the very best.

satisficing

Choosing an option that is acceptable, although not necessarily the best or perfect.

Satisficing is choosing the first option that is minimally acceptable or adequate. When you satisfice, you compare your choice against your goal, not against other options. Satisficing means that a search for alternatives stops after you find one that is okay. You do not expend the time or energy to gather more information. Instead you make the expedient decision based on readily available information.

Let's say you are purchasing new equipment, and your goal is to avoid spending too much money. You would be maximizing if you checked out all your options and their prices and then bought the cheapest one that met your performance requirements. But you would be satisficing if you bought the first adequate option that was within your budget and failed to look for less expensive options. Satisficing is sometimes a result of laziness; other times, there is no other known option because time is short, information is unavailable, or other constraints make maximizing impossible. When the consequences are not huge, satisficing can even be the ideal approach. But in other situations, when managers satisfice, they fail to consider options that might be better.

optimizing

Achieving the best possible balance among several goals.

Optimizing means that you achieve the best possible balance among several goals. Perhaps, in purchasing equipment, you are interested in quality and durability as well as price. So instead of buying the cheapest piece of equipment that works, you buy the one with the best combination of attributes, even though there may be options that are better on the price criterion and others that are better on the quality and durability criteria. The same idea applies to achieving business goals: One marketing strategy could maximize sales, whereas a different strategy might maximize profit. An optimizing strategy is the one that achieves the best balance among multiple goals. The nearby "Social Enterprise" box discusses how a social entrepreneur decided to optimize the impact of his organization.

Implementing the Decision

The decision-making process does not end once a choice is made. The chosen alternative must be implemented. Sometimes the people involved in making the choice must put it into

Social Enterprise

Saul Garlick's Social Enterprise: Nonprofit or For-Profit?

When visiting Mpumalanga, South Africa, as a boy, Saul Garlick was shocked at the village's lack of basic resources: "The small rural village had nothing—no classrooms, no electricity, no water." He decided he wanted to help. While still in high school, Garlick founded Student Movement for Real Change (SMRC), a nonprofit whose mission was to fight poverty by encouraging entrepreneurship in villages in Africa. The organization recruited students to "live with local families, hunt for water sources, farm alongside villagers and absorb day-to-day nuances of life in a developing country with the goal of building social businesses along with the local residents."

As a nonprofit, the organization was funded through an intermittent stream of donations from friends, family members, and donors. SMRC started to grow. Even with extra help from a small staff, Garlick was under constant pressure to raise enough funds to keep the operation functioning when in fact he wanted to spend more time doing the core work of the organization.

Garlick needed a business model that could sustain itself. He believed that a market-based solution was his best hope to help him reduce poverty in Africa, resulting in his decision to buy out his nonprofit, SMRC, and launch a for-profit social enterprise, ThinkImpact.

By borrowing an initial $450,000, Garlick developed a growth strategy to set ThinkImpact on a profitable course. The for-profit social enterprise developed an eight-week program that brings students, corporations, conference communities, and enterprise incubators to Ghana, Kenya, Rwanda, and South Africa. The curriculum is designed to spark the creative talents of individuals while developing their problem-solving skills. ThinkImpact has expanded into other revenue-generating areas, including offering a course to assist university faculty and administrators develop experiential education in social entrepreneurship.

Based in Denver, ThinkImpact now generates sales revenue of over $1 million. Garlick is committed to ThinkImpact's success: "These other platforms help people develop a fresh entrepreneurial mindset and a new way of tackling significant problems here and abroad. I want to become the best in the world at delivering this process."[28]

Questions

- What are the advantages and disadvantages of market-based solutions to problems in developing countries?
- Would you consider attending a ThinkImpact learning program in an international location? Why or why not?

---

effect. At other times, they delegate the responsibility for implementation to others, such as when a top management team changes a policy or operating procedure and has operational managers carry out the change. At Capterra, implementation of the decision to add customer reviews included 10 months of software development, followed by invitations to vendors to encourage their customers to submit reviews. Notice that the implementation took into account the concerns about negative reviews by giving the vendors some control over who submitted the initial reviews.[29]

Unfortunately, sometimes people make decisions but don't take action. Implementing may fail to occur when talking a lot is mistaken for doing a lot; if people just assume that a decision will happen; when people forget that merely making a decision changes nothing; when meetings, plans, and reports are seen as actions, even if they have no effect on what people actually do; and if managers don't check to ensure that what was decided was actually done.[30]

Managers should plan implementation carefully. Adequate planning requires several steps:[31]

1. Determine how things will look when the decision is fully operational.
2. Chronologically order, perhaps with a flow diagram, the steps necessary to achieve a fully operational decision.
3. List the resources and activities required to implement each step.
4. Estimate the time needed for each step.
5. Assign responsibility for each step to specific individuals.

Decision makers should assume that things will *not* go smoothly during implementation. It is useful to take a little extra time to *identify potential problems* and *identify*

Bottom Line

It's easy to become so focused on maximizing one goal that you lose sight of other important goals. You're optimizing if you make sure that no important result suffers too much unnecessarily. *What could be the negative consequences of making decisions that maximize only innovation?*

EXHIBIT 3.6
Questions to Ask When
Implementing Decisions

What problems could this action cause?
What can we do to prevent the problems?
What unintended benefits or opportunities could arise?
How can we make sure they happen?
How can we be ready to act when the opportunities come?

potential opportunities associated with implementation. Then you can take actions to prevent problems and be ready to seize unexpected opportunities. Exhibit 3.6 lists several useful questions that should be asked in the implementation stage of decision making.

Many of the chapters in this book are concerned with implementation issues: how to implement strategy, allocate resources, organize for results, lead and motivate people, manage change, and so on. View the chapters from that perspective and learn as much as you can about how to implement properly.

> Decision makers should assume that things will *not* go smoothly during implementation.

Evaluating the Decision

The final phase in the decision-making process is evaluating the decision. It involves collecting information on how well the decision is working. Quantifiable goals—a 20 percent increase in sales, a 95 percent reduction in accidents, 100 percent on-time deliveries—can be set before the solution to the problem is implemented. Then objective data can be gathered to determine its success or failure accurately.

Decision evaluation is useful whether the conclusion is positive or negative. Feedback that suggests the decision is working implies that the decision should be continued and perhaps applied elsewhere in the organization. Negative feedback means that either (1) implementation will require more time, resources, effort, or thought or (2) the decision was a bad one. The feedback for Capterra was positive. In the first year of offering customer reviews, the site gathered about 500 reviews. Another year after that, the site had 2,000 reviews, with about 40 percent of them unsolicited. Most of the reviews are positive. Even though some are less than glowing, traffic to the site has grown so much that vendors see the review feature as a benefit because they are getting more business. Revenues to Capterra have jumped and Ortner and Chilakapati are finally in agreement: Customer reviews were a great idea.[32]

If the decision appears inappropriate, it's back to the drawing board. Then the process cycles back to the first phase: (re)defining the problem. The decision-making process begins anew, preferably with more information, new suggestions, and an approach that attempts to eliminate the mistakes made the first time around.

The Best Decision

 LO 3

vigilance

A process in which a decision maker carefully executes all stages of decision making.

How can managers tell whether they have made the best decision? Although nothing can guarantee a "best" decision, managers should at least be confident that they followed proper *procedures* that will yield the best possible decision under the circumstances. This means that the decision makers were appropriately vigilant in making the decision. **Vigilance** occurs when the decision makers carefully and conscientiously execute all six phases of decision making, including making provisions for implementation and evaluation.[33]

Author and CEO Luda Kopeikina says managers can learn to make better decisions by improving the processes they use. First, your decisions will get better if you learn to manage stress, get enough rest, and put distractions aside when you need to make important decisions. Next, you should define the consequences you are trying to achieve and make sure the data you gather match the goals for your decision. Along with this comes the vision of how your decision can play out when you implement it. Finally, you need to develop the strength of character to take responsibility for the consequences of your decision. Encourage debate so you can see all the alternatives; but if you are the decision maker, you must eventually end the debate, exercise courage, and act on your responsibility as decision maker.[34]

Even if managers reflect on their decision-making activities and conclude that they executed each step conscientiously, they still will not know whether the decision will work; after all, nothing guarantees a good outcome. But they *will* know that they did their best to make the best possible decision. As you read "Management in Action: Progress Report," ask yourself whether you think this is how the managers at Boeing felt about their decision to develop the Dreamliner.

Barriers to Effective Decision Making

Vigilance and full execution of the six-phase decision-making process are the exception rather than the rule. But when managers use such rational processes, better decisions result.[35] Managers who make sure they engage in these processes are more effective.

But, it is easy to neglect or improperly execute these processes. The problem may be improperly defined or goals misidentified. Not enough solutions may be generated, or they may be evaluated incompletely. A satisficing rather than maximizing choice may be made. Implementation may be poorly planned or executed, or monitoring may be inadequate or nonexistent. And decisions are influenced by subjective psychological biases, time pressures, and social realities.

Psychological Biases

Decision makers are far from objective in the way they gather, evaluate, and apply information in making their choices. People have biases that interfere with objective rationality. The examples that follow represent only a few of the many documented subjective biases.[36]

The **illusion of control** is a belief that one can influence events even when one has no control over what will happen. Gambling is one example: some people believe they have the skill to beat the odds, even though most of the time they cannot. In business, such overconfidence can lead to failure because decision makers ignore risks and fail to evaluate the odds of success objectively.

In addition, managers may believe they can do no wrong or hold a general optimism about the future that can lead them to believe they are immune to risk and failure.[37] In addition, managers may overrate the value of their experience. They may believe that a previous project met its goals because of their decisions, so they can succeed by doing everything the same way on the next project.

Framing effects refer to how problems or decision alternatives are phrased or presented and how these subjective influences can override objective facts. In one example, managers indicated a desire to invest more money in a course of action that was reported to have a 70 percent chance of profit than in one said to have a 30 percent chance of loss.[38] The choices were equivalent in their chances of success; it was the way the options were framed that determined the managers' choices.

Managers may be quick to frame a problem as being similar to problems they have already handled, so they don't search for new alternatives. For example, when CEO Richard Fuld tackled financial problems at Lehman Brothers as the mortgage market tumbled, he assumed that the situation was much the same as when he had handled a previous financial crisis in the late 1990s. Unfortunately for Lehman Brothers, the recent crisis was far worse. In late 2008, the firm declared bankruptcy—the largest in U.S. history—helping to send global financial markets into a tailspin. Similarly, when the head of the operations center of the Department of Homeland Security prepared for Hurricane Katrina as it headed for

illusion of control

People's belief that they can influence events even when they have no control over what will happen.

framing effects

A decision bias influenced by the way in which a problem or decision alternative is phrased or presented.

Management in Action

BOEING'S DECISION TO INNOVATE

For Alan Mulally, getting the approval from Boeing's board of directors to build the 787 Dreamliner was far from a sure thing. Boeing had made cutbacks in new-product investments, and Mulally's previous project, development of the 777, had run far over budget (although it did make money for the company). However, the Dreamliner's design was so impressive that the directors believed the project would succeed even if Mulally's projections turned out to be too rosy.

Mulally recognized, however, that he must address concerns about cost overruns. He had an idea to minimize that risk: Design and construction wouldn't be centralized within Boeing. Rather, the company would work with a global network of suppliers. They would share in the costs and use their own investments in factories and equipment to build components of the aircraft. With this arrangement, Boeing hoped to keep the costs of developing the aircraft around $5 billion. With the average jetliner selling for around $100 million, the program could cost far more and still make money.

Implementing the decision was both difficult and rewarding. Coordinating the work of a network of suppliers proved to be far more difficult to manage than anyone seems to have anticipated. Meanwhile, leadership at the top changed: Boeing hired James McNerney, a board member with broad business experience, to be its new CEO, rather than Mulally, whose background was in aircraft engineering. Shortly afterward, Mulally left Boeing to run Ford. Without Mulally, who pushed hard to keep work on schedule, the plane's development fell further and further behind. McNerney struggled to find a successful replacement at the head of the commercial-aircraft division, appointing three managers to that post.

Nevertheless, airline customers loved the idea of a plane that would please passengers while saving money due to its increased fuel efficiency. Robert Milton was CEO of Air Canada's parent company when it ordered 60 Dreamliners. Milton noted that "issues" are bound to arise whenever a company introduces "an airplane so radically different." Customers placed orders totaling 848, a record for a new jetliner.[39]

- Evaluate how well Boeing's managers performed at each phase of the decision-making process. How could they have improved the process?
- Do you think the board's decisions about the Dreamliner were the best it could have made? Explain.

New Orleans, he assumed the storm would be like Florida hurricanes he had prepared for in the past. As information came in, he focused on the data that fit his expectations, but Katrina turned out to be far more devastating.[40]

Often, decision makers **discount the future.** That is, in their evaluation of alternatives, they weigh short-term costs and benefits more heavily than longer-term costs and benefits. Consider your own decision about whether to go for a dental checkup. The choice to go poses short-term financial costs, anxiety, and perhaps physical pain. The choice not to go will inflict even greater costs and more severe pain if dental problems worsen. How do you choose? Many people decide to avoid the short-term costs by not going for regular checkups, but end up facing greater pain in the long run.

The same bias applies to students who don't study, weight watchers who sneak dessert or skip an exercise routine, and people who take the afternoon off to play golf when they really need to work. It can also affect managers who hesitate to invest funds in research and development programs that may not pay off until far into the future. In all these cases, the avoidance of short-term costs or the seeking of short-term rewards results in negative long-term consequences.

Asian managers tend to think with a longer-term outlook than do American managers, and many believe that this provides competitive advantage for long-term success.[41] Western myopia is driven in part by Wall Street's focus on quarterly earnings, causing managers to make decisions based primarily on short-run considerations and to neglect long-term problems and opportunities.

In contrast, when U.S. companies sacrifice present value to invest for the future—such as when Weyerhaeuser incurs enormous costs for its reforestation efforts that won't

discounting the future

A bias weighting short-term costs and benefits more heavily than longer-term costs and benefits.

Bottom Line

As in this example, when you want to pursue sustainability, think in terms of the *long-term consequences* of your decisions.
What might be the long-term consequences of not investing in energy efficiency?

lead to harvest until 60 years in the future—it seems the exception rather than the rule. Discounting the future partly explains governmental budget deficits, environmental destruction, and decaying urban infrastructure.[42]

Time Pressures

In today's rapidly changing business environment, the premium is on acting quickly and keeping pace. The most conscientiously made business decisions can become irrelevant and even disastrous if managers take too long to make them.

How can managers make decisions quickly? Some natural tendencies, at least for North Americans, might be to skimp on analysis (not be too vigilant), suppress conflict, and make decisions on one's own without consulting other managers.[43] These strategies may speed up decision making, but they reduce decision quality. Carl Camden, president and CEO of Kelly Services, believed that rapid-fire decisions were the sign of a dynamic executive until he saw how this approach could hurt decision quality.[44]

The speed trap can be as dangerous as moving too slowly.[45] In an Internet start-up that went bankrupt, fast decisions initially helped the firm achieve its growth objectives. Early on, the founders did everything they could to create a sense of urgency: They planned a meeting to "light a fire under the company," calling it a "state-of-emergency address" with the purpose of creating "the idea of panic with an emerging deadline." Speed became more important than content. They failed to consider multiple alternatives, used little information, didn't fully acknowledge competing views, and didn't consult outside advisers. They never considered slowing down to be an option.

Can managers under time pressure make decisions that are timely and of high quality? A study of effective decision-making processes in microcomputer firms—a high-tech, fast-paced industry—revealed the tactics that such companies use.[46] First, instead of relying on old data, long-range planning, and futuristic forecasts, they focus on real-time information: current information obtained with little or no time delay. For example, they constantly monitor daily operating measures such as work in process rather than checking periodically the traditional accounting-based indicators such as profitability.

Second, they involve people more effectively and efficiently in the decision-making process. They rely heavily on trusted experts, and this yields both good advice and the confidence to act quickly despite uncertainty. They also take a realistic view of conflict; they value differing opinions, but they know that if disagreements are not resolved, the top executive must make the final choice in the end. Slow-moving firms, in contrast, are stymied by conflict. Like the fast-moving firms, they seek consensus; but when disagreements persist, they fail to decide.

Social Realities

Many decisions are made by a group rather than by an individual manager. In slow-moving firms, interpersonal factors decrease decision-making effectiveness. Even the manager acting alone is accountable to the boss and to others and must consider the preferences and reactions of many people. Important managerial decisions are marked by conflict among interested parties. Therefore, many decisions are the result of intensive social interactions, bargaining, and politicking.

The remainder of this chapter focuses on the social context of decisions, including decision making in groups and the realities of decision making in organizations.

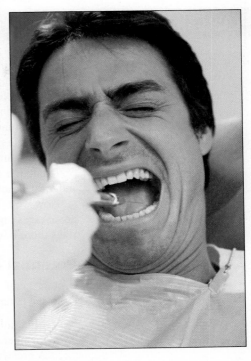

Delaying dental checkups can have a negative impact on the future. It may save money today but lead to larger costs (and pain) later.

© *Ingram Publishing*

The speed trap can be as dangerous as moving too slowly.

Bottom Line

You'll feel pressure to make quick decisions, but then it becomes easier to make mistakes. Fortunately, you can be vigilant while moving quickly, and you can avoid the speed trap. *When you are under time pressure, what can you do to avoid mistakes?*

Decision Making in Groups

 Sometimes a manager finds it necessary to convene a group of people for the purpose of making an important decision. Some advise that in today's complex business environment, significant problems should *always* be tackled by groups.[47] As a result, managers must understand how groups operate and how to use them to improve decision making. You will learn much more about how groups work later in the book.

The basic philosophy behind using a group to make decisions is captured by the adage, "two heads are better than one." But is this statement really valid? Yes, it is—potentially.

If enough time is available, groups usually make higher-quality decisions than most individuals acting alone. However, groups often are inferior to the *best* individual.[48]

How well the group performs depends on how effectively it capitalizes on the potential advantages and minimizes the potential problems of using a group. Exhibit 3.7 summarizes these issues.

Potential Advantages of Using a Group

If other people have something to contribute, using groups to make a decision offers at least five potential advantages:[49]

1. More information is available when several people are making the decision. If one member doesn't have all the facts or the pertinent expertise, another member might.
2. A greater number of perspectives on the issues, or different approaches to solving the problem, are available. The problem may be new to one group member but familiar to another. Or the group may need to consider other viewpoints—financial, legal, marketing, human resources, and so on—to achieve an optimal solution.
3. Group discussion provides an opportunity for intellectual stimulation. It can get people thinking and unleash their creativity to a far greater extent than would be possible with individual decision making.

These three potential advantages of using a group improve the odds that a more fully informed, higher-quality decision will result. Thus managers should involve people with different backgrounds, perspectives, and access to information. They should not involve only their cronies who think the same way they do.

4. People who participate in a group discussion are more likely to understand why the decision was made. They will have heard the relevant arguments both for the chosen alternative and against the rejected alternatives.
5. Group discussion typically leads to a higher level of commitment to the decision. Buying into the proposed solution translates into high motivation to ensure that it is executed well.

The last two advantages improve the chances that the decision will be implemented successfully. Therefore, managers should involve the people who will be responsible for implementing the decision as early in the deliberations as possible.

Potential Problems of Using a Group

Things can go wrong when groups make decisions. Most of the potential problems concern the process through which group members interact with one another:[50]

Bottom Line

Using a group may seem to slow down decision making. If one person dominates the discussion, it may feel like you're speeding up the decision making. But one dominant person reduces decision quality, and most of you will have wasted your time.

When you're meeting with a group, how can you help to make sure everyone is contributing?

EXHIBIT 3.7
Pros and Cons of Using a Group to Make Decisions

Potential Advantages	Potential Disadvantages
1. Larger pool of information.	1. One person dominates.
2. More perspectives and approaches.	2. Satisficing.
3. Intellectual stimulation.	3. Groupthink.
4. People understand the decision.	4. Goal displacement.
5. People are committed to the decision.	5. Social loafing.

1. Sometimes one group member dominates the discussion. When this occurs—such as when a strong leader makes his or her preferences clear—the result is the same as it would be if the dominant individual made the decision alone. Individual dominance has two disadvantages. First, the dominant person does not necessarily have the most valid opinions—and may even have the most unsound ideas. Second, even if that person's preference leads to a good decision, convening as a group will have been a waste of everyone else's time.

Heated arguments can arise when team members have differing opinions and are more concerned with winning the dispute than resolving the initial problem.

© *Ingram Publishing*

2. Satisficing is more likely with groups. Most people don't like meetings and will do what they can to end them. This may include criticizing members who want to continue exploring new and better alternatives. The result is a satisficing rather than an optimizing or maximizing decision.

3. Pressure to avoid disagreement can lead to a phenomenon called groupthink. **Groupthink** occurs when people choose not to disagree or raise objections because they don't want to break up a positive team spirit. Some groups want to think as one, tolerate no dissension, and strive to remain cordial. Such groups are overconfident, complacent, and perhaps too willing to take risks. Pressure to go along with the group's preferred solution stifles creativity and the other behaviors characteristic of vigilant decision making.

4. Goal displacement often occurs in groups. The goal of group members should be to come up with the best possible solution to the problem. But when **goal displacement** occurs, new goals emerge to replace the original ones. It is common for two or more group members to have different opinions and present their conflicting cases. Attempts at rational persuasion become heated disagreement. Winning the argument becomes the new goal. Saving face and defeating the other person's idea become more important than solving the problem.

5. When members of a group do not feel their contribution is important, they may engage in social loafing by working less hard when in a group.[51] This tendency to not pull one's own weight while working in groups poses many problems. Social loafing reduces cohesiveness between group members, resulting in lower group performance and higher absenteeism.[52] Chapter 14 discusses how managers can address social loafing and other barriers to building effective teams.

groupthink

A phenomenon that occurs in decision making when group members avoid disagreement as they strive for consensus.

goal displacement

A decision-making group loses sight of its original goal and a new, less important goal emerges.

Effective managers pay close attention to the group process; they manage it carefully. You have just read about the pros and cons of using a group to make decisions, and you are about to read how to manage the group's decision-making process. Chapter 12, on leadership, helps you decide when to use groups to make decisions.

Managing Group Decision Making

As Exhibit 3.8 illustrates, effectively managing group decision making has three requirements: (1) an appropriate leadership style, (2) the constructive use of disagreement and conflict, and (3) the enhancement of creativity.

LO 5

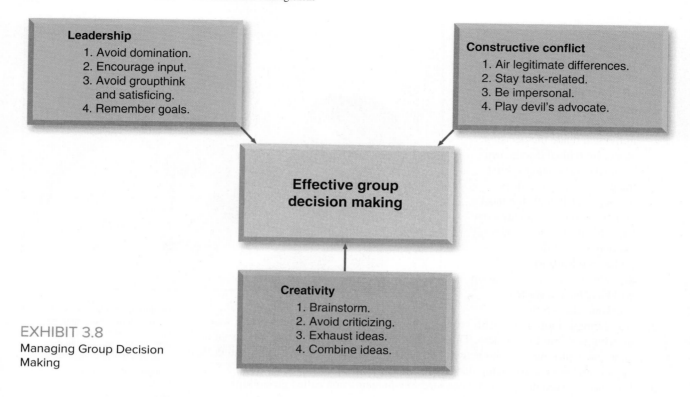

EXHIBIT 3.8
Managing Group Decision Making

Leadership Style

The leader of a decision-making group must attempt to minimize process-related problems. The leader should avoid dominating the discussion or allowing another individual to dominate. Less vocal group members should be encouraged to air their opinions and suggestions, and all members should be asked for dissenting viewpoints.

First, don't lose sight of the problem and your goals. Second, make a decision!

At the same time, the leader should not allow the group to pressure people into conforming. The leader should be alert to the dangers of groupthink and satisficing. Also, she should be attuned to indications that group members are losing sight of the primary objective: to come up with the best possible solution to the problem.

These suggestions have two implications. First, don't lose sight of the problem and your goals. Second, make a decision! Slow-moving organizations whose group members can't come to an agreement will be standing still while their competitors move ahead.

Constructive Conflict

cognitive conflict

Issue-based differences in perspectives or judgments.

affective conflict

Emotional disagreement directed toward other people.

Total and consistent agreement among group members can be destructive. It can lead to groupthink, uncreative solutions, and a waste of the knowledge and diverse viewpoints that individuals bring to the group. Therefore, a certain amount of constructive conflict should exist.[53] Pixar, which depends on creativity to make its animated films great, encourages constructive conflict with a standard for production meetings: Whenever someone wants to criticize an idea, the critic must attach an idea for improvement. In this way, good ideas can become great, and great ideas can become amazing. The practice is so much a part of Pixar's culture, it even has a name, "plussing."[54]

The most constructive type of conflict is **cognitive conflict,** or differences in perspectives or judgments about issues. In contrast, **affective conflict** is emotional and directed at other people. Affective conflict is likely to be destructive to the group because it can lead to anger, bitterness, goal displacement, and lower-quality decisions. Cognitive conflict, in contrast, can air legitimate differences of opinion and develop better ideas and problem solutions. Conflict, then, should be task-related rather than personal.[55] But even task-related conflict is good only when managed properly.[56]

Conflict can be generated formally through structured processes.[57] Two techniques that purposely program cognitive conflict into the decision-making process are devil's advocacy and the dialectic method.

A **devil's advocate** has the job of criticizing ideas. The group leader can formally assign people to play this role. Requiring people to point out problems can lessen inhibitions about disagreeing and make the conflict less personal and emotional.

An alternative to devil's advocacy is the dialectic. The **dialectic** goes a step beyond devil's advocacy by requiring a structured debate about two conflicting courses of action.[58] The philosophy of the dialectic stems from Plato and Aristotle, who advocated synthesizing the conflicting views of a thesis and an antithesis. Structured debates between plans and counterplans can be useful prior to making a strategic decision. For example, one team might present the case for acquiring a firm while another team advocates not making the acquisition.

Constructive conflict does not need to be generated on such a formal basis and is not solely the leader's responsibility. Any team member can introduce cognitive conflict by being honest with opinions, by being unafraid to disagree with others, by pushing the group to action if it is taking too long or making the group slow down if necessary, and by advocating long-term considerations if the group is too focused on short-term results. Introducing constructive conflict is a legitimate and necessary responsibility of all group members interested in improving the group's decision-making effectiveness.

devil's advocate

A person who has the job of criticizing ideas to ensure that their downsides are fully explored.

dialectic

A structured debate comparing two conflicting courses of action.

Encouraging Creativity

As you've already learned, ready-made solutions to a problem can be inadequate or unavailable. In such cases, custom-made solutions are necessary, so the group must be creative in generating ideas.

LO 6

Some have said we are in the midst of the next great business revolution: the "creative revolution."[59] Said to transcend the agricultural, industrial, and information revolutions, the most fundamental unit of value in the creativity revolution is ideas. Creativity is more than just an option; it is essential to survival. Allowing people to be creative may be one of the manager's most important and challenging responsibilities.

You might be saying to yourself, "I'm not creative." But even if you are not an artist or a musician, you do have potential to be creative in countless other ways. Exhibit 3.9 describes ideas of actual college student entrepreneurs who turned their creativity into businesses.[60] You don't need to be a genius in school either—Thomas Edison and Albert Einstein were not particularly good students. Nor does something need to change the world to be creative; the little things can always be done in new, creative ways that add value to the product and for the customer.

Creation
- How? Bring a new thing into being.
- *Example: Develop a new energy drink from a family recipe.*

Synthesis
- How? Join two previously unrelated things.
- *Example: Personalize multimedia online assignments to teach Mandarin to college students.*

Modification
- How? Improve something or give it a new application.
- *Example: Refurbish cell phones and sell them on e-Bay.*

EXHIBIT 3.9   Some Ways to Be Creative

Brainstorming is a technique used to generate as many ideas as possible to solve a problem. You have probably engaged in brainstorming sessions for various class or work projects.

© Blend Images/SuperStock

brainstorming

A process in which group members generate as many ideas about a problem as they can; criticism is withheld until all ideas have been proposed.

Bottom Line

Most creative ideas come not from the lone genius in the basement laboratory, but from people talking and working together.

Why is listening part of stimulating creativity?

How do you get creative?[61] Recognize the almost infinite little opportunities to be creative. Assume you can be creative if you give it a try. Escape from work once in a while. Read widely and try new experiences. Take a course or find a good book about creative thought processes; plenty are available. Exchange information and seek feedback about your ideas.[62] And be aware that creativity is social; your creativity will be affected by your social relationships at work, including your connections with other people outside your immediate close network.[63] Talk to people, often, about the issues and ideas with which you are wrestling.

How do you get creativity out of other people?[64] Give creative efforts the credit they are due and don't punish creative failures. Avoid extreme time pressure if possible.[65] Stimulate and challenge people intellectually. Listen to employees' ideas and allow enough time to explore different ideas. Put together groups of people with different styles of thinking and behaving. Get your people in touch with customers. Experiment with ways to stimulate fresh modes of thinking: Some companies are asking employees to put down their electronic devices and doodle on paper or whiteboards, and a software company called Citrix Systems stocks its meeting room with craft supplies for modeling ideas.[66] And strive to be creative yourself—you'll set a good example.

People are likely to be more creative if they believe they are capable, if they know that their coworkers expect creativity, and if they believe that their employer values creativity.[67] As a manager, you can do much to help employees develop these beliefs by how you listen, what you allow, and what you reward and punish. At a large consumer products company, management signals that it values creativity by inviting managers to post stories on the company's intranet about ideas their employees have suggested and the results of implementation. The company also awards innovation bonuses linked to how these innovations have benefited the organization.[68]

Brainstorming

A common technique used to elicit creative ideas is brainstorming. In **brainstorming,** group members generate as many ideas about a problem as they can. As the ideas are presented, they are posted so that everyone can read them, and people can use the ideas as building blocks. The group is encouraged to say anything that comes to mind, with one exception: no criticism of other people or their ideas is allowed.

In the proper brainstorming environment—free of criticism—people are less inhibited and more likely to voice their unusual, creative, or even wild ideas. By the time people have exhausted their ideas, a long list of alternatives has been generated. Only then does the group turn to the evaluation stage. At that point, many ideas can be considered, modified, or combined into a creative, custom-made solution to the problem.

Brainstorming isn't necessarily as effective as some people think. Sometimes in a brainstorming session, people are inhibited and anxious, they conform to others' ideas, they set low standards, and they engage in noncreative behaviors including cocktail party–type conversations—complimenting one another, repeating ideas, telling stories—that are nice but don't promote creativity. Exhibit 3.10 shows how McKinsey creates effective brainstorming sessions.[69] Other techniques that help include brainwriting (taking time to write down ideas silently), using trained facilitators, setting high performance goals, brainstorming electronically so that people aren't competing for air time, and even building a playground with fun elements that can foster creativity.[70] The nearby Multiple Generations at Work box discusses an Internet-based approach to soliciting ideas and feedback from customers anywhere in the world.

Multiple Generations at Work

Crowdsourcing: An Inexpensive Way to Get Creative Ideas

When faced with a difficult work problem to solve, a Baby Boomer manager's first impulse is to seek the opinion of experts who have significant experience and a proven track record in the area in question. For example, if a Boomer marketing manager wants to develop a new slogan for her product line of snacks, she may hire a team of experts specializing in consumer goods from an advertising agency. In contrast, a Millennial employee may be more inclined to *crowdsource* or solicit ideas, opinions, and suggestions from members of large online networks. He may run an online contest to see which fan or customer can create the best tag line. Whoever creates the winning entry may be awarded a modest cash prize or free merchandise. The cost of crowdsourcing to generate a creative slogan is typically much lower than seeking guidance from experts, in this case an advertising company.

A variety of individuals are using crowdsourcing to their advantage. Anyone from cash-starved entrepreneurial ventures to charities to large companies can use crowdsourcing (and crowdfunding) to help them accomplish a variety of objectives and goals. Here is a sample of how organizations are tapping into the creativity and funding of online crowds:

1. Gustin, a premium menswear store, received $450,000 in crowdfunding through the Kickstarter funding platform. Now 8 years old, the firm uses crowdsourcing to ask customers what types of handcrafted jeans they want the store to sell. The reduced inventory and marketing costs are then passed to customers in the form of lower prices.
2. PepsiCo turned to the crowd for help naming the newest flavor of Frito-Lay potato chips. After launching the "Do Us a Flavor" online contest,

© *The McGraw-Hill Companies, Inc./Roberts Publishing Services*

PepsiCo received 3.8 million chip flavor ideas. Celebrity chefs and other experts narrowed the list to three finalists. An online fan vote resulted in Cheesy Garlic being named the winner.

3. Chip maker Intel has partnered with Zooppa, a company that helps clients collect crowdsourced content, to tap the collective creativity of its 185,000-member online community. An online contest was run to see who could "create a print ad or a video up to 60 seconds long expressing their perception of the technology firm."

Inspired by the Millennial generation, crowdsourcing provides managers with a virtually limitless source of creative ideas for solving problems, building brands, and co-creating products and services with customers around the world.[71]

1. Consider what your organization is willing to accept when generating new ideas.	**EXHIBIT 3.10**
2. Use well-thought-out questions as a platform to spark new ideas.	Improving the Effectiveness of Brainstorming Sessions
3. Choose participants based on their expertise and knowledge of the challenge.	
4. Break up large groups into focused problem-solving subgroups of 3–5 people.	
5. Ask subgroups to think deeply to generate 2–3 solutions for each key question explored.	
6. Do not have the full group evaluate the winning ideas, but rather ask subgroups to identify their top 2 or 3 ideas. Describe next steps (e.g., top management team will evaluate ideas).	
7. Act quickly on key ideas and provide feedback to all participants.	

Organizational Decision Making

Individuals and groups make decisions constantly throughout every organization. To understand decision making in organizations, a manager must consider (1) the constraints decision makers face, (2) organizational decision processes, and (3) decision making during a crisis.

Constraints on Decision Makers

Organizations—or, more accurately, the people who make important decisions—cannot do whatever they wish. They face various constraints—financial, legal, market, human, and organizational—that inhibit certain actions. Capital or product markets may make an expensive new venture impossible. Legal restrictions may constrain the kinds of international business activities in which a firm can participate. Labor unions may defeat a contract proposed by management, and managers and investors may block a takeover attempt. In strategic alliances, the allies should pursue rational decisions collaboratively, not separately.[72] Even brilliant ideas must take into account the practical matters of implementation.[73]

Suppose you have a great idea that will provide a revolutionary service for your bank's customers. You won't be able to put your idea into action immediately. You will have to sell it to the people who can give you the go-ahead and to those whose help you will need to carry out the project. You might start by convincing your boss of your idea's merit. Next, the two of you may have to hash it out with a vice president. Then maybe the president has to be sold. At each stage, you must listen to these individuals' opinions and suggestions and often incorporate them into your original concept. Ultimately, you will have to derive a proposal acceptable to others.

In addition, ethical and legal considerations must be thought out carefully. Decision makers must consider ethics and the preferences of many constituent groups—the realities of life in organizations. You will have plenty of opportunity to think about ethical issues in Chapter 5.

Organizational Decision Processes

Just as with individuals and groups, organizational decision making historically was described with rational models like the one depicted earlier, in Exhibit 3.3. But Nobel laureate Herbert Simon challenged the rational model and proposed an important alternative called bounded rationality. According to Simon's **bounded rationality,** decision makers cannot be truly rational because (1) they have imperfect, incomplete information about alternatives and consequences; (2) the problems they face are so complex; (3) human beings simply cannot process all the information to which they are exposed; (4) there is not enough time to process all relevant information fully; and (5) people, including managers within the same firm, have conflicting goals.

When these conditions hold—and they do for most consequential managerial decisions—perfect rationality will give way to more biased, subjective, messier decision processes. For example, the **incremental model** of decision making occurs when decision makers make small decisions, take little steps, move cautiously, and move in piecemeal fashion toward a bigger solution. The classic example is the budget process, which traditionally begins with the budget from the previous period and makes incremental decisions from that starting point.

The **coalitional model** of decision making arises when people disagree on goals or compete with one another for resources. The decision process becomes political as groups of individuals band together and try collectively to influence the decision. Two or more coalitions form, each representing a different preference, and each tries to use power and negotiations to sway the decision.

Bottom Line

You may be an innovator if you come up with a creative idea. But you're not yet, until you implement it.

Say you're a manager who dreamed up a great process for cutting costs. Whose buy-in might you need to implement this innovation?

---

bounded rationality

A less-than-perfect form of rationality in which decision makers cannot be perfectly rational because decisions are complex and complete information is unavailable or cannot be fully processed.

---

incremental model

Model of organizational decision making in which major solutions arise through a series of smaller decisions.

---

coalitional model

Model of organizational decision making in which groups with differing preferences use power and negotiation to influence decisions.

Organizational politics, in which people try to influence organizational decisions so that their own interests will be served, can reduce decision-making effectiveness.[74] One of the best ways to reduce such politics is to create common goals for members of the team—that is, make the decision-making process a collaborative, rather than a competitive, exercise by establishing a goal around which the group can rally. In one study, top management teams with stated goals such as "build the biggest financial war chest" for an upcoming competitive battle, or "create *the* computer firm of the decade," or "build the best damn machine on the market" were less likely to have dysfunctional conflict and politics between members.[75] On a personal level, if you find yourself in a conflict, you and your adversary may be focused on the wrong goals. Work to find common ground in the form of an important goal that you both want to achieve.

The **garbage can model** of decision making occurs when people aren't sure of their goals, or disagree about the goals, and likewise are unsure of or in disagreement about what to do. This situation occurs because some problems are so complex that they are not well understood and because decision makers move in and out of the decision process because they have so many other things to attend to as well. This model implies that some decisions are chaotic and almost random. You can see that this is a dramatic departure from rationality in decision making.

garbage can model

Model of organizational decision making depicting a chaotic process and seemingly random decisions.

Decision Making in a Crisis

In crises, managers must make decisions under a great deal of pressure.[76] You may know some of the most famous recent crises: the explosion of BP's oil rig in the Gulf of Mexico, the devastation of hurricanes along the East Coast, the financial crisis that brought turmoil to the housing industry, and the political crises that have shaken many governments in the Middle East and northern Africa.

In two famous cases from the past, Union Carbide's gas leak in Bhopal, India, killed thousands of people, and several people were killed in the cyanide poisonings from using Johnson & Johnson's Tylenol. As outlined in Exhibit 3.11, Union Carbide and J&J handled their crises in very different ways. Today, J&J is still known for its effective handling of the crisis, as outlined in the table.

Information technology is a new arena for crises. Businesses, homes, government agencies, hospitals, and other organizations send critical information through the Internet and private networks around the clock, and any technical failure—sometimes accidental, sometimes maliciously intentional—could be magnified by the speed and widespread use of information technology. One vulnerable area is the electrical grid, which links utilities and carries power to each user. Information technology systems allow utility employees to control the grid remotely. Hackers have gained access to the U.S. electrical grid, enabling them to interfere with the grid's operations.[77] Such programs can be purged, but the biggest challenge is preventing or catching each attempt to gain unauthorized access to the system.

Superstorm Sandy hit the East Coast with fierce devastation. Managers had to make critical decisions to keep people safe.

© Patsy Lynch/FEMA

The response to IT-related crises must involve senior executives in online communication, both to protect the firm's reputation and to communicate with outside experts, news sources,

EXHIBIT 3.11   Two Companies, Two Disasters

Decision Criteria	Union Carbide Gas Leak	Johnson & Johnson Tylenol Poisonings
Identified as a crisis to the public.	No. Public perceived company as negligent, uncaring killer.	Yes. Public perception that Tylenol was unsafe and J&J was not in control.
Planned before reacting.	No. CEO went to India to inspect damage. All executives involved.	Yes. CEO picked one executive to head crisis team. Rest of company involved on a need-to-know basis.
Set clear goals to guide efforts.	Set no goals.	Set goals to stop killings, find reasons for killings, provide assistance to victims, and restore Tylenol's credibility.
Took appropriate actions to resolve crisis.	No. Engaged in damage control/stonewalling by distancing itself, misrepresenting safety conditions, not informing spokespeople, and adopting a bunker mentality.	Yes. Gave complete information by working with authorities, removing Tylenol from shelves (first-year cost was $150 million), launching a hard-to-modify caplet, and reissued Tylenol with tamper-proof packaging.
Outcome of crisis.	Chronic problems continued including low public confidence, costly litigation, and no formal crisis plan for future incidents.	Crisis was resolved leading to restored public confidence, high sales levels, and well-documented crisis management plan.

and key external and internal stakeholders. Managers can use IT to monitor and respond immediately to problems, including scandals, boycotts, rumors, cyberattacks, and other crises.[78]

Although many companies don't concern themselves with crisis management, it is imperative for it to be on management's agenda. An effective plan for crisis management (CM) should include the following elements:[79]

1. *Strategic actions* such as integrating CM into strategic planning and official policies.
2. *Technical and structural actions* such as creating a CM team and dedicating a budget to CM.
3. *Evaluation and diagnostic actions* such as conducting audits of threats and liabilities and establishing tracking systems for early warning signals.
4. *Communication actions* such as providing training for dealing with the media, local communities, and police and government officials.
5. *Psychological and cultural actions* such as showing a strong top management commitment to CM and providing training and psychological support services regarding the human and emotional impacts of crises.

Ultimately, management should be able to answer the following questions:[80]

What kinds of crises could your company face?
Can your company detect a crisis in its early stages?
How will it manage a crisis if one occurs?
How can it benefit from a crisis after it has passed?

With effective crisis management, old as well as new problems can be resolved, new strategies and competitive advantages may appear, and positive change can emerge. And if someone steps in and manages the crisis well, a hero is born. As you read "Management in Action: Onward," ask yourself who emerged as heroes during Boeing's management of the battery fire crisis.

And if someone steps in and manages the crisis well, a hero is born.

As a leader during a crisis, don't pretend that nothing happened (as did managers at one firm after a visitor died in the hallway despite employees' efforts to save him).[81] Communicate and reinforce

Management in Action

BOEING CONTENDS WITH A CRISIS

To reduce fuel consumption, Boeing designed its Dreamliner with lightweight but strong composite materials and with many systems running on electricity instead of hydraulic and pneumatic controls. Unfortunately, the complex electrical systems had problems. Most dramatically, in a 787 sold to Japan Airlines, the 63-pound lithium-ion battery caught fire while the plane was parked in Boston, and an All Nippon Airways plane experienced a battery fire during a flight. Following cockpit warnings, the pilot was able to land the second aircraft safely.

The Dreamliners were grounded by the Federal Aviation Administration (FAA), and the Japanese and the U.S. governments launched investigations. Deborah Hersman, chairman of the National Transportation Safety Board, said the NTSB would review the design and the testing that had led to FAA approval for the Dreamliner to carry passengers. Today's safety standard for onboard fires is zero. The FAA approval was based on Boeing's estimate that the chance of a battery meltdown was about one in 10 million flights—not exactly zero but much safer than industry-standard jet engines that malfunction once out of about 100,000 flights. (So far, the actual performance has been two battery fires in fewer than 50,000 flights.)

Boeing, too, responded with an investigation. It assigned engineers and technical experts to focus on identifying and correcting the problems so the aircraft could be returned to service as soon as possible. Boeing also stated its commitment to cooperate fully with investigators.

Boeing's decision to produce the Dreamliner using a network of suppliers complicated its decision making during this crisis. Boeing did not make the batteries in question; they came from GS Yuasa Corporation, a Japanese supplier. Another complication was the technology's sophistication. The first weeks of study yielded no clear answers about the cause of the fires, and few people at the NTSB and Japan Transport Safety Board had expertise in the technology, so they were learning about the batteries while investigating them. Even if Boeing solved the problem itself, it would have to convince these investigators that its solution was valid.

As the investigation continued, so did management decisions. Chairman and CEO James McNerney reportedly sent handwritten letters of apology to the heads of the affected airlines. Separately, he said he was doing the one thing that would make him confident: "dive in deeply with the people doing the scientific and technical work." Meanwhile, Boeing maintained its production schedule.[82]

- Compare Boeing's decision making during a crisis (the battery fire) with its process of deciding to make the Dreamliner. How does a crisis make the process harder?
- What principles of group decision making could help Boeing make decisions during this crisis?

the organization's values. Try to find ways for people to support one another and remember that people will take cues from your behavior. You should be optimistic but brutally honest. Show emotion, but not fear. "You have to be cooler than cool," says Gene Krantz of *Apollo 13* ground control fame. But don't ignore the problems or downplay them and reassure too much; don't create false hopes. Give people the bad news straight—you'll gain credibility, and when the good news comes, it will really mean something.

KEY TERMS

affective conflict, p. 90	devil's advocate, p. 91	maximizing, p. 82
bounded rationality, p. 94	dialectic, p. 91	nonprogrammed decisions, p. 77
brainstorming, p. 92	discounting the future, p. 86	optimizing, p. 82
certainty, p. 77	framing effects, p. 85	programmed decisions, p. 77
coalitional model, p. 94	garbage can model, p. 95	ready-made solutions, p. 79
cognitive conflict, p. 90	goal displacement, p. 89	risk. p. 78
conflict, p. 78	groupthink, p. 89	satisficing, p. 82
contingency plans, p. 81	illusion of control, p. 85	uncertainty, p. 77
custom-made solutions, p. 79	incremental model, p. 94	vigilance, p. 84

RETAINING WHAT YOU LEARNED

In Chapter 3, you learned that most managers make less than perfectly rational decisions because they lack the necessary information, time, or structure. The ideal decision-making process includes six steps (see Exhibit 3.3 below) and requires managers to ask themselves questions at each stage. The best decision hinges on the manager's ability to be vigilant at all stages of the decision-making process. Barriers can diminish the effectiveness of the decision-making process. While there are advantages and disadvantages of making decisions in groups, a good leader can manage the challenges by using the right leadership style, allowing constructive conflict, encouraging creativity, and brainstorming.

Decision making in organizations is complex and individuals are often bounded by multiple constraints. Decisions can be made incrementally, through coalitions, or in a chaotic garbage can manner. Decision making during organizational crises is particularly challenging.

LO 1 Describe the kinds of decisions you will face as a manager.

- Most important managerial decisions lack structure and are characterized by uncertainty, risk, and conflict.
- Despite these challenges, managers are expected to make rational decisions in a timely manner.

LO 2 Summarize the steps in making "rational" decisions.

- The ideal decision-making process involves six phases. The first, identifying and diagnosing the problem (or opportunity), requires recognizing a discrepancy between the current state and a desired state and then delving below surface symptoms to uncover the underlying causes of the problem.
- The second phase, generating alternative solutions, requires adopting ready-made or designing custom-made solutions.
- The third, evaluating alternatives, means predicting the consequences of different alternatives, sometimes through building scenarios of the future.
- Fourth, a solution is chosen; the solution might maximize, satisfice, or optimize.
- Fifth, people implement the decision; this phase requires more careful planning than it often receives.
- Finally, managers should evaluate how well the decision is working. This means gathering objective, valid information about the impact the decision is having. If the evidence suggests the problem is not getting solved, either a better decision or a better implementation plan must be developed.

LO 3 Recognize the pitfalls you should avoid when making decisions.

- Situational and human limitations lead most decision makers to satisfice rather than maximize or optimize.
- Psychological biases, time pressures, and the social realities of organizational life may prevent rational execution of the six decision-making stages.
- Vigilance and an understanding of how to manage decision-making groups and organizational constraints will improve the process and result in better decisions.

LO 4 Evaluate the pros and cons of using a group to make decisions.

- Advantages of using groups include more information, perspectives, and approaches brought to bear on problem solving; intellectual stimulation; greater understanding by all of the final decision; and higher commitment to the decision once it is made.
- Potential dangers or disadvantages of using groups include individual domination of discussions, satisficing, groupthink, goal displacement, and social loafing.

LO 5 Identify procedures to use in leading a decision-making group.

- Effective leaders in decision-making teams avoid dominating the discussion; encourage people's input; avoid groupthink and satisficing; and stay focused on the group's goals.
- They encourage constructive conflict via devil's advocacy and the dialectic, posing opposite sides of an issue or solutions to a problem.

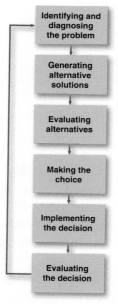

EXHIBIT 3.3   The Phases of Decision Making

LO 6 | **Explain how to encourage creative decisions.**

- When creative ideas are needed, leaders should set a good example by being creative themselves. They should recognize the almost infinite little opportunities for creativity and have confidence in their own creative abilities.
- They can inspire creativity in others by pushing for creative freedom, rewarding creativity, and not punishing creative failures.
- Leaders should encourage interaction with customers, stimulate discussion, and protect people from managers who might squelch the creative process.
- Brainstorming is one of the most popular techniques for generating creative ideas.

LO 7 | **Discuss the processes by which decisions are made in organizations.**

- Decision making in organizations is often a highly complex process. Individuals and groups are constrained by a variety of factors and constituencies. In practice, decision makers are boundedly rational rather than purely rational.
- Some decisions are made on an incremental basis. Coalitions form to represent different preferences. The process is often chaotic, as depicted in the garbage can model.
- Politics can also enter the process, decisions are negotiated, and crises come and go.

LO 8 | **Describe how to make decisions in a crisis.**

- Crisis conditions make sound, effective decision making more difficult. However, it is possible for crises to be managed well.
- A strategy for crisis management can be developed beforehand, and the mechanisms readied, so that if crises do arise, decision makers are prepared.

DISCUSSION QUESTIONS

1. Discuss Boeing's Dreamliner in terms of risk, uncertainty, and how its managers handled the company's challenges. What is the current news on this company?
2. Identify some risky decisions you have made. Why did you take the risks? How did they work out? Looking back, what did you learn?
3. Identify a decision you made that had important unexpected consequences. Were the consequences good, bad, or both? Should you, and could you, have done anything differently in making the decision?
4. What effects does time pressure have on your decision making? In what ways do you handle it well and not so well?
5. Recall a recent decision that you had difficulty making. Describe it in terms of the characteristics of managerial decisions.
6. What do you think are some advantages and disadvantages to using computer technology in decision making?
7. Do you think that when managers make decisions they follow the decision-making steps as presented in this chapter? Which steps are apt to be overlooked or given inadequate attention? What can people do to make sure they do a more thorough job?
8. Discuss the potential advantages and disadvantages of using a group to make decisions. Give examples from your experience.
9. Suppose you are the CEO of a major corporation and one of your company's oil tanks has ruptured, spilling thousands of gallons of oil into a river that empties into the ocean. What do you need to do to handle the crisis?
10. Identify some problems you want to solve. Brainstorm with others a variety of creative solutions.

EXPERIENTIAL EXERCISES

3.1 DECISION MAKING IN ACTION

OBJECTIVE

Learn how to improve your ability to make good decisions.

INSTRUCTIONS

Refer back to Exhibit 3.3 in the chapter. Think back to a recent expensive purchase you made. It could have been a bike, mobile device, suit for interviews, and so forth. In order to evaluate the quality of your decision, please think about your purchase when answering each of the questions below.

Decision Making Worksheet

1. What problem did you hope to solve by making this purchase?

2. What alternative (or competing) products did you consider?

3. How did you evaluate the different alternative (or competing) products? Did you identify each product's strengths and weaknesses?

_____

4. When you made the final choice, was it a maximizing, satisficing, or optimizing outcome?

_____

5. After purchasing the product, how frequently did you test it out?

_____

6. Was your decision to make the purchase a positive or negative one? Did it satisfy your original need(s)?

_____

3.2 GROUP PROBLEM SOLVING AT A SOCIAL ENTERPRISE

OBJECTIVE

To understand the dynamics of group decision making through role-playing a meeting between a president and her employees.

INSTRUCTIONS

1. Identify 5 students to play the roles of the employees. Ask these 5 individuals to read their roles below.

2. Identify 1 student to play the role of the president of the social enterprise. Ask this individual to read his/her role below.

3. Set up a table with 6 chairs at the front of the classroom.

4. Ask the remaining students in the audience to observe how the 6 individuals behave and then answer the discussion questions (below).

5. When everyone is ready, Taylor Johnson joins the others at the table in her office, and the scene commences.

6. The meeting continues until there is a successful close unless an argument develops and no progress is made after 10–15 minutes.

DISCUSSION QUESTIONS

1. How did each member frame the problem? What did each member discuss?

2. How effectively did the group generate and evaluate alternatives?

3. What was its final decision?

4. Evaluate the effectiveness of the group's decision making?

5. How could the group's effectiveness be enhanced?

OVERVIEW

The role-play exercise is based on a meeting between a manager of a social enterprise and her 5 employees. Each character's role is designed to re-create a realistic business meeting. Each character brings to the meeting a unique perspective on a major problem confronting the social enterprise as well as some personal views of the other characters developed over several years of knowing them in business and social contexts.

CAST OF CHARACTERS

Taylor Johnson, the president, founded the enterprise 10 years ago as a way to connect outstanding teachers who have recently earned their teaching degrees with students in schools located in economically disadvantaged areas. The new teachers agree to serve in the disadvantaged schools for a 3-year period in exchange for a reasonably good salary and forgiveness of up to $30,000 of their student loans. Taylor is well known for her hard driving, selfless style of leadership. A charismatic leader, she is highly skilled at bringing diverse stakeholders together. However, Taylor admits that she lacks knowledge related to online classroom and teaching technologies. In the old days, this wouldn't be an issue. However, Taylor's competitors are beginning to overtake the social enterprise by offering new teachers training, mobile devices, and online learning tools (e.g., online homework, interactive videos, eBooks, and so forth) to help them create high-performance classrooms. She doesn't know whether the enterprise should continue doing what it does best (placing new teachers into traditional face-to-face teaching environments) or begin preparing its recruits to teach online and hybrid (combining face-to-face with online modules) classes.

Amit Patel, head of information technology, has worked for the enterprise for 6 months. A recent college graduate, Amit reports directly to Taylor. She is on a mission to modernize the way the enterprise does its work. She feels strongly that the enterprise should be shifting more of its IT operations to the cloud. Also, Amit feels that a great deal of insight could be mined from 10 years of data currently stored in antiquated servers at the enterprise. Amit believes she could make these changes without spending a lot of funds. Unfortunately, Amit's zeal for rapid change has been a cause of concern for Felipe and Taylor who prefer a more methodical approach to change.

Felipe Rodriguez, director of fund-raising, reports directly to Johnson. He has held this position for 8 years and is a very close friend of Taylor's. Donations and grants for the most recent year are down by 10 percent. Prior to joining the enterprise, he worked as a fund-raiser for a major university in the region. The university offered a wide variety of online and hybrid courses. Felipe would often refer to these innovations when seeking donations from alumni. He was widely viewed as successful at his work.

Mike Clarke, manager in charge of recruiting new teachers, works for Felipe. After working for the enterprise as an entry-level recruiter for two years, Mike was recently promoted to this position. Though a persuasive recruiter of new teachers, he has noticed a recent decline in the number of recruits willing to teach in traditional face-to-face learning environments. He is progressive in his thinking and believes that the enterprise needs to change how it does business in order to keep up with the competitors. Mike and Amit feel they are agents of change and want to modernize the enterprise.

TODAY'S MEETING

Taylor has called the meeting with these three managers to decide whether the social enterprise should begin preparing its new recruits to teach not only traditional face-to-face classes, but also hybrid and online classes. This decision has to be made within 15 minutes because the enterprise's largest client just called and asked to meet with Taylor immediately. Taylor is concerned that the school may be on the verge of discontinuing the contract with the enterprise. If that's the case, Taylor wants the managers to help her decide on a counteroffer to win back the client school. Losing this client school is not an option given that it makes up 40 percent of the enterprise's revenue.

SOURCE: Adapted from Judith R. Gordon, *A Diagnostic Approach to Organizational Behavior* (1983, Upper Saddle River, NJ: Pearson Education, Inc.).

CONCLUDING CASE

SOARING EAGLE SKATE COMPANY

As a child, Stan Eagle just knew he loved riding his skateboard and doing tricks. By the time he was a teenager, he was so proficient at the sport that he began entering professional contests and taking home prize money. By his twenties, Eagle was so successful and popular that he could make skateboarding his career. A skateboard maker sponsored him in competitions and demonstrations around the world.

The sponsorship and prize money paid enough to support him for several years. But then interest in the sport waned, and Eagle knew he would have to take his business in new directions. He believed skateboarding would return to popularity, so he decided to launch into designing, building, and selling skateboards under his own brand. To finance Soaring Eagle Skate Company, he pooled his own personal savings with money from a friend, Pete Williams, and came up with $75,000. Sure enough, new young skaters began snapping up the skateboards, attracted in part by the products' association with a star.

As the company prospered, Eagle considered ideas for expansion. Another friend had designed a line of clothing he thought would appeal to Eagle's skateboarding fans, and Eagle's name on the product would lend it credibility. At the friend's urging, Eagle branched out into clothing for skateboarders. However, he discovered that the business of shorts and shirts is far different from the business of sports equipment. The price markups were tiny, and the sales channels were entirely different. Three years into the expansion, Soaring Eagle had invested millions of dollars in the line but was still losing money. Eagle decided to sell off that part of the business to a clothing company and cut his losses.

Soon after that experiment, cofounder Williams proposed another idea: They should begin selling other types of sports equipment—inline roller skates and ice skates. Selling equipment for more kinds of sports would produce more growth than the company could obtain by focusing on just one sport. Eagle was doubtful. He was considered one of the most knowledgeable people in the world about skateboarding. He knew nothing about inline skating and ice skating. Eagle argued that the company would be better off focusing on the sport in which it offered the most expertise. Surely there were ways to seek growth within that sport—or at least to avoid the losses that came from investing in industries in which the company lacked experience.

Williams continued to press Eagle to try his idea. He pointed out that unless the company took some risks and expanded into new areas, there was little hope that Williams and Eagle could continue to earn much of a return on the money they had invested. Eagle was troubled. The attempt at clothing delivered, he thought, a message that they needed to be careful about expansion. But he seemed unable to persuade Williams to accept his point of view. He could go along with Williams and take the chance of losing money again, or he could use money he had earned from his business to buy Williams's ownership share in the company and then continue running Soaring Eagle on his own.

DISCUSSION QUESTIONS

1. How do the characteristics of management decisions—uncertainty, risk, conflict, and lack of structure—affect the decision facing Stan Eagle?

2. What steps can Eagle take to increase the likelihood of making the best decision in this situation?

Zappos Eliminates All Managers and Titles

Recently, Zappos' CEO Tony Hsieh surprised many observers in the business world by announcing to his 1,500 or so employees that the e-retailer famous for its shoes was doing away with job titles, managers, and other artifacts associated with traditional top-down management and replacing it with a system where employees are expected to act like mini entrepreneurs. This new approach or holacracy encourages employees to self-manage and self-organize, thus eliminating the need for bosses. One of the management system's overarching goals is to "create a dynamic workforce where everyone has a voice and bureaucracy doesn't stifle innovation."

How does a holacracy function? Based on the work of Brian Robertson, who developed the idea while running his start-up, Ternary Software, a holacracy organizes employees into circles of responsibility—similar to functional areas like marketing and customer service, and employee special interest areas like career development and so forth. Though democratic and self-governing, the circles do not operate in a vacuum as they are arranged in a hierarchy (circles report to higher-level circles) and follow detailed procedures for running meetings and making decisions. Employees are free to choose which circles to which they want to belong and on what projects they would like to work. The circles are responsible for achieving a specific set of responsibilities. At meetings, employees are encouraged to address and resolve in a proactive manner "tensions" or problems related to internal (e.g., unfair workloads) or external (e.g., a way to enhance the customer experience) issues. Rather than reporting to a manager with the power to hire or fire, as is the case in hierarchically organized companies, a "lead link" helps employees accomplish the circle's responsibilities and communicates between circles.

Zappos is not the first company in history to experiment with employee self-management. For example, Gore & Associates (maker of Gore-Tex) has no formal chain of command and provides its associates with freedom to self-select work projects and choose associates with relevant expertise to assist in the development of those projects. Semco Partners, a Brazilian industrial machinery manufacturer, engages its 3,000-plus employees through participative management, where employees set their own work hours and pay levels, hire and review their supervisors, and decide which new businesses in which to enter. Johnsonville Sausage Company eliminated its hierarchy and introduced "self-managed, self-organizing teams throughout the company." Ralph Styer, the CEO who championed this radical change, believed that "helping human beings fulfill their potential is of course a moral responsibility, but it's also good business practice." He believed in the connection between employee happiness and organizational performance: "Learning, striving people are happy people and good workers."

Are the employees at Zappos happy about their expanded responsibilities and freedom to self-govern? How are the managers accepting this change? It's mixed. In a recent e-mail to all staff at the company, Hsieh said that everyone had a choice to make: either embrace the new holacratic system or accept a three-month severance package and resign. Two hundred and ten (or 14 percent) of the staff resigned. Of those who left the company, 20 (or 7 percent) were managers. Does that mean that the 86 percent of staff who decided to stay did so because they believe in the new holacratic approach? Time will tell. One may speculate that the individuals who chose to remain at Zappos did so because they are either "believers" or lack the interest or motivation to switch jobs at the moment.

Some of the employees who are staying have shared concerns about the new management approach like using the complicated new lingo, adjusting to the rapidly changing work roles and expectations, and the "ever-expanding number of circles and the endless meetings" that take employees away from achieving their work goals. On the upside, holacracy promotes employees' ownership and encourages even the lowest-paid employees to add items to meeting agendas that are subsequently discussed and acted upon.

What will become of the 267 ex-managers at Zappos? Though no one knows for sure, the company has created a new circle titled "Reinventing Yourself" to help these individuals find "new roles that might be a good match for their passions, skills, and experience." John Bunch, the employee who is helping Zappos transition to a holacracy, suggests, "most managers will be able to grow into new areas of technical work to replace the time they were doing people management."

There may be an irony in the way that Zappos shifted from a hierarchical management structure to one that is based on democratic, self-organizing circles. The mandate for this change came from Tony Hsieh, the CEO. Those employees and managers who did not agree with the "top-down" change were asked to leave the company. This irony suggests that even for visionary business leaders like Hsieh, radical change may not be easy to accomplish in a consensus-driven manner.

As Zappos and its employees continue to adapt to the new holacratic system of management, Bunch has admitted the company will need to refine salary processes as well as the decision process for assigning projects throughout the company. He is patient and is taking the long view: "We believe that, over time, the ability for people to be empowered and entrepreneurial will make people happy."

DISCUSSION QUESTIONS

1. To what degree do you think that Zappos' new hola-cratic approach to organizing will enhance its competi-tive advantage in innovation, quality, service, speed, and cost competitiveness? Explain.

2. Referring back to Exhibit 2.13 in Chapter 2, which type of culture (group, hierarchy, adhocracy, or ratio-nal) does Zappos want to create by moving to a holacracy?

SOURCES: Adapted from Y. Noguchi, "Zappos: A Workplace Where No One and Everyone Is the Boss," *NPR*, July 21, 2015, http://www.npr.org; D. Gelles, "At Zappos, Pushing Shoes and a Vision," *The New York Times,* July 17, 2015, http://www.nytimes.com; R. Feloni, "7% of Zappos' Managers Quit After Recent CEO Ultimatum to Embrace Self-Management or Leave," *Business Insider,* June 9, 2015, http://www.buisnessinsider.com; R. Silverman, "At Zappos, Banishing Bosses Brings Confusion," *The Wall Street Journal,* May 20, 2015, http://www.wsj.com; G. Petriglieri, "Making Sense of Zappos' War on Manager," *Harvard Business Review,* May 19, 2015, http://www.hbr.org; S. Denning, "Zappos Says Goodbye to Bosses," *Forbes,* January 15, 2015, http://www.forbes.com; L. Fisher, "Ricardo Semler Won't Take Control," *Strategy + Business* November 29, 2005, http://www.strategy-business.com.

CASE INCIDENTS

Employee Raiding

Litson Cotton Yarn Manufacturing Company, located in Murray, New Jersey, decided as a result of increasing labor costs to relocate its plant in Fairlee, a southern commu-nity of 4,200. Plant construction was started, and a human resources office was opened in the state employment office, located in Fairlee.

Because of ineffective HR practices in the other three textile mills located within a 50-mile radius of Fairlee, Litson was receiving applications from some of the most highly skilled and trained textile operators in the state. After receiv-ing applications from approximately 500 people, employ-ment was offered to 260 male and female applicants. These employees would be placed immediately on the payroll with instructions to await final installation of machinery, which was expected within the following six weeks.

The managers of the three other textile companies, faced with resignations from their most efficient and best-trained employees, approached the Litson managers with the complaint that their labor force was being "raided." They registered a strong protest to cease such practices and demanded an immediate cancellation of the employment of the 260 people hired by Litson.

Litson managers discussed the ethical and moral consid-erations involved in offering employment to the 260 peo-ple. Litson clearly faced a tight labor market in Fairlee, and management thought that if the 260 employees were dis-charged, the company would face cancellation of its plans and large construction losses. Litson management also felt obligated to the 260 employees who had resigned from their previous employment in favor of Litson.

The dilemma was compounded when the manager of one community plant reminded Litson that his plant was part of a nationwide chain supplied with cotton yarn from Litson. He implied that Litson's attempts to continue opera-tions in Fairlee could result in cancellation of orders and the possible loss of approximately 18 percent market share. It was also suggested to Litson managers that actions taken by the nationwide textile chain could result in cancellation of orders from other textile companies. Litson's president held an urgent meeting of his top subordinates to (1) decide what to do about the situation in Fairlee, (2) formulate a written policy statement indicating Litson's position regard-ing employee raiding, and (3) develop a plan for implement-ing the policy.

How would you prepare for the meeting, and what would you say at the meeting?

SOURCE: J. Champion and J. James, *Critical Incidents in Management: Decision and Policy Issues,* 6th ed. McGraw-Hill/Irwin, 1989. Copyright © 1989 The McGraw-Hill Companies.

Effective Management

Dr. Sam Perkins, a graduate of the Harvard University College of Medicine, had a private practice in internal medi-cine for 12 years. Fourteen months ago, he was persuaded by the Massachusetts governor to give up private practice to be director of the State Division of Human Services.

After one year as director, Perkins recognized he had made little progress in reducing the considerable ineffi-ciency in the division. Employee morale and effectiveness seemed even lower than when he had assumed the posi-tion. He realized his past training and experiences were of a clinical nature with little exposure to effective management techniques. Perkins decided to research literature on the subject of management available to him at a local university.

Perkins soon realized that management scholars are divided on the question of what constitutes effective man-agement. Some believe people are born with certain identi-fiable personality traits that make them effective managers. Others believe a manager can learn to be effective by treat-ing subordinates with a personal and considerate approach and by giving particular attention to their need for favorable working conditions. Still others emphasize the importance of developing a management style characterized by an authoritarian, democratic, or laissez-faire approach. Perkins was further confused when he learned that a growing num-ber of scholars advocate that effective management is con-tingent on the situation.

Because a state university was located nearby, Perkins contacted the dean of its college of business administra-tion. The dean referred him to the director of the college's management center, Professor Joel McCann. Discussions between Perkins and McCann resulted in a tentative agreement that the management center would organize a series of management training sessions for the State Division of Human Services. Before agreeing on the price tag for the management conference, Perkins asked McCann to prepare a proposal reflecting his thoughts on the following questions:

1. How will the question of what constitutes effective management be answered during the conference?
2. What will be the specific subject content of the conference?
3. Who will the instructors be?

4. What will be the conference's duration?
5. How can the conference's effectiveness be evaluated?
6. What policies should the State Division of Human Services adopt regarding who the conference participants should be and how they should be selected? How can these policies be implemented best?

SOURCE: J. Champion and J. James, *Critical Incidents in Management: Decision and Policy Issues,* 6th ed. McGraw-Hill/Irwin, 1989. Copyright © 1989 The McGraw-Hill Companies.

CHAPTER 4

Planning and Strategic Management

Manage your destiny, or someone else will.

—JACK WELCH, FORMER CEO, GENERAL ELECTRIC

Management in Action

HOW WALT DISNEY COMPANY SCRIPTS ITS OWN SUCCESS

Mickey Mouse, mascot of the Walt Disney Company, may be a tiny creature, but the company he represents might be better portrayed as the massive and many-tentacled giant squid. With revenues approaching $49 billion per year, the company is one of the largest in the entertainment industry, competing with Comcast, News Corp, and others.

Walt Disney is not merely huge in terms of sales volume; it has five business divisions, involved in nearly every kind of commercial entertainment. It all began with Walt Disney Studios, which today produces movies, music, and stage shows under the banners of Disney, Pixar, Marvel Studios, Lucasfilm, Touchstone Pictures, and Hollywood Records. The Media Networks group covers publishing, radio, and broadcast and cable television, including Disney/ABC Television and ESPN. The Parks and Resorts group encompasses 11 theme parks and 44 resorts around the world as well as a cruise line. Disney Interactive offers entertainment on digital platforms, including console games and the Internet. And Disney Consumer Products extends the business value of characters and story lines by operating Disney Stores and licensing its creations for use on toys, clothing, art objects, and a wide variety of other consumer goods.

The man in charge of keeping the magic alive through activities carried out by more than 175,000 employees is Disney's chief executive officer, Robert Iger. Iger and his executive team must define an overall direction and goal for the company and keep an eye on how well each business group is contributing to achievement of that goal. Iger does this by spotting

© Photos 12/Alamy

opportunities for growth in the industry—hence the expansion into cable television and, more recently, into interactive entertainment. He also looks for characters and brands Disney can make more valuable because of its access to more channels. For example, Disney could pay generously for Pixar and Marvel because those companies' characters generate sales in products as diverse as theme parks, videogames, and sweatshirts. Another coup for Iger was the purchase of ESPN, the most valuable cable channel in terms of revenues.

Iger meets weekly with the heads of the business units. Although he keeps an eye on the company's overall direction, he gives each unit's head wide latitude. This pattern was evident when he planned the purchase of Pixar in 2006. Acknowledging that Pixar had become the dominant animation studio, he not only left its executives in charge after the acquisition but also placed them at the helm of the Disney animation studios. *Frozen,* the highest grossing animated film of all time, and sales of movie-themed toys, contributed to a 19 percent increase in profits in first quarter 2015. However, challenges remain for Iger. Disney Interactive is struggling to turn a profit. Somehow, the CEO from the television era has to ensure that Mickey remains a star of the Internet age.[1]

As you read this chapter, think about the challenge of providing direction to a massive enterprise offering entertainment to all ages around the globe. What planning methods could help managers at all levels zero in on the best opportunities?

To imagine Disney—or any organization—dealing with the significant challenges it faces without developing a plan beforehand is almost impossible. Planning describes what managers decide to do and how they will do it. It provides the framework, focus, and direction required for a meaningful effort. Without planning, any improvements in an organization's innovation, speed, quality, service, and cost will be accidental, if they occur at all. This chapter examines the most important concepts and processes involved in planning and strategic management. By learning these concepts and reviewing the steps outlined, you will be on your way to understanding the current approaches to the strategic management of today's organizations.

An Overview of Planning Fundamentals

The importance of formal planning in organizations has grown dramatically. Until the mid-1900s, most planning was unstructured and fragmented, and formal planning was restricted to a few large corporations. Although management pioneers such as Alfred Sloan of General Motors instituted formal planning processes, planning became a widespread management function only during the past few decades. Initially, larger organizations adopted formal planning, but today even small firms operated by aggressive, opportunistic entrepreneurs engage in formal planning.[2]

As discussed in Chapter 1, planning is the conscious, systematic process of making decisions about goals and activities that an individual, group, work unit, or organization will pursue in the future. Planning is not an informal or haphazard response to a crisis; it is a purposeful effort that is directed and controlled by managers and often draws on the knowledge and experience of employees throughout the organization. Planning provides individuals and work units with a clear map to follow in their future activities; at the same time, this map may be flexible enough to allow for individual circumstances and changing conditions.

The Basic Planning Process

Because planning is a decision process—you're deciding what to do and how to go about doing it—the important steps followed during formal planning are similar to the basic decision-making steps we discussed in Chapter 3. Exhibit 4.1 summarizes the similarities between decision making and planning—including the fact that both move not just in one direction but in a cycle. The outcomes of decisions and plans are evaluated, and if necessary, they are revised.

We now describe the basic planning process in more detail. Later in this chapter, we will discuss how managerial decisions and plans fit into the larger purposes of the organization—its ultimate strategy, mission, vision, and goals.

situational analysis

A process planners use, within time and resource constraints, to gather, interpret, and summarize all information relevant to the planning issue under consideration.

Step 1: Situational Analysis   As the contingency approach advocates, planning begins with a **situational analysis.** Within their time and resource constraints, planners should gather, interpret, and summarize all information relevant to the planning issue in question. A thorough situational analysis studies past events, examines current conditions, and attempts to forecast future trends. It focuses on the internal forces at work in the organization or work unit and, consistent with the open-systems approach (see Chapter 2), examines influences from the external environment. The outcome of this step is the identification and diagnosis of planning assumptions, issues, and problems.

A thorough situational analysis will provide information about the planning decisions you need to make. For example, if you are a manager in a magazine company considering the launch of a sports publication for the teen market, your analysis will include such factors as the number of teens who subscribe to magazines, the appeal of the teen market to advertisers, your firm's ability to serve this market effectively, current economic conditions, the level of teen interest in sports, and any sports magazines already serving this

General decision-making stages	Specific formal planning steps
Identifying and diagnosing the problem	Situational analysis
Generating alternative solutions	Alternative goals and plans
Evaluating alternatives	Goal and plan evaluation
Making the choice	Goal and plan selection
Implementing	Implementation
Evaluation	Monitor and control

EXHIBIT 4.1

Decision-Making Stages (Chapter 3) and Formal Planning Steps (Chapter 4)

market and their current sales. Such a detailed analysis will help you decide whether to proceed with the next step in your magazine launch.

Step 2: Alternative Goals and Plans   Based on the situational analysis, the planning process should generate alternative goals that may be pursued in the future and the alternative plans that may be used to achieve those goals. This step in the process should stress creativity and encourage managers and employees to think in broad terms about their jobs. Once a range of alternatives has been developed, the merits of these different plans and goals will be evaluated. Continuing with our magazine publishing example, the alternatives you might want to consider could include whether the magazine should be targeted at young men, young women, or both groups, and whether it should be sold mainly online, through subscriptions, or on newsstands.

Goals are the targets or ends the manager wants to reach. As shown in Exhibit 4.2, effective goals tend to have certain qualities, which can be remembered by the acronym SMART.

Starbucks is applying several of these criteria as it plans to open 3,400 stores in China by 2020. To date, the specialty coffee retailer has opened 1,400 stores in 84 cities with more than 3 million transactions per week.[3] Belinda Wong, president of Starbucks China, is leading the charge. At the recent opening of the company's flagship three-story building in the city of Chengdu, Wong linked the event to Starbucks' goals in China: "This is a reflection of our continued focus to highlight our coffee passion and create a locally-relevant Starbucks Experience through each moment of connection for our customers."[4] Ideally, SMART goals not only point individual employees in the direction they should be going but also tend to be accepted by the managers and employees who are charged with achieving them. Thus they both direct employees and motivate them. (For more on the importance of motivation, see Chapter 13.)

Plans are the actions or means the manager intends to use to achieve goals. At a minimum, planning should outline alternative actions that may lead to the attainment of each

goal

A target or end that management desires to reach.

plans

The actions or means managers intend to use to achieve organizational goals.

Specific	• Describe precisely what behavior and outcomes are desired so employees can direct their efforts. • *Example: Increase sales by landing 3–4 new clients from companies with more than 500 employees.*

Measurable	• Quantify what the goal should achieve. • *Example: Increase sales revenue by 5% or $50,000.*

Attainable (but challenging)	• The goal should challenge employees to work hard and creatively, but not be so difficult that they become discouraged. • *Example: Last year's increase in sales revenue was 4% or $40,000. An increase of 5% this year is achievable.*

Relevant	• Each goal should contribute to the organization's overall mission while being consistent with its mission, values, and ethical standards. Goals are relevant when they are consistent among and within teams and groups. • *Example: To support the organization's mission to help more customers each year, all sales units are asked to increase revenue by 5%.*

Time-bound	• Effective goals have a deadline or target date for completion. • *Example: Each sales employee needs to achieve the 5% increase in sales by December 31.*

EXHIBIT 4.2

SMART Goals Are Motivational

Bottom Line

Contingency plans that keep service levels high during a crisis can seal a company's reputation for caring about customers. But this commitment requires highly dedicated and creative employees, and access to the necessary resources can be expensive. Managers must decide how crucial service is to their strategy—and how willing customers will be to forgive them for service lapses under pressure. *During a major storm, what services do you expect to be able to receive without interruption? Would you pay more to make these services more reliable?*

goal, the resources required to reach the goal through those means, and the obstacles that may develop. After General Motors declared bankruptcy and borrowed billions from the U.S. government in 2009, management made plans for a return to profitability. The plans included reducing costs by producing fewer trucks, eliminating several brands, introducing smaller vehicles, keeping fewer vehicles in inventory, and closing hundreds of dealerships. So besides cutting costs, GM introduced cars it hoped would be more popular, including the Cruze compact and the Sonic subcompact. Despite obstacles such as difficulty meeting demand with a reduced workforce and the lower profitability of smaller vehicles, the company moved back into the black a year after the bankruptcy, and in two years it reported its strongest financial performance in over a decade.[5]

In this chapter, we will talk about various types of plans. Some plans, called *contingency plans,* might be referred to as "what if" plans. They include sets of actions to be taken when a company's initial plans have not worked well or if events in the external environment require a sudden change. Disasters of recent years, including the 2001 terrorist attacks and Hurricanes Katrina, Rita, and Sandy, have reminded many businesses how important contingency planning can be. Wal-Mart stores in the United States, with over 140 million customer visits per week, has several crisis plans in place to keep stores open and stocked with food, water, pharmaceutical supplies, and so forth in the aftermath of natural disasters.[6]

Most major corporations now have contingency plans in place to respond to a major disaster—to make sure vital data are backed up and can be recovered in an emergency, for instance, or that employees know what to do when a crisis occurs. But contingency plans are important for more common situations as well. For example, many businesses are affected by snowstorms, increases in gasoline prices, computer breakdowns, or changes in consumer tastes. JetBlue initially achieved success as an airline that would "bring humanity back to air travel" by caring about its customers and employees. But the airline was humiliated by its inability to cope with a February snowstorm during which at least one plane notoriously sat on a runway for 10 hours; the company took days to recover, canceling a thousand flights.[7]

Step 3: Goal and Plan Evaluation

Next, managers will evaluate the advantages, disadvantages, and potential effects of each alternative goal and plan. They must prioritize those goals and even eliminate some of them. Also, managers will consider carefully the implications of alternative plans for meeting high-priority goals. In particular, they will pay a great deal of attention to the cost of any initiative and the investment return that is likely to result. In our magazine publishing example, your evaluation might determine that newsstand sales alone wouldn't be profitable enough to justify the launch. Perhaps you could improve profits with an online edition supplemented by podcasts. To decide, you would estimate the costs and expected returns of such alternatives, trying to follow the decision steps advised in Chapter 3.

The Hard Rock Café carries its strategy—to be identified with rock 'n' roll—through to its hotel signs.
© *Richard Cummins/Corbis*

Step 4: Goal and Plan Selection

Once managers have assessed the various goals and plans, they will select the one that is most appropriate and feasible. The evaluation process will identify the priorities and trade-offs among the goals and plans. For example, if your plan is to launch a number of new online publications, and you're trying to choose among them, you might weigh the different up-front investment each requires, the size of each market, which one fits best with your existing product line or company image, and so on. Experienced judgment always plays an important role in this process. However, as you will discover later in the chapter, relying on judgment alone may not be the best way to proceed.

Typically, a formal planning process leads to a written set of goals and plans that are appropriate and feasible for a particular set of circumstances. In some organizations, the alternative generation, evaluation, and selection steps generate planning **scenarios,** as discussed in Chapter 2. A different contingency plan is attached to each scenario. The manager pursues the goals and implements the plans associated with the most likely scenario. However, the manager will also be prepared to switch to another set of plans if the situation changes and another scenario becomes relevant. This approach helps the firm anticipate and manage crises and allows greater flexibility and responsiveness.

scenario

A narrative that describes a particular set of future conditions.

Step 5: Implementation

Once managers have selected the goals and plans, they must implement the plans designed to achieve the goals. Even the best plans are useless if they are not implemented properly. Managers and employees must understand the plan, have the resources to implement it, and be motivated to do so. Including employees in the previous steps of the planning process paves the way for the implementation phase. As we mentioned earlier, employees usually are better informed, more committed, and more highly motivated when a goal or plan is one they helped develop.

Finally, successful implementation requires a plan to be linked to other systems in the organization, particularly the budget and reward systems. If the manager does not have a budget with financial resources to execute the plan, the plan is probably doomed. Similarly, goal achievement must be linked to the organization's reward system. Many organizations use incentive

> Even the best plans are useless if they are not implemented properly.

Social Enterprise

Novo Nordisk Monitors Progress Regarding Its Triple Bottom Line

While some companies discuss the importance of operating in a more socially and environmentally conscious manner, others like Novo Nordisk put this philosophy into action. Headquartered in Denmark, Novo Nordisk is a leading global provider of diabetes care solutions. The firm follows a Triple Bottom Line (TBL) strategy, meaning decisions are based on the belief that "a healthy economy, environment, and society are fundamental to long-term business success." Novo Nordisk's goal is to operate its business so that diabetes solutions benefit both the business and patients, while meeting societal expectations in the process. To ensure that the TBL philosophy would stick, Novo Nordisk took the uncommon step of incorporating it into its company bylaws.[8]

In addition to standard financial performance measures, Novo Nordisk monitors multiple short- and long-term goals within the social and environmental areas. The 2014 Integrated Annual Report Emphasizing Long-term Thinking highlights the company's social and environmental performance:[9]

Social impact
- Diabetes care products reached 24.4 million people with the disease.
- Over 3,000 new jobs were added in the company.

Environmental impact
- Continued to reduce CO_2 emissions from energy consumption for production (45 percent reduction since 2004).
- Decreased energy consumption by 1 percent over previous year.

Novo Nordisk is breaking with traditional profit-only business models by setting and monitoring meaningful social and environmental goals. The TBL model seems to be working. With the diabetes drug market expected to reach $58 billion by 2018, the company is positioned to perform well financially while making a significant, multilevel impact.[10]

Questions

- According to Novo Nordisk, only four companies have incorporated Triple Bottom Line goals into their bylaws. Why do you think so few companies take this step?

- Assume you want your employer to consider adopting a Triple Bottom Line philosophy. How would you pitch the idea? With whom would you speak?

---

programs to encourage employees to achieve goals and to implement plans properly. Commissions, salaries, promotions, bonuses, and other rewards are based on successful performance.

New York Community Bancorp (NYCB) looked at the possible ways to compete for customers: convenient locations, interest rates on savings, and customer service. With branches expensive to open and interest rates highly competitive, NYCB decided it would become known for exceptional customer service. NYCB's training department used service standards to create a classroom training program that teaches employees how to deliver excellent service. The trainers also visit NYCB's business units to practice the jobs and see firsthand what issues are important to success, using these experiences to make improvements to the employee training program. NYCB reinforces the program with coaching, and it has a system of rewards and recognition for meeting the service standards. Since implementing the goal-oriented training, coaching, and rewards, NYCB has seen its overall score for customer service rise from 89.5 percent to 97.5 percent.[11]

Step 6: Monitor and Control   Although it is sometimes ignored, the sixth step in the formal planning process—monitoring and controlling—is essential. Without it, you

Bottom Line

Tying plans to a firm's financials is a key element of success.
How might a plan to improve employees' job satisfaction be tied to a company's financial measures?

will never know whether your plan is succeeding. As we mentioned earlier, planning works in a cycle; it is an ongoing, repetitive process. Managers must continually monitor the actual performance of their work units against the units' goals and plans. They also need to develop control systems to measure that performance and allow them to take corrective action when the plans are implemented improperly or when the situation changes. The nearby "Social Enterprise" box discusses how Novo Nordisk monitors progress toward achieving important organizational goals. We will discuss the important issue of control systems in greater detail later in this chapter and in Chapter 16.

Levels of Planning

LO 2

In Chapter 1, you learned about the three major types of managers: top-level (strategic managers), middle-level (tactical managers), and frontline (operational managers). Because planning is an important management function, managers at all three levels use it. However, the scope and activities of the planning process at each level of the organization often differ.

Strategic Planning

Strategic planning involves making decisions about the organization's long-term goals and strategies. Strategic plans have a strong external orientation and cover major portions of the organization. Senior executives are responsible for the development and execution of the strategic plan, although they usually do not formulate or implement the entire plan personally.

Strategic goals are major targets or results that relate to the long-term survival, value, and growth of the organization. Strategic managers—top-level managers—usually establish goals that reflect both effectiveness (providing appropriate outputs) and efficiency (a high ratio of outputs to inputs). Typical strategic goals include growth, increasing market share, improving profitability, boosting return on investment, fostering both quantity and quality of outputs, increasing productivity, improving customer service, and contributing to society.

Organizations usually have a number of mutually reinforcing strategic goals. For example, a computer manufacturer may have as its strategic goals the launch of a specified number of new products in a particular time frame, of higher quality, with a targeted increase in market share. Each of these goals supports and contributes to the others.

A **strategy** is a pattern of actions and resource allocations designed to achieve the goals of the organization. As Exhibit 4.3 illustrates, an effective strategy provides a basis for answering five broad questions about how the organization will meet its objectives.[12] Former Procter & Gamble CEO A. G. Lafley and consultant Roger Martin emphasize that the answers to the "where" and "how" questions should be aimed at winning (question 3), which requires offering a better "value proposition" than the competition. Merely matching the competition, they say, is neither strategic nor a path to success. For example, P&G gave new life to its Oil of Olay skin care brand by addressing the concerns of middle-aged women and by improving the active ingredients in its product. In addition, P&G used its strength in selling to mass-market retailers to persuade them to set up attractive displays

strategic planning

A set of procedures for making decisions about the organization's long-term goals and strategies; see also *planning*.

strategic goals

Major targets or end results relating to the organization's long-term survival, value, and growth.

strategy

A pattern of actions and resource allocations designed to achieve the organization's goals.

1. Where will we be active?
2. How will we get there (e.g., by increasing sales or acquiring another company)?
3. How will we win in the market (e.g., by keeping prices low or offering the best service)?
4. How fast will we move and in what sequence will we make changes?
5. How will we obtain financial returns (low costs or premium prices)?

EXHIBIT 4.3
Effective Strategies
Answer Five Questions

for Oil of Olay. With the value proposition of an affordable, attractive, widely available product serving a previously ignored market segment, P&G could meet its strategic goal of leadership in the skin care market.[13]

In setting a strategy, managers try to match the organization's skills and resources to the opportunities found in the external environment. Every organization has certain strengths and weaknesses, so the actions, or strategies, the organization implements should help build on strengths in areas that satisfy the wants and needs of consumers and other key factors in the organization's external environment. Also, some organizations may implement strategies that change or influence the external environment, as discussed in Chapter 2.

Tactical and Operational Planning

Once the organization's strategic goals and plans are identified, they serve as the foundation for planning done by middle-level and frontline managers. As you can see in Exhibit 4.4, goals and plans become more specific and involve shorter periods of time as they move from the strategic level to the tactical level and then to the operational level. A strategic plan will typically have a time horizon of from three to seven years—but sometimes even decades, as with the successful plan to land a probe on Titan, Saturn's moon. Tactical plans may have a time horizon of a year or two, and operational plans may cover a period of months.

Tactical planning translates broad strategic goals and plans into specific goals and plans that are relevant to a definite portion of the organization, often a functional area like marketing or human resources, as discussed in Chapter 10. Tactical plans focus on the major actions a unit must take to fulfill its part of the strategic plan. For example, if the strategy calls for the rollout of a new product line, the tactical plan for the manufacturing unit might involve the design, testing, and installation of the equipment needed to produce the new line.

Operational planning identifies the specific procedures and processes required at lower levels of the organization. Frontline managers usually focus on routine tasks such as production runs, delivery schedules, and human resource requirements, as we discuss in Chapters 16 and 17.

The planning model we have been describing is a hierarchical one, with top-level strategies flowing down through the levels of the organization into more specific goals and plans and an ever-more-limited timetable. But in today's complex organizations, the planning sequence is often not as rigid as this traditional view. As we will see later in this chapter, managers throughout an organization may be involved in developing the strategic plan and contributing critical elements to it. Also, in practice, lower-level managers may be making decisions that shape strategy, whether or not top executives realize it. When Intel senior adviser Andy Grove suggested that the company exit the computer memory business, Intel

---

tactical planning

A set of procedures for translating broad strategic goals and plans into specific goals and plans that are relevant to a distinct portion of the organization, such as a functional area like marketing.

---

operational planning

The process of identifying the specific procedures and processes required at lower levels of the organization.

Bottom Line

Ideally, strategic plans integrate all the bottom-line practices of the firm. *What could be the consequences if a company's innovation practices were not aligned with its strategy?*

EXHIBIT 4.4
Hierarchy of Goals and Plans

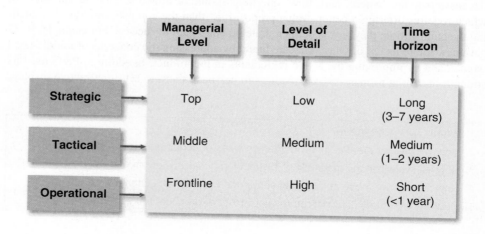

	Managerial Level	Level of Detail	Time Horizon
Strategic	Top	Low	Long (3–7 years)
Tactical	Middle	Medium	Medium (1–2 years)
Operational	Frontline	High	Short (<1 year)

was directing about one-third of its research dollars to memory-related projects. However, on a practical level, the company had already been exiting the business; only 4 percent of its total sales were for computer memory products. Why was this occurring if it wasn't yet a defined strategy? Manufacturing managers had been directed by finance executives to set up factories in a way that would generate the biggest margins (revenues minus costs) per square inch of microchips produced. As computer memory became a money-losing commodity, manufacturing made fewer of those products. So when Intel announced it would get out of the memory business, its strategy was catching up with its operational planning, which had been driven by tactical plans.[14] The lesson for top managers is to make sure they are communicating strategy to all levels of the organization *and* paying attention to what is happening at all levels in the organization.

Aligning Tactical, Operational, and Strategic Planning

To be fully effective, the organization's strategic, tactical, and operational goals and plans must be aligned—that is, they must be consistent, mutually supportive, and focused on achieving the common purpose and direction. Whole Foods Market, for example, links its tactical and operational planning directly to its strategic planning. The firm describes itself on its website as a mission-driven company that aims to set the standards for excellence for food retailers. The firm measures its success in fulfilling its vision by "customer satisfaction, team member excellence and happiness, return on capital investment, improvement in the state of the environment, and local and larger community support."

Whole Foods' strategic goal is "to sell the highest-quality products that also offer high value for our customers." Its operational goals focus on ingredients, freshness, taste, nutritional value, safety, and appearance that meet or exceed its customers' expectations, including guaranteeing product satisfaction. Tactical goals include store environments that are "inviting, fun, unique, informal, comfortable, attractive, nurturing, and educational" and safe and inviting work environments for its employees.

One method for aligning the organization's strategic and operational goals is a *strategy map*. A strategy map provides a tool managers can use to communicate their strategic goals and enable members of the organization at every level to understand the parts they will play in helping to achieve them. The map illustrates the four key drivers (or "balanced scorecard") of a firm's long-term success: the skills of its people and their ability to grow and learn; the effectiveness of its internal processes; its ability to deliver value to customers; and ultimately its ability to grow its financial assets. The map shows how specific plans and goals in each area link to the others and can generate real improvements in an organization's performance.

Exhibit 4.5 shows how a strategy map might be built and how the various goals of the organization relate to each other to create long-term value for the firm. As an example, let us assume that a company's primary financial goal is "to increase revenues by enhancing the value we offer to existing customers by making our prices the lowest available." (Target and Walmart might be good examples of companies with this kind of strategy.) The company will then have corresponding goals and plans in the other sections of the map to support that strategy. Its learning and growth goals might include bringing in the most efficient production technologies or work processes and training the staff to use them. These in turn will lead to the internal goals of improved production speed and lower cost, which in turn lead to the customer goal of competitive pricing, making the original financial goal feasible. On the other hand, a financial strategy of revenue growth through new products might lead to people and technology goals that speed up product design, to internal processes that lead to innovation, and to a customer goal of perceived product leadership. Whatever the strategy, the strategy map can be used to develop the appropriate measures and standards in each operational area for that strategy and to show how they are all linked.[15]

Whole Foods has operational goals that focus on high quality and appearance among other qualities.

© *Rubberball/Getty Images*

Bottom Line

The strategy map shows the relationship between a firm's practices and its long-term success.
Where do a company's quality practices show up in the strategy map (Exhibit 4.5)?

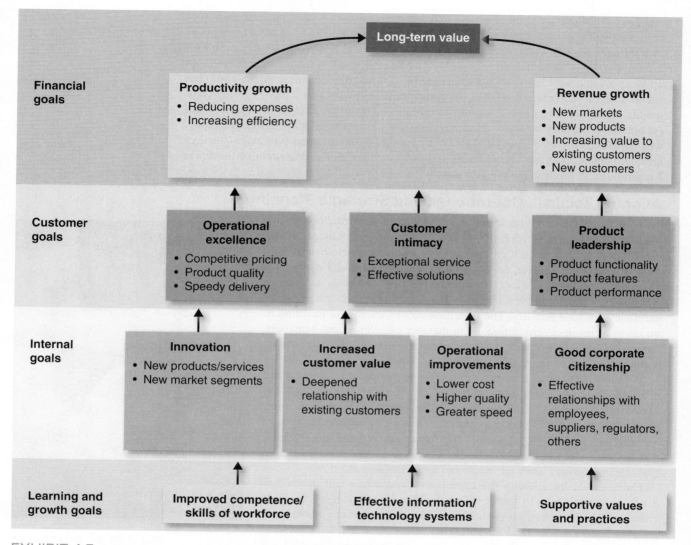

EXHIBIT 4.5   The Strategy Map: Creating Value by Aligning Goals

SOURCE: Adapted from R. Kaplan and Norton, "Plotting Success with Strategy Maps," *Optimize*, February 2004, online; and R. Kaplan and Norton, "Having Trouble with Your Strategy? Then Map It," *Harvard Business Review*, September–October 2000.

As you read "Management in Action: Progress Report," consider how well tactical, operational, and strategic planning are aligned at Walt Disney Company, particularly with regard to its Disney Interactive unit.

Strategic Planning

Strategic decision making is one of the most exciting and controversial topics in management today. In fact, many organizations currently are changing the ways they develop and execute their strategic plans.

Traditionally, strategic planning emphasized a top-down approach—senior executives and specialized planning units developed goals and plans for the entire organization. Tactical and operational managers received those goals and plans, and their own planning activities were limited to specific procedures and budgets for the units.

Management in Action

PLANNING A TURNAROUND FOR DISNEY INTERACTIVE

Walt Disney Company's corporate strategy is to lead in providing entertainment and information. The company's top ranking in the industry and recent profits of $9 billion suggest it is succeeding. Despite years of operating at a loss and recent layoffs, Disney Interactive Media is the fastest growing business segment in the company's portfolio.

Disney Interactive, founded in 2008, has as its ambitious goal to "entertain kids, families, and Disney enthusiasts everywhere with world-class products that push the boundaries of technology and imagination." Its tactical plans include development of games for every digital media platform, including mobile and social media as well as the major gaming consoles.

Measured by those standards, performance has been less than stellar. The slow pace at which it crafts movies is unsuitable for game creation. The six years required to go from concept to release of Epic Mickey, created only for the Nintendo Wii, meant the release came in 2010, after that console's popularity had peaked. At one point, Disney ran six development studios creating games for consoles, which became a problem when players switched to online games and began using mobile devices.

A basic element of Disney's digital strategy has been its entertainment website, Disney.com, successor to the Go.com web portal, which closed in 2001. However, the company has struggled to make it relevant. One challenge is that the brand aims to serve the diverse interests of toddlers and parents as well as game players of all ages in between. Mostly, the site has focused on cross-promoting its entertainment and licensed merchandise.

James A. Pitaro, president of Disney Interactive Media, is pivoting the unit in two significant ways. First, it is focusing more on mobile gaming that can be played on tablets and smartphones. In Japan, the mobile game Tsumu Tsumu is a big hit with over 8 million downloads. And second, Disney Interactive Media is seeking brand sponsors for its Disney Online website that has grown in popularity to nearly 53 million unique visitors per month.[16] Pitaro believes that brand sponsors will generate more revenue than the website advertising model currently being used.

- At which steps of the planning process would you say Disney Interactive most needs improvement? Why?
- How can Pitaro ensure that strategic, tactical, and operational management are well aligned?

Over the years, managers and consulting firms innovated with a variety of analytical techniques and planning approaches, many of which have been critical for analyzing complex business situations and competitive issues. In many instances, however, senior executives spent too much time with their planning specialists to the exclusion of line managers in the rest of the organization. As a result, a gap often developed between strategic managers and tactical and operational managers, and managers and employees throughout the organization became alienated and uncommitted to the organization's success.[17]

Today, however, senior executives increasingly are involving managers throughout the organization in the strategy formation process.[18] The problems just described and the rapidly changing environment of the past 25 years have forced executives to look to all levels of the organization for ideas and innovations to make their firms more competitive. Although the CEO and other top managers continue to furnish the strategic direction, or "vision," of the organization, tactical and even operational managers often provide valuable inputs to the organization's strategic plan. In some cases, these managers also have substantial autonomy to formulate or change their own plans. This authority increases flexibility and responsiveness, critical requirements for success in today's organizations.

Because of these trends, firms often use the term *strategic management* to describe the process. **Strategic management** involves managers from all parts of the organization in the formulation and implementation of strategic goals and strategies. It integrates strategic planning and management into a single process. Strategic planning becomes an ongoing activity in which all managers are encouraged to think strategically and focus on long-term, externally oriented issues as well as short-term tactical and operational issues.

Bottom Line

New ideas from managers throughout the organization can contribute to a plan's effectiveness.
What experiences might give frontline managers ideas that top-level executives haven't thought of?

---

strategic management

A process that involves managers from all parts of the organization in the formulation and implementation of strategic goals and strategies.

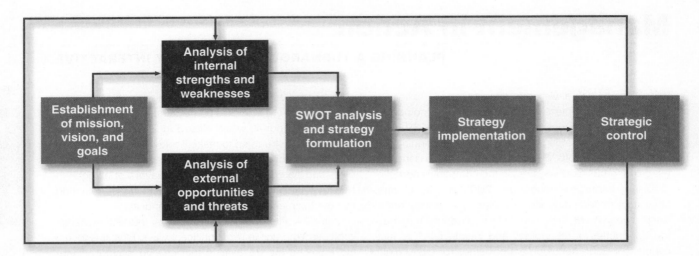

EXHIBIT 4.6
The Strategic Management Process

As shown in Exhibit 4.6, the strategic management process has six major components:

1. Establishment of mission, vision, and goals.
2. Analysis of external opportunities and threats.
3. Analysis of internal strengths and weaknesses.
4. SWOT (strengths, weaknesses, opportunities, and threats) analysis and strategy formulation.
5. Strategy implementation.
6. Strategic control.

Because this process is a planning and decision process, it is similar to the planning framework discussed earlier. Although organizations may use different terms or emphasize different parts of the process, the components and concepts described in this section are found either explicitly or implicitly in every organization. Even a small entrepreneurial firm can benefit from the kind of planning framework we describe here.

Step 1: Establishment of Mission, Vision, and Goals

The first step in strategic planning is establishing a mission, a vision, and goals for the organization. The **mission** is a clear and concise expression of the basic purpose of the organization. It describes what the organization does, for whom it does it, its basic good or service, and its values. Here are some mission statements from firms you will recognize:[19]

mission

An organization's basic purpose and scope of operations.

> *McDonald's:* "To be our customers' favorite place and way to eat."
> *Uber:* "Evolve the way the world moves."
> *United Way:* "Improve lives by mobilizing the caring power of communities around the world to advance the common good."

Smaller organizations, of course, may have missions that aren't as broad as these. For example, the local bar found next to most campuses has this implicit mission: "to sell large quantities of inexpensive beer to college students in a noisily enjoyable environment."

The mission describes the organization as it currently operates. The **strategic vision** points to the future—it provides a perspective on where the organization is headed and what it can become. Ideally, the vision statement clarifies the long-term direction of the company and its strategic intent. Here are some actual vision statements:[20]

strategic vision

The long-term direction and strategic intent of a company.

> *NASA Armstrong Flight Research Center:* "To fly what others only imagine."
> *City of Redmond, Washington:* "Together we create a community of good neighbors."
> *Samsung:* "Inspire the world. Create the future."

The most effective vision statements inspire organization members. They offer a worthwhile target for the entire organization to work together to achieve. Often these statements are not strictly financial because financial targets alone may not motivate all organization members. For example, NASA's Armstrong Flight Research Center focuses on the future of flight and exploration. Similarly, Samsung's vision refers to inspiring the world and creating the future.

> The strategic vision points to the future—where the organization is headed and what it can become.

Strategic goals evolve from the mission and vision of the organization. The chief executive officer of the organization, with the input and approval of the board of directors, establishes the mission, vision, and major strategic goals. The concepts and information within the mission statement, vision statement, and strategic goals statement may not be identified as such, but they should be communicated to everyone who has contact with the organization. Large firms generally provide public formal statements of their missions, visions, goals, and even values. For example, in support of its vision that "creating a community of good neighbors" is best done "together" with all sectors of the community, the City of Redmond has established goals such as these:

- Enhance citizen engagement in city issues.
- Sustain the natural systems and beauty of the community.
- Sustain a safe community with a coherent, comprehensive, cohesive approach to safety.
- Maintain economic vitality.

Different city departments would contribute to various aspects of this vision in the way they carry out their operational plans with an emphasis on collaborating with local businesses and residents.

Lofty words in a vision and mission statement cannot be meaningful without strong leadership support. At McDonald's, the commitment of past and present CEOs has played a large role in the success of the company's strategy implementation. Several years ago, the company was floundering as it lost sight of its commitment to quality, value, speed, and convenience. Under the leadership of James Cantalupo, the company created the mission statement quoted earlier, which placed the emphasis on the customer's experience. In a "Plan to Win," strategic goals such as revamping restaurants for a better drive-through experience and improving the quality of the menu supported the mission. When Jim Skinner took the job of chief executive, he enthusiastically backed the mission statement and its supporting Plan to Win, not hesitating to share credit for the company's continued success.[21]

Where leadership is strong, statements of visions and goals clarify the organization's purpose to key constituencies outside the organization. They also help employees focus their talent, energy, and commitment in pursuit of the organization's goals. When the time comes for you to seek employment with a firm, reviewing the firm's statements of mission, vision, and goals is a good first step in determining whether the firm's purposes and values will be compatible with your own.

Step 2: Analysis of External Opportunities and Threats

The mission and vision drive the second component of the strategic management process: analysis of the external environment. Successful strategic management depends on an accurate and thorough evaluation of the competitive environment and macroenvironment. The various components of these environments were introduced in Chapter 2.

The important activities in an environmental analysis include the ones listed in Exhibit 4.7. The analysis begins with an examination of the industry. Next, organizational stakeholders are examined. **Stakeholders** are groups and individuals who affect and are affected by the achievement of the organization's mission, goals, and strategies. They include buyers, suppliers, competitors, government and regulatory agencies, unions and employee groups, the financial community, owners and shareholders, and trade associations. The environmental analysis provides a map of these stakeholders and the ways they influence the organization.[22]

stakeholders

Groups and individuals who affect and are affected by the achievement of the organization's mission, goals, and strategies.

EXHIBIT 4.7
Environmental Analysis

Industry and Market Analysis

Industry profile: major product lines and significant market segments in the industry.

Industry growth: growth rates for the entire industry, growth rates for key market segments, projected changes in patterns of growth, and the determinants of growth.

Industry forces: threat of new industry entrants, threat of substitutes, economic power of buyers, economic power of suppliers, and internal industry rivalry (recall Chapter 2).

Competitor Analysis

Competitor profile: major competitors and their market shares.

Competitor analysis: goals, strategies, strengths, and weaknesses of each major competitor.

Competitor advantages: the degree to which industry competitors have differentiated their products or services or achieved cost leadership.

Political and Regulatory Analysis

Legislation and regulatory activities and their effects on the industry.

Political activity: the level of political activity that organizations and associations within the industry undertake (see Chapter 5).

Social Analysis

Social issues: current and potential social issues and their effects on the industry.

Social interest groups: consumer, environmental, and similar activist groups that attempt to influence the industry (see Chapters 5 and 6).

Human Resources Analysis

Labor issues: key labor needs, shortages, opportunities, and problems confronting the industry (see Chapters 10 and 11).

Macroeconomic Analysis

Macroeconomic conditions: economic factors that affect supply, demand, growth, competition, and profitability within the industry.

Technological Analysis

Technological factors: scientific or technical methods that affect the industry, particularly recent and potential innovations (see Chapter 17).

Since some states require the use of renewable sources to generate power, it is up to these companies to turn the negative aspect of higher costs into an overall positive outcome.

© Kim Steele/Getty Images

The environmental analysis also should examine other forces in the environment, such as economic conditions and technological factors. One critical task in environmental analysis is forecasting future trends. As noted in Chapter 2, forecasting techniques range from simple judgment to complex mathematical models that examine systematic relationships among many variables. Even simple quantitative techniques outperform the intuitive assessments of experts. Judgment is susceptible to bias, and managers have a limited ability to process information. Managers should use subjective judgments as inputs to quantitative models or when they confront new situations.

Frequently, the difference between an opportunity and a threat depends on how a company positions itself strategically. For example, some states have required electric utilities to get a certain share of their power from renewable sources such as wind and solar energy rather than from fossil fuels, including coal, oil, and natural gas. This requirement poses an obvious threat to utilities because the costs of fossil fuel energy are less, and customers demand low prices. However, some companies see strategic opportunities in renewable power. For over 10 years, Ocean Renewable Power Company (ORPC) has been developing technology that uses "ocean and river currents to produce clean, predictable electricity to power our homes and businesses while protecting the environment." At the Bay of Fundy on the border between Maine and Canada, ORPC operates the first commercial tidal power system in the United States. The system converts ocean energy to electricity that is then delivered to the public electricity grid. ORPC's goal is to increase output to the point where the system will power approximately 2,000 homes and businesses in Maine with clean tidal energy. ORPC has similar renewable energy generation projects under way in Alaska and Nova Scotia.[23] Similarly, overflowing landfills are an expensive challenge for many municipalities, but a growing number are seeing an opportunity in the form of energy generation. As garbage decomposes, it produces methane gas, which is used as a fuel to power generators. In East Brunswick, New Jersey, for example, the Edgeboro landfill generates electricity that powers the county's wastewater treatment plant.[24]

In some environments, it takes an especially creative mind to see opportunities among severe threats. For Farif Ali Abood, who opened a shop to make commercial signs in his hometown of Najaf, Iraq, the difficulties have included sporadic electrical service, lack of funds to borrow, and even occasional sniper fire in the area. Despite these challenges, Abood has managed to keep the business running by using a generator when the power goes out. As conditions in the city have stabilized, business has grown enough for Abood to hire several full-time employees and earn a modest profit.[25] The brave few who, like Abood, can fill needs amidst such difficult threats are well positioned to benefit from the business relationships they create with loyal customers.

Step 3: Analysis of Internal Strengths and Weaknesses

As managers conduct an external analysis, they will also assess the strengths and weaknesses of major functional areas inside their organization. Exhibit 4.8 lists some of the major components of this internal resource analysis. For example, is your firm strong enough financially to handle the lengthy and costly investment new projects often require? Can your existing staff carry out its part of the plan, or will additional training or hiring be needed? Is your firm's image compatible with the strategy, or will it have to persuade key

EXHIBIT 4.8
Internal Resource Analysis

Financial Analysis

Examines financial strengths and weaknesses through financial statements such as a balance sheet and an income statement and compares trends to historical and industry figures (see Chapter 18).

Marketing Audit

Examines strengths and weaknesses of major marketing activities and identifies markets, key market segments, and the competitive position (market share) of the organization within key markets.

Operations Analysis

Examines the strengths and weaknesses of the manufacturing, production, or service delivery activities of the organization (see Chapters 9, 16, and 17).

Other Internal Resource Analyses

Examine, as necessary and appropriate, the strengths and weaknesses of other organizational activities, such as research and development (product and process), management information systems, engineering, and purchasing.

Human Resources Assessment

Examines strengths and weaknesses of all levels of management and employees and focuses on key human resources activities, including recruitment, selection, placement, training, labor (union) relationships, compensation, promotion, appraisal, quality of work life, and human resources planning (see Chapters 10 and 11).

stakeholders that a change in direction makes sense? This kind of internal analysis gives strategic decision makers an inventory of the organization's existing functions, skills, and resources as well as its overall performance level. Many of your other business courses will prepare you to conduct an internal analysis.

resources

Inputs to a system that can enhance performance.

Resources and Core Capabilities   Without question, strategic planning has been strongly influenced in recent years by a focus on internal resources. **Resources** are inputs to production (recall systems theory) that can be accumulated over time to enhance the performance of a firm. Resources can take many forms, but they tend to fall into two broad categories: (1) tangible assets such as real estate, production facilities, raw materials, and so on, and (2) intangible assets such as company reputation, culture, technical knowledge, and patents as well as accumulated learning and experience. The Walt Disney Company, for example, has developed its strategic plan on combinations of tangible assets (e.g., hotels and theme parks) as well as intangible assets (brand recognition, talented crafts-people, culture focused on customer service).[26]

Effective internal analysis provides a clearer understanding of how a company can compete through its resources. Resources are a source of competitive advantage only under certain circumstances. First, if the resource is instrumental for creating customer value—that is, if it increases the benefits customers derive from a good or service relative to the costs they incur—the resource can lead to a competitive advantage.[27] For example, Amazon's powerful search technology and its ability to track customer preferences and offer personalized recommendations each time its site is accessed, as well as its quick product delivery system, are clearly valuable resources that enhance Amazon's competitiveness.

Second, resources are a source of advantage if they are rare and not equally available to all competitors. Even for extremely valuable resources, if all competitors have equal access, the resource cannot provide a source of competitive advantage. For companies such as W.L. Gore, Intel, DuPont, Dow Chemical, and others, patented formulas represent important resources that are both rare and valuable. Amazon, too, sought a patent for its one-click shopping technique.

Third, if resources are difficult to imitate, they provide a source of competitive advantage. Online retailer Zappos.com seeks a competitive advantage in the form of service that makes customers say "Wow!" The company hires customer service employees based on their match with its values, gives them seven weeks of training, and empowers them to do whatever it takes to delight a customer, whether that be spending hours on the phone, issuing a refund, or sending a package of free cookies. Zappos frees reps from using scripted replies, promotes positive relationships with colleagues through mentoring programs and fun activities, and provides on-site coaching to help employees achieve their career and personal goals.[28] As in this example, where success relies on a combination of hiring, training, motivation, and job design, not just a policy of free returns, resources tend to be harder to imitate if they are complex, with many interdependent variables and no obvious links between easily explained behaviors and desired outcomes.[29]

Bottom Line

Amazon's key customer benefits are speed and excellence of service. *What are some resources Amazon needs to deliver these benefits?*

Finally, resources can enhance a firm's competitive advantage when they are well organized. For example, Coca-Cola's well-organized and global network of bottlers allows the company to introduce a new soft drink worldwide quickly and to distribute it more efficiently than any competitor. IBM, known primarily for computer hardware until it became more of a commodity than a source of competitive advantage.

As shown in Exhibit 4.9, when resources are valuable, rare, inimitable, and organized, they can be viewed as a company's core capabilities. Simply stated, a **core capability** (also referred to as "competence") is something a company does especially well relative to its competitors. Honda, for example, has a core competence in small engine design and manufacturing; Netflix has a core competence in delivering Internet TV and movies; and Federal Express has a core competence in logistics and customer service. As in these examples, a core competence typically refers to a set of skills or expertise in some activity rather than physical or financial assets.

core capability

A unique skill and/or knowledge an organization possesses that gives it an edge over competitors.

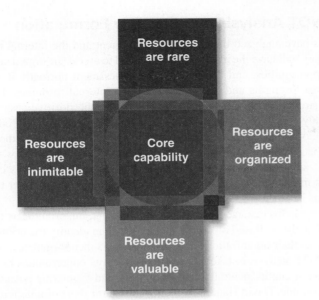

EXHIBIT 4.9
Resources and Core
Capability

Benchmarking   To assess and improve performance, some companies use benchmarking, the process of assessing how well one company's basic functions and skills compare with those of another company or set of companies. The goal of benchmarking is to understand the "best practices" of other firms thoroughly and to undertake actions to achieve both better performance and lower costs.

According to consulting firm Accenture, benchmarking consists of four stages:[30]

1. Decide what needs to be measured and which metrics will be used.
2. Collect and validate the data; compile initial findings.
3. Assess initial findings to see if additional data need to be collected.
4. Analyze results and make final recommendations to key stakeholders.

Benchmarking programs have helped a myriad of companies, such as Ford, Corning, Hewlett-Packard, Xerox, and Anheuser-Busch, make great strides in eliminating inefficiencies and improving competitiveness.

Depending on how it is applied, benchmarking may be of limited help in that it only helps a company perform as well as its competitors; strategic management ultimately is about surpassing those companies. Besides benchmarking against leading organizations in other industries, companies may address this problem by engaging in internal benchmarking. That approach involves benchmarking their different internal operations and departments against one another to disseminate the company's best practices throughout the organization and thereby gain a competitive advantage.

One company that has experienced the pros and cons of benchmarking is AXA Canada, an insurance company. The company turned to benchmarking as a way to identify how it could improve its processes and lower its costs. AXA Canada used internal benchmarking to compare results among its regions. However, employees objected that in a country as vast as Canada, the differences among regions were so great that performance couldn't really be compared. More energy went to arguing about the numbers than looking for ways to close performance gaps. The company made similar efforts to compare Canadian performance with insurers in other countries, and it ran into even greater difficulty making comparisons. The most success came from an arrangement with the Ward Group to gather performance data from several insurance companies, analyze it, and report on areas of strength and weakness. Using this benchmarking information, AXA Canada has found areas where it can operate more efficiently by applying other companies' practices. The company uses the benchmarking data primarily for cutting costs and identifying potential new markets.[31]

Bottom Line

Aligning a firm's bottom-line practices with best practices can improve its competitiveness.
In some famous benchmarking examples, businesses have learned from pit crews for race car teams. What kinds of bottom-line practices could such an organization demonstrate?

Step 4: SWOT Analysis and Strategy Formulation

Once managers have analyzed the external environment and the internal resources of the organization, they will have the information they need to assess the organization's strengths, weaknesses, opportunities, and threats. Such an assessment normally is referred to as a **SWOT analysis.** Strengths and weaknesses refer to internal resources. For example, an organization's strengths might include skilled management, positive cash flow, and well-known and highly regarded brands. Weaknesses might be lack of spare production capacity and the absence of reliable suppliers. Opportunities and threats arise in the macroenvironment and competitive environment. Examples of opportunities are a new technology that could make the supply chain more efficient and a market niche that is currently underserved. Threats might include the possibility that competitors will enter the underserved niche once it has been shown to be profitable.

SWOT analysis helps managers summarize the relevant, important facts from their external and internal analyses. Based on this summary, they can identify the primary and secondary strategic issues their organization faces. The managers then formulate a strategy that will build on the SWOT analysis to take advantage of available opportunities by capitalizing on the organization's strengths, neutralizing its weakness, and countering potential threats.

To take an example, David Handmaker enjoyed several years of unfettered growth since opening his printing company, Next Day Flyers, in Los Angeles in 2004. However, over time he noticed that his competitors were more adept at finding and serving online customers. Handmaker needed a plan to restore healthy business growth by migrating parts of his marketing and printing services online before it was too late. But, Next Day Flyers originally aimed at local customers, which raised questions about whether the company could serve the needs of geographically dispersed customers.

Handmaker and his team need to analyze what the firm does well and in what areas it needs improvement relative to the printing marketplace. Exhibit 4.10 summarizes these points in a format commonly used for a basic SWOT analysis. The company's strategy

SWOT analysis

A comparison of strengths, weaknesses, opportunities, and threats that helps executives formulate strategy.

EXHIBIT 4.10

Sample SWOT Analysis: Next Day Flyers

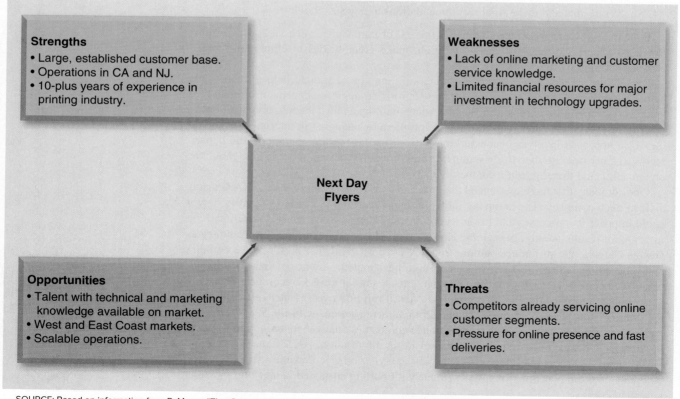

Strengths
- Large, established customer base.
- Operations in CA and NJ.
- 10-plus years of experience in printing industry.

Weaknesses
- Lack of online marketing and customer service knowledge.
- Limited financial resources for major investment in technology upgrades.

Next Day Flyers

Opportunities
- Talent with technical and marketing knowledge available on market.
- West and East Coast markets.
- Scalable operations.

Threats
- Competitors already servicing online customer segments.
- Pressure for online presence and fast deliveries.

SOURCE: Based on information from R. Myers, "That Sounds Like a Plan," *Inc.,* no. 36 (2014), pp. 90–92; and Next Day Flyers company website, "About Next Day Flyers," http://www.nextdayflyers.com.

Multiple Generations at Work

Perceived Strengths and Weaknesses of Each Generation

Ernst & Young, an accounting and consulting firm, recently asked managers and employees across multiple generations and industries to describe the strengths and weaknesses commonly associated with workers from other generational cohorts. The following exhibit includes some of the findings:

Baby Boomers	Gen Xers	Millennials
Strengths • *Loyal* • *Mentoring others* • *Hardworking* **Weaknesses** • *Slower to adapt to change and collaborate with others*	**Strengths** • *Revenue generators* • *Adaptable* • *Problem-solvers* **Weaknesses** • *Displaying executive presence and being cost effective*	**Strengths** • *Tech savvy* • *Skilled at leveraging social media* • *Enthusiastic* **Weaknesses** • *Team player and hardworking*

The results reflect respondents' perceptions of the strengths and weaknesses of different generations at work. Of course, caution is advised when generalizing to all members of a given generation of workers. However, when individuals do a self-SWOT analysis, they may want to compare their results to those of the stereotypical traits identified above. This information may prove useful for overcoming or leveraging stereotypes. If a Millennial has a track record of being hardworking (e.g., working full-time while in college to pay for tuition), then the individual should highlight this fact during interviews. Gen Xers who want to advance into executive positions may want to observe how current executives dress, communicate, plan, and make decisions. A Boomer can overcome the stereotype of being slow to adapt to change by embracing new technology at work.[32]

calls for it to hire talent with the skills, knowledge, and experience to help Next Day Flyers establish a professional presence on the web, including simple online ordering; free online design services; free printing templates; blog with design and marketing tips; and customer support by phone, e-mail, and live chat.[33]

In the real world, as a company is formulating strategy, so are its competitors. As a result, the process must be continually evolving through contingency planning. The more uncertainty that exists in the external environment, the more the strategy needs to focus on building internal capabilities through practices such as knowledge sharing and continuous process improvement.[34] Yet at a basic level, strategy formulation moves from analysis to devising a coherent course of action. In this way, the organization's online customer engagement will keep Next Day Flyers competitive.

Before we continue our strategy discussion, we note that many individuals seeking a job or a career change can find a self-SWOT analysis helpful. What are you particularly good at? What weaknesses might you need to overcome to improve your employment chances? What firms offer the best opportunity to market your skills to full advantage? How are individuals from your generation perceived in the workplace (see the nearby "Multiple Generations at Work" box)? Will you have a lot of competition from other job seekers? As with companies, this kind of analysis can be the beginning of a plan of action and can improve the plan's effectiveness.

corporate strategy

The set of businesses, markets, or industries in which an organization competes and the distribution of resources among those entities.

Corporate Strategy   A **corporate strategy** identifies the set of businesses, markets, or industries in which the organization competes and the distribution of resources among those businesses. Exhibit 4.11 shows four basic alternatives for a corporate strategy,

LO 5

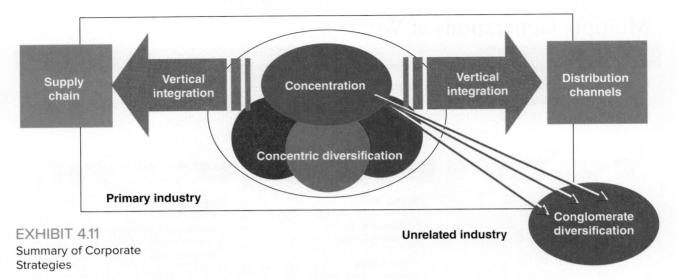

EXHIBIT 4.11
Summary of Corporate Strategies

concentration

A strategy employed for an organization that operates a single business and competes in a single industry.

vertical integration

The acquisition or development of new businesses that produce parts or components of the organization's product.

concentric diversification

A strategy used to add new businesses that produce related products or are involved in related markets and activities.

conglomerate diversification

A strategy used to add new businesses that produce unrelated products or are involved in unrelated markets and activities.

ranging from very specialized to highly diverse. A **concentration** strategy focuses on a single business competing in a single industry. In the food retailing industry, Kroger, Safeway, and A&P all pursue concentration strategies. Frequently, companies pursue concentration strategies to gain entry into an industry when industry growth is good or when the company has a narrow range of competencies. An example is C. F. Martin & Company, which pursues a concentration strategy by focusing on making the best possible guitars and guitar strings, a strategy that has enabled the family-owned business to operate successfully for more than 150 years.

A **vertical integration** strategy involves expanding the domain of the organization into supply channels or to distributors. At one time, Henry Ford had fully integrated his company from the ore mines needed to make steel all the way to the showrooms where his cars were sold. Vertical integration generally is used to eliminate uncertainties and reduce costs associated with suppliers or distributors.

A strategy of **concentric diversification** involves moving into new businesses that are related to the company's original core business. William Marriott expanded his original restaurant business outside Washington, DC, by moving into airline catering, hotels, and fast food. Each of these businesses within the hospitality industry is related in terms of the services it provides, the skills necessary for success, and the customers it attracts. Often companies such as Marriott pursue a strategy of concentric diversification to take advantage of their strengths in one business to gain advantage in another. Because the businesses are related, the products, markets, technologies, or capabilities used in one business can be transferred to another. Success in a concentric diversification strategy requires adequate management and other resources for operating more than one business. Guitar maker C. F. Martin once tried expanding through purchases of other instrument companies, but management was stretched too thin to run them all well, so the company eventually divested the acquisitions and returned to its concentration strategy.[35]

In contrast to concentric diversification, **conglomerate diversification** is a corporate strategy that involves expansion into unrelated businesses. For example, General Electric Corporation has diversified from its original base in electrical and home appliance products to such wide-ranging industries as health, finance, insurance, truck and air transportation, and even media with its ownership of NBC (now owned with Comcast). Typically, companies pursue a conglomerate diversification strategy to minimize risks due to market fluctuations in one industry.

The diversified businesses of an organization are sometimes called its business *portfolio.* One of the most popular techniques for analyzing a corporation's strategy for managing its portfolio is the BCG matrix, developed by the Boston Consulting Group. The BCG matrix is shown in Exhibit 4.12. Each business in the corporation is plotted on the matrix

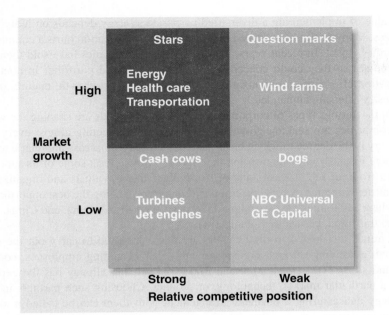

on the basis of the growth rate of its market and the relative strength of its competitive position in that market (market share). The business is represented by a circle whose size depends on the business's contribution to corporate revenues.

High-growth, weak-competitive-position businesses are called *question marks*. They require substantial investment to improve their position; otherwise divestiture is recommended. High-growth, strong-competitive-position businesses are called *stars*. These businesses require heavy investment, but their strong position allows them to generate the needed revenues. Low-growth, strong-competitive-position businesses are called *cash cows*. These businesses generate revenues in excess of their investment needs and therefore fund other businesses. Finally, low-growth, weak-competitive-position businesses are called *dogs*. The remaining revenues from these businesses are realized, and then the businesses are divested.

The BCG matrix is not intended as a substitute for management judgment, creativity, insight, or leadership. But it is a tool that can, along with other techniques, help managers of the firm as a whole and of its individual businesses evaluate their strategy alternatives.[36] This approach can help a company such as General Electric that needs to weigh the relative merits of many business units and product lines. When GE struggled to generate acceptable returns in some of its widely diversified businesses, such as NBC Universal and GE Capital, the company refocused on its strength as a manufacturer, targeting three industries: energy, health care, and transportation. Not only do these industries offer significant growth potential, but GE already dominates the markets for electric turbines and jet engines. Therefore, besides selling the NBC unit and scaling back the financial business, GE has acquired wind farms in Europe and purchased Avio, an Italian aerospace company with jet engine expertise and customers beyond the aviation industry.[37]

Trends in Corporate Strategy   Corporate America is periodically swept by waves of mergers and acquisitions (M&As). The targets chosen for mergers and acquisitions depend on the organization's corporate strategy of either concentrating in one industry or diversifying its portfolio. Many recent deals have been aimed at helping companies expand their market share and product offerings within related industries. For example, General Electric's acquisition of France-based Alstom gives the American company access to nuclear plant servicing technology and renewable energy assets in Europe. By purchasing DirecTV, AT&T gained 38 million customers in the United States and Latin America. Holcim's acquisition of Lafarge will create the largest cement manufacturer in the world.[38]

Bottom Line

Companies that integrate vertically often do so to reduce their costs. *Why might buying from a division of your company be less costly than buying on the open market?*

The value of implementing a diversified corporate strategy depends on individual circumstances. Many critics have argued that unrelated diversification hurts a company more often than it helps it. In recent years, many diversified companies have sold their peripheral businesses so they could concentrate on a more focused portfolio. In contrast, the diversification efforts of an organization competing in a slow-growth, mature, or threatened industry often are applauded.

Within the various types of corporate strategies, other trends are shaping the ways that today's companies are seeking growth. One major trend affecting almost every company's strategy is the degree to which business today takes place across national boundaries. Today, there is hardly any organization that does not buy at least some of its supplies and equipment from, or sell at least some of its products to, individuals and organizations in other countries. In terms of strategy, companies are often finding the best opportunities for growth where economies are expanding the fastest, as in Brazil, India, and China. Chapter 6 explores this trend, known as globalization.

Other trends are related to the business arrangements used to carry out the strategy. Rather than expanding through organic growth—that is, adding employees, equipment, offices, and so on—an organization can find a partner that already has the expertise it needs in a particular market, technology, or product. Choosing such partners in support of a strategy and entering a business arrangement with them can be called a joint venture, strategic partnership, or strategic alliance, depending on the details of the arrangement. Chapter 9 describes how some organizations use strategic alliances to become more agile, and Chapter 17 tells how joint ventures can give companies quick access to new technology.

LO 6

business strategy

The major actions by which a business competes in a particular industry or market.

low-cost strategy

A strategy an organization uses to build competitive advantage by being efficient and offering a standard, no-frills product.

differentiation strategy

A strategy an organization uses to build competitive advantage by being unique in its industry or market segment along one or more dimensions.

Bottom Line

Low-price strategies usually require low production costs. *How do you think Walmart keeps costs low?*

Business Strategy   After the top management team and board make the corporate strategic decisions, executives must determine how they will compete in each business area. **Business strategy** defines the major actions by which an organization builds and strengthens its competitive position in the marketplace. A competitive advantage typically results from one of two generic business strategies introduced here and elaborated in Chapter 7.[39]

First, organizations such as Walmart and Southwest Airlines pursue competitive advantage through **low-cost strategies.** Businesses using a low-cost strategy attempt to be efficient and offer a standard, no-frills product. Walmart Stores expresses its low-price strategy with the slogan "save money, live better." The company uses the power of its giant size to negotiate favorable prices from suppliers, enabling it to sell at prices below those of most competing retailers. Recently, when gasoline prices soared, the company promoted its stores as a place where consumers can save on transportation costs by purchasing everything they need at low prices in one trip.[40] Companies that succeed with a low-cost strategy often are large and try to take advantage of economies of scale in production or distribution. In many cases, their scale allows them to buy and sell their goods and services at a lower price, which leads to higher market share, volume, and ultimately profits. To succeed, an organization using this strategy generally must be the cost leader in its industry or market segment. However, even a cost leader must offer a product that is acceptable to customers compared with competitors' products.

Second, an organization may pursue a **differentiation strategy.** With a differentiation strategy, a company attempts to be unique in its industry or market segment along some dimensions that customers value. This unique or differentiated position within the industry often is based on high product quality, excellent marketing and distribution, or superior service.

Nordstrom's commitment to quality and customer service in the retail apparel industry is an excellent example of a differentiation strategy. For example, Nordstrom's personal shoppers are available online, by phone, or in stores to select items for shoppers' consideration at no charge. Innovation, too, is an important ingredient of a differentiation strategy. In the market for toilet paper, Scott Paper Company once determined that it could not afford to compete for institutional sales based on price. Instead, the company began offering institutions a free dispenser that would hold larger rolls of paper, saving its customers the labor cost of replacing empty rolls more frequently. Scott initially was the only company selling the larger rolls, so it gained market share while competitors scrambled to catch up.[41]

Whatever strategy managers adopt, the most effective strategy is one that competitors are unwilling or unable to imitate. If the organization's strategic plan is one that could easily be adopted by industry competitors, it may not be sufficiently distinctive or, in the long run, contribute significantly to the organization's competitiveness. For example, a strategy to gain market share and profits by being the first mover to offer an innovative product may or may not succeed, depending in part on competitive responses. In some industries, such as computers, technology advances so fast that the first company to provide a new product is quickly challenged by later entrants offering superior products.[42]

Functional Strategy   The final step in strategy formulation is to establish the major functional strategies. **Functional strategies** are implemented by each functional area of the organization to support the business strategy. The typical functional areas include production, human resources, marketing, research and development, finance, and distribution. For example, Bloomin' Brands, the parent company of restaurant chains including Outback Steakhouse, Bonefish Grill, and Carrabba's Italian Grill, recently set a business strategy with targets for aggressive growth and greater efficiency built on the chains' reputation for offering good food at affordable prices. To achieve this, functional strategies include creation of a lunch menu, methods aimed at improving the productivity of its employees, and deals signed in advance for large purchases of beef, a major expense for the Outback restaurants. Another functional strategy is the use of a team of data analysts to keep an eye on consumer behavior, environmental trends, and other information that can support informed decisions about menu items, new restaurant locations, and more.[43]

Functional strategies typically are developed by functional area executives with input of and approval from the executives responsible for business strategy. Senior strategic decision makers review the functional strategies to ensure that each major department is operating consistently with the business strategies of the organization. For example, automated production techniques—even if they saved money—would not be appropriate for a piano company like Steinway, whose products are strategically positioned (and priced) as high-quality and handcrafted. At companies that compete based on product innovation, strategies for research and development are especially critical. But in the recession of 2001, General Electric cut back on research in lighting technology just as other companies were making advances in LED lighting. When the economy recovered, customers were looking for innovative lighting, but GE had fallen behind. Based on that experience, GE committed itself to an R&D strategy of maintaining budgets even when sales slow down. In the latest economic downturn, the company continued to fund a project in which it developed new aircraft engines with Honda Motor Company.[44]

functional strategies

Strategies implemented by each functional area of the organization to support the organization's business strategy.

Employees at Bonefish Grill strive to meet the company's business strategy to achieve greater efficiency.

© *Mark Gail/The Washington Post/ Getty Images*

Step 5: Strategy Implementation

As with any plan, simply formulating a good strategy is not enough. Strategic managers also must ensure that the new strategies are implemented effectively and efficiently. Recently, corporations and strategy consultants have been paying more attention to implementation. They realize that clever techniques and a good plan do not guarantee success. This greater appreciation is reflected in two major trends.

First, organizations are adopting a more comprehensive view of implementation. Successful strategy execution depends on building human and organizational resources

EXHIBIT 4.13

4 A's Model of Execution
Capability

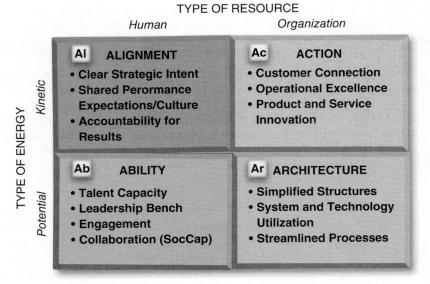

SOURCE: Carrig, Snell, and Onozuka (2014).

that can be energized to achieve organizational goals. Exhibit 4.13 suggests that energy is either potential or kinetic (in motion) in nature. When applied to human or organizational resources, four "A's" result: ability and architecture are sources of potential energy, while alignment and activation are sources of kinetic energy that sparks performance.[45]

Second, many organizations are extending the more participative strategic management process to implementation. Managers at all levels are involved with formulating strategy and identifying and executing ways to implement it. Senior executives still may oversee the implementation process, but they are placing much greater responsibility and authority in the hands of others. In general, strategy implementation involves four related steps:

Step 1: Define strategic tasks. Articulate in simple language what a particular business must do to create or sustain a competitive advantage. Define strategic tasks to help employees understand how they contribute to the organization, including redefining relationships among the parts of the organization.

Step 2: Assess organization capabilities. Evaluate the organization's ability to implement the strategic tasks. A task force typically interviews employees and managers to identify specific issues that help or hinder effective implementation. Then the results are summarized for top management. In the course of your career, you will likely be asked to participate in a task force. We discuss working effectively in teams in Chapter 14.

Step 3: Develop an implementation agenda. Management decides how it will change its own activities and procedures; how critical interdependencies will be managed; what skills and individuals are needed in key roles; and what structures, measures, information, and rewards might ultimately support the needed behavior. A philosophy statement, communicated in terms of value, is the outcome of this process.

Step 4: Create an implementation plan. The top management team, the employee task force, and others develop the implementation plan. The top management team then monitors progress. The employee task force continues its work by providing feedback about how others in the organization are responding to the changes.

This process, though straightforward, does not always go smoothly. Exhibit 4.14 shows six barriers to strategy implementation and provides a description of some key principles for overcoming these silent killers. By paying closer attention to the processes by which strategies are implemented, executives, managers, and employees can make sure that strategic plans are actually carried out.[46]

EXHIBIT 4.14
Attacking the Six
Barriers to Strategy
Implementation

The Silent Killers	Change starts with the leader Principles for Engaging and Changing the Silent Killers
Top-down or laissez-faire senior management style	With the top team and lower levels, the CEO/general manager creates a partnership built around the development of a compelling business direction, the creation of an enabling organizational context, and the delegation of authority to clearly accountable individuals and teams.
Unclear strategy and conflicting priorities	The top team, as a group, develops a statement of strategy, and priorities that members are willing to stand behind are developed.
An ineffective senior management team	The top team, as a group, is involved in all steps in the change process so that its effectiveness is tested and developed.
Poor vertical communication	An honest, fact-based dialogue is established with lower levels about the new strategy and the barriers to implementing it.
Poor coordination across functions, businesses, or borders	A set of businesswide initiatives and new organizational roles and responsibilities are defined that require "the right people to work together on the right things in the right way" to implement the strategy.
Inadequate down-the-line leadership skills and development	Lower-level managers develop skills through newly created opportunities to lead change and drive key business initiatives. They are supported with just-in-time coaching, training, and targeted recruitment. Those who still are not able to make the grade must be replaced.

SOURCE: From M. Beer and R. A Eisenstat, "The Silent Killers of Strategy Implementation and Learning Barriers," *MIT Sloan Management Review,* Summer 2000, Vol. 4 #4, pp. 29–40. Copyright © 2000 by Massachusetts Institute of Technology. All rights reserved. Distributed by Tribune Media Services.

Step 6: Strategic Control

The final component of the strategic management process is strategic control. A **strategic control system** is designed to support managers in evaluating the organization's progress with its strategy and, when discrepancies exist, taking corrective action. The system must encourage efficient operations that are consistent with the plan while allowing flexibility to adapt to changing conditions. As with all control systems, the organization must develop performance indicators, an information system, and specific mechanisms to monitor progress. Spirit Airlines has a low-cost strategy, captured in the "Bare Fare" flights slogan, that depends on cutting costs wherever possible so the airline can remain profitable while winning passengers with the lowest fare. According to Spirit's CEO, Ben Baldanza, this makes productivity a key performance indicator for every function. For example, the company purchases airplanes with the maximum number of seats allowed by the Federal Aviation Administration, so it minimizes the amount of fuel required to transport each passenger. In marketing, Spirit relies heavily on e-mail advertising because that medium costs relatively little, yet recipients will pass along messages they find funny or thought-provoking.[47]

strategic control system

A system designed to support managers in evaluating the organization's progress regarding its strategy and, when discrepancies exist, taking corrective action.

Management in Action

WALT DISNEY COMPANY'S STRATEGY UNDER ROBERT IGER

Reportedly, Walt Disney Company's mission statement once was "Make people happy." The corporate website now offers a longer statement: "to be one of the world's leading producers and providers of entertainment and information, using its portfolio of brands to differentiate its content, services and consumer products." The statement adds, "The company's primary financial goals are to maximize earnings and cash flow, and to allocate capital toward growth initiatives that will drive long-term shareholder value."

In pursuit of this two-part objective, Disney has made decisions about its large portfolio of businesses. As it repositions itself for a global marketplace and a social, mobile Internet, it continues making strategic decisions about where to invest and what to divest.

Disney's largest sources of revenues are cable networks and theme parks, with cable providing by far the greatest profits. ESPN alone delivers 45 percent of operating income. Recently, Disney entered into a media rights contract with the NFL and a deal to air NBA games on ESPN and ABC. The company has rolled out apps based on WatchESPN to let cable subscribers watch programming on mobile devices. In the theme park arena, profitability during a sluggish economy lets Disney build when construction costs are low, so it has renovated Disney California Adventure, expanded Hong Kong Disneyland, and added a cruise ship to its fleet. In 2016, it plans to open a theme park in Shanghai, China.

Disney Interactive is by far the smallest business unit in terms of revenues and has not been profitable. Still, it matters because children are spending ever more time online, and winning the hearts of children has been the basis for the company's growth. Disney Interactive will continue to engage fans through mobile games like Frozen Free Fall and Disney Tsum Tsum, as well as connect with parents via Disney.com.

Disney's movie studios, though a relatively small unit, are a core business. To increase the brand's appeal with teenage boys, this unit purchased Lucasfilm, producer of *Star Wars*. Disney also signed a deal giving Netflix the right to stream movies soon after release on DVD, when cable channels air movies. Dealing directly with Netflix signals that movie streaming is an important trend for Disney. And Disney created Keychest, which gives buyers of its DVDs and Blu-ray discs automatic access to streamed versions.

China is a huge growth market, so Iger is heavily investing in a new theme park, Shanghai Disney. The venture is risky; Disney's resort in Hong Kong is just breaking even after a 2005 opening. But it offers access to a billion consumers, and the effort is supported by use of the Disney Channel to build consumer relationships in China and 166 other countries.[48]

- How clear is Walt Disney Company's mission? How well does its strategy support the mission?
- In the BCG matrix (see again Exhibit 4.12), where would you place Disney's main businesses? How well is Disney matching its strategic moves to businesses' positions in the matrix?

Bottom Line

Firms that follow low-cost strategies exert downward pressure on competitors' prices.

What is the best way to compete against a low-cost strategy so that a firm can continue to charge higher prices for its products or services?

Most strategic control systems include a budget to monitor and control major financial expenditures. In fact, as a first-time manager, you will most likely confront your work unit's budget—a key aspect of your organization's strategic plan. Your executive team may give you budget assumptions and targets for your area, reflecting your part in the overall plan, and you may be asked to revise your budget once all the budgets in your organization have been consolidated and reviewed.

The dual responsibilities of a control system—efficiency and flexibility—often seem contradictory with respect to budgets. The budget usually establishes spending limits, but changing conditions or the need for innovation may require different financial commitments during the period. To solve this dilemma, some companies have created two budgets: strategic and operational. For example, managers at Texas Instruments control two budgets under the OST (objectives–strategies–tactics) system. The strategic budget is used to create and maintain long-term effectiveness, and the operational budget is tightly monitored to achieve short-term efficiency. In "Management in Action: Onward," consider the significance of budgets and budgetary controls to Disney's decisions about its portfolio of businesses. The topic of control in general—and budgets in particular—is discussed in more detail in Chapter 16.

KEY TERMS

RETAINING WHAT YOU LEARNED

In Chapter 4, you learned that managerial planning is a conscious, systematic process of deciding which goals and activities the organization will pursue in the future. Directed and controlled by managers, this purposeful effort draws on the experience and knowledge of employees throughout the organization. As shown in Exhibit 4.1, general decision making is linked closely to the formal planning process. Strategic planning should be integrated with tactical and operational planning. Before formulating a strategy, managers should analyze the external environment and internal resources, such as core capabilities. Corporate strategies can be narrow,

or include suppliers and buyers. A firm may broaden its strategy via related or unrelated diversification. Companies can achieve competitive advantage by being unique and differentiated, or by focusing on efficiency and lower prices. Effective implementation is critical to the success of any strategy.

LO 1   **Summarize the basic steps in any planning process.**

- The planning process begins with a situation analysis of the external and internal forces affecting the

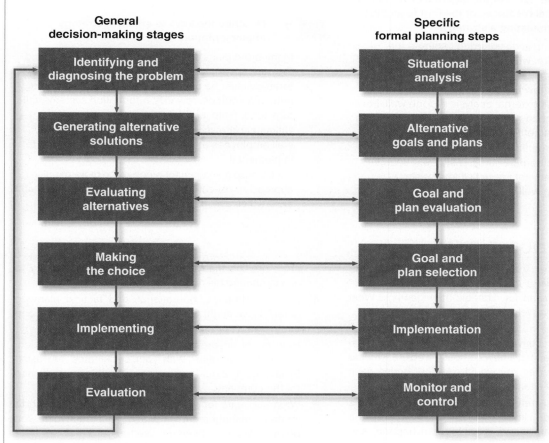

**General
decision-making stages**

Identifying and
diagnosing the problem

Generating alternative
solutions

Evaluating
alternatives

Making
the choice

Implementing

Evaluation

**Specific
formal planning steps**

Situational
analysis

Alternative
goals and plans

Goal and
plan evaluation

Goal and
plan selection

Implementation

Monitor and
control

EXHIBIT 4.1

Decision-Making Stages (Chapter 3) and Formal Planning Steps (Chapter 4)

organization. This examination helps identify and diagnose issues and problems and may bring to the surface alternative goals and plans for the firm.

- The advantages and disadvantages of these goals and plans should be evaluated against one another.
- Once a set of goals and a plan have been selected, implementation involves communicating the plan to employees, allocating resources, and making certain that other systems such as rewards and budgets support the plan.
- Planning requires instituting control systems to monitor progress toward the goals.

LO 2   Describe how strategic planning should be integrated with tactical and operational planning.

- Strategic planning is different from operational planning in that it involves making long-term decisions about the entire organization.
- Tactical planning translates broad goals and strategies into specific actions to be taken within parts of the organization.
- Operational planning identifies the specific short-term procedures and processes required at lower levels of the organization.

LO 3   Identify elements of the external environment and internal resources of the firm to analyze before formulating a strategy.

- Strategic planning is designed to leverage the strengths of a firm while minimizing the effects of its weaknesses.
- It is difficult to know the potential advantage a firm may have unless external analysis is done well. For example, a company may have a talented marketing department or an efficient production system.
- However, the organization cannot determine whether these internal characteristics are sources of competitive advantage until it knows something about how well the competitors stack up in these areas.

LO 4   Define core capabilities and explain how they provide the foundation for business strategy.

- A core competence is something a company does especially well relative to its competitors.
- When this competence, say, in engineering or marketing, is in some area important to market success, it becomes the foundation for developing a competitive advantage.
- It can provide a sustainable advantage if it is valuable, rare, difficult to imitate, and well organized.

LO 5   Summarize the types of choices available for corporate strategy.

- Corporate strategy identifies the breadth of a firm's competitive domain.
- Corporate strategy can be kept narrow, as in a concentration strategy, or can move to suppliers and buyers via vertical integration.
- Corporate strategy also can broaden a firm's domain via concentric (related) diversification or conglomerate (unrelated) diversification.

LO 6   Discuss how companies can achieve competitive advantage through business strategy.

- Companies gain competitive advantage in two primary ways. They can attempt to be unique in some way by pursuing a differentiation strategy, or they can focus on efficiency and price by pursuing a low-cost strategy.

LO 7   Describe the keys to effective strategy implementation.

- Many good plans are doomed to failure because they are not implemented correctly.
- Strategy must be supported by structure, technology, human resources, rewards, information systems, culture, leadership, and so on.
- Ultimately, the success of a plan depends on how well employees at low levels are able and willing to implement it.
- Participative management is one of the more popular approaches executives use to gain employees' input and ensure their commitment to strategy implementation.

DISCUSSION QUESTIONS

1. This chapter opened with a quote from former CEO of GE Jack Welch: "Manage your destiny, or someone else will." What does this mean for strategic management? What does it mean when Welch adds, "or someone else will"?

2. List the six steps in the formal planning process. Suppose you are a top executive of a home improvement chain and you want to launch a new company website. Provide examples of activities you would carry out during each step to create the site.

3. Your friend is frustrated because he's having trouble selecting a career. He says, "I can't plan because the future is too complicated. Anything can happen, and

there are too many choices." What would you say to him to change his mind?

4. How do strategic, operational, and tactical planning differ? How might the three levels complement one another in an organization?

5. How might an organization such as Urban Outfitters use a strategy map? With your classmates and using Exhibit 4.5 as a guide, develop a possible strategy map for the company.

6. What accounts for the shift from strategic planning to strategic management? In which industries would you be most likely to observe these trends? Why?

7. Review Exhibit 4.7, which lists the components of an environmental analysis. Why would this analysis be important to a company's strategic planning process?

8. In your opinion, what are the core capabilities of Harley-Davidson Motor Company motorcycles? How do these capabilities help Harley-Davidson compete against foreign competitors such as Yamaha and Suzuki?

9. How could SWOT analysis help newspaper companies remain competitive in the new media environment?

10. What are the key challenges in strategy implementation? What barriers might prevent strategy implementation?

EXPERIENTIAL EXERCISES

4.1 BUSINESS STRATEGIES NEED ADJUSTING

OBJECTIVE
To study why and how a company adjusts its business strategy to adapt to changing external environments.

INSTRUCTIONS
Using an Internet browser or a college's library research portal, identify a recent article from such business news outlets as *The Wall Street Journal, Bloomberg Business, Forbes,* or *Fast Company* that describes a company that is changing its short-and long-term business strategies. Please read the article and provide answers the following questions:

1. How would you describe the company's former business strategy?

_____

_____

_____

_____

_____

_____

_____

2. Why is the company changing its strategy? What external forces are encouraging it to change?

_____

_____

_____

_____

_____

_____

3. How would you describe the new business strategy?

_____

_____

_____

_____

_____

_____

4. What strategic goals or major targets does the company hope to achieve?

_____

_____

_____

_____

_____

_____

_____

5. How does the company intend to translate its new strategic goals into tactical or operational plans? Which levels of management will carry out these plans?

_____

_____

_____

_____

_____

_____

_____

_____

6. To what extent do you think the new strategy will be successful in addressing or adapting to the external forces? Explain.

_____

_____

_____

_____

_____

_____

_____

_____

_____

SOURCE: Adapted from R. R. McGrath Jr., *Exercises in Management Fundamentals*, 1st, p. 15.

CONCLUDING CASE

WISH YOU WOOD TOY STORE

Wish You Wood is a toy boutique located in the main shopping strip of a resort town near Piney Lake. People who own cabins near the lake or come to visit the local state park enjoy browsing through the town's stores, where they pick up pottery, landscape paintings, and Wish You Wood's beautifully crafted wooden toys. For these shoppers, Wish You Wood is more than a store; it is a destination they associate with family and fun.

The store's owners, Jim and Pam Klein, personally select the toys from craftspeople and toymakers around the world. They enjoy their regular customers but believe selling mostly to vacationers has limited the company's growth.

They decided that the lowest-cost way to expand would be to sell toys online. However, after several years, they had to admit that traffic to the store's website was unimpressive. Thanks to e-mail and Facebook reminders, they were luring some of their loyal in-store shoppers to the site to make off-season purchases, but few other people looking for toys ever found Wish You Wood online.

Jim and Pam concluded that the next-best way to sell online would be to partner with Amazon.com. Amazon's Marketplace service lets other retailers sell products on Amazon. The Kleins signed an agreement to list the store's most popular items with Amazon. For example, if a shopper is searching for wooden dollhouses, Wish You Wood's dollhouses will be included in the search results. A customer who chooses to buy from Wish You Wood places the order right on Amazon's website. Under Amazon's participation agreement, the listings must be honest and may not link to Wish You Wood's own website or invite phone calls from customers. In exchange for giving the products exposure on the site, Amazon charges a monthly fee plus a commission on each sale.

Initially, Jim and Pam were thrilled about their decision to partner with Amazon. They tracked each month's sales and compared them with in-store sales. In the first five months, sales jumped 45 percent, mainly because of sales on Amazon. Then, suddenly, sales of popular toy train sets, which were particularly profitable, stopped altogether. Puzzled, Jim visited Amazon to make sure the train sets were still listed. To his surprise, he found that the train set was there, at the usual price of $149, listed right after the same set available directly from Amazon, at $129. He and Pam concluded that shoppers were now buying the product directly from Amazon. It appeared that their store had helped Amazon identify a product consumers value.

The Kleins worried that they needed a new strategy. If they matched Amazon's price, they would lose most of the profit on their most popular items. Wish You Wood was too small of a business to negotiate better prices from its suppliers. If the store didn't match Amazon's price, it would continue to lose sales at the Amazon site. Jim and Pam wondered whether they should pull out of Amazon altogether or find a way to continue working with the partner that had become a competitor. They also considered rethinking which toys to offer on Amazon.

DISCUSSION QUESTIONS

1. Prepare a SWOT analysis for Wish You Wood, based on the information given.

2. Using the SWOT analysis, what general corporate strategy would you recommend for Wish You Wood? Should the store continue or change its current approach?

CHAPTER 5

Ethics, Corporate Responsibility, and Sustainability

> It is truly enough said that a corporation has no conscience; but a corporation of conscientious men is a corporation with a conscience.
>
> —HENRY DAVID THOREAU

Management in Action

HOW CAN GINNI ROMETTY ENSURE THAT IBM DOES WELL WHILE DOING GOOD?

The standard for principled leadership is set high for IBM's chief executive, Ginni Rometty. She took charge of IBM upon the retirement of the widely admired Sam Palmisano, who saw an opportunity for the company to distinguish itself by applying its data-processing expertise to delivering customized business solutions. Rather than jumping straight into corporate restructuring or marketing campaigns, Palmisano started with values. He set up a three-day "values jam," during which employees throughout the global company were asked to contribute thoughts about what IBM's values should be. Out of that process came a commitment to helping clients and building relationships based on trust and personal responsibility.

In a further expression of Palmisano's vision, IBM began to use the tagline "Smarter Planet." Employees are helping companies, cities, and communities around the world make better decisions aimed at improving business results, living conditions, and even the health of planet Earth. This goal was based on the realization that computers have extraordinary power to gather and analyze data, but applying the data also requires creative thinking, productive processes, and open communication. IBM would offer not just computer hardware but also decision-making and analytic expertise to bring all these requirements together.

Palmisano's vision set IBM on course for years of strong growth as businesses, city governments, and nongovernmental organizations saw how the company could help them meet their goals. When he prepared to retire, Palmisano threw his support behind Rometty, who had started as a systems engineer at IBM in the 1980s and worked her way up to senior vice president

© *Feature Photo Service for IBM via AP Images*

and group executive for sales, marketing, and strategy. In a recent speech, Rometty signaled that she sees the Smarter Planet strategy as positioning IBM for a future in which data will drive more decisions, cloud computing will transform how industries operate, and mobile and social media will facilitate personalized user engagement.

Rometty's strategy expertise and technical background prepared her to guide IBM through an unprecedented shift away from legacy hardware and services to new business initiatives such as business analytics, cloud computing, and mobile apps. This change has not been an easy one. IBM's sales revenue has declined even as profit margins have increased. Change takes time. Rometty believes there is money to be made in caring about the needs of cities, the business community, and the planet.[1]

> For IBM's Sam Palmisano and Ginni Rometty, business success can grow out of values that emphasize focusing on the needs of others. As you read this chapter, think about how well IBM's values-driven approach positions the company to be both ethical and successful.

How would you measure the success of a company such as IBM? By this quarter's profits and its value in the stock market? By the degree of trust people place in its managers and consultants? By the good it does in improving quality of life by helping people make better decisions? Although a company might enjoy high profits in one quarter without quality, trust, or contributions to society, many people would argue that in the long run, all these measures of success are interdependent.

This chapter addresses the values and manner of doing business adopted by managers as they carry out their corporate and business strategies. In particular, we will explore ways of applying **ethics,** the system of rules that governs the ordering of values. We do so based on the premise that managers, their organizations, and their communities thrive over the long term when the managers apply ethical standards that direct them to act with integrity.

In addition, we consider the idea that organizations may have a responsibility to meet social obligations beyond earning profits within legal and ethical constraints. As you study this chapter, consider what kind of manager you want to be. What reputation do you hope to have? How would you like others to describe your behavior as a manager?

ethics

The system of rules that governs the ordering of values; see also *corporate social responsibility*.

It's a Big Issue

Recent scandals have engulfed company executives, independent auditors, politicians and regulators, and shareholders and employees.[2] In some, executives at public companies have made misleading statements to inflate stock prices, undermining the public's trust in the integrity of the financial markets. Often the scandals are perpetrated by a number of people cooperating with one another, and many of the guilty parties had been otherwise upstanding individuals. Lobbyists have been accused—and some convicted—of buying influence with lavish gifts to politicians. Executives have admitted to bribing representatives of foreign governments in order to secure large contracts. What other news disturbs you about managers' behavior? Tainted products in the food supply . . . actions that harm the environment . . . Internet scams . . . employees pressured to meet sales or production targets by any means? The list goes on, and the public becomes cynical. According to a survey by the public relations firm Edelman, only about one-fifth of people trust business leaders to make ethical decisions and tell uncomfortable truths.[3] Try to imagine the challenge of leading employees who don't trust you. The nearby "Multiple Generations at Work" box discusses trust in the workplace.

Temptations exist in every organization.

Sadly, when corporations behave badly, it's often not the top executives but the rank-and-file employees who suffer most. For example, a recent discovery that $3 billion was stolen from Brazil's state-run oil company, Petroleo Brasilieiro (a.k.a., Petrobras), has led to layoffs of thousands of employees.[4] In the United States, scandals at Enron, Arthur Andersen, WorldCom, and AIG had similar devastating effects on employees.

Still, simply talking about Petrobras and other famous cases as examples of lax company ethics doesn't get at the heart of the problem. Clearly, these cases involve bad guys, and the ethical lapses are obvious. But saying "I would never do things like that" becomes too easy. The fact is that temptations exist in every organization. Many of the decisions you will face as a manager will pose ethical dilemmas, and the right thing to do is not always evident.

It's a Personal Issue

"Answer true or false: 'I am an ethical manager.' If you answered 'true,' here's an uncomfortable fact: You're probably not."[5] These sentences are the first in a *Harvard Business Review* article called "How (Un)Ethical Are You?" The point is that most of us think we are good decision makers, ethical, and unbiased. But the fact is, most people have unconscious biases that favor themselves and their own group. For example, managers often hire people who are like them, think they are immune to conflicts of interest, take more credit than they deserve, and blame others when they deserve some blame themselves. Knowing that you have biases may help you try to overcome them, but usually that's not enough.

Multiple Generations at Work

Do Millennials Lack Trust?

According to research by the Pew Research Center, Millennials on average may be less trusting than older generational cohorts. Surveyed in 2007 and 2012, members of four generations were asked: "Generally speaking, would you say that most people can be trusted or that you can't be too careful in dealing with people?" As shown below, only 19 percent of Millennials agree with the statement compared with 31 percent of Gen Xers, 40 percent of Boomers, and 37 percent of Silents.[6]

Lack of trust appears to be an issue in society as a whole. It is reasonable to assume that this distrust extends to the workplace. Given that the highest level of agreement is only 40 percent, managers should make it a priority to build trust across all generations by being a good role model and behaving in an ethical manner. Also, managers should try to be open and transparent when communicating with employees. Given the especially low level of trust among early career employees, managers should make a strong effort to earn Millennials' trust by keeping their promises and engaging them in an honest manner.

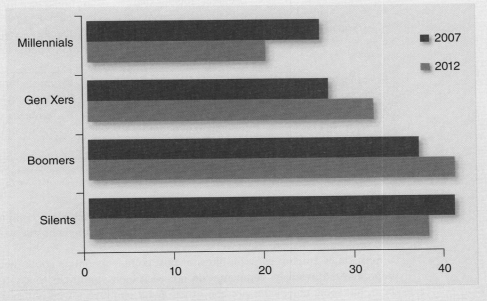

Percentage of respondents agreeing with "trust" question

Knowing that you have biases may help you try to overcome them, but usually that's not enough. Consider the basic ethical issue of telling a lie. Many people lie—some more than others, and in part depending on the situation, usually presuming that they will benefit from the lie. At a basic level, we all can make ethical arguments against lying and in favor of honesty. Yet it is useful to think thoroughly about the real consequences of lying.[7] Exhibit 5.1 summarizes the possible outcomes of telling the truth or lying in different situations. People often lie or commit other ethical transgressions somewhat mindlessly, without realizing the full array of negative personal consequences.

Ethics issues are not easy, and they are not just for newsworthy corporate CEOs. For example, people at work use computers with Internet access. If the employer pays for the computer and the time you spend sitting in front of it, is it ethical for you to use the computer to do tasks unrelated to your work?

But what if you stream video of games for your own and your co-workers' enjoyment or take a two-hour lunch to locate the best deal on a flat-panel TV?

EXHIBIT 5.1

Possible Outcomes of Lying and Telling the Truth

Reason for the Lie	Results of Lying	Results of Telling the Truth
Negotiation	• Short-term gain and economically positive. • Harms long-term relationship. • Must rationalize to oneself.	• Supports high-quality, long-term relationship. • Develops reputation of integrity. • Models behavior to others.
Conflicting expectations	• Easier to lie than to address the underlying conflict. • Does not solve underlying problem. • Liar must rationalize the lie to preserve positive self-concept.	• Emotionally more difficult than lying. • May correct underlying problem. • Develops one's reputation as an honest person.
Keeping a confidence (that may require at least a lie of omission)	• Maintains relationship with the party for whom confidence is kept. • May project deceitfulness to the deceived party.	• Violates a trust to the confiding party. • Makes one appear deceitful to all parties in the long run.
Reporting your own performance (within an organization)	• Might advance oneself or one's cause. • Develops dishonest reputation over time.	• Creates a reputation of honesty and integrity. • Performance report may not always be positive.

SOURCE: Adapted from *Academy of Management Executive: The Thinking Manager's Source* by S. L. Gover, "The Truth, the Whole Truth, and Nothing but the Truth: The Causes and Management of Workplace Lying." Copyright © 2005. Reproduced with permission of Academy of Management via Copyright Clearance Center.

Besides lost productivity, employers are most concerned about computer users introducing viruses, leaking confidential information, and creating a hostile work environment by downloading inappropriate web content.

Sometimes employees write blogs or post comments online about their company and its products. Obviously, companies do not want their employees to say bad things about them, but some companies are concerned about employees who are overly enthusiastic. When employees plug their companies and products on comments pages, this practice is considered spamming at best and deceptive if the employees don't disclose their relationship with their company. Another practice considered deceptive is when companies create fictional blogs as a marketing tactic without disclosing their sponsorship. And in a practice known as "astroturfing"—because the "grassroots" interest it builds is fake—businesses pay bloggers to write positive comments about them. A New York company, Zamdel, was fined for posting over 1,500 fake reviews on Yelp and Google Places. National bus charter company, US Coachways, also received a fine for astroturfing. Some companies think this unethical behavior is worth the risk; for example, a one-point increase in an online review score (of 1–5 points) for a hotel allows the hotel to increase its prices by over 10 percent.[8]

Are these examples too small to worry about? This chapter will help you think through decisions with ethical ramifications.

Ethics

The aim of ethics is to identify both the rules that should govern people's behavior and the "goods" that are worth seeking. Ethical decisions are guided by the underlying values of the individual. Values are principles of conduct such as caring, being honest, keeping promises, pursuing excellence, showing loyalty, being fair, acting with integrity, respecting others, and being a responsible citizen.[9]

Most people would agree that all of these values are admirable guidelines for behavior. However, ethics becomes a more complicated issue when a situation dictates that one value overrules others. An **ethical issue** is a situation, problem, or opportunity in which an individual must choose among several actions that must be evaluated as morally right or wrong.[10]

> Ethics becomes a more complicated issue when a situation dictates that one value overrules others.

Ethical issues arise in every facet of life; we concern ourselves here with business ethics in particular. **Business ethics** comprises the moral principles and standards that guide behavior in the world of business.[11]

Ethical Systems

Moral philosophy refers to the principles, rules, and values people use in deciding what is right or wrong. This is a simple definition in the abstract but often terribly complex and difficult when facing real choices. How do you decide what is right and wrong? Do you know what criteria you apply and how you apply them?

Ethics scholars point to various major ethical systems as guides (see Exhibit 5.2).[12] The first ethical system, **universalism,** states that all people should uphold certain values, such as honesty, that society needs to function. Universal values are principles so fundamental to human existence that they are important in all societies—for example, rules against murder, deceit, torture, and oppression.

Some efforts have been made to establish global, universal ethical principles for business. The Caux Roundtable, a group of international executives based in Caux, Switzerland, worked with business leaders from Japan, Europe, and the United States to create the **Caux Principles.** Two basic ethical ideals underpin the Caux Principles: *kyosei* and human dignity. *Kyosei* means living and working together for the common good, allowing cooperation and mutual prosperity to coexist with healthy and fair competition. Human dignity concerns the value of each person as an end, not a means to the fulfillment of others' purposes.

---

ethical issue

Situation, problem, or opportunity in which an individual must choose among several actions that must be evaluated as morally right or wrong.

business ethics

The moral principles and standards that guide behavior in the world of business. See also *ethics.*

moral philosophy

Principles, rules, and values people use in deciding what is right or wrong.

universalism

The ethical system stating that all people should uphold certain values that society needs to function.

Caux Principles

Ethical principles established by international executives based in Caux, Switzerland, in collaboration with business leaders from Japan, Europe, and the United States.

Universalism	A multinational company treats all of its employees who work in different countries with fairness and dignity.
Egoism	An entrepreneur builds a successful company for personal growth and financial gain; and ultimately, employs thousands of employees.
Utilitarianism	Employees of a charity, facing the loss of a federal grant, accept a 10 percent reduction in salary so no one has to be laid off.
Relativism	A college student refuses to share answers with a fellow student during an exam because her friends would disapprove.
Virtue ethics	A manager believes that it is critical to stand up for what is right and not be unduly influenced by organizational pressures or politics.

EXHIBIT 5.2

Examples of Decisions Made under Different Ethical Systems

Employees sometimes feel that "borrowing" a few office supplies from their company helps compensate for any perceived inequities in pay or other benefits.

© Inspirestock/Corbis

---

egoism

An ethical system defining acceptable behavior as that which maximizes consequences for the individual.

---

utilitarianism

An ethical system stating that the greatest good for the greatest number should be the overriding concern of decision makers.

---

relativism

Philosophy that bases ethical behavior on the opinions and behaviors of relevant other people.

Universal principles can be powerful and useful, but what people say, hope, or think they would do is often different from what they *really* do, faced with conflicting demands in real situations. Different individuals in different circumstances apply different moral philosophies. Consider each of the following moral philosophies and the actions to which they might lead.[13]

Egoism and Utilitarianism   According to **egoism,** acceptable behavior is that which maximizes benefits for the individual. "Doing the right thing," the focus of moral philosophy, is defined by egoism as "do the act that promotes the greatest good for oneself." If everyone follows this system, according to its proponents, the well-being of society as a whole should increase. This notion is similar to Adam Smith's concept of the invisible hand in business. Smith argued that if every organization follows its own economic self-interest, the total wealth of society will be maximized.

Unlike egoism, **utilitarianism** directly seeks the greatest good for the greatest number of people. Consider whether utilitarianism would help guide ethical decision making with regard to student loan programs. New York's attorney general investigated 100 colleges and half a dozen lenders for arrangements in which the lenders allegedly offered payments, stock grants, and perks to schools, and the schools listed the companies as "preferred lenders" in information given to students who wanted to borrow tuition money from private sources. The attorney general called the arrangements "kickbacks"; some schools replied that they were not being corrupted but used the money to add to the financial aid they could award to students.[14]

Whereas ethics based on egoism would accept actions that allow the lenders to maximize their earnings and the financial aid officers to pursue whatever arrangements benefit themselves and their schools, utilitarianism requires a broader view. Most obviously, there is the question of what these arrangements cost students who make borrowing decisions on the possibly mistaken assumption that preferred lenders will give students the best deals. But other students benefited if payments from lenders were used to augment the financial aid given to other students. The utilitarian approach might consider how many students benefited—and by how much—and how many students paid extra for loans and how much more they paid. One company responded to the allegations by agreeing to a code of conduct that forbids gifts in exchange for preferred status.[15]

Relativism   Perhaps it seems that an individual makes ethical choices on a personal basis, applying personal perspectives. But this is not necessarily the case. **Relativism** defines ethical behavior based on the opinions and behaviors of relevant other people. In the previous example of student loans, U.S. business, government, and society largely agree that bribes, kickbacks, and conflicts of interest would not be acceptable behaviors for people in the lending industry—perhaps even less so for those charged with serving students. Those standards help explain the rapid actions taken by the organizations when they found out about the situation.

Relativism acknowledges the existence of different ethical viewpoints. For example, *norms,* or standards of expected and acceptable behavior, vary from one culture to another. A study of Russian versus U.S. managers found that all followed norms of informed consent about chemical hazards in work situations and paying wages on time. But in Russia more than in the United States, businesspeople were likely to consider the interests of a broader set of stakeholders (in this study, keeping factories open for the sake of local employment), to keep double books to hide information from tax inspectors and criminal organizations, and to make personal payments to government officials in charge of awarding contracts.[16] Relativism defines ethical behavior according to how others behave.

Virtue ethics   The moral philosophies just described apply different types of rules and reasoning. **Virtue ethics** is a perspective that goes beyond the conventional rules of society by suggesting that what is moral must also come from what a mature person with good "moral character" would deem right. Society's rules provide a moral minimum, and then moral individuals can transcend rules by applying their personal virtues such as faith, honesty, and integrity.

Individuals differ in this regard. **Kohlberg's model of cognitive moral development** classifies people into categories based on their level of moral judgment.[17] People in the *preconventional* stage make decisions based on rewards and punishments and immediate self-interest. People in the *conventional* stage conform to the expectations of ethical behavior held by groups or institutions such as society, family, or peers. People in the *principled* stage see beyond authority, laws, and norms and follow their self-chosen ethical principles.[18] Some people forever reside in the preconventional stage, some move into the conventional stage, and some develop further yet into the principled stage. Over time, and through education and experience, people may change their values and ethical behavior.[19]

These major ethical systems underlie personal moral choices and ethical decisions in business.

virtue ethics

Perspective that what is moral comes from what a mature person with "good" moral character would deem right.

Kohlberg's model of cognitive moral development

Classification of people based on their level of moral judgment.

Business Ethics

Insider trading, sweatshops and modern slavery,[20] bribery and kickbacks, famous court cases, and other scandals have created a perception that business leaders use illegal means to gain competitive advantage, increase profits, or improve their personal positions. Neither young managers nor consumers believe top executives are doing a good job of establishing high ethical standards.[21] Some even joke that *business ethics* is a contradiction in terms.

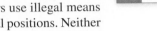

Most employees rate their supervisors' performance as ethical and professional.[22] However, many people feel ethically conflicted, stressed, and exhausted as companies sometimes encourage them to behave in ways that differ from their own sense of right and wrong.[23] Many managers and their organizations must deal frequently with ethical dilemmas, and the issues are becoming increasingly complex. For example, many people seek spiritual renewal in the workplace, in part reflecting a broader religious awakening in America, whereas others argue that this trend violates religious freedom and the separation of church and boardroom.[24]

Exhibit 5.3 shows some other important examples of ethical dilemmas in business. Think about how you would address each of these issues as a manager. What ethical principles are you applying?

Should pharmaceutical companies be allowed to advertise directly to the consumer if the medicine can be obtained only with a prescription from a doctor? When patients request a particular product, doctors are more likely to prescribe it—even if the patients haven't reported the corresponding symptoms.

© *The McGraw-Hill Companies, Inc./John Flournoy, photographer*

The Ethics Environment

Responding to a series of corporate scandals—particularly the high-profile cases of Enron and WorldCom—Congress passed the **Sarbanes-Oxley Act** in 2002 to improve and maintain investor confidence. The law requires companies to have more independent board directors (not just company insiders), to adhere strictly to accounting rules, and to have senior managers personally sign off on financial results. Violations can result in heavy fines and criminal prosecution. One of the biggest impacts of the law was the requirement for companies and their auditors to provide reports to financial statement users about the effectiveness of internal controls over the financial reporting process.

Companies that make the effort to meet or exceed these requirements can reduce their risks by lowering the likelihood of misdeeds and the consequences if an employee does

Sarbanes-Oxley Act

An act passed into law by Congress to establish strict accounting and reporting rules in order to make senior managers more accountable and to improve and maintain investor confidence.

EXHIBIT 5.3
Current Ethical Issues in
Business

CEO pay	What is a fair level of pay for a top executive? Twenty times what the average company worker earns? Whatever other companies pay their top executives?
Climate	What is a company's responsibility for its impact on the climate? For example, if operations in one country contribute to rising global temperatures that lead to greater floods in another country, how should the company respond?
Globalization	When a company operates in countries with lower costs, what are its obligations, if any, to the workers in those countries? What standards should it meet for pay rates?
Health care	With health care costs outpacing inflation, employers struggle to cover the cost of health insurance for workers. Are they ethically obligated to provide this benefit?
Obesity	As an obesity epidemic threatens health and adds to health care costs, what role, if any, should employers play in encouraging healthy employee lifestyles?
Online privacy	What obligations do employers have in protecting the privacy of employee information and information about customers?
Politics	Since 2010, businesses and labor unions in the United States have wide latitude for making anonymous contributions to political candidates. What are the ethical limits of such contributions?
Social media	What ethical obligations do employees have in commenting about their employer on social media? What ethical obligations do employers have concerning their employees' privacy on social media?
Telework	When employees work at home or in other remote locations, how can they and their employer ensure that these arrangements are fair to the employees, their co-workers, and the company?
Wages	When adjusted for inflation, the median wage in the United States has fallen over the past few decades. What should employers do to promote a sense that their compensation is fair?

break the law.[25] But some executives say Sarbanes-Oxley distracts from their real work and makes them more risk-averse. Some complain about the time and money needed to comply with the internal control reporting—millions of dollars at big businesses. But as companies have implemented tighter controls, many have discovered that the effort is helping them avoid mistakes and improve efficiency. Regardless of managers' attitudes toward Sarbanes-Oxley, it creates legal requirements intended to improve ethical behavior.

Ethics are not shaped only by laws and by individual virtue. They also may be influenced by the company's work environment. Unethical corporate behavior may be the responsibility of an unethical individual, but it often also reveals a company culture that is ethically lax.[26]

Maintaining a positive ethical climate is always challenging, but it is especially complex for organizations with international activities. Different cultures and countries may have different standards of behavior, and managers have to decide when relativism is appropriate, rather than adherence to firm standards. Exhibit 5.4 gives examples of real situations when ethics-related decisions have arisen in an international context.

The **ethical climate** of an organization refers to the processes by which decisions are evaluated and made on the basis of right and wrong.[27] For example, General Electric's top executives have demonstrated a commitment to promoting high levels of integrity without sacrificing the company's well-known commitment to business results. The measures taken by GE to maintain a positive ethical climate include establishing global standards

ethical climate

In an organization, the processes by which decisions are evaluated and made on the basis of right and wrong.

EXHIBIT 5.4
Ethical Decision Making in
the International Context

What would you do in each of these true-life situations, and why?

- You are a sales representative for a construction company in the Middle East. Your company wants very much to land a particular project. The cousin of the minister who will award the contract informs you that the minister wants $20,000 in addition to the standard fees. If you do not make this payment, your competition certainly will—and will get the contract.

- You are the international vice president of a multinational chemical corporation. Your company is the sole producer of an insecticide that will effectively combat a recent infestation of West African crops. The minister of agriculture in a small, developing African country has put in a large order for your product. Your insecticide is highly toxic and is banned in the United States. You inform the minister of the risks of using your product, but he insists on using it and claims it will be used "intelligently." The president of your company believes you should fill the order, but the decision ultimately is yours.

- You are a new marketing manager for a large automobile tire manufacturer. Your company's advertising agency has just presented plans for introducing a new tire into the Southeast Asia market. Your tire is a truly good product, but the proposed advertising is deceptive. For example, the "reduced price" was reduced from a hypothetical amount that was established only so it could be "reduced," and claims that the tire was tested under the "most adverse" conditions ignore the fact that it was not tested in prolonged tropical heat and humidity. Your superiors are not concerned about deceptive advertising, and they are counting on you to see that the tire does extremely well in the new market. Will you approve the ad plan?

SOURCE: N. Adler, *International Dimensions of Organizational Behavior,* 2nd ed. (Boston: Kent, 1997).

for behavior to prevent ethical problems such as conflicts of interest and money laundering. As managers monitor the external environment, they are expected to consider legal and ethical developments, along with other concerns, so that the company can be prepared for new issues as they arise. Managers at all levels are rewarded for their performance in meeting both integrity and business standards, and when violations occur, even managers who were otherwise successful are disciplined, sending a powerful message that ethical behavior is truly valued at GE.[28]

Danger Signs   Maintaining consistent ethical behavior by all employees is an ongoing challenge. What are some danger signs that an organization may be allowing or even encouraging unethical behavior? Exhibit 5.5 lists many factor that could create a climate conducive to unethical behavior:[29]

Regardless of your employer's ethical climate, you are responsible for the decisions you make.

It's been said that your reputation is your most precious asset. Here's a suggestion: Set a goal for yourself to be seen by others as both a moral person and as a moral manager, someone who influences others to behave ethically. When you are both personally moral and a moral manager, you will truly be an **ethical leader**.[30] You can have strong personal character, but if you pay more attention to other things, and ethics is managed by benign neglect, you won't have a reputation as an ethical leader.

Corporate Ethical Standards   To create a culture that encourages ethical behavior, managers must be more than ethical people. They also should lead others to behave ethically.[31] At General Electric, chief executive Jeffrey Immelt demonstrates his concern for ethical leadership by beginning and ending each annual meeting with a statement of the company's integrity principles, emphasizing that "GE's business success is built on our reputation with all stakeholders for lawful and ethical behavior."[32]

ethical leader

One who is both a moral person and a moral manager influencing others to behave ethically.

EXHIBIT 5.5

Seven Danger Signs of Unethical Behavior at Your Organization

1. Excessive emphasis on short-term revenues over longer-term considerations.
2. Failure to establish a written code of ethics.
3. A desire for simple, quick fix solutions to ethical problems.
4. An unwillingness to take an ethical stand that may impose financial costs.
5. Consideration of ethics solely as a legal issue or a public relations tool.
6. Lack of clear procedures for handling ethical problems.
7. Responding to the demands of shareholders at the expense of other constituencies.

IBM uses a guideline for business conduct that asks employees to determine whether, under the full glare of examination by associates, friends, and family, they would remain comfortable with their decisions. One suggestion is to imagine how you would feel if you saw your decision and its consequences on the front page of the newspaper.[33] This "light of day" or "sunshine" ethical framework can be powerful.

> Fear of exposure compels people more strongly in some cultures than in others.

Such fear of exposure compels people more strongly in some cultures than in others. In some Asian countries, anxiety about losing face often makes executives resign immediately if they are caught in ethical transgressions or if their companies are embarrassed by revelations in the press. By contrast, in the United States, exposed executives might respond with indignation, intransigence, pleading the Fifth Amendment, stonewalling, and an everyone-else-does-it self-defense or by not admitting wrongdoing and giving no sign that resignation ever crossed their minds. Partly because of legal tradition, the attitude often is never explain, never apologize, don't admit the mistake, and do not resign, even if the entire world knows exactly what happened.[34]

Ethics Codes   The Sarbanes-Oxley Act requires public companies periodically to disclose whether they have adopted a code of ethics for senior financial officers—and if not, why not. Often the statements are just for show, but when implemented well, they can change a company's ethical climate for the better and truly encourage ethical behavior. Executives say they pay most attention to their company's code of ethics when they feel that stakeholders (customers, investors, lenders, and suppliers) try to influence them to do so, and their reasons for paying attention to the code are that doing so will help create a strong ethical culture and promote a positive image.[35]

Ethics codes must be carefully written and tailored to individual companies' philosophies. Exhibit 5.6 reprints the Commitments section of The Hershey Company's code of ethics. Most ethics codes address subjects such as employee conduct, community and environment, shareholders, customers, suppliers and contractors, political activity, and technology. The nonprofit Ethics Resource Center conducts research and assists companies interested in establishing a corporate code of ethics.[36]

To make an ethics code effective, do the following: (1) involve those who have to live with it in writing the statement; (2) focus on real-life situations that employees can relate to; (3) keep it short and simple, so it is easy to understand and remember; (4) write about values and shared beliefs that are important and that people can really believe in; and (5) set the tone at the top, having executives talk about and live up to the statement.[37] When reality differs from the statement—as when a motto says people are our most precious asset or a product is the finest in the world, but in fact people are treated poorly or product quality is weak—the statement becomes a joke to employees rather than a guiding light.

Ethics Programs   Corporate ethics programs commonly include formal ethics codes that articulate the company's expectations regarding ethics: ethics committees that develop policies, evaluate actions, and investigate violations; ethics communication systems that give employees a means of reporting problems or getting guidance; ethics officers or

We have each made a commitment to operate ethically and to lead with integrity. This commitment is embedded in the Hershey values. Our Code of Ethical Business Conduct ("Code") shows us how to uphold this commitment as we interact with the various groups that have a stake in our Company's success.

OUR COMMITMENT TO FELLOW EMPLOYEES

We treat one another fairly and with respect, valuing the talents, experiences and strengths of our diverse workforce.

OUR COMMITMENT TO CONSUMERS

We maintain the trust consumers place in our brands, providing the best products on the market and adhering to honest marketing practices.

OUR COMMITMENT TO THE MARKETPLACE

We deal fairly with our business partners, competitors and suppliers, acting ethically and upholding the law in everything we do.

OUR COMMITMENT TO STOCKHOLDERS

We act honestly and transparently at all times, maintaining the trust our stockholders have placed in us.

OUR COMMITMENT TO THE GLOBAL COMMUNITY

We comply with all global trade laws, protecting our natural resources and supporting the communities where we live, work and do business.

SOURCE: The Hershey Company, "Code of Ethical Business Conduct," accessed March 20, 2015, http://www.thehersheycompany.com. Reprinted with permission.

ombudspersons who investigate allegations and provide education; ethics training programs; and disciplinary processes for addressing unethical behavior.[38]

Ethics programs can range from compliance-based to integrity-based.[39] **Compliance-based ethics programs** are designed by corporate counsel to prevent, detect, and punish legal violations. Program elements include establishing and communicating legal standards and procedures, assigning high-level managers to oversee compliance, auditing and monitoring compliance, reporting criminal misconduct, punishing wrongdoers, and taking steps to prevent offenses in the future.

Such programs should reduce illegal behavior and help a company stay out of court. But Richard Breeden, former chair of the Securities and Exchange Commission, said, "It is not an adequate ethical standard to aspire to get through the day without being indicted."

Integrity-based ethics programs go beyond the mere avoidance of illegality; they are concerned with the law but also with instilling in people a personal responsibility for ethical behavior. With such a program, companies and people govern themselves through a set of guiding principles that they embrace.

For example, the Americans with Disabilities Act (amended in 2008) required companies to change the physical work environment so it will allow people with disabilities to function on the job. Mere compliance would involve making the changes necessary to avoid legal problems. Integrity-based programs would go further by training people to understand and perhaps change attitudes toward people with disabilities and sending clear signals that people with disabilities also have valued abilities. This effort goes far beyond taking action to stay out of trouble with the law.[40]

compliance-based ethics programs

Company mechanisms typically designed by corporate counsel to prevent, detect, and punish legal violations.

integrity-based ethics programs

Company mechanisms designed to instill in people a personal responsibility for ethical behavior.

Ethical Decision Making

We've said it's not easy to make ethical choices. Such decisions are complex. For starters, you may face pressures that are difficult to resist. Furthermore, it's not always clear that a problem has ethical dimensions; they don't hold up signs that say "Hey, I'm an ethical issue, so think about me in moral terms!"[41]

LO 3

Making ethical decisions takes moral awareness (realizing the issue has ethical implications), moral judgment (knowing what actions are morally defensible), and moral character (the strength and persistence to act in accordance with your ethics despite the challenges).[42]

The philosopher John Rawls created a thought experiment based on the "veil of ignorance."[43] Imagine that you are making a decision about a policy that will benefit or disadvantage some groups more than others. For example, a policy might provide extra vacation time for all employees but eliminate flextime, which allows parents of young children to balance their work and family responsibilities. Or you're a university president considering raising tuition or cutting financial support for study abroad.

Now pretend that you belong to one of the affected groups, but you don't know which one—for instance, those who can afford to study abroad or those who can't, or a young parent or a young single person. You won't find out until after the decision is made. How would you decide? Would you be willing to risk being in the disadvantaged group? Would your decision be different if you were in a group other than your own? Rawls maintained that only a person ignorant of his own identity can make a truly ethical decision. A decision maker can apply the veil of ignorance to help minimize personal bias.

Thinking before deciding, and having an ethics-oriented conversation with others, can help you and others make more ethical decisions.[44] You can use the process illustrated in Exhibit 5.7. Understand the various moral standards (universalism, relativism, etc.), as described earlier in the chapter. Go through the problem-solving model from Chapter 3 and recognize the impacts of your alternatives: Which people do they benefit and harm, which are able to exercise their rights, and whose rights are denied? You now know the full scope of the moral problem.

Excuses are often bogus.

Excuses are often bogus.[45] "I was told to do it" implies a person has no thought and blindly obeys. "Everybody's doing it" often really means that someone is doing it, but it's rarely everybody; regardless, following convention doesn't mean correctness. "Might equals right" is just a rationalization. "It's not my problem" is sometimes a wise perspective, if it's a battle you can't win, but sometimes it's a cop-out. "I didn't mean for that to happen, it just felt right at the time" can be prevented with more forethought and analysis.

You must also consider legal requirements to ensure full compliance, and the economic outcomes of your options, including costs and potential profits.[46] Some are obvious: fines and penalties. Others, such as corrective actions and lower morale, are less obvious. Ultimately, the effects on customers, employees, and government reactions can be huge. Being fully aware of the potential costs can help prevent people from straying into unethical terrain.

EXHIBIT 5.7
A Process for Ethical Decision Making

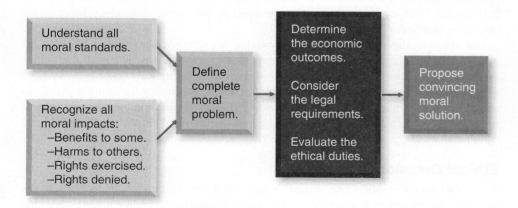

SOURCE: L. T. Hosmer, *The Ethics of Management*, 4th ed. McGraw-Hill/Irwin, 2003, p. 32. Fig. 5.1A. © 2003 The McGraw-Hill Companies. Reprinted with permission.

Courage

Behaving ethically requires not just moral awareness and moral judgment but also moral character, including the courage to take actions consistent with your ethical decisions. Think about how hard it can be to do the right thing.[47] On the job, how hard would it be to walk away from lots of money just to stick to your ethics? To tell colleagues or your boss that you believe they've crossed an ethical line? To disobey a boss's order? To go over your boss's head to someone in senior management with your suspicions about accounting practices? To go outside the company to alert others if someone is being hurt and management refuses to correct the problem?

Courage plays a role in the moral awareness involved in identifying an act as unethical, the moral judgment to consider the repercussions fully, and the moral character to take the ethical action. Consider, for example, how difficult it is to deliver unpleasant news, even if you agree that honesty is important and is the way you would want to be treated. This was a hurdle for some Hilton Worldwide managers as they made staffing decisions for their call centers. Hilton, which operates call centers in five countries and contracts with call centers in the Philippines, reportedly sent employees from its Hemet, California, center to a new call center in Manila to train employees in handling reservation changes and other customer service activities. Only afterward were the California employees told that the

Management in Action

THE STATE OF ETHICS AT IBM

One advantage IBM has in meeting its standards for trust is that it is part of a relatively trusted industry. In the Edelman Trust Barometer, an annual survey of public attitudes toward a variety of institutions, people from around the world rated the technology industry as the industry they most often trust to do what is right—mainly because they see tech companies as able to benefit society. Ginni Rometty, CEO of IBM, recently reinforced how important it is to protect people's privacy and security.

IBM is addressing these issues. It has a set of policies aimed at building trust, including a policy for business conduct and ethics and a policy for protecting data privacy. The ethics policy states, "It is IBM's policy to conduct itself ethically and lawfully in all matters and to maintain IBM's high standards of business integrity." It puts employees on notice that there are consequences for unethical conduct. IBM's policies call for fairness, equity, a commitment to quality, and compliance with laws, including employment and anti-corruption laws. Its data privacy laws call for employees to collect only relevant personal information, keep it as accurate as possible, and take measures to keep it secure, among other requirements.

Compliance with ethical standards is most likely when managers and employees at all levels are committed to the standards. Thus, it should help IBM that its strategy and culture changes under Sam Palmisano started with an all-employee values jam. An outcome of that process was a statement of three values:

1. Dedication to every client's success
2. Innovation that matters, for our company and the world
3. Trust and personal responsibility in all relationships

These statements appear on the company's website, where any employee or concerned citizen can be reminded of what IBM is striving to achieve.

Even with formal statements and consequences for behavior, maintaining ethical conduct is a challenge, especially for a global company, because employees encounter differences in standards and practices in other countries. Thus, IBM was charged by the Securities and Exchange Commission with bribing government officials in South Korea and China over more than 10 years. In its settlement, IBM must file monthly reports with the SEC to demonstrate its efforts to avoid future violations of the Foreign Corrupt Practices Act. Living up to its own code of ethics will require continued vigilance at IBM.[48]

- Besides the measures described, how else can IBM promote ethical conduct by its employees?
- In a company operating where bribing government officials is expected, how can employees find the moral courage to forgo bribery at the risk of losing a big sale?

company would be closing the Hemet facility, located southeast of Los Angeles, and laying off the workers there unless they chose to relocate to jobs in Texas or Florida. Perhaps the managers feared that telling employees they were training their replacements would have hurt performance; honesty takes courage when it is risky, and the risks of complete honesty are real.[49]

The road for whistleblowers is rocky.

Behaving ethically in an ethical climate is complicated enough, but even more courage is necessary when you decide that the only ethical course of action is *whistleblowing*—telling others, inside or outside the organization, of wrongdoing. The road for whistleblowers is rocky. When whistleblowers go public, they are often seen as acting against the company's interests. Many, perhaps most, whistleblowers suffer consequences such as being ostracized, treated rudely, or given undesirable assignments.

For this reason, and in response to the revised sentencing guidelines under the Sarbanes-Oxley Act, organizations set up channels for employees to report ethics problems so the organization can respond without the matter becoming a scandal. Ideally, the reporting method should keep the whistleblower's identity secret, management should investigate and respond quickly, and there should be no retaliation against whistleblowers who use proper channels.[50]

From the manager's perspective, of course, the goal is to lead employees to maintain high ethical standards, which creates an environment in which whistleblowing is unnecessary. As you read "Management in Action: Progress Report," consider how IBM promotes ethical conduct and how this might reinforce employees' moral courage.

Corporate Social Responsibility

stewardship

Contributing to the long-term welfare of others.

Stewardship means contributing to the long-term welfare of others.[51] Does business ever operate this way? Consider the following examples:

- Google's employees volunteered over 150,000 hours in the past three years to support nonprofits in local communities.
- Burt's Bees helped develop the Natural Standard for personal products, which created guidelines for what can be deemed natural.
- Pedigree dog food built its brand by focusing on the need to adopt homeless dogs.
- Whole Foods created Whole Planet Foundation to fight poverty through microlending to microentrepreneurs in rural communities around the world.
- Ford Motor Company fights HIV/AIDS in South Africa.
- Kickboard empowers teachers to use data to improve student performance in high-poverty areas in the United States.
- Green Mountain Coffee promotes fair trade coffee around the world.
- Bank Boston fosters economic development in communities of moderate income and in the inner city.
- McDonald's and Bank of America support sustainable development in a variety of strategic ways.[52]

corporate social responsibility (CSR)

Obligation toward society assumed by business. See also *ethics*.

Should business be responsible for social concerns beyond its own economic well-being? Do social concerns affect a corporation's financial performance? The extent of business's responsibility for noneconomic concerns has been hotly debated for years. In the 1960s and 1970s, the political and social environment became more important to U.S. corporations as society turned its attention to issues such as equal opportunity, pollution control, energy and natural resource conservation, and consumer and worker protection.[53] Public debate addressed these issues and the ways business should respond to them. This controversy focused on the concept of corporate social responsibility.

Corporate social responsibility (CSR) is the obligation toward society assumed by business.[54] Corporate social responsibility reflects the social imperatives and the social consequences of business success and consists broadly of policies and practices that reflect business responsibility for some of the wider societal good. CSR actions and policies take into account stakeholders' expectations and often consider the **triple bottom line** of economic, social, and environmental performance.[55] The precise policies and practices underlying this responsibility lie at the discretion of the corporation. Some companies refer to their CSR practices in terms of sustainability, on the grounds that these efforts maintain positive long-term relationships with communities, employees, customers, governments, and the natural environment.[56]

Social responsibilities can be categorized[57] as shown in Exhibit 5.8. The **economic responsibilities** of business are to produce goods and services that society wants at a price that perpetuates the business and satisfies its obligations to investors. For Smithfield Foods, the largest pork producer in the United States, this means selling bacon, ham, and other products to customers at prices that maximize Smithfield's profits and keep the company growing over the long term. Economic responsibility may also extend to offering certain products to needy consumers at a reduced price.

Legal responsibilities are to obey local, state, federal, and relevant international laws. Laws affecting Smithfield cover a wide range of requirements, from filing tax returns to meeting worker safety standards. **Ethical responsibilities** include meeting other societal expectations, not written as law. Smithfield took on this level of responsibility when it responded to requests by major customers, including McDonald's and Walmart, that it discontinue the practice of using gestation crates to house its sows. The customers were reacting to pressure from animal rights advocates who consider it cruel for sows to live in the two-foot by seven-foot crates during their entire gestation period, which means they cannot walk, turn around, or stretch their legs for months at a time.[58]

Green Mountain Coffee promotes fair trade coffee around the world as part of its corporate social responsibility.

© Alison Yin/AP Images for Green Mountain Coffee

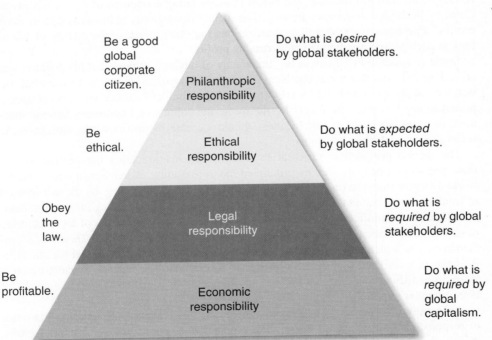

Be a good global corporate citizen.

Do what is *desired* by global stakeholders.

Philanthropic responsibility

Be ethical.

Do what is *expected* by global stakeholders.

Ethical responsibility

Obey the law.

Do what is *required* by global stakeholders.

Legal responsibility

Be profitable.

Do what is *required* by global capitalism.

Economic responsibility

SOURCE: From *Academy of Management Executive: The Thinking Manager's Source* by A. Carroll, "Management Ethically with Global Stakeholders: A Present and Future Challenge." Copyright © 2004. Reproduced with permission of Academy of Management via Copyright Clearance Center.

triple bottom line

Economic, social, and environmental performance.

economic responsibilities

To produce goods and services that society wants at a price that perpetuates the business and satisfies its obligations to investors.

ethical responsibilities

Meeting other social expectations, not written as law.

legal responsibilities

To obey local, state, federal, and relevant international laws.

EXHIBIT 5.8

Pyramid of Global Corporate Social Responsibility and Performance

philanthropic responsibilities

Additional behaviors and activities that society finds desirable and that the values of the business support.

transcendent education

An education with five higher goals that balance self-interest with responsibility to others.

Smithfield was not legally required to make the change (except in two states), and the arrangement was costly, but the company's decision helped its public image—that is, until it backed out of the plan, citing economic woes.

Finally, **philanthropic responsibilities** are additional behaviors and activities that society finds desirable and that the values of the business support. Examples include supporting community projects and making charitable contributions. Philanthropic activities can be more than mere altruism; managed properly, strategic philanthropy can become not an oxymoron but a way to build goodwill in a variety of stakeholders and even add to shareholder wealth.[59]

Robert Giacalone, who teaches business ethics at the University of Denver, believes that a 21st-century education must help students think about responsibilities beyond self-interest and profitability. A real education, he says, teaches students to leave a legacy that extends beyond the bottom line—a transcendent education.[60] A **transcendent education** has five higher goals that balance self-interest with responsibility to others: *empathy* (feeling your decisions as potential victims might feel them, to gain wisdom); *generativity* (learning how to give as well as take, to others in the present as well as to future generations); *mutuality* (viewing success not merely as personal gain, but a common victory); *civil aspiration* (thinking not just in terms of don'ts [lie, cheat, steal, kill], but also in terms of positive contributions); and *intolerance of ineffective humanity* (speaking out against unethical actions).

> A real education, he says, teaches students to leave a legacy that extends beyond the bottom line—a transcendent education.

Contrasting Views

Two basic and contrasting views describe principles that should guide managerial responsibility. The first holds that managers act as agents for shareholders and, as such, are obligated to maximize the present value of the firm. This tenet of capitalism is widely associated with the early writings of Adam Smith in *The Wealth of Nations* and more recently with Milton Friedman, the Nobel Prize–winning economist of the University of Chicago. With his now-famous dictum, "The social responsibility of business is to increase profits," Friedman contended that organizations may help improve the quality of life as long as such actions are directed at increasing profits.

Some considered Friedman to be "the enemy of business ethics," but his position was ethical: he believed that it was unethical for unelected business leaders to decide what was best for society and unethical for them to spend shareholders' money on projects unconnected to key business interests.[61] Furthermore, the context of Friedman's famous statement includes the qualifier that business should increase its profits while conforming to society's laws and ethical customs.

The second perspective, different from the profit maximization perspective, is that managers should be motivated by principled moral reasoning. Adam Smith wrote about a world different from the one we are in now, driven in the 18th century by the self-interest of small owner-operated farms and craft shops trying to generate a living income for themselves and their families. This self-interest was quite different from that of top executives of modern corporations.[62] It is noteworthy that Adam Smith also wrote *A Theory of Moral Sentiments,* in which he argued that "sympathy," defined as a proper regard for others, is the basis of a civilized society.[63] Smith argued further that "the wise and virtuous man is at all times willing that this own private interest should be sacrificed to public interest" if circumstances require it.[64]

Advocates of corporate social responsibility argue that organizations have a wider range of responsibilities that extend beyond the production of goods and services at a profit. As members of society, organizations should actively and responsibly participate in the community and in the larger environment. From this perspective, many people criticized insurance companies after Hurricanes Katrina and Rita devastated homes and businesses along the Gulf Coast. From a social responsibility perspective, it was wrong for companies to watch out for their bottom line and avoid paying claims where they could make a case that the damage wasn't covered; the insurers should have been more concerned about their devastated customers.

Reconciliation

Profit maximization and corporate social responsibility used to be regarded as antagonistic, leading to opposing policies. But the two views can converge.[65] The Coca-Cola Company has set a goal to be "water neutral" by 2020. The company is improving water efficiency in the production process and treating its wastewater.[66] From a practical perspective, Coca-Cola's strategic planners have identified water shortages as a strategic risk; from a values perspective, water is, in the words of executive Neville Isdell, "at the very core of our ethos," so "responsible use of that resource is very important to us."[67]

Earlier attention to corporate social responsibility focused on alleged wrongdoing and how to control it. More recently, attention has also been centered on the possible competitive advantage of socially responsible actions. DuPont has been incorporating care for the environment into its business in two ways it hopes will put it ahead of the competition. First, the company has been reducing its pollution. It hopes these efforts will give it an advantage in a future when the government more heavily regulates emissions, requiring competitors to play catch-up. Second, DuPont has been developing products that are sustainable, meaning they don't deplete the earth's resources. Examples include corn-based fabrics and new applications of its Tyvek material to make buildings more energy-efficient. DuPont expects these innovations to give the company profitable access to the growing market for environmentally friendly products.[68]

The real relationship between corporate social performance and corporate financial performance is highly complex; socially responsible organizations are not necessarily more or less successful in financial terms.[69] But on net, the accumulated evidence indicates that social responsibility is associated with better financial performance.[70] Some advantages are clear. For example, socially responsible actions can have long-term benefits. Companies can avoid unnecessary and costly regulation if they are socially responsible. Honesty and fairness may pay great dividends to the conscience, to the personal reputation, and to the public image of the company as well as in the market response.[71] In addition, society's problems can offer business opportunities, and profits can be made from systematic and vigorous efforts to solve these problems. Firms can perform cost–benefit analyses to identify actions that will maximize profits while satisfying the demand for corporate social responsibility from multiple stakeholders.[72] In other words, managers can treat corporate social responsibility as they would treat all investment decisions. This has been the case as firms attempt to reconcile their business practices with their effect on the natural environment.

The Natural Environment and Sustainability

Most large corporations developed in an era of abundant raw materials, cheap energy, and unconstrained waste disposal.[73] But many of the technologies developed during this era are contributing to the destruction of ecosystems. Industrial-age systems follow a linear flow of extract, produce, sell, use, and discard—what some call a take–make–waste approach.[74] But perhaps no time in history has offered greater possibilities for a change in business thinking than the 21st century. Some maintain that ecological sustainability is now the key driver of innovation.[75] And, whereas some are pessimistic about the planet's future, many are both resolute about creating a healthier planet, and more optimistic now than in recent years for many of the reasons to follow. One such optimist is the new CEO of RFX trucking (featured in the nearby "Social Enterprise" box).[76]

Business used to look at environmental issues as a no-win situation; you either help the environment and hurt your business or help your business at a cost to the environment. But

Social Enterprise

Can a Former Yoga Instructor Clean Up the Trucking Business?

While growing up, joining the family's trucking business was never an option for Caitlin Welby. Founded in 1952 by Welby's grandfather, Refrigerated Food Express (RFX) was passed to Welby's father, who died when she was a senior in high school.

Her teen years were spent as a punk rock artist who did not want anything to do with her father's "dirty business" that she felt was destroying the environment. This stage was followed by years of traveling and studying in art schools in Europe and the United States. Eventually, Caitlin began teaching yoga, but as a result of repeated requests from interim CEO Jim Morse, started to show an interest in the family business. Faced with the pending retirement of Morris and no other successor, Caitlin eventually had a change of heart. At age 32, Caitlin Welby was named the new president and CEO of RFX Trucking.

One of her major challenges is how to reconcile being part of an industry that creates considerable pollution with her values of wanting a sustainable and healthy planet. Other trucking companies such as UPS, YRC Worldwide, and J.B. Hunt are pursuing goals to reduce fuel usage, increase use of alternative energy, or cut carbon emissions.

How is Welby going to pivot RFX so that it can become more environmentally sustainable while remaining profitable? Her training as a yoga instructor and traveler will help bring a new perspective to a legacy industry.

Courtesy of Caitlin Welby, president and CEO, RFX Global Companies

She describes the trucking industry as convoluted and overcomplicated: "Nature doesn't work like that. It's the appropriate amount of energy in the right direction that makes things efficient." Time will tell whether shifting from a yoga instructor to CEO of a trucking company is too much of a stretch.[77]

Questions

- Do you think Welby can help change the trucking industry for the better? Why or why not?
- If you were Welby, how would you go about making RFX into a more environmentally and socially responsible company?

now a paradigm shift is taking place in corporate environmental management: the deliberate incorporation of environmental values into competitive strategies and into the design and manufacturing of products.[78] Why? In addition to philosophical reasons, companies go green to satisfy consumer demand, to react to a competitor's actions, to meet requests from customers or suppliers, to comply with guidelines, and to create competitive advantage.

> Business used to look at environmental issues as a no-win situation, but now a paradigm shift is taking place.

General Electric CEO Jeff Immelt used to view environmental rules as a burden and a cost. Now he sees environmentally friendly technologies as one of the global economy's most significant business opportunities. Under a business initiative called Ecomagination, GE is looking for business opportunities from solving environmental problems. Ecomagination solutions include wind turbines, materials for solar energy cells, and energy-efficient home appliances. Ecomagination has delivered many billions in revenues. It also has built a green image for the GE brand and positioned the company as a leader in many rapidly growing markets, including high-efficiency jet engines and locomotives.[79]

A Risk Society

We live in a risk society. That is, the creation and distribution of wealth generate by-products that can cause injury, loss, or danger to people and the environment. The fundamental sources of risk in modern society are the excessive production of hazards and ecologically unsustainable consumption of natural resources.[80] Risk has proliferated through population explosion, industrial pollution, and environmental degradation.[81]

Industrial pollution risks include air pollution, smog, global warming, ozone depletion, acid rain, toxic waste sites, nuclear hazards, obsolete weapons arsenals, industrial accidents, and hazardous products. Tens of thousands of uncontrolled toxic waste sites have been documented in the United States alone. The situation is far worse in other parts of the world. The pattern, for toxic waste and many other risks, is one of accumulating risks and inadequate remedies.

The institutions that create environmental and technological risk (corporations and government agencies) are responsible for controlling and managing the risks.[82] For example, as a manufacturer, 3M acknowledges that its activities result in pollution, so the company has committed itself to reducing its impact on the environment. A combination of reduced energy use, improvements in manufacturing processes, redesign of products, and the use of pollution control equipment have enabled the company to cut its global emissions of greenhouse gases dramatically. 3M recently installed charging stations for electric vehicles at its headquarters in St. Paul, Minnesota.[83]

Some of the world's worst environmental problems are in China because of its rapid industrialization and its huge population and size. About one-third of China's rural population—hundreds of millions of people—drink unhealthful, unclean water. At least the problem is recognized; local authorities are beginning to experience pressure from the central government to clean up or shut down dirty factories.[84] Still, most cleanup efforts focus on big cities while rural areas get worse.

Developing countries are often seen as sustainability laggards, focused solely on raising people out of poverty. Regulatory agencies can be weak and hesitant to impose restrictions, but visionary individuals the world over can pioneer successful sustainability efforts.[85]

Ecocentric Management

Ecocentric management has as its goal the creation of sustainable economic development and improvement of quality of life worldwide for all organizational stakeholders.[86] **Sustainable growth** is economic growth and development that meet the organization's present needs without harming the ability of future generations to meet their needs.[87] Sustainability is fully compatible with the natural ecosystems that generate and preserve life.[88]

Businesses are both a cause of and a solution to environmental degradation, and clearly have a major role to play in sustainability debates and strategies.[89]

Increasingly, firms are paying attention to the total environmental impact throughout the life cycle of their products.[90] **Life-cycle analysis (LCA)** is a process of analyzing all inputs and outputs, through the entire cradle-to-grave life of a product, to determine the total environmental impact of the production and use of a product. LCA quantifies the total use of resources and the releases into the air, water, and land. Reporting worldwide **carbon footprints** is a big step in environmental reporting in that industry. Apparel maker Patagonia uses LCA to analyze the carbon footprint at each stage of its supply chain from farm to factory.[91]

LCA considers the extraction of raw materials, product packaging, transportation, and disposal. Consider packaging alone. Goods make the journey from manufacturer to wholesaler to retailer to customer; then they are recycled back to the manufacturer. They may be packaged and repackaged several times, from bulk transport, to large crates, to cardboard boxes, to individual consumer sizes. Repackaging not only creates waste but also costs time. The design of initial packaging in sizes and formats adaptable to the final customer can minimize the need for repackaging, cut waste, and realize financial benefits.

Rather than the linear take–make–waste production model described earlier, a fully sustainable model applies a circular borrow–use–return approach.[92] Whereas the former model engages in harmful extraction, generates huge quantities of waste and pollution, and depletes natural resources (a process in which resources move from cradle to grave),

ecocentric management

Its goal is the creation of sustainable economic development and improvement of quality of life worldwide for all organizational stakeholders.

sustainable growth

Economic growth and development that meets present needs without harming the needs of future generations.

life-cycle analysis (LCA)

A process of analyzing all inputs and outputs, through the entire "cradle-to-grave" life of a product, to determine total environmental impact.

carbon footprint

The output of carbon dioxide and other greenhouses gases.

Timberland has paid particular attention to life-cycle analysis, as implied by what is printed on its recycled material shoe boxes.

© *The McGraw-Hill Companies, Inc./Jill Braaten, photographer*

the cradle-to-cradle approach is ecologically benign and restorative. In its ideal form, this sustainable approach extracts energy and raw materials without harm, phases out the use of nonrenewable resources, designs processes and products that recirculate so they don't cause environmental or socioeconomic harm, keeps toxic substances in closed-loop industrial cycles, and recirculates biological materials back into nature without harm.[93]

Profitability need not suffer and may be positively affected by ecocentric philosophies and practices. Some, but not all, research has shown a positive relationship between corporate environmental performance and profitability.[94] Of course, whether the relationship is positive, negative, or neutral depends on the strategies chosen and the effectiveness of implementation.

Companies can integrate green practices with strategy in a variety of ways. Certainly they develop and market green products; Toyota's bold move to develop the Prius paid off handsomely with market dominance.[95] Companies also can emphasize green attributes in their marketing but need to avoid misleading claims (greenwashing) and public backlash. For instance, Arm & Hammer positioned its baking soda brand as "the number one environmentally sensible alternative for cleaning and deodorizing" and "committed to the environment since 1846." On the other hand, the company ignored a major problem: it used animal testing. The blogosphere began touting equally green but cruelty-free Bob's Red Mill baking soda.[96]

Companies also can acquire other companies with sustainability (and image) in mind. L'Oréal bought The Body Shop, Colgate-Palmolive bought Tom's of Maine, Unilever bought Ben & Jerry's, and Group Danone bought Stonyfield's.[97] When Clorox bought Burt's Bees, which had decades of leadership and experience with sustainability, it did so for growth and to convince environmental stakeholders that the company's strategic change was genuine, but also to acquire knowledge about the green product space.[98]

For those interested in reading more about this subject, Appendix B of this chapter discusses in greater detail the reasons for managing with the environment in mind, some history of the environmental movement, economic issues, and a wide array of green examples pertaining to strategy, public affairs, legal issues, operations, marketing, accounting, and finance.

You also can check out the Global Reporting Initiative (GRI) list of sustainability performance indicators. This useful resource, at www.globalreporting.org, aims to help companies improve their sustainability practices, including transparent reporting.

Environmental Agendas for the Future

In the past, most companies were oblivious to their negative environmental impact. More recently, many began striving for low impact. Now some strive for positive impact, eager to sell solutions to the world's problems. Siemens, a major electronics and electrical engineering company headquartered in Switzerland, produces energy-efficient equipment for power generation and transmission, including smart grids. In addition, Siemens Building Technologies is tackling energy efficiency in buildings, which account for 40 percent of energy consumption. For example, in Oregon, a Siemens project is helping Sky Lakes Medical Center save $3 million in energy expenses over 12 years with advanced lighting, heating, and cooling systems.[99]

Or consider climate change and the world's shortage of clean water. When Dow Chemical's Freeport, Texas, site had trouble getting enough water to run its processes during droughts, it installed technology to monitor the water system 24/7 and reduced water consumption by a billion gallons a year.[100] Marriott is pursuing a goal to reduce energy and water consumption by 20 percent per occupied hotel room.[101] Nestlé saves up to 1,375 cubic meters of water per year since improving how it collects and transports milk from farmers.

You don't have to be a manufacturer or a utility to jump on the green bandwagon. Web search giant Google is working hard to reduce its carbon footprint and purchasing offsets—funding projects that reduce greenhouse gas emissions elsewhere.[102]

Collaborative efforts will be essential—for example, the energy industry and environmentalists working with rather than against one another.[103] Networks of companies with a common ecological vision can combine their efforts into high-leverage, impactful action.[104] In cities such as San Antonio, Texas, and Columbus, Ohio, federal partner agencies work closely with city governments, utilities, and multiple manufacturers to reduce pollutants and energy consumption and to increase energy savings. In Kalundborg, Denmark, such

Management in Action

IBM TAKES RESPONSIBILITY

Given that disclosure builds the kind of trust IBM wants as the basis for its relationships, the company publishes its values and policies online along with an annual Corporate Responsibility Report. IBM's understanding of its role in corporate citizenship includes practices related to the natural environment and the communities it serves. IBM defines its social role this way:

1. We identify and act upon new opportunities to apply our technology and expertise to societal problems.
2. We scale our existing programs and initiatives to achieve maximum benefit.
3. We empower our employees and others to serve their communities.
4. We integrate corporate citizenship and social responsibility into every aspect of our company.

These statements apply IBM's resources as a large global technology company (over 431,000 employees in almost 170 countries) to the communities where it operates.

Especially in its concern for the natural environment, IBM unites a commitment to be responsible with the business opportunities available to a company specializing in data analysis, cloud computing solutions, and planning. In fact, IBM has had policies for protecting the environment and conserving resources since 1967. IBM's product recycling programs are designed to resell, refurbish, or recycle at least 97 percent of its end-of-life products. The company also requires its suppliers to demonstrate that they are taking responsibility for their impact on the environment.

Moreover, environmental protection is now part of IBM's Smarter Planet strategy. IBM's consultants and systems help cities, businesses, and building owners manage the data required to operate as efficiently as possible. For example, IBM is helping San Francisco figure out how to keep all of its waste out of landfills by directing it to recycling and other uses. IBM's Smarter Building initiative installs sensors and building automation software to gather data on building systems and uses, applying the data to conserve energy and water.

IBM's corporate citizenship also involves supporting selected nonprofit causes, including economic development, education, and health. Its biggest philanthropy is its Smarter Cities challenge, which awards grants to cities to help them improve in a specified area of performance. IBM sends a six-member team of its own experts to each city to help leaders analyze problems and develop solutions. By the end of 2013, IBM had sent teams to 100 cities around the world to address such challenges as improving urban planning, managing traffic, encouraging entrepreneurship, improving energy efficiency, and much more.[105]

- How is IBM's commitment to corporate social responsibility good for IBM as a business? Explain.
- Improving energy efficiency saves IBM millions of dollars, but recycling its used electronics requires hiring hundreds of people. Is the recycling program justifiable? Why or why not?

MANAGER'S BRIEF

PROGRESS REPORT

ONWARD

Bottom Line

Packaging isn't the most glamorous of business topics, but it holds great potential for reducing costs and increasing speed while helping the environment. You can always find opportunities to improve results in unexpected places where others haven't tried.

Think of a product you recently purchased. How could its packaging have been more environmentally friendly?

a collaborative alliance exists among an electric power generating plant, an oil refiner, a biotech production plant, a plasterboard factory, cement producers, heating utilities, a sulfuric acid producer, and local agriculture and horticulture. Chemicals, energy (for both heating and cooling), water, and organic materials flow among companies. Resources are conserved, waste materials generate revenues, and water, air, and ground pollution all are reduced.

Mark Tercek, president and CEO of the Nature Conservancy and former managing director and partner at Goldman Sachs, states, "individuals, businesses, and nations have long acted as if 'society will always have the resources it needs, and if anything runs short, then creative businesses can simply replace it with something else that is not so scarce.' [But] for the first time in human history, these assumptions are open to serious question at a global scale."[106] Natural resources no longer are free goods.[107]

In 2010, the World Bank launched a project to help developing countries arrive at valuations of their natural capital. Then-president Robert Zoellik said, "The natural wealth of nations should be a capital asset, valued in combination with its financial capital, manufactured capital, and human capital."[108] Now, nonprofit organizations and accounting firm PricewaterhouseCoopers offer methodologies that value ecosystems. Dow Chemical pledged $10 million for scientists from the Nature Conservancy to help Dow develop ecosystem service valuation methods.

States Dow CEO Andrew Liveris, "Companies that value and integrate biodiversity and ecosystem services into their strategic plans are best positioned for the future."[109] In addition to the benefits to the world of sustainable practices, many now believe that preparing for and adapting to climate change is a big and fast-arriving challenge,[110] and that solving environmental problems is one of the biggest opportunities in the history of commerce.[111]

KEY TERMS

business ethics, p. 143

carbon footprint, p. 157

Caux Principles, p. 143

compliance-based ethics programs, p. 149

corporate social responsibility (CSR), p. 152

ecocentric management, p. 157

economic responsibilities, p. 153

egoism, p. 144

ethical climate, p. 146

ethical issue, p. 143

ethical leader, p. 147

ethical responsibilities, p. 153

ethics, p. 140

integrity-based ethics programs, p. 149

Kohlberg's model of cognitive moral development, p. 145

legal responsibilities, p. 153

life-cycle analysis (LCA), p. 157

moral philosophy, p. 143

philanthropic responsibilities, p. 154

relativism, p. 144

Sarbanes-Oxley Act, p. 145

stewardship, p. 152

sustainable growth, p. 157

transcendent education, p. 154

triple bottom line, p. 153

universalism, p. 143

utilitarianism, p. 144

virtue ethics, p. 145

RETAINING WHAT YOU LEARNED

In Chapter 5, you learned that ethics is an important and personal issue that affects employee and organizational behavior. Ethical decisions are influenced by individuals' values and which ethical system they use to frame a given problem. Companies attempt to influence their ethics environment by establishing ethical programs or codes. Codes prescribe guidelines for how various stakeholders should behave. Making ethical decisions requires moral awareness, moral judgment, and moral character. A model of ethical decision making is shown in Exhibit 5.7 (which is repeated on the next page). Corporate social responsibility suggests that corporations have not only economic but also legal, ethical, and philanthropic responsibilities. While most companies used to view the natural environment as a source of raw materials and profit, now more companies are adopting a greener agenda for philosophical reasons and personal commitment to sustainable development. Ecocentric managers attempt to minimize negative environment impact, create sustainable economic development, and improve the quality of life worldwide.

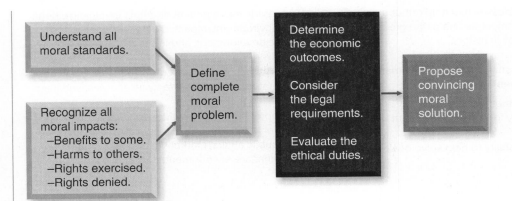

SOURCE: L. T. Hosmer, *The Ethics of Management,* 4th ed. McGraw-Hill/Irwin, 2003, p. 32. Fig. 5.1A. © 2003 The McGraw-Hill Companies, Reprinted with permission.

EXHIBIT 5.7
A Process for Ethical
Decision Making

LO 1   **Describe how different ethical perspectives guide decision making.**

- The purpose of ethics is to identify the rules that govern human behavior and the "goods" that are worth seeking.
- Ethical decisions are guided by the individual's values or principles of conduct such as honesty, fairness, integrity, respect for others, and responsible citizenship.
- Different ethical systems include universalism, egoism and utilitarianism, relativism, and virtue ethics.
- These philosophical systems, as practiced by different individuals according to their level of cognitive moral development and other factors, underlie the ethical stances of individuals and organizations.

LO 2   **Explain how companies influence their ethics environment.**

- Different organizations apply different ethical perspectives and standards.
- Ethics codes sometimes are helpful, although they must be implemented properly.
- Ethics programs can range from compliance-based to integrity-based.
- Ethics codes address employee conduct, community and environment, shareholders, customers, suppliers and contractors, political activity, and technology.

LO 3   **Outline a process for making ethical decisions.**

- Making ethical decisions requires moral awareness, moral judgment, and moral character.
- When faced with ethical dilemmas, the veil of ignorance is a useful metaphor.
- As shown in Exhibit 5.7, you can know various moral standards (universalism, relativism, and so on), use the problem-solving model described in Chapter 3, identify the positive and negative effects of your

alternatives on different parties, consider legal requirements and the costs of unethical actions, and then evaluate your ethical duties.

LO 4   **Summarize the important issues surrounding corporate social responsibility.**

- Corporate social responsibility is the extension of the corporate role beyond economic pursuits. It includes not only economic but also legal, ethical, and philanthropic responsibilities.
- Advocates believe managers should consider societal and human needs in their business decisions because corporations are members of society and carry a wide range of responsibilities.
- Critics of corporate responsibility believe managers' first responsibility is to increase profits for the shareholders who own the corporation.
- The two perspectives are potentially reconcilable, especially if managers choose to address areas of social responsibility that contribute to the organization's strategy.

LO 5   **Discuss reasons for businesses' growing interest in the natural environment.**

- In the past, most companies viewed the natural environment as a resource to be used for raw materials and profit. But consumer, regulatory, and other pressures arose. Executives often viewed these pressures as burdens, constraints, and costs to be borne.
- Now more companies view the interface between business and the natural environment as a potential win–win opportunity.
- Some are adopting a greener agenda for philosophical reasons and personal commitment to sustainable development.
- Many also are recognizing the potential financial benefits of managing with the environment in mind and are integrating environmental issues into corporate and business strategy.

- Some see entering businesses that help rather than harm the natural environment as one of the great commercial opportunities in history.

LO 6   Identify actions managers can take to manage with the environment in mind.

- Organizations have contributed risk to society and have some responsibility for reducing risk to the environment.
- They also have the capability to help solve environmental problems.

- Ecocentric management attempts to minimize negative environment impact, create sustainable economic development, and improve the quality of life worldwide.
- Relevant actions are described in the chapter, including strategic initiatives, life-cycle analysis, and interorganizational alliances.
- A chapter appendix provides a wide variety of specific examples of strategic, operations, finance, legal and public affairs, marketing, and accounting practices that are environmentally friendly.

DISCUSSION QUESTIONS

1. Consider the various ethical systems described early in the chapter. Identify concrete examples from your own past decisions or the decisions of others you have seen or read about.

2. Choose one or more topics from Exhibit 5.3 and discuss their current status and the ethical issues surrounding them.

3. What would you do in each of the scenarios described in Exhibit 5.4?

4. Identify and discuss illegal, unethical, and socially responsible business actions in the current news.

5. Does your school have a code of ethics? If so, what does it say? Is it effective? Why or why not?

6. You have a job you like at which you work 40 to 45 hours per week. How much off-the-job volunteer work would you do? What kinds of volunteer work? How will you react if your boss makes it clear he or she wants you to cut back on the outside activities and devote more hours to your job?

7. What are the arguments for and against the concept of corporate social responsibility? Where do you stand and why? Give your opinions, specifically, with respect to the text examples.

8. What do you think of the concept of a transcendent education as described in the chapter? What can be done to implement such a vision for education?

9. What is the current status of the Sarbanes-Oxley Act? What do executives think of it now? What impact has it had?

10. A company in England slaughtered 70,000 baby ostrich chicks each year for their meat. It told a teen magazine that it would stop if it received enough complaints. Analyze this policy, practice, and public statement using the concepts discussed in the chapter.

11. A Nike ad in the U.S. magazine *Seventeen* showed a picture of a girl, aged perhaps 8 or 9. The ad read,

    If you let me play . . .
    I will like myself more.
    I will have more self-confidence.
    I will suffer less depression.
    I will be 60 percent less likely to get breast cancer.
    I will be more likely to leave a man who beats me.
    I will be less likely to get pregnant before I want to.
    I will learn what it means to be strong.
    If you let me play sports.

    Assess this ad in terms of chapter concepts surrounding ethics and social responsibility. What questions would you ask in doing this analysis?

12. Should companies be held accountable for actions of decades past, then legal but since made illegal, as their harmful effects became known? Why or why not?

13. Discuss courage as a requirement for ethical behavior. What personal examples can you offer, either as an actor or as an observer? What examples are in the news?

14. See additional discussion questions in Appendix B.

EXPERIENTIAL EXERCISES

5.1 MEASURING YOUR ETHICAL WORK BEHAVIOR

OBJECTIVES

1. To explore a range of ethically perplexing situations.
2. To understand your own ethical attitudes.

INSTRUCTIONS

Make decisions in the situations described in the Ethical Behavior Worksheet. You will not have all the background information on each situation; instead, you should make whatever assumptions you feel you would make if you were actually confronted with the decision choices described. Select the decision choice that most closely represents the decision you feel you would make personally. You should choose decision options even though you can envision other creative solutions that were not included in the exercise.

Ethical Behavior Worksheet

SITUATION 1

You are taking a very difficult chemistry course, which you must pass to maintain your scholarship and to avoid damaging your application for graduate school. Chemistry is not your strong suit, and, because of a just-below-failing average in the course, you will have to receive a grade of 90 or better on the final exam, which is two days away. A janitor, who is aware of your plight, informs you that he found the master for the chemistry final in a trash barrel and has saved it. He will make it available to you for a price, which is high but which you could afford. What would you do?

_____(a) I would tell the janitor thanks, but no thanks.

_____(b) I would report the janitor to the proper officials.

_____(c) I would buy the exam and keep it to myself.

_____(d) I would not buy the exam myself, but I would let some of my friends, who are also flunking the course, know that it is available.

SITUATION 2

You have been working on some financial projections manually for two days now. It seems that each time you think you have them completed, your boss shows up with a new assumption or another what-if question. If you only had a copy of a spreadsheet software program for your personal computer, you could plug in the new assumptions and revise the estimates with ease. Then a colleague offers to let you make a copy of some software that is copyrighted. What would you do?

_____(a) I would accept my friend's generous offer and make a copy of the software.

_____(b) I would decline to copy it and plug away manually on the numbers.

_____(c) I would decide to go buy a copy of the software myself, for $300, and hope I would be reimbursed by the company in a month or two.

_____(d) I would request another extension on an already overdue project date.

SITUATION 3

Your small manufacturing company is in serious financial difficulty. A large order of your products is ready to be delivered to a key customer when you discover that the product is simply not right. It will not meet all performance specifications, will cause problems for your customer, and will require rework in the field; however, this, you know, will not become evident until after the customer has received and paid for the order. If you do not ship the order and receive the payment as expected, your business may be forced into bankruptcy. And if you delay the shipment or inform the customer of these problems, you may lose the order and go bankrupt. What would you do?

_____(a) I would not ship the order and place my firm in voluntary bankruptcy.

_____(b) I would inform the customer and declare voluntary bankruptcy.

_____(c) I would ship the order and inform the customer after I received payment.

_____(d) I would ship the order and not inform the customer.

SITUATION 4

You are the cofounder and president of a new venture, manufacturing products for the recreational market. Five months after launching the business, one of your suppliers informs you it can no longer supply you with a critical raw material because you are not a large-quantity user. Without the raw material, the business cannot continue. What would you do?

_____(a) I would grossly overstate my requirements to another supplier to make the supplier think I am a much larger potential customer to secure the raw material from that supplier, even though this would mean the supplier will no longer be able to supply another, noncompeting small manufacturer who may thus be forced out of business.

_____(b) I would steal raw material from another firm (noncompeting) where I am aware of a sizable stockpile.

_____(c) I would pay off the supplier because I have reason to believe that the supplier could be persuaded to meet my needs with a sizable under-the-table payoff that my company could afford.

_____(d) I would declare voluntary bankruptcy.

SITUATION 5

You are on a marketing trip for your new venture for the purpose of calling on the purchasing agent of a major prospective client. Your company is manufacturing an electronic system that you hope the purchasing agent will buy. During your conversation, you notice on the cluttered desk of the purchasing agent several copies of a cost proposal for a system from one of your direct competitors. This purchasing agent has previously reported mislaying several of your own company's proposals and has asked for additional copies. The purchasing agent leaves the room momentarily to get you a cup of coffee, leaving you alone with your competitor's proposals less than an arm's length away. What would you do?

_____(a) I would do nothing but await the man's return.

_____(b) I would sneak a quick peek at the proposal, looking for bottom-line numbers.

_____(c) I would put the copy of the proposal in my briefcase.

_____(d) I would wait until the man returns and ask his permission to see the copy.

5.2 ETHICAL STANCE

Are the following actions ethical or unethical in your opinion? Why? Consider the actions individually and discuss them in small groups.

- Calling in sick when you really are not
- Taking office supplies home for personal use
- Cheating on a test
- Turning someone in for cheating on a test or paper
- Overcharging on your company expense report
- Trying to flirt your way out of a speeding ticket
- Splicing cable from your neighbor
- Surfing the net on company time
- Cheating on income tax

- Lying (exaggerating) about yourself to influence someone of the opposite sex
- Looking at pornographic sites on the web through the company network
- Lying about your education on a job application
- Lying about experience in a job interview
- Making a copy of a rental DVD before returning it to the store

SOURCE: Suzanne C. de Janasz, Karen O'Dowd, and Beth Z. Schneider, *Interpersonal Skills in Organizations,* McGraw-Hill, 2002, p. 211. Copyright 2002 The McGraw-Hill Companies. Reprinted with permission.

CONCLUDING CASE

MA EARTH SKIN CARE TRIES TO STAY NATURAL

Heather Franklin is a marketing manager for Ma Earth Skin Care. Four years ago, when she was hired to help with the paperwork for promotional campaigns, she was thrilled to become a part of this company because she loved Ma Earth's lotions, soaps, and cosmetics. Besides smelling heavenly and offering exquisite colors for eye shadow and lipstick, the products spoke to Heather's values: Ma Earth promised to use all natural ingredients, sustainably grown or mined, and to operate with minimal adverse impact on the planet. So for Heather, going to work was almost like carrying out a mission, promoting both beauty and concern for the planet's well-being. No doubt, her commitment and enthusiasm helped pave the way when the position of marketing manager opened up.

Currently, Heather and her team are preparing a promotional campaign for a new product line, Oré Essentials, which includes lipsticks, foundation, and eye shadows tinted with a plant extract called orellana. The exciting feature of Oré Essentials is that orellana is harvested deep in the Amazon rain forest, and because of its sustainable practices, Ma Earth will obtain this special ingredient in a socially responsible manner. The company set up a contract with a tribe living in a remote village. The people of the tribe are supposed to grow and harvest the orellana, which is naturally part of the area's ecosystem, and Ma Earth has promised to pay a fair price to the whole tribe so the people can use the money to maintain their village and their way of life. Consumers will get a beautiful product and the pleasure of knowing that they are helping preserve an endangered ecology—and an endangered way of life for the rain forest people.

But when Heather sat down for a meeting with the photography crew that traveled to the village, some concerns began to surface. She was looking at stunning photos of tribe members arrayed in grass skirts as they stood behind a pile of fruit from the orellana tree. As she was selecting her favorite shots, one of the photographers commented that the translator had made some surprising remarks on the return trip from the village. Apparently the pile of orellana fruit had been gathered just for the photo shoot. The tribe doesn't really bother with growing and harvesting orellana; the people of this area aren't primarily farmers, and there aren't actually many orellana trees within a day's walk of the village. The first year they had tried selling orellana to Ma Earth, they grew only enough to earn a few hundred dollars, not really worth the effort. Heather felt confused by these statements and planned to take a closer look at spending on her product later that day.

Hours later, when the other employees had gone home, Heather finally had a chance to spend some time researching her product on the company's employee website. She found purchasing transactions for "orellana/annatto," and after a little research learned that under either name, the product is just an inexpensive dye. Under the latter name, it is used as a common food coloring. It turns out that Ma Earth made most of its purchases from a mainstream supplier, which is cheaper than persuading remote villagers to provide orellana.

That evening Heather went home feeling betrayed and upset. The next day she asked her boss, the divisional vice president, why the company pretended to care about a remote village if it was just a front for a brand. Heather's boss, Megan McDonough, said, "But we *do* care! We send them tens of thousands of dollars every year. Sure, they don't actually grow that stuff for us, but they could, and we'll buy it if they do. Anyway, our aid has provided a school and a health clinic, not to mention food and clothing. We've helped the tribe members stay healthy and preserve their language and culture."

Heather considered what Megan said. "So," she asked, "does this mean we're using their culture to build an image for our brand, and in exchange, they get money from us to keep that culture alive?" She thought about the traditional designs the marketing department had copied from the tribe as decorations for the Oré Essentials packaging.

Megan nodded encouragingly. "That's exactly what I'm saying. It's a win–win situation." Heather felt relieved but not quite sure that her original idealism would withstand her deeper knowledge of how Ma Earth defined its mission.

DISCUSSION QUESTIONS

1. What ethical issues is Heather facing in this situation? What possible marketing claims about the company's relationship with the Amazonian tribe would cross a line into unethical territory? What claims could it make ethically?

2. How could Ma Earth create an ethical climate that would help managers such as Heather ensure that they are behaving ethically?

3. How effectively do you think Ma Earth is practicing corporate social responsibility in this situation? Explain the reasoning behind your evaluation.

Managing in Our Natural Environment

BUSINESS AND THE ENVIRONMENT: CONFLICTING VIEWS

Some people believe everyone wins when business tackles environmental issues.[1] Others disagree.

Business used to look at environmental issues as a no-win situation; you either help the environment and hurt your business or help your business only at a cost to the environment. Fortunately, things have changed. "When Americans first demanded a cleanup of the environment during the early 1970s, corporations threw a tantrum. Their response ran the psychological gamut from denial to hostility, defiance, obstinacy, and fear. But today, when it comes to green issues, many U.S. companies have turned from rebellious underachievers to active problem solvers."[2] This appendix gives examples of things U.S. corporations are doing to help solve environmental problems.

Johan Piet said, "Only win–win companies will survive, but that does not mean that all win–win ideas will be successful."[3] In other words, rigorous analysis is essential. Thus some companies maintain continuous improvement in environmental performance but fund only projects that meet financial objectives.

Most people understand that business has the resources and the competence to bring about constructive change and that this creates great opportunity—if well managed—for both business and the environment.

WHY MANAGE WITH THE ENVIRONMENT IN MIND?

Business is turning its full attention to environmental issues for many reasons, including legal compliance, cost-effectiveness, competitive advantage, public opinion, and long-term thinking.

Legal Compliance Government regulations and liability for damages provide strong economic incentives to comply with environmental guidelines. Most industries already have made environmental protection regulation and liability an integral part of their business planning.[4] The U.S. Justice Department has handed out tough prison sentences to executives whose companies violate hazardous waste requirements.

Some businesspeople consider the regulations to be too rigid, inflexible, and unfair. In response to this concern, regulatory reform may become more creative. The Aspen Institute Series on the Environment in the Twenty-First Century has tried to increase the cost-effectiveness of compliance measures through more flexibility in meeting standards and relying on market-based incentives. Such mechanisms, including tradable permits, pollution charges, and deposit refund systems, provide positive financial incentives for good environmental performance.[5]

Cost-Effectiveness Environmentally conscious strategies can be cost-effective.[6] In the short run, company after company is realizing cost savings from repackaging, recycling, and other approaches. General Motors generates $1 billion per year by reusing, selling, or recycling manufacturing materials that would otherwise be trashed. The company views waste as a "resource out of place." Recently, GM diverted over 2.5 million metric tons of waste, from cardboard boxes to scrap steel, from landfills.[7]

Environmentally conscious strategies offer long-run cost advantages as well. Companies that are functioning barely within legal limits today may incur big costs—being forced to pay damages or upgrade technologies and practices—when laws change down the road.

A few of the other cost savings include fines, cleanups, and litigation; lower raw materials costs; reduced energy use; less expensive waste handling and disposal; lower insurance rates; and possibly higher interest rates.

Competitive Advantage Corporations gain a competitive advantage by channeling their environmental concerns into entrepreneurial opportunities and by producing higher-quality products that meet consumer demand. Business opportunities abound in pollution protection equipment and processes, waste cleanup, low-water-use plumbing, new light bulb technology, and marketing of environmentally safe products such as biodegradable plastics. With new pools of venture capital, government funding, and specialized investment funds available, environmental technology has become a major sector of the venture capital industry.[8]

In addition, companies that fail to innovate in this area will be at a competitive disadvantage. Environmental protection is not only a universal need; it is also a major export industry. U.S. trade suffered as other countries—notably Germany—took the lead in patenting and exporting anti–air pollution and other environmental technologies. If the United States does not produce innovative, competitive new technologies, it will forsake a growth industry and see most of its domestic spending for environmental protection go to imports.[9]

In short, competitive advantage can be gained by maintaining market share with old customers and by creating new products for new market opportunities. And if you are an environmental leader, you may set the standards for future regulations—regulations that you are prepared to meet while your competitors are not.

Public Opinion The majority of the U.S. population believes business must clean up; few people think it is doing its job well. Gallup surveys have shown that more than 80 percent of U.S. consumers consider environmentalism in making purchases. An international survey found that majorities gave priority to environmental protection even at the risk of slowing economic growth. Consumers seem to have reached the point of routinely expecting companies to come up with environmentally friendly alternatives to current products and practices.[10]

Companies also receive pressure from local communities and from their own employees. Sometimes the pressure is informal and low-key, but much pressure is exerted by environmental organizations; aroused citizen groups, societies and associations; international codes of conduct; and environmentally conscious investors.[11]

Another important reason for paying attention to environmental impact is TRI, the Toxic Release Inventory.[12] The EPA requires all the plants of approximately 10,000 U.S. manufacturers to report annual releases of 650 toxic chemicals into the air, ground, and water. The substances include Freon, PCBs, asbestos, and lead compounds. Hundreds of others have been added to the list. The releases are not necessarily illegal, but they provide the public with an annual environmental benchmark. TRI continues to provide a powerful incentive to reduce emissions.

Finally, it is useful to remember that companies recover very slowly in public opinion from the impact of an environmental disaster. Adverse public opinion may affect sales as well as the firm's ability to attract and retain talented people. You can see why companies such as P&G consider concern for the environment a consumer need, making it a basic and critical business issue.

Long-Term Thinking Long-term thinking about resources helps business leaders understand the nature of their responsibilities with regard to environmental concerns. For example, you read about sustainable growth in the chapter.[13] Seventh Generation is named after, and operates under, the ideals set by the Iroquois Indians—every decision must consider the impact it will have on the next (seven) generations. Economic arguments and the tragedy of the commons highlight the need for long-term thinking.

Economic arguments In Chapter 3, we discussed long-term versus short-term decision making. We stated that it is common for managers to succumb to short-term pressure for profits and to avoid spending now when the potential payoff is years down the road. In addition, some economists maintain that it is the responsibility of management to maximize returns for shareholders, implying the preeminence of the short-term profit goal.

But other economists argue that such a strategy caters to immediate profit maximization for stock speculators and neglects serious investors who are with the company for the long haul. Attention to environmental issues enhances the organization's long-term viability because the goal is the long-term creation of wealth for the patient, serious investors in the company[14]—not to mention the future state of our planet and the new generations of humans and other species who will inhabit it.

The tragedy of the commons In a classic article in *Science,* Garrett Hardin described a situation that applies to all business decisions and social concerns regarding scarce resources such as clean water, air, and land.[15] Throughout human history, a commons was a tract of community land on which people grazed their animals. A commons has limited

carrying capacity, or the ability to sustain a population, because it is a finite resource. For individual herders, short-term interest lies in adding as many animals to the commons as they can. But problems develop as more herders add more animals to graze the commons. This leads to tragedy: As each herder acts in his short-term interest, the long-run impact is the destruction of the commons. The solution is to make choices according to long-run rather than short-run consequences.

In many ways, we are witnessing this **tragedy of the commons.** Carrying capacities are shrinking as precious resources, water chief among them, become scarcer. Inevitably, conflict arises—and solutions are urgently needed.

The Environmental Movement The 1990s were labeled the earth decade, when a new environmentalism with new features emerged.[16] For example, proponents of the new environmentalism asked companies to reduce their wastes, use resources prudently, market safe products, and take responsibility for past damages. These requests are updated and formalized in the CERES Roadmap for Sustainability.

The new environmentalism combined many diverse viewpoints, but initially it did not blend easily with traditional business values. Some of the key aspects of this philosophy are noted in the following discussion of the history of the movement.[17]

Conservation and Environmentalism A strand of environmental philosophy that is not at odds with business management is **conservation**. The conservation movement is anthropocentric (human centered), technologically optimistic, and concerned chiefly with the efficient use of resources. The movement seeks to avoid waste, promote the rational and efficient use of natural resources, and maximize long-term yields, especially of renewable resources.

The **environmental movement,** in contrast, historically has posed dilemmas for business management. Following the lead of early thinkers such as George Perkins Marsh (1801–1882), it has shown that the unintended negative effects of human economic activities on the environment often are greater than the benefits. For example, there are links between forest cutting and soil erosion and between the draining of marshes and lakes and the decline of animal life.

Other early environmentalists, such as John Muir (1838–1914) and Aldo Leopold (1886–1948), argued that humans are not above nature but a part of it. Nature is not for humans to subdue but is sacred and should be preserved not simply for economic use but for its own sake—and for what people can learn from it.

Science and the Environment Rachel Carson's 1962 best-selling book, *Silent Spring,* helped ignite the modern environmental movement by alerting the public to the dangers of unrestricted pesticide use.[18] Carson brought together the findings of toxicology, ecology, and epidemiology in a form accessible to the public. Blending scientific, moral, and political arguments, she connected environmental politics and values with scientific knowledge.

Barry Commoner's *Science and Survival* (1963) continued in this vein. Commoner expanded the scope of ecology to include everything in the physical, chemical, biological, social, political, economic, and philosophical worlds.[19] He argued that all of these elements fit together and have to be understood as a whole. According to Commoner, the symptoms of environmental problems are in the biological world, but their source lies in economic and political organizations.

Economics and the Environment

Economists promote growth for many reasons: to restore the balance of payments, to make nations more competitive, to create jobs, to reduce the deficit, to provide for the elderly and the sick, and to reduce poverty. Environmentalists criticize economics for its notions of efficiency and its emphasis on economic growth.[20] For example, environmentalists argue that economists do not adequately consider the unintended side effects of efficiency such as negative production externalities, which occur when a firm's production harms the environment or reduces the well-being of others who receive no benefit. Environmentalists hold that economists need to supplement estimates of the economic costs and benefits of growth with estimates of other factors that historically were not measured in economic terms.[21]

Economists and public policy analysts argue that the benefits of eliminating risk to the environment and to people must be balanced against the costs. Reducing risk involves determining how effective the proposed methods of reduction are likely to be and how much they will cost. There are many ways to consider cost factors. Analysts can perform cost-effectiveness analyses, in which they attempt to figure out how to achieve a given goal with limited resources, or they can conduct more formal risk–benefit and cost–benefit analyses, in which they quantify both the benefits and the costs of risk reduction.[22]

Qualitative Judgments in Cost–Benefit Analysis

Formal, quantitative approaches to balancing costs and benefits do not eliminate the need for qualitative judgments. For example, how does one assess the value of a magnificent vista obscured by air pollution? What is the loss to society if a particular genetic strain of grass or animal species becomes extinct? How does one assess the lost opportunity costs of spending vast amounts of money on air pollution that could have been spent on productivity enhancement and global competitiveness?

Fairness cannot be ignored when doing cost–benefit analysis.[23] For example, the costs of air pollution reduction may have to be borne disproportionately by the poor in the form of higher gasoline and automobile prices. Intergenerational fairness also plays a role.[24] Future generations have no representatives in the current market and political processes. To what extent should the current generation hold back on its own consumption for the sake of posterity? This question is particularly poignant because

few people in the world today are well off. To ask the poor to reduce their life's chances for the sake of a generation yet to come is asking for a great sacrifice.

International Perspectives Environmental problems present a different face in various countries and regions of the world. The United States and Great Britain lagged behind Germany and Japan in mandated emissions standards.[25] In Europe, the Dutch, the Germans, and the Danes are among the most environmentally conscious. Italy, Ireland, Spain, Portugal, and Greece are in earlier stages of developing environmental policies. Poland, Hungary, the Czech Republic, and former East Germany are among the most polluted of the world's industrialized nations.[26]

U.S. companies need to realize that there is a large market in western Europe for environmentally friendly products. U.S. managers also need to be fully aware of the environmental movement in western Europe. Environmentalists in Europe have been successful in halting many projects, and consumers generally have been much more resistant to genetically modified foods than in the United States.[27] China has been paying a high ecological price for its rapid economic growth. In addition to widespread thick smog in many Chinese cities, it is estimated that a fifth of the country's agricultural land and 60 percent of its groundwater are polluted. In 2014, China's Environmental Protection Law was strengthened to more effectively address these problems.[28]

WHAT MANAGERS CAN DO

To be truly green—that is, a cutting-edge company with respect to environmental concerns—legal compliance is not enough. Progressive companies stay abreast and ahead of the laws by going beyond marginal compliance and anticipating future requirements and needs.[29] But companies can go further still by experimenting continually with innovations that protect the environment. McDonald's, for example, conducted tests and pilot projects in composting food scraps and in offering refillable coffee mugs and starch-based (biodegradable) cutlery.[30]

Systems Thinking

The first thing managers can do to understand environmental issues in their companies better is to engage in systems thinking. Environmental considerations relate to the organization's inputs, processes, and outputs.[31] Inputs include raw materials and energy. Environmental pressures are causing prices of some raw materials, such as metals, to rise. This greatly increases the costs of production. Higher energy costs are causing firms to switch to more efficient sources.

Firms are considering new processes or methods of production that will reduce water pollution, air pollution, noise and vibration, and waste. They are incorporating technologies that sample and monitor (control) these by-products of business processes. Chemical plants have computerized systems that flash warnings when a maximum allowable pollution level is soon to be reached. Many companies keep only minimal stocks of hazardous materials, making serious accidents less likely.

Outputs have environmental impact, whether the products themselves or the waste or by-products of processes. To reduce the impact of its outputs, Herman Miller recycles or reuses nearly all waste from the manufacturing process. It sells fabric scraps to the auto industry, leather trim to luggage makers, and vinyl to stereo and auto manufacturers. It buys back its old furniture, refurbishes it, and resells it. Its corporatewide goal is to send zero waste to landfills. As their environmental manager stated, "There is never an acceptable level of waste at Miller. There are always new things we can learn."[32]

Strategic Integration Systems thinking reveals that environmental issues permeate the firm and therefore should be addressed in a comprehensive, integrative fashion. Start with the proper mind-set. Does your firm see environmental concerns merely in terms of a business versus environment trade-off, or does it see a potential source of competitive advantage and an important part of a strategy for long-term success? The latter attitude, of course, is more likely to set the stage for the following strategic actions.

These ideas help integrate environmental considerations strategically into the firm's ongoing activities:[33]

1. *Develop a mission statement and strong values supporting environmental advocacy.* See P&G, Starbucks, Bayer, or other examples online.

2. *Establish a framework for managing environmental initiatives.* Some industries have created voluntary codes of environmental practice, such as the chemical industry's Responsible Care Initiative. Not all standard practices are adopted by all companies, however.[34] At J&J, Environmental Regulatory Affairs uses external audit teams to conduct environmental audits.[35] The Community Environmental Responsibility Program includes strategy and planning and the development of products and processes with neutral environmental impact.

3. *Engage in green process and design.* Herman Miller's leading Aeron desk chair had 200 components made from more than 800 chemical compounds. Upon learning this, it created the award-winning Mirra desk chair, using far fewer materials that are 96 percent recyclable.[36] The surface of Chicago City Hall's landscaped green roof is 70 degrees cooler in the summer than those of nearby buildings, and the air temperature just above is 15 degrees cooler. Green roofs help clean the air, serve as a wildlife habitat, and absorb and filter rain that would otherwise flood storm drains and streets.[37]

4. *Establish environmentally focused stakeholder relationships.* The E3 Initiative is a coordinated federal and local technical assistance initiative that helps manufacturers adapt and thrive in a sustainability era. It became official in September 2010. To defray costs as well as develop new ideas, small companies such as WHYCO Chromium Company establish environmental management partnerships with firms such as IBM and GM.[38]

5. *Provide internal and external education.* Engage employees in environmental actions. Dow's WRAP

program has cut millions of pounds of hazardous and solid waste and emissions and achieved annual cost savings of over $10 million, all through employee suggestions.[39] At the same time, inform the public of your firm's environmental initiatives. For example, ecolabeling can urge consumers to recycle and communicate the environmental friendliness of your product. But don't greenwash—that is, engage in deceptive communication practices that do not accurately reflect the company's behavior.[40]

Implementation How can companies implement greening strategies? One tactic you read about in the chapter is life-cycle analysis.[41] That and other approaches begin with a commitment by top management. Specific actions could include commissioning an environmental audit in which an outside company checks for environmental hazards, drafting (or reviewing) the organization's environmental policy, communicating the policy and making it highly visible throughout the organization, having environmental professionals within the company report directly to the president or CEO, allocating sufficient resources to support the environmental effort, and building bridges between the organization and other companies, governments, environmentalists, and local communities.

Companies can employ all areas of the organization to meet the challenges posed by pollution and environmental challenges. A variety of companies have responded creatively to these challenges[42] and may serve as models for other organizations. The following sections describe specific actions companies can take to address environmental issues.

Strategy Actions companies can take in the area of strategy include the following:

1. *Cut back on environmentally unsafe businesses.* DuPont, the leading producer of CFCs, voluntarily pulled out of this $750 million business.[43]

2. *Carry out R&D on environmentally safe activities.* GM is spending millions to develop hydrogen-powered cars that don't emit carbon dioxide. GE is doing research on earth-friendly hydrogen and lower-emission locomotives and jet engines.[44]

3. *Develop and expand environmental cleanup services.* Building on the expertise gained in cleaning up its own plants, Du Pont formed a safety and environmental resources division to help industrial customers clean up their toxic wastes.[45] Global Research Technologies LLC is trying to use solvents to grab carbon dioxide out of the air to isolate it for disposal.[46]

4. *Compensate for environmentally risky projects.* AES has a long-standing policy of planting trees to offset its power plants' carbon emission.[47]

5. *Make your company accountable to others.* Royal Dutch Shell and Bristol-Myers Squibb are trendsetters in green reporting.[48] Danish health care and enzymes company Novo Nordisk purposely asked for feedback from environmentalists, regulators, and other

interested bodies from around Europe. Its reputation has been enhanced, its people have learned a lot, and new market opportunities have been identified.[49]

6. *Make every new product environmentally better than the last.* Intel is developing ultra-energy-efficient chips.[50] IBM uses recyclable materials, reduces hazardous materials, reduces emissions, and uses natural energy and resources in packaging.[51]

7. *Invest in green businesses.* American Electric Power Co. invested in renewable energy in Chile and retrofitted Bulgarian schools for greater efficiency.[52]

Public affairs In the area of public affairs, companies can take a variety of actions:

1. *Attempt to gain environmental legitimacy and credibility.* The cosponsors of Earth Day included Apple Computer, Hewlett-Packard, and the Chemical Manufacturers Association. McDonald's has tried to become a corporate environmental educator. Ethel M. Chocolates, in public tours of its Las Vegas factory, showcases effective handling of its industrial wastes. 1% for the Planet has inspired members of the business community to contribute 1 percent of sales to environmental groups around the world.[53]

2. *Work to improve standing in the Dow Jones Sustainability Index,* which assesses the sustainability performance of the largest companies on the Dow Jones Global Total Stock Market Index. Companies are evaluated on long-term economic, social, and environmental asset management plans.

3. *Try to avoid losses caused by insensitivity to environmental issues.* As a result of Exxon's apparent lack of concern after the *Valdez* oil spill, 41 percent of Americans polled said they would consider boycotting the company.[54] MacMillan Bloedel lost a big chunk of sales almost overnight when it was targeted publicly as a clear-cutter and chlorine user.[55] The BP Gulf oil spill in 2010 was a disaster on many levels, including the company's inadequate and insensitive communications with the public.

4. *Collaborate with environmentalists.* Executives at Pacific Gas & Electric seek discussions and joint projects with any willing environmental group.

The legal area Actions companies can take in the legal area include the following:

1. *Try to avoid confrontation with state or federal pollution control agencies.* Browning-Ferris, Waste Management Inc., and Louisiana-Pacific were charged with pollution control violations, damaging their reputations.

2. *Comply early.* Because compliance costs only increase over time, the first companies to act will have lower costs. The European Union's Restriction of Hazardous Substances Directive, which regulates the use of lead in electronics products, took effect in July 2006. Hewlett-Packard realized in the previous decade that lead is toxic and governments would one day ban lead

solders. Experiments begun in the early 1990s led to new solders that are an amalgam of tin, silver, and copper. HP was able to comply with the directive immediately, long before others. HP and Cisco try to comply with the most stringent legal standards in the world, thus positioning themselves to be ahead of the requirements of other countries.[56]

3. *Take advantage of innovative compliance programs.* The EU started a carbon-cutting and trading system in 2005.[57] Instead of source-by-source reduction, the EPA's bubble policy allows factories to reduce pollution at different sources by different amounts, provided the overall result is equivalent. Therefore, 3M installed equipment on only certain production lines at its tape-manufacturing facility in Pennsylvania, thereby lowering its compliance costs.[58] *Joint implementation* involves companies in industrialized nations working with businesses in developing countries to help them reduce greenhouse gas emissions. The company lending a hand then receives credit toward fulfilling its environmental obligations at home. The developing country receives investment, technology, and jobs; the company giving a lending hand receives environmental credits; and the world gets cleaner air.[59]

4. *Don't deal with fly-by-night subcontractors for waste disposal.* They are more likely to cut corners, break laws, and do a poor job. Moreover, the result for you could be bad publicity and legal problems.[60]

Operations The actions companies can take in the area of operations include the following:

1. *Promote new manufacturing technologies.* Louisville Gas and Electric took the lead in installing smokestack scrubbers, Consolidated Natural Gas pioneered the use of clean-burning technologies, and Nucor developed state-of-the-art steel mills.

2. *Practice reverse logistics.* Firms move packaging and other used goods from the consumer back up the distribution channel to the firm. Make them not just costs but a source of revenue—inputs to production. Fuji Australia believes that remanufacturing has generated returns in the tens of millions of dollars.[61]

3. *Encourage technological advances that reduce pollution from products and manufacturing processes.* Cinergy and AEP are working on technologies that capture carbon as coal is burned and pump it deep into the ground to be stored for thousands of years.[62] 3M's Pollution Prevention Pays has saved the company approximately $1.2 billion.[63] Pollution prevention, more than pollution control, is related to both better environmental performance and better manufacturing performance, including cost and speed.[64]

4. *Develop new product formulations.* The Chicago Transit Authority and Union Pacific Corporation replaced traditional wood railroad ties with plastic ties. Other companies experimented with making recycled cross-ties of old tires, grocery bags, milk jugs, and

Styrofoam cups.[65] Weyerhaeuser, recognizing the decreasing supply of timber and growing demand, is working to produce high-quality wood on fewer, continuously regenerated acres.[66] Electrolux has developed a sun-powered lawn mower and a chainsaw that runs on vegetable oil.[67]

5. *Eliminate manufacturing wastes.* The city of San Francisco has targeted zero waste by 2020. 3M replaced volatile solvents with water-based ones, thereby eliminating the need for costly air pollution control equipment. DuPont, consistent with its "zero waste" commitment, shed its carpet and nylon businesses, in part because of their big eco-footprints.[68] Walmart's Sustainability 360 established goals to purchase 100 percent renewable energy, create zero waste, and slash greenhouse gas emissions.[69]

6. *Reduce waste and recycle.* In Canada, most beer bottles are refillable, and return rates approach 100 percent.[70] Most bottles are reused 15 to 20 times before recycling. FedEx has developed dozens of software programs to optimize aircraft schedules and flight routes and uses hybrid vans and efficient aircraft to reduce fuel consumption.[71]

7. *Find alternative uses for wastes.* When DuPont halted ocean dumping of acid iron salts, it discovered that the salts could be sold to water treatment plants at a profit. A Queensland sugarcane facility powers production via sugarcane waste.[72]

8. *Insist that your suppliers have strong environmental performance.* Scott Paper discovered that many of its environmental problems were imported through the supply chain. Scott dropped the worst performers and announced that the best performers would in the future receive preference in its purchasing decisions.[73] Unilever will soon be purchasing palm oil and tea exclusively from sustainable sources.[74] Staples gets materials for most of its paper-based products from sustainable-yield forests.[75] McDonald's shows its commitment to global fish stocks because the Marine Stewardship Council certifies that its Filet-O-Fish sandwiches use fish from sustainable fisheries.[76]

9. *Assemble products with the environment in mind.* Make them easy to snap apart, sort, and recycle, and avoid glues and screws.

Marketing Companies can also take action in the marketing area:

1. *Cast products in an environment-friendly light.* Most Americans believe a company's environmental reputation influences what they buy.[77] Seventh Generation Products are not tested on animals, are kosher-certified, and use hydrogen peroxide rather than chlorine bleach and plant-derived cleaning agents rather than petroleum-based cleaners. A Chinese entrepreneur is making underwear out of soybean by-products.[78] Other eco-friendly fibers are made from hemp and bamboo, which require little pesticide.

2. *Avoid attacks by environmentalists for unsubstantiated or inappropriate claims.* When Hefty marketed biodegradable garbage bags, that claim was technically true, but it turned out that landfill conditions didn't allow decomposition to occur.[79] The extensive public backlash affected not only Hefty bags but also other Hefty products. Hefty didn't lie, but it did exaggerate. Its tactics overshadowed well-intentioned greening actions.

3. *Differentiate your product via environmental services.* Teach customers how to use and dispose of products; for instance, farmers inadvertently abuse pesticides. Make education part of a firm's after-sales service. Waste Management, formerly just a waste-trucking company, set up a unit to generate value from waste; it now shows customers how to reduce waste and recover value from waste.[80]

4. *Take advantage of the net.* The EcoMall (www.ecomall.com/biz/) promotes a number of environmentally oriented firms. Firms can target green consumers globally, effectively, and efficiently.[81]

Accounting Actions companies can take in the accounting area include the following:

1. *Collect useful data.* The best reporters of environmental information include Dow Europe, Danish Steel, BSO/Origin, 3M, and Monsanto.[82]

2. *Make polluters pay.* CIBA-GEIGY has a "polluter pays" principle throughout the firm, so managers have the incentive to combat pollution at the sources they can influence.[83]

3. *Demonstrate that antipollution programs pay off.* 3M's Pollution Prevention Pays program is based on the premise that only if the program pays will there be the motivation to carry it out. Every company needs to be cost-effective in its pollution reduction efforts.

4. *Use an advanced waste accounting system.* Do this in addition to standard management accounting, which can hinder investment in new technologies. Waste accounting makes sure all costs are identified and better decisions can be made.

5. *Adopt full-cost accounting.* This approach ensures that the price of a product reflects its full environmental cost.[84] Puma, of the French PPR Group (which includes Yves Saint Laurent and Stella McCartney among others), commissioned PricewaterhouseCoopers to develop the EP&L statement, calling it "hard-nosed economics."[85]

6. *Show the overall impact of the pollution reduction program.* Companies have an obligation to account for the costs and benefits of their pollution reduction programs. 3M has saved billions from pollution prevention efforts.

Finance In the area of finance, companies can do the following:

1. *Gain the respect of the socially responsible investment community.* Deutsche Asset Management, CalPERS, and Nikko Asset management are integrating sustainability into investment decision making in all asset classes.[86] The Ariel Fund screens for environmental impact, tobacco, weapons, nuclear energy, and lack of diversity. Orientation has shifted from negative (problem companies) to positive (companies that are most environmentally viable in the long run). Terminology has shifted from "socially responsible" companies to "sustainable investing."[87]

2. *Recognize true liability.* Investment houses often employ environmental analysts who search for companies' true environmental liability in evaluating their potential performance. Bankers look at environmental risks and environmental market opportunities when evaluating a company's credit rating.[88] The Securities and Exchange Commission in New York requires some companies to report certain environmental costs.

3. *Fund and then assist green companies.* Ann Winblad was one of the first venture capitalists to coach green entrepreneurs to increase their business skills and chances of success.[89]

4. *Recognize financial opportunities.* Worldwide, one of these great opportunities is water. Water must be purified and delivered reliably to everyone worldwide. Billions of people lack sanitary sewage facilities and have poor access to drinking water. Infrastructures in big cities, including those in the United States, are seriously deteriorating. Supplying clean water to people and companies is a huge industry. Companies are aggressively pursuing this market. They are betting that water in the 21st century will be like oil in the 20th century.

KEY TERMS

carrying capacity   The ability of a finite resource to sustain a population, p. 167

conservation   The environmental destruction that results as individuals and businesses consume finite resources (the commons) to serve their short-term interests without regard for the long-term consequences, p. 167

environmental movement   An environmental philosophy that seeks to avoid waste, promote the rational and efficient use of natural resources, and maximize long-term yields, especially of renewable resources, p. 167

tragedy of the commons   An environmental philosophy postulating that the unintended negative effects of human economic activities on the environment are often greater than the benefits, and that nature should be preserved, p. 167

DISCUSSION QUESTIONS

1. To what extent can and should we rely on government to solve environmental problems? What are some of government's limitations? Take a stand on the role and usefulness of government regulations on business activities.

2. To what extent should managers today be responsible for cleaning up mistakes from years past that have hurt the environment?

3. How would you characterize the environmental movement in western Europe? How does it differ from the U.S. movement? What difference will this make to a multinational company that wants to produce and market goods in many countries?

4. What business opportunities can you see in meeting environmental challenges? Be specific.

5. You are appointed environmental manager of XYZ Company. Describe some actions you will take to address environmental challenges. Discuss obstacles you are likely to encounter in the company and how you will manage them.

6. Interview a businessperson about environmental regulations and report your findings to the class. How would you characterize his or her attitude? How constructive is his or her attitude?

7. Interview a businessperson about actions he or she has taken that have helped the environment. Report your findings to the class and discuss.

8. Identify and discuss some examples of the tragedy of the commons. How can the tragedies be avoided?

9. Discuss the status of recycling efforts in your community or school, your perspectives on it as a consumer, and what business opportunities could be available.

10. What companies currently come to mind as having the best and worst reputations with respect to the environment? Why do they have these reputations?

11. Choose one product and discuss its environmental impact through its entire life cycle.

12. What are you, your college or university, and your community doing about the environment? What would you recommend doing?

CHAPTER 6

International Management

It was once said that the sun never set on the British Empire. Today, the sun does set on the British Empire, but not on the scores of global empires, including those of IBM, Unilever, Volkswagen, and Hitachi.

—LESTER BROWN

Management in Action

HOW LENOVO IS BECOMING A GLOBAL BRAND

Sales in China have fueled growth that propelled Lenovo onto the world stage. Today, the electronics company led by chief executive Yang Yuanqing is the world's largest PC maker. With its recent acquisition of IBM's low-end server unit, Lenovo will compete directly with Hewlett-Packard in computers and servers. *The Wall Street Journal* has called Lenovo "the first Chinese global consumer brand."

Until 2005, Lenovo was a Chinese manufacturer serving Chinese customers. But China is a huge marketplace, and sales there brought in a lot of revenue as the company developed its expertise in the high-tech sector. That cash came in handy when IBM decided to get out of the business of selling laptop computers. Lenovo surprised the Western world by purchasing IBM's laptop division, including the ThinkPad brand name.

© Justin Chin/Bloomberg via Getty Images

Lenovo assumed it would need Western-style management to compete in the West, so it hired an American executive to run the laptop business. But by 2009, sales had slumped. Businesses, which had been the ThinkPad's main customers, were cutting back in the Great Recession, and Lenovo lacked strong relationships with retailers. Yang, who rose through the ranks after starting as a Lenovo salesperson, took back the reins with one of Lenovo's founders, Liu Chuanzhi, who returned as chair. Together, they crafted Lenovo's strategy for international expansion—start by targeting fast-growing developing economies and use the revenues to enter additional markets as the brand and company strengthened.

Lenovo focused on expanding its presence through retailers in the BRIC nations, Brazil, Russia, India, and China. This strategy generated sales growth in computers even while the worldwide market for PCs slumped as consumers in North America switched to tablet computers and smartphones, and European customers struggled with economic stagnation in their region. Lenovo is the top brand in the high-potential market of India, where less than 10 percent of the population owns a personal computer. Brazil, too, has a large population with rising incomes, and Lenovo expects that market to represent one of its biggest in the future.

Lenovo's strategy for smartphones is similar. In China, Lenovo is among the top brands in the biggest market for the devices. In just one recent quarter, Lenovo sold 9 million smartphones in China. The company has recently moved into India, Indonesia, and Russia, where the market for smartphones, like the market for PCs, is potentially huge. In just one year, Lenovo doubled its sales from 22 to 44 million units. While others in the PC industry are struggling in mature markets, Lenovo has recently boasted record profits, even profiting in the highly competitive market for smartphones.[1]

How well can Lenovo's commitment to meeting the needs of developing economies appeal to consumers around the world? As you read this chapter, consider what qualities of the international business environment present threats and opportunities for this company.

The direction of Lenovo's growth resembles that of many successful businesses in recent decades. The company started out by satisfying customers in a local market. As sales increased, the company began serving a larger region. Eventually, it began selling goods to and running operations in other countries. Now it boasts sales and develops managers around the globe.

Today's corporate giants—and many ambitious, creative small businesses—need employees and sales in other countries to meet their objectives. U.S. multinational corporations now employ almost one-third of their workers outside the United States, and the overseas share is growing. Sales of some product categories also are growing faster outside the United States. That's why GE, for example, earns 60 percent of its revenues outside the United States (versus 30 percent in 2000) and has over half its workforce outside the United States (54 percent, up from 46 percent in 2000).[2] Or consider Walt Disney Company. After years of negotiations, the iconic U.S. company is building a $5.5 billion theme park and resort in Shanghai. Expected to open in 2016, the deal is complex because the Chinese government insisted on Chinese ownership, but for Disney it was worthwhile because it wants to bring its brand of entertainment to China's vast population and rapidly developing economy.[3]

Because of such trends, today's managers need to be able to plan how their company will enter markets around the world. That planning begins with understanding the importance of the global economy and the opportunities and threats of the fast-changing global environment.

Managing in a (Sometimes) Flat World

The global economy matters precisely because it *is* global—because your customers, employees, and suppliers could be located anywhere in the world. Several years ago, *New York Times* columnist Thomas Friedman wrote a best seller about this phenomenon. His book, *The World Is Flat,* described how such trends as the Internet and trade agreements between more and more nations have made international business the norm today. Whether you are a large or small company looking for financing, supplies, employees, machinery, natural resources, or transportation services, you can readily go online and find the mix of price and quality that is right for you. In that way, according to Friedman, the business environment has become a level playing field—in a word, flat.

But if "flat" is taken to mean everyone has the same advantages or buys the same products, it hardly describes the real world. Internet connectivity doesn't necessarily make us more aware of every idea or interested in every global trend. Sometimes individuals go online to connect with people they already know and to buy products that are tailored to their own particular tastes. And sometimes a local government still makes it hard for a business to grow, or a community lacks the resources to encourage development. In that sense, the world is not always flat; it is often bumpy.[4] For managers, that makes the business environment more complex and exciting than ever: a global economy with threats and opportunities around the world, accompanied by a requirement to know their customers' specific needs and values, which may vary considerably from place to place.

Later in this chapter, we will describe how managers can select strategies for the world's bumpiness. But first, let's see how the ever-greater interconnection, or integration, of the world economy is shaping the way business is done today.

Implications of a Flat World

LO 1   As you will see later in the chapter, increasing prosperity and the lowering of trade barriers have increased the extent to which the economies of different nations are integrated into one global economy. The increasing integration of the global economy has had many consequences. First, even as the world's economic output has grown, the volume of exports has increased much faster. The severe global recession of 2009 caused a one-year dip in output and trade, but exports surged the following year and have continued to climb since then.[5] Years of emphasis on international commerce by major industrial countries, liberalized trading brought about by free trade agreements, and market reforms in China have resulted in lowering the barriers to the free flow of goods, services, and capital among nation–states. The impact of these trends is staggering. The dollar value of international trade (merchandise exports and commercial services) is over $18.8 trillion—up from just a few hundred billion dollars in the 1960s and 1970s. For example, Exhibit 6.1 shows how international trade of the United States (exports of goods and services) increased relative to the country's output since the 1990s. Despite some dips during recessions, the percentage of goods and services exported to other countries has risen from 10 percent to 14 percent of U.S. gross domestic product. And for durable goods (manufactured goods such as computers and machinery designed to last for several years), more than 20 percent of these products shipped are now exports. Most experts expect competition to increase as trade is liberalized, and as is often the case, the more efficient players will survive. To succeed in this industrial climate, managers need to study opportunities in existing markets as well as work to enhance the competitiveness of their firms.

A second consequence of increased global integration is that foreign direct investment (FDI) is playing an ever-increasing role in the global economy as companies of all sizes invest overseas. In 2013, global FDI inflows reached nearly $1.5 trillion (a 9 percent increase over 2012), with relatively larger increases to firms in developing countries.[6] While the United States attracted $188 billion in investments in 2013, China, Russia, Hong Kong, and Brazil received a total of $344 billion in the same year.[7] In recent years, the United States has received more foreign direct investment than any other country.[8] To give two examples, Deutsche Boerse, a German provider of securities trading, arranged to buy the parent company of the New York Stock Exchange, and a Chinese company called Geely bought the Volvo business unit from Ford Motor Company.[9] In recent years, China's role as an export powerhouse has allowed the Chinese government to amass about $1 trillion in foreign exchange reserves, of which it is expected to invest hundreds of billions of dollars.[10]

A third consequence of an increasingly integrated global economy is that imports are penetrating deeper into the world's largest economies. For example, high percentages of the clothing and textile products, paper, cut diamonds, and electronics consumed in the United States are imported. Until recently, most of the canned peaches sold in the United States were cling peaches grown in California, but China's share of this market has been skyrocketing and now represents more than 1 out of every 10 cans sold. And in the automobile industry, over half of the new cars sold in the United States in 2014 were from automakers based in other countries, primarily in Asia.[11] Exhibit 6.2 shows how the world

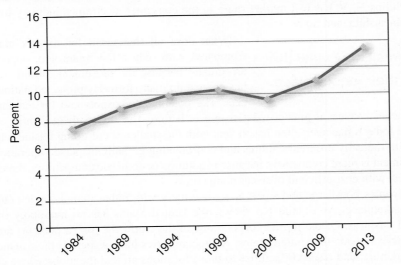

EXHIBIT 6.1

U.S. Exports as a Share of U.S. GDP (goods and services)

SOURCE: World Bank, "World Development Indicators," World DataBank, http://databank.worldbank.org.

EXHIBIT 6.2

Relative Growth in World
Merchandise Exports by
Major Product Group,
1950–2011

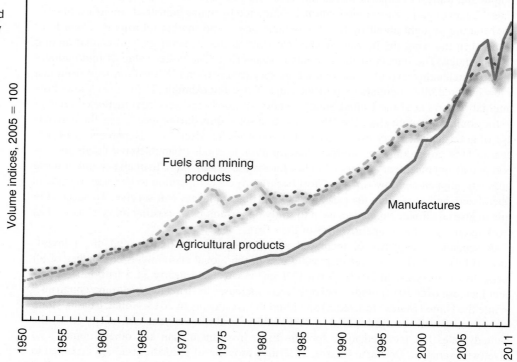

SOURCE: World Trade Organization, "Appendix: Historical Trends," *International Trade Statistics 2012,* Table A1,
p. 204, available at http://www.wto.org.

trade of manufactured merchandise has grown relative to other product groups. The growth
of imports is a natural by-product of the growth of world trade and the trend toward the
manufacture of component parts, or even entire products, overseas before shipping them
back home for final sale.

Finally, the growth of world trade, FDI, and imports implies that companies around the
globe are finding their home markets under attack from foreign competitors. This is true
in the United States, where Japanese automakers have captured market share from General
Motors, Ford, and Chrysler, and in western Europe, where the once-dominant Dutch company Philips N. V. has lost market share in the consumer electronics industry to Japan's
JVC, Matsushita, and Sony.

> Companies both large and small now view the
> world as their marketplace.

What does all this mean for today's managers?
Compared with only a few years ago, opportunities
are greater because the movement toward free trade
has opened up many formerly protected national markets. The potential for export and for making direct
investments overseas is greater today than ever before. The environment is more complex
because today's manager often has to deal with the challenges of doing business in countries with radically different cultures and coordinating globally dispersed operations. The
environment is more competitive because in addition to domestic competitors, the manager
must deal with cost-efficient overseas competitors.

Companies both large and small now view the world, rather than a single country, as
their marketplace. As Exhibit 6.3 shows, the United States has no monopoly on international business. Of the top 25 corporations in the world, 18 (or 72 percent) are based
in countries outside the United States. Also, companies have dispersed their manufacturing, marketing, and research facilities to those locations around the globe where cost and
skill conditions are most favorable. This trend is now so pervasive in industries such as

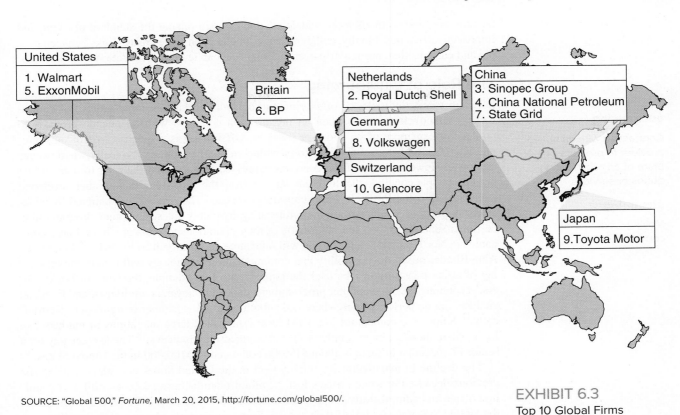

SOURCE: "Global 500," *Fortune,* March 20, 2015, http://fortune.com/global500/.

EXHIBIT 6.3
Top 10 Global Firms

automobiles, aerospace, and electronics that it is becoming increasingly irrelevant to talk about "American products" or "Japanese products" or "German products."

For example, the headquarters of an automaker no longer says much about where a particular car is made. According to the National Highway Traffic Safety Administration, the 2014 Ford F-150 and 2014 Honda Ridgeline tied for first place for being the "most American"; each had 75 percent content from the United States or Canada, and was assembled in the United States.[12] A U.S. headquarters doesn't limit a U.S. car company either. General Motors reports that it employs more people, sells more cars, and sees its best growth prospects outside the United States.[13]

Such internationalization is not limited to the largest corporations. An increasing number of medium-size and small firms also engage in international trade. Some companies have limited their involvement to exporting, whereas others source from or set up production facilities overseas. New York Dehli started off as a local spice business in London. Nina Uppal, the founder, decided to branch out and begin exporting spiced nuts and snacks. Within three years, exports increased from 2 to 45 percent of total sales. The flavorful nuts and snacks are marketed to airlines, bars, and hotels in 25 different countries.[14] In another example, Cakes and Kids, a party supply company in Concord, California, purchases products from vendors in China. The owner, Julie Degnan, sources products from overseas due to lower price points (higher profit margins) and a greater variety of products.[15]

Some of the reasons managers collaborate with their overseas counterparts on trade are obvious. Other countries offer expanded markets for one's own products. In turn, they might have natural resources, products, or cost structures that managers need but that aren't available in the home country. But there are other, perhaps less obvious, benefits to collaborating with other countries on trade. Because trade allows each country to obtain more efficiently what it cannot as easily produce on its own, it lowers prices overall and makes more goods more widely available. This in turn raises living standards—and may broaden the market for a manager's own products, both locally and abroad. Trade also makes new technologies and methods more widely available, again raising the standard of living and improving efficiency. Finally, collaborating with others on trade creates links between people and cultures that, particularly over the long run, can lead to cooperation in other areas.

The Role of Outsourcing

outsourcing

Contracting with an outside provider to produce one or more of an organization's goods or services.

offshoring

Moving work to other countries.

In recent years, the issues of offshoring and outsourcing have become sources of controversy. **Outsourcing** occurs when an organization contracts with an outside provider to produce one or more of its goods or services. **Offshoring** is a specific type of outsourcing whereby companies move jobs to providers in another country, typically where wages are lower. However, most of the concerns expressed about offshoring refer to outsourcing because people conclude that high-paying jobs from the United States and other developed countries are being lost to low-cost countries overseas. The concern is prompted by widespread reports of major corporations relocating assembly lines, computer programming, customer service centers, and other parts of their operations to India or China. Large companies in North America and Europe will outsource 3.7 million jobs by 2017.[16] Economist Alan Blinder raised the possibility that communication technology will lead to the offshoring of at least 30 million jobs over the longer term. For example, the work of bookkeepers, accounting clerks, computer programmers, data entry keyers, radiologists, and financial analysts can be performed anywhere and submitted to the customer or employer electronically.[17] Some tech companies like IBM have established large operations in markets like India where there's a large supply of IT and engineering graduates.[18] The average pay for a senior IT specialist in India is about $17,000 compared to $100,000 in the United States.[19]

The decline in manufacturing employment in the United States is evident. During the previous decade, the United States lost 2 million manufacturing jobs as well as 1.6 million office and administrative support jobs. During the recession in 2009, more workers in the United States were laid off than abroad. Some economists blame certain conditions in the United States for making the business climate relatively unfavorable: taxes, declining infrastructure, inadequate education, and barriers to hiring skilled immigrant workers.[20] However, considerable evidence suggests that the cause of this job decline is not offshoring but innovation. Because of new technology and processes, managers simply need fewer workers to produce the same quantity of goods. Even as manufacturing employment has declined, manufacturing output in the United States has grown. In addition, technology and trade enable the creation of new jobs. Even as manufacturing jobs have been lost, the United States has gained millions of new jobs, including 3.2 million service jobs, 2.5 million professional jobs, and 1.3 million managerial jobs. Thus the important question may not be how to prevent offshoring from taking jobs but how to prepare the workforce for the types of jobs that will be needed in the United States of the future—jobs requiring personal interaction (such as the work of doctors or counselors), hands-on activity (plumbers, janitors), and tailoring to particular situations (identifying clients' needs rather than following a routine).[21]

The statistics on offshoring often overlook that the job transfers from offshoring represent a small fraction of the 135 million jobs in the United States. Most jobs require workers to be close to their markets—people still shop at their local supermarkets and appliance dealers, visit their doctors, and attend a community school. Perhaps most important, as offshoring increases efficiency, it frees funds for expansion and additional employment. The challenge is primarily one in which individual workers are deeply affected when their jobs are lost. Some organizations determine that they have a social responsibility to participate in retraining programs to help these displaced workers identify and prepare for jobs that are less likely to move overseas. The controversy over offshoring also overlooks the extent to which foreign companies hire workers in the United States—for example, InBev (owner of Anheuser-Busch), Toyota, Tata Group, and Nestlé are all large employers. In fact, it is estimated that these and other foreign-owned firms employ 5.3 million Americans.[22]

One less positive effect of offshoring has been wage stagnation in industries where offshoring is common because workers in those areas compete with their lower-wage counterparts abroad. On the other hand, wages, energy costs, and other expenses in some of those other countries have started to rise, reducing the benefits of offshoring.[23] Some firms have looked for lower costs outside India and China by heading for Bangladesh, Vietnam, and Indonesia, whereas others are testing the potential of operations in African countries.

In recent years, automation has reduced the percentage of product costs that can be attributed to labor, making it less necessary to consider moving jobs overseas. Also, managers who offshore to achieve wage savings are often surprised by increasing wage rates and the unexpected additional costs in travel, training, supply chain disruption, quality control, language barriers, and the resistance of some customers who prefer to deal with local personnel. These drawbacks, along with political pressure, have led some companies to engage in **inshoring,** or moving work back to the United States. For example, a large domestic insurer may stop using a call center in Bangalore in favor of one based in the United States. Deloitte Consulting found that one-fourth of companies that outsourced to international locations soon after inshored the operations due to quality and cost concerns.[24]

Using the same example, if the domestic insurer were to create an internal (or in-house) call center staffed with its own employees and managers, that would be an example of **insourcing.**[25]

In short, in deciding whether to offshore, managers should not start out with the assumption that it will be cheaper for them to do so. Instead, here are some of the factors they might take into account:

What is the competitive advantage of the products they offer? If, say, rapid delivery, reliability, and customer contact are paramount, then offshoring is a less attractive option. But if the product is widely available and standardized, like a calculator, and the only competitive advantage is price, the lowest possible production cost becomes essential and offshoring becomes something managers will consider.

Is the business in its early stages? If so, offshoring may well be inappropriate because managers need to stay close to the business and its customers to solve problems and make sure everything is going according to plan. When the business is more mature, managers can afford to consider moving some operations overseas.

Can production savings be achieved locally? Automation can often achieve significant labor cost savings and eliminate the advantage of moving production abroad. Where automation savings are not feasible, as with computer call centers, then offshoring becomes a more attractive option.

Can the entire supply chain be improved? As we discussed in Chapter 2, enormous productivity savings are possible when managers develop an efficient supply chain, from suppliers to manufacturing to customers. These improvements permit both lower cost and high customer responsiveness. If the supply chain is not a major consideration, or is already highly efficient or routine, and more savings are needed, then offshoring may be one way for managers to achieve additional efficiencies.[26]

These considerations lead to a variety of decisions about where to operate. The high costs of transporting heavy appliances are one reason GE decided to move some of its appliance manufacturing back to the United States. Master Lock, based in Milwaukee, Wisconsin, also found that returning production to the United States from China had become more cost-effective. Fortunately for the company, it still had some production facilities and employees in the United States; companies that previously outsourced all production have found that their options for bringing manufacturing home are now more limited.[27]

An increasing number of American companies are outsourcing and offshoring divisions and departments of their organizations to save money. Many call centers are now located in India, where wages are still much lower than in the United States. Here is a photo of a typical call center in Hyderabad, India.

© AP Photo/Mustafa Quraishi

inshoring

Moving work from other countries back to the headquarters country. Work may be done by a domestic provider or in-house.

insourcing

Producing in-house one or more of an organization's goods or services.

The Global Environment

 As we saw in Chapter 2, an organization's external environment includes its economic, technological, legal/regulatory, demographic, social, and natural environments. When today's managers think about, for example, the economic potential of a market, the laws that protect their property, and the resources they need for making products, they should be thinking about these in terms of where the best opportunities lie anywhere in the world. The simple fact is that technology and an integrated economy are making international business inescapable. Exhibit 6.4 provides examples of current issues we will consider in each area of this international environment.

> The global economy is becoming more integrated than ever before.

The global economy is becoming more integrated than ever before. For example, the World Trade Organization (WTO), formed in 1995, now has 160 member countries involved in most of the world's trade. The newest members are Laos, Montenegro, the Russian Federation, Samoa, Tajikistan, and Vanuatu. (The International Monetary Fund, set up by the United Nations in 1945, serves a similar purpose and includes 188 countries.) The WTO provides a forum for nations to negotiate trade agreements and procedures for administering the agreements and resolving disputes. Issues that are currently under negotiation because they have been difficult for the parties to resolve include objections to environmental regulations and subsidies to farmers in developed countries, on the grounds that they conflict with free trade. To follow how these issues are playing out, you can explore the "Trade Topics" section of the WTO website, http://www.wto.org.

The global economy is dominated by countries in three regions: North America, western Europe, and Asia. However, other developing countries and regions represent important areas for economic growth as well.

European Unification

Europe is integrating economically to form the biggest market in the world. Under the Maastricht Treaty, which formally established the European Union (EU), the euro was adopted as a common currency among 13 member countries. Currencies with a long history like the franc and the mark are now relics of the past. The EU allows most goods, services, capital, and human resources to flow freely across its national borders. The EU was originally formed after World War II to foster cooperation through trade in place of military conflict, but the efforts have also created an economic superpower. Its 28 members now boast a population of more than 507 million and a GDP (gross domestic product) exceeding that of the United States.[28]

The pace of European unification accelerated in 2004 with the addition of former Eastern-bloc countries, including Poland and Hungary, and since 2007, Bulgaria, Romania,

EXHIBIT 6.4
Key Issues of the Global Environment

Economic environment	Foreign investment; growth of developing nations; rising wages in developing nations
Technological environment	Internet and wireless technology
Legal/regulatory environment	Free trade agreements; anticorruption laws
Demographics	Aging population in developed nations; growing population worldwide, especially in the developing world
Social issues	Cultural differences; bribery concerns
Natural environment	Intensifying demand for resources, including oil, water, and food; growing desire for sustainable products and operations; increasingly endangered species; climate change

and Croatia have joined. Many of these new members offer a particular challenge to full integration because as former communist countries they do not have extensive experience as modern market economies. Other even less wealthy countries—Albania, Macedonia, and Turkey—have also applied to join the EU.

In addition to the difficulty of integrating widely divergent economies, certain structural issues within Europe need to be corrected for the EU to function effectively. In particular, western Europeans on average work fewer hours, earn more pay, take longer vacations, and enjoy far more social entitlements than do their counterparts in North America and Asia. To be competitive in a global economy, Europeans must increase their level of productivity. Other problems will present even greater challenges, such as Europe's aging population, low birthrates, and low immigration, all of which are threatening to cause Europe's population to drop, even as America's is increasing. Recently, EU relationships were tested by the global financial crisis and recession, which hit some member nations harder than others. For example, Ireland, which had been enjoying impressive growth in the banking and insurance sectors, suffered the near-collapse of those industries. With tax revenues falling even as citizens needed more help, the governments of Portugal, Ireland, and Greece found themselves petitioning other EU nations for financial assistance. The economically stronger nations were reluctant to ask their own citizens to support a bailout of other countries but eventually agreed to provide loans through the EU and International Monetary Fund. That assistance is accompanied by requirements that the less stable governments bring more discipline to their spending habits. That, in the end, may make the EU even more potent than it was before.[29]

Still, unification is creating a more competitive Europe, one that U.S. managers will increasingly have to take into account. The economic difficulties in the region have brought down the costs of investing and hiring workers there, and the region boasts a highly skilled workforce. Dow Chemical, for example, has taken advantage of the opportunity to build a research center to study water desalination in Spain; in Ireland, Microsoft is building a data center, and Eli Lilly expects to erect a facility for making biopharmaceuticals. Also, companies like Netflix and Box, an online business data storage company, are expanding their presence in Europe.[30] Companies such as these are hoping Europe will recover from its financial woes, and they will be ready for the next surge in demand.[31]

The EU also presents a regulatory challenge to the United States and other countries. For example, the EU has supported excluding genetically engineered food products from American firms, over objections from the WTO. After a five-year investigation, the EU is considering slapping Google with an antitrust fine for allegedly abusing its "dominant position [80 percent] in the Internet search market to direct users to its own in-house products and services." Fines can reach up to 10 percent of a company's global revenue.[32]

The EU's more competitive and regulatory environment clearly presents new challenges to managers and their employees. Managers in U.S. companies that wish to export to that market must become more knowledgeable about the new business environment the EU is creating. Management and labor will have to work cooperatively to achieve high levels of quality to make U.S. goods and services attractive to consumers in Europe and other markets around the world. The United States needs managers who will stay on top of worldwide developments and manage high-quality, efficient organizations as well as a well-educated, well-trained, and continually *retrained* labor force to remain competitive with the Europeans and other formidable competitors.

Asia: China's and India's Ascent

Among the Pacific Rim countries, and particularly in the United States, Japan dominated world attention toward the end of the last century. Today Japan is America's fourth-largest export market, after Canada, China, and Mexico, as you can see in Exhibit 6.5. And Japan is in fourth place as a source of U.S. imports. Japanese companies such as Toyota are both a major source of goods and, as competitors, a growing influence in the ways U.S. managers seek quality and efficiency.

EXHIBIT 6.5

Top U.S. Trading Partners, Based on Total Imports and Exports

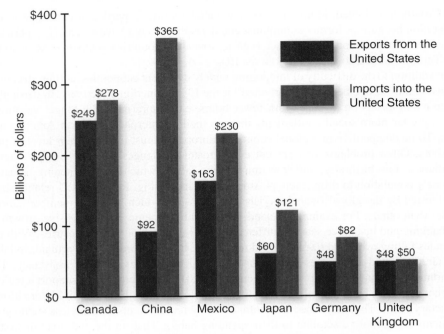

SOURCE: U.S. Bureau of the Census, *Statistical Abstract of the United States: 2012*, Table 1307, http://www.census.gov.

Today, however, a bigger force is rising in Asia: China. With the world's largest population and increasing industrialization, China is on its way to becoming the largest producer and consumer of many of the world's goods. Its large and growing demand for oil is a cost factor that managers everywhere must consider in their long-range planning. The country has also become the world's largest consumer of basic raw materials, such as steel and cement, as well as the world's largest cell phone market. Not only is China the largest source of imports to the United States (see Exhibit 6.5), but it has surged ahead of Germany to become the world's largest exporter and is the number two importer after the United States.[33]

As a consuming nation, China's appeal to managers lies in its large population of 1.37 billion people and its rapid economic growth. As more and more Chinese people earn engineering and science degrees and as labor demand pushes up wages, Chinese companies are branching out into more complex manufacturing operations, such as auto parts, optical devices, and other advanced electronics. Rising incomes create a paradox for business expansion: Newly middle-class consumers in China are purchasing more products, both foreign and domestic, and low-cost manufacturers are now looking away from China to set up operations in lower-wage countries, such as Vietnam.[34] Other companies are staying in China to serve the huge market there. General Motors, for example, is setting up research and design facilities in China so it can introduce innovations aimed at satisfying the demands of Chinese consumers, starting with battery power.[35]

Even with its growing consumption, China has had an even greater global impact in its role as an exporting nation. The enormous size of its labor force, combined with its low labor costs, has given it a competitive advantage in manufacturing. Just a few years ago, estimates place labor costs in China at less than $2.00 an hour, compared with $6.36 for manufacturing workers in Mexico and $35.67 for manufacturing workers in the United States.[36] These low wage rates led many managers to relocate operations to China or to import an increasing number and variety of Chinese products instead of continuing to do business with local manufacturers. This trend is one reason the value of U.S. imports from China is more than five times the value of U.S exports to China.

This type of trade imbalance may well have contributed to the loss of manufacturing jobs in the United States and Europe. But it has also led to the continuing availability of comparatively low-priced goods, helping consumers everywhere and leading to overall economic and job growth at home. Yet jobs in certain industries, such as textiles, may have been transferred abroad permanently to lower-cost producers such as China and India. Those affected workers and communities experience real hardships. We will be discussing the effects of outsourcing or offshoring in more detail later in this chapter.

Threats to China's growing dominance include political instability as the growing prosperity of its cities and industrial enclaves leaves millions of poor rural residents further behind. Also, countries that have experienced job loss may face growing pressure to restrict Chinese imports, particularly in the EU, with its strong labor unions. But for the foreseeable future, China's growing presence in the world economy, as an importer *and* exporter, is one that you as a manager will increasingly have to take into account.

This Chevy Volt electric car is charging in the parking lot in Shanghai at General Motors headquarters.

© Peter Parks/AFP/Getty Images

Besides China, India has become an important player in the global marketplace. The nation is still developing, and its poverty is often severe, but its 1.25 billion people (the world's second-largest population), many of them entering the working and professional classes, make India an essential market for more and more companies. For many U.S. companies, India is seen as a provider of online support for computer software, software development, and other services. In fact, so many companies have set up shop there that the demand for Indian workers with strong technical and English language skills is exceeding the supply. Companies such as Wipro, Infosys, and Tata Group are responding with expanded training programs.[37] Thanks to India's fast-growing economy and huge population, more U.S. businesses are beginning to see the country as a source of customers as well as workers. Uber, for example, plans to expand its taxi business in India. In 2015, the start-up entered into a $24 million deal with the Times of India to market the firm's services to local customers.[38]

Other rapidly growing countries in the region that have strong trade relationships with the United States include South Korea, Taiwan, and Singapore. These countries are important trading partners not merely because of their wage rates but because many of their companies have developed competitive advantages in areas such as engineering and technological know-how. South Korea's Samsung has the largest share of the world's markets for flat-screen televisions and flash memory cards, and Taiwan's Hon Hai is the leader in contract manufacturing of electronics. The reason you may not have heard of Hon Hai is that it specializes in making components for brand-name products of other companies, including Sony (PlayStations), Apple (iPods), and Dell (computers).[39]

These Asian countries and others have joined with the United States, Australia, and Russia to form the 21-member Asia-Pacific Economic Cooperation (APEC) trade group. Combined, APEC members' economies account for more than half of world output (GDP) and 54 percent of world trade.[40] In recent years, the APEC countries have been working to establish policies that encourage international commerce and reduce trade barriers. APEC members address these objectives through dialogue and nonbinding commitments rather than treaties.

Another international organization, the Association of Southeast Asian Nations (ASEAN), brings together 10 developing nations, including Indonesia, Malaysia, and the Philippines. Along with economic development, ASEAN is aimed at promoting cultural development and political security.

The Americas

North and South America constitute a mix of industrialized countries, such as Canada and the United States, as well as countries with growing economies, such as Argentina, Brazil, Chile, and Mexico. The winter fruit you eat may come from Chile, the coffee you drink from Jamaica, and the shirt you wear from Honduras. Increasingly, businesses are looking to establish freer trade among countries in the Western Hemisphere—and with other parts of the world.

The **North American Free Trade Agreement (NAFTA)** combined the economies of the United States, Canada, and Mexico into the world's largest trading bloc with nearly 444 million U.S., Canadian, and Mexican consumers and a total output of $17 trillion. By 2008, virtually all U.S. industrial exports into Mexico and Canada were duty-free. Although the United States has had a longer-standing agreement with Canada, Mexico has quickly emerged as the United States's third-largest trading partner as a result of NAFTA. U.S. industries that have benefited in the short run include capital goods suppliers, manufacturers of consumer durables, grain producers and distributors, construction equipment manufacturers, the auto industry, and the financial industry, which now has privileged access into a previously protected market. Besides importing and exporting, companies in the NAFTA countries have invested in facilities across national borders. Mexico-based CEMEX, the world's third-largest cement company, is actually the largest cement supplier in the United States. Twenty-two percent of CEMEX's employees and 27 percent of its sales are in the United States, and it conducts management meetings in English because the majority of its employees do not speak Spanish.[41]

Leading the growth following the Great Recession was Brazil, especially in the agricultural and energy sectors. Bright spots in Brazil have included the production of ethanol and potential leadership in wind power from harnessing its steady trade winds at wind farms built on land being auctioned by the government. As Brazil's economy matures, investors looking for fresh growth are turning their attention to other South American markets, including Colombia and Peru, both of which have posted solid economic growth in recent years.[42] As in Asia, more South American companies are relying on innovation and technology rather than simply cost to compete in the global marketplace. "Start-Up Chile," an innovative program to attract immigrant entrepreneurs to Chile, provides start-up funds to founders of promising businesses. Since its inception in 2010, entrepreneurs from 37 countries have participated.[43]

Other agreements have been proposed to promote trade with Central and South America. In 2005, President George W. Bush signed into law U.S. participation in a Central America–Dominican Republic–United States Free Trade Agreement (CAFTA-DR). Other nations that have agreed to participate include Costa Rica, the Dominican Republic, El Salvador, Guatemala, Honduras, and Nicaragua. CAFTA-DR creates the second-largest free trade zone with the United States (NAFTA being the largest). As part of the negotiations for CAFTA-DR, Central American nations promised to protect workers' rights in their countries. Complaints that some countries have not delivered on this promise have led the U.S. government to request consultations with Guatemala on "apparent violations of its obligations."[44] Other trade agreements have been negotiated on a country-by-country basis with Chile, Peru, Colombia, and Panama. In addition, the countries of South America formed their own trading bloc, called Mercosur, to promote trade among nations of that continent.

Africa and the Middle East

We can't begin to discuss fully all the important developments, markets, and competitors shaping the global environment. These trends leave huge and promising areas of the world—the Middle East, parts of South America, and much of Africa—that have not yet participated as much in globalization. These regions account for a major share of the world's natural resources, and managers are watching the global environment, looking for areas with potential.

The economy of the Middle East is, of course, best known for its export of oil. Although oil exploration and drilling take place in many parts of the world, the oil-rich countries of the Middle East supply by far the most oil to the world's buyers, most of it going to buyers in Asia. The main Middle Eastern supplier of U.S. oil imports is Saudi Arabia,[45] with other major suppliers being Canada, Mexico, and Venezuela. In recent years, United States' dependence on foreign oil has decreased. Since the shale oil boom in Texas, North Dakota,

Social Enterprise

Student Social Entrepreneurs Compete for $1 Million

The Hult Prize Foundation is a student business competition and start-up accelerator that awards $1 million to talented social entrepreneurs from universities around the world. The annual competition identifies and provides seed funding to promising "start-up social enterprises that tackle grave issues faced by billions of people." Each year, about 10,000 students from 150 countries around the world participate in the Hult Prize and spend over 2 million hours on solving the world's most pressing issues. Since its founding in 2009, students from 600 schools have competed for the Hult Prize. Former president Bill Clinton of the Clinton Global Initiative presents the prize money to the student winners.

Here are some recent start-ups that were awarded the Hult Prize:

NanoHealth from the Indian School of Business won for its work in providing affordable, holistic medical services for impoverished "slum-dwellers" who suffer from chronic diseases.

Sweet Bites from the University of Pennsylvania aims to improve the health and quality of life of millions of impoverished people globally who can't afford dental care. Sweet Bites is 100% xylitol chewing gum that stops the progression of tooth decay.

Bee Healthy from HEC Paris uses bees to revolutionize disease detection for underprivileged people around the world. The bees' olfactory system is used to detect diseases such as diabetes, cancer, and tuberculosis on a person's breath.

© Jason Decrow/AP Images for Hult Prize

Are student social entrepreneurs who compete for the Hult Prize making a difference? Yes. According to Muhammad Yunus, Nobel Peace Prize winner for his pioneering work in microlending: "If you can create a real business, the beginning of a prototype, you can change the world."[46]

Questions

- Of the three recent award-winning start-ups mentioned, which do you find most likely to succeed? Why?
- The Hult Prize has been awarded to new social enterprises from all over the world. Why do you think the competition has a global focus?

and Alaska, imports of foreign oil have dropped from 60 percent of overall consumption in 2005 to 32 percent in 2013.[47] Nevertheless, U.S. businesses remain concerned about the Middle East because activities there can shape the price of oil, which is important not only for transportation but also for the manufacture of many products, including fertilizer and plastic.

Africa has long been seen only as a place of dire poverty. Indeed, the continent is still plagued by an epidemic of AIDS and many unstable political situations, including outright wars. Nevertheless, a reduction in severe poverty and growth in the middle class in many countries have provided exciting opportunities for businesses willing to learn the needs of the population and make the effort of navigating a sometimes challenging environment. The nearby "Social Enterprise" box discusses how student social entrepreneurs are tackling some of the world's toughest challenges. As part of its Smarter Planet initiative (described in the "Management in Action" for Chapter 5), IBM learns about the continent's huge potential by sending in teams to help local governments solve problems. As it gets to know the region, IBM has begun selling services, setting up partnerships with local companies, and opening research facilities in Kenya, Senegal, South Africa, and other countries. Although African sales are still a small part of IBM's total, the company expects them to double over the next few years.[48]

Global Strategy

 LO 3

One of the critical tasks an international manager faces is to identify the best strategy for competing in a global marketplace. To approach this issue, managers can plot a company's position on an integration–responsiveness grid, such as that shown in Exhibit 6.6. The vertical axis measures pressures for global integration, and the horizontal axis measures pressures for local responsiveness. Borrowing language from early in this chapter, we might say that much of the pressure for global integration comes from today's business world being flat, whereas the pressure for local responsiveness reflects the world's bumpiness.

Pressures for Global Integration

Managers may have several reasons to want or need a common global strategy rather than one tailored to individual markets. These factors include the existence of universal needs, pressures to reduce costs, or the presence of competitors with a global strategy.

Universal needs create strong pressure for a global strategy. Universal needs exist when the tastes and preferences of consumers in different countries with regard to a product are similar. Products that serve universal needs require little adaptation across national markets; thus global integration is facilitated. This is the case in many industrial markets. For example, electronic products such as semiconductor chips meet universal needs. Certain basic foodstuffs (such as colas) and appliances (such as can openers) are also increasingly available and regarded in similar ways globally.

> Universal needs create strong pressure for a global strategy.

Competitive pressures to reduce costs may cause managers to seek to integrate manufacturing globally. Cost can be particularly important in industries in which price is the main competitive weapon and competition is intense (e.g., as with smartphones). It is also important if key international competitors are based in countries where labor and other operating costs are low. In these cases, products are more likely to be standardized and perhaps produced in a few locations to capture economies of scale.

The presence of competitors engaged in global strategic coordination is another factor that creates pressures for global integration. For example, a competitor that centrally coordinates the purchase of raw materials worldwide may achieve significant price reductions compared with firms that allow subsidiaries to handle purchases locally. Global competition can often create pressures to centralize in corporate headquarters certain decisions being made by different national subsidiaries. And once one multinational company adopts global strategic coordination, its competitors may be forced to do the same.

Bottom Line

The need to lower costs is a key globalization driver. *What is one way in which a global strategy can help reduce costs?*

EXHIBIT 6.6
Organizational Models

SOURCES: C. A. Bartlett and S. Ghoshal, *Managing across Borders: The Transnational Solution* (Boston: Harvard Business School Press, 1991); and A. W. Harzing, "An Empirical Analysis and Extension of the Bartlett and Ghoshal Typology of Multinational Companies," *Journal of International Business Studies* 31, no. 1 (2000), pp. 101–20.

Pressures for Local Responsiveness

In some circumstances, managers need to make sure their companies can adapt to different needs in different locations. Strong pressures for local responsiveness emerge when consumer tastes and preferences differ significantly among countries. In such cases, products and/or marketing messages have to be customized. In the automobile industry, for example, U.S. consumers' demand for pickup trucks is strong in the South and West, where many families have a pickup truck as a second or third vehicle. In contrast, in Europe pickup trucks are viewed as utility vehicles and are purchased primarily by companies rather than by individuals. As a result, automakers must tailor their marketing messages to these differences in consumer demand.

Pressures for local responsiveness also emerge when there are differences in traditional practices among countries. For example, in Great Britain people drive on the left side of the road, creating a demand for right-hand-drive cars, whereas in neighboring France, people drive on the right side of the road. Obviously, automobiles must be customized to accommodate this difference in traditional practices.

Differences in distribution channels and sales practices among countries also may create pressures for local responsiveness. L'Oréal, the French cosmetics maker, has achieved success by adapting its brands to different cultures and markets: French (L'Oréal Paris), American (Maybelline), and Italian (Giorgio Armani).[49] Cinnabon had to adjust its approach to retailing when it moved into the Middle East and Russia. The company had found customers in the United States by setting up in malls, but Middle Eastern and Russian consumers have less of a culture of entertaining themselves with a visit to the mall. So in those locations, Cinnabon shops are more likely to be storefronts in shopping districts.[50]

Finally, economic and political demands that host-country governments impose may necessitate a degree of local responsiveness. Most important, threats of protectionism, economic nationalism, and local content rules (rules requiring that a certain percentage of a product be manufactured locally) dictate that international companies manufacture locally. For example, countries may impose tariffs (taxes on imports) or quotas (restrictions on the number of imports allowed into a country) to protect domestic industries from foreign competition perceived to be unfair or not in the nation's interests. Recently, the United States began imposing tariffs on solar panels imported from China and Taiwan. The U.S. government justified the tariffs as a response to complaints that the Chinese and Taiwanese companies were selling the solar panels below the cost of the raw materials, presumably because the Chinese government was subsidizing the industry. Others interpret this and other protectionist actions as being motivated primarily by political objectives.[51] Whatever the reasons for them, tariffs and quotas influence managers' decisions about whether it is economically advantageous, or even possible, to operate locally or rely on exporting.

Choosing a Global Strategy

As Exhibit 6.6 shows, managers can use four approaches to international competition, depending on their company's position on the integration–responsiveness grid: the international model, the multinational model, the global model, and the transnational model. Organizations in each model compete globally, but they differ in the strategy they use and in the structure and systems that drive their operations.

The International Model

In the **international model,** managers use their organization's existing core capabilities to expand into foreign markets. As the grid suggests, it is most appropriate when there are few pressures for economies of scale *or* local responsiveness. Pfizer is an example of a company operating in the international model. It is in an industry that doesn't compete on cost, and its drugs obviously don't need to be tailored for local tastes. The international model uses subsidiaries in each country in which the company does business, with ultimate control exercised by the parent company. In particular, although subsidiaries may have some latitude to adapt products to local conditions, core functions such as research and development tend to be centralized in the parent company. Consequently, the dependence of subsidiaries on the parent company for new

international model

An organizational model that is composed of a company's overseas subsidiaries and characterized by greater control by the parent company over the research function and local product and marketing strategies than is the case in the multinational model.

products, processes, and ideas requires a great deal of coordination and control by the parent company.

The advantage of this model is that it facilitates the transfer of skills and know-how from the parent company to subsidiaries around the globe. For example, IBM and Xerox profited from the transfer of their core skills in technology and research and development (R&D) overseas. The overseas successes of Kellogg, Coca-Cola, Heinz, and Procter & Gamble are based more on marketing know-how than on technological expertise. Toyota and Honda successfully penetrated U.S. markets from their base in Japan with their core competencies in manufacturing relative to local competitors. Still other companies have based their competitive advantage on general management skills. These factors explain the growth of international hotel chains such as Hilton International, Intercontinental, and Sheraton.

One disadvantage of the international model is that it does not provide maximum latitude for responding to local conditions. In addition, it frequently does not provide the opportunity to achieve a low-cost position via scale economies.

The Multinational Model   Where global efficiency is not required but adapting to local conditions offers advantages, the multinational model is appropriate. The **multinational model,** sometimes referred to as *multidomestic,* uses subsidiaries in each country in which the company does business and provides a great deal of discretion to those subsidiaries to respond to local conditions. Each local subsidiary is a self-contained unit with all the functions required for operating in the host market. Thus each subsidiary has its own manufacturing, marketing, research, and human resources functions. Because of this autonomy, each multinational subsidiary can customize its products and strategies according to the tastes and preferences of local consumers; the competitive conditions; and political, legal, and social structures.

A good example of a multinational firm is Heineken, a Netherlands-based brewing company. Heineken has three major global brands—Heineken, Amstel, and Murphy's Stout—but it also offers regional and local brands. The company understands that every country is unique, with its own culture and business practices. So it attempts to adapt its products to local attitudes and tastes while maintaining its high quality. As a result, the company produces more than 170 brands around the world, from its international brands to local and specialty brews. The localized portfolio includes such brands as Primus and Star in Africa, Vitamalt and Piton in the Caribbean, and Tiger in Asia. Individual countries have considerable autonomy in the beer that is brewed locally.[52]

A major disadvantage of the multinational form is higher manufacturing costs and duplication of effort. Although a multinational can transfer core skills among its international operations, it cannot realize scale economies from centralizing manufacturing facilities and offering a standardized product to the global marketplace. Moreover, because a multinational approach tends to decentralize strategy decisions (discussed further in Chapters 8 and 9), launching coordinated global attacks against competitors is difficult. This can be a significant disadvantage when competitors have this ability.

The Global Model   The **global model** is designed to enable a company to market a standardized product in the global marketplace and to manufacture that product in a limited number of locations where the mix of costs and skills is most favorable. The global model has been adopted by companies that view the world as one market and assume that no tangible differences exist among countries with regard to consumer tastes and preferences. Procter & Gamble, for example, has been successful in Europe against Unilever because it has approached the entire continent as a unified whole. As part of its effort to improve efficiency while broadening its appeal, Ford recently launched a line of compact cars under the Ford Focus brand as the company's first truly global product. The Focus models include hybrid, plug-in hybrid, and electric cars, and promotional plans are built around a unified advertising campaign highlighting technology features.[53] The strategy is paying off. In 2012 and 2013, the Focus was the best-selling car (by units) in the world.[54]

Companies that adopt the global model tend to construct global-scale manufacturing facilities in a few selected locations so they can realize scale economies. These scale economies come from spreading the fixed costs of investments in new product development, plants and equipment, and the like over worldwide sales. By using centralized manufacturing facilities and global marketing strategies, Sony was able to push down its unit costs to the point where it became the low-cost player in the global television market. This advantage enabled Sony to take market share away from Philips, RCA, and Zenith, all of which used traditionally based manufacturing operations in each major national market (a characteristic of the multinational approach). Because operations are centralized, subsidiaries usually are limited to marketing and service functions.

On the downside, because a company pursuing a purely global approach tries to standardize its goods and services, it may be less responsive to consumer tastes and demands in different countries. Attempts to lower costs through global product standardization may result in a product that fails to satisfy anyone. For example, although Procter & Gamble has been quite successful using a global approach, the company experienced problems when it tried to market Cheer laundry detergent in Japan. Unfortunately for P&G, the product did not suds up as promoted in Japan because the Japanese use a great deal of fabric softener, which suppresses suds. Moreover, the claim that Cheer worked in all water temperatures was irrelevant in Japan, where most washing is done in cold water. The global model also requires a great deal of coordination, with significant additional management and paperwork costs.

The Transnational Model   In today's global economy, achieving a competitive advantage often requires managers to pursue local responsiveness, transfer of know-how, and cost economies simultaneously.[55] The transnational model is designed to help them do just that. It is an approach that enables managers to "think globally but act locally."

In companies that adopt the **transnational model,** functions are centralized where it makes sense to do so, but a great deal of decision making also takes place at the local level. In addition, the experiences of local subsidiaries are shared worldwide to improve the firm's overall knowledge and capabilities. For example, research, training, and the overall development of the organization's strategy and global brand image tend to be centralized at home. Other functions may be centralized as well, but not necessarily in the home country.

To achieve cost economies, companies may base global-scale production plants for labor-intensive products in low-wage countries such as Mexico, Poland, and China and locate production plants that require a skilled workforce in high-skill countries such as Germany and Japan. Increasingly, companies are able to find locations where the workforce includes the optimal balance of needed skills and relatively low costs. Thus, although wages have begun rising in India, the level of technical skill of its workforce has made that country an attractive place to locate many kinds of knowledge-based operations such as loan approvals, legal research, and biotech R&D. These types of skilled occupations are growing faster in India than jobs in call centers, the work that once brought India to prominence as an offshoring location.[56]

Marketing, service, and final assembly functions tend to be based in the national subsidiaries to facilitate greater local responsiveness. Thus major components may be manufactured in centralized production plants to realize scale economies and then shipped to local plants, where the final product is assembled and customized to fit local needs.

Panasonic's experience in China has made it more of a transnational company.[57] Panasonic, a Japanese company, initially saw China primarily as a low-cost site for manufacturing its home appliances. In the early years, Panasonic conducted extensive consumer research in Japan but none in China; it served the Chinese market by removing features to make low-cost versions of its appliances. But as China's economy developed, consumers began buying new products from Chinese producers—who were also capturing market share from Panasonic elsewhere. Panasonic's management realized it needed to see China as more than a source of cheap labor. It set up a business unit called Panasonic Corporation of China to provide research and development and marketing support, as

Management in Action

LENOVO'S GLOBAL STRATEGY

When Lenovo's chief executive, Yang Yuanqing, crafted the strategy to build outward from China, he had to consider how the company would compete in a fast-changing industry selling to developing markets. A core part of his strategy is to acquire brands that can fuel future growth. Not long after acquiring IBM's PC business, Lenovo purchased IBM's low-end server business and Motorola's mobile phone brand. Selling high-tech products requires constant innovation; selling in communities where people are newly entering the middle class requires high efficiency and low prices.

Yang and Gerry Smith, executive vice president of Lenovo's supply chain, explored the most efficient and responsive ways to make electronics. They concluded that Lenovo could win on both counts by handling more of its own manufacturing. In contrast to U.S.-based electronics companies, Lenovo does about half of its own manufacturing, outsourcing the other half. Its 4,000-employee facility in Brazil helps Lenovo cut costs, including taxes, related to serving the Latin American market. Lenovo facilities in the United States (North Carolina), Japan, and India keep production close to those regions' buyers and their needs and tastes.

The company-owned factories were an advantage when floods in Thailand interrupted production of computer hard drives. Lenovo and other computer makers competed fiercely for the limited supply. As hard drives became available, Lenovo made prompt adjustments to its production lines, focusing on the most profitable models using the hard drives available. Companies that outsourced were less agile, and Lenovo gained market share at their expense.

Another challenge is the importance of brand image. By prioritizing developing economies such as Brazil, Lenovo has the advantage of arriving early and establishing a reputation before Hewlett-Packard, Apple, and other competitors move in. In countries such as Russia and India, the company established a good reputation for PCs, which now elevates the brand's reputation in servers and smartphones. The situation is trickier when products are rolled out to developed economies such as the United States, where consumers expect their electronic devices to be exciting. In 2013, Lenovo opened its North Carolina factory, which it hopes will further raise the brand's profile in the United States.[58]

- Where in this example do you see pressures for global integration? Where do you see pressures for local responsiveness?
- Which global strategy (international, multinational, global, or transnational) do you think is most appropriate for Lenovo? Why?

well as back-office services, to the manufacturing facilities in China. It also set up the China Lifestyle Research Center to learn more about the tastes and lifestyles of Chinese consumers.

These new units formalized two-way communication. The Japanese managers shared their knowledge of technology and production efficiency. Their Chinese colleagues helped Panasonic identify and meet the needs of this huge consumer market. Managers brought together engineers from different facilities to work together on understanding how they could meet the identified needs better. As the efforts helped Panasonic develop successful new products, the company began to spread this collaborative approach to other markets—for example, by opening research centers in Germany and India. To ensure that lessons learned in one location were shared, when appropriate, to improve operations in others, Panasonic also set up a global marketing organization to share knowledge about its best practices. Such efforts are critical for Panasonic, whose performance has suffered from efforts to remain profitable in the highly competitive market for electronics such as televisions. Perhaps the most important distinguishing characteristic of the transnational organization is the fostering of communications among subsidiaries and the ability to integrate the efforts of subsidiaries when doing so makes sense. Achieving such communications across subsidiaries requires elaborate formal mechanisms, such as transnational committees staffed by people from the various subsidiaries who are responsible for monitoring coordination among subsidiaries. Equally important is to transfer managers among subsidiaries on a regular basis. This enables international managers to establish a global network of personal contacts in different subsidiaries with whom they can share information as the need arises. Finally, achieving coordination among subsidiaries requires the head office to play a proactive role in coordinating their activities.

Now that you have seen examples of the need to balance global integration and local responsiveness, consider how those pressures apply to Lenovo's situation as described in "Management in Action: Progress Report."

Entry Mode

LO 4

When considering global expansion, international managers must decide on the best means of entering an overseas market. The five basic ways to expand overseas are exporting, licensing, franchising, entering into a joint venture with a host-country company, and setting up a wholly owned subsidiary in the host country.[59] Exhibit 6.8 compares the entry modes.

Exporting

Most manufacturing companies begin global expansion as exporters and later switch to one of the other modes for serving an overseas market. The advantages of exporting are that it (1) provides scale economies by avoiding the costs of manufacturing in other countries and (2) is consistent with a pure global strategy. By manufacturing the product in a centralized location and then exporting it to other national markets, the company may be able to realize substantial scale economies from its global sales volume.

However, exporting has a number of drawbacks. First, exporting from the company's home base may be inappropriate if other countries offer lower-cost locations for manufacturing the product. An alternative is to manufacture in a location where the mix of factor costs and skills is most favorable and then export from that location to other markets to achieve scale economies. Several U.S. electronics companies have moved some manufacturing operations to parts of Asia where low-cost, high-skill labor is available and export from that location to other countries, including the United States.

A second drawback of exporting is that high transportation costs can make it uneconomical, particularly in the case of bulk products. Chemical companies get around this by manufacturing their products on a regional basis, serving several countries in a region from one facility.

Bottom Line
Exporting offers scale economies.
Can services be exported? Why or why not?

EXHIBIT 6.8
Comparison of Entry Modes

Exporting	Licensing	Franchising	Joint Venture	Wholly Owned Subsidiary
Advantages				
Scale economies	Lower development costs	Lower development costs	Local knowledge	Maintains control over technology
Consistent with pure global strategy	Lower political risk	Lower political risk	Shared costs and risk	Maintains control over operations
			May be the only option	
Disadvantages				
No low-cost sites	Loss of control over technology	Loss of control over quality	Loss of control over technology	High cost
High transportation costs			Conflict between partners	High risk
Tariff barriers				

A third drawback is that host countries can impose (or threaten to impose) tariff barriers. Trade arrangements described earlier, including the World Trade Organization, NAFTA, and APEC, work to minimize this risk. However, tariffs continue to affect trade between particular countries in various industries. Examples include U.S.-imposed tariffs on sugar imported from Mexico and, as mentioned earlier, solar panels imported from China. The U.S. government recently proposed tariffs of 18 to 81 percent on Chinese-made tires for passenger cars and light trucks after concluding that Chinese companies were dumping them in the U.S. market, or selling them below cost to gain an unfair competitive advantage.[60]

In six years, Cold Stone Creamery has expanded its franchises into 17 countries outside the United States, including South Korea, shown here.

© Kazuhiro Nogi/AFP/Getty Images

Licensing

International licensing is an arrangement by which a licensee in another country buys the rights to manufacture a company's product in its own country for a negotiated fee (typically royalty payments on the number of units sold). The licensee then puts up most of the capital necessary to get the overseas operation going. The advantage of licensing is that the company need not bear the costs and risks of opening up an overseas market.

However, a problem arises when a company licenses its technological expertise to overseas companies. Technological know-how is the basis of the competitive advantage of many multinational companies. But RCA Corporation lost control over its color TV technology by licensing it to a number of Japanese companies. The Japanese companies quickly assimilated RCA's technology and then used it to enter the U.S. market, eventually gaining a bigger share of the U.S. market than RCA held.

Franchising

In many respects, franchising is similar to licensing. However, whereas licensing is a strategy pursued primarily by manufacturing companies, franchising is used primarily by service companies. McDonald's, Hilton International, and many other companies have expanded overseas by franchising. For example, 7-Eleven has expanded through franchising to the point where it has 39,000 stores in Europe, Australia, and Asia.[61]

In franchising, the company sells limited rights to use its brand name to franchisees in return for a lump-sum payment and a share of the franchisee's profits. However, unlike most licensing agreements, the franchisee has to agree to abide by strict rules regarding how it does business. Thus, when McDonald's enters into a franchising agreement with an overseas company, it expects the franchisee to run its restaurants in a manner identical to that used under the McDonald's name elsewhere in the world.

The advantages of franchising as an entry mode are similar to those of licensing. The franchisees put up capital and assume most of the business risk. However, local laws can limit this advantage. Until recently, China required franchisors to operate at least two company-owned outlets in that country profitably for at least a year before they would be allowed to offer franchises to Chinese entrepreneurs. Relaxation of that requirement made franchising in China's high-growth market far more attractive to businesses such as Ruby Tuesday, all of whose restaurants are operated by franchisees with knowledge of their local markets.[62]

The most significant disadvantage of franchising concerns quality control. The company's brand name guarantees consistency in the company's product. Thus a business traveler booking into a Hilton International hotel in Hong Kong can reasonably expect the same quality of room, food, and service that he or she would receive in New York. But if overseas franchisees are less concerned about quality than they should be, the impact can

Bottom Line

Franchising is one way to maintain standards globally. *Why does quality control pose a risk in franchising?*

go beyond lost sales in the local market to a decline in the company's reputation worldwide. If a business traveler has an unpleasant experience at the Hilton in Hong Kong, she or he may decide never to go to another Hilton hotel—and urge colleagues to do likewise. To make matters worse, the geographic distance between the franchisor and its overseas franchisees makes poor quality difficult to detect.

Joint Ventures

Establishing a joint venture (a formal business agreement discussed in more detail in Chapter 17) with a company in another country has long been a popular means of entering a new market. Joint ventures benefit a company through (1) the local partner's knowledge of the host country's competitive conditions, culture, language, political systems, and business systems and (2) the sharing of development costs and/or risks with the local partner. Duke University and Wuhan University recently opened a joint venture in China, Duke Kunshan University (DKU). DKU offers programs in global health, medical physics, and management studies. Approved by the Chinese Ministry of Education, DKU joins other high-profile partnerships that have been created between Western and Chinese institutions of higher education. Many of the new ventures focus on "advanced business studies, especially targeting the Chinese MBA market, and most are taught partly or entirely in English." Fueling this trend in cross-border ventures is China's goal to become a major education hub and the fact that several state-owned enterprises (SOEs) in China want to modernize the way they do business. One way to accomplish both of these goals is by attracting students and scholars from premier learning institutions.[63] In addition, many countries' political considerations make joint ventures the only feasible entry mode. Before China opened its borders to trade, many U.S. companies, including Eastman Kodak, AT&T, Ford, and GM, did business in the country via joint ventures.

But as attractive as they sound, joint ventures have their problems. First, as in the case of licensing, a company runs the risk of losing control over its technology to its venture partner. For example, Japan's Kawasaki Heavy Industries and Germany's Siemens entered into joint ventures with Chinese partners to build China's high-speed rail network, but now those Chinese companies are using some of the technology they learned from the venture to compete with Kawasaki and Siemens for contracts elsewhere.[64] Second, companies may find themselves at odds with one another. For example, one joint venture partner may want to move production to a country where demand is growing, but the other would prefer to keep its factories at home running at full capacity. Conflict over who controls what within a joint venture is a primary reason many fail.[65] In fact, many of the early joint ventures American and European companies entered into with companies in China lost money or failed precisely because of conflicts over control. To offset these disadvantages, experienced managers strive to iron out technology, control, and other potential conflicts up front, when they first negotiate the joint venture agreement.

Wholly Owned Subsidiaries

Establishing a wholly owned subsidiary—that is, an independent company owned by the parent corporation—is the most costly method of serving an overseas market. Companies that use this approach must bear the full costs and risks associated with setting up overseas operations (as opposed to joint ventures, in which the costs and risks are shared, or licensing, in which the licensee bears most of the costs and risks).

Nevertheless, setting up a wholly owned subsidiary offers two clear advantages. First, when a company's competitive advantage is based on technology, a wholly owned subsidiary normally is the preferred entry mode because it reduces the risk of losing control over the technology. Wholly owned subsidiaries are thus the preferred mode of entry in the semiconductor, electronics, and pharmaceutical industries. However, this advantage is limited by the extent to which the government of the country where the subsidiary is located will protect intellectual property such as patents and trademarks. Seven years after SI Group, a U.S. chemical company, began making rubber-bonding resins in China for the local tire industry, a competitor hired away SI Group's plant manager and began making a product that was virtually identical. After aggressive efforts to find relief in the Chinese legal system failed, SI Group took its complaint to the U.S. International Trade Commission (ITC). The ITC could restrict the sale of the Chinese competitor's products in the United States if it finds the company stole trade secrets.[66]

Setting up a wholly owned subsidiary offers two clear advantages.

Second, a wholly owned subsidiary gives a company tight control over operations in other countries, which is necessary if the company chooses to pursue a global strategy. Establishing a global manufacturing system requires world headquarters to have a high degree of control over the operations of national affiliates. Unlike licensees or joint venture partners, wholly owned subsidiaries usually accept centrally determined decisions about how to produce, how much to produce, and how to price output for transfer among operations.

Managing across Borders

LO 5

expatriates

Parent-company nationals who are sent to work at a foreign subsidiary.

host-country nationals

Natives of the country where an overseas subsidiary is located.

third-country nationals

Natives of a country other than the home country or the host country of an overseas subsidiary.

Bottom Line

Expatriate hiring increases cost; training raises quality. *How might training an expatriate manager differ from training a local manager?*

When establishing operations overseas, headquarters executives have a choice among sending **expatriates** (individuals from the parent country), using **host-country nationals** (natives of the host country), and deploying **third-country nationals** (natives of a country other than the home country or the host country). Although most corporations use some combination of all three types of employees, there are advantages and disadvantages for each. Colgate-Palmolive and Procter & Gamble, for example, use expatriates to get their products to market abroad more quickly. AT&T and Toyota have used expatriates to transfer their corporate cultures and best practices to other countries—in Toyota's case, to its U.S. plants.

Because sending employees abroad can cost three to four times as much as employing host-country nationals, other companies, including Texas Instruments, have made more limited use of expatriates. Moreover, in many countries—particularly developing countries in which firms are trying to get an economic foothold—the personal security of expatriates is an issue. As a result, more firms may send their expatriates on shorter assignments and engage in telecommuting, teleconferencing, and other electronic means to facilitate communications between their international divisions. In fact, working internationally can be very stressful, even for experienced globalites. Exhibit 6.9 shows some of the primary stressors for expatriates at different stages of their assignments. It also shows ways for executives to cope with the stress as well as some of the things companies can do to help with the adjustment.

Although developing a valuable pool of expatriates is important, local employees are more available, tend to be familiar with the culture and language, and usually cost less because they do not have to be relocated. In addition, local governments often provide incentives to companies that create good jobs for their citizens, or they may place restrictions on the use of expatriates. Such advantages, coupled with the often-inadequate educational systems of developing nations, combine to create stiff competition for local management talent. The result is that China, India, and Latin America do not have enough qualified talent to fill the demand for local executives. For example, in China, recruiting firm Russell Reynolds finds that local managers offer technical skills but often lack conceptual skills and a strategic perspective. Motorola Mobility meets the challenge in mainland China with a mix of executives—about one-third from mainland China, one-third from other Asian countries, and one-third from the West.[67]

It is estimated that nearly 15 percent of all employee transfers are to an international location.

Stage	Primary Stressors	Executive Coping Response	Employer Coping Response
Expatriate selection	Cross-cultural unreadiness.	Engage in self-evaluation.	Encourage expatriate's self- and family evaluation. Perform an assessment of potential and interests.
Assignment acceptance	Unrealistic evaluation of stressors to come. Hurried time frame.	Think of assignment as a growth opportunity rather than an instrument to vertical promotion.	Do not make hard-to-keep promises. Clarify expectations.
Pre- and postarrival	Ignorance of cultural differences.	Do not make unwarranted assumptions of cultural competence and cultural rules.	Provide pre-, during-, and postassignment training. Encourage support-seeking behavior.
Arrival	Cultural shock. Stressor reevaluation. Feelings of lack of fit and differential treatment.	Do not construe identification with the host and parent cultures as mutually exclusive. Seek social support.	Provide postarrival training. Facilitate integration in expatriate network.
Novice	Cultural blunders or inadequacy of coping responses. Ambiguity owing to inability to decipher meaning of situations.	Observe and study functional value of coping responses among locals. Do not simply replicate responses that worked at home.	Provide follow-up training. Seek advice from locals and expatriate network.
Transitional	Rejection of host or parent culture.	Form and maintain attachments with both cultures.	Promote culturally sensitive policies in host country. Provide Internet access to family and friends at home. Maintain constant communication and periodic visits to parent organization.
Mastery	Frustration with inability to perform boundary-spanning role. Bothered by living with a cultural paradox.	Internalize and enjoy identification with both cultures and walking between two cultures.	Reinforce rather than punish dual identification by defining common goals.
Repatriation	Disappointment with unfulfilled expectations. Sense of isolation. Loss of autonomy.	Realistically reevaluate assignment as a personal and professional growth opportunity.	Arrange prerepatriation briefings and interviews. Schedule postrepatriation support meetings.

SOURCE: From *Academy of Management Executive,* J. Sanchez, P. Spector, and C. Cooper, May 2000, pp. 96–106. Copyright © 2000. Reproduced with permission of Academy of Management via Copyright Clearance Center.

Skills of the Global Manager

failure rate

The number of expatriate managers of an overseas operation who come home early.

It is estimated that nearly 15 percent of all employee transfers are to an international location. However, the **failure rate** among expatriates (defined as those who come home early) is considerably higher for American expatriates compared to those international assignees from Europe and Asia.[68] The cost of each of these failed assignments ranges from tens of thousands to hundreds of thousands of dollars.[69] Typically, the causes for failure overseas extend beyond technical capability and include personal and social issues. In a recent survey of human resource managers around the globe, two-thirds said the main reason for the failures is family issues, especially dissatisfaction of the employee's spouse or partner.[70] The problem may be compounded in this era of dual-career couples, in which one spouse may have to give up his or her job to accompany the expatriate manager to the new location. To ensure that an overseas posting will succeed, managers can encourage an employee to talk to her or his spouse about what he or she will do in the foreign country. For both the expatriate and the spouse, adjustment requires flexibility, emotional stability, empathy for the culture, communication skills, resourcefulness, initiative, and diplomatic skills.[71] When Kent Millington took the position of vice president of Asia operations for an Internet hosting company, his wife Linda quit her job to move with him to Japan. Especially for Linda Millington, the first three months were difficult because she didn't speak Japanese, found the transit system confusing, and even struggled to buy food because she couldn't translate the labels. But she persevered and participated in classes and volunteer activities. Eventually, she and her husband learned to enjoy the experience and appreciated the chance to see just how well they could tackle a challenge.[72]

Companies such as Levi Strauss, Bechtel, Monsanto, Whirlpool, and Dow Chemical have worked to identify the characteristics of individuals that will predict their success abroad. Exhibit 6.10 shows skills that can be used to identify candidates who are likely to succeed in a global environment. Interestingly, in addition to such characteristics as cultural sensitivity, technical expertise, and business knowledge, an individual's success abroad may depend greatly on his or her ability to learn from experience.[73]

Companies such as BPAmoco, Global Hyatt, and others with large international staffs have extensive training programs to prepare employees for international assignments. Exhibit 6.11 suggests ways to improve their likelihood of success. Other organizations, such as Coca-Cola, Motorola, Chevron, and Mattel, have extended this training to include employees who may be located in the United States but who also deal in international markets. These programs focus on areas such as language, culture, and career development.

Managers who are sent on an overseas assignment usually wonder about the effect such an assignment will have on their careers. Certainly their selection for a post overseas is usually an indication that they are being groomed to become more effective managers in an era of globalization. In addition, they will often have more responsibility, challenge, and operating leeway than they might have at home. Yet they may be concerned that they will soon be out of the loop on key developments back home. Good companies and managers address that issue with effective communication between subsidiaries and headquarters and by a program of visitations to and from the home office. Communication technology now makes it easy for expatriates to keep in touch with colleagues in their home country on a daily or even more frequent basis, through e-mail and phone calls. Alan Paul, an American journalist working in China, says Internet phone service, a webcam, and podcasts of favorite radio programs also enable him to stay in touch with family and friends back home, even to the extent that he has to work hard to have "a fully engaged existence in China."[74]

Understanding Cultural Issues

In many ways, cultural issues represent the most elusive aspect of international business. In an era when modern transportation and communication technologies have created a global village, it is easy to forget how deep and enduring the differences among nations

End-State Dimensions	Survey Items
1. Sensitivity to cultural differences	When working with people from other cultures, works hard to understand their perspective.
2. Business knowledge.	Has a solid understanding of the company's products and services.
3. Courage to take a stand.	Is willing to take a stand on issues.
4. Brings out the best in people.	Has a special talent for dealing with people.
5. Acts with integrity.	Can be depended on to tell the truth regardless of circumstances.
6. Is insightful.	Is good at identifying the most important part of a complex problem.
7. Is committed to success.	Clearly demonstrates commitment to seeing the organization succeed.
8. Takes risks.	Takes personal as well as business risks.

Learning-Oriented Dimensions	Survey Items
1. Uses feedback.	Has changed as a result of feedback.
2. Is culturally adventurous.	Enjoys the challenge of working in countries other than his or her own.
3. Seeks opportunities to learn.	Takes advantage of opportunities to do new things.
4. Is open to criticism.	Does not appear brittle—as if criticism might cause him or her to break.
5. Seeks feedback.	Pursues feedback even when others are reluctant to give it.
6. Is flexible.	Doesn't get so invested in things that he or she cannot change when something doesn't work.

EXHIBIT 6.10
Identifying International Executives

SOURCE: Copyright © 1997 by the American Psychological Association. G. M. Spreitzer, M. W. McCall, and J. D. Mahoney, "Early Identification of International Executive Potential," *Journal of Applied Psychology* 82, no. 1 (1997), pp. 6–29.

can be. The fact that people everywhere drink Coke, wear blue jeans, and drive Toyotas doesn't mean we are all becoming alike. Each country is unique for reasons rooted in history, culture, language, geography, social conditions, race, and religion. These differences complicate any international activity and represent the fundamental issues

- Structure assignments clearly: Develop clear reporting relationships and job responsibilities.
- Create clear job objectives.
- Develop performance measurements based on objectives.
- Use effective, validated selection and screening criteria (both personal and technical attributes).
- Prepare expatriates and families for assignments (briefings, training, support).
- Create a vehicle for ongoing communication with expatriates.
- Anticipate repatriation to facilitate reentry when they come back home.
- Consider developing a mentor program that will help monitor and intervene in case of trouble.

EXHIBIT 6.11
How to Prevent Failed Global Assignments

In this era, when people from all over the globe are collaborating on business issues, it is important to continue learning about and respecting different cultures in order to succeed.

© Digital Vision/Getty Images

ethnocentrism

The tendency to judge others by the standards of one's group or culture, which are seen as superior.

culture shock

The disorientation and stress associated with being in a foreign environment.

that inform and guide how a company should conduct business across borders. For example, while working in Hong Kong, Geoffrey Fowler discovered that his co-workers there choose topics for small talk—people's weight, salary, and the size of their apartment—that would horrify Americans. At the same time, Chinese workers are put off by the American custom of combining lunch with a business meeting, meaning junior employees are chewing away while a superior in the company is talking.[75] As the nearby "Multiple Generations at Work" box emphasizes, international experience helps employees build successful careers.

Ironically, although most of us would guess that the trick to working abroad is learning about a foreign culture, in reality our problems often stem from our being oblivious to our own cultural conditioning. Most of us pay no attention to how culture influences our everyday behavior, and because of this, we tend to adapt poorly to situations that are unique or foreign to us. Without realizing it, some managers may even act out of **ethnocentrism**—a tendency to judge foreign people or groups by the standards of one's own culture or group and to see one's own standards as superior. Such tendencies may be totally unconscious—for example, the assumption that "in England, they drive on the *wrong* side of the road" rather than merely on the left. Or they may reflect a lack of awareness of the values underlying a local culture—for example, an assumption that the culture is backward because it does not air American or European television programming, when it is actually focused on maintaining its traditional values and norms.

Assumptions such as these are one reason people traveling abroad frequently experience **culture shock**—the disorientation and stress associated with being in a foreign environment. Managers are better able to navigate this transition if they are sensitive to their surroundings, including social norms and customs, and readily able to adjust their behavior to such circumstances.[76] Employers can help by identifying some of the cultural norms to expect and by establishing performance measures for behaviors that contribute to success in the host country (for example, the types of communication and direction employees will expect from their manager).

A wealth of cross-cultural research has been conducted on the differences and similarities among various countries. Geert Hofstede, for example, has identified four dimensions along which managers in multinational corporations tend to view cultural differences:

Power distance: the extent to which a society accepts the fact that power in organizations is distributed unequally.
Individualism/collectivism: the extent to which people act on their own or as a part of a group.
Uncertainty avoidance: the extent to which people in a society feel threatened by uncertain and ambiguous situations.
Masculinity/femininity: the extent to which a society values quantity of life (e.g., accomplishment, money) over quality of life (e.g., compassion, beauty).

Exhibit 6.12 offers a graphic depiction of how 40 nations differ on the dimensions of individualism/collectivism and power distance. Of course, this depiction exaggerates the differences between national traits to some extent. Many Americans prefer to act as part of a group, just as many Taiwanese prefer to act individualistically. And globalization may have already begun to blur some of these distinctions. Still, to suggest no cultural differences exist is equally simplistic. Clearly, cultures such as the United States, which emphasize rugged individualism, differ significantly from collectivistic cultures such as those of Pakistan, Taiwan, and Colombia. To be effective in cultures that exhibit a greater power distance, managers often must behave more autocratically, perhaps being less participative

Multiple Generations at Work

Do Millennials Need International Work Experience?

According to the results of a survey of working Millennials from six countries, the answer is yes. PricewaterhouseCoopers asked early career employees the following question: "Thinking of working outside your home country, do you agree/disagree that you need international experience to further your career?" The percentage of respondents who agree that they need international experience is illustrated below.

A large majority of Millennial respondents from emerging economies Brazil, China, and India view international experience as important for their career. In contrast, just over half of respondents from the United States and Germany, both developed economies, think international experience will benefit their careers. Given the dramatic increase in globalization and international competition in recent decades, employees of all ages and economies should be looking for opportunities to acquire international business skills. By working with people from different cultures, employees learn how cultural programming influences their behaviors and attitudes. That is the first step in being able to function effectively in international business situations.[77]

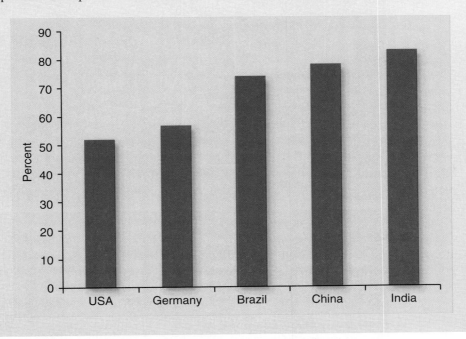

in decision making. Conversely, in Scandinavian cultures such as Sweden's, for instance, where power distance is low, the very idea that management would make decisions on its own may be questioned. Here, managers tend to work more toward creating processes that reflect an industrial democracy.

Cross-cultural management extends beyond U.S. employees going abroad. It also includes effective management of **inpatriates**—foreign nationals who are brought in to work at the parent company. These employees provide a valuable service to global companies because they bring extensive knowledge about how to operate effectively in their home countries. They will also be better prepared to communicate their organization's products and values when they return. But they often have the same types of problems as expatriates and may be even more neglected because parent–company managers either are more focused on their expatriate program or unconsciously see the home country as normal—requiring no period of adjustment. Yet the language, customs, expense, and lack of local community support in the United States are at least as daunting to inpatriates as the experience of American nationals abroad. Culture shock works both ways.

inpatriate

A foreign national brought in to work at the parent company.

EXHIBIT 6.12

Positions of 40 Countries on the Power Distance and Individualism Scales

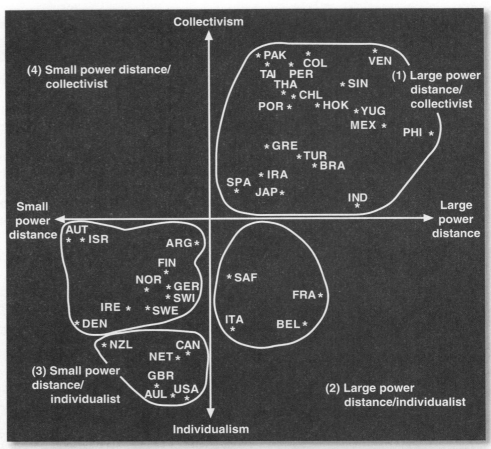

ARG Argentina	FRA France	JAP Japan	SIN Singapore
AUL Australia	GBR Great Britain	MEX Mexico	SPA Spain
AUT Austria	GER Germany (West)	NET Netherlands	SWE Sweden
BEL Belgium	GRE Greece	NOR Norway	SWI Switzerland
BRA Brazil	HOK Hong Kong	NZL New Zealand	TAI Taiwan
CAN Canada	IND India	PAK Pakistan	THA Thailand
CHL Chile	IRA Iran	PER Peru	TUR Turkey
COL Colombia	IRE Ireland	PHI Philippines	USA United States
DEN Denmark	ISR Israel	POR Portugal	VEN Venezuela
FIN Finland	ITA Italy	SAF South Africa	YUG Yugoslavia

SOURCE: G. Hofstede, "Motivation, Leadership, and Organization: Do American Theories Apply Abroad?" *Organizational Dynamics* 9, no. 1 (Summer 1980), pp. 42–63. Reprinted by permission.

Effective managers are sensitive to these issues and take them into account in dealing with foreign-national employees. In contrast to American-born employees, co-workers or customers from other countries might tend to communicate less directly, place more emphasis on hierarchy and authority, or make decisions more slowly. For example, an American manager working in Japan sent an e-mail to her American supervisor and Japanese colleagues in which she pointed out flaws in the process they were working on. The supervisor appreciated the alert, but her colleagues were embarrassed by behavior they considered rude; she should have inquired indirectly—say, by wondering what might happen if such a problem did exist. In another situation, a manager from Mexico showed respect for authority by phrasing ideas as questions when he was in a meeting with superiors. Instead of seeing him as appropriately humble, his American colleagues concluded that he was indecisive. In general, managers of international groups can manage these types of misunderstandings by acknowledging cultural differences frankly and finding ways to work around them by modifying the group (e.g., assigning tasks to subgroups), by setting rules to correct problems that are upsetting group members, or by removing group members who demonstrate they cannot work effectively within a particular situation.[78]

In addition, when working in the United States, foreign nationals will encounter a number of work-related differences. Alert managers help their employees adjust. A few basic categories include the following:

Meetings: Americans tend to have specific views about the purpose of meetings and how much time can be spent. International workers may have different preconceptions about the nature and length of meetings, and managers should make sure foreign nationals are comfortable with the American approach.

Work(aholic) schedules: Workers from other countries can work long hours but, in countries with strong labor organizations, often get many more weeks of vacation than American workers. And Europeans in particular may balk at working on weekends. Obviously, matters such as these are most helpfully raised and addressed at the beginning of the work assignment.

E-mail: Parts of the world have not yet embraced e-mail and voice mail the way U.S. workers have. Often others prefer to communicate face to face. Particularly when potential language difficulties exist, managers will probably want to avoid using e-mail for important matters at the outset.

Fast-trackers: Although U.S. companies may put a young MBA graduate on the fast track to management, most other cultures still see no substitute for the wisdom gained through experience. (This is something U.S. managers working abroad will also want to keep in mind.) More experienced managers are often a better choice for mentoring inpatriates.

Feedback: Everyone likes praise, but the use of excessive positive feedback tends to be less prevalent in other cultures than in the United States—a useful fact for managers when they give foreign nationals their performance reviews.[79]

Ethical Issues in International Management

If managers are to function effectively in a foreign setting, they must understand how culture influences both how they are perceived and how others behave. One of the most sensitive issues in this regard is how culture plays out in terms of ethical behavior.[80] Issues of right and wrong get blurred as we move from one culture to another, and actions that may be normal and customary in one setting may be unethical—even illegal—in another. The use of bribes, for example, is perceived to be an accepted part of commercial transactions in many Asian, African, Latin American, and Middle Eastern cultures; and even in cultures that view bribery as a form of corruption, some companies offer bribes when they think that it is part of the culture.[81]

In the United States, of course, such behavior is illegal, but what should a U.S. businessperson do when working abroad? Failure to sweeten the deal with bribes can result in lost business. Although the Foreign Corrupt Practices Act of 1977 prohibits U.S. employees from bribing foreign officials, one study published in the United States found that fewer than half of U.S. managers said bribes were unacceptable, and 20 percent actually said they were always acceptable. (Small business gifts or grease payments to lower-level officials are permissible under the act if the dollar amount of the payments would not influence the outcome of the negotiations.) Internationally, countries of the Organisation for Economic Co-operation and Development (OECD), including the United States, have also prohibited bribes since 1977.[82] Companies that conduct business in Britain are also subject to that country's Bribery Act, which prohibits not only bribes of foreign officials but also bribes between businesspeople.[83] That sweeping law took effect in 2011; as of this writing, it is not yet clear how aggressive the British government will be in pursuing cases involving small bribes and companies based outside Britain.

Britain's law comes at a time when other governments are getting tough on bribery and other forms of corruption. Other European countries have recently strengthened their laws against bribery, and China has begun to prosecute corporations for bribery. In the United States, the Justice Department has been charging more firms with violating the Foreign Corrupt Practices Act (FCPA). In one case, for example, IBM paid $10 million to settle charges by the Securities and Exchange Commission that its people had been engaging in bribery to win contracts. (That settlement was actually small; fines in FCPA cases can exceed $100 million.) In this case, IBM neither admitted wrongdoing nor denied it, and the company said it was taking remedial action to ensure that violations didn't occur in the future.[84]

Without an understanding of local customs, ethical standards, and applicable laws, an expatriate may be woefully unprepared to work internationally. To safeguard against the problems and mitigate the punishment if an organization should be found guilty of bribery, the U.S. Sentencing Commission has deemed it essential for firms to establish effective ethics programs and see that they are enforced. Companies such as Coca-Cola, Nikon, Kellogg, and Novartis established official codes of conduct for their employees years ago. In addition, many other companies have hired official ethics officers and increased their efforts to ensure ethical conduct. UPS couples an international code of conduct (available in 12 languages) with tools to ensure compliance: a corporate compliance department headed by a senior vice president, ethics training for all managers and employees, a toll-free line for requesting guidance or reporting problems, and regular audits of compliance with the code. In developing the international code of ethics, the compliance department sought input from employees in many positions and countries to ensure that the policies would be relevant throughout the company. Employees are invited to submit any ideas they have for improving the code's current language.[85]

To put teeth into the corporate ethics initiative, companies with global operations should be at least as engaged in establishing and enforcing standards for ethical behavior as domestic corporations. In Chapter 5, we identified a number of steps organizations should take. They include establishing and communicating the company's values, measuring performance in meeting ethical standards, rewarding employees at all levels for meeting those standards, and taking swift but fair action when violations occur. The primary difference in the international context is that these activities must be carried out with foreign business partners and employees in any subsidiary, franchise, or other company operation.

Interestingly, despite some obvious differences across cultures, research suggests that regardless of nationality or religion, most people embrace a set of five core values: compassion, fairness, honesty, responsibility, and respect for others. These values lie at the heart of human rights issues and seem to transcend more superficial differences among Americans, Europeans, and Asians. Finding shared values such as these allows companies to build more effective partnerships and alliances, especially across cultures. Perhaps as long as people understand that there is a set of core values, they can permit all kinds of differences in strategy and tactics.[86]

To a large extent, the challenge of managing across borders comes down to the philosophies and systems used to manage people. In moving from domestic to international management, managers need to develop a wide portfolio of behaviors along with the capacity to adjust their behavior for a particular situation. This adjustment, however, should not compromise the values, integrity, and strengths of their home country. When managers can transcend national borders and move among different cultures, they can leverage the strategic capabilities of their organization and take advantage of the opportunities that our global economy has to offer.

Taking these management principles beyond national borders is an exciting challenge that should be irresistible to today's and tomorrow's leaders. As we saw in the early sections of this chapter, the business environment is spreading wider. The implications are

Management in Action

MANAGING LENOVO ACROSS NATIONAL BOUNDARIES

To implement its strategy of keeping production in-house, growing through acquisition, and expanding to new markets as it builds market share, Lenovo needs managers who understand local markets and can run an efficient manufacturing operation. Examples include host-country nationals such as Amar Babu, the managing director of Lenovo's business in India, and third-country nationals such as American Dan Stone, whose background in business strategy helps him succeed as the head of Lenovo's Brazilian business unit. In India, Babu notes that consumers are just beginning to make the move from a basic cell phone to a smartphone, whereas demand for PCs is likely to remain strong because people want a computer with a full screen for educational applications.

Of course, electronics companies also need to dream up, or at least keep up with, the next great ideas. Lenovo's chief executive, Yang Yuanqing, admits that Lenovo has not exactly been a leader in design, but he has plenty of experience in catching up. In the 1980s, when Yang was a Lenovo salesperson, he used a bicycle to deliver products, and support services such as advertising agencies were unavailable. As he persevered then, he is persevering today in leading innovation. Recent attempts include the IdeaPad Yoga, whose keyboard can be positioned for using the computer as a tablet or laptop and the IdeaTab, a low-cost tablet on which to play movies and videos.

China, where the market is huge and the brand is already respected and popular, provides fertile ground for launching new ideas such as the Smart HD TV, an Internet-connected television. China is an important locale for the expansion of its mobile phone business. In 2014, Lenovo reported that revenue from mobile devices accounted for a quarter of the firm's revenue, a significant increase over the previous year. Lenovo has overtaken Samsung as the largest smartphone manufacturer in China and the fourth-largest exporter worldwide.

Yang is patient in building Lenovo's brand in the United States. According to Yang, the company intends to use its reputation as the maker of business computers as the basis for selling high-end PCs to consumers. Yang said recent prototypes have been exciting, but the final versions suffered from compromises made to lower costs. Yang intends to shift the focus toward favoring the design. Also, during some recent quarters, Lenovo has ranked as the world's biggest seller of PCs, which Lenovo hopes will further raise the brand's profile worldwide.[87]

- What advantages does Lenovo have from its choice of entry modes?
- What cultural issues should an American-born manager at Lenovo be prepared to handle?

evident at Lenovo, as described in "Management in Action: Onward" and the earlier parts of this continuing case. People around the world are seizing the chance to get an education, launch a business, and enjoy a higher standard of living. The opportunities to serve their needs are enormous. Thanks to modern technology, the ability to learn about needs and meet them globally is available even to small, local businesses. Whether you are addressing unique desires in a bumpy world or delivering your product to all continents in a flat one, you must pay attention to what is happening far beyond your neighborhood.

KEY TERMS

culture shock, p. 200

ethnocentrism, p. 200

expatriates, p. 196

failure rate, p. 198

global model, p. 190

host-country nationals, p. 196

inpatriate, p. 201

inshoring, p. 181

insourcing, p. 181

international model, p. 189

multinational model, p. 190

North American Free Trade Agreement (NAFTA), p. 186

offshoring, p. 180

outsourcing, p. 180

third-country nationals, p. 196

transnational model, p. 191

RETAINING WHAT YOU LEARNED

In Chapter 6, you learned how globalization is changing the competitive landscape and influencing the behavior of companies and their managers. The lowering of trade barriers is fueling the movement toward increased globalization. Managers today find themselves in a more complex and competitive marketplace than years ago. Companies use different strategies to compete, including: international, multinational, global, and transnational. Each strategy emphasizes a different mix of global integration and local responsiveness. The five methods of entering an overseas market are exporting, licensing, franchising, entering into a joint venture, and setting up a wholly owned subsidiary. When staffing an overseas operation, companies can deploy expatriates from the headquarters' country, host-country nationals, and third-country nationals. To decrease the risk of failure, expatriates should possess not only technical capability but also personal and social skills. Resourcefulness, cultural adaptability, sensitivity, team-building skills, and mental ability are especially important for international managers. By recognizing cultural differences, people can find it easier to work together collaboratively and benefit from the exchange.

LO 1   Discuss what integration of the global economy means for individual companies and their managers.

- In recent years, rapid growth has occurred in world trade, foreign direct investment, and imports.
- One consequence is that companies around the globe are now finding their home markets under attack from international competitors.
- The global competitive environment is becoming a much tougher place in which to do business. However, companies now have access to markets that previously were denied to them.

LO 2   Describe how the world economy is becoming more integrated than ever before.

- The gradual lowering of barriers to free trade is making the world economy more integrated.
- This means that the modern manager operates in an environment that offers more opportunities but is also more complex and competitive than that faced by the manager of a generation ago.

LO 3   Define the strategies organizations use to compete in the global marketplace.

- The international corporation builds on its existing core capabilities in R&D, marketing, manufacturing, and so on to penetrate overseas markets.
- A multinational is a more complex form that usually has fully autonomous units operating in multiple countries. Subsidiaries are given latitude to address local issues such as consumer preferences, political pressures, and economic trends in different regions of the world.
- The global organization pulls control of overseas operations back into the headquarters and tends to approach the world market as a unified whole by combining activities in each country to maximize efficiency on a global scale.
- A transnational attempts to achieve both local responsiveness and global integration by using a network structure that coordinates specialized facilities positioned around the world.

LO 4   Compare the various entry modes organizations use to enter overseas markets.

- There are five ways to enter an overseas market: exporting, licensing, franchising, entering into a joint venture, and setting up a wholly owned subsidiary.
- Each mode has advantages and disadvantages.

LO 5   Explain how companies can approach the task of staffing overseas operations.

- Most executives use a combination of expatriates, host-country nationals, and third-country nationals.
- Expatriates sometimes are used to establish new country operations quickly, transfer the company's culture, and bring in a specific technical skill.
- Host-country nationals have the advantages that they are familiar with local customs and culture, may cost less, and are viewed more favorably by local governments.
- Third-country nationals often are used as a compromise in politically touchy situations or when home-country expatriates are not available.

LO 6   Summarize the skills and knowledge managers need to manage globally.

- The causes for failure overseas extend beyond technical capability and include personal and social issues as well.
- Success depends on a manager's core skills, such as having a multidimensional perspective; having proficiency in line management and decision making; and having resourcefulness, cultural adaptability, sensitivity, team-building skills, and mental maturity.
- In addition, helpful augmented skills include computer literacy, negotiating skills, strategic vision, and the ability to delegate.

LO 7   Identify ways in which cultural differences across countries influence management.

- Culture influences our actions and perceptions as well as the actions and perceptions of others. Unfortunately, we are often unaware of how culture influences us, and this can cause problems.
- Today, managers must be able to change their behavior to match the needs and customs of local cultures. For example, in various cultures, employees expect a manager to be either more or less autocratic or participative.
- By recognizing their cultural differences, people can find it easier to work together collaboratively and benefit from the exchange.

DISCUSSION QUESTIONS

1. Why is the world economy becoming more integrated? What are the implications of this integration for international managers?

2. Imagine you were the CEO of a major company. What approach to global competition would you choose for your firm: international, multinational, global, or transnational? Why?

3. Why have franchises been so popular as a method of international expansion in the fast-food industry? Contrast this with high-tech manufacturing, where joint ventures and partnerships have been more popular. What accounts for the differences across industries?

4. What are the pros and cons of using expatriates, host-country nationals, and third-country nationals to run overseas operations? If you were expanding your business, what approach would you use?

5. If you had entered into a joint venture with a foreign company but knew that women were not treated fairly in that culture, would you consider sending a female expatriate to handle the start-up? Why or why not?

6. What are the biggest cultural obstacles that we must overcome if we are to work effectively in Mexico? Are there different obstacles in France? Japan? China?

EXPERIENTIAL EXERCISES

6.1 GLOBAL INTEGRATION—LOCAL RESPONSIVENESS WORKSHEET

OBJECTIVE

To understand how companies compete in the global marketplace.

INSTRUCTIONS

An effective way to learn how companies respond to the competing pressures to be globally integrated and locally responsive is to study them in action. Referring back to Exhibit 6.6, search online for examples of companies that are currently using a global, transnational, international, or multinational organizational model. Please provide answers to the following questions:

PART I: GLOBAL MODEL

Name of company using a *global* organizational model:

_____

URL of website/article describing the company's *global* strategy:

_____

Explain why the company uses a *global* strategy to complete:

_____

_____

_____

PART II: TRANSNATIONAL MODEL

Name of company using a *transnational* organizational model:

_____

URL of website/article describing the company's *transnational* strategy:

_____

Explain why the company uses a *transnational* strategy to complete:

_____

_____

_____

_____

PART III: INTERNATIONAL MODEL

Name of company using an *international* organizational model:

_____

URL of website/article describing the company's *international* strategy:

_____

Explain why the company uses an *international* strategy to complete:

_____

_____

_____

_____

_____

PART IV: MULTINATIONAL MODEL

Name of company using a *multinational* organizational model:

_____

URL of website/article describing the company's *multinational* strategy:

_____

Explain why the company uses a *multinational* strategy to complete:

_____

_____

_____

_____

SOURCE: Adapted from R. R. McGrath Jr., *Exercises in Management Fundamentals*, 1st, p. 177. Copyright 1985.

6.2 CROSS-CULTURAL ANTHROPOLOGIST

Assume you are a cross-cultural anthropologist. In this role, please visit multiple public places that are frequented by one or more ethnic or cultural groups. Observe four to five behaviors that strike you as unique or different compared to what you consider to be "normal." After you make your observations, walk to a quiet location and record what you observed in a notebook or mobile device. Think about why these behaviors caught your attention in the first place and then analyze them from the perspective of Hofstede's cultural dimensions (individualism, power distance, uncertainty avoidance and masculinity).

LEARNING OBJECTIVES

1. To help students interpret in a more culturally neutral manner nonverbal communication.

2. To encourage students to understand their own reactions to different cultural behaviors.

3. To reinforce the importance of observation skills in cross-cultural encounters.

STEPS

1. Visit multiple public places where you can observe the behaviors of one or more ethnic or cultural groups. Examples include major airports, ethnic associations, foreign consulates, religious entities, cultural centers, museums, and cultural or affinity groups at universities.

2. Bring a notebook or mobile device and:
   a. On the *left* side of the page, make a column titled: **"Observation/description."**
      i. In this section, describe what you saw. Any behavior that strikes you as different, frustrating, funny, or confusing is appropriate. Stick to the facts when describing these behaviors. Write down 5–10 observed behaviors.
   b. On the *right* side of the page, make a column titled: **"How This Observation Relates to Hofstede's Dimensions."**

i. In this section, interpret the behaviors by using Hofstede's dimensions (individualism/collectivism, uncertainty avoidance, power distance, and masculinity). How can these dimensions help explain what you observed? Explain.

3. Type and hand-in your anthropologist's analysis. This should include:

   a. Your name, date, and the name of each public place you visited.

b. Include 5–10 observed behaviors (left side of notebook) that you made while visiting the place(s) and describe how these observations relate to Hofstede's cultural dimensions (right side of notebook).

SOURCE: Adapted from L. R. Kohls and J. M., Knight, *Cross-Cultural Journal in Developing Intercultural Awareness: A Cross-cultural Training Handbook* (Yarmouth, ME: Intercultural Press, 1994), p. 67.

CONCLUDING CASE

A GLOBAL LAUNCH FOR NET-WORK DOCS

Nina Jones and Matt Smith have been raising capital for their start-up, Net-Work Docs. The company will help business clients create and manage their documents electronically. Net-Work Docs will help companies create easily searchable electronic versions of their safety manuals, human resource manuals, training guides, operating instructions, and more. For clients who wish, the company will help in embedding video, audio, and pop-up content along with the basic text and will develop apps for companies that want to make the content available through mobile devices. They also will provide consulting services such as helping clients shop for cloud storage of their documents.

As Nina and Matt developed their business plan, they found themselves expanding their idea of the geographic market they could serve. Initially, they intended to start by working with businesses in their city. But they realized they will be selling a product that can be made anywhere and shipped anywhere. Software and electronic documents can be transported over the Internet at essentially no cost, and a website gives a company an immediate global presence. With that in mind, Nina and Matt have concluded that they are unnecessarily limiting themselves by targeting geographic markets.

Thus, the plan is now to launch Net-Work Docs as a global company, serving clients in any country. After all, reason Nina and Matt, companies everywhere have policies and procedures they need to document. They will describe their services on their website, make initial contacts via e-mail, and set up a PayPal service to handle online payments. They can travel to meet major clients, but routine jobs may not require face-to-face meetings, and cost-conscious clients should appreciate the savings of conducting business online.

One hitch with this plan is that some potential investors have expressed doubts about operating globally before the company has built experience and a reputation serving clients locally. One investor asked Matt and Nina whether they really were prepared to understand the needs of business clients located hundreds or thousands of miles away—and whether they could assess a faraway client's likelihood to pay for services. He asked, "Can you really serve overseas clients without any overseas employees?" The company's founders believe they can because they will start with an English-only website, so they will initially have only English-speaking clients.

DISCUSSION QUESTIONS

1. What are some possible advantages of Net-Work Docs serving a global market?

2. How are the founders balancing pressures for global integration and local responsiveness? Is their global strategy likely to succeed? Why or why not?

3. What skills of a global manager could help Net-Work Docs succeed?

CHAPTER 7

Entrepreneurship

> A man is known by the company he organizes.
>
> —Ambrose Bierce

After studying Chapter 7, you will be able to:

LO 1 Describe why people become entrepreneurs and what it takes, personally.

LO 2 Summarize how to assess opportunities to start new businesses.

LO 3 Identify common causes of success and failure.

LO 4 Discuss common management challenges.

LO 5 Explain how to increase your chances of success, including good business planning.

LO 6 Describe how managers of large companies can foster entrepreneurship.

Management in Action

HOW POPCHIPS BECAME KEITH BELLING'S NEXT BIG IDEA

Keith Belling was no stranger to business start-ups when he got an idea for making snacks better. A corporate attorney until age 27, Belling had already built and run the Oh La La chain of coffee stores and the Paragon restaurant group; in addition, his web portal for small companies, Allbusiness.com, earned him and his business partner $225 million when he eventually sold it to NBC Interactive. After the experience of running those enterprises, it might not seem so crazy to take on industry giants such as PepsiCo to sell a new line of snacks, branded Popchips.

Belling had been looking for a healthy-food company to run with his business partner, Pat Turpin. They toured a possible facility, a factory for making rice cakes, located near Los Angeles. Belling was intrigued by the process, cooking rice under high pressure to make it pop the way popcorn does. He investigated the possibility of popping other starchy foods and concluded that making snacks this way preserved flavor in a reduced-fat snack. It sounded like the next great thing for diet-conscious Americans, so he and Turpin had the idea they were looking for.

Belling and Turpin bought the Los Angeles rice cake factory in 2005, and two years later, Popchips, with Belling as CEO, was making popped, seasoned potato chips and selling them at Safeway stores on the West Coast. (Later, the company introduced popped tortilla and veggie chips.) By 2008, Popchips was reporting sales of $6.5 million. To expand, Popchips generated publicity. The company sent samples to all the employees at selected companies (for example, Amazon.com and J. Crew) and to influential people at Mercedes-Benz Fashion Week. With the attention earned, Popchips won shelf space in Jamba Juice, Target, and Whole Foods.

© Zuma Press, Inc./Alamy

Along the way, Belling pursued a creative idea for publicity: Sign agreements with celebrities in which they not only pitch the brand in advertisements but actually become investors. Each celebrity invests in Popchips, gets involved in developing a new flavor, and becomes a spokesperson for the flavor. First was Ashton Kutcher, who also was a party to the company's first big marketing embarrassment: In one ad, he portrayed an awkward Indian stereotype of a Bollywood producer to promote the snack's chili-lime flavor. After complaints of racism, the ads were canceled. Meanwhile, however, sales continued rising, and Popchips has signed up other celebrities, including Jillian Michaels, Heidi Klum, Sean "Diddy" Combs, David Ortiz of the Red Sox, and Katy Perry. Sales have continued to soar—to $93 million in 2012. By a recent count, Popchips snacks are now available for sale in 30,000 stores in the United States and beyond.[1]

Keith Belling took an existing method for preparing snacks and built a company by applying that method in tasty new ways. As you read about the qualities of successful entrepreneurs and the challenges they must overcome, think about which of these you see in Belling and his experience with Popchips.

entrepreneurship

The pursuit of lucrative opportunities by enterprising individuals.

small business

A business having fewer than 100 employees, independently owned and operated, not dominant in its field, and not characterized by many innovative practices.

entrepreneurial venture

A new business having growth and high profitability as primary objectives.

Bottom Line

Entrepreneurship is inherently about innovation—creating a new venture where one didn't exist before.
How is entrepreneurship different from inventing a new product?

As Keith Belling and countless others have demonstrated, great opportunity is available to talented entrepreneurs who are willing to work hard to achieve their dreams. **Entrepreneurship** occurs when an enterprising individual pursues a lucrative opportunity.[2] To be an entrepreneur is to initiate and build an organization rather than being only a passive part of one.[3] The entrepreneurial process involves discovering, evaluating, and capitalizing on opportunities to create new and future goods and services.[4]

Creating value is a central objective of entrepreneurship, just as it is in strategic management. Wealth may be an entrepreneur's ultimate goal, but it won't come without providing value for other individuals, organizations, and/or society.[5]

How does entrepreneurship differ from managing a small business?[6] A **small business** is often defined as having fewer than 100 employees, being independently owned and operated, not dominant in its field, and not characterized by many innovative practices. Small-business owners tend not to manage particularly aggressively, and they expect normal, moderate sales, profits, and growth. In contrast, an **entrepreneurial venture** has growth and high profitability as primary objectives. Entrepreneurs manage aggressively and develop innovative strategies, practices, and products. They and their financial backers usually seek rapid growth, immediate and high profits, and sometimes a quick sellout with large capital gains.

The Excitement of Entrepreneurship   Consider these words from Jeffry Timmons, a leading entrepreneurship scholar and author: "During the past 30 years, America has unleashed the most revolutionary generation the nation has experienced since its founding in 1776. This new generation of entrepreneurs has altered permanently the economic and social structure of this nation and the world. . . . It will determine more than any other single impetus how the nation and the world will live, work, learn, and lead in this century and beyond."[7] Timmons had written previously, "We are in the midst of a silent revolution—a triumph of the creative and entrepreneurial spirit of humankind throughout the world. I believe its impact on the 21st century will equal or exceed that of the Industrial Revolution on the 19th and 20th."[8]

Overhype? Well, partly, because the rate of new business formation may be slowing down.[9] Given that 99 percent of companies in the United States are small businesses, a slowdown could lower employment rates.[10] But let's hope the slowdown is temporary, because entrepreneurship has transformed economies all over the world and the global economy in general.[11] In the United States in the quarter century since 1980, more than 95 percent of the wealth was created by entrepreneurs.[12] It's been estimated that since World War II, small entrepreneurial firms have generated 95 percent of all radical innovation in the United States. The Small Business Administration has found that in states with more small-business start-ups, statewide economies tend to grow faster, and employment levels tend to be higher than in states with less entrepreneurship.[13]

The self-employed love the entrepreneurial process, and they report the highest levels of pride, satisfaction, and income. Importantly, entrepreneurship is not about the privileged descendants of the Rockefellers and the Vanderbilts—it provides opportunity and upward mobility for anyone who performs well.[14]

Myths about Entrepreneurship   Simply put, entrepreneurs generate new ideas and turn them into business ventures.[15] But entrepreneurship is not simple, and it is frequently misunderstood. Review Exhibit 7.1 to start thinking about the myths and realities of this important career option.

Here is another myth, not in the exhibit: Being an entrepreneur is great because you can get rich quick and enjoy a lot of leisure time while your employees run the company. But the reality is much more difficult. During the start-up period, you are likely to have a lot of bad days. It's exhausting. Even if you don't have employees, you should expect communications breakdowns and other people problems with agents, vendors, distributors, family, subcontractors, lenders, and whomever. Software entrepreneur Dan Bricklin advises that the most important thing to remember is this: "You are not your business. On those darkest days when things aren't going so well—and trust me, you will have them—try to

EXHIBIT 7.1
Some Myths about
Entrepreneurs

Myth 1—Entrepreneurs are born, not made.

Reality—Although entrepreneurs are born with certain native intelligence, a flair for creating, and energy, these talents by themselves do not guarantee success. Adaptive entrepreneurs accumulate the relevant skills, know-how, experiences, and contacts over a period of years. The creative capacity to envision and then pursue an opportunity is earned from at least 10 or more years of experience that lead to pattern recognition.

Myth 2—Anyone can start a business.

Reality—Entrepreneurs who recognize the difference between an idea and an opportunity, and who think big enough, start businesses that have a better chance of succeeding. And the easiest part is starting. What is hardest is surviving, sustaining, and building a venture so its founders can realize a harvest. Perhaps only 1 in 10 to 20 new businesses that survive five years or more results in a capital gain for the founders.

Myth 3—Entrepreneurs are gamblers.

Reality—Successful entrepreneurs take very careful, calculated risks. They try to influence the odds, often by getting others to share risk with them and by avoiding or minimizing risks if they have the choice. Often they slice up the risk into smaller, quite digestible pieces; only then do they commit the time or resources to determine whether that piece will work.

Myth 4—Entrepreneurs want the whole show to themselves.

Reality—Owning and running the whole show effectively puts a ceiling on growth. Solo entrepreneurs usually make a living. It is extremely difficult to grow a higher-potential venture by working single-handedly. Higher-potential entrepreneurs build a team, an organization, and a company.

Myth 5—Entrepreneurs are their own bosses and completely independent.

Reality—Entrepreneurs are far from independent and have to serve many constituencies, including partners, investors, customers, suppliers, creditors, employees, families, and those involved in social and community obligations. Entrepreneurs, however, can make free choices of whether, when, and what they care to respond to.

Myth 6—Entrepreneurs work longer and harder than managers in big companies.

Reality—There is no evidence that all entrepreneurs work more than their corporate counterparts. Some do, some do not. Some actually report that they work less.

Myth 7—Entrepreneurs experience a great deal of stress and pay a high price.

Reality—Being an entrepreneur is stressful and demanding. But there is no evidence that it is any more stressful than numerous other highly demanding professional roles, and entrepreneurs find their jobs very satisfying. They have a high sense of accomplishment, are healthier, and are much less likely to retire than those who work for others.

Myth 8—If an entrepreneur is talented, success will happen in a year or two.

Reality—An old maxim among venture capitalists says it all: The lemons ripen in two and a half years, but the pearls take seven or eight. Rarely is a new business established solidly in less than three or four years.

Myth 9—Entrepreneurs are lone wolves and cannot work with others.

Reality—The most successful entrepreneurs are leaders who build great teams and effective relationships working with peers, directors, investors, key customers, key suppliers, and the like.

Myth 10—Unless you attained 600 or higher on your GMATs, you'll never be a successful entrepreneur.

Reality—Entrepreneurial IQ is a unique combination of creativity, motivation, integrity, leadership, team building, analytical ability, and ability to deal with ambiguity and adversity.

SOURCE: Adapted from S. Spinelli Jr., and R. J. Adams, *New Venture Creation: Entrepreneurship for the 21st Century,* 9th ed., 2012, pp. 46–47. Copyright 2012 The McGraw Hill Companies, Inc. Reprinted with permission.

intrapreneurs

New venture creators working inside big companies.

entrepreneur

Individual who establishes a new organization without the benefit of corporate sponsorship.

remember that your company's failures don't make you an awful person. Likewise, your company's successes don't make you a genius or superhuman."[16]

As you read this chapter, you will learn about two primary sources of new venture creation: independent entrepreneurship and intrapreneurship. **Entrepreneurs** are individuals who establish a new organization without the benefit of corporate support. **Intrapreneurs** are new venture creators working inside big companies; they are corporate entrepreneurs, using their company's resources to build a profitable line of business based on a fresh new idea.[17] Thus, although people tend to think of new, young ventures when they consider entrepreneurship, really it is an activity that should contribute to mature organizations as well. Entrepreneurship is vitally important across the entire life cycle of an organization.[18]

Entrepreneurship

 LO 1

Exhibit 7.2 lists some extraordinary entrepreneurs. The companies they founded are famously successful—and all of the founders started in their 20s. Two young entrepreneurs who started a highly successful business are Tony Hsieh and Nick Swinmurn. In 1999, Swinmurn had the then-new idea to sell shoes online, but he needed money to get started. Hsieh, who at age 24 had already just sold his first start-up, agreed to take a chance on the new venture. It was a smart decision. Ten years later, Amazon purchased Zappos for $1.2 billion.[19]

Swinmurn has moved on, but Hsieh remains at the helm of the company as the CEO of Zappos.com. The real, more complete story of entrepreneurship is not about the famous people in Exhibit 7.2—it's mostly about people you've probably never heard of. Often it's about young people, and definitely it's about people of all ages and ethnic groups.[20]

They have built companies, thrived personally, created jobs, and made positive contributions to their communities through their businesses. Or they're just starting out.

Why Become an Entrepreneur?

Bottom Line

Today's concern for sustainability presents a tremendous variety of opportunities to entrepreneurs who care about the environment. *What are some environmentally friendly start-ups you've heard about? Do you think they have great profit potential?*

Jessica Mah was an entrepreneur before she even finished school. At the age of 13, she went into business using eBay to sell computer parts and templates for websites. While in college at the University of California–Berkeley, she and another student, Andy Su, founded a business they called InternshipIN, which provided information about internship opportunities. When she graduated, Mah was ready to launch another venture. With support from Y

EXHIBIT 7.2
Successful Entrepreneurs Who Started in Their 20s

Entrepreneurial Company	Founder(s)
Apple	Steve Jobs and Steve Wozniak
Facebook	Mark Zuckerberg
Sun Media	Yang Lan
Google	Sergey Brin and Larry Page
Instagram	Kevin Systrom
Microsoft	Bill Gates and Paul Allen
Pinterest	Ben Silbermann and Evan Sharp
The Huffington Post	Arianna Huffington
Spotify	Daniel Ek
Zero Waste Solutions	Shavila Singh
Wal-Mart	Sam Walton

SOURCES: R. Borison, "10 Entrepreneurs Who Can't Be Overshadowed by Men–Even in Silicon Valley," *Inc.* (online), December 18, 2014, http://www.inc.com; Brock Blake, "Why 20-Somethings Are the Most Successful Entrepreneurs," *Forbes*, November 30, 2012, http://www.forbes.com; Burt Helm, "Inside Spotify's U.S. Invasion," *Inc.*, July 2, 2012, http://www.inc.com; "30 under 30 2011: Where Are They Now?" *Inc.*, 2011, http://www.inc.com (slideshow); Lizette Chapman, "'Pivoting' Pays Off for Tech Entrepreneurs," *The Wall Street Journal*, April 26, 2012, http://online.wsj.com; Christine Lagorio, "Introducing the Two Young Men Who Made Pinterest," *Inc.*, July 2, 2012, http://www.inc.com.

Combinator, which provides funds and advice to selected start-ups, Mah again partnered with Su, this time founding inDinero, a company that helps small-business owners manage their money. Customers give inDinero their bank and credit card account numbers, and inDinero keeps track of transactions and analyzes where their money is going. The idea for inDinero came from Mah's own experience that for some people excited about starting a new business, working with customers and products is more exciting and easier to learn than handling money.[21]

Why do Jessica Mah and other entrepreneurs do what they do? Entrepreneurs start their own firms because of the challenge, the profit potential, and the enormous satisfaction they hope lie ahead. People starting their own businesses are seeking a better quality of life than they might have at big companies. They seek independence and a feeling of being part of the action. They feel tremendous satisfaction in building something from nothing, seeing it succeed, and watching the market embrace their ideas and products.

People also start their own companies when they see their progress or ideas blocked at big corporations. When people are laid off, they often try to start businesses of their own. And when employed people believe they will not receive a promotion or are frustrated by bureaucracy or other features of corporate life, they may quit and become entrepreneurs. Years ago, Philip Catron became disillusioned with his job as a manager at ChemLawn because he concluded that the lawn care company's reliance on pesticides contributed to illness in its employees, its customers' pets, and even in the lawns themselves. Catron left the company to start NaturaLawn of America, based on the practice of integrated pest management, which uses natural and nontoxic products as much as possible, reducing pesticide use on lawns by 85 percent. Catron built NaturaLawn into 64 franchises worth $46 million—and helped integrated pest management become mainstream, as even his former employer, now part of TruGreen, has changed many of its practices.[22]

© AP Photo/Paul Sakuma

Immigrants also may find conventional paths to economic success closed to them and turn to entrepreneurship.[23] For example, the Cuban community in Miami has produced many successful entrepreneurs, as has the Vietnamese community throughout the United States. Sometimes the immigrant's experience gives him or her useful knowledge about foreign suppliers or markets that present an attractive business opportunity. Elon Musk grew up in Pretoria, South Africa. At age 20, he immigrated to the United States to study at the University of Pennsylvania. After graduation, Musk cofounded an online payments company, X.com (renamed PayPal), acquired for $1.5 billion by eBay. Next, he cofounded an electric automobile company, Tesla Motors. Musk also founded SpaceX which shuttles supplies to the International Space Station. What's next for this serial entrepreneur? Musk plans to build a new form of transportation called a "hyperloop" connecting Los Angeles and San Francisco. He envisions people traveling through tubes at speeds greater than 700 miles per hour.[24]

What Does It Take to Succeed?

What can we learn from the people who start their own companies and succeed? What enables entrepreneurs to succeed? We show this in general terms with Exhibit 7.3. Successful entrepreneurs are innovators who also have good knowledge and skills in management, business, and networking.[25] In contrast, inventors may be highly creative but often lack the skills to turn their ideas into a successful business. Manager–administrators may be great at ensuring efficient operations but aren't necessarily innovators. Promoters have a different set of marketing and selling skills—useful for entrepreneurs, but those skills can be hired, whereas innovativeness and business management skills remain the essential combination for successful entrepreneurs.

EXHIBIT 7.3
Who Is the Entrepreneur?

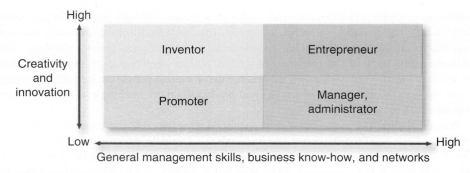

SOURCE: J. A. Timmons and S. Spinelli Jr., *New Venture Creation: Entrepreneurship for the 21st Century,* 7th ed., 2007, pp. 67–68. Copyright 2007 The McGraw-Hill Companies, Inc. Reprinted with permission.

What Business Should You Start?

LO 2

You need a good idea, and you need to find or create the right opportunity. The following discussion offers some general considerations for choosing a type of business.

The Idea   Many entrepreneurs and observers say that in contemplating your business, you must start with a great idea. A great product, a viable market, and good timing are essential ingredients in any recipe for success.

Many great organizations have been built on a different kind of idea: the founder's desire to build a great organization rather than to offer a particular product.[26] Examples abound. Bill Hewlett and David Packard decided to start a company and then figured out what to make. J. Willard Marriott knew he wanted to be in business for himself but didn't have a product in mind until he opened an A&W root beer stand. Masaru Ibuka had no specific product idea when he founded Sony in 1945. Sony's first product attempt, a rice cooker, didn't work, and its first product (a tape recorder) didn't sell. The company stayed alive by making and selling crude heating pads.

Many now-great companies had early failures. But the founders persisted; they believed in themselves and in their dreams of building great organizations. Be prepared to kill or revise an idea, but never give up on your company—this has been a prescription for success for many great entrepreneurs and business leaders. Think about Sony, Disney, Hewlett-Packard, Procter & Gamble, IBM, and Walmart: their founders' greatest achievements—their greatest ideas—are their organizations.[27]

Limor Fried, Adafruit Industries, combined both her academic knowledge and personal interests to prove her capabilities as an entrepreneur.

© Brian Ach/Getty Images for TechCrunch

The Opportunity   Entrepreneurs spot, create, and exploit opportunities in a variety of ways.[28] Entrepreneurial companies can explore domains that big companies avoid and introduce goods or services that capture the market because they are simpler, cheaper, more accessible, or more convenient. Limor Fried spotted her opportunity when she got involved with a hobby that flew under the radar of most traditional businesses: building clever do-it-yourself electronic gadgets. When Fried was at MIT, earning a master's degree in computer science and electrical engineering, she relaxed by ordering parts to build home-made MP3 players, programmable jewelry, and other fun gadgets. As she posted her creations on her personal website, she began attracting requests from people wanting her to sell them kits so they could make the same items themselves. Fried took some personal funds and started Adafruit Industries, now a 50-employee business racking up $10 million in sales annually.[29]

To spot opportunities, think carefully about events and trends as they unfold. Consider, for example, the following possibilities:[30]

Technological discoveries. Start-ups in biotechnology, microcomputers, artificial intelligence, robotics, and nanotechnology followed technological advances. Johnson & Johnson will collaborate with Google to develop advanced robots to aid in surgeries.[31]

Demographic changes. All kinds of health care organizations have sprung up to serve an aging population, from exercise studios to assisted-living facilities. One business that targets the aging American population is fitness center company, Welcyon, which provides senior-friendly low-impact cardio machines, background music at lower volumes, and some fitness classes that can be taken while seated.[32] The service assists those who are pressed for time or have difficulty getting around.[33]

Lifestyle and taste changes. Start-ups have capitalized on new clothing and music trends, desire for fast food, and growing interest in sports. In recent years, more consumers want to help take care of the environment, and more businesses are concerned about showing consumers that they care, too.

Economic dislocations, such as booms or failures. Rising oil prices spurred a variety of developments related to alternative energy or energy efficiency.

Calamities such as wars and natural disasters. The terrorist attacks of September 2001 spurred concern about security, and entrepreneurs today are still pursuing ideas to help government agencies prevent future attacks. Destructive hurricanes, floods, and tornadoes raised awareness of the importance of preparing for emergencies.

Government initiatives and rule changes. Deregulation spawned new airlines and trucking companies. Whenever the government tightens energy efficiency requirements, opportunities become available for entrepreneurs developing ideas for cutting energy use.

Franchises   One important type of opportunity is the franchise. You may know intuitively what franchising is. Or you can at least name some prominent franchises: Subway, Supercuts, Baskin-Robbins—add your favorites here. **Franchising** is an entrepreneurial alliance between two organizations: the franchisor and the franchisee.[34] The franchisor is the innovator who has created at least one successful store and seeks partners to operate the same concept in other local markets. For the franchisee, the opportunity is wealth creation via a proven (but not failureproof) business concept, with the added advantage of the franchisor's expertise. For the franchisor, the opportunity is wealth creation through growth. The partnership is manifest in a trademark or brand, and together the partners' mission is to maintain and build the brand. The Panera Bread chain of bakery-cafés has expanded rapidly in recent years. In 2014, there were nearly 1,900 stores in 45 states.[35]

franchising

An entrepreneurial alliance between a franchisor (an innovator who has created at least one successful store and wants to grow) and a franchisee (a partner who manages a new store of the same type in a new location).

People often assume that buying a franchise is less risky than starting a business from scratch, but the evidence is mixed. One study that followed businesses for six years found the opposite of the popular assumption: 65 percent of the franchises studied were operating at the end of the period, whereas 72 percent of independent businesses were still operating.[36] One reason may be that the franchises involved mostly a few, possibly riskier, industries. A study that compared only restaurants over a three-year period found that 43 percent of the franchises and 39 percent of independent restaurants remained in business.[37]

© RosalreneBetancourt 6/Alamy

If you are contemplating a franchise, consider its market presence (local, regional, or national), market share and profit margins, national programs for marketing and purchasing, the nature of the business, including required training and degree of field support, terms of the license agreement (e.g., 20 years with automatic renewal versus less than 10 years or no renewal), capital required, and franchise fees and royalties.[38]

Although some people think success with a franchise is a no-brainer, would-be franchisees have a lot to consider. Luckily, plenty of useful sources exist for learning more, including the International Franchise Association (http://www.franchise.org), the Small Business Administration (http://www.sba.gov), Franchise Chat (http://www.franchise-chat.com), and *Entrepreneur* magazine's online Franchises page (http://www.entrepreneur.com), which includes rankings as well as articles profiling franchisors and franchisees. In addition, the Federal Trade Commission investigates complaints of deceptive claims by franchisors and publishes information about those cases. Take your time in investigating business opportunities, consulting with an accountant or lawyer who has experience.

The Next Frontiers   The next frontiers for entrepreneurship—where do they lie? Throughout history, aspiring entrepreneurs have asked this question. The editors of *Entrepreneur* magazine recently identified opportunities arising from new technology and changing consumer tastes.[39] The powerful potential of big data to improve decision making is opening up tremendous opportunities for businesses that can help their clients collect, store, manage, and analyze data. Sectors and product categories that have recently enjoyed huge growth are health care, education, and, of course, mobile apps.[40]

One fascinating opportunity for entrepreneurs is outer space. Historically, the space market was driven by the government and was dominated by big defense contractors such as Boeing and Lockheed Martin. But now, with demand for satellite launches and potential profits skyrocketing, smaller entrepreneurs are entering the field. SpaceX has been transporting cargo to the International Space Station for NASA and is developing the capability to transport astronaut crews. NASA also has granted a cargo-shuttling contract to Orbital Sciences Corporation. More futuristic still is the concept of entrepreneur Robert Bigelow. His company, Bigelow Aerospace, has created a residence module for living in space. The module is made out of a synthetic fiber rather than a metal structure, so it can be compressed for more efficient transportation and then expanded upon its arrival. Bigelow received a $17.8 million contract from NASA to send a module into space for a two-year mission.[41]

Changes have been coming fast in the health care sector in the United States, and where there is change, smart entrepreneurs spot opportunities. Driven by advances in technology coupled with incentives in the Affordable Care Act, health care providers have been digitizing their data for patient care, medication management, and treatment outcomes—a trend that yields opportunities for hardware and software businesses that understand the needs of these clients. In addition, rising costs for health care and health insurance create opportunities for entrepreneurs with ideas for restraining those costs. For example, mobile-device apps that promote fitness or help patients manage chronic conditions can appeal to consumers, insurance companies, and employers. GE's healthymagination program recently partnered with an entrepreneurship support group called Startup Health to fund promising start-ups in the health care field. Among the companies the partners funded are BrainScope, which develops imaging biomarkers to better detect and diagnose brain injuries, and Care at Hand, which analyzes data about elderly patients receiving home care to alert nurses when data signal a possible disease requiring attention.[42]

The International Space Station is a habitable artificial satellite. Currently the largest artificial body in orbit, it can be seen at certain times with the naked eye from earth.

© *NASA*

The Internet   The Internet is a business frontier that continues to expand. With Internet commerce, as with any start-up, entrepreneurs need sound business models and practices.

During the heady days of the Internet rush, many entrepreneurs and investors thought revenues and profits were unimportant and all that mattered was to attract visitors to their websites (capture eyeballs). But you need to watch costs carefully, and you want to break even and achieve profitability as soon as possible.[43]

At least five successful business models have proven successful in the e-commerce market: transaction fee, advertising support, intermediary, affiliate, and subscription models.[44] In the **transaction fee model,** companies charge a fee for goods or services. Amazon.com and online travel agents are prime examples. In the **advertising support model,** advertisers pay the site operator to gain access to the demographic group that visits the operator's site.

The **intermediary model** has eBay as the premier example, bringing buyers and sellers together and charging a commission for each sale. With the **affiliate model,** sites pay commissions to other sites to drive business to their own sites. Zazzle.com, Spreadshirt.com, and CafePress.com are variations on this model. They sell custom-decorated gift items such as mugs and T-shirts. Designers are the affiliates; they choose basic, undecorated products (such as a plain shirt) and add their own designs, creating the customized products offered to consumers.[45] Finally, websites using the **subscription model** charge a monthly or annual fee for site visits or access to site content. Newspapers and magazines are good examples.

What about businesses whose primary focus is not e-commerce? Start-ups and established small companies can create attractive websites that add to their professionalism, give them access to more customers, and bring them closer to suppliers, investors, and service providers. Companies can move much more quickly than in the past and save money on activities including customer service/support, technical support, data retrieval, public relations, investor relations, selling, requests for product literature, and purchasing. Setting up shop online costs less than it ever did.

Social Entrepreneurship   Social entrepreneurship has been around for decades, but is surging in popularity and impact and as a focus for academic research.[46] **Social entrepreneurship** has been defined in many ways, but most fundamentally it refers to leveraging resources to address social problems.[47]

It does so by using market-based methods.[48] Organizations that do this are **social enterprises.** Social entrepreneurship creates social value by stimulating social change or meeting social needs.[49]

One of the best-known examples of social entrepreneurship is the Nobel Prize–winning work of Dr. Muhammad Yunus, formerly of Grameen Bank, which began helping women in South Asia obtain microloans.[50] Another is Fabio Rosa's Agroelectric System of Appropriate Technology (STA), which established low-cost electrification and irrigation in rural Brazil.[51] Additional examples include Basic Needs, which provides treatment for mentally ill people across 12 developing countries;[52] Sproxil, which developed a mobile app that enables consumers in Kenya, Ghana, Nigeria, and India to verify the pharmaceutical product they are purchasing is authentic;[53] and Clínicas del Azúcar (Sugar Clinics) which provides affordable care to low- and middle-income patients who suffer from diabetes.[54]

Social entrepreneurship is not charity, and it is different from corporate social responsibility (CSR),[55] which you read about in Chapter 5. CSR is not necessarily practiced with profit as a guiding principle, and corporations often relegate it to a side activity. As described in the nearby "Social Enterprise" box, social entrepreneurship fully incorporates social as well as economic value into mainstream thinking and decision making. It provides dual, shared value: creating economic value plus social or societal benefit simultaneously.[56] See Exhibit 7.4 for examples.

Combining social and commercial goals isn't new; consider hospitals, universities, and arts organizations.[57] And, not all social problems can be solved by entrepreneurial solutions. But pursuing the dual goal of both economic and social value may be developing as the new norm, with positive social outcomes as key to long-term success. States Pierre

---

transaction fee model

Charging fees for goods and services.

advertising support model

Charging fees to advertise on a site.

intermediary model

Charging fees to bring buyers and sellers together.

affiliate model

Charging fees to direct site visitors to other companies' sites.

subscription model

Charging fees for site visits.

---

social entrepreneurship

Leveraging resources to address social problems.

social enterprise

Organization that applies business models and leverages resources in ways that address social problems.

Social Enterprise

Empowering Latina Entrepreneurs

When she was 5 years old, Nely Galan and her family left their native Cuba and began a new life in the United States. As a young person, Galan admired Sherry Lansing, the first female president of Paramount Pictures movie studio. After leaving the entertainment business, Lansing started an "encore career" by pursuing a variety of philanthropic activities.

Galan is following in Lansing's footsteps. Galan became the first Latina president of the Miami-based TV network Telemundo. The "Tropical Tycoon" went on to found her own business, Galan Entertainment, which launched TV channels in Latin America and produced original programming from sitcoms to *telenovelas* (soap operas).

Being an entertainment mogul was not enough. Galan founded Adelante (http://theadelantemovement.com), a movement "designed to empower Latinas in the U.S. economically through inspiration, training, and resources on entrepreneurship." Galan feels that helping Latinas become more financially successful will have a positive impact on their communities and families. The potential ripple effect is significant when considering that the Latina population in the United States is expected to grow to about 13 percent of the United States' population by 2050. In 2013, Latina-owned businesses earned about $66 billion in revenue.

Galan is not working alone. She has joined forces with Coca-Cola's worldwide effort to empower 5 million women entrepreneurs by 2020. Citing a personal goal to train 30,000 Latinas in the United States to became entrepreneurs, Galan sums up her passion this way: "I am a woman that believes in ownership and entrepreneurship as the way for most women to have financial freedom and become actualized."[58]

© Imeh Akpanudosen/Getty Images

Questions

- What factors are motivating Galan to help Latinas become successful entrepreneurs?
- Why do you think Coca-Cola, a global consumer products company, is collaborating with Galan to empower women entrepreneurs?

Omidyar, founder of eBay: "you really can make the world better in any sector—in non-profits, in business, or in government. It's not a question of one sector's struggling against another, or of 'giving back' versus 'taking away.' That's old thinking. A true philanthropist will use every tool he can to make an impact. Today business is a key part of the equation, and the sectors are learning to work together."[59]

Opportunities exist to make substantial positive impact on virtually every societal need and to make a profit doing so. Profit is likely to make societal value creation more sustainable over the long run.

What Does It Take, Personally?

Many people assume that there is an entrepreneurial personality. No single personality type predicts entrepreneurial success, but you are more likely to succeed as an entrepreneur if you exhibit certain characteristics:[60]

1. *Commitment and determination:* Successful entrepreneurs are decisive, tenacious, disciplined, willing to sacrifice, and able to immerse themselves in their enterprises. Entrepreneurial passion[61] can play an important role in all of these things.

Company Name	Description
40K Plus Education	Sets learning "pods" in rural villages that offer tablet-based after-school tutoring to students of government and low-cost private schools.
Barrier Break	Employs deaf people to provide services for those who are hearing impaired online, utilizing an innovative "Sign-and-Talk" business over video-enabled web connections.
Buy42.com	Promotes sustainable living and resells goods collected from individuals and businesses online with a proportion of the revenue being used to fund charity projects.
Edom Nutritional Solutions	Manufactures organically fortified staple flours cost effectively and sells them at affordable prices to the malnourished in East Africa.
Healthy-TX	Sells a mobile platform that automates patient education around post, chronic and preventive care. The physician-designed technology platform and programs greatly improve the quality of care for patients.
Jack and Jake's	Has developed a local/organic wholesale company, sourcing food from within a 100-mile radius of New Orleans to provide healthy food for hospitals and schools.
Kweli	Provides a mobile marketplace for fishermen to access centralized data on market-competitive prices. The goal is to help create a fair marketplace for fishermen.
Not Mass Produced	Is an online marketplace for local, independent businesses in the UK; their flagship site sources local food for UK restaurants, wholesale purchasers, and retail consumers.
PEURegen	Sells a sponge-like scaffold, which is placed inside a deep skin defect to help with wound healing. The product helps patients retain their quality of life through improved healing outcomes after a wound or surgery.
Solidarium	Partners with Walmart and JCPenney to sell ethically produced, fair trade consumer products, selling over 100,000 units and paying its producers 50% more than competitors.

EXHIBIT 7.4
Examples of Social Enterprises

SOURCE: Courtesy of Village Capital.

2. *Leadership:* They are self-starters, team builders, superior learners, and teachers. Communicating a vision for the future of the company—an essential component of leadership that you'll learn more about in Chapter 12—has a direct impact on venture growth.[62]
3. *Opportunity obsession:* They have an intimate knowledge of customers' needs, are market driven, and are obsessed with value creation and enhancement.
4. *Tolerance of risk, ambiguity, and uncertainty:* They are calculated risk takers and risk managers, tolerant of stress, and able to resolve problems.
5. *Creativity, self-reliance, and ability to adapt:* They are open-minded, restless with the status quo, able to learn quickly, highly adaptable, creative, skilled at conceptualizing, and attentive to details.
6. *Motivation to excel:* They have a clear results orientation, set high but realistic goals, have a strong drive to achieve, know their own weaknesses and strengths, and focus on what can be done rather than on the reasons things can't be done.

Making Good Choices   Success is a function not only of personal approaches but also of making good choices about the business you start. Exhibit 7.5 presents a model for

EXHIBIT 7.5
Entrepreneurial Strategy
Matrix

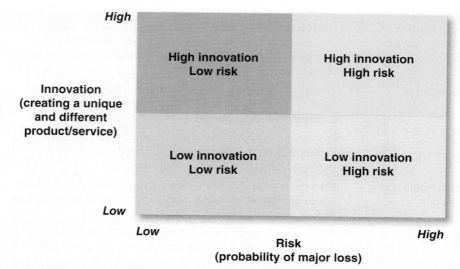

SOURCE: Reprinted from *Business Horizons*, May–June 1997, Sonfield and Lussier, "Entrepreneurial Strategy Matrix: A Model of New and Ongoing Ventures," Copyright © 1997, with permission from Elsevier.

conceptualizing entrepreneurial ventures and making the best possible choices. It depicts ventures along two dimensions: innovation and risk. The new venture may involve high or low levels of innovation or the creation of something new and different. It can also be characterized by low or high risk. Risk refers primarily to the probability of major financial loss. But it also is more than that; it is psychological risk as perceived by the entrepreneur, including risk to reputation and ego.[63]

The upper-left quadrant, high innovation/low risk, depicts ventures of truly novel ideas with little risk. As examples, the inventors of Lego building blocks and Velcro fasteners could build their products by hand at little expense. A pioneering product idea from Google might fit here if there are no current competitors and because, for a company of that size, the financial risks of new product investments can seem relatively small.

In the upper-right quadrant, high innovation/high risk, novel product ideas are accompanied by high risk because the financial investments are high and the competition is great. A new drug or a new automobile would likely fall into this category.

Most small-business ventures are in the low innovation/high risk cell (lower right). They are fairly conventional entries in well-established fields. New restaurants, retail shops, and commercial outfits involve high investment for the small-business entrepreneur and face direct competition from similar businesses. Finally, the low innovation/low risk category includes ventures that require minimal investment and/or face minimal competition for strong market demand. Examples are some service businesses having low start-up costs and those involving entry into small towns if there is no competitor and demand is adequate.

How is this matrix useful? It helps entrepreneurs think about their ventures and decide whether they suit their particular objectives. It also helps identify effective and ineffective strategies. You might find one cell more appealing than others. The lower-left cell is likely to have relatively low payoffs but to provide more security. The higher risk/return trade-offs are in other cells, especially the upper right. So you might place your new venture idea in the appropriate cell and determine whether that cell is the one in which you would prefer to operate. If it is, the venture is one that perhaps should be pursued, pending fuller analysis. If it is not, you can reject the idea or take steps to move it toward a different cell.

The matrix also can help entrepreneurs remember a useful point: successful companies do not always require a cutting-edge technology or an exciting new product. Even companies offering the most mundane products—the type that might reside in the lower-left cell—can gain competitive advantage by doing basic things differently from and better than competitors.

Success and Failure

Success or failure lies ahead for entrepreneurs starting their own companies as well as for those starting new businesses within bigger corporations. Entrepreneurs succeed or fail in private, public, and not-for-profit sectors; in nations at all stages of development; and in all nations, regardless of their politics.[64]

Estimated failure rates for start-ups vary. Most indicate that failure is more the rule than the exception. The failure rate is high for certain businesses such as restaurants and lower for successful franchises. Start-ups have at least two major liabilities: newness and smallness.[65] New companies are relatively unknown and need to learn how to be better than established competitors at something that customers value. Regarding smallness, the odds of surviving improve if the venture reaches a critical mass of at least 10 or 20 people, has revenues of $2 million or $3 million, and is pursuing opportunities with growth potential.[66]

To understand further the factors that influence success and failure, we'll consider risk, the economic environment, various management-related hazards, and initial public stock offerings (IPOs).

Risk You learned about risk in Chapter 3. It's a given: starting a new business is risky. Entrepreneurs with plenty of business experience are especially aware of this. When Chris McGill was evaluating his idea for Mixx.com, a news website that could be personal-ized based on recommendations by users, he was *USA Today*'s vice president of strategy. To make Mixx succeed, McGill knew he would be leaving a well-paying job for an uncertain future in which he had to line up financing and hire talented people in a turbulent business environment. But McGill also concluded that his experience at *USA Today* and prior management experience with *Yahoo News* gave him the knowledge and connections for a suc-cessful Internet business.[67] He sold Mixx.com in 2011 to UberMedia.

© Web Pix/Alamy

Successful entrepreneurs are realistic about risk. They anticipate difficulties and cushion their business to help it weather setbacks. Susan Petersen needed a way to sup-port her young, growing family. In 2006, she learned how to sew baby blankets and began selling them through her online Etsy page. Building on her experience, she decided to make footwear for infants. Petersen bought a bag of scrap leather at a garage sale. Working with her infant son as a Moc-tester, she designed colorful leather moccasins for infants. Her new start-up, Freshly Picked, was born. By 2014, the company had grown to $5.4 million in sales and had 12 employees.[68]

The Role of the Economic Environment Entrepreneurial activity stems from the economic environment as well as the behavior of individuals. For example, money is a critical resource for all new businesses. Increases in the money supply and the supply of bank loans, real economic growth, and improved stock market performance lead to both improved prospects and increased sources of capital. In turn, the prospects and the capital increase the rate of business formation. Under favorable conditions, many aspiring entre-preneurs find early success. But economic cycles can quickly change favorable conditions into downturns. To succeed, entrepreneurs must have the foresight and talent to survive when the environment becomes more hostile.

> Economic cycles can quickly change favorable conditions into downturns.

Although good economic times may make it easier to start a company and to survive, bad times can offer an opportunity to expand. Ken Hendricks of ABC Supply found a business opportunity in a grim economic situation: a serious downturn in the manufacturing economy of the Midwest contributed to the shutdown of his town's largest employer, the Beloit Corporation. Hendricks purchased the company's buildings and lured a diverse group of new employers to town despite the economic challenges. In fact, Hendricks turned around struggling suppliers that ABC acquired.[69] Another silver lining in difficult economic times is that it's easier to recruit talent.

business incubators

Protected environments for new, small businesses.

Business Incubators   The need to provide a nurturing environment for fledgling enterprises led to the creation of business incubators. **Business incubators,** often located in industrial parks or abandoned factories, are protected environments for new, small businesses. Incubators offer benefits such as low rents and shared costs. Shared staff costs, such as for receptionists and secretaries, avoid the expense of a full-time employee but still provide convenient access to services. The staff manager is usually an experienced businessperson or consultant who advises the new business owners. Incubators often are associated with universities, which provide technical and business services for the new companies.

The heyday of business incubators came in the 1990s, when around 700 of them were financing start-ups, mainly emphasizing technology. Eight out of 10 shut down following the collapse of the Internet bubble, but the idea of nurturing new businesses persists. For example, the Houston Technology Center (HTC) focuses on two critical areas: energy and nanotechnology. HTC has launched 1,000 entrepreneurs who have raised $1 billion in funding. The Center works with 60 companies at a time. Successful graduates include NanoRidge Materials, which makes carbon nanotubes to make metal alloys 10 times stronger than steel, and Hydro Green Energy, which produces hydro-electricity using the energy generated by the natural flow of a river or stream.[70]

business accelerator

Organization that provides support and advice to help young businesses grow.

Business incubators hatch new businesses. Once a young business begins gaining a foothold and establishing itself, **business accelerators** can provide additional support and advice. These still-young firms are more mature but still in their formative years, and they now face the challenges of sustaining growth and achieving their full market potential.[71]

Common Management Challenges

As an entrepreneur, you are likely to face several common challenges that you should understand before you face them and then manage effectively when the time comes. We next discuss several such challenges.

You Might Not Enjoy It   Some managers and employees can specialize in what they love, whether it's selling or accounting. But entrepreneurs usually have to do it all, at least in the beginning. If you love product design, you also have to sell what you invent. If you love marketing, get ready to manage the money too. This last challenge was almost a stumbling block for Elizabeth Busch, Anne Frey-Mott, and Beckie Jankiewicz when they launched The Event Studio to run business conferences for their clients. All three women had experience with some aspect of running conferences, but when they started their company, they didn't fully think out all the accounting decisions they would need for measuring their income and cash flow. With some practical advice, they learned some basic accounting lessons that helped them avoid tax troubles later on.[72] If they hadn't been willing to learn new skills, entrepreneurship might not have been the right career path for them.

Survival Is Difficult   Companies without much of a track record tend to have more trouble lining up lenders, investors, and customers. When economic conditions cool or competition heats up, a small start-up serving a niche market may have limited options for survival. Failure can be devastating.

Founders of a start-up must make key decisions in so many areas of business that mistakes are a potentially devastating risk. Several months after starting Zipcar, a car-sharing service, founder Robin Chase evaluated the early financial data and discovered that the company had made a mistake in setting prices. The daily rental fees had been set too low to make the company profitable. Chase concluded that the only way she could keep Zipcar in business was to own up to her error, disclose it to her customers, and explain that the rate would be rising by 25 percent. Only two customers complained, and Zipcar grew into a multimillion-dollar business.[73]

Growth Creates New Challenges   Just one in three *Inc.* 500 companies keeps growing fast enough to make this list of fastest-growing companies two years running. The reason: They are facing bigger challenges, competing with bigger firms, stretching the founders' capacities, and probably burning cash. Consultant Doug Tatum calls this phase of a company's growth "no man's land."[74] It's a difficult transition.

In the beginning, entrepreneurs keep their business afloat with dogged determination to win customers and keep them happy. They work long hours at low pay, deliver great service, and get good word-of-mouth advertising, and their business grows. When keeping up with all the work becomes physically impossible, entrepreneurs feel they need to bring in help. Julie Ladd, founder of CopyShark.net, says she got ready to contract for help after she spent six months doing everything alone: "I was working 70-plus hours a week and wasn't able to get the turnaround time that my clients needed."[75] The challenge, of course, is that you not only have to come up with the money to keep paying people for the long haul but also have to figure out who will bring the necessary skills and a level of motivation that can bring them close to the business owner's commitment to the company.

Growth seems to be a consuming goal for most entrepreneurs. But some company founders reach the size where they're happy and don't want to grow any further. Reaching a golden mean is possible.[76] Other founders pursue slow growth. Jason Fried, cofounder of Basecamp (formerly known as 37signals), refuses to grow so fast that the workload and stress would push employees to the point of quitting: "I like the people who work here too much. I don't want them to burn out." With a relatively small staff of 43 people, Basecamp is successful with nearly 15 million individual and 7,000 company subscribers.[77]

It's Hard to Delegate   As the business grows, entrepreneurs often hesitate to delegate to other people work that they are used to doing. Leadership deteriorates into micromanagement, in which managers monitor too strictly, to the minutest detail. For example, during the Internet craze, many company founders with great technical knowledge but little experience became instant experts in every phase of business, including branding and advertising.[78] Turns out, they didn't know as much as they thought, and their companies crashed. Fortunately, many entrepreneurs observe the consequences of their behavior and figure out how to manage more effectively. Kit Hickey and her business partners had a good problem on their hands. Within a month of launching Ministry of Supply, they sold 6,000 shirts and acquired 4,000 customers. The leadership team had to scale production from 300 to 6,000 shirts per month. Their solution was to divide responsibilities and then empower each other to make customers as happy as possible. For example, one partner was in charge of product development and technology, another was the head of Customer Advocacy, and so forth. These decisions, combined with agile problem solving and transparent communication, helped Ministry of Supply grow rapidly to meet surging customer demand.[79]

Misuse of Funds   Many unsuccessful entrepreneurs blame their failure on inadequate financial resources. Yet failure due to a lack of financial resources doesn't necessarily indicate a real lack of money; it could mean a failure to use the available money properly. A lot of start-up capital may be wasted—on expensive locations, great furniture, and fancy stationery. Entrepreneurs who fail to use their resources wisely usually make one of two mistakes: They apply financial resources to the wrong uses, or they maintain inadequate control over their resources.

This problem may be more likely when a lucky entrepreneur gets a big infusion of cash from a venture capital firm or an initial offering of stock. For most start-ups, where the money on the line comes from the entrepreneur's own assets, he or she has more incentive to be careful. Tripp Micou, founder of Practical Computer Applications, says, "If all the money you spend is based on what you're bringing in [through sales], you very quickly focus on the right things to spend it on."[80] Micou, an experienced entrepreneur, believes that this financial limitation is actually a management advantage.

Poor Controls   Entrepreneurs, in part because they are very busy, often fail to use formal control systems. One common entrepreneurial malady is an aversion to record keeping. Expenses mount, but records do not keep pace. Pricing decisions are based on intuition without adequate reference to costs. As a result, the company earns inadequate margins to support growth.

Sometimes an economic slowdown provides a necessary alarm, warning business owners to pay attention to controls. When Servatii Pastry Shop and Deli's sales deteriorated even as the prices of ingredients were rising, owner Gary Gottenbusch set goals and monitored progress. One problem Gottenbusch tackled was the price of baking commodities, such as shortening and flour. He partnered with other local bakeries to form a purchasing association that buys in bulk and passes along the savings. Keeping costs down helped Servatii stay profitable when customers were trimming their budgets for baked goods.[81] Blinded by the light of growing sales, many entrepreneurs fail to maintain vigilance over other aspects of the business.

Even in high-growth companies, great numbers can mask brewing problems. In the absence of controls, the business veers out of control. So don't get overconfident; keep asking critical questions. Is our success based on just one big customer? Is our product just a fad that can fade away? Can other companies easily enter our domain and hurt our business? Are we losing a technology lead? Do we really understand the numbers, know where they come from, and have any hidden causes for concern?

Mortality and Succession   One long-term measure of an entrepreneur's success is the fate of the venture after the founder's death. Founding entrepreneurs often fail to plan for succession. When death occurs, estate tax problems or the lack of a skilled replacement for the founder can lead to business failure. In the United States and around the world, the large majority of family-owned businesses fail before the founder's grandchildren have taken charge.[82]

Management guru Peter Drucker offered the following advice to help family-managed businesses survive and prosper.[83] Family members working in the business must be at least as capable and hard-working as other employees; at least one key position should be filled by a nonfamily member; and someone outside the family and the business should help plan succession. Family members who are mediocre performers are resented by others; outsiders can be more objective and contribute expertise the family might not have. Issues of management succession are often the most difficult of all, causing serious conflict and possible breakup of the firm.

Going Public
Sometimes companies reach a point at which the owners want to go public. **Initial public stock offerings (IPOs)** offer a way to raise capital through federally registered and underwritten sales of shares in the company.[84] You need lawyers and accountants who know current regulations. The reasons for going public include raising more capital, reducing debt or improving the balance sheet and enhancing net worth, pursuing otherwise unaffordable opportunities, and improving credibility with customers and other stakeholders—you're in the big leagues now. Disadvantages include the expense, time, and effort involved; the tendency to become more interested in the stock price and capital gains than in running the company properly; and the creation of a long-term relationship with an investment banking firm that won't necessarily always be a good one.[85]

Many entrepreneurs prefer to avoid going public, feeling they'll lose control if they do. That's a viewpoint that has persisted into the second generation of ownership at Half Price Books, a retail chain that was founded four decades ago by Pat Anderson and Ken Gjemre and remains a family business run by Anderson's daughter, Sharon Anderson Wright. Wright sees retaining private ownership as a necessary part of maintaining the company's commitment to employees, pointing out that "not everyone comes out well" when a business is sold. The company, which has more than 120 stores in 16 states, prides itself on hiring bright people and rewarding them with training, a good benefits package, and

Bottom Line

You probably will pay close attention to costs at the beginning, but success sometimes brings neglect. Don't fall into that trap. *An entrepreneur who loves selling delegates bookkeeping to an accountant. What danger does this pose to the business?*

initial public offering (IPO)

Sale to the public, for the first time, of federally registered and underwritten shares of stock in the company.

Management in Action

CAN POPCHIPS STAY HEALTHY?

Cofounders Keith Belling and Pat Turpin can be proud to see Popchips generate $93.7 million in sales and report a distribution network of 30,000 retailers across the United States, but their company does face some formidable challenges. For one thing, although $93 million is a lot of money, it represents roughly 0.1 percent of the $90 *billion* global market for snacks. Among the hundreds of snack makers in the United States alone, Popchips is competing with such giants as PepsiCo's Frito-Lay products and Mondelez (formerly part of Kraft Foods). In fact, Kellogg's has introduced Popcorn Chips, and Quaker has introduced its Popped brand of snacks. Consumers who are now snapping up Popchips as a way to enjoy crunchy snacks without the fat could abandon the brand as soon as someone new offers an alternative.

Belling (now chair) has hired a new CEO, Paul Davis, to help boost sales and build brand awareness on a national level. Davis is a snack food industry veteran, having served as CEO of Kettle and a senior executive with Frito-Lay. He's ready for the challenge: "I'm thrilled to be joining the team and helping take the brand to the next level."

To reach a broader audience, Popchips recently launched its first national advertising campaign. The campaign no longer uses Millennial-friendly celebrities like Katy Perry and Ashton Kutcher and instead focuses on convincing "mainstream, fried-snack-addicted Americans that a healthier option can actually taste good."

Popchips is making other changes. The company has redesigned its website, beefed up its social media presence, and increased by 15 percent the amount of chips in its packages (without boosting prices). Even if consumers haven't always appreciated the taste of Popchips advertising, the company hopes they will continue to get excited about the taste of its popped snacks.[86]

- What do you think are the most significant risks affecting Popchips?
- Do you think Popchips would be a good candidate for an initial public offering (IPO)? Why or why not?

---

opportunities for advancement. Concern for employees fits in well with Half Price Books' general commitment to sustainability: 70 percent of the stores' inventory consists of used books, magazines, and music, a business model that promotes reusing rather than throwing out these items. Also, it encourages customers to use reusable tote bags when checking out from stores, purchases recycled office supplies for office needs, and uses low-flow power-assisted commodes to conserve water. Wright's desire to run an ecofriendly business is another value she can insist on when she is both owner and CEO of the company.[87]

Executing IPOs and other approaches to acquiring capital are complex, legalistic, and beyond the scope of this chapter. Sources for more information include the National Venture Capital Association (www.nvca.org), the Small Business Administration's Community page (http://www.sba.gov/community), and the SBA's Small Business Learning Center (http://www.sba.gov/sba-learning-center). In the case of Popchips founder Keith Belling, he didn't opt for an IPO with his earlier venture, Allbusiness.com; instead, he exited after selling it to NBC. As you read "Management in Action: Progress Report," think about whether Popchips would be a good candidate for an IPO.

Increasing Your Chances of Success

Entrepreneurs need to think through their business idea carefully to help ensure its success. We discuss here the importance of good planning and a variety of resources.

Planning   So you think you have identified a business opportunity. And you have the personal drive to make it a success. Now what? Where should you begin?

The Business Plan   Your excitement and intuition may convince you that you are on to something. But they might not convince anyone else. You need more thorough planning and analysis. This effort will help convince other people to get on board and help you avoid costly mistakes.

EXHIBIT 7.6
Opportunity Analysis

What market need does my idea fill?
What personal observations have I experienced or recorded with regard to that market need?
What social condition underlies this market need?
What market research data can be marshaled to describe this market need?
What patents might be available to fulfill this need?
What competition exists in this market? How would I describe the behavior of this competition?
What does the international market look like?
What does the international competition look like?
Where is the money to be made in this activity?

SOURCE: R. Hisrich and M. Peters, *Entrepreneurship: Starting, Developing, and Managing a New Enterprise*, p. 41. Copyright © 1998 by The McGraw-Hill Companies, Inc. Reprinted with permission.

opportunity analysis

A description of the good or service, an assessment of the opportunity, an assessment of the entrepreneur, specification of activities and resources needed to translate your idea into a viable business, and your source(s) of capital.

business plan

A formal planning step that focuses on the entire venture and describes all the elements involved in starting it.

The first formal planning step is to do an opportunity analysis. An **opportunity analysis** includes a description of the good or service, an assessment of the opportunity, an assessment of the entrepreneur (you), a specification of activities and resources needed to translate your idea into a viable business, and your source(s) of capital.[88] Exhibit 7.6 shows the questions you should answer in an opportunity analysis.

The opportunity analysis, or opportunity assessment plan, focuses on the opportunity, not the entire venture. It provides the basis for making a decision on whether to act. Then the **business plan** describes all the elements involved in starting the new venture.[89] The business plan describes the venture and its market, strategies, and future directions. It often has functional plans for marketing, finance, manufacturing, and human resources.

Exhibit 7.7 shows an outline for a typical business plan. The business plan (1) helps determine the viability of your enterprise, (2) guides you as you plan and organize, and (3) helps you obtain financing. It is read by potential investors, suppliers, customers, and others. Get help in writing up a sound plan!

Key Planning Elements   A successful business needs enough cash to cover start-up expenses and keep the company running during slow periods. The initial budget should cover one-time costs, such as the fee to form a corporation, and ongoing expenses such as supplies and rent for the first few months. The company's founders may start the business with their own money, or they may seek financing in the form of debt (taking out a loan from family, friends, or a bank) or equity (taking money in exchange for an ownership share in the company). Typically, start-ups get most of their money from the owners, their families, and loans and credit lines from banks. Other kinds of investors, such as venture capital firms, generate a lot of publicity for splashy deals but provide a very small share of start-up funds.[90]

Under these circumstances, raising money to start a business can be one of the entrepreneur's greatest challenges. Since the Great Recession, some entrepreneurs and small-business owners have had a difficult time convincing banks to loan them funds. Peer-to-peer loans are an alternative to using a bank. Using online platforms like Lending Club or Prosper, individual investors loan up to $35,000 to small businesses. For example, Hannah Attwood wanted to raise money to open a cloth diaper supply and cleaning service. After four banks rejected her, Attwood secured from investors a three-year loan to help launch her new business. Combining the loan with her own savings, Attwood was able to purchase industrial washers and dryers.[91]

Just as the Internet has transformed every other aspect of business, it is poised to remake the challenge of raising start-up money. This trend started with the use of social media tools to link would-be entrepreneurs with people who want to make great ideas

EXHIBIT 7.7   Outline of a Business Plan

I.   EXECUTIVE SUMMARY

Description of the Business Concept and the Business

Opportunity and Strategy

Target Market and Projections

Competitive Advantages

Costs

Sustainability

The Team

The Offering

II.   THE INDUSTRY AND THE COMPANY AND ITS PRODUCT(S) OR SERVICE(S)

The Industry

The Company and the Concept

The Product(s) or Service(s)

Entry and Growth Strategy

III.   MARKET RESEARCH AND ANALYSIS

Customers

Market Size and Trends

Competition and Competitive Edges

Estimated Market Share and Sales

Ongoing Market Evaluation

IV.   THE ECONOMICS OF THE BUSINESS

Gross and Operating Margins

Profit Potential and Durability

Fixed, Variable, and Semivariable Costs

Months to Breakeven

Months to Reach Positive Cash Flow

V.   MARKETING PLAN

Overall Marketing Strategy

Pricing

Sales Tactics

Service and Warranty Policies

Advertising and Promotion

Distribution

VI.   DESIGN AND DEVELOPMENT PLANS

Development Status and Tasks

Difficulties and Risks

Product Improvement and New Products

Costs

Proprietary Issues

VI.   MANUFACTURING AND OPERATIONS PLAN

Operating Cycle

Geographical Location

Facilities and Improvements

Strategy and Plans

Regulatory and Legal Issues

VIII.   MANAGEMENT TEAM

Organization

Key Management Personnel

Management Compensation and Ownership

Other Investors

Employment and Other Agreements and Stock Option and Bonus Plans

Board of Directors

Other Shareholders, Rights, and Restrictions

Supporting Professional Advisers and Services

IX.   OVERALL SCHEDULE

X.   CRITICAL RISKS, PROBLEMS, AND ASSUMPTIONS

XI.   THE FINANCIAL PLAN

Actual Income Statements and Balance Sheets

Pro Forma Income Statements

Pro Forma Balance Sheets

Pro Forma Cash Flow Analysis

Breakeven Chart and Calculation

Cost Control

Highlights

XII.   PROPOSED COMPANY OFFERING

Desired Financing

Offering

Capitalization

Use of Funds

Investor's Return

XIII.   APPENDIXES

happen. At crowdfunding websites, such as AngelList, Crowdfunder.com, FundersClub, and Kickstarter, the entrepreneurs post their ideas, and anyone can donate to the cause. Until recently, crowdfunding was mostly limited to small contributions from people who gave in exchange for a company-provided experience, discount, or product sample; the funders don't receive equity in the business. The main reason is that the Securities and Exchange Commission, which regulates investing, needs to ensure that investors on these sites have the same protections available to traditional investors. In 2012, however, Congress passed the Jumpstart Our Business Startups Act (JOBS Act), which makes it easier for start-ups to receive funding from online investors (crowdfunding) and to go public. Early results are promising. In 2014, the number of IPOs increased by 70 percent over the previous year and high-tech company IPOs are expected to reach their highest level in over 10 years.[92]

Most business plans devote so much attention to financial projections that they neglect other important information—information that matters greatly to astute investors. In fact, financial projections tend to be overly optimistic. Investors know this and discount the figures. In addition to the numbers, the best plans convey—and make certain that the entrepreneurs have carefully thought through—five key factors: the people, the opportunity, the competition, the context, and risk and reward.[93]

The people should be energetic and have skills and expertise directly relevant to the venture. For many astute investors, the people are the most important variable, more important even than the idea. Arthur Rock, a legendary venture capitalist who helped start Intel, Teledyne, and Apple, stated, "I invest in people, not ideas. If you can find good people, if they're wrong about the product, they'll make a switch."[94]

> The opportunity should provide a competitive advantage that can be defended.

The opportunity should provide a competitive advantage that can be defended. Customers are the focus here: Who is the customer? How does the customer make decisions? How will the product be priced? How will the venture reach all customer segments? How much does it cost to acquire and support a customer and to produce and deliver the product? How easy or difficult is it to retain a customer?

It is also essential to consider the competition fully. The plan must identify current competitors and their strengths and weaknesses, predict how they will respond to the new venture, indicate how the new venture will respond to the competitors' responses, identify future potential competitors, and consider how to collaborate with or face off against actual or potential competitors. The original plan for Zappos was for its website to compete with other online shoe retailers by offering a wider selection than they did. However, most people buy shoes in stores, so Zappos cofounders Nick Swinmurn and Tony Hsieh soon realized that they needed a broader view of the competition. They began focusing more on service and planning a distribution method that would make online shopping as successful as visiting a store.[95]

The environmental context should be a favorable one from regulatory and economic perspectives. Such factors as tax policies, rules about raising capital, interest rates, inflation, and exchange rates will affect the viability of the new venture. The context can make it easier or harder to get backing and to succeed. Importantly, the plan should make clear that you know that the context inevitably will change, forecast how the changes will affect the business, and describe how you will deal with the changes.

The risk must be understood and addressed as fully as possible. The future is always uncertain, and the elements described in the plan will change over time. Although you cannot predict the future, you must contemplate head-on the possibilities of key people

Entrepreneurs should carefully consider the five key factors when developing a business plan: the people, the opportunity, the competition, the context, and risk and reward. Typically, financial projections dominate the plan while these other important factors are overlooked or undervalued.

© John Lund/Marc Romanelli/ Getty Images/RF

leaving, interest rates changing, a key customer leaving, or a powerful competitor responding ferociously. Then describe what you will do to prevent, avoid, or cope with such possibilities. You should also speak to the end of the process: how to get money out of the business eventually. Will you go public? Will you sell or liquidate? What are the various possibilities for investors to realize their ultimate gains?[96]

Selling the Plan   Your goal is to get investors to support the plan, so the elements of a great plan, as just described, are essential. It's also important whom you decide to try to convince to back your plan.

Many entrepreneurs want passive investors who will give them money and let them do what they want. Doctors and dentists generally fit this image. Professional venture capitalists do not—they demand more control and more of the returns. But when a business goes wrong—and chances are, it will—nonprofessional investors are less helpful and less likely to advance more (needed) money. Sophisticated investors have seen sinking ships before and know how to help. They are more likely to solve problems, provide more money, and navigate financial and legal waters.[97]

View the plan as a way for you to figure out how to reduce risk, maximize reward, and convince others that you understand the entire new venture process. Don't put together a plan built on naïveté or overconfidence or one that cleverly hides major flaws. You might not fool others, and you certainly would be fooling yourself.

Nonfinancial Resources   Also crucial to the success of a new business are nonfinancial resources, including legitimacy in the minds of the public and the various ways in which other people can help. The nearby "Multiple Generations at Work" box suggests start-ups are more likely to gain legitimacy and success by employing multiple generations.

Legitimacy   An important resource for the new venture is **legitimacy**—people's judgment of a company's acceptance, appropriateness, and desirability.[98] When the market confers legitimacy, it helps overcome the liability of newness that creates a high percentage of new venture failure.[99] Legitimacy helps a firm acquire other resources such as top managers, good employees, financial resources, and government support. In a three-year study tracking business start-ups, the likelihood that a company would succeed at selling products, hiring employees, and attracting investors depended most on how skillfully entrepreneurs demonstrated that their business was legitimate.[100]

A business is legitimate if its goals and methods are consistent with societal values. You can generate legitimacy by visibly conforming to rules and expectations created by governments, credentialing associations, and professional organizations; by visibly endorsing widely held values; and by visibly practicing widely held beliefs.[101]

legitimacy

People's judgment of a company's acceptance, appropriateness, and desirability, generally stemming from company goals and methods that are consistent with societal values.

Networks   The entrepreneur is aided greatly by having a strong network of people. **Social capital**—being part of a social network and having a good reputation—helps entrepreneurs gain access to useful information, gain trust and cooperation from others, recruit employees, form successful business alliances, receive funding from venture capitalists, and become more successful.[102] Social capital provides a lasting source of competitive advantage.[103]

social capital

Goodwill stemming from your social relationships; a competitive advantage in the form of relationships with other people and the image other people have of you.

Top Management Teams   The top management team is another crucial resource. For example, Sudhin Shahani's start-ups include MyMPO, whose digital media services include Musicane, which lets musicians sell audio and video files and ringtones online at storefronts they create for themselves. The company's head of marketing was singer Will.i.am.[104] Having a musician in that top spot may help Musicane build client relationships with other artists. Also, in companies that have incorporated, a board of directors improves the company's image, develops longer-term plans for expansion, supports day-to-day activities, and develops a network of information sources.

Multiple Generations at Work

Fast-Growth Start-Up Realizes That Three Generations Are Better Than One

Greg Skloot is a 24-year-old cofounder of an event management software company, Attend.com. Initially, he was excited when his start-up began to grow rapidly until he realized that he and his cofounder lacked the managerial and organizational skills needed to scale his business. Skloot described his challenge this way:

Young, creative team members give start-ups great energy, but they've likely never dealt with investors or overseen the hiring process. That's why any new company looking to scale needs to find experienced senior executives to guide the business forward, particularly when product-market is found and the start-up is ready for serious growth.

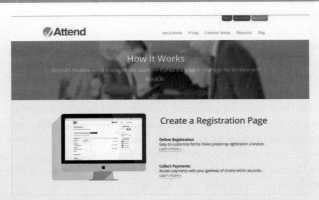

Despite retirements, Boomers still comprise one-third of the workforce and represent the largest source of experienced talent in the marketplace. The Kaufmann Foundation reports one-quarter of all new entrepreneurs in 2012 were 55- to 64-year-olds. These data suggest there is a large pool of "seniorpreneurs" who are available and willing to lend decades of experience to Millennial and Gen X founders of start-ups.

Here are some areas in which Boomers can help start-ups achieve scalability and success:

1. Angel investors and advisers. Boomers can bring much needed funding and advice with regard to business plan development and marketing strategies.

2. Partnership or executive positions. Boomers may be willing to work with founders for an equity stake in the business. This can create a win–win for the cash-starved start-up that needs experienced personnel.

3. Talent management issues. Boomers have decades of experience dealing with talent management issues such as hiring, firing, training, compensation, and performance evaluation. This can free up the founders to focus on the core activity of the start-up.

By handling the above tasks, Boomers can empower the founders and other employees to focus on developing and improving products, sales and marketing (traditional and social media) to Millennial and Gen X customers.[105]

Advisory Boards   Whether or not the company has a formal board of directors, entrepreneurs can assemble a group of people willing to serve as an advisory board. Board members with business experience can help an entrepreneur learn basics such as how to do cash flow analysis; identify needed strategic changes; and build relationships with bankers, accountants, and attorneys.

Partners   Often two people go into business together as partners. Partners can help one another access capital, spread the workload, share the risk, and share expertise. One of the strengths of JLW Homes and Communities, the Atlanta construction business described earlier, is that the three founding partners bring different areas of expertise to the business. Gregory Wynn was a master homebuilder, Komichel Johnson was a financial expert, and Robert A. Jones III was a successful salesperson. Johnson explains the advantage this way: "We don't all agree on the same issues, and we've had some heated arguments. . . . But we realize that through communication and laying out the facts, we can overcome any issues that may arise within our organization."[106]

Despite the potential advantages of finding a compatible partner, partnerships are not always marriages made in heaven. "Mark" talked three of his friends into joining him in

> Partnerships are not always marriages made in heaven.

starting his own telecommunications company because he didn't want to try it alone. He learned quickly that while he wanted to put money into growing the business, his three partners wanted the company to pay for their cars and meetings in the Bahamas. The company collapsed. "I never thought a business relationship could overpower friendship, but this one did. Where money's involved, people change."

To be successful, partners need to acknowledge one another's talents, let each other do what they do best, communicate honestly, and listen to one another. Partners also must learn to trust each other by making and keeping agreements. If they must break an agreement, it is crucial that they give early notice and clean up after their mistakes.

Corporate Entrepreneurship

Large corporations are more than passive bystanders in the entrepreneurial explosion. Even established companies try to find and pursue new and profitable ideas—and they need in-house entrepreneurs (sometimes called intrapreneurs) to do so.

Building Support for Your Idea

A manager who has a new idea to capitalize on a market opportunity will need to get others in the organization to buy in or sign on. In other words, you need to build a network of allies who support and will help implement the idea.

If you need to build support for a project idea, the first step involves clearing the investment with your immediate boss or bosses.[107] At this stage, you explain the idea and seek approval to look for wider support.

Higher executives often want evidence that the project is backed by your peers before committing to it. This involves making cheerleaders—people who will support the manager before formal approval from higher levels.

Next, horse trading begins. You can offer promises of payoffs from the project in return for support, time, money, and other resources that peers and others contribute.

Finally, you should get the blessing of relevant higher-level officials. This usually involves a formal presentation. You will need to guarantee the project's technical and political feasibility. Higher management's endorsement of the project and promises of resources help convert potential supporters into an enthusiastic team. At this point, you can go back to your boss and make specific plans for going ahead with the project. Along the way, expect resistance and frustration—and use passion and persistence, as well as business logic, to persuade others to get on board.

Building Intrapreneurship

Success in fostering a culture in which intrapreneurs flourish comes from making an intentional decision to foster entrepreneurial thinking and behavior, creating new venture teams, and changing the compensation system so that it encourages, supports, and rewards creative and innovative behaviors. In other words, building intrapreneurship derives from careful and deliberate strategy.

Two common approaches used to stimulate intrapreneurial activity are skunkworks and bootlegging. **Skunkworks** are project teams designated to produce a new product. A team is formed with a specific goal within a specified time frame. A respected person is chosen to be manager of the skunkworks. In this approach to corporate innovation, risk takers are not punished for taking risks and failing—their former jobs are held for them. The risk takers also have the opportunity to earn large rewards.

Bootlegging refers to informal efforts—as opposed to official job assignments—in which employees work to create new products and processes of their own choosing and initiative. Informal can mean secretive, such as when a bootlegger believes the company or the boss will frown on those activities. But companies should tolerate some bootlegging,

Bottom Line
Recall from Chapter 3 that creativity spawns good new ideas, but innovation requires actually implementing those ideas so they become realities. If you work in an organization and have a good idea, you must convince other people to get on board.
What skills would you need to get people on board with a new idea?

skunkworks

A project team designated to produce a new, innovative product.

bootlegging

Informal work on projects, other than those officially assigned, of employees' own choosing and initiative.

and some even encourage it. To a limited extent, they allow people freedom to pursue pet projects without asking what they are or monitoring progress, figuring bootlegging will lead to some lost time but also to learning and to some profitable innovations.

W.L. Gore, maker of Gore-Tex fabric, encourages all employees to be intrapreneurs. Employees spend 10 percent of their day (called "dabble time") developing new product ideas. One employee, Dave Myers, learned that the coating from the company's cable product could make guitar strings hold their tone longer and be more comfortable to use. The idea was a success. Gore launched ELIXIR Strings which are now a top-selling product.[108] At Gore, as elsewhere, intrapreneurship derives from deliberate strategic thinking and execution.

Management Challenges

Organizations that encourage intrapreneurship face an obvious risk: the effort can fail. One author noted, "There is considerable history of internal venture development by large firms, and it does not encourage optimism."[109] However, this risk can be managed. In fact, failing to foster intrapreneurship may represent a subtler but greater risk than encouraging it. The organization that resists entrepreneurial initiative may lose its ability to adapt when conditions dictate change.

The most dangerous risk in corporate entrepreneurship is the risk of overreliance on a single project. Many companies fail while awaiting the completion of one large, innovative project.[110] The successful entrepreneurial organization avoids overcommitment to a single project and relies on its entrepreneurial spirit to produce at least one winner from among several projects.

Organizations also court failure when they spread their entrepreneurial efforts over too many projects.[111] If there are many projects, each effort may be too small in scale. Managers will consider the projects unattractive because of their small size. Or those recruited to manage the projects may have difficulty building power and status within the organization.

The hazards in intrapreneurship, then, are related to scale. One large project is a threat, as are too many underfunded projects. But a carefully managed approach to this strategically important process will upgrade an organization's chances for long-term survival and success.

Entrepreneurial Orientation

Earlier in this chapter, we described the characteristics of individual entrepreneurs. To conclude the chapter, we do the same for companies: we describe how companies that are highly entrepreneurial differ from those that are not. CEOs play a crucial role in promoting entrepreneurship within large corporations.[112]

Entrepreneurial orientation is the tendency of an organization to engage in activities designed to identify and capitalize successfully on opportunities to launch new ventures by entering new or established markets with new or existing goods or services.[113] Entrepreneurial orientation is determined by five tendencies: to allow independent action, innovate, take risks, be proactive, and be competitively aggressive. Entrepreneurial orientation should enhance the likelihood of success and may be particularly important for conducting business internationally.[114]

To allow independent action is to grant to individuals and teams the freedom to exercise their creativity, champion promising ideas, and carry them through to completion. Innovativeness requires the firm to support new ideas, experimentation, and creative processes that can lead to new products or processes; it requires a willingness to depart from existing practices and venture beyond the status quo. Risk taking comes from a willingness to commit significant resources, and perhaps borrow heavily, to venture into the unknown. The tendency to take risks can be assessed by considering whether people are bold or cautious, whether they require high levels of certainty before taking or allowing action, and whether they tend to follow tried-and-true paths.

entrepreneurial orientation

The tendency of an organization to identify and capitalize successfully on opportunities to launch new ventures by entering new or established markets with new or existing goods or services.

Management in Action

THE PEOPLE AND PASSION OF POPCHIPS

Despite his own track record as a successful entrepreneur, Keith Belling never tried to start Popchips alone. He partnered with Pat Turpin, whose experience included investment banking and management of Costco's private-label (store brand) products. Before the Popchips venture, she had worked for Belling at the Allbusiness.com portal. As president of Popchips, Turpin focuses on manufacturing and finance.

Belling's experience also gave him time to build a network of valuable relationships. A key contact early on was someone he knew socially, Alex Panos, managing director of an investment firm called TSG Consumer Partners. When Panos heard about Belling's idea for Popchips, he thought it sounded similar to another product TSG had successfully invested in, Vitaminwater, so he was interested in a financial stake in the start-up. TSG eventually took 30 percent ownership in exchange for a $25 million investment. It helped that Panos knew Belling as an entrepreneur who had successfully started companies in the past.

But networking was hardly just about money. Through TSG, Belling met Rohan Oza, who had been the chief marketing officer at Vitaminwater. Oza, too, loved the idea for Popchips, so he invested, offered advice, and helped the company recruit former Vitaminwater employees to market Popchips.

As Popchips has built its sales, the value of the business has grown. TSG recently sold its ownership share to another investment firm, Verlinvest, based in Brussels. Verlinvest paid $670 million—a handsome return for TSG and a vote of confidence in the future of Popchips.

With a strong network, consistent access to funds, and a new CEO with extensive experience in the snack food industry, can Popchips keep growing, or will it be gobbled up by another business?[115]

- What actions described in this case increase Popchips' chances of long-term success?
- Why do you think the innovation of popped snacks came from an entrepreneur like Keith Belling instead of from a big snack company? How could a large company increase the odds that it will be the source of the next great snack idea?

To be proactive is to act in anticipation of future problems and opportunities. A proactive firm changes the competitive landscape; other firms merely react. Proactive firms are forward thinking and fast to act and are leaders rather than followers. Similarly, some individuals are more likely to be proactive, to shape and create their own environments, than others who more passively cope with the situations in which they find themselves.[116] Proactive firms encourage and allow individuals and teams to be proactive.

Finally, competitive aggressiveness is the tendency of the firm to challenge competitors directly and intensely to achieve entry or improve its position. In other words, it is a competitive tendency to outperform one's rivals in the marketplace. This might take the form of striking fast to beat competitors to the punch, to tackle them head-to-head, and to analyze and target competitors' weaknesses.

What makes a firm entrepreneurial is its engagement in an effective combination of independent action, innovativeness, risk taking, proactiveness, and competitive aggressiveness.[117] The relationship between these factors and the performance of the firm is a complicated one that depends on many things. Still, you can imagine how the opposite profile—too many constraints on action, business as usual, extreme caution, passivity, and a lack of competitive fire—will undermine entrepreneurial activities. And without entrepreneurship, how would firms survive and thrive in a constantly changing competitive environment? Thus management can create environments that foster more entrepreneurship. If your bosses are not doing this, consider trying some entrepreneurial experiments on your own.[118] Seek out others with an entrepreneurial bent. What can you learn from them, and what can you teach others? Sometimes it takes individuals and teams of experimenters to show the possibilities to those at the top. Ask yourself and ask others: Between the bureaucrats and the entrepreneurs, who is having a more positive impact? And who is having more fun?

KEY TERMS

advertising support model, p. 219

affiliate model, p. 219

bootlegging, p. 233

business accelerator, p. 224

business incubators, p. 224

business plan, p. 228

entrepreneur, p. 214

entrepreneurial orientation, p. 234

entrepreneurial venture, p. 212

entrepreneurship, p. 212

franchising, p. 217

initial public offering (IPO), p. 226

intermediary model, p. 219

intrapreneurs, p. 214

legitimacy, p. 231

opportunity analysis, p. 228

skunkworks, p. 233

small business, p. 212

social capital, p. 231

social enterprise, p. 219

social entrepreneurship, p. 219

subscription model, p. 219

transaction fee model, p. 219

RETAINING WHAT YOU LEARNED

In Chapter 7, you learned that people become entrepreneurs for a variety of reasons. Successful entrepreneurs are innovators, but also possess management, business, and networking skills. While there is no single entrepreneurial personality, certain characteristics contribute to their success. To start a new business, it is important to monitor the current business environment and other indicators. Choosing a business idea to pursue should be based on planning, trial and error, and fit with risk preferences and personal interests. Effective planning and getting advice from experienced experts are helpful in preventing failure. Common challenges include getting started, warding off competitors, managing growth, and controlling finances. Developing and executing a comprehensive business plan will increase the chances of the venture being successful. Successful entrepreneurs develop social capital and a network of customers, partners, boards, and other talented people. Managers of large companies can encourage intrapreneurship by using skunkworks and allowing bootlegging. A portfolio of projects should be chosen carefully and funded appropriately. An entrepreneurial orientation in a company comes from encouraging independent action, innovativeness, risk taking, proactive behavior, and competitive aggressiveness.

LO 1   Describe why people become entrepreneurs and what it takes, personally.

- People become entrepreneurs because of the profit potential, the challenge, and the satisfaction they anticipate (and often receive) from participating in the process, and sometimes because they are blocked from more traditional avenues of career advancement.
- As shown in Exhibit 7.3 (on the next page), successful entrepreneurs are innovators, and they have good knowledge and skills in management, business, and networking.
- Although there is no single entrepreneurial personality, certain characteristics are helpful: commitment and determination; leadership skills; opportunity obsession; tolerance of risk, ambiguity, and uncertainty; creativity; self-reliance; the ability to adapt; and motivation to excel.

LO 2   Summarize how to assess opportunities to start new businesses.

- You should always be on the lookout for new ideas, monitoring the current business environment and other indicators of opportunity.
- Franchising offers an interesting opportunity, and the potential of the Internet is being tapped (after entrepreneurs learned some tough lessons from the dot-bomb era).

- Trial and error and preparation play important roles. Assessing the business concept on the basis of how innovative and risky it is, combined with your personal interests and tendencies, will also help you make good choices.
- Ideas should be carefully assessed via opportunity analysis and a thorough business plan.

LO 3   Identify common causes of success and failure.

- New ventures are inherently risky. The economic environment plays an important role in the success or failure of the business, and the entrepreneur should anticipate and be prepared to adapt in the face of changing economic conditions.
- How you handle a variety of common management challenges also can mean the difference between success and failure, as can the effectiveness of your planning and your ability to mobilize nonfinancial resources, including other people who can help.

LO 4   Discuss common management challenges.

- When new businesses fail, the causes often can be traced to some common challenges that entrepreneurs face and must manage well. You might not enjoy the entrepreneurial process.
- Survival—including getting started and fending off competitors—is difficult.

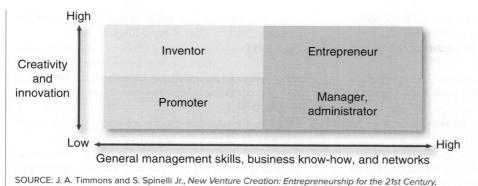

SOURCE: J. A. Timmons and S. Spinelli Jr., *New Venture Creation: Entrepreneurship for the 21st Century,* 7th ed., 2007, pp. 67–68. Copyright 2007 The McGraw-Hill Companies, Inc. Reprinted with permission.

- Growth creates new challenges, including reluctance to delegate work to others. Funds may be put to improper use, and financial controls may be inadequate.
- Many entrepreneurs fail to plan well for succession.
- When needing or wanting new funds, initial public offerings provide an option, but they represent an important and difficult decision that must be considered carefully.

LO 5   Explain how to increase your chances of success, including good business planning.

- The business plan helps you think through your idea thoroughly and determine its viability. It also convinces (or fails to convince) others to participate.
- The plan describes the venture and its future, provides financial projections, and includes plans for marketing, manufacturing, and other business functions.
- The plan should describe the people involved in the venture, a full assessment of the opportunity (including customers and competitors), the environmental context (including regulatory and economic issues),

and the risk (including future risks and how you intend to deal with them).
- Successful entrepreneurs also understand how to develop social capital, which enhances legitimacy and helps develop a network of others including customers, talented people, partners, and boards.

LO 6   Describe how managers of large companies can foster entrepreneurship.

- Intrapreneurs work within established companies to develop new goods or services that allow the corporation to reap the benefits of innovation.
- To facilitate intrapreneurship, organizations use skunkworks—special project teams designated to develop a new product—and allow bootlegging—informal efforts beyond formal job assignments in which employees pursue their own pet projects.
- Organizations should select projects carefully, have an ongoing portfolio of projects, and fund them appropriately.
- Ultimately, a true entrepreneurial orientation in a company comes from encouraging independent action, innovativeness, risk taking, proactive behavior, and competitive aggressiveness.

DISCUSSION QUESTIONS

1. On a 1 to 10 scale, what is your level of personal interest in becoming an entrepreneur? Why did you rate yourself as you did?

2. How would you assess your capability of being a successful entrepreneur? What are your strengths and weaknesses? How would you increase your capability?

3. Most entrepreneurs learn the most important skills they need after age 21. How does this affect your outlook and plans?

4. Identify and discuss new ventures that fit each of the four cells in the entrepreneurial strategy matrix.

5. Brainstorm a list of ideas for new business ventures. Where did you get the ideas? Which ones are most and least viable, and why?

6. Identify some businesses that recently opened in your area. What are their chances of survival, and why? How would you advise the owners or managers of those businesses to ensure their success?

7. Assume you are writing a story about what it's really like to be an entrepreneur. To whom would you talk, and what questions would you ask?

8. Conduct interviews with two entrepreneurs, asking whatever questions most interest you. Share your findings with the class. How do the interviews differ from one another, and what do they have in common?

9. Read Exhibit 7.1 Which myths did you believe? Do you still? Why or why not? Interview two entrepreneurs by asking each myth as a true-or-false question. Then ask them to elaborate on their answers. What did they say? What do you conclude?

10. With your classmates, form small teams of skunkworks. Your charge is to identify an innovation that you think would benefit your school and to outline an action plan for bringing your idea to reality.

11. Identify a business that recently folded. What were the causes of the failure? What could have been done differently to prevent the failure?

12. Does franchising appeal to you? What franchises would most and least interest you, and why?

13. The chapter specified some of the changes in the external environment that can provide business opportunity (technological discoveries, lifestyle and taste changes, and so on). Identify some important recent changes or current trends in the external environment and the business opportunities they might offer.

14. Choose an Internet company with which you are familiar and brainstorm ideas for how its services or approach to business can be improved. How about starting a new Internet company altogether—what would be some possibilities?

15. Find some inspiring examples of social entrepreneurship and describe them to your class.

16. Brainstorm some new ideas for social enterprise. What challenges do you foresee, and how would you proceed?

EXPERIENTIAL EXERCISES

7.1 TAKE AN ENTREPRENEUR TO DINNER

OBJECTIVES

1. To get to know what an entrepreneur does, how she or he got started, and what it took to succeed.

2. To interview a particular entrepreneur in depth about his or her career and experiences.

3. To acquire a feeling for whether you might find an entrepreneurial career rewarding.

INSTRUCTIONS

1. Identify an entrepreneur in your area you would like to interview.

2. Contact the person you have selected and make an appointment. Be sure to explain why you want the appointment and to give a realistic estimate of how much time you will need.

3. Identify specific questions you would like to have answered and the general areas about which you would like information. (See the following suggested interview questions, although there probably won't be time for all of them.) Using a combination of open-ended questions—such as general questions about how the entrepreneur got started, what happened next, and so forth—and closed-ended questions—such as specific questions about what his or her goals were, if he or she had to find partners, and so forth—will help keep the interview focused yet allow for unexpected comments and insights.

4. Conduct the interview. If both you and the person you are interviewing are comfortable, using a small voice recorder during the interview can be of great help to you later. Remember, too, that you most likely will learn more if you are an interested listener.

5. Evaluate what you have learned. Write down the information you have gathered in some form that will be helpful to you later on. Be as specific as you can. Jotting down direct quotes is more effective than statements such as "highly motivated individual." Also be sure to make a note of what you did not find out.

6. Write a thank-you note. This is more than a courtesy; it will also help the entrepreneur remember you favorably should you want to follow up on the interview.

Suggested Interview

QUESTIONS FOR GATHERING INFORMATION

• *Would you tell me about yourself before you started your first venture?*

Were your parents, relatives, or close friends entrepreneurial? How so?

Did you have any other role models?

What was your education/military experience? In hindsight, was it helpful? In what specific ways?

What was your previous work experience? Was it helpful? What particular chunks of experience were especially valuable or relevant?

In particular, did you have any sales or marketing experience? How important was this in starting your company?

• *How did you start your venture?*

How did you spot the opportunity? How did it surface?

What were your goals? What were your lifestyle or other personal requirements? How did you fit these factors together?

How did you evaluate the opportunity in terms of the critical elements for success? The competition? The market?

Did you find or have partners? What kind of planning did you do? What kind of financing did you have?

Did you have a start-up business plan of any kind? Please tell me about it.

How much time did it take from conception to the first day of business? How many hours a day did you spend working on it?

How much capital did it take? How long did it take to reach a positive cash flow and break-even sales volume? If you did not have enough money at the time, what were some ways in which you "bootstrapped" the venture (i.e., bartering, borrowing, and the like)? Tell me about the pressures and crises during that early survival period.

What outside help did you get? Did you have experienced advisers? Lawyers? Accountants? Tax experts? Patent experts? How did you develop these networks and how long did it take?

What was your family situation at the time?

What did you perceive to be your own strengths? Weaknesses?

What did you perceive to be the strengths of your venture? Weaknesses?

What was your most triumphant moment? Your worst moment?

Did you want to have partners or do it solo? Why?

- *Once you got going . . .*

What were the most difficult gaps to fill and problems to solve as you began to grow rapidly?

When you looked for key people as partners, advisers, or managers, were there any personal attributes or attitudes you were especially seeking because you knew they would fit with you and were important to success? How did you find them?

Are there any attributes among partners and advisers that you would definitely try to avoid?

Have things become more predictable? Or less?

Do you spend more/same/less time with your business now than in the early years?

Do you feel more managerial and less entrepreneurial now?

In terms of the future, do you plan to harvest? To maintain? To expand?

Do you plan ever to retire? Would you explain?

Have your goals changed? Have you met them?

QUESTIONS FOR CONCLUDING
(CHOOSE ONE)

- What do you consider your most valuable asset—the thing that enabled you to make it?
- If you had it to do over again would you do it again in the same way?
- Looking back, what do you feel are the most critical concepts, skills, attitudes, and know-how you needed to get your company started and grown to where it is today? What will be needed for the next five years? To what extent can any of these be learned?
- Some people say there is a lot of stress being an entrepreneur. What have you experienced? How would you say it compares with other hot-seat jobs, such as the head of a big company or a partner in a large law, consulting, or accounting firm?
- What are the things that you find personally rewarding and satisfying as an entrepreneur? What have been the rewards, risks, and trade-offs?
- Who should try to be an entrepreneur? Can you give me any ideas there?
- What advice would you give an aspiring entrepreneur? Could you suggest the three most important lessons you have learned? How can I learn them while minimizing the tuition?

SOURCE: J. A. Timmons, *New Venture Creation,* 3rd ed. 1994. Copyright © 1994 The McGraw-Hill Companies. Reprinted with permission.

7.2 STARTING A NEW BUSINESS

OBJECTIVES

1. To introduce you to the complexities of going into business for yourself.
2. To provide hands-on experience in making new business decisions.

INSTRUCTIONS

1. Your instructor will divide the class into teams and assign each team the task of investigating the start-up of one of the following businesses:
   a. Submarine sandwich shop
   b. Day care service
   c. Bookstore
   d. Gasoline service station
   e. Other

2. Each team should research the information necessary to complete the New Business Start-Up Worksheet. The following agencies or organizations might be of assistance:
   a. Small Business Administration
   b. Local county/city administration agencies
   c. Local chamber of commerce
   d. Local small-business development corporation
   e. U.S. Department of Commerce
   f. Farmer's Home Administration
   g. Local realtors
   h. Local businesspeople in the same or a similar business
   i. Banks and S&Ls

3. Each team presents its findings to the class.

New Business Start-Up Worksheet

1. *Product*

    What customer need will we satisfy?

    How can our product be unique?

2. *Customer*

    Who are our customers? What are their profiles?

    Where do they live/work/play?

    What are their buying habits?

    What are their needs?

3. *Competition*

    Who/where is the competition?

    What are their strengths and weaknesses?

    How might they respond to us?

4. *Suppliers*

    Who/where are our suppliers?

    What are their business practices?

    What relationships can we expect?

5. *Location*

    Where are our customers/competitors/suppliers?

    What are the location costs?

    What are the legal limitations to location?

6. *Physical Facilities/Equipment*

    Rent/own/build/refurbish facilities?

    Rent/lease/purchase equipment?

    Maintenance?

7. *Human Resources*

    Availability?

    Training?

    Costs?

8. *Legal/Regulatory Environment*

    Licenses/permits/certifications?

    Government agencies?

    Liability?

9. *Cultural/Social Environment*

    Cultural issues?

    Social issues?

10. *International Environment*

    International issues?

11. *Other*

CONCLUDING CASE

ROLLING OUT SCROLLCO

Mandy Toberman had enjoyed her engineering job at Acme Electronics, but she began to grow restless. Most of her work for the past five years had involved designing minor adjustments to existing products. She worried she would lose her edge in a fast-changing industry, and work just didn't engage her imagination or problem-solving skills the way it once did. In the evenings, she found herself pursuing new ideas, researching some of the latest technology, and testing out some possible inventions. As the weeks passed, Mandy became increasingly interested in one idea: an e-reader made with flexible materials that could be rolled up and stuffed into a satchel, backpack, or purse. At first she doubted it could be made, but with some investigation, Mandy began to develop a design for the device, which she called the Scroll.

The more Mandy considered the Scroll, the more she thought it would be an exciting new product for Acme to offer. It would open up a whole new area of sales for the company, which had not seen much growth for the past few years. It would generate tremendous publicity for Acme and excitement in her division. So Mandy collected a few of the drawings she had created, estimated the manufacturing costs, and prepared a proposal. She invited her supervisor, Tom Ringsack, and two of her colleagues to a meeting, saying only that she had an idea she wanted to bring up.

At the meeting, Mandy started her laptop to show her drawings and describe her idea for the Scroll. The other engineers' eyes were wide, and Mandy could sense their eagerness to explore the concept. However, Tom sighed and said, "Mandy, you know our situation, right? In the present economy, we can't get a lot of financing for risky new projects. We have to focus on the product enhancements that will increase our profit margins, and the budget for anything else is tight—well, really, nonexistent." Mandy could tell the discussion was over, so she shut down her computer with a quiet sigh.

That weekend, Mandy spent hours at her desk at home, beginning to plan her escape from Acme Electronics. She perused the Small Business Administration website, looking for advice on writing a business plan, and explored her LinkedIn network, looking for contacts who might give her advice—and possibly funding—for her start-up, which she intended to name ScrollCo. By the end of the weekend, feeling more than a little nervous, Mandy had drafted the outline of a business plan.

DISCUSSION QUESTIONS

1. What actions could Acme Electronics take to foster intrapreneurship? What consequences does it suffer from failing to foster it?
2. What information should Mandy include in her business plan?
3. Describe three nonfinancial resources likely to be important for the future of ScrollCo. How can Mandy ensure that her business has those resources?

PART TWO   SUPPORTING CASE

Will Foxconn Remain Apple's Top Supplier of iGadgets?

Apple is famous for its attractive and highly prized electronics, including iPhone and iTouch portable devices, iPod and iTunes for music, and iMac and iPad computers. However, Apple doesn't actually make any of its products. Rather, it develops ideas, designs devices, and promotes the products and its brand. To put the devices together, Apple relies on a set of contractors.

One key contractor is an electronics firm called Foxconn, based in Taiwan. With factories located in China, Foxconn has combined manufacturing expertise with low-cost labor to win deals to make computers and key components such as motherboards. As consumers have slowed their spending on laptop computers in favor of smaller devices such as the iPad tablet computer and smartphones, Foxconn has benefited. Until recently, it was the only company making Apple's iPad and one of just two makers of Apple's iPhone. Workers at Foxconn facilities also produce the Sony

PlayStation 3, the Nintendo Wii, and Amazon's Kindle Fire. It also produces TVs for Sony, Sharp, and Toshiba. In China alone, Foxconn employs almost 1.3 million workers, making it one of the largest employers in the world. Many of those workers live in on-site dormitories, eat in company-run dining halls, and relax in bookstores and gyms located right at their workplace.

In recent years, Foxconn has been running into some tragic problems. In 2010, the company drew international media attention when it came to light that several workers at Foxconn's plant in Shenzhen (a city in southern China) had committed suicide. Questions arose about whether working conditions were so horrible as to drive workers to kill themselves. Apple sent executives accompanied by suicide prevention experts to the plant to investigate. Although Apple requires its contract partners to meet specific standards in its code of conduct, and it visits over 100 facilities a year to ensure compliance, it had failed to uncover any problems at Foxconn before the suicides came to light.

In the following year, Foxconn was again in the news about a tragedy when an explosion in its Chengdu, China, plant killed 3 workers and injured 15. Initial investigations suggested that the explosion was the result of a fairly basic manufacturing safety problem: because of improper ventilation, dust collected in the air of a metal-polishing shop, and the dust ignited. If such a problem occurred in the United States, regulators would quickly shut down the facility for violating safety requirements.

Embarrassed by the media and pressured by important customers such as Apple, Foxconn acted to improve working conditions. At the Shenzhen plant, it brought in counselors, improved training of managers and the staff answering calls on the employee hotline, and launched a morale-boosting program called Care–Love, which sponsors employee outings. In the factories in Chengdu and elsewhere, the company took measures to improve ventilation. Along with these changes, Foxconn began giving out raises. In Shenzhen, workers' wages more than doubled.

Since Foxconn launched the effort to improve morale, employee turnover has fallen, and the suicides seem to have ended. Unfortunately, the payoff for the company is difficult to measure. Higher costs have erased profits, and Foxconn's stock price has tumbled. So now the company is looking for lower-cost locations. It opened facilities in China's interior cities, where wage rates are about one-third below those of Shenzhen. Making matters more challenging for Foxconn is the fact that Apple CEO Tim Cook has shifted some of the production of iPhones and iPad minis to Pegatron, another Taiwan-based electronics manufacturer. Pegatron also makes products for Microsoft, Dell, and Hewlett-Packard.

DISCUSSION QUESTIONS

1. What threats, opportunities, strengths, and weaknesses can you identify at Foxconn? How is it addressing these with its strategy?

2. If Foxconn's management hired you to offer advice on improving its ethical decision making and corporate social responsibility, what measures would you suggest? Why?

3. Why do you think Tim Cook, after years of using Foxconn for most of Apple's production needs, shifted some production to Pegatron?

SOURCES: M. Gold and Y. Lee, "Apple Supplier Foxconn to Shrink Workforce as Sales Growth Stalls," Reuters, January 27, 2015, http://www.reuters.com; E. Dou, "Apple Shifts Supply Chain Away from Foxconn to Pegatron," *The Wall Street Journal* (online), May 29, 2013, http://www.wsj.com; M. Kan, "Foxconn Builds Products for Many Vendors, But Its Mud Sticks to Apple," *MacWorld* (online), October 24, 2012, http://www.macworld.com; T. Culpan, Z. Lifei, and B. Einhorn, "Foxconn: How to Beat the High Cost of Happy Workers," *Bloomberg Businessweek,* May 5, 2011, http://www.businessweek.com; D. Nystedt, "Apple: Foxconn 'Saved Lives' with Suicide Prevention Efforts," *PC World,* February 15, 2011, http://www.pcworld.com; J. Bussey, "Measuring the Human Cost of an iPad Made in China," *The Wall Street Journal,* June 3, 2011, http://online.wsj.com; "Apple Report Details Response to Foxconn Suicides," *eWeek,* February 15, 2011, Business & Company Resource Center, http://galenet.galegroup.com; and J. Dalrymple, "Apple Reports on Foxconn, Supplier Workplace Standards," *CNET News,* February 14, 2011, http://news.cnet.com.

Information for Entrepreneurs

If you are interested in starting or managing a small business, you have access to many sources of useful information.

PUBLISHED SOURCES

The first step is a complete search of materials in libraries and on the Internet. You can find a huge amount of published information, databases, and other sources about industries, markets, competitors, and personnel. Some of this information will have been uncovered when you searched for ideas. Listed here are additional sources that should help get you started.

Guides and Company Information

Valuable information is available in special issues and on the websites of *Bloomberg Business, Forbes, Inc., The Economist, Fast Company,* and *Fortune,* as well as online in the following:

- Hoovers.com
- ProQuest.com
- Investext.com

Valuable Sites on the Internet

- Entrepreneurship (http://www.kauffman.org/what-we-do/entrepreneurship), the website of the Kauffman Center for Entrepreneurial Leadership, Ewing Marion Kauffman Foundation
- *Fast Company* (http://www.fastcompany.com)
- Ernst & Young (http://www.ey.com)
- *Inc.* magazine (http://www.inc.com)
- Entrepreneur.com and magazine (http://www.entrepreneur.com)
- EDGAR database (http://www.sec.gov)—subscription sources, such as ThomsonResearch (http://www.thomsonfinancial.com), provide images of other filings as well
- Thomson Venture Economics (https://vx.thomsonib.com/VxComponent/vxhelp/VentureXpert_Fact_Sheet.pdf)

Journal Articles via Computerized Indexes

- Factiva with Dow Jones, Reuters, *The Wall Street Journal*
- EBSCOhost
- FirstSearch
- Ethnic News Watch
- LEXIS/NEXIS
- *The New York Times* (http://www.nytimes.com)
- InfoTrac from Gale Group
- ABI/Inform and other ProQuest databases
- RDS Business Reference Suite
- *The Wall Street Journal* (http://www.wsj.com)

Statistics

- Stat-USA (https://www.usa.gov/statistics)—U.S. government subscription site for economic, trade, and business data and market research
- U.S. Bureau of the Census (http://www.census.gov)—the source of many statistical data, including
  - *Statistical Abstract of the United States*
  - *American FactFinder*—population data
  - Economic programs (http://www.census.gov/econ/www/index.html)—data by sector
  - County business patterns
  - Zip code business patterns
- Knight Ridder . . . *CRB Commodity Yearbook*
- Manufacturing USA, Service Industries USA, and other sector compilations from Gale Group
- Economic Statistics Briefing Room (https://www.whitehouse.gov/administration/eop/cea/economic-indicators)
- *Federal Reserve Bulletin*
- Survey of Current Business
- Bureau of Labor Statistics (http://www.bls.gov)
- Global Insight, formerly DRI-WEFA
- International Financial Statistics—International Monetary Fund
- World Development Indicators—World Bank
- Bloomberg Database

Consumer Expenditures

- New Strategist Publications

Projections and Forecasts

- ProQuest
- InfoTech Trends
- Guide to Special Issues and Indexes to Periodicals *(Grey House Directory of Special Issues)*
- RDS Business Reference Suite
- Value Line Investment Survey

Market Studies

- LifeStyle Market Analyst
- MarketResearch.com
- Scarborough Research
- Simmons Market Research Bureau

Consumer Expenditures

- New Strategist Publications
- Consumer Expenditure Survey
- Euromonitor

Other Sources

- Wall Street transcript
- Brokerage house reports from Investext, Multex, and so on
- Company annual reports and websites

OTHER INTELLIGENCE

Everything entrepreneurs need to know will not be found in libraries because this information needs to be highly specific and current. This information is most likely available from people—industry experts, suppliers, and the like. Summarized here are some useful sources of intelligence.

Trade Associations

Trade associations, especially the editors of their publications and information officers, are good sources of information. Trade shows and conferences are prime places to discover the latest activities of competitors.

Employees

Employees who have left a competitor's company often can provide information about the competitor, especially if the employee departed on bad terms. Also, a firm can hire people away from a competitor. Although consideration of ethics in this situation is important, the number of experienced people in any industry is limited, and competitors must prove that a company hired a person intentionally to get specific trade secrets to challenge any hiring legally. Students who have worked for competitors are another source of information.

Consulting Firms

Consulting firms frequently conduct industry studies and then make this information available. Frequently, in such fields as computers or software, competitors use the same design consultants, and these consultants can be sources of information.

Market Research Firms

Firms doing market studies, such as those listed under the previously mentioned published sources, can be sources of intelligence.

Key Customers, Manufacturers, Suppliers, Distributors, and Buyers

These groups are often a prime source of information.

Public Filings

Federal, state, and local filings, such as filings with the Securities and Exchange Commission (SEC), Patent and Trademark Office, or Freedom of Information Act filings, can reveal a surprising amount of information. There are companies that process inquiries of this type.

Reverse Engineering

Reverse engineering can be used to determine costs of production and sometimes even manufacturing methods. An example of this practice is the experience of Advanced Energy Technology, Inc., of Boulder, Colorado, which learned firsthand about such tactics. No sooner had it announced a new product, which was patented, than it received 50 orders, half of which were from competitors asking for only one or two of the items.

Networks

The networks mentioned in this chapter can be sources of new venture ideas and strategies.

Other

Classified ads, buyers' guides, labor unions, real estate agents, courts, local reporters, and so on can all provide clues.

The U.S. government is engaging in new and more extensive outreach efforts so that small-business owners will use government resources more and understand them more easily. In 2009, the U.S. Small Business Administration launched a community forum, the first government-sponsored online community built specifically for small-business owners, on the Business Gateway site of Business.gov. The forum combines discussion threads, blogs, and resource articles. The goals for the SBA and 21 other federal agencies that cosponsor the site are to engage in dialogue with the public, leverage the expertise that exists in both the public and private sectors, and help government serve entrepreneurs better.

SOURCES: J. A. Timmons and S. Spinelli, *New Venture Creation,* 7th ed. (Burr Ridge, IL: McGraw-Hill/Irwin, 2007), pp. 103–4; and K. Klein, "Government Resources for Entrepreneurs," *BusinessWeek,* March 3, 2009.

CHAPTER 8

Organization Structure

Take my assets—but leave me my organization and in five years I'll have it all back.

—ALFRED P. SLOAN JR.

Management in Action

LEADERSHIP AND STRUCTURAL CHANGE AT GENERAL MOTORS

The history of General Motors shows that size and longevity do not guarantee success. GM once dominated the U.S. auto industry with a "price ladder" strategy in which Chevrolet, Pontiac, GMC, Oldsmobile, Buick, and Cadillac catered to specific slices of the consumer market. But after GM's U.S. market share peaked in 1962 at 51 percent, the company steadily began losing share to smaller, more nimble, and more innovative competition. By 2008, GM's U.S. market share was less than half what it was in 1962, and when customer demand and bank lending dried up in the 2008 financial crisis, GM nearly collapsed. The federal government stepped in with money to keep GM alive through a Chapter 11 managed bankruptcy. In July 2009, after restructuring, the old General Motors Corporation reemerged as General Motors Company. Daniel Akerson, a Navy veteran with experience turning around companies in other industries, was named to the new company's Board of Directors. In September 2010, Akerson was named chair and CEO and led the company's initial public offering—the largest in U.S. history—in November of that year.

In 2011, GM posted record earnings and reclaimed its spot as the world's automotive sales leader, but its stock price slid as investors questioned the company's long-term potential. In the years leading up to bankruptcy, GM had become known for a culture in which managers were slow to act, reluctant to speak up, and averse to change. Akerson set out to change that. Among Akerson's challenges was teaching a 213,000-employee multinational company selling millions of vehicles annually to be more nimble, more innovative, and more customer-centric.

© Richard Lautens/Toronto Star via Getty Images

Akerson drove change by assembling a management team of seasoned industry insiders. GM also assembled a diverse board of 14 directors, mostly current and retired executives from other organizations, including representatives from Fortune 100 companies (Walmart, Coca-Cola, Conoco-Phillips, Burlington Northern Santa Fe, etc.), the financial and telecom industries, academia, and a former chair of the U.S. Joint Chiefs of Staff.

The company reported 2013 earnings of $8.6 billion on revenue of more than $155 billion, enabling significant reinvestments for growth. GM also boasted the largest market share in China, fueled by record sales of 3.2 million. GM's ability to meet it goals depended on offering attractive new products while continuing to improve vehicle safety, quality, customer service, and global efficiency.[1]

Ex-Chair and CEO Dan Akerson believed that the way employees are organized into departments and divisions played a role in how fast and effectively they could seize new opportunities. As you read this chapter, notice the options available for an organization's structure, and consider whether GM's management has made the right choices to enable continued growth and a more responsive culture.

Since its emergence from bankruptcy, General Motors has been running neck and neck with Toyota and Volkswagen to keep its spot as the world's biggest auto company, even as its U.S. market share slips and it struggles with investor doubts about its ability to operate efficiently. How could the company respond to this situation? The way in which a company organizes itself to address an issue such as declining market share may well be the most important factor in determining whether its strategy will succeed. GM, like many other companies, is working hard to make certain that its strategy and structure are aligned.

This chapter focuses on the vertical and horizontal dimensions of organization structure. We begin by covering basic principles of differentiation and integration. Next we discuss the vertical structure, which includes issues of authority, hierarchy, delegation, and decentralization. We continue on to describe the horizontal structure, which includes functional, divisional, and matrix forms. Finally, we illustrate the ways in which organizations can integrate their structures: coordination by standardization, coordination by plan, and coordination by mutual adjustment.

In the next chapter, we continue with the topic of organization structure but take a different perspective. In that chapter, we focus on the flexibility and responsiveness of an organization—that is, how capable it is of changing its form and adapting to strategy, technology, the environment, and other challenges it confronts.

Fundamentals of Organizing

 LO 1

organization chart

The reporting structure and division of labor in an organization.

differentiation

An aspect of the organization's internal environment created by job specialization and the division of labor.

integration

The degree to which differentiated work units work together and coordinate their efforts.

division of labor

The assignment of different tasks to different people or groups.

specialization

A process in which different individuals and units perform different tasks.

To get going, let's start simple. We often begin to describe a firm's structure by looking at its organization chart. The **organization chart** depicts the positions in the firm and the way they are arranged. The chart provides a picture of the reporting structure (who reports to whom) and the various activities that are carried out by different individuals. Most companies have official organization charts drawn up to give people this information.

Exhibit 8.1 shows a traditional organization chart. Note the various types of information that are conveyed in a very simple way:

1. The boxes represent different work.
2. The titles in the boxes show the work performed by each unit.
3. Reporting and authority relationships are indicated by solid lines showing superior–subordinate connections.
4. Levels of management are indicated by the number of horizontal layers in the chart. All persons or units that are at the same rank and report to the same person are on one level.

Although the organization chart presents some important structural features, other design issues related to structure—while not so obvious—are no less significant. Two fundamental concepts around which organizations are structured are differentiation and integration. **Differentiation** means that the organization is composed of many units that work on different kinds of tasks, using different skills and work methods. **Integration** means that these differentiated units are put back together so that work is coordinated into an overall product.[2]

Differentiation

Several related concepts underlie the idea of structural differentiation. For example, differentiation is created through division of labor and job specialization. **Division of labor** means the work of the organization is subdivided into smaller tasks. Various individuals and units throughout the organization perform different tasks. **Specialization** refers to the fact that different people or groups often perform specific parts of the larger task. The two concepts are, of course, closely related. Administrative assistants and accountants specialize in, and perform, different jobs; similarly, marketing, finance, and human resources

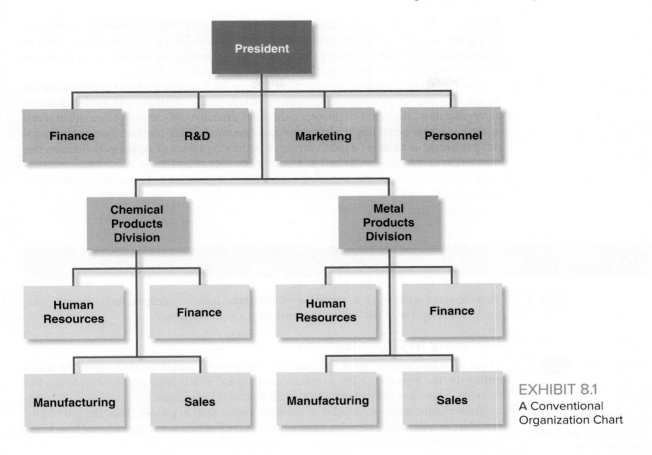

EXHIBIT 8.1
A Conventional
Organization Chart

tasks are divided among the respective departments. The many tasks that must be carried out in an organization make specialization and division of labor necessities. Otherwise, the complexity of the overall work of the organization would be too much for any individual.[3]

Differentiation is high when an organization has many subunits and many kinds of specialists who think differently. Harvard professors Lawrence and Lorsch found that organizations in complex, dynamic environments (plastics firms in their study) developed a high degree of differentiation to cope with the complex challenges. Companies in simple, stable environments (container companies) had low levels of differentiation. Companies in intermediate environments (food companies) had intermediate differentiation.[4]

> As organizations differentiate their structures, managers must simultaneously consider issues of integration.

Integration

As organizations differentiate their structures, managers must simultaneously consider issues of integration. All the specialized tasks in an organization cannot be performed completely independently. Because the different units are part of the larger organization, some degree of communication and cooperation must exist among them. Integration and its related concept, **coordination,** refer to the procedures that link the various parts of the organization to achieve the organization's overall mission.

Integration is achieved through structural mechanisms that enhance collaboration and coordination. Any job activity that links different work units performs an integrative function. Remember, the more highly differentiated your firm, the greater the need for integration among the different units. Lawrence and Lorsch found that highly differentiated firms were successful if they also had high levels of integration. Organizations are more likely to fail if they exist in complex environments and are highly differentiated but fail to integrate their activities adequately.[5] In contrast, focusing on integration may slow innovation, at

coordination

The procedures that link the various parts of an organization for the purpose of achieving the organization's overall mission.

least for a while. In a study tracking the outcomes at information technology companies that acquired other firms, companies with more structural integration were less likely to introduce new products soon after the acquisition, but integration had less of an impact on product launches involving more experienced target companies.[6]

These concepts permeate the rest of the chapter. First we discuss vertical differentiation within organization structure. This concept includes issues pertaining to authority within an organization, the board of directors, the chief executive officer, and hierarchical levels as well as issues pertaining to delegation and decentralization. Next we turn to horizontal differentiation in an organization's structure, exploring issues of departmentalization that create functional, divisional, and matrix organizations. Finally, we cover issues pertaining to structural integration, including coordination, organizational roles, interdependence, and boundary spanning.

The Vertical Structure

To understand issues such as reporting relationships, authority, responsibility, and the like, we need to begin with the vertical dimension of a firm's structure.

Authority in Organizations

authority

The legitimate right to make decisions and to tell other people what to do.

At the most fundamental level, the functioning of every organization depends on the use of **authority,** the legitimate right to make decisions and to tell other people what to do. For example, a boss has the authority to give an order to a subordinate.

Traditionally, authority resides in positions rather than in people. Thus the job of vice president of a particular division has authority over that division, regardless of how many people come and go in that position and who currently holds it.

In private business enterprises, the owners have ultimate authority. In most small, simply structured companies, the owner also acts as manager. Sometimes the owner hires another person to manage the business and its employees. The owner gives this manager some authority to oversee the operations, but the manager is accountable to—that is, reports and defers to—the owner. Thus the owner still has the ultimate authority.

Formal position authority is generally the primary means of running an organization. An order that a boss gives to a lower-level employee is usually carried out. As this occurs throughout the organization day after day, the organization can move forward and achieve its goals.[7] However, authority in an organization is not always position-dependent. People with particular expertise, experience, or personal qualities may have considerable *informal* authority—for example, people who carry themselves with confidence, can deliver valuable information, or work face to face with those who have high positions.[8] Effective managers are aware of informal authority as a factor that can help or hinder their achievement of the organization's goals; we will say more about informal authority in the next chapter and Chapter 12. For now, we discuss the formal authority structure of the organization from the top down, beginning with the board of directors.

Board of Directors   In corporations, the owners are the stockholders. But because there are numerous stockholders and these individuals generally lack timely information, few are directly involved in managing the organization. Stockholders elect a board of directors to oversee the organization. The board, led by the chair, makes major decisions affecting the organization, subject to corporate charter and bylaw provisions. Boards perform at least three major sets of duties: (1) selecting, assessing, rewarding, and perhaps replacing the CEO; (2) determining the firm's strategic direction and reviewing financial performance; and (3) ensuring ethical, socially responsible, and legal conduct.[9]

The board's membership usually includes some top executives—called *inside directors.* Outside members of the board tend to be executives at other companies. The trend in recent years has been toward reducing the number of insiders and increasing the number of outsiders. Today, most companies have a majority of outside directors. Boards made up of strong, independent outsiders are more likely to provide different information and perspectives and to prevent big mistakes. Successful boards tend to be those who are active, critical participants in determining company strategies. Even so, in the wake of scandals and lawsuits, many boards have shifted their focus to compliance issues, such as audits, financial reporting, and laws against discrimination. These issues are critically important, but a board staffed mainly with legal and regulatory experts cannot always give management the necessary direction on strategy.[10]

The job of CEO typically consists of leading the board of directors, encouraging employees, and promoting positive change while being accountable for the overall success of the company.

© Tom Merton/age fotostock

The owner and managers of a small business may need the expertise of a board of directors at least as much as a large company does. To obtain some of these benefits without the expense or loss of day-to-day control, small-business leaders may seek advisers who will hold them accountable for their goals and performance. Some owners set up a board of advisers, such as owners of noncompeting companies, retired executives, and perhaps their banker or accountant. Others seek the advice of peers by joining organizations that facilitate regular meetings of business owners with different areas of expertise. Members of peer advisory groups, like The Alternative Board, can share problems and exchange solutions with fellow members in a confidential setting.[11] University of Windsor, Canada, professor Roger Hussey found that privately owned companies were more profitable during the recent recession if they had a board of directors that included people from outside the company. One important reason was their ability to be more objective about what the company could do during difficult times.[12]

Chief Executive Officer   The authority officially vested in the board of directors is assigned to a chief executive officer (CEO), who occupies the top of the organizational pyramid. The CEO is personally accountable to the board and to the owners for the organization's performance.

In some corporations, one person holds all three positions of CEO, chair of the board of directors, and president.[13] More commonly, however, one person holds two of those positions, with the CEO serving also as either the chair of the board or the president of the organization. When the CEO is president, the chair may be honorary and may do little more than conduct meetings. In other cases, the chair may be the CEO, and the president is second in command.

In recent years, the trend has been to separate the position of CEO and chair of the board. Sometimes this change is related to improved corporate governance; board oversight is easier when the CEO is not quite as dominant a figure. In other cases, the board has acted to reduce an unpopular CEO's power or to help prepare for a successor to the CEO.

Top Management Team   Increasingly, CEOs share their authority with other key members of the top management team or C-suite (the "C" stands for Chief). Top management teams typically are composed of the CEO, president, chief operating officer, chief financial officer, chief human resources officer, and other key executives. Rather than make critical decisions on their own, CEOs at companies such as Shell, Honeywell, and Merck regularly meet with their top management teams to make decisions as a unit.[14]

Hierarchical Levels

In Chapter 1, we discussed the three broad levels of the organizational pyramid, commonly called the **hierarchy.** The CEO occupies the top position and is the senior member of top management. The top managerial level also includes presidents and vice presidents. They are the strategic managers in charge of the entire organization.

The key responsibilities at this top level include **corporate governance**—a term describing the oversight of the firm by its executive staff and board of directors. In recent years, as a result of corporate scandals and extremely generous executive pay packages, the public's trust in corporate governance has eroded significantly. As we mentioned in Chapter 5, Congress responded by passing the Sarbanes-Oxley Act, which, along with requirements by the Securities and Exchange Commission, imposed much tighter corporate governance rules. For example, company CEOs and CFOs (chief financial officers) now have to certify the accuracy of their firm's financial statements personally.

The second broad level of the organization is middle management. At this level, managers are in charge of plants or departments. The lowest level is made up of lower management and workers. It includes office managers, sales managers, supervisors, and other first-line managers as well as the employees who report directly to them. This level is also called the *operational level* of the organization.

An authority structure is the glue that holds these levels together. Generally, but not always, people at higher levels have the authority to make decisions and tell lower-level people what to do. For example, middle managers can give orders to first-line supervisors; first-line supervisors, in turn, direct operative-level workers.

A powerful trend for U.S. businesses over the past few decades has been to reduce the number of hierarchical layers. General Electric used to have 29 levels; today it has only a handful of layers, and its hierarchical structure is basically flat. Most executives today believe that fewer layers create a more efficient, fast-acting, and cost-effective organization. This also holds true for the **subunits** of major corporations. A study of 234 branches of a financial services company found that branches with fewer layers tended to have higher operating efficiency than did branches with more layers.[15]

This trend and research might seem to suggest that hierarchy is a bad thing, but it offers benefits as well. A hierarchy provides management career paths that help organizations retain and develop ambitious, talented people, giving them gradually more challenging experiences as they prepare for executive positions. In contrast, where there is little hierarchy, employees who see no chance of promotion may leave to find better opportunities elsewhere. Also, a well-designed hierarchy can ensure that managers have a reasonable number of people to monitor, as described in the next section.[16]

Span of Control

The number of people under a manager is an important feature of an organization's structure. The number of subordinates who report directly to an executive or supervisor is called the **span of control.** The implications of differences in the span of control for the shape of an organization are straightforward. Holding size constant, narrow spans build a tall organization that has many reporting levels. Wide spans create a flat organization with fewer reporting levels. The span of control can be too narrow or too wide. The optimal span of control maximizes effectiveness because it is (1) narrow enough to permit managers to maintain control over subordinates but (2) not so narrow that it leads to overcontrol and an excessive number of managers who oversee a small number of subordinates.

What is the optimal number of subordinates? Five, according to Napoleon Bonaparte.[17] Some managers today still consider five a good number. At one Japanese bank, in contrast, several hundred branch managers report to the same boss. In a study by the Corporate Executive Board, the average span of control at large companies increased from 7 direct reports to 12 between 2008 and 2012.

As shown in Exhibit 8.2, the optimal span of control depends on a number of factors.

---

hierarchy

The authority levels of the organizational pyramid.

corporate governance

The role of a corporation's executive staff and board of directors in ensuring that the firm's activities meet the goals of the firm's stakeholders.

Bottom Line

A structure with fewer horizontal layers saves time and money.
Why not eliminate all middle layers to save the most time and money?

subunits

Subdivisions of an organization.

LO 4

span of control

The number of subordinates who report directly to an executive or supervisor.

Factors	Use a Wide Span of Control
The nature of the work	Work is clearly defined and unambiguous.
Subordinates' preparation	Subordinates are highly trained and have access of information.
Managers' capabilities	Managers are capable and supportive of subordinates.
Comparability of subordinates' jobs	Subordinates have similar jobs and are rated on comparable performance measures.
Subordinates' supervisory preferences	Subordinates prefer autonomy and independence.
Organizational size	The organization is small.

EXHIBIT 8.2
When Is a Wide Managerial Span of Control Preferable?

Note: If the opposite conditions exist, a narrow span of control may be more appropriate.
SOURCES: Adapted from "Span of Control: What Factors Should Determine How Many Direct Reports a Manager Has?" Society for Human Resource Management, April 25, 2013, http://www.shrm.org; P. Jehiel, "Information Aggregation and Communication in Organizations," *Management Science* 45, no. 5 (May 1999), pp. 659–69; and A. Altaffer, "First-Line Managers: Measuring Their Span of Control," *Nursing Management* 29, no. 7 (July 1998), pp. 36–40.

Delegation

As we look at organizations and recognize that authority is spread out over various levels and spans of control, the issue of delegation becomes paramount. **Delegation** is the assignment of authority and responsibility to a subordinate at a lower level. It often requires the subordinate to report back to his or her boss about how effectively the assignment was carried out. Delegation is perhaps the most fundamental feature of management because it entails getting work done through others. Thus delegation is important at all hierarchical levels. The process can occur between any two individuals in any type of structure with regard to any task.

delegation

The assignment of new or additional responsibilities to a subordinate.

Some managers are comfortable fully delegating an assignment to subordinates; others are not. Consider how the two office managers in the following example gave out the same assignment. Are both of these statements examples of delegation?

Manager A: "Call Tom Burton at Cavalier Computer. Ask him to give you the price list on an upgrade for our personal computers. I want to move up to a quad-core processor with 8 gigs of RAM and at least a 1.5-terabyte hard drive. Ask them to give you a demonstration of the Windows 8 operating system and Microsoft Office 365. I want to be able to establish collaboration capability for the entire group. Invite Cochran and Snow to the demonstration and let them try it out. Have them write up a summary of their needs and the potential applications they see for the new systems. Then prepare me a report with the costs and specifications of the upgrade for the entire department. Oh, yes, be sure to ask for information on service costs."

Manager B: "I'd like to do something about our personal computer system. I've been getting some complaints that the current systems are too slow, can't run current software, and don't allow for networking. Could you evaluate our options and give me a recommendation on what we should do? Our budget is around $2,000 per person, but I'd like to stay under that if we can. Feel free to talk to some of the managers to get their input, but we need to have this done as soon as possible."

Responsibility, Authority, and Accountability   When delegating work, it is helpful to keep in mind the important distinctions among the concepts of authority, responsibility, and accountability. **Responsibility** means that a person is assigned a task that he or she is supposed to carry out. When delegating work responsibilities, the manager also should delegate to the subordinate enough authority to get the job done. Authority, recall, means that the person has the power and the right to make decisions, give orders, draw on

responsibility

The assignment of a task that an employee is supposed to carry out.

resources, and do whatever else is necessary to fulfill the responsibility. Ironically, it is quite common for people to have more responsibility than authority; they must perform as well as they can through informal influence tactics instead of relying purely on authority. More will be said about informal power and how to use it in Chapter 12.

As the manager delegates responsibilities, subordinates are held accountable for achieving results. **Accountability** means that the subordinate's manager has the right to expect the subordinate to perform the job and the right to take corrective action if the subordinate fails to do so. The subordinate must report upward on the status and quality of his or her performance of the task.

However, the ultimate responsibility—accountability to higher-ups—lies with the manager doing the delegating. Managers remain responsible and accountable not only for their own actions but also for the actions of their subordinates. Managers should not resort to delegation to others as a means of escaping their own responsibilities. In many cases, however, managers refuse to accept responsibility for subordinates' actions. Managers often pass the buck or take other evasive action to ensure they are not held accountable for mistakes.[18] Ideally, however, empowering employees to make decisions or take action results in an increase in employee responsibility.

accountability

The expectation that employees will perform a job, take corrective action when necessary, and report upward on the status and quality of their performance.

 Advantages of Delegation   Delegating work offers important advantages, particularly when it is done effectively. Effective delegation leverages the manager's energy and talent and those of his or her subordinates. It allows managers to accomplish much more than they would be able to do on their own. Conversely, lack of delegation, or ineffective delegation, sharply reduces what a manager can achieve, and lowers employee morale. The manager also saves one of his or her most valuable assets—time—by giving some of his or her responsibility to somebody else. He or she is then free to devote energy to important, higher-level activities such as planning, setting objectives, and monitoring performance.

Another very important advantage of delegation is that it helps develop effective subordinates. Look again at the different ways the two office managers gave out the same assignment. The approach that is more likely to empower subordinates and help them develop will be obvious to you. (You may also quickly conclude which of the two managers you would prefer to work for.) Delegation essentially gives the subordinate a more important job. The subordinate acquires an opportunity to develop new skills and to demonstrate potential for additional responsibilities and perhaps promotion. In essence, the subordinate receives a vital form of on-the-job training that could pay off in the future. In addition, there is evidence that, at least for some employees, delegation promotes a sense of being an important, contributing member of the organization, so these employees tend to feel a stronger commitment, perform their tasks better, and engage in more innovation.[19]

Through delegation, the organization also receives payoffs. Allowing managers to devote more time to important managerial functions while lower-level employees carry out assignments means that jobs are done more efficiently and cost-effectively. In addition, as subordinates develop and grow in their own jobs, their ability to contribute to the organization increases as well.

It is important to note that not all managers like to delegate. For example, Steve Jobs, cofounder of Apple, preferred to micromanage and be heavily involved with each product (e.g., iPhone) the company designed.[20] This approach worked for Apple, but many organizations rely heavily on delegation.

Bottom Line

Effective delegation raises the quality of subordinates and the service they provide to customers or co-workers. *Under what conditions might an effort at delegation backfire?*

How Should Managers Delegate?   To achieve the advantages we have just discussed, delegation must be done properly. As Exhibit 8.3 shows, effective delegation proceeds through several steps.[21]

The first step in the delegation process, defining the goal, requires the manager to have a clear understanding of the outcome he or she wants. Then the manager should select a person who is capable of performing the task. Delegation is especially beneficial if you can

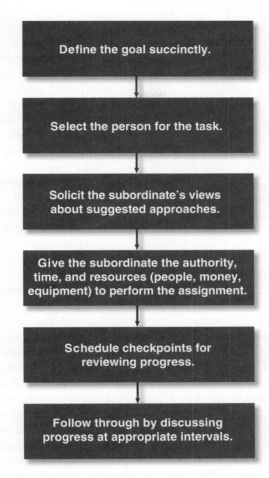

Define the goal succinctly.

Select the person for the task.

Solicit the subordinate's views about suggested approaches.

Give the subordinate the authority, time, and resources (people, money, equipment) to perform the assignment.

Schedule checkpoints for reviewing progress.

Follow through by discussing progress at appropriate intervals.

EXHIBIT 8.3
The Steps in Effective Delegation

identify an employee who would benefit from developing skills through the experience of taking on the additional responsibility.

The person who gets the assignment should be given the authority, time, and resources to carry out the task successfully. The required resources usually involve people, money, and equipment, but often they may also involve critical information that will put the assignment in context. Throughout the delegation process, the manager and the subordinate must work together and communicate about the project. The manager should know the subordinate's ideas at the beginning and inquire about progress or problems at periodic meetings and review sessions. Thus, even though the subordinate performs the assignment, the manager is available and aware of its current status. These checkups also provide an important opportunity to offer encouragement and praise.

Some tasks, such as disciplining subordinates and conducting performance reviews, should not be delegated. But when managers err, it usually is because they delegated too little rather than too much. The manager who wants to learn how to delegate more effectively should remember this distinction: If you are not delegating, you are merely doing things; but the more you delegate, the more you are truly building and managing an organization.[22]

Decentralization

The delegation of responsibility and authority *decentralizes* decision making. In a **centralized organization,** important decisions usually are made at the top. In **decentralized organizations,** more decisions are made at lower levels. Ideally, decision making occurs at the level of the people who are most directly affected and have the most intimate knowledge about the problem. This is particularly important when the business environment is fast-changing and decisions

centralized organization

An organization in which high-level executives make most decisions and pass them down to lower levels for implementation.

decentralized organization

An organization in which lower-level managers make important decisions.

LO 6

The delegation of responsibility and authority *decentralizes* decision making.

At times, decentralizing decision making or allowing decisions to be made by middle and lower-level managers can be an advantage to higher-level executives. These are the managers who deal directly with the problem and know the best solution for the company and the employees.

© Squaredpixels/Getty Images

Bottom Line

Decentralization often speeds decision making. *What makes centralized decision making slower?*

must be made quickly and well. Balanced against these criteria, centralization may be valuable when departments have different priorities or conflicting goals, which need to be mediated by top management. For example, when researchers modeled the search for new ideas in organizations, they found that the worst performance occurred in decentralized organizations where the search for new ideas was carried out at lower levels, because ideas were presented for approval only if they benefited the particular department doing the search.[23]

Sometimes organizations change their degree of centralization, depending on the particular challenges they face. Tougher times often cause senior management to take charge, whereas in times of rapid growth, decisions are pushed further down the chain of command. Time Warner Cable (TWC) tried to decentralize marketing as a way to let regional teams move quickly in response to opportunities in local markets. However, competition for online entertainment and from satellite companies is putting cable companies such as TWC in an increasingly tight spot. In that environment, TWC reversed its decision and returned to a centralized marketing structure.[24] Unfortunately for TWC, research suggests that decentralizing tends to go more smoothly than a change toward greater centralization; in that study, teams that became more centralized failed to make the efficiency gains typically associated with a centralized organization.[25]

Most American executives today understand the advantages of pushing decision-making authority down to the point of the action. The level that deals directly with problems and opportunities has the most relevant information and can foresee the consequences of decisions best. Executives also see how the decentralized approach allows people to take faster action.[26]

Paul Bulcke, CEO of global food giant Nestlé, empowers employees in over 100 countries to be responsive to local consumers. He believes that a decentralized approach in which local employees can make decisions is the key to growing the company's global market share. When discussing the Japanese market, he explains: "We are decentralized, so we give them power. You cannot organize Japan from here, in Lake Geneva. You have to be there. You have to live the culture from day to day."[27]

The Horizontal Structure

line departments

Units that deal directly with the organization's primary goods and services.

Up to this point, we've talked primarily about vertical aspects of organization structure. Issues of authority, span of control, delegation, and decentralization are important because they give us an idea of how managers and employees relate to one another at different levels. Yet separating discussion of vertical differentiation from horizontal differentiation is a bit artificial because the elements work simultaneously.

As the tasks of organizations become increasingly complex, the organization inevitably must be subdivided—that is, *departmentalized*—into smaller units or departments. One of the first places this can be seen is in the distinction between line and staff departments. **Line departments** are those that have responsibility for the principal activities of the firm. Line units deal directly with the organization's primary goods or services; they make things, sell things, or provide customer service. At General Motors, for example, line departments include product design, fabrication, assembly, distribution, and the like. Line managers typically have much authority and power in the organization. They have the ultimate responsibility for making major operating decisions. They also are accountable for the bottom-line results of their decisions.

Staff departments are those that provide specialized or professional skills that support line departments. They include research, legal, accounting, public relations, and human resources departments. Each of these specialized units often has its own vice president, and some are vested with a great deal of authority, as when accounting or finance groups approve and monitor budgetary activities.

In traditionally structured organizations, conflicts could arise between line and staff departments. One reason was that career paths and success in many staff functions have depended on being an expert in that particular functional area, whereas success in line functions is based more on knowing the organization's industry. Thus, although line managers might be eager to pursue new products and customers, staff managers might seem to stifle these ideas with a focus on requirements and procedures. Line managers might seem more willing to take risks for the sake of growth, whereas staff managers seem more focused on protecting the company from risks. But in today's organizations, staff units tend to be less focused on monitoring and controlling performance and more interested in moving toward a new role focused on strategic support and expert advice.[28] For example, human resource managers have broadened their focus from merely creating procedures that meet legal requirements to helping organizations plan for, recruit, develop, and keep the kinds of employees who will give the organization a long-term competitive advantage.[29] This type of strategic thinking not only makes staff managers more valuable to their organizations but also can reduce the conflict between line and staff departments.

As organizations divide work into different units, we can detect patterns in the way departments are clustered and arranged. The three basic approaches to **departmentalization** are functional, divisional, and matrix. We will talk about each and highlight some of their similarities and differences.

The Functional Organization

In a **functional organization**, jobs (and departments) are specialized and grouped according to business functions and the skills they require: production, marketing, human resources, research and development, finance, accounting, and so forth. Exhibit 8.4 illustrates a basic functional organization chart.

Functional departmentalization is common in both large and small organizations. Large companies may organize along several functional groupings, including groupings unique to their businesses. For example, Carmike Cinema, which operates nearly 2,900 screens in 274 theaters in 41 states, has vice presidents of finance, concessions, film, and entertainment and digital cinema as well as a general manager of theater operations. Kiva, a nonprofit organization, also uses a functional grouping (see the nearby "Social Enterprise" box).

staff departments

Units that support line departments.

departmentalization

Subdividing an organization into smaller subunits.

functional organization

Departmentalization around specialized activities such as production, marketing, and human resources.

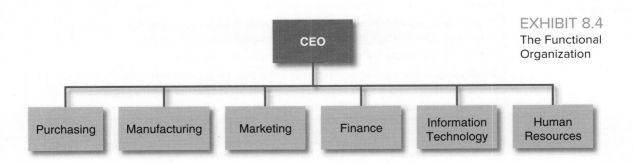

EXHIBIT 8.4
The Functional Organization

Social Enterprise

Kiva Organizes by Function

Imagine having an idea to start a food stand or car cleaning business. Also imagine that you and your family live in poverty and don't even have $50 to spare to buy the initial supplies to launch the business. Where can you turn, to the local bank? It is unlikely a bank will provide a small, unsecured loan to you.

Kiva, a nonprofit organization, is trying to meet this need. Kiva connects via the Internet a global network of lenders with entrepreneurs in impoverished communities. Individuals can lend as little as $25 to help empower a budding entrepreneur to start a business to feed his or her family. Over the past 10 years 1.3 million lenders have made it possible for Kiva to make over $692.5 million in loans to individuals in 86 different countries. With an average repayment rate of nearly 99 percent, this social enterprise is making an impact on the lives of countless individuals, their families, and their communities.

While some nonprofits may choose to organize around the clients they serve or the regions they operate in, Kiva takes a different approach. Kiva's organizational structure is unique in how it contributes to the enterprise's efficiency and effectiveness.

Given the global complexity of Kiva's operations, the organization hopes to achieve economies of scale by grouping employees and volunteers with similar training and skills into eight functional areas.[30] Other benefits of functional departmentalization are listed in Exhibit 8.5.

Questions

- Why do you think Kiva is using a functional approach to structuring its organization?
- Referring to the eight areas illustrated, which would be considered staff activities? Line activities?

Development | Marketing & Communications | Global Partnerships | Engineering

People | Finance | Legal | Product & User Experience

Bottom Line

When like functions are grouped, savings often result.

Why might a company centralize its information technology (IT) department?

As shown in Exhibit 8.5, the traditional functional approach to departmentalization has a number of potential advantages for an organization.

The functional form does have disadvantages, however. People may care more about their own function than about the company as a whole, and their attention to functional tasks may make them lose focus on overall product quality and customer satisfaction. Managers develop functional expertise but do not acquire knowledge of the other areas of the business; they become specialists but not generalists. Between functions, conflicts arise, and communication and coordination fall off. In short, although functional differentiation may exist, functional integration may not.

EXHIBIT 8.5

Advantages of Functional Approach to Departmentalization

Economies of scale can be realized. When people with similar skills are grouped, more efficient equipment can be purchased, and discounts for large purchases can be used.

People have greater opportunity for specialized training and in-depth skill development.

Performance standards are better maintained. People with similar training and interests may develop a shared concern for performance in their jobs.

Technical specialists are relatively free of administrative work.

Monitoring of the environment is more effective. Each functional group is more closely attuned to developments in its own field and therefore can adapt more readily.

Decision making and lines of communication are simple and clearly understood.

SOURCES: Adapted from R. Cross and L. Baird, "Technology Is Not Enough: Improving Performance by Building Organizational Memory," *Sloan Management Review* 41, no. 3 (Spring 2000), pp. 69–78; and R. Duncan, "What Is the Right Organizational Structure?" *Organizational Dynamics* 7 (Winter 1979), pp. 59–80.

As a consequence, the functional structure may be most appropriate in rather simple, stable environments. If the organization becomes fragmented (or *dis*integrated), it may have difficulty developing and bringing new products to market and responding quickly to customer demands and other changes. Particularly when companies are growing and business environments are changing, organizations need to integrate work areas more effectively so they can be more flexible and responsive. Other forms of departmentalization can be more flexible and responsive than the functional structure.

One organization that has capitalized on the benefits of integrating functions is San Francisco Federal Credit Union (SFFCU). Several years ago, management could see the organization was losing members but didn't have the tools to understand why or to plan for growth. So SFFCU purchased a software system called Connections Online that gives employees in all functions access to information about the credit union's strategy and its progress toward goals. That visibility pushed management to launch regular cross-functional discussions about SFFCU's strategic plan. With everyone understanding priorities and engaged in getting results, the credit union has upgraded its technology, improved its marketing, and is watching membership and lending rates climb again.[31]

Demands for total quality, customer service, innovation, and speed have made clear the shortcomings of the functional form for some firms. Functional organizations are highly differentiated and create barriers to coordination across functions. Cross-functional coordination is essential for total quality, customer service, innovations, and speed. The functional organization will not disappear, in part because functional specialists will always be needed, but functional managers will make fewer decisions. The more important units will be cross-functional teams that have integrative responsibilities for products, processes, or customers.[32]

The Divisional Organization

The discussion of a functional structure's weaknesses leads us to the **divisional organization.** As organizations grow and become increasingly diversified, they find that functional departments have difficulty managing a wide variety of products, customers, and geographic regions. In this case, organizations may restructure to group all functions into a single division and duplicate each of the functions across all the divisions. In the divisional organization chart in Exhibit 8.6, Division A has its own operations, marketing,

divisional organization

Departmentalization that groups units around products, customers, or geographic regions.

EXHIBIT 8.6
The Divisional Organization

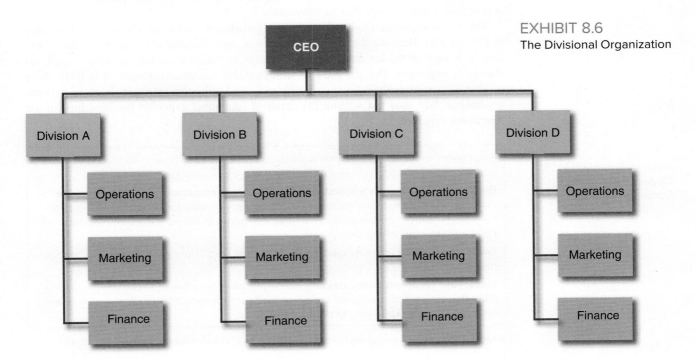

EXHIBIT 8.7
Examples of Functional and Divisional Organization

Functional Organization	Divisional Organization
Chain of pharmacies with departments for cosmetics, photos, greetings cards, human resources, operations, and finance, responsible for all store locations.	Chain of pharmacies with one division for each region (e.g., Northeast, Midwest, and Southeast) of the country managing all functions in that region.
Automotive manufacturer with departments for research and development, engineering, purchasing, production, and sales, managing all automotive products.	Automotive manufacturer with product groups (e.g., SUV or truck), each staffed with employees to manage that automobile's development, engineering, purchasing, production, and sales.
One marketing department serving the needs of all the domestic and international subsidiaries of a multinational company, reporting to the corporate leadership.	A marketing department at the offices of each subsidiary in which the multinational firm operates, reporting to the leadership in charge of that subsidiary's operations.

SOURCE: Adapted from George Strauss and Leonard R. Sayles, Strauss and Sayles's *Behavioral Strategies for Managers,* © 1980, p. 221.

and finance departments, Division B has its own operations, marketing, and finance departments, and so on. In this structure, separate divisions may act almost as separate businesses or profit centers and work autonomously to accomplish the goals of the entire enterprise. Exhibit 8.7 presents examples of how the same tasks would be organized under functional and divisional structures.

Organizations create a divisional structure in several ways. It can be created around products, customers, or geographic regions. Each of these is described in the following sections.

Product Divisions   In the product organization, all functions that contribute to a given product are organized under one manager. In the product organization, managers in charge of functions for a particular product report to a product manager. Johnson & Johnson is one example of this form. J&J is organized into three broad product categories: consumer health care, medical devices, and pharmaceuticals. Within these categories are 275 independent company divisions, many of which are responsible for particular product lines. For example, Ethicon develops and sells surgical equipment, whereas McNeil-PPC's products include Listerine and Plax mouthwashes.[33]

The product approach to departmentalization offers a number of advantages (illustrated in Exhibit 8.8). Because the product structure is more flexible than the functional structure, it is best suited for unstable environments in which an ability to adapt rapidly to change is important. But the product structure also has disadvantages. It is difficult to coordinate across product lines and divisions. And although managers learn to become generalists, they may not acquire the depth of functional expertise that develops in the functional structure.

EXHIBIT 8.8
Product Approach to Departmentalization: Some Advantages

Employees are focused solely on a particular product line. They have a keen understanding of how their jobs fit into the larger organization.

Employees have a clear understanding of their task responsibilities. Managers are more empowered to make decisions and take responsibility for performance because they often control needed resources. Also, the output of different divisions can be compared by contrasting their profits.

Information needs are managed more efficiently. Less information is required because people work closely on one product.

Employees receive broader training. Managers develop a broad set of skills, and they learn that they will be assessed based on their performance. Many managers received meaningful early experience in product structures.

SOURCE: Adapted from R. Boehm and C. Phipps, "Flatness Forays," *McKinsey Quarterly* 3 (1996), pp. 128–43.

Furthermore, functions are not centralized at headquarters, where they are done for all product lines or divisions. Such duplication of effort is expensive. Also, decision making is decentralized in this structure, so top management can lose some control over decisions made in the divisions. Proper management of all the issues surrounding decentralization and delegation, as discussed earlier, is essential for this structure to be effective.[34]

Customer and Geographic Divisions   Some companies build divisions around groups of customers or around different geographic areas. IT firm EMC helps customers of all sizes and industries around the world transition to cloud computing and manage their data. While many similar IT firms focus on engineering or marketing, EMC invests heavily in R&D, nearly $17 billion over the past decade, to develop products to solve customers' problems.[35] Similarly, a hospital may organize its services around child, adult, psychiatric, and emergency cases. Bank loan departments commonly have separate groups handling consumer and business needs.

In contrast to customers, divisions can be structured around geographic regions. Sears, for example, was a pioneer in creating geographic divisions. Geographic distinctions include district, territory, region, and country. Macy's Group, formerly Federated Department Stores, has geographic divisions for its operations serving particular states or regions of the United States: Macy's Northwest, North Central, Northeast, Mid-Atlantic, Southeast, South Central, and Southwest as well as Macys.com for online shoppers. Avon Products, in an attempt to improve weak sales of its cosmetic products in North America, is restructuring its sales force to focus more on Hispanic women. In 2014, this customer segment spent on average 11 percent more per order than non-Hispanic customers. More Avon representatives are being assigned to areas with higher concentrations of Hispanics.[36]

The primary advantage of both the product and customer/regional approaches to departmentalization is the ability to focus on customer needs and provide faster, better service.

> ## Bottom Line
> Customer and geographic divisions often serve customers faster.
> *Suppose your international company sells scientific equipment to high schools, universities, and businesses. Would you set up customer divisions or geographic divisions? Why?*
>
>

Management in Action

GENERAL MOTORS EXPERIENCES A CRISIS AND LEADERSHIP CHANGE

Through 2013, ex-CEO Daniel Akerson's plans to make General Motors more nimble included a corporate reorganization to create more of a functional structure. Over the past few decades, GM had moved from a structure based on product lines (Chevrolet, Buick, Cadillac, and so on) toward one based on regions (North America, South America, Europe, and International Operations). But the main result seems to have been that the company moved from one set of independently operating groups (the brand groups) to another (the geographic groups), and the company still was not operating as a unified whole with a common mission. Efforts to save money by globally applying product designs broke down as regional executives insisted on making their own decisions for their regions.

A functional structure placed more authority in the hands of the functional executives, who could set up companywide systems and identify designs to use for models created to sell in several or all geographic markets.

The effectiveness of Akerson's corporate restructuring at GM was eclipsed by two major events in 2014. In January of that year, Akerson retired earlier than expected for family reasons. Mary Barra, with 33 years of experience at GM, took over as CEO. Barra is known for her candid style and ability to improve efficiencies. Later in 2014, GM had to recall over 30 million cars and trucks at a cost of $4.1 billion. Nearly 3 million of the recalls were attributed to a faulty ignition switch that has been linked to 67 deaths as of the writing of this book. Evidence suggests that GM managers knew about this problem for over 10 years, but waited until 2014 to address it.[37]

- Review the advantages and drawbacks of functional organizations and geographic divisions. Which ones may have contributed to the decision to finally address the faulty ignition switch issue?
- What do you think will be the impact of GM's effort to create more centralized structure based on functional groups?

MANAGER'S BRIEF

PROGRESS REPORT

ONWARD

But again, duplication of activities across many customer groups and geographic areas is expensive. As you read "Management in Action: Progress Report," consider how well the advantages and drawbacks of these divisional structures might apply to General Motors.

The Matrix Organization

LO 8

matrix organization

An organization composed of dual reporting relationships in which some employees report to two superiors—a functional manager and a divisional manager.

A **matrix organization** is a hybrid form of organization in which functional and divisional forms overlap. Managers and staff personnel report to two bosses—a functional manager and a divisional manager. Thus matrix organizations have a dual rather than a single line of command. In Exhibit 8.9, for example, each project manager draws employees from each functional area to form a group for the project. The employees working on those projects report to the individual project manager as well as to the manager of their functional area.

A good example of the matrix structure can be found at Time Inc., the top magazine publisher in the United States and United Kingdom. At major Time Inc. titles such as *Time, Sports Illustrated, Fortune,* and *People,* production managers who are responsible for getting the magazines printed report both to the individual publishers and editors of each title *and* to a senior corporate executive in charge of production. At the corporate level, Time Inc. achieves enormous economies of scale by buying paper and printing in bulk and making sure production activities in the company as a whole are coordinated. At the same time, production managers working at each title make sure the different needs and schedules of their individual magazines are being met. Similar matrix arrangements are in place for other key managers such as circulation and finance. In this way, the company attempts to gain the benefits of both the divisional and functional organization structure.

The matrix form originated in the aerospace industry, first with TRW in 1959 and then with NASA. Applications now occur in hospitals and health care agencies, entrepreneurial organizations, government laboratories, financial institutions, and multinational corporations.[38] Other companies that have used or currently use the matrix form include IBM, Boeing, Procter & Gamble, Nokia, Cisco, Schlumberger, Bechtel, and Dow Corning.

Pros and Cons of the Matrix Form   Like other organization structures, the matrix has both strengths and weaknesses. Exhibit 8.10 summarizes the advantages of using a matrix structure. The major potential advantage is a higher degree of flexibility and adaptability.

EXHIBIT 8.9
Matrix Organizational
Structure

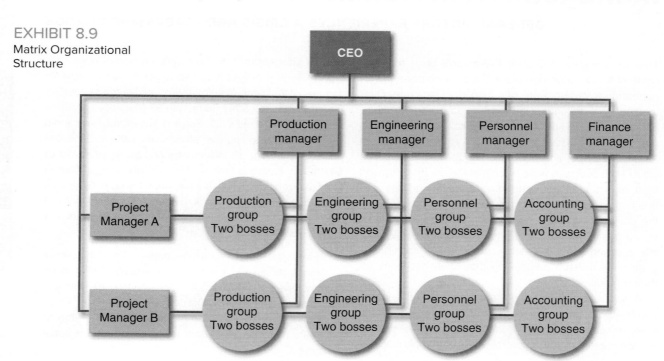

Advantages
• Linkage of employees at all levels and in all functions to the company's goals and strategy.
• More information shared across functions.
• Communication fostered—especially valuable for complex assignments where different groups depend on each other.
• Greater responsiveness to customers from bringing together information about customer needs and organizational capabilities.
• Creative ideas from cross-functional work.
• Loyalty to the organization as a whole rather than to a function or division.

Disadvantages
• Unclear responsibilities and competing priorities.
• Violation of the unity-of-command principle.
• Accountability difficult to define.
• Accountability for results under other matrix members' control.
• Possible conflict and stress for employees who must manage a dual reporting role.
• Additional time required for meetings and other communications to coordinate work.
• Extensive collaboration needed but not always easy to reward.

EXHIBIT 8.10
Strengths and Weaknesses of the Matrix Design

SOURCES: Based on E. Krell, "Managing the Matrix," *HR Magazine,* April 2011, pp. 69–71; R. Lash, "Cracking the Matrix Code," *Canadian HR Reporter,* March 28, 2011, pp. 16, 18; and M. North and C. Coors, "Avoiding Death by Dotted Line," *Healthcare Financial Management,* January 2010, pp. 120–21.

Exhibit 8.10 also summarizes the potential shortcomings of the matrix form. Many of the disadvantages stem from the matrix's inherent violation of the **unity-of-command principle,** which states that a person should have only one boss. Reporting to two superiors can create confusion and a difficult interpersonal situation unless steps are taken to prevent these problems from arising.

unity-of-command principle

A structure in which each worker reports to one boss, who in turn reports to one boss.

Matrix Survival Skills   The value of collaboration is particularly pronounced in a matrix organization. For example, in the kind of structure illustrated in Exhibit 8.9, project group members may not be permanently assigned to the project manager. They will return to their functional area once the project has been completed. For this group to work effectively, the traditional command-and-control management style may not be the most appropriate; it might gain compliance from group members but not their full commitment, making it harder to achieve the project's goals. Also, because the matrix organization draws on members of functional groups to tap their expertise, it is very important to get their full contribution. A collaborative process, in which the manager and participants develop a shared sense of ownership for the work they are doing, will generate better ideas, participation, and commitment to the project and its outcomes.

To a large degree, problems can be avoided if the key managers in the matrix learn the behavioral skills demanded in the matrix structure.[39] These skills vary depending on the job in the four-person diamond structure shown in Exhibit 8.11.

The top executive, who heads the matrix, must learn to balance power and emphasis between the product and functional orientations. Product or division managers and functional managers must learn to collaborate and manage their conflicts constructively. Finally, the two-boss managers or employees at the bottom of the diamond must learn how to be responsible to two superiors. This means prioritizing multiple demands and sometimes even reconciling

The key to managing today's matrix is the realization that the matrix is a process.

EXHIBIT 8.11
The Matrix Diamond

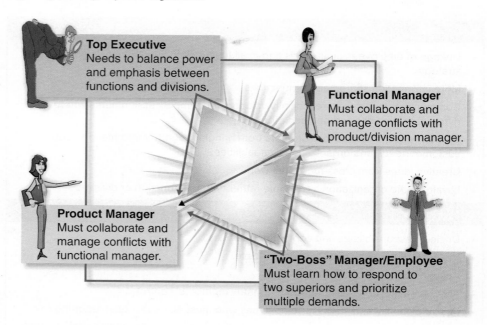

EXHIBIT 8.11
The Matrix Diamond

Top Executive
Needs to balance power and emphasis between functions and divisions.

Functional Manager
Must collaborate and manage conflicts with product/division manager.

Product Manager
Must collaborate and manage conflicts with functional manager.

"Two-Boss" Manager/Employee
Must learn how to respond to two superiors and prioritize multiple demands.

Bottom Line

The matrix structure can speed decisions and cut costs. *How might a matrix structure increase speed?*

conflicting orders. Some people function poorly under this ambiguous, conflictual circumstance; sometimes this signals the end of their careers with the company. Others learn to be proactive, communicate effectively with both superiors, rise above the difficulties, and manage these work relationships constructively.

The Matrix Form Today   The popularity of the matrix form waned during the late 1980s, when many companies had difficulty implementing it. But recently it has come back strong. Reasons for this resurgence include pressures to consolidate costs and be faster to market, creating a need for better coordination across functions in the business units and a need for coordination across countries for firms with global business strategies. Many of the challenges created by the matrix are particularly acute in an international context, mainly because of the distances involved and the differences in local markets.[40]

The key to managing today's matrix is not the formal structure itself but the realization that the matrix is a process. Managers who have appropriately adopted the matrix structure because of the complexity of the challenges they confront, but have had trouble implementing it, often find that they haven't changed the employee and managerial relationships within their organizations in ways that make the matrix effective. It is not enough to create a flexible organization merely by changing its structure. To create an environment that allows information to flow freely throughout the organization, managers must also attend to the norms, values, and attitudes that shape how people within their organizations behave.[41] We will address these issues in the next chapter and in Part 4 of the book, which focuses on how to lead and manage people.

The Network Organization

So far, the structures we have been discussing are variations of the traditional, hierarchical organization, within which all the business functions of the firm are performed. In contrast, the **network organization** is a collection of independent, mostly single-function firms that collaborate to produce a good or service. As depicted in Exhibit 8.12, the network organization describes not one organization but the web of relationships among many firms. Network organizations are flexible arrangements among designers, suppliers, producers, distributors, and customers where each firm is able to pursue its own distinctive competence yet work effectively with other members of the network. Often, members of the network communicate electronically and share information to be able to respond quickly to customer demands. As the nearby "Multiple Generations at Work" box suggests, Millennials

network organization

A collection of independent, mostly single-function firms that collaborate on a good or service.

Multiple Generations at Work

Will Online Networks Replace Traditional Hierarchies?

According to journalist and author Malcolm Gladwell, the United States is reaching a "generational tipping point" in which Millennials may bring dramatic changes in the structure and function of organizations. During several recent speeches to industry groups, Gladwell discussed how Baby Boomers and other older generations prefer to organize around the concept of a hierarchy where strong leadership, expertise, strategy, and a guiding ideology are common.

In comparison, Gladwell points out that Millennials have a different worldview: "[Millennials] take a profoundly different attitude toward authority and toward expertise." As the first generation to grow up with unfettered access to social networking sites, online gaming, and smartphones, these "digital natives" prefer to organize around and seek information from their peers via online social networks. Given that as children, Millennials were accustomed to such "open, leaderless platforms," they naturally gravitate toward organizations that are open and collaborative in nature. In comparison to Boomers, Millennials tend to bristle when working for bosses who exert their authority by micromanaging and imposing too much structure (and rules) on employees. Perhaps this mismatch partially explains

© Robert A Tobiansky/Getty Images for SXSW

why approximately 60 percent of Millennial employees quit their jobs within three years.

What does this generational shift mean for organizations that use hierarchical structures? They may want to begin shifting their cultures and designing jobs and teams in a way that encourages collaborative, network-driven engagement. Organizations may want to make these adjustments soon given that by 2025, approximately 75 percent of workers in the United States will be from the Millennial generation.[42]

are especially well-suited for network organizations. In effect, the normal boundary of the organization becomes blurred or porous as managers within the organization interact closely with network members outside it. The network as a whole, then, can display the technical specialization of the functional structure, the market responsiveness of the product structure, and the balance and flexibility of the matrix.[43]

A very flexible version of the network organization is the **dynamic network**—also called the *modular* or *virtual* corporation. It is composed of temporary arrangements

dynamic network

Temporary arrangements among partners that can be assembled and reassembled to adapt to the environment.

EXHIBIT 8.12
A Network Organization

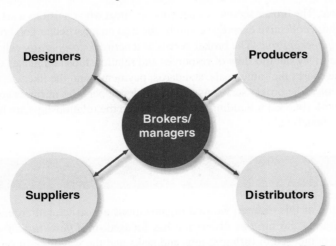

SOURCE: From Raymond E. Miles and Charles C. Snow, "Organizations: New Concepts for New Forms," in *California Management Review* 28, no. 3 (Spring 1986), pp. 62–73. Copyright 1986 by the Regents of the University of California. Reprinted by permission of University of California Press.

Bottom Line

Networks can improve cost, quality, service, speed, sustainability, and innovation. *Which functions would you include in a network to improve sustainability?*

among members that can be assembled and reassembled to meet a changing competitive environment. The members of the network are held together by contracts that stipulate results expected (market mechanisms) rather than by hierarchy and authority. Poorly performing firms can be removed and replaced.

Such arrangements are common in the electronics, toy, and apparel industries, each of which creates and sells trendy products at a fast pace. Dynamic networks also are suited to organizations in which much of the work can be done independently by experts. For example, Philip Rosedale set up a virtual company called SendLove to commercialize a software tool of the same name: an online communication system that allows co-workers to recognize each other with brief positive messages. The primary difference from a microblogging service like Twitter is that the system is completely transparent; everyone in the system sees the messages. Thus in a company using SendLove for employee recognition, everyone sees a message of appreciation, with the intent that public acknowledgment builds morale. For such a transparent application, Rosedale and his partners decided to build a completely transparent company. They launched an online bulletin board where they posted a list of all the tasks to be done for SendLove. Freelancers bid on a job by describing how they would carry out the task and what they would charge. For any collaboration required, the freelancers communicate online at the company's chat room or via e-mail and Skype. Rosedale started this virtual arrangement for programming tasks, and it was so successful in delivering great prices and fast turnaround that the company expanded to support tasks such as recruiting contracts and processing payments.[44]

Successful networks potentially offer flexibility, innovation, quick responses to threats and opportunities, and reduced costs and risk. But for these arrangements to be successful, several things must occur:

The firm must choose the right specialty. It must be something (good or service) that the market needs and that the firm is better at providing than other firms.

The firm must choose collaborators that also are excellent at what they do and that provide complementary strengths.

The firm must make certain that all parties fully understand the strategic goals of the partnership.

Each party must be able to trust all the others with strategic information and trust that each collaborator will deliver quality products even if the business grows quickly and makes heavy demands.

broker

A person who assembles and coordinates participants in a network.

The role of managers shifts in a network from that of command and control to more like that of a **broker**. Broker/managers serve several important boundary roles that aid network integration and coordination:

Designer role. The broker serves as a network architect who envisions a set of groups or firms whose collective expertise could be focused on a particular good or service.

Process engineering role. The broker serves as a *network co-operator* who takes the initiative to lay out the flow of resources and relationships and makes certain that everyone shares the same goals, standards, payments, and the like.

Nurturing role. The broker serves as a network developer who nurtures and enhances the network (like team building) to make certain the relationships are healthy and mutually beneficial.[45]

Organizational Integration

LO 9   At the beginning of this chapter, we said organizations are structured around differentiation and integration. So far, our discussion has focused on *differentiation*—the way the organization is composed of different jobs and tasks and the way they fit on an organization chart. But as organizations differentiate their structures, they also need to be concerned about *integration* and *coordination*—the way all parts of the organization will work

Slack resources are simply extra resources on which organizations can rely in a pinch so that if they get caught off guard, they can still adjust. Inventory, for example, is a type of slack resource that provides extra stock on hand in case it is needed. With extra inventory, an organization does not need as much information about sales demand, lead time, and so on.

Like slack resources, creating self-contained tasks allows organizations to reduce the need for some information. Creating self-contained tasks refers to changing from a functional organization to a product or project organization and giving each unit the resources it needs to perform its task. Information-processing problems are reduced because each unit has its own full complement of specialties instead of functional specialties that have to share their expertise among a number of different product teams. Communications then flow within each team rather than among a complex array of interdependent groups.

Option 2: Increasing Information-Processing Capability   Instead of reducing the need for information, an organization may take the approach of increasing its information-processing capability. It can invest in information systems, which usually means employing or expanding computer systems. But increasing an organization's information-processing capability also means what we referred to in Chapter 1 as knowledge management—capitalizing on the intellect and experience of the organization's human assets to increase collaboration and effectiveness. One way to do that is by creating horizontal relationships between units to foster coordination. Such horizontal relationships are effective because they increase integration, which Lawrence and Lorsch suggest is necessary for managing complex environments. As uncertainty increases, the following horizontal processes may be used, ranging from the simplest to the most complex:[50]

1. *Direct contact (mutual adjustment)* among managers who share a problem. In a university, for example, a residence hall adviser might call a meeting to resolve differences between two feuding students who live in adjacent rooms.
2. *Liaison roles,* or specialized jobs to handle communications between two departments. A fraternity representative is a liaison between the fraternity and the interfraternity council, the university, or the local community.
3. *Task forces,* or groups of representatives from different departments, brought together temporarily to solve a common problem. For example, students, faculty, and administrators may be members of a task force charged with bringing distinguished speakers to campus for a current events seminar.
4. *Teams,* or permanent interdepartmental decision-making groups. An executive council made up of department heads might meet regularly to make decisions affecting a college of engineering or liberal arts.
5. *Product, program, or project managers* who direct interdisciplinary groups with a common task to perform. In a college of business administration, a faculty administrator might head an executive education program of professors from several disciplines.
6. *Matrix organizations,* composed of dual relationships in which some managers report to two superiors. Your instructors, for example, may report to department heads in their respective disciplines and to a director of undergraduate or graduate programs.

Several of these processes are discussed further in Chapter 14, where we examine managing teams and intergroup relations.

> **Bottom Line**
> Cross-unit coordination can lead to effective problem solutions.
> *Why does more information tend to improve solutions?*
>
>

Looking Ahead

The organization chart, differentiation, integration, authority, delegation, coordination, and the like convey fundamental information about an organization's structure. However, the information so far has provided only a snapshot. The real organization is more like a motion picture—it moves! More flexible and innovative—even virtual—forms of organizations

Management in Action

REGROUPING AND CHANGING THE CULTURE AT GENERAL MOTORS

GM is weathering the recall fiasco and reported a 27 percent increase in operating income in the last quarter of 2014. The end-of-year rebound was attributable to an overall increase in car sales in the United States and strong company sales in China. Despite record global sales, revenue remained stable at $155 billion. Barra stated: "A strong fourth quarter helped us deliver very good core operating results in 2014 despite significant challenges we faced."

What changes does Barra have in mind for 2015 and forward? Her last position as senior vice president of global product development, whose decisions shaped how fast new products came to market, may provide some clues. Her streamlining of the product development group's structure was an important first step. Barra, who joined GM as an electrical engineer and worked her way up, also simplified systems. Instead of letting managers constantly tweak their four-year plans, she held twice-yearly meetings at which the plans were reviewed. Her audit of processes in product development showed that the people in her own group were the ones slowing development by coming up with a stream of revision ideas. Under Barra, such conduct was not tolerated.

Barra has the daunting task of changing the way managers and employees behave at GM. She has made it clear that GM's inward-looking culture and slow responses to safety issues and product defects will no longer be tolerated. She has pledged to hold people accountable for their actions. Barra refuses to sweep the tragic events of 2014 under the rug. She wants GM decision makers to remember the pain that the ignition switch problem (and 10-year delay) caused for victims and the company: "I never want to put this behind us. I want to put this painful experience permanently in our collective memories."

Changing a company's culture is difficult, and past efforts at reorganizing GM have not always gone as planned. Helping Barra in this change effort are executives like Michael Arena, GM's Chief Talent Officer. Arena uses an evidence-based approach to drive organizational performance, leveraging such concepts as predictive analytics and network analysis to empirically determine talent needs across the pipeline. Recent declines in GM's stock price show that investors continue to worry. But executives remain confident that they have begun matching GM's structure to its strategy.[51]

- How might Barra's efforts at changing the culture at GM increase the chances that the structural changes will be effective in the long-term?
- What personal factors are likely to affect GM's success in achieving greater organizational integration?

are evolving. Today's organizations are far removed, in many of their fundamental characteristics, from the traditional forms they once had. They may be more networked, flexible, and global, using electronic sharing of information to move faster than 20th-century managers could have envisaged.

No organization is merely a set of static work relationships. Because organizations are composed of people, they are hotbeds of social relationships. Networks of individuals cutting across departmental boundaries interact with one another. Various friendship groups or cliques band together to form *coalitions*—members of the organization who jointly support a particular issue and try to ensure that their viewpoints determine the outcome of policy decisions.

Thus the formal organization structure does not describe everything about how the company really works. Even if you know departments and authority relationships, you still have much to understand. How do things really get done? Who influences whom, and how? Which managers are the most powerful? How effective is the top leadership? Which groups are most and which are least effective? What is the nature of communication patterns throughout the organization? These issues are discussed throughout the rest of the book.Now you are familiar with the basic organizing concepts discussed in this chapter. In the next chapter, we will discuss the current challenges of designing the modern organization with which the modern executive constantly grapples. As you read "Management In Action: Onward," consider how the organizing concepts from the chapter help you evaluate the challenges facing General Motors, but also notice where personal relationships and other human factors come into play.

KEY TERMS

accountability, p. 254

authority, p. 250

broker, p. 266

centralized organization, p. 255

coordination, p. 249

coordination by mutual adjustment, p. 268

coordination by plan, p. 267

corporate governance, p. 252

decentralized organization, p. 255

delegation, p. 253

departmentalization, p. 257

differentiation, p. 248

division of labor, p. 248

divisional organization, p. 259

dynamic network, p. 265

formalization, p. 267

functional organization, p. 257

hierarchy, p. 252

integration, p. 248

line departments, p. 256

matrix organization, p. 262

network organization, p. 264

organization chart, p. 248

responsibility, p. 253

span of control, p. 252

specialization, p. 248

staff departments, p. 257

standardization, p. 267

subunits, p. 252

unity-of-command principle, p. 263

RETAINING WHAT YOU LEARNED

In Chapter 8, you learned that the structure of organizations is affected by their degree of differentiation and integration. People and groups are assigned specialized tasks, and these tasks are coordinated to achieve the organizations' overall mission. Bosses exercise authority throughout an organizations' hierarchy, even though owners or stockholders have ultimate authority. Boards of directors report to stockholders, advise management, consider the firms legal interests, and protect stockholders rights. Span of control refers to the number of people who report directly to a manager. Delegation, the assignment of tasks and responsibilities, offers a variety of benefits but must be managed carefully. In centralized organizations, top managers make the most important decisions whereas in decentralized organizations, many decisions are delegated to lower levels. Organizations can be structured in a variety of ways, including function, division (product, customers, or geographic), matrix, and network. Matrix structures allow a company to adapt to changing conditions, but presents unique challenges to managers and employees. Managers can coordinate interdependent units through standardization, plans, and mutual adjustment.

LO 1   Explain how differentiation and integration influence an organization's structure.

- Differentiation means that organizations have many parts. Specialization means that various individuals and units throughout the organization perform different tasks. The assignment of tasks to different people or groups often is referred to as the division of labor. But the specialized tasks in an organization cannot all be performed independently of one another.
- Coordination links the various tasks to achieve the organizations overall mission.
- An organization with many specialized tasks and work units is highly differentiated; the more differentiated the organization is, the more integration or coordination is required.

LO 2   Summarize how authority operates.

- Authority is the legitimate right to make decisions and tell other people what to do. It is exercised throughout the hierarchy because bosses have the authority to give orders to subordinates.
- Through the day-to-day operation of authority, the organization proceeds toward achieving its goals. Owners or stockholders have ultimate authority.

LO 3   Define the roles of the board of directors and the chief executive officer.

- Boards of directors report to stockholders. The board of directors controls or advises management, considers the firms legal and other interests, and protects stockholders' rights.
- The chief executive officer reports to the board and is accountable for the organizations' performance.

LO 4   Discuss how span of control affects structure and managerial effectiveness.

- Span of control is the number of people who report directly to a manager. Narrow spans create tall organizations, and wide spans create flat ones.
- No single span of control is always appropriate; the optimal span is determined by characteristics of the work, the subordinates, the manager, and the organization.

LO 5   Explain how to delegate effectively.

- Delegation the assignment of tasks and responsibilities has many potential advantages for the manager, the subordinate, and the organization.
- But to be effective, the process must be managed carefully. The manager should define the goal, select the person, solicit opinions, provide resources, schedule checkpoints, and discuss progress periodically.

LO **6** **Distinguish between centralized and decentralized organizations.**

- In centralized organizations, top managers make the most important decisions.
- In decentralized organizations, many decisions are delegated to lower levels.

LO **7** **Summarize ways organizations can be structured.**

- Organizations can be structured on the basis of function, division (product, customers, or geographic), matrix, and network.
- Each form has advantages and disadvantages.

LO **8** **Identify the unique challenges of the matrix organization.**

- The matrix is a complex structure with a dual authority organization. A well-managed matrix enables organizations to adapt to change.

- But it can also create confusion and interpersonal difficulties. People in all positions in the matrix top executives, product and function managers, and two-boss employees must acquire unique survival skills.

LO **9** **Describe important integrative mechanisms.**

- Managers can coordinate interdependent units through standardization, plans, and mutual adjustment.
- Standardization occurs when routines and standard operating procedures are put in place. They typically are accompanied by formalized rules.
- Coordination by plan is more flexible and allows more freedom in how tasks are carried out but keeps interdependent units focused on schedules and joint goals.
- Mutual adjustment involves feedback and discussions among related parties to accommodate each others needs. It is at once the most flexible and simple to administer, but it is time-consuming.

DISCUSSION QUESTIONS

1. Based on the description of General Motors in this chapter, give some examples of differentiation in that organization. In other words, what specialized tasks have to be performed, and how is labor divided at General Motors? Also, how does General Motors integrate the work of these different units? Based on what you have learned in this chapter, would you say General Motors has an effective structure? Why or why not?

2. What are some advantages and disadvantages of being in the CEO position?

3. Would you like to sit on a board of directors? Why or why not? If you did serve on a board, what kind of organization would you prefer? As a board member, in what kinds of activities do you think you would most actively engage?

4. Interview a member of a board of directors, and discuss that member's perspectives on his or her role.

5. Pick a job you have held and describe it in terms of span of control, delegation, responsibility, authority, and accountability.

6. Why do you think managers have difficulty delegating? What can be done to overcome these difficulties?

7. Consider an organization in which you have worked, draw its organization chart, and describe it by using terms in this chapter. How did you like working there, and why?

8. Would you rather work in a functional or divisional organization? Why?

9. If you learned that a company had a matrix structure, would you be more or less interested in working there? Explain your answer. How would you prepare yourself to work effectively in a matrix?

10. Brainstorm a list of methods for integrating interdependent work units. Discuss the activities that need to be undertaken and the pros and cons of each approach.

EXPERIENTIAL EXERCISES

8.1   THE BUSINESS SCHOOL ORGANIZATION CHART

OBJECTIVES

1. To clarify the factors that determine organization structure.
2. To provide insight into the workings of an organization.
3. To examine the working relationships within an organization.

INSTRUCTIONS

1. Draw an organization chart for your school of business. Be sure to identify all the staff and line positions in the school. Specify the chain of command and the levels of administration. Note the different spans of control. Are there any advisory groups, task forces, or committees to consider?

2. Review the chapter material on organization structure to help identify both strong and weak points in your school's organization. Now draw another organization chart for the school, incorporating any changes you believe would improve the quality of the school. Support the second chart with a list of recommended changes and reasons for their inclusion.

DISCUSSION QUESTIONS

1. Is your business school well organized? Why or why not?
2. In what ways is the school's structure designed to suit the needs of students, faculty, staff, the administration, and the business community?

8.2 DESIGNING A STUDENT-RUN ORGANIZATION THAT PROVIDES CONSULTING SERVICES

OBJECTIVES

1. To appreciate the importance of the total organization on group and individual behavior.

2. To provide a beginning organization design experience that will be familiar to students.

BACKGROUND

The Industry Advisory Council for your school has decided to sponsor a student-run organization that will provide business consulting services to nonprofit groups in your community. The council has donated $20,000 toward start-up costs and has agreed to provide office space, computer equipment, and other materials as needed. The council hopes that the organization will establish its own source of funding after the first year of operation.

TASK 1

The dean of the school wants you to develop alternative designs for the new organization. Your task is to identify the main design dimensions or factors to be dealt with in establishing such an organization and to describe the issues that must be resolved for each factor. For example, you might provide an organization chart to help describe the structural issues involved. Before jumping ahead with your design,

you may also have to think about (1) groups in the community that could use your help and (2) problems they face. Remember, though, your task is to create the organization that will provide services, not to provide an in-depth look at the types of services provided.

You and your team are to brainstorm design dimensions to be dealt with and to develop a one- or two-page outline that can be shared with the entire class. You have one hour to develop the outline. Select two people to present your design. Assume that you will all be involved in the new organization, filling specific positions.

TASK 2

After the brainstorming period, the spokespersons will present the group designs or preferred design and answer questions from the audience.

TASK 3

The instructor will comment on the designs and discuss additional factors that might be important for the success of this organization.

SOURCE: A. B. (Rami) Shani and James B. Lau, *Behavior in Organizations: An Experimental Approach,* p. 369. Copyright 2005 The McGraw-Hill Companies. Reprinted with permission.

8.3 WHEN SHOULD A COMPANY DECENTRALIZE?

OBJECTIVE

To explore the conditions under which a company should decentralize its structure and decision making.

INSTRUCTIONS

The following scenarios describe situations faced by hypothetical companies that currently have a *centralized* organization structure. As you review each of the scenarios, provide your opinion as to whether the company should move to a more *decentralized* organization structure.

1. Company X produces one specialized product line for heart surgeons in the United States.
   - Maintain current centralized organization structure

      or

   - Move to a more decentralized organization structure

      Defend your choice:

   _____

   _____

2. Company Y makes over 100 electronic products and has to respond rapidly to the moves of its competitors.
   - Maintain current centralized organization structure

      or

   - Move to a more decentralized organization structure

      Defend your choice:

   _____

   _____

3. Company Z's managers are becoming increasingly comfortable with delegating tasks and responsibilities to subordinates in order to develop their decision making skills.

- Maintain current centralized organization structure

  or

- Move to a more decentralized organization structure

  Defend your choice:

_____

_____

SOURCE: Adapted from R. R. McGrath Jr., *Exercises in Management Fundamentals* (Englewood Cliffs, NJ: Prentice Hall, 1985), pp. 59–60.

CONCLUDING CASE

STANLEY LYNCH INVESTMENT GROUP

The Stanley Lynch Investment Group is a large investment firm headquartered in New York. The firm has 12 major investment funds, each with analysts operating in a separate department. Along with knowledge of the financial markets and the businesses it analyzes, Stanley Lynch's competitive advantage comes from its advanced and reliable computer systems. Thus an effective information technology (IT) division is a strategic necessity, and the company's chief information officer (CIO) holds a key role at the firm.

When the company hired J. T. Kundra as a manager of technology, he learned that the IT division at Stanley Lynch consists of 68 employees, most of whom specialize in serving the needs of a particular fund. The IT employees serving a fund operate as a distinct group, each of them led by a manager who supervises several employees. (Five employees report to J. T.)

He also learned that each group sets up its own computer system to store information about its projects. The problems with that arrangement quickly became evident. As J. T. tried to direct his group's work, he would ask for documentation of one program or another. Sometimes, no one was sure where to find the documentation; it might turn out to be stored in an obscure place such as only on someone's flash drive. Other times, he would quickly get three different responses from three different people with three different versions of the documentation. And if he was interested in another group's project or a software program used in another department, getting information was next to impossible. He lacked the authority to ask employees in another group to drop what they were doing to hunt down information he needed.

J. T. concluded that the entire IT division could serve the firm much better if all authorized people had easy access to the work that had already been done and the software that was available. The logical place to store that information was online. From experience at a previous company,

he believed that the easiest way to compile the information would be to set up a shared web project called a wiki—an online document created through the collaboration of its users, who can look up or contribute information according to their knowledge and needs. The challenge would be how to get everyone to contribute, given that he had authority over so few of the IT workers.

J. T. started by working with his five employees to build a wiki offering basic information presented in a consistent format. Then he met with two higher-level managers who report to the CIO. He showed them the wiki and explained that fast access to information would improve the IT group's quality and efficiency. He suggested that the managers require all the IT employees to put their documentation on the wiki, and he even persuaded them that this behavior should be measured for performance appraisals. This last tactic was especially significant because at an investment company, bonuses for meeting performance targets are a big part of employees' compensation.

The IT employees quickly came to appreciate that the wiki would help them perform better. When they visited it, they could see from the original information that it would be useful. Adoption of the wiki was swift, and before long, the IT employees came to think of it as one of their most important software systems.

DISCUSSION QUESTIONS

1. Give an example of differentiation in Stanley Lynch's organization structure and an example of integration in this structure.

2. What role did authority play in the adoption of the wiki by the IT division at Stanley Lynch?

3. Describe how the IT division used coordination to achieve greater integration.

CHAPTER 9

Organizational Agility

> I came to the conclusion long ago that limits to innovation have less to do with technology or creativity than organizational agility. Inspired individuals can only do so much.
>
> —RAY STATA, FOUNDER OF ANALOG DEVICES

Management in Action

HOW JEFFREY IMMELT TRIES TO KEEP GENERAL ELECTRIC NIMBLE

As General Electric's CEO, Jeffrey Immelt once was asked to identify GE's core capability. Immelt's reply echoed his predecessor, the legendary Jack Welch: "Evaluating people." Evaluation—needed for identifying, developing, and keeping the best leaders—is a powerful core capability, especially for GE, which requires excellence in so many areas. Unlike specialized or regional companies, GE operates eight large industrial businesses and a financial business, all operating worldwide. It has to be able to do *many* things right.

Recently, however, some observers have wondered whether GE has been losing its core capability. The recent financial crisis hit GE hard, especially because it had relied heavily on GE Capital's lending and investments for a significant part of GE's earnings. Although GE Capital managed to turn a profit every year, 2009's profits were less than one-sixth of 2008's, and the numbers climbed back slowly over the next few years. The recession slowed purchases from GE's business and government customers, and in the United States, the rising cost of health care hit demand for GE's imaging equipment such as X-ray machines and MRI scanners. GE's stock price tumbled, and its credit rating slipped. Immelt responded by focusing the company more on infrastructure, such as transportation and energy systems, and scaling back GE Capital, especially its real estate investments.

Can a behemoth such as GE be nimble enough for today's business world? Immelt says yes. He sees GE as a 305,000-employee team with operations in 175 countries, united by a mission to "build, move, power and cure the world." He expects strong growth from its oil and gas and its power and water business units, especially as a result of demand for infrastructure in developing economies. As economies compete for increasingly scarce (and costly) energy resources, Immelt sees potential for GE's energy management business, which helps customers conserve energy. The company hopes efficiency projects will also spur demand in its other industrial businesses: aviation, transportation, health care, and home and business solutions.

© *Prashanth Vishwanathan/Bloomberg via Getty Images*

Few businesses could maintain a lead in so many arenas, but Immelt sees GE as having the resources to do just that. In recessions as well as expansions, customers want to save money, so GE invests heavily in research for making jet engines more efficient, cutting waste from energy systems, and upgrading its equipment for the era of big data. In a recent letter to shareholders, Immelt maintains, "Today, GE is a different company—a company in motion; a company that is well-positioned to seize this moment, and lead as we always have."[1]

GE is trying to maintain its position as one of the world's great industrial companies with an organization that enables innovation and demands high performance. As you read this chapter, consider whether GE can remain competitive in a fast-changing world.

Like GE, today's successful companies can't afford to rest on their previous accomplishments. If they do, they can all too easily become vulnerable—to a competitor's new product, shifts in customer preferences, or other changes in their environment. Instead they need to proactively seek new ways to remain flexible, innovative, efficient, and responsive to their customers. One of the most important ways they have of doing that is to make sure that their organization structures and systems remain *adaptable*—prepared to meet the complex and ever-changing challenges that managers and their organizations constantly confront.

In Chapter 8, we described the formal structure of the organization. Businesses and other organizations are complex; they use the elements of the formal structure, including hierarchical levels, division of labor, and coordination, to manage that complexity. Adding to the complexity is that many people do many things at the same time. The behavior of organizations does not just pop out of a chart; it emerges from the processes, systems, and relationships.

Therefore, the task of organizing extends to the issues described in this chapter: the design of processes, information flows, and technology. When these are well designed, the organization is flexible and agile enough to succeed in a changing world. Such an organization is often called ambidextrous. As some people have the gift of writing with either hand, an ambidextrous organization is simultaneously good at *exploitation* (efficiently and quickly meeting needs in areas where it currently excels) and *exploration* (seeking and recognizing new ways to meet future needs).[2] In this chapter, we will see ways to organize people, information, and work that have helped organizations excel at both exploitation and exploration.

The Responsive Organization

 LO 1

Bottom Line

Speed is vital to an organization's survival.
How can lack of speed kill an organization?

mechanistic organization

A form of organization that seeks to maximize internal efficiency.

organic structure

An organizational form that emphasizes flexibility.

The formal structure is put in place to control people, decisions, and actions. But in today's fast-changing business environment, responsiveness—quickness, agility, the ability to adapt to changing demands—is more vital than ever to a firm's survival.[3]

Many years after Max Weber wrote about the concept of bureaucracy, two British management scholars (Burns and Stalker) described what they called the **mechanistic organization.**[4] The common mechanistic structure they described was similar to Weber's bureaucracy, but they went on to suggest that in the modern corporation, the mechanistic structure is not the only option. The **organic structure** stands in stark contrast to the mechanistic organization. It is much less rigid and, in fact, emphasizes flexibility. The organic structure can be described as follows:

1. Jobholders have broader responsibilities that change as the need arises.
2. Communication occurs through advice and information rather than through orders and instructions.
3. Decision making and influence are more decentralized and informal.
4. Expertise is highly valued.
5. Jobholders rely more heavily on judgment than on rules.
6. Commitment to the organization's goals is more important than obedience to authority.
7. Employees depend more on one another and relate more informally and personally.

Exhibit 9.1 contrasts the formal structure of an organization—epitomized by the organization chart—to the informal structure, which is much more organic. As you compare these two charts, what do you notice that should concern this company's managers? Astute managers are keenly aware of the network of interactions among the organization's members, and they work within this network to increase agility. People in organic organizations work more as teammates than as subordinates who take orders from the boss, thus breaking away from the traditional bureaucratic form.[5]

EXHIBIT 9.1
Formal and Informal
Organizational Structures

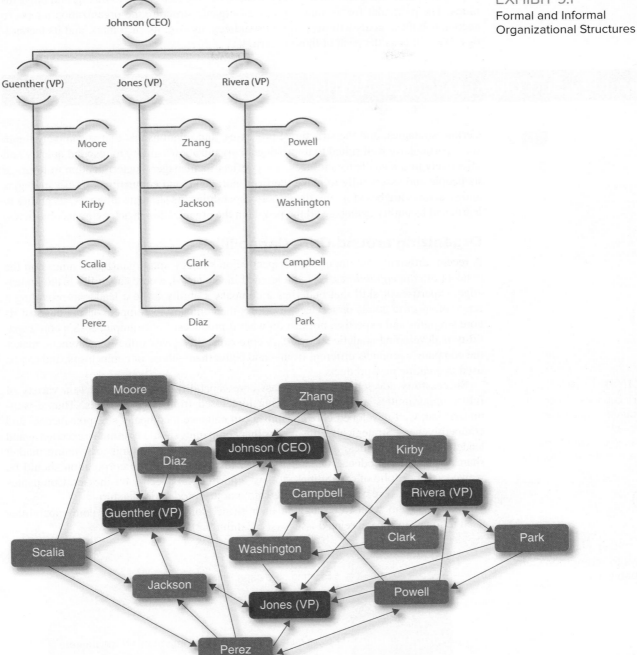

SOURCE: Adapted from *Harvard Business Review*. Adapted from "Information Networks: The Company Behind the Chart," by D. Krackhardt and J. R. Hanson, July–August 1993, pp. 104–111. Copyright 1993 by the Harvard Business School Publishing Corporation; all rights reserved.

The ideas underlying the organic structure and networks are the foundation for the newer forms of organization described in this chapter. The more organic a firm is, the more responsive it will be to changing competitive demands and market realities. Managers in progressive companies place a premium on being able to act fast. They want to satisfy customers' changing needs and address other outside pressures. They want to take actions to prepare for an uncertain future. They want to be able to respond to threats and opportunities. The particular form—and degree—of organic structure the organization adopts to accomplish these goals will depend on its strategy, its size, its customers, and its technology. We will consider each of these in turn.

Strategy and Organizational Agility

Certain strategies, and the structures, processes, and relationships that accompany them, seem particularly well suited to improving an organization's ability to respond quickly and effectively to the challenges it faces. They reflect its managers' determination to leverage its people and assets fully to make the firm more agile and competitive. These strategies and structures are based on the firm's core capabilities, its strategic alliances, its ability to learn, and its ability to engage all the people in the organization in achieving its objectives.

Organizing around Core Capabilities

A recent, different, and important perspective on strategy and organization hinges on the concept of *core capabilities*.[6] As you learned in Chapter 4, a core capability is the knowledge, expertise, or skill that underlies a company's ability to be a leader in providing a range of specific goods or services. It allows the company to compete on the basis of its core strengths and expertise, not just on what it produces. For example, SAS's core capability is developing analytic software. A core capability gives value to customers, makes the company's products different from—and better than—those of competitors, and can be used in creating new products.

Successfully developing a world-class core capability opens the door to a variety of future opportunities; failure means being foreclosed from many markets. Thus a well-understood, well-developed core capability can enhance a company's responsiveness and competitiveness. Strategically, this means that companies should commit to excellence and leadership in capabilities, and strengthen them, before they commit to winning market share for specific products. Organizationally, this means that the corporation should be viewed as a portfolio of capabilities, not just a portfolio of specific businesses. Companies should strive for core competence leadership, not just product leadership.

Managers who want to strengthen their firms' competitiveness via core capabilities need to focus on several related issues (see Exhibit 9.2).

Bottom Line
Core capabilities can be a source of quality and innovation.
Does your school have a core capability? If so, what is it?

EXHIBIT 9.2
Ways to Strengthen Core Capabilities

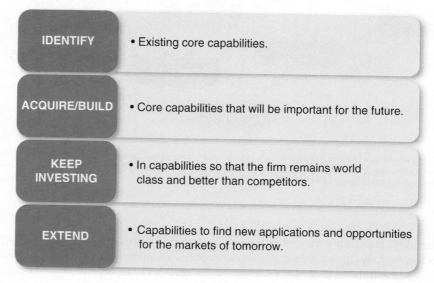

IDENTIFY • Existing core capabilities.

ACQUIRE/BUILD • Core capabilities that will be important for the future.

KEEP INVESTING • In capabilities so that the firm remains world class and better than competitors.

EXTEND • Capabilities to find new applications and opportunities for the markets of tomorrow.

SOURCE: Adapted from G. Hamel and C. K. Prahalad, *Competing for the Future* (Boston: Harvard Business School Press, 1994).

Multiple Generations at Work

Changing Internal Structures to Accommodate Millennial Employees

Many managers are expressing concerns over their ability to find Millennial talent and then, once hired, to motivate and retain them. Some estimates suggest that the average length of time these early career employees stay in a professional job, where training is provided, is about three years. This tendency to job-hop is very different from the way older generations approached jobs.

What are some workplace strategies that can help attract and retain Millennial employees?

1. *Flexible work arrangements.* While many Traditionalists and Boomers are generally comfortable being at work Monday–Friday from 9 to 5 p.m., many Millennials find this approach stifling and rigid. Having grown up in a mobile and connected world, Millennials want some flexibility with regard to where and when they do their work. When possible, managers should be flexible but also set clear performance expectations.

2. *Involvement in decision making.* Raised by parents who encouraged and valued their opinions, Millennials want to be heard even without the benefit of having substantive experience. Managers should look for ways to engage them in suitable projects that build their knowledge of the organization and customers.

3. *Different types of recognition.* Whereas a handwritten note may be an effective way to recognize older employees' efforts, this approach may have less impact on Millennial employees. Many younger employees prefer near instantaneous feedback delivered either electronically or verbally.

Each generational cohort in the workplace has its own view of how jobs, reporting relationships, co-worker interactions, and so forth should be structured. A pressing challenge for managers is how to modify internal organization structures so they are more Millennial-friendly without alienating older generations.[7]

Keep in mind that it's not enough for an organization to have valuable resources that provide capabilities; those resources have to be managed in a way that gives the organization an advantage over competitors.[8] That means managers have to do three things. First, they must accumulate the right resources (such as talented people) by determining what resources they need, acquiring and developing those resources, and eliminating resources that don't provide value. Next, they combine the resources in ways that give the organization capabilities, such as researching new products or resolving problems for customers. These combinations may involve knowledge sharing and alliances between departments or with other organizations. Finally, managers need to leverage or exploit their resources. They do this by identifying the opportunities where their competencies deliver value to customers—say, by creating new products or by delivering existing products better than competitors—and then by coordinating and deploying the employees and other resources needed to respond to those opportunities. The nearby "Multiple Generations at Work" box discusses further how modifying internal structures can boost the ROI from human capital.

Strategic Alliances

As we discussed in Chapter 8, the modern organization has a variety of links with other organizations. These links are more complex than the standard relationships with traditional stakeholders such as suppliers and clients. Today even fierce competitors are working together at unprecedented levels to achieve their strategic goals. For example, Starbucks makes coffee and tea pods for Keurig Green Mountain single-server brewers.[9] TAG Heuer, Google, and Intel announced recently that they will collaborate to develop a smartwatch.[10] In these and other examples, strategic alliances allow participants to respond to customer demands or environmental threats far faster and less expensively than each would be able to do on its own.

A **strategic alliance** is a formal relationship created with the purpose of joint pursuit of mutual goals. In a strategic alliance, individual organizations share administrative

strategic alliance

A formal relationship created among independent organizations with the purpose of joint pursuit of mutual goals.

Faster Wi-Fi and coffee—a wonderful strategic alliance. Recently, Starbucks switched from AT&T to Google to provide free wireless Internet in its 7,000 U.S. stores. This move allows customers to surf the Internet up to 10 times faster.

© The McGraw-Hill Companies, Inc./John Flournoy, photographer

Bottom Line

Alliances can increase speed and innovation and lower costs.

How might an alliance increase innovation?

authority, form social links, and accept joint ownership. They occur between companies and their competitors, governments, and universities. As with the TAG Heuer–Google–Intel collaboration, partnering often crosses national and cultural boundaries. Companies form strategic alliances to develop new technologies, enter new markets, and reduce manufacturing costs. Not only can alliances enable companies to move ahead faster and more efficiently, but they also are sometimes the only practical way to bring together the variety of specialists needed for operating in today's complex environment. Rather than hiring experts who understand the technology and market segments for each new product, companies can form alliances with partners that already have those experts on board.[11]

Managers typically devote plenty of time to screening potential partners in financial terms. But for the alliance to work, the partners also must consider one another's areas of expertise and the incentives involved in the structure of the alliance. A comparison of research and development alliances found that the most innovation occurred when the partners were experts in moderately different types of research. If the partners were very different, they shared ideas and innovated more when the alliance was set up through equity (stock) ownership; for similar partners, a contract to do the research was associated with more innovation.[12]

Managers also must foster and develop the human relationships in the partnership. Asian companies seem to be the most comfortable with the nonfinancial, people side of alliances; European companies the next so; and U.S. companies the least. Thus U.S. companies may need to pay extra attention to the human side of alliances. Exhibit 9.3 shows some recommendations for how to do this. In fact, most of the ideas apply not only to strategic alliances but to any type of relationship.[13]

The Learning Organization

Being responsive requires continually changing and learning new ways to act. Some experts have stated that the only sustainable advantage is learning faster than the competition. This has led to a new term that is now part of the vocabulary of most managers: the learning

EXHIBIT 9.3   How I's Can Become We's

The best alliances are true partnerships that meet these criteria:
1. *Individual excellence:* Both partners add value, and their motives are positive (pursue opportunity) rather than negative (mask weaknesses).
2. *Importance:* Both partners want the relationship to work because it helps them meet long-term strategic objectives.
3. *Interdependence:* The partners need each other; each helps the other reach its goal.
4. *Investment:* The partners devote financial and other resources to the relationship.
5. *Information:* The partners communicate openly about goals, technical data, problems, and changing situations.
6. *Integration:* The partners develop shared ways of operating; they teach each other and learn from each other.
7. *Institutionalization:* The relationship has formal status with clear responsibilities.
8. *Integrity:* Both partners are trustworthy and honorable.

SOURCE: Reprinted by permission of *Harvard Business Review.* Adapted from "Collaborative Advantage: The Art of Alliances," by R. M. Kanter, July–August 1994, pp. 96–108. Copyright © 1994 by the Harvard Business School Publishing Corporation; all rights reserved.

organization.[14] A **learning organization** is an organization skilled at creating, acquiring, and transferring knowledge and at modifying its behavior to reflect new knowledge and insights.[15] Google, Toyota, and IDEO are good examples of learning organizations. Such organizations are skilled at solving problems, experimenting with new approaches, learning from their own experiences, learning from other organizations, and spreading knowledge quickly and efficiently.

How do firms become true learning organizations? They make sure a few important activities are happening at all levels and in all functions:[16]

1. Engaging in disciplined thinking and paying attention to details, so decisions are based on data and evidence, not guesswork and assumptions
2. Searching constantly for new knowledge and ways to apply it, looking for broader horizons and opportunities, not just quick fixes for current problems
3. Valuing and rewarding individuals who expand their knowledge and skill in areas that benefit the organization
4. Reviewing successes and failures carefully to find lessons and deeper understanding
5. Benchmarking—that is, identifying and implementing the best business practices of other organizations, stealing ideas shamelessly
6. Sharing ideas throughout the organization via reports, information systems, informal discussions, site visits, education, training, and mentoring of less experienced employees by more experienced ones

These efforts are ideally aimed at the two areas of learning we mentioned at the beginning of this chapter.[17] The first is exploitation, or continuously learning ways to operate more efficiently and effectively in the company's first domain. We will see ideas for this kind of learning throughout the remainder of this chapter. The second is exploration, or uncovering new areas in which the company can excel. Chapter 17 will say more about this kind of learning with regard to technology and innovation.

The High-Involvement Organization

Participative management is becoming increasingly popular as a way to create a competitive advantage. Particularly in high-technology companies facing stiff international competition, the aim is to generate high levels of commitment and involvement as employees and managers work together to achieve organizational goals.

In a **high-involvement organization,** top management ensures that there is a consensus about the direction in which the business is heading. The leader seeks input from his or her top management team and from lower levels of the company. Task forces, study groups, and other techniques are used to foster participation in decisions that affect the entire organization. Also fundamental to the high-involvement organization is continual feedback to participants regarding how they are doing compared with the competition and how effectively they are meeting the strategic agenda.

Structurally, this usually means that even lower-level employees have a direct relationship with a customer or supplier and thus receive feedback and are held accountable for a good or service delivery. The organizational form is a flat, decentralized structure built around a customer, good, or service. Employee involvement is particularly powerful when the environment changes rapidly, work is creative, complex activities require coordination, and firms need major breakthroughs in innovation and speed— in other words, when companies need to be more responsive.[18]

Participative management is becoming increasingly popular as a way to create competitive advantage.

Organizational Size and Agility

One of the most important characteristics of an organization—and one of the most important factors influencing its ability to respond effectively to its environment—is its size. Large organizations are typically less organic and more bureaucratic. For example, Unilever, whose many consumer brands include Axe, Hellman's, Ben & Jerry's, Lipton, Vaseline, Dove, and Slim-Fast, has more than 170,000 employees worldwide. In many countries, the company has operated as three independent business lines—food, personal care, and ice cream and frozen food—each with its own supply chain and marketing budget.[19]

In large organizations, jobs become more specialized. More distinct groups of specialists get created because large organizations can add a new specialty at lower proportional expense. The complexity created by these numerous specialties makes the organization harder to control. As a result, in the past, management added more levels to keep spans of control from becoming too large. To cope with complexity, large companies tend to become more bureaucratic. Rules, procedures, and paperwork are introduced.

Thus with size comes greater complexity, and complexity brings a need for increased control. In response, organizations adopt bureaucratic strategies of control. The conventional wisdom is that bureaucratization increases efficiency but decreases a company's ability to innovate. So are larger companies more responsive to competitive demands or not? Let's see.

The Case for Big

Bigger was better after World War II, when foreign competition was limited and growth seemed limitless. To meet high demand for its products, U.S. industry embraced high-volume, low-cost manufacturing methods. IBM, General Motors (GM), and Sears all grew into behemoths during those decades.

Alfred Chandler, a pioneer in strategic management, noted that big companies were the engine of economic growth throughout the 20th century.[20] Size creates scale economies—that is, lower costs per unit of production. And size can offer specific advantages such as lower operating costs, greater purchasing power, and easier access to capital. Walmart, among the largest companies in America, has the purchasing power to buy merchandise in larger volumes and sell it at lower prices than its competitors can. Size also creates **economies of scope;** materials and processes employed in one product can be used to make related products. With such advantages, huge companies with lots of money may be the best at taking on large foreign rivals in huge global markets.

The Case for Small

But a huge, complex organization can find it hard to manage relationships with customers and among its own units. Bureaucracy can run rampant. Too much success can breed complacency, and the resulting inertia hinders change. Experts suggest that this is a sure-fire formula for being left in the dust by hungry competitors. As consumers demand a more diverse array of high-quality, customized products supported by excellent service, giant companies have begun to stumble. Some evidence exists, for example, that as firms get larger and their market share grows, customers begin to view their products as having lower quality. Also, once a company has captured a big share of the market, future growth is complicated because winning over more customers requires costlier efforts or a fresh approach. Walmart's low-price strategy helped it become the largest U.S. corporation in terms of sales, but sales growth has flattened out. The company's response—cutting labor costs—has helped profits in the short term but may drive away shoppers frustrated with unstocked shelves and difficulty finding help. Walmart recently placed last in the American Customer Satisfaction Index for department and discount stores.[21]

Larger companies also are more difficult to coordinate and control. Although size may enhance efficiency by spreading fixed costs over more units, it also may create administrative difficulties that inhibit efficient performance. Unilever not only has three organizations selling different product lines in each country it serves, but until recently it was run by two chairmen–CEOs, an artifact of a merger that took place decades ago. This cumbersome structure has held back Unilever's efficiency and agility, making competition more difficult.[22] To describe this type of problem, a new term has entered the business vocabulary: *diseconomies of scale,* or the costs of being too big. "Small is beautiful" has become a favorite phrase of entrepreneurial business managers.[23]

Smaller companies can move fast, provide quality goods and services to targeted market niches, and inspire greater involvement from their people. Nimble small firms frequently outmaneuver big bureaucracies. They introduce new and better products, and they steal market share. The premium now is on flexibility and responsiveness—the unique potential strengths of the small firm. An extreme example is Kobold Watch, staffed by founder Michael Kobold and three employees. The small company makes and sells premium mechanical wristwatches priced at thousands of dollars each. Kobold advertises online and through word of mouth generated by sales to celebrities, including former president Bill Clinton and celebrities Kiefer Sutherland, and Bruce Springsteen. When sales surge, Kobold calls on two other watchmakers to help out as needed. He intentionally limits production to 2,500 watches a year—not just to keep his company lean but also to maintain the prestige of his brand.[24]

© AP Photo/Paul Sakuma

Being Big and Small

Small *is* beautiful for unleashing energy and speed. But in buying and selling, size offers market power. The challenge, then, is to be both big and small to capitalize on the advantages of each.

When Intuit grew from a software start-up to an established company selling popular accounting software, the company brought in a CEO recruited from General Electric, Steve Bennett, to mesh big-company skills with Intuit's entrepreneurial energy. Managers had plenty of new ideas but needed to build their skill in choosing and implementing the best ideas. Bennett helped the company reevaluate its strategy to find areas of new growth. After popular Intuit products such as QuickBooks and TurboTax captured most of the market for accounting and tax preparation software, the company expanded into the online banking market with QuickenLoans. In 2014, QuickenLoans was the largest online lender in the United States.[25]

From a different angle, companies such as Starbucks and Amazon are very large companies that work hard to act small and maintain a sense of intimacy with employees and customers. Both are considered among the best-managed companies in the world. To avoid problems of growth and size, they decentralize decision making and organize around small, adaptive, team-based work units. In a similar vein, many social enterprises need to grow in order to expand their impact. The nearby "Social Enterprise" box discusses some unique issues related to scaling SEs.

> The challenge is to be both big and small to capitalize on the advantages of each.

Downsizing

As large companies attempt to regain the responsiveness of small companies, they often face the dilemma of downsizing. **Downsizing** is the planned elimination of positions or jobs. Common approaches to downsizing include eliminating functions, hierarchical levels, or even whole units.[26] Another growing trend has been to replace full-time employees with less expensive part-time or temporary workers.

downsizing

The planned elimination of positions or jobs.

Social Enterprise

Making More Impact: Scaling Social Enterprises

Social enterprises typically begin as small, grassroots efforts whose goal is to create a sustainable organization that helps solve important social problems. For example, Living Goods, a U.S.-based nonprofit, sells essential products such as high-efficiency stoves, fortified foods, and pharmaceuticals "through an Avon-like network of microfranchises in Uganda." Sautil, based in Brazil, uses a web-based platform to provide free health care information to over 100,000 impoverished Brazilians.

What happens when social enterprises want to scale their operations to impact the lives of more people? How can they expand globally? What unique issues do social enterprises face when planning for growth?

Here are some issues for the leaders of SEs to consider:

1. *Consider alliances with governments.* Governments are the largest consumers of social investment. If a social enterprise's mission aligns with a government's social investment priorities, a productive alliance could be formed. Currently, the G8 governments view social enterprises as a way of "tackling social problems, driving innovation and helping economic growth."
2. *Partner with big businesses.* Big businesses can bring considerable resources to bear on social problems. For this to happen, social enterprises need to develop a viable business model that big businesses are willing to support. Network for Good, an online giving and fund-raising platform was founded with the help of AOL, the Cisco Foundation, and Yahoo!. Since 2001, the social enterprise has processed over $1 billion for more than 100,000 nonprofits.
3. *Do not lose sight of what matters.* As a social enterprise grows in size and complexity, there is a "risk

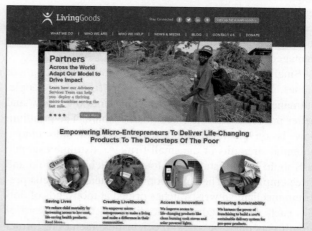

© The McGraw-Hill Companies, Inc./Roberts Publishing Services

that it will become detached and unresponsive to the grassroots." Selco Solar, a provider of sustainable energy solutions, manages this risk of becoming too big by "incubating others who can replicate their model in other geographic areas, rather than scaling themselves." Like for-profit companies, social enterprises need to strike the right balance between being big and small.[27]

Questions

- As social enterprises try to get larger, what unique challenges do they face?
- What are some of the drawbacks associated with partnering with governments or big businesses? If you ran an SE, which of these options would you pursue?

Recognizing that people will be unemployed, frightened, and perhaps unable to pay their bills, managers usually opt for downsizing only in response to some kind of pressure. Traditionally, companies have downsized when demand falls and seems unlikely to rebound in the short run. Laying off workers is a way to avoid paying people who aren't needed to produce goods or services, as well as to lower costs so that the company remains profitable—or at least viable—until the next upturn in business. More recently, however, global competition forced companies to cut costs even when sales were strong, and technological advances made it possible to produce the same amount of work with fewer employees. As a result, in recent decades, many companies have used downsizing as a way to become more efficient. This trend changed the types of positions that were eliminated. Downsizing in response to a slowdown in demand has tended to have the most impact on operating-level jobs in manufacturing firms. Downsizing to improve efficiency has focused on eliminating layers of management and bureaucratic structures, so those layoffs target white-collar middle managers.

The recent recession has forced widespread downsizing across a variety of industries, not just manufacturing. Although companies have rehired workers during the recovery, many find that tough competition requires them to stay as lean as possible. In the movie industry, the success or failure of a few releases can drastically affect the amount of money available to pay employees to work on new films. Recently, DreamWorks Animation announced that it would be cutting about 25 percent of its workforce and reducing the number of movies it releases each year by one-third. The layoffs are in response to under-performing movies released over the past two years, including *Mr. Peabody & Sherman, Rise of the Guardians,* and *Turbo.*[28]

Done appropriately, with inefficient layers eliminated and resources focused more on adding customer value than on wasteful internal processes, downsizing can indeed lead to a more agile, flexible, and responsive firm. In that case, downsizing can be called **rightsizing**—arrival at the size at which the company performs most effectively. But even under the best circumstances, downsizing can be traumatic for an organization and its employees. What can be done to manage downsizing effectively, to help make it more effective?

> **rightsizing**
>
> A successful effort to achieve an appropriate size at which the company performs most effectively.

First, firms should avoid excessive (cyclical) hiring to help reduce the need to engage in major or multiple downsizings. But beyond that, firms must avoid common mistakes such as making slow, small, frequent layoffs; implementing voluntary early retirement programs that entice the best people to leave; and laying off so many people that the company's work can no longer be performed. Instead firms can engage in a number of positive practices to ease the pain and increase the effectiveness of downsizing (see Exhibit 9.4).

The management practices of high-involvement organizations, described earlier in this chapter, also play a role. In general, the negative consequences of downsizing are greater at high-involvement organizations—but not as bad if the organization continues the high employee involvement after the layoffs.[29]

Interestingly, the people who lose their jobs because of downsizing are not the only ones deeply affected. Those who survive the process—who keep their jobs—tend to exhibit what has become known as **survivor's syndrome.**[30] They struggle with heavier workloads; wonder who will be next to go; try to figure out how to survive; lose commitment to the company and faith in their bosses; and become narrow-minded, self-absorbed, and risk-averse. As a consequence, morale and productivity usually drop. You will learn more about some of these ideas in later chapters on human resources management, leadership, motivation, communication, and managing change. You might also refer back to our discussion in Chapter 1 about some of the things you can do to manage your own career successfully in an era where downsizing is a normal occurrence. And for an example of a company that has made downsizing one element of its efforts to enjoy the advantages of being both big and small, see "Management in Action: Progress Report."

> **survivor's syndrome**
>
> Loss of productivity and morale in employees who remain after a downsizing.

Use downsizing only as a last resort, when other methods of improving performance by innovating or changing procedures have been exhausted.
Give special attention and help to those who have lost their jobs.
Identify and protect talented people.
Choose positions to be eliminated by engaging in analysis and strategic thinking.
Train people to cope with the new situation.
Communicate constantly with people about the process and invite ideas for alternative ways to operate more efficiently.
Identify how the organization will operate more effectively in the future and emphasize this positive future and the remaining employees' new roles in attaining it.

EXHIBIT 9.4
Ways to Increase the Effectiveness of Downsizing

SOURCES: Adapted from W. F. Cascio, "Strategies for Responsible Restructuring," *Academy of Management Executive* 19, no. 4 (2005), pp. 39–50; W. F. Cascio, "Downsizing: What Do We Know? What Have We Learned?" *Academy of Management Executive* 7 (February 1993); S. J. Freeman, "The Gestalt of Organizational Downsizing: Downsizing Strategies as Package of Change," *Human Relations* 52, no. 12 (December 1999); and M. Hitt, B. Keats, H. Harback, and R. Nixon, "Rightsizing: Building and Maintaining Strategic Leadership and Long-Term Competitiveness," *Organizational Dynamics,* Fall 1994, pp. 18–31.

Management in Action

GE'S ADVANTAGES OF BEING BIG—AND TRYING TO ACT SMALL(ER)

Writing to stakeholders on the company website, GE chief executive Jeffrey Immelt states: "We are confident that creating a simpler GE will position us to deliver superior outcomes around our core capabilities." Immelt is referring to the reduction in its financial business and renewed focus on what it does best, developing industrial solutions for customers around the globe. The company operates in several industries, and when it wants to launch new products, it has the resources to do so. Thanks to its 50,000 engineers and scientists, GE ranks in the top 10 companies for U.S. patent applications. In terms of the total value of its stock, GE is the world's seventh-largest company.

Consider GE's response to the role big data has begun to play. Companies are analyzing detailed data about their customers, employees, and operations so they can identify how to make significant improvements in efficiency and quality. GE got on board by setting up its GE Global Research in California, near Silicon Valley, and hiring hundreds of software and statistical experts to make GE's equipment and systems part of the big-data revolution. Applications include jet engines that monitor their own performance, sensors on hospital equipment to streamline operations, and systems for automating train traffic.

Another example is GE's creation of an energy-efficient battery for heavy-duty use. Applying technology from more than 30 patents it already owned, GE set up a team Immelt calls "a start-up within the Company." GE staffed the team with its own experts from several industries and consulted with customers around the globe. Potential applications such as powering cell phone towers and electric buses, and storing energy at wind farms could make the battery a billion-dollar business.

Despite the advantages of bigness, Immelt is concerned about the downside, that people in a giant corporation can be more attuned to its rules and habits than to customers' needs. His solution is to focus on measuring whether GE is delivering on its purpose—its mission to "build, move, power and cure the world." GE sold unrelated businesses, such as NBC Universal, and downsized others, such as GE Capital. The focused approach is also shaping the way GE develops managers. In the past, high-potential managers moved from one industry to another on their way up GE's hierarchy. Today they are likelier to specialize in an industry. GE's recent split of its energy business into three units (Power and Water, Oil and Gas, and Energy Management) opened up more paths for developing leaders within those related industries, even as it removed layers of management from the former energy unit.[31]

- How does GE benefit from being large?
- How can GE also reap some of the benefits of smallness?

Customers and the Responsive Organization

LO 5

So far we have discussed how an organization's agility, adaptability, and structure are influenced by its strategy and size. But in the end, the point of structuring a responsive, agile organization lies in enabling it to meet and exceed the expectations of its customers—the people it must attract to purchase a good or service and whose continued patronage and involvement with the organization constitute the fundamental driver of sustained, long-term competitiveness and success.

Recall from Chapter 2 that an organization's environment is composed of many parts—government, suppliers, competitors, and the like. Perhaps no other aspect of the environment has had a more profound impact on organizing in recent years than a focus on customers. Dr. Kenichi Ohmae points out that any business unit must take into account three key players: the company itself, the competition, and the customer. These components form what Ohmae refers to as the *strategic triangle*, as shown in Exhibit 9.5. Managers need to balance the strategic triangle, and successful organizations use their strengths to create value by meeting customer requirements better than competitors do. In this section, we will discuss how organizations maintain and extend a competitive advantage with their customers.

Bottom Line

Today's customers demand excellent service and new high-quality, low-cost products—fast.
How does a rigid bureaucracy make it difficult to meet all these challenges at once?

EXHIBIT 9.5
The Strategic Triangle

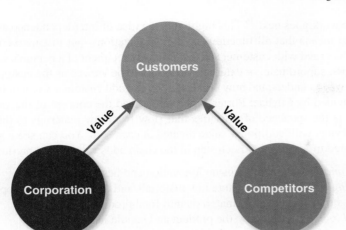

SOURCE: From K. Ohmae et al., *The Mind of the Strategist: The Art of Japanese Business,* 1982, p. 92. Copyright 1982 The McGraw-Hill Companies, Inc. Reprinted with permission.

Customer Relationship Management

Customer relationship management (CRM) is a multifaceted process, typically mediated by a set of information technologies, that focuses on creating two-way exchanges with customers so that firms have an intimate knowledge of their needs, wants, and buying patterns. Firms can acquire this knowledge by applying predictive analytical techniques to the voluminous amounts of data (aka, big data) that have been collected from customers. The goal of this analysis is to identify patterns from current and historical data sets in order to make business decisions. Ideally, the organization can use the predictive analysis to figure out how to deliver exactly what customers want.[32] For example, Netflix used insights mined from subscriber data to create its hit show *House of Cards*.[33] Thus at companies that use CRM effectively, it helps them understand, as well as anticipate, the needs of current and potential customers. And in that way, it is part of a business strategy for managing customers to maximize their long-term value to an enterprise.[34]

As discussed throughout this book, customers want quality goods and services, low cost, innovative products, and speed. Traditional thinking considered these basic customer wants as a set of potential trade-offs. For instance, customers wanted high quality or low costs passed along in the form of low prices. But world-class companies today know that the trade-off mentality no longer applies. Customers want it *all,* and they are learning that an organization exists somewhere that will provide it all.

But if all companies seek to satisfy customers, how can a company realize a competitive advantage? World-class companies have learned that almost any advantage is temporary because competitors will strive to catch up. Simply stated—although obviously not simply done—a company attains and retains competitive advantage by continuing to improve. This concept—*kaizen,* or continuous improvement—is an integral part of Japanese operations strategy.

In the realm of customer relations, continuous improvement includes continually changing to connect with customers, even without waiting for customers to make the first move. Coca-Cola, Philips, the American Red Cross, and other organizations have adopted Salesforce.com's Service Cloud application, which lets companies find customers who take their questions and problems to Facebook, Twitter, or other social networking communities. Customer service agents can locate messages about their products and then offer to help, potentially saving a customer relationship.[35]

As organizations focus on responding to customer needs, they soon find that the traditional meaning of a customer expands to include internal customers. The word *customer* now refers to the next process, or

customer relationship management (CRM)

A multifaceted process focusing on creating two-way exchanges with customers to foster intimate knowledge of their needs, wants, and buying patterns.

World-class companies know that the trade-off mentality no longer applies.

wherever the work goes next.[36] This highlights the idea of interdependence among related functions and means that all functions of the organization—not just marketing people—have to be concerned with customer satisfaction. Any recipient of a person's work, whether coworker, boss, subordinate, or external party, should be viewed as the customer.

A deeper way to understand how organizations can add customer value to their products has been provided by Michael Porter, who popularized the concept of the value chain. A **value chain** is the sequence of activities that flow from raw materials to the delivery of a good or service, with additional value created at each step. You can see a generic value chain illustrated in Exhibit 9.6. Each step in the chain adds value to the product or service:

> *Research and development* focus on innovation and new products.
> *Inbound logistics* receive and store raw materials and distribute them to operations.
> *Operations* transform the raw materials into final product.
> *Outbound logistics* warehouse the product and handle its distribution.
> *Marketing and sales* identify customer requirements and get customers to purchase
> the product.
> *Service* offers customer support, such as repair, after the item has been bought.

When the total value created—that is, what customers are willing to pay—exceeds the cost of providing the good or service, the result is the organization's profit margin.[37]

Managers can add customer value and build competitive advantage by paying close attention to their organization's value chain—not only each step in it, but the way each step interacts with the others. For example, they can achieve economies of scale, as Walmart has, so that their materials and operations costs are lowered, or they can develop innovative distribution channels, as Amazon has done, and add customer value that way. They can also create structures and systems that link the elements of the value chain in innovative ways.

One of the most effective ways to leverage an organization's value chain is to bring together elements of the chain to collaborate to add customer value and build competitive advantage. For example, long-term relationships can be established with suppliers to encourage investment in new technologies and practices that speed product development and turnaround. Nike chooses its suppliers—what it calls its strategic partners—to that end and shares its business plans and strategies with them to reinforce close collaboration. Sales staff can communicate with operations staff, before the manufacturing process even starts, to develop products jointly that customers will value highly. Service managers can

value chain

The sequence of activities that flow from raw materials to the delivery of a good or service, with additional value created at each step.

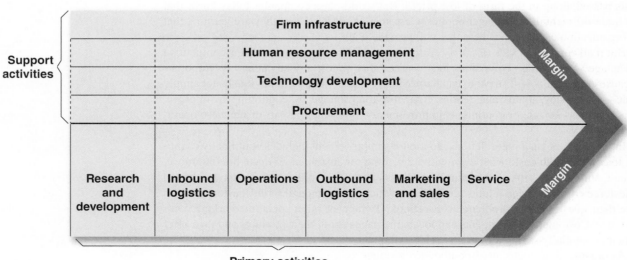

EXHIBIT 9.6
Generic Value Chain

SOURCE: M. Porter, *Competitive Advantage: Creating and Sustaining Superior Performance* (New York: Free Press, 1985).

constantly report back to operations about defects and work with operations and suppliers to reduce and eliminate them. When managers create that type of collaboration, their organization's agility and responsiveness increase significantly.

Quality Initiatives

Often the effort to be more responsive has brought managers face to face with the need to ensure consistently high quality. Systematic ways of meeting that need include total quality management, six sigma, and ISO 9001 standards.

Total quality management (TQM) is a way of managing in which everyone is committed to continuous improvement of his or her part of the operation. In business, success depends on having high-quality products. As described in Chapter 1 and throughout the book, TQM is a comprehensive approach to improving product quality and thereby customer satisfaction. It is characterized by a strong orientation toward customers (external and internal) and has become an umbrella theme for organizing work. TQM reorients managers toward involving people across departments in improving all aspects of the business. Continuous improvement requires integrative mechanisms that facilitate group problem solving, information sharing, and cooperation across business functions. As a consequence, the walls that separate stages and functions of work tend to come down, and the organization operates more in a team-oriented manner.[38]

One of the founders of the quality management movement was W. Edwards Deming. When he started, his work was largely ignored by American companies, but it was adopted eagerly by Japanese firms that wanted to shed their products of their post–World War II reputation for shoddiness. The quality emphasis of Japanese car manufacturing was one direct result of Deming's work, which has since been adopted by many American and other companies worldwide. As listed in Exhibit 9.7, Deming's "14 points" of quality emphasized a holistic approach to management that demands intimate understanding of the process—the delicate interaction of materials, machines, and people that determines productivity, quality, and competitive advantage.

total quality management (TQM)

An integrative approach to management that supports the attainment of customer satisfaction through a wide variety of tools and techniques that result in high-quality goods and services.

Bottom Line
High quality requires organizationwide commitment.
What happens when the commitment to quality is weak at the top of an organization?

At six sigma, a product or process is defect-free 99.99966 percent of the time.

EXHIBIT 9.7
Deming's 14 Points of Quality

1. Create constancy of purpose—strive for long-term improvement rather than short-term profit.
2. Adopt the new philosophy—don't tolerate delays and mistakes.
3. Cease dependence on mass inspection—build quality into the process on the front end.
4. End the practice of awarding business on price tag alone—build long-term relationships.
5. Improve constantly and forever the system of production and service—at each stage.
6. Institute training and retraining—continually update methods and thinking.
7. Institute leadership—provide the resources needed for effectiveness.
8. Drive out fear—people must believe it is safe to report problems or ask for help.
9. Break down barriers among departments—promote teamwork.
10. Eliminate slogans, exhortations, and arbitrary targets—supply methods, not buzzwords.
11. Eliminate numerical quotas—they are contrary to the idea of continuous improvement.
12. Remove barriers to pride in workmanship—allow autonomy and spontaneity.
13. Institute a vigorous program of education and retraining—people are assets, not commodities.
14. Take action to accomplish the transformation—provide a structure that enables quality.

six sigma quality

A method of systematically analyzing work processes to identify and eliminate virtually all causes of defects, standardizing the processes to reach the lowest practicable level of any cause of customer dissatisfaction.

One of the most important contributors to total quality management has been the introduction of statistical tools to analyze the causes of product defects, in an approach called **six sigma quality.** Sigma is the Greek letter used to designate the estimated standard deviation or variation in a process. (The higher the sigma level, the lower the amount of variation.) The product defects analyzed may include anything that results in customer dissatisfaction—for example, late delivery, wrong shipment, or poor customer service as well as problems with the product itself. When the defect has been identified, managers then engage the organization in a determined, comprehensive effort to eliminate its causes and reduce it to the lowest practicable level. At six sigma, a product or process is defect-free 99.99966 percent of the time—fewer than 3.4 defects or mistakes per million. Reaching that goal almost always requires managers to restructure their internal processes and relationships with suppliers and customers in fundamental ways. For example, managers may have to create teams from all parts of the organization to implement the process improvements that will prevent defects from arising. Motorola, where six sigma was developed, and General Electric, whose success with six sigma helped to make the technique popular, credit the method with helping them improve efficiency and quality. Today many companies are combining six sigma's drive to improve quality with a method of improving efficiency known as lean manufacturing, described later in this chapter. This hybrid effort, often called *lean six sigma,* is powerful because it helps an organization to be simultaneously responsive and agile. We will discuss six sigma in more detail in Chapter 16.

Commitment to total quality requires a thorough, extensive, integrated approach to organizing. To encourage American companies to make that commitment and achieve excellence, the Malcolm Baldrige National Quality Award was established in 1987. Named after a former U.S. Secretary of Commerce, the award is given every year to companies and nonprofit organizations that have met specified criteria in seven areas: (1) leadership; (2) strategic planning; (3) customer and market focus; (4) measurement, analysis, and knowledge management; (5) workforce focus; (6) process management; and (7) business results. Recent winners include PricewaterhouseCoopers' Public Sector Practice, which received high scores over the past four years from federal, state, and local governments for its Engagement Management Process, and St. David's Healthcare, a Texas hospital system, which has been ranked for the past five years in the top 10 percent of hospitals nationally for treating all diseases.[39]

A company can both improve its responsiveness to customers and demonstrate to them that it has done so by being certified for meeting widely recognized standards set by outside organizations. For example, the International Organization for Standardization (known globally as ISO) sets a wide variety of exacting standards for parts, materials, products, and organizational processes, each identified by number.

In the quality arena, a particularly important family of standards is ISO 9000, which defines good quality management practices. The requirements for a quality management system that will ensure such practices are spelled out in **ISO 9001.** Meeting this standard enables any type or size of organization to improve its total quality for the benefit of producers and consumers by addressing eight principles:[40]

ISO 9001

A series of quality standards developed by a committee working under the International Organization for Standardization to improve total quality in all businesses for the benefit of producers and consumers.

1. *Customer focus*—learning and addressing customer needs and expectations.
2. *Leadership*—establishing a vision and goals, establishing trust, and providing employees with the resources and inspiration to meet goals.
3. *Involvement of people*—establishing an environment in which employees understand their contribution, engage in problem solving, and acquire and share knowledge.
4. *Process approach*—defining the tasks needed to carry out each process successfully and assigning responsibility for them.
5. *System approach to management*—putting processes together into efficient systems that work together effectively.
6. *Continual improvement*—teaching people how to identify areas for improvement and rewarding them for making improvements.
7. *Factual approach to decision making*—gathering accurate performance data, sharing the data with employees, and using the data to make decisions.
8. *Mutually beneficial supplier relationships*—working in a cooperative way with suppliers.

U.S. companies first became interested in ISO 9001 because overseas customers, particularly those in the European Union, embraced it. Companies that comply with the quality guidelines of ISO 9001 can apply for official certification; some countries and companies demand certification as an acknowledgment of compliance before they will do business. Now some U.S. customers as well are making the same demand.

Certification is not the end of the quality effort but a beginning step. Rather than defining how to operate perfectly, ISO 9001 standards establish practices that enable the organization to keep improving—assuming that it continues to follow those practices.

Reengineering

Extending from TQM and a focus on organizing around customer needs, organizations also have embraced the notion of reengineering (introduced in Chapter 1). The principal idea of reengineering is to revolutionize key organizational systems and processes to answer this question: "If you were the customer, how would you like us to operate?" The answer to this question forms a vision for how the organization should run, and then decisions are made and actions are taken to make the organization operate like the vision. Processes such as product development, order fulfillment, customer service, inventory management, billing, and production are redesigned from scratch as if the organization were brand new and just starting out.

> **Bottom Line**
> Effective reengineering can cut costs significantly.
> *What other drivers of success can reengineering improve?*

For example, Procter & Gamble used reengineering to make its products more competitive. The company learned that the average family buying its products rather than private-label or lower-price brands paid an extra $725 per year. That figure, P&G realized, was far too high and warned that the company's high prices could drive the company to extinction. Other data also signaled the need for P&G to change. Market shares of famous brands such as Comet, Mr. Clean, and Ivory had been dropping for 25 years. P&G was making 55 price changes *daily* on about 80 brands, and inaccurate billings were common. Its plants were inefficient, and the company had the highest overhead in the business. It clearly had to cut prices, and to do that, it had to cut costs.

> Reengineering often requires a fundamental change in the way the parts of the organization work together.

In response, P&G reengineered. The company tore down and rebuilt nearly every activity that contributed to its high costs. It redesigned the way it develops, manufactures, distributes, prices, markets, and sells products. After the changes, price changes became rare, factories became far more efficient, inventory levels fell, and sales and profits rose. P&G was able to price its brands nearer to the prices of store brands. P&G might have reinvented itself as a leader in the industry once again and created for itself a long-term competitive advantage that others have scrambled to match.[41]

The kind of reengineering that P&G undertook requires much more than a management directive from the top, a change in the formal organization structure, the introduction of new technology, or even a well-communicated change in strategy. Rather, to be fully effective and successful, reengineering often requires a fundamental change in the way the parts of the organization work together. They need to see each other as partners in a common effort rather than as members of a particular department or unit. Teams made up of all levels of the organization may be involved in the reengineering effort, and information on problems and possible solutions needs to be fully shared between them. Customers and other stakeholders may be interviewed to get their feedback. Often several teams will be working simultaneously. In this way, all the information that is available within and outside the organization can be brought to bear on a problem—and the solution developed will have wider acceptance and can be implemented faster.

As you can see, reengineering is not about making minor organizational changes here and there. It is about completely overhauling the operation, in revolutionary ways, to achieve the greatest possible benefits to the customer and to the organization.

Technology and Organizational Agility

technology

The systematic application of scientific knowledge to a new product, process, or service.

small batch

Technologies that produce goods and services in low volume.

large batch

Technologies that produce goods and services in high volume.

continuous process

A process that is highly automated and has a continuous production flow.

We have discussed the strategic, size, and customer influences on organizational design and agility. We now turn to one more critical factor affecting an organization's structure and responsiveness: its technology.

Broadly speaking, **technology** can be viewed as the methods, processes, systems, and skills used to transform resources (inputs) into products (outputs). Although we will discuss technology—and innovation—more fully in Chapter 17, in this chapter we want to highlight some of the important influences technology has on organizational design.

Types of Technology Configurations

Research by Joan Woodward laid the foundation for understanding technology and structure. According to Woodward, three basic technologies characterize how work is done: small batch, large batch, and continuous process technologies. These three classifications are equally useful for describing either service or manufacturing technologies. Each differs in terms of volume produced and variety of goods/services offered. Each also has a different influence on how managers organize and structure the work of their organizations.[42]

Small Batch Technologies   When goods or services are provided in very low volume or **small batches,** a company that does such work is called a *job shop*. A fairly typical example of a job shop is PMF Industries, a small custom metalworking company in Williamsport, Pennsylvania, that produces stainless steel assemblies for medical and other uses. In the service industry, restaurants or doctors' offices are examples of job shops because they provide a high variety of low-volume, customized services.

In a small batch organization, structure tends to be very organic. There tend not to be a lot of rules and formal procedures, and decision making tends to be decentralized. The emphasis is on mutual adjustment among people.

Large Batch Technologies   As volume increases, product variety usually decreases. Companies with higher volumes and lower varieties than a job shop tend to be characterized as **large batch,** or mass production technologies. Examples of large batch technologies include the auto assembly operations of General Motors, Ford, and Chrysler. In the service sector, McDonald's and Burger King are good examples. Their production runs tend to be more standardized, and all customers receive similar (if not identical) products. Machines tend to replace people in the physical execution of work. People run the machines.

With a large batch technology, structure tends to be more mechanistic. There tend to be more rules and formal procedures, and decision making tends to be centralized with higher spans of control. Communication tends to be more formal in companies where hierarchical authority is more prominent.

Dell has revolutionized the concept of mass customization. The production process from order to delivery is managed electronically, which allows Dell to build servers very efficiently and its customers to know where their server is during each step of the process.

© AP Photo/Paul Sakuma

Continuous Process Technologies   At the very-high-volume end of the scale are companies that use **continuous process** technologies—technologies that do not stop and start. Domino Sugar and Shell Chemical, for example, use continuous process technologies by which a very limited number of products are produced. People are completely removed from the work itself. It is done entirely by machines and/or computers. In some cases, people run the computers that run the machines.

Ironically, with continuous process technology, structure can return to a more organic form because less monitoring and supervision are needed. Communication tends to be more informal in companies where fewer rules and regulations are established.

Organizing for Flexible Manufacturing

Although issues of volume and variety often have been seen as trade-offs in a technological sense, today organizations are trying to produce both high-volume and high-variety products at the same time. This is referred to as **mass customization**.[43] Automobiles, clothes, computers, and other products are increasingly being manufactured to match each customer's taste, specifications, and budget. Although this seemed only a fantasy a few years ago, mass customization is quickly becoming more prevalent among leading firms. You can now buy clothes cut to your proportions, supplements with the exact blend of the vitamins and minerals you like, CDs with the music tracks you choose, and textbooks whose chapters are picked out by your professor.

How do companies organize to pull off this type of customization at low cost? As shown in Exhibit 9.8, they organize around a dynamic network of relatively independent operating units.[44] Each unit performs a specific process or task—called a *module*—such as making a component, performing a credit check, or performing a particular welding method. Some modules may be performed by outside suppliers or vendors.

mass customization

The production of varied, individually customized products at the low cost of standardized, mass-produced products.

EXHIBIT 9.8
Key Features in Mass Customization

Products	High Variety and Customization
Product design	Collaborative design; significant input from customers.
	Short product development cycles.
	Constant innovation.
Operations and processes	Flexible processes.
	Business process reengineering (BPR).
	Use of modules.
	Continuous improvement (CI).
	Reduced setup and changeover times.
	Reduced lead times.
	JIT delivery and processing of materials and components.
	Production to order.
	Shorter cycle times.
	Use of information technology (IT).
Quality management	Quality measured in customer delight.
	Defects treated as capability failures.
Organizational structure	Dynamic network of relatively autonomous operating units.
	Learning relationships.
	Integration of the value chain.
	Team-based structure.
Workforce management	Empowerment of employees.
	High value on knowledge, information, and diversity of employee capabilities.
	New product teams.
	Broad job descriptions.
Emphasis	Low-cost production of high-quality, customized products.

SOURCE: Reprinted with permission of APICS—The Educational Society for Resource Management, *Production and Inventory Management* 41, no. 1, 2000, pp. 56–65.

computer-integrated manufacturing (CIM)

The use of computer-aided design and computer-aided manufacturing to sequence and optimize a number of production processes.

flexible factories

Manufacturing plants that have short production runs, are organized around products, and use decentralized scheduling.

lean manufacturing

An operation that strives to achieve the highest possible productivity and total quality, cost-effectively, by eliminating unnecessary steps in the production process and continually striving for improvement.

Different modules join forces to make the good or provide a service. How and when the various modules interact with one another are dictated by the unique requests of each customer. The manager's responsibility is to make it easier and less costly for modules to come together, complete their tasks, and then recombine to meet the next customer demand. The ultimate goal of mass customization is a never-ending campaign to expand the number of ways a company can satisfy customers. The Internet has also made it easy for customers to choose their product preferences online and for companies to take an order straight to the manufacturing floor.

Computer-Integrated Manufacturing   One technological advance that has helped make mass customization possible is **computer-integrated manufacturing (CIM),** which links computerized production efforts. Two major elements are computer-aided design and computer-aided manufacturing, which share data needed for product design, testing, manufacturing, and quality control.

These systems can produce high-variety and high-volume products at the same time.[45] They may also offer greater control and predictability of production processes, reduced waste, faster throughput times, and higher quality. But managers cannot buy their way out of competitive trouble simply by investing in superior technology alone. They must also ensure that their organization has the necessary strategic and people strengths.

Flexible Factories   CIM can make it practical to set up **flexible factories,** which serve customers needing fast turnaround on relatively small orders. In contrast to traditional factories, flexible factories have short production runs, organize work flow around products, and use decentralized scheduling.[46] Instead of moving large orders of standard products through assembly lines, flexible factories set up work cells or teams to focus on one product at a time. Scheduling decisions are made on the shop floor by the people doing the work, which aims to keep the schedules adaptable to change.

Lean Manufacturing   Another organizing approach is **lean manufacturing,** based on a commitment to making an operation both efficient and effective; it strives to achieve the highest possible productivity and total quality, cost-effectively, by eliminating unnecessary steps in the production process and continually striving for improvement. Rejects are unacceptable, and staff, overhead, and inventory are considered wasteful. In a lean operation, the emphasis is on quality, speed, and flexibility more than on cost, efficiency, and hierarchy. If an employee spots a problem, the employee is authorized to halt the operation and signal for help to correct the problem at its source so that processes can be improved and future problems avoided. With a well-managed lean production process, a company can develop, produce, and distribute products with half or less of the human effort, space, tools, time, and overall cost.[47]

The lean approach is also used in the services industry. For example, lean principles are adopted by banks to support their growth strategies, energy companies to lower costs, and retailers to increase customer service in stores.[48] Wipro, an Indian software developer, uses lean methods to "deliver projects that perform better and with lower variation."[49]

Toyota receives much of the credit for modeling and teaching a commitment to think lean. Many manufacturing companies have tried to adopt a similar lean approach, but Toyota and others have also applied lean methods to nonmanufacturing processes, including product development. For example, early in the design process, teams bring together experts from various functions to identify potential problems and identify as many solutions as they can to avoid the need to make design changes later in the process. Further adding to efficiency and quality, the company uses standard parts, procedures, and skill sets wherever possible; detailed checklists help engineers ensure they are using best practices. As technology has advanced, Toyota has used these advances in the service of its lean approach. What makes Toyota's use of lean so effective is that when a new technology, such advanced bar coding for keeping track of components, comes along, the company does not simply assume more automation or more data collection will be better.

| People are broadly trained rather than specialized. |
| Communication is informal and horizontal among line workers. |
| Equipment is general-purpose. |
| Work is organized in teams, or cells, that produce a group of similar products. |
| Supplier relationships are long-term and cooperative. |
| Product development is concurrent, not sequential, and is done by cross-functional teams. |

EXHIBIT 9.9
Conditions That Increase
Lean Manufacturing
Effectiveness

SOURCES: F. Sahin, "Manufacturing Competitiveness: Different Systems to Achieve the Same Results," *Production and Inventory Management Journal* 41, no. 1 (First Quarter 2000), pp. 56–65; and G. S. Vasilash, "Flexible Thinking: How Need, Innovation, Teamwork & a Whole Bunch of Machining Centers Have Transformed TRW Tillsonburg into a Model of Lean Manufacturing," *Automotive Manufacturing & Production* 111, no. 10 (October 1999), pp. 64–65.

Rather, it looks at the entire process to see whether technology, with or without other changes, will make it more efficient.[50]

For the lean approach to result in more effective operations, many of the conditions specified in Exhibit 9.9 must be met.

In recent years, many companies have tried to become leaner by cutting overhead costs, laying off operative-level workers, eliminating layers of management, and utilizing capital equipment more efficiently. But if the move to lean manufacturing is simply a harsh, haphazard cost-cutting approach, the result will be chaos, overworked people, and low morale.

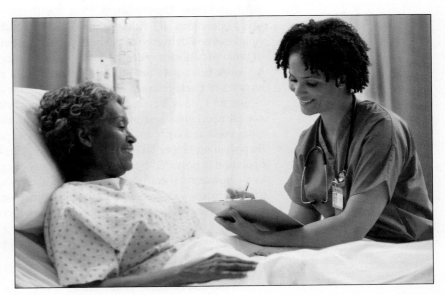

Some hospitals have been using lean principles to reduce costs and patient waiting times while improving safety.

© *Blend Images/Getty Images*

Organizing for Speed: Time-Based Competition

Companies worldwide have devoted so much energy to improving product quality that high quality is now the standard attained by all top competitors. Competition has driven quality to such heights that quality products no longer are enough to distinguish one company from another. Time has emerged as the key competitive advantage that can separate market leaders from also-rans.[51]

Companies today must learn what the customer needs and meet those needs as quickly as possible. **Time-based competition (TBC)** refers to strategies aimed at reducing the total time needed to deliver the good or service. TBC has several key organizational elements: logistics, just-in-time (JIT), and concurrent engineering. JIT production systems reduce the time to manufacture products. Logistics speed the delivery of products to customers. Both are essential steps toward bringing products to customers in the shortest time possible. In today's world, speed is essential.

> Time has emerged as the key competitive advantage that can separate market leaders from also-rans.

time-based competition (TBC)

Strategies aimed at reducing the total time needed to deliver a good or service.

Logistics The movement of resources into the organization (inbound) and products from the organization to its customers (outbound) is called **logistics.** Like the supply chain, which we discussed in Chapter 2, an organization's logistics are often a critical element in its responsiveness and competitive advantage.

The world of logistics includes the great mass of parts, materials, and products moving via trucks, trains, planes, and ships from and to every region of the globe. Depending

logistics

The movement of the right goods in the right amount to the right place at the right time.

on the product, duplication and inefficiency in distribution can cost far more than making the product itself, and slowdowns can cause products to go out of stock so that consumers choose alternatives. One technological advance that is helping some companies improve logistics efficiency and speed is the use of radio frequency identification (RFID) tags. When manufacturers label their products with RFID tags, automated readers can easily track where each product is in the distribution system, including which particular items are selling in each store. Macy's uses RFID tags on apparel and shoes within its stores for inventory tracking; this system ensures that items are replenished and in front of customers during peak selling periods. Walmart, in contrast, is trying to keep its well-known leadership role in distribution by asking suppliers to use RFID, but many of them are finding they cannot afford to institute the new system at this stage of its development while also meeting Walmart's demands to keep prices at a minimum.[52]

just-in-time (JIT)

A system that calls for subassemblies and components to be manufactured in very small lots and delivered to the next stage of the production process just as they are needed.

Just-in-Time Operations An additional element of TBC involves **just-in-time (JIT)** operations. JIT calls for subassemblies and components to be manufactured in very small lots and delivered to the next stage in the process precisely at the time needed, or just in time. A customer order triggers a factory order and the production process. The supplying work centers do not produce the next lot of product until the consuming work center requires it. Even external suppliers deliver to the company just in time.

Just-in-time is a companywide philosophy oriented toward eliminating waste throughout all operations and improving materials throughout. In this way, excess inventory is eliminated and costs are reduced. The ultimate goal of JIT is to serve the customer better by providing higher levels of quality and service. An example of an effective just-in-time operation is provided by Dell, which does not begin production of a computer customized to a consumer's specifications until after the customer's order has been received. Contrast this approach with traditional production methods, which require extremely costly warehousing of inventory and parts, uncertain production runs, considerable waste, no customizing capability, and lengthy delivery times.

JIT represents a number of key production and organizational concepts, including the following:

Elimination of waste. Eliminate all waste from the production process, including waste of time, people, machinery, space, and materials.

Perfect quality. Produce perfect parts even when lot sizes are reduced, and produce the product exactly when it is needed in the exact quantities that are needed.

Reduced cycle times. Accomplish the entire manufacturing process more rapidly. Reduce setup times for equipment, move parts only short distances (machinery is placed in closer proximity), and eliminate all delays. The goal is to reduce action to the time spent working on the parts. For most manufacturers today, the percentage of time parts are worked on is about 5 percent of the total production time. JIT seeks to eliminate the other 95 percent—that is, to reduce to zero the time spent not working on the parts.

Employee involvement. In JIT, employee involvement is central to success. The workers are responsible for production decisions. Managers and supervisors are coaches. Top management pledges that there will never be layoffs due to improved productivity.

Value-added manufacturing. Do only those things (actions, work, etc.) that add value to the finished product. If it doesn't add value, don't do it. For example, inspection does not add value to the finished product, so make the product correctly the first time and inspection will not be necessary.

Discovery of problems and prevention of recurrence. Foolproofing, or fail-safing, is a key component of JIT. To prevent problems from arising, their cause(s) must be known and acted on. Thus, in JIT operations, people try to find the weak link in the chain by forcing problem areas to the surface so that preventive measures may be determined and implemented.

As organizations have seen the advantages of JIT, they have found applications beyond the factory floor. For example, in the area of training, CHG Healthcare Services encourages employees to view mobile learning videos (on demand) and reach out to fellow employees with questions via online chat.[53]

However, JIT has limits. It's not the most efficient choice when the costs of delivery exceed the costs of storage. And if suppliers have any problems fulfilling orders, the whole system breaks down. JIT requires close ties with suppliers, so finding replacements can be difficult. These weaknesses became painfully clear when a massive earthquake and tsunami hit Japan in 2011. Big manufacturers there, including Toyota, Canon, and Sony, began experiencing supply disruptions not only from their suppliers but from the supplier's suppliers. With the potential to lose millions of sales, the companies quickly began learning more about the entire supply chains feeding into their companies and diversifying their networks of suppliers.[54] The Automotive Experience group at Johnson Controls used to have arrangements in which one plant served one customer to deliver products just in time to the customer's assembly plant. But now the company's Lerma, Mexico, facility designs standard seats that a variety of customers can use; robots switch between the assembly of seats for the Dodge Journey, Ford Fiesta, and Chrysler PT Cruiser.[55]

Concurrent Engineering   JIT is a vital component of TBC, but JIT traditionally concentrates on reducing time in only one function: manufacturing. TBC attempts to deliver speed in *all* functions—product development, manufacturing, logistics, and customer service. Customers will not be impressed if you manufacture quickly but it takes weeks for them to receive their products or get a problem solved.

Many companies are turning to concurrent (sometimes called simultaneous) engineering as the cornerstone of their TBC strategy. **Concurrent engineering**—also an important component of total quality management—is a major departure from the old development process in which tasks were assigned to various functions in sequence. When R&D completed its part of the project, the work was passed over the wall to engineering, which completed its task and passed it over the wall to manufacturing, and so on. This process was highly inefficient, and errors took a long time to correct.

In contrast, concurrent engineering incorporates the issues and perspectives of all the functions—and customers and suppliers—from the beginning of the process. This team-based approach results in a higher-quality product that is designed for efficient manufacturing *and* customer needs.[56] When concurrent engineering brings the perspective of manufacturing employees into the design process, the company can find significant cost savings and reduce error rates. Every time manufacturing employees can identify how to reduce the use of different parts, they reduce the need to order those parts, maintain an inventory of them, and keep track of which parts to use in which application. R. A. Jones & Co., which makes machines used for packaging, found a way to realize these benefits. Every time the company's engineers would design a new model of its machines, they would devise all new parts for the machine. Jones & Co. moved the engineers' work stations to the factory floor, so the engineers would routinely interact with the production employees. With more communication during the design process, they found they could readily use many standard parts in their new designs.[57]

Some managers resist the idea of concurrent engineering. Why should marketing, product planning and design, and R&D allow manufacturing to get involved in their work? The answer is because the decisions made during the early, product concept stage determine most of the manufacturing cost and quality. Furthermore, manufacturing can offer ideas about the product because of its experience with the prior generation of the product and with direct customer feedback. Also, the other functions must know early on what manufacturing can and cannot do. Finally, when manufacturing is in from the start, it is a full and true partner and will be more committed to decisions it helped make.

concurrent engineering
A design approach in which all relevant functions cooperate jointly and continually in a maximum effort aimed at producing high-quality products that meet customers' needs.

Bottom Line
Time-based competition brings speed to all organization processes. *Give an example of a situation in which speed would be important for a book publisher.*

When relevant functions interact with each other on a regular basis, the greater the opportunity to improve processes, maximize efficiency, and reduce cost.
© *Glow Images*

Final Thoughts on Organizational Agility

As we pointed out in the previous chapter, *any* approach to organizing has its strengths and limitations. The advantages of even the innovative, leading-edge structures and systems we have discussed in this chapter are likely to be short-lived if they become fixed rather than remain flexible. Smart managers and smart competitors soon catch up. Today's advantages are tomorrow's table stakes—the minimum requirements that need to be met if an organization expects to be a major player.

To retain or gain a competitive edge, managers may want to keep in mind the principle with which we opened this chapter: successful organizations—and that includes the successful managers within them—do not sit still. They do not follow rigid models but maintain structures, systems, organizational designs, and relationships that are adaptive—always sensitive to changes in their environment and able to respond quickly, efficiently, and effectively to them. Their managers focus constantly on exceeding customer expectations and on continuous quality improvement, designing their systems and structures to help them do just that.

The emphasis on agility, quality, flexibility, learning, and leanness to which you have been exposed in this chapter is likely to be a constant in your managerial career—ideally in your own organization, but perhaps as well in the competition you confront. When Jack Welch was chairman of GE, he saw his goal as the creation of the boundaryless organization, one in which there were no meaningful barriers between the organization and its environment. In such an organization, structures, technologies, and systems are perfectly aligned with the external challenges and opportunities it confronts. Many forward-thinking managers have embraced this goal.[58]

MANAGER'S BRIEF

PROGRESS REPORT

ONWARD

Management in Action

GE'S PURSUIT OF HIGH QUALITY AND LEANNESS

GE tries to be responsive to customers in multiple ways. To improve quality, GE applies six sigma, and to improve efficiency by eliminating waste, it uses lean initiative methods. These methods are not just for manufacturing, either; six sigma has been used for finance, human resources, and other key areas within the company.

GE considers six sigma part of its culture, not just a process tacked on. Employees must apply the concepts of six sigma to all GE's processes and in the design of its products. Six sigma is the latest initiative in a series of efforts beginning in the 1980s. Then it launched a program called Work-Out to empower employees, hear ideas from employees at all levels, and eliminate bureaucracy and boundaries that got in the way of making improvements. The Work-Out initiative continues to create a learning environment in which quality improvement can proceed more effectively. GE trains all its employees in the six sigma practices, with the most basic training being quality overview seminars. Employees also learn to participate on six sigma teams, and some learn the statistical and quality-control techniques needed to become six sigma Green Belts, Black Belts, and Master Black Belts.

Lean gets credit for enabling GE to move some of its appliance manufacturing back to the United States from China and Mexico, according to Chip Blankenship, chief executive

of GE Appliances and Lighting. GE seeks input from employees at all levels about how to make its processes more efficient. At the GE Appliances facility in Louisville, Kentucky, one outcome of the lean initiative is that all functions related to manufacturing—design, product development, engineering, production, and quality control—are located at the same facility. When an employee learns of customer concerns or a production problem, everyone is at hand to respond.

GE continues experimenting with methods for being more responsive. For example, GE Aviation used a concurrent engineering process, working with its suppliers, to develop wing components for the Airbus A350 XWB. And a few years ago, GE software developers began trying out a technique known as Agile software development. This method entails developing new software with customers by creating a minimally viable product and making adjustments as they work. In one project for GE Healthcare, the Agile process cut development time by about half. [59]

- How else might GE become more responsive to its customers?
- Based on the information in the three parts of this case, how would you rate GE's organizational agility? Summarize your reasons for this rating.

KEY TERMS

computer-integrated manufacturing (CIM), p. 296

concurrent engineering, p. 299

continuous process, p. 294

customer relationship management, (CRM), p. 289

downsizing, p. 285

economies of scope, p. 284

flexible factories, p. 296

high-involvement organization, p. 283

ISO 9001, p. 292

just-in-time (JIT), p. 298

large batch, p. 294

lean manufacturing, p. 296

learning organization, p. 283

logistics, p. 297

mass customization, p. 295

mechanistic organization, p. 278

organic structure, p. 278

rightsizing, p. 287

six sigma quality, p. 292

small batch, p. 294

strategic alliance, p. 281

survivor's syndrome, p. 287

technology, p. 294

time-based competition (TBC), p. 297

total quality management, (TQM), p. 291

value chain, p. 290

RETAINING WHAT YOU LEARNED

In Chapter 9, you learned that organizations exert control internally through formal structures and respond to fast-changing demands in their environments. Organic structures, which are flexible in nature, are decentralized, informal, and guided by the actions of people with broad responsibilities. Strategies and concepts increase an organization's responsiveness, including core capabilities, strategic alliances, learning organizations, and high-involvement organizations. Small firms have certain advantages over their larger counterparts, including the ability to act quickly, respond to customer demands, and serve small niches. The ideal organization today harnesses the power of large firms while staying flexible. Driven to meet customer needs, firms adopt the principles of continuous improvement, total quality management, and six sigma quality (often combined with lean manufacturing). Reengineering efforts are directed at completely overhauling processes to provide world-class customer service. To organize for flexible manufacturing, organizations pursue mass customization via computer-integrated manufacturing and lean manufacturing. To organize for time-based competition, firms emphasize their logistics operations, just-in-time operations, and concurrent engineering.

LO 1 Discuss why it is critical for organizations to be responsive.

- Organizations have a formal structure to help control what goes on within them.
- But to survive today, firms need more than control—they need responsiveness. They must act quickly and adapt to fast-changing demands.

LO 2 Describe the qualities of an organic organization structure.

- The organic form emphasizes flexibility. Organic organizations are decentralized, informal, and dependent on the judgment and expertise of people with broad responsibilities.
- The organic form is not a single formal structure but a concept that underlies all the new forms discussed in this chapter.

LO 3 Identify strategies and dynamic organizational concepts that can improve an organization's responsiveness.

- New and emerging organizational concepts and forms include core capabilities, strategic alliances, learning organizations, and high-involvement organizations.

LO 4 Explain how a firm can be both big and small.

- Historically, large organizations have had important advantages over small organizations. Today small size has advantages, including the ability to act quickly, respond to customer demands, and serve small niches.
- The ideal firm today combines the advantages of both. It creates many small, flexible units, while the corporate levels add value by taking advantage of its size and power.

LO 5 Summarize how firms organize to meet customer requirements.

- Firms have embraced principles of continuous improvement, total quality management, and six sigma quality (often combined with lean manufacturing) to respond to customer needs.
- Baldrige criteria and ISO 9001 standards help firms organize to meet better quality specifications.
- Extending these, reengineering efforts are directed at completely overhauling processes to provide world-class customer service.

LO 6 Identify ways that firms organize around different types of technology.

- Organizations tend to move from organic structures to mechanistic structures and back to organic structures as they transition from small batch to large batch and continuous process technologies.
- To organize for flexible manufacturing, organizations pursue mass customization via computer-integrated manufacturing and lean manufacturing.
- To organize for time-based competition, firms emphasize their logistics operations, just-in-time operations, and concurrent engineering.

DISCUSSION QUESTIONS

1. Discuss evidence you have seen of the imperatives for change, flexibility, and responsiveness faced by today's firms.

2. Describe large, bureaucratic organizations with which you have had contact that have not responded flexibly to customer demands. Also describe examples of satisfactory responsiveness. What do you think accounts for the differences between the responsive and nonresponsive organizations?

3. Considering the potential advantages of large and small size, would you describe the feel of your college or university as big, small, or small within big? Why? What might make it feel different?

4. What is a core capability? What would you say are the core capabilities of Toyota, Walmart, and Apple? Brainstorm some creative new products and markets to which these capabilities could be applied.

5. If you were going into business for yourself, what would be your core capabilities? What capabilities do you have now, and what capabilities are you going to develop? Describe what your role would be in a network organization and the capabilities and roles of other firms you would want in your network.

6. Using an Internet search engine, search for "strategic alliance" and identify three recently formed alliances. For each alliance, identify whether the companies' other products are generally competitors or complementary products. What are the goals of each alliance? What brought them together? Discuss whether you think a strategic alliance is an effective way for these organizations to meet their goals.

7. What skills will you need to work effectively in (a) a learning organization and (b) a high-involvement organization? Be specific, generating long lists. Would you enjoy working in these environments? Why or why not? What can you do to prepare yourself for these eventualities?

EXPERIENTIAL EXERCISES

9.1 MECHANISTIC AND ORGANIC STRUCTURES

OBJECTIVES

1. To think about your own preferences when it comes to working in a particular organizational structure.

2. To examine aspects of organizations by using as an example this class you are a member of.

INSTRUCTIONS

1. Complete the Mechanistic and Organic Worksheet here.

2. Meet in groups of four to six persons. Share your data from the worksheet. Discuss the reasons for your responses and analyze the factors that probably encouraged your instructor to choose the type of structure that now exists.

Mechanistic and Organic Worksheet

1. Indicate your general preference for working in one of these two organizational structures by circling the appropriate response:

Mechanistic   1   2   3   4   5   6   7   8   9   10   **Organic**

2. Indicate your perception of the form of organization that is used in this class by circling the appropriate response for each item:

A. **Task role definition**

| **Rigid** | 1 | 2 | 3 | 4 | 5 | 6 | 7 | 8 | 9 | 10 | **Flexible** |

B. **Communication**

| **Vertical** | 1 | 2 | 3 | 4 | 5 | 6 | 7 | 8 | 9 | 10 | **Multidirectional** |

C. **Decision making**

| **Centralized** | 1 | 2 | 3 | 4 | 5 | 6 | 7 | 8 | 9 | 10 | **Decentralized** |

D. **Sensitivity to the environment**

| **Closed** | 1 | 2 | 3 | 4 | 5 | 6 | 7 | 8 | 9 | 10 | **Open** |

SOURCE: From Keith Davis and John W. Newstrom, *Human Behavior at Work*, p. 346. Copyright 1993. Reprinted with permission of the McGraw-Hill Companies.

9.2   THE WOODY MANUFACTURING COMPANY

OBJECTIVE

To apply the concepts learned about structure and agility at the individual, group, and organizational levels in designing the Woody Manufacturing Company.

TASK 1 (INDIVIDUAL ASSIGNMENT)

a. Read the following case study of the Woody Manufacturing Company.
b. Review the chapter carefully and choose the organizational design orientation that you feel can best guide you in developing the design for Mr. Woody.
c. Write down your thoughts on alternative management structures, pay systems, and allocation of work to individuals and groups.

TASK 2 (TEAM ASSIGNMENT)

a. Get together with your team and develop a proposal for Mr. Woody that, if followed, would help him fulfill his vision.
b. Prepare a five-minute presentation. Your typewritten team proposal is due prior to your team presentation in Mr. Woody's conference room.

Designing a New Furniture Company

Mr. Woody, the owner/operator of a small furniture company specializing in the manufacture of high-quality bar stools, has experienced a tremendous growth in demand for his products. He has standing orders for $750,000. Consequently, Mr. Woody has decided to expand his organization and attack the market aggressively. His stated mission is "to manufacture world-class products that are competitive in the world market in quality, reliability, performance, and profitability." He would like to create a culture where "pride, ownership, employment security, and trust" are a way of life. He just finished a set of interviews, and he has hired 32 new workers with the following skills:

Four skilled craftspeople.

Ten people with some woodworking experience.

Twelve people with no previous woodworking experience or other skills.

One nurse.

One schoolteacher.

One bookkeeper.

Three people with some managerial experience in nonmanufacturing settings.

Mr. Woody (with your help) must now decide how to design his new organization. This design will include the management structure, pay system, and the allocation of work to individuals and groups. The bar stool–making process has 15 steps:

1. Wood is selected.
2. Wood is cut to size.
3. Defects are removed.
4. Wood is planed to exact specifications.
5. Joints are cut.
6. Tops are glued and assembled.
7. Legs/bases are prepared.
8. Legs/bases are attached to tops.
9. Bar stools are sanded.
10. Stain is applied.
11. Varnish is applied.
12. Bar stools are sanded.
13. Varnish is reapplied.
14. Bar stools are packaged.
15. Bar stools are delivered to the customer.

Mr. Woody currently manufactures three kinds of bar stools (pedestal, four-legged corner, and four-legged recessed). There is no difference in the difficulty of making the three types of bar stools. Major cost variations have been associated with defective wood, imprecise cuts, and late deliveries to customers. Mr. Woody must decide how to organize his company to maintain high quality and profits.

He has thought about several options. He could have some individuals perform the first step for all types of bar stools; he could have an individual perform several steps for one type of bar stool; or he could have a team perform some combination of steps for one or more bar stools. He wonders whether how he organized would affect quality or costs. He's also aware that although the demand for all types of bar stools has been roughly equal over the long run, there were short periods where one type of bar stool was in greater demand than the others. Because Mr. Woody wants to use his people effectively, he has committed an expert in work design to help him set up an optimal organization.

SOURCE: A. B. (Rami) Shani and James B. Lau, *Behavior in Organizations: An Experimental Approach*, 2005, p. 370. Copyright 2005 Reprinted with permission of The McGraw-Hill Companies.

CONCLUDING CASE

DIY STORES

DIY Stores is a nationwide chain that offers every tool and supply for repairing and maintaining a home. Shoppers at DIY can find paints and paintbrushes, screwdrivers and lumber, pliers and electrical conduit, spades and shrubs, and much more. Besides the wide variety under one roof, what sets DIY apart is its sales associates. The company hires avid do-it-yourselfers and retired trade workers, assigns them to work in departments where their know-how is relevant, provides training in new products and creative methods, and pays them a little more than they could earn by working for another retailer. The company also makes available fact sheets and lists of tips and building ideas. Together these efforts make DIY Stores a place where shoppers can go to get ideas and advice, so they get more than supplies for a project—they get all the ingredients they need for their project to succeed.

Over the past couple of decades, however, consumers have found an alternative to getting advice in a store: many prefer to do their research online, comfortably seated at a computer. If consumers can use a search engine or chat in an online community to figure out the best way to fix a leaky toilet or make a small bedroom look airy and bright, why would they trek into a store to ask? The answer, DIY's management feared, was that they wouldn't bother. If true, that trend placed DIY's competitive advantage at risk. The retailer needed to change with the times.

DIY's solution was to go where the consumers were: online. Management decided the company needed to supplement its in-store experts with online experts, employees who shared the same kinds of information on the Internet as they did in the stores. The company's corporate communications department was charged with developing a plan for this effort.

The department's people were used to thinking of corporate communications as something that originates at headquarters, so they initially thought the most efficient approach would be to hire a team of writers to work in offices at headquarters, blogging about new products and maintenance tips. But when they presented this plan to top management, one of the vice presidents raised a question: The company's salespeople were its base of knowledge. Why bring in new people? Why not figure out a way to use the human assets the company already had?

The corporate communications people went back to work on the plan. Probably some of the sales associates already were using the Internet themselves and knew how to write a blog and participate in social networking. Probably some of them had the necessary combination of helpfulness and writing skills. So they considered identifying those employees and inviting them to take jobs at headquarters. But as the group discussed this idea, they realized it had a flaw. If employees left the stores, they would no longer be seeing, selling, and watching customers' reactions to products. They would lose the hands-on and face-to-face experiences that kept them up to date and in touch with consumers. Also, consumers would quickly figure out that the online exchanges were not with a real DIY sales associate but with someone who had become a call center employee or professional communicator.

So the team arrived at an unusual plan. The company would identify Internet-savvy sales associates, but it wouldn't remove them from the stores. Rather, the associates who accepted the new position would work three days a week in a store and two days a week in an office, with their schedules staggered so that the online community would be active seven days a week. The company's executives were enthusiastic about this plan.

DIY contacted store managers in cities where it has regional offices. The store managers recommended employees they thought would deliver effective help online, and a team of recruiters interviewed these candidates and selected two dozen to provide an online presence. The typical employee selected had eight years of experience with DIY and submitted an excellent writing sample. Meanwhile, the company built an online "Do It with Us" web page where customers can submit questions, read tips, share ideas, and find links to information about new products available at DIY's stores.

After a three-day training program, the sales associates started the online conversation with DIY. Within months, they and the site's visitors had started thousands of conversation threads. And in an unexpected development, the sales associates have also become a valued source of knowledge for DIY's other employees. In stores, at headquarters, and in the regional offices, if someone wants product or project information, they often start their search at the "Do It with Us" web page.

DISCUSSION QUESTIONS

1. As DIY Stores built its online presence, how well did it organize around its core capabilities?

2. DIY Stores is a large national chain. What impact did its size have on its agility?

3. How could DIY increase its agility in responding to the importance of the Internet?

CHAPTER 10

Human Resources Management

> You can get capital and erect buildings, but it takes people to build a business.
>
> —THOMAS J. WATSON, FOUNDER, IBM

Management in Action

HOW GOOGLE LANDS THE BEST EMPLOYEES IN A TOUGH JOB MARKET

Year after year, we hear that U.S. schools are not preparing enough engineers and software developers to meet employers' demand for skilled technology workers. Yet Google, the software company known for its popular search engine, gets about a million job applicants a year and hires the cream of the crop.

How does Google win the competition for talent? An obvious place to find answers is in how the 40,000-employee company treats its workers. It pays them well, and knowing they hold demanding jobs, it makes the workplace comfortable. Uncommon benefits include exercise facilities, extended time off to pursue passions, permission to bring pets to work, and free food in all company cafeterias. Google offers flexibility with on-site child care and arrangements for job sharing and telecommuting. These qualities help Google land at the top of *Fortune*'s list of the 100 Best Companies to Work For.

More significant is the excitement of being part of something meaningful. At least since the name Google became synonymous with searching the web, people with a passion for technology have considered the company a cool place to work, both because its software is advanced and because it makes the Internet a powerful tool. In a survey of young professionals, Google was by far the top choice for an ideal employer. Universum, which conducted the survey, noted that young professionals value working for companies they already like as consumers.

Because Google is an attractive employer, it can be picky about whom it hires. The company selects people who are excited about what computers can do and value intellectual excellence. It retains them by creating a work environment in which employees can

© *Simon Dawson/Bloomberg via Getty Images*

contribute creatively and continue to develop. Such people appreciate the hours of training Google provides its employees each year.

These decisions about hiring, training, and employee benefits are far from random. Rather, under the leadership of Chief People Officer Laszlo Bock, Google applies its prowess in analyzing data to figure out how to acquire, develop, and keep talented people. Every year, Google conducts its Googlegeist employee survey to measure employee attitudes about work, and the company carefully tracks all kinds of people-related measures such as managers' effectiveness. Prasad Setty, who as the director of people analytics reports to Bock, says Google tries to "bring the same level of rigor to people decisions that we do to engineering decisions," so all decisions are based on hard data.[1]

> In receiving roughly 2 million job applications each year, Google has a huge challenge as well as an opportunity. It has to figure out which of these people to hire, how to bring out the best in them, and how to keep them around. As you read this chapter, think about how the strategic use of people is essential to Google's success.

**human resources
management (HRM)**

Formal systems for the
management of people
within an organization.

The opening quote by Thomas Watson, founder of IBM, summarizes our view of the importance of people to any organization. Google's practice of wooing bright people with exciting challenges and generous perks has differentiated the company in important ways. **Human resources management (HRM),** historically known as personnel management, deals with formal systems for managing people at work. For that reason, it is one of the fundamental aspects of organizational and managerial life. Your first formal interaction with an organization you wish to join will likely involve some aspect of its human resources function, and throughout your career as a manager you will interact with your organization's human resources management.

We begin this chapter by describing HRM as it relates to strategic management. We will also discuss more of the nuts and bolts of HRM: staffing, training, performance appraisal, rewards, and labor relations. Throughout the chapter, we discuss legal issues that influence each aspect of HRM. In the next chapter, we expand this focus to address related issues of managing a diverse workforce.

Strategic Human Resources Management

 HRM has assumed a vital strategic role in recent years as organizations attempt to compete through people. Recall from Chapter 4 that firms can create a competitive advantage when they possess or develop resources that are valuable, rare, inimitable, and organized. We can use the same criteria to talk about the strategic impact of human resources:

1. *Creates value.* People can increase value through their efforts to decrease costs or provide something unique to customers or some combination of the two. Empowerment programs, total quality initiatives, and continuous improvement efforts at companies such as Corning and Xerox are intentionally designed to increase the value that employees bring to the bottom line.

2. *Is rare.* People are a source of competitive advantage when their skills, knowledge, and abilities are not equally available to all competitors. Top companies invest a great deal to hire and train the best and the brightest employees to gain advantage over their competitors. Dow Chemical went to court to stop General Electric from hiring away its engineers. This case shows that some companies recognize both the value and the rarity of certain employees.

> People are a source of competitive advantage when their skills, knowledge, and abilities are not equally available to all competitors.

3. *Is difficult to imitate.* People are a source of competitive advantage when their capabilities and contributions cannot be copied by others. IDEO, Pixar, and Whole Foods are known for creating unique cultures that get the most from employees (through teamwork) and are difficult to imitate.

4. *Is organized.* People are a source of competitive advantage when organizations know how to deploy them as needed based on their experience, skills, and potential. Johnson & Johnson, Colgate, and other companies have formal systems for identifying future management needs and developing high-potential employees so the company can promote from within. This way, they fill openings with people who are well acquainted with the company's culture, customers, and industry.

These four criteria highlight the importance of people and show the closeness of HRM to strategic management. At a growing number of companies, HR experts are participating in strategy meetings to identify key issues where they can analyze data and propose how new methods of acquiring, training, and keeping talent will help the company meet its goals.[2] The evidence is growing that this focus brings positive business results. For example, a study by Deloitte associated the use of effective human resources practices with higher valuation of a company in the stock market.[3] Global trends make this focus even more important. Competition is intensifying. Rising educational standards and access to technology are increasingly available worldwide. *Innovation*—useful new ideas that emerge from the focused creativity of organization members—has become ever more critical to gaining and maintaining competitive advantage. Because employee skills, knowledge, and abilities are among the most distinctive and renewable resources on which a company can draw, their strategic management is more important than ever. Increasingly, organizations are recognizing that their success depends on what people know— that is, their knowledge and skills. The term **human capital** (or, more broadly, *intellectual capital*) often is used today to describe the strategic value of employee knowledge and abilities.

Southwest Airlines is known for creating a unique culture that gets the most from employees. Southwest rewards its employees for excellent performance and maintains loyalty by offering free airfare, profit sharing, and other incentives. What benefits would you need to stay motivated?

© Ned Dishman/NBAE/Getty Images

human capital

The knowledge, skills, and abilities of employees that have economic value.

As more executives have come to appreciate that their employees can be their organization's most valuable resources, human resources managers have played a greater role in contributing to the organization's strategic planning. That means human resources (HR) specialists are challenged to know their organization's business, and line managers are challenged to excel at selecting and motivating the best people. As contributors to the organization's strategy, HR managers also face greater ethical challenges. When they were merely a specialized staff function, they could focus on, say, legal requirements for hiring decisions. But strategy decisions require them to be able to link decisions about staffing, training, and other HR matters to the organization's business success. For example, as members of the top management team, HR managers may be faced with the need for drastic downsizing of the workforce while still retaining top executives through generous salaries or bonuses, or they may fail to investigate and challenge corrupt practices of colleagues aggressively. Such dilemmas are complex and challenging. In the long run, however, organizations are best served when HR leaders are a strong advocate for at least four sets of values: strategic, ethical, legal, and financial.[4]

Managing human capital to sustain a competitive advantage is perhaps the most important part of an organization's HR function. But on a day-to-day basis, HR managers also have many other concerns regarding their workers and the entire personnel puzzle. These concerns include attracting talent; maintaining a well-trained, highly motivated, and loyal workforce; managing diversity; devising effective compensation systems; managing layoffs; and containing health care and pension costs. Balancing these issues is difficult, and the best approach varies depending on the circumstances of the organization. An oil and natural gas producer facing a cutback in business may need human resources activities to assist with layoffs, whereas a semiconductor company may need more staff to produce enough microchips to meet the demands of the consumer electronics market. The emphasis on different HR activities depends on whether the organization is growing, declining, or standing still. This leads to the practical issues involved in HR planning.

The HR Planning Process

"Get me the right kind and the right number of people at the right time." It sounds simple enough, but meeting an organization's staffing needs requires strategic human resources planning: an activity with a strategic purpose derived from the organization's plans.

The HR planning process occurs in three stages: planning, programming, and evaluating. First, HR managers need to know the organization's business plans to ensure that the

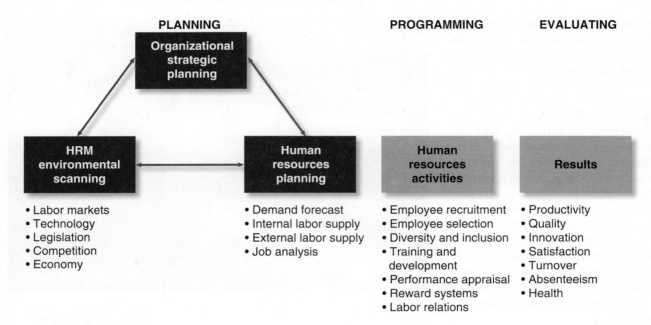

EXHIBIT 10.1

An Overview of the HR
Planning Process

right number and types of people are available—where the company is headed, in what businesses it plans to be, what future growth is expected, and so forth. Few actions are more damaging to morale than having to lay off recently hired college graduates because of inadequate planning for future needs. Hiring enough employees to scale an organization can be challenging too (see the nearby "Social Enterprise" box). Second, the organization conducts programming of specific human resources activities, such as recruitment, training, and performance appraisals. In this stage, the company's plans are implemented. Third, human resources activities are evaluated to determine whether they are producing the results needed to contribute to the organization's business plans. Exhibit 10.1 illustrates the components of the human resources planning process. In this chapter, we focus on human resources planning and programming. Many of the other factors listed in Exhibit 10.1 are discussed in later chapters.

Demand Forecasts   Perhaps the most difficult part of human resources planning is conducting demand forecasts—that is, determining how many and what type of people are needed. Demand forecasts for people needs are derived from organizational plans. As Ford Motor Company increased production and prepared to launch new products following the recession of 2009, it hired more than 8,100 workers for manufacturing and engineering positions associated with the greater production volume. It then planned to hire 2,200 salaried workers to carry out work related to introducing new models, including engineering and software jobs. Similarly, companies selling an existing product consider current sales and projected future sales growth as they estimate the plant capacity needed to meet future demand, the sales force required, the support staff needed, and so forth. They calculate the number of labor-hours required to operate a plant, sell the product, distribute it, serve customers, and so forth. These estimates are used to determine the demand for different types of workers.

Labor Supply Forecasts   Along with forecasting demand, managers must forecast the *supply of labor*—that is, how many and what types of employees the organization actually will have. In performing a supply analysis, the organization estimates the number and quality of its current employees as well as the available external supply of workers. To estimate internal supply, the company typically relies on its experiences with turnover,

Social Enterprise

Are Business School Graduates Willing to Work for Social Enterprises?

According to a recent study, many social enterprises in the United States are operating at a suboptimal level where "approximately 40 percent of these businesses have fewer than five employees." In addition, about half of social enterprises' revenues do not exceed $250,000.

Scaling is an important goal for many social enterprises. A larger organization with more resources and employees generally equates to making more impact with regard to the enterprise's mission. For example, Mason Arnold had a burning desire to improve the food system by delivering fresh, nutritious food to consumers in a way that did not damage the environment. His Austin, Texas–based social enterprise, Greenling, purchases food from farms that use chemical-free land in order to have sustainable food for generations. As Greenling grows, so will its impact on consumers, farmers, and the environment.

The social enterprise industry in the United States is larger than one might imagine. One estimate suggests that it employs over 10 million people and generates annual revenues of $500 billion. To fuel additional growth, more individuals will be needed to work for organizations that use commercial strategies to support social initiatives. There is good news on this front. A study of MBA students found that over 97 percent of them were "willing to forgo financial benefits to work for an organization with a better reputation for corporate social responsibility and ethics." On average, the MBAs were willing to give up 14 percent of their expected income.

© Getty Images

Taken together, it appears that many business school graduates are willing to work for organizations that are socially responsible and managed in an ethical manner.[5]

Questions

- Assume you are the manager of a social enterprise like Greenling. How would you go about attracting individuals to work for your organization?
- To what degree would you or your fellow students consider working for a social enterprise?

---

terminations, retirements, promotions, and transfers. A computerized human resources information system assists greatly in supply forecasting.

Externally, organizations have to look at workforce trends to make projections. Worldwide, as we discussed in Chapter 6, the highly skilled, higher-paid jobs have been generated mostly in the cities of the industrialized world, where companies have scrambled to find enough qualified workers. At the same time, companies in industrialized nations have used offshoring to move much of their routine and less skilled work to nations with a large population willing to work for lower pay.

In the United States, demographic trends have contributed to a shortage of workers with the appropriate skills and education level. Traditional labor-intensive jobs, in agriculture, mining, and assembly-line manufacturing, are making way for jobs in technical, financial, and customized goods and service industries. These jobs often require much more training and schooling than the jobs they are replacing—or that the education system may currently be producing. Demand for highly qualified employees continues to outpace supply—one reason some jobs are being transferred overseas. Some demographic trends we discussed in Chapter 2 may worsen this situation. For example, the upcoming retirement of the baby boomer generation will remove a large number of educated and trained employees from the workforce.[6] And in math, science, and engineering graduate schools, fewer than half of the students receiving graduate degrees are American born. (To fill U.S. jobs, companies must hire U.S. citizens or immigrants with permission to work in the United States.)

One response managers have made to deal with this skills shortage has been to increase significantly the remedial and training budgets within their own organizations.[7] For example, Caspers Company, which operates 53 McDonald's stores in Tampa, Florida, pays for its non-English-speaking employees to take an intensive English language class. Employees who choose to participate not only provide better customer service but also are able to move into positions of greater responsibility. And several companies like Target, Valero Energy, and Verizon set up internships to address the shortage of IT workers.[8] A related approach to training current employees is to retrain and hire workers who were downsized.

Another response has been to increase the labor supply by recruiting workers from other countries. The supply of legal immigrant labor is restricted by various laws and regulations. For example, each year the U.S. government awards H-1B visas to 65,000 college-educated workers in high-skilled, highly demanded jobs such as engineers and college instructors. Those people are permitted to work temporarily in the United States. Managers at high-tech companies, including Microsoft and Google, complain that the number of H-1B visas is too small to enable companies to meet the demand for science and technology workers, and some companies address that challenge by aggressively hiring early each year, before the quota has been met.[9] Immigrant workers are also attractive to companies with a low-cost strategy because strong labor demand in the United States enables U.S. workers to insist on higher pay.

On the plus side, earlier forecasts of a diverse workforce have become fact, adding greatly to the pool of available talent. The business world is no longer the exclusive domain of white males. In fact, two-career families have become the norm. Minorities, women, immigrants, older and disabled workers, and other groups have made the management of diversity a fundamental activity of the modern manager. Because of the importance of managing the new workforce, the next chapter is devoted entirely to this topic.

Reconciling Supply and Demand   Once managers have a good idea of the supply of and the demand for various types of employees, they can start developing approaches for reconciling the two. In some cases, organizations find they need more people than they currently have (i.e., a labor deficit). In such cases, organizations can hire new employees, promote current employees to new positions, or outsource work to contractors. In other cases, organizations may find that they have more people than they need (i.e., a labor surplus). If this is detected far enough in advance, organizations can use attrition—the normal turnover of employees—to reduce the surplus. In other instances, the organization may lay off employees or transfer them to other areas.

When managers do need to hire, one tool they can use is their organization's compensation policy. Large companies in particular spend a lot of time gathering information about pay scales for the various jobs they have available and making sure their compensation system is fair and competitive. We discuss pay issues later in this chapter.

Job Analysis   Although issues of supply and demand are fairly macro activities—conducted at an organizational level—HR planning also has a micro side called *job analysis*. **Job analysis** does two things.[10] First, it tells the HR manager about the job itself: the essential tasks, duties, and responsibilities involved in performing the job. This information is called a *job description*. The job description for an accounting manager might specify that the position will be responsible for monthly, quarterly, and annual financial reports, getting bills issued and paid, preparing budgets, ensuring the company's compliance with laws and regulations, working closely with line managers on financial issues, and supervising an accounting department of 12 people.

Second, job analysis describes the skills, knowledge, abilities, and other characteristics needed to perform the job. This is called the *job specification*. For our accounting manager example, the job requirements might include a degree in accounting or business,

job analysis

A tool for determining what is done on a given job and what should be done on that job.

knowledge of computerized accounting systems, prior managerial experience, and excellent communication skills.

Job analysis provides the information required by virtually every human resources activity. It assists with the essential HR programs: recruitment, training, selection, appraisal, and reward systems. It may also help organizations defend themselves in lawsuits involving employment practices—for example, by clearly specifying what a job requires if someone claims unfair dismissal.[11] Ultimately, job analysis helps increase the value added by employees to the organization because it clarifies what is really required to perform effectively.

> Job analysis provides the information required by virtually every human resources activity.

Staffing the Organization

Once HR planning is completed, managers can focus on staffing the organization. The staffing function consists of three related activities: recruitment, selection, and outplacement.

Recruitment

Recruitment activities help increase the pool of candidates that might be selected for a job. Recruitment may be internal to the organization (considering current employees for promotions and transfers) or external. Each approach has advantages and disadvantages.[12]

recruitment
The development of a pool of applicants for jobs in an organization.

Internal Recruiting   The advantages of internal recruiting are that employers know their employees, and employees know their organization. External candidates who are unfamiliar with the organization may find they don't like working there. Also, the opportunity to move up within the organization may encourage employees to remain with the company, work hard, and succeed. Recruiting from outside the company can be demoralizing to employees. Many companies, such as Bain, H-E-B, and Cameron Oil, prefer internal to external recruiting for these reasons.

Internal staffing has some drawbacks. If existing employees lack skills or talent, internal recruitment yields a limited applicant pool, leading to poor selection decisions. Also, an internal recruitment policy can inhibit a company that wants to change the nature or goals of the business by bringing in outside candidates. In changing from a rapidly growing, entrepreneurial organization to a mature business with more stable growth, Dell went outside the organization to hire managers who better fit those needs.

Many companies that rely heavily on internal recruiting use a job-posting system. A *job-posting system* is a mechanism for advertising open positions, typically on a bulletin board or the company's intranet. W.L. Gore, Patagonia, and insurance provider Acuity use job posting. Employees complete a request form indicating interest in a posted job. The posted job description includes a list of duties and the minimum skills and experience required.

Bottom Line
Outside hires often bring new ideas to the organization.
How might an organization identify candidates with innovative ideas?

External Recruiting   External recruiting brings in new blood to a company and can inspire innovation. Among the most frequently used sources of outside applicants are Internet job boards, company websites, employee referrals, newspaper advertisements, and college campus recruiting.

Recent surveys suggest that employers place the greatest emphasis on referrals by current employees and online job boards.[13] Some companies actively encourage employees to refer their friends by offering cash rewards. In fact, surveys show word-of-mouth recommendations are the way most job positions get filled. Not only is this recruitment method relatively inexpensive, but employees also tend to know who will be a good fit with the company. Web job boards such as CareerBuilder, SimplyHired, Glassdoor, and Monster are widely used because they easily reach a large pool of job seekers. For specialized

© NetPhotos/Alamy

positions, however, a growing number of companies are opting to look on professional networking sites such as LinkedIn, Sales Gravy, or Mashable, or to hire a recruiter because the job boards generate many unqualified leads that are overwhelming to process. Many companies accept applications and may post job openings at their corporate websites. When it is worthwhile to pay an outside organization to narrow down the pool of applicants, employers may turn to employment agencies or, for important management positions, an executive search firm. Campus recruiting can be helpful for companies looking for applicants who have up-to-date training and innovative ideas. However, companies that rely heavily on campus recruiting and employee referrals have to take extra care to ensure that these methods do not discriminate by generating pools of applicants who are, say, mostly women or primarily white.[14]

Most companies use some combination of the methods we have been discussing, depending on the particular job or situation. For example, they might use internal recruiting for existing jobs that need replacements and external recruiting when the firm is expanding or needs to acquire some new skill.

Selection

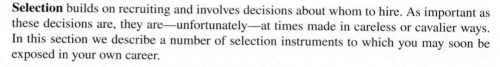

Selection builds on recruiting and involves decisions about whom to hire. As important as these decisions are, they are—unfortunately—at times made in careless or cavalier ways. In this section we describe a number of selection instruments to which you may soon be exposed in your own career.

selection

Choosing from among qualified applicants to hire into an organization.

Applications and Résumés
Application blanks and résumés provide basic information to prospective employers. To make a first cut through candidates, employers review the profiles and backgrounds of various job applicants. Applications and résumés typically include information about the applicant's name, educational background, citizenship, work experiences, certifications, and the like. Their appearance and accuracy also say something about the applicant—spelling mistakes, for example, are almost always immediately disqualifying (something to keep in mind when preparing your own). Although providing important information, applications and résumés tend not to be extremely useful for making final selection decisions.

Interviews
The most popular selection tool is interviewing, and every company uses some type of interview. However, employment interviewers must be careful about what they ask and how they ask it. As we will explain later in the chapter, federal law requires employers to avoid discriminating against people based on criteria such as sex and race; questions that distinguish candidates according to protected categories may be seen as evidence of discrimination.

In an unstructured (or nondirective) interview, the interviewer asks different interviewees different questions. The interviewer may also use probes—that is, ask follow-up questions to learn more about the candidate.[15]

structured interview

Selection technique that involves asking all applicants the same questions and comparing their responses to a standardized set of answers.

In a **structured interview,** the interviewer conducts the same interview with each applicant. There are two basic types of structured interview. The first approach—called the *situational interview*—focuses on hypothetical situations. Zale Corporation, a major jewelry chain, uses this type of structured interview to select sales clerks. Here is a sample question: "A customer comes into the store to pick up a watch he had left for repair. The watch is not back yet from the repair shop, and the customer becomes angry. How would you handle the situation?" An answer that says "I would refer the customer to my supervisor" might suggest that the applicant felt incapable of handling the situation on his or her own. The second approach—called the *behavioral description interview*—explores what candidates have actually done in the past. In selecting wait staff, a hiring manager at a restaurant might ask how candidates have handled demanding or upset customers in a previous job.[16] Because behavioral questions are based on real events, they often provide useful information about how the candidate will actually perform on the job.

Each of these interview techniques offers a manager different advantages and disadvantages, and many interviewers use more than one technique during the same interview. Unstructured interviews can help establish rapport and provide a sense of the applicant's personality, but they may not provide the manager with specific information about the candidate's ability. Structured interviews tend to be more reliable predictors of job performance because they are based on the job analysis that has been done for the position. They are also more likely to be free of bias and stereotypes. And because the same questions are being asked of all candidates for the job, an interview that is at least partially structured allows the manager to compare responses across different candidates.[17]

During an interview, employers may opt to hold unstructured interviews, where they ask each potential employee different questions, or they may choose to hold structured interviews where the employer asks all potential employees the same questions.

© Chris Ryan/Getty Images

Reference Checks   Résumés, applications, and interviews rely on the honesty of the applicant. To make an accurate selection decision, employers have to be able to trust the words of each candidate. Unfortunately, some candidates may hide criminal backgrounds that could pose a risk to the employer or exaggerate their qualifications. In a highly publicized incident, the dean of admissions at the Massachusetts Institute

> Many interviewers use more than one technique during the same interview.

of Technology resigned after nearly three decades on the job because the school learned that she had provided false information about her educational background.[18] Although she had certainly demonstrated an ability to perform the job functions, she could no longer claim the level of integrity required by that position. This is not an isolated incident. Scott Thompson was removed as CEO of Yahoo! after it was discovered that he listed a nonexistent computer science degree on his résumé.[19] Once lost, a reputation is hard to regain.

Because these and more ambiguous ethical gray areas arise, employers supplement candidate-provided information with other screening devices, including reference checks. Virtually all organizations contact references or former employers and educational institutions listed by candidates. Although checking references makes sense, reference information is becoming increasingly difficult to obtain because individuals have won costly lawsuits against former employers who spoke negatively about them. Nevertheless, HR experts encourage prospective employers to make a practice of checking references.[20] One reason is that it does occasionally raise a red flag: past employers will usually just verify dates of employment, job title, and sometimes pay, but sometimes they will advise caution when asked if the candidate is hirable. Checking references also provides a defense for an employer in the event that one of its employees causes harm. It demonstrates that the company was diligent about making the decision to hire that person.

Background Checks   For a higher level of scrutiny, background investigations also have become standard procedure for many companies. Some state courts have ruled that companies can be held liable for negligent hiring if they fail to do adequate background checks. The different types of checks include Social Security verification, past employment and education verification, and a criminal records check. A number of other checks can be conducted if they pertain to the job being hired for, including a motor vehicle record check (for jobs involving driving) and a credit check (for money-handling jobs).

EXHIBIT 10.2
Online Tools Used to
Screen Job Applicants

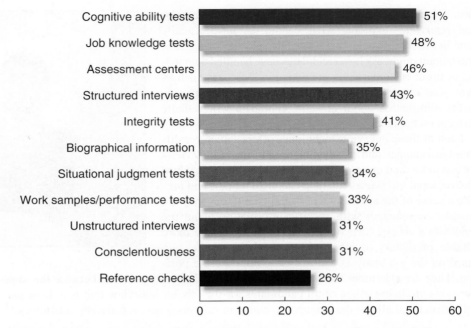

SOURCE: http://answers.mheducation.com/management/human-resource-management/personnel-selection.

Internet tools have made basic background checks fast and easy to perform. Recent surveys of hiring managers found that roughly half are using social networking sites, especially Facebook and LinkedIn, to learn about job candidates; some prospective employers even ask candidates for user names and passwords.[21] Many companies have chosen not to extend job offers to candidates based on content they have found online. Internet users are advised to remember that anything that carries their name online may become information for potential employers, even years down the road.

Exhibit 10.2 shows which screening tools are used most often.

Personality Tests   The popularity of using tests to measure candidates' personalities has risen and fallen, but it currently seems to be on the upswing.[22] Companies that use personality tests include Alton Lane, Lowe's, and Xerox.[23] Concerns that have discouraged the use of personality tests include the possibility they might be seen as discriminatory or might not accurately predict job performance—perhaps because candidates will cheat by trying to guess the right answers or even retaking the test with different answers later if they fail the first screening. However, tests can be constructed using past performance data to find associations between traits and job performance. Some personality types have been associated with greater job satisfaction and performance, especially in situations in which the organization can build groups of people with similar positive traits.[24]

A number of well-known inventories measure personality traits such as conscientiousness, extraversion, sociability, adjustment, and energy. Typical questions are "Do you like to socialize with people?" and "Do you enjoy working hard?" Some personality tests try to determine the type of working conditions that the candidate prefers, to see whether he or she would be motivated and productive in the particular job. For example, if the candidate prefers making decisions on his or her own but the job requires gaining the cooperation of others, another candidate might be a better fit. Today many personality tests are taken online rather than with paper and pencil. These online tests can be constructed to deliver certain questions based on answers to preceding questions, so that the test is tailored to the individual test taker.

Drug Testing   Drug testing is now a frequently used screening instrument. Since the passage of the Drug-Free Workplace Act of 1988, applicants and employees of federal contractors and Department of Defense contractors and those under Department of Transportation regulations have been subject to testing for illegal drugs. To avoid discrimination against individuals with disabilities, companies typically wait to conduct drug testing until after they have made a conditional job offer. According to statistics from the federal government, about one in four full-time employees is tested when hired, and almost one in three is subject to random drug tests once they have started working.[25]

Drug testing has become more complicated for employers in the growing number of states that have legalized the use of marijuana for medical purposes or recreational use.[26] Companies that fire a worker for failing a drug test because of medical marijuana use worry that they could be found guilty of discriminating against a disabled person. For many jobs, however, it is also critical that workers not be under the influence of any substance, legal or illegal. So far, most state medical marijuana laws do not include employment protections for workers, but because these developments are new and the laws vary from state to state, employers are in a legal gray area for the time being.

Cognitive Ability Tests   Among the oldest employment selection devices are cognitive ability tests. These tests measure a range of intellectual abilities, including verbal comprehension (vocabulary, reading) and numerical aptitude (mathematical calculations). About 20 percent of U.S. companies use cognitive ability tests for selection purposes.[27]

Performance Tests   In a performance test, the test taker performs a sample of the job. Most companies use some type of performance test, typically for administrative assistant and clerical positions. The most widely used performance test is the typing test. However, performance tests have been developed for almost every occupation, including managerial positions. Assessment centers are the most notable offshoot of the managerial performance test.[28]

Assessment centers originated during World War II. A typical **assessment center** consists of 10 to 12 candidates who participate in a variety of exercises or situations; some of the exercises involve group interactions, and others are performed individually. Each exercise taps a number of critical managerial dimensions, such as leadership, decision-making skills, and communication ability. Assessors, generally line managers from the organization, observe and record information about the candidates' performance in each exercise. The first organization to use assessment centers was AT&T. Since then, a number of large organizations have used or currently are using the assessment center technique, including the FBI, Ford Motors, and Sears.

assessment center

A managerial performance test in which candidates participate in a variety of exercises and situations.

Integrity Tests   To assess job candidates' honesty, employers may administer integrity tests. Two forms of integrity tests are polygraphs and paper-and-pencil honesty tests. Polygraphs, or lie detector tests, have been banned for most employment purposes.[29] Paper-and-pencil honesty tests are more recent instruments for measuring integrity. These tests include questions such as whether a person has ever thought about stealing and whether he or she believes other people steal ("What percentage of people take more than $1 from their employer?"). Although companies, including Payless ShoeSource, reported that losses due to theft declined following the introduction of integrity tests, the accuracy of these tests is still debatable.[30]

Reliability and Validity   Regardless of the method used to select employees, two crucial issues that need to be addressed are a test's reliability and its validity. **Reliability** refers to the consistency of test scores over time and across alternative measurements. For example, if three interviewers talked to the same job candidate but drew very different conclusions about the candidate's abilities, we might suspect that there were problems with the reliability of the interview questions or procedures.

Validity moves beyond reliability to assess the accuracy of the selection test. The most common form of validity, *criterion-related validity*, refers to the degree to which a test

reliability

The consistency of test scores over time and across alternative measurements.

validity

The degree to which a selection test predicts or correlates with job performance.

actually predicts or correlates with job performance. Questions about validity are one reason (along with ethical and public policy concerns) employers were recently criticized for making current employment a requirement for being hired. At a time when unemployment rates were high and employers were flooded with applications, some companies were screening out people based on their unemployed status. Critics of this practice doubted that being jobless during a recession was highly correlated with poor performance.[31] In general, validity is usually established through studies comparing test performance and job performance for a large enough sample of employees to enable a fair conclusion to be reached.

Another form of validity, *content validity,* concerns the degree to which selection tests measure a representative sample of the knowledge, skills, and abilities required for the job. The best-known example of a content-valid test is a keyboarding test (which measures proficiency in word processing, spreadsheets, and so forth) for administrative assistants, because keyboarding is a task a person in that position almost always performs. However, to be completely content-valid, the selection process also should measure other skills the assistant would be likely to perform, such as answering the telephone, copying and collating documents, and dealing with customers. Content validity is more subjective (less statistical) than evaluations of criterion-related validity but is no less important, particularly when one is defending employment decisions in court.

Workforce Reductions

Unfortunately, staffing decisions do not simply focus on hiring employees. As organizations evolve and markets change, the demand for certain employees rises and falls. Also, some employees simply do not perform at a level required to justify continued employment. For these reasons, managers sometimes must make difficult decisions to terminate their employment.

Layoffs   As a result of the massive restructuring of American industry brought about by mergers and acquisitions, divestiture, and increased competition, many organizations have been downsizing—laying off large numbers of managerial and other employees. Over the past two decades, IBM, Citigroup, and Sears Roebuck have laid off a combined 160,000 employees.[32] As mentioned in Chapter 9, dismissing any employee is tough, but when a company lays off a substantial portion of its workforce, the results can rock the foundations of the organization.[33] The victims of restructuring face all the difficulties of being let go—loss of self-esteem, demoralizing job searches, and the stigma of being out of work. To some extent, employers can help employees with these problems by offering **outplacement,** the process of helping people who have been dismissed from the company regain employment elsewhere. Even then, the impact of layoffs goes further than the employees who leave. For many of the employees who remain with the company, disenchantment, distrust, and lethargy overshadow the comfort of still having a job. In many respects, how management deals with dismissals will affect the productivity and satisfaction of those who remain. A well-thought-out dismissal process eases tensions and helps remaining employees adjust to the new work situation.

Organizations with strong performance evaluation systems benefit because the survivors are less likely to believe the decision was arbitrary. In addition, if care is taken during the actual layoff process—that is, if workers are offered severance pay and help in finding a new job—remaining workers will be comforted. Companies also should avoid stringing out layoffs by dismissing a few workers at a time.

Termination   People sometimes get fired for poor performance or other reasons. Should an employer have the right to fire a worker? In 1884, a Tennessee court ruled, "All may dismiss their employee(s) at will for good cause, for no cause, or even for cause morally wrong." The concept that an employee may be fired for any reason is known as **employment-at-will** or *termination-at-will* and was upheld in a 1908 Supreme Court

outplacement

The process of helping people who have been dismissed from the company regain employment elsewhere.

employment-at-will

The legal concept that an employee may be terminated for any reason.

ruling.[34] The logic is that if the employee may quit at any time, the employer is free to dismiss at any time.

Since the mid-1970s, courts in most states have made exceptions to this doctrine. Under the public policy exception (i.e., a ruling designed to protect the public from harm), employees cannot be fired for such actions as refusing to break the law, taking time off for jury duty, or whistleblowing to report illegal company behavior. For example, if a worker reports an environmental violation to a regulatory agency and the company fires him or her, the courts may argue that the firing was unfair because the employee acted for the good of the community. Union contracts that limit an employer's ability to fire without cause are another major exception to the employment-at-will doctrine.

> How management deals with dismissals will affect the productivity and satisfaction of those who remain.

Employers can avoid the pitfalls associated with dismissal by developing progressive and positive disciplinary procedures.[35] By *progressive,* we mean that a manager takes graduated steps in attempting to correct a workplace behavior. For example, an employee who has been absent receives a verbal reprimand for the first offense. A second offense invokes a written reprimand. A third offense results in employee counseling and probation, and a fourth results in a paid leave day to think over the consequences of future rule infractions. The employer is signaling to the employee that this is the last straw. Arbitrators are more likely to side with an employer that fires someone when they believe the company has made sincere efforts to help the person correct his or her behavior.

The **termination interview,** in which the manager discusses the company's position with the employee, is a stressful situation for both parties. Most experts believe that the immediate superior should be the one to deliver the bad news to employees. However, it is a wise precaution to have a third party, such as an HR manager, present to provide guidance and take notes on the meeting. Because announcing a termination is likely to upset the employee and occasionally leads to a lawsuit, the manager should prepare carefully. Preparation should include knowing all the facts of the situation and reviewing any documents to make sure they are consistent with the reason for the termination. During the termination interview, ethics and common sense dictate that the manager should be truthful but respectful, stating the facts and avoiding arguments.[36] Exhibit 10.3 provides some other guidelines for conducting a termination interview.

termination interview

A discussion between a manager and an employee about the employee's dismissal.

Legal Issues and Equal Employment Opportunity   Many laws have been passed governing employment decisions and practices. They will directly affect a good part of your day-to-day work as a manager as well as the human resource function of your organization. Most of these laws are designed to protect job candidates and employees against discrimination or sexual harassment and to establish standards of pay and hours worked for certain classes of employee. For example, the 1938 *Fair Labor Standards Act (FLSA),* among other provisions, creates two employee categories: exempt and nonexempt. Employees are normally exempt from overtime pay if they have considerable discretion in how they carry out their jobs and if their jobs require them to exercise independent judgment. Managers usually fall in this category. Nonexempt employees are usually paid by the hour and must be paid overtime if they work more than 40 hours in a week. As a manager, you will almost certainly need to specify the exempt or nonexempt status of anyone you hire.

The 1964 *Civil Rights Act* prohibits discrimination in employment based on race, sex, color, national origin, and religion. Title VII of the act specifically forbids discrimination in such employment practices as recruitment, hiring, discharge, promotion, compensation, and access to training.[37] The *Americans with Disabilities Act,* passed in 1990 (amended in 2008), prohibits employment discrimination against people with disabilities. Recovering alcoholics and drug abusers, cancer patients in remission, and

EXHIBIT 10.3
Advice on Termination

Do's	Don'ts
• Make termination the last step in a clear and fair process, being certain you have the facts.	• Don't spring a termination on an employee as a total surprise.
• Be sure the person terminating the employee is the employee's direct supervisor.	• Don't start a meeting unprepared, causing the terminated employee to wait awkwardly while you find answers or call in an HR representative.
• Be prepared with answers to basic questions such as the official end date and any severance benefits.	• Don't beat around the bush; state the termination simply and briefly.
• Consult with the human resource department to identify any benefits available; give the employee a written list of information about benefits and policies.	• Don't get caught up in responding to the employee's emotions or views about fairness; focus on practical realities—the need to move on.
• Invite a trained HR representative to attend the meeting.	• Don't argue with the employee or apologize.
• Listen respectfully.	• Don't offer to help the employee find another job, assuming you cannot honestly give a glowing reference.

SOURCES: Ron Ashkenas, "If You Have to Fire an Employee—Here's How to Do It Right," *Forbes*, March 11, 2013, http://www.forbes.com; Jeff Haden, "The Best Way to Fire an Employee," *Inc.*, March 19, 2012, http://www.inc.com; Melissa Korn, "The Best Ways to Fire Somebody," *The Wall Street Journal*, October 26, 2012, http://online.wsj.com.

AIDS patients are covered by this legislation. The 1991 *Civil Rights Act* strengthened all these protections and permitted punitive damages to be imposed on companies that violate them.

Failure to comply with any of these laws may expose the organization to charges of unfair practices, expensive lawsuits, and civil and even criminal penalties in some cases. For example, Bank of America was recently fined $2.2 million for discriminating against African American job candidates over a 20-year period.[38] In another case, AutoZone was hit with a $185 million punitive award for gender and pregnancy discrimination.[39]

adverse impact

When a seemingly neutral employment practice has a disproportionately negative effect on a protected group.

One common reason employers are sued is **adverse impact**—when a seemingly neutral employment practice has a disproportionately negative effect on a group protected by the Civil Rights Act.[40] For example, if equal numbers of qualified men and women apply for jobs but a particular employment test results in far fewer women being hired, the test may be considered to cause an adverse impact and, therefore, be subject to challenge on that basis.

Because of the importance of these issues, many companies have established procedures to ensure compliance with labor and equal opportunity laws. For example, companies frequently monitor and compare salaries by race, gender, length of service, and other categories to make sure employees across all groups are being fairly paid. Written policies, when implemented and followed, can also help ensure fair and legal practices in the workplace. In this sense, smart and effective management practices not only help managers motivate employees to do their best work but often help provide legal protection as well. For example, managers who provide their employees with regular, specific evaluations can often prevent misunderstandings that can lead to lawsuits. And a written record of those evaluations is often useful in demonstrating fair and objective treatment.

Many other important staffing laws affect employment practices. For example, the *Age Discrimination in Employment Act* of 1967 and its amendments in 1978 and 1986 prohibit discrimination against people age 40 and over. One reason for this legislation was

EXHIBIT 10.4   U.S. Equal Employment Laws

Act	Major Provisions	Enforcement and Remedies
Fair Labor Standards Act (1938)	Creates exempt (salaried) and nonexempt (hourly) employee categories, governing overtime and other rules; sets minimum wage, child labor laws.	Enforced by Department of Labor, private action to recover lost wages; civil and criminal penalties also possible.
Equal Pay Act (1963)	Prohibits gender-based pay discrimination between two jobs substantially similar in skill, effort, responsibility, and working conditions.	Fines up to $10,000, imprisonment up to 6 months, or both; enforced by Equal Employment Opportunity Commission (EEOC); private actions for double damages up to 3 years' wages, liquidated damages, reinstatement, or promotion.
Title VII of Civil Rights Act (1964)	Prohibits discrimination based on race, sex, color, religion, or national origin in employment decisions: hiring, pay, working conditions, promotion, discipline, or discharge.	Enforced by EEOC; private actions, back pay, front pay, reinstatement, restoration of seniority and pension benefits, attorneys' fees and costs.
Executive Orders 11246 and 11375 (1965)	Requires equal opportunity clauses in federal contracts; prohibits employment discrimination by federal contractors based on race, color, religion, sex, or national origin.	Established Office of Federal Contract Compliance Programs (OFCCP) to investigate violations; empowered to terminate violator's federal contracts.
Age Discrimination in Employment Act (1967)	Prohibits employment discrimination based on age for persons over 40 years; restricts mandatory retirement.	EEOC enforcement; private actions for reinstatement, back pay, front pay, restoration of seniority and pension benefits; double unpaid wages for willful violations; attorneys' fees and costs.
Vocational Rehabilitation Act (1973)	Requires affirmative action by all federal contractors for persons with disabilities; defines disabilities as physical or mental impairments that substantially limit life activities.	Federal contractors must consider hiring disabled persons capable of performance after reasonable accommodations.
Americans with Disabilities Act Amendments Act (2008)	Extends affirmative action provisions of Vocational Rehabilitation Act to private employers; requires workplace modifications to facilitate disabled employees; prohibits discrimination against disabled.	EEOC enforcement; private actions for Title VII remedies.
Civil Rights Act (1991)	Clarifies Title VII requirements: disparate treatment impact suits, business necessity, job relatedness; shifts burden of proof to employer; permits punitive damages and jury trials.	Punitive damages limited to sliding scale only in intentional discrimination based on sex, religion, and disabilities.
Family and Medical Leave Act (1991)	Requires 12 weeks' unpaid leave for medical or family needs: paternity, family member illness.	Private actions for lost wages and other expenses, reinstatement.

the common practice of dismissing older workers to replace them with younger workers who were not as highly paid. The *Worker Adjustment and Retraining Notification Act* of 1989, commonly known as the *WARN Act* or *Plant Closing Bill,* requires covered employers to give affected employees 60 days' written notice of plant closings or mass layoffs. Exhibit 10.4 summarizes many of these major employment laws.

Developing the Workforce

LO 4

Bottom Line

Training improves employee quality.

How might you measure quality improvements from training salespeople?

Q

Today's competitive environment requires managers to upgrade the skills and performance of employees continually—and their own. Such constant improvement increases both personal and organizational effectiveness. It makes organization members more useful in their current jobs and prepares them to take on new responsibilities. And it helps the organization as a whole handle new challenges and take advantage of new methods and technologies that emerge. Developing the workforce in this way involves training and development activities. It also involves appraising employees' performance and giving them effective feedback so they will be motivated to perform at their best. We will discuss each of these activities in turn.

Training and Development

Cold Stone Creamery spends a portion of its training budget in developing computerized simulations to show how employee actions affect store performance. The company uses computer games because they are familiar and attractive to its young employees.

© Corey Lowenstein/Raleigh News & Observer/MCT via Getty Images

---

training

Teaching lower-level employees how to perform their present jobs.

---

development

Helping managers and professional employees learn the broad skills needed for their present and future jobs.

---

needs assessment

An analysis identifying the jobs, people, and departments for which training is necessary.

U.S. businesses spend more than $164 billion annually to provide their employees with formal training. The greatest share of that spending goes to training that the organization itself delivers to its employees. The remainder is spent on training by outsiders, including payments for training companies and tuition reimbursement.[41]

Fortune 500 companies such as General Electric and Procter & Gamble have invested heavily in training. IBM's annual training costs have at times exceeded Harvard University's annual operating expenses. But competitive pressures require companies to consider the most efficient training methods. That means traditional classroom settings are often giving way to computerized methods.

The average amount spent per employee on training is around $1,200, which has remained flat over the past several years.[42] This lack of commitment is a great concern because today's jobs require more education, but the education level of U.S. workers has not kept pace. What's more, companies need to ensure that employees who have survived layoffs can lead their organizations through tough times.

Overview of the Training Process   Although we use the general term *training* here, training sometimes is distinguished from development. **Training** usually refers to teaching lower-level employees how to perform their present jobs, whereas **development** involves teaching managers and professional employees broader skills needed for their present and future jobs.

Phase one of training usually starts with a **needs assessment.** Managers conduct an analysis to identify the jobs, people, and departments for which training is necessary. Job analysis and performance measurements are useful for this purpose.

Phase two involves the design of training programs. Based on needs assessment, training objectives and content can be established. For example, in support of Verizon's corporate goals for operational excellence, the company's learning and development team set a goal to make the sales support team "an industry-leading technical sales support team capable of selling/supporting complex solutions" for Verizon's business customers. The team would do this by developing and presenting a training program in which the employees earn a Data Solutions Certification by mastering 11 competencies—technical skills needed for selling data solutions to businesses.[43]

Phase three involves decisions about the training methods to be used and whether the training will be provided on or off the job. Common training methods include lectures, role-playing, business simulation, behavior modeling (watching a video and imitating what is observed), conferences, vestibule training (practicing in a simulated job environment), and apprenticeships. The method should be well suited to the objectives defined in phase two. Verizon sales support employees earning a Data Solutions Certificate participated in 45 hours of technical training presented through a combination of instructor-led training (both in classrooms and virtually, over the Internet) and online training, and they prepared a sales presentation, which they presented to management. Besides this, the employees had to meet or exceed their sales quota for the period.[44] As shown in Exhibit 10.5, a major share of training is conducted electronically (for example, with online videos, games, and quizzes). Computer-based training is easy and inexpensive to deliver, can be provided anywhere an employee has access to a computer, and can be tailored to a trainee's responses. Well-designed computer training also can get trainees highly involved in learning. A study found that trainees learned better from an interactive video game than they did from other forms of instruction.[45] Another popular training method is job rotation, by which employees are assigned to different jobs in the organization to broaden their experience and improve their skills. It is frequently applied to managers as well as lower-level employees. In fact, smart managers often request assignment to jobs where they can be challenged and their skills broadened.

Finally, *phase four* of training should evaluate the program's effectiveness. Measures of effectiveness include employee reactions (surveys), learning (tests), improved behavior on the job, and bottom-line results (e.g., an increase in sales or reduction in defect rates following the training program).

Types of Training   Companies invest in training to enhance individual performance and organizational productivity. Programs to improve an employee's computer, technical, or communication skills are quite common, and some types of training have become fairly standard across many organizations. **Orientation training** is typically used to familiarize new employees with their new jobs, work units, and the organization in general. Done well, orientation training has a number of benefits, including lower employee turnover, increased morale, better productivity, and lower recruiting and training costs. The need for soft skills training, especially among early career employees, is discussed in the nearby "Multiple Generations at Work" box.

Team training has taken on more importance as organizations reorganize to facilitate individuals working together. Team training teaches employees the skills they need to work together and facilitates their interaction. After General Mills acquired Pillsbury, it used a team training program called Brand Champions to combine the marketing expertise of the two companies and share knowledge among employees handling various functions such as sales and research and development. Most of the time, trainees engaged in team exercises to analyze brands, target customers, and develop marketing messages.[46]

orientation training

Training designed to introduce new employees to the company and familiarize them with policies, procedures, culture, and the like.

team training

Training that provides employees with the skills and perspectives they need to collaborate with others.

EXHIBIT 10.5
Training Delivery Methods: Percentage of Total Hours

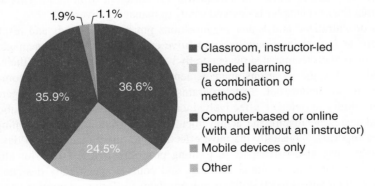

1.9%   1.1%

36.6%

35.9%

24.5%

■ Classroom, instructor-led

■ Blended learning (a combination of methods)

■ Computer-based or online (with and without an instructor)

■ Mobile devices only

■ Other

SOURCE: Based on data from "2014 Training Industry Report," *Training*, November/December 2014, *Training Magazine*, http://www.trainingmag.com.

Multiple Generations at Work

Developing Soft Skills Will Help College Students' Career Prospects

A recent study suggests that many college students expect their newly acquired hard skills, like the ability to design a website, develop a recruiting plan, or use the latest accounting software, to be enough to achieve success with employers. While these tangible skills are very important, two-thirds of respondents (corporate recruiters, business leaders, college students, and so forth) in the study believe that hard and soft skills are equally important for success in the workplace.

As illustrated below, business leaders ranked integrity, professionalism, and positive attitude as the top three attributes desired in new hires. Strong oral communication and teamwork skills were also important to the respondents.

College students can take steps to acquire or refine their soft skills. For example, internships can provide them with exposure to professional organizational settings. Also, individuals can join student organizations and leadership groups, or attend functions from their universities' career services division, such as career fairs, etiquette dinners, and dress for success seminars. Students who display excellent soft skills, combined with the requisite hard skills, will increase their chances of having promising careers.[46]

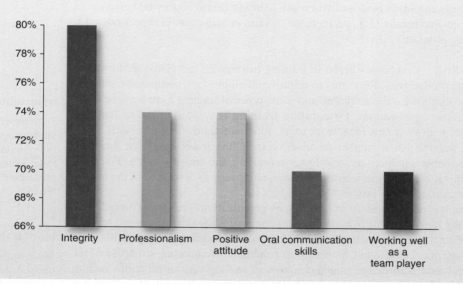

diversity training

Programs that focus on identifying and reducing hidden biases against people with differences and developing the skills needed to manage a diversified workforce.

Diversity training focuses on building awareness of diversity issues and providing the skills employees need to work with others who are different from them. This topic is so important that the next chapter is devoted solely to managing diversity.

Today's decentralized and leaner organizations put more demands and responsibility on managers, as has an increasingly competitive environment. And as managers rise in the organization, their technical skills generally become less important than their ability to motivate others. For these reasons, management training programs have become another widely used development tool. Such programs often seek to improve managers' people skills—their ability to delegate effectively, increase the motivation of their subordinates, and communicate and inspire the achievement of organization goals. Coaching—being trained by a superior—is usually the most effective and direct management development tool. Managers may also participate in training programs that are used for all employees, such as job rotation, or attend seminars and courses specifically designed to help them improve their supervisory skills or prepare them for future promotion. As you read "Management in Action: Progress Report," consider how Google's management training and coaching complement its methods for hiring.

Management in Action

HOW GOOGLE HIRES AND TRAINS

The Google search engine provides a model for how the company has successfully grown and continued attracting the best talent. Much as the search engine sorts through vast amounts of data to deliver the most relevant information, its human resource strategy involves analyzing data about employees and the impact of how they are managed.

In terms of hiring, Google's strategy is to position the company as a highly attractive place to work, receive a flood of applications, and make collaborative decisions about which applicants will fit best with Google's demanding and creative culture. In the tight labor market for experts in computer programming and online marketing, even a popular employer such as Google must recruit actively. Google has expanded its recruiting on college campuses and offers generously paid summer internships. It hosts regular open houses, provides speakers about its projects, and posts information about Google jobs on YouTube, blogs, and Twitter feeds.

The selection process is famously demanding and occasionally quirky. Candidates interview with several Google employees. The interviewers compile an extensive file of information to use in making a group decision, a process aimed at avoiding selection of candidates that merely resemble the interviewer. What does Google look for when hiring candidates? According to Laszlo Bock, Chief People Officer, it boils down to the following attributes: (1) ability to learn and apply knowledge to solve problems;

(2) willingness to lead and follow others; (3) humility when faced with new or opposing information; and (4) desire to take ownership and defend ideas. In the past, a candidate might undergo a dozen interviews or more; data showed that interviews beyond four provide little value, so five is now the maximum number.

With regard to training, data-driven decisions match topics to particular employees for whom the training will deliver meaningful results. For management training, Laszlo Bock's People Operations group studied data from employee surveys, managers' performance appraisals, and nominations for best-manager awards. They identified eight management behaviors associated with success in leading teams and retaining employees. They developed training programs for each behavior, and they recommend programs to individual managers based on each manager's performance. Management training courses also are recommended based on data showing the skills that are relevant in particular functions or at particular stages of a manager's career. Formal training sessions are backed up with customized reminders and recommendations related to events in the manager's department.[48]

- Discuss why you think Google wants to hire people who possess the four attributes mentioned above.
- How could Google's approach to management training address the training needs of its nonmanagement employees?

Performance Appraisal

One of the most important responsibilities you will have as a manager is **performance appraisal (PA),** the assessment of an employee's job performance. Done well, it can help employees improve their performance, pay, and chances for promotion; foster communication between managers and employees; and increase the employees' and the organization's effectiveness. Done poorly, it actually can have a negative effect—it can cause resentment, reduce motivation, diminish performance, and even expose the organization to legal action.

Performance appraisal has two basic purposes. First, appraisal serves an administrative purpose. It provides managers with the information they need to make salary, promotion, and dismissal decisions; helps employees understand and accept the basis of those decisions; and, if necessary, provides documentation that can justify those decisions in court. Second, and at least as important, appraisal serves a developmental purpose. The information gathered in the appraisal can be used to identify and plan the additional training, learning, experience, or other improvement employees require. In addition, the

LO 5

performance appraisal (PA)

Assessment of an employee's job performance.

manager's feedback and coaching based on the appraisal help employees improve their day-to-day performance and can help prepare them for greater responsibilities in the future.

What Do You Appraise?

Performance appraisals can assess three basic categories of employee performance: traits, behaviors, and results. Trait appraisals involve subjective judgments about employee characteristics related to performance. They contain dimensions such as initiative, leadership, and attitude, and they ask raters to indicate how much of each trait an employee possesses. Usually the manager will use a numerical ratings scale to specify the extent to which an employee possesses the particular traits being measured. For example, if the measured trait is attitude, the employee might be rated anywhere from 1 (very negative attitude) to 5 (very positive attitude). Trait scales are quite common because they are simple to use and provide a standard measure for all employees. But they are often not valid as performance measures. Because they tend to be ambiguous as well as highly subjective—does the employee really have a bad attitude, or is he or she just shy?—they often lead to personal bias and may not be suitable for providing useful feedback.

Behavioral appraisals, although still subjective, focus more on observable aspects of performance. They were developed in response to the problems of trait appraisals. These scales focus on specific, prescribed behaviors that can help ensure that all parties understand what the ratings are really measuring. Because they are less ambiguous, they also can help provide useful feedback. Exhibit 10.6 contains an example of a behaviorally anchored rating scale (BARS) for evaluating quality.

Another common behaviorally focused approach is the critical incident technique. In this technique, the manager keeps a regular log and records each significant behavior by

EXHIBIT 10.6
Example of BARS Used for Evaluating Quality

Performance dimension: total quality management. This area of performance concerns the extent to which a person is aware of, endorses, and develops proactive procedures to enhance product quality, ensure early disclosure of discrepancies, and integrate quality assessments with cost and schedule performance measurement reports to maximize clients' satisfaction with overall performance.

OUTSTANDING	7	Uses measures of quality and well-defined processes to achieve project goals. Defines quality from the client's perspective.
	6	Looks for/identifies ways to continually improve the process.
	5	Clearly communicates quality management to others. Develops a plan that defines how the team will participate in quality.
		Appreciates TQM as an investment.
AVERAGE	4	Has measures of quality that define tolerance levels.
	3	Views quality as costly. Legislates quality.
	2	Focuses his/her concerns only on outputs and deliverables, ignoring the underlying processes.
POOR	1	Blames others for absence of quality. Gives lip service only to quality concerns.

SOURCE: Landy, Jacobs, and Associates. Used with permission.

the subordinate that reflects the quality of his or her performance. ("Juanita impressed the client with her effective presentation today." "Joe was late with his report.") This approach can be subjective as well as time-consuming, and it may give some employees the feeling that everything they do is being recorded. But it does have the advantage of reminding managers in advance of a performance review what the employee actually did.

Results appraisals tend to be more objective and can focus on production data such as sales volume (for a salesperson), units produced (for a line worker), or profits (for a manager). One approach to results appraisals—called **management by objectives (MBO)**—involves a subordinate and a supervisor agreeing in advance on specific performance goals (objectives). They then develop a plan that describes the time frame and criteria for determining whether the objectives have been reached. The aim is to agree on a set of objectives that are clear, specific, and reachable. For example, an objective for a salesperson might be "Increase sales by 25 percent during the following year."

MBO has several important advantages. First, it avoids the biases and measurement difficulties of trait and behavioral appraisals. At the end of the review period, the employee either has or has not achieved the specified objective. The employee is judged on actual job performance. Second, because the employee and manager have agreed on the objective at the outset, the employee is likely to be more committed to the outcome, and there is less chance for misunderstanding. Third, because the employee is directly responsible for achieving the objective, MBO can be useful when managers want to empower employees to adapt their behavior to achieve the desired results. But the approach has disadvantages as well. It can result in unrealistic objectives being set, frustrating the employee and the manager. The objectives can also be too rigid, leaving the employee with insufficient flexibility should circumstances change. Finally, MBO often focuses too much on short-term achievement at the expense of long-term goals.

None of these performance appraisal systems is easy to conduct properly, and all have drawbacks that must be guarded against. In choosing an appraisal method, the following guidelines may prove helpful:

1. Base performance standards on job analysis.
2. Communicate performance standards to employees.
3. Evaluate employees on specific performance-related behaviors rather than on a single global or overall measure.
4. Document the PA process carefully.
5. If possible, use more than one rater (discussed in the next section).
6. Develop a formal appeal process.
7. Always take legal considerations into account.[49]

Who Should Do the Appraisal?

Just as multiple methods can be used to gather performance appraisal information, several sources can provide PA information. Managers and supervisors are the traditional source of appraisal information because they are often in the best position to observe an employee's performance. However, companies are also turning to peers and team members to provide input to the performance appraisal. Peers and team members often see different dimensions of performance and are often best at identifying leadership potential and interpersonal skills.

One increasingly popular source of appraisal is a person's subordinates. Appraisal by subordinates has been used by companies such as Xerox and IBM to give superiors feedback on how their employees view them. Often this information is given in confidence to the manager and not shared with superiors. Even so, this approach can make managers uncomfortable initially, but the feedback they get is often extremely useful and can help them significantly improve their management style. Because this process gives employees power over their bosses, it is generally used for development purposes only, not for salary or promotion decisions.

management by objectives (MBO)

A process in which objectives set by a subordinate and a supervisor must be reached within a given time period.

Internal and external customers also are used as sources of performance appraisal information, particularly for companies, such as Ford and Honda, that are focused on total quality management. External customers have been used for some time to appraise restaurant employees, but internal customers can include anyone inside the organization who depends on an employee's work output. Finally, it is usually a good idea for employees to evaluate their own performance. Although self-appraisals may be biased upward, the process of self-evaluation helps increase the employee's involvement in the review process and is a starting point for establishing future goals.

Because each source of PA information has some limitations, and because different people may see different aspects of performance, Shell, PepsiCo, and many other companies have used approaches that involve more than one source for appraisal information. In a process known as **360-degree appraisal,** feedback is obtained from subordinates, peers, and superiors—every level involved with the employee.[50] Often the person being rated can select the appraisers, subject to a manager's approval, with the understanding that the individual appraisals are kept confidential; returned forms might not include the name of the appraiser, for example, and the results may be consolidated for each level.

The 360-degree appraisal offers many advantages. It provides a much fuller picture of the employee's strengths and weaknesses, and it often captures qualities other appraisal methods miss. For example, an employee may have a difficult relationship with his or her supervisor yet be highly regarded by peers and subordinates. The approach can lead to significant improvement, with employees often very motivated to improve their ratings. Improvements in management performance following 360-degree appraisals have been observed in various countries, but cultural differences can affect the impact of this method. Using the cultural measures defined by Geert Hofstede (described in Chapter 6), researchers found that 360-degree appraisals were most effective with managers in cultures that were individualistic and had relatively low power distance.[51] On the downside, employees are often unwilling to rate their colleagues harshly, so a certain uniformity of ratings may result. In addition, the 360-degree appraisal is less useful than more objective criteria, such as financial targets, in measuring performance. Its objective is usually the employee's development, not to provide a basis for administrative decisions such as raises. For those, appraisal methods like MBO are more appropriate.[52]

360-degree appraisal

Process of using multiple sources of appraisal to gain a comprehensive perspective on one's performance.

How Do You Give Employees Feedback?

Appraisals are most effective when they are based on an ongoing relationship with employees and not just a top-down formal judgment issued once a year. Managers of sports teams do not wait until the season is over to perform an appraisal. Instead they work with team members throughout the season, and with the team as a whole, to improve the team's performance. Similarly, in high-functioning organizations informal appraisal and feedback are constantly taking place. Managers discuss the goals of the organization regularly and often to create a shared understanding of the job performance those goals require. They try to create an atmosphere in which they and their employees are working together on a common agenda. And they communicate with their employees on a day-to-day basis, praising or coaching as appropriate and together assessing progress toward goals. When managers and employees have open communication and employees feel fairly and effectively managed, the kind of appraisal they receive should rarely come as a surprise to them.

> In high-functioning organizations, informal appraisal and feedback are constantly taking place.

Giving PA feedback can be a stressful task for both managers and subordinates. The purposes of PA conflict to some degree. Providing growth and development requires understanding and support; however, the manager must be impersonal and be able to make tough decisions. Employees want to know how they are doing, but typically they are uncomfortable about getting feedback. Finally, the organization's need to make HR decisions conflicts with the individual employee's need to

1.	**Summarize** the employee's specific performance. Describe the performance in behavioral or outcome terms, such as sales or absenteeism. Don't say the employee has a poor attitude; rather, explain which employee behaviors indicate a poor attitude.
2.	**Describe** the expectations and standards and be specific.
3.	**Determine** the causes for the low performance; get the employee's input.
4.	**Discuss** solutions to the problem and have the employee play a major role in the process.
5.	**Agree** to a solution. As a supervisor, you have input into the solution. Raise issues and questions but also provide support.
6.	**Agree** to a timetable for improvement.
7.	**Document** the meeting.

EXHIBIT 10.7
Useful PA Interview Format to Use with an Underperforming Employee

maintain a positive image.[53] These conflicts often make a PA interview difficult; therefore, managers should conduct such interviews thoughtfully.

There is no one best way to do a PA interview. In general, appraisal feedback works best when it is specific and constructive—related to clear goals or behaviors and clearly intended to help the employee rather than simply criticize. Managers have an interest not just in rating performance but in raising it, and effective appraisals take that into account. In addition, the appraisal is likely to be more meaningful and satisfying when the manager gives the employee an opportunity to discuss his or her performance and respond to the appraisal.

One of the most difficult interviews takes place with an employee who is performing poorly. Exhibit 10.7 contains a useful PA interview format to use when an employee is performing below acceptable standards.

Follow-up meetings may be needed. Here are some guidelines for giving feedback to an average employee:

1. Summarize the employee's performance and be specific.
2. Explain why the employee's work is important to the organization.
3. Thank the employee for doing the job.
4. Raise any relevant issues, such as areas for improvement.
5. Express confidence in the employee's future good performance.

Bottom Line
Effective feedback raises employee performance. *What kind of feedback is most likely to be effective?*

Designing Reward Systems

Another major set of HRM activities involves reward systems. Most of this section will be devoted to monetary rewards such as pay and fringe benefits. (We discuss other motivational tools in Chapter 13.) Although traditionally pay has been the primary monetary reward considered, in recent years benefits have received increased attention. Benefits currently make up a far greater percentage of the total payroll than they did in past decades.[54] The typical employer today pays about 30 percent of payroll costs in benefits.[55] Throughout most of the past two decades, benefits costs have risen faster than wages and salaries, fueled by the rapidly rising cost of medical care. Accordingly, employers are attempting to reduce benefits costs, even as their value to employees is rising. Benefits are also receiving more management attention because of their increased complexity. Many new types of benefits are now available, and tax laws affect myriad fringe benefits such as health insurance and pension plans.

LO 6

The typical employer today pays about 30 percent of payroll costs in benefits.

Pay Decisions

Reward systems can serve the strategic purposes of attracting, motivating, and retaining people. The wages paid to employees are based on a complex set of forces. Beyond the body of laws governing compensation, a number of basic decisions must be made in choosing the appropriate pay plan. Exhibit 10.8 illustrates some of the factors that influence the wage mix.

Three types of decisions are crucial for designing an effective pay plan: pay level, pay structure, and individual pay.

Pay level refers to the choice of whether to be a high-, average-, or low-paying company. Compensation is a major cost for any organization, so low wages can be justified on a short-term financial basis. But being the high-wage employer—the highest-paying company in the region—ensures that the company will attract many applicants. Being a wage leader may be important during times of low unemployment or intense competition.

The *pay structure* decision is the choice of how to price different jobs within the organization. Jobs that are similar in worth usually are grouped into job families. A pay grade, with a floor and a ceiling, is established for each job family. Exhibit 10.9 illustrates a hypothetical pay structure.

Finally, *individual pay decisions* concern different pay rates for jobs of similar worth within the same family. Differences in pay within job families are decided in two ways. First, some jobs are occupied by individuals with more seniority than others. Second, some people may be better performers who are therefore deserving of a higher level of pay. Setting an individual's pay lower than that of coworkers—like choosing an overall low pay level—may become more difficult for employers to sustain in the future as more employees use online resources such as Salary.com and PayScale to check whether their pay is above or below the average amount for similar job titles.[56]

Unlike many other types of decisions in organizations, decisions about pay, especially at the individual level, often are kept confidential. Is that practice advantageous for organizations? Surprisingly, there is little evidence about this practice even though it affects almost every private sector employee.[57] Some possible ways the organization may benefit from keeping pay decisions secret are by avoiding conflicts, protecting individuals' privacy, and reducing the likelihood that employees will leave to seek better pay if they are earning less than the average for their position. However, if decisions about pay are kept secret, employees may worry that decisions are unfair and may be less motivated because the link between performance and pay is unclear. Also, in an economic sense, labor markets are less efficient when information is unavailable, which can reduce organizations' ability to get the best workers at the optimum rate of pay. Finally, as a practical matter, younger employees today are used to living in a world where most data are readily retrievable online (including pay data on websites such as Glassdoor.com), and many

EXHIBIT 10.8

Factors Affecting the Wage Mix

SOURCE: Snell, S.A., and Bohlander, G.W. *Managing Human Resources,* 16th ed. Copyright © 2012. Cincinnati, OH: Cengage Learning, Inc. Reproduced by permission. www.cengage.com/permissions

EXHIBIT 10.9
Pay Structure

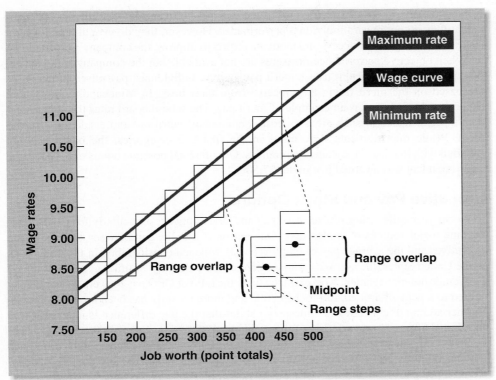

SOURCE: From Arthur Sherman, George Bohlander, and Scott Snell, *Managing Human Resources,* 11th ed. Copyright 1998 South-Western, a part of Cengage Learning, Inc. Reproduced by permission. www.cengage.com/permissions

are dismissive of requests for confidentiality. Given these possible pros and cons of pay secrecy, do you think this practice is wise? Is it ethical? And what about you—do you want to know how much your coworkers earn?

Incentive Systems and Variable Pay

Various incentive systems have been devised to encourage and motivate employees to be more productive.[58] (See Chapter 13 for more discussion of rewarding performance.) Individual incentive plans are the most common type of incentive plan. An individual incentive system consists of an objective standard against which a worker's performance is compared. Pay is determined by the employee's performance. Individual incentive plans are used frequently in sales jobs—for example, a salesperson will receive extra compensation for exceeding a sales target. Another widely used individual incentive tool is management bonuses. If effectively designed, individual incentive plans can be highly motivating. Some companies, including Walmart, apply them for nonmanagers. Walmart hopes that using bonuses to reward hourly employees for meeting sales, profit, and inventory targets at their stores each quarter will build employees' job satisfaction and reduce turnover.[59]

Several types of group incentive plans, in which pay is based on group performance, are increasingly used today. The idea behind these plans is to give employees a sense of shared participation and even ownership in the performance of the firm. Gainsharing plans concentrate on rewarding employees for increasing productivity or saving money in areas under their direct control.[60] For example, if the usual waste allowance in a production line has been 5 percent and the company wants production employees to try to reduce that number, the company may offer to split any savings gained with the employees.

Profit-sharing plans are usually implemented in the division or organization as a whole, although some incentives may still be tailored to unit performance. In most companies, the profit-sharing plan is based on a formula for allocating an annual amount to each employee

Bottom Line

Incentives can help raise all aspects of organization performance.
Think about the activities of a store employee. What could a Walmart employee do to earn a bonus for meeting quarterly profit goals?

if the company exceeds a specified profit target. One disadvantage of profit-sharing plans is that they do not reward individual performance. However, they do give all employees a stake in the company's success and motivate efforts to improve the company's profitability.

When objective performance measures are not available but the company still wants to base pay on performance, it uses a merit pay system. Individuals' pay raises and bonuses are based on the merit rating they receive from their boss. In Minneapolis, the school superintendent's bonus is an example of merit pay. The school board rates the superintendent's performance in such areas as cost containment, nutrition, and academic achievement. While improvements were made in the first two categories, the board was not satisfied with the district's academic progress. Out of a total possible bonus of $40,000, the superintendent was awarded just under $7,500.[61]

Executive Pay and Stock Options

In recent years, the issues of executive pay and stock options, particularly for CEOs, have become major sources of controversy. One reason is that the gap between the pay of top executives and the average pay of employees has widened considerably. In the mid-1960s in the United States, the average company paid its CEO roughly 20 times as much as it paid its average nonmanagement worker. Since then, the ratio of CEO pay to average-worker pay soared to a peak of around 400-to-1 in 2000 and more recently has been around 250-to-1. Further adding to concern is a widespread belief that the pay difference is much wider in the United States. However, some of those claims may be exaggerated. A recent analysis of companies in countries where corporations must disclose executive pay found a difference among countries, but it was a relatively modest 26 percent advantage for U.S. CEOs, down from 58 percent in 2003.[62]

Besides the difference between executive and average-worker pay, the sheer size and growth of CEO compensation have also contributed to criticism by shareholders and the general public. Top-earning CEOs today can make tens of millions of dollars a year—sometimes even at companies that have performed poorly and even, recently, at companies that received government help during the financial crisis. Still, it's important to keep in mind that the huge awards that make headlines are not necessarily typical. In a recent year, CEOs of companies in the Standard & Poor's stock index earned on average $4.5 million, but the median was $2.5 million because a few executives with far higher earnings pushed the average higher. Also, if we consider only the biggest companies, those in the Standard & Poor's 500, CEO pay averaged $10.5 million because CEOs of the biggest companies tend to earn more than most CEOs.[63]

Even with these considerations, $10.5 million or even $2.5 million is a lot of money to earn in one year, and the amount of compensation paid to top executives is growing. Although salaries and bonuses have risen at a moderate pace, the fastest-growing part of executive compensation comes from stock grants and stock options. Such options give the holder the right to purchase shares of stock at a specified price. For example, if the company's stock price is $8 a share, the company may award a manager the right to purchase a specific number of shares of company stock at that price. If the price of the stock rises to, say, $10 a share after a specified holding period—usually three years or more—the manager can exercise the option. He or she can purchase the shares from the company at $8 per share, sell the shares on the stock market at $10, and keep the difference. (Of course, if the stock price never rises above $8, the options will be worthless.) For many top managers, large option grants became a major source of additional compensation. Adding to the scrutiny over this practice is the striking number of situations in which options were dated just before the company's stock price rose, increasing their value—and the suspicion that at least some of these options were backdated unethically to make them more valuable rather than give executives the incentive to improve the company's performance in the stock market.[64]

Companies issue options to managers to align their interests with those of the company's owners, the shareholders. The assumption is that managers will become even more focused on making the company successful, leading to a rise in its stock price. Assuming that the executives continue to own their stock year after year, the amount of their wealth that is tied to the company's performance—and their incentive to work hard for the company—should continually increase.[65] However, many critics have suggested that excessive use of options encouraged executives to focus on short-term results to drive up the price of their stock at the expense of their firm's long-run competitiveness. Others suggested that lucrative options motivated questionable or even unethical behavior, as we mentioned in Chapter 2. More recently, a plunging stock market highlighted another problem with stock options: many options became essentially worthless, so they failed to reward employees.[66] Evidence suggests, however, that corporations readily adjust executives' total compensation packages accordingly. A review of compensation to the five highest-paid executives at 3,000 companies found that after the financial crisis, performance-based pay continued to rise, becoming a majority of the pay package, but shifted away from options toward stock grants and bonuses.

Traditionally, companies incurred no expense when they issued stock options. This was another reason options were considered an attractive incentive tool and were sometimes even issued to nonmanagers. However, because of corporate scandals and to curb excessive use of options, the rules were changed in 2004 so that options have to be treated as an expense by companies that issue them. This means that compensation committees have to focus more on whether options motivate executives to focus on what is important for the company's future.

Employee Benefits

Like pay systems, employee benefit plans are subject to regulation. Employee benefits are divided into those required by law and those optional for an employer.

The three basic required benefits are workers' compensation, Social Security, and unemployment insurance. Workers' compensation provides financial support to employees suffering a work-related injury or illness. Social Security, as established in the Social Security Act of 1935, provides financial support to retirees; in subsequent amendments, the act was expanded to cover disabled employees. The funds come from payments made by employers, employees, and self-employed workers. Unemployment insurance provides financial support to employees who are laid off for reasons they cannot control. Companies that have terminated fewer employees pay less into the unemployment insurance fund; thus organizations have an incentive to keep terminations at a minimum.

A large number of benefits are not required to be employer-provided. The most common are pension plans and medical and hospital insurance. Both of these are undergoing significant change. For decades, most Americans under the retirement age were covered by health insurance plans provided by their employers. But as the cost of providing this benefit has soared far faster than other compensation costs, employers started dropping it or providing very limited policies. In 2010 the federal government responded to concern about the rising number of uninsured people and the high cost of care by passing the Patient Protection and Affordable Care Act. Among its many provisions, the law requires that, employers (except small businesses) must either provide their employees with health insurance or pay a fee to offset the cost of government subsidies for individuals buying their own insurance. Organizations have responded to the law in different ways. Some have offset these higher costs by delaying hiring or shifting more health care costs to employees through higher premiums, co-payments, or deductibles.[67] Some large retailers such as Walmart, Home Depot, Trader Joe's, and Target have cut back on providing health insurance, especially for part-time staff. Instead, part-time employees are encouraged to seek individual coverage from health insurance exchanges.[68] Many small businesses are also dropping health coverage for workers. Defined as having fewer than 50 employees, small businesses provide medical coverage to approximately 20 million people. That seems to be changing. During 2014, Anthem, the largest provider of health insurance to small businesses, lost about 300,000 plan members. After several consecutive years of

Bottom Line
Organizations today seek new ways to reduce benefits costs.
What benefits have you received from an employer? Did you ever consider the cost of those benefits?

Employee benefits include those required by law, such as workers' compensation, Social Security, and unemployment insurance, and those decided by the employer. Retirement plans and paid vacation time are examples of employer-provided, nonrequired benefits.

© Digital Vision

dealing with rising health care costs, many people like Jim Dunn, owner of three Italian Oven restaurants, are encouraging their managers and employees to purchase their own coverage on health insurance exchanges.[69] Despite this trend, some observers expect a continuation of this benefit because employees place a high value on health insurance, so employers view it as a necessary means of attracting and retaining employees—and of enabling them to stay healthy and productive.[70]

At the same time, retirement benefits have been shifting away from guaranteed pension payments. Whereas a promised monthly payout used to be the norm, only about 7 percent of companies offer this approach to new employees today.[71] Instead, in many companies, the employer, and perhaps the employee, may contribute to an individual retirement account or 401(k) plan, which is invested. When the employee retires, he or she gets the total amount that has accumulated in the account.

Because of the wide variety of possible benefits and the considerable differences in employee preferences and needs, companies often use **cafeteria** or **flexible benefit programs.** In this type of program, employees are given credits that they spend on benefits they desire. Then employees use their credits toward individualized packages of benefits—medical and dental insurance, dependent care, life insurance, and so on.

Legal Issues in Compensation and Benefits

Several laws affect employee compensation and benefits. We have already mentioned the FLSA, which in addition to distinguishing between exempt and nonexempt employees also sets minimum wage, maximum hour, and child labor provisions.[72] The *Equal Pay Act (EPA)* of 1963, now enforced by the EEOC, prohibits unequal pay for men and women who perform equal work. Equal work means jobs that require equal skill, effort, and responsibility and are performed under similar working conditions. The law does permit exceptions in which the difference in pay is due to a seniority system, a merit system, an incentive system based on quantity or quality of production, or any other factor other than sex, such as market demand. Although equal pay for equal work may sound like common sense, many employers have fallen victim to this law by rationalizing that men, traditionally the breadwinners, deserve more pay than women or by giving equal jobs different titles (senior assistant versus office manager) as the sole basis for pay differences.

One controversy concerns male and female pay differences within the same company. **Comparable worth** doctrine implies that women who perform *different* jobs of *equal* worth as those performed by men should be paid the same wage.[73] In contrast to the equal-pay-for-equal-work notion, comparable worth suggests that the jobs need *not* be the same to require the same pay. For example, nurses (predominantly female) were found to be paid considerably less than skilled craftworkers (predominantly male), even though the two jobs were found to be of equal value or worth.[74] Under the Equal Pay Act, this would not constitute pay discrimination because the jobs are very different. But under the comparable worth concept, these findings would indicate discrimination because the jobs are of equal worth. To date, no federal law requires comparable worth, and the Supreme Court has made no decisive rulings about it. However, some states, including Iowa, Minnesota, and Washington have comparable worth laws for public sector employees.

Some laws influence mostly benefit practices. The *Pregnancy Discrimination Act* of 1978 states that pregnancy is a disability and qualifies a woman to receive the same benefits that she would with any other disability. The *Employee Retirement Income Security Act*

cafeteria benefit program

An employee benefit program in which employees choose from a menu of options to create a benefit package tailored to their needs.

flexible benefit programs

Benefit programs in which employees are given credits to spend on benefits that fit their unique needs.

comparable worth

Principle of equal pay for different jobs of equal worth.

(ERISA) of 1974 protects private pension programs from mismanagement. ERISA requires that retirement benefits be paid to those who vest or earn a right to draw benefits and ensures retirement benefits for employees whose companies go bankrupt or who otherwise cannot meet their pension obligations.

Health and Safety

The *Occupational Safety and Health Act (OSHA)* of 1970 requires employers to pursue workplace safety. Employers must maintain records of injuries and deaths caused by workplace accidents and submit to onsite inspections. Large-scale industrial accidents and nuclear power plant disasters worldwide have focused attention on the importance of workplace safety.

Coal mining is one of many industries that benefit from safety laws. Mining is one of the five most dangerous jobs to perform, according to the U.S. Bureau of Labor Statistics. Nearly every coal miner can name a friend or family member who has been killed, maimed, or stricken with black lung disease. "You die quick or you die slow," reports one mine worker. Mine safety tragically returned to American consciousness in April 2010, when a coal mine explosion at the Massey Energy Company's Upper Big Branch Mine killed 29 workers. An independent investigation found that the accident could have been prevented by standard mine safety practices that evidently had been disregarded by management and missed by regulators.[75] However, according to the Mine Safety and Health Administration, mines have become safer. In the 1960s, hundreds of coal miners died in mine accidents every year; beginning in the mid-1980s, that number fell below 100 per year. During the past decade, even in the year of the Massey disaster, the number of annual fatalities was less than 50.[76]

Another area of concern is the safety of young immigrant workers. A recent study found that Latino immigrants have a 50 percent higher workplace fatality rate than all other workers. Reasons for the higher fatality rate included lack of safety training, and language and cultural barriers.[77]

Labor Relations

Labor relations is the system of relations between workers and management. Labor unions recruit members, collect dues, and ensure that employees are treated fairly with respect to wages, working conditions, and other issues. When workers organize for the purpose of negotiating with management to improve their wages, hours, or working conditions, two processes are involved: unionization and collective bargaining. These processes have evolved since the 1930s in the United States to provide important employee rights.[78]

Labor Laws

Try to imagine what life would be like with unemployment at 25 percent. Pretty grim, you would say. Legislators in 1935 felt that way too. Therefore, organized labor received its Magna Carta with the passage of the National Labor Relations Act.

The *National Labor Relations Act* (also called the *Wagner Act* after its legislative sponsor) ushered in an era of rapid unionization by (1) declaring labor organizations legal, (2) establishing five unfair employer labor practices, and (3) creating the National Labor Relations Board (NLRB). Prior to the act, employers could fire workers who favored unions, and federal troops were often provided to put down strikes. Today the NLRB conducts unionization elections, hears complaints of unfair labor practices, and issues injunctions against offending employers. The Wagner Act greatly assisted the growth of unions by enabling workers to use the law and the courts to organize and collectively bargain for better wages, hours, and working conditions. Many of the improvements all of us take for granted in the workplace, including minimum wages, health benefits, maternity leave, the

LO 7

labor relations
The system of relations between workers and management.

Since 2000, unions have aggressively tried to organize workers at Walmart, the world's largest employer with over 2 million employees. So far, the company remains union-free except in China. For a manager, what would be the pros and cons of a union?

© Robyn Beck/AFP/Getty Images

35-hour workweek, and worker protections in general were largely the result of collective bargaining over many years by unions.

Public policy began on the side of organized labor in 1935, but over the next 25 years, the pendulum swung toward the side of management. The *Labor-Management Relations Act,* or *Taft-Hartley Act* (1947), protected employers' free speech rights, defined unfair labor practices by unions, and permitted workers to decertify (reject) a union as their representative.

Finally, the *Labor-Management Reporting and Disclosure Act,* or *Landrum-Griffin Act* (1959), swung the public policy pendulum midway between organized labor and management. By declaring a bill of rights for union members, establishing control over union dues increases, and imposing reporting requirements for unions, Landrum-Griffin was designed to curb abuses by union leadership and rid unions of corruption.

Unionization

How do workers join unions? Through a union organizer or local union representative, workers learn what benefits they may receive by joining.[79] The union representative distributes authorization cards that permit workers to indicate whether they want an election to be held to certify the union to represent them. The National Labor Relations Board will conduct a certification election if at least 30 percent of the employees sign authorization cards. Management has several choices at this stage: to recognize the union without an election, to consent to an election, or to contest the number of cards signed and resist an election.

If an election is warranted, an NLRB representative will conduct the election by secret ballot. A simple majority of those voting determines the winner. Thus apathetic workers who do not show up to vote in effect support the union. If the union wins the election, it is certified as the bargaining unit representative.

During the campaign preceding the election, management and the union each try to persuade the workers how to vote. Most workers, though, are somewhat resistant to campaign efforts, having made up their minds well before the NLRB appears on the scene. If the union wins the election, management and the union are legally required to bargain in good faith to obtain a collective bargaining agreement or contract.

Why do workers vote for a union? The four factors that play a significant role are presented in Exhibit 10.10.[80] First, economic factors are important, especially for workers in low-paying jobs; unions attempt to raise the average wage rate for their members. Second, job dissatisfaction encourages workers to seek out a union. Poor supervisory practices, favoritism, lack of communication, and perceived unfair or arbitrary discipline and discharge are specific triggers of job dissatisfaction. Third, the belief that the union can obtain desired benefits can generate a pro-union vote. Finally, the image of the union can determine whether a dissatisfied worker will seek out the union. Headline stories of union corruption and dishonesty can discourage workers from unionization.

Collective Bargaining

In the United States, management and unions engage in a periodic ritual (typically every three years) of negotiating an agreement over wages, benefits, hours, and working

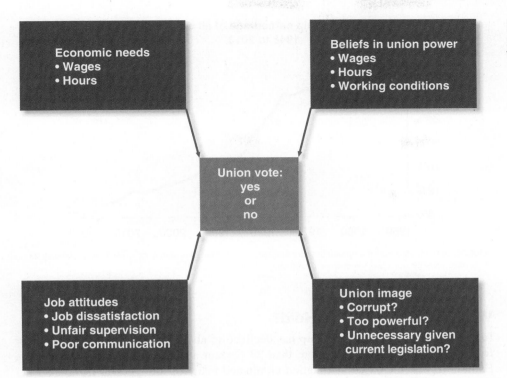

EXHIBIT 10.10
Determinants of Union
Voting Behavior

conditions. Two types of disputes can arise during this process. First, before an agreement is reached, the workers may go on strike to compel agreement on their terms. Such an action is known as an *economic strike* and is permitted by law. However, strikes today are less likely to be used as a bargaining tool, although they sometimes occur as a last resort. Strikers are not paid if they are on strike, and few workers want to undertake this hardship unnecessarily. In addition, managers may legally hire replacement workers during a strike, offsetting some of the strike's effect. Finally, workers are as aware as managers of the tougher competition companies face today, and if treated fairly, they will usually share management's interest in coming to an agreement.

Once an agreement is signed, management and the union sometimes disagree over *interpretation* of the agreement. Usually they settle their disputes through arbitration. **Arbitration** is the use of a neutral third party, typically jointly selected, to resolve the dispute. U.S. companies use arbitration while an agreement is in effect to avoid *wildcat strikes* (in which workers walk off the job in violation of the contract) or unplanned work stoppages.

What does a collective bargaining agreement contain? In a **union shop,** a union security clause specifies that workers must join the union after a set period of time. **Right-to-work** states, through restrictive legislation, do not permit union shops; that is, workers have the right to work without being forced to join a union. The southern United States has many right-to-work states. The wage component of the contract spells out rates of pay, including premium pay for overtime and paid holidays. Individual rights usually are specified in terms of the use of seniority to determine pay increases, job bidding, and the order of layoffs.

A feature of any contract is the grievance procedure. Through the grievance procedure, unions perform a vital service for their membership by giving workers a voice in what goes on during contract negotiations and administration.[81] In about 50 percent of discharge cases that go to arbitration, the arbitrator overturns management's decision and reinstates the worker.[82] Unions have a legal duty of fair representation, which means they must represent all workers in the bargaining unit and ensure that workers' rights are protected.

arbitration

The use of a neutral third party to resolve a labor dispute.

union shop

An organization with a union and a union security clause specifying that workers must join the union after a set period of time.

right-to-work

Legislation that allows employees to work without having to join a union.

EXHIBIT 10.11
Decline in Union
Membership—1948 to 2013

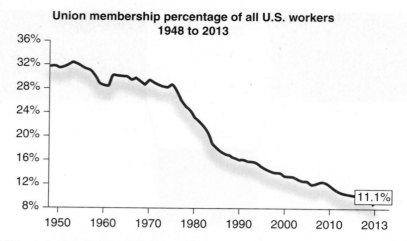

**Union membership percentage of all U.S. workers
1948 to 2013**

SOURCE: Data adapted from the Bureau of Labor Statistics, "Union Members Summary," press release, January 23, 2015, http://www.bls.gov/news.release/union2.nr0.htm.

What Does the Future Hold?

In recent years, union membership has declined to about 11 percent of the U.S. labor force—down from a peak of more than 33 percent at the end of World War II (see Exhibit 10.11). Increased automation eliminated many of the types of manufacturing jobs that used to be union strongholds. Employees in today's white-collar office jobs are less interested in joining unions and are also more difficult to organize. Tough global competition has made managers much less willing to give in to union demands, and as a result, the benefits of unionization are less clear to many workers—particularly young, skilled workers who no longer expect to stay with one company all their lives. Some people applaud unions' apparent decline. Others hope for an eventual reemergence. Unions may play a different role in the future, one that is less adversarial and more cooperative with management. Unions are adapting to changing workforce demographics; they are paying more attention to women, older workers, government employees, and people who work at home. Elimination of inefficient work rules, the introduction of profit sharing, and a guarantee of no layoffs were seen as big steps toward a fundamentally different, cooperative long-term relationship.

> In recent years, union membership has declined to about 11 percent of the U.S. labor force.

What seems clear is that when companies recognize that their success depends on the talents and energies of employees, the interests of unions and managers may begin to converge. Rather than one side exploiting the other, unions and managers can find common ground in developing, valuing, and involving employees. Particularly in knowledge-based companies, the balance of power is shifting toward employees. Whether or not employees belong to a union, they, not companies, own their own human capital. And these employees are free, within limits, to leave the organization, taking their human capital with them. This leaves organizations in a particularly vulnerable position if they manage poorly. To establish a strong competitive capability, organizations are searching for ways to obtain, retain, and engage their most valuable resources: human resources. "Management in Action: Onward" explores why and how this is a critical issue for Google today. The processes and practices outlined in this chapter form the foundation for effective people management. In the next chapter, we discuss one particularly important people-related issue: managing a diverse workforce.

Management in Action

GOOGLE GEARS UP FOR MORE LABOR MARKET COMPETITION

Google's recruiting and selection practices have contributed to its mystique, helping it meet its goals for hiring the best talent, but that human resource strategy has been shaken by the appeal of up-and-coming high-tech firms. Google risks becoming the boring, established brand. High-tech workers still love Google, but many are drawn to opportunities at F5 Networks, LinkedIn, Dropbox, and other rising stars. Thus, even as Google is adding thousands to its ranks, it must keep current employees from leaving.

One way to keep people is to ensure that they feel well compensated. Google has increased its budget for compensation. For Google, this is an investment: to enter new, growing areas of the high-tech industry, it needs talented people.

But it's not just about money. One reason tech workers leave for start-ups is that they want to enjoy the excitement of building something new. Big-company bureaucracy can be boring. Google's founders originally held weekly meetings during which engineers presented their projects to the leaders. As the company grew, the list of presenters got so long that the founders lost interest and limited technical reviews to a select group.

Google therefore tries to be worker-friendly in its own data-driven way. The effort to measure and improve management effectiveness was conceived partly as a way to create a more positive work environment. It helps that managers' performance is measured both by the manager's boss and by his or her employees. The same goal and approach apply to decisions about employee benefits. For example, Google determines what kind of advice helps employees get the most value from their retirement plans and how to structure an increase in pay so employees will appreciate it most. (It concluded that a raise in base pay is better than a bonus.)

Or consider the case of the disappearing women. Google's People Operations (POPS) department tracked turnover rates and noticed that female employees were leaving at a high rate—an expensive problem, given the costs to recruit, hire, and train replacements. Digging deeper, POPS analysts determined that the attrition was led by women quitting after giving birth. Google's parental-leave policy was standard for its industry, but the evidence showed that was not enough. So Google began offering mothers 18 months off at full pay—time they may schedule however they want. Turnover among new mothers dropped by half, matching the rate of all employees. That improvement lowered the expense of replacing employees enough to make up for the cost of the benefit.[83]

- How is Google's approach to employee benefits more effective than a simple decision to offer the biggest benefits package?
- Do you think Google's HR strategy will enable it to maintain a competitive advantage? Why or why not?

KEY TERMS

RETAINING WHAT YOU LEARNED

In Chapter 10, you learned that by aligning their human resources and strategies, organizations can achieve a competitive advantage. Hiring the right number and types of employees requires effective planning. Organizations should design their HR systems to reinforce key employee behaviors. There are advantages and disadvantages associated with internal and external recruitment. Companies use a variety of selection methods when choosing whom to hire, including interviews and cognitive ability tests. It is important that organizations use methods that are valid and reliable. In order to maintain a competitive edge, companies need talented, flexible workers who engage in continuous training. While supervisors typically provide performance appraisals for their subordinates, organizations may seek this information from multiple sources. An organization's reward system consists of pay and benefits. Paying above the going rate is an advantage, but can be more costly. Labor relations involve the interactions between workers and management. In addition to negotiating agreements with management, unions also develop grievance procedures to protect certain rights of members. Labor laws seek to protect the rights of both employees and managers.

LO 1 **Discuss how companies use human resources management to gain competitive advantage.**

- To succeed, companies must align their human resources to their strategies. Effective planning is necessary to make certain that the right number and types of employees are available to implement a company's strategic plan.
- It is clear that hiring the most competent people is a very involved process.
- Companies that compete on cost, quality, service, and so on also should use their staffing, training,

appraisal, and reward systems to elicit and reinforce the kinds of behaviors that underlie their strategies.

LO 2 **Give reasons companies recruit both internally and externally for new hires.**

- Some companies prefer to recruit internally to make certain that employees are familiar with organizational policies and values.
- In other instances, companies prefer to recruit externally, such as through employee referrals, job boards, newspaper advertising, and campus visits, to find individuals with new ideas and fresh perspectives.
- External recruiting is also necessary to fill positions when the organization is growing or needs skills that do not exist among its current employees.

LO 3 **Identify various methods for selecting new employees.**

- There are myriad selection techniques from which to choose. Interviews and reference checks are the most common. Personality tests and cognitive ability tests measure an individual's aptitude and potential to do well on the job. Other selection techniques include assessment centers and integrity tests. Background and reference checks verify that the information supplied by employees is accurate.
- Regardless of the approach used, any test should be able to demonstrate reliability (consistency across time and different interview situations) and validity (accuracy in predicting job performance).
- In addition, selection methods must comply with equal opportunity laws, which are intended to ensure that companies do not discriminate in any employment practices.

PLANNING

Organizational strategic planning

HRM environmental scanning

Human resources planning

- Labor markets
- Technology
- Legislation
- Competition
- Economy

- Demand forecast
- Internal labor supply
- External labor supply
- Job analysis

PROGRAMMING

Human resources activities

- Employee recruitment
- Employee selection
- Diversity and inclusion
- Training and development
- Performance appraisal
- Reward systems
- Labor relations

EVALUATING

Results

- Productivity
- Quality
- Innovation
- Satisfaction
- Turnover
- Absenteeism
- Health

EXHIBIT 10.1   An Overview of the HR Planning Process

4   **Evaluate the importance of spending on training and development.**

- People cannot depend on a set of skills for all of their working lives. In today's changing, competitive world, old skills quickly become obsolete, and new ones become essential for success.
- Refreshing or updating an individual's skills requires a great deal of continuous training, designed with measurable goals and methods that will achieve those goals.
- Companies understand that gaining a competitive edge in quality of service depends on having the most talented, flexible workers in the industry.

LO 5   **Explain alternatives for who appraises an employee's performance.**

- Many companies are using multiple sources of appraisal because different people see different sides of an employee's performance. Typically, a superior is expected to evaluate an employee, but peers and team members are often well positioned to see aspects of performance that a superior misses. Even an employee's subordinates are being asked more often today to give their input to get yet another perspective on the evaluation.
- Particularly in companies concerned about quality, internal and external customers also are surveyed.
- Finally, employees should evaluate their own performance, if only to get them thinking about their own performance as well as to engage them in the appraisal process.

LO 6   **Describe the fundamental aspects of a reward system.**

- Reward systems include pay and benefits.
- Pay systems have three basic components: pay level, pay structure, and individual pay determination. To achieve an advantage over competitors, executives may want to pay a generally higher wage to their company's employees, but this decision must be weighed against the need to control costs. (Pay level decisions often are tied to strategic concerns such as these.)
- To achieve internal equity (paying people what they are worth relative to their peers within the company), managers must look at the pay structure, making certain that pay differentials are based on knowledge, effort, responsibility, working conditions, seniority, and so on.
- Individual pay determination is often based on merit or the different contributions of individuals. In these cases, it is important to make certain that men and women receive equal pay for equal work, and managers may wish to base pay decisions on the idea of comparable worth (equal pay for an equal contribution).

LO 7   **Summarize how unions and labor laws influence human resources management.**

- Labor relations involve the interactions between workers and management. One mechanism by which this relationship is conducted is unions.
- Unions seek to present a collective voice for workers, to make their needs and wishes known to management. Also, they negotiate agreements with management regarding a range of issues such as wages, hours, working conditions, job security, and health care.
- One important tool that unions can use is the grievance procedure established through collective bargaining. This mechanism gives employees a way to seek redress for wrongful action on the part of management. In this way, unions make certain that the rights of all employees are protected.
- Labor laws seek to protect the rights of both employees and managers so that their relationship can be productive and agreeable.

DISCUSSION QUESTIONS

1. How will changes in the labor force affect HRM practices for the next decade?
2. Describe the major regulations governing HRM practices.
3. Define job analysis. Why is job analysis relevant to each of the six key HRM activities discussed in the chapter (i.e., planning, staffing, training, performance appraisal, reward systems, labor relations)?
4. What are the various methods for recruiting employees? Why are some better than others? In what sense are they better?
5. What is a test? Give some examples of tests used by employers.
6. What purpose does performance appraisal serve? Why are there so many methods of appraisal?
7. What are some key ideas to remember when conducting a performance appraisal?
8. How would you define an effective reward system? What role do benefits serve in a reward system?
9. Why do workers join unions? What implications would this have for an organization that wishes to remain nonunion?
10. Discuss the advantages and disadvantages of collective bargaining for the employer and the employee.

EXPERIENTIAL EXERCISES

10.1 THE LEGAL INTERVIEW

OBJECTIVES

1. To introduce you to the complexities of employment law.
2. To identify interview practices that might lead to discrimination in employment.

INSTRUCTIONS

1. Working alone, review the text material on interviewing and discrimination in employment.
2. In small groups, complete the Legal Interview Worksheet.
3. After the class reconvenes, group spokespersons present group findings.

Legal Interview Worksheet

The employment interview is one of the most critical steps in the employment selection process. It also may be an occasion for discriminating against individual employment candidates. The following represents questions that interviewers often ask job applicants. Identify the legality of each question by circling L (legal) or I (illegal) and briefly explain your decision.

Interview Question	Legality	Explanation
1. Could you provide us with a photo for our files?	L I	_____
2. Have you ever used another name (previous married name or alias)?	L I	_____
3. What was your maiden name?	L I	_____
4. What was your wife's maiden name?	L I	_____
5. What was your mother's maiden name?	L I	_____
6. What is your current address?	L I	_____
7. What was your previous address?	L I	_____
8. What is your Social Security number?	L I	_____
9. Where was your place of birth?	L I	_____
10. Where were your parents born?	L I	_____
11. What is your national origin?	L I	_____
12. Are you a naturalized citizen?	L I	_____
13. What languages do you speak?	L I	_____
14. What is your religious/church affiliation?	L I	_____
15. What is your racial classification?	L I	_____
16. How many dependents do you have?	L I	_____
17. What are the ages of your dependent children?	L I	_____
18. What is your marital status?	L I	_____
19. How old are you?	L I	_____
20. Do you have proof of your age (birth certificate or baptismal record)?	L I	_____
21. Whom do we notify in case of an emergency?	L I	_____
22. What are your height and weight?	L I	_____
23. Have you ever been arrested?	L I	_____
24. Do you own your own car?	L I	_____
25. Do you own your own house?	L I	_____
26. Do you have any charge accounts?	L I	_____
27. Have you ever had your salary garnished?	L I	_____
28. To what organizations do you belong?	L I	_____
29. Are you available to work on Saturdays and Sundays?	L I	_____
30. Do you have any form of disability?	L I	_____

10.2 THE PAY RAISE

OBJECTIVES

1. To further your understanding of salary administration.
2. To examine the many facets of performance criteria, performance criteria weighting, performance evaluation, and rewards.

INSTRUCTIONS

1. Working in small groups, complete the Pay Raise Worksheet.
2. After the class reconvenes, group spokespersons present group findings.

Pay Raise Worksheet

April Knepper is the new supervisor of an assembly team. It is time for her to make pay raise allocations for her subordinates. She has been budgeted $30,000 to allocate among her seven subordinates as pay raises. There have been some ugly grievances in other work teams over past allocations, so Knepper has been advised to base the allocations on objective criteria that can be quantified, weighted, and computed in numerical terms. After she makes her allocations, Knepper must be prepared to justify her decisions. All of the evaluative criteria available to Knepper are summarized as follows:

Employee	Seniority	Output Rating*	Absent Rate	Supervisory Ratings			
				Skills	Initiative	Attitude	Personal
David Bruce	15 yrs.	0.58	0.5%	Good	Poor	Poor	Nearing retirement. Wife just passed away. Having adjustment problems.
Eric Cattalini	12 yrs.	0.86	2.0	Excellent	Good	Excellent	Going to night school to finish his BA degree.
Chua Li	7 yrs.	0.80	3.5	Good	Excellent	Excellent	Legally deaf.
Marilee Miller	1 yr.	0.50	10.0	Poor	Poor	Poor	Single parent with three children.
Victor Munoz	3 yrs.	0.62	2.5	Poor	Average	Good	Has six dependents. Speaks little English.
Derek Thompson	11 yrs.	0.64	8.0	Excellent	Average	Average	Married to rich wife. Personal problems.
Sarah Vickers	8 yrs.	0.76	7.0	Good	Poor	Poor	Women's activist. Wants to create a union.

* Output rating determined by production rate less errors and quality problems.

CONCLUDING CASE

INVINCIBILITY SYSTEMS

The 17,000 employees of Invincibility Systems design and make aerospace and defense equipment such as rockets, spacecraft propulsion systems, and missile propulsion systems. Along with cutting-edge engineering, the company stands out for its cutting-edge human resource management. Invincibility has hired quantitative experts to analyze HR data with the same care it uses to analyze rocket trajectories.

A few years ago, the company hired a statistician and an HR planner to join a team that would collect and analyze data, looking for factors that would predict human resource needs. The team started by looking for ways to improve recruiting. They collected data on the various sources of candidates that the company was using and the candidates actually selected. Then they used a statistical method called regression analysis to identify which sources of candidates generated the most hires—as well as the sources that generated hires who went on to perform well. Using the results of the analysis, Invincibility made its recruiting effort more efficient. By focusing on the most productive sources of top employees, it saves time and money that formerly had gone toward recruiting through channels that were less fruitful.

Next the HR team turned its efforts toward workforce planning. For each department of Invincibility, the team collects data describing the workforce—for example, job categories, years with the company, and labor force projections. It runs regression analysis to predict the likelihood that employees will leave the company in the coming year. The results, coupled with sales forecasts, enable the company to predict how many new employees will need to be hired in each department.

Other companies do this kind of planning, but the extent of the analysis at Invincibility is unusual. For one thing, the analysis is conducted on the level of individual employees. Thus it shows not only that turnover may rise or fall, but also which employees are most likely to leave. That level of analysis is important to Invincibility because unlike organizations where many people perform the same type of work and can step in when someone leaves, employees at Invincibility typically fill highly specialized, highly skilled roles. If an engineer with years of experience in developing high-caliber ammunition suddenly departs, there may be no one else on the team with that person's knowledge and skill set.

Another unusual quality of Invincibility's HR planning is the variety of factors that the planners consider when they run their regression analyses. For example, the company has run regressions to determine whether turnover is related to changes in employee benefits and even the month of the year. If the analysis shows that a factor has been significant in the past, the planners take it into account in their forecasts. In one situation, the planners found that retirements in a department rose after the company announced that it would be phasing out health insurance benefits for retirees. More experienced workers left before the phase-out took effect. When the company prepared to phase out similar benefits in another division, the planners knew they would need to step up recruiting efforts there in preparation for an uptick in retirements.

Some of the data Invincibility uses for planning are unsuitable for other kinds of HR decisions. For example, the company has found that employees' ages and marital status are relevant for predicting whether they are likely to leave the company. Turnover rates are higher among unmarried employees and recently hired employees (who tend to be younger). Thus the company plans greater recruiting efforts in departments where it has higher levels of young and unmarried employees. It also may consider stepping up its efforts to mentor and train employees in these departments. However, it does not make employment decisions such as hiring and promotion based on these factors.

DISCUSSION QUESTIONS

1. Besides the factors identified, what other factors should Invincibility Systems take into account in its HR planning?

2. What legal concerns does the data analysis at Invincibility raise? How should the company address those issues?

3. Besides its use for HR planning and recruiting, how might Invincibility's data analysis be applied to improving the company's training programs?

CHAPTER 11

Managing the Diverse Workforce

e pluribus unum

Management in Action

HOW BRIAN FRANCE IS CHANGING THE FACE OF NASCAR

What does a NASCAR fan look like? A NASCAR driver? If you pictured a white, male Southerner in answer to both questions, you have just illustrated a concern of NASCAR's chief executive, Brian France. Even as America's population is becoming more diverse, the sport of auto racing has tended to draw its drivers and fans from one segment of the population. If a sport is off the radar of the rest of the population, its growth potential is limited.

But France sees a different future. Years ago, he told Richard Lapchick, founder of the National Consortium for Academics and Sports, that he wanted NASCAR to "look like America." And since then, he has moved aggressively to begin making that happen.

Under France's leadership, NASCAR established its Drive for Diversity (D4D) development program to recruit female and minority group drivers and members of pit crews. The program selects the best for training and support, which includes guidance in marketing and media opportunities. Participants enter D4D's Rev Racing competitions, seeking to move up to other competitive levels, including the top level, the Sprint Cup Series. Since the program was established in 2004, NASCAR has supported more than 30 drivers in competitions at the grassroots level. In 2013, Kyle Larson, who is Japanese-American, became the first Drive for Diversity driver to win a national series race (the Truck Series race held at Rockingham Speedway). In 2014, Darrell Wallace Jr., an African American, earned four NASCAR wins in the Camping World Truck Series hosted at the Homestead-Miami Speedway. Other graduates of D4D have signed developmental contracts with NASCAR teams. In the pit crew training program, participants develop the technical and athletic skills to serve as tire changers, fuelers, and jackmen.

Diversity efforts are not just for show out on the track. NASCAR also seeks to develop talent for its business and leadership roles. It partners with about 20 universities to identify talented students for internships and jobs in marketing and other business areas.

© Sean Gardner/Getty Images

It also brought in the Teamwork Leadership Institute, a program of the National Consortium for Academics and Sports, to train all its employees in valuing and managing diversity. The institute's program supports NASCAR's goal of making diversity a value in all of NASCAR's relationships—within the organization and with its fans, vendors, and sponsors.[1]

When Brian France talks about NASCAR "looking like America," he may be thinking of a variety of the characteristics that define people—their age and sex, their place of birth and economic status, their racial and ethnic identities. As you read this chapter, think about how bringing together a diverse group and leading it toward a common purpose can be challenging but also a source of opportunity.

In Chapter 10, we described the laws that require equal opportunity and fair treatment in the workplace. In this chapter, we discuss why a proactive approach to developing and managing a diverse workforce has become not only a legal or moral obligation but a fundamental business requirement as well. NASCAR's Brian France considers diversity an essential ingredient for his sport's future growth. Managers who lack the ability to work with and effectively manage individuals of different colors, cultures, ages, abilities, and backgrounds will be at a significant disadvantage in their careers. And organizations that do not take the issue of managing diversity seriously will leave their organizations not only open to legal challenge but also far less able to compete effectively at home and abroad.

In the United States, the number of racial and ethnic minorities is increasing at a far faster rate than the growth in the white, nonminority population, and women make up a sizable share of the workforce. American workers, customers, and markets are already highly diverse and becoming even more so every day. In addition, as we discussed in Chapter 6, businesses are increasingly global. Managers need to be much more aware of, and sensitive to, cultural differences to succeed in a world economy. We have also discussed throughout this book how vital creativity and innovation have become for organization success. These qualities are fostered in an atmosphere where different perspectives and bright people from all walks of life are included. Few societies have access to the range of talents available in the United States, with its immigrant tradition and racially and ethnically diverse population. Yet getting people from widely divergent backgrounds to work together effectively is not easy. For this reason, managing diversity is one of America's biggest challenges—and opportunities.

managing diversity

Managing a culturally diverse workforce by recognizing the characteristics common to specific groups of employees while dealing with employees as individuals and supporting, nurturing, and utilizing their differences to the organization's advantage; see also *diversity*.

Managing diversity involves, first, such basic activities as recruiting, training, promoting, and using to full advantage individuals with different backgrounds, beliefs, capabilities, and cultures. But it means more than just hiring women and minorities and making sure they are treated equally and encouraged to succeed. It also means understanding and deeply valuing employee differences to build a more effective and profitable organization.

This chapter examines the meaning of diversity and the management skills and organizational processes involved in managing the diverse workforce effectively. We also explore the social and demographic changes and economic and employment shifts that are creating this changing U.S. workforce.

Diversity: A Brief History

Managing diversity is not a new management issue. From the late 1800s to the early 1900s, most of the groups that immigrated to the United States were from Italy, Poland, Ireland, and Russia. Members of those groups were considered outsiders because most did not speak English and had different customs and work styles. They struggled, often violently, to gain acceptance in industries such as steel, coal, automobile manufacturing, insurance, and finance. In the 1800s, it was considered poor business practice for white Protestant–dominated insurance companies to hire Irish, Italians, Catholics, or Jews. As late as the 1940s, and in some cases even later than that, colleges routinely discriminated against immigrants, Catholics, and Jews, establishing strict quotas that limited their number, if any were admitted at all. The employment prospects of these groups were severely diminished by this kind of discrimination, and it wasn't until the 1960s that the struggle for acceptance by the various white ethnic and religious groups had on the whole succeeded.

Women's struggle for acceptance in the workplace was in some ways even more difficult. When the women's rights movement was launched in Seneca Falls in 1848, most occupations were off-limits to women, and colleges and professional schools were totally closed to them. Women could not vote and lost all property rights once they were married.

In the first part of the 20th century, when women began to be accepted into professional schools, they were subject to severe quotas. There was also a widespread, persistent assumption that certain jobs were done only by men, and other jobs only by women. Even into the 1970s, less than 40 years ago, classified ad sections in newspapers listed different jobs by sex, with sections headed "Help Wanted—Males" and "Help Wanted—Females." Women who wanted a bank loan needed a male cosigner, and married women were not issued credit cards in their own name.[2] Only when the Civil Rights Act of 1964 (see Chapter 10) and other legislation began to be enforced was this kind of sex discrimination gradually eliminated. As we shall see, women are still underrepresented at the most senior levels of corporate life, and major disparities in other areas, such as pay, still exist. But most jobs today once considered the exclusive province of men—including frontline military units as well as the executive suite—are now open to and occupied by increasing numbers of women.

Many of the rights all of us take for granted today—equal opportunity, fair treatment in housing, the illegality of religious, racial, and sex discrimination—received their greatest impetus from the civil rights movement.

© *Associated Press*

The most difficult and wrenching struggle for equality involved America's nonwhite minorities. Rigid racial segregation remained a fact of American life for 100 years after the end of the Civil War. Black voting rights, particularly in the South, were often viciously suppressed, and racial discrimination in education, employment, and housing throughout the United States was a harsh daily reality. Years of difficult, courageous protest and struggle gradually began to eat away at both legal and social barriers to equality. Organizations such as the NAACP, formed by a group of blacks and whites, began to use America's court system and the Constitution to bring equality to African Americans and other people of color. The unanimous *Brown v. Board of Education* Supreme Court decision in 1954 declared segregation unconstitutional, setting the stage for other legislation we discussed in the previous chapter, including the Civil Rights Act of 1964. The consequences of America's bitter racial legacy are still with us; the struggle for equality is far from complete. But many of the rights all of us take for granted today—equal opportunity, fair treatment in housing, the illegality of religious, racial, and sex discrimination—received their greatest impetus from the civil rights movement.

Today nearly half of the U.S. workforce consists of women, 16 percent of U.S. workers identify themselves as Hispanic or Latino, and 12 percent are black. Two-thirds of all global migration is into the United States. One-third of all businesses in the United States are owned by women, employing about 20 percent of America's workers.[3]

The traditional American image of diversity has been one of assimilation. The United States was considered the melting pot of the world, a country in which ethnic and racial differences were blended into an American purée. In real life, many ethnic

> The traditional American image of diversity has been one of assimilation.

and most racial groups retained their identities, but they did not express them at work. Employees often abandoned most of their ethnic and cultural distinctions while at work to keep their jobs and get ahead. Many Europeans came to the United States, Americanized their names, perfected their English, and tried to enter the mainstream as quickly as possible.

Today's immigrants typically want to be part of an integrated team, but they understandably do not want to sacrifice their cultural identities to get ahead. Nor will they have to do so. Companies are recognizing that they should be more accommodating of differences, and that doing so pays off in business. Managers are also realizing that their customers have become increasingly diverse and that retaining a diversified workforce can provide a significant competitive advantage in the marketplace.

Diversity Today

LO 1

Today *diversity* refers to far more than skin color and gender. It is a broad term used to refer to all kinds of differences, as summarized in Exhibit 11.1. These differences include education, political belief, religion, and income in addition to gender, race, ethnicity, and nationality.[4]

Although members of different groups (white males, people born during the Depression, gay men and lesbians, Iraq and Afghanistan war veterans, Hispanics, Asians, women, African Americans, etc.) share within their groups many common values, attitudes, and perceptions, much diversity also exists within each of these categories. Every group is made up of individuals who are unique in personality, education, and life experiences. There may be more differences among, say, three Asians from Thailand, Hong Kong, and Korea than among a white, an African American, and an Asian all born in Chicago. And not all white males share the same personal or professional goals and values or behave alike.

Thus managing diversity may seem a contradiction within itself. It means being acutely aware of characteristics common to a group of employees while also managing these employees as individuals. Managing diversity means not just tolerating or accommodating all sorts of differences, but supporting, nurturing, integrating, and using these differences to the organization's advantage. JCPenney, for example, tries to match up the demographics of its workforce with the demographics of the communities in which its stores operate. The retailer reported improvements in productivity, customer satisfaction, and earnings as a result.[5] U.S. businesses will not have a choice of whether to have a diverse workforce; if they want to survive, they must learn to manage a diverse workforce sooner or better than their competitors do.

Although many companies initially instituted diversity programs to prevent discrimination, more are seeing these programs as a crucial way to expand their pool of talent and customer bases worldwide. These potential benefits are making diversity initiatives standard practice among industry-leading companies. A recent study of the large, mostly multinational companies in the Standard & Poor's 100 stock index found that 95 percent have at least one or two initiatives to develop a diverse workforce. Exhibit 11.2 shows how widespread those initiatives are.

EXHIBIT 11.1

Components of a Diversified Workforce

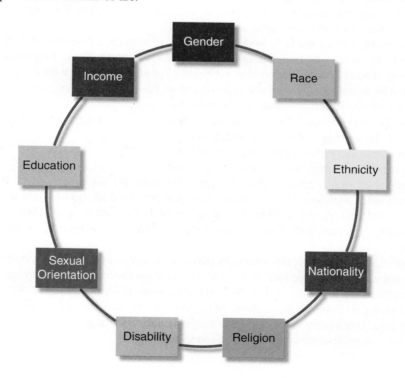

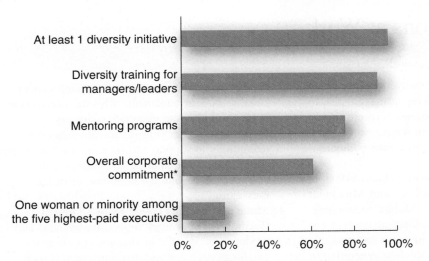

EXHIBIT 11.2
Examples of Diversity
Programs in S&P 100
Companies

SOURCE: Based on data in Christine DeGroot, Aditi Mohapatra, and Jamie Lippman, "Examining the Cracks in the Ceiling: A Survey of Corporate Diversity Practices of the S&P 100," Calvert Investments, March 2015 Supplement, http://www.calvert.com.
*Refers to corporate structures that govern inclusion strategies across all operations, including board oversight of diversity programs, an established diversity council, CEO and/or chair involvement in inclusion initiatives, and compensation plans tied to diversity objectives.

The Workforce of the Future

Until recently, white American-born males dominated the U.S. workforce. Businesses catered to their needs. However, although this group still constitutes the largest percentage of workers—about 80 percent of U.S. workers are white, and more than half of them are male—its share of the labor force is declining. Although the number of white male workers is expected to continue growing, the numbers of Asian American, African American, and Hispanic workers are expected to grow faster.[6] This significant change in the workforce parallels trends in the overall U.S. population. Recently the census bureau announced that, for the first time, about one in three residents of the United States is a racial or ethnic minority—a unique milestone in the nation's history. The largest and fastest-growing minority group is Hispanics, closely followed by Asian Americans. In several states—California, Hawaii, New Mexico, and Texas—and the District of Columbia, these minority groups plus Asians, Native Americans, and Pacific Islanders combine to make a population that is "majority minority."[7] These population trends affect not only the nature of the workforce but also the varied customers and markets managers must attract.

Gender Issues   One of the most important developments in the U.S. labor market has been the growing number of women working outside the home. Social changes during the 1960s and 1970s coupled with financial necessity caused women to enter the workforce and redefine their roles. Consider this:

Women make up about 47 percent of the workforce.
The overall labor force participation rate of women rose throughout the 1970s through the 1990s, but has edged down slightly in recent years as has men's participation rates.
Approximately 53 percent of marriages are dual-earner marriages.
Nearly one of every three married women in two-income households earns more than her husband does.
The percentage of women in the labor force earning college degrees has more than tripled over the past 40 years.[8]

For many women, as well as their spouses, balancing work life with family responsibilities and parenting presents an enormous challenge. Although men's roles in our society

Multiple Generations at Work

Flexibility and Work–Life Balance

In addition to offering family-friendly benefits, many companies provide flexible working arrangements to recruit and retain Millennial employees. A recent survey suggests that these early career employees value work flexibility and work–life balance more than compensation growth or skill development.

Other factors that are driving the trend toward flexible work arrangements include technology and Millennial employees' affinity for using it. Mobile technology, cloud computing services, and high-speed Internet are enabling employees to collaborate in teams and with clients from non-office locations. As the first generation to come of age as "digital natives," Millennials are comfortable working in this virtual, flexible environment. The traditional Monday–Friday, 9–5 p.m. work schedule can be perceived as too restrictive for this generation that is used to integrating work and leisure during "off hours."

Here are some tips for making your job more flexible:[9]

1. **Identify** which type of flexible work arrangement you desire. Is it telecommuting, job sharing, flexible work hours, and so forth?

2. **Review** your company's existing policies about flexible work arrangements. This information can help you shape your negotiation strategy.

3. **Research** whether your organization has the technology to support virtual workers. For example, does it have VoIP phones, teleconferencing software, cloud-based computing, or instant messaging?

4. **Make** a compelling case for why adding more flexibility to your work is good for business and productivity. It could be that you commute for two hours each day and that time could be better spent working on projects.

5. **Be Prepared** for "pushback." Your manager may resist granting a flexible schedule for fear that you will use the time outside the office for nonwork activities. A counterpoint may be that you'll likely put in longer hours (and be more productive) and that your online work and e-communication time stamps will provide consistent evidence of time worked.

Irene Rosenfeld has broken through the glass ceiling as CEO of Mondelez International, overseeing the company with revenues of over $35 billion.

© Jon Gress/Reuters/Corbis

have been changing, women still adopt the bulk of family responsibilities, including homemaking, child care, and care of elderly parents. Yet some companies may still expect their employees, particularly at the managerial level, to put in long hours and sacrifice their personal lives for the sake of their jobs, organizations, and careers. Not only may these expectations put many women at a disadvantage in the workplace, but they also may cause companies to lose valuable talent. Companies that offer their employees the opportunity to balance work and family commitments are better able to recruit and retain women. These companies are offering family-friendly benefits such as onsite child care, in-home care for elderly family members, increased maternity leave, job sharing, and flexible work schedules, and they are taking advantage of newer technologies to permit more work from home. The nearby "Multiple Generations at Work" box discusses how organizations are offering flexible work arrangements.

The desire for flexible scheduling is often cited as a reason significant pay disparities still exist between men and women. The average full-time working woman earns about 82 percent as much as men in the same job (recall the discussion in Chapter 10 about equal pay and comparable worth). However, the gap has shrunk most years since the 1970s; women's earnings were just 62 percent of men's in 1979. Still, research by the AAUW has found a persistent gap between male and female workers' earnings that grows over time, even after adjusting for age, marital status, geographic region, college major and GPA, type and selectivity of undergraduate school, type of occupation, economic sector, number of hours worked, and months between graduation and starting work. While interruptions to womens' careers to care for family lowers long-term earnings,[10] another possible explanation for the wage gap is that women are not negotiating pay as effectively as men seeking the same positions. This hurdle is complicated by evidence that some negotiation tactics that work for men can backfire when women use them, but women may benefit from greater skill at researching pay scales and expressing their pay requirements in a pleasant tone, backed up with evidence of their worth.[11]

> The average full-time working woman earns about 82 percent as much as men in the same job.

Another concern involving female workers is the low representation of women in top jobs. As women—along with minorities—move up the corporate ladder, they encounter a glass ceiling. The *glass ceiling* is an invisible barrier that makes it difficult for women and minorities to move beyond a certain level in the corporate hierarchy. For example, just 25 women are chief executives of Fortune 500 companies—that's 25 out of 500. Looking at all board members of those companies, 17 percent are white women, and 3 percent are minority women.[12] Still, one positive trend is that women's leadership is beginning to be seen at a broader range of companies. Besides Ginni Rometty at the helm of IBM and Mary Barra at General Motors, the executive ranks now include the likes of DuPont chair Ellen Kullman and Yahoo! chief executive officer Marissa Mayer. Exhibit 11.3 lists top women executives and the companies for which they work.

Some companies are helping women break through the glass ceiling. Accenture sponsors monthly networking events for its female employees and offers flexible schedules and part-time arrangements. Employers also sometimes match employees with mentors to help the employees navigate the business environment. Frustratingly, the very roadblocks that can make this guidance important may come from female managers. Researchers have observed what they call the queen bee syndrome, in which a female manager, perhaps out of insecurity, insults and demeans women who report to her.[13] Of course, managerial bullies are as likely to be men, but there is evidence that a queen bee targets mainly women. Whatever the source of the obstacles, corporate efforts to empower female employees can help. For example, Exhibit 11.4 lists 10 companies where women are thriving as a result of proactive leadership, mentoring programs, and hiring initiatives.

As women have gained more presence and power in the workforce, some have drawn attention to the problem of **sexual harassment,** which is unwelcome sexual conduct that is a term or condition of employment. Sexual harassment falls into two categories. The first, *quid pro quo harassment,* occurs when submission to or rejection of sexual conduct is used as a basis for employment decisions. The second type of harassment, *hostile environment,* occurs when unwelcome sexual conduct "has the purpose or effect of unreasonably interfering with job performance or creating an intimidating, hostile, or offensive working environment." Behaviors that can cause a hostile work environment include persistent or pervasive displays of pornography, lewd or suggestive remarks, or demeaning taunts or jokes. Both categories of harassment violate Title VII of the Civil Rights Act of 1964,

sexual harassment

Conduct of a sexual nature that has negative consequences for employment.

EXHIBIT 11.3
Top Ten Most Powerful Women Executives

Rank	Name	Company	Title
1	Ginni Rometty	IBM	Chairman, CEO, and president
2	Mary Barra	General Motors	CEO
3	Indra Nooyi	PepsiCo	Chairman and CEO
4	Marillyn Hewson	Lockheed Martin	Chairman, CEO, and president
5	Ellen Kullman	DuPont	Chairman and CEO
6	Meg Whitman	Hewlett-Packard	Chairman, CEO, and president
7	Irene Rosenfeld	Mondelez International	Chairman and CEO
8	Pat Woertz	Archer Daniels Midland	Chairman, CEO, and president
9	Abigail Johnson	FMR	President
10	Sheryl Sandberg	Facebook	Chief operating officer

SOURCE: From "The Most Powerful Women in Business," 2014 *Fortune*, http://www.fortune.com.

EXHIBIT 11.4
Excellent Companies for
Women

Abbott	KPMG
Ernst & Young	Marriott
General Mills	Mass Mutual Financial
IBM	P&G
Johnson & Johnson	State Farm Insurance

SOURCE: Based on data from National Association for Female Executives and S. Adams, "10 Great Companies for Women In 2015," *Forbes* (online), March 3, 2015, http://www.forbes.com.

regardless of the sex of the harasser and the victim; in a recent year, more than 15 percent of complaints filed with the federal government came from males. If an employee files a complaint of sexual harassment with the Equal Employment Opportunity Commission (EEOC), the commission may investigate and, if it finds evidence for the complaint, may request mediation, seek a settlement, or file a lawsuit with the potential for stiff fines—and negative publicity that may damage the company's ability to recruit the best employees in the future.

Harassment by creation of a hostile work environment is now more typical than quid pro quo harassment. But because it may involve more subjective standards of behavior, it puts an extra burden on managers to maintain an appropriate work environment by ensuring that all employees know what conduct is and is not appropriate and that there are serious consequences for this behavior. In fact, even when managers do not themselves engage in harassment, if they fail to prevent it or to take appropriate action after receiving legitimate complaints about it, they may still be held liable, along with their companies, if a lawsuit is filed. It is also important for managers to know that the "hostile work environment" standard applies to same-sex harassment as well as to non-gender-related cases, such as a pattern of racial or ethnic slurs. Teenaged workers are a particularly vulnerable population because they are inexperienced, tend to hold lower-status jobs, and often feel hesitant or embarrassed to speak up. For example, a restaurant chain in Wisconsin lost a case over sexual harassment of teenage employees by an adult male manager.[14] The federal EEOC has made this concern a priority and launched a teen-focused page called "Youth at Work" on its website (http://www.youth.eeoc.gov). The National Restaurant Association and National Retail Federation also have stepped up efforts to protect teens from harassment.[15]

A strong commitment to diversity leads to fewer problems with sexual harassment.

One way managers can help their companies prevent harassment from arising, or avoid punitive damages if a lawsuit is filed, is to make sure their organizations have an effective and comprehensive policy on harassment in place. Exhibit 11.5 shows the basic components of such a policy. Companies such as Avon, Corning, and PwC have found that a strong commitment to diversity leads to fewer problems with sexual harassment.[16]

Before moving on, it is important to note that gender issues and the changing nature of work do not apply just to women. In some ways, the changing status of women has given men the opportunity to redefine their roles, expectations, and lifestyles. Some men are deciding that there is more to life than corporate success and are choosing to scale back work hours and commitments to spend time with their families. Worker values are shifting toward personal time, quality of life, self-fulfillment, and family. Workers today, both men and women, are looking to achieve a balance between career and family.

In addition, a growing number of employers are thinking about gender in terms of the issues facing their employees who are lesbian, gay, bisexual, or transgender (LGBT). These employees may be concerned about work-related issues such as avoiding harassment, obtaining benefits for a same-sex spouse or domestic partner, or simply feeling free not to be secretive about this aspect of who they are. Treatment of LGBT employees is an area of ongoing change, both in societal attitudes and in the law. For example, a few years ago, a person in a same-sex relationship would automatically be legally categorized

EXHIBIT 11.5
Basic Components of
an Effective Sexual
Harassment Policy

1. **Develop a comprehensive organizationwide policy** on sexual harassment and present it to all current and new employees. Stress that sexual harassment will not be tolerated under any circumstances. Emphasis is best achieved when the policy is publicized and supported by top management.

2. **Hold training sessions with supervisors** to explain Title VII requirements, their role in providing an environment free of sexual harassment, and proper investigative procedures when charges occur.

3. **Establish a formal complaint procedure** in which employees can discuss problems without fear of retaliation. The complaint procedure should spell out how charges will be investigated and resolved.

4. **Act immediately when employees complain of sexual harassment.** Communicate widely that investigations will be conducted objectively and with appreciation for the sensitivity of the issue.

5. When an investigation supports employee charges, **discipline the offender at once.** For extremely serious offenses, discipline should include penalties up to and including discharge. Discipline should be applied consistently across similar cases and among managers and hourly employees alike.

6. **Follow up on all cases** to ensure a satisfactory resolution of the problem.

SOURCE: Snell, S.A., and Bohlander, G.W. *Managing Human Resources,* 16th ed. Copyright © 2012. Cincinnati, OH: Cengage Learning, Inc. Reproduced by permission. www.cengage.com/permissions.

as single, but today some states have laws allowing these people to marry or register as domestic partners and to adopt children together. Over 90 percent of Fortune 500 companies have policies protecting employees on the basis of sexual orientation. Also an executive order was signed recently by the president of the United States prohibiting federal contractors from discriminating against LGBT workers.[17] In situations such as this, where laws, policies, and social norms are in a state of flux, employers must be especially attentive to understand what is required and how employees, customers, and other stakeholders are affected by company policies and practices.

Minorities and Immigrants   In addition to gender issues, the importance and scope of diversity are evident in the growth of racial minorities and immigrants in the workforce. Consider these facts:

African American, Asian, and Hispanic workers are about one-third of the labor force in the United States.

Asian and Hispanic workforces are growing the fastest in the United States, followed by the African American workforce.

By 2022, more than 19 percent of the workforce is expected to be people of Hispanic origin.

In 2012, for the first time, the census bureau estimated that a majority of children under age 1 in the United States were members of racial or ethnic minority groups.

Four states (California, Hawaii, New Mexico, and Texas) and the District of Columbia have become majority minority, meaning a majority of the population consists of members of racial and ethnic minorities.

Foreign-born workers make up more than 16 percent of the U.S. civilian labor force. Close to half of these workers are Hispanic, and nearly one-fourth are Asian.[18]

These numbers indicate that the term *minority,* as it is used typically, may soon become outdated. Particularly in urban areas where white males do not predominate, managing diversity means more than eliminating discrimination; it means capitalizing on the wide variety of skills available in the labor market. Organizations that do not take full advantage of the skills and capabilities of minorities and immigrants are severely limiting their potential talent pool and their ability to understand and capture minority markets. Those markets are growing rapidly. As the minority share of the population expands, so does its share of purchasing power. And if you sell to businesses, you are likely to deal with some minority-owned companies because the number of businesses started by Asian American, African American, and Hispanic entrepreneurs is growing much faster than the overall growth in new companies in the United States. For example, more than half of the companies that started in California's high-tech Silicon Valley were founded by immigrants, and in a recent year, one-fourth of patent applications in the United States identified an immigrant as the inventor or a co-inventor.[19]

In many urban areas with large Asian, Hispanic, or African American populations, banks have deliberately increased the diversity of their managers and tellers to reflect the population mix in the community and attract additional business. If they did not, customers would readily notice and switch to other banks in the area where they would feel more welcome and comfortable. Such diversity—and collaboration among employees—permits increased customer service, helping banks maintain their competitiveness. For example, tellers approached by new immigrants who do not yet speak English immediately call on their bilingual colleagues for help. The bilingual colleagues are also in a better position to assist the bank customers with special problems such as income transfers from abroad.

Even so, the evidence shows some troubling disparities in employment and earnings. Unemployment rates are higher for black and Hispanic workers than for whites—twice as high in the case of black men. Earnings of black and Hispanic workers have consistently trailed those of white workers; recent figures put the median earnings for African American employees at 78 percent of median earnings for white workers and the median earnings of Hispanics at just 72 percent. African Americans and Hispanic Americans are also underrepresented in management and professional occupations.[20] This underrepresentation may itself help perpetuate the problem because it can leave many aspiring young minorities with fewer role models or mentors that are so helpful in an executive career.

This disparity may exist even for similar jobs. There is also considerable evidence that discrimination may account for at least some of the disparities in employment and earnings. For example, in one recent study, fictitious résumés were used to respond to help-wanted ads in Boston and Chicago newspapers. Each résumé used either African American names such as Lakisha and Jamal or white-sounding names such as Emily and Greg. The résumés with white-sounding names were 50 percent more likely to get a callback for an interview than the same résumés with African American names. Despite equivalence in credentials, the often unconscious assumptions about different racial groups are very difficult to overcome.[21]

Nevertheless, significant progress has been made. As you can see from the examples in Exhibit 11.6, talented members of minority groups are among the executives running companies and their divisions in a wide variety of industries. And some individuals and groups are highly successful. Average pay and employment rates for Asian Americans actually exceed those for white workers.

In addition, virtually every large organization today has policies and programs dedicated to increasing minority representation—including compensation systems that reward managers for increasing the diversity of their operations. Major companies such as FedEx, Xerox, Shell, PNC Financial, and Sun Microsystems have corporate diversity officers who assist organization managers in their efforts to attract, retain, and promote minority and women executives. Many organizations are also working to ensure a continuing supply of minority candidates by supporting minority internships and MBA programs. Microsoft, for example, sponsors summer internship programs for minority undergraduate college minority students pursuing computer science or software

According to a recent survey, Ernst & Young has been named as one of the best companies for valuing diversity, based on how it ranked in four key areas—CEO commitment, human capital, corporate and organizational communications, and supplier diversity.

© Lars Niki

EXHIBIT 11.6   Examples of Executives of Color

Name	Company	Title
Ajay Banga	MasterCard	President and CEO
Denice Torres	McNeil Consumer Health Care	President
David P. Bozeman	Caterpillar	Senior vice president, Caterpillar Enterprise System Group
Ursula Burns	Xerox	Chairman and CEO
Jin Sook and Do Won Chang	Forever 21	Cofounders and owners
Kenneth Chenault	American Express	Chairman and CEO
Gisel Ruiz	Walmart	Executive vice president and COO
John Thompson	Microsoft	Chairman
Marvin Ellison	JCPenney	President and CEO
Kenneth Frazier	Merck	CEO and chairman
Roger Ferguson	TIAA-CREF	President and CEO
Francisco D'Souza	Cognizant Technology Solutions	CEO
Rosalind Brewer	Sam's Club	President and CEO
Oprah Winfrey	Harpo	Chairman and CEO
Oscar Munoz	CSX	Chairman and CEO

SOURCES: J. Krell, "McDonald's CEO Exit Erodes Diversity among Fortune 500 Execs," *Fortune* (online), January 29, 2015; CSX Corporation, "Oscar Munoz Named President, CSX Corporation," press release, February 11, 2015, http://www.csx.com; C. Zillman, "Microsoft's New CEO: One Minority Exec in a Sea of White," *Fortune* (online), February 4, 2014; K. Curiel, "50 Latinas Who Rock Fortune 500 Companies," *Latina* (online), June 10, 2013, http://www.latina.com; "The 100 Most Powerful African Americans in Corporate America," *Black Business Profile* (online), accessed April 23, 2015; "5 Asian CEOs You Should Know," *Diversity Best Practices* (online), http://www.diversitybestpractices.com, accessed April 23, 2015.

engineering degrees. Lockheed Martin has partnered with the American Management Association's Operation Enterprise to establish two-week paid summer internship programs for high school and college students. These internship programs help students and organizations learn about one another and, ideally, turn into full-time employment opportunities. Exhibit 11.7 shows the top 10 companies for diversity according to DiversityInc. com. For all these companies, developing, hiring, and retaining minority executives is critical for their ability to manage an ever-more-diverse workforce and to serve an increasing number of clients and customers with varied backgrounds.

Mentally and Physically Disabled People   The largest unemployed minority population in the United States is people with disabilities. It is composed of people of all ethnic backgrounds, cultures, and ages. The share of the population with a disability is growing as the average worker gets older and heavier.[22] According to U.S. government statistics, people with disabilities represent 10 percent of the working-age civilian population. Many of these people are not in the labor force (meaning they are neither working nor looking for a job), but of the nearly 6 million persons with disabilities who are in the labor force, 13.2 percent were unemployed in 2013. That rate was far above the 7.4 percent

1.	Novartis	6.	MasterCard Worldwide
2.	Sodexo	7.	Procter & Gamble
3.	Ernst & Young	8.	Prudential Financial
4.	Kaiser Permanente	9.	Johnson & Johnson
5.	PricewaterhouseCoopers	10.	AT&T

EXHIBIT 11.7
Top Ten Companies for Diversity

SOURCE: "The DiversityInc Top 50 Companies for Diversity," *DiversityInc,* 2014, http://www.diversityinc.com.

unemployment rate for the general population.[23] Persons with a disability are more likely to have jobs if they have higher levels of education, and they are more likely than workers without disabilities to have a part-time job because they can't find full-time work.[24]

The Americans with Disabilities Act Amendments Act (ADAAA), mentioned in Chapter 10, defines a disability as a physical or mental impairment that substantially limits one or more major life activities. Examples of such physical or mental impairments include those resulting from conditions such as orthopedic, visual, speech, and hearing impairments; cerebral palsy; epilepsy; multiple sclerosis; HIV infections; cancer; heart disease; diabetes; mental retardation; psychological illness; specific learning disabilities; drug addiction; and alcoholism.[25]

New assistive technologies are making it easier for companies to comply with the ADA and for those with disabilities to be productive on the job. In many cases, state governments will pay for special equipment or other accommodations that workers need. Companies are discovering that making these accommodations can result in unanticipated fringe benefits, too. The National Industries for the Blind (NIB), a Wisconsin company that markets products under the Skilcraft brand name, is a case in point. Seventy-five percent of NIB employees are visually impaired. Because the company's warehouse pickers have trouble reading instructions on paper, NIB installed a voice technology system that conveys instructions to workers through headsets. An added benefit is that the technology has raised the productivity of the entire operation. Accuracy has improved, and workers—both blind and sighted—are able to pick and ship orders faster using the headsets.

For most businesses, people with mental and physical disabilities represent an unexplored but fruitful labor market. Frequently employers have found that employees with disabilities are more dependable than other employees, miss fewer days of work, and exhibit lower turnover. Tax credits are also available to companies that hire workers with disabilities. In addition, managers who hire and support employees with disabilities are signaling to other employees and outside stakeholders their strong interest in creating an inclusive organization culture.

Education Levels   When the United States was primarily an industrial economy, many jobs required physical strength, stamina, and skill in a trade, rather than college and professional degrees. In today's service and technology economy, more positions require a college education and even a graduate or professional degree. Today's prospective employees have responded by applying to college in record numbers. The proportion of the workforce with at least some college education has been growing steadily. In 1947, about 5 percent of workers had at least a bachelor's degree; the percentage passed 15 percent in the 1970s and stands at 30 percent today. These numbers include rising shares of African American, Hispanic, and female graduates. People with degrees in science and technology are in especially high demand. Employers often expand their search for scientists and computer professionals overseas, but visa requirements limit that supply. At the other end of the spectrum, in the current labor pool, almost 25 percent of foreign-born workers have not completed high school, compared with just 5 percent of native-born workers.[26]

The share of workers with a bachelor's degree has more than doubled since 1970.

The Age of the Workforce

The baby boom generation (those born between 1946 and 1964) is aging. The Pew Research Center states that approximately 10,000 Boomers are retiring each day in the United States.[27] Industries most at risk include health care (hospitals and nursing facilities), transportation, social assistance, and mining and construction.[28] As a result of these trends, the Bureau of Labor Statistics projects that entry-level workers will be in short supply.

On the plus side, almost 70 percent of workers between the ages of 45 and 74 told researchers with AARP (formerly the American Association of Retired Persons) that they intend to work in retirement. Retirees often return to the workforce at the behest of their employers, who can't afford to lose the knowledge accumulated by longtime employees, their willingness to work nontraditional shifts, and their reliable work habits, which have a positive effect on the entire work group.

To prevent an exodus of talent, employers need strategies to help retain and attract skilled and knowledgeable older workers. Phased retirement plans that allow older employees to work fewer hours per week is one such strategy. Other strategies include making workplace adaptations to help older workers cope with the physical problems they experience as they age, such as poorer vision, hearing, and mobility. This trend is a significant change from the practice in recent decades, when older workers were given incentives to leave to allow companies to reduce overhead and perhaps hire less expensive replacements. A recent study found 87 percent of employers view their older workers as valuable resources for training, mentoring, and sharing institutional knowledge.[29] These companies save on turnover and training costs and capitalize on the experience of their older employees.

At the same time, companies need to compete hard for the smaller pool of young talent, being prepared for applicants who know the job market and are ready to demand the working conditions they value and the praise they were raised to expect. Bruce Tulgan, founder of Rainmaker Thinking, which specializes in researching generational differences, says Generation Y—today's young workers—tend to be "high-maintenance" but also "high-performing," having learned to process the flood of information that pours in over the Internet.[30] Many of these workers were raised by highly involved parents who filled their lives with quality experiences, so employers are scrambling to design work arrangements that are stimulating, involve teamwork, keep work hours reasonable to allow for outside activities, and provide for plenty of positive feedback. Employers are also updating their recruiting tactics to reach young workers where they are—online. For example, online retailer Zappos attracts Millennial applicants by posting videos on YouTube about the company's values and how fun it is to work for the company. Others like Panera Bread, Starbucks, and Uber use LinkedIn to find qualified candidates. In the government sector, the Central Intelligence Agency and National Security Agency have set up pages on Facebook, where members who register for access can read information about job openings.[31]

Managing Diversity versus Affirmative Action

For many organizations, the original impetus to diversify their workforces was social responsibility and legal necessity (recall Chapters 5 and 10). To correct the past exclusion of women and minorities, companies introduced **affirmative action**—special efforts to recruit and hire qualified members of groups that have been discriminated against in the past. The intent is not to prefer these group members to the exclusion of others but to correct for the long history of discriminatory practices and exclusion. Viewed from this perspective, amending these wrongs is seen as the moral, ethical, and legal approach.

affirmative action

Special efforts to recruit and hire qualified members of groups that have been discriminated against in the past.

Such efforts, along with legal remedies to end discrimination, have had a powerful impact, transforming our society and organizations in positive ways that would have been unimaginable only a few decades ago. Today the immigrant nature of American society is virtually taken for granted—even seen as a source of pride. And women, African Americans, Hispanics, and other minorities routinely occupy positions that in years past would have been totally closed to them.

Nevertheless, as we have seen, a legislated approach tends to result in fragmented efforts that have not yet fully achieved the integrative goals of diversity. Employment discrimination still persists, and even after decades of government legislation, equal employment opportunity (EEO) and affirmative action laws have not adequately improved the upward mobility of women and minorities. To move beyond correcting past wrongs to truly inclusive organizations requires a change in organization culture—one in which diversity is seen as contributing directly to the attainment of organization goals.

Managing diversity involves organizations making changes to remove obstacles that may keep people from reaching their full potential.

© Beathan/Corbis

Seen in this way, affirmative action and diversity are complementary, not the same. In contrast to EEO and affirmative action programs, managing diversity means moving beyond legislated mandates to embrace a proactive business philosophy that sees differences as a positive value. In the end, *all* employees are different. These differences may include the fundamental attributes of race, ethnicity, age, and gender we have been discussing, but they also may include less obvious attributes such as employees' place of origin, their education, or their life experience. All these elements add to the richness of talents and perspectives managers can draw on. Managing diversity in this broader sense involves organizations making changes in their systems, structures, and practices to eliminate barriers that may keep people from reaching their full potential. It means treating people as individuals—*equally* but not necessarily the *same*—recognizing that each employee has different needs and will need different things to succeed. But it also asks managers to recognize and value the uniqueness of each employee and to see the different ideas and perspectives each brings to the organization as a source of competitive advantage. In short, managing diversity is not just about getting more minorities and women into the organization. It is about creating an environment in which employees from *every* background listen to each other and work better together so that the organization as a whole will become more effective. This emphasis on coming together to benefit the whole has led many companies now to refer to diversity and *inclusion* as their objectives.

> Affirmative action and diversity are complementary, not the same.

Competitive Advantage through Diversity and Inclusion

Today many organizations are approaching diversity and inclusion from a more practical, business-oriented perspective. Increasingly, diversity can be a powerful tool for building competitive advantage. Various studies have found links between diversity in an organization's upper ranks and superior financial performance. Some evidence suggests that this correlation may result from investors' preferences for organizations with a policy of inclusion rather than from superior management of diverse companies. Nevertheless, diversity does not stand in the way of high performance, and it may provide an organizational strength—especially if organizations know how to leverage it.[32]

There are many advantages—and some obvious challenges—to managing a diverse workforce. We discuss some of them in this section.

Ability to Attract and Retain Motivated Employees   For companies facing changing demographics and business needs, diversity makes good sense. Companies with a reputation for providing opportunities for diverse employees will have a competitive advantage in the labor market and will be sought out by the most qualified employees. In addition, when employees believe their differences are not merely tolerated but valued, they may become more loyal, productive, and committed.

Better Perspective on a Differentiated Market   Companies such as Ford, General Mills, IBM, Target, and Kroger are committed to diversity because as the composition of the American workforce changes, so does the customer base of these companies. Just as women and minorities may prefer to work for an employer that values diversity, they may prefer to patronize such organizations.

Many Asian Americans, African Americans, Hispanic Americans, and women have entered the middle class and now control consumer dollars. Similarly, each new generation has its own set of values and experiences, so diversity in ages can help the organization relate to more age groups of customers. A diverse workforce can provide a company with

Bottom Line

Diversity can help an organization succeed in new markets.

What are some new or diverse markets that Toys "R" Us can serve best with a diverse workforce?

greater knowledge of the preferences and consuming habits of this diversified marketplace. This knowledge can assist companies in designing products and developing marketing campaigns to meet those consumers' needs. In addition, for at least some goods and services, a multicultural sales force may help an organization sell to diverse groups. A diverse workforce also can give a company a competitive edge in a global economy by facilitating understanding of other customs, cultures, and marketplace needs.

Ability to Leverage Creativity and Innovation in Problem Solving   Work team diversity promotes creativity and innovation because people from different backgrounds hold different perspectives on issues. Diverse groups have a broader base of experience from which to approach a problem; when effectively managed, they invent more options and create more solutions than homogeneous groups do. In addition, diverse work groups are freer to deviate from traditional approaches and practices. The presence of diversity also can help minimize "groupthink" (recall Chapter 3).[33]

Many law firms now routinely have diverse legal teams working together on a case. Fresh "out of the box" ideas are often required in complex cases, and a group of lawyers from the same background who all think the same way may not be able to be as innovative as a team that is more diverse. In addition, in jury trials, the impression that a legal team makes on a jury can help or badly hurt the client, and diverse jurors are more likely to be receptive to a visibly diverse team, with different kinds of lawyers participating. The increased importance of legal team diversity has caused some law firms to form alliances with minority firms so they can collaborate on cases.

Enhancement of Organizational Flexibility   A diverse workforce can enhance organizational flexibility because managing diversity successfully requires a corporate culture that tolerates many styles and approaches. Less restrictive policies and procedures and less standardized operating methods enable organizations to become more flexible and thus better able to respond quickly to environmental changes (recall Chapters 2 and 9). Procter & Gamble, for example, values diversity as an important part of fulfilling its strategy: "Everyone valued, everyone included, everyone performing at their peak."[34]

Challenges of Diversity and Inclusion

We have discussed the laws guaranteeing equal opportunity and the significant and growing business advantages of diversity and inclusion. Yet every year thousands of lawsuits are filed over issues of discrimination and fair treatment, some involving even the largest and most respected firms.[35] Recent examples of settled governmental EEOC lawsuits include Walgreen's firing a longtime employee with diabetes for eating a bag of chips during a diabetes-related episode; McCormick & Schmick's Seafood Restaurants for discriminating against black workers in hiring and work assignments; and DSW for unfairly firing employees who were over 40 years old as part of a workforce reduction effort.[36] Even when there is no overt discrimination in hiring and pay, managing diversity can be difficult. Often minorities and women who have been hired find themselves in an organization culture or environment that does not give them the opportunity to do their best work. And managers with all the goodwill in the world find it harder than they expected to get people from different backgrounds to work together for a common goal.[37]

To become effective managers of the diverse organization, we first have to identify and overcome a number of challenges. These include unexamined assumptions, lower cohesiveness, communication problems, mistrust and tension, and stereotyping.

Unexamined Assumptions   For most of us, seeing the world from someone else's perspective is difficult because our own assumptions and viewpoints seem so normal and familiar. For example, heterosexuals may not even think about whether to put a picture of their loved ones on their desks; it is a routine, even automatic decision, repeated in a million workplaces across the country. But for gay employees in many companies, displaying such a picture may cause considerable anxiety—if they feel able to consider it at all.

Bottom Line

Diversity can bring new ideas to the organization.
What kinds of innovation are a strength in your generation? In a generation older than yours?

Bottom Line

A diverse workforce can lead to greater responsiveness.
Why might a customer who wants something new get a faster response from a company that tolerates different styles?

 LO 4

Other unexamined assumptions involve the roles of men and women; for example, many people assume that women will shoulder the burden of caring for children, even if it conflicts with the demands of work. In a recent study, researchers sent employers résumés that were identical except that some bore a male name and others a female name, and half implied that the person submitting the résumé was a parent. Employers were less likely to invite the fictional candidate for an interview when the résumé implied the candidate was a parent—but only if the name was female.[38] Because the résumés were otherwise identical, the results suggest that people make assumptions about mothers that do not apply to fathers or to childless women.

In an organization that is oblivious to these different perspectives and does not take an active role in making people from diverse backgrounds feel welcome and valued, managers may find it more difficult to develop an enthusiastically shared sense of purpose.

Lower Cohesiveness   Diversity can create a lack of cohesiveness. *Cohesiveness* refers to how tightly knit the group is and the degree to which group members perceive, interpret, and act on their environment in similar or mutually agreed-upon ways. Because of their lack of similarity in language, culture, and/or experience, diverse groups typically are less cohesive than homogeneous groups. Often mistrust, miscommunication, stress, and attitudinal differences reduce cohesiveness, which in turn can diminish productivity. This may be one explanation for the results of a study that showed greater turnover among store employees who feel they are greatly outnumbered by coworkers from other racial or ethnic groups.[39] In a diverse group, managers are challenged to take the lead in building cohesiveness by establishing common goals and values. Group cohesiveness will be discussed in greater detail in Chapter 14.

Communication Problems   Perhaps the most common negative effect of diversity is communication problems. These difficulties include misunderstandings, inaccuracies, inefficiencies, and slowness. Speed is lost when not all group members are fluent in the same language or when additional time is required to explain things. Sometimes diversity may decrease communication, as when white male managers feel less comfortable giving feedback to women or minorities for fear of how criticism may be received. The result may be employees who do not have a clear idea of what they need to do to improve their performance.

Diversity can also lead to errors and misunderstandings. Group members may assume they interpret things similarly when they in fact do not, or they may disagree because of their different frames of reference.[40] For example, if managers do not actively encourage and accept the expression of different points of view, some employees may be afraid to speak up at meetings, leaving the manager with a false impression that consensus has been reached. We discuss other problems in communication and how to avoid them in Chapter 15.

Mistrust and Tension   People prefer to associate with others who are like themselves. This is a normal, understandable tendency. But it can often lead to misunderstanding, mistrust, and even fear of those who are different because of a lack of contact and low familiarity. For example, if women and minority group members are routinely excluded, as they sometimes are, from joining white male colleagues at business lunches or after-hour gatherings, they may come to feel isolated from their colleagues. Similarly, tension often develops between people of different ages—for example, what one generation might see as a tasteless tattoo may be a creative example of body art for a member of a different generation. Such misunderstandings can cause stress, tension, and even resentment, making it more difficult to reach agreement on solutions to problems.

Stereotyping   We learn to see the world in a certain way on the basis of our backgrounds and experiences. Our interests, values, and cultures act as filters and distort, block, and select what we see and hear. We see and hear what we expect to see and hear. Group members often inappropriately stereotype their different colleagues rather than accurately perceiving and evaluating those individuals' contributions, capabilities, aspirations, and motivations. Such stereotypes are usually negative or condescending. Women may be stereotyped as not dedicated to their careers, older workers as unwilling to learn new skills, minority group members as less educated or capable. But even so-called positive stereotypes can be burdensome. For example, the common stereotype that Asians are good at math may leave unrecognized other attributes that a particular Asian employee might have. Many women and minorities dislike being stereotyped as members of groups that need special help or support, preferring to be treated as individuals.

Stereotypes may lead organizations to miss the opportunity to hire qualified candidates. A recent study submitted over 9,000 résumés for jobs in several cities from fictitious, recently graduated job candidates. All of the résumés were essentially identical, except for the names of the applicants. Half the résumés had "typically black names" and the other half had "typically white names." The researchers found that black applicants received 14 percent fewer interview requests from recruiters than their otherwise identical white counterparts.[41]

Stereotypes may cost the organization dearly by stifling employees' ambition so that they don't fully contribute. Research supports the idea that people perform better when they expect that they can. In a study in which undergraduate students were purportedly pretesting a new graduate admissions test, half the subjects were told that males had greater ability in the test's subject matter. Although all subjects were told they received the same score, the females exposed to the biased message rated their abilities in the subject lower than the males who heard the message, and they set lower goals for their future performance in that area.[42] In a corporate setting, managers want their employees to perform to their full ability; stereotypes that dampen individual employees' ambition and performance also detract from the organization's success.

Unless managers are aware of their stereotypes, either their own or those held by others, the stereotypes can directly affect how people in their organizations are treated. Employees stereotyped as unmotivated or emotional will be given less stress-provoking (and perhaps less important) jobs than their coworkers. Those job assignments will create frustrated employees, perhaps resulting in lower commitment, higher turnover, and underused skills.[43]

The Challenge Ahead   For all these reasons, and more, managing diversity is not easy. As illustrated by the example of NASCAR in the following "Management in Action: Progress Report," U.S. organizations are not isolated from the continuing effects of America's racial legacy or the remaining barriers to equal opportunity. Nor are managers immune to the biases, stereotypes, lack of experience, and tensions that make communication, teamwork, and leadership in a diverse workforce much more challenging. Yet managers very much need to confront these issues. They need to develop the skills and strategies diversity requires if they and their organizations are to succeed in our increasingly multicultural business environment.

One constructive way to begin is with what Martin Davidson has called "leveraging difference." This approach sees diversity not as a problem to be tolerated or solved but as a resource the organization can capitalize on, even though doing so is sometimes difficult. Leveraging difference starts with the recognition that we all bring something different to an organization. Along with surface differences such as sex and race, we contribute different ways of thinking and problem solving, different strengths and values, and so on. To capitalize on these differences, as shown in Exhibit 11.8, people in the organization have to begin by seeing them. Then individuals must make the effort to understand the differences by asking questions and listening carefully. The next step is to value the differences not only through the organization's recruitment and recognition programs but also through willingness to persist despite conflict and to incorporate new perspectives into one's own thinking. This effort provides the information needed to leverage the differences by applying them to the whole spectrum of organization activities, such as innovating, learning, working as a team, and interacting with customers.[44] The remainder of this chapter provides further thinking on how to meet the challenges of diversity and leverage it for organizational success.

Management in Action

NASCAR'S DRIVE FOR DIVERSITY CAN BE A GRUELING RIDE

The driver development program of NASCAR's Drive for Diversity (D4D) effort aims to "give minority and female drivers the opportunity to compete with a NASCAR team." It does so by recruiting minority and female drivers, training them, and letting them compete in the K&N Pro Series East and Whelen All-American Series. Also, according to NASCAR, the program "seeks opportunities for program graduates to advance within various NASCAR series; provides media training and marketing guidance to developing drivers; and exposes participating drivers to media opportunities outside the sport."

The program is open to candidates who are between the ages of 15 and 26, citizens or those legally able to work in the United States, and female or a member of one of several minority groups: African American, Asian, Hispanic, Native Hawaiian or Pacific Islander, and American Indian. However, not just anyone in these groups qualifies. All applicants must have experience and skill in racing at the local or regional level (for example, in go-karts, sprint cars, or stock cars). Out of more than 200 applicants, NASCAR selects about 30 to compete in an evaluation program called the Combine. NASCAR observes their on-track performance and interactions with sponsors and the media. It then chooses 6 to 10 drivers for the program, based on driving ability, physical stamina, knowledge about cars, and

whether they are marketable. Drivers chosen for the 2015 class came from New Mexico, Nevada, Florida, Wisconsin, Oklahoma, and Vermont.

According to Max Siegel, CEO of Rev Racing, D4D is an all-encompassing development program aimed at having its drivers eventually win one of NASCAR's three national series. D4D drivers such as Kyle Larson and Darrell Wallace Jr. credit the program with giving them the kinds of experiences they need to reach their full potential and introduce the sport to a wider audience. Veteran driver Kyle Busch agrees that diversity can benefit the whole organization, saying it "widens our fan base."

Participants in the program are grateful for the experience, training, and mentoring. However, they acknowledge that there's a downside. Although few applicants make the cut and the training is rigorous, D4D drivers have admitted they hear criticism that NASCAR is giving them an unfair advantage. However, drivers who benefited from D4D such as Ryan Gifford and Katie Hagar say their best answer is to learn all aspects of the sport, get out on the track, ride near the front, and win.[45]

- Does the D4D program sound more like managing diversity or affirmative action? Why?
- How should NASCAR address criticism that it gives minority and female drivers an unfair advantage?

EXHIBIT 11.8 Beyond Affirmative Action: Key Practices to Leverage Employee Differences

	Key Individual Practices	Key Organizational Practices
Seeing	• Adopt a stance that relevant differences are ubiquitous. • Attend to points of conflict. • Observe silence.	• Attend to intergroup tension. • Reduce the climate of secrecy.

Understanding	• Build skill in acquiring data.
	  – Listen.
	  – Ask questions.
	  – Learn and share your own story.
	• Include people who are different in your inner circle or network.
		• Acquire information via survey and other data gathering.
		• Create and institutionalize inclusive structures.

Valuing	• Lower the levels of unnecessary carefulness when dealing with differences. • Be willing to persist in the midst of conflict and its accompanying discomfort. • Incorporate data into your worldview.	• Reward and hold employees accountable for engaging in difference-related activities. • Recruit and develop people who add diversity to the organization.

SOURCE: M. N. Davidson, *The End of Diversity as We Know It: Why Diversity Efforts Fail and How Leveraging Difference Can Succeed* (San Francisco: Berrett-Kohler Press, 2011).

Multicultural Organizations

To capitalize on the benefits and minimize the costs of a diverse workforce, perhaps one of the first things managers need to do is examine their organization's prevailing assumptions about people and cultures. Exhibit 11.9 shows some of the fundamental assumptions that may exist. Based on these assumptions, we can classify organizations as one of three types and describe their implications for managers.

Some organizations are **monolithic.** This type of organization has very little cultural integration; in other words, it employs few women, minorities, or any other groups that differ from the majority. For example, in its hiring, an organization might favor alumni of the same college, perhaps even more specifically targeting members of fraternities who are enthusiastic about the school's football team. Such an organization is highly homogeneous in terms of its employee population. In monolithic organizations, if groups other than the norm are employed, they are found primarily in low-status jobs. Minority group members must adopt the norms of the majority to survive. This fact, coupled with small numbers, keeps conflicts among groups low. Discrimination and prejudice typically prevail, informal integration is almost nonexistent, and minority group members do not identify strongly with the company.

Most large U.S. organizations made the transition from monolithic to pluralistic organizations in the 1960s and 1970s because of changing demographics as well as societal forces such as the civil rights and women's movements. **Pluralistic organizations** have a more diverse employee population and take steps to involve persons from different gender, racial, or cultural backgrounds. These organizations use an affirmative action approach to managing diversity: They actively try to hire and train a diverse workforce and to ensure against any discrimination against minority group members. They typically have much more integration than do monolithic organizations, but like monolithic organizations, they often have minority group members clustered at certain levels or in particular functions within the organization.

monolithic organization

An organization that has a low degree of structural integration—employing few women, minorities, or other groups that differ from the majority—and thus has a highly homogeneous employee population.

pluralistic organization

An organization that has a relatively diverse employee population and makes an effort to involve employees from different gender, racial, or cultural backgrounds.

EXHIBIT 11.9   Diversity Assumptions and Their Implications for Management

Common and Misleading Assumptions		Less Common and More Appropriate Assumptions	
Homogeneity	*Melting pot myth:* We are all the same.	**Heterogeneity**	*Image of cultural pluralism:* We are not all the same; groups within society differ across cultures.
Similarity	*Similarity myth:* "They" are all just like me.	**Similarity and difference**	*They are not just like me:* Many people differ from me culturally. Most people exhibit both cultural similarities and differences when compared with me.
Parochialism	*Only-one-way myth:* Our way is the only way. We do not recognize any other way of living or working.	**Equifinality**	*Our way is not the only way:* There are many culturally distinct ways of reaching the same goal, of working, and of living one's life.
Ethnocentrism	*One-best-way myth:* Our way is the best way. All other approaches are inferior versions of our way.	**Culture contingency**	*Our way is one possible way:* There are many and equally good ways to reach the same goal. The best way depends on the culture of the people involved.

SOURCE: From "Diversity Assumptions and Their Implications for Management" by Nancy J. Adler, *Handbook of Organization,* 1996. Reprinted courtesy of Marcel Dekker Inc., New York.

multicultural organization

An organization that values cultural diversity and seeks to utilize and encourage it.

ambicultural organization

An organization that embraces and unites opposites (e.g., majority and minority) in order to achieve balance and long-term success.

Because of greater cultural integration, affirmative action programs, and training programs, the pluralistic organization has some acceptance of minority group members into the informal network, much less discrimination, and less prejudice. Improved employment opportunities create greater identification with the organization among minority group members. Often the resentment of majority group members, coupled with the increased number of women and minorities, creates more conflict than exists in the monolithic organization.

The pluralistic organization fails to address the cultural aspects of integration. In contrast, in **multicultural organizations** diversity not only exists but is valued. These organizations fully integrate gender, racial, and minority group members both formally and informally. But managers in such organizations do not focus primarily on the visible differences between employees, such as race or sex. Rather, managers value and draw on the different experience and knowledge employees bring to the organization and help it achieve agreed-upon strategies and goals.[46] The multicultural organization is marked by an absence of prejudice and discrimination and by low levels of intergroup conflict. Such an organization creates a synergistic environment in which all members contribute to their maximum potential, and the advantages of diversity can be fully realized.[47]

Building on some of the best attributes of multiculturalism is the **ambicultural organization.** Professor Ming-Jer Chen of the University of Virginia suggests that managers and organizations that embrace, overcome, and unite "opposites" are more likely to achieve long-term success. Examples of opposites include for-profit and nonprofit, majority and minority, local and global, short-term and long-term, and so forth. Dr. Chen notes that visionary business leaders like Carlos Ghosn of Renault-Nissan and Ruimin Zhang of Haier have instilled ambicultural thinking into "their integrative, balanced, relational approach to management."

Lincoln Electric, a U.S.-based welding equipment manufacturer, has practiced ambicultural management for decades. The 3,000-employee organization strikes a balance between "internal competition and cooperation, social welfare and individual interest, and tradition and entrepreneurship." The company's philosophy is to treat employees very well while demanding outstanding performance. This balanced approach is very successful. Not only has Lincoln Electric remained the dominant firm in the global electric welding industry since the 1930s, but it has not laid off a single employee in 65 years. As members of the company's profit sharing plan, employees recently made an average of $81,366 in wages/salary plus bonus.[48]

How Organizations Can Cultivate a Diverse Workforce

An organization's plans for becoming multicultural and making the most of its diverse workforce should include (1) securing top management's leadership and commitment, (2) assessing the organization's progress toward goals, (3) attracting employees, (4) training employees in diversity, and (5) retaining employees. A study examining the performance of hundreds of companies over a 30-year period found that organizations that assigned responsibility for achieving diversity targets to certain individuals or groups made the most progress in increasing the share of female and black workers on their payrolls. Moderate change occurred in companies that set up programs for mentoring and networking, but formal diversity training programs had little effect unless the organizations also use the other methods.[49] Thus cultivating diversity needs to be a well-planned, organizationwide effort in which each element is supported by the personal commitment of individual managers, who address this issue as seriously as they do other management challenges. These managers actively seek to develop the skills, understanding, and practices that enable people of every background to do their best work in the common pursuit of the organization's goals.

Social Enterprise

Managing Diversity at Change.org

When Jen Dulski took over as chief operating officer of the online petition platform, Change.org, there was only one female employee in the engineering department. For an organization that serves diverse stakeholders in 196 countries, this lack of diversity did not align with the organization's mission.

Change.org's mission is to "empower people everywhere to create the change they want to see." The company is currently helping 40 million global users launch approximately 1,000 online petitions per day. Tens of thousands of online signatures on petitions have resulted in the following changes: Bank of America dropped a $5 per month surcharge for customers using its debit card, Jamba Juice replaced its Styrofoam cups for an eco-friendly alternative, and 1-800-Flowers shifted its sourcing away from potentially exploited workers overseas to fair-trade and transparent sourcing.

Dulski and other leaders have realigned its internal culture and employee composition with that of its customers. The leaders are "embracing openness," which means working toward gender equality while also embracing employees with different perspectives—international workers, older employees, and individuals with different career experiences.

Dulski suggests the following steps to embrace employee diversity and inclusiveness:

1. *Make everyone part of the mission.* Make diversity a part of your firm's core values and celebrate those employees who embody those values.
2. *Improve the hiring process.* Cast a wider recruitment net to find qualified, diverse applicants.

© *Linda Davidson*/The Washington Post *via Getty Images*

3. *Create the right culture.* Encourage open communication between managers and employees and provide rewards that employees value.

Have these initiatives helped increase diversity at Change.org? The company's engineering team of nearly 50 people is 27 percent female and over half the company's total employees are women. In terms of leadership positions, women hold 40 percent of the positions and non-Americans occupy 43 percent of them.[50]

Questions

- What internal and external forces drove Jen Dulski and other managers at Change.org to reexamine their commitment to diversity?

- Why was it important for the company to hire more female and international employees?

Top Management's Leadership and Commitment

Obtaining top management's leadership and commitment is critical for diversity programs to succeed. Otherwise the rest of the organization will not take the effort seriously. One way to communicate this commitment to all employees—as well as to the external environment—is to incorporate the organization's attitudes toward diversity into the corporate mission statement and into strategic plans and objectives. Managerial compensation can be linked directly to accomplishing diversity goals. Adequate funding must be allocated to the diversity effort to ensure its success. Also, top management can set an example for other organization members by participating in diversity programs and making participation mandatory for all managers. The nearby "Social Enterprise" box discusses how Change.org manages diversity.

As we mentioned earlier, some organizations have established corporate offices or committees to coordinate the companywide diversity effort and provide feedback to top management. The City of Boston hired a chief diversity officer, and Avon, a director of multicultural planning and design. Other companies prefer to incorporate diversity management into the function of director of affirmative action or EEO.

Michael Jordan, Basketball Hall of Fame inductee, is one of the high-profile minority team owners in the NBA.

© Streeter Lecka/Getty Images

The work of managing diversity cannot be done by top management or diversity directors alone. Many companies rely on minority advisory groups or task forces to monitor organizational policies, practices, and attitudes; assess their impact on the diverse groups within the organization; and provide feedback and suggestions to top management.

For example, at Equitable Life Assurance Society, employee groups meet regularly with the CEO to discuss issues pertaining to women, African Americans, and Hispanics and make recommendations for improvement. At Honeywell, employees with disabilities formed a council to discuss their needs. They proposed and accepted an accessibility program that went beyond federal regulations for accommodations of disabilities.

As you can see, progressive companies are moving from asking managers what they think minority employees need and toward asking the employees themselves what they need.

Organizational Assessment

The next step in managing diversity is to establish an ongoing assessment of the organization's workforce, culture, policies, and practices in areas such as recruitment, promotions, benefits, and compensation. As part of this assessment, managers may evaluate whether they are attracting their share of diverse candidates from the labor pool and whether the needs of their customers are being addressed by the current composition of their workforce. The objective is to identify areas where there are problems or opportunities and to make recommendations where changes are needed. Etsy, the social commerce website for handcrafted and vintage items, determined that 80 percent of its customers are women but only about 3 percent of its engineers were women. Marc Hedlund, former senior vice president of engineering, was concerned this mismatch was making it harder to attract and serve customers. Hedlund determined that Etsy needed to bring more female engineers on board and develop their skills.[51]

Many women and Asians can be at a disadvantage when aggressiveness is a valued part of an organization's culture. Analysis might reveal that this value exists and that it excludes employees who do not share it from full participation. Managers can then decide that the organizational values need to be changed so that other styles of interacting are equally acceptable. Managers can also change their own behaviors to reflect this change—for example, by calling on all individuals in a meeting for their ideas instead of letting more assertive participants dominate. Corporate values and norms should be identified and critically evaluated regarding their necessity and their impact on the diverse workforce.

Attracting Employees

Companies can attract a diverse, qualified workforce by using effective recruiting practices, accommodating employees' work and family needs, and offering alternative work arrangements.

Recruitment   A company's image can be a strong recruiting tool. Companies with reputations for hiring and promoting all types of people have a competitive advantage. Xerox gives prospective minority employees reprints of an article that rates the company as one of the best places for African Americans to work. Hewlett-Packard ensures that its female candidates are familiar with its high rating by *Working Woman* magazine.

Many employers are implementing policies to attract more women, ensure that women's talents are used to full advantage, and avoid losing their most capable female employees. With over 80 percent of its customers being female, Etsy's solution was to increase the pool of software engineers, at the same time positioning itself as a company that values women. It offers female engineers $5,000 scholarships to the Hacker School's three-month programming course, which brought a flood of Etsy-appreciating women to learn the kinds of skills Etsy needs. Also, it shifted its focus from hiring senior engineers to hiring junior engineers and training them to lead. The focus on diversity not only has increased the share of female engineers at Etsy, but it also has attracted the kinds of male engineers who value the company's culture and work well on group projects. In less than two years, the number of women in engineering positions grew from four to 20. [52]

Many minority group members, persons with disabilities, and those who are economically disadvantaged are physically isolated from job opportunities. Companies can bring information about job opportunities to the source of labor, or they can transport the labor to the jobs. Polycast Technology in Stamford, Connecticut, contracts with a private van company to transport workers from the Bronx in New York City to jobs in Stamford. Days Inn recruits homeless workers in Atlanta and houses them in a motel within walking distance of their jobs. Burger King has done a lot to recruit and hire immigrants in its fast-food restaurants.

Accommodating Work and Family Needs   More job seekers are putting family needs first. Corporate work and family policies are now one of the most important recruiting tools. SAS, a business analytics software company in North Carolina, keeps turnover to less than 3 percent by providing free "work–life" counseling, which helps employees more effectively manage the stresses of everyday life. Also, employees can burn stress by working out in a large gymnasium, swimming laps in a heated pool, or taking advantage of deeply discounted child care.[53]

© AP Photo/Karl DeBlaker

Employers that offer onsite child care report decreased turnover and absenteeism and improved morale. In addition to providing child care, many companies now assist with care for elderly dependents, offer time off to care for sick family members, provide parental leaves of absence, and offer a variety of benefits that can be tailored to individual family needs. Some companies are accommodating the needs and concerns of dual-career couples by limiting relocation requirements or providing job search assistance to relocated spouses.

Alternative Work Arrangements   Another way managers accommodate diversity is to offer flexible work schedules and arrangements. Stiff demand for engineering talent is motivating manufacturing companies to accommodate the needs of employees with family responsibilities. General Electric Aviation offers flexible work options to engineers like Sharon Crall. Crall, who struggles to balance busy work and home lives, can develop and submit a plan to reduce her work hours and work offsite. Approval of the flexible work plan depends on her job duties and the business's ability to accommodate the request.[54]

Other creative work arrangements include compressed workweeks (e.g., four 10-hour days) and job sharing, in which two part-time workers share one full-time job. Another option to accommodate working mothers and employees with disabilities is teleworking (working from home) or telecommuting (working from home via computer hookup to the main work site). This option has been slow to catch on, but the organizations that have tried it report favorable results.

Training Employees

As you learned in Chapter 10, employees can be developed in a variety of ways. Traditionally, most management training was based on the unstated assumption that managing means managing a homogeneous, often white-male, full-time workforce. But gender, race, culture, age, educational, and other differences create an additional layer of complexity.[55] Diversity training programs attempt to identify and reduce hidden biases and develop the skills needed to manage a diversified workforce effectively.

The majority of U.S. organizations sponsor some sort of diversity training. Typically, diversity training has two components: awareness building and skill building.

Awareness Building   Awareness building is designed to increase awareness of the meaning and importance of valuing diversity.[56] Its aim is not to teach specific skills but to sensitize employees to the assumptions they make about others and the way those assumptions affect their behaviors, decisions, and judgment. For example, male employees who have never reported to a female manager may feel awkward the first time they are required to do so. Awareness building can reveal this concern in advance and help the managers address it.

To build awareness, trainers teach people to become familiar with myths, stereotypes, and cultural differences as well as the organizational barriers that inhibit the full contributions of all employees. They develop a better understanding of corporate culture, requirements for success, and career choices that affect opportunities for advancement.

In most companies, the rules for success are ambiguous, unwritten, and perhaps inconsistent with written policy. A common problem for women, minorities, immigrants, and young employees is that they are unaware of many of the unofficial rules that are obvious to people in the mainstream. For example, organizations often have informal networks and power structures that may not be apparent or readily available to women and minority group members. As a result, these employees are less likely to know where to go when they need to get something approved or when they want to build support and alliances. For managers, valuing diversity means teaching the unwritten rules or cultural values to those who need to know them and changing the rules when necessary to benefit employees and hence the organization. It also requires inviting outsiders in and giving them access to information and meaningful relationships with people in power.

Skill Building   Diversity training that merely identifies problems without giving participants the tools they need to be able to act on what they have learned may leave participants feeling that the training was not useful or worthwhile. For this reason, many organizations include skill building as part of a diversity program. Skill building is designed to allow all employees and managers to develop the skills they need to deal effectively with one another and with customers in a diverse environment. Most of the skills taught are interpersonal, such as active listening, coaching, and giving feedback. Ideally, the skills taught are based on the organizational assessment, so the training can be tailored to the specific business issues managers have identified. For example, if too many women and minorities believe they are not getting enough helpful feedback, the skills-building program can be designed to address that issue. Likewise, training in flexible scheduling can help managers meet the company's needs while accommodating and valuing workers who want to be able to set aside time to advance their education, participate in community projects, or look after elderly parents. Tying the training to specific, measurable business goals increases its usefulness and allows managers to assess whether it is working.

Experiential exercises, online training videos, and software often are used in the training programs to help expose stereotypes and encourage employees to discuss fears, biases, and problems. Again, the best exercises are related to the actual problems employees are likely to encounter in the workplace. For example, employees in a hospital diversity training program may practice how to handle a white patient who asks to be treated only by a white doctor or a male patient who wants to be treated only by a male doctor. Training ABC, and American Training Resources are among the companies that offer such products. Exhibit 11.10 provides a set of guidelines for designing effective diversity training.

Awareness and skill building are critical first steps in becoming an effective 21st-century manager. However, it's also important for managers and employees to engage or actively participate in bridging differences between people's attitudes, thoughts, and behaviors. Active engagement will help make the world a smaller place.

Retaining Employees

As replacing qualified and experienced workers becomes more difficult and costly, retaining good workers will become much more important. A recent study found that 84 percent of executives believe a "lack of attention on diversity and inclusion contributes to employee turnover."[57] A number of policies and strategies, such as the following, can be used to increase retention of all employees, especially those who are different from the norm.[58]

Bottom Line

Retaining qualified employees increases workforce quality. *What makes you feel that your employer values who you are and what you contribute?*

EXHIBIT 11.10
Guidelines for Diversity
Training

1. **Position training in your broad diversity strategy.** Training is one important element of managing diversity, but on its own it will probably fail. Culture change means altering underlying assumptions and systems that guide organizational behavior. Training programs must be internally consistent with, and complement, other initiatives focused on culture change.

2. **Do a thorough needs analysis.** Do not start training prematurely. As with any training program, eagerness to "do something" may backfire unless you have assessed what specific aspects of diversity need attention first. Focus groups help identify what employees view as priority issues.

3. **Distinguish between education and training.** Education helps build awareness and understanding but does not teach usable skills. Training involves activities that enhance skills in areas such as coaching, conducting performance appraisals, and adapting communication styles. Education and training are both important, but they're not the same.

4. **Use a participative design process.** Tap a multitude of parties to ensure that the content and tone of the program are suitable to everyone involved. Outside consultants often provide fresh perspectives and have credibility. Insiders have specific company knowledge, sensitivity to local issues, and long-standing relationships with company members. Balance these various sources.

5. **Test the training thoroughly before rollout.** Given the sensitivity, even volatility, of diversity issues, use diversity councils and advocacy groups to pilot the programs. Build in ample feedback time to allow these groups to address sensitive concerns and refine the training.

6. **Incorporate diversity programs into the core training curriculum.** One-time programs do not have a lasting impact. Blend the program's content into other training programs such as performance appraisal, coaching, and so on.

SOURCE: From *Training: The Human Side of Business.* 1993. Copyright 1993. The Lakewood Media Group.

Support Groups   Companies can help form minority networks and other support groups to promote information exchange and social support. Support groups, sometimes called affinity groups, provide emotional and career support for members who traditionally have not been included in the majority's informal groups. They also can help diverse employees understand work norms and the corporate culture.

At Apple headquarters in Cupertino, California, support groups include a Jewish cultural group, a gay/lesbian group, an African American group, and a technical women's group. Avon encourages employees to organize into African American, Hispanic, and Asian networks by granting them official recognition and assigning a senior manager to provide advice. These groups help new employees adjust and provide direct feedback to management on problems that concern the groups.

Mentoring   Many people have been puzzled at the apparent inability of women and minorities to move up beyond a certain point on the corporate ladder (the glass ceiling). To help these groups enter the informal network that provides exposure to top management and access to information about organizational politics, many companies have implemented formal mentoring programs. **Mentors** are higher-level managers who help ensure that high-potential people are introduced to top management and socialized into the norms and values of the organization.

In Canada, Ernst & Young makes mentorship an important part of employee development. In fact, the tax and consulting firm has established several mentoring programs aimed at the needs of particular employee groups, including women, minorities, and immigrants. Mentors work with employees to help them develop relevant experience, add skills, and make contact with senior leaders. Ernst & Young sees these mentorships not only

mentors

Higher-level managers who help ensure that high-potential people are introduced to top management and socialized into the norms and values of the organization.

as a way to increase what employees can offer but also as a way to fill its talent pipeline with future leaders. In a related but distinct effort, Ernst & Young identifies high-potential employees and has company leaders sponsor them. Sponsorship is similar to mentorship except that the sponsor is more actively involved in the employee's development. Finally, in an unusual twist on mentorship, Ernst & Young has a reverse mentoring program in which women and minority employees counsel leaders on issues related to diversity at the company.[59]

Career Development and Promotions   Because they are hitting a glass ceiling, many of the most talented women and minority group members are leaving their organizations in search of better opportunities elsewhere. In response, companies such as Deloitte & Touche and Honeywell have established teams to evaluate the career progress of women, minorities, and employees with disabilities and to devise ways to move them up through the ranks. One extremely important step is to make sure deserving employees get a chance at line positions. Women in particular are often relegated to staff positions, such as human resources, with less opportunity to demonstrate how they can earn money for their employers. Career development programs that give a wide range of employees exposure and experience in line jobs can make senior management positions more available to them.

Systems Accommodation   Managers can support diversity by recognizing cultural and religious holidays, differing modes of dress, and dietary restrictions as well as accommodating the needs of individuals with disabilities. One important disabling condition is AIDS. Under the ADA Amendments Act (ADAAA), organizations must accommodate employees with AIDS as they would persons with any other disability, permitting and even encouraging them to continue working for as long as they are able and, if warranted, allowing flexible scheduling. Also, accommodations for disability may become increasingly important in the future as the median age of the workforce continues to rise. In addition, the rise in the *weight* of the average U.S. worker may raise disability concerns. Not only are the familiar health consequences such as heart disease, joint problems, and diabetes associated with increased weight, but one study found that workers who were obese (with a body mass index of 25 or more) had many more workplace injury claims and absences related to injuries.[60] This pattern suggests that managers of the future will be even more concerned than in the past with keeping their workers of all sizes on the job by maintaining safe workplaces and offering benefits that encourage healthy lifestyles (possibly through company-sponsored fitness programs).

Accountability   As we noted at the beginning of this section, one of the most effective ways to ensure that diversity efforts succeed is to hold managers accountable for hiring and developing a diverse workforce. Organizations must ensure that their performance appraisal and reward systems reinforce the importance of effective diversity management. At PepsiCo, each executive reporting to the CEO is assigned responsibility for employee development of a different group—for example, the company's women or Latinos or gay and lesbian employees. The executive responsible for that group must identify leadership talent, learn group members' concerns, identify areas where support is needed, and identify plans for addressing these issues.[61] PepsiCo has earned several awards in recent years for its diversity management efforts.[62]

For decades, U.S. corporations were striving to integrate their workforces because of regulatory and social responsibility pressures. Today globalization, changing demographics, and the expansion of ethnic markets at home have made managing a diverse workforce a bottom-line issue. Managers at organizations such as NASCAR realize that to remain competitive in the coming years, they will have to make managing diversity a strategic priority to attract, develop, keep, and apply the knowledge of their top talent.

Management in Action

ON DIVERSITY, NASCAR LEADERS SHOW THEY MEAN BUSINESS

Participants in NASCAR's Drive for Diversity program say it works. For example, NASCAR partners with Virginia State University (and other schools) to recruit marketing interns. One of them, Adenike Mustapha, told a reporter that the internship "exposed me to something I would never have been exposed to before." The more people who are exposed, they agree, the more who will become fans. That's also what NASCAR hopes will happen when D4D graduate and Mexico native Daniel Suarez uses his Twitter account to generate buzz as he competes in the NASCAR Nationwide Series.

The commitment to diversity was tested when a NASCAR driver, Jeremy Clements, let slip a racial slur while talking to a blogger for MTV News. Clements was not using the ugly term to refer to a colleague; it slipped out as he made a general remark about overly aggressive drivers. Some organizations might have tried to downplay the situation, but NASCAR suspended Clements for two weeks.

Beyond punishing Clements, NASCAR directed him to meet with Richard Lapchick, cofounder of a diversity training program of the National Consortium for Academics and Sports. That program, the Teamwork Leadership Institute (TLI), provides diversity training to the National Basketball Association, Major League Baseball, and many college athletics departments as well as to NASCAR employees. After the suspension, Clements said the counseling from Lapchick helped him think more carefully about himself and the impact of his words.

Lest anyone think this incident signals a weak commitment to diversity at NASCAR, Lapchick argues that the opposite is true. Over the course of a decade and a half, Lapchick says, he has consistently seen from CEO Brian France a sincere commitment to making NASCAR "look like America." Lapchick's TLI has provided more training, he says, to NASCAR "than any other [sports] league or college." It has brought in TLI to train all its employees, at a cost of more than $500,000. TLI training includes discussion and exercises related to self-identity and the use of stereotypes, using examples drawn from sports.

Besides bringing in female and minority drivers, NASCAR has hired diverse employees at its headquarters. The 26 members of its board and officers include eight women and two persons of color. Lapchick credited the work of Marcus Jadotte, former vice president of public affairs and multicultural development. Jadotte ensured that NASCAR's leaders received regular training and kept diversity and inclusion on the executive agenda.[63]

- Assess NASCAR's response to a driver's use of a racial slur. What did it do right? What else should it have done?
- Assess NASCAR's leadership and commitment concerning diversity. What else should it do?

KEY TERMS

affirmative action, p. 359	mentors, p. 371	pluralistic organization, p. 365
ambicultural organization, p. 366	monolithic organization, p. 365	sexual harassment, p. 353
managing diversity, p. 348	multicultural organization, p. 366	

RETAINING WHAT YOU LEARNED

In Chapter 11, you learned that the U.S. workforce is becoming more diverse. A skills gap exists because typical workers often lack the skills to fill jobs that are currently being created. To fill this gap and achieve competitive advantage, managers need to recruit, develop, motivate, and retain a diverse workforce. Affirmative action is used to correct past exclusion of women and minorities from organizations. Managing diversity takes a broader approach aimed at supporting, nurturing, and using employee differences to the organization's advantage. Managing diversity can result in enhanced talent management practices, marketing strategies to reach diverse consumers, innovation and problem solving, and organizational flexibility. Challenges associated with managing a diverse workforce include decreased group cohesiveness, communication problems, mistrust and tension, and stereotyping. Based on prevailing assumptions about people and cultures, organizations take one of the following forms: (1) monolithic, (2) pluralistic, or (3) multicultural. In order to cultivate diversity, managers and organizations need to support and commit to it. A thorough assessment needs to be completed before programs can be designed to attract, develop, motivate, and retain a diverse workforce.

1 **Describe how changes in the U.S. workforce make diversity a critical organizational and managerial issue.**

- The labor force is getting older and more racially and ethnically diverse, with a higher proportion of women. Exhibit 11.1 (below) illustrates the components of a diversified workforce.
- In addition, the jobs that are being created frequently require higher skills than the typical worker can provide; thus we are seeing a growing skills gap.
- To be competitive, organizations can no longer take the traditional approach of depending on white males to form the core of the workforce.
- Today managers must look broadly to make use of talent wherever it can be found. As the labor market changes, organizations that can recruit, develop, motivate, and retain a diverse workforce will have a competitive advantage.

LO 2 **Distinguish between affirmative action and managing diversity.**

- Affirmative action is designed to correct past exclusion of women and minorities from U.S. organizations.
- But despite the accomplishments of affirmative action, it has not eliminated barriers that prevent individuals from reaching their full potential.
- Managing diversity goes beyond hiring people who are different from the norm and seeks to support, nurture, and use employee differences to the organization's advantage.

LO 3 **Explain how diversity, if well managed, can give organizations a competitive edge.**

- Managing diversity is a bottom-line issue. If managers are effective at managing diversity, they will have an easier time attracting, retaining, and motivating the best employees.
- Also, managers will be more effective at marketing to diverse consumer groups in the United States and globally. They will have a workforce that is more creative, more innovative, and better able to solve problems.

- In addition, they are likely to increase the flexibility and responsiveness of the organization to environmental change.

LO 4 **Identify challenges associated with managing a diverse workforce.**

- The challenges for managers created by a diverse workforce include decreased group cohesiveness, communication problems, mistrust and tension, and stereotyping.
- These challenges can be turned into advantages by means of training and effective management.

LO 5 **Define monolithic, pluralistic, and multicultural organizations.**

- These categories are based on the organization's prevailing assumptions about people and cultures.
- Monolithic organizations have a low degree of structural integration, so their population is homogeneous.
- Pluralistic organizations have a relatively diverse employee population and try to involve various types of employees (e.g., engaging in affirmative action and avoiding discrimination).
- Multicultural organizations not only have diversity but value it, and they fully integrate men and women of various racial and ethnic groups as well as people with different types of expertise.
- Conflict is greatest in a pluralistic organization.

LO 6 **List steps managers and their organizations can take to cultivate diversity.**

- To be successful, organizational efforts to manage diversity must have top management support and commitment.
- Organizations should first undertake a thorough assessment of their cultures, policies, and practices as well as the demographics of their labor pools and customer bases.
- Only after this diagnosis has been completed is a company in position to initiate programs designed to attract, develop, motivate, and retain a diverse workforce.

EXHIBIT 11.1   Components of a Diversified Workforce

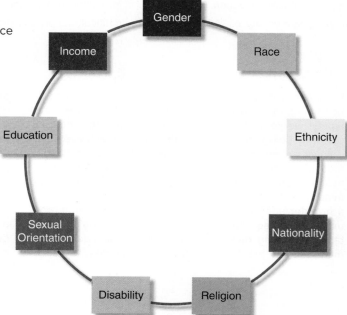

DISCUSSION QUESTIONS

1. What opportunities do you see as a result of changes in our nation's workforce?

2. Is prejudice declining in our society? In our organizations? Why or why not?

3. What distinctions can you make between affirmative action and managing diversity?

4. How can managers overcome obstacles to diversity such as mistrust and tension, stereotyping, and communication problems?

5. How can organizations meet the special needs of different groups (e.g., work and family issues) without appearing to show favoritism to those particular sets of employees?

6. How can diversity give a company a competitive edge? Can diversity really make a difference in the bottom line? How?

EXPERIENTIAL EXERCISES

11.1   BEING DIFFERENT

OBJECTIVES

1. To increase your awareness of the feeling of being different.

2. To understand better the context of being different.

INSTRUCTIONS

1. Working alone, complete the Being Different Worksheet.

2. In small groups, compare worksheets and prepare answers to the discussion questions.

3. When the class reconvenes, group spokespersons present group findings.

DISCUSSION QUESTIONS

1. Were there students who experienced being different in situations that surprised you?

2. How would you define 'being different'?

3. How can this exercise be used to good advantage?

Being Different Worksheet

Think back to a recent situation in which you experienced 'being different' and answer the following questions:

1. Describe the situation in which you experienced 'being different.

_____

_____

2. Explain how you felt.

_____

_____

3. What did you do as a result of 'being different'? (That is, in what way was your behavior changed by the feeling of 'being different'?)

_____

_____

4. What did others in the situation do? How do you think they felt about the situation?

_____

_____

5. How did the situation turn out in the end?

_____

_____

6. As a result of that event, how will you probably behave differently in the future? In what way has the situation changed you?

_____

_____

11.2 GENDER STEREOTYPES

PART I

Your instructor will divide the group into smaller groups based on gender, resulting in male-only and female-only groups. Groups are to brainstorm a list in response to the following statements. It is not necessary for all members to agree with everything the group generates. Add all inputs to the list.

FEMALE GROUPS COMPLETE THE FOLLOWING:

• All men are _____

• Men think all women are _____

MALE GROUPS COMPLETE THE FOLLOWING:

• All women are _____

• Women think all men are _____

PART II

After generating your lists, your groups will present a role-play to the class based on the following scenarios by switching gender roles (females portray males, and males portray females):

Two friends (of the same gender) meeting each other back at school for the first time this year.

A person flirting with a member of the opposite sex at a party. (Females play a male flirting with a female; males play a female flirting with a male.)

QUESTIONS

1. What aspects of the role-plays were accurate, distorted, or inaccurate?

2. How did you feel portraying the opposite gender, and how did it feel to see your gender portrayed?

3. On what stereotypes or experiences were these role-plays based?

PART III

Your group will now write its brainstorm lists on the board for discussion. Remember that these lists are a product of a group effort and are generally based on stereotypes and not necessarily the view of any one individual.

Analyze the lists for positive and negative results in both personal and professional settings. Generate a list of ways to dispel, reduce, or counter negative stereotypes.

QUESTIONS

1. What similarities, patterns, or trends developed from the groups?

2. How do you feel about the thoughts presented about your gender?

3. What implications do these thoughts have on actions and situations in the work environment?

4. What can you do to reduce the negative effects of these stereotypes? What can you do to help dispel these stereotypes? (Brainstorm with your group or class.)

SOURCE: Portions of this exercise were adapted from concepts in S. F. Fritz, W. Brown, J. Lunde, and E. Banset, *Interpersonal Skills for Leadership* (Englewood Cliffs, NJ: Prentice Hall, 1999); and A. B. Shani and J. B. Lau, *Behavior in Organizations: An Experiential Approach,* 6th ed. (New York: Irwin, 1996).

11.3 HE WORKS, SHE WORKS

INSTRUCTIONS

1. Complete the He Works, She Works Worksheet. In the appropriate spaces, write what you think the stereotyped responses would be. Do not spend too much time considering any one item. Rather, respond quickly and let your first impression or thought guide your answer.

2. Compare your individual responses with those of other class members or participants. It is interesting to identify and discuss the most frequently used stereotypes.

He Works, She Works Worksheet

The family picture is on *his* desk: *He's a solid, responsible family man.*

   His desk is cluttered: _____

   He's talking with coworkers: _____

   He's not at his desk: _____

   He's not in the office: _____

The family picture is on *her* desk: *Her family will come before her career.*

   Her desk is cluttered: _____

   She's talking with co-workers: _____

   She's not at her desk: _____

   She's not in the office: _____

The family picture is on *his* desk: *He's a solid, responsible family man.*

   He's having lunch with the boss: _____

   The boss criticized *him:* _____

   He got an unfair deal: _____

   He's getting married: _____

   He's going on a business trip: _____

   He's leaving for a better job: _____

The family picture is on *her* desk: *Her family will come before her career.*

   She's having lunch with the boss: _____

   The boss criticized *her:* _____

   She got an unfair deal: _____

   She's getting married: _____

   She's going on a business trip: _____

   She's leaving for a better job: _____

SOURCE: F. Luthans, *Organizational Behavior.* 1989. Copyright © 1989 The McGraw-Hill Companies. Reproduced with permission.

CONCLUDING CASE

NICHE HOTEL GROUP

Monique Johnson was thrilled about her new position as vice president of human resources for Niche Hotel Group (NHG). The hotel chain has distinctive properties in major cities throughout the United States, attracting a young, international clientele with super-fast Wi-Fi, casual but elegant surroundings, and popular sushi bars. Besides the chance to stay at these establishments as she toured the country, Monique would have opportunities to meet the members of NHG's enthusiastic, talented, and racially diverse workforce. In addition, she was proud to advance NHG's practice of valuing employees' and customers' diversity, including respect for all people regardless of age, sex, race, ethnicity, nationality, disability status, and sexual orientation. She felt sure those values would be upheld because the commitment came from the top. In fact, NHG's chief executive, Mike Jepsen, had asked Monique to meet with him every Thursday to review the company's performance in attracting and developing talent.

For several weeks, Monique's work progressed much as she had expected. Then she heard some disturbing news. One of the hotel's managers, April Lee, called her to say she had received complaints that an assistant manager in the hotel's sushi bar had been embarrassing some of the male servers. When April met with the servers to investigate, they described being teased because they were gay, but said they had not bothered to complain. Two of the servers admitted that they believed complaining would be futile. As white, male employees, they said, they doubted they would be taken seriously, because NHG's management tended to favor its female and minority employees. April worried that the servers might quit, take legal action, or both before the situation could be sorted out. Meanwhile, she wondered how top management would help her deal with the situation. Monique reviewed with April the basic legal requirements and company policy for handling this type of problem, and she offered to fly out to April's hotel with one of her staff members after her Thursday meeting with the CEO.

That Thursday, Monique briefed Mike about the situation at April's hotel. Mike sighed, "Here we go again." In response to Monique's puzzled look, he explained, "We've had mandatory diversity training three times for every single NHG employee. But it's never enough. Sooner or later, someone hurts someone else's feelings, and we have to bring back the trainers. I guess we just have to keep doing it until everyone respects everyone else's differences."

"You've done diversity training three times without creating a positive climate for diversity?" replied Monique. Mike nodded his head ruefully and then asked if she had a better idea. "Maybe. Hmm, maybe it's time to stop focusing so much on categorizing people and start thinking about how each of us individually is working as part of a team, how each of us is contributing to our mission. Maybe we need to train in something else—say, communication—how we talk and how well we listen."

DISCUSSION QUESTIONS

1. How can promoting a diverse workforce help Niche Hotel Group succeed as a business?
2. Why do you think diversity training has not always prevented problems at NHG?
3. What should NHG do to improve its climate for diversity?

PART THREE   SUPPORTING CASE

Zappos

At the turn of the millennium, Zappos, a Las Vegas–based Internet retailer, was a start-up struggling to survive. The company wanted to be *the* online destination for buying shoes, but customers hesitated to pick out shoes online. The company hired a 27-year-old business consultant named Tony Hsieh to figure out what would save Zappos.

Hsieh, a first-generation Taiwanese American with a degree in computer science, already had a couple of successful business start-ups under his belt. Undeterred by Zappos' weak performance, he set an ambitious goal: Zappos would become the largest shoe retailer on the Internet. How? Not by focusing on mainly price or even selection, but by enhancing a company culture designed to make employees happy. Happy employees, Hsieh believed, would deliver superior service. And when customers take a chance on picking out shoes from a website, they want to trust that the seller will ensure they are satisfied with everything about the purchase, from shoe style and fit to fast delivery and an easy returns policy.

The approach quickly began to stimulate sales, and just a year after he started advising Zappos, Hsieh was named chief executive. He works for the startlingly small salary of $36,000. That arrangement doesn't bother Hsieh because he is more motivated by creating a great organization than by earning money. After all, his previous business, LinkExchange, brought him $265 million when he sold it to Microsoft.

The Zappos culture is built on 10 core values:

1. Deliver WOW (an emotional impact and powerful story to tell) through service.
2. Embrace and drive change.
3. Create fun and a little weirdness.
4. Be adventurous, creative, and open-minded.
5. Pursue growth and learning.
6. Build open and honest relationships with communication.
7. Build a positive team and family spirit. ("Family" refers to Zappos co-workers.)
8. Do more with less.
9. Be passionate and determined.
10. Be humble.

These somewhat unconventional values are essential hiring criteria, and the company's career website directs potential applicants to read the values—which are described in whimsical terms—and apply for a job only if they want to be part of this "best thing about the Zappos family." In fact, at the end of the orientation process, employees are offered $3,000 to quit if they feel they aren't a good fit with the company values, and displaying a lack of the values is grounds for being discharged. According to Hsieh, hiring people who share the core values makes it easy to form real friendships, and those relationships, in turn, create an environment in which people think creatively.

The Zappos human resources department, under the leadership of Hollie Delaney, a Salt Lake City native, ensures that job candidates start to experience and participate in this unconventional, fun culture during the application and selection process. An online application invites them to submit video cover letters with their applications, and interviews are conducted in a room that looks like the set of a TV talk show, where candidates might answer a question such as "What's your theme song?" Employees evaluating candidates consider not only work history but also the way candidates interact during lunch. They even take into account the observations of the shuttle drivers who take visiting job candidates back to their hotel. Once on board, employees might discover that fun and a little weirdness at the company includes an opportunity to dye Hsieh's or another manager's hair blue or shave his or her head at the annual Bald & Blue Day. And the commitment to wowing customers spills over into work relationships: Given a chance to reward colleagues' good behavior with a $50 monthly bonus, many employees held off, waiting to see exceptional behavior.

Recently performance appraisals also were brought into line with the focus on values. Employees are rated not just on task accomplishment but also on how well they represent the core values. Managers are expected to describe specific instances of employees demonstrating the values at work, and employees who score low on a measure have the chance to receive training in that value. Outside the formal appraisal process, employees also continue to receive regular feedback on task-related measures such as percentage of hours spent talking to customers.

Delaney acknowledges that the company's values result in a work environment that is loud, hardworking, and full of change—conditions that aren't for everyone. Pay also isn't necessarily high, especially for call center workers. But for those who share the values, this kind of workplace is exhilarating. There also are plenty of rewards and perks, including profit sharing, a nap room, and access to a life coach who counsels employees as they sit on a velvet throne.

With this approach to human resources management, Hsieh helped Zappos grow into a billion-dollar company, which was eventually acquired by Amazon for $1.2 billion. Hsieh negotiated a deal in which Amazon promised to let Zappos continue operating independently, in accordance with its distinctive culture.

Unfortunately, although the 2008 financial crisis didn't keep sales at Zappos from rising, the ongoing economic slowdown eventually hurt, and Zappos laid off some of its workers, letting them down as gently as it could with generous severance packages. Even so, Zappos, unlike many businesses, hasn't outsourced its call center, located in Kentucky, because those employees need to be a part of the company culture. After all, they are the ones who talk directly with customers, and they're trained to wow customers—for example, encouraging them to try multiple sizes because shipping is free in both directions. What's next for this innovative e-retailer? Several reports are emerging that Zappos is moving away from using a hierarchical, traditional management approach with titles and detailed employee job descriptions. Instead, a holacracy approach will likely be implemented which will organize employees into "functional self-organizing circles." Zappos hopes this innovative approach to empowering its diverse employees will keep it at the forefront of employees' minds as a great place to work.

QUESTIONS

1. Evaluate whether you think Zappos is a responsive organization. How do you expect its recent downsizing to affect its responsiveness?

2. How does human resources management reinforce Zappos' core values?

3. How well do you think Zappos' human resource strategy supports the valuing of employee diversity? What diversity issues does Zappos need to address?

SOURCES: R. Greenfield, "Zappos CEO Tony Hsieh: Adopt Holacracy or Leave," *Fast Company* (online), March 30, 2015, http://www.fastcompany .com; G. Rodriguez, "The Great Zappos 'Circles' Experiment and Why It Really Matters," *Forbes* (online), January 15, 2014, http://www.forbes.com; H. Blodget, "Zappos CEO Tony Hsieh Making $36,000 a Year Working for Amazon," *Yahoo Finance*, September 10, 2010, http://finance.yahoo.com; Zappos, Jobs webpage, http://about.zappos.com/jobs/; K. Gurchiek, "Delivering HR at Zappos," *HR Magazine*, June 2011, http://www.shrm.org; J. M. O'Brien, "Zappos Knows How to Kick It," *Fortune*, January 22, 2009, http://money .cnn.com; and R. Pyrillis, "The Reviews Are In," *Workforce Management*, May 1, 2011, Business & Company Resource Center, http://galenet.galegroup.com.

CHAPTER 12

Leadership

Every soldier has a right to competent command.

—JULIUS CAESAR

LEARNING OBJECTIVES

After studying Chapter 12, you will be able to:

LO 1 Discuss what it means to be a leader.

LO 2 Summarize what people want and organizations need from their leaders.

LO 3 Explain how a good vision helps you be a better leader.

LO 4 Identify sources of power in organizations.

LO 5 List personal traits and skills of effective leaders.

LO 6 Describe behaviors that will make you a better leader, and identify when the situation calls for them.

LO 7 Distinguish between charismatic and transformational leaders.

LO 8 Describe types of opportunities to be a leader in an organization.

LO 9 Discuss how to further your own leadership development.

CHAPTER OUTLINE

Management in Action

MEG WHITMAN'S LEADERSHIP CHALLENGE AT HEWLETT-PACKARD

One of the great legends of the computer age tells of how William Hewlett and David Packard, two recent graduates with degrees in electrical engineering, set up shop in a Palo Alto, California, garage to make electronic instruments in the 1930s. Through technological expertise, management innovation, and respect for their highly skilled workers, the two founders built their garage enterprise, Hewlett-Packard Company, into a Silicon Valley leader serving businesses and individuals. Consumers have known HP's brand most for its calculators, personal computers, and printers.

Beginning in the 1990s, however, HP has struggled to live up to its earlier reputation. It remains an industry giant, ranked number 17 on the Fortune 500, but it seems to have lost its direction. The company fell behind in innovation in the market for computers, especially mobile devices. Market share, profits, and the company's stock market valuation have been sliding for years. It announced a tablet PC and then pulled it from the market after poor initial reviews; scared off loyal PC customers by publicly flirting with the idea of selling off that product line; and tried to expand into the software business by acquiring software maker Autonomy for $11 billion, a price widely viewed as too high. Meanwhile, there have been persistent reports of poor morale throughout HP and turmoil in the top ranks. In just over a decade, the company pushed out four chief executives.

Desperate for a turnaround, HP's board of directors hired former eBay chief executive. She placed HP on a 5-year turnaround plan that included restructuring and cost-cutting, spinning off the computer and printer businesses, and focusing on faster-growing cloud, security, and data analysis segments. Whitman herself had been a member of HP's board for several months, so she had seen the company's difficulties from the inside. Her track

© ChinaFotoPress/ChinaFotoPress via Getty Images

record with eBay showed that she could perform well in Silicon Valley.

Will Whitman's bold turnaround plan reverse HP's sliding performance? She is confident that the iconic company will regain its stride. In a likely nod to founders William Hewlett and David Packard, she states: "Success hinges on consistency of leadership, focus, execution, and most importantly, great products and services."[1]

Observers agree that Hewlett-Packard's people need a compelling vision and inspiration to bring that vision to life. HP's directors chose Meg Whitman as a person they believe can deliver this kind of leadership. As you read this chapter, compare Whitman's approach with the kinds of practices recommended for successful leadership.

People get excited about the topic of leadership. They want to know what makes a great leader like HP's founders, Bill Hewlett and David Packard. Managers in all industries are interested in this question. They believe the answer will bring improved organizational performance and personal career success. They hope to acquire the skills that will transform an average manager into a true leader.

Based on the idea that leadership can be learned, many large organizations such as Home Depot, Cintas, USAA, and Union Pacific actively recruit retired military personnel in the belief that military training and experience prepare those individuals to lead. Of course you don't have to join the armed services to acquire leadership skills. According to one source, "Leadership seems to be the marshaling of skills possessed by a majority but used by a minority. But it's something that can be learned by anyone, taught to everyone, denied to no one."[2]

What is leadership? To start, a leader is one who influences others to attain goals. The greater the number of followers, the greater the influence. And the more successful the attainment of worthy goals, the more evident the leadership. But we must explore beyond this bare definition to capture the excitement and intrigue that devoted followers and students of leadership feel when they see a great leader in action, to understand what organizational leaders really do, and to learn what it really takes to become a truly outstanding leader.

Outstanding leaders combine good strategic substance and effective interpersonal processes to formulate and implement strategies that produce results and sustainable competitive advantage.[3] They may launch enterprises, build organization cultures, win wars, or otherwise change the course of events.[4] They are strategists who seize opportunities others overlook, but "they are also passionately concerned with detail—all the small, fundamental realities that can make or mar the grandest of plans."[5]

What Do We Want from Our Leaders?

What do people want from their leaders? Broadly speaking, they want help in achieving their goals.[6] These goals include not just more pay and promotions but support for their personal development; clearing obstacles so they can perform at high levels; and treatment that is respectful, fair, and ethical. Leaders serve people best when they help them develop their own initiative and good judgment, enable them to grow, and help them become better contributors. People want competence and proper management—the kinds of things you will read about in this chapter and that are found in other chapters in this book. The "Multiple Generations at Work" box discusses additional expectations Millennials have of their leaders.

Organizations need people at all levels to be leaders.

What do organizations need? Organizations need people at all levels to be leaders. Leaders throughout the organization are needed to do the things that their people want, but also to help create and implement strategic direction. Thus organizations place people in formal leadership roles so these leaders will achieve not their personal goals, but the organization's goals. At Illinois Tool Works (ITW), general counsel Maria Green has learned to create a listening environment so members of the legal staff contribute ideas. In the past, Green admits, she would have been eager to deliver answers showcasing her own extensive legal and business knowledge. However, a mentor helped her understand that ITW needs Green, as a leader, to draw out the full potential of the entire group.[7]

These two perspectives—what people want and what organizations need—are neatly combined in a set of five key behaviors identified by James Kouzes and Barry Posner, two well–known authors and consultants (see Exhibit 12.1).

You will read about these and other aspects of leadership in this and the following chapters. The topics we discuss will not only help you become a better leader but give you benchmarks that will help you assess the competence and fairness with which your boss manages you.

Multiple Generations at Work

Millennials are Redefining the Nature of Leadership

Approximately two-thirds of Millennials want to be leaders in the next five years. This generational cohort defines a good leader as one who "mentors others to reach their personal achievements, achieves his/her goals, and affects change in the community." This view of leadership is very different from viewing a leader as someone who takes charge, issues orders, and gets the job done.

Parents, teachers, coaches, and other influences empowered Millennials to think for themselves, ask questions, challenge conventional wisdom, and take leadership roles. As employees, they expect the same type of mentoring and coaching from their bosses. Also, Millennials want to have a positive impact on their communities and social causes. As seen in the "Social Enterprise" boxes throughout this textbook, Millennials are applying their leadership skills to help people and communities around the world.

As a generation, Millennials share some common leadership characteristics, including:

1. *Transparency.* As leaders, Millennials tend to be open and share information willingly with their bosses, team members, and clients.
2. *Relevancy.* Millennials want to make a meaningful contribution to their organizations and communities.
3. *Autonomy and flexibility.* Millennials want choice over when and where they get their work done. As leaders, this generational cohort will encourage and trust their employees to use creative work arrangements.[8]

---

1. **Challenge the process.** They challenge conventional beliefs and practices, and they create constructive change.
2. **Inspire a shared vision.** They appeal to people's values and motivate them to care about an important mission.
3. **Enable others to act.** They give people access to information and give them the power to perform to their full potential.
4. **Model the way.** They don't just tell people what to do—they are living examples of the ideals they believe in.
5. **Encourage the heart.** They show appreciation, provide rewards, and use various approaches to motivate people in positive ways.

EXHIBIT 12.1
What Do the Best Leaders Do?

SOURCE: Adapted from J. Kouzes and B. Posner, *The Leadership Challenge,* 2nd ed. (San Francisco: Jossey-Bass, 1995).

Vision

"The leader's job is to create a vision," stated Robert L. Swiggett, former chair of Kollmorgen Corporation.[9] Until a few years ago, *vision* was not a word one heard managers utter. But today, having a vision for the future and communicating that vision to others are known to be essential components of great leadership. Tony Hsieh, CEO of Zappos, is "more of an architect; he designs the big vision and then gets out of the way so that everyone can make things happen."[10] Howard Schultz, CEO of Starbucks, states: "our vision at Starbucks has been to create a 'third place' between home and work where people can come together to enjoy the peace and pleasure of coffee and community."[11] Practicing businesspeople are not alone in this belief; academic research shows that a clear vision and communication of that vision lead to higher venture growth in entrepreneurial firms.[12]

A **vision** is a mental image of a possible and desirable future state of the organization. It expresses the leaders ambitions for the organization.[13] A leader can create a vision that describes high performance aspirations, the nature of corporate or business strategy, or

 LO 3

vision

A mental image of a possible and desirable future state of the organization.

Imagine trying to complete a challenging jigsaw puzzle without the vision of what you're working toward.

© *Tetra Images/Getty Images*

Bottom Line

You can't perform in the long run if you don't have a vision of what you want to accomplish.

Do you have to be a top-level executive to have a vision?

Bottom Line

Imagine a world with clean air, clean water, and enough food for all. In many businesses around the world, managers with vision are working toward making parts of that fantasy a reality.

What is your vision for a better future?

even the kind of workplace worth building. The best visions are both ideal and unique.[14] If a vision conveys an *ideal,* it communicates a standard of excellence and a clear choice of positive values. If the vision is also *unique,* it communicates and inspires pride in being different from other organizations. The choice of language is important; the words should imply a combination of realism and optimism, an action orientation, and resolution and confidence that the vision will be attained.[15]

Visions can be small or large and can exist at any organizational level as well as at the very top. The important points are that (1) a vision is necessary for effective leadership; (2) a person or team can develop a vision for any job, work unit, or organization; and (3) many people, including managers who do not develop into strong leaders, do not develop a clear vision—instead they focus on performing or surviving on a day-by-day basis.

Put another way, leaders must know what they want.[16] And other people must understand what that is. The leader must be able to articulate the vision, clearly and often. Other people throughout the organization should understand the vision and be able to state it clearly themselves. Thats a start. But the vision means nothing until the leader and followers take action to turn the vision into reality.[17]

One leader who articulated and modeled a clear vision was George Buckley, chief executive of 3M Company, the innovative manufacturer best known for its Scotch tape, Post-It notes, and sandpaper. When the economy turned sour, other manufacturers slashed spending on research and development (R&D), but Buckley wanted to retain 3M's commitment to innovation. So even as he tied R&D spending to revenues (R&D spending fell, but not faster than revenues), he challenged his R&D staff to target their efforts toward making products cheaper to produce—and even convinced them that the effort could be satisfying. He accomplished this by recognizing that what drives researchers is a belief that what they do is intellectually stimulating and significant. For example, when Buckley asked the leader of 3M's abrasives business what innovations were in the pipeline, the unit's head commented that abrasives were "not considered sexy." Buckley replied, "Why not? I think abrasives are sexy. Why can't abrasives be sexy?" Eventually, as researchers saw how their innovations were helping the company serve its markets, they grew enthusiastic about Buckley's vision.[18]

A metaphor reinforces the important concept of vision.[19] Putting a jigsaw puzzle together is much easier if you have the picture on the box cover in front of you. Without the picture, or vision, the lack of direction is likely to result in frustration and failure. That is what communicating a vision is all about: making clear where you are heading.

Not just any vision will do. Visions can be inappropriate, or fail, for a variety of reasons (see Exhibit 12.2).[20] First, an inappropriate vision may reflect merely the leader's personal needs. Such a vision can be unethical, or it may fail because of lack of acceptance by the market or by those who must implement it. Second (and related to the first), an inappropriate vision may ignore stakeholder needs. Third, the leader must stay abreast of environmental changes. Although effective leaders maintain confidence and persevere despite obstacles, the time may come when the facts dictate that the vision must change. You will learn more about change and how to manage it later in the book.

Where do visions come from?[21] Leaders should be sensitive to emerging opportunities, develop the right capabilities or worldviews, and not be overly invested in the status quo. You also can capitalize on networks of insightful individuals who have ideas about the future. Some visions are accidental; a company may stumble into an opportunity, and the leader may get credit for foresight. Some leaders and companies launch many new initiatives and, through trial and error, occasionally hit home runs. If the company learns from these successes, the vision emerges.

> Not just any vision will do.

EXHIBIT 12.2
Reasons Why Visions Fail

SOURCE: Adapted from J. A. Conger, "The Dark Side of Leadership," *Organizational Dynamics* 19 (Autumn 1990), pp. 44–55.

Leading and Managing

Effective managers are not necessarily true leaders. Many administrators, supervisors, and even top executives perform their responsibilities successfully without being great leaders. But these positions afford an opportunity for leadership. The ability to lead effectively, then, will set the excellent managers apart from others.

Whereas management must deal with the ongoing, day-to-day complexities of organizations, true leadership includes effectively orchestrating important change.[22] Managing requires planning and budgeting routines; leading includes setting the direction (creating a vision) for the firm. Management requires structuring the organization, staffing it with capable people, and monitoring activities; leadership goes beyond these functions by inspiring people to attain the vision. Great leaders keep people focused on moving the organization toward its ideal future, motivating them to overcome whatever obstacles lie in the way.

Good leadership, unfortunately, is all too rare. Managers may focus on the activities that earn them praise and rewards, such as actions that cause a rise in the company's stock price, rather than making tough ethical choices or investing in long-term projects. Some new managers, learning that quick wins will help them establish their credibility as leaders, push a pet project while neglecting the impact on the very people they were assigned to lead. This approach tends to backfire because employees distrust this type of manager and lose any commitment they might have had to the team's long-term success. Successful leaders, in contrast, enlist the team in scoring collective wins that result from working together toward a shared vision.[23]

It is important to be clear here about several things. First, management and leadership are both vitally important. To highlight the need for more leadership is not to minimize the importance of management or managers. But leadership involves unique processes that are distinguishable from basic management processes.[24] Moreover, just because they involve different processes does not mean that they require different, separate people. The same individual can exemplify effective managerial processes, leadership processes, both, or neither.

Some people dislike the idea of distinguishing between management and leadership, maintaining that it is artificial or derogatory toward the managers and the management processes that make organizations run. An alternative distinction is between supervisory

> Good leadership, unfortunately, is all too rare.

EXHIBIT 12.3
Behaviors of Effective
Followers

1.	**Volunteering** to handle tasks or help accomplish goals.
2.	**Accepting** assignments in a willing manner.
3.	**Exhibiting** loyalty to the group.
4.	**Voicing** differences of opinions, but supporting the group's decisions.
5.	**Offering** suggestions.
6.	**Maintaining** a positive attitude, even in confusing or trying times.
7.	**Working** effectively as a team member.

SOURCE: Adapted from Holden Leadership Center, University of Oregon, http://leadership.uoregon.edu/resources/
exercises_tips/skills/followership.

supervisory leadership

Behavior that provides
guidance, support, and
corrective feedback for day-
to-day activities.

strategic leadership

Behavior that gives
purpose and meaning to
organizations, envisioning
and creating a positive
future.

and strategic leadership.[25] **Supervisory leadership** is behavior that provides guidance, support, and corrective feedback for day-to-day activities. **Strategic leadership** gives purpose and meaning to organizations. Strategic leadership involves anticipating and envisioning a viable future for the organization and working with others to initiate changes that create such a future.[26] For example, Indian business leaders prioritize their top responsibilities[27] as providing input for business strategy (which you studied thoroughly in Part I of this book); keeper of the organizational culture (introduced in Chapter 2); and guiding, teaching, and serving as a role model for employees (employees being the focus of this part of the book).

Leading and Following

Organizations succeed or fail not only because of how well they are led but because of how well followers follow. Just as managers are not necessarily good leaders, people are not always good followers. One leadership scholar stated, "Executives are given subordinates; they have to earn followers."[28] But it's also true that good followers help produce good leaders.

As a manager, you will be asked to play the roles of both leader and follower. As you lead the people who report to you, you will report to your boss. You will be a member of some teams and task forces, and you may head others. Although the leadership roles get the glamour and therefore are the roles that many people covet, followers must perform their responsibilities conscientiously and well. Good followership doesn't mean merely obeying orders, although some bosses may view it that way. The most effective followers are capable of independent thinking and at the same time are actively committed to organizational goals.[29] Exhibit 12.3 lists additional behaviors of effective followers. Robert Townsend, who led a legendary turnaround at Avis, said that the most important characteristic of a follower may be the willingness to tell the truth.[30]

They master skills that are useful to their organizations, and they hold performance standards that are higher than required. Effective followers may not get the glory, but they know their contributions to the organization are valuable. And as they make those contributions, they study leaders in preparation for their own leadership roles.[31] Effective followers also distinguish themselves from ineffective ones by their enthusiasm and commitment to the organization and to a person or purpose—an idea, a product—other than themselves or their own interests.

Power and Leadership

power

The ability to influence
others.

LO 4

Central to effective leadership is **power**—the ability to influence other people. In organizations, this influence often means the ability to get things done or accomplish one's goals despite resistance from others.

EXHIBIT 12.4
Sources of Leader Power

SOURCE: Adapted from J. R. P. French and B. Raven, "The Bases of Social Power," in *Studies in Social Power,* ed. D. Cartwright (Ann Arbor, MI: Institute for Social Research, 1959).

Sources of Power

One of the earliest and still most useful approaches to understanding power suggests that leaders have five important potential sources of power in organizations.[32] Exhibit 12.4 shows those power sources.

Legitimate Power   The leader with *legitimate power* has the right, or the authority, to tell others what to do; employees are obligated to comply with legitimate orders. For example, a supervisor tells an employee to remove a safety hazard, and the employee removes the hazard because he has to obey the authority of his boss. In contrast, when a staff person lacks the authority to give an order to a line manager, the staff person has no legitimate power over the manager. As you might guess, managers have more legitimate power over their direct reports than they do over their peers, bosses, and others inside or outside their organizations.[33]

Reward Power   The leader who has *reward power* influences others because she controls valued rewards; people comply with the leader's wishes to receive those rewards. For example, a manager works hard to achieve her performance goals to get a positive performance review and a big pay raise from her boss. On the other hand, if company policy dictates that everyone receive the same salary increase, a leader's reward power decreases because he or she is unable to give higher raises.

Coercive Power   The leader with *coercive power* has control over punishments; people comply to avoid those punishments. For instance, a manager implements an absenteeism policy that administers disciplinary actions to offending employees. A manager has less coercive power if, say, a union contract limits her ability to punish. In general, lower-level managers have less legitimate, coercive, and reward power than do middle and higher-level managers.[34]

Referent Power   The leader with *referent power* has personal characteristics that appeal to others; people comply because of admiration, personal liking, a desire for approval, or a desire to be like the leader. For example, young, ambitious managers emulate the work habits and personal style of a successful, charismatic executive. An executive who is incompetent, disliked, and less respected has little referent power.

Expert Power   The leader who has *expert power* has certain expertise or knowledge; people comply because they believe in, can learn from, or can otherwise gain from that expertise. For example, a seasoned sales manager gives her salespeople some tips on how to close a deal. The salespeople then alter their sales techniques because they respect the manager's expertise. However, this manager may lack expert power in other areas, such as finance; thus her salespeople may ignore her advice concerning financial matters.

People who are in a position that gives them the right to tell others what to do, who can reward and punish, who are well liked and admired, and who have expertise on which other people can draw will be powerful members of the organization. All of these sources of power are potentially important. Although it is easy to assume that the most powerful bosses are those who have high legitimate power and control major rewards and punishments, it is important not to underestimate the more personal sources such as expert and referent power.

Additional personal sources of power that do not necessarily stem from one's position or level within an organization include access to information and the strength of one's informal network.[35]

Traditional Approaches to Understanding Leadership

Three traditional approaches to studying leadership are the trait approach, the behavioral approach, and the situational approach.

Leader Traits

trait approach

A leadership perspective that attempts to determine the personal characteristics that great leaders share.

The **trait approach** is the oldest leadership perspective; it focuses on individual leaders and attempts to determine the personal characteristics (traits) that great leaders share. What set Winston Churchill, Alexander the Great, Gandhi, and Martin Luther King Jr. apart from the crowd? The trait approach assumes the existence of a leadership personality and assumes that leaders are born, not made.

From 1904 to 1948, researchers conducted more than 100 leadership trait studies.[36] At the end of that period, management scholars concluded that no particular set of traits is necessary for a person to become a successful leader. Enthusiasm for the trait approach diminished, but some research on traits continued. By the mid-1970s, a more balanced view emerged: Although no traits ensure leadership success, certain characteristics are potentially useful. The current perspective is that some personality characteristics—many of which a person need not be born with but can strive to acquire—contribute to leader effectiveness (see Exhibit 12.5).[37]

1. *Drive.* Drive refers to a set of characteristics that reflect a high level of effort. Drive includes high need for achievement, constant striving for improvement, ambition, energy, tenacity (persistence in the face of obstacles), and initiative. In several countries, the achievement needs of top executives have been shown to be related to the growth rates of their organizations.[38] But the need to achieve can be a drawback if leaders focus on personal achievement and get so personally involved with the work that they do not delegate enough authority and responsibility.

2. *Leadership motivation.* Great leaders not only have drive; they *want to lead.* In this regard, it helps to be extroverted—extroversion is consistently related to both leader emergence and leader effectiveness.[39] However—and this is a huge point—introverts have great strengths that can contribute to effective leadership, and extroversion can backfire. For example, the assertiveness of extroverted leaders can

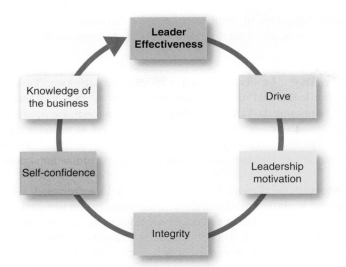

EXHIBIT 12.5
Personality Characteristics
That Increase Leader
Effectiveness

quash the contributions of group members. Extroverts sometimes should adopt a more reserved, quiet style.[40]

Also important is a high need for power, a preference to be in leadership rather than follower positions.[41] A high power need induces people to attempt to influence others and sustains interest and satisfaction in the process of leadership. When the power need is exercised in moral and socially constructive ways, rather than to the detriment of others, leaders inspire more trust, respect, and commitment to their vision.

3. *Integrity.* Integrity is the correspondence between actions and words. Honesty and credibility, in addition to being desirable characteristics in their own right, are especially important for leaders because these traits inspire trust in others.

4. *Self-confidence.* Self-confidence is important for a number of reasons. The leadership role is challenging, and setbacks are inevitable. Self-confidence allows a leader to overcome obstacles, make decisions despite uncertainty, and instill confidence in others. Of course you don't want to overdo this; arrogance and cockiness have triggered more than one leader's downfall.

5. *Knowledge of the business.* Effective leaders have a high level of knowledge about their industries, companies, and technical matters. Leaders must have the intelligence to interpret vast quantities of information. Advanced degrees are useful in a career, but ultimately less important than acquired expertise in matters relevant to the organization.[42]

Finally, one personal skill may be the most important: the ability to perceive the needs and goals of others and to adjust one's personal leadership approach accordingly.[43] Effective leaders do not rely on one leadership style; rather, they are capable of using different styles as the situation warrants.[44] This quality is the cornerstone of the situational approaches to leadership, which we will discuss shortly.

> Arrogance and cockiness have triggered more than one leader's downfall.

Leader Behaviors

The **behavioral approach** to leadership attempts to identify what good leaders do. Should leaders focus on getting the job done or on keeping their followers happy? Should they make decisions autocratically or democratically? In the behavioral approach, personal characteristics are considered less important than the actual behaviors that leaders exhibit.

behavioral approach

A leadership perspective that attempts to identify what good leaders do—that is, what behaviors they exhibit.

Bottom Line

Task performance behaviors focus on achieving work goals. *What shows you that a manager cares about task performance?*

task performance behaviors

Actions taken to ensure that the work group or organization reaches its goals.

group maintenance behaviors

Actions taken to ensure the satisfaction of group members, develop and maintain harmonious work relationships, and preserve the social stability of the group.

EXHIBIT 12.6

Questions Assessing Task Performance and Group Maintenance Leadership

Three general categories of leadership behavior have received particular attention: behaviors related to task performance, group maintenance, and employee participation in decision making.

Task Performance   Leadership requires getting the job done. **Task performance behaviors** are the leader's efforts to ensure that the work unit or organization reaches its goals. This dimension is variously referred to as *concern for production, directive leadership, initiating structure,* or *closeness of supervision.* It includes a focus on work speed, quality and accuracy, quantity of output, and following the rules.[45] This type of leader behavior improves leader job performance and group and organizational performance.[46]

Group Maintenance   Leadership is inherently an interpersonal, group activity.[47] In exhibiting **group maintenance behaviors,** leaders take action to ensure the satisfaction of group members, develop and maintain harmonious work relationships, and preserve the social stability of the group. This dimension is sometimes referred to as *concern for people, supportive leadership,* or *consideration.* It includes a focus on people's feelings and comfort, appreciation of them, and stress reduction.[48] This type of leader behavior has a strong positive impact on follower satisfaction, motivation, and leader effectiveness.[49]

What specific behaviors do performance- and maintenance-oriented leadership imply? To help answer this question, assume you are asked to rate your boss on these two dimensions. If a leadership study were conducted in your organization, you would be asked to fill out a questionnaire similar to the one in Exhibit 12.6. The behaviors indicated in the first set of questions represent performance-oriented leadership; those indicated in the second set represent maintenance-oriented leadership.

Task Performance Leadership

1. Is your superior strict about observing regulations?
2. To what extent does your superior give you instructions and orders?
3. Is your superior strict about the amount of work you do?
4. Does your superior urge you to complete your work by a specified time?
5. Does your superior try to make you work to your maximum capacity?
6. When you do an inadequate job, does your superior focus on the inadequate way the job is done?
7. Does your superior ask you for reports about the progress of your work?
8. How precisely does your superior work out plans for goal achievement each month?

Group Maintenance Leadership

1. Can you talk freely with your superior about your work?
2. Does your superior generally support you?
3. Is your superior concerned about your personal problems?
4. Do you think your superior trusts you?
5. Does your superior give you recognition when you do your job well?
6. When a problem arises in your workplace, does your superior ask your opinion about how to solve it?
7. Is your superior concerned about your future benefits, such as promotions and pay raises?
8. Does your superior treat you fairly?

SOURCE: Reprinted from J. Misumi and M. Peterson, "The Performance-Maintenance (PM) Theory of Leadership: Review of a Japanese Research Program," *Administrative Science Quarterly* 30, no. 2 (June 1985). Reprinted with permission of Sage Publications, Inc.

Leader–member exchange (LMX) theory highlights the importance of leader behaviors not just toward the group as a whole but toward individuals on a personal basis.[50] The focus in the original formulation, which has since been expanded, is primarily on the leader behaviors historically considered group maintenance.[51] According to LMX theory, and as supported by research evidence, maintenance behaviors such as trust, open communication, mutual respect, mutual obligation, and mutual loyalty form the cornerstone of relationships that are satisfying and perhaps more productive.[52]

Remember, though, the potential for cross-cultural differences. Maintenance behaviors are important everywhere, but the specific behaviors can differ from one culture to another.[53] For example, in the United States, maintenance behaviors include dealing with people face to face; in Japan, written memos are preferred over giving directions face to face, thus avoiding confrontation and permitting face-saving in the event of disagreement.[54]

Participation in Decision Making   How should a leader make decisions? More specifically, to what extent should leaders involve their people in making decisions?[55] As a dimension of leadership behavior, **participation in decision making** can range from autocratic to democratic. **Autocratic leadership** makes decisions and then announces them to the group. **Democratic leadership** solicits input from others. Democratic leadership seeks information, opinions, and preferences, sometimes to the point of meeting with the group, leading discussions, and using consensus or majority vote to make the final choice.

The Effects of Leader Behavior   How the leader behaves influences people's attitudes and performance. Studies of these effects focus on autocratic versus democratic decision styles or on performance- versus maintenance-oriented behaviors.

Decision Styles   The classic study comparing autocratic and democratic styles found that a democratic approach resulted in the most positive attitudes, whereas an autocratic approach resulted in somewhat higher performance.[56] A **laissez-faire** style, in which the leader essentially made no decisions, led to more negative attitudes and lower performance. These results seem logical and probably represent the prevalent beliefs among managers about the general effects of these approaches.

Democratic styles, appealing though they may seem, are not always the most appropriate. When speed is of the essence, democratic decision making may be too slow, or people may want decisiveness from the leader.[57] Whether a decision should be made autocratically or democratically depends on the characteristics of the leader, the followers, and the situation.[58] Thus a situational approach to leader decision styles, discussed later in the chapter, is appropriate.

Performance and Maintenance Behaviors   The performance and maintenance dimensions of leadership are independent of each other. In other words, a leader can behave in ways that emphasize one, both, or neither of these dimensions. Some research indicates that the ideal combination is to engage in both types of leader behaviors.

A team of Ohio State University researchers investigated the effects of leader behaviors in a truck manufacturing plant of International Harvester.[59] Generally, supervisors who were high on maintenance behaviors (which the researchers termed *consideration*) had fewer grievances and less turnover in their work units than supervisors who were low on this dimension. The opposite held for task performance behaviors (which the research team called *initiating structure*). Supervisors high on this dimension had more grievances and higher turnover rates.

> A leader can behave in ways that emphasize one, both, or neither of these dimensions.

When maintenance and performance leadership behaviors were considered together, the results were more complex. But one conclusion was clear: when a leader is high on performance-oriented behaviors, he or she should also be maintenance oriented. Otherwise, the leader will face high rates of employee turnover and grievances.

---

leader-member exchange (LMX) theory

Highlights the importance of leader behaviors not just toward the group as a whole but toward individuals on a personal basis.

participation in decision making

Leader behaviors that managers perform in involving their employees in making decisions.

autocratic leadership

A form of leadership in which the leader makes decisions on his or her own and then announces those decisions to the group.

democratic leadership

A form of leadership in which the leader solicits input from subordinates.

laissez-faire

A leadership philosophy characterized by an absence of managerial decision making.

At about the same time the Ohio State studies were being conducted, a research program at the University of Michigan was studying the impact of the same leader behaviors on groups' job performance.[60] Among other things, the researchers concluded that the most effective managers engaged in what they called task-oriented behavior: planning, scheduling, coordinating, providing resources, and setting performance goals. Effective managers also exhibited more relationship-oriented behavior: demonstrating trust and confidence, being friendly and considerate, showing appreciation, keeping people informed, and so on. As you can see, these dimensions of leader behavior are essentially the task performance and group maintenance dimensions.

After the Ohio State and Michigan findings were published, it became popular to talk about the ideal leader as one who is always both performance and maintenance oriented. The best-known leadership training model to follow this style is Blake and Mouton's Leadership Grid.[61] In grid training, managers are rated on their performance-oriented behavior (called *concern for production*) and maintenance-oriented behavior (*concern for people*). Then their scores are plotted on the grid shown in Exhibit 12.7. The highest score is a 9 on both dimensions.

As the figure shows, joint scores can fall at any point on the grid. Managers who did not score a 9,9—for example, those who were high on concern for people but low on concern for production—would then receive training on how to become a 9,9 leader.

For a long time, grid training was warmly received by U.S. business and industry. Later, however, it was criticized for embracing a simplistic, one-best-way style of leadership and ignoring the possibility that 9,9 is not best under all circumstances. For example, even 1,1 can be appropriate if employees know their jobs (and therefore don't need to receive directions).

EXHIBIT 12.7
The Leadership Grid

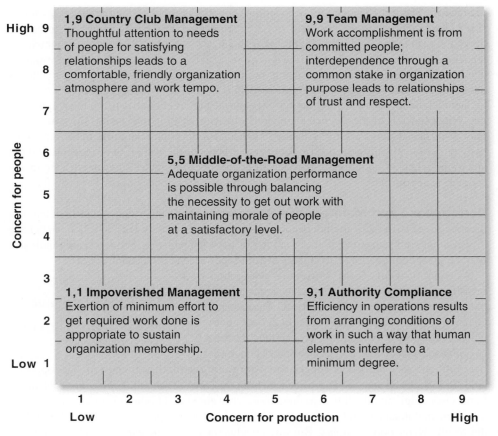

Also, they may enjoy their jobs and their co-workers enough that whether the boss shows personal concern for them is not very important. Nonetheless, if the manager is uncertain how to behave, it probably is best to exhibit behaviors that are related to both task performance and group maintenance.[62]

In fact, a wide range of effective leadership styles exists. Organizations that understand the need for diverse leadership styles will have a competitive advantage in the modern business environment over those that believe there is only one best way.

Situational Approaches to Leadership

According to proponents of the **situational approach** to leadership, universally important traits and behaviors don't exist. They believe effective leader behaviors vary from situation to situation. The leader should first analyze the situation and then decide what to do. In other words, look before you lead.

A head nurse in a hospital described her situational approach to leadership:

> My leadership style is a mix of all styles. In this environment I normally let people participate. But in a code blue situation where a patient is dying I automatically become very autocratic: "You do this; you do that; you, out of the room; you all better be quiet; you, get Dr. Mansfield." The staff tell me that's the only time they see me like that. In an emergency like that, you don't have time to vote, talk a lot, or yell at each other. It's time for someone to set up the order.
>
> I remember one time, one person saying, "Wait a minute, I want to do this." He wanted to do the mouth-to-mouth resuscitation. I knew the person behind him did it better, so I said, "No, he does it." This fellow told me later that I hurt him so badly to yell that in front of all the staff and doctors. It was like he wasn't good enough. So I explained it to him: "That's the way it is. A life was on the line. I couldn't give you warm fuzzies. I couldn't make you look good because you didn't have the skills to give the very best to that patient who wasn't breathing anymore."[63]

Look before you lead.

This nurse has her own intuitive situational approach to leadership. She knows the potential advantages of the participatory approach to decision making, but she also knows that in some circumstances she must make decisions herself.

The first situational model of leadership was proposed in 1958 by Tannenbaum and Schmidt. In their classic *Harvard Business Review* article, these authors described how managers should consider three factors before deciding how to lead: forces in the manager, forces in the subordinate, and forces in the situation.[64]

Forces in the manager include the manager's personal values, inclinations, feelings of security, and confidence in subordinates. Forces in the subordinate include his or her knowledge and experience, readiness to assume responsibility for decision making, interest in the task or problem, and understanding and acceptance of the organization's goals. Forces in the situation include the type of leadership style the organization values, the degree to which the group works effectively as a unit, the problem itself and the type of information needed to solve it, and the amount of time the leader has to make the decision.

Consider which of these forces makes an autocratic style most appropriate and which dictates a democratic, participative style. By engaging in this exercise, you are constructing a situational theory of leadership.

Although the Tannenbaum and Schmidt article was published more than a half-century ago, most of its arguments remain valid. Since that time, other situational models have emerged. We will focus here on four: the Vroom model for decision making, Fiedler's contingency model, Hersey and Blanchard's situational theory, and path–goal theory.

Nurses experience situational leadership on a daily basis. How would you handle a leadership role under pressure?

© Jupiterimages/Imagesource

Vroom model

A situational model that
focuses on the participative
dimension of leadership.

The Vroom Model of Leadership   This situational model follows in the tradition of Tannenbaum and Schmidt. The **Vroom model** emphasizes the participative dimension of leadership: how leaders go about making decisions. The model uses the basic situational approach of assessing the situation before determining the best leadership style.[65]

The Vroom model operates like a funnel. You answer the questions one at a time, choosing high or low for each, sometimes skipping questions as you follow the appropriate path. Eventually you reach one of 14 possible endpoints. For each endpoint, the model states which of five decision styles is most appropriate. Several decision styles may work, but the style recommended is the one that takes the least amount of time.

The five leader decision styles—decide, consult individually, consult the group, facilitate, and delegate—indicate that there are several shades of participation, not just autocratic or democratic.

Of course not every managerial decision warrants this complicated analysis. But the model becomes less complex after you work through it a couple of times. Also, using the model for major decisions ensures that you consider the important situational factors and alerts you to the most appropriate style to use.

**Fiedler's contingency
model of leadership
effectiveness**

A situational approach to
leadership postulating that
effectiveness depends on
the personal style of the
leader and the degree to
which the situation gives the
leader power, control, and
influence over the situation.

Fiedler's Contingency Model   According to **Fiedler's contingency model of leadership effectiveness,** effectiveness depends on two factors: the personal style of the leader and the degree to which the situation gives the leader power, control, and influence over the situation.[66] Exhibit 12.8 illustrates the contingency model. The upper half of the figure shows the situational analysis, and the lower half indicates the appropriate style. In the upper portion, three questions are used to analyze the situation:

1. Are leader–member relations good or poor? (To what extent is the leader accepted and supported by group members?)
2. Is the task structured or unstructured? (To what extent do group members know what their goals are and how to accomplish them?)
3. Is the leader's position power strong or weak (high or low)? (To what extent does the leader have the authority to reward and punish?)

EXHIBIT 12.8   Fiedler's Analysis of Situations in Which the Task- or Relationship-Motivated Leader Is More Effective

Leader–member relations	Good				Poor			
Task structure	Structured		Unstructured		Structured		Unstructured	
Leader position power	High	Low	High	Low	High	Low	High	Low
Favorable for leader	→ Unfavorable for leader							
Type of leader most effective in the situation	Task-motivated	Task-motivated	Task-motivated	Relation-ship-motivated	Relation-ship-motivated	Relation-ship-motivated	Relation-ship-motivated	Task-motivated

These three sequential questions create a decision tree (from top to bottom in the figure) in which a situation is classified into one of eight categories. The lower the category number, the more favorable the situation is for the leader; the higher the number, the less favorable the situation. Fiedler originally called this variable "situational favorableness," and later "situational control." Situation 1 is the best: relations are good, task structure is high, and power is high. In the least favorable situation (8), in which the leader has very little situational control, relations are poor, tasks lack structure, and the leader's power is weak.

Different situations dictate different leadership styles. Fiedler measured leadership styles with an instrument assessing the leader's least preferred co-worker (LPC); that is, the attitude toward the follower the leader liked the least. This was considered an indication more generally of leaders' attitudes toward people. If a leader can single out the person she likes the least, but her attitude is not all that negative, she would receive a high score on the LPC scale. Leaders with more negative attitudes toward others would receive low LPC scores.

Based on the LPC score, Fiedler considered two leadership styles. **Task-motivated leadership** places primary emphasis on completing the task and is more likely exhibited by leaders with low LPC scores. **Relationship-motivated leadership** emphasizes maintaining good interpersonal relationships and is more likely from high-LPC leaders. These leadership styles correspond to task performance and group maintenance leader behaviors, respectively.

The lower part of Exhibit 12.8 indicates which style is situationally appropriate. For situations 1, 2, 3, and 8, a task-motivated leadership style is more effective. For situations 4 through 7, relationship-motivated leadership is more appropriate.

Fiedler's theory was not always supported by research. It is better supported if three broad rather than eight specific levels of situational control are assumed: low, medium, and high. The theory was quite controversial in academic circles; among other arguable things, it assumed that leaders cannot change their styles but must be assigned to situations that suit their styles. However, the model has withstood the test of time and still receives attention. Most important, it initiated and continues to emphasize the importance of finding a fit between the situation and the leader's style.

Hersey and Blanchard's Situational Theory   Hersey and Blanchard developed a situational model that added another factor the leader should take into account before deciding whether task performance or maintenance behaviors are more important. Originally called the *life-cycle theory of leadership,* **Hersey and Blanchard's situational theory** highlights the maturity of the followers as the key situational factor.[67] **Job maturity** is the level of the follower's skills and technical knowledge relative to the task being performed; **psychological maturity** is the follower's self-confidence and self-respect. High-maturity followers have both the ability and the confidence to do a good job.

The theory proposes that the more mature the followers, the less the leader needs to engage in task performance behaviors. The required amount of maintenance behavior is a bit more complex; maintenance behaviors are not important with followers of low or high levels of maturity but are important for followers of moderate maturity. For low-maturity followers, the emphasis should be on performance-related leadership; for moderate-maturity followers, performance leadership is somewhat less important and maintenance behaviors become more important; and for high-maturity followers, neither dimension of leadership behavior is important.

Little academic research has been done on this situational theory, but the model is popular in management training seminars. Regardless of its scientific validity, Hersey and Blanchard's model provides a reminder that it is important to treat different people differently. Moreover, it suggests the importance of treating the same individual differently from time to time as he or she changes jobs or acquires more maturity in her or his particular job.[68]

Path–Goal Theory   Perhaps the most comprehensive and generally useful situational model of leadership effectiveness is path–goal theory. Developed by Robert House,

task-motivated leadership

Leadership that places primary emphasis on completing a task.

relationship-motivated leadership

Leadership that places primary emphasis on maintaining good interpersonal relationships.

Hersey and Blanchard's situational theory

A life-cycle theory of leadership postulating that a manager should consider an employee's psychological and job maturity before deciding whether task performance or maintenance behaviors are more important.

job maturity

The level of the employee's skills and technical knowledge relative to the task being performed.

psychological maturity

An employee's self-confidence and self-respect.

path–goal theory

A theory that concerns how leaders influence subordinates' perceptions of their work goals and the paths they follow toward attainment of those goals.

path–goal theory gets its name from its concern with how leaders influence followers' perceptions of their work goals and the paths they follow toward goal attainment.[69]

The key situational factors in path–goal theory are (1) personal characteristics of followers and (2) environmental pressures and demands with which followers must cope to attain their work goals. These factors determine which leadership behaviors are most appropriate.

The four pertinent leadership behaviors are as follows:

1. *Directive leadership,* a form of task performance-oriented behavior.
2. *Supportive leadership,* a form of group maintenance-oriented behavior.
3. *Participative leadership,* or decision style.
4. *Achievement-oriented leadership,* or behaviors geared toward motivating people, such as setting challenging goals and rewarding good performance.

These situational factors and leader behaviors are merged in Exhibit 12.9. As you can see, appropriate leader behaviors—as determined by characteristics of followers and the work environment—lead to effective performance.

The theory also specifies which follower and environmental characteristics are important. There are three key follower characteristics. *Authoritarianism* is the degree to which individuals respect, admire, and defer to authority. *Locus of control* is the extent to which individuals see the environment as responsive to their own behavior. People with an *internal* locus of control believe that what happens to them is their own doing; people with an *external* locus of control believe that it is just luck or fate. Finally, *ability* is people's beliefs about their own abilities to do their assigned jobs.

Path–goal theory states that these personal characteristics determine the appropriateness of various leadership styles. For example, the theory makes the following propositions:

- A directive leadership style is more appropriate for highly authoritarian people because such people respect authority.
- A participative leadership style is more appropriate for people who have an internal locus of control because these individuals prefer to have more influence over their own lives.
- A directive style is more appropriate when subordinates' ability is low. The directive style helps people understand what has to be done.

Appropriate leadership style is also determined by three important environmental factors: people's tasks, the formal authority system of the organization, and the primary work group:

- Directive leadership is inappropriate if tasks already are well structured.
- If the task and the authority or rule system are dissatisfying, directive leadership will create greater dissatisfaction.
- If the task or authority system is dissatisfying, supportive leadership is especially appropriate because it offers one positive source of gratification in an otherwise negative situation.
- If the primary work group provides social support to its members, supportive leadership is less important.

EXHIBIT 12.9
The Path–Goal Framework

Path–goal theory offers many more propositions. In general, the theory suggests that the functions of the leader are to (1) make the path to work goals easier to travel by providing coaching and direction, (2) reduce frustrating barriers to goal attainment, and (3) increase opportunities for personal satisfaction by increasing payoffs to people for achieving performance goals. The best way to do these things depends on your people and on the work situation. Again, analyze and then adapt your style accordingly.

Substitutes for Leadership   Sometimes leaders don't have to lead, or situations constrain their ability to lead effectively. The situation may be one in which leadership is unnecessary or has little impact. **Substitutes for leadership** can provide the same influence on people that leaders otherwise would have.

Certain follower, task, and organizational factors are substitutes for task performance and group maintenance leader behaviors.[70] For example, group maintenance behaviors are less important and have less impact if people already have a closely knit group, they have a professional orientation, the job is inherently satisfying, or there is great physical distance between leader and followers. Thus physicians who are strongly concerned with professional conduct, enjoy their work, and work independently do not need social support from hospital administrators.

Task performance leadership is less important and will have less of a positive effect if people have a lot of experience and ability, feedback is supplied to them directly from the task or by computer, or the rules and procedures are rigid. If these factors are operating, the leader does not have to tell people what to do or how well they are performing.

The concept of substitutes for leadership does more than indicate when a leader's attempts at influence will and will not work. It provides useful and practical prescriptions for how to manage more efficiently.[71] If the manager can develop the work situation to the

substitutes for leadership

Factors in the workplace that can exert the same influence on employees as leaders would provide.

Management in Action

IS MEG WHITMAN'S LEADERSHIP STYLE RIGHT FOR HEWLETT-PACKARD?

MANAGER'S BRIEF

PROGRESS REPORT

ONWARD

HP's board of directors certainly thinks so; they appointed Whitman chairman of the board in 2014. Described as "blunt, folksy, and persistent," she is a decisive leader and team builder who realizes that turning around HP requires a long-term commitment to making several adjustments and improvements, and not betting on a magical silver bullet. In her own words: "We are in a multi-year journey to turn HP around, and we have put in place a plan to restore HP to growth. We know where we need to go, and we're making progress."

Some of the decisions that Whitman has made to achieve the turnaround plan include:

– *Reduce costs.* Since taking over as CEO in 2011, HP has conducted over 34,000 layoffs and may not stop there: "there may be more opportunity for efficiency." Inventory has been managed more carefully and capital spending has been reduced.
– *Realign resources toward high-growth markets like corporate hardware and services operations.* Separate mature computer and printer businesses.

– *Reinvigorate innovation.* HP is making a significant effort to make inroads into the emerging areas of cloud computing, security, and data analysis.

Now with just one year remaining to achieve her turnaround plan, Whitman's leadership style is showing some glimmers of success. Despite a four-year slide in revenue, HP's long-term debt was reduced by 22 percent, cash reserves have doubled to $16 billion, and earnings per share rose 10 percent. While none of this means HP will experience fast revenue growth in the near term, it does suggest Whitman's turnaround efforts are showing signs of progress.[72]

• What leader traits and behaviors has Meg Whitman used? Are they likely to be effective?
• How well suited to HP's situation is Whitman's leadership style, as described here?

point that a number of these substitutes for leadership are operating, less time will need to be spent in direct attempts to influence people. The leader will be free to spend more time on other important activities.

Research indicates that substitutes for leadership may be better predictors of commitment and satisfaction than of performance.[73] These substitutes are helpful, but you can't put substitutes in place and think you've completed your job as leader. Consider, for example, whether these substitutes would be enough to turn around performance at Hewlett-Packard (see "Management in Action: Progress Report"). And as a follower, consider this: if you're not getting good leadership, and if these substitutes are not in place, create your own substitute for leadership—self-leadership. Take the initiative to motivate yourself, lead yourself, create positive change, and lead others.

Contemporary Perspectives on Leadership

LO 7

So far you have learned the major classic approaches to understanding leadership, all of which remain useful today. Now we will discuss a number of newer developments that are revolutionizing our understanding of this vital aspect of management.

charismatic leader

A person who is dominant, self-confident, convinced of the moral righteousness of his or her beliefs, and able to arouse a sense of excitement and adventure in followers.

Charismatic Leadership

Like many great leaders, Ronald Reagan had charisma. So does Barack Obama. Thomas Watson, Alfred Sloan, Oprah Winfrey, Steve Jobs, and Richard Branson are good examples of charismatic leaders in industry.

Charisma is a rather elusive concept; it is easy to spot but hard to define. What *is* charisma, and how does one acquire it? According to one definition, "Charisma packs an emotional wallop for followers above and beyond ordinary esteem, affection, admiration, and trust. . . . The charismatic is an idolized hero, a messiah, and a savior."[74] As you can see from this quotation, many people, particularly North Americans, value charisma in their leaders. But some people don't like the term *charisma;* it can be associated with the negative charisma of evil leaders whom people follow blindly.[75] Nevertheless, charismatic leaders who display appropriate values and use their charisma for appropriate purposes serve as ethical role models for others.[76]

Charismatic leaders are dominant and exceptionally self-confident and have a strong conviction in the moral righteousness of their beliefs.[77] They strive to create an aura of competence and success and communicate high expectations for and confidence in followers. Ultimately, charismatic leaders satisfy other peoples' needs.[78] Even people who have direct contact with a leader can perceive him or her as charismatic, because other followers spread the word.[79] And guess what: People can learn to be more charismatic.[80]

The charismatic leader articulates ideological goals and makes sacrifices in pursuit of those goals.[81] Martin Luther King Jr. had a dream for a better world, and John F. Kennedy spoke of landing a human on the moon. In other words, such leaders have a compelling vision. The charismatic leader also arouses a sense of excitement and adventure. He or she is an eloquent speaker who exhibits superior verbal skills, which help communicate the vision and motivate followers. Steve Jobs inspired extraordinary performance from employees, had the fortitude to take innovative risks, and was exceptionally skilled at envisioning and designing products.[82]

Martin Luther King was a brilliant, charismatic leader who had a compelling vision, a dream for a better world.

© *Associated Press*

Leaders who possess these characteristics or do these things inspire in their followers trust, confidence, acceptance, obedience, emotional involvement, affection, admiration, and higher performance.[83] For example, a study of firefighters found them to be happier when working for charismatic officers who expressed positive attitudes.[84] Having charisma not only helps CEOs inspire other employees in the organization but also may enable them to influence external stakeholders, including customers and investors.[85] Evidence for the positive effects of charismatic leadership has been found in a wide variety of groups, organizations, and management levels, and in countries including India, Singapore, the Netherlands, China, Japan, and Canada.[86]

Charisma has been shown to improve corporate financial performance, particularly under conditions of uncertainty—that is, in risky circumstances or when environments are changing and people have difficulty understanding what they should do.[87] Uncertainty is stressful, and it makes people more receptive to the ideas and actions of charismatic leaders. By the way, too, as an organization's performance improves under a person's leadership, that person becomes seen as more charismatic as a result of the higher performance.[88]

Transformational Leadership

Charisma contributes to transformational leadership. **Transformational leaders** motivate people to transcend their personal interests for the sake of the larger community.[89] They generate excitement and revitalize organizations. At Amazon, chief executive Jeff Bezos generates excitement with his zeal to create a great customer experience coupled with determination to focus on the long term, no matter how hard investors press for quick profits. His vision keeps employees innovating and gives them a sense of purpose greater than quarterly financial performance.[90]

The transformational process moves beyond the more traditional *transactional* approach to leadership. **Transactional leaders** view management as a series of transactions in which they use their legitimate, reward, and coercive powers to give commands and exchange rewards for services rendered. Unlike transformational leadership, transactional leadership is dispassionate; it does not excite, transform, empower, or inspire people to focus on the interests of the group or organization. However, transactional approaches may be more effective for individualists than for collectivists (recall Chapter 6).[91]

Generating Excitement   Transformational leaders generate excitement in several ways.[92] First, they are charismatic, as described earlier. Second, they give their followers individualized attention. Transformational leaders delegate challenging work to deserving people, keep lines of communication open, and provide one-on-one mentoring to develop their people. They do not treat everyone alike because not everyone *is* alike.

Third, transformational leaders are intellectually stimulating. They arouse in their followers an awareness of problems and potential solutions. They articulate the organization's opportunities, threats, strengths, and weaknesses. They stir the imagination and generate insights. Therefore, problems are recognized, and high-quality solutions are identified and implemented with the full commitment of followers.

Additional Strategies   At least four additional strategies contribute to transformational leadership.[93] First, transformational leaders have a vision—a goal, an agenda, or a results orientation that grabs people's attention. Second, they communicate their vision; through words, manner, or symbolism, they relate a compelling image of the ultimate goal. Transformational leadership is most effective in motivating followers when they can see directly the meaningful consequences of the leader's vision, such as by interacting with those who benefit from their work.[94]

Third, transformational leaders build trust by being consistent, dependable, and persistent. They position themselves clearly by choosing a direction and staying with it, thus projecting integrity. Finally, they have a positive self-regard. They do not feel self-important or complacent; rather, they recognize their personal strengths, compensate for their weaknesses, nurture and continually develop their talents, and know how to learn from failure. They strive for success rather than merely try to avoid failure.

Transformational leadership has been identified in industry, the military, and politics.[95] Besides Amazon's Jeff Bezos, mentioned earlier, examples of transformational leaders in

transformational leader

A leader who motivates people to transcend their personal interests for the good of the group.

transactional leaders

Leaders who manage through transactions, using their legitimate, reward, and coercive powers to give commands and exchange rewards for services rendered.

Transformational leaders strive for success rather than merely try to avoid failure.

business include Indra Nooyi (CEO of PepsiCo), Richard Branson (founder and CEO of Virgin Group), and Brad Smith (CEO of Intuit).[96] Transformational leadership exhibited by CEOs predicts firm performance, at least for small and midsized firms.[97]

As with studies of charisma, transformational leadership and its positive impact on follower satisfaction and performance have been demonstrated in countries the world over, including Egypt, Germany, China, England, and Japan.[98] A study of employees in mainland China found that transformational leadership predicted employee creativity.[99] Under transformational leadership, people view their jobs as more intrinsically motivating (see Chapter 13 for more on this) and are more strongly committed to work goals.[100] And top management teams agree more clearly about important organizational goals, which translates into higher organizational performance.[101]

Transforming Leaders   Importantly, transformational leadership is not the exclusive domain of presidents and chief executives. In the military, leaders who received transformational leadership training had a positive impact on followers' personal development. They also were successful as indirect leaders: military recruits under the transformational leaders' direct reports were stronger performers.[102] Don't forget, though: The best leaders are those who can display both transformational and transactional behaviors.[103]

Ford Motor Company, in collaboration with the University of Michigan School of Business, put thousands of middle managers through a program designed to stimulate transformational leadership.[104] The training included analysis of the changing business environment, company strategy, and personal reflection and discussion about the need to change. Participants assessed their own leadership styles and developed a specific change initiative to implement after the training—a change that would make a needed and lasting difference for the company.

Over the next six months, the managers implemented change on the job. Almost half of the initiatives resulted in transformational changes in the organization or work unit; the rest of the changes were smaller, more incremental, or more personal. Whether managers made small or transformational changes depended on their attitude going into the training, their level of self-esteem, and the amount of support they received from others on the job for their efforts. Thus some managers did not respond as hoped. But almost half embraced the training, became more transformational in orientation, and tackled significant transformational changes for the company.

Level 5 leadership, a term well-known among executives, is considered by some to be the ultimate leadership style. Level 5 leadership is a combination of strong professional will (determination) and personal humility that builds enduring greatness.[105] Thus a Level 5 leader is relentlessly focused on the organization's long-term success while behaving with modesty, directing attention toward the organization rather than him- or herself. Examples include Tim Cook, CEO of Apple, John Chambers, CEO of Cisco Systems, and IBM's former chief executive Louis Gerstner. Gerstner is widely credited for turning around a stodgy IBM by shifting its focus from computer hardware to business solutions. Following his retirement, Gerstner wrote a memoir that details what happened at the company but says little about himself. Level 5 leadership is seen as a way to transform organizations to make them great and requires the leader to exhibit a combination of transactional and transformational styles.[106]

Authenticity

Consider **authentic leadership** to be rooted in the ancient Greek philosophy "To thine own self be true."[107] In your own leadership, strive for authenticity in the form of honesty, genuineness, reliability, integrity, and trustworthiness. Authentic transformational leaders care about public interests (community, organizational, or group), not just their own.[108] They are willing to sacrifice their own interests for others, and they can be trusted. They are ethically mature; people view leaders who exhibit moral reasoning as more transformational than leaders who do not.[109] Importantly, ethical leadership flows down from one organizational level to the next[110]—your actions as a leader have an impact beyond your immediate, direct reports.

Level 5 leadership

A combination of strong professional will (determination) and humility that builds enduring greatness.

authentic leadership

A style in which the leader is true to himself or herself while leading.

Pseudotransformational leaders are the opposite: they talk a good game, but they ignore followers' real needs as their own self-interests (power, prestige, control, wealth, fame) take precedence.[111]

Opportunities for Leaders

A common view of leaders is that they are superheroes acting alone, swooping in to save the day. But especially in these complex times, leaders cannot and need not act alone. Effective leadership must permeate the organization, not reside in one or two superstars at the top. The leader's job becomes one of spreading leadership abilities throughout the firm.[112] Make people responsible for their own performance. Create an environment in which each person can figure out what needs to be done and then do it well. Point the way and clear the path so that people can succeed. Give them the credit they deserve. Make heroes out of *them*.

Thus what is now required of leaders is less the efficient management of resources and more the effective unleashing of people and their intellectual capital.

This perspective uncovers a variety of nontraditional leadership roles that are emerging as vitally important.[113] The term **servant–leader** was coined by Robert Greenleaf, a retired AT&T executive. The term is paradoxical in the sense that "leader" and "servant" are usually opposites; the servant–leader's relationship with employees is more like that of serving customers. For the individual who wants to both lead and serve others, servant-leadership is a way of relating to others to serve their needs and enhance their personal growth while strengthening the organization.[114]

For example, at Mississippi Health Services, CEO John Heer had himself and the other executives assessed for servant leadership qualities, including humility, honesty, integrity, and a focus on results. The executives then created action plans for improving in the areas with the lowest scores and met to share their results and plans. Asking for help with weaknesses felt uncomfortable, but the process freed everyone to be more honest and led to greater satisfaction among employees, doctors, and patients. Even market share improved.[115] The nearby "Social Enterprise" box describes how Richard Murphy used his leadership to serve the needs of tens of thousands of disadvantaged youth in New York City.

A number of other roles provide leadership opportunities. **Intergroup leaders** lead collaborative performance between different groups or organizations.[116] Examples are interdepartmental cooperation, joint ventures, public/private partnerships, and collaborations that cross national, cultural, and religious boundaries.

With work often being team-based (see Chapter 14), **shared leadership** occurs when leadership rotates to the person with the key knowledge, skills, and abilities for the issue facing the team at a particular time.[117] Shared leadership is most important when tasks are interdependent, are complex, and require creativity. High-performing teams engaged in such work exhibit more shared leadership than poorly performing teams. In consulting teams, the higher the shared leadership, the higher their clients rated the teams' performance.[118] The role of vertical leader remains important—the formal leader still designs the team, manages its external boundaries, provides task direction, emphasizes the importance of the shared leadership approach, and engages in the transactional and transformational activities described in this chapter. But at the same time, the metaphor of geese in V-formation adds strength to the group; the lead goose periodically drops to the back, and another goose steps up and takes its place at the forefront.

Lateral leadership does not involve a hierarchical, superior–subordinate relationship but instead invites colleagues at the same level to solve problems together.[119] You alone can't provide a solution to every problem, but you can create processes through which people work collaboratively. If you can get people working to improve methods collaboratively, you can help create an endless stream of innovations. In other words, it's not about you providing solutions to problems; it's about creating better interpersonal processes for finding solutions. Strategies and tactics can be found throughout this book, including the chapters on decision making, organization structure, teams, communication, and change.

pseudotransformational leaders

Leaders who talk about positive change but allow their self-interest to take precedence over followers' needs.

servant–leader

A leader who serves others' needs while strengthening the organization.

intergroup leader

A leader who leads collaborative performance between groups or organizations.

shared leadership

Rotating leadership, in which people rotate through the leadership role based on which person has the most relevant skills at a particular time.

lateral leadership

Style in which colleagues at the same hierarchical level are invited to collaborate and facilitate joint problem solving.

Social Enterprise

Richard L. Murphy Served Thousands

Like many people, Richard Murphy held a variety of jobs after graduating from college. In the late 1960s, he was hired as a part-time social worker in New York City. He soon learned that "as many as 200,000 students were skipping school each day, many of them getting into trouble." He believed that these young people, in order to stay out of trouble, needed a place to hang out.

With financing from a city agency, Murphy established the Rheedlen Center for Children and Families (now known as the Harlem Children's Zone). While its original goal was to help truant students finish school, it currently provides after-school programs and other educational services to 12,000 youth and their families from all over Harlem.

Murphy made another vision into a reality. Appointed NYC Commissioner of Youth Services by a former mayor, David Dinkins, Murphy instituted a program to keep open several public schools after 3 p.m. The schools were used as community centers to provide young people tutoring, exercise classes, and other enriching activities. Murphy's vision was to "create dozens of 'small universes' in which young people could learn, dream, and grow." This model of using schools as community centers has been replicated in several cities throughout the United States.

Paul Schmitz, a social innovator and author, learned a great deal from Richard Murphy's selfless approach to leadership, including:

1. *Scale ideas, not just programs and organizations.* Murphy wanted others to take, use, and build upon his ideas so that more young people and their families could be helped.
2. *Build and support other leaders.* Murphy multiplied his impact by mentoring countless diverse leaders from such organizations as Carnegie Corporation and Good Shepard Services.
3. *Take chances on people.* Murphy hired people who he believed could be effective leaders, including someone who had left youth work due to a battle with addiction. Murphy hired him back into the field. This individual went on to a long, successful career in helping others.[120]

Questions

- What made Richard Murphy such an effective leader? Explain.

- In addition to being a servant–leader, to what degree was Murphy a Level 5 leader?

A Note on Courage

To be a good leader, you need the courage to create a vision of greatness for your unit; identify and manage allies, adversaries, and fence sitters; and execute your vision, often against opposition. This does not mean you should commit career suicide by alienating too many powerful people; it does mean taking reasonable risks, with the good of the firm at heart, to produce constructive change.

For example, Alan Mulally needed courage when he left Boeing to take charge of Ford Motor Company in 2006, a point at which a series of poor decisions had made Ford a money-losing company. Many of Ford's managers were skeptical of Mulally as their new CEO because he came from outside the automobile industry. Nevertheless, Mullaly plunged ahead with decisions that were controversial at the time. He borrowed heavily and determined that the company would go forward with greater focus by offering fewer brands and models, with each being the best in its class. A few years later, Mulally's courageous efforts looked brilliant; Ford's borrowing gave the company resources to draw on when other automakers were accepting government loans to survive a financial crisis, and within a few years, Ford was recording record profits.[121]

Specifically, fulfilling your vision will require some of the following acts of courage:[122] (1) seeing things as they are and facing them head-on, making no excuses and harboring no wishful illusions; (2) saying what needs to be said to those who need to hear it; and (3) persisting despite resistance, criticism, abuse, and setbacks. Courage includes stating the realities, even when they are harsh, and publicly stating what you will do to help and what you want from others. This means laying the cards on the table honestly: Here is what I want from you . . . what do you want from me?[123]

Developing Your Leadership Skills

As with other things, you must work at developing your leadership abilities. Great musicians and great athletes don't become great on natural gifts alone. They pay their dues by practicing, learning, and sacrificing. Leaders in a variety of fields, when asked how they became the best leader possible, offered the following comments:[124]

- "I've observed methods and skills of my bosses that I respected."
- "By taking risks, trying, and learning from my mistakes."
- "Reading autobiographies of leaders I admire to try to understand how they think."
- "Lots of practice."
- "By making mistakes myself and trying a different approach."
- "By being put in positions of responsibility that other people counted on."

How Do I Start?

How do you go about developing your leadership abilities? You don't have to wait until you land a management job or even finish your education. You can begin establishing credibility by behaving with integrity, learning from your mistakes, and becoming competent in your chosen field. You should look for—and then seize—opportunities to take actions that will help the groups you already belong to. Even before you are a supervisor, you can practice empowering others by listening carefully when you are in a group and by sharing what you know so that the whole group will be better informed. Finally, begin building a network of personal contacts by reaching out to others to offer help, not just to request it.[125]

When you are searching for your next job, look for a position with an employer that is committed to developing leadership talent. Ideally, leadership development is connected to opportunities to practice the skills you are learning about, so ask about chances to lead a project or a team, even for short periods of time.[126] Companies that excel at leadership development include Microsoft, Unilever, 3M, and IBM.[127]

More specifically, here are some developmental experiences you should seek:[128]

Challenges expand knowledge and experiences. Being open to new ideas allows managers to learn, grow, and succeed even though the challenge may be out of their comfort zone.

© Karl Weatherly/Getty Images

- *Assignments:* Building something from nothing; fixing or turning around a failing operation; taking on project or task force responsibilities; accepting international assignments.
- *Other people:* Having exposure to positive role models; increasing visibility to others; working with people of diverse backgrounds.
- *Hardships:* Overcoming ideas that fail and deals that collapse; confronting others' performance problems; breaking out of a career rut.
- *Other events:* Formal courses; challenging job experiences; supervision of others; experiences outside work.

What Are the Keys?

The most effective developmental experiences have three components: assessment, challenge, and support.[129] Assessment includes information that gives you an understanding of where you are now, what your strengths are, your current levels of performance and leadership effectiveness, and your primary development needs. You can think about what your past feedback has been, what previous successes and failures you have had, how people have reacted to your ideas and actions, what your personal goals are, and what strategies you should implement to make progress. You can seek answers from your peers at work, bosses, family, friends, customers, and anyone else who knows you and how you work. The information you collect will help clarify what you need to learn, improve, or change.[130]

Management in Action

HP'S FUTURE ACCORDING TO MEG WHITMAN

Four years into Meg Whitman's tenure as chief executive of Hewlett-Packard, some observers remain skeptical that she will achieve a successful turnaround. In her defense, Whitman pointed to her original forecast that a turnaround would take five years and insisted that employees, customers, and business partners see signs of a turnaround. Although the sliding stock price showed the doubts of investors, others interpreted her stance as evidence of courage, consistency, and an admirably long view of corporate performance.

Whitman had shown courage before joining HP. Early in her career, she was a junior partner at Bain Consulting. Colleagues were intimidated by her boss, Tom Tierney, but Whitman met with him privately and asked whether he wanted feedback from the staff about his leadership style. When Tierney said yes, she told him he was like a steamroller and inhibited his staff. After the initial shock, Tierney took her counsel to heart and now praises her courage.

At HP, Whitman has been fearless in making tough decisions. In 2015, she took the bold step to split HP into two publicly traded companies, HP Enterprise (focusing on corporate customers) and HP Inc. (focused on the printer and PC businesses). Whitman will lead the former and Dion Weisler will head up the latter.

Whitman also has demonstrated concern for what it is like to be an HP employee. She has sought to restore a culture more like the one that prevailed under the founders—one where technology is revered and technology workers are valued. She eliminated the fenced-off executive parking lot and executive suites, working in a cubicle like everyone else. When she travels, she stays at a Courtyard Marriott, and when she works evenings, she orders from Chipotle or the local pizza company. Whitman certainly values the power of symbols. HP's renovated meeting center at headquarters in Palo Alto has a courtyard built around an oak tree planted by Bill Hewlett and Dave Packard in the 1960s. Meg told a *Bloomberg Businessweek* reporter, "This is symbolic of the rebirth of Hewlett-Packard anchored by the foundation of that oak tree."[131]

- What evidence, if any, do you see that Whitman is a charismatic leader? A transformational leader? An authentic leader? A servant–leader?
- Look up recent business news to learn how well HP is performing today and whether Whitman remains CEO. Has she been a successful leader of HP? Why or why not?

The most potent developmental experiences provide challenge—they stretch you. We all think and behave in habitual, comfortable ways. This is natural and perhaps sufficient to survive. But you've probably heard people say how important it can be to get out of your comfort zone—to tackle situations that require new skills and abilities, that are confusing or ambiguous, or that you simply would rather not deal with. Sometimes the challenge comes from lack of experience; other times, it requires changing old habits. It may be uncomfortable, but this is how great managers learn. Remember, some people don't bother to learn or refuse to learn. Make sure you think about your experiences along the way and reflect on them afterward, introspectively and in discussion with others.

You receive support when others send the message that your efforts to learn and grow are valued. Without support, challenging developmental experiences can be overwhelming. With support, it is easier to handle the struggle, stay on course, open up to learning, and actually learn from experiences. Support can come informally from other people; more formally through the procedures of the organization; and through learning resources in the forms of training, constructive feedback, talking with others, and so on. What develops in leadership development? Through such experiences, you can acquire more self-awareness and self-confidence, a broader perspective on the organizational system, creative thinking, the ability to work more effectively in complex social systems, and the ability to learn from experience.

KEY TERMS

authentic leadership, p. 400

autocratic leadership, p. 391

behavioral approach, p. 389

charismatic leader, p. 398

democratic leadership, p. 391

Fiedler's contingency model of
    leadership effectiveness, p. 394

group maintenance behaviors, p. 390

Hersey and Blanchard's situational
    theory, p. 395

intergroup leader, p. 401

job maturity, p. 395

laissez-faire, p. 391

lateral leadership, p. 401

leader–member exchange (LMX)
    theory, p. 391

Level 5 leadership, p. 400

participation in decision making, p. 391

path–goal theory, p. 396

power, p. 386

pseudotransformational
    leaders, p. 401

psychological maturity, p. 395

relationship-motivated
    leadership, p. 395

servant–leader, p. 401

shared leadership, p. 401

situational approach, p. 393

strategic leadership, p. 386

substitutes for leadership, p. 397

supervisory leadership, p. 386

task-motivated leadership, p. 395

task performance behaviors, p. 390

trait approach, p. 388

transactional leaders, p. 399

transformational leader, p. 399

vision, p. 383

Vroom model, p. 394

RETAINING WHAT YOU LEARNED

In Chapter 12, you learned what it means to be a leader. You also learned that leaders are needed at all levels of organizations and that people want leaders to help them achieve their goals. The best leaders have and share effectively a compelling vision that motivates others to achieve more than they thought was possible. Having and using power are important tools for any leader. Leaders can draw on five types of power—legitimate, reward, coercive, referent, and expert—to influence others. While there are several characteristics associated with leaders, the most important skill is the ability to perceive the situation accurately and then change behavior accordingly. There are several leadership theories that describe the interaction of leaders and the situation at hand, including Vroom's model, Fiedler's contingency model, Hersey and Blanchard's situation theory, and House's path–goal theory. Charismatic leaders are dominant and self-confident, and communicate high expectations for and confidence in their followers. Transformational leaders translate vision into reality by inspiring followers to transcend their individual interests for the good of the larger community. There are several nontraditional opportunities to be a leader such as servant, intergroup, shared, or lateral leadership. Also, you can ask for development assignments or activities that include assessment, challenge, and support.

LO 1 Discuss what it means to be a leader.

- A leader is one who influences others to attain goals.
- Leaders orchestrate change, set direction, and motivate people to overcome obstacles and move the organization toward its ideal future.

LO 2 Summarize what people want and organizations need from their leaders.

- People want help in achieving their goals, and organizations need leaders at all levels.
- The best leaders challenge the process, inspire a shared vision, enable others to act, model the way, and encourage the heart.

LO 3 Explain how a good vision helps you be a better leader.

- Outstanding leaders have vision. A vision is a mental image that goes beyond the ordinary and perhaps beyond what others thought possible.
- The vision provides the direction in which the leader wants the organization to move and inspiration for people to pursue it.

LO 4 Identify sources of power in organizations.

- Having power and using it appropriately are essential to effective leadership. Managers at all levels of the organization have five potential sources of power.
- Legitimate power is the company-granted authority to direct others.
- Reward power is control over rewards valued by others in the organization.
- Coercive power is control over punishments that others in the organization want to avoid.
- Referent power consists of personal characteristics that appeal to others, so they model their behavior on the leader's and seek the leader's approval.
- Expert power is expertise or knowledge that can benefit others in the organization.

LO 5 List personal traits and skills of effective leaders.

- Important leader characteristics include drive, leadership, motivation, integrity, self-confidence, and knowledge of the business.
- Perhaps the most important skill is the ability to perceive the situation accurately and then change behavior accordingly.

6 **Describe behaviors that will make you a better leader, and identify when the situation calls for them.**

- Important leader behaviors include task performance behaviors, group maintenance, and decision making.
- According to the Vroom model, the leadership style should involve individual decisions, consultation with followers, facilitation, or delegation depending on qualities such as the significance of the decision and the importance of followers' commitment.
- Fiedler's contingency model says that a task-motivated leader is more successful when leader–member relations are good and the task is highly structured, or with an unstructured task but low position power for the leader, or with poor leader–member relations when the task structure and leader's position power are both low. In other situations, a relationship-oriented leader will perform better.
- Hersey and Blanchard's situational theory says that task performance behaviors become less important as the follower's job maturity and psychological maturity increase.
- Path–goal theory assesses characteristics of the followers, the leader, and the situation; it then indicates the appropriateness of directive, supportive, participative, or achievement-oriented leadership behaviors.

LO 7 **Distinguish between charismatic and transformational leaders.**

- To have charisma is to be dominant and self-confident, to have a strong conviction of the righteousness of your beliefs, to create an aura of competence and success, and to communicate high expectations for and confidence in your followers. Charisma is one component of transformational leadership.
- Transformational leaders translate a vision into reality by inspiring people to transcend their individual interests for the good of the larger community.

- They do this through charisma, individualized attention to followers, intellectual stimulation, formation and communication of their vision, building of trust, and positive self-regard.

LO 8 **Describe types of opportunities to be a leader in an organization.**

- There's plenty of opportunity to be a leader; being a manager of others who report to you is just the traditional one.
- You can also take or create opportunities to be a servant–leader or intergroup leader and engage in shared leadership and lateral leadership. A servant–leader serves others' needs while strengthening the organization.
- An intergroup leader leads collaborative performance between different groups or organizations.
- Shared leadership involves taking on a leadership role when your skills are most relevant to a particular situation.
- Lateral leadership is inspiring people to work collaboratively and solve problems together.

LO 9 **Discuss how to further your own leadership development.**

- You can develop your own leadership skills not only by understanding what effective leadership is all about but also by seeking challenging developmental experiences.
- Such important life experiences come from taking challenging assignments, through exposure in working with other people, by overcoming hardships and failures, by taking formal courses, and by other actions.
- The most important elements of a good developmental experience are assessment, challenge, and support.

DISCUSSION QUESTIONS

1. What do you want from your leader?
2. Is there a difference between effective management and effective leadership? Explain your views and learn from others' views.
3. Identify someone you think is an effective leader. What makes him or her effective?
4. Do you think most managers can be transformational leaders? Why or why not?
5. In your own words, define courage. What is the role of courage in leadership? Give examples of acts of leadership you consider courageous.
6. Do you think men and women differ in their leadership styles? If so, how? Do men and/or women prefer different styles in their bosses? What evidence do you have for your answers?
7. Who are your heroes? What makes them heroes, and what can you learn from them?

8. Assess yourself as a leader based on what you have read in this chapter. What are your strengths and weaknesses?
9. Identify the developmental experiences you have had that may have strengthened your ability to lead. What did those experiences teach you? Also identify some developmental experiences you need to acquire and how you will seek them. Be specific.
10. Consider a couple of decisions you are facing that could involve other people. Use Fiedler's contingency model to decide what approach to use to make the decisions.
11. Consider a job you hold or held in the past. Consider how your boss managed you. How would you describe him or her as a leader? What substitutes for leadership would you have enjoyed seeing put into place?

12. Consider an organization of which you are a leader or a member. What could great transformational leadership accomplish in the organization?

13. Name some prominent leaders whom you would describe as authentic and inauthentic and discuss.

14. Name some leaders you consider servant–leaders and discuss.

15. Identify some opportunities for you to exhibit shared leadership and lateral leadership.

EXPERIENTIAL EXERCISES

12.1   USING THE FIVE SOURCES OF POWER AT WORK

OBJECTIVE

To explore how power can be applied to organizational challenges to create positive outcomes.

INSTRUCTIONS

Read each of the scenarios (below) and choose one of the five sources of power to resolve the challenge in each scenario.

Five Sources of Power Worksheet

Five Sources of power:

1. *Authority*
2. *Rewards*
3. *Punishments*
4. *Appealing personal characteristics*
5. *Expertise*

Scenario #1:

Assume you are a supervisor of an IT department at a website hosting company. You want your staff to complete a large project within the next two months. Usually, such a project would take about three months to accomplish. To persuade your staff to rise to this challenge, you offer each of them three additional paid vacation days. Your staff enjoys taking three-day weekends, so the incentive should motivate them to finish the project within the shorter time frame.

As the supervisor, you are using _____ power to motivate your staff.

Scenario #2:

Assume you work at a local retail store. As a part-time employee working your way through college, you are not interested in becoming a manager. Even so, sometimes you wish you were in charge. Just yesterday, your boss asked if you would be willing to work two extra days per week for a month. After you explained that you could work only your usual three days per week due to college and other commitments, your boss threatened to cut your hours indefinitely. Given how much you need the money, you begrudgingly accepted to work the two extra days per week.

Your manager is using _____ power to persuade you to work the two extra days per week.

Scenario #3:

Assume you were recently promoted to assistant manager of the bank in your hometown. You are friends with the employees who now report to you. You notice that they still treat you like a buddy and do not seem to respect you in your new role. You decide that it will be in everyone's best interest if you assert yourself by reminding them that you are now their manager (and not their buddy). This is a challenging transition, but you feel the need to have their respect now that you are the manager.

You are using _____ power to encourage employees to respect you in your new role as assistant manager.

Scenario #4:

Assume you are an experienced marketer of outdoor adventure trips. You recently changed jobs. While working for your previous employer, Outdoor Adventures, you created several successful marketing programs that resulted in a 30 percent increase in sales over a three-year period. Now that you recently joined Eco Tours & Adventures, none of your co-workers knows the extent of your marketing knowledge. Your goal is to increase your power within the company. You decide to develop a really impactful and creative marketing campaign unlike any used by Eco Tours & Adventures in the past.

You are using _____ power to increase your influence at Eco Tours & Adventures.

Scenario #5:

Assume you are a salesperson and just found out that your organization's largest client is thinking about moving its business to one of your competitors. If this happens, you will lose about 30 percent of your commission this year, not to mention the loss of revenue to your company. You decide to rush over to see your contact at the client company. You spend two hours listening to why the client might leave and ask repeatedly what your company can do to make things right. You are nervous, but still use your charm and sense of humor to convince your contact that you and your company deserve one more chance. Your contact agrees to get you a meeting with the CEO and to put in a good word for your company. She says she is doing this because she likes you (professionally) and doesn't want to see you lose the business.

You are using _____ power to convince your contact that you and your company deserve another chance.

CONCLUDING CASE

BREITT, STARR & DIAMOND LLC

Josh Breitt, Rachel Starr, and Justin Diamond started an advertising agency to serve the needs of small businesses selling in and around their metropolitan area. Breitt contributed clever ideas and a talent for writing scripts and wooing clients. Starr brought a wealth of media contacts, and Diamond handled the artwork. Their quirky ad campaigns soon attracted a stream of projects from car dealers, community banks, and a carpet store. Since the agency's first year, these clients have kept the bills paid while the three win contracts from other companies. Breitt, Starr & Diamond (BS&D) prospered by helping clients keep up with the times, and the agency grew to meet the demand, adding a bookkeeper, a graphic artist, a web designer, two salespeople, a social media expert, and a retired human resource manager, who works 10 hours per week.

As the firm grew, the three partners felt they were constantly being pulled away from their areas of expertise to answer questions and solve problems about how to coordinate work, define jobs, and set priorities. They realized that none of them had any management training—and none of them had ever wanted to be a manager. They decided to hire a manager for a position they would call general manager of operations. That person would be responsible for supervising the employees, making sure expenses didn't go over budget, and planning the resources (including people) needed for further growth.

The partners interviewed several candidates and hired Brad Howser, a longtime administrator for a four-physician medical office. Howser spent the first few weeks quietly studying BS&D's financial data and observing employees at work. Then he became more outspoken and assertive. Although the partners had never cared to monitor what time employees came or left, Howser began requiring all employees to start by 9:00 each morning. The graphic artist and one of the salespeople complained that flexible hours were necessary for their child care arrangements, but Howser was unyielding. He also questioned whether the employees had been shopping carefully for supplies, indicating that from then on, he would be making all purchases, and only after the employees submitted their requests on a form of his design. Finally, to promote what he called team spirit, Howser began scheduling weekly Monday-morning staff meetings. He would offer motivational thoughts based on his experience at his previous job and invite the employees to share any work-related concerns or ideas they might have. Generally, the employees chose not to share.

Initially, the partners were impressed with Howser's vigorous approach to his job. They felt more productive than they had been in years because Howser was handling employee concerns himself. Then the top salesperson quit, followed by the social media expert. The bookkeeper asked if she might meet with the partners. "Is it something you should be discussing with Brad?" Rachel asked her. The bookkeeper replied that, no, it was *about* Brad. All the employees were unhappy with him, and more were likely to leave.

DISCUSSION QUESTIONS

1. Assume that hiring a general manager of operations was a good idea. What leadership style would be most effective in this position? Why?

2. What leader behaviors did Brad Howser exhibit? How well do they fit the needs of the ad agency?

3. Consider your own leadership style. What are some of your tendencies, and how might you change your perspective?

CHAPTER 13

Motivating for Performance

> The worst mistake a boss can make is not to say well done.
> —John Ashcroft, Business Executive
>
> The reward of a thing well done is to have done it.
> —Ralph Waldo Emerson

LEARNING OBJECTIVES

After studying Chapter 13, you will be able to:

LO 1 Identify the kinds of behaviors managers need to motivate in people.

LO 2 List principles for setting goals that motivate employees.

LO 3 Summarize how to reward good performance effectively.

LO 4 Describe the key beliefs that affect people's motivation.

LO 5 Discuss ways in which people's individual needs affect their behavior.

LO 6 Define ways to create jobs that motivate.

LO 7 Summarize how people assess fairness and how to achieve fairness.

LO 8 Identify causes and consequences of a satisfied workforce.

CHAPTER OUTLINE

Motivating for Performance

Setting Goals

Goals That Motivate

Stretch Goals

Limitations of Goal Setting

Set Your Own Goals

Reinforcing Performance

(Mis)Managing Rewards and Punishments

Managing Mistakes

Providing Feedback

Performance-Related Beliefs

The Effort-to-Performance Link

The Performance-to-Outcome Link

Impact on Motivation

Managerial Implications of Expectancy Theory

Understanding People's Needs

Maslow's Need Hierarchy

Alderfer's ERG Theory

McClelland's Needs

Need Theories: International Perspectives

Designing Motivating Jobs

Job Rotation, Enlargement, and Enrichment

Herzberg's Two-Factor Theory

The Hackman and Oldham Model of Job Design

Empowerment

Achieving Fairness

Assessing Equity

Restoring Equity

Procedural Justice

Job Satisfaction

Quality of Work Life

Psychological Contracts

Management in Action

WHAT MAKES SAS A GREAT PLACE TO WORK?

SAS (named after its first product, Statistical Analysis Software) has grown since its 1976 founding into the world's leader in data analytics software—a $3.1 billion company with nearly 14,000 employees in 55 countries. Along the way, SAS has ranked as one of the 100 Best Companies to Work For in America every year since the Great Place to Work Institute began handing out that recognition in *Fortune* magazine—and in the top five every year since 2010. In 2012, the institute created its first list of the World's Best Multinational Workplaces, and SAS took the number one spot. Both rankings are based on a combination of employee surveys and an analysis by the institute.

Photo by SAS Software Co.

What does SAS do to earn this prestigious recognition? Certainly, the company is famous for the perks it offers its employees. Along with medical insurance, vacation time, profit sharing, and retirement savings accounts, SAS employees have access to adoption assistance, parental leave, and a college scholarship program for their children. At the Cary, North Carolina, headquarters, employees can use the on-site fitness center, health clinic, and day care center. Stress management programs include yoga, massage, and exercise programs. Those seeking to juggle home and work responsibilities can seek flexibility through options such as telecommuting, job sharing, or unpaid sabbaticals.

An employee summed up his appreciation of the company this way: "SAS does so much for the employees. I always feel this is my second home. I want to give my best to this company and would like to help in any way possible to make this company more successful."

However, if you talk to SAS's leaders, you hear less about benefits and more about the company's values, which shape its work environment. As Jack Poll, SAS's director of recreation and employee services, told a reporter for *Fast Company,* "When people are treated as if they're important and truly make a difference, their loyalty and engagement soar." The kind of treatment Poll is referring to emphasizes appreciating what workers contribute, building their trust, and empowering them to make decisions in their area of responsibility. Poll and SAS's founder and chief executive, James Goodnight, believe this treatment is the primary way SAS unleashes creativity. Creativity, in the hypercompetitive world of computer software, is essential for staying relevant. That SAS gets it right is evident in the company's sales, which have risen every year of the company's existence.[1]

SAS stands out as a company that offers generous benefits to its workers. As you read this chapter, consider whether generosity is enough to bring out employees' best work, aimed at the company's goals and priorities. If not, what other efforts should managers make?

This chapter tackles an age-old question: How can a manager motivate people to work hard and perform at their best levels? SAS demonstrates that treating employees as valued contributors to the organization can be a key part of motivating them.

A sales manager in one company had a different approach to this question. Each month, the person with the worst sales performance took home a live goat for the weekend. The manager hoped the goat-of-the-month employee would be so embarrassed that he or she would work harder the next month to increase sales.[2] This sales manager may get high marks for creativity. But if he is graded by results, as he grades his salespeople, he will fail. He may succeed in motivating a few of his people to increase sales, but some good people will be motivated to quit the company.

Motivating for Performance

 Understanding why people do the things they do on the job is not an easy task for a manager. Predicting their response to management's latest productivity program is harder yet. Fortunately, enough is known about motivation to give the thoughtful manager practical, effective techniques for increasing people's effort and performance.

motivation

Forces that energize, direct, and sustain a person's efforts.

Motivation refers to forces that energize, direct, and sustain a person's efforts. All behavior, except involuntary reflexes such as eye blinks (which have little to do with management), is motivated. A highly motivated person will work hard toward achieving performance goals. With adequate ability, understanding of the job, and access to the necessary resources, such a person will be highly productive.

To be effective motivators, managers must know what behaviors they want to motivate people to exhibit. Although productive people appear to do a seemingly limitless number of things, most of the important activities can be grouped into five general categories.[3] As shown in Exhibit 13.1, managers must motivate people to (1) join the organization, (2) remain in the organization, and (3) come to work regularly. On these points, you should reject the common recent notion that loyalty is dead and accept the challenge of creating an environment that will attract and energize people so that they commit to the organization.[4]

Of course, companies also want people to (4) perform—that is, once employees are at work, they should work hard to achieve high output and high quality. Finally, managers

EXHIBIT 13.1
Managers Must Motivate People to Engage in Key Behaviors

want employees to (5) exhibit good citizenship. Good citizens of the organization are committed, satisfied employees who perform above and beyond the call of duty by doing extra things that can help the company. The importance of citizenship behaviors may be less obvious than performance, but these behaviors help the organization function smoothly. They also make managers' lives easier.

Many ideas have been proposed to help managers motivate people to engage in these constructive behaviors. The most useful of these ideas are described in the following pages. We start with the most fundamental processes that influence the motivation of all people. These processes—described by goal-setting, reinforcement, and expectancy theories— suggest basic and powerful actions for managers to take. Then we discuss the content of what people want and need from work, how individuals differ from one another, and how understanding people's needs leads to powerful prescriptions about designing motivating jobs and empowering people to perform at the highest possible levels. Finally, we discuss the most important beliefs and perceptions about fairness that people hold toward their work, and the implications for job satisfaction.

Setting Goals

Providing work-related goals for people is an extremely effective way to stimulate motivation. In fact, it is perhaps the most important, valid, and useful single approach to motivating performance. Therefore, we discuss it first.

Goal-setting theory states that people have conscious goals that energize them and direct their thoughts and behaviors toward a particular end.[5] Keeping in mind the principle that goals matter, managers set goals for employees or collaborate with employees on goal setting. For example, in order to protect the United States against terrorist attacks, the IT division of the Federal Bureau of Investigation (FBI) sets goals for improving analysis, collaboration, and information sharing.[6] Goal setting works for any job in which people have control over their performance.[7] You can set goals for performance quality and quantity, and behavioral goals such as cooperation or teamwork.[8] In fact, you can set goals for whatever is important.[9]

Goals That Motivate

The most powerful goals are meaningful; noble purposes that appeal to people's higher values add extra motivating power.[10] Patagonia makes outdoor apparel, but also cares deeply about the environment. Whole Foods sells organic and natural food products but also wants to improve people's health and well-being. ServiceMaster, the cleaning and maintenance company, and Chick-fil-A have religious commitments that appeal to their employees, and Huntsman Chemical has goals of paying off corporate debt but also relieving human suffering—it sponsors cancer research and a number of charities. Meaningful goals also may be based on data about competitors; exceeding competitors' performance can stoke people's competitive spirit and desire to succeed in the marketplace.[11] This point is not just about the values companies espouse and the lofty goals they pursue; it's also about leadership at a more personal level. Followers of transformational leaders view their work as more important and as highly congruent with their personal goals compared with followers of transactional leaders[12] (recall Chapter 12).

More specifically, much is known about how to manage goals in ways that motivate high job performance. Goals should be acceptable to employees. This means, among other things, that they should not conflict with people's personal values and that people have reasons to pursue the goals. Allowing people to participate in setting their work goals—as opposed to having the boss set goals for them—is often a great way to generate goals that people accept and pursue willingly.

Acceptable, maximally motivating goals are challenging but attainable. In other words, they should be high enough to inspire better performance but not so high that people can

LO 2

Bottom Line
You can set goals for cost, quality, speed, service, innovation, sustainability— anything that's important. *What is one goal you have set for yourself as a student? If you haven't set any goals, you could start by setting one now for this course.*

goal-setting theory

A motivation theory stating that people have conscious goals that energize them and direct their thoughts and behaviors toward a particular end.

EXHIBIT 13.2
SMART Goals Motivate

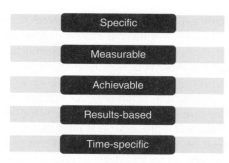

SOURCE: Adapted from K. N. Shaw, "Changing the Goal-Setting Process at Microsoft," *Academy of Management Executive* 4 (November 2004), pp. 139–43.

never reach them. For instance, setting challenging sales goals for district business units results in higher unit sales performance unless employees don't trust their manager.[13]

Ideal goals do not merely exhort employees in general terms to improve performance, start doing their best, increase productivity, or decrease the length of time customers must wait to receive service. Rather, the goals should specify what the employee should do and within what time frame. At the Quick Lane Tire & Auto Center that serves Olathe Ford near Kansas City, Missouri, each service adviser is given a monthly goal for revenues from service orders and receives daily feedback about sales to see what categories of products need extra attention. In addition, whenever a customer chooses to postpone needed repairs, these are assigned a red or yellow code. The service center's receptionist has specific goals of calling each red-code customer within seven days and sending a letter within 90 days to each customer who has a yellow code.[14] Such deadlines and measurable performance goals are specific, quantifiable goals that employees are motivated to achieve. Microsoft uses the acronym SMART (see Exhibit 13.2) to create motivating goals: specific, measurable, achievable, results-based, and time-specific.[15]

> Goals can generate manipulative game-playing and unethical behavior.

Stretch Goals

stretch goals

Targets that are particularly demanding, sometimes even thought to be impossible.

Some firms today set **stretch goals**—targets that are exceptionally demanding and that some people would never even think of. There are two types of stretch goals: vertical stretch goals, aligned with current activities including productivity and financial results, and horizontal stretch goals, which involve people's professional development such as attempting and learning new, difficult things.[16] Impossible though stretch goals may seem to some, they often are in fact attainable.

Stretch goals can generate a major shift away from mediocrity and toward tremendous achievement. But if someone tries in good faith but doesn't meet their stretch goals, don't punish—remember how difficult they are! Base your assessment on how much performance has improved, how the performance compares with others, and how much progress has been made.[17]

Limitations of Goal Setting

Goal setting is an extraordinarily powerful management technique. But even specific, challenging, attainable goals work better under some conditions than others. For example, if people lack relevant ability and knowledge, a better course to follow might be simply urging them to do their best or setting a goal to learn rather than a goal to achieve a specific performance level.[18] Individual performance goals can be dysfunctional if people work in a group and cooperation among team members is essential to team performance.[19] Individualized goals can create competition and reduce cooperation. In groups, individual goals aimed at maximizing individual performance will hurt group performance; groupcentric goals aimed at maximizing the individual's contributions to the group's performance have a positive effect.[20] If cooperation is important, performance goals should be established for the team.

Goals can generate manipulative game-playing and unethical behavior. For example, people can sometimes find ingenious ways to set easy goals and convince their bosses that they are difficult.[21] Or they may find ways to meet goals simply to receive a reward, without necessarily performing in desirable ways. For example, in big law firms it's common for lawyers to keep detailed records of their time and to be rewarded for billing, say, 2,000 hours per year. This system is an invitation to work inefficiently and a dismal, demotivating environment for any lawyer who chose the profession out of concern for clients or love of the law.[22] In addition, people who don't meet their goals are more likely to engage in unethical behavior than are people who are trying to do their best but have no specific performance goals.[23] This is true regardless of whether they have financial incentives, and it is particularly true when people fall just short of reaching their goals.[24]

Another familiar example comes from the pages of financial reports. Some executives have mastered the art of earnings management—precisely meeting Wall Street analysts' earnings estimates or beating them by a single penny.[25] The media trumpet, and investors reward, the company that meets or beats the estimates. People sometimes meet this goal by either manipulating the numbers or initiating whispering campaigns to persuade analysts to lower their estimates, making them more attainable. The marketplace wants short-term, quarterly performance, but long-term viability is ultimately more important to a company's success.

It is important *not* to establish a single productivity goal if there are other important dimensions of performance.[26] For instance, if the acquisition of knowledge and skills is important, you can also set a specific and challenging learning goal such as "identify 10 ways to develop relationships with end users of our products." Productivity goals will likely enhance productivity, but they may also cause employees to neglect other areas, such as learning, tackling new projects, or developing creative solutions to job-related problems. A manager who wants to motivate creativity can establish creativity goals along with productivity goals for individuals or for brainstorming teams.[27]

Setting unprecedented goals can push an individual to reach a higher level of achievement.

© Brand X/Jupiterimages

Set Your Own Goals

Goal setting works for yourself as well—it's a powerful tool for self-management. Set goals for yourself; don't just try hard or hope for the best. Create a statement of purpose for yourself comprising three elements: an inspiring distant vision, a mid-distant goal along the way (worthy in its own right), and near-term objectives to start working on immediately.[28] So if you are going into business, you might articulate your goal for the type of businessperson you want to be in five years, the types of jobs that could create the opportunities and teach you what you need to know to become that businessperson, and the specific schoolwork and job search activities that can get you moving in those directions. And on the job, apply SMART and other goal-setting advice for yourself.

law of effect

A law formulated by Edward Thorndike in 1911 stating that behavior that is followed by positive consequences will likely be repeated.

reinforcers

Positive consequences that motivate behavior.

Reinforcing Performance

Goals are universal motivators. So are the processes of reinforcement described in this section. In 1911, psychologist Edward Thorndike formulated the **law of effect:** behavior that is followed by positive consequences probably will be repeated.[29] This powerful law of behavior laid the foundation for countless investigations into the effects of the positive consequences, called **reinforcers,** that motivate behavior. **Organizational behavior modification** (or **OB mod**) attempts to influence people's behavior, and improve performance,[30] by systematically managing work conditions and the consequences of people's actions.

 LO 3

organizational behavior modification (OB mod)

The application of reinforcement theory in organizational settings.

Four key consequences of behavior either encourage or discourage people's behavior (see Exhibit 13.3):

positive reinforcement

Applying consequences that increase the likelihood that a person will repeat the behavior that led to it.

1. **Positive reinforcement**—applying a positive consequence that increases the likelihood that the person will repeat the behavior that led to it. Examples of positive reinforcers include a boss thanking an employee, letters of commendation, favorable performance evaluations, and pay raises.[31]

negative reinforcement

Removing or withholding an undesirable consequence.

2. **Negative reinforcement**—removing or withholding an undesirable consequence. For example, a manager takes an employee (or a school takes a student) off probation because of improved performance.

punishment

Administering an aversive consequence.

3. **Punishment**—administering an aversive consequence. Examples include criticizing or shouting at an employee, assigning an unappealing task, and sending a worker home without pay. Negative reinforcement can involve the *threat* of punishment and not delivering the punishment when employees perform satisfactorily. Punishment is the actual delivery of the aversive consequence.

Managers use punishment when they think it is warranted or when they believe others expect them to, and they usually concern themselves with following company policy and procedure.[32] It also may be that managers who catch employees behaving badly prefer to punish more severely when the managers have a lot of power and have clear opinions about what is right and wrong.[33]

extinction

Withdrawing or failing to provide a reinforcing consequence.

4. **Extinction**—withdrawing or failing to provide a reinforcing consequence. When this occurs, motivation is reduced and the behavior is *extinguished,* or eliminated. Ways that managers may unintentionally extinguish desired behaviors include not giving a compliment for a job well done, forgetting to say thanks for a favor, and setting impossible performance goals so a person never experiences success.

Extinction may be used to end undesirable behaviors, too. The manager might ignore long-winded observations during a meeting or fail to acknowledge unimportant e-mails in the hope that the lack of feedback will discourage the employee from continuing.

The first two consequences, positive and negative reinforcement, are positive for the person receiving them—the person either gains something or avoids something negative. Therefore, the person who experiences these consequences will be motivated to behave in the ways that led to the reinforcement. The last two consequences, punishment and extinction, are negative outcomes for the person receiving them: motivation to repeat the behavior that led to the undesirable results will be reduced.

Managers should be careful to match consequences to what employees will actually find desirable or undesirable. A supervisor once made the mistake of punishing an employee for tardiness by suspending him for three days during fishing season. The employee was delighted.[34]

EXHIBIT 13.3
Behavior, Consequences, and Outcomes

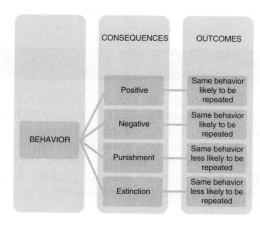

(Mis)Managing Rewards and Punishments

You've learned about the positive effects of a transformational leadership style, but giving rewards to high-performing people is also essential.[35] Unfortunately, sometimes organizations and managers reinforce the wrong behaviors.[36] For example, compensation plans that include stock options are intended to reinforce behaviors that add to the company's value, but stock options also can reinforce decisions that artificially deliver short-term gains in stock prices, even if they hurt the company in the long run. Likewise, programs that punish employees for absenteeism beyond a certain limit may actually encourage them to be absent. People may use up all their allowable absences and fail to come to work regularly until they reach the point at which their next absence will result in punishment. Sometimes employees are reinforced with admiration for multitasking. This behavior may look efficient and send a signal that the employee is busy and valuable, but multitasking actually slows down the brain's efficiency and can contribute to mistakes.[37] Scans of brain activity show that the brain is not able to concentrate on two tasks at once; it needs time to switch among the multitasker's activities. As a result, managers who praise the hard work of multitaskers may be unintentionally reinforcing inefficiency and failure to think deeply about problems.

> Sometimes organizations and managers reinforce the wrong behaviors.

To use reinforcement effectively, managers must identify which kinds of behaviors they reinforce and which they discourage (see Exhibit 13.4). The reward system has to support the firm's strategy, defining people's performance in ways that pursue strategic objectives.[38] Reward employees for developing themselves in strategically important ways—for building new skills that are critical to strengthening core competencies and creating value. Managers should be creative in their use of reinforcers. QuikTrip, which operates a chain of convenience stores in 11 states, has a creative way of making sure new employees at headquarters feel welcome. On an employee's first day, a tub of candy appears on his or her desk. The treats reward co-workers for coming over to introduce themselves. The company also offers above-average pay for the industry and enjoys its industry's lowest rate of employee turnover.[39]

Innovative managers use nonmonetary rewards, including intellectual challenge, greater responsibility, autonomy, recognition, flexible benefits, and greater influence over decisions. These and other rewards for high-performing employees, when creatively devised and applied, can continue to motivate when pay and promotions are scarce. Employees at Brown Flynn—a firm that provides services to help companies exercise social

EXHIBIT 13.4
The Greatest Management Principle in the World

"The things that get rewarded get done" is what one author called The Greatest Management Principle in the World. With this in mind, Michael LeBoeuf offered prescriptions for effectively motivating high performance. Companies, and individual managers, should reward the following:

1. *Solid solutions* instead of quick fixes.
2. *Risk taking* instead of risk avoiding.
3. *Applied creativity* instead of mindless conformity.
4. *Decisive action* instead of paralysis by analysis.
5. *Smart work* instead of busywork.
6. *Simplification* instead of needless complication.
7. *Quietly effective behavior* instead of squeaky wheels.
8. *Quality work* instead of fast work.
9. *Loyalty* instead of turnover.
10. *Working together* instead of working against.

SOURCE: From *The Greatest Management Principle in the World* by Michael LeBoeuf. Copyright © 1985 by Michael LeBoeuf. Reprinted with permission.

Managers who inappropriately yell at their staff or overuse punishment often create a climate of fear and anxiety in the workplace. How would you deal with a situation like this?

responsibility—receive practical benefits such as profit sharing and creative ones such as jewelry and shopping sprees, but the intangibles may be what matter most. Employees describe Brown Flynn as offering challenges and rewards, mutual respect, recognition for hard work, and opportunities to exercise leadership.[40]

Managing Mistakes

How a manager reacts to people's mistakes has a big impact on motivation. Punishment is sometimes appropriate, as when people violate the law, ethical standards, safety rules, or standards of interpersonal treatment, or when they perform like a slacker. But sometimes managers punish people when they shouldn't—when poor performance isn't the person's fault or when managers take out their frustrations on the wrong people.

Managers who overuse punishment or use it inappropriately create a climate of fear in the workplace.[41] Fear causes people to focus on the short term, sometimes creating problems in the longer run. Fear also creates a focus on oneself rather than on the group and the organization. B. Joseph White, president emeritus of the University of Illinois, recalls consulting for a high-tech entrepreneur who heard a manager present a proposal and responded with brutal criticism: "That's the . . . stupidest idea I ever heard in my life. I'm disappointed in you." According to White, this talented manager was so upset she never again felt fully able to contribute.[42] To avoid such damage, managers should think about how they handle mistakes.

Recognize that everyone makes mistakes and that mistakes can be dealt with constructively by discussing and learning from them. Don't punish, but praise, people who deliver bad news to their bosses. Treat failure to act as a failure but don't punish unsuccessful, good-faith efforts. If you're a leader, talk about your failures with your people and show how you learned from them. Give people second chances and maybe third chances. (Donald Trump claims to give second chances, but never third.) Encourage people to try new things and don't punish them if what they try doesn't work out.

Providing Feedback

Most managers don't provide enough useful feedback, and most people don't ask for feedback enough.[43] As a manager, you should consider all potential causes of poor performance, pay full attention when employees ask for feedback or want to discuss performance issues, and give feedback according to the guidelines you read about in Chapter 10.

Feedback can be offered in many ways.[44] Customers sometimes give feedback directly; you also can request customer feedback and give it to the employee. You can provide statistics on work that the person has directly influenced. A manufacturing firm—high tech or otherwise—can put the phone number or website of the production team on the product so customers can contact the team directly. Performance reviews, described in Chapter 11, should be conducted regularly. And bosses should give more regular, ongoing feedback—it helps correct problems immediately, provides immediate reinforcement for good work, and prevents surprises when the formal review comes.

For yourself, try not to be afraid of receiving feedback; in fact, you should actively seek it. But whether or not you seek the feedback, when you get it, don't ignore it. Try to avoid negative emotions such as anger, hurt, defensiveness, or resignation. Think, It's up to me to get the feedback I need; I need to know these things about my performance and my behavior; learning what I need to know about myself will help me identify needs and create new opportunities; it serves my interest best to know rather than not know; taking initiative on this gives me more power and influence over my career.[45]

Bottom Line

Make sure that you reward the right things, not the wrong things. Sound obvious? You'd be surprised how often this principle is violated!

What is rewarding about feedback from your manager?

Try not to be afraid of receiving feedback; in fact, you should actively seek it.

Performance-Related Beliefs

In contrast to reinforcement theory, which describes the processes by which factors in the work environment affect people's behavior, expectancy theory considers some of the cognitive processes that go on in people's heads. According to **expectancy theory,** the person's work efforts lead to some level of performance.[46] Then performance results in one or more outcomes for the person. This process is shown in Exhibit 13.5. People develop two important beliefs linking these three events: expectancy, which links effort to performance, and instrumentality, which links performance to outcomes.

The Effort-to-Performance Link

The first belief, **expectancy,** is people's perceived likelihood that their efforts will enable them to attain their performance goals. An expectancy can be high (up to 100 percent), such as when a student is confident that if she studies hard, she can get a good grade on the final. An expectancy can also be low (down to a 0 percent likelihood), such as when a suitor is convinced that his dream date will never go out with him.

All else equal, high expectancies create higher motivation than do low expectancies. In the preceding examples, the student is more likely to study for the exam than the suitor is to pursue the dream date, even though both want their respective outcomes.

Expectancies can vary among individuals, even in the same situation. For example, a sales manager might initiate a competition in which the top salesperson wins a free trip to Hawaii. In such cases, the few top people, who have performed well in the past, will be more motivated by the contest than will the historically average and below-average performers. The top people will have higher expectancies—stronger beliefs that their efforts can help them win the competition.

The Performance-to-Outcome Link

The example of the sales contest illustrates how performance results in some kind of **outcome,** or consequence, for the person. Actually, it often results in several outcomes. For example, turning in the best sales performance could lead to (1) a competitive victory, (2) the free trip to Hawaii, (3) feelings of achievement, (4) recognition from the boss, (5) prestige throughout the company, and (6) resentment from other salespeople.

But how certain is it that performance will result in all of those outcomes? Will winning the contest really lead to resentment? Will it really lead to increased prestige?

These questions address the second key belief described by expectancy theory: instrumentality.[47] **Instrumentality** is the perceived likelihood that performance will be followed by a particular outcome. Like expectancies, instrumentalities can be high (up to 100 percent) or low (approaching 0 percent). For example, you can be fully confident that

expectancy theory

A theory proposing that people will behave based on their perceived likelihood that their effort will lead to a certain outcome and on how highly they value that outcome.

---

expectancy

Employees' perception of the likelihood that their efforts will enable them to attain their performance goals.

---

outcome

A consequence a person receives for his or her performance.

---

instrumentality

The perceived likelihood that performance will be followed by a particular outcome.

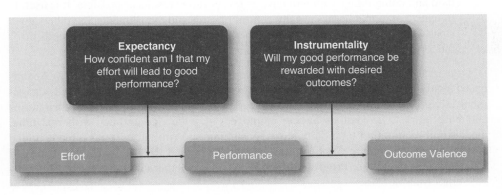

EXHIBIT 13.5
Basic Concepts of Expectancy Theory

Winning a competition for a free trip to Hawaii would be great, but what about all the losers?

© Robert Glusic/Getty Images

valence

The value an outcome holds for the person contemplating it.

if you do a good job, you'll get a promotion; or you can feel that no matter how well you do, the promotion will go to someone else.

Also, each outcome has an associated valence. **Valence** is the value the person places on the outcome. Valences can be positive, as a Hawaiian vacation would be for most people, or negative, as in the case of the other salespeople's resentment.

Impact on Motivation

For motivation to be high, expectancy, instrumentalities, and total valence of all outcomes must all be high. A person will not be highly motivated if any of the following conditions exist:

1. He believes he can't perform well enough to achieve the positive outcomes that he knows the company provides to good performers (high valence and high instrumentality but low expectancy).
2. He knows he can do the job and is fairly certain what the ultimate outcomes will be (say, a promotion and a transfer). However, he doesn't want those outcomes or believes other, negative outcomes outweigh the positive (high expectancy and high instrumentality but low valence).
3. He knows he can do the job and wants several important outcomes (a favorable performance review, a raise, and a promotion). But he believes that no matter how well he performs, the outcomes will not be forthcoming (high expectancy and positive valences but low instrumentality).

Managerial Implications of Expectancy Theory

Expectancy theory helps the manager zero in on key leverage points for influencing motivation. Three implications are crucial:

1. *Increase expectancies.* Provide a work environment that facilitates good performance and set realistically attainable performance goals. Provide training, support, required resources, and encouragement so that people are confident they can perform at the levels expected of them. Recall from Chapter 12 that some leaders excel at boosting their followers' confidence.
2. *Identify positively valent outcomes.* Understand what people want to get out of work. Think about what their jobs provide them and what is not, but could be, provided. Consider how people may differ in the valences they assign to outcomes. Know the need theories of motivation, described in the next section, and their implications for identifying important outcomes.
3. *Make performance instrumental toward positive outcomes.* Make sure that good performance is followed by personal recognition and praise, favorable performance reviews, pay increases, and other positive results. Also, make sure that working hard and doing things well will have as few negative results as possible. It is useful to realize, too, that bosses usually control rewards and punishments, but others do so as well. Peers, direct reports, customers, and others tend to provide rewards in the form of compliments, help, and social punishments.

Organizations may set up formal reward systems as well. Founded in 2012, Austin-based YouEarnedIt created an app designed to increase employee happiness and engagement at work. The app empowers employees to recognize one another's contributions and hard work. The idea of having employees provide one another with real-time, meaningful recognition on a daily basis is catching on. YouEarnedIt has already added several clients, including Conde Nast, Tempur-Pedic, and Rent-2-Own.[48] As you read "Management in Action: Progress Report," consider whether similar ideas would motivate employees at SAS.

Management in Action

GETTING EMPLOYEES TO BACK THE MISSION OF SAS

James Goodnight, a statistician, founded SAS with colleagues from North Carolina State University. Since his first experiences of programming a computer while in college, Goodnight had recognized the joy of creating something that would benefit others. Goodnight expected that his employees too would feel rewarded by their accomplishments. On SAS's website, Goodnight describes SAS's culture as one that "rewards innovation, encourages employees to try new things and yet doesn't penalize them for taking chances."

To see how this works, consider how SAS has recently innovated in a couple of important areas of computing. One is the rapid switch of the computer industry to cloud computing. SAS grew up when big organizations invested in large, powerful computers, and its software was written for those systems. With the rise of the Internet, data has streamed in from many sources in real time, and computing systems are being reworked to process the data in parallel on multiple computers that do not necessarily reside at the organization using the data. Some observers wondered whether SAS could rewrite its software for this new era of computing. But because SAS attracts the best people (thanks to its reputation for treating employees well), hires for creativity, and makes it easy to stay on the job (thanks to corporate perks such as subsidized cafeterias and on-site haircuts), SAS has no trouble convincing employees to push hard toward reaching ambitious goals. SAS impressed observers by announcing new, cloud-ready software with graphics that even nonexperts can view on their laptop or tablet computers. Recent sales revenue from cloud services has grown rapidly.

SAS also has smoothly entered the social media era by introducing a networking site for its employees. The company found that its employees, especially the younger ones, were sharing work information with each other on sites such as Facebook. Although some companies were cracking down on social media use, SAS got busy creating software that would be so useful and easy to learn that employees wouldn't be able to resist. The result was the Hub, which enrolled more than 1,400 employees even before its official launch. Rather than micromanaging how the Hub would be used, SAS's information systems division showed off some relevant features, gently pointed out advantages to nonusers, and trusted them to behave professionally. Before long, about two-thirds of SAS employees were trading information on the Hub.[49]

- What kinds of reinforcement and feedback do you think would be most effective with SAS employees?
- How should SAS's managers apply the implications of expectancy theory (listed just before this case) to keep the company innovative?

Understanding People's Needs

So far, we have focused on processes underlying motivation. The manager who appropriately applies goal-setting, reinforcement, and expectancy theories is creating essential motivating elements in the work environment. But motivation also is affected by characteristics of the person. The second type of motivation theory, *content theories,* indicates the kinds of needs that people want to satisfy. People have different needs energizing and motivating them toward different goals and reinforcers. The extent to which and the ways in which a person's needs are met or not met at work affect his or her behavior on the job.

LO 5

The most important theories describing the content of people's needs are Maslow's need hierarchy, Alderfer's ERG theory, and McClelland's needs.

Maslow's Need Hierarchy

Abraham Maslow organized five major types of human needs into a hierarchy, as shown in Exhibit 13.6.[50] **Maslow's need hierarchy** illustrates his conception of people satisfying their needs in a specified order, from bottom to top. The needs, in ascending order, are

1. *Physiological* (food, water, sex, and shelter).
2. *Safety or security* (protection against threat and deprivation).

Maslow's need hierarchy

A conception of human needs organizing needs into a hierarchy of five major types.

EXHIBIT 13.6
Maslow's Need Hierarchy

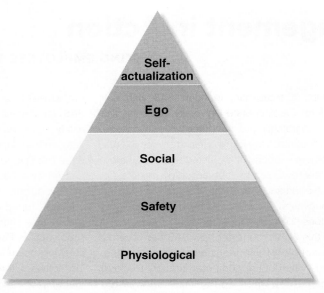

SOURCE: D. Organ and T. Bateman, *Organizational Behavior,* 4th ed., 1991. Copyright 1991. The McGraw-Hill Companies, Inc. Reprinted with permission.

3. *Social* (friendship, affection, belonging, and love).
4. *Ego* (independence, achievement, freedom, status, recognition, and self-esteem).
5. *Self-actualization* (realizing one's full potential, becoming everything one is capable of being).

According to Maslow, people are motivated to satisfy the lower needs before they try to satisfy the higher needs. In today's workplace, physiological and safety needs generally are well satisfied, making social, ego, and self-actualization needs important. But safety issues are still very important in manufacturing, mining, health care, and other work environments. And long after the terrorist attacks of September 2001, employees still felt fear, denial, and anger—especially among people with children, women, and those close to the events.[51] To deal with such safety issues, managers can show what the firm will do to improve security and manage employee risk, including crisis management plans as discussed in Chapter 3.

> Safety issues are still very important in manufacturing, mining, health care, and other work environments.

Once a need is satisfied, it is no longer a powerful motivator. For example, labor unions negotiate for higher wages, benefits, safety standards, and job security. These bargaining issues relate directly to the satisfaction of Maslow's lower-level needs. Only after these needs are reasonably satisfied do the higher-level needs—social, ego, and self-actualization—become dominant concerns.

Maslow's hierarchy, however, is a simplistic and not altogether accurate theory of human motivation.[52] For example, not everyone progresses through the five needs in hierarchical order. But Maslow made three important contributions. First, he identified important need categories, which can help managers create effective positive reinforcers. Second, it is helpful to think of two general levels of needs, in which lower-level needs must be satisfied before higher-level needs become important. Third, Maslow alerted managers to the importance of personal growth and self-actualization.

Self-actualization is the best-known concept arising from this theory. According to Maslow, the average person is only 10 percent self-actualized. In other words, most of us are living our lives and working at our jobs with a large untapped reservoir of potential. The implication is clear: Managers should help create a work environment that provides training, resources, autonomy, responsibilities, and challenging assignments. This type of environment gives people a chance to use their skills and abilities in creative ways and allows them to achieve more of their full potential (see "Multiple Generations at Work").

Multiple Generations at Work

Millennials Want to Fulfill Higher-Order Needs

A recent survey found that 60 percent of Millennials leave their organizations in less than three years. Turnover has both direct (e.g., lost productivity) and indirect (e.g., lost productivity) costs. Many companies are trying to attract, motivate, and retain this generation of employees by offering flexible work arrangements, additional vacation time, and relaxed dress codes. For some firms, these measures may not be enough to motivate and retain high performers.

David Glickman, CEO of mobile carrier Ultra Mobile, believes that Millennials are motivated by jobs that fulfill their higher-order needs. Eighty percent of Ultra Mobile's 300-plus employees and contractors are Millennials. Over the past two years, the company has grown rapidly to over $100 million in sales revenue and reports 100 percent retention.

Glickman suggests that many Baby Boomers at younger ages were willing to accept jobs that fulfilled basic needs like a constant paycheck, modest home, and so forth. Glickman states that Millennials are "less interested in job promotion than in becoming an entrepreneur and who will quit if they feel they do not have freedom" to grow and develop.

He offers the following tips for motivating and retaining Millennials:[53]

1. *Focus on results, not time in the office.* After they have proven themselves, provide Millennial

© Ryan Miller/Getty Images

employees with the freedom and trust to get at least some of their work done offsite.

2. *Make your organization a cool place to work.* Do fun things (e.g., invite a pet shelter to bring in kittens and puppies for an hour for possible adoption) for employees so they have something to brag about on social media.

3. *Leverage their passions.* Get to know what really matters to each employee and then try to design jobs and volunteer opportunities that tap into those passions.

Glickman concludes: "Provide the belonging and self-actualization needs they crave, and Millennials will knock your socks off with astounding performance."

So treat people not merely as a cost to be controlled but an asset to be developed. Many companies have embarked on programs that provide personal growth experiences for their people. For example, associates at W.L. Gore are encouraged to reach their full potential by developing their talents, enjoying their work, and directing their own work activities.[54]

Organizations gain by making full use of their human resources. Employees also gain by capitalizing on opportunities to meet their higher-order needs on the job. Wegmans Food Markets is known for its high-quality workforce. The company invests heavily in training and developing its employees. It sends staff around the world to become experts in their products, trains cashiers for 40 hours before allowing them to interact with customers, and doesn't lay off employees.[55] Employees feel secure in their jobs, enjoy friendships with co-workers and customers, and experience a sense of achievement.

Alderfer's ERG Theory

A theory of human needs that is more advanced than Maslow's is Alderfer's ERG theory.[56] Maslow's theory has general applicability, but Alderfer aims his theory expressly at understanding people's needs at work.

Alderfer's ERG theory postulates three sets of needs: existence, relatedness, and growth. Existence needs are all material and physiological desires. Relatedness needs involve relationships with other people and are satisfied through the process of mutually

Alderfer's ERG theory

A human needs theory postulating that people have three basic sets of needs that can operate simultaneously.

sharing thoughts and feelings. Growth needs motivate people to change themselves or their environment productively or creatively. Satisfaction of the growth needs comes from fully using personal capacities and developing new capacities.

What similarities do you see between Alderfer's and Maslow's needs? Roughly speaking, existence needs subsume physiological and security needs, relatedness needs are similar to social and esteem needs, and growth needs correspond to self-actualization.

ERG theory proposes that several needs can be operating at once. Thus, whereas Maslow would say that self-actualization is important to people only after other sets of needs are satisfied, Alderfer maintains that people—particularly working people in our postindustrial society—can be motivated to satisfy existence, relatedness, and growth needs at the same time.

Consider which theory best explains the motives identified by Diane Schumaker-Krieg to describe her successful career in the financial services industry. Schumaker-Krieg says she was "driven . . . by fear" in October 1987, when she was working for investment firm Dillon Read at the time of the stock market crash. Layoffs were spreading throughout the industry, jobs were scarce, and she was supporting her son following a divorce. Out of determination to take care of her son, Schumaker-Krieg reacted to being laid off by writing a plan for a new business. She persuaded Dillon Read to fund the idea for a year, began building the business, moved it to Credit Suisse, and within years was earning $150 million in profits for her employer. During that time, she remarried and earned enough to retire, but she continues working, now as a managing director at Wells Fargo. She sees her current motivation as enjoyment of her accomplishments, her business relationships, and opportunities to continue innovating.[57] Certainly lower-level needs dominated the early years of Schumaker-Krieg's career, but did the basis for her motivation move one step at a time through all the levels of Maslow's hierarchy?

Maslow's theory is better known to American managers than Alderfer's, but ERG theory has more scientific support.[58] Both have practical value in that they remind managers of the types of reinforcers or rewards that can be used to motivate people. Regardless of whether a manager prefers the Maslow or the Alderfer theory of needs, he or she can motivate people by helping them satisfy their needs, particularly by offering opportunities for self-actualization and growth.

McClelland's Needs

David McClelland also identified a number of basic needs that guide people. The most important needs for managers, according to McClelland, are the needs for achievement, affiliation, and power.[59] Different needs predominate for different people. As you read about these needs, think about yourself—which ones are most and least important to you?

The need for achievement is characterized by a strong orientation toward accomplishment and an obsession with success and goal attainment. Most managers and entrepreneurs in the United States have high levels of this need and like to see it in their employees.

The need for affiliation reflects a strong desire to be liked by other people. Individuals who have high levels of this need are oriented toward getting along with others and may be less concerned with performing at high levels.

The need for power is a desire to influence or control other people. This need can be a negative force—termed *personalized power*—if it is expressed through the aggressive manipulation and exploitation of others. People high on the personalized power need want power purely for the pursuit of their own goals. But the need for power also can be a positive motive—called *socialized power*—because it can be channeled toward the constructive improvement of organizations and societies.

Low need for affiliation and moderate to high need for power are associated with managerial success for both higher- and lower-level managers.[60] One reason the need for affiliation is not necessary for leadership success is that people high on this need have difficulty making tough but necessary decisions that will make some people unhappy.

Need Theories: International Perspectives

How do the need theories apply abroad?[61] Whereas managers in the United States care most strongly about achievement, esteem, and self-actualization, managers in Greece and Japan are motivated more by security. Social needs are most important in Sweden, Norway, and Denmark. "Doing your own thing"—the phrase from the 1960s that describes an American culture oriented toward self-actualization—is not even translatable into Chinese. "Achievement," too, is difficult to translate into most other languages. Researchers in France, Japan, and Sweden would have been unlikely even to conceive of McClelland's achievement motive because people of those countries traditionally tend to be more group-oriented than individually oriented.

Clearly, achievement, growth, and self-actualization are profoundly important in the United States, Canada, and Great Britain. But these needs are not universally important. Every manager must remember that need importance varies from country to country and that people may not be motivated by the same needs. One study found that employees in many countries are highly engaged at companies that have strong leadership, work–life balance, a good reputation, and opportunities for employees to contribute; another found variations from country to country:[62] Employees in Canada were attracted by competitive pay, work–life balance, and opportunities for advancement; workers in Germany by autonomy; in Japan by high-quality co-workers; in the Netherlands by a collaborative work environment; and in the United States by competitive health benefits. Generally, no single way is best, and managers can customize their approaches by considering how individuals differ.[63]

Designing Motivating Jobs

Here's an example of a company that gave a reward that didn't motivate. One of Mary Kay Ash's former employers gave her a sales award: a flounder-fishing light. Unfortunately, she didn't fish. Fortunately, she later was able to design her own organization, Mary Kay Cosmetics, around intrinsic as well as extrinsic motivators that mattered to her people.[64] **Extrinsic rewards** are given to people by the boss, the company, or some other person. An **intrinsic reward** is a reward the person derives directly from performing the job itself. An interesting project, an intriguing subject that is fun to study, a completed sale, helping a co-worker achieve a difficult task, and the discovery of the perfect solution to a difficult problem all can give people the feeling that they have done something well. This is the essence of the motivation that comes from intrinsic rewards. The "Social Enterprise" box discusses how one organization is giving veterans a renewed sense of purpose.

Intrinsic rewards are essential to the motivation underlying creativity.[65] A challenging problem, a chance to create something new, and work that is exciting in and of itself can provide intrinsic motivation that inspires people to devote time and energy to the task. So do managers who allow people some freedom to pursue the tasks that interest them most. The opposite situations result in routine, habitual behaviors that interfere with creativity.[66] A study in manufacturing facilities found that employees initiated more applications for patents, made more novel and useful suggestions, and were rated by their managers as more creative when their jobs were challenging and their managers did not control their activities closely.[67]

> Intrinsic rewards are essential to the motivation underlying creativity.

extrinsic reward

Reward given to a person by the boss, the company, or some other person.

intrinsic reward

Reward a worker derives directly from performing the job itself.

Conversely, some managers and organizations create environments that quash creativity and motivation.[68] The classic example of a demotivating job is the highly specialized assembly line job; each worker performs one boring operation before passing the work along to the next worker. Such specialization, the mechanistic approach to job design, was the prevailing practice through most of the 20th century.[69] But jobs that are too simple and routine result in employee dissatisfaction, absenteeism, and turnover.

Social Enterprise

Giving Veterans a Renewed Sense of Purpose

Shortly after returning from his deployments in Iraq and Afghanistan, Marine veteran Jake Wood cofounded Team Rubicon. Staffed by veterans, his organization bridges the gap between the moment a natural disaster happens and the time at which conventional aid organizations respond. Wood seeks to solve two problems. The first is that many aid organizations are not equipped or trained to respond rapidly during the "crucial window" of time immediately following a disaster. The second is the inadequate way that many veterans are reintegrated into society after serving in the military. Veterans have a unique set of skills and experiences that are ideal for disaster relief situations.

© Justin Sullivan/Getty Images

Team Rubicon provides veterans with three things they lose after leaving the military:

1. *Purpose:* Doing work with a higher purpose, in this case helping survivors of natural disasters, is motivational for veterans.
2. *Community:* Veterans are accustomed to serving with and protecting their team members.
3. *Self-worth:* Helping others in crisis provides veterans with a sense of self-worth and accomplishment.

Since its founding in 2011, Team Rubicon has made a positive impact on survivors immediately following several disasters around the world, including Hurricane Sandy in New York and New Jersey, a tsunami in Chile, floods in Pakistan, an earthquake in Haiti, and tornadoes in Missouri and Arkansas.

Disaster relief missions are highly motivating for veterans, and their skills bring victims badly needed assistance, medical supplies, and other forms of relief until organizations like the Red Cross arrive. Team Rubicon staff and volunteers know how to get their jobs done: "When we arrive on site after a disaster in a foreign country, all eyes and hope have turned to us, expecting immediate action and results. Disasters are no-excuse, results-only zones."[70]

Questions:

- Of those veterans who would like to work for Team Rubicon, what types of rewards are likely to keep them motivated: extrinsic, intrinsic, or both?
- To what degree do you think Team Rubicon will make a positive impact on natural disaster victims? Explain.

Bottom Line

Intrinsic rewards and the freedom to be creative are keys to innovation.

Why might an employee be more innovative when a job is intrinsically rewarding?

---

job rotation

Changing from one task to another to alleviate boredom.

---

job enlargement

Giving people additional tasks at the same time to alleviate boredom.

Especially in industries that depend on highly motivated knowledge workers, keeping talented employees may require letting them design their own jobs so their work is more interesting than it would be elsewhere.[71] Jobs can be designed in the following ways to increase intrinsic rewards and therefore motivation.

Job Rotation, Enlargement, and Enrichment

With **job rotation,** workers who spend all their time in one routine task can instead move from one task to another. Rather than working in a single section of a department store for an entire month, an employee might be rotated through housewares, shoes, and toys. Job rotation is intended to alleviate boredom by giving people different things to do at different times.

As you may guess, however, the person may just be changing from one boring job to another. But job rotation can benefit everyone when done properly, with people's input and career interests in mind. Starbucks hires MBAs straight out of school to join its Rotational Development Program, a full-time, two-year program that focuses on developing future leaders.[72]

Job enlargement is similar to job rotation in that people are given different tasks to do. But whereas job rotation involves doing one task at one time and changing to a different task at a different time, job enlargement means that the worker has multiple tasks at the same time. Thus an assembly worker's job is enlarged if he or she is given two tasks rather than one to perform. In a study of job enlargement in a financial services organization, enlarged jobs led to higher job satisfaction, better error detection by clerks, and improved customer service.[73]

With job enlargement, the person's additional tasks are at the same level of responsibility. More profound changes occur when jobs are enriched. **Job enrichment** means that jobs are restructured or redesigned by adding higher levels of responsibility. This practice includes giving people not only more tasks but higher-level ones, such as when decisions are delegated downward and authority is decentralized. Herzberg's two-factor theory was the first approach to job enrichment, followed by the Hackman and Oldham model.

job enrichment

Changing a task to make it inherently more rewarding, motivating, and satisfying.

Herzberg's Two-Factor Theory

Frederick Herzberg's **two-factor theory** distinguished between two broad categories of factors that affect people working on their jobs.[74] The first category, **hygiene factors,** are characteristics of the workplace: company policies, working conditions, pay, co-workers, supervision, and so forth. These factors can make people unhappy if they are poorly managed. If they are well managed and viewed as positive by employees, the employees will no longer be dissatisfied. However, no matter how good these factors are, they will not make people truly satisfied or motivated to do a good job.

According to Herzberg, the key to true job satisfaction and motivation to perform lies in the second category: the motivators. The **motivators** describe the job itself—that is, what people *do* at work. Motivators are the nature of the work itself, the actual job responsibilities, opportunity for personal growth and recognition, and the feelings of achievement the job provides. When these factors are present, jobs are presumed to be both satisfying and motivating for most people.

Herzberg's theory has been criticized by many scholars, and for that reason we will not go into more detail about his original theory. But Herzberg was a pioneer in the area of job design and still is a respected name among American managers. Furthermore, even if the specifics of his theory do not hold up to scientific scrutiny, he made several very important contributions. First, Herzberg's theory highlights the important distinction between extrinsic rewards (from hygiene factors) and intrinsic rewards (from motivators). Second, it reminds managers not to count solely on extrinsic rewards to motivate workers but to focus on intrinsic rewards as well. Third, it set the stage for later theories, such as the Hackman and Oldham model, that explain more precisely how managers can enrich people's jobs.

two-factor theory

Herzberg's theory describing two factors affecting people's work motivation and satisfaction.

hygiene factors

Characteristics of the workplace, such as company policies, working conditions, pay, and supervision, that can make people dissatisfied.

motivators

Factors that make a job more motivating, such as additional job responsibilities, opportunities for personal growth and recognition, and feelings of achievement.

The Hackman and Oldham Model of Job Design

Following Herzberg's work, Hackman and Oldham proposed a more complete model of job design.[75] Exhibit 13.7 illustrates their model. As you can see, well-designed jobs lead to high motivation, high-quality performance, high satisfaction, and low absenteeism and turnover. These outcomes occur when people experience three critical psychological states (noted in the middle column of the figure):

1. They believe they are doing something meaningful because their work is important to other people.
2. They feel personally responsible for how the work turns out.
3. They learn how well they perform their jobs.

These psychological states occur when people are working on enriched jobs—that is, jobs that offer the following five core job dimensions:

1. *Skill variety*—different job activities involving several skills and talents. When cleaning employees in hospitals were given some freedom in how they carried out their work, the employees themselves added skill variety to their work through extra efforts such as engaging patients in small talk and figuring out ways they could make nurses' jobs easier. After adding this skill variety, the employees reported being more satisfied with their jobs.[76]

EXHIBIT 13.7

The Hackman and Oldham Model of Job Enrichment

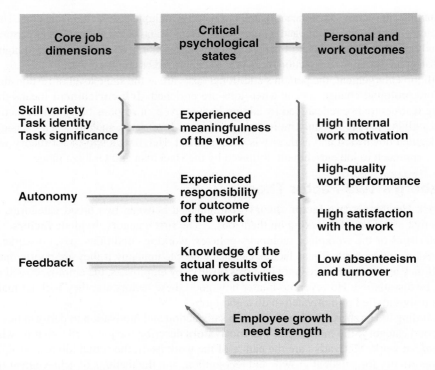

SOURCE: From J. Richard Hackman, Greg R. Oldham, Robert Janson, and Kenneth Purdy, "A New Strategy for Job Enrichment," in *California Management Review* 17, no. 4 (Summer 1975), pp. 57–71. Copyright © 1975 by the Regents of the University of California. Reprinted by permission of University of California Press.

2. *Task identity*—the completion of a whole, identifiable piece of work. At State Farm Insurance, agents are independent contractors who sell and provide service for State Farm products exclusively. They have built and invested in their own businesses. As a result, agent retention and productivity are far better than industry norms.[77]

3. *Task significance*—an important, positive impact on the lives of others. A study of lifeguards found dramatic improvements in their performance if they were taught about how lifeguards make a difference by preventing deaths. Lifeguards in the study who simply were told that the job can be personally enriching showed no such improvements.[78] Similarly, James Perry, an expert on motivation of government employees, says these workers generally have a strong commitment to serving the public good, including public welfare and stewardship of public resources.[79]

4. *Autonomy*—independence and discretion in making decisions. In China, a GE Healthcare team was given the autonomy to develop an inexpensive ultrasound device to serve poorly funded health clinics. The device was successful and inspired the development of other innovative products throughout the division.[80]

5. *Feedback*—information about job performance. Many companies post charts or provide computerized data indicating productivity, number of rejects, and other data. The Parasole restaurant group, which operates a variety of casual restaurants and steakhouses in Minnesota, uses customer feedback on social media—hundreds of comments every day—as a powerful source of motivation. Employees see that today's customers comment about their experiences online and that the employees' treatment of customers has a direct impact on what they post.[81]

The most effective job enrichment increases all five core dimensions.

A person's growth need strength will help determine just how effective a job enrichment program might be. **Growth need strength** is the degree to which individuals want

growth need strength

The degree to which individuals want personal and psychological development.

personal and psychological development. Job enrichment would be more successful for people with high growth need strength. But very few people respond negatively to job enrichment.[82]

Empowerment

Today one frequently hears managers talk about empowering their people. Individuals may—or may not—feel empowered, and groups can have a culture of empowerment that predicts work unit performance.[83] **Empowerment** is the process of sharing power with employees, thereby enhancing their confidence in their ability to perform their jobs and their belief that they are influential contributors to the organization. Unfortunately, empowerment doesn't always live up to its hype. One problem is that managers undermine it by sending mixed messages such as "Do your own thing—the way we tell you."[84] But empowerment can be profoundly motivating when done properly.[85]

Empowerment results in changes in employees' beliefs—from feeling powerless to believing strongly in their own personal effectiveness.[86] The result is that people take more initiative and persevere in achieving their goals and their leader's vision even in the face of obstacles.[87] Specifically, empowerment encourages the following beliefs among employees.[88] First, they perceive meaning in their work: Their job fits their values. Second, they feel competent, or capable of performing their jobs with skill. Third, they have a sense of self-determination, of having some choice in regard to the tasks, methods, and pace of their work. Fourth, they have an impact—that is, they have some influence over important strategic, administrative, or operating decisions or outcomes on the job.

When speaking of times when they felt disempowered, people mentioned the following:[89]

- I had no input into a hiring decision of someone who was to report directly to me. I didn't even get to speak to the candidate.
- They treated us like mushrooms. They fed us and kept us in the dark.
- I worked extremely hard—long hours and late nights—on an urgent project, and then my manager took full credit for it.
- My suggestions, whether good or bad, were either not solicited or, worse, ignored.
- The project was reassigned without my knowledge or input.

In contrast, people felt empowered in the following examples:

- I was able to make a large financial decision on my own. I got to write a large check without being questioned.
- After having received a memo that said, "Cut travel," I made my case about why it was necessary to travel for business reasons, and I was told to go ahead.
- I was five years old, and my dad said, "You'll make a great mechanic one day." He planted the seed. Now I'm an engineer.
- My president supported my idea without question.
- All the financial data were shared with me.

To foster empowerment,[90] management must create an environment in which all the employees feel they have real influence over performance standards and business effectiveness within their areas of responsibility. An empowering work environment provides people with information necessary for them to perform at their best, knowledge about how to use the information and how to do their work, power to make decisions that give them control over their work, and the rewards they deserve for the contributions they make.[91] Such an environment reduces costs because fewer people are needed to supervise, monitor, and coordinate. It improves quality and service because high performance is inspired at the source—the people who do the work. It also allows quick action because people on the spot see problems, solutions, and opportunities for innovation on which they are empowered to act.

It is essential to give people clear strategic direction but to leave some room for flexibility and calculated risk taking. For example, Google empowers its employees to ask questions. TGIF is a weekly, companywide event where employees ask senior leadership about business issues. If employees have an issue about anything, they can log it into Google

empowerment

The process of sharing power with employees, thereby enhancing their confidence in their ability to perform their jobs and their belief that they are influential contributors to the organization.

Bottom Line

Job enrichment and empowerment don't work magic overnight; people may resist the new approaches and make mistakes along the way. But done right, their potential to achieve real results is undeniable. *Name two ways to ensure that empowerment is done right.*

Universal Ticketing Systems (GUTS) which is monitored for patterns.[92] More-specific actions include increasing signature authority at all levels; reducing the number of rules and approval steps; assigning nonroutine jobs; allowing independent judgment, flexibility, and creativity; defining jobs more broadly as projects rather than tasks; and providing more access to resources and people throughout the organization.[93]

You should not be surprised when empowerment causes some problems, at least in the short term. This often occurs with virtually any change, including changes for the better. It's important to remember that with empowerment comes responsibility, and employees don't necessarily like the accountability at first.[94] People may make mistakes at first, especially until they have had adequate training. And because more training is needed, costs are higher. Also, because people acquire new skills and make greater contributions, they may demand higher wages. But if they are well-trained and truly empowered, they will deserve them—and both they and the company will benefit.

Achieving Fairness

Ultimately, one of the most important issues in motivation surrounds how people view their contributions to the organization and what they receive from the organization. Ideally, they will view their relationship with their employer as a well-balanced, mutually beneficial exchange. As people work and realize the outcomes or consequences of their actions, they assess how fairly the organization treats them.

The starting point for understanding how people interpret their contributions and outcomes is equity theory.[95] **Equity theory** proposes that when people assess how fairly they are treated, they consider two key factors: outcomes and inputs. Outcomes, as in expectancy theory, refer to the various things the person receives on the job: recognition, pay, benefits, satisfaction, security, job assignments, punishments, and so forth. Inputs refer to the contributions the person makes to the organization: effort, time, talent, performance, extra commitment, good citizenship, and so forth. People have a general expectation that the outcomes they receive will reflect, or be proportionate to, the inputs they provide—a fair day's pay (and other outcomes) for a fair day's work (broadly defined by how people view all their contributions).

equity theory

A theory stating that people assess how fairly they have been treated according to two key factors: outcomes and inputs.

But this comparison of outcomes to inputs is not the whole story. People also pay attention to the outcomes and inputs others receive. At salary review time, for example, most people—from executives on down—try to pick up clues that will tell them who got the high raises. As described in the following section, they compare ratios, try to restore equity if necessary, and derive more or less satisfaction based on how fairly they believe they have been treated.

Assessing Equity

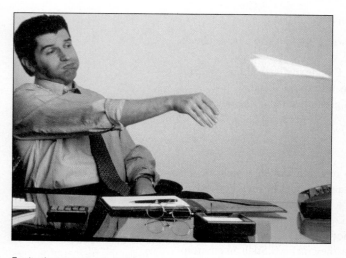

Equity theory suggests that people compare the ratio of their outcomes to inputs against the outcome-to-input ratio of some comparison person. How would you deal with someone you perceive to be a slacker who gets promoted over you?

© Tom & Dee Ann McCarthy/Corbis

Equity theory suggests that people compare the ratio of their own outcomes to inputs against the outcome-to-input ratio of some comparison person. The comparison person can be a fellow student, a co-worker, a boss, or an average industry pay scale. Stated more succinctly, people compare their own outcomes and inputs to those of a comparison person (see Exhibit 13.8). If the ratios are equivalent, people believe the relationship is equitable, or fair. Equity causes people to be satisfied with their treatment. But the person who believes his or her ratio is lower than another's will feel inequitably treated. Inequity causes dissatisfaction and leads to an attempt to restore balance to the relationship.

EXHIBIT 13.8   Equity Theory

Comparing Your Ratio to Other's Ratio	Your Likely Perception	Actions You May Take to Restore Equity
$\dfrac{\text{Your Outcomes}}{\text{Your Inputs}} = \dfrac{\text{Other's Outcomes}}{\text{Other's Inputs}}$	Equitably treated.	No action necessary.
$\dfrac{\text{Your Outcomes}}{\text{Your Inputs}} < \dfrac{\text{Other's Outcomes}}{\text{Other's Inputs}}$	Inequitably treated. Feel underrewarded.	Reduce your inputs (e.g., exert less effort). Try to increase your outcomes (e.g., ask for a raise). Change your perception of inputs or outcomes (e.g., maybe so-and-so really did deserve the bonus).
$\dfrac{\text{Your Outcomes}}{\text{Your Inputs}} > \dfrac{\text{Other's Outcomes}}{\text{Other's Inputs}}$	Inequitably treated. Feel overrewarded.	Increase your inputs by putting in extra effort. Help other person increase her outcomes (e.g., urge her to ask for a larger bonus).

Inequity and the negative feelings it creates may appear anywhere. As a student, perhaps you have been in the following situation. You stay up all night and get a C on the exam. Meanwhile another student studies a couple of hours, goes out for the rest of the evening, gets a good night's sleep, and gets a B on the exam. You perceive your inputs (time spent studying) as much greater than the other student's, but your outcomes (exam grade) are lower. You are displeased at the seeming unfairness. In business, the same thing sometimes happens with pay raises. One manager puts in 60-hour weeks, has a degree from a prestigious university, and believes she is destined for the top. When her archrival—whom she perceives as less deserving ("she never comes into the office on weekends, and all she does when she is here is butter up the boss")—gets the higher raise or the promotion, she experiences severe feelings of inequity.

In recent years, many people have felt inequity when they learn about large sums paid to high-profile CEOs. Fair pay is an increasingly public issue at U.S. companies because the Dodd-Frank Wall Street Reform and Consumer Protection Act requires greater disclosure of performance-based pay details.[96]

Assessments of equity are not made objectively. They are subjective perceptions or beliefs. In the preceding examples, the person who got the higher raise probably felt she deserved it. Even if she admits she doesn't put in long workweeks, she may convince herself she doesn't need to because she's so talented. The student who got the higher grade may believe it was a fair, equitable result because (1) she kept up all semester, while the other student did not, and (2) she's smart. (Ability and experience, not just time and effort, can be seen as inputs.)

Restoring Equity

People who feel inequitably treated and dissatisfied are motivated to do something to restore equity. They have a number of options to change the ratios or reevaluate the situation and decide it is equitable after all.

The equity equation shown earlier indicates a person's options for restoring equity. People who feel inequitably treated can reduce their inputs by giving less effort, performing at lower levels, or quitting. ("Well, if that's the way things work around here, there's no way I'm going to work that hard [or stick around].") Or they can attempt to increase their outcomes. ("My boss [or teacher] is going to hear about this. I deserve more; there must be some way I can get more.") On the positive side, employees may also put forth extra effort to keep a situation equitable for the group. When employees see their colleagues working hard to meet an important deadline, they may be inclined to work harder themselves.

Other ways of restoring equity focus on changing the other person's ratio. A person can decrease others' outcomes. For example, an employee may sabotage work to create problems for his company or his boss.[97] A person can also change her perceptions of inputs or outcomes. ("That promotion isn't as great a deal as he thinks. The pay is not that much better, and the headaches will be unbelievable.") It is also possible to increase others' inputs, particularly by changing perceptions. ("The more I think about it, the more I see he deserved it. He's worked hard all year, he's competent, and it's about time he got a break.")

Thus a person can restore equity in a number of ways by behaviorally or perceptually changing inputs and outcomes.

Procedural Justice

procedural justice

Using fair processes in decision making and making sure others know that the process was as fair as possible.

Inevitably, managers make decisions that have outcomes more favorable for some than for others. Those with favorable outcomes will be pleased; those with worse outcomes, all else equal, will be more displeased. But managers desiring to put salve on the wounds—say, of people they like or respect or want to keep and motivate—still can take actions to reduce the dissatisfaction. The key is for people to believe that managers provide **procedural justice**—using fair process in decision making and helping others know that the process was as fair as possible. When people perceive procedural fairness, they are more likely to support decisions and decision makers.[98] For example, nurses who perceived their performance evaluations as fair were more likely to remain in their jobs.[99]

Even if people believe that their outcome was inequitable and unfair, they are more likely to view justice as having been served if the process was fair. You can increase people's beliefs that the process was fair by making the process open and visible; stating decision criteria in advance rather than after the fact; making sure that the most appropriate people—those who have valid information and are viewed as trustworthy—make the decisions; giving people a chance to participate in the process; and providing an appeal process that allows people to question decisions safely and receive complete answers.[100] However, the impact of procedural justice can differ by country and culture—for instance, the impact is strongest among nations characterized by individualism, femininity, uncertainty avoidance, and low power distance (recall Chapter 6).[101]

At an elevator plant in the United States, an army of consultants arrived one day, unexplained and annoying.[102] The rumor mill kicked in; employees thought the plant was to be shut down or that some of them would be laid off. Three months later, management unveiled its new plan, involving a new method of manufacturing based on teams. As the changes were implemented, management did not adequately answer questions about the purpose of the changes, employees resisted, conflicts arose, and the formerly popular plant manager lost the trust of his people. Costs skyrocketed, and quality plummeted.

Concerned, management conducted an employee survey. Employees were skeptical that the survey results would lead to any positive changes and were worried that management would be angry that people had voiced their honest opinions. But management reacted by saying, "We were wrong, we screwed up, we didn't use the right process." They went on to share with employees critical business information, the limited options available, and the dire consequences if the company didn't change. Employees saw the dilemma and came to view the business problem as theirs as well as management's, but they were scared that some of them would lose their jobs. Management retained the right to lay people off if business conditions grew worse but also made several promises: no layoffs as a result of changes made; cross-training programs for employees; no replacements of departing people until conditions improved; a chance for employees to serve in new roles as consultants on quality issues; and sharing of sales and cost data on a regular basis.

The news was bad, but people understood it and began to share responsibility with management. This was the beginning of the restoration of trust and commitment and of steady improvements in performance.

Job Satisfaction

If people feel fairly treated from the outcomes they receive and the processes used, they will be satisfied. A satisfied worker is not necessarily more productive than a dissatisfied one; sometimes people are happy with their jobs because they don't have to work hard! But job dissatisfaction, aggregated across many individuals, creates a workforce that is more likely to exhibit (1) higher turnover; (2) higher absenteeism; (3) less good citizenship among employees;[103] (4) more grievances and lawsuits; (5) strikes; (6) stealing, sabotage, and vandalism; (7) poorer mental and physical health (which can mean higher job stress, higher insurance costs, and more lawsuits);[104] (8) more injuries;[105] (9) poor customer service;[106] and (10) lower productivity and profits.[107] All of these consequences of dissatisfaction, either directly or indirectly, are costly to organizations. Sadly, a survey of U.S. households found that a majority of workers are dissatisfied with their jobs, with the greatest amount of dissatisfaction among lower wage earners and workers aged 25 and younger.[108]

Job satisfaction is especially important for relationship-oriented service employees such as realtors, hair stylists, and stockbrokers. Customers develop (or don't develop) a commitment to a specific service provider. Satisfied service providers are less likely to quit the company and more likely to provide an enjoyable customer experience.[109]

Quality of Work Life

Quality of work life (QWL) programs create a workplace that enhances employee well-being and satisfaction. The general goal of QWL programs is to satisfy the full range of employee needs. People's needs apparently are well met at Plante Moran, an accounting firm with offices in 18 midwestern cities. Cofounder Frank Moran's goal was for the business to be a "people firm disguised as an accounting firm," and he brought that vision to life by allowing any flexible work arrangement that is satisfactory to the employee's clients. The firm's website, which promises a "jerk-free" workplace, describes challenging jobs with varied assignments and buddies assigned to new employees so they can more wisely navigate their careers. In the end, what employees say they appreciate most are the interesting assignments that bring them into direct contact with key people at client companies.[110]

QWL has eight categories:[111]
1. Adequate and fair compensation
2. A safe and healthy environment
3. Jobs that develop human capacities
4. A chance for personal growth and security
5. A social environment that fosters personal identity, freedom from prejudice, a sense of community, and upward mobility
6. Constitutionalism, or the rights of personal privacy, dissent, and due process
7. A work role that minimizes infringement on personal leisure and family needs
8. Socially responsible organizational actions

Organizations differ drastically in their attention to QWL. Critics claim that QWL programs don't necessarily inspire employees to work harder if the company does not tie rewards directly to individual performance. Advocates of QWL claim that it improves organizational effectiveness and productivity. The term *productivity,* as applied by QWL programs, means much more than each person's quantity of work output.[112] It also includes turnover, absenteeism, accidents, theft, sabotage, creativity, innovation, and especially the quality of work.

Bottom Line
A single satisfied person doesn't necessarily produce well on every performance dimension. But an organization full of people with high job satisfaction will likely perform well in many ways.
In an organization with a strategy focused on low cost, is employee satisfaction important? Why or why not?

quality of work life (QWL) programs

Programs designed to create a workplace that enhances employee well-being.

Plante Moran promises applicants a "jerk-free" workplace on its website.

All in all, people's satisfaction and well-being have many important consequences, beneficial to both employees and employers.[113] These range from better attitudes and health to work behaviors and performance and ultimately include business outcomes.[114] In a well-managed workplace, win–win solutions are indeed possible.

Psychological Contracts

psychological contract

A set of perceptions of what employees owe their employers, and what their employers owe them.

The relationship between individuals and employing organizations typically is formalized by a written contract. But in employees' minds, there also exists a **psychological contract**—a set of perceptions of what they owe their employers and what their employers owe them.[115] This contract, whether it is seen as being upheld or violated—and whether the parties trust one another or not—has important implications for employee satisfaction and motivation and the effectiveness of the organization. Experiencing significant breach of psychological contract also can adversely affect physical and mental health.[116]

Historically, in many companies, the employment relationship was stable and predictable. Now mergers, layoffs, and other disruptions have torn asunder the old deal.[117] As one executive put it, "The 'used-to-be's' must give way to the realities of 'What is and what will be.'"[118] The fundamental used-to-be of traditionally managed organizations was that employees were expected to be loyal, and employers would provide secure employment. Today the implicit contract goes something like this:[119] If people stay, do their own jobs plus someone else's (who has been downsized), and do additional things such as participating in task forces, the company will try to provide a job (if it can), provide gestures that it cares, and keep providing more or less the same pay (with periodic small increases). The likely result of this not-very-satisfying arrangement: uninspired people and a business trying to survive. Career advisors tell disillusioned employees to think of themselves as free agents and to change jobs when a new option beckons.

But a better deal is possible, for both employers and employees.[120] Ideally, your employer will provide continuous skill updating and an invigorating work environment in which you can use your skills and are motivated to stay even though you may have other job options.[121] The employer says, in essence, "If you make us more valuable, we'll make you more valuable," and the employee says, "If you help me grow, I'll help the company grow." The company benefits from your contributions, and you thrive in your work while you also become more marketable if and when you decide to look elsewhere. Employment is an alliance—perhaps temporary, perhaps long term—aimed at helping both employer and employee succeed.[122] The results of such a contract are much more likely to be a mutually beneficial and satisfying relationship and a high-performing, successful organization.

Consider how business coach Ram Charan assumed this new psychological contract in advising a frustrated human resource (HR) manager.[123] The manager had asked Charan for guidance in coping with bureaucratic red tape that was frustrating to him as a leader and to the employees in his group. Charan encouraged the manager to reframe the situation as a need for learning, creativity, and leadership. The manager, said Charan, should investigate what the managers in other departments need from HR so that his people would truly be serving business needs and helping to solve business problems. Charan also encouraged the manager to learn about his employees' career goals and interests so that he can focus on ways to develop his people's strengths through assignments and greater decision-making authority within the department. If the HR manager accepts Charan's guidance, he and his people will face more interesting challenges than they would by simply defining themselves as a static part of a bureaucracy.

Finally, consider how these ideas for motivation apply at SAS. Read the "Management in Action: Onward" feature and ask yourself whether old-fashioned stable employment relationships can—or should—be the norm.

Management in Action

HOW SAS MAKES WORK MOTIVATING

Jennifer Mann, SAS's vice president of human resources, says everyone there "is working toward the same vision and inspiring each other to do their best work." Mann sees this as evidence that the company's culture is yielding great results. Other signs of success include employee turnover below 3 percent (versus the industry average of more than 20 percent), tens of thousands of job applicants to fill hundreds of open positions, and steadily growing revenues.

What convinces employees that SAS values their contributions? We have already talked about employee benefits, but these are mere symbols of underlying beliefs. The managers rewarded at SAS are those who advocate for and develop their people. CEO James Goodnight (also an owner of the privately held company) puts his time and money on the line for his people. Each month, he presides at a breakfast meeting where any employee may join in and ask questions or share ideas. In 2008, as financial crisis gave way to Great Recession, other software companies announced major layoffs, and SAS employees became nervous. Goodnight spoke to all of them via webcast, saying there would be no layoffs; they just needed to be frugal. Not only did the company weather that economic downturn, it continued growing and developed new products to launch as the economy recovered.

Another quality of the SAS culture is trust in employees. The company's standard workweek is just 35 hours, and its onsite facilities and beautiful grounds make it easy for employees to take a break to work out, get a haircut or massage, or go for a hike. Managers don't worry that employees will goof off; they find that trust motivates employees to work hard to please customers and help the company succeed. In fact, great subsidized food (some of it grown on an SAS-owned organic farm) and other services can make staying at work easier than going home. A similar attitude of trust applies to sick days at SAS, which are unlimited.

Finally, SAS ensures that work is meaningful. Goodnight reminds employees that SAS software is useful to people all over the world. Programmers' work is designed so they feel ownership of their creations. Even the landscapers at headquarters are assigned to particular plots, so these employees enjoy imparting beauty to that parcel and feel the same identification with the company as any programmer does.[124]

- How does SAS make its jobs motivating? What other principles of job design could enhance motivation at SAS?
- What elements of SAS's approach to motivation do you think would contribute more to job satisfaction than to performance? Why?

KEY TERMS

Alderfer's ERG theory, p. 423

empowerment, p. 429

equity theory, p. 430

expectancy, p. 419

expectancy theory, p. 419

extinction, p. 416

extrinsic reward, p. 425

goal-setting theory, p. 413

growth need strength, p. 428

hygiene factors, p. 427

instrumentality, p. 419

intrinsic reward, p. 425

job enlargement, p. 426

job enrichment, p. 427

job rotation, p. 426

law of effect, p. 415

Maslow's need hierarchy, p. 421

motivation, p. 412

motivators, p. 427

negative reinforcement, p. 416

organizational behavior modification (OB mod), p. 415

outcome, p. 419

positive reinforcement, p. 416

procedural justice, p. 432

psychological contract, p. 434

punishment, p. 416

quality of work life (QWL) programs, p. 433

reinforcers, p. 415

stretch goals, p. 414

two-factor theory, p. 427

valence, p. 420

RETAINING WHAT YOU LEARNED

In Chapter 13, you learned that managers motivate employees for a variety of reasons and in a variety of ways. Goals that are specific, quantifiable, and challenging are powerful tools for motivating individuals and teams. Organizations develop programs that use different types of reinforcement to influence employees' behaviors. Managers should reinforce appropriate behaviors, manage mistakes properly,

and provide useful feedback. Expectancy theory suggests that employees are motivated when they believe they can perform a job well and their performance will be rewarded with a valued outcome. People's desire to fulfill needs affects their behaviors at work. Maslow and Alderfer suggested that individuals are motivated by their needs. McClelland said people vary in the extent to which they need achievement, affiliation, and power. Managers can create jobs that are motivational by making them intrinsically rewarding. Jobs can be enriched by building in more skill variety, task identity, task significance, autonomy, and feedback. Employees with jobs that have the necessary information, knowledge, power, and rewards feel empowered. Equity theory explores how an individual's perceptions of fairness can lead to either feeling satisfied or dissatisfied at work. A satisfied workforce has many advantages for the firm, including lower absenteeism and turnover; fewer grievances, lawsuits, and strikes; lower health costs; and higher-quality work. A psychological contract is a set of perceptions of what employees think they owe their organizations and vice versa. If these perceptions are violated or changed unfairly, employees' satisfaction or motivation may decrease.

LO 1   Identify the kinds of behaviors managers need to motivate in people.

- All important work behaviors are motivated.
- Managers need to motivate employees to join and remain in the organization and to exhibit high attendance, job performance, and citizenship.

LO 2   List principles for setting goals that motivate employees.

- Goal setting is a powerful motivator. Specific, quantifiable, and challenging but attainable goals motivate high effort and performance.
- Goal setting can be used for teams as well as for individuals.
- Care should be taken to avoid setting single goals to the exclusion of other important dimensions of performance.
- Managers also should keep sight of the other potential downsides of goals.

LO 3   Summarize how to reward good performance effectively.

- Organizational behavior modification programs influence behavior at work by arranging consequences for people's actions.
- Most programs use positive reinforcement as a consequence, but other important consequences are negative reinforcement, punishment, and extinction.
- Care must be taken to reinforce appropriate, not inappropriate, behavior.
- Innovative managers use a wide variety of rewards for good performance.
- They also understand how to manage mistakes and provide useful feedback.

LO 4   Describe the key beliefs that affect people's motivation.

- Expectancy theory describes three important work-related beliefs.
- Motivation is a function of people's: (1) expectancies, or effort-to-performance links; (2) instrumentalities, or performance-to-outcome links; and (3) the valences people attach to the outcomes of performance.

LO 5   Discuss ways in which people's individual needs affect their behavior.

- According to Maslow, important needs arise at five levels of a hierarchy: physiological, safety, social, ego, and self-actualization needs.
- Focusing more on the context of work, Alderfer's ERG theory describes three sets of needs: existence, relatedness, and growth.
- McClelland says people vary in the extent to which they have needs for achievement, affiliation, and power.
- Because people are inclined to satisfy their various needs, these theories suggest to managers the kinds of rewards that motivate people.

LO 6   Define ways to create jobs that motivate.

- One approach to satisfying needs and motivating people is to create intrinsic motivation through the improved design of jobs.
- Jobs can be enriched by building in more skill variety, task identity, task significance, autonomy, and feedback.
- Empowerment, the most recent development in the creation of motivating jobs, includes the perceptions of meaning, competence, self-determination, and impact. These qualities come from an environment in which people have necessary information, knowledge, power, and rewards.

LO 7   Summarize how people assess fairness and how to achieve fairness.

- Equity theory states that people compare their inputs and outcomes to the inputs and outcomes of others.
- Perceptions of equity (fairness) are satisfying; feelings of inequity (unfairness) are dissatisfying and motivate people to change their behavior or their perceptions to restore equity.
- In addition to fairness of outcomes, as described in equity theory, fairness is also appraised and managed through procedural justice.

LO 8   Identify causes and consequences of a satisfied workforce.

- A satisfied workforce has many advantages for the firm, including: lower absenteeism and turnover; fewer grievances, lawsuits, and strikes; lower health costs; and higher-quality work.
- One general approach to generating higher satisfaction for people is to implement a quality of work life program. QWL seeks to provide a safe and healthy environment, opportunity for personal growth, a positive social environment, fair treatment, and other improvements in people's work lives.
- These and other benefits from the organization, exchanged for contributions from employees, create a psychological contract.
- Over time, how the psychological contract is upheld or violated, and changed unfairly or fairly, will influence people's satisfaction and motivation.

DISCUSSION QUESTIONS

1. Think of a significant mistake made by someone on a job. How did the boss handle it, and what was the effect?

2. Why do you think it is so difficult for managers to empower their people?

3. Think of a job you hold currently or held in the past. How would you describe the psychological contract? How does (did) this affect your attitudes and behaviors on the job?

4. If a famous executive or sports figure were to give a passionate motivational speech, trying to persuade people to work harder, what do you think the impact would be? Why?

5. Give some examples of situations in which you wanted to do a great job but were prevented from doing so. What was the impact on you, and what would this suggest to you in your efforts to motivate other people to perform?

6. Discuss the similarities and differences between setting goals for other people and setting goals for yourself. When does goal setting fail, and when does it succeed?

7. Identify four examples of people inadvertently reinforcing the wrong behaviors or punishing or extinguishing good behaviors.

8. Assess yourself on McClelland's three needs. On which need are you highest, and on which are you lowest? What are the implications for you as a manager?

9. Identify a job you have held and appraise it on Hackman and Oldham's five core job dimensions. Also describe the degree to which it made you feel empowered. As a class, choose one job and discuss together how it could be changed to be more motivating and empowering.

10. Using expectancy theory, analyze how you have made and will make personal choices, such as a major area of study, a career to pursue, or job interviews to seek.

11. Describe a time when you felt unfairly treated and explain why. How did you respond to the inequity? What other options might you have had?

12. Provide examples of how outcomes perceived as unfair can decrease motivation. Then discuss how procedural justice, or fair process, can help overcome the negative effects.

13. What are the implications for your career of, and how will you prepare for, the psychological contracts described at the end of the chapter?

14. Set some goals for yourself, considering the discussion of goal setting in the chapter.

EXPERIENTIAL EXERCISES

13.1 ASSESSING YOURSELF

Circle the response that most closely correlates with each of the following items:

	Agree	Neither Agree nor Disagree		Disagree	
1. I have developed a written list of short and long-term goals I would like to accomplish.	1	2	3	4	5
2. When setting goals for myself, I give consideration to what my capabilities and limits are.	1	2	3	4	5
3. I set goals that are realistic and attainable.	1	2	3	4	5
4. My goals are based on my hopes and beliefs, not on those of my parents, friends, or significant other.	1	2	3	4	5
5. When I fail to achieve a goal, I get back on track.	1	2	3	4	5
6. My goals are based on my personal values.	1	2	3	4	5
7. I have a current mission statement and have involved those closest to me in formulating it.	1	2	3	4	5
8. I regularly check my progress toward achieving the goals I have set.	1	2	3	4	5
9. When setting goals, I strive for performance, not outcomes.	1	2	3	4	5
10. I have a support system in place—friends, family members, and/or colleagues who believe in me and support my goals.	1	2	3	4	5
11. I apply SMART characteristics to my goals.	1	2	3	4	5
12. I prioritize my goals, focusing only on the most important or valuable ones at a particular point in time.	1	2	3	4	5
13. I reward myself when I achieve a goal or even when I reach a particular milestone.	1	2	3	4	5
14. I revisit my goals periodically and add and modify goals as appropriate.	1	2	3	4	5

Sum your circled responses. If your total is 42 or higher, you might want to explore ways to improve your skill in the area of goal setting.

SOURCE: Suzanne C. de Janasz, Karen O'Dowd, and Beth Z. Schneider, *Interpersonal Skills in Organizations,* McGraw-Hill, 2002, p. 211. Copyright 2002. The McGraw-Hill Companies, Inc. Reprinted with permission.

13.2   PERSONAL GOAL SETTING

1. In the spaces provided, brainstorm your goals in the following categories. Write down as many as you wish, including goals that are short-, mid-, and long-term.

   Academic, intellectual

   Health, fitness

   Social: family, friends, significant other, community

   Career, job

   Financial

   Other

2. Of the goals you have listed, select from each of the six categories the two most important goals that you would like to pursue in the short term (next 6–12 months). Write these here.

   a. _____

   b. _____

   c. _____

   d. _____

   e. _____

   f. _____

   g. _____

   h. _____

   i. _____

   j. _____

   k. _____

   i. _____

3. From the 12 goals listed, choose the 3 that are the most important to you at this time: the 3 you commit to work on in the next few months. Write a goal statement for each one, using the following guidelines:

   Begin each with the word "To . . ."

   Be specific.

Quantify the goal if possible.

Each goal statement should be realistic, attainable, and within your control.

Each goal statement should reflect your aspirations—not those of others such as parents, roommates, significant others, and the like.

   a. _____

   _____

   b. _____

   _____

   c. _____

   _____

4. On a separate sheet of paper, develop an action plan for each goal statement. For each action plan,

   List the steps you will take to accomplish the goal.

   Include dates (by when) and initials (who's responsible) for each step.

   Visualize completing the goal and, working backward, specify each step necessary between now and then to reach the goal.

   Identify any potential barriers you might experience in attaining the goal. Problem-solve around these obstacles and convert them into steps in your action plan.

   Identify the resources you will need to accomplish these goals and build in steps to acquire the necessary information into your action plan.

5. Transfer the dates of each step for each goal in your action plan to a daily calendar.

6. Keep an ongoing daily or weekly record of the positive steps you take toward meeting each goal.

SOURCE: Suzanne C. de Janasz, Karen O'Dowd, and Beth Z. Schneider, *Interpersonal Skills in Organizations*, McGraw-Hill, 2002, p. 211. Copyright 2002. The McGraw-Hill Companies, Inc. Reprinted with permission.

13.3   WHAT DO STUDENTS WANT FROM THEIR JOBS?

OBJECTIVES

1. To demonstrate individual differences in job expectations.
2. To illustrate individual differences in need and motivational structures.
3. To examine and compare extrinsic and intrinsic rewards.

INSTRUCTIONS

1. Working alone, complete the "What I Want from My Job" survey.
2. In small groups, compare and analyze differences in the survey results and prepare group responses to the discussion questions.

3. After the class reconvenes, group spokespersons present group findings.

DISCUSSION QUESTIONS

1. Which items received the highest and lowest scores from you? Why?
2. On which items were there most and least agreement among students? What are the implications?
3. Which job rewards are extrinsic, and which are intrinsic?
4. Were more response differences found in intrinsic or in extrinsic rewards?
5. In what ways do you think blue-collar workers' responses would differ from those of college students?

What I Want from My Job

Determine what you want from a job by circling the level of importance of each of the following job rewards:

	Very Important	Important	Indifferent	Unimportant	Very Unimportant
1. Advancement opportunities	5	4	3	2	1
2. Appropriate company policies	5	4	3	2	1
3. Authority	5	4	3	2	1
4. Autonomy and freedom on the job	5	4	3	2	1
5. Challenging work	5	4	3	2	1
6. Company reputation	5	4	3	2	1
7. Fringe benefits	5	4	3	2	1
8. Geographic location	5	4	3	2	1
9. Good coworkers	5	4	3	2	1
10. Good supervision	5	4	3	2	1
11. Job security	5	4	3	2	1
12. Money	5	4	3	2	1
13. Opportunity for self-development	5	4	3	2	1
14. Pleasant office and working conditions	5	4	3	2	1
15. Performance feedback	5	4	3	2	1
16. Prestigious job title	5	4	3	2	1
17. Recognition for doing a good job	5	4	3	2	1
18. Responsibility	5	4	3	2	1
19. Sense of achievement	5	4	3	2	1
20. Training programs	5	4	3	2	1
21. Type of work	5	4	3	2	1
22. Working with people	5	4	3	2	1

CONCLUDING CASE

BIG BISON RESORTS: FINDING THE KEY TO WHAT EMPLOYEES VALUE

Frank Schuman, vice president of human resources for Big Bison Resorts, heard laughter as he approached the chief executive's office door. As he stepped into the room, he saw CEO Janette Briggs seated behind her desk, regaling two other executives with a story that the three were obviously enjoying immensely.

"Oh, Frank! Good!" exclaimed Janette when she saw him enter. "I was just telling Pedro and Marlys about my great adventure in TV land." Janette had been away from the office for the past two weeks, taping the popular reality TV show *Executive in Disguise* instead of running her company, a regional chain of indoor water parks.

"How did it go?" asked Frank. "From the laughter I heard outside your door, it must have been hilarious."

"Well, funny, yes," replied Janette. "But mainly it was eye-opening. After spending all that time in our kitchens and cleaning the guest rooms and pools, I see our people and their jobs in a totally new way."

"Is that why you called me here? I was expecting you wanted to review our plans for the Employee of the Month program we're unrolling next month. That is, until I saw—" He waved his hand toward the other two people seated in the room, Pedro Gutierrez, head of operations, and finance chief Marlys Higgenbotham. "Or at least I was guessing they're not here to nominate the first employee of the month."

"No, see, that's the issue. After working directly with our frontline staff, I'm having my doubts about putting resources into Employee of the Month," replied the CEO. Frank swallowed. Employee of the Month had been a pet idea of Janette's, so he had poured most of his time into developing the program. Each month, a manager at each resort was going to nominate a top-performing employee to be the Employee of the Month and enjoy the glory, not to mention a premium parking space and a framed photo posted in the lobby of the resort where he or she worked. Now it appeared that Janette shared what, he had to admit, were his own doubts about whether the program would really do much to improve performance or lower turnover. Janette continued, "Have a seat, Frank, and let me tell you about what I saw the past two weeks." Frank settled into a chair next to Marlys.

Janette brought Frank up to date: "I've been telling Marlys and Pedro what it was like to work in one of our kitchens. The pace is unbelievable. The workload is unbelievable. And the teamwork is out of this world. Frank, I was amazed, and you would be, too. I know how to make a grilled cheese sandwich, but these folks do a lot more than cook. They're planning and controlling on the fly: How many salads? How many pancakes? How can we make all that without any waste? There's no supervisor on the line; they're *all* thinking like managers—how to please customers, control costs. Honestly, our managers could take lessons from them on teamwork and quality control."

"It sounds like we have a lot of Employees of the Month," Frank said hopefully. Maybe the program wouldn't be canceled after all, and his group's efforts wouldn't have been wasted.

"No, no, no!" broke in Marlys. "The point is, we've tried so many programs to boost productivity. As you know, we were looking at bonuses last year, till the economy got so bad. We simply couldn't justify paying more when occupancy rates were diving. But we have to do something. Now that business is picking up in our market area, other hotels and resorts are going to start recruiting away our best people. The question is, what can we do that will keep employees working as hard as they are now without burning out and leaving us? We thought people would just like a little recognition, but Janette is saying she doubts it now."

"Exactly," said Janette. "And that's why I called you in. We need your expertise about human relations. What do people want? I thought it would be pay, prizes, that sort of thing. And you went along with me. But really, Frank, can that be it? The people I worked with the past two weeks—they have so much skill at what they do, and they're constantly thinking up ways to make our guests happy. They already take pride in what they accomplish. We need to decide what will make their jobs better so they can accomplish more without us getting in their way with, well, Employee of the Month ceremonies."

"OK," replied Frank, "now that you've put it that way, I have to ask if maybe what we *don't* want to do is decide what will make their jobs better."

As Janette and Marlys gazed at Frank quizzically, Pedro spoke up. "That's great, Frank. You're saying we shouldn't make their jobs better? I came up through the ranks at Big Bison, and I can recall that those hourly jobs aren't exactly perfect the way they are."

"What I mean," replied Frank, "is that we need to *listen* before we *decide*."

DISCUSSION QUESTIONS

1. What kinds of behavior would an Employee of the Month program, as described here, reinforce at Big Bison Resorts? How might the company apply the principles of reinforcement more effectively?

2. How might Big Bison Resorts get input from employees to make the company's jobs more motivating? What impact would this effort have on the company's performance?

3. How would Big Bison's employees perceive the equity of the Employee of the Month program? Compare their reactions to that program with the response you would expect from an effort to involve employees in improving their jobs.

4. Think about a previous job you have held or hold currently. If you had the power to make such decisions, what would you do to make the job more motivating for employees?

CHAPTER 14

Teamwork

> "No one can whistle a symphony. It takes an orchestra to play it."
>
> —HALFORD E. LUCCOCK

Management in Action

HOW TEAMS WORK AT WHOLE FOODS MARKET

Whole Foods Market has a purpose beyond profits, and even a purpose beyond selling gorgeous vegetables and great cheeses. The chain of more than 400 health-food stores in the United States, Canada, and the United Kingdom seeks to do no less than "contribute to the well-being of people and the planet." This mission shapes the selection of merchandise grown organically and sustainably, including fresh produce, meats and fish, and whole grains, all attractively displayed. It also shapes the way the company treats its 80,000-plus employees.

Management of employees is based on key values: personal responsibility, valuing diversity, and commitment to the organization's purpose. To sustain this combination of values, the company operates as a set of teams, with every employee being a team member. A team may have between six and a hundred members, with the large teams divided into subteams. The leader of each team in a store is a member of the store's leadership team, and the head of each store leadership team is a member of a regional team. At the top of the Whole Foods hierarchy is an executive team. Each employee is responsible for participating in decisions related to his or her team's work. Team members have a vote in which employees are part of the team and what benefits will be included in their compensation packages.

Team spirit and empowerment at Whole Foods has laid a strong foundation for business success. Teamwork starts at the top where John Mackey and Walter Robb share the role of CEO. Mackey says

© David Paul Morris/Bloomberg via Getty Images

living out the store's values creates a climate that frees employees to innovate without fear, and the creative, fear-free environment feels great to shoppers. It is one of a handful of companies that has attained a spot on *Fortune*'s list of Best Companies to Work For in every year the list has been compiled. Whole Foods reports employee turnover of just 10 percent per year (the industry average is ten times that). Mark Ehrnstein, global vice president of Team Member Services, attributes the low turnover to the company's ability to foster a strong, team-oriented culture. And after year upon year of strong growth, Whole Foods has become the world's largest supermarket chain specializing in natural and organic foods, with investors seeing far more room to grow in the future.[1]

Whole Foods Market expresses a strong commitment to its employees, empowers them to make decisions, and expects a high level of commitment to serving customers. As you read this chapter, consider whether these ingredients are enough to ensure truly effective teamwork.

Sometimes teams work, and sometimes they don't. The goal of this chapter is to help make sure that your teams (and you) succeed. Empowerment at Whole Foods Market illustrates one way a company can apply teamwork with extraordinary results.

Teams transform the ways organizations do business.[2] Almost all companies now use teams to produce goods and services, to manage projects, and to make decisions and run the company.[3] For you, this has two vital implications. First, you will be working in and perhaps managing teams. Second, the ability to work in and lead teams is valuable to your employer and important to your career. Fortunately, coursework focusing on team training can enhance students' teamwork knowledge and skills.[4]

The Contributions of Teams

Used properly, teams can be powerfully effective as a building block for organization structure. Organizations such as Semco, W.L. Gore, and Kollmorgen are structured entirely around teams. 3M's breakthrough products emerge through the use of teams that are small entrepreneurial businesses within the larger corporation.

Teams can increase productivity, improve quality, and reduce costs. At Massachusetts-based manufacturer FLEXcon, teams of employees applying the lean principles described in Chapter 9 have significantly increased productivity and decreased energy consumption.[5] At Nucor's steel plant in Decatur, Alabama, the general manager credits teamwork for high productivity and improved safety.[6]

Teams also can enhance speed and be powerful forces for innovation, creativity,[7] and change. Boeing, 3M, Google, and many other companies use teams to create new products faster. General Mills uses a team approach to make decisions about the packaging for its products. For product divisions such as Big G cereals or Yoplait yogurt teams bring together employees from brand design, engineering, production, research and development, and other relevant functions to figure out how packaging can reduce waste, cut costs, send a clearer marketing message, and find ways to work more efficiently with suppliers.[8]

Teams also provide many benefits for their members.[9] The team is a very useful learning mechanism. Members learn about the company and themselves, and they acquire new skills and performance strategies. The team can satisfy important personal needs, such as affiliation and esteem. Other needs are met as team members receive tangible organizational rewards that they could not have achieved working alone. Moreover, teams help individuals develop their networks.[10]

Team members can provide one another with feedback; identify opportunities for growth and development; and train, coach, and mentor.[11] A marketing representative can learn about financial modeling from a colleague on a new product development team, and the financial expert can learn about consumer marketing. Experience working together in a team, and developing strong problem-solving capabilities, is a vital supplement to specific job skills or functional expertise. And the skills are transferable to new positions.

Bottom Line

Well-managed teams are powerful forces that can deliver all desired results. *What do you think makes a team more powerful than a set of individuals?*

Teams also can enhance speed and be powerful forces for innovation, creativity, and change.

work teams

Teams that make or do things like manufacture, assemble, sell, or provide service.

Types of Teams

Your organization may have hundreds of groups and teams, and the variety of different types is vast.[12] Following are a few of the best-known examples.[13] **Work teams** make or do things such as manufacture, assemble, sell, or provide service. They typically are well defined; a clear part of the formal organization structure; and composed of a full-time, stable membership. Work teams are what most people think of when they think of teams in organizations.[14]

Project and development teams work on long-term projects, often over a period of years. They have specific assignments, such as research or new product development, and members usually must contribute expert knowledge and judgment. These teams work toward a one-time product, disbanding once their work is completed. Then new teams are formed for new projects.

Parallel teams operate separately from the regular work structure of the firm on a temporary basis. Members often come from different units or jobs and are asked to do work that is not normally done by the standard structure. Their charge is to recommend solutions to specific problems. They usually do not have authority to act, however. Examples include task forces and quality or safety teams formed to study a particular problem. In response to complaints from victims of Hurricane Sandy regarding how some insurance companies assessed damage after the storm, four U.S. senators from New York and New Jersey formed a task force. The task force is working with the Federal Emergency Management Agency (FEMA) to review up to 142,000 claims.[15]

Management teams coordinate and provide direction to the subunits under their jurisdiction and integrate work among subunits.[16] The management team is based on authority stemming from hierarchical rank and is responsible for the overall performance of the business unit. Managers responsible for different subunits form a team together, and at the top of the organization resides the executive management team that establishes strategic direction and manages the firm's overall performance.

Transnational teams are work teams composed of multinational members whose activities span multiple countries.[17] Such teams differ from other work teams not only by being multicultural but also by often being geographically dispersed, being psychologically distant, and working on highly complex projects having considerable impact on company objectives.

Transnational teams tend to be **virtual teams,** communicating electronically more than face to face, although other types of teams may operate virtually as well. Virtual teams face difficult challenges: building trust, cohesion, and team identity, and overcoming the isolation of virtual team members.[18] Exhibit 14.1 suggests ways that managers can improve the effectiveness of virtual teams. As discussed in "Multiple Generations at Work," universities are experimenting with ways to train students to work effectively in global virtual teams.

In today's fast-changing, unpredictable environment, **teaming** is a strategy of teamwork on the fly.[19] In teaming, organizations create many temporary, changing teams, and you might feel like you are in a shifting series of temporary pick-up basketball games, working with different teammates and facing different challenges. You will leave one team when it has achieved (or failed at) its goal and join new teams when new opportunities arise. Because

project and development teams

Teams that work on long-term projects but disband once the work is completed.

parallel teams

Teams that operate separately from the regular work structure and exist temporarily.

management teams

Teams that coordinate and provide direction to the subunits under their jurisdiction and integrate work among subunits.

transnational model

An organizational model characterized by centralizing certain functions in locations that best achieve cost economies; basing other functions in the company's national subsidiaries to facilitate greater local responsiveness; and fostering communication among subsidiaries to permit transfer of technological expertise and skills.

virtual teams

Teams that are physically dispersed and communicate electronically more than face-to-face.

teaming

A strategy of teamwork on the fly, creating many temporary, changing teams.

One example of a project and development team is the Omnica product development team. The 27-person team is responsible for producing medical and high-tech products for their clients faster and more efficiently than they could by any other means.
Courtesy of Omnica Corporation

Multiple Generations at Work

Preparing for Global Virtual Teamwork

Approximately 1.3 billion people worldwide soon will be engaged in virtual work. IBM estimates that nearly half of its 400,000 employees and contractors already work remotely, many from dispersed locations. Companies are equipping their employees for virtual work with advanced videoconferencing software as well as mobile devices like smartphones and tablets.

Employees all need to master the necessary skills to collaborate effectively with international stakeholders in virtual settings. The skills fall into two broad areas: (1) using online sharing tools like Google Docs and Drop Box and communication technology like online chat text; and (2) cross-cultural skills such as adapting to language and value differences, overcoming stereotypes, and coordinating across different time zones.[20]

To prepare students to work effectively in global virtual teams, instructors from several universities in multiple countries engaged in a large-scale collaboration project. Over 6,000 business students were assigned to mostly seven-member, multinational teams. Working together virtually, the teams were tasked with developing a proposal for creating a new product for a client company and analyzing how the product would be brought to market. Instructors graded the projects and feedback was collected from the students regarding how much they learned. The global virtual team assignments helped students:[21]

1. Improve their understanding of the challenges associated with global virtual teamwork;
2. Change their attitudes toward different cultures (reduction in perceived differences); and
3. Use more effective behaviors with regard to team leadership, coordination, and communication.

Are you ready to be an effective member or leader of a global virtual team?

---

no two projects are alike, people need to get up to speed quickly on brand-new topics again and again. Because solutions can come from anywhere, team members can, too.

Self-Managed Teams

traditional work groups

Groups that have no managerial responsibilities.

Today many types of work teams exist, with different labels.[22] **Traditional work groups** have no managerial responsibilities. The frontline manager plans, organizes, staffs, directs, and controls them, and other groups provide support activities, including quality control and maintenance.

self-managed teams

Autonomous work groups in which workers are trained to do all or most of the jobs in a unit, have no immediate supervisor, and make decisions previously made by frontline supervisors.

But the trend is toward giving teams more autonomy so that workers are trained to do all or most of the jobs in the unit, and they make decisions previously made by frontline supervisors.[23] People sometime resist **self-managed teams,** in part because they don't want so much responsibility and the change is difficult.[24] In addition, people often don't like to do performance evaluation of teammates or to fire people, and poorly managed conflict may be a particular problem in self-managed teams.[25] But compared with traditionally managed teams, self-managed teams appear to be more productive, have lower costs,

---

EXHIBIT 14.1

Best Practices of Virtual Team Leaders

1. Establish and maintain trust through the use of communication technology.
2. Ensure diversity in the team is understood, appreciated, and leveraged.
3. Manage virtual work cycle and meetings.
4. Monitor team progress through the use of technology.
5. Enhance external visibility of the team and its members.
6. Ensure individuals benefit from participating in virtual teams.

SOURCE: Adapted from: A. Malhotra, A. Majchrzak, and B. Rosen, "Leading Virtual Teams," *Academy of Management Perspectives,* February 2007, pp. 60–70. Reproduced with permission of Academy of Management via Copyright Clearance Center.

Management in Action

SELF-MANAGED TEAMS AT WHOLE FOODS MARKET

To spur innovation and strengthen commitment, Whole Foods Market empowers employees to participate in planning and decision making with their teams. Within a store, members of teams are involved in decisions concerning product selection and merchandising (the way products are displayed to entice buyers) as well as efforts to improve efficiency. They also contribute to decisions about hiring and compensation.

The company is widely known for team member involvement in hiring decisions, but employees support rather than control the entire hiring process. A human resource employee at each store or other facility screens job applications and selects candidates with the necessary skills and concern for customer service. Candidates who pass the initial screening may be interviewed by one or more store leaders. (Applicants to lead teams generally interview with a group.) Each employee hired then begins an orientation period, during which he or she has probationary status. After the new employee has worked with the team for one to three months, the team meets to decide whether to keep the person on the team, based on whether he or she meets the job requirements, follows company policies and procedures, provides excellent customer service, and works well with the team. Two-thirds must vote in favor of the employee; otherwise, the person can try to join another team or will have to leave the company.

Whole Foods recognizes that for empowerment to succeed, employees need information and other resources to support them in carrying out their responsibilities. Managers share information about the company's financial performance, and everyone can see a list of the gross pay of every team member, including top executives. The company also provides key information for decisions about benefits, starting with the total amount the company will allocate to that expense. Every three years, employees vote on which benefits they want to receive as part of their compensation package. The company provides a list of possible benefits, identifying the cost of each one. Then the employees set priorities within the spending limit.

Rewards, too, are linked to teamwork. Most incentive pay, such as bonuses, is tied to team performance. As Co-CEO John Mackey has said, "We have a shared fate. We either succeed together or we fail together."[26]

- What advantages does teamwork offer to Whole Foods Market?
- Why do you think human resource professionals conduct the initial screening process for new hires? What might be the consequences of having the store teams carry out the entire process of hiring and rewarding team members?

---

provide better customer service, provide higher quality, have better safety records, and are more satisfying for members.

Autonomous work groups control decisions about and execution of a complete range of tasks—acquiring raw materials and performing operations, quality control, maintenance, and shipping. They are fully responsible for an entire product or an entire part of a production process. **Self-designing teams** do all of that and go one step further—they also have control over the design of the team. They decide themselves whom to hire, whom to fire, and what tasks the team will perform.

When teams reach the point of being truly self-managed, results have included lower costs and greater levels of team productivity, quality, and customer satisfaction.[27] Autonomous teams are known to improve the organization's financial and overall performance.[28] For example, at Lockheed Martin's Missiles and Fire Control facility in Troy, Alabama, all members of the workforce are assigned to self-directed work teams, and many also participate in performance management teams, which set goals and monitor progress. The teams have achieved 100 percent on-time delivery, 99 percent of first-pass production meeting quality standards, and a 43 percent cut in energy consumption per unit produced.[29]

In trying to take such practices to operations outside the United States, managers need to recognize that cultural differences such as those described in Chapter 6 may affect how employees react to being given decision-making authority. As you learn more about the self-managed teams at Whole Foods Market, described in "Management in Action: Progress Report," consider whether this kind of employee empowerment would continue to be effective if the company expanded into other countries with different cultures.

autonomous work groups

Groups that control decisions about and execution of a complete range of tasks.

self-designing teams

Teams with the responsibilities of autonomous work groups, plus control over hiring, firing, and deciding what tasks members perform.

Teams at Lockheed Martin have achieved success in terms of on-time delivery and production standards, allowing the company to meet customer demand.

© NU Collection/Alamy

How Groups Become Real Teams

The words *group* and *team* often are used interchangeably.[30] Modern managers sometimes use the word *teams* to the point that it has become a cliché; they talk about teams while skeptics perceive no real teamwork.

Therefore making a distinction between groups and teams can be useful. A *working group* is a collection of people who work in the same area or have been drawn together to undertake a task but do not necessarily come together as a unit and achieve significant performance improvements. A real **team** is formed of people (usually a small number) with complementary skills who trust one another and are committed to a common purpose, common performance goals, and a common approach for which they hold themselves mutually accountable.[31]

Groups become true teams via basic group processes, critical periods, and the management practices described throughout this chapter.

Group Processes

Assume you are the leader of a newly formed group—actually a bunch of people. What will you face as you attempt to develop your group into a high-performing team? If groups are to develop successfully, they will engage in various processes, including the broad categories detailed in Exhibit 14.2

Virtual teams also go through these stages of group development.[32] The forming stage is characterized by unbridled optimism: "I believe we have a great team and will work well

team

A small number of people with complementary skills who are committed to a common purpose, set of performance goals, and approach for which they hold themselves mutually accountable; see also *groups.*

Forming	Group members attempt to lay the ground rules for what types of behavior are acceptable.
Storming	Hostilities and conflict arise, and people jockey for positions of power and status.
Norming	Group members agree on their shared goals, and norms and closer relationships develop.
Performing	The group channels its energies into performing its tasks.

EXHIBIT 14.2
Categories of Team
Development

SOURCE: Adapted from: B. W. Tuckman, "Developmental Sequence in Small Groups," *Psychological Bulletin* 63 (1965), pp. 384–99.

together. We all understand the importance of the project and intend to take it seriously." Optimism turns into reality shock in the storming stage: "No one has taken a leadership role. We have not made the project the priority that it deserves." The norming stage comes at about the halfway point in the project life cycle, in which people refocus and recommit: "You must make firm commitments to a specific time schedule." The performing stage is the dash to the finish as teammates show the discipline needed to meet the deadline.

Groups don't necessarily go through those processes in that particular sequence, but all the processes are important. From a leadership perspective, it is particularly useful to know the two most fundamental phases of team functioning: a transition phase of planning and establishing the group's mission, goals, and processes, and an action phase in which the team executes the work activities that contribute directly to it performance goals.[33] Think about how often groups dive into their work without adequately tackling the transition phase and the problems that arise when they neglect that phase.

Critical Periods

Groups pass through critical periods, or times when they are particularly open to formative experiences.[34] The first such critical period is in the forming stage, at the first meeting, when rules and roles are established that set longer-lasting precedents. A second critical period is the midway point between the initial meeting and a deadline (e.g., completing a project or making a presentation). At this point, the group has enough experience to understand its work; it comes to realize that time is becoming a scarce resource and it must get on with it; and there is enough time left to change its approach if necessary.

In the initial meeting, the group should establish desired norms, roles, and other determinants of effectiveness, which are discussed throughout this chapter. At the second critical period (the midpoint), groups should renew or open lines of communication with outside constituencies. The group can use fresh information from its external environment to revise its approach to performing its task and ensure that it meets the needs of customers and clients. Without these activities, groups may get off on the wrong foot from the beginning, and members may never revise their behavior in the appropriate direction.[35]

Teaming Challenges

In today's era of teaming, fast-forming, fast-acting, temporary groups do not have the luxury of time to allow all necessary team processes to develop slowly and naturally. Practices that are particularly helpful in this context[36] include (1) emphasizing the team's purpose, including why it exists, what's at stake, and what its shared values are; (2) building psychological safety, making clear that people need to and can freely speak up, be honest, disagree, offer ideas, raise issues, share their knowledge, ask questions, or show fallibility without fear that others will think less of them or criticize them; (3) embracing failure, understanding that mistakes are inevitable, errors should be acknowledged, and learning as we go is a way to create new knowledge while we execute; and (4) putting conflict to work by explaining how we arrive at our views, expressing interest in one another's thinking and analyses, and attempting fully to understand and capitalize on others' diverse perspectives.[37]

The leader, and team members who want to help the team perform well, should ask for, expect, and model these behaviors.

Why Groups Sometimes Fail

Team building does not necessarily progress smoothly and culminate in a well-oiled team and superb performance.[38] Some groups never do work out. Such groups can be frustrating for managers and members, who may feel teams are a waste of time and that the difficulties outweigh the benefits.

It is not easy to build high-performance teams. *Teams* is often just a word management uses to describe merely putting people into groups. "Teams" sometimes are launched with little or no training or support systems. For example, both managers and group members need new skills to make a group work. These skills include negotiating goals that everyone can get behind, delivering on promises made, speaking up in groups to share ideas and build cooperation, recognizing and getting along with people's different work styles, and finding constructive ways to deal with conflict.[39] Giving up some control is very difficult for managers from traditional systems, but they have to realize they will gain control in the long run by creating stronger, better-performing units.

Teams should be empowered,[40] as discussed in Chapter 13. The benefits of teams are reduced when they are not allowed to make important decisions—in other words, when management doesn't trust them with important responsibilities. If teams must acquire permission for every innovative idea, they will revert to making safe, traditional decisions.[41]

Empowerment enhances team performance even among virtual teams. Empowerment for virtual teams includes thorough training in using the technologies and strong technical support from management. Some virtual teams have periodic face-to-face interactions, which help performance; empowerment is particularly helpful for virtual teams that don't often meet face to face.[42]

> Empowerment enhances team performance even among virtual teams.

In today's fast-moving business environment, the difference between success and failure often lies with whether people can rapidly form and contribute to one team after another as new opportunities and challenges arise. Teamwork fails when individuals have not considered what they bring to a team and how to bring out the best in others. To be successful, team members must apply clear thinking and appropriate practices.[43] That is what this entire chapter is about.

Building Effective Teams

All the considerations just described form the building blocks of an effective work team. But what does it really mean for a team to be effective? Team effectiveness is defined by three criteria.[44]

1. *Team productivity.* The output of the team meets or exceeds the standards of quantity and quality expected by the customers, inside and outside the organization, who receive the team's goods or services.

2. *Member satisfaction.* Team members realize satisfaction of their personal needs.

3. *Member commitment.* Team members remain committed to working together again; that is, the group doesn't burn out and disintegrate after a grueling project. Looking back, the members are glad they were involved. In other words, effective teams remain viable and have good prospects for repeated success in the future.[45]

Performance Focus

The key element of effective teamwork is commitment to a common purpose.[46] The best teams are those that have been given an important performance challenge by management and then have reached a common understanding and appreciation of their purpose. Without such understanding and commitment, a group will be just a bunch of individuals.

The best teams also work hard at developing a common understanding of how they will work together to achieve their purpose.[47] They discuss and agree on such details as how tasks will be allocated and how they will make decisions. The team should examine its performance strategies and be open to changing them when appropriate. For example, work teams usually standardize at least some processes, but they should be willing to try creative new ideas if the situation calls for them.[48] With a clear, strong, motivating purpose and effective performance strategies, people will pull together into a powerful force that has a chance to achieve extraordinary things.

The team's general purpose should be translated into specific, measurable performance goals.[49] You learned in Chapter 13 about how goals motivate individual performance. Performance can be defined by collective end products instead of an accumulation of individual products.[50] Team-based performance goals help define and distinguish the team's product, encourage communication within the team, energize and motivate team members, provide feedback on progress, signal team victories (and defeats), and ensure that the team focuses clearly on results. It is not simple in practice, but teams with both difficult goals and incentives to attain them tend to achieve the highest performance levels.[51]

The best team-based measurement systems inform top management of the team's level of performance and help the team understand its own processes and gauge its own progress. Ideally, the team plays the lead role in designing its own measurement system. This responsibility is a great indicator of whether the team is truly empowered.[52]

Teams, like individuals, need feedback on their performance. Feedback from customers is especially crucial. Some customers for the team's products are inside the organization. Teams should be responsible for satisfying customers and should be given or should seek performance feedback.

Better yet, wherever possible, teams should interact directly with external customers who make the ultimate buying decisions about their goods and services. External customers typically provide the most honest, and most crucial and useful, performance feedback of all.[53]

Motivating Teamwork

Sometimes individuals work less hard and are less productive when they are members of a group. Such **social loafing** occurs when individuals believe that their contributions are not important, others will do the work for them, their lack of effort will go undetected, or they will be the lone sucker if they work hard but others don't. Perhaps you have seen social loafing in some of your student teams.[54] Conversely, sometimes individuals work harder when they are members of a group than when they are working alone. This **social facilitation effect** occurs because individuals usually are more motivated when others are present, they are concerned with what others think of them, and they want to maintain a positive self-image.

A social facilitation effect is maintained—and a social loafing effect can be avoided—when group members know each other, they can observe and communicate with one another, clear performance goals exist, the task is meaningful to the people working on it, they believe that their efforts matter and others will not take advantage of them, and the culture supports teamwork.[55] Thus, under ideal circumstances, everyone works

social loafing

Working less hard and being less productive when in a group.

social facilitation effect

Working harder when in a group than when working alone.

Accountability to one another, rather than just to the boss, is an essential aspect of good teamwork.

hard, contributes in concrete ways to the team's work, and is accountable to other team members. Accountability to one another, rather than just to the boss, is an essential aspect of good teamwork. Accountability inspires mutual commitment and trust.[56] Trust in your teammates—and their trust in you—may be the ultimate key to effectiveness.

Team effort is also generated by designing the team's task to be motivating. Techniques for creating motivating tasks appear in the guidelines for job enrichment discussed in Chapter 13. Tasks are motivating when they use a variety of member skills and provide high task variety, identity, significance, autonomy, and performance feedback.

Ultimately, teamwork is motivated by tying rewards to team performance.[57] Furthermore, combining individual and shared rewards can reduce social loafing and increase team performance.[58] If team performance can be measured validly, team-based rewards can be given accordingly.

It is not easy to move from a system of rewards based on individual performance to one based on team performance and cooperation. It also may not be appropriate unless people are truly interdependent and must collaborate to attain true team goals.[59] Team-based rewards are often combined with regular salaries and rewards based on individual performance. At the National Information Solutions Cooperative, which provides utilities with accounting and billing services, rewards for teamwork include bonuses based on the company's and division's financial performance. In addition, individual performance reviews (which affect compensation decisions) include an assessment of how well employees collaborate. Although NISC meets industry standards for salaries, employees say what engages them most is experiencing NISC's supportive climate, encouragement of new ideas, and concern for helping customers.[60]

If team performance is difficult to measure validly, then desired behaviors, activities, and processes that indicate good teamwork can be rewarded. Individuals in teams can be given differential rewards based on teamwork indicated by active participation, cooperation, leadership, and other contributions to the team.

If team members are to be rewarded differentially, such decisions are better *not* left only to the boss.[61] They should be made by the team itself through peer ratings or multirater evaluation systems. Why? Team members are in a better position to observe, know, and make valid reward allocations. Finally, the more teams the organization has, and the more a full team orientation exists, the more valid and effective it will be to distribute rewards via gainsharing and other organizationwide incentives.

Member Contributions

Team members should be selected and trained so that they become effective contributors to the team. The teams themselves often hire their new members. MillerCoors Brewing Company and Eastman Chemical teams select members based on the results of tests designed to predict how well they will contribute to team success in an empowered environment. At website design firm Geonetric, team members are responsible for budgets and revenues, and present companywide project updates each month.[62]

Generally, the skills required by teams include technical or functional expertise, problem-solving and decision-making skills, and interpersonal skills. Some managers and teams mistakenly overemphasize some skills, particularly technical or functional ones, and underemphasize the others. A study found that groups in which members shared sad feelings performed better at analytical tasks and difficult decisions, and groups did better at creative tasks if they shared positive emotions.[63] Learning to share emotions appropriately can therefore be an important skill for team success. For the best team performance, all three types of skills should be represented, and developed, among team members.

The "Social Enterprise" box discusses an innovative way that individuals contribute to one another's success.

Social Enterprise

Paying for Co-working Space with Social Capital

Freelancers, entrepreneurs, and remote workers who prefer not to work at home frequently turn to nontraditional work locations to get their work done. Cafés or coffee houses are one option, but can be crowded, loud, and often lack critical tools for virtual workers like high-speed Wi-Fi, printers, and a more work-focused "vibe." Growing in popularity since the mid-2000s, co-working spaces provide all of these attributes and more; they offer a space on a temporary basis (hourly, daily, weekly, and so forth) from which to work and connect people. Such interactions can lead to exchanging business or project ideas, providing strategic advice, or acquiring new projects.

One question that is important to co-working companies is how much to charge individuals for this service. While many co-working firms like New York–based WeWork, NextSpace in California, and WorkBar in Boston all charge workers for daily use of their workspaces, this is not the case for some co-working companies in Europe. For example, Netherlands-based Seats2Meet offers "nearly 80,000 seats across its locations in exchange for nothing more than 'social capital,' or the sharing of knowledge and expertise." The seats are located in train stations, hospitals, libraries, and schools where there is underutilized space. How does Seats2Meet earn revenue? It offers another 240,000 (or 80 percent) seats in meeting rooms and private offices at a cost of $22–$65 per day.

Customers who receive the seats at no cost complete an online profile before arriving at the location. The profile, which captures "who they are, what they're working

© Mandel Ngan/AFP/Getty Images

on that day, and what they consider their area of expertise," is used to assign individuals to a desk with individuals with similar interests, skills, and projects. These customers are expected to give strategic advice in their expertise area to paying and nonpaying customers. The model is gaining traction. Since its founding in 2005 by Ronald van den Hoff, Seats2Meet has opened new operations throughout the Netherlands and in Ecuador, Egypt, Brazil, Japan, and the United Kingdom.[64]

Questions

- Do you think the model used by Seats2Meet would work in the United States? Why or why not?

- In what ways can social capital help you in running a start-up firm or doing freelance projects?

Norms

Norms are shared beliefs about how people should think and behave. For example, some people like to keep information and knowledge to themselves, but teams should try to establish a norm of knowledge sharing because it can improve team performance.[65] Teams perform better when they think and talk about their tasks (duties, equipment, and resources) and about how they interact with and depend on one another.[66] From the organization's standpoint, norms can be positive or negative. In some teams, everyone works hard; in other groups, employees are antimanagement and do as little work as possible. Some groups develop norms of taking risks, others of being conservative.[67] A norm could dictate that employees speak either favorably or critically of the company. Team members may show concern about poor safety practices, drug and alcohol abuse, and employee theft, or they may not care about these issues (or may even condone such practices). Health consciousness is the norm among executives at some companies, but smoking is the norm at tobacco companies. Some groups have norms of distrust and of being closed toward one another; but as you might guess, norms of trust and open discussion about conflict are better for group performance.[68]

norms

Shared beliefs about how people should think and behave.

The mission of Cassini Imaging Science Team is to guide the cameras that take photos of the outer reaches of space. Though the team is widely dispersed (members' locations include New York, California, and Belgium), they are united by a shared sense of purpose and a high value placed on scientific knowledge and technical excellence.

© NASA, ESA, and A. Nota

roles

Different sets of expectations for how different individuals should behave.

task specialist role

An individual who has more advanced job-related skills and abilities than other group members possess.

team maintenance role

Individual who develops and maintains team harmony.

cohesiveness

The degree to which a group is attractive to its members, members are motivated to remain in the group, and members influence one another.

A professor described his consulting experiences at two companies that exhibited different norms in their management teams.[69] At Federal Express Corporation, a young manager interrupted the professor's talk by proclaiming that a recent decision by top management ran counter to the professor's point about corporate planning. He was challenging top management to defend its decision. A hot debate ensued, and after an hour everyone went to lunch without a trace of hard feelings. But at another corporation, the professor opened a meeting by asking a group of top managers to describe the company's culture. There was silence. He asked again. More silence. Then someone passed him an unsigned note that read, "Dummy, can't you see that we can't speak our minds? Ask for the input anonymously, in writing." As you can see, norms are important and can vary greatly from one group to another.

Roles

Roles are different sets of expectations for how different individuals should behave. Whereas norms apply generally to all team members, different roles exist for different members within the norm structure.

Two important sets of roles must be performed.[70] **Task specialist roles** are filled by individuals who have particular job-related skills and abilities. These employees keep the team moving toward accomplishment of the objectives. **Team maintenance roles** develop and maintain harmony within the team. They boost morale, give support, provide humor, soothe hurt feelings, and generally exhibit a concern with members' well-being.

Note the similarity between these roles and the important task performance and group maintenance leadership behaviors you learned about in Chapter 12. As suggested in that chapter, some of these roles will be more important than others at different times and under different circumstances. But these behaviors need not be carried out only by one or two leaders; any member of the team can assume them at any time. Both types of roles can be performed by different individuals to maintain an effectively functioning work team.

Beyond what you read about in Chapter 12, what roles should team leaders perform? Superior leaders are better at relating, scouting, persuading, and empowering than are average team leaders.[71] Relating includes exhibiting more social and political awareness, caring for team members, and building trust. Scouting means seeking information from managers, peers, and specialists, and investigating problems systematically. Persuading means not only influencing the team members but also obtaining external support for teams. Empowerment includes delegating authority, being flexible regarding team decisions, and coaching. Leaders also should roll up their sleeves and do real work to accomplish team goals, not just supervise.[72]

Finally, recall from Chapter 12 the importance of team leadership, in which group members rotate or share leadership roles.[73]

Cohesiveness

One of the most important properties of a team is cohesiveness.[74] **Cohesiveness** refers to how attractive the team is to its members, how motivated members are to remain in the team, and the degree to which team members influence one another. In general, it refers to how tightly knit the team is.

The Importance of Cohesiveness Cohesiveness is important for two primary reasons. First, it contributes to member satisfaction. In a cohesive team, members communicate and get along well with one another. They feel good about being a part of the team. Even if their jobs are unfulfilling or the organization is oppressive, people gain some satisfaction from enjoying their co-workers.

Second, cohesiveness has a major impact on performance. A study of manufacturing teams showed that performance improvements in both quality and productivity occurred in the most cohesive unit, whereas conflict within another team prevented any quality or productivity improvements.[75] Sports fans read about this all the time. When teams are winning, players talk about the team being close, getting along well, and knowing one another's games. In contrast, losing is attributed to infighting and divisiveness.

Cohesiveness clearly can have a positive effect on performance.[76] But this interpretation is simplistic; exceptions to this intuitive relationship occur. Tightly knit work groups can also be disruptive to the organization, such as when they sabotage the assembly line, get their boss fired, or enforce low performance norms. When does high cohesiveness lead to good performance, and when does it result in poor performance? The ultimate outcome depends on the task and on whether the group has high or low performance norms.

The Task   If the task is to make a decision or solve a problem, cohesiveness can lead to poor performance. Groupthink (discussed in Chapter 3) occurs when a tightly knit group is so cooperative that agreeing with one another's opinions and refraining from criticizing others' ideas become norms. For a cohesive group to make good decisions, it should establish a norm of constructive disagreement. This type of debating is important for groups up to the level of boards of directors.[77] In top management teams it has been shown to improve the financial performance of companies.[78]

But the effect of cohesiveness on performance can be positive, particularly if the task is to produce some tangible output. In day-to-day work groups for which decision making is not the primary task, cohesiveness can enhance performance. However, that depends on the group's performance norms.[79]

Performance Norms   Some groups are better than others at ensuring that their members behave the way the group prefers. Cohesive groups are more effective than noncohesive groups at norm enforcement. But the next question is, Do they have norms of high or low performance?

As Exhibit 14.3 shows, the highest performance occurs when a cohesive team has high-performance norms. But if a highly cohesive group has low-performance norms, that group will have the worst performance. In the group's eyes, however, it will have succeeded in achieving its goal of poor performance. Noncohesive groups with high-performance norms can be effective from the company's standpoint. However, they won't be as productive as they would be if they were more cohesive. Noncohesive groups with low-performance norms perform poorly, but they will not ruin things for management as effectively as can cohesive groups with low-performance norms.

Bottom Line

Cohesive groups are better than noncohesive groups at attaining the goals they want to attain; as a manager, you need to ensure that your team's goals represent good business results. *What happens if a team leader builds a cohesive team but fails to set the right goals?*

Performance norms

		Low	High
Cohesiveness	**High**	High goal attainment (group's perspective) and lowest task performance (management's perspective)	High goal attainment and task performance
	Low	Poor goal attainment and task performance	Moderate goal attainment and task performance

EXHIBIT 14.3
Cohesiveness, Performance Norms, and Group Performance

Building Cohesiveness and High-Performance Norms

As Exhibit 14.3 suggests, managers should build teams that are cohesive and have high-performance norms. The following actions can help create such teams:[80]

1. *Recruit members with similar attitudes, values, and backgrounds.* Similar individuals are more likely to get along with one another. Don't do this, though, if the team's task requires heterogeneous skills and inputs. For example, a homogeneous committee or board might make poor decisions because it will lack different information and viewpoints and may succumb to groupthink. Research has shown that educational diversity and national diversity provide more benefits than limitations to groups' use and application of information.[81]

2. *Maintain high entrance and socialization standards.* Teams and organizations that are difficult to get into have more prestige. Individuals who survive a difficult interview, selection, or training process will be proud of their accomplishment and feel more attachment to the team.

3. *Keep the team small* (but large enough to get the job done). The larger the group, the less important members may feel. Small teams make individuals feel like large contributors. Amazon uses a two-pizza rule when deciding how many people should be on a team. If two pizzas can feed the team (usually between 5–8 members), then the team is not too big.[82]

4. *Help the team succeed, and publicize its successes.* You read about empowerment in the previous chapter; you can empower teams as well as individuals.[83] Be a path–goal leader who facilitates success; the experience of winning brings teams closer together. Then, if you inform superiors of your team's successes, members will believe they are part of an important, prestigious unit. Teams that get into a good performance track continue to perform well as time goes on; groups that don't often enter a downward spiral in which problems compound over time.[84]

5. *Be a participative leader.* Participation in decisions gets team members more involved with one another and striving toward goal accomplishment. Too much autocratic decision making from above can alienate the group from management.

6. *Present a challenge from outside the team.* Competition with other groups makes team members band together to defeat the enemy (witness what happens to school spirit before a big game against an archrival). Some of the greatest teams in business and in science have been focused on winning a competition.[85]

   But don't *you* become the outside threat. If team members dislike you as a boss, they will become more cohesive—but their performance norms will be against you, not with you.

7. *Tie rewards to team performance.* To a large degree, teams are motivated just as individuals are—they do the activities that are rewarded. Make sure that high-performing teams get the rewards they deserve and that poorly performing groups get fewer rewards. Bear in mind that not just monetary rewards but also recognition for good work are powerful motivators. Recognize and celebrate team accomplishments. The team will become more cohesive and perform better to reap more rewards. Performance goals will be high, the organization will benefit from higher team motivation and productivity, and the individual needs of team members will be better satisfied. Ideally, being a member of a high-performing team, recognized as such throughout the organization, will become a badge of honor.[86]

But keep in mind that strong cohesiveness encouraging agreeableness can be dysfunctional. For problem solving and decision making, the team should establish norms promoting an open, constructive atmosphere including honest disagreement over issues without personal conflict and animosity.[87]

Managing Lateral Relationships

Teams do not function in a vacuum; they are interdependent with other teams. For example, **boundary-spanning** teams are responsible for interfacing with other teams to eliminate production bottlenecks and implement new processes and for working with suppliers on quality issues.[88] Boundary-spanning activities[89] crucial to the team are those that entail dealing with people outside the group.

Managing Outward

Several vital roles (see Exhibit 14.4) link teams to their external environments—that is, to other individuals and groups both inside and outside the organization. A specific type of role that spans team boundaries is the **gatekeeper,** a team member who stays abreast of current information in scientific and other fields and informs the group of important developments. Information useful to the group can also include information about resources, trends, and political support throughout the corporation or the industry.[90]

The team's strategy dictates the team's mix of internally versus externally focused roles and how the mix changes over time. General team strategies include informing, parading, and probing.[91] The **informing** strategy entails making decisions with the team and then telling outsiders of the team's intentions. **Parading** means the team's strategy is to emphasize internal team building and achieve external visibility simultaneously. **Probing** involves a focus on external relations. This strategy requires team members to interact frequently with outsiders; diagnose the needs of customers, clients, and higher-ups; and experiment with solutions before taking action.

The appropriate balance between an internal and external strategic focus and between internal and external roles depends on how much the team needs information, support, and resources from outside. When teams have a high degree of dependence on outsiders, probing is the best strategy. Parading teams perform at an intermediate level, and informing teams are likely to fail. They are too isolated from the outside groups on which they depend.

Informing or parading strategies may be more effective for teams that are less dependent on outside groups—for example, established teams working on routine tasks in stable external environments. But for most important work teams—task forces, new product teams, and strategic decision-making teams tackling unstructured problems in rapidly changing external environments—effective performance in roles that involve interfacing with the outside will be vital.

boundary-spanning

Interacting with people in other groups, thus creating linkages between groups.

gatekeeper

A team member who keeps abreast of current developments and provides the team with relevant information.

informing

A team strategy that entails making decisions with the team and then informing outsiders of its intentions.

parading

A team strategy that entails simultaneously emphasizing internal team building and achieving external visibility.

probing

A team strategy that requires team members to interact frequently with outsiders, diagnose their needs, and experiment with solutions.

EXHIBIT 14.4

Teams Link to the External Environment in Different Ways

SOURCE: Adapted from D. G. Ancona, "Outward Bound: Strategies for Team Survival in an Organization," *Academy of Management Journal* 33 (1990), pp. 334–65.

Lateral Role Relationships

Teams do not function in a vacuum; they are interdependent with other teams. These inter-dependencies require coordination and leadership.[92] To help understand the process and make it more productive, we can identify and examine the different types of lateral role relationships and take a strategic approach to building constructive relationships.

> Different teams, like different individuals, have roles to perform.

Different teams, like different individuals, have roles to perform. As teams carry out their roles, several distinct patterns of working relationships develop:[93]

1. *Work flow relationships* emerge as materials are passed from one group to another. A group commonly receives work from one unit, processes it, and sends it to the next unit in the process. Your group, then, will come before some groups and after others in the process.

2. *Service relationships* exist when top management centralizes an activity to which a large number of other units must gain access. Common examples are technology services, libraries, and clerical staff. Such units assist other people to help them accomplish their goals.

3. *Advisory relationships* are created when teams with problems call on centralized sources of expert knowledge. For example, staff members in the human resources or legal department advise work teams.

4. *Audit relationships* develop when people not directly in the chain of command evaluate the methods and performances of other teams. Financial auditors check the books, and technical auditors assess the methods and technical quality of the work.

5. *Stabilization relationships* involve auditing before the fact. In other words, teams sometimes must obtain clearance from others—for example, for large purchases—before they take action.

6. *Liaison relationships* involve intermediaries between teams. Managers often are called on to mediate conflict between two organizational units. Public relations people, sales managers, purchasing agents, and others who work across organizational boundaries serve in liaison roles as they maintain communications between the organization and the outside world.

By assessing each working relationship with another unit (from whom do we receive work, and to whom do we send work? what permissions do we control, and to whom must we go for authorizations?), teams can better understand whom to contact and when, where, why, and how to do so. Coordination throughout the working system improves, problems are avoided or short-circuited before they get too serious, and performance improves.[94]

Managing Conflict

The complex maze of interdependencies throughout organizations provides many oppor-tunities for conflict to arise among groups and teams. Some conflict is constructive for the organization, as we discussed in Chapter 3. Typically, conflict can foster creativity when it is about ideas rather than personalities. In contrast, team members can be committed to maintaining harmony during meetings, but unresolved differences can spill over into nasty remarks outside the office.[95]

Many factors cause great potential for destructive conflict: the sheer number and variety of contacts, ambiguities in jurisdiction and responsibility, differences in goals, competition for scarce resources, different perspectives held by members of different units, varying time horizons in which some units attend to long-term considerations and others focus on short-term needs, and others. For many reasons, and very commonly, subgroups form.[96]

Both demographic and cross-functional heterogeneity initially lead to problems such as stress, lower cooperation, and lower cohesiveness.[97] Transformational leadership (recall Chapter 13), effective diversity management (recall Chapter 11), and constructive conflict management (see the following) can reduce the problems and help realize the often-untapped potential benefits of diversity in teams.[98]

Conflict Styles

Teams inevitably face conflicts and must decide how to manage them. The aim should be to make the conflict productive—that is, to make those involved believe they have benefited rather than lost from the conflict.[99] People believe they have benefited from a conflict when (1) a new solution is implemented, the problem is solved, and it is unlikely to emerge again, and (2) work relationships have been strengthened and people believe they can work together productively in the future.

Teams inevitably face conflicts and must decide how to manage them.

© *Juice Images/Glow Images*

People handle conflict in different ways. You have your own style; others' styles may be similar or may differ. Styles depend in part on the home country's cultural norms. For example, as you learned in Chapter 6, people from some cultures are more concerned with collective than with individual interests, and they are more likely than managers in the United States to turn to higher authorities to make decisions rather than resolve conflicts themselves.[100] But culture aside, any team or individual has several options regarding how to deal with conflicts.[101] These personal styles of dealing with conflict, shown in Exhibit 14.5, are distinguished based on how much people strive to satisfy their own concerns (the assertiveness dimension) and how much they focus on satisfying the other party's concerns (the cooperation dimension).

For example, a common reaction to conflict is **avoidance.** Here, people do nothing to satisfy themselves or others. They either ignore the problem by doing nothing at all or address it by merely smoothing over or deemphasizing the disagreement. This, of course, fails to solve the problem or clear the air. In a large retail company, employees in the marketing department decided they were tired of dealing with the limits placed on them by the security team of the company's information technology (IT) department. Marketing wanted more communication with consumers, while IT security was obsessed with protecting the company's data from unauthorized access. To avoid the conflict, the marketing group set up a website without telling anyone in IT security.[102]

avoidance

A reaction to conflict that involves ignoring the problem by doing nothing at all or deemphasizing the disagreement.

Cooperation

Uncooperative		Cooperative
Assertive Competing		Collaborating
	Compromising	
Unassertive Avoiding		Accommodating

Assertiveness

EXHIBIT 14.5
Conflict Management Strategies

SOURCE: K. Thomas, "Conflict and Conflict Management." In *Handbook of Industrial and Organizational Psychology,* ed. M. D. Dunnette. Copyright © 1976. Reprinted by permission of the author.

accommodation

A style of dealing with conflict involving cooperation on behalf of the other party but not being assertive about one's own interests.

compromise

A style of dealing with conflict involving moderate attention to both parties' concerns.

competing

A style of dealing with conflict involving strong focus on one's own goals and little or no concern for the other person's goals.

collaboration

A style of dealing with conflict emphasizing both cooperation and assertiveness to maximize both parties' satisfaction.

superordinate goals

Higher-level goals taking priority over specific individual or group goals.

mediator

A third party who intervenes to help others manage their conflict.

Accommodation means cooperating on behalf of the other party but not being assertive about one's own interests. **Compromise** involves moderate attention to both parties' concerns, being neither highly cooperative nor highly assertive. This style results in satisficing but not optimizing solutions. **Competing** is a highly competitive response in which people focus strictly on their own wishes and are unwilling to recognize the other person's concerns. Finally, **collaboration** emphasizes both cooperation and assertiveness. The goal is to maximize satisfaction for both parties. At the retail company in the previous example, a consulting firm called Solutionary discovered the website secretly created by the marketing group during a routine test of the company's computer network. Using basic techniques, the consultants were able to hack into the company's network and alter information, such as store prices, very easily. Knowing this would be simple for an outsider to do, the consultants then called together the IT security people and the marketing people to work out a solution that would meet marketing goals without compromising the data in the computer system.[103]

So imagine you and a friend want to go to a movie together, and you have different movies in mind. If he insists that you go to his movie, he is showing the competing style. If you agree, even though you prefer another movie, you are accommodating. If one of you mentions a third movie that neither of you is excited about but both of you are willing to live with, you are compromising. If you realize you don't know all the options, do some research, and find another movie that you're both enthusiastic about, you are collaborating.

Different approaches are necessary at different times.[104] For example, competing can be necessary for cutting costs or dealing with other scarce resources. Compromise may be useful when people are under time pressure, when they need to achieve a temporary solution, or when collaboration fails. People should accommodate when they learn they are wrong or to minimize loss when they are outmatched. Even avoiding may be appropriate if the issue is trivial or resolving the conflict should be someone else's responsibility.

But when the conflict concerns important issues, when both sets of concerns are valid and important, when a creative solution is needed, and when commitment to the solution is vital to implementation, collaboration is the ideal approach. Collaboration can be achieved by airing feelings and opinions, addressing all concerns, and not letting personal attacks interfere with problem solving. An important technique is to invoke **superordinate goals**—higher-level organizational goals toward which everyone should be striving and that ultimately need to take precedence over personal or unit preferences.[105] A superordinate identity can reduce differences and enhance performance.[106] Collaboration offers the best chance of reaching mutually satisfactory solutions based on the ideas and interests of all parties and of maintaining and strengthening work relationships.

Being a Mediator

Managers spend a lot of time trying to resolve conflict between other people. You already may have served as a **mediator,** a third party intervening to help settle a conflict between other people. Third-party intervention, done well, can improve working relationships and help the parties improve their own conflict management, communication, and problem-solving skills.[107]

Some insight comes from a study of human resource (HR) managers and the conflicts with which they deal.[108] HR managers encounter every type of conflict imaginable: interpersonal difficulties from minor irritations to jealousy to fights; operations issues, including union issues, work assignments, overtime, and sick leave; discipline over infractions ranging from drug use and theft to sleeping on the job; sexual harassment and racial bias; pay and promotion issues; and feuds or strategic conflicts among divisions or individuals at the highest organizational levels.

In the study, the HR managers successfully settled most of the disputes. These managers typically follow a four-stage strategy, summarized in Exhibit 14.6. They investigate by interviewing the disputants and others and gathering more information. While talking with the disputants, they seek

HR managers encounter every type of conflict imaginable.

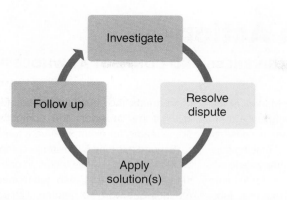

EXHIBIT 14.6
A Four-Stage Model of
Dispute Resolution

SOURCE: Adapted from M. Blum and J. A. Wall Jr., "HRM: Managing Conflicts in the Firm," *Business Horizons,* May–June 1997, pp. 84–87.

both parties' perspectives, remaining as neutral as possible. The discussion should stay issue oriented, not personal. They decide how to resolve the dispute, often in conjunction with the disputants' bosses. In preparing to decide what to do, blame should not be assigned prematurely; at this point they should be exploring solutions. They take action by explaining their decisions and the reasoning, and advise or train the disputants to avoid future incidents. And they follow up by making sure everyone understands the solution, documenting the conflict and the resolution, and monitoring the results by checking back with the disputants and their bosses. Throughout, the objectives of the HR people are to be fully informed so that they understand the conflict; to be active and assertive in trying to resolve it; to be as objective, neutral, and impartial as humanly possible; and to be flexible by modifying their approaches according to the situation.

Here are some other recommendations for more effective conflict management.[109] Don't allow dysfunctional conflict to build, or hope or assume that it will go away. Address it before it escalates. Try to resolve it, and if the first efforts don't work, try others. And remember the earlier discussion (Chapter 13) of procedural justice. Even if disputants are not happy with your decisions, there are benefits to providing fair treatment, making a good-faith effort, giving them a voice in the proceedings, and so on. Caring about others' goals as well as your own will help ensure a collaborative process. Remember, too, that you may be able to ask HR specialists to help with difficult conflicts.

Electronic and Virtual Conflict

When teams are geographically dispersed, as is often the case for virtual teams, team members tend to experience more conflict and less trust.[110] Conflict management affects the success of virtual teams.[111] In a recent study, avoidance hurt performance. Accommodation—conceding to others to maintain harmony rather than assertively attempting to negotiate integrative solutions—had no effect on performance. Collaboration had a positive effect on performance. The researchers also uncovered two surprises: compromise hurt performance, and competition helped performance. Compromises hurt because they often are watered-down, middle-of-the-road, suboptimal solutions. Competitive behavior was useful because the virtual teams were temporary and under time pressure, so having some individuals behave dominantly and impose decisions to achieve efficiency was more useful than detrimental.

When people have problems in business-to-business e-commerce (e.g., costly delays), they tend to behave competitively and defensively rather than collaboratively.[112] Technical problems and recurring problems test people's patience. The conflict will escalate unless people use more cooperative, collaborative styles. Try to prevent conflicts before they arise; for example, make sure your information system is running smoothly before linking with others. Monitor and reduce or eliminate problems as soon as possible. When problems arise, express your willingness to cooperate, and then actually be cooperative. Even technical problems require the social skills of good management.

Management in Action

COHESIVENESS AND CONFLICT AT WHOLE FOODS MARKET

What unifies employees at Whole Foods Market is the sense of mission and shared values. Serving on a team fulfilling a mission gives each team member a sense of purpose, and the team monitors performance, making sure everyone contributes. In addition, unlike many retailers, Whole Foods schedules most of its employees for full-time work, which enables them to learn more about their jobs, build stronger team relationships, and develop a greater commitment to the organization.

A challenge to cohesiveness, however, is one of the very values the company espouses: appreciation of diversity. Whole Foods stresses its commitment to hiring employees from many different backgrounds. Compared with other supermarkets, its dress code offers wide latitude for personal style. To counteract misunderstandings that can occur when people come from different backgrounds and express themselves differently, the company expects team members to communicate frequently and respectfully and to show appreciation for what others contribute.

Co-CEO John Mackey sees a role for competition as well as collaboration. The company encourages teams to compete with one another to be best at what they do. For example, the produce teams might strive to have the biggest sales increase in their region or among all the company's stores. The glory of being the best Whole Foods produce team is a compelling motivator, with or without a bonus. As team members collaborate in trying to outdo other teams, they build the sense of identity Mackey sees in what he considers the company's strongest teams. Some teams, for example, invent team names.

Beyond this kind of desirable competition among teams, conflicts do occur within teams. In one incident that recently made national news, two team members at a store in Albuquerque were suspended (with pay) after they became upset during a team meeting. At the meeting, discussion turned to the men's use of Spanish at work. The two men interpreted statements by the team leader to mean they were forbidden from speaking Spanish while on the job, and they became angry. Management saw their anger as "rude and disrespectful both in an office and in the store in front of customers," so the two were suspended. Through official statements, Whole Foods said it uses English as its "default" language, especially for safety matters, but does not forbid the speaking of other languages. It added that its leadership team would soon review the company's language policy.[113]

- How does Whole Foods promote team cohesiveness? What else can it do?
- How should Whole Foods manage the conflict in its Albuquerque store? What should it do to minimize similar conflicts in the future?
- If you were in this situation, would your conflict management styles involve avoidance, accommodation, compromise, competition, or collaboration? Why?

In the end, of course, conflicts are part of human relationships, whether they occur online or face to face. Members of a virtual team at a software company and members of a deli team at the nearest Whole Foods Market need relevant skills, such as the ability to communicate and cooperate. As you read "Management in Action: Onward," think about the skills needed to keep diverse employees working constructively at Whole Foods.

KEY TERMS

RETAINING WHAT YOU LEARNED

In Chapter 14, you learned that teams can help organizations be more effective, productive, and innovative. Compared to the past, teams now have more authority and may be self-managed. Teams come in several shapes and sizes, including work teams, project and development teams, parallel teams, management teams, transnational teams, and virtual teams. Groups typically experience four stages of development: forming, storming, norming, and performing. A group generally becomes a team when team members commit to a purpose, pursue goals, and hold themselves accountable to one another. Moving from a traditional structure to a team-based approach tends to be challenging for many companies. There are several ways to build high-performance teams, including establishing a common purpose, setting measurable goals, and making sure everyone works hard and contributes in meaningful ways. Team members perform important roles such as gatekeeping, informing, parading, and probing. Inevitably, conflict arises on teams. Five basic interpersonal approaches to managing conflict can be used: avoidance, accommodation, compromise, competition, and collaboration. Techniques for managing conflict between other parties include acting as a mediator and managing virtual conflict.

LO 1 Discuss how teams can contribute to an organization's effectiveness.

- Teams are building blocks for organization structure and forces for productivity, quality, cost savings, speed, change, and innovation.
- They have the potential to provide many benefits for both the organization and individual members.

LO 2 Describe different types of teams.

- Compared with traditional work groups that were closely supervised, today's teams have more authority and often are self-managed.

- Teams now are used in many more ways, for many more purposes, than in the past. Generally, types of teams include work teams, project and development teams, parallel teams, management teams, transnational teams, and virtual teams.
- Types of work teams range from traditional groups with low autonomy to self-designing teams with high autonomy.

LO 3 Summarize how groups become teams.

- Groups carry on a variety of important developmental processes, including forming, storming, norming, and performing (see Exhibit 14.2).
- A true team has members who complement one another; who are committed to a common purpose, performance goals, and approach; and who hold themselves accountable to one another.

LO 4 Explain why groups sometimes fail.

- Teams do not always work well. Some companies underestimate the difficulties of moving to a team-based approach.
- Teams require training, empowerment, and a well-managed transition to make them work.
- Groups may fail to become effective teams unless managers and team members commit to the idea, understand what makes teams work, and implement appropriate practices.

LO 5 Describe how to build an effective team.

- Create a team with a high-performance focus by establishing a common purpose, translating the purpose into measurable team goals, designing the

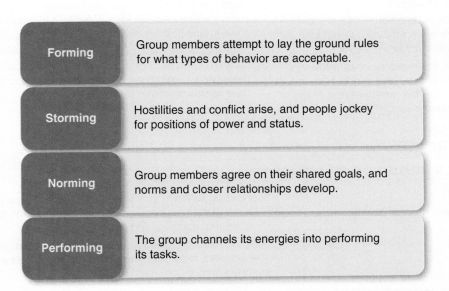

EXHIBIT 14.2
Categories of Team Development

Forming	Group members attempt to lay the ground rules for what types of behavior are acceptable.
Storming	Hostilities and conflict arise, and people jockey for positions of power and status.
Norming	Group members agree on their shared goals, and norms and closer relationships develop.
Performing	The group channels its energies into performing its tasks.

SOURCE: Adapted from B. W. Tuckman, "Development Sequence in Small Groups," *Psychological Bulletin* 63 (1965), pp. 384–99.

team's task so it is intrinsically motivating, designing a team-based performance measurement system, and providing team rewards.

- Work to develop a common understanding of how the team will perform its task. Make it clear that everyone has to work hard and contribute in concrete ways.
- Establish mutual accountability and build trust among members.
- Examine the team's strategies periodically and be willing to adapt.
- Make sure members contribute fully by selecting them appropriately, training them, and checking that all important roles are carried out.
- Take a variety of steps to establish team cohesiveness and high-performance norms.

LO 6   List methods for managing a team's relationships with other teams.

- Don't just manage inwardly. Manage the team's relations with outsiders, too.
- Perform important roles such as gatekeeping, informing, parading, and probing.

- Identify the types of lateral role relationships you have with outsiders. This can help coordinate efforts throughout the work system.

LO 7   Identify ways to manage conflict.

- Managing lateral relationships well can prevent some conflict. But conflict arises because of the sheer number of contacts, ambiguities, goal differences, competition for scarce resources, and different perspectives and time horizons.
- Depending on the situation, five basic interpersonal approaches to managing conflict can be used: avoidance, accommodation, compromise, competition, and collaboration.
- Superordinate goals offer a focus on higher-level organizational goals that can help generate a collaborative relationship.
- Techniques for managing conflict between parties include acting as a mediator and managing virtual conflict.

DISCUSSION QUESTIONS

1. Why do you think some people resist the idea of working in teams? How would you deal with their resistance?

2. Consider a job you have held. To what extent did you work in teams, and how effective was the teamwork? What affected the effectiveness?

3. Experts say that teams are a means, not an end. What do you think they mean? What do you think happens in a company that creates teams just for the sake of having teams because it's a fad or because it sounds good? How can this pitfall be avoided?

4. Choose a sports team with which you are familiar. Assess its effectiveness and discuss the factors that contribute to its level of effectiveness.

5. Assess the effectiveness, as in Question 4, of a student group with which you have been affiliated. Could anything have been done to make it more effective?

6. Consider the various roles members have to perform for a team to be effective. Which roles would play to your strengths, and which to your weaknesses? How can you become a better team member?

7. Discuss personal examples of virtual conflict and how they were managed, well or poorly.

8. What do you think are your own most commonly used approaches to handling conflict? Least common? What can you do to expand your repertoire and become more effective at conflict management?

9. Generate real examples of how superordinate goals have helped resolve a conflict. Identify some current conflicts and provide some specific ideas for how superordinate goals could be used to help.

10. Have you ever been part of a group that was self-managed? What was good about it, and what not so good? Why do many managers resist this idea? Why do some people love the idea of being a member of such a team, while others don't?

11. How might self-managed teams operate differently in different cultures? What are the advantages, disadvantages, and implications of homogeneous versus highly diverse self-managed teams?

EXPERIENTIAL EXERCISES

14.1 STUDENT PROJECT GROUP DEVELOPMENT

OBJECTIVE

To explore how students' project groups develop through various stages.

INSTRUCTIONS

1. Think about the last time you were assigned to a student group to complete a course-related project.

2. Next, write down how your group experienced (if at all) each of the four stages of group development: forming, storming, norming, and performing.

3. The instructor assigns students into groups of three and asks team members to share their answers with one another.

Student Project Group Processes Worksheet

Process (refer to page 463 for definitions)	To what degree did your student project group experience this stage? Explain.
Forming	_____
	_____
	_____
Storming	_____
	_____
	_____
Norming	_____
	_____
	_____
Performing	_____
	_____
	_____
	_____

14.2 WHICH STYLE OF CONFLICT RESOLUTION WOULD YOU USE?

OBJECTIVE

To explore which conflict styles students would use in a variety of workplace scenarios.

INSTRUCTIONS

1. Read each of the following workplace scenarios.

2. Next, choose the conflict style being used by the individual in the scenario.

3. Describe why you think the conflict style will (or will not) help resolve the situation.

Conflict Styles (see pages 459–460 for definitions):

- *Avoidance*
- *Accommodation*
- *Compromise*
- *Competing*
- *Collaboration*

CONFLICT STYLE WORKSHEET

Scenario #1: While at work, Maria and her co-worker notice that a laptop is missing from an employee's cubicle (note that the employee is on vacation). Maria's first impulse is to report the missing laptop to the manager. However, her co-worker thinks there may be an innocent reason for the missing laptop. He wants Maria to join him in speaking with employees who are in the office. Maria agrees to team up with her co-worker but insists that if after one hour they haven't found the missing laptop, they would inform the manager.

Maria is using the _____ conflict style.

To what degree will this style help (or not help) resolve the situation?

_____

_____

_____

Scenario #2: Assume Paul is waiting to hear from his boss whether he is finally going to receive the promotion that he has been promised. Paul's boss just found out that the budget for the new position for which Paul was slotted has been cut. Consequently, he will not receive the promotion. His boss thinks she can get Paul a job transfer and promotion in another division in the company. She needs a few days to make it happen and doesn't want to discuss the situation with Paul until it is a done deal. Paul's boss intends to keep him busy with projects over the next few days until she finds out whether Paul receives the alternate promotion.

Paul's boss is using the _____ conflict style until she hears back from her contact in the other division.

To what degree will this style help (or not help) resolve the situation?

_____

_____

_____

CONCLUDING CASE

EXCEL PRO DRILLING SYSTEMS

Based in Alabama, Excel Pro Drilling Systems sells drilling equipment around the world. Its factories in Brazil, China, the Czech Republic, India, and South Africa run three shifts to keep up with strong demand in developing nations. Excel Pro enjoys profitability, but environmental groups have expressed concern about its impact on climate change. As executives explored their response, they saw that achieving more sustainable resource use also could make the company more efficient and create a more favorable business environment for the long term.

The executives decided to form a group called the Excel Pro Green Team, made up of representatives in each of its locations. Each facility's managers chose three employees, one each from engineering, production, and finance, with leadership skills, English-language ability, and interest in the topic of environmental sustainability. These 18 employees formed the Green Team.

To save money as well as fuel, the Green Team operates as a virtual team. Its members meet by videoconferencing once a month. Between meetings, they share thoughts via e-mail and in a social-media-style page Excel Pro created for this purpose.

Initially, all the Green Team members were enthusiastic. The Czech and Brazilian representatives even came to the first meeting with specific ideas. Other team members were inspired to prepare ideas for the next meeting, but several were concerned that the team needed a plan establishing goals and a time line before the team addressed specific actions. Most of the third meeting was devoted to debating whether to establish an action plan or refine the ideas already submitted. Frustrated, the South African representatives took one idea to their facility's management for approval and began to implement it without telling the rest of the team.

By the fourth meeting, the representatives in India and the Czech Republic were openly complaining that meetings were always scheduled at times convenient for the headquarters employees. The Chinese team members agreed; in fact, one had quietly stopped attending meetings, although she did continue to participate in the exchange of e-mail ideas. The debate about whether headquarters should always schedule meetings lasted for 45 minutes, after which no one was in any mood to discuss sustainability.

Two of the Alabama team representatives took their frustration to their managers. The executive team investigated and decided the team needed to be unified behind a common goal. They directed the team to present three resource-saving ideas by the end of the year, and they offered a reward system to promote teamwork. The team members are each allocated 100 points a month. Whenever one team member appreciates another's actions, he or she gives that person points. All team members' point scores are viewable by the whole team at a shared website. At the end of the year, the points earned by each employee will be exchanged for cash rewards in the local currency. The executives hope the program will motivate greater cooperation.

DISCUSSION QUESTIONS

1. What went wrong in the formation of the Green Team? What should Excel Pro have done differently?

2. What conditions contribute to this team's cohesiveness? What reduces cohesiveness?

3. What do you think of the points plan? How should Excel Pro's management help the Green Team manage its conflict?

CHAPTER 15

Communicating

> The single biggest problem with communication is the illusion that it has taken place.
>
> —G. B. SHAW

Management in Action

HOW YAHOO'S MARISSA MAYER TRIED TO GET EMPLOYEES TALKING

Before Google, there was Yahoo, one of the most popular Internet search engines of the 1990s. The company, founded by two Stanford graduate students, was innovative and fun, its employees calling themselves Yahoos. But then Yahoo became—at least in Internet years—a stodgy old-timer. Despite hanging onto 700 million users, Yahoo had falling revenues and market share and a shrinking workforce. It was launching no hit products for mobile devices or social media.

To bring new life to Yahoo, its board of directors turned to today's most popular Internet search firm, Google, and recruited away Marissa Mayer. Mayer, Google's vice president of location and local services, was one of its original employees (its first female engineer). She has a reputation for being brilliant, hardworking, and highly successful at developing people.

© David Paul Morris/Bloomberg via Getty Images

One of Mayer's chief concerns when she arrived at Yahoo was that employees seemed detached and demoralized. At other big-name Internet companies and hot start-ups, employees labor through the night, but Yahoo's parking lots emptied out promptly at five. Mayer was determined to reignite the company's former enthusiasm. She started with a memo announcing her long-standing respect for Yahoo and determination to make it "the absolute best place to work," and she set up weekly Friday meetings to bring everyone up to speed on her plans and Yahoo's performance. Yahoo also began offering free food in its cafeteria and gave its employees new smartphones.

Mayer's next move sparked controversy. She decided to bring people close together by requiring their presence in the workplace. In a memo from HR director Jackie Reses, Yahoo announced that employees would no longer be allowed work-from-home arrangements; they must be at the office with their colleagues. Reses wrote, "We need to be one Yahoo!, and that starts with physically being together." She went on to state how important spontaneous communication can be: "Some of the best decisions and insights come from hallway and cafeteria discussions, meeting new people, and impromptu team meetings."

Most critics predicted demotivation or saw hypocrisy in a CEO who had recently given birth imposing restrictions that could make scheduling more difficult for working parents. However, Mayer insisted the new policy is not about motivation or child care, but about bringing employees close together so they can communicate more easily. Employees who happen to pass by each other's desks or sit near one another at lunch are likelier to build ties, ask questions, and trade ideas. Those interactions, Mayer believes, will open the door to more innovation and camaraderie.[1]

Marissa Mayer values spontaneous workplace conversations so much that she risked criticism by banning the practice of working from home. As you read this chapter, consider how communication among employees can build commitment and nourish creativity.

As Yahoo's Marissa Mayer is well aware, effective communication is a fundamental component of work performance and organizational effectiveness.[2] It is a primary means by which managers carry out the responsibilities described throughout this book, such as making group decisions, sharing a vision, coordinating individuals and work groups, hiring and motivating employees, and leading teams. In these and other areas, managers have to be able to share thoughts clearly and convincingly, and they have to listen effectively to others. In this chapter, we present important communication concepts and some practical guidelines for improving your effectiveness. We also discuss communication at the organizational level.

Interpersonal Communication

communication

The transmission of information and meaning from one party to another through the use of shared symbols.

Communication is the transmission of information and meaning from one party to another through the use of shared symbols. Exhibit 15.1 shows a general model of how one person communicates with another.

The sender initiates the process by conveying information to the receiver—the person for whom the message is intended. The sender has a meaning he or she wishes to communicate and encodes the meaning into symbols (the words chosen for the message). Then the sender transmits, or sends, the message through some channel, such as a verbal or written medium.

The receiver decodes the message (e.g., reads it) and attempts to interpret the sender's meaning. The receiver may provide feedback to the sender by encoding a message in response to the sender's message.

The communication process often is hampered by noise, or interference in the system, that blocks perfect understanding. Noise could be anything that interferes with accurate communication: vibrating cell phones, thoughts about other things, or simple fatigue or stress. The model in Exhibit 15.1 is more than a theoretical treatment of the communication process: it points out the key ways in which communications can break down. Mistakes can be made at each stage of the model. A manager who is alert to potential problems can perform each step carefully to ensure more effective communication. The model also helps explain the topics discussed next: the differences between one-way and two-way communication, communication pitfalls, misperception, and the various communication channels.

one-way communication

A process in which information flows in only one direction—from the sender to the receiver, with no feedback loop.

One-Way versus Two-Way Communication

In **one-way communication,** information flows in only one direction—from the sender to the receiver, with no feedback loop (see Exhibit 15.1). A manager sends an e-mail to a subordinate without asking for a response. An employee phones the information technology (IT) department and leaves a message requesting repairs for her computer. A supervisor scolds a production worker about defects and then storms away.

two-way communication

A process in which information flows in two directions—the receiver provides feedback, and the sender is receptive to the feedback.

When receivers respond to senders—Person B becomes the sender and Person A the receiver—**two-way communication** has occurred. One-way communication in situations like those just described can become two-way if the manager's e-mail invites the receiver to reply with any questions, the IT department returns the employee's call and asks for

EXHIBIT 15.1
A Model of One-Way
Communication

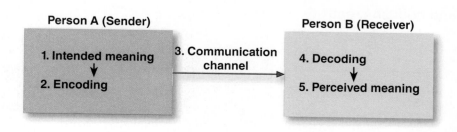

details about the computer problem, and the supervisor calms down and listens to the production worker's explanation of why defects are occurring.

True two-way communication means not only that the receiver provides feedback but also that the sender is receptive to the feedback. In these constructive exchanges, information is shared between both parties rather than merely delivered from one person to the other.

Because it is faster and easier for the sender, one-way communication is much more common than it should be. A busy executive finds it easier to dash off an e-mail message than to discuss a nagging problem with a subordinate. Also, he doesn't have to deal with questions or be challenged by someone who disagrees.

Two-way communication is more difficult and time-consuming than one-way communication. However, it is more accurate; fewer mistakes occur, and fewer problems arise. When receivers have a chance to ask questions, share concerns, and make suggestions or modifications, they understand more precisely what is being communicated and what they should do with the information.[3] Effectively sharing information among teammates is a prime contributor to performance.[4]

These advantages of two-way communication are why Cisco manager Randy Pond wants to see and hear the people he is meeting with. If some participants are in remote locations, Pond, who is Cisco's executive vice president of operations, processes, and systems, uses a videoconference. During one such meeting, when Pond made a statement, he watched his colleagues on his computer screen and noticed that one put his head in his hands. Pond reminded the participants that he could see them, adding, "If you disagree, tell me." This prodding opened up a fuller discussion of the ideas under consideration.[5]

Communication Pitfalls

As we know from personal experience, the sender's intended message does not always get across to the receiver. You are operating under an illusion if you think there is a perfect correlation between what you say and what people hear.[6] Errors can occur in all stages of the communication process. In the encoding stage, words can be misused, decimal points entered in the wrong places, facts left out, or ambiguous phrases inserted. In the transmission stage, a message may get lost on a cluttered desk, the words on the screen could be too small to read from the back of the room, or words might be spoken with ambiguous inflections.

Decoding problems arise when the receiver doesn't listen carefully or reads too quickly and overlooks a key point. And of course receivers can misinterpret the message: A reader draws the wrong conclusion from an unclear text message, a listener takes a general statement by the boss too personally, or a sideways glance is taken the wrong way.

More generally, people's perceptual and filtering processes create misinterpretations. **Perception** is the process of receiving and interpreting information. As you know, such processes are not perfectly objective. They are subjective because people's self-interested motives and attitudes toward the sender and toward the message create biased interpretations. People often assume that others share their views and naturally pay more attention to their own views than to those of others.[7] But perceptual differences get in the way of shared consensus. To remedy this situation, it helps to remember that others' viewpoints are legitimate and to incorporate others' perspectives into your interpretation of issues.[8] Generally, adopting another person's viewpoint is fundamental to working collaboratively. And your ability to take others' perspectives—for instance, really to understand the viewpoints of customers or suppliers—can result in higher assessments of your performance.[9]

Filtering is the process of withholding, ignoring, or distorting information. Senders do this, for example, when they tell the boss what they think the boss wants to hear or give unwarranted compliments rather than honest criticism. Receivers also filter information; they may fail to recognize an important message or attend to some aspects of the message but not others.

A manager at a magazine who tended to phrase the assignments she gave her reporters as questions—"How would you like to do the X project with Y?" and "I was thinking of

perception
The process of receiving and interpreting information.

filtering
The process of withholding, ignoring, or distorting information.

Social Enterprise

Confusion Still Surrounds the "Social Enterprise" Concept

If you tell someone that you work for a social enterprise, chances are good that they won't know whether your employer is a charity, nonprofit, or for-profit company. One recent survey found that only 21 percent of respondents could correctly identify the nature of a social enterprise. About one-third of the respondents who missed the correct definition believed that social enterprises relied on grants and donations for income (as opposed to supporting themselves with revenue).

The Twin Cities chapter of the Social Enterprise Alliance and social enterprise practitioners in Minneapolis–St. Paul worked together to identify a simple definition of social enterprise: "an organization that sells products and services in order to achieve its social purpose." Any organization that refers to itself as a social enterprise must meet the following criteria:

1. *It must officially have a social purpose.* This is typically a nonprofit with tax-exempt status from the IRS like online educator Khan Academy. The Academy's mission is to "provide a free, world-class education for anyone, anywhere." A corporation may qualify if there is a social purpose included in their Articles of Incorporation. For example, Novo Nordisk states that it follows the triple bottom line business principle (financial, social, and environmental responsibilities) in its bylaws.

2. *It must sell products or services.* Whereas the Khan Academy wouldn't qualify for this criterion, Novo Nordisk does sell diabetes-related products. Cookie Cart, a nonprofit organization, provides leadership and job training to at-risk teenagers. Since they meet both criteria these organizations would qualify as a social enterprise.

Many different types of organizations can make a social impact. It is important to communicate clearly how your organization is legally defined and how you engage customers and other important stakeholders.[10]

Questions

- Can you identify some organizations that fit both of the criteria above?

- Assume that Khan Academy wanted to move from being a nonprofit to a social enterprise. What products or services could it sell?

---

putting you on the X project; is that okay?"—was criticized by her male boss, who told her she did not assume the proper demeanor with her staff.[11] Another, the owner of a retail operation, told one of her store managers to do something by saying, "The bookkeeper needs help with the billing. How would you feel about helping her out?" He said fine but didn't do it. Whereas the boss thought he meant he would do it, he said he meant to indicate how he would feel about helping. He decided he had better things to do.[12]

Because of such filtering and perceptual differences, you cannot assume the other person means what you think he means or understands the meanings you intend. Managers need to excel at reading interactions and adjusting their communication styles and perceptions to the people with whom they interact.[13] The very human tendencies to filter and perceive subjectively underlie much of the need for more effective communication practices that you will read about in the rest of this chapter.

Mixed Signals and Misperception

A common thread underlying the discussion so far is that people's perceptions can undermine attempts to communicate. People do not pay attention to everything going on around them. They inadvertently send mixed signals that can undermine the intended messages. Different people attend to different things, and people interpret the same thing in different ways. All of this creates problems in communication (see the "Social Enterprise" box example).

If the communication is between people from different cultures, these problems are magnified.[14] Communication breakdowns often occur when business transactions take place between people from different countries.[15] Chapter 6 introduced you to the importance of these cultural issues.

The following example highlights the operation of mixed signals and misperceptions. A bank CEO knew that to be competitive he had to downsize his organization, and the employees who remained would have to commit to customer service, become more empowered, and really earn customer loyalty.[16] Knowing that his employees would have doubts and concerns about the coming reorganization, he decided to make a promise to them that he would do his best to guarantee employment to the survivors.

What signals did the CEO communicate to his people by his promises? One positive signal was that he cared about his people. But he also signaled that *he* would take care of *them,* thus undermining his goal of giving them more responsibility and empowering them. The employees wanted management to take responsibility for the market challenge that *they* needed to face—to handle things for them when in fact *they* needed to learn the new ways of doing business. Inadvertently, the CEO spoke to their backward-looking need for security when he had meant to make them see that the bank's future depended on their

efforts. However, the CEO did avoid one common pitfall at companies that announce plans for downsizing or outsourcing: ignoring the emotional significance of the message.[17] Sometimes managers are so intent on delivering the business rationale for the changes that they fail to acknowledge the human cost of layoffs. When employees hear a message that neglects to address their feelings, they generally interpret the message to mean that managers don't care.

Consider how many problems can be avoided—and how much more effective communication can be—if people take the time to (1) ensure that the receivers attend to the message they are sending, (2) consider the other party's frame of reference and attempt to convey the message with that viewpoint in mind, (3) take concrete steps to minimize perceptual errors and improper signals in both sending and receiving, and (4) send consistent messages. You should make an effort to predict people's interpretations of your messages and think in terms of how they could misinterpret your messages. It helps to say not only what you mean but also what you don't mean. Every time you say "I am not saying *X,* I am saying *Y,*" you eliminate a possible misinterpretation.[18]

Any interpersonal situation holds potential for perceptual errors, filtering, and other communication breakdowns.

© *BananaStock Ltd.*

Oral and Written Channels

Communication can be sent through a variety of channels (step 3 in the Exhibit 15.1 model), including oral, written, and electronic. Each channel has advantages and disadvantages.

Oral communication includes face-to-face discussions, phone conversations, meetings, and formal presentations and speeches. Advantages are that questions can be asked and answered, feedback is immediate and direct, the receiver(s) can sense the sender's sincerity (or lack thereof), and oral communication is more persuasive and sometimes less expensive than written. However, oral communication also has disadvantages: it can lead to spontaneous, ill-considered statements (and regret), and there is no permanent record of it (unless an effort is made to record it).

Written communication includes e-mail, memos, letters, reports, computer files, and other written documents. Advantages to using written messages are that the message can be revised several times, it is a permanent record that can be saved, the message stays the same even if relayed through many people, and the receiver has more time to analyze the message. Disadvantages are that the sender has no control over where, when, or if the message is read; the sender does not receive immediate feedback; the receiver may not understand parts of the message; and the message must be longer to contain enough information to answer anticipated questions.[19]

E-mail is one of the most convenient forms of communication, but what are some of the pitfalls? How often have you sent an e-mail, whether personal or professional, and found that someone misinterpreted the message?

© Comstock/PunchStock

You should weigh these considerations when deciding whether to communicate orally or in writing. Also, sometimes use both channels, such as following up a meeting with a confirming memo or writing an e-mail to prepare someone for your phone call.

Electronic Media

Among other things, electronic media and online software provide opportunities for individuals to multicommunicate: engage in more than one conversation at the same time.[20] Employees at 97 percent of Fortune 500 companies are using Box, a platform that empowers people to simultaneously access and upload files while collaborating and sharing content online.[21] Other means of electronic communication include teleconferencing, in which groups of people in different locations interact over telephone lines and perhaps also see one another on television monitors as they participate in group discussions (videoconferencing). And you probably are intimately familiar with e-mail, instant messaging, text messaging, and blogging.

Recently, as we shall see, social media have made their way into the workplace as well.

E-mail is a fundamental tool of workplace communication. In fact, for some kinds of work, employees spend a substantial part of each workday reading and replying to e-mail messages. For short messages and to get a quick reply, workers also may use texting or instant messaging (IMing). And employers are catching up with consumers in their use of social media. Close to four in ten companies communicate on video-sharing sites and blogs, and roughly a quarter use wikis (publications with contributions from many authors and users) and microblogging (such as Twitter).[22] Generally, social media invite comments from an entire network of users. Suppose a company uses a blog to communicate with the external environment (for example, sharing information about products or corporate social responsibility) or with employees (for example, posts about company initiatives or employee accomplishments). The blog's audience typically can comment in reply to each blog post.

Advantages   Advantages of electronic communication are numerous and dramatic. Within firms, the advantages include the sharing of more information and speed and efficiency in delivering routine messages to large numbers of people across vast geographic areas. Discussing ideas with colleagues in other cities is much faster and less expensive with teleconferencing or corporate social media than when the colleagues must travel to be at the same location.

For example, Microsoft's SharePoint allows companies to create websites that enable employees to collaborate on web pages, documents, lists, calendars, and data. Hitachi Solutions Europe helps client companies create SharePoint platforms to quickly respond to changing business needs and reduce their training costs.[23] Groupon, IBM, and Blue Cross/Blue Shield use an online platform called Candor to help generate anonymous ideas from participants before meeting in person to discuss them.[24] This approach tends to yield a wider range of potential solutions.

Some research indicates more data sharing and critical argumentation, and higher-quality decisions, with a group decision support system than is found in face-to-face meetings.[25] Others are concerned that anonymity tempts participants to make careless, rude, or ill-advised statements, so they require identities to be revealed, or they limit access to social networking technologies. However, a growing number of companies see services such as LinkedIn, Twitter, and Facebook as necessary for staying in touch with the hundreds of millions of people who use these services—especially the younger generations of co-workers and customers, who are likelier to check tweets and texts than voice mail and e-mail.[26] Fueling this trend is how employees use their own mobile devices and applications in the workplace (see "Multiple Generations at Work").

Bottom Line

Imagine how much time you would lose if you couldn't communicate electronically; imagine the savings of money and natural resources you could create if your company and its people sought and used the most cost-effective ways to communicate.
What forms of electronic communication do you use (on the job or for personal use)?

Multiple Generations at Work

Bring Your Own Device to Work (But Keep It Safe!)

Many employees view their mobile devices as indispensible tools for both fun and work activities. According to Cheryl Tang, a senior manager for Symantec: "Today, work is no longer a place I go to, it's something I do." Organizations are adjusting to the changing times: nearly two-thirds of firms currently allow employees to use personal smartphones and tablets for work-related activities. VMware, a cloud-computing software company, has taken the next step by requiring all 6,000 employees in the United States to use personal smartphones for work.

There are several advantages and disadvantages of allowing employees to use their own devices for work:

Advantages	Disadvantages
1. Reduces a company's equipment costs.	1. Increases risk of security breach and data loss.
2. Reduces training time since employee knows device.	2. Increases cost of supporting various devices.
3. Improves employee job satisfaction and morale.	3. Shifts purchase cost of devices to employees.
4. Boosts innovation as new applications are used.	4. Enables nonwork-related activities.

A related trend known as "bring your own app" (BYOA) is when employees use their own applications for work-related purposes. For example, employees may find that transferring large files via Dropbox is faster and easier than using their company e-mail accounts. Though good for employee morale and innovation, unsecured devices and applications are vulnerable to security threats like hacking, lost data, or theft of the device. Employee attitudes toward security matters, too. A recent study found that 70 percent of Millennials "admitted to bringing outside applications into the enterprise in violation of IT policies, compared to just 31 percent of Baby Boomers."

Mobile devices and boundaryless work are here to stay. A major goal for managers will continue to be how to balance employee independence and innovation with effective security policies.[27]

Disadvantages   Disadvantages of electronic communication include the difficulty of solving complex problems that require more extended, face-to-face interaction and the inability to pick up subtle, nonverbal, or inflectional clues about what the communicator is thinking or conveying. Perhaps partly for this reason, people are more willing to lie online.[28] In online bargaining—even before it begins—negotiators distrust one another more than in face-to-face negotiations. After the negotiation (compared with face-to-face negotiators), people usually are less satisfied with their outcomes, even when the outcomes are economically equivalent.[29]

Although organizations rely heavily on computer-aided communication for group decision making, face-to-face groups generally develop more trust among members, take less time, make higher-quality decisions, and are more satisfying for members.[30] E-mail is most appropriate for routine messages that do not require the exchange of large quantities of complex information. It is less suitable for confidential information, resolving conflicts, or negotiating.[31] Employees have reported being laid off via e-mail and even text messages.[32] Not only do these more impersonal forms of communication cause hurt feelings, but an upset employee can also easily forward messages, and forwarding often has a snowball effect that can embarrass everyone involved.

Companies are worried about leaks and negative portrayals, and they may require employees to agree to specific guidelines before they post information on blogs or networking sites or use a microblogging service such as Twitter.

Unisys, Sprint, and Hewlett-Packard provide training programs to help employees use social media in a productive manner. Guidelines for social media use include the following: (1) use reasonable etiquette, (2) identify and represent yourself (not the organization),

Cisco employees in New York, left, and San Jose, California, on screen, meeting via monitor. What are the advantages and disadvantages to using this type of technology to communicate?

© Ariel Skelley/Blend Images LLC

(3) be factual and don't violate company disclosure policies, (4) be respectful, and (5) review the message before posting it (it will become permanent record).[33]

Two results of electronic communication are a proliferation of negative and nasty messages, and misinterpretations. People hurl insults, vent frustration, snitch on co-workers to the boss, and otherwise breach protocol. The lack of nonverbal cues can result in kidding remarks being taken seriously, causing resentment and regret.[34] People see negative meanings in neutral messages[35] and are more likely to lie electronically and to feel justified in doing so.[36] Also, it is not unheard of for confidential messages—including details about people's personal lives and insulting, embarrassing remarks—to become public knowledge through electronic leaks.

Other downsides to electronic communication are important to know.[37] Different people and sometimes different working units latch onto different channels as their medium of choice. For example, many Generation Y workers and customers (born in 1980 or later) tend to ignore voice mail and infrequently check e-mail because they expect these messages to be mostly spam.[38] Another disadvantage is that electronic messages sometimes are seen by those for whom they are not intended. Be careful with whether you click Reply or Reply to All, set your message notifications not to pop up when you're using your computer for a presentation, and remember that any message you put online might be reposted or forwarded to others. Many companies use software to monitor electronic messages. And the messages can be used in court cases to indict individuals or companies. Electronic messages sent from work and on company-provided devices are private property—but they are private property of the system's owner, not of the sender.

> **Electronic messages are private property of the system's owner, not of the sender.**

Here's a golden rule (like the sunshine rule in the ethics chapter): Don't hit Send or post a comment unless you'd be comfortable having the contents on the front page of a newspaper, being read by your mother or a competitor.

Managing the Electronic Load   Electronic communication media are essential these days, but the sheer volume and variety of sources (e.g., e-mails, texts, LinkedIn, and Skype notifications) of communication can be overwhelming.[39] Fortunately, a few rules of thumb can help; by one estimate, workers can improve their productivity in e-mail use alone by as much as 30 percent.[40] For the problem of information overload, the challenge is to separate the truly important from the routine. Take control over your time by deciding how often you need to check e-mail, texts, and tweets and turn off the notifications when you are doing other things.[41] When you check messages, reply immediately if you can, so you only handle each message once, and use the organizational tools such as file folders that come with the software. And, of course, avoid burdening others by copying them on messages they do not need to see. Some employees are finding that social media offer more efficient communication tools than e-mail. At IBM Software Group, for example, Luis Suarez posts answers to business questions on a social media site, where it is far simpler to address the usual follow-up questions and forwarding of information that accompany e-mail discussions.[42]

Of course, management also has a role to play. Often employees check messages constantly because they believe (perhaps correctly) that this is what their bosses or customers expect of them. Managers can help employees by establishing a "standard response time" policy that sets acceptable guidelines.[43]

Some companies are recognizing the downsides of electronic media overuse. At Atos, a French IT company, internal e-mail has been banned and replaced by an instant messaging software. Other companies like Reliable PSD and Graystone Industries are experimenting with "going e-mail free" for part of each workday or week.[44] And JPMorgan recently announced that it would be dropping voice-mail service for its retail banking employees. The move is expected to save about $3.2 million annually.[45]

The Virtual Office   Based on the philosophy that management's focus should be on what people do, not where they are, the **virtual office** is a mobile office in which people can work anywhere—their home, car, airport, coffee houses, customers' offices—as long as they have the tools to communicate with customers and colleagues. Deloitte gives many of its employees the choice to work up to five days a week outside the office. When desired, employees can reserve a workspace at the company for the day.[46]

In the short run, at least, the benefits of virtual offices appear substantial. Saving money on rent and utilities is an obvious advantage. In the earlier example, consulting firm Deloitte saved 30 percent in office rental and energy costs.[47] A virtual office also gives employees access to whatever information they need from the company, whether they are in a meeting, visiting a client, or working from home.[48] Hiring and retaining talented people is easier because virtual offices support scheduling flexibility and may make it possible to keep an employee who wants to relocate—for example, with a spouse taking a new job in another city.

Web-hosting company Automattic, based in San Francisco, takes the virtual office to an extreme, and its people love it. Employees work at their homes in 28 states and almost as many countries. For meetings, participants sign in to the Skype or Google+ Hangouts video chat service. If a topic is sensitive or a misunderstanding occurs, employees place a phone call (the traditional way or using Skype). For an informal chat, they often use the ICQ instant-messaging system.

Automattic has not abandoned face-to-face communication. Teams are encouraged to meet at least once a year in mutually agreed-on locations. And at a different location each year, the company hosts a weeklong grand meetup for everyone to gather, get acquainted, and talk strategy.[49]

But what will be the longer-term impact on productivity and morale? We may be in danger of losing too many human moments, those authentic encounters that happen only when two people are physically together.[50] Some people hate working at home. Some send texts, e-mail, and tweets in the middle of the night—and others receive them. Some work around the clock and still feel they are not doing enough. The long hours of being constantly close to the technical tools of work can cause burnout. And some companies are learning that direct supervision at the office is necessary to maintain the quality of work, especially when employees are inexperienced and need guidance. The virtual office requires changes in human beings and presents technical challenges; so although it is much hyped and useful, it will not completely replace real offices and face-to-face work.

virtual office
A mobile office in which people can work anywhere, as long as they have the tools to communicate with customers and colleagues.

EXHIBIT 15.2
Examples of Media
Richness

More rich
Face-to-face conversation,
videoconference, and phone call

Less rich
E-mail, text, blog post, and
memo

Media Richness

media richness

The degree to which a
communication channel
conveys information.

Some communication channels convey more information than others. The amount of information a medium conveys is called **media richness**.[51] (See Exhibit 15.2 for a comparison.) The more information or cues a medium sends to the receiver, the richer the medium is.[52] The richest media are more personal than technological, provide quick feedback, allow lots of descriptive language, and send different types of cues. Thus face-to-face communication is the richest medium because it offers a variety of cues in addition to words: tone of

MANAGER'S BRIEF

PROGRESS REPORT

ONWARD

Management in Action

GOING FACE TO FACE AT YAHOO

Marissa Mayer's decision to insist that employees work together, not from home, was an endorsement of the value of face-to-face communication. Ironically, it also pointed to the limitations of the very channels of communication that Yahoo provides, e-mail and instant messaging as well as other forms of electronic communication. The assumption is that workers who encounter one another in physical space will share more ideas than workers who don't make those physical connections. As Jackie Reses's message stated, "Some of the best decisions and insights come from hallway and cafeteria discussions, meeting new people, and impromptu team meetings."

When Yahoo's memo reached the media, it opened the way to a flood of comments. Some people acknowledged research supporting Mayer's decision. One professor told a reporter that teams with face-to-face contact experience greater cohesiveness and trust, and another said that most of the information people receive in a spoken message comes from facial expressions and the speaker's tone of voice. A research scientist who runs Sociometric Solutions has collected detailed data about people's interactions and learned that people who have the most face-to-face communication and friendships at work are not only more productive but also happier.

Nevertheless, critics of Mayer's decision note that telecommuters have been shown to work longer hours than in-office workers. (However, this points to a downside of telecommuting; if these workers are spending *more* time on the job, working from home does not actually help with work–life balance, as is popularly believed.) Others point to the strangeness of an Internet company not trusting its employees to communicate effectively through electronic channels. To some, the change in policy looked like a step backward by a company trying to signal it was finally moving forward. Richard Branson, CEO of Virgin, commented that Mayer's policy is misguided and may not help the company's productivity.

Another aspect of this decision, of course, was the way Yahoo's management implemented it. Mayer could have presented the idea to employees at one of her Friday meetings, or she could have held a conversation about policy ideas on social media. Instead, she arranged for the head of human resources to send all employees a memo announcing the decision via e-mail.[53]

- What impacts on communication would most likely result from Yahoo's directive to end work-at-home arrangements?
- Was an e-mailed memo the most appropriate communication channel to use for sending this message? Why or why not?

voice, facial expression, body language, and other nonverbal signals. It also allows more descriptive language than, say, an e-mail does. In addition, it affords more opportunity for the receiver to give feedback to and ask questions of the sender, turning one-way into two-way communication.

A phone conversation is less rich than face-to-face communication, and e-mail and texts are less rich yet. In general, you should send difficult and unusual messages through richer media, transmit simple and routine messages through less rich media, and use multiple media for important messages that you want to ensure people attend to and understand.[54] You should also consider factors such as which medium your receiver prefers, the preferred communication style in your organization, and cost.[55] Also, as you read "Management in Action: Progress Report," consider how Yahoo's policy requiring employees to work at company facilities affects the media richness of their communications.

Improving Communication Skills

Employers are dismayed by college graduates' poor communication skills. A demonstrated ability to communicate effectively makes a job candidate more attractive and distinguishes him or her from others. You can do many things to improve your communication skills, both as a sender and as a receiver.

LO 4

Improving Sender Skills

To start, be aware that honest, direct, straight talk is important but all too rare. CEOs are often coached on how to slant their messages for different audiences—the investment community, employees, or the board. That's not likely to be straight talk. The focus of the messages can differ, but they can't be inconsistent. People should be able to identify your perspective, your reasoning, and your intentions.[56]

Beyond this basic point, senders can improve their skills in making persuasive presentations, writing, using effective language, and sending nonverbal messages. Exhibit 15.3 offers some useful tips on formal presentations; the following discussion focuses more on other keys to persuasion.

Presentation and Persuasion Skills   Throughout your career, you will be called on to state your case on a variety of issues. You will have information and perhaps an opinion or proposal to present to others. Typically, your goal will be to sell your idea. In other words, your challenge will be to persuade others to go along with your personal recommendation. As a leader, you will find that some of your toughest challenges arise when people do not want to do what has to be done. Leaders have to be persuasive to get people on board.[57]

Your attitude in presenting ideas and persuading others is important. Persuasion is not what many people think: merely selling an idea or convincing others

Persuasion is not what many people think.

to see things your way. Don't assume that it takes a "my way or the highway" approach, with a one-shot effort to make a hard sell and resisting compromise.[58] It usually is more constructive to consider persuasion a process of learning from each other and negotiating a shared solution. Persuasive speakers are seen as authentic, which happens when speakers are open with the audience, make a connection, demonstrate passion, and show they are listening as well as speaking. As a speaker, you can practice this kind of authenticity by noticing and adopting the type of body language you use when you're around people you're comfortable with, planning how to engage directly with your listeners, identifying the reasons you care about your topic, and watching for nonverbal cues as well as fully engaging yourself when you listen to audience comments and questions.[59]

The most powerful and persuasive messages are simple and informative, are told with stories and anecdotes, and convey excitement.[60] People are more likely to remember and

EXHIBIT 15.3
Ten Ways to Add Power to Your Presentations

"All the great speakers were bad speakers at first." Ralph Waldo Emerson

1. *Spend adequate time on the **content** of your presentation.* It's easy to get so distracted with PowerPoint slides or concern about delivery skills that the actual content of a presentation is neglected. Know your content inside and out; you'll be able to discuss it conversationally and won't be tempted to memorize. If you believe in what you're saying and *own* the material, you will convey enthusiasm and will be more relaxed.

2. *Clearly understand the **objective** of your presentation.* Answer this question with one sentence: "What do I want the audience to believe following this presentation?" Writing down your objective will help you focus on your bottom line. Everything else in a presentation—the structure, the words, the visuals—should support your objective.

3. ***Tell** the audience the **purpose** of the presentation.* As the saying goes, "Tell them what you're going to tell them, then tell them, then tell them what you've told them." Use a clear preview statement early on to help the audience know where you're taking them.

4. *Provide **meaning**, not just data.* Today information is widely available; you won't impress people by overloading them with data. People have limited attention spans and want presenters to help clarify the meaning of data.

5. ***Practice, practice, practice.*** Appearing polished and relaxed during a presentation requires rehearsal time. Practice making your points in a variety of ways. Above all, don't memorize a presentation's content.

6. *Remember that a presentation is more like a **conversation** than a speech.* Keep your tone conversational, yet professional. Audience members will be much more engaged if they feel you are talking with them rather than at them. Rely on PowerPoint slides or a broad outline to jog your memory.

7. *Remember the incredible power of **eye contact**.* Look at individual people in the audience. Try to have a series of one-on-one conversations with people in the room. This will calm you and help you connect with your audience.

8. ***Allow imperfection.*** If you forget what you were going to say, simply pause, look at your notes, and go on. Don't break character and effusively apologize or giggle or look mortified. Remember that an audience doesn't know your material nearly as well as you do and won't notice many mistakes.

9. *Be prepared to **answer tough questions**.* Try to anticipate the toughest questions you might receive. Plan your answers in advance. If you don't have an answer, acknowledge the fact and offer to get the information later.

10. *Provide a **crisp wrap-up** to a question-and-answer session.* Whenever possible, follow the Q&A period with a brief summary statement. Set up the Q&A session by saying, "We'll take questions for 10 minutes and then have a few closing remarks." This prevents your presentation from just winding down to a weak ending. Also, if you receive hostile or hard-to-answer questions, you'll have a chance to have the final word.

SOURCE: Lynn Hamilton, University of Virginia, class handout (with permission).

buy into your message if you can express it as a story that is simple, unexpected, concrete, and credible and that includes emotional content. For example, the Chicago energy company Exelon wanted to build employee support for its corporate values. To teach about diversity, the company posted videos of its executives making personal statements about what diversity means to them. A finance executive told about being from a working-class family in England and feeling like an outsider when he took a job in a bank where most of the employees came from the upper class. When this manager asserted, "I never want anyone else to feel that way," his openness about his own life made his statement more powerful.[61] Then, to be credible, a communicator backs up the message with actions consistent with the words.

Writing Skills   Effective writing is more than correct spelling, punctuation, and grammar (although these help). Good writing above all requires clear, logical thinking.[62] The act of writing can be a powerful aid to thinking because you have to think about what you really want to say and what the logic is behind your message.[63]

You want people to find your e-mail and reports readable and interesting. Strive for clarity, organization, readability, and brevity.[64] Brevity is much appreciated by readers who are overloaded with documents, including e-mail. Help e-mail recipients manage the flood of information by providing specific subject lines, putting your main point at the beginning of the message, limiting paragraphs to five lines or less, and avoiding sarcasm or caustic humor (which can be misinterpreted, especially when readers are scanning messages in a hurry).[65]

Your first draft rarely is as good as it could be. If you have time, revise it. Take the reader into consideration. Go through your entire attachment, e-mail, memo, or report and delete all unnecessary words, sentences, and paragraphs. Use specific, concrete words rather than abstract phrases. Instead of saying, "A period of unfavorable weather set in," say, "It rained every day for a week."

Language   Word choice can enhance or interfere with communication effectiveness. For example, jargon is actually a form of shorthand and can make communication more effective when both the sender and the receiver know the buzzwords. But when the receiver is unfamiliar with the jargon, misunderstandings result. When people from different functional areas or disciplines communicate with one another, misunderstandings often occur because of language barriers. As in writing, simplicity usually helps.

Therefore, whether speaking or writing, you should consider the receiver's background—cultural as well as technical—and adjust your language accordingly. When you are receiving, don't assume that your understanding is the same as the speaker's intentions. Cisco CEO John Chambers, whose background is in business, simply asks the engineering managers in his high-tech company to explain any jargon. He says, "They do it remarkably well."[66] At the same time, Chambers shows respect and enhances his credibility by being truly interested in their work. Whenever Chambers travels with or reviews engineers, he asks them to teach him a topic—and he listens.

Global teams fail when members have difficulty communicating because of language, cultural, and geographic barriers. What could you do to overcome these barriers?

© Chris Ryan/age fotostock

The meaning of word choices also can vary by culture. Japanese people use the simple word *hai* (yes) to convey that they understand what is being said; it does not necessarily mean that they agree. Asian businesspeople rarely use the direct "no," using more subtle or tangential ways of disagreeing.[67] Similarly, Japanese speakers apologize more often than Americans; the Japanese focus on the potential of an apology to repair damage in relationships, whereas U.S. speakers interpret apologies as admissions of guilt and therefore avoid them. Global teams fail when members have difficulties communicating because of language, cultural, and geographic barriers. Heterogeneity harms team functioning at first. But when they develop ways to interact and communicate, teams develop a common identity and perform well.[68]

When conducting business overseas, try to learn something about the other country's language and customs. Americans are less likely to do this than people from some other cultures; most Americans do not consider a foreign language necessary for doing business abroad, and a significant majority of U.S. firms do not require employees sent abroad to know the local language.[69] But those who do will have a big edge over their competitors who do not.[70] Making the effort to

Those who learn local languages and customs will have a big edge over their competitors who do not.

© Sam Edwards/age fotostock

learn the local language builds rapport, sets a proper tone for doing business, aids in adjustment to culture shock, and especially can help you get inside the other culture.[71] You will learn more about how people think, feel, and behave, both in their lives and in their business dealings.

Nonverbal Skills   As you know, people send and interpret signals other than those that are spoken or written. Nonverbal messages can support or undermine the stated message. Often nonverbal cues make a greater impact than other signals. In employees' eyes, managers' actions often speak louder than the words managers choose. To show confidence, managers (and employees, too) should make eye contact, use a firm handshake, dress professionally, and speak in an appropriate tone of voice.[72]

In conversation, except when you intend to convey a negative message, you should give nonverbal signals that express warmth, respect, concern, a feeling of equality, and a willingness to listen. Negative nonverbal signals show coolness, disrespect, lack of interest, and a feeling of superiority.[73] The following suggestions can help you send positive nonverbal signals.

First, use time appropriately. Avoid keeping your employees waiting to see you. Devote sufficient time to your meetings with them and communicate frequently with them to signal your interest in their concerns. Second, make your office arrangement conducive to open communication. A seating arrangement that avoids separation of people helps establish a warm, cooperative atmosphere (in contrast, an arrangement in which you sit behind your desk and your subordinate sits before you creates a more intimidating, authoritative environment).[74] Third, remember your body language. Facial expression and tone of voice can account for much of the communication between two people.[75] Several nonverbal body signals convey a positive attitude toward the other person: assuming a position close to the person; gesturing frequently; maintaining eye contact; smiling; having an open body orientation, such as facing the other person directly; uncrossing the arms; and leaning forward to convey interest in what the other person is saying.

Silence is an interesting nonverbal signal. The average American is said to spend about twice as many hours per day in conversation as the average Japanese.[76] North Americans tend to talk to fill silences. Japanese allow long silences to develop, believing they can get to know people better. Japanese believe that two people with good rapport will know each other's thoughts. The need to use words implies a lack of understanding.

Improving Receiver Skills

Once you become effective at sending oral, written, and nonverbal messages, you are halfway toward becoming a complete communicator. However, you must also develop adequate receiving capabilities. Receivers need good listening, reading, and observational skills.

Listening   In today's demanding work environment, managers need excellent listening skills. Although people frequently assume that good listening is easy and natural, in fact it is difficult and not nearly as common as needed. Consultant Bernard Ferrari saw this challenge in a meeting of an industrial company's chief marketing officer (CMO) and the team that had introduced a new product. The new product was not selling, even though the engineers on the team described it as delivering many important benefits. The CMO listened carefully to the engineers and then asked, given that the product was great and the engineers convincingly described its worth, what customers were saying that might explain the lack of orders. The engineers admitted they had not spoken with any customers; rather, they had been careful not to leak any information while the product was under development and assumed that customers would plainly see its value. Because the CMO took time to listen to the engineers, instead of jumping to conclusions about the source of the problem, she and the engineers could arrive at a plan for them to begin talking to technical people at the customer firms, and orders soon began flowing in.[77]

A basic technique called *reflection* will help a manager listen effectively.[78] **Reflection** is a process by which a person states what he or she believes the other person is saying. This technique places a greater emphasis on listening than on talking, and the result is more accurate two-way communication.

Besides using reflection, you can improve how well you listen by practicing the techniques described in Exhibit 15.4. (Note the date of the citation; some things don't change!) For managers, the stakes are high; failure to listen not only causes managers to miss good ideas but can even drive employees away.[79]

Listening begins with personal contact. Staying in the office, keeping the door closed, and eating lunch at your desk are sometimes necessary to get pressing work done, but that is no way to stay on top of what's going on. Better to walk the halls, initiate conversations, and go to lunch even with people outside your area.[80] Reed Hastings, CEO of Netflix, doesn't have an office. He stays connected by talking with employees as he works at empty desks around headquarters.[81]

When a manager takes time to really listen to and get to know people, those same people think, "She's showing an interest in me" or "He's letting me know that I matter" or "She values my ideas and contributions." Trust develops. Listening and learning from others are even more important for innovation than for routine work. Successful change and innovation come through lots of human contact.

> **reflection**
> Process by which a person states what he or she believes the other person is saying.

EXHIBIT 15.4
Ten Keys to Effective Listening

1. *Find an area of interest.* Even if you decide the topic is dull, ask yourself, "What is the speaker saying that I can use?"

2. *Judge content, not delivery.* Don't get caught up in the speaker's personality, mannerisms, speaking voice, or clothing. Instead, try to learn what the speaker knows.

3. *Hold your fire.* Rather than getting immediately excited by what the speaker seems to be saying, withhold evaluation until you understand the speaker's message.

4. *Listen for ideas.* Don't get bogged down in all the facts and details; focus on central ideas.

5. *Be flexible.* Have several systems for note taking and use the system best suited to the speaker's style. Don't take too many notes or try to force everything said by a disorganized speaker into a forma l outline.

6. *Resist distraction.* Close the door, shut off the radio, move closer to the person talking, or ask him or her to speak louder. Don't look out the window or at papers on your desk.

7. *Exercise your mind.* Some people tune out when the material gets difficult. Develop an appetite for a good mental challenge.

8. *Keep your mind open.* Many people get overly emotional when they hear words referring to their most deeply held convictions—for example, *union, subsidy, import, Republican* or *Democrat,* and *big business.* Try not to let your emotions interfere with comprehension.

9. *Capitalize on thought speed.* Take advantage of the fact that most people talk at a rate of about 125 words per minute, but most of us think at about four times that rate. Use those extra 400 words per minute to think about what the speaker is saying rather than turning your thoughts to something else.

10. *Work at listening.* Spend some energy. Don't just pretend you're paying attention. Show interest. Good listening is hard work, but the benefits outweigh the costs.

SOURCE: Ralph G. Nichols, "Listening Is a 10-Part Skill," *Nation's Business* 45 (July 1957), pp. 56–60. Cited in R. C. Huseman, C. M. Logue, and D. L. Freshley, eds., *Readings in Interpersonal and Organizational Communication* (Boston: Allyn & Bacon, 1977).

Reading   Illiteracy is a significant problem in the United States as well as in other countries. Even if illiteracy is not a problem in your organization, reading mistakes are common and costly. As a receiver, for your own benefit, read memos and e-mail as soon as possible, before it's too late to respond. You may skim most of your reading materials, but read important messages, documents, and passages slowly and carefully. Note important points for later referral. Consider taking courses to increase your reading speed and comprehension skills. Finally, don't limit your reading to items about your particular job skill or technical expertise; read materials that fall outside your immediate concerns. You never know when a creative idea that will help you in your work will be inspired by a novel, a biography, a sports story, or an article about a problem in another business or industry.

Observing   Effective communicators are also capable of observing and interpreting nonverbal communications. (As Yogi Berra said, "You can observe a lot by watching.") For example, by reading nonverbal cues, a presenter can determine how her talk is going and adjust her approach if necessary. Some companies train their sales forces to interpret the nonverbal signals of potential customers. People can also decode nonverbal signals to determine whether a sender is being truthful or deceitful. Deceitful communicators tend to maintain less eye contact, make either more or fewer body movements than usual, and smile either too much or too little. Verbally, they offer fewer specifics than do truthful senders.[82]

A vital source of useful observations comes from personally visiting people, plants, and other locations to get a firsthand view.[83] Many corporate executives rely heavily on reports from the field and don't travel to remote locations to observe firsthand what is going on. Reports are no substitute for actually seeing things happen in practice. Frequent visits to the field and careful observation can help a manager develop deep understanding of current operations, future prospects, and ideas for how to exploit capabilities fully.[84] Tools like the Rapid Plant Assessment are available for visiting managers to evaluate a plant's performance on such factors as safety, scheduling, teamwork, and inventory.[85]

Of course, you must accurately interpret what you observe. An American employee working at Razorfish, a firm based in Shanghai, was surprised to discover how much he was expected to socialize with his Chinese boss. Beyond attending occasional happy hours and lunches, the employee observed: "In China, it's really expected that you become friends with your boss and you go out and socialize in a way that doesn't happen in the U.S."[86]

The Japanese are particularly skilled at interpreting every nuance of voice and gesture, putting most Westerners at a disadvantage.[87] When one is conducting business in Asia or other countries, local guides can be invaluable not only to interpret language but to decode behavior at meetings, what subtle hints and nonverbal cues mean, who the key people are, and how the decision-making process operates.

Organizational Communication

Being a skilled communicator is essential to being a good manager and team leader. But communication must also be managed throughout the organization. Every minute of every day, countless bits of information are transmitted through an organization. The flow of information affects how well people and units perform. Communications travel downward, upward, horizontally, and informally within the organization.

Downward Communication

downward communication

Information that flows from higher to lower levels in the organization's hierarchy.

Downward communication refers to the flow of information from higher to lower levels in the organization's hierarchy. Examples include a manager giving an assignment to an assistant, a supervisor making an announcement to his subordinates, and a company president delivering a talk to her management team. Downward communication that provides relevant information enhances employee identification with the company, supportive attitudes, and decisions consistent with the organization's objectives.[88]

© Fuse/Getty Images

People must receive the information they need to perform their jobs and become—and remain—loyal members of the organization. But they often lack adequate information.[89] One problem is information overload; they are bombarded with so much information that they fail to absorb everything. Much of the information is not very important, but its volume causes a lot of relevant information to be lost.

A second problem is a lack of openness between managers and employees. Managers may believe "No news is good news," "I don't have time to keep them informed of everything they want to know," or "It's none of their business, anyway." Some managers withhold information even if sharing it would be useful.

A third problem is filtering, introduced earlier in the chapter. When messages are passed from one person to another, some information is left out. When a message passes through many people, each transmission may cause further information losses. The message can also be distorted as people add their own words or interpretations.

Filtering poses serious problems in organizations. As messages are communicated downward through many organizational levels, much information is lost. The data in Exhibit 15.5 suggest that by the time messages reach the people for whom they are intended, the receivers may get very little useful information. The smaller the number of authority levels through which communications must pass, the less information will be lost or distorted. Flatter organization offers the advantage of fewer problems caused by filtering of information as it cascades through many layers.

> As messages are communicated downward through many organizational levels, much information is lost.

Coaching   Some of the most important downward communications occur when managers give performance feedback to their direct reports. We discussed earlier the importance of giving feedback and positive reinforcement when it is deserved. It is also important to discuss poor performance explicitly and areas that can be improved.

EXHIBIT 15.5
Information Loss in Downward Communication

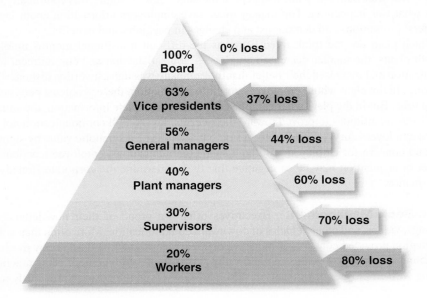

100% Board — 0% loss
63% Vice presidents — 37% loss
56% General managers — 44% loss
40% Plant managers — 60% loss
30% Supervisors — 70% loss
20% Workers — 80% loss

coaching

Dialogue with a goal of
helping another be more
effective and achieve his or
her full potential on the job.

Coaching is dialogue with a goal of helping another be more effective and achieve his or her full potential on the job.[90] When done properly, coaching develops executives and enhances performance.[91] Even CEOs desire coaching, especially in the areas of managing conflict, delegating, building teams, and mentoring.[92]

When people have performance problems or exhibit behaviors that need to be changed, coaching is often the best way to help a person change and succeed. And coaching is not just for poor performers; as even the greatest athletes know, it is for anyone who is good and aspires to excellence. Although coaches for executives sometimes are hired from the outside, coaches from outside your organization may not understand fully the context in which you are working.[93] So don't take advice automatically. The best use of coaches is as sounding boards, helping you think through the potential impact of your ideas, generate new options, and learn from experience.

Companies such as Coca-Cola use coaching as an essential part of their executive development process. When done well, coaching is true dialogue between two committed people engaged in joint problem solving. Good coaching requires achieving real understanding of the problem, the person, and the situation; jointly generating ideas for what to do; and encouraging the person to improve. Good coaches ask a lot of questions, listen well, provide input, and encourage others to think for themselves. Effective coaching requires honesty, calmness, and supportiveness—all aided by a sincere desire to help. The ultimate and longest-lasting form of help is to help people think through and solve their own problems.

Downward Communication in Difficult Times   Managers frequently need to deliver bad news,[94] and proper downward communication can be particularly valuable during difficult times. During corporate mergers and acquisitions, employees are anxious as they wonder how the changes will affect them. Ideally—and ethically—top management should communicate with employees about the change as early as possible.

But some argue against that approach, maintaining that informing employees about the reorganization might cause them to quit too early. Then too, top management often isolates itself, prompting rumors and anxiety. CEOs and other senior execs are surrounded by lawyers, investment bankers, and so on—people who are paid merely to make the deal happen, not to make it work.

Yet with the people who are affected by the deal, you must increase, not decrease, communication.[95]

In a merger of two Fortune 500 companies, two plants received very different information.[96] All employees at both plants received the initial letter from the CEO announcing the merger. But after that, one plant was kept in the dark while the other was continually filled in on what was happening. Top management gave employees information about layoffs; transfers; promotions and demotions; and changes in pay, jobs, and benefits.

Which plant do you think fared better as the difficult transitional months unfolded? In both plants, the merger decreased employees' job satisfaction and commitment to the organization and increased their belief that the company was untrustworthy, dishonest, and uncaring. In the plant whose employees got little information, these problems persisted for a long time. But in the plant where employees received complete information, the situation stabilized and attitudes improved toward their normal levels. Full communication not only helped employees survive an anxious period but also served a symbolic value by signaling care and concern for employees. Without such communications, employee reactions to a merger or acquisition may be so negative that they undermine the corporate strategy and performance.

open-book management

Practice of sharing with
employees at all levels
of the organization vital
information previously meant
for management's eyes only.

Open-Book Management   Executives often are proud of their newsletters, staff meetings, videos, and other vehicles of downward communication. More often than not, the information provided concerns company sports teams, birthdays, and new copy machines. But here is a more unconventional philosophy. **Open-book management** is the practice of sharing with employees at all levels of the organization vital information previously meant for management's eyes only. This information includes financial goals, income statements, budgets, sales, forecasts, and other relevant data about company performance and prospects. This practice is dramatically different from the traditional closed-book approach in which people may or may not have a clue about how the company is doing, may or may not believe the things that management tells them, and may or may not believe that their personal performance makes a difference.

Open-book management is controversial because many managers prefer to keep such information to themselves. Sharing strategic plans and financial information with employees could lead to leaks to competitors or to employee dissatisfaction with compensation. Father of scientific management Frederick Taylor, early in the 20th century, would have considered opening the books to all employees idiotic.[97]

Rob Tolleson at CPO Commerce credits it with saving his company from collapse. Due to a major IT malfunction, the online vendor of power tools struggled to figure out how to fulfill customers' orders. Employees, who had full access to company information, were able to work together for weeks to develop creative solutions until the company could stabilize itself.[98] Similarly, at Hilcorp Energy Company, senior managers assemble the 280-plus employees once a month to share data about the company's performance and listen to ideas from the workers. This is much more than going through the motions. One employee commented: "When you suggest an idea to upper management they really listen to you and most of the time they will go along with the idea you suggested."[99]

Upward Communication

Upward communication travels from lower to higher ranks in the hierarchy. Adequate upward communication is important for several reasons.[100] First, managers learn what's going on. Management gains a more accurate picture of subordinates' work, accomplishments, problems, plans, attitudes, and ideas. Second, employees gain from the opportunity to communicate upward. People can relieve some of their frustrations and achieve a stronger sense of participation in the enterprise. Third, effective upward communication facilitates downward communication as good listening becomes a two-way street.

The problems common in upward communication are similar to those for downward communication. Managers, like their subordinates, are bombarded with information and may neglect or miss information from below. Furthermore, some employees are not always open with their bosses; in other words, filtering occurs upward as well as downward. People tend to share only good news with their bosses and suppress bad news because they (1) want to appear competent; (2) mistrust their boss and fear that if he or she finds out about something they have done they will be punished; (3) fear the boss will punish the messenger, even if the reported problem is not that person's fault; or (4) believe they are helping their boss if they shield him or her from problems.

For these and other reasons,[101] managers may not learn about important problems. As one leadership expert put it, "If the messages from below say you are doing a flawless job, send back for a more candid assessment."[102]

Managing Upward Communication   Generating useful information from below requires managers to both facilitate and motivate upward communication. For example, they could have an open-door policy and encourage people to use it, have lunch or coffee with employees, use surveys, institute a program for suggestions, or have town hall meetings. They can ask for advice, make informal visits to plants, really think about and respond to employee suggestions, and distribute summaries of new ideas and practices inspired by employee suggestions and actions.[103]

Some executives practice MBWA (management by wandering around). That term, coined by Ed Carlson of United Airlines, refers simply to getting out of the office, walking around, and talking frequently and informally with employees.[104] Over his 40-year career with Marriott Corporation, Bill Marriott would walk through many of the firm's hotels to speak with employees and to ensure they were delivering consistent, high-quality service to customers.[105]

Bottom Line

The more management communicates cost, quality, sustainability, and other data, the more people will care about and pay attention to performance and find new ways to improve.

For employees to be motivated by open-book management, what kinds of information would they need besides sales and profit numbers?

upward communication

Information that flows from lower to higher levels in the organization's hierarchy.

Useful upward communication must be reinforced and not punished. The person who tries to talk to the manager about a problem must not be brushed off consistently. An announced open-door policy must truly be open-door. Also, people must trust their supervisor and know that the manager will not hold a grudge if they deliver negative information. To get honesty, managers must truly listen, not punish the messenger for being honest, and act on valid comments.

Horizontal Communication

horizontal communication

Information shared among people on the same hierarchical level.

Much information needs to be shared among people on the same hierarchical level. Such **horizontal communication** can take place among people in the same work team or in different departments. For example, a purchasing agent discusses a problem with a production engineer, and a task force of department heads meets to discuss a particular concern. Communicating with others outside the firm, including potential investors, is another vital type of horizontal communication.[106]

Horizontal communication has several important functions.[107] First, it allows sharing of information, coordination, and problem solving among units. Second, it helps solve conflicts. Third, by allowing interaction among peers, it provides social and emotional support to people. All these factors contribute to morale and effectiveness. For example, National Public Radio has brought together groups of a few dozen employees from different departments to share ideas for new projects. On one of these Serendipity Days, the employees put together a program for training staff members in using social media. And a study at the University of Michigan found that researchers were significantly more likely to collaborate on research projects with a colleague if they both worked in the same building and had walking patterns that overlapped.[108]

Managing Horizontal Communication   The need for horizontal communication is similar to the need for integration, discussed in Chapter 8. Particularly in complex environments, in which decisions in one unit affect another, information must be shared horizontally. An example of good horizontal communication is Google Cafés, which are designed to encourage interactions between employees within and across teams.[109]

Applied Materials, a semiconductor equipment manufacturer in Santa Clara, California, took a sophisticated approach to managing horizontal communication. To improve the caliber and efficiency of its information technology (IT) group, the company outsourced routine tasks, cut the in-house IT workforce, and focused the remaining IT employees on supporting strategy. As a result, the IT workers were expected to collaborate with each other (and with customers) to develop and implement creative projects. To improve this kind of collaboration, Applied Materials conducted a survey of the IT staff to determine the existing patterns of communication. Survey results showed that about half of the IT employees were, in effect, communication hubs—many of their colleagues consulted with them for ideas and questions. Those highly networked employees weren't necessarily managers; they were people at all levels whom others trusted and respected. The company assembled a team of 12 highly networked IT employees and had them share insights about what conditions affected collaboration in the company. This team identified barriers, and Applied Materials used that information to provide coaching in better communication. A follow-up survey showed that more employees had become highly networked.[110]

Informal Communication

LO 6

Organizational communications differ in formality. Formal communications are official, organization-sanctioned episodes of information transmission. They can move upward, downward, or horizontally and often are prearranged and necessary for performing some task.

Informal communication is more unofficial. People gossip; employees complain about their bosses; people talk about their favorite sports teams; work teams tell newcomers how to get by.[111]

The **grapevine** is the social network of informal communications. Informal networks provide people with information, help them solve problems, and teach them how to do their work successfully. You should develop a good network of people willing and able to help.[112] However, the grapevine can be destructive when irrelevant or erroneous gossip and rumors proliferate and harm operations.[113]

What does this mean for you personally? Don't engage in e-gossip. Embarrassing episodes become public, and lawsuits based on defamation of character and invasion of privacy have used e-mail evidence. But don't avoid the grapevine, either.[114] Listen, but evaluate before believing what you hear. Who is the source? How credible is he or she? Does the rumor make sense? Is it consistent or inconsistent with other things you know or have heard? Seek more information. Don't stir the pot.

grapevine

Informal communication network.

Managing Informal Communication   Rumors start over any number of topics, including who's leaving, who's getting a promotion, salaries, job security, and costly mistakes. Rumors can destroy people's faith and trust in the company—and in each other. But the grapevine cannot be eliminated. Therefore, managers need to work with the grapevine.

The grapevine can be managed in several ways.[115] First, if a manager hears a story that could get out of hand, he or she should talk to the key people involved to get the facts and their perspectives. Don't allow malicious gossip.

Second, suggestions for preventing rumors from starting include explaining events that are important but have not been explained, dispelling uncertainties by providing facts, and working to establish open communications and trust over time. These efforts are especially important during times of uncertainty, such as after a merger or layoff or when sales slow down, because rumors increase along with anxiety.

Third, neutralize rumors once they have started. Disregard a rumor if it is ridiculous; openly confirm any parts that are true; make public comments ("no comment" is seen as a confirmation of the rumor); deny the rumor if the denial is based in truth (don't make false denials); make sure communications about the issue are consistent; select a spokesperson of appropriate rank and knowledge; and hold town meetings if needed.[116]

It's hard to know how rumors get started, but we do know they happen. The grapevine can be managed if you talk to the key people involved and neutralize rumors once they've started.

© Bill Varie/Corbis

Boundarylessness

Many executives and management scholars today consider free access to information in all directions to be an organizational imperative. Jack Welch, when he was CEO of General Electric, coined the term *boundarylessness*. A **boundaryless organization** is one in which no barriers to information flow exist. Instead of separating people, jobs, processes, and places with boundaries, ideas, information, decisions, and actions move to where they are most needed.[117] This free flow does not imply a random free-for-all of unlimited communication and information overload. It implies information available *as needed* moving quickly and easily enough that the organization functions far better as a whole than as separate parts.

GE's chief learning officer used the metaphor of the organization as a house having three kinds of boundaries: the floors and ceilings, the walls that separate the rooms, and the outside walls. These barriers correspond in organizations to the boundaries between different organizational levels, different units and departments, and the organization and its external stakeholders—for example, suppliers and customers. GE adds a fourth wall: global boundaries separating domestic from global operations.[118]

boundaryless organization

Organization in which there are no barriers to information flow.

Management in Action

FORMAL AND INFORMAL COMMUNICATION AT YAHOO

Marissa Mayer's initial months at Yahoo showed her to be concerned about formal and informal communication. Some of her earliest actions established downward communication and invited upward communication. For example, upon arriving, she sent employees a memo expressing her excitement to be at Yahoo, encouraging them to "keep moving" on their "important work," and inviting them to share their ideas with her. Soon after, she set up Friday town hall meetings.

The announcement of the policy ending work-at-home arrangements was aimed at increasing informal communication. Aiming for a positive tone, HR executive Jackie Reses started by recalling some of the benefits Yahoo had previously delivered and said, "We want everyone to participate in our culture and contribute to the positive momentum." The memo next explained the rationale for the decision: fostering communication and collaboration so Yahoo could "become the absolute best place to work."

The announcement generated unintended informal communication when angry employees shared the memo with journalists, even though it was marked "proprietary and confidential." One employee affected by the decision called it "outrageous and a morale killer." A possible reason for the anger was that employees received an order to come to the workplace, rather than incentives or a message encouraging them. Also, the decision may have come as a surprise, given that it reversed earlier policy and stands in contrast to flexible work arrangements allowed at Google, Facebook, LinkedIn, Hewlett-Packard, IBM, Microsoft, and Cisco, among other companies. At those companies, working at home is not necessarily encouraged, but it is available with the assumption that workers and their managers can take responsibility for being productive. One Silicon Valley observer suggested that Yahoo made the policy change to shake up the culture and revitalize communication but will likely relax the rules eventually.

Has the boost in informal communication among employees contributed to Yahoo's financial performance? It may be too early to tell. In 2014, revenue fell to $1.04 billion from $1.09 billion in the previous year. However, its search business and advertising revenues have increased. Even with these mixed results, the company's board recently praised Mayer's performance: "She significantly improved the company's reputation and revitalized the company's employee base."[119]

- How could Mayer make her downward communication more effective?
- How could Yahoo make informal communication among employees more constructive?

GE's famous Workout program is a series of meetings for business members across multiple hierarchical levels, characterized by extremely frank, tough discussions that break down vertical boundaries. Workout has involved hundreds of thousands of GE people; in any given week thousands may be participating in a Workout program.[120] Workout is also done with customers and suppliers, breaking down outside boundaries. GE has also reached out to the community by providing this expertise to nonprofits, such as CommonBond Communities, a provider of affordable housing. A GE employee led a Workout session in which CommonBond employees identified how to improve processes and horizontal communication.[121]

GE uses plenty of other techniques to break down boundaries as well. It relentlessly benchmarks competitors and companies in other industries to learn best practices all over the world. GE places different functions together physically, such as engineering and manufacturing. It shares services across units. And it sometimes shares physical locations with its customers.

Boundaryless organizations intentionally create dialogue across boundaries, turning barriers into permeable membranes. As the GE people put it, people from different parts of the organization need to learn "how to talk."[122] They must also learn "how to walk." That is, dialogue is essential, but it must be followed by commensurate action. As you read "Management in Action: Onward," consider whether Yahoo under Marissa Mayer meets the description of a boundaryless organization.

KEY TERMS

boundaryless organization, p. 489

coaching, p. 486

communication, p. 470

downward communication, p. 484

filtering, p. 471

grapevine, p. 489

horizontal communication, p. 488

media richness, p. 478

one-way communication, p. 470

open-book management, p. 486

perception, p. 471

reflection, p. 483

two-way communication, p. 470

upward communication, p. 487

virtual office, p. 477

RETAINING WHAT YOU LEARNED

In Chapter 15, you learned that there are key differences between one-way and two-way communication flows. One-way communication is faster and easier than two-way communication, but two-way communication is more accurate and results in better performance. Problems in communication can occur in all stages: encoding, transmission, decoding, and interpreting. Noise can complicate communication. Subjective perceptions and filtering are potential sources of error. Communications are sent through oral, written, and electronic channels. People should weigh the advantages and disadvantages of each channel before sending a message. Electronic media have a major impact on interpersonal and organizational communications. Media richness is one factor to consider as you decide which channels to use and how to use them. There are several ways you can improve your writing and speaking skills. Actively manage downward, upward, and horizontal communication. The informal flow of communication (the grapevine) is important and needs to be managed actively. Boundaries exist between different organizational levels, units, and organizations and external stakeholders. The ideal boundaryless organization is one in which no barriers to information flow exist.

LO 1 Discuss important advantages of two-way communication.

- One-way communication flows from the sender to the receiver with no feedback loop.
- In two-way communication, each person is both a sender and a receiver as both parties provide and react to information.
- One-way communication is faster and easier but less accurate than two-way; two-way communication is slower and more difficult but is more accurate and results in better performance.

LO 2 Identify communication problems to avoid.

- The communication process involves a sender who conveys information to a receiver.
- Problems in communication can occur in all stages: encoding, transmission, decoding, and interpreting.

- Noise in the system further complicates communication, creating more distortion. Moreover, feedback may be unavailable or misleading.
- Subjective perceptions and filtering add to the possibility of error.

LO 3 Describe when and how to use the various communication channels.

- Communications are sent through oral, written, and electronic channels. All have important advantages and disadvantages that should be considered before choosing a channel.
- Electronic media have a huge impact on interpersonal and organizational communications and make possible the virtual office.
- Key advantages of electronic media are speed, cost, and efficiency, but the downsides are also significant, including information overload.
- Media richness, or how much and what sort of information a channel conveys, is one factor to consider as you decide which channels to use and how to use them both efficiently and effectively.

LO 4 Summarize ways to become a better sender and receiver of information.

- Practice writing, be critical of your work, and revise.
- Train yourself as a speaker. Use language carefully and well and work to overcome cross-cultural language differences. Be alert to the nonverbal signals that you send, including your use of time as perceived by other people.
- Know the common bad listening habits and work to overcome them. Read widely and engage in careful, firsthand observation and interpretation.

LO 5 Explain how to improve downward, upward, and horizontal communication.

- Actively manage communications in all directions. Engage in two-way communication more than one-way. Make information available to others.
- Useful approaches to downward communication include coaching, special communications during difficult periods, and open-book management.

- You should also both facilitate and motivate people to communicate upward.
- Many mechanisms exist for enhancing horizontal communications.

LO 6 Summarize how to work with the company grapevine.

- The informal flow of information can contribute as much as formal communication can to organizational effectiveness and morale.
- Managers must understand that the grapevine cannot be eliminated and should be managed actively.
- Many of the suggestions for managing formal communications apply also to managing the grapevine. Moreover, managers can take steps to prevent rumors or neutralize the ones that arise.

LO 7 Describe the boundaryless organization and its advantages.

- Boundaries—psychological if not physical—exist between different organizational levels, units, and organizations and external stakeholders.
- The ideal boundaryless organization is one in which no barriers to information flow exist. Ideas, information, decisions, and actions move to where they are most needed.
- Information is available as needed and freely accessible so that the organization as a whole functions far better than as separate parts.

DISCUSSION QUESTIONS

1. Think of an occasion when you faced a miscommunication problem. What do you think caused the problem? How do you think it should have been handled better?

2. Have you ever *not* given someone information or opinions that perhaps you should have? Why? Was it the right thing to do? Why or why not? What would cause you to be glad that you provided (or withheld) negative or difficult information? What would cause you to regret providing/withholding it?

3. Think back to discussions you have heard or participated in. Consider the differences between one-way and two-way communication. How can two one-ways be turned into a true two-way?

4. Share with the class some of your experiences—both good and bad—with electronic media.

5. Report examples of mixed signals you have received (or sent). How can you reduce the potential for misunderstanding and misperception as you communicate with others?

6. What makes you want to say to someone, "You're not listening"?

7. What do you think about the practice of open-book management? What would you think about it if you were running your own company?

8. Discuss organizational rumors you have heard: what they were about, how they got started, how accurate

they were, and how people reacted to them. What lessons can you learn from these episodes?

9. Refer to the "The Virtual Office" section. What do you think will be the long-term impact of the mobile office on job satisfaction and performance? If you were a manager, how would you maximize the benefits and minimize the drawbacks? If you worked in this environment, how would you manage yourself to maximize your performance and avoid burnout?

10. Have you ever made or seen mistakes due to people not speaking a common language well? How do you or will you deal with others who do not speak the same language as you?

11. Have you ever tried to coach someone? What did you do well, and what mistakes did you make? How can you become a better coach?

12. Have you ever been coached by someone? What did he or she do well, and what mistakes were made? How was it for you to be on the receiving end of the coaching, and how did you respond? What is required to be successful as the receiver of someone else's coaching attempts?

13. Think about how companies communicate with Wall Street and the media and how analysts on TV communicate with viewers. What concepts from the chapter apply, and how can you become a more astute consumer of such information?

EXPERIENTIAL EXERCISES

15.1 INTERPRETING NONVERBAL COMMUNICATION

OBJECTIVE

To become more skilled at interpreting meanings associated with nonverbal communication.

INSTRUCTIONS

Assume your boss exhibits each of the five behaviors listed below over the course of a month. Read each behavior and then record your interpretation of what it most likely means.

Nonverbal Communication Interpretation Worksheet

Your boss . . .	You interpret this behavior to mean . . .
Arrives at the office earlier than usual and has a worried look on her face.	_____ _____ _____
Spends more time than any other manager when training new employees.	_____ _____ _____
Wears the same old jeans, tee shirt, and sneakers to work each day.	_____ _____ _____
Looks at her phone to read texts and e-mails several times per hour, even during meetings and one-on-one conversations.	_____ _____ _____

SOURCE: Adapted from Laurence R. Jauch, Arthur G. Bedian, Sally A. Coltin, and William F. Glueck, *The Managerial Experience: Cases, Exercises, and Readings,* 5th ed. Copyright © 1989. South-Western, a part of Cengage Learning, Inc.

15.2 LISTENING SKILLS SURVEY

OBJECTIVES

1. To measure your skills as a listener.
2. To gain insight into the factors that determine good listening habits.
3. To demonstrate how you can become a better listener.

INSTRUCTIONS

1. Working alone, complete the Listening Skills Survey.
2. In small groups, compare scores, discuss survey test items, and prepare responses to the discussion questions.

3. After the class reconvenes, group spokespersons present group findings.

DISCUSSION QUESTIONS

1. In what ways did students' responses on the survey agree or disagree?
2. What do you think accounts for the differences?
3. How can the results of this survey be put to practical use?

Listening Skills Survey

To measure your listening skills, complete the following survey by circling the degree to which you agree with each statement.

	Strongly Agree	Agree	Neither Agree nor Disagree	Disagree	Strongly Disagree
1. I tend to be patient with the speaker, making sure she or he is finished speaking before I respond in any fashion.	5	4	3	2	1
2. When listening, I don't doodle or fiddle with papers and things that might distract me from the speaker.	5	4	3	2	1
3. I attempt to understand the speaker's point of view.	5	4	3	2	1
4. I try not to put the speaker on the defensive by arguing or criticizing.	5	4	3	2	1
5. When I listen, I focus on the speaker's feelings.	5	4	3	2	1
6. I let a speaker's annoying mannerisms distract me.	5	4	3	2	1
7. While the speaker is talking, I watch carefully for facial expressions and other types of body language.	5	4	3	2	1
8. I never talk when the other person is trying to say something.	5	4	3	2	1

(continued)

	Strongly Agree	Agree	Neither Agree nor Disagree	Disagree	Strongly Disagree
9. During a conversation, a period of silence seems awkward to me.	5	4	3	2	1
10. I want people to just give me the facts and allow me to make up my own mind.	5	4	3	2	1
11. When the speaker is finished, I respond to his or her feelings.	5	4	3	2	1
12. I don't evaluate the speaker's words until she or he is finished talking.	5	4	3	2	1

15.3 ACTIVE LISTENING

This exercise involves triads. Each triad counts off into threes: 1, 2, 3, 1, 2, 3, and so on. In the first round, all the 1s in their respective triads take the pro position (see the topics given later in exercise), all the 2s take the con position, and all the 3s act as observers. After a topic is given, two individuals representing opposing viewpoints have one minute to collect their thoughts and then five to seven minutes to arrive at a mutually agreeable position on that topic.

The observer should use the form here to capture actual examples of what the individuals said or did that indicated active and less-than-active listening. When time is called, the pro individuals share their opinion of which listening behaviors they performed well and which ones

they'd like to improve. Then the con individuals do the same. Finally, the observers share their observations and insights, using examples to reinforce their feedback.

If additional rounds are used, rotate the roles so that each person plays a speaking role and, if possible, an observing role.

Round 1:
Topic selected: _____
Notes:

Round 2:
Topic selected: _____
Notes:

Listening Feedback Form

Indicators of Active Listening	Pro	Con
1. Asked questions for clarification		
2. Paraphrased the opposing view		
3. Responded to nonverbal cues (e.g., body posture, tone of voice)		
4. Appeared to move toward a mutually satisfying solution		
Indicators of Less-Than-Active Listening		
5. Interrupted before allowing the other person to finish		
6. Was defensive about her or his position		
7. Appeared to dominate the conversation		
8. Ignored nonverbal cue		

Potential topics to be used:

1. Gun control
2. Capital punishment
3. Race as a criterion for college admission
4. Prison reform
5. U.S. intervention in wars outside the United States
6. Legalization of marijuana
7. Mandatory armed forces draft
8. Interracial adoption
9. Premarital and extramarital sex
10. Prayer in schools
11. Diversity in the workplace
12. Pornography on the Internet

QUESTIONS

1. Did you arrive at a mutually agreeable solution? What helped you get there?
2. What were some factors that hindered this process?
3. How comfortable did you feel arguing the position you were given? How did this influence your ability to listen actively?
4. If the position you were given was exactly opposite your values or beliefs, do you see this topic differently now than before the exercise?
5. What steps can you take to improve your ability to listen actively to friends or associates, especially when you don't agree with their viewpoint?

CONCLUDING CASE

BEST TRUST BANK

Best Trust Bank attracts accounts from households and businesses based on its broad name recognition and reputation for integrity. In this way, Best Trust has grown to one of the world's top 25 banks. Its 73,000 employees work at headquarters and in facilities located in 47 countries.

One of those employees is Paul Wysinsky, who in the 1970s took an entry-level job as a bank teller. As he developed a track record of satisfying customers, working efficiently, and cooperating well with others on his team, Paul moved up to teller supervisor, branch manager, and operations manager. He took business courses during the evening, earned a master's degree, and worked his way up through middle management positions. Twenty years later, he was offered a vice president's job in the human resources division, responsible for recruiting and retaining Best Trust's employees in Houston. Eager to learn about a new part of the company, Paul tackled the new responsibilities so well that when there was an opening for a new executive vice president in charge of corporate human resources, Paul was tapped to run all of HR.

The nature of Paul's work communications changed considerably as he rose through the ranks. When Paul was a teller, he looked forward to chatting with his co-workers during breaks; their enjoyment of each other's company made the days pass pleasantly. His supervisor checked in with him regularly to make sure Paul understood his job. His favorite responsibility, though, was greeting customers and listening to them carefully, trying to guess the unspoken needs that Best Trust might be able to meet. When customers were upset about a problem, he used to get nervous; but with experience, he became an expert at listening attentively, helping the customer find the best possible solution, and speaking in a respectful tone that almost always soothed any frayed nerves.

Now that Paul is an executive vice president, he rarely talks with Best Trust's customers, and more of his communications are structured and formal. Although he cares about attracting, motivating, and retaining employees in all positions, he knows he cannot possibly have a dialogue with 73,000 people in dozens of countries. In fact, he can't even have personal conversations with all of the HR employees—Best Trust has more than 800 of them, including several at each facility.

Consequently, Paul looks for a variety of ways to communicate. He meets weekly with all the department and functional heads involved in formulating strategy. The meeting's agenda includes reviewing HR issues such as leadership development, succession planning, diversity management, and employee satisfaction. Paul is well prepared because he meets at least weekly with each of the managers who report directly to him. In these one-on-one meetings, Paul and the manager review progress on the issues handled by that manager. Paul also uses those meetings to learn what challenges the manager is facing so he can offer coaching and encouragement. And Paul looks for ways to meet with as many employees outside HR as he can. For example, he attends an annual employee recognition gathering held to honor the company's 800 top-performing employees. There he talks to as many people as he can. He asks open-ended questions such as "What are you happy about at Best Trust? What could we do better?"

Talking one on one to employees can feel like an escape from one of the chief annoyances of his job: poorly written messages from many of the bank's middle managers. It seems that Best Trust has excelled at finding people with strong analytic and customer service skills, but many of these people stumble at presenting an idea or summarizing their progress in e-mails and reports. Paul feels intense time pressure, and if he gets a suggestion but can't figure out the main idea in the first couple of sentences, he simply passes it to one of his managers for a possible follow-up. Paul suspects that good ideas and real problems are being missed. Rambling reports and presentations loaded with jargon seem to have become a norm at Best Trust, and Paul is thinking about adding a new training program to improve writing skills.

To get out the word about the bank's policies, benefits, and other initiatives, Paul uses a variety of media. He gives presentations at events such as the employee recognition gathering and at branches around the world. Four times a year, he records a video that is posted on the bank's intranet. Topics range from a summary of HR resources to interviews with key leaders at Best Trust. Also on the intranet, Paul leads regular town hall meetings, a live video feed that allows employees to post questions and ideas, which Paul and other executives answer immediately on the video.

Promotions to the executive level are not the only reason communication has changed for Paul at Best Trust. Another source of change is technology. When Paul was a teller, the Internet was just a concept, and transmitting data online was a major undertaking that required computer experts. Now the Internet is a basic tool. On the plus side, it helps Paul deliver information efficiently and keep up with far-flung colleagues. But Paul also has a whole set of policy concerns related to the Internet, such as whether to allow employees to access social networking sites and how closely to monitor blogs and other public information for company-related posts. When Paul thinks about it, he realizes that his communication skills have barely grown as fast as the communication demands of his work.

QUESTIONS

1. How has the media richness of Paul's communications changed since the days when he was a teller?

2. What sender and receiver skills are described in this case? Which ones need improvement? Offer one suggestion for improving the weak skills.

3. How might Paul improve upward communication and the communication culture more generally at Best Trust?

PART FOUR SUPPORTING CASE

Leading and Motivating When Disaster Strikes: Magna Exteriors and Interiors

The name of Magna Exteriors and Interiors Corporation captures its product mix of vehicle components that give each car or truck model its distinctive look. Some of Magna's exterior products are trim, roof systems, body panels, and front and rear end fascia; interior products include trim, cockpit systems, and cargo management systems. Nowadays auto companies don't make all these components but, instead, create the designs and handle the final assembly of components from suppliers such as Magna, delivered to the auto company as needed to meet production plans.

Magna Exteriors and Interiors is a unit of Magna International, which describes itself as "the most diversified automotive supplier in the world." Magna has 263 manufacturing operations plus sales and engineering centers in 26 countries of North America, South America, Africa, Europe, and Asia. These meet the needs of more than two dozen customers, including General Motors, Ford, Chrysler, Toyota, Mack, Harley-Davidson, Freightliner, and Volkswagen. The customers sell very different kinds of vehicles, and it is expensive to build and transport large components, so Magna's factories need to be close to customers both geographically and in their working relationships.

Meeting these requirements suddenly became a problem for Magna's factory in Howell, Michigan, on a recent Wednesday evening in March. A fire started on an assembly line at the facility, which makes interior trim such as rear window trays, door panels, and skins for instrument panels. Fortunately the hundred workers who were finishing up the afternoon shift all escaped safely.

The Howell facility employs about 450 workers. Its customers include 16 GM, Ford, Chrysler, Nissan, and Mazda assembly plants. Forecasting a shortage of parts, some of its customers slowed production and canceled shifts in the days immediately after the fire. Magna's managers knew they needed to scramble, or employees would be out of work and important customers would be lost. Robert Brownlee, president of Magna Exteriors and Interiors North America, decided the Howell facility should be running again within just two days. Meeting that goal would require an all-out effort.

While the firefighters were still battling the blaze, Brownlee conferred by phone with his top managers, figuring out what they should do first. Because they couldn't yet assess the extent of the damages, they had to work with a worst-case scenario: destruction of the entire building. They identified four Magna facilities making similar products, where they could ship the Howell plant's tooling on flatbed trucks if need be. That night, Brownlee directed all four of the plants to increase production and build up their inventories in case they would be needed for the Howell plant's customers.

Next the managers set up a reconstruction team, including electricians, pipe fitters, millwrights, mechanics, toolmakers, and information technology specialists. The team assembled in Howell with a structural engineer, awaiting permission to enter the damaged building. On Thursday night, about 24 hours after the fire, the fire department let the team enter the plant. The structural engineer determined that the fire had been contained in one part of the plant. About 30 percent of the plant, representing one out of four production sectors, was destroyed beyond repair. One of the four remaining production sectors had largely escaped damage.

Now the clock was ticking on Brownlee's two-day recovery goal. On Friday morning, workers pulled damaged tooling out of the rubble and had it moved to Brighton, a city 12 miles away, where they cleaned it and set up a temporary assembly line in a Magna warehouse. Back in Howell, the reconstruction team was building a temporary wall to seal off the undamaged part of the facility and repairing the roof. The heating and electrical systems were destroyed, so they brought in a dozen diesel generators to power heaters and lighting. Until the roof was repaired, they coped with Michigan's wintry March weather by wearing snowmobile suits while clearing out debris and damaged products, working around the clock.

The next morning, spirits rose when power was restored to the least-damaged sector, and the lights came back on. Workers continued to repair, clean, and rewire the tooling. By Saturday night, workers were able to restart some of the machinery and do test runs. Unfortunately they ran into problems with each attempt. Managers were scrambling to keep on top of the plant reconstruction and the attempts to restart machinery. Brownlee saw that this was too much responsibility. He called together the managers, put each one in charge of relaunching one product line, and directed them to put a subordinate in charge of every other duty, including reconstruction.

The efforts to restart continued as representatives from every customer monitored the progress. Magna gave customers daily updates, and as each assembly line resumed, the relevant customer's representative signed off as part of the quality-control practices. By Sunday, limited production had begun at the Howell plant. Six days after the fire department determined that the fire was extinguished, the Howell plant was running at 80 percent of capacity, and its temporary line in Brighton handled the remaining production.

In a statement to the media, the company publicly thanked "the Magna Howell employees who continue to do whatever it takes to meet customer requirements; the Magna group office employees and Magna employees from numerous other divisions who have come to support the effort," the company's contractors and customers, the community's firefighters, and others who helped after the fire.

QUESTIONS

1. As a leader, what vision did Robert Brownlee offer? What combination of task performance and group maintenance behaviors did he use? Was this the appropriate combination after the fire? Why or why not?

2. What do you think the Magna managers and employees were motivated by most after the fire? Why?

3. Management set up a cross-functional reconstruction team, but there is no evidence that this was a self-managed team. Would a self-managed team have been more effective? Why or why not?

SOURCES: D. Sedgwick, "Five-Alarm Planning," *Crain's Detroit Business*, April 18, 2011, Business & Company Resource Center, http://galenet. galegroup.com; Magna International, "About Magna Exteriors and Interiors," http://www.magna.com; T. Van Alphen, "Magna Plant Resumes Full Deliveries after Fire," *Toronto Star*, March 10, 2011, http://www.thestar.com; and Magna International, "Magna Atreum Howell Plant Back in Business Six Days after Fire," news release, March 9, 2011, http://www.magna.com.

CHAPTER 16

Managerial Control

More than at any time in the past, companies will not be able to hold themselves together with the traditional methods of control: hierarchy, systems, budgets, and the like. . . . The bonding glue will increasingly become ideological.

—COLLINS AND PORRAS[1]

Use your good judgment in all situations.

—NORDSTROM'S EMPLOYEE MANUAL

Management in Action

CAN BETTER CONTROLS HELP BEST BUY SURVIVE IN THE INTERNET AGE?

Best Buy once had other stores' managers running scared. Founder Richard Schulze built a St. Paul, Minnesota, electronics store into a retailing giant; today more than 125,000 employees sell $40 billion of merchandise a year. Consumers who once bought a television set at a department or discount store flocked to Best Buy for its wide selection and knowledgeable salespeople. Today, however, consumers have alternatives. They can find product specifications and reviews online, from the comfort of their homes. Those who bother to visit a store are likely to be just taking a look at preselected items; after making their choice, they will return to the Internet and order from the lowest-priced seller.

© Brendan Smialowski/AFP/Getty Images

Best Buy is struggling to stay relevant in this environment. Its revenues at stores open a year or more have been sliding, and it has posted one unprofitable quarter after another. Its market share, though it represents close to one-third of U.S. sales of consumer electronics, is falling. Competing on price with online retailers such as Amazon is difficult because Best Buy has many large stores to maintain.

Management has tried several responses. Trying to keep prices low, the company launched a program to match prices available online. It cut costs by laying off employees. It lured in younger shoppers with low-priced items such as CDs and expanded into services with the Geek Squad. It pressed customers to buy extended warranties, which are very profitable. To its credit, Best Buy has stayed in business while its competitors, Circuit City and Radio Shack, declared bankruptcy.

One of management's most attention-getting efforts was the decision to abandon a policy called Results Only Work Environment (ROWE). The policy granted employees at headquarters freedom to set work hours; managers, dubbed "results coaches," evaluated these employees only on their achievements, not their attendance. Facilitators were used to help move the organization from a "face time culture to a workplace that is focused on work outcomes." The policy had been announced to great fanfare, with its sponsors saying ROWE helped the company save money that would have been lost to employee turnover. However, CEO Hubert Joly saw ROWE as a failure to lead decisively at a time when Best Buy needs all hands on deck. Eliminating ROWE was just one part of a major restructuring plan, called "Renew Blue," aimed at "enhancing the company's core business, removing management layers, and eliminating operational inefficiencies." Joly's first step was to save $725 million in costs by cutting about 400 jobs from Best Buy headquarters resulting in the elimination of $150 million in administrative costs.[2]

Survival is difficult in the retailing industry because consumer tastes and habits can change abruptly. Best Buy won over a huge base of customers and is now struggling to keep them without sacrificing profits. As you read this chapter, think about the kinds of control measures and processes that can help a company manage in a turbulent environment.

LO 1

Bottom Line

Control is essential for the attainment of any management objective. *What happens in the absence of control?*

control

Any process that directs the activities of individuals toward the achievement of organizational goals.

Financial measures are signaling Best Buy's managers that they need to make changes to improve performance. Another company that uses measurements to help it improve is La-Z-Boy, where teams of employees constantly find ways to improve productivity and quality. La-Z-Boy also uses systems to prevent problems. It assigns a production engineer to design teams to make sure that new products can be produced efficiently, reducing defects as well as costs.[3] These examples are two sides of one coin: control—a means or mechanism for regulating the behavior of organization members. Left on their own, people may act in ways that they perceive to be beneficial to them individually but that may work to the detriment of the organization as a whole. Even well-intentioned people may not know whether they are directing their efforts toward the activities that are most important. Thus control is one of the fundamental forces that keep the organization together and heading in the right direction.

Control is defined as any process that directs the activities of individuals toward the achievement of organizational goals. It is how effective managers make sure that activities are going as planned. Some managers don't want to admit it (see Exhibit 16.1), but control problems—the lack of controls or the wrong kinds of controls—frequently cause irreparable damage to organizations. Ineffective control systems result in problems ranging from employee theft to peeling tire tread problems. BP has spent billions of dollars to repair damage to the Gulf of Mexico following the Deepwater Horizon disaster; years later, it was still in court, defending charges of negligence. The damage to its reputation could hardly help the company as it more recently responded to safety questions related to oil leaks in Lake Michigan and off the coast of Norway.[4] Employees simply wasting time cost U.S. employers billions of dollars each year![5]

Control has been called one of the conjoined twins of management. The other twin is planning. Some means of control are necessary because once managers form plans and strategies, they must ensure that the plans are carried out. They must make sure that other people are doing what needs to be done and not doing inappropriate things. If plans are not carried out properly, management must take steps to correct the problem. This process is the primary control function of management. By ensuring creativity, enhancing quality, and reducing cost, managers must figure out ways to control the activities in their organizations.

Control has been called one of the conjoined twins of management.

Not surprisingly, effective planning facilitates control, and control facilitates planning. Planning lays out a framework for the future and, in this sense, provides a blueprint for control. Control systems, in turn, regulate the allocation and use of resources and, in so doing, facilitate the process of the next phases of planning. In today's complex organizational environment, both functions have become more difficult to implement while they have become more important in every department of the organization. Managers today

EXHIBIT 16.1

Symptoms of an Out-of-Control Company

- **Lax top management**—senior managers do not emphasize or value the need for controls, or they set a bad example.

- **Absence of policies**—the firm's expectations are not established in writing.

- **Lack of agreed-upon standards**—organization members are unclear about what needs to be achieved.

- **"Shoot the messenger" management**—employees feel their careers would be at risk if they reported bad news.

- **Lack of periodic reviews**—managers do not assess performance on a regular, timely basis.

- **Bad information systems**—key data are not measured and reported in a timely and easily accessible way.

- **Lack of ethics in the culture**—organization members have not internalized a commitment to integrity.

must control their people, inventories, quality, and costs, to mention just a few of their responsibilities.

According to William Ouchi of the University of California at Los Angeles, managers can apply three broad strategies for achieving organizational control: bureaucratic control, market control, and clan control.[6] **Bureaucratic control** is the use of rules, regulations, and formal authority to guide performance. It includes such items as budgets, statistical reports, and performance appraisals to regulate behavior and results. **Market control** involves the use of pricing mechanisms to regulate activities in organizations as though they were economic transactions. Business units may be treated as profit centers and trade resources (services or goods) with one another via such mechanisms. Managers who run these units may be evaluated on the basis of profit and loss. **Clan control** (also known as *cultural control*), unlike the first two types, does not assume that the interests of the organization and individuals naturally diverge. Instead clan control is based on the idea that employees may share the values, expectations, and goals of the organization and act in accordance with them. When members of an organization have common values and goals—and trust one another—formal controls may be less necessary. Clan control is based on many of the interpersonal processes described in the organization culture section of Chapter 2, in Chapter 12 on leadership, and in Chapter 14 on groups and teams (e.g., group norms and cohesiveness).

Exhibit 16.2 summarizes the main features of bureaucratic, market, and clan controls. We use this framework as a foundation for our discussions throughout the chapter.

bureaucratic control

The use of rules, regulations, and authority to guide performance; see also *control systems*.

market control

Control based on the use of pricing mechanisms and economic information to regulate activities within organizations.

clan control

Control based on the norms, values, shared goals, and trust among group members.

EXHIBIT 16.2

Characteristics of Controls

System Control	Features and Requirements
Bureaucratic control	Uses formal rules, standards, hierarchy, and legitimate authority. Works best where tasks are certain and workers are independent.
Market control	Uses prices, competition, profit centers, and exchange relationships. Works best where tangible output can be identified and a market can be established between parties.
Clan control	Involves culture, shared values, beliefs, expectations, and trust. Works best where there is no one best way to do a job, and employees are empowered to make decisions.

SOURCES: W. G. Ouchi, "A Conceptual Framework for the Design of Organizational Control Mechanisms," *Management Science* 25 (1979), pp. 833–48; W. G. Ouchi, "Markets, Bureaucracies, and Clans," *Administrative Science Quarterly* 25 (1980), pp. 129–41; and R. D. Robey and C. A. Sales, *Designing Organizations* (Burr Ridge, IL: Richard D. Irwin, 1994).

Bureaucratic Control Systems

Bureaucratic (or formal) control systems are designed to measure progress toward set performance goals and, if necessary, to apply corrective measures to ensure that performance achieves managers' objectives. Control systems detect and correct significant variations, or discrepancies, in the results of planned activities.

The Control Cycle

As Exhibit 16.3 shows, a typical control system has four major steps:

1. Setting performance standards.
2. Measuring performance.
3. Comparing performance against the standards and determining deviations.
4. Taking action to correct problems and reinforce successes.

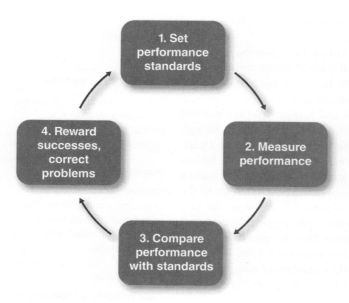

EXHIBIT 16.3
The Control Process

standard

Expected performance for a given goal: a target that establishes a desired performance level, motivates performance, and serves as a benchmark against which actual performance is assessed.

Bottom Line

Standards must be set for all bottom-line practices. *Give an example of a standard for sustainability.*

Step 1: Setting Performance Standards

Every organization has goals: profitability, innovation, satisfaction of customers and employees, and so on. A **standard** is the level of expected performance for a given goal. Standards are targets that establish desired performance levels, motivate performance, and serve as benchmarks against which to assess actual performance. Standards can be set for any activity—financial activities, operating activities, legal compliance, charitable contributions,[7] and social impact (see the "Social Enterprise" box).

We have discussed setting performance standards in other parts of the text. For example, employee goal setting for motivation is built around the concept of specific, measurable performance standards. Such standards should be challenging and should aim for improvement over past performance. Typically, performance standards are derived from job requirements, such as increasing market share by 10 percent, reducing costs 20 percent, and answering customer complaints within 24 hours. But performance standards don't apply just to people in isolation—they frequently reflect the integration of both human and system performance.

HealthPartners, a Bloomington, Minnesota, nonprofit organization that operates clinics and a hospital and offers health insurance plans, sets ambitious standards for patient care. To achieve a goal of reducing diabetes complications by 30 percent, HealthPartners measured existing practices and results and then set up a standard protocol for exams and treatments, including the requirement that any abnormal results receive an immediate response. To encourage its physicians to follow the protocol, HealthPartners offers financial incentives for compliance. In little more than a decade, HealthPartners exceeded its goal for improved diabetes care. HealthPartners has similar programs for treatment of cardiovascular disease and depression and for improving the health status of patients who are obese or smoke.[8] In a recent year, HealthPartners estimated it saved more than $3.6 million through programs aimed at eliminating health complications that bring patients back to the hospital after being discharged.

Performance standards can be set with respect to (1) quantity, (2) quality, (3) time used, and (4) cost. For example, production activities include volume of output (quantity), defects (quality), on-time availability of finished goods (time use), and dollar expenditures for raw materials and direct labor (cost). Many important aspects of performance, such as customer service, can be measured by the same standards—adequate supply and availability of products, quality of service, speed of delivery, and so forth.

One word of caution: The downside of establishing performance targets and standards is that they may not be supported by other elements of the control system. Each piece of the system is important and depends on the others. Otherwise the system can get terribly out of balance.

Step 2: Measuring Performance

The second step in the control process is to measure performance levels. For example, managers can count units produced, websites viewed, days absent, samples distributed, and dollars earned. Performance data commonly are obtained from three sources: written reports, oral reports, and personal observations.

Written reports include computer-generated reports. Thanks to computers' data-gathering and analysis capabilities and decreasing costs, both large and small companies can gather huge amounts of performance data.

One common example of oral reports occurs when a salesperson contacts his or her immediate manager at the close of each business day to report the accomplishments, problems, or customers' reactions during the day. The manager can ask questions to gain

Social Enterprise

Beyond Counting: Alternative Ways to Measure Social Impact

Many social enterprises set ambitious goals such as ending hunger or eradicating diseases in the world. Mohammed Yunus, former recipient of a Nobel Peace Prize and founder of Grameen Bank, set a high standard when he declared that "social business" could lead to a "world without poverty." Before progress toward such objectives can be assessed, social enterprises need to measure more fully the impact they are having on social challenges.

A popular approach among social enterprises is to count the number of people that received the enterprise's product or service. For example, TOMS counts the number of shoes it donates annually to impoverished children (over 35 million in 70 countries at last count). Root Capital has made loans to 600,000 small-scale farmers and over 3 million individuals. Both organizations are certainly making a social impact, but the questions remain: How much of an impact are they making on their recipients? Did all of the recipients wear the shoes or use the loan money as intended? To what degree did the recipients fare better than comparable individuals who didn't receive free shoes or a loan?

Despite its popularity, counting outcomes is an incomplete measure. Progress is being made to develop more comprehensive assessments of social impact, including the following measures:

1. *Impact Value Chain (IVC).* Developed by Professor Catherine Clark, the IVC takes a holistic approach to measuring social impact. She recommends that social enterprises measure their impact by evaluating the entire process or value chain of their enterprise, including inputs, outputs, and outcomes.
2. *Progress Out of Poverty Index (PPI).* Created by the Grameen Foundation, the PPI "provides a relatively low-cost and efficient way to evaluate the poverty level of a given community."

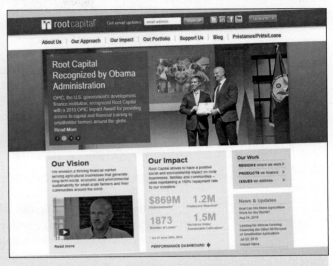

© The McGraw-Hill Companies, Inc./Roberts Publishing Services

3. *B Impact Assessment (BIA).* Developed by B-Lab, a nonprofit that certifies benefit corporations, the BIA evaluates an organization's "impact on its workers, community, environment, and customers."

With better measures, we will all know when a social enterprise changes the world.[9]

Questions

• Assume the role of devil's advocate: Why is counting outcomes, like in the case of TOMS, an adequate way of assessing a social enterprise's social impact?

• If you ran a social enterprise to reduce poverty in India, which of the three measures (IVC, PPI, or BIA) would you likely use to measure your enterprise's social impact?

additional information or clear up any misunderstandings. When necessary, tentative corrective actions can be worked out during the discussion.

Personal observation involves going to the area where activities take place and watching what is occurring. The manager can directly observe work methods, employees' nonverbal signals, and the general operation. Personal observation gives a detailed picture of what is going on, but it also has some disadvantages. It does not provide accurate quantitative data; the information usually is general and subjective. Also, employees can misunderstand the purpose of personal observation as mistrust or lack of confidence. Still, many managers believe in the value of firsthand observation. As you learned in earlier chapters, personal contact can increase leadership visibility

At the Baccarat factory in France, the workers in the quality control area are responsible for the quality and selection of these fine cut crystal glasses.
© Chamussy/Sipa via AP Images

and upward communication. It also provides valuable information about performance to supplement written and oral reports.

Regardless of the performance measure used, the information must be provided to managers on a timely basis. For example, consumer goods companies such as General Foods carefully track new product sales in selected local markets first so they can make any necessary adjustments well before a national rollout. Information that is not available is of little or no use to managers.

Step 3: Comparing Performance with the Standard

The third step in the control process is comparing performance with the standard. In this process, the manager evaluates the performance. For some activities, relatively small deviations from the standard are acceptable, whereas in others a slight deviation may be serious. In many manufacturing processes, a significant deviation in either direction (e.g., drilling a hole that is too small or too large) is unacceptable. In other cases, a deviation in one direction, such as sales or customer satisfaction that fall below the target level, is a problem, but a deviation in the other, exceeding the sales target or customer expectations, is a sign employees are getting better-than-expected results. As a result, managers who perform the oversight must analyze and evaluate the results carefully.

> Managers can save much time and effort if they apply the principle of exception.

principle of exception

A managerial principle stating that control is enhanced by concentrating on the exceptions to or significant deviations from the expected result or standard.

The managerial **principle of exception** states that control is enhanced by concentrating on the exceptions to, or significant deviations from, the expected result or standard. In other words, in comparing performance with the standard, managers need to direct their attention to the exception—for example, a handful of defective components produced on an assembly line or the feedback from customers who are upset or delighted with a service. Virginia-based Accurid Pest Solutions installed GPS tracking software on company-issued smartphones used by its drivers. After monitoring the location and movement of the staff, the owner of the company discovered that two drivers were taking off several hours from work each day (without permission). Consequently, the drivers were let go.[10]

With the principle of exception, only exceptional cases require corrective action. This principle is important in controlling. The manager is not concerned with performance that equals or closely approximates the expected results. Managers can save much time and effort if they apply the principle of exception.

Step 4: Taking Action to Correct Problems and Reinforce Successes

The last step in the control process is to take appropriate action when there are significant deviations. This step ensures that operations are adjusted to achieve the planned results—or to continue exceeding the plan if the manager determines that is possible. In cases in which significant variances are discovered, the manager usually takes immediate and vigorous action.

McDonald's has an extra challenge in introducing corrective action: When it identifies a problem in its restaurants, it has to persuade franchise owners that they should make changes. Most McDonald's restaurants have independent owners (franchisees), so the company cannot simply direct them as it would direct employees.

Recently, McDonald's addressed the problem that its sales had begun to fall after years of solid growth. In looking for the source of the problem, management observed that the data it gathers about customer satisfaction showed an increase in complaints about speed and quality of service.

McDonald's responded by sharing this information with its franchisees. It told them that a survey by the National Restaurant Association showed that customers care almost as much about high-quality service as about value for the price. McDonald's urged franchisees to schedule more employees for peak hours, and it began providing equipment and training for a new dual-point ordering system. Under the system, one employee takes a customer's order and provides a receipt showing an order number. The customer moves to the other end of the counter to pick up the order when the order number displays on a monitor.[11]

When corrective action is needed to solve a systemic problem, such as major delays in work flow, often a team approach is most effective. A corrective action is more likely to have greater acceptance in the organization if it is based on a common effort and takes into account multiple points of view. As we discussed in Chapter 14, teams often bring a greater diversity of resources, ideas, and perspectives to problem solving. Knowledgeable team members can often prevent managers from implementing simplistic solutions that don't address the underlying causes of a problem. They are more likely to take into account the effects of any solution on other parts of the organization, preventing new problems from arising later. And they may well develop solutions that managers might not have considered on their own. As a result, any corrective action that is finally adopted will probably be more effective. An important added benefit of bringing employees together to develop corrective actions is that it helps managers build and reinforce an organizationwide culture of high standards.

The selection of the corrective action depends on the nature of the problem. The corrective action may involve a shift in marketing strategy (if, say, the problem is lower-than-expected sales), a disciplinary action, a new way to check the accuracy of manufactured parts, or a major modification to a process or system. Sometimes managers learn they can get better results if they adjust their own practices. Each year, FedEx surveys employees about their job satisfaction and feelings about management's leadership performance. After the results are tabulated, managers hold feedback sessions to discuss the survey findings with employees. Problems are identified and action plans are developed to resolve them. The survey and subsequent action plans have become a problem-solving tool that operates both horizontally and vertically throughout the organization.[12]

After trying corrective action, a growing number of organizations conduct an **after-action review,** a frank and open-minded discussion of the four questions shown in Exhibit 16.4, aimed at continuous improvement.[13] The process was developed by the U.S. Army to help soldiers learn from their experiences, and many companies find that the method applies equally well to businesses that want to improve. Employees at the J. M. Huber Corporation conduct a review after every planned project and major unplanned event and then post the lessons learned in a database available online. In the public sector, emergency response teams have improved their performance as a result of using after-action reviews. This type of review is most effective if the reviews are scheduled consistently, participation is mandatory, and all participants in the project are included.

Approaches to Bureaucratic Control

The three approaches to bureaucratic control are feedforward, concurrent, and feedback. **Feedforward control** takes place before operations begin and includes policies, procedures, and rules designed to ensure that planned activities are carried out properly. Examples include inspection of raw materials and proper selection and training of employees. **Concurrent control** takes place while plans are being carried out. It includes directing, monitoring, and fine-tuning activities as they occur. **Feedback control** focuses on the use of information about results to correct deviations from the acceptable standard after they arise.

after-action review

A frank and open-minded discussion of four basic questions aimed at continuous improvement.

feedforward control

The control process used before operations begin, including policies, procedures, and rules designed to ensure that planned activities are carried out properly.

concurrent control

The control process used while plans are being carried out, including directing, monitoring, and fine-tuning activities as they are performed.

feedback control

Control that focuses on the use of information about previous results to correct deviations from the acceptable standard.

EXHIBIT 16.4
Questions for an After-Action Review

1. What were our intended results?	2. What were our actual results?	3. What caused our results?	4. What will we sustain? Improve?
(What was planned?)	(What really happened?)	(Why did it happen?)	(What can we do better next time?)

Feedforward Control Feedforward control (sometimes called *preliminary control*) is future oriented; its aim is to prevent problems before they arise. Instead of waiting for results and comparing them with goals, a manager can exert control by limiting activities in advance. For example, companies have policies defining the scope within which decisions are made. A company may dictate that managers must adhere to clear ethical and legal guidelines when making decisions. Formal rules and procedures also prescribe people's actions before they occur. For example, legal experts advise companies to establish policies forbidding disclosure of proprietary information or making clear that employees are not speaking for the company when they post messages on blogs, microblogging sites such as Tumblr or Twitter, or social networking sites such as LinkedIn or Facebook. Human resource policies defining what forms of body art are acceptable to display at work can avoid awkward case-by-case conversations about a tattoo that offends co-workers or piercings that are incompatible with the company's image.[14]

Recently more managers have grown concerned about the organizational pitfalls of workplace romances, and some have sought a solution in feedforward controls. As wonderful as it is to find love, problems can arise if romantic activities between a supervisor and subordinate create a conflict of interest or charges of sexual harassment. Other employees might interpret the relationship wrongly—that the company sanctions personal relationships as a path to advancement. In addition, romantic ups and downs can spill over into the workplace and affect everyone's mood and motivation. Controls aimed at preventing such problems in an organization include training in appropriate behavior (including how to avoid sexual harassment) and even requiring executives and their romantic interests to sign love contracts in which they indicate that the relationship is voluntary and welcome. A copy of the contract goes into the company's personnel files in case the attachment disintegrates and an unhappy employee wants to blame the company for having allowed it in the first place.[15]

Concurrent Control Concurrent control, which takes place while plans are carried out, is the heart of any control system. On a manufacturing floor, all efforts are directed toward producing the correct quantity and quality of the right products in the specified amount of time. In an airline terminal, the baggage must get to the right airplanes before flights depart. In factories, materials must be available when and where needed, and breakdowns in the production process must be repaired immediately. Concurrent control also is in effect when supervisors watch employees to ensure they work efficiently and avoid mistakes.

Advances in information technology have created powerful concurrent controls. Computerized systems give managers immediate access to data from the most remote corners of their companies. For example, managers can update budgets instantly based on a continuous flow of performance data. In production facilities, monitoring systems that track errors per hour, machine speeds, and other measures allow managers to correct small production problems before they become disasters. Point-of-sale terminals in store checkout lines send sales data back to a retailer's headquarters to show which products are selling in which locations.

Concurrent control also can be applied to service settings. As part of its efforts to transform safety, quality, and efficiency, Virginia Mason Medical Center authorized employees to issue personal safety alerts (PSAs). If any employee has a concern or question about a patient's safety, that employee may call an alert. The PSA system not only has improved the hospital's safety performance, it also has lowered its costs for professional liability insurance.[16]

> Timing is an important aspect of feedback control.

Feedback Control Feedback control is involved when performance data have been gathered and analyzed and the results have been returned to someone (or something) in the process to make corrections. When supervisors monitor behavior, they are exercising

Multiple Generations at Work

Is Annual Performance Feedback a Thing of the Past?

Some companies are doing away with annual performance evaluations in favor of continuous coaching and development of employees. Some attribute this change to Millennial employees' desire for greater responsibility and a "feedback-rich" culture in which learning is continuous. Others suggest that today's fast-changing business environment requires more frequent dialogue between managers and employees to ensure alignment between employees' skills and the firm's business strategy.

Tata Consulting Services (TCS) of India has a workforce of 240,000 employees of which over 70 percent are Millennials. Ajoy Mukherjee, the director of human resources, responded to this pressure for change by having managers provide feedback on performance more quickly and giving junior employees more responsibility sooner.

Software maker Adobe used to spend over 80,000 hours per year on administering traditional performance evaluations. After trying to modify the system, the firm decided "it was inconsistent with Adobe's strong culture of teamwork and collaboration." The new feedback system is more effective. Every three months, a manager or employee requests a "check-in" to discuss ways to improve the employee's performance. Prior to the meeting, feedback about his/her performance is collected from

© E. Audras/PhotoAlto

a group of fellow employees. Adobe's goal is to "make coaching and developing a continuous, collaborative process between managers and employees." Since launching the new performance feedback system, Adobe reported a 30 percent reduction in its voluntary employee turnover.

If organizations want to align their highly skilled talent with evolving business strategies, then managers must provide employees with continuous coaching and developmental feedback.[17]

concurrent control. When they point out and correct improper performance, they are using feedback as a means of control.

Timing is an important aspect of feedback control. Long time lags often occur between performance and feedback, such as when actual spending is compared with the quarterly budget, instead of weekly or monthly, or when an employee's annual performance is compared to goals set a year earlier. Yet if feedback on performance is not timely, managers cannot quickly identify and eliminate the problem and prevent more serious harm.[18] The "Multiple Generations at Work" box discusses the trend toward more frequent, timely performance feedback.

Some feedback processes are under real-time (concurrent) control, such as a computer-controlled robot on an assembly line. Such units have sensors that continually determine whether they are in the correct position to perform their functions. If they are not, a built-in control device makes immediate corrections.

In other situations, feedback processes require more time. The feedback used by Hertz includes customer ratings of the company's service and the quality of the cars it rents. Patterns of praise and complaints can help the company reinforce or correct practices at particular facilities or throughout the organization, and if a customer is upset about something, Hertz wants to know as soon as possible so it can correct the problem. In the past, gathering and interpreting customer feedback from surveys and online comments could take about three weeks. Now, however, analytic software collects and tallies data as it flows into the company, and it delivers daily reports to local managers. Armed with the information, the managers are expected to respond to any problems within 24 hours. With these changes, customer satisfaction with Hertz has been rising consistently.[19]

The Role of Six Sigma   One of the most important quality control tools to emerge is six sigma, which we first discussed in Chapter 9. It is a particularly robust and powerful application of feedback control. Six sigma is designed to reduce defects in all organization processes—not just product defects but anything that may result in customer dissatisfaction. The system was developed at Motorola in the late 1980s, when the company found it was being beaten consistently in the competitive marketplace by foreign firms that were able to produce higher-quality products at a lower cost. Since then, the technique has been widely adopted and even improved on by many companies, such as GE, AlliedSignal, Ford, and Xerox.

Sigma is the Greek letter used in statistics to designate the estimated standard deviation, or variation, in a process. It indicates how often defects in a process are likely to occur. The higher the sigma number, the lower the level of variation or defects. For example, as you can see in Exhibit 16.5, a two-sigma-level process has more than 300,000 defects per million opportunities (DPMO)—not a very well-controlled process. A three-sigma-level process has 66,807 DPMO, which is roughly a 93 percent level of accuracy. Many organizations operate at this level, which on its face does not sound too bad, until we consider its implications—for example, 7 items of airline baggage lost for every 100 processed. The additional costs to organizations of such inaccuracy are enormous. As you can see in the exhibit, even at just above a 99 percent defect-free rate, or 6,210 DPMO, the accuracy level is often unacceptable.[20]

At a six-sigma level, a process is producing fewer than 3.4 defects per million, which we saw in Chapter 9 is a 99.99966 percent level of accuracy. Six-sigma companies have not only close to zero product or service defects but also substantially lower production costs and cycle times and much higher levels of customer satisfaction. The methodology isn't just for the factory floor, either. Accountants have used six sigma to improve the quality of their audits investigating risks faced by their clients.[21]

The six-sigma approach is based on an intense statistical analysis of business processes that contribute to customer satisfaction. For example, a business process could be assembling a product or delivering products to customers. For the given process, the effort begins by defining the outputs and information that flow through each stage of the process and then measuring performance at each stage. A variety of tools are available for analyzing the results. These might include looking for all the root causes of any problem. Suppose some customers are dissatisfied with a company's customer service. Asking "why?" over and over could reveal that customers are dissatisfied because phone calls go unanswered, which happens because support staff cannot keep up with the call volume, which happens because the department is understaffed, which is the result of frozen hiring levels, the result of budget cuts. Any solution will have to address the budget restrictions, either by increasing the budget or by finding a way that a small department can satisfy customers. After the problems are analyzed, process improvements are identified and implemented, and the new process is evaluated again. This cycle continues until the desired quality level is achieved. In this way, the six-sigma process leads to continuous improvement in an organization's operations.

Bottom Line

Six sigma aims for defect-free performance.
What impact would achieving six-sigma quality have on a company's costs?

EXHIBIT 16.5

Relationship between Sigma Level and Defects per Million Opportunities

Sigma Level	DPMO	Is Four Sigma Good Enough?
2σ	308,537	Consider these everyday examples of four-sigma quality . . .
3σ	66,807	• 20,000 lost articles of mail per hour.
4σ	**6,210**	• Unsafe drinking water 15 minutes per day.
5σ	233	• 5,000 incorrect surgical operations per week.
6σ	3.4	• 200,000 wrong prescriptions each year.
		• No electricity for 7 hours each month.

SOURCE: Tom Rancour and Mike McCracken, "Applying 6 Sigma Methods for Breakthrough Safety Performance," *Professional Safety* 45, no. 10 (October 2000), pp. 29–32. Reprinted with permission.

Six sigma has come under some criticism for not always delivering business results.[22] One likely reason six sigma doesn't always improve the bottom line is that it focuses only on how to eliminate defects in a process, not whether the process is the best one for the organization. So, for example, at 3M, a drive to improve efficiency through six sigma has been blamed for slowing the flow of innovative ideas. At Home Depot, six sigma has been credited with improving such processes as customer checkout and deciding where to place products in stores, but some say the effort took store workers away from customers. One way managers can apply the strengths of six sigma and minimize the drawbacks is by setting different goals and control processes for the company's mature products than for its areas of innovation.

Management Audits

Over the years, **management audits** have developed as a means of evaluating the effectiveness and efficiency of various systems within an organization, from social responsibility programs to accounting control. Management audits may be external or internal. Managers conduct external audits of other companies and internal audits of their own companies. Some of the same tools and approaches are used for both types of audit.[23]

External Audits   An **external audit** occurs when one organization evaluates another organization. Typically an external body such as a CPA firm conducts financial audits of an organization (accounting audits are discussed later). But any company can conduct external audits of competitors or other companies for its own strategic decision-making purposes. This type of analysis (1) investigates other organizations for possible merger or acquisition, (2) determines the soundness of a company that will be used as a major supplier, or (3) discovers the strengths and weaknesses of a competitor to maintain or better exploit the competitive advantage of the investigating organization. Publicly available data usually are used for these evaluations.[24]

External audits provide essential feedback control when they identify legal and ethical lapses that could harm the organization and its reputation. They also are useful for preliminary control because they can prevent problems from occurring. If a company seeking to acquire other businesses gathers adequate, accurate information about possible candidates, it is more likely to acquire the most appropriate companies and avoid unsound acquisitions.

Internal Audits   An organization may assign a group to conduct an **internal audit** to assess (1) what the company has done for itself and (2) what it has done for its customers or other recipients of its goods or services. The company can be evaluated on a number of factors, including financial stability, production efficiency, sales effectiveness, human resources development, earnings growth, energy use, public relations, civic responsibility, and other criteria of organizational effectiveness. The audit reviews the company's past, present, and future, including any risks the organization should be prepared to face.[25] A recent study found that the stock prices of companies with highly rated audit committees tended to rise faster than shares of companies with lower-rated internal auditors. It is likely that the higher-rated audit committees do a better job of finding and eliminating undesirable practices.[26]

To perform a management audit, auditors compile a list of desired qualifications and weight each qualification. Among the most common undesirable practices uncovered by a management audit are the performance of unnecessary work, duplication of work, poor inventory control, uneconomical use of equipment and machines, procedures that are more costly than necessary, and wasted resources. At Coca-Cola, an internal assessment revealed nearly 33 percent of its bottling operations and 24 percent of the suppliers audited had violations related to employee overtime and rest days. This rate increases to nearly 1 in 2 workplaces in some developing countries. To ensure that employees receive adequate time off, Coca-Cola recommends that managers map out production flow and pinpoint "bottlenecks, increase staffing levels to cover peak periods, and provide cross training to employees."[27]

management audit
An evaluation of the effectiveness and efficiency of various systems within an organization.

external audit
An evaluation conducted by one organization, such as a CPA firm, on another.

internal audit
A periodic assessment of a company's own planning, organizing, leading, and controlling processes.

Sustainability Audits and the Triple Bottom Line   Companies that are serious about goals for sustainability conduct audits to evaluate how effectively they are serving all stakeholders and protecting the environment. These sustainability audits typically evaluate performance in terms of a triple bottom line—that is, the company's financial performance, environmental impact, and impact on people in the company and the communities where it operates. Adapting a slogan coined by Shell in the 1990s, an easy way to remember the three bottom lines is with the terms *profit, planet,* and *people.*[28] In practice, reporting a triple bottom line is not standardized and regulated the way financial reporting is. A company might report its profitability in the traditional way, its environmental impact in terms of trends in efficiency of resource use, and its human impact in terms of general policies. As we saw Chapter 13, we can expect the impact of a sustainability audit to be greatest where there are specific goals and rewards for achieving them. However, committing to issue a report based on a sustainability audit can be a first step toward measuring and reinforcing sustainable business practices.

Budgetary Controls

Budgetary control is one of the most widely recognized and commonly used methods of managerial control. It ties together feedforward control, concurrent control, and feedback control, depending on the point at which it is applied. Budgetary control is the process of finding out what's being done and comparing the results with the corresponding budget data to verify accomplishments or remedy differences. Budgetary control is commonly called **budgeting.**

budgeting

The process of investigating what is being done and comparing the results with the corresponding budget data to verify accomplishments or remedy differences; also called budgetary controlling.

Fundamental Budgetary Considerations   In private industry, budgetary control begins with an estimate of sales and expected income. Exhibit 16.6 shows a budget with a forecast of expected sales (the sales budget) on the top row, followed by several categories of estimated expenses for the first three months of the year. In the bottom row, the profit estimate is determined by subtracting each month's budgeted expenses from the sales in that month's sales budget. Columns next to each month's budget provide space to enter the actual accomplishments so that managers can readily compare expected amounts and actual results.

Although this discussion of budgeting focuses on the flow of money into and out of the organization, budgeting information is not confined to finances. The entire enterprise and any of its units can create budgets for their activities, using units other than dollars if appropriate. For example, many organizations use production budgets forecasting physical units produced and shipped, and labor can be budgeted in skill levels or hours of work required.

EXHIBIT 16.6   A Sales Expense Budget

	January		February		March	
	Expectancy	Actual	Expectancy	Actual	Expectancy	Actual
Sales	$1,200,000		$1,350,000		$1,400,000	
Expenses						
General overhead	310,000		310,000		310,000	
Selling	242,000		275,000		288,000	
Producing	327,000		430,000		456,800	
Research	118,400		118,400		115,000	
Office	90,000		91,200		91,500	
Advertising	32,500		27,000		25,800	
Estimated gross profit	80,100		97,900		112,900	

A primary consideration of budgeting is the length of the budget period. All budgets are prepared for a specific time period. Many budgets cover one, three, or six months or one year. The length of time selected depends on the primary purpose of the budgeting. The period chosen should include the enterprise's complete normal cycle of activity. For example, seasonal variations should be included for production and for sales. The budget period commonly coincides with other control devices such as managerial reports, balance sheets, and statements of profit and loss. In addition, the extent to which reasonable forecasts can be made should be considered in selecting the length of the budget period.

Budgetary control proceeds through several stages. Establishing *expectancies* starts with the broad plan for the company and the estimate of sales, and it ends with budget approval and publication. Next, the budgetary operations stage deals with finding out what is being accomplished and comparing the results with expectancies. The last stage, as in any control process, involves responding appropriately with some combination of reinforcing successes and correcting problems.

Although practices differ widely, a member of top management often serves as the chief coordinator for formulating and using the budget. Usually the chief financial officer (CFO) has these duties. He or she needs to be less concerned with the details than with resolving conflicting interests, recommending adjustments when needed, and giving official sanction to the budgetary procedures. In a small company, budgeting responsibility generally rests with the owner.

Types of Budgets   There are many types of budgets. Some of the more common types are as follows:

- *Sales budget.* Usually data for the sales budget include forecasts of sales by month, sales area, and product.
- *Production budget.* The production budget commonly is expressed in physical units. Required information for preparing this budget includes types and capacities of machines, economic quantities to produce, and availability of materials.
- *Cost budget.* The cost budget is used for areas of the organization that incur expenses but no revenue, such as human resources and other support departments. Cost budgets may also be included in the production budget. Costs may be fixed, or independent of the immediate level of activity (such as rent), or variable, rising or falling with the level of activity (such as raw materials).
- *Cash budget.* The cash budget is essential to every business. It should be prepared after all other budget estimates are completed. The cash budget shows the anticipated receipts and expenditures, the amount of working capital available, the extent to which outside financing may be required, and the periods and amounts of cash available.
- *Capital budget.* The capital budget is used for the cost of fixed assets such as plants and equipment. Such costs are usually treated not as regular expenses but as investments because of their long-term nature and importance to the organization's productivity.
- *Master budget.* The master budget includes all the major activities of the business. It brings together and coordinates all the activities of the other budgets and can be thought of as a budget of budgets.

Traditionally, budgets were often imposed top-down, with senior management setting specific targets for the entire organization at the beginning of the budget process. In today's more complex organizations, the budget process is much more likely to be bottom-up, with top management setting the general direction but with lower-level and middle-level managers actually developing the budgets and submitting them for approval. When the budgets are consolidated, senior managers can then determine whether the budget objectives of the organization are being met. The budget will then be either approved or sent back down the organization for additional refinement.

accounting audits

Procedures used to verify accounting reports and statements.

activity-based costing (ABC)

A method of cost accounting designed to identify streams of activity and then to allocate costs across particular business processes according to the amount of time employees devote to particular activities.

Bottom Line

Activity-based costing can highlight overspending. *If one activity costs the most, how would you decide whether this is a case of overspending?*

Accounting records must be inspected periodically to ensure they were properly prepared and are correct. **Accounting audits,** which are designed to verify accounting reports and statements, are essential to the control process. This audit is performed by members of an outside firm of public accountants. Knowing that accounting records are accurate, true, and in keeping with generally accepted accounting practices (GAAP) creates confidence that a reliable base exists for sound overall controlling purposes.

Activity-Based Costing   Traditional methods of cost accounting may be inappropriate in today's business environment because they are based on outdated methods of rigid hierarchical organization. Instead of assuming that organizations are bureaucratic machines that can be separated into component functions such as human resources, purchasing, and maintenance, companies such as Hewlett-Packard and GE have used **activity-based costing (ABC)** to allocate costs across business processes.

ABC starts with the assumption that organizations are collections of people performing many different but related activities to satisfy customer needs. The ABC system is designed to identify those streams of activity and then to allocate costs across particular business processes. The basic procedure involves assigning expenses to particular processes or areas of activity. In a manufacturing company, for example, a group of employees might process sales orders, buy parts, and request engineering changes. The expenses for their salaries and fringe benefits would be divided among these activities according to the amount of time spent on each activity. A similar approach, illustrated in Exhibit 16.7, is to allocate expenses of providing support services to the functions served. In this example, a medical clinic, administrative expenses such as office workers' salaries, rent, and utilities are divided among the doctors' practices and the clinic's laboratory and radiology services. Options for allocating these expenses include the number of employees served in each group, the number of patients seen, and the square footage occupied by each group. Traditional and ABC systems reach the same bottom line. However, because the ABC method allocates costs across business processes, it provides a more accurate picture of how costs should be charged to products and services.[29]

This heightened accuracy can give managers a more realistic picture of how the organization is actually allocating its resources. It can highlight where wasted activities are occurring or whether activities cost too much relative to the benefits provided. Managers can then take action to correct the problem.

EXHIBIT 16.7
Activity-Based Costing Example: ABC Medical Clinic

Administrative expenses		Laboratory	Radiology	Dr. Kent (240 visits)	Dr. Olson (200 visits)	Dr. Lane (160 visits)
Office salaries						
Direct	1,500			600	500	400
Payroll and personnel	1,000	119	39	337	254	251
Supervision	2,000	238	79	673	508	502
Unutilized*	500					
Advertising	600			200	200	200
Rent	1,000	125	125	250	250	250
Utilities	200	25	25	50	50	50
Office supplies	300			100	100	100
Building insurance	100	12	13	25	25	25
Telephone	600			200	200	200
Depreciation	300			100	100	100
Total	8,100	519	281	2,535	2,187	2,078

*Not allocated.

Expenses allocated to services provided

SOURCE: Based on Pam Schuneman, "Master the 'ABCs' of Activity-Based Costing," *Managed Care,* May 1997, http://www.managedcaremag.com.

Financial Controls

In addition to budgets, businesses commonly use other statements for financial control. Two financial statements that help control overall organizational performance are the balance sheet and the profit and loss statement.

The Balance Sheet   The **balance sheet** shows the financial picture of a company at a given time. This statement itemizes three elements: (1) assets, (2) liabilities, and (3) stockholders' equity. **Assets** are the values of the various items the corporation owns. **Liabilities** are the amounts the corporation owes to various creditors. **Stockholders' equity** is the amount accruing to the corporation's owners. The relationship among these three elements is as follows:

$$\text{Assets} = \text{Liabilities} + \text{Stockholders' equity}$$

Exhibit 16.8 shows an example of a balance sheet. During the year, the company grew because it enlarged its building and acquired more machinery and equipment by means of long-term debt in the form of a first mortgage. Additional stock was sold to help finance the expansion. At the same time, accounts receivable were increased, and work in process was reduced. Observe that Total assets ($3,053,367) = Total liabilities ($677,204 + $618,600) + Stockholders' equity ($700,000 + $981,943 + $75,620).

Summarizing balance sheet items over a long period of time uncovers important trends and gives a manager further insight into overall performance and areas in which adjustments need to be made. For example, at some point, the company might decide that it would be prudent to slow down its expansion plans.

The Profit and Loss Statement   The **profit and loss statement** is an itemized financial statement of the income and expenses of a company's operations. Exhibit 16.9 shows a comparative statement of profit and loss for two consecutive years. In this illustration, the operating revenue of the enterprise has increased. Expense also has increased but at a lower rate, resulting in a higher net income. Some managers draw up tentative profit and loss statements and use them as goals. Then performance is measured against these goals or standards. From comparative statements of this type, a manager can identify trouble areas and correct them.

Controlling by profit and loss is most commonly used for the entire enterprise and, in the case of a diversified corporation, its divisions. However, if controlling is by departments, as in a decentralized organization in which department managers have control over both revenue and expense, a profit and loss statement is used for each department. Each department's output is measured, and a cost, including overhead, is charged to each department's operation. Expected net income is the standard for measuring a department's performance.

Financial Ratios   An effective approach for checking on the overall performance of an enterprise is to use key financial ratios. Ratios help indicate possible strengths and weaknesses in a company's operations. Key ratios are calculated from selected items on the profit and loss statement and the balance sheet. We will briefly discuss three categories of financial ratios—liquidity, leverage, and profitability:

- *Liquidity ratios.* Liquidity ratios indicate a company's ability to pay short-term debts. The most common liquidity ratio is *current assets to current liabilities,* called the **current ratio** or *net working capital ratio.* This ratio indicates the extent to which current assets can decline and still be adequate to pay current liabilities. Some analysts set a ratio of 2 to 1, or 2.00, as the desirable minimum. For example, referring back to Exhibit 16.8, the liquidity ratio there is about 2.86 ($1,918,455/$667,204). The company's current assets are more than capable of supporting its current liabilities.
- *Leverage ratios.* Leverage ratios show the relative amount of funds in the business supplied by creditors and shareholders. An important example is the **debt–equity ratio,** which indicates the company's ability to meet its long-term

LO 4

balance sheet

A report that shows the financial picture of a company at a given time and itemizes assets, liabilities, and stockholders' equity.

assets

The values of the various items the corporation owns.

liabilities

The amounts a corporation owes to various creditors.

stockholders' equity

The amount accruing to the corporation's owners.

profit and loss statement

An itemized financial statement of the income and expenses of a company's operations.

current ratio

A liquidity ratio that indicates the extent to which short-term assets can decline and still be adequate to pay short-term liabilities.

debt–equity ratio

A leverage ratio that indicates the company's ability to meet its long-term financial obligations.

EXHIBIT 16.8
A Comparative Balance
Sheet

Comparative Balance Sheet for the Years Ending December 31		
	This Year	Last Year
Assets		
Current assets:		
Cash	$161,870	$119,200
U.S. Treasury bills	250,400	30,760
Accounts receivable	825,595	458,762
Inventories:		
Work in process and finished products	429,250	770,800
Raw materials and supplies	251,340	231,010
Total current assets	1,918,455	1,610,532
Other assets:		
Land	157,570	155,250
Building	740,135	91,784
Machinery and equipment	172,688	63,673
Furniture and fixtures	132,494	57,110
Total other assets before depreciation	1,202,887	367,817
Less: Accumulated depreciation and amortization	67,975	63,786
Total other assets	1,134,912	304,031
Total assets	$3,053,367	$1,914,563
Liabilities and stockholders' equity		
Current liabilities:		
Accounts payable	$287,564	$441,685
Payrolls and withholdings from employees	44,055	49,580
Commissions and sundry accruals	83,260	41,362
Federal taxes on income	176,340	50,770
Current installment on long-term debt	85,985	38,624
Total current liabilities	667,204	622,021
Long-term liabilities:		
15-year, 9 percent loan, payable in each of the years 2005–2018	210,000	225,000
5 percent first mortgage	408,600	
Registered 9 percent notes payable		275,000
Total long-term liabilities	618,600	500,000
Stockholders' equity:		
Common stock: authorized 1,000,000 shares, outstanding last year 492,000 shares, outstanding this year 700,000 shares at $1 par value	700,000	492,000
Capital surplus	981,943	248,836
Earned surplus	75,620	51,706
Total stockholders' equity	1,757,563	792,542
Total liabilities and stockholders' equity	$3,053,367	$1,914,563

Comparative Statement of Profit and Loss for the Years Ending June 30			
	This Year	Last Year	Increase or Decrease
Income:			
Net sales	$253,218	$257,636	$4,418*
Dividends from investments	480	430	50
Other	1,741	1,773	32*
Total	255,439	259,839	4,400*
Deductions:			
Cost of goods sold	180,481	178,866	1,615
Selling and administrative expenses	39,218	34,019	5,199
Interest expense	2,483	2,604	121*
Other	1,941	1,139	802
Total	224,123	216,628	7,495
Income before taxes	31,316	43,211	11,895*
Provision for taxes	3,300	9,500	6,200*
Net income	$ 28,016	$ 33,711	$5,695*

* Decrease

EXHIBIT 16.9

A Comparative Statement of Profit and Loss

financial obligations. If this ratio is less than 1.5, the amount of debt is not considered excessive. In Exhibit 16.8, the debt–equity ratio is only 0.35 ($618,600/$1,757,563). The company has financed its expansion almost entirely by issuing stock rather than by incurring significant long-term debt.

- *Profitability ratios.* Profitability ratios indicate management's ability to generate a financial return on sales or investment. For example, **return of investment (ROI)** is a ratio of profit to capital used, or a rate of return from capital (equity plus long-term debt). This ratio allows managers and shareholders to assess how well the firm is doing compared with other investments. For example, if the net income of the company in Exhibit 16.8 were $300,000 this year, its return on capital would be 12.6 percent [$300,000/($1,757,563/$618,600)]—normally a very reasonable rate of return.

return on investment (ROI)

A ratio of profit to capital used, or a rate of return from capital.

Using Financial Ratios   Although ratios provide both performance standards and indicators of what has occurred, exclusive reliance on financial ratios can have negative consequences. Because ratios usually are expressed in compressed time horizons (monthly, quarterly, or yearly), they often cause **management myopia**—managers focus on short-term earnings and profits at the expense of their longer-term strategic obligations.[30] Control systems using long-term (e.g., three- to six-year) performance targets can reduce management myopia and focus attention further into the future.

A second negative outcome of ratios is that they relegate other important considerations to a secondary position. Research and development, management development, progressive human resource practices, and other considerations may receive insufficient attention. Therefore, the use of ratios should be supplemented with other control measures. Organizations can hold managers accountable for market share, number of patents granted, sales of new products, human resource development, and other performance indicators. As you read "Management in Action: Progress Report," consider the advantages and limits of financial ratios in helping Best Buy's managers figure out how to improve performance.

management myopia

Focusing on short-term earnings and profits at the expense of longer-term strategic obligations.

Management in Action

BEST BUY AIMS FOR BETTER NUMBERS

Best Buy's financial numbers have raised concern. The company has recently posted losses, with flat sales and falling market share, even after Circuit City closed and RadioShack filed for bankruptcy. A key measure in retailing is same-store sales, the total sales made only at the company's stores that have been open at least one year. By ignoring any other stores, managers can see whether performance has changed within stores, in contrast to sales growth or declines from opening or closing stores. At Best Buy, same-store sales have increased for three straight quarters, but the growth rate in the latest quarter was only 0.6 percent. Sales of smartphones and big screen televisions are helping to keep same-store sales in the black.

To sell more, Best Buy cut prices, but to preserve profits, it must cut costs, too. On the price side, the company promised to match the lowest price charged by any competitor, and it increased the value of rewards issued to customers with loyalty cards. On the cost side, CEO Hubert Joly has cut more than $1 billion since Renew Blue was announced a couple of years ago. In 2015, he announced that he "plans to reduce expenses by another $400 million in the next three years." The cost-cutting measures, along with the sale of higher margin products like smartphones and televisions, have helped the firm turn a small profit. Also, in competing with online retailers, Best Buy remains at a disadvantage. Selling from a warehouse is cheaper

than selling from a store, and most of Best Buy's customers shop in its stores, not at its website. To counter this challenge, Best Buy is experimenting with shipping customers' online orders directly from stores.

Another way to sell more is to use persuasive salespeople. In its early years, Best Buy was known for skillful selling, and managers emphasized sales targets. Best Buy recently increased training and began offering incentive pay linked to sales. The ratio of closed to attempted sales did not improve, but surveys showed greater customer satisfaction.

Another way Joly is trying to boost sales is by pursuing a "store within a store" business model. Best Buy will be opening another 60 Pacific Kitchen & Home "stores" that sell premium appliances. Also, 20 more Magnolia design centers will be opened where sales staff help customers design home entertainment theaters.

Management also considered geography. The worst performance has been in Best Buy's European stores, so the company arranged to sell its European operations.[31]

- How well do you think Best Buy's management has analyzed and corrected its performance? Why?

- Besides the measures described here, what other financial measures could help with controlling performance at Best Buy?

The Downside of Bureaucratic Control

So far you have learned about control from a mechanical viewpoint. But organizations are not strictly mechanical; they are composed of people. Although control systems are used to constrain people's behavior and make their future behavior predictable, people are not machines that automatically fall into line as the designers of control systems intend. In fact,

> A control system cannot be effective without consideration of how people will react to it.

control systems can lead to dysfunctional behavior. A control system cannot be effective without consideration of how people will react to it. For effective control of employee behavior, managers should consider three types of potential responses to control: rigid bureaucratic behavior, tactical behavior, and resistance.[32]

Rigid Bureaucratic Behavior Often people act in ways that will help them look good on the control system's measures. This tendency can be useful because it focuses people on the behaviors management requires. But it can result in rigid, inflexible behavior geared toward doing *only* what the system requires. For example, in the earlier discussion of six sigma, we noted that this control process emphasizes efficiency over innovation. After 3M began using six sigma extensively, it slipped from its goal of having at least one-third of sales come from newly released products. When George Buckley took the CEO post, only one-fourth of sales were coming from new products, and Buckley began relying less extensively on efficiency controls. Buckley explained to a reporter, "Invention is by its very nature a disorderly process."[33] The control challenge, of course, is for 3M to be both efficient and creative.

Rigid bureaucratic behavior occurs when control systems prompt employees to stay out of trouble by following the rules. Unfortunately, such systems often lead to poor customer service and make the entire organization slow to act. (Recall the discussion of bureaucracy in Chapter 10.) General Motors is notorious for having a lumbering bureaucracy, which has often been blamed for making the company unresponsive to changes in consumer tastes. For example, several years ago, GM kept engineers at work on the design for a new Hummer SUV even though many of them doubted the vehicles would ever be built. Their pessimism was correct; GM shut down the Hummer group. The company has been trying to change. For its head of vehicle development, GM selected Mary Barra, who has a background in both manufacturing and human resources as well as a reputation for speaking out and pressing for action. She quickly eliminated layers of management between herself and the top engineer and aggressively supports designers who want to make changes consumers are asking for.[34] Now as CEO, Barra continues to pursue her mission to make GM more responsive and efficient (see the Management in Action boxes in Chapter 8).

We have all been victimized at some time by rigid bureaucratic behavior. Reflect for a moment on this now classic story of a nightmare at a hospital:

> At midnight, a patient with eye pains enters an emergency room at a hospital. At the reception area, he is classified as a nonemergency case and referred to the hospital's eye clinic. Trouble is, the eye clinic doesn't open until the next morning. When he arrives at the clinic, the nurse asks for his referral slip, but the emergency room doctor had forgotten to give it to him. The patient has to return to the emergency room and wait for another physician to screen him. The physician refers him back to the eye clinic and to a social worker to arrange payment. Finally, a third doctor looks into his eye, sees a small piece of metal, and removes it—a 30-second procedure.[35]

Stories such as these have, of course, given bureaucracy a bad name. Some managers will not even use the term *bureaucratic control* because of its potentially negative connotation. That is unfortunate because the control system itself is not the problem. The problems occur when the systems are no longer viewed as tools for running the business but instead as rules for dictating rigid behavior.

Tactical Behavior   Control systems will be ineffective if employees engage in tactics aimed at beating the system. The most common type of tactical behavior is to manipulate information or report false performance data. People may produce two kinds of invalid data: about what *has* been done and about what *can* be done. False reporting about the past is less common because it is easier to identify someone who misreports what happened than someone who gives an erroneous prediction or estimate of what might happen. Still, managers sometimes change their accounting systems to smooth out the numbers. Also, people may intentionally feed false information into a management information system to cover up errors or poor performance. In 2014, allegations surfaced that some employees of the U.S. Department of Veterans Affairs were falsifying records regarding how many days it took for veterans to receive medical help.[36] According to guidelines, new patients were entitled to see a physician within 14 days of completing the necessary paperwork. According to one investigation of the VA medical center in Phoenix, 1,700 veterans were kept waiting an average of 115 days for their first primary care appointment.[37] The VA's inspector general discovered that officials at the medical center hid this fact by falsifying the records.

President Barack Obama and other officials meet to discuss how to correct problems at the U.S. Department of Veterans Affairs.

© Saul Loeb/AFP/Getty Images

Additional evidence of alleged wrongdoing has been linked to other VA medical units in multiple cities.[38] One U.S. senator summed up the scandal: "Poor management is costing the department billions of dollars more and compromising veterans' access to medical care."[39]

More commonly, people falsify their predictions or requests for the future. When asked to give budgetary estimates, employees usually ask for larger amounts than they need. On the other hand, they sometimes submit unrealistically *low* estimates when they believe a low estimate will help them get a budget or a project approved. Budget-setting sessions can become tugs of war between subordinates trying to get slack in the budget and superiors attempting to minimize slack. Similar tactics are exhibited when managers negotiate unrealistically low performance standards so that subordinates will have little trouble meeting them; when salespeople project low forecasts so that they will look good by exceeding them; and when workers slow down the work pace while time-study analysts are setting work pace standards. In these and other cases, people are concerned only with their own performance figures rather than with the overall performance of their departments or companies.

Resistance to Control   Often people strongly resist control systems. They do so for several reasons. First, comprehensive control systems increase the accuracy of performance data and make employees more accountable for their actions. Control systems uncover mistakes, threaten people's job security and status, and decrease people's autonomy.

Second, control systems can change expertise and power structures. For example, management information systems can make the costing, purchasing, and production decisions previously made by managers much quicker. Those individuals may fear a loss of expertise, power, and decision-making authority as a result.

Third, control systems can change the social structure of an organization. They can create competition and disrupt social groups and friendships. People may end up competing against those with whom they formerly had comfortable, cooperative relationships. Because people's social needs are so important, they will resist control systems that reduce social need satisfaction.

Fourth, control systems may be seen as an invasion of privacy, lead to lawsuits, and cause low morale.

Designing Effective Control Systems

Effective control systems maximize potential benefits and minimize dysfunctional behaviors. To achieve this, management needs to design control systems that

1. Establish valid performance standards.
2. Provide adequate information to employees.
3. Ensure acceptability to employees.
4. Maintain open communication.
5. Use multiple approaches.

Establish Valid Performance Standards   An effective control system must be based on valid and accurate performance standards. The most effective standards, as discussed earlier, tend to be expressed in quantitative terms; they are objective rather than subjective. Also, the measures should not be capable of being easily sabotaged or faked. Moreover, the system must incorporate all important aspects of performance. For example, a company that just focused on sales volume without also looking at profitability might soon go out of business. As you learned earlier, unmeasured behaviors are neglected. Often performance standards for delivering training and other HR programs emphasize trainee satisfaction as reported on surveys. But the Philadelphia Department of Licenses and Inspections instead verified that its training actually improved employee performance. The department was notorious for its long lines and rude workers, so it turned for help to the Philadelphia Ritz-Carlton Hotel—part of a chain known for its superb customer service. The hotel's area general manager provided training initially to 40 department workers in how to improve their service skills. As part of its posttraining measurement process, the department checked the wait times for license applicants, which dropped from 82 minutes to 14 minutes. The department is continuing its partnership program with Ritz-Carlton through additional employee training and attendance at each other's management meetings.[40]

But management also must defend against another problem: too many measures that create overcontrol and employee resistance. To make many controls tolerable, managers can devote attention to a few key areas while setting satisfactory performance standards in others. Or they can establish simple priorities. The purchasing agent may have to meet targets in the following sequence: quality, availability, cost, inventory level. Finally, managers can set tolerance ranges. For example, in financial budgeting, optimistic, expected, and minimum levels sometimes are specified.

Many companies' budgets set cost targets only. This causes managers to control spending but also to neglect earnings. At Emerson Electric, profit and growth are key measures. If an unanticipated opportunity to increase market share arises, managers can spend what they need to go after it. The phrase "it's not in the budget" is less likely to stifle people at Emerson than it is at most other companies.

This principle applies to nonfinancial aspects of performance as well. At many customer service call centers, control aims to maximize efficiency by focusing on the average amount of time each agent spends handling each phone call. But the business objectives of call centers should also include other measures such as cross-selling products or improving customer satisfaction and repeat business. Customer service agents at TD bank are trained to solve customers' problems the first time they call. The agents are evaluated by their ability to "achieve first-call issue resolution and receive favorable customer feedback—not by how quickly they can get the customer off the phone."[41]

Business consultant Michael Hammer summarizes these points in terms of what he calls seven "deadly sins" of performance measurement to avoid:[42]

1. *Vanity*—using measures that are sure to make managers and the organization look good. For example, a company might measure order fulfillment in terms of whether products are delivered by the latest date promised by the organization, rather than by the tougher and more meaningful measure of when the customers request to receive the products.

2. *Provincialism*—limiting measures to functional or departmental responsibilities rather than the organization's overall objectives. If a company's transportation department measures only shipping costs, it won't have an incentive to consider that shipping reliability (delivery on a given date) will affect performance at the company's stores or distribution centers.

3. *Narcissism*—measuring from the employee's, manager's, or company's point of view, rather than the customer's. For example, a maker of computer systems measured on-time shipping of each component; if 90 percent of the system's components arrived at the customer on time, it was 90 percent on time. But from the customer's point of view, the system wasn't on time at all because the customer needed *all* the components to use the system.

4. *Laziness*—not expending the effort to analyze what is important to measure. An electric power company simply assumed customers cared about installation speed, but in fact, customers really cared more about receiving an accurate installation schedule.

5. *Pettiness*—measuring just one component of what affects business performance. An example would be clothing manufacturers that assume they should consider just manufacturing cost rather than the overall costs of making exactly the right products available in stores when customers demand them.

6. *Inanity*—failing to consider the way standards will affect real-world human behavior and company performance. A fast-food restaurant targeted waste reduction and was surprised when restaurant managers began slowing down operations by directing their employees to hold off on cooking anything until orders were placed.

7. *Frivolity*—making excuses for poor performance rather than taking performance standards seriously. In some organizations, more effort goes to blaming others than to correcting problems.

According to Hammer, the basic correction to these "sins" is to select standards carefully that look at entire business processes, such as product development or order fulfillment, and identify which actions make those processes succeed. Then managers should measure performance against these standards precisely, accurately, and practically, making individuals responsible for their achievement and rewarding success.

Provide Adequate Information   Management must communicate to employees the importance and nature of the control system. Then people must receive feedback about their performance. Feedback motivates people and provides information that enables them to correct their own deviations from performance standards. Allowing people to initiate their own corrective action encourages self-control and reduces the need for outside supervision. Open-book management, described in Chapter 15, is a powerful use of this control principle.

Information should be as accessible as possible, particularly when people must make decisions quickly and frequently. For example, a national food company with its own truck fleet had a difficult problem. The company wanted drivers to go through customer sales records every night, insert new prices from headquarters every morning, and still make their rounds—an impossible set of demands. To solve this control problem, the company installed personal computers in more than 1,000 delivery trucks. Now drivers use their PCs for constant communication with headquarters. Each night drivers send information about the stores, and each morning headquarters sends prices and recommended stock mixes.

In general, a manager designing a control system should evaluate the information system in terms of the following questions:

1. Does it provide people with data relevant to the decisions they need to make?
2. Does it provide the right amount of information to decision makers throughout the organization?
3. Does it provide enough information to each part of the organization about how other, related parts of the organization are functioning?[43]

Ensure Acceptability to Employees   Employees are less likely to resist a control system and exhibit dysfunctional behaviors if they accept the system. They are more likely to accept systems that have useful performance standards but are not overly controlling. Employees also will find systems more acceptable if they believe the standards are possible to achieve.

The control system should emphasize positive behavior rather than focusing on controlling negative behavior alone. In more than two decades, Johnson & Johnson's Ethicon San Lorenzo facility has never had to recall a product. The company makes sutures, meshes, and other supplies for surgery—an industry in which quality must be perfect but recalls have been all too common. To achieve these outstanding results, the company set up a system it calls the Do It Right Framework, which includes training, employee involvement in process improvements, and open communication about company objectives and the reasons for changes. Most important, employees understand that their work matters. Every employee sees a video about Ethicon's work, highlighted by a cardiovascular surgeon describing how he uses the products and why their quality affects patients' recovery. Thus, doing the job right is something employees genuinely care about.[44]

One of the best ways to establish reasonable standards and thus gain employee acceptance of the control system is to set standards participatively. As we discussed in Chapter 4, participation in decision making secures people's understanding and cooperation and results in better decisions. Allowing employees to collaborate in control system decisions that affect their jobs directly will help overcome resistance and foster acceptance of the system. In addition, employees on the front line are more likely to know which standards are most important and practical, and they can inform a manager's judgment on these issues. Finally, if standards are established in collaboration with employees, managers will more easily obtain cooperation on solving the problem when deviations from standards occur.

Maintain Open Communication   When deviations from standards occur, it is important for employees to feel able to report the deviations so that the problem can be addressed. If employees come to feel that their managers want to hear only good news or, worse, if they fear reprisal for reporting bad news, even if it is not their fault, then any controls that are in place will be much less likely to be effective. Problems may go unreported or, even worse, may reach the point at which they become much more expensive or difficult to solve. But if managers create an environment of openness and honesty, one in which employees feel comfortable sharing even negative information and are appreciated for doing so in a timely fashion, then the control system is much more likely to work effectively.

Nevertheless, managers may sometimes need to discipline employees who are failing to meet important standards. In such cases, an approach called *progressive discipline* is usually most effective. In this approach, clear standards are established, but failure to meet them is dealt with in a progressive or step-by-step process. For example, the first time an employee's sales performance has been worse than it should have been, the supervising manager may offer verbal counseling or coaching. If problems persist, the next step might be a written reprimand. This type of reasonable and considered approach signals to all employees that the manager is interested in improving their performance, not in punishing them.

Use Multiple Approaches   Multiple controls are necessary. For example, banks need controls on risk so that they don't lose a lot of money from defaulting borrowers, as well as profit controls including sales budgets that aim for growth in accounts and customers.

As you learned earlier in this chapter, control systems generally should include both financial and nonfinancial performance targets and incorporate aspects of preliminary, concurrent, and feedback control. In recent years, a growing number of companies are using **strategy maps** to show how they plan to convert their various assets into desired outcomes. Related to these maps is the **balanced scorecard** which holds managers responsible for a combination of four sets of performance measures (see Exhibit 16.10): (1) financial, (2) customer satisfaction, (3) business processes (quality and efficiency), and (4) learning and growth.[45] The goal is generally to broaden management's horizon beyond short-term financial results so that the company's long-term success is more likely. Michael Boo, chief strategy officer of the National Marrow Donor Program (NMDP), wanted to develop new ways of reaching the nonprofit's vision of 10,000 bone marrow transplants per year. Such transplants can prolong the lives of individuals with leukemia and other life-threatening diseases. He and colleagues developed a Balanced Scorecard with four perspectives: stakeholder, financial performance, processes, and people/knowledge/technology. The NMDP has achieved 60 percent of its goal, averaging nearly 500 transplants each month.[46]

Effective control will also require managers and organizations to use many of the other techniques and practices of good management. For example, compensation systems will grant rewards for meeting standards and impose consequences if they are not met. And to gain employee acceptance, managers may also rely on many of the other communication and motivational tools that we discussed in earlier chapters, such as persuasion and positive reinforcement.

strategy map

A visual depiction that shows how an organization plans to convert its various assets into desired outcomes

balanced scorecard

Control system combining four sets of performance measures: financial, customer, business process, and learning and growth.

EXHIBIT 16.10   A Strategy Map and Balanced Scorecard for Performance Improvement at a Hospital

Strategy Map

Balanced Scorecard

				Objectives	Measurement	Target
Financial	Steady growth	Return on investor capital	Productivity		Grow sales revenue Increase profit	Balance sheet Profit and loss statement	10% annually 5% annually
Customer	Service leadership	Patient satisfaction	Operational excellence		Increase satisfaction Attract repeat patients	Satisfaction surveys Track in database	90% highly satisfied 80% return rate
Internal	Improve quality and timeliness of services	Continuously improve staff's skills	Improve patient value		Increase expertise of staff Reduce error rates	Completion rate of online training modules Number of incorrect dosages	90% passed with score of 85% or higher 2% or lower
Learning & Growth	Promote culture of quality service	Align employee competencies with strategy	Implement technology to support innovation		Communicate importance of high quality Develop succession plan	Number of e-mails and mentions during meetings Percent completed and times updated	One e-mail and mention per week 90% by year-end and one time per month

SOURCES: Adapted from R. S. Kaplan and D. P. Norton, "Having Trouble with Your Strategy? Then Map It," *Harvard Business Review* (September–October 2000), pp. 167–72; and R. S. Kaplan and D. P. Norton, *The Balanced Scorecard: Translating Strategy into Action* (Boston: Harvard Business School Press, 1996), p. 76.

The Other Controls: Markets and Clans

Although the concept of control has always been a central feature of organizations, the principles and philosophies underlying its use are changing. In the past, control was focused almost exclusively on bureaucratic (and market) mechanisms. Generations of managers were taught that they could maximize productivity by regulating what employees did on the job—through standard operating procedures, rules, regulations, and close supervision. To increase output on an assembly line, for example, managers in the past tried to identify the one best way to approach the work and then to monitor employees' activities to make certain that they followed standard operating procedures. In short, they controlled work by dividing and simplifying tasks, a process we referred to in Chapter 1 as *scientific management.*

> Although formal bureaucratic control systems are perhaps the most pervasive in organizations, they are not always the most effective.

Although formal bureaucratic control systems are perhaps the most pervasive in organizations (and the most talked about in management textbooks), they are not always the most effective. Market controls and clan controls may both represent more flexible, though no less potent, approaches to regulating performance.

Market Control

In contrast to bureaucratic controls, market controls involve the use of economic forces— and the pricing mechanisms that accompany them—to regulate performance. The system works like this: when output from an individual, department, or business unit has value to other people, a price can be negotiated for its exchange. As a market for these transactions becomes established, two effects occur:

- Price becomes an indicator of the value of the good or service.
- Price competition has the effect of controlling productivity and performance.

The basic principles that underlie market controls can operate at the corporate level, the business unit (or department) level, and the individual level. Exhibit 16.11 shows a few ways in which market controls are used in an organization.

Market Controls at the Corporate Level

In large, diversified companies, market controls often are used to regulate independent business units. Particularly in large conglomerate firms that act as holding companies, business units typically are treated as profit centers that compete with one another. Top executives may place very few bureaucratic controls on business unit managers but use profit and loss data for evaluating performance. Although decision making and power are decentralized to the business units, market controls ensure that business unit performance is in line with corporate objectives.

Use of market control mechanisms in this way has been criticized by those who insist that economic measures do not reflect the complete value of an organization adequately. Employees often suffer as diversified companies are repeatedly bought and sold based on market controls.

Market Controls at the Business Unit Level

Market control also can be used within business units to regulate exchanges among departments and functions. Transfer pricing is one method that organizations use to try to reflect market forces for internal transactions. A **transfer price** is the charge by one unit in the organization for a good or service that it supplies to another unit of the same organization. For example, in automobile manufacturing, a transfer price may be affixed to components and subassemblies before they are shipped to subsequent business units for final assembly. Ideally, the transfer price reflects the price that the receiving business unit would have to pay for that product or service in the marketplace.

transfer price

Price charged by one unit for a good or service provided to another unit within the organization.

EXHIBIT 16.11
Examples of Market
Control

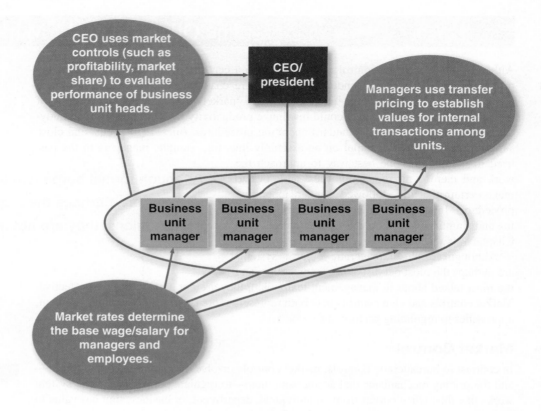

As organizations have more options to outsource goods and services to external part-ners, market controls such as transfer prices provide natural incentives to keep costs down and quality up. Managers stay in close touch with prices in the marketplace to make sure their own costs are in line, and they try to improve the service they provide to increase their department's value to the organization. Consider the situation in which training and development activities can be done internally by the human resources department or out-sourced to a consulting firm. If the human resources department cannot supply quality training at a reasonable price, there may be no reason for that department to exist inside the firm. Similarly, Penske Truck Leasing Company began outsourcing many of its finance processes to a company called Genpact, not only for lower prices but also for the exper-tise developed by that specialized firm to compete in the marketplace. Penske's chief financial officer, Frank Cocuzza, says the department spends $20 million less per year than it did to perform the same functions in-house while it has improved its rate of collections and learned thousands of ways to make his own operation more efficient, modeled after Genpact's lean practices.[47]

Market Controls at the Individual Level   Market controls also are used at the indi-vidual level. For example, when organizations are trying to hire employees, the supply and demand for particular skills influence the wages employees can expect to receive and the rate organizations are likely to pay. Employees or job candidates who have more valuable skills tend to be paid a higher wage. Of course, wages don't always reflect market rates—sometimes they are based (perhaps arbitrarily) on internal resource considerations—but the market rate is often the best indicator of an employee's potential worth to a firm.

Market-based controls such as these are important in that they provide a natural incen-tive for employees to enhance their skills and offer them to potential firms. Even after individuals gain employment, market-based wages are important as controls in that persons with higher economic value may be promoted faster to higher positions in the organization.

Market controls often are used by boards of directors to manage CEOs of major corporations. Ironically, CEOs usually are seen as the ones controlling everyone else in the company; but the CEO is accountable to the board of directors, and the board must devise ways to ensure that the CEO acts in its interest. Absent board control, CEOs may act in ways that make them look good personally (such as making the company bigger or more diversified) but that do not lead to higher profits for the firm. And as recent corporate scandals have shown, without board control, CEOs may also artificially inflate the firm's earnings or not fully declare expenses, making the firm look much more successful than it really is.

Traditionally, boards have tried to control CEO performance mainly through the use of incentive plans in addition to base salary. These typically include some type of bonus tied to short-term profit targets. In large U.S. companies, most CEO compensation is now at risk, meaning it depends mainly on the performance of the company. In addition to short-term incentives, boards use some type of long-term incentives linked to the firm's share price, usually through stock options, which we discussed in Chapter 10. Also, balanced scorecards are intended to keep CEOs focused on the company's longer-term health. And under the Sarbanes-Oxley Act, described in Chapter 5, board members are expected to exercise careful control over the company's financial performance, including oversight of the CEO's compensation package.

As much as it would seem that market controls play a significant role in the salary of a professional baseball player or any other professional athlete, are the sometimes ridiculously high salaries that are paid for players today truly indicative of a player's skill—or something else? If the player doesn't live up to the expectation of the previously perceived skill level or, put another way, has a bad year, should the organization be allowed to cut his pay?

© imac/Alamy

Clan Control: The Role of Empowerment and Culture

Increasingly, managers are discovering that control systems based solely on bureaucratic and market mechanisms are insufficient for directing today's workforce. There are several reasons for this:

- *Employees' jobs have changed.* The nature of work is evolving. Employees working with computers, for example, have more variability in their jobs, and much of their work is intellectual and therefore invisible. Because of this, there is no one best way to perform a task, and programming or standardizing jobs becomes extremely difficult. Close supervision is also unrealistic because it is nearly impossible to supervise activities such as reasoning and problem solving.
- *The nature of management has changed.* The role of managers is evolving, too. Managers used to know more about the job than employees did. Today it is typical for employees to know more about their jobs than anyone else does. We refer to this as the shift from touch labor to knowledge work. When real expertise in organizations exists at the very lowest levels, hierarchical control becomes impractical.[48]
- *The employment relationship has changed.* The social contract at work is being renegotiated. It used to be that employees were most concerned about issues such as pay, job security, and the hours of work. Today, however, more and more employees want to be more fully engaged in their work, taking part in decision making, devising solutions to unique problems, and receiving assignments that are challenging and involving. They want to use their brains.

For these three reasons, the concept of *empowerment* not only has become more popular in organizations but has become a necessary aspect of a manager's repertoire of control. With no one best way to approach a job and no way to scrutinize what employees do every day, managers must empower employees to make decisions and trust that they will act in the best interests of the firm. But this does not mean giving up control. It means creating a strong culture of high standards and integrity so that employees will exercise effective control on their own.

Recall our extensive discussion of organization culture in Chapter 2. If the organization's culture encourages the wrong behaviors, then an effort to impose effective controls will be severely hindered. But if managers create and reinforce a strong culture that encourages correct behavior, one in which everyone understands management's values and expectations and is motivated to act in accordance with them, then clan control can be a very effective control tool.[49] As we noted at the beginning of this chapter, clan control involves creating relationships built on mutual respect and encouraging each individual to take responsibility for his or her actions. Employees work within a guiding framework of values, and they are expected to use good judgment. For example, at NetApp, an IT company specializing in data storage and protection, a commitment to employee empowerment prompted the switch from a 12-page travel policy to some simple guidelines for employees who need to go on a business trip: "We are a frugal company. But don't show up dog-tired to save a few bucks. Use your common sense."[50] The emphasis in an empowered organization is on satisfying customers, not on pleasing the boss. Mistakes are tolerated as the unavoidable by-product of dealing with change and uncertainty and are viewed as opportunities to learn. And team members learn together. Exhibit 16.12 provides a set of guidelines for managing in an empowered world.

The resilience and time investment of clan control are a double-edged sword. Clan control takes a long time to develop and an even longer time to change. This gives an organization stability and direction during periods of upheaval in the environment or the organization (e.g., during changes in the top management). "Management in Action: Onward" provides an example of a company trying to cope with upheaval in the retail industry; consider whether clan control could help Best Buy. Yet if managers want to establish a new culture—a new form of clan control—they must help employees unlearn the old values and embrace the new. We will talk about this transition process more in the final chapter of this book.

Bottom Line

Clan control empowers employees to meet performance standards. *Would you expect more clan control with standardized jobs or creative positions?*

EXHIBIT 16.12
Management Control in an Empowered Setting

1. **Put control where the operation is.** Layers of hierarchy, close supervision, and checks and balances are quickly disappearing and being replaced with self-guided teams. For centuries even the British Empire—as large as it was—never had more than six levels of management, including the queen.

2. **Use real-time rather than after-the-fact controls.** Issues and problems must be solved at the source by the people doing the actual work. Managers become a resource to help out the team.

3. **Rebuild the assumptions underlying management control to build on trust rather than distrust.** Today's high-flex organizations are based on empowerment, not obedience. Information must facilitate decision making, not police it.

4. **Move to control based on peer norms.** Clan control is a powerful thing. Workers in Japan, for example, have been known to commit suicide rather than disappoint or lose face within their team. Although this is extreme, it underlines the power of peer influence. The Japanese have a far more homogeneous culture and set of values than we do. In North America, we must build peer norms systematically and put much less emphasis on managing by the numbers.

5. **Rebuild the incentive systems to reinforce responsiveness and teamwork.** The twin goals of adding value to the customer and team performance must become the dominant raison d'être of the measurement systems.

SOURCE: Gerald. H. B. Ross, "Revolution in Management Control," *Management Accounting,* November 1990, pp. 23–27. Reprinted by permission.

Management in Action

WAS ROWE A PROBLEM FOR BEST BUY—OR PART OF THE SOLUTION?

When Hubert Joly became Best Buy's CEO in 2012, he focused on basic ideas: a company whose name points to great deals should offer customers the merchandise they want at the lowest price. That requires operating efficiently and selling effectively in stores and on the web.

As simple as the principles are, they are extremely hard to carry out in the Internet age. Nevertheless, Joly sees his role as being the leader who points to the basics and the need to be fully engaged. In December 2012, when Joly called "All hands on deck," sending office employees into stores during the evening and weekend hours, he expressed a spirit he wanted to permeate the company.

For Joly, the Results Oriented Work Environment (ROWE) was inconsistent with "all hands on deck." If employees could work wherever and whenever they wanted, perhaps they would not be at the office when needed or would be unavailable in a crisis. Ending ROWE would put employees "in the office as much as possible," to quote Best Buy spokesman Matt Furman. Joly also said ROWE delegates decisions that managers should be involved in making.

The creators of the ROWE policy dispute this understanding. Cali Ressler and Jody Thompson, former Best Buy employees, came up with the idea as a way to improve efficiency while motivating workers. They say Best Buy saved more than $2 million in the first two years of ROWE because employee turnover plummeted and productivity rose. (Based on the interest in ROWE, the two women left Best Buy to spread the idea through a consulting firm,

CultureRx.) They explain that under ROWE, employees discussed goals and work arrangements with their managers and were responsible for achieving the mutually agreed-upon goals. Flexibility involved only the details of *how* they achieved their goals. Also, ROWE applied only to Best Buy's office employees, not to the store workers.

ROWE's emphasis on flexibility contrasts with commentary about decision making and change at Best Buy. According to the *Minneapolis Star Tribune*, former executives say Best Buy developed a bureaucratic style that slowed down its responses to a changing environment. Perhaps more ROWE-style flexibility would have made Best Buy nimbler; clearly, Joly disagrees. In contrast to the bottom-up creation of ROWE, the program's elimination was a swift, top-down decision.

In the three years since Joly's announcement, Best Buy's revenues stopped falling, and its stock price took a long-awaited upward turn. Several other factors have contributed to the improved financial results at Best Buy, most notably the "Renew Blue" plan that resulted in $1 billion in cost reductions, the offering of high-margin smartphones, and the growth of the store-within-a-store concept.[51]

- How well did ROWE meet the criteria of an effective performance system? Will eliminating it be more or less effective? Why?
- How can clan control help Best Buy improve its performance?

KEY TERMS

accounting audits, p. 512

activity-based costing (ABC), p. 512

after-action review, p. 505

assets, p. 513

balance sheet, p. 513

balanced scorecard, p. 521

budgeting, p. 510

bureaucratic control, p. 501

clan control, p. 501

concurrent control, p. 505

control, p. 500

current ratio, p. 513

debt–equity ratio, p. 513

external audit, p. 509

feedback control, p. 505

feedforward control, p. 505

internal audit, p. 509

liabilities, p. 513

management audit, p. 509

management myopia, p. 515

market control, p. 501

principle of exception, p. 504

profit and loss statement, p. 513

return on investment (ROI), p. 515

standard, p. 502

stockholders' equity, p. 513

strategy map, p. 521

transfer price, p. 523

RETAINING WHAT YOU LEARNED

In Chapter 16, you learned that companies develop control systems in order to keep employees focused on achieving organizational goals. The basic bureaucratic control system includes setting, measuring, and comparing performance standards and, when necessary, eliminating unfavorable deviations. Performance standards should cover issues such as quantity, quality, time, and cost. Budgets are a control mechanism that act as an initial guide for allocating resources and using funds. Many companies are changing how they prepare budgets to eliminate waste and improve business processes. Balance sheets compare the value of company assets to the obligations the company owes to owners and creditors. Profit and loss statements show company income relative to costs incurred. Ratios provide a goal for managers as well as a standard against which to evaluate performance. Managers use a variety of procedures to maximize the effectiveness of control systems. Market controls can be used at the level of the corporation, the business unit or department, or the individual. To be responsive to customers, companies are increasingly using clan control to harness the expertise of employees and give them the freedom to act on their own initiative.

LO 1   Explain why companies develop control systems for employees.

- Left to their own devices, employees may act in ways that do not benefit the organization.
- Control systems are designed to eliminate idiosyncratic behavior and keep employees directed toward achieving the goals of the firm.
- Control systems are a steering mechanism for guiding resources and for helping each individual act on behalf of the organization.

LO 2   Summarize how to design a basic bureaucratic control system.

- The design of a basic control system involves four steps: (1) setting performance standards, (2) measuring performance, (3) comparing performance with the standards, and (4) eliminating unfavorable deviations by taking corrective action.
- Performance standards should be valid and should cover issues such as quantity, quality, time, and cost.
- Once performance is compared with the standards, the principle of exception suggests that the manager needs to direct attention to the exceptional cases that have significant deviations. Then the manager takes the action most likely to solve the problem.

LO 3   Describe the purposes for using budgets as a control device.

- Budgets combine the benefits of feedforward, concurrent, and feedback controls. They are used as an initial guide for allocating resources, a reference point for using funds, and a feedback mechanism for comparing actual levels of sales and expenses with their expected levels.

- Recently companies have modified their budgeting processes to allocate costs over basic processes (such as customer service) rather than to functions or departments.
- By changing the way they prepare budgets, many companies have discovered ways to eliminate waste and improve business processes.

LO 4   Define basic types of financial statements and financial ratios used as controls.

- The basic financial statements are the balance sheet and the profit and loss statement.
- The balance sheet compares the value of company assets to the obligations the company owes to owners and creditors.
- The profit and loss statement shows company income relative to costs incurred. In addition to these statements, companies look at liquidity ratios (whether the company can pay its short-term debts), leverage ratios (the extent to which the company is funding operations by going into debt), and profitability ratios (profit relative to investment). These ratios provide a goal for managers as well as a standard against which to evaluate performance.

LO 5   List procedures for implementing effective control systems.

- To maximize the effectiveness of controls, managers should (1) establish valid performance standards, (2) provide adequate information to employees, (3) ensure acceptability, (4) maintain open communication, and (5) see that multiple approaches are used (such as bureaucratic, market, and clan control).

LO 6   Identify ways in which organizations use market control mechanisms.

- Market controls can be used at the level of the corporation, the business unit or department, or the individual.
- At the corporate level, business units are evaluated against one another based on profitability. At times, less profitable businesses are sold while more profitable businesses receive more resources.
- Within business units, transfer pricing may be used to approximate market mechanisms to control transactions among departments.
- At the individual level, market mechanisms control the wage rate of employees and can be used to evaluate the performance of individual managers.

LO 7   Discuss the use of clan control in an empowered organization.

- Approaching control from a centralized, mechanistic viewpoint is increasingly impractical. In today's organizations, it is difficult to program one best way to approach work, and it is often difficult to monitor performance.

- To be responsive to customers, companies must harness the expertise of employees and give them the freedom to act on their own initiative.
- To maintain control while empowering employees, companies should (1) use self-guided teams, (2) allow decision making at the source of the problems, (3) build trust and mutual respect, (4) base control on a guiding framework of norms, and (5) use incentive systems that encourage teamwork.

DISCUSSION QUESTIONS

1. What controls can you identify in the management of your school or at a company where you now work (or recently worked)? If you can, interview a manager or employee of the organization to learn more about the controls in use there. How might the organization's performance change if those controls were not in place?

2. How are leadership and control different? How are planning and control different? How are structure and control different?

3. Imagine you are the sales manager of a company that sells medical supplies to hospitals nationwide. You have 10 salespeople reporting to you. You are responsible for your department achieving a certain level of sales each year. In general terms, how might you go about taking each step in the control cycle?

4. In the situation described in Question 3, what actions would you need to take if sales fell far below the budgeted level? What, if any, actions would you need to take if sales far exceeded the sales budget? If sales are right on target, does effective controlling require any response from you? (Would your answer differ if the department were on target overall, but some salespeople fell short and others exceeded their targets?)

5. Besides sales and expenses, identify five other important control measures for a business. Include at least one nonfinancial measure.

6. What are the pros and cons of bureaucratic controls such as rules, procedures, and supervision?

7. Suppose a company at which executives were rewarded for meeting targets based only on profits and stock price switches to a balanced scorecard that adds measures for customer satisfaction, employee engagement, employee diversity, and ethical conduct. How, if at all, would you expect executives' performance to change in response to the new control system? How, if at all, would you expect the company's performance to change?

8. Google offers Google Apps, such as Gmail, Google Calendar, and Docs & Spreadsheets, as collaboration tools for employees. Describe how the company could use market controls to determine whether Google employees will use these software programs or competing software (e.g., Word and Excel).

9. How effective is clan control as a control mechanism? What are its strengths? Its limitations? When would a manager rely on clan control the most?

10. Does empowerment imply the loss of control? Why or why not?

11. Some people use the concept of personal control to describe the application of business control principles to individual careers. Thinking about your school performance and career plans, which steps of the control process (Exhibit 16.3) have you been applying effectively? How do you keep track of your performance in meeting your career and life goals? How do you measure your success? Does clan control help you meet your personal objectives?

EXPERIENTIAL EXERCISES

16.1   SAFETY PROGRAM

OBJECTIVE

To understand some of the specific activities that fall under the management functions of planning, organizing, controlling and staffing, and directing.

INSTRUCTIONS

Read the following case and then evaluate the likely success of this managerial control effort. Specifically, how well did the manager review the source of the problems? How well designed is the new control system? How effectively is the manager building employee commitment to using the control mechanisms? How could this manager improve the control process? Summarize your findings and recommendations in a paragraph or two.

MANAGING THE VAMP CO. SAFETY PROGRAM

If there are specific things that a manager does, how are they done? What does it look like when one manages? The following describes a typical situation in which a manager performs managerial functions:

As production manager of the Vamp Stamping Company, you've become quite concerned over the metal stamping shop's safety record. Accidents that resulted in operators' missing time on the job have increased quite rapidly in the past year. These more serious accidents have jumped from 3 percent of all accidents reported to a current level of 10 percent.

Because you're concerned about your workers' safety as well as the company's ability to meet its customers' orders, you want to reduce this downtime accident rate to its previous level or lower within the next six months.

You call the accident trend to the attention of your production supervisors, pointing out the seriousness of the situation and their continuing responsibility to enforce the gloves and safety goggles rules. Effective immediately, every supervisor will review his or her accident reports for the past year, file a report summarizing these accidents with you, and state their intended actions to correct recurring causes of the accidents. They will make out weekly safety reports as well as meet with you every Friday to discuss what is being done and any problems they are running into.

You request the union steward's cooperation in helping the safety supervisor set up a short program on shop safety practices.

Because the machine operators are having the accidents, you encourage your supervisors to talk to their workers and find out what they think can be done to reduce the downtime accident rate to its previous level.

While the program is going on, you review the weekly reports, looking for patterns that will tell you how effective the program is and where the trouble spots are. If a supervisor's operators are not decreasing their accident rate, you discuss the matter in considerable detail with the supervisor and his or her key workers.

SOURCE: From Theodore T. Herbert, *The New Management: Study Guide,* 4th ed., p. 41.

16.2 PRELIMINARY, CONCURRENT, AND FEEDBACK CONTROL

OBJECTIVES

1. To demonstrate the need for control procedures.
2. To gain experience in determining when to use preliminary, concurrent, and feedback controls.

INSTRUCTIONS

1. Read the text materials on preliminary, concurrent, and feedback control.
2. Read the Control Problem Situation and be prepared to resolve those control problems in a group setting.
3. Your instructor will divide the class into small groups. Each group completes the Preliminary, Concurrent, and Feedback Control Worksheet by achieving consensus on the types of control that should be applied in each situation. The group also develops responses to the discussion questions.
4. After the class reconvenes, group spokespersons present group findings.

DISCUSSION QUESTIONS

1. For which control(s) was it easier to determine application? For which was it harder?
2. Would this exercise be better assigned to groups or to individuals?

CONTROL PROBLEM SITUATION

Your management consulting team has just been hired by Technocron International, a rapidly growing producer of electronic surveillance devices that are sold to commercial and government end users. Some sales are made through direct selling, and some through industrial resellers. Direct-sale profits are being hurt by what seem to be exorbitant expenses paid to a few of the salespeople, especially those who fly all over the world in patterns that suggest little planning and control. There is trouble among the resellers because standard contracts have not been established and each reseller has an entirely different contractual relationship. Repayment schedules vary widely from customer to customer. Also, profits are reduced by the need to customize most orders, making mass production almost impossible. However, no effort has been made to create interchangeable components. There are also tremendous inventory problems. Some raw materials and parts are bought in such small quantities that new orders are being placed almost daily. Other orders are so large that there is hardly room to store everything. Many of these purchased components are later found to be defective and unusable, causing production delays. Engineering changes are made that make large numbers of old components still in storage obsolete. Some delays result from designs that are very difficult to assemble, and assemblers complain that their corrective suggestions are ignored by engineering. To save money, untrained workers are hired and assigned to experienced worker-buddies who are expected to train them on the job. However, many of the new people are too poorly educated to understand their assignments, and their worker-buddies wind up doing a great deal of their work. This, along with the low pay and lack of consideration from engineering, is causing a great deal of worker unrest and talk of forming a union. Last week alone nine new worker grievances were filed, and the U.S. Equal Employment Opportunity Commission has just announced intentions to investigate two charges of discrimination on the part of the company. There is also a serious cash flow problem because a number of long-term debts are coming due at the same time. The cash flow problem could be relieved somewhat if some of the accounts payable could be collected.

The CEO manages corporate matters through five functional divisions: operations, engineering, marketing, finance, and human resources management and general administration.

Preliminary, Concurrent, and Feedback Control Worksheet

Technocron International is in need of a variety of controls. Complete the following matrix by noting the preliminary, concurrent, and feedback controls that are needed in each of the five functional divisions.

Divisions	Preliminary Controls	Concurrent Controls	Feedback Controls
HRM and general administration	_____	_____	_____
Operations	_____	_____	_____
Engineering	_____	_____	_____
Marketing	_____	_____	_____
Finance	_____	_____	_____

CONCLUDING CASE

THE GRIZZLY BEAR LODGE

Diane and Rudy Conrad own a small lodge outside Yellowstone National Park. Their lodge has 15 rooms that can accommodate up to 40 guests, with some rooms set up for families. Diane and Rudy serve a continental breakfast on weekdays and a full breakfast on weekends, included in the room rates they charge. Their busy season runs from May through September, but they remain open until Thanksgiving and reopen in April for a short spring season. They currently employ one cook and two waitpersons for the breakfasts on weekends, handling the other breakfasts themselves. They also have several housekeeping staff members, a groundskeeper, and a front-desk employee. The Conrads take pride in the efficiency of their operation, including the loyalty of their employees, which they attribute to their own form of clan control. If a guest needs something—whether it's a breakfast catered to a special diet or an extra set of towels—Grizzly Bear workers are empowered to supply it.

The Conrads are considering expanding their business. They have been offered the opportunity to buy the property next door, which would give them the space to build an annex containing an additional 20 rooms. Currently their annual sales total $300,000. With expenses running at $230,000—including mortgage, payroll, maintenance, and so forth—the Conrads' annual income is $70,000. They want to expand and make improvements without cutting back on the personal service they offer to their guests. In fact, in addition to hiring more staff to handle the larger facility, they are considering collaborating with more local businesses to offer guided rafting, fishing, hiking, and horseback riding trips. They also want to expand their food service to include dinner during the high season, which means renovating the restaurant area of the lodge and hiring more kitchen and wait staff. Ultimately, the Conrads would like the lodge to be open year-round, offering guests opportunities to cross-country ski, ride snowmobiles, or hike in the winter. They hope to offer holiday packages for Thanksgiving, Christmas, and New Year's celebrations in the great outdoors. The Conrads report that their employees are enthusiastic about their plans and want to stay with them through the expansion process. "This is our dream business," says Rudy. "We're only at the beginning."

QUESTIONS

1. Discuss how Rudy and Diane can use feedforward, concurrent, and feedback controls both now and in the future at the Grizzly Bear Lodge to ensure their guests' satisfaction.

2. What might be some of the fundamental budgetary considerations the Conrads would have as they plan the expansion of their lodge?

3. Describe how the Conrads could use market controls to plan and implement their expansion.

CHAPTER 17

Managing Technology and Innovation

> The imperatives of technology and organization, not the images of ideology, are what determine the shape of economic society.
>
> —JOHN KENNETH GALBRAITH

Management in Action

HOW TESLA MOTORS DRIVES IN TECHNOLOGY'S FAST LANE

For the average manager, competing against the dominant car makers with a start-up would be unthinkable, but Elon Musk is far from average. Musk, who made his fortune starting the Internet ventures Zip2 and PayPal, believes he can compete by offering better vehicles—that run on electricity. To do so, his company, Tesla Motors, must overcome technological hurdles and convince car buyers to imagine driving in a new way. According to Musk, the vehicle industry someday must switch from gasoline to battery power, and he wants to drive that change.

As Musk sees it, being outside the auto-making establishment gives Tesla an advantage. Whereas the established car companies have labored to redesign vehicles to run on electrical power along with or in place of gasoline, Tesla's pure goal is to build an electric vehicle that is a pleasure to drive. Its first vehicle, the $109,000 Roadster sports car, sold few units but provided lessons for Tesla's more competitively priced entrant into the luxury market, the Model S sedan. The engineers placed the Model S's battery pack in the base of the vehicle, adding stability and safety while freeing up space for other uses—a spacious trunk, a storage compartment under the front hood, and room for seats to fold down in the back, allowing the car to carry seven people. In place of a gear shift console, a 17-inch touch screen displays controls and maps. And the super-efficient engine can take the car from 0 to 60 miles per hour in a few seconds.

Even as Musk persisted, observers doubted, seeing Tesla struggle with delays and quarterly losses while developing and troubleshooting its vehicles. Recently, however, developments suggest Tesla can succeed

© Johannes Eisele/AFP/Getty Images

financially by leaving the competition in the dust technologically. By December 2012, the company reached full production of the Model S. Soon glowing reviews made news: *Motor Trend* named it Car of the Year, calling it "a truly remarkable automobile." *Road and Track* said of the Model S, "For the first time since automobiles had fins, the world stands in awe of a car from the United States." And *Consumer Reports* said it was the best car it had ever tested.

In the first quarter of 2013, Tesla delivered 4,750 units of the Model S and recorded its first and only quarterly profit since it went public in 2010. Despite the fact that the auto maker increased its deliveries to nearly 32,000 units in 2014, that is far from the hundreds of thousands of hybrids sold by Honda and Toyota. Even so, investors—and drivers—are beginning to believe Tesla can make the electric car the vehicle of choice.[1]

Although more companies are introducing electric vehicles, most cars still run on gasoline. As you read this chapter, think about the issues that Tesla's managers must consider as they decide how to make electric vehicles an attractive and affordable option.

Although some visionaries such as Tesla's Elon Musk seem fearless, technological innovation is daunting in its complexity and pace of change. Nevertheless, it also is vital for a firm's competitive advantage. Not long ago, new products took years to plan and develop, were standardized and mass produced, and were pushed onto the market through extensive selling and promotional campaigns. With sales lives for these products measured in decades, production processes used equipment dedicated to making only those standardized products and achieved savings through economies of scale. But today's customers often demand products that have yet to be designed. Product development is now a race to become the first to introduce innovative products—products whose lives often are measured in months as they are quickly replaced by other, even more technologically sophisticated products. For example, robotics technology used to be limited to repetitive, programmable tasks like in manufacturing. Nowadays, robots are being used in a variety of human–machine contexts, from nursing to customer service roles in big box retailers.[2]

Today's managers and organizations depend on effective management of technology not only to carry out their basic tasks but, even more important, to ensure the continuing competitiveness of their goods or services. In a marketplace where technology and rapid innovation are critical for success, managers must understand how technologies emerge, develop, and change the ways organizations compete and the ways people work. This chapter discusses how technology can affect an organization's competitiveness and how to integrate technology into the organization's competitive strategy. Then we assess the technological needs of the organization and the means by which these needs can be met.

Bottom Line

Innovation is a key to competitiveness.

Why does innovation matter for a service business?

Technology and Innovation

LO 1

In Chapter 9, we defined **technology** as the methods, processes, systems, and skills used to transform resources into products. More broadly speaking, we can think of technology as the commercialization of science: the systematic application of scientific knowledge to a new product, process, or service. In this sense, technology is embedded in every product, service, and procedure used or produced.[3]

When technology is used to create a new product or service to sell or a new way of working, what has taken place is a form of innovation. Innovation differs from invention, or making a new idea manifest, which may or may not add value to any organization. In the context of management, **innovation** is any new way of working that creates value. Innovation can result from combining things that are new or from combining existing things in new ways. The resulting innovation can be any one of these three fundamental types:[4]

technology

The systematic application of scientific knowledge to a new product, process, or service.

innovation

The introduction of new goods and services; a change in method or technology; a positive, useful departure from previous ways of doing things.

1. *Product innovation* is a change in the outputs (goods or services) the organization produces. If BP's research into biofuels resulted in a new kind of fuel to sell, this would be an example of product innovation.

2. *Process innovation* is a change in the way outputs (goods or services) are produced. If BP's research into biofuels resulted in a more efficient way to produce fuel from sugarcane, this would be an example of process innovation. Other examples of process innovation are flexible manufacturing processes discussed in Chapter 9, including mass customization, just-in-time, and concurrent engineering.

3. *Business model innovation* refers to a change in the way the organization creates and delivers value. The change may affect any element of a company's business model: its customer value proposition (the basic problem it solves, such as ecofriendly fuel for about the same cost as fossil fuels), its profit formula (the financial road map for its success), its key resources (people, technology, facilities, brand, etc.), and its key processes. (See Exhibit 17.1 for additional examples.)

Social Enterprise

Detecting Landmines and Saving Lives

Despite the fact that 160 countries signed the 1997 Mine Ban Treaty, approximately 4,000 people die each year from buried explosives. It is estimated that 60 countries around the world still have thousands of active landmines, many of which are located near civilian populations. Countries with the most landmine casualties include Afghanistan, Colombia, Cambodia, and Syria. Children are not immune from danger, given their natural curiosity to pick up objects while playing in fields.

Selene Biffi wanted to help solve this problem. Lacking financing, credibility, and an infrastructure, she used innovative, low-cost technology to start Bibak (pronounce "be back"). The goal of the social enterprise is to "help communities take brave steps from landmines to land security." Working with a team of entrepreneurs, Biffi developed the "podtector" that houses a metal detector, ground-penetrating radar, and sensor for vapors from explosives. It can detect mines made of metal, plastic, and wood. The "podtector" is made from a portable water container and other off-the-shelf components. It can be carried on the end of a rake or stick, or by a tractor.

Bibak does more than make and distribute a life-saving device; it trains communities on how to assemble and use the device to detect mines. The device has other uses, too. According to Biffi: "Once demining is done, they can upcycle the technology to generate energy, improve local agriculture, or access clean water."

© Prakash Singh/AFP/Getty Images

What's next for this young social enterprise? Bibak is seeking funding and plans to roll out the "podtector" to several communities in Afghanistan. Reflecting on the role that technology is playing in her enterprise, Biffi commented: "Technology proved to be a safe passage to creating change despite having limited resources and support."[5]

Questions

- How would you classify Bibak's work? Does it represent a process or product innovation (or both)?
- To what degree has Bibak created an innovative business model?

These categories cover a multitude of creative new ideas (see the nearby "Social Enterprise" box), which in businesses can involve changes in product offerings, the basic platforms or common features and processes that underlie product creation, the customer problems the organization can solve, the types of customers the organization serves, the nature of the experience provided by the organization, the way the organization earns money from what it does, the efficiency and effectiveness of its processes, the structure of the organization, the supply chain through which it delivers goods and services, the

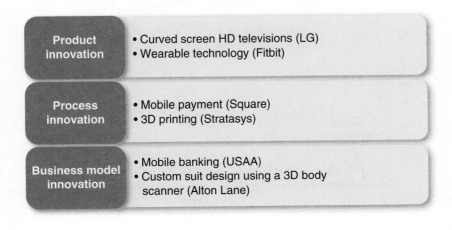

Product innovation
- Curved screen HD televisions (LG)
- Wearable technology (Fitbit)

Process innovation
- Mobile payment (Square)
- 3D printing (Stratasys)

Business model innovation
- Mobile banking (USAA)
- Custom suit design using a 3D body scanner (Alton Lane)

EXHIBIT 17.1
Examples of Different Types of Innovation

physical or virtual points at which it interacts with customers, the ways the organization communicates, and the brand associated with the organization and its products.[6]

There are definable and predictable patterns in the way technologies emerge, develop, and are replaced. Critical forces converge to create new technologies, which then follow well-defined life-cycle patterns. Understanding the forces driving technological development and the patterns they follow can help a manager anticipate, monitor, and manage technologies more effectively.

1. There must be a need, or demand, for the technology. Without this need driving the process, there is no reason for technological innovation to occur.
2. Meeting the need must be theoretically possible, and the knowledge to do so must be available from basic science.
3. We must be able to convert the scientific knowledge into practice in both engineering and economic terms. If we can theoretically do something but doing it is economically impractical, the technology cannot be expected to emerge.
4. The funding, skilled labor, time, space, and other resources needed to develop the technology must be available.
5. Entrepreneurial initiative is needed to identify and pull all the necessary elements together.

Technology Life Cycle

technology life cycle

A predictable pattern followed by a technological innovation, from its inception and development to market saturation and replacement.

Technological innovations typically follow a relatively predictable pattern called the **technology life cycle.** Exhibit 17.2 depicts the pattern. The cycle begins with the recognition of a need and a perception of a means by which the need can be satisfied through applied science or knowledge. The knowledge and ideas are brought together and developed, culminating in a new technological innovation. Early progress can be slow in these formative years as competitors continually experiment with product design and operational characteristics to meet consumer needs. This stage is where the rate of product innovation tends to be highest. For example, during the early years of the auto industry, companies tried a wide range of machines, including electric and steam-driven cars, to determine which product would be most effective. Eventually the internal combustion engine emerged as the dominant design, and the number of product innovations leveled off.

Once early problems are resolved and a dominant design emerges, improvements come more from process innovations to refine the technology. At this point managers can gain an advantage by pursuing process efficiencies and cost competitiveness. In the auto example, as companies settled on a product standard, they began leveraging the benefits

> Once early problems are resolved and a dominant design emerges, improvements come more from process innovations.

EXHIBIT 17.2
The Technology Life Cycle

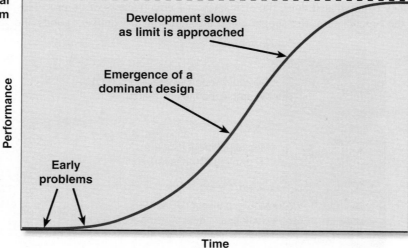

of mass production and vertical integration to improve productivity. These process innovations were instrumental in lowering production costs and bringing the price of automobiles in line with consumer budgets.[7]

Eventually the new technology begins to reach the upper limits of both its performance capabilities and the spread of its usage. Development slows and becomes increasingly costly, and the market becomes saturated (i.e., there are few new customers). The technology can remain in this mature stage for some time—as in the case of autos—or can be replaced quickly by another technology offering superior performance or economic advantage. The life cycles can take decades or even centuries, as in the case of iron- and steel-making technologies. A dramatic example of technology evolution can be found in the recorded music industry, which moved from the relatively primitive device Thomas Edison invented through the vinyl record to the cassette tape to the digitally recorded CD and then to highly miniaturized but memory-intensive MP3 players such as the iPod, which are now being challenged by services, such as Pandora or Spotify, that allow users to stream songs from the Internet on their smartphones or computers.

As this example shows, a technology life cycle can be made up of many individual product life cycles. Each of these products performs a similar task—delivering recorded music to a listener—yet each product is an improvement over its predecessors. In this way, technological development involves significant innovations, often representing entirely new technologies, followed by a large number of small, incremental innovations. Ongoing development of a technology increases the benefits gained through its use, makes the technology easier to use, and allows more applications. In the process, the use of the technology expands to new adopters.

Diffusion of Technological Innovations

Like the technology life cycle, the adoption of new technology over time follows an S-shaped pattern (see the top line in Exhibit 17.3). The percentage of people using the technology is small in the beginning but increases dramatically as the technology succeeds and spreads through the population. Eventually the number of users peaks and levels off when the market for the technology is saturated. This pattern, first observed in 1903, has been verified with many new technologies and ideas in a wide variety of industries and settings.[8]

The adopters of a new technology fall into five groups (see the bottom line in Exhibit 17.3). Each group presents different challenges and opportunities to managers who want to market a new technology or product innovation.

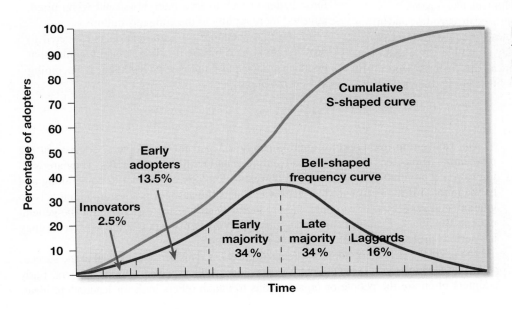

EXHIBIT 17.3
Technology Dissemination Pattern and Adopter Categories

Multiple Generations at Work

Using Gamification to Boost Employee Engagement

Gamification is a process of digitally motivating people to achieve their goals. A well-designed system not only helps the individual, but also benefits the company in question. In 2015, about 25 percent of companies were using gamification to build brand loyalty among customers. Some examples include: Starbucks Cards earn patrons rewards and free drinks; Marriott's reward program earns customers points that can be redeemed for discounts and charitable contributions; and Nike+ FuelBand helps users set and measure daily activity goals, as well as reinforcing exercise habits by sending motivational badges and feedback to customers.

Innovators and early adopters of gamification are experimenting by using this technology to increase the engagement level of their employees. Motivating and retaining employees is a major challenge for organizations. A recent Gallup poll found that only 31.5 percent of employees in the United States are engaged in their jobs. When analyzed by generational segment, Millennials were the least engaged cohort of workers. The hope is that organizations can incorporate "game elements into existing processes to boost productivity, improve skills and drive performance."

One of the areas where gamification is taking root is in employee learning and development. Using Badgeville's gamification platform, Deloitte's Leadership Academy motivates its employees through the use of missions, badges, and leaderboards to carve time out of their busy schedules to keep their knowledge up to date by completing online coursework. According to Frank Farral, lead partner of Deloitte Digital: "If you can gamify the process, you are rewarding the behavior and it's like a dopamine release in the brain. Humans like a game."

Gamification is also being used in recruiting and hiring. Prior to hiring job candidates, PricewaterhouseCoopers Hungary allows them to play an online game that "tests their readiness for working at the firm by working in teams to solve real world business problems." Noemi

© Craig F. Walker/The Denver Post via Getty Images

Biro, PwC's regional recruitment manager, found that candidates who completed the 1½-hour virtual game fared better in face-to-face interviews, and when hired, adjusted more rapidly to the company culture.

Given that spending on gamification is expected to grow to about $5.5 billion by 2018, creating games that boost customer and employee engagement is becoming serious business.[9]

The first group, representing approximately 2.5 percent of adopters, consists of the *innovators*. Typically, innovators are adventurous and willing to take risks. They are willing to pay a premium for the latest and newest technology or product to come along and to champion it if it meets with their approval. The enthusiasm of innovator–adopters is no guarantee of success—for example, the product may still be too expensive for the general market. But a lack of enthusiasm among this group is often a sign that the new technology has serious problems and more development is needed.

The next 13.5 percent of adopters are *early adopters*. This group is critical to the success of a new technology because its members include well-respected opinion leaders. Early adopters often are the people or organizations to which others look for leadership, ideas, and up-to-date technological information. Innovators and early adopters are extremely important in new product launches, and marketing managers often spend heavily in promotion among these groups to generate a groundswell of enthusiasm. For example, companies are increasingly using gamification to engage their customers and employees (see "Multiple Generations at Work").

The next group, representing 34 percent of adopters, is the *early majority*. These adopters are more deliberate and take longer to decide to use something new. Often they are important members of a community or industry, but typically not the leaders. It may take a while for the technology or new product to spread to this group, but once it does, use will begin to proliferate into the mainstream.

Representing the next 34 percent are the *late majority*. Members of this group are more skeptical of technological change and approach innovation with great caution, often adopting only out of economic necessity or increasing social pressure.

The final 16 percent are *laggards*. Often isolated and highly conservative in their views, laggards are extremely suspicious of innovation and change.

The speed with which an innovation spreads depends largely on five attributes. An innovation will spread quickly if it

- Has a great advantage over its predecessor.
- Is compatible with existing systems, procedures, infrastructures, and ways of thinking.
- Has less rather than greater complexity.
- Can be tried or tested easily without significant cost or commitment.
- Can be observed and copied easily.

Designing products with these technological considerations in mind can make a critical difference in their success.

Technological Innovation in a Competitive Environment

LO 3

Discussions about technology life cycles and diffusion patterns may imply that technological change occurs naturally or automatically. Just the opposite is true: Change is neither easy nor natural in organizations. (We discuss change more fully in the next chapter.) Decisions about technology and innovation are very strategic, and managers need to approach them in a systematic way.

In Chapter 4, we discussed two generic strategies a company can use to position itself in the market: low cost and differentiation. With low-cost leadership, the company maintains an advantage because it has a lower cost than its competitors. With a differentiation strategy, the advantage comes from having a unique good or service for which customers are willing to pay a premium price.[10] Technological innovations can support either of these strategies: They can be used to gain cost advantage through pioneering lower-cost product designs and creating low-cost ways to perform needed operations, or they can support differentiation by pioneering unique goods or services that increase buyer value and thus command premium prices.

In some cases, technology can completely change the rules of competition within an industry. Clayton Christensen coined the term **disruptive innovation** to describe situations in which a simple application is adopted at the lower end of a market and then swiftly takes over the market.[11] For example, computer users initially mocked tablet computers because they offer less computing power than a laptop and more bulk than a smartphone. Nevertheless, Apple's iPad quickly helped tablets carve out a big share of the market for portable computers. The power of disruptive innovation creates a dilemma for companies: Should they continue on with the superior technology (and possibly lose the advantages of early adoption) or switch over to the new technology (and find themselves with an inferior product that may or may not succeed)? In practice, the tendency is to innovate to the point

Bottom Line
Innovation can improve any bottom-line practice.
How can innovation support a low-cost strategy?

disruptive innovation

A process by which a product, service, or business model takes root initially in simple applications at the bottom of a market and then moves "up market," eventually displacing established competitors.

that products or services become too sophisticated or expensive for buyers' tastes, creating new opportunities for the next disruptive innovation. To be a disruptive innovator, focus on the users of a product and look for customers whose needs are being ignored—say, because they want something that costs less or is easier to use.

But industries seldom are transformed overnight. Typically, signals of a new technology's impact are visible well in advance, leaving time for companies and people to respond. For example, almost every competitor in the telecommunications industry fully understood the value of cellular technology. Often the key issue is not whether to adopt a new technology but when to adopt it and how to integrate the change with the organization's operating practices and strategies.

Technology Leadership

The adage "timing is everything" is applied to many things, ranging from financial investments to telling jokes. It also applies to the development and exploitation of new technologies. Industry leaders such as 3M, Amazon, Nike, and Merck built and now maintain their competitive positions through early development and application of new technologies. However, technology leadership imposes costs and risks, and it is not the best approach for every organization (see Exhibit 17.4).[12] Apple is well known for its technology leadership, beginning with its Macintosh computer, which pioneered the use of a mouse and graphical desktop icons instead of strings of typed computer commands, and advancing through the wildly popular iPod and iPhone. Time will tell if Apple can repeat its success with such innovations as the Apple Watch and "force of touch" technology being added to the forthcoming iPhone.[13]

> Often the key issue is not whether to adopt a new technology but when to adopt it.

Advantages of Technology Leadership   What makes innovators and technology leadership attractive is the potential for high profits and first-mover advantages. Being the first to market with new technologies can provide significant competitive advantage. If technology leadership increases an organization's efficiency relative to competitors, it achieves a cost advantage. The organization can use the advantage to reap greater profits than competitors or attract more customers by charging lower prices. Similarly, if a company is first to market with a new technology, it may be able to charge a premium price because it faces no competition. Higher prices and greater profits can defray the costs of developing new technologies.

EXHIBIT 17.4
Advantages and Disadvantages of Technology Leadership

Advantages	Disadvantages
First-mover advantage	Greater risks
Little or no competition	Cost of technology development
Greater efficiency	Costs of market development and customer education
Higher profit margins	Infrastructure costs
Sustainable advantage	Costs of learning and eliminating defects
Reputation for innovation	Possible cannibalization of existing products
Establishment of entry barriers	
Occupation of best market niches	
Opportunities to learn	

This one-time advantage of being the technology leader can be turned into a sustainable advantage. Sustainability of a lead depends on competitors' ability to duplicate the technology and the organization's ability to keep building on the lead quickly enough to outpace competitors. It can do this in several ways. The reputation for being an innovator can create an ongoing advantage and even spill over to the company's other products. For example, 3M's reputation for innovation and quality differentiates some of its standard products, such as adhesive tape, and allows a product to command a premium price. A competitor may be able to copy the product but not the reputation. Patents and other institutional barriers also can be used to block competitors and maintain leadership. The big players in the pharmaceutical industry invest heavily in research and development; they depend on patents to give them several years of selling new drugs without competition before generic versions of their drugs are permitted. For example, the cholesterol-lowering drug Crestor, which had recent annual sales of over $6 billion, is protected by patent until 2016.[14] As additional blockbuster drug patents expire over the next few years, pharmaceutical companies are facing a tremendous challenge to develop new drugs.

The first mover can also preempt competitors by occupying the best market niches. If it can establish high switching costs (recall Chapter 2) for repeat customers, these positions can be difficult for competitors to capture. Microsoft dominates the software market with its Windows operating system because of the large library of software that is packaged with it. Although other companies can offer more advanced software, their products are not as attractive because they are not bundled as the Windows-based systems is.

Technology leadership can provide a significant learning advantage. Although competitors may be able to copy or adopt a new technology, ongoing learning by the technology leader can keep a company ahead by generating minor improvements that are difficult to imitate. Many Japanese manufacturers use several small, incremental improvements generated with their *kaizen* programs (recall Chapter 9) to upgrade the quality of their products and processes continuously. All these minor improvements cannot be copied easily by competitors, and collectively they can provide a significant advantage.[15]

Top pharmaceutical companies depend on patents to allow them several years of selling new drugs without competition before cheaper generic versions of their drugs are released. Their competitive strategy is to develop new drugs in the meantime to sustain their success.

© Thinkstock/Jupiterimages

> The first mover can also preempt competitors by occupying the best market niches.

Disadvantages of Technology Leadership   Being the first to develop or adopt a new technology does not always lead to immediate advantage and high profits, however. Although such potential may exist, technology leadership does impose high costs and risks that followers do not have to bear. Being the leader thus can be more costly than being the follower. (There's good reason the forefront of technology is often called the bleeding edge.) These costs include educating buyers unfamiliar with the new technology, building an infrastructure to support the technology, and developing complementary products to achieve the technology's full potential. For example, when the personal computer was first developed in the 1970s, dozens of computer companies entered the market. Almost all of them failed, usually because they lacked the financial, marketing, and sales ability required to attract and service customers. Also, many new products require regulatory approval. For example, developing a new drug, including testing and obtaining FDA approval, can take 10 years or more and cost upward of $60 million to $1 billion or more. After that, developers enjoy a profitable period of patent protection until competitors move in with low-cost generics. Although these followers do not get the benefits of being first to market, they can copy the drug for a fraction of the cost once the original patents expire. This strategy can be highly profitable.[16]

Being a pioneer carries other risks. If raw materials and equipment are new or have unique specifications, a ready supply at a reasonable cost may not be available. Or the technology may not be fully developed and may have problems yet to be resolved. In addition, the unproved market for the technology creates uncertainty in demand. Finally, the new technology may have an adverse impact on existing structures or business. It may cannibalize current products or make existing investments obsolete.

Technology Followership

Not all organizations are equally prepared to be technology leaders, nor would leadership benefit each organization equally. In deciding whether to be a technology leader or follower, managers will consider their company's competitive strategy, the benefits gained through use of the technology, and the characteristics of their organization.[17]

Interestingly, technology followership also can be used to support both low-cost and differentiation strategies. If the follower learns from the leader's experience, it can avoid the costs and risks of technology leadership, thereby establishing a low-cost position. The makers of generic drugs use this type of strategy. Followership also can support differentiation. By learning from the leader, the follower can adapt the products or delivery systems to fit buyers' needs more closely. Microsoft is famous for having built a successful company on this type of followership. The company's products, including music players, video game consoles, spreadsheet and word-processing software, and web browsers, have been launched after technology leaders have paved the way. Likewise, Facebook came to dominate the realm of social networking only after other services such as Friendster and MySpace had burned through money introducing the concept. Newer competitors, such as Google, and photo- and video-sharing apps like Instagram, Snapchat, and WhatsApp continue to enter the market with the hope that they can lure away users with a service that improves on Facebook's strengths while avoiding its weaknesses. This follower strategy is more challenging once an industry leader has established widespread customer loyalty.

A manager's decision on when to adopt new technology also depends on the potential benefits of the new technology as well as the organization's technology skills. As discussed earlier, technologies do not emerge in their final state; rather, they exhibit ongoing development (see Exhibit 17.5). Such development eventually makes the technology easier to use and more adaptable to various strategies. For example, the development of high-bandwidth communication networks has enabled many more companies to work with suppliers located abroad. At the same time, complementary products and technologies may be developed and introduced that make the main technology more useful. For example, tablet computers are becoming more of an asset at work—and therefore more common—as wireless speeds increase and developers offer business-friendly apps and adapt popular business software for use on mobile devices.

These complementary products and technologies combine with the gradual diffusion of the technology to form a shifting competitive impact from the technology. The appropriate time for an organization to adopt technological innovations is when the costs and risks of switching to the technology are outweighed by the benefits. This point will be different

Bottom Line

Following the technology leader can save development expense. *How can being a follower help reduce costs?*

EXHIBIT 17.5

Dynamic Forces of a Technology's Competitive Impact

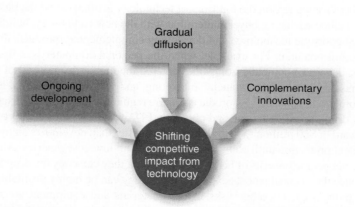

SOURCE: D. M. Schroeder, "A Dynamic Perspective on the Impact of Process Innovation upon Competitive Strategies," *Strategic Management Journal* 11 (January 1990), pp. 25–42. Reprinted with permission.

for each organization, with some organizations benefiting from a leadership, early adopter role, and others from a followership role, depending on each organization's characteristics and strategies.[18]

Assessing Technology Needs

The biggest industry sector in the U.S. economy is health care services, where spending is soaring, much to the dismay of the insurers and patients paying the medical bills. One reason U.S. health care costs so much is that the industry has been slower than others to adopt types of technology that can make day-to-day operations more efficient. According to a RAND Corporation study, Americans could save $81 billion a year if health care providers made better investments in information technology. To reach this level of savings, the study recommends (1) making patient information stored in one IT system retrievable by other health care systems, (2) allowing patients to have ready online access to their medical information, and (3) engineering health information systems so they are mobile-friendly and easy to use.[19]

In today's increasingly competitive environment, failure to assess the technology needs of the organization correctly can fundamentally impair the organization's effectiveness. Assessing the technology needs of the organization involves measuring current technologies as well as external trends affecting the industry.

LO 4

Measuring Current Technologies

Before organizations can devise strategies for developing and exploiting technological innovation, they must gain a clear understanding of their current technology base. A **technology audit** helps clarify the key technologies on which an organization depends. The most important dimension of a new technology is its competitive value. One technique for measuring competitive value categorizes technologies as emerging, pacing, key, and base:[20]

technology audit

Process of clarifying the key technologies on which an organization depends.

- *Emerging technologies* are still under development and thus are unproved. They may, however, significantly alter the rules of competition in the future. Managers will want to monitor the development of emerging technologies but may not yet need to invest in them until they have been more fully developed.
- *Pacing technologies* have yet to prove their full value but have the potential to alter the rules of competition by providing significant advantage. For example, when first installed, computer-aided manufacturing (see Chapter 9) was a pacing technology. Its full potential was not yet widely realized, but companies that used it effectively developed significant speed and cost advantages. Managers will want to focus on developing or investing in pacing technologies because of the competitive advantages they can provide.
- *Key technologies* have proved effective, but they also provide a strategic advantage because not everyone uses them. Knowledge and dissemination of these technologies are limited, and they continue to provide some first-mover advantages. For example, a more powerful, proprietary processing chip by Intel is a key technology for that organization. Eventually, alternatives to key technologies can emerge. But until then key technologies can give organization managers a significant competitive edge and make it much more difficult for new entrants to threaten the organization.
- *Base technologies* are those that are commonplace in the industry; everyone must have them to be able to operate. Thus they provide little competitive advantage. Managers have to invest only to ensure their organization's continued competence in the technology.

The most important dimension of a new technology is its competitive value.

Technologies can evolve rapidly through these categories. For example, electronic word processing was considered an emerging technology in the late 1970s. By the early 1980s, it could have been considered pacing. Although promising advantages, the technology's cost and capabilities restricted its usefulness to a limited number of applications. With continued improvements and more powerful computer chips, electronic word processing quickly became a key technology. Its costs dropped, its usage spread, and it demonstrated the capacity to enhance productivity. By the late 1980s, it was considered a base technology in most applications. Word-processing technology is now used so widely that it is viewed as a routine activity in almost every office.

Assessing External Technological Trends

Just as with any planning, decisions about technology must balance internal capabilities (strengths and weaknesses) with external opportunities and threats. Managers can use several techniques to understand better how technology is changing within an industry.

Bottom Line

Benchmarking can lower cost and raise speed, quality, sustainability, and customer service.

What are some limits on benchmarking as a source of technology ideas?

Benchmarking   As mentioned in Chapter 4, benchmarking is the process of comparing the organization's practices and technologies with those of other companies. The ability to benchmark technologies against those of competitors varies among industries. Although competitors understandably are reluctant to share their secrets, information trading for benchmarking is not uncommon and can prove highly valuable. For example, Harley-Davidson's recovery of its reputation for manufacturing quality motorcycles began only after company executives toured Honda's plant and witnessed firsthand the weaknesses of Harley's manufacturing technologies and the vast potential for improvement.

Benchmarking against potential competitors in other nations is also important. Companies may find key or pacing technologies in use that can be imported easily and offer significant advantage. Also, overseas firms may be more willing to share their knowledge if they are not direct competitors and if they are eager to exchange information to benefit both companies.

After Harley-Davidson executives toured a Honda plant, they were able to identify the weaknesses within their own company and use that knowledge to improve and boost their reputation.

© AP Photo/Nati Harnak

Scanning

Whereas benchmarking focuses on what is being done currently, scanning focuses on what can be done and what is being developed. In other words, benchmarking examines key and perhaps some pacing technologies, whereas scanning seeks out pacing and emerging technologies—those just being introduced and still in development. For example, IBM's million-neuron TrueNorth chip may be a game changer in the computer industry. Still in development, the neuromorphic chip is hundreds of times more powerful than current chips and will likely empower the next level of artificial intelligence where computers will be designed to "anticipate and learn."[21]

Scanning typically involves a number of tactics, many of them the same as those used in benchmarking. However, scanning places greater emphasis on identifying and monitoring the sources of new technologies for an industry. It also may dictate that executives read more cutting-edge research journals and attend research conferences and seminars. The extent to which scanning is done depends largely on how close to the cutting edge of technology an organization needs to operate.

Key Factors to Consider in Technology Decisions

Once managers have thoroughly analyzed their organization's current technological position, they can plan how to either develop or exploit emerging technological innovations for the future. Managers must balance many interrelated factors in their decisions, such as the technology's potential to support the organization's strategic needs and the organization's skills and capabilities to exploit the technology successfully. The organization's competitive strategy, the technical abilities of its employees to deal with the new technology, the fit of the technology with the company's operations, and the company's ability to deal with the risks and ambiguities of adopting a new technology all must be considered in conjunction with the dynamic forces of a developing technology. This process does not always mean waiting for the technology to develop. Often it requires changing the capabilities and strategies of the organization to match the needs of the technology, including hiring new people, training existing employees, changing internal policies and procedures, and changing strategies. These considerations are discussed next.

Anticipated Market Receptiveness

The first consideration that needs to be addressed in developing a strategy around technological innovation is market potential. In many cases, innovations are stimulated by external demand for new goods and services. For example, a Boston company called Rethink Robotics believes the problem of repetitive-motion injuries will drive demand for robots that can safely work near humans to perform repetitive tasks such as picking, sorting, and arranging items. The company has responded by developing its Baxter robot with plastic, padded arms and sensors in the joints so workers can safely stand nearby and program the six-foot-tall robot. To help production workers control the robot, Baxter has a display screen on which expressive eyes signal the robot's status.[22]

In assessing market receptiveness, executives need to make two determinations:

1. In the short run, the new technology should have an immediate, valuable application.
2. In the long run, the technology must be able to satisfy market needs.

For example, retailers are always looking for ways to get the right goods on their shelves at the right time at a lower cost. They were therefore immediately interested in the introduction of a new technology for tracking inventory, radio frequency identification (RFID). Over a decade ago, Walmart adopted RFID technology to increase the efficiency of its supply chain. Walmart asked its suppliers to put RFID tags on individual products so store employees can measure exactly what is in stock with the wave of a scanner. Retailers like Macy's also use RFID technology. As more customers stand in stores and comparative shop on their mobile devices, Macy's wants to make sure "that what its website says is in the store is actually in the store." This alignment leads to a higher number of closed sales. Hospitals are beginning to place RFID tags on equipment, supplies, and even patients' bracelets so they can ensure adequate supplies and efficiently deliver the right services. And when art collectors transport valuable pieces, they often mark each work with an RFID tag as one of their many security measures.[23]

© Marc F. Henning/Alamy

Technological Feasibility

In addition to market receptiveness, managers must consider the feasibility of technological innovations. Visions can stay unrealized for a long time. Technical obstacles may represent barriers to progress. For example, security experts have for years wanted reliable face recognition systems; if a computer or mobile device can correctly associate a face with the correct person's identity, this would prevent many of the problems that arise from stolen ID cards, passwords, and other fallible protection systems. But a recent study by the National Research Council found that face recognition technology cannot be improved to the point of making zero errors. Some of the stumbling blocks that are too complex for the computer systems of today and the foreseeable future are picking out facial features from a picture with other details, accounting for differences in a person's posture or facial expression, and accounting for differences in lighting levels and time (because people's faces change as they age). Improving performance in one of these areas tends to reduce performance in another. Even testing these systems is difficult; if, say, the lighting is adjusted, the results will diverge from test results under different conditions. Despite these challenges, progress is being made. The National Institute of Standards and Technology (NIST) reported that accuracy of facial recognition programs has improved up to 30 percent over the past few years.[24]

Other industries face technological hurdles as well. In the oil industry, for example, technological barriers prevent exploration and drilling in the deepest parts of the ocean. In medicine, scientists and doctors work continuously to identify the causes of and cures for diseases such as cancer and AIDS. Makers of electronic devices are constantly challenged by how to keep their processors cool enough to function properly even as they get smaller and more powerful. GE recently applied jet engine technology to send high-velocity jets of air across electronic components, replacing fans with a system that can be as small as 4 millimeters high.[25] As time passes, however, electronics manufacturers will surely be looking for something even smaller. Each of these potentially valuable innovations is slowed by the technical limits of currently available technologies.

Economic Viability

Closely related to technological feasibility is economic viability. Apart from whether a firm can pull off a technological innovation, executives must consider whether there is a good financial incentive for doing so. The use of hydrogen-powered fuel cell technology for automobiles is almost feasible technically, but its costs are still too high. In addition, even if those costs were brought down to more acceptable levels, the absence of a supporting infrastructure in the society as a whole—such as the lack of hydrogen refueling stations—would represent another barrier to economic viability. However, if organizations can find niche markets for a high-priced new technology, they often can advance the technology to the point that applications become more affordable. For example, three-dimensional (3D) printers can read plans and translate them into physical objects by spraying out extremely thin layers of plastic or other materials to create the physical object. With advances in computer software, a skilled designer can create a 3D model of a part in a matter of hours and then direct the printer to finish the job. If the design disappoints, changes are easy to make with the software's commands, and no machinery needs to be retooled. A factory might invest in a high-end printer for $100,000 or more, but the price of basic printers has fallen below $1,500, putting them in reach of entrepreneurs and inventors.[26]

> Closely related to technological feasibility is economic viability.

Less futuristic innovations also require a careful assessment of economic viability and costs. New technologies often represent an expensive and long-term commitment of resources. And integrating them effectively within an organization can require a great deal of management time. Once an organization commits to a technological innovation, a change in direction becomes extremely difficult and costly. For these reasons, a careful, objective analysis of technology costs versus benefits is essential. Of course, benefits can be substantial as well. Fast-food restaurants can adopt a system called HyperActive Bob. The system scans the parking lot to count vehicles that are arriving; compiles that data with information about time of day, cooking times, ordering patterns, and so on; and then issues orders to employees, telling them which items and how many to begin cooking. Employees touch a screen to indicate when they accept a task and when they are finished. The system, made by HyperActive Technologies, costs $5,000 to install and $3,000 a year for software licensing, but it saves thousands a year in reduced food waste plus much more in reduced employee turnover—because Bob is an alternative to being shouted at by an anxious supervisor.[27]

The issue of economic viability takes us back to our earlier discussion of adoption timing. Earlier adopters may have first-mover advantages, but costs are associated with this strategic approach. The development costs of a particular technological innovation may be quite high, as in pharmaceuticals, chemicals, and software. Patents and copyrights often help organizations recoup the costs of their investments in technological innovations. Without such protection, the investments in research and development might not be justifiable.

Unfortunately, the exploding growth in piracy or even fakery of patented pharmaceuticals, software, and other products has added new barriers to economic viability. Globalization has created a worldwide market for goods produced by low-cost counterfeiters and pirates overseas, who have the added advantage that they do not have to incur research and development expense. In addition, technology has made it easy to copy software without paying for it. Ugg boots, iPhones, Pfizer's anti-impotence drug Viagra, Rolex watches, Prada handbags, LEGO building sets, and countless music and movie recordings—all these and much more have been counterfeited or illegally copied and sold. In one year alone, U.S. Customs and Border Protections seized counterfeit or pirated goods worth $1.2 billion in lost sales, and that amount does not count the goods that slipped through customs undetected. A major contributor to the problem is China, which in recent years has accounted for more than three-quarters of the fake or pirated goods seized by the U.S. government. All these measures are designed to help organizations—and countries—maintain the economic viability of their innovations.[28]

HyperActive Bob applies robotics technology (computer vision and artificial intelligence) to fast-food operations to make them more efficient. Using this technology is economically feasible because it reduces waste, improves customer satisfaction, and reduces employee turnover.

Courtesy of HyperActive Technologies

Anticipated Capability Development

We have stated repeatedly in this text that organizations should (and do) build their strategies based on core capabilities. This advice applies to technology and innovation strategies as well. Frequently we can view technological innovations that are the tangible product of intangible—or tacit—knowledge and skill that make up a firm's core capabilities. Merck, Apple, and Intel are examples of companies in which core capabilities in research and development lead to new technological innovations. Even in these cases, research capabilities are not always a good match with market opportunities. Pharmaceutical companies such as Merck are finding that many of the best new opportunities for fighting disease are in biotechnology, but the companies had developed expertise in chemistry-based drugs. Often these companies add new capabilities by acquiring or setting up ventures with biotechnology start-ups.

Some innovations are competency enhancing, exploiting or strengthening a core capability, whereas others are competency destroying. Continuing the example of Merck, biotechnology is changing the pharmaceutical industry. Currently, most core capabilities in the industry are in chemistry-based drugs. The shift to biotech requires firms to develop or acquire a capability in biology-based therapeutics. For most firms, that is not an easy shift.[29]

A firm may not be technology oriented, but it still must pay attention to changing technology because it sometimes will need new capabilities to survive. For example, when Amazon.com changed the face of e-retailing in the 1990s, traditional brick-and-mortar bookstores had to adapt quickly. To regain competitiveness, they had to bolster their information technology capabilities, which wasn't always an easy thing to do.

The upshot of this is that although certain technologies may have tremendous market applicability, managers must have (or develop) the internal capabilities needed to execute their technology strategies. Without the skills needed to implement an innovation, even promising technological advances may prove disastrous.

Organizational Suitability

The final issues that tend to be addressed in deciding on technological innovations have to do with the culture of the organization, the interests of managers, and the expectations of stakeholders. Companies such as 3M and Google, which are seen as proactive technology-push innovators, tend to have cultures that are more outward-looking and opportunistic. Executives in these *prospector* firms give considerable priority to developing and exploiting technological expertise, and decision makers tend to have bold intuitive visions of the future. Typically they have technology champions who articulate competitively aggressive, first-mover technological strategies. In many cases, executives are more concerned about the opportunity costs of not taking action than they are about the potential to fail.

By contrast, *defender* firms, such as Kroger and Safeway, tend to adopt a more circumspect posture toward innovation. These firms tend to operate in stable environments. As a result, their strategies are focused more on deepening their capability base through complementary technologies that extend rather than replace their current ones. Strategic decisions are likely to be based on careful analysis and experience in the industry setting. In the United States, supermarkets have competed for decades by emphasizing low-cost distribution over large distances. That strategy has helped the companies survive low-cost pressure from Walmart but has not always translated well when U.S.-based supermarket chains have tried to expand into other parts of the world.[30]

A hybrid *analyzer* firm, such as Microsoft, needs to stay technologically competitive but tends to allow others to demonstrate solid demand in new arenas before it responds. Microsoft's Xbox game console, Office software, and Zune music player all contain innovations, but other companies pioneered the original path-breaking product concepts. As we noted earlier, these types of firms tend to adopt an early follower strategy to grab a dominant position more from their strengths in marketing and manufacturing than through technological innovation.

Every company has different capabilities to deal with new technology. As discussed previously, early adopters have characteristics different from those of late adopters. Early adopters of new technologies tend to be larger, more profitable, and more specialized. Therefore, they are in an economic position to absorb the risks associated with early adoption while profiting more from its advantages. In addition, the people involved in early adoption are more highly educated, have a greater ability to deal with abstraction, can cope with uncertainty more effectively, and have strong problem-solving capabilities. Thus early adopters can more effectively manage the difficulties and uncertainty of a less fully developed technology.[31]

One additional consideration managers need to take into account when introducing new technology is the impact the new technology will have on employees. Often new technology brings with it work flow and other changes that directly affect the organization's work environment. When managers communicate well in advance about the new technology, explain its purpose, and provide the necessary training, the process of integrating the new technology into the organization's existing processes becomes easier. The cooperation of employees is often a major factor in determining how difficult and costly the introduction of new technology will be. We discuss the issue of managing change in more detail in the next chapter.

Licensing

Certain technologies that are not easily purchased as part of a product can be licensed for a fee. Companies like Epic Games in North Carolina that develop video games often license technology, including the software that models the physics behind the activities depicted in the game. The artwork, characters, and music for a particular game may be unique, but the basic laws of real-world physics apply to the action shown in most of today's sophisticated games, so there is no advantage to programming that aspect of each game. Licensing is more economical.[35]

Technology Trading

Another way to gain access to new technologies is with technology trading. Representatives from Scotsman Ice Systems have studied other manufacturers' information technology applications. Whether or not those companies were in the same industry, their experiences have provided Scotsman with lessons that would have been expensive to learn from trial and error. Similarly, Mary Jo Cartwright, a director of plant operations at Batesville Casket Company, adopted Toyota's manufacturing philosophy of lean production and continuous improvement. The company has been able to decrease manufacturing costs by 25 percent and the number of hours to make a coffin by 40 percent. Prior to adopting the "Toyota way," 20 percent of manufactured coffins needed repair. That rate has been cut to 1 percent.[36]

Sometimes even rival companies use technology trading. Not all industries are amenable to this kind of sharing, but technology trading is becoming increasingly common because of the high cost of developing advanced technologies independently.[37]

Research Partnerships and Joint Ventures

Research partnerships are arrangements designed to pursue specific new technology development jointly. Typically each member enters the partnership with different skills or resources needed for development to succeed. One effective combination is an established company and a start-up. Joint ventures are similar in most respects to research partnerships, but they tend to have greater permanence, and their outcomes result in entirely new companies.[38] But as we described in our discussion on strategic alliances in Chapter 9, sometimes even powerful competitors collaborate on projects. Nestlé Health Sciences and Chi-Med, a health care group in China, established a joint venture that will develop and market "innovative nutritional and medicinal products derived from botanical plants." This venture brings together Nestlé's knowledge of marketing to global customers and Chi-Med's expertise in traditional Chinese medicine (and its collection of more than 50,000 extracts from 1,200 different herbal plants).[39]

> Sometimes even powerful competitors collaborate on projects.

Acquisition of an Owner of the Technology

If a company lacks the needed technology but wishes to acquire proprietary ownership of it, one option is to purchase the company that owns the technology. This transaction can take a number of forms, ranging from an outright purchase of the entire company to a minority interest sufficient to gain access to the technology. Twitter has recently been buying privately owned tech companies at a rapid clip. Among its recent acquisitions were Vine, creator of a service that lets people post short videos; Lucky Sort, which built software for identifying patterns in live data streams such as social-media posts and news reports; and Bluefin Labs, which developed a service that gathers data from social media to measure what TV shows and ads people are talking about.[40] Each acquisition gave Twitter new technological capabilities related to its main service of hosting microblogs and delivering ads to users.

EXHIBIT 17.7
Technology Acquisition
Options

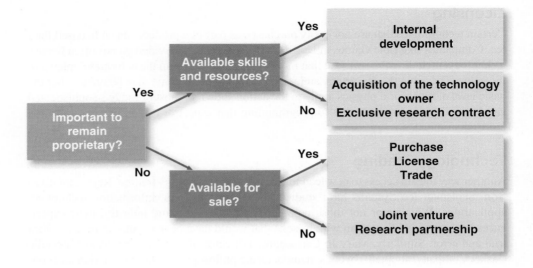

Choosing among these alternatives is simpler if managers ask the following basic questions:

1. Is it important (and possible) in terms of competitive advantage for the technology to remain proprietary?
2. Are the time, skills, and resources for internal development available?
3. Is the technology readily available outside the company?

As Exhibit 17.7 illustrates, the answers to these questions guide the manager to the most appropriate technology acquisition option.

If the preferred decision is to acquire a company, managers take additional steps to ensure the acquisition will make sense for the long term. For example, they try to make sure that key employees will remain with the firm instead of leaving and perhaps taking essential technical expertise with them. Similarly, as with any large investment, managers carefully assess whether the financial benefits of the acquisition will justify the purchase price.

Technology and Managerial Roles

chief information officer (CIO)

Executive in charge of information technology strategy and development.

In organizations, technology traditionally has been the responsibility of vice presidents for research and development. These executives are directly responsible for corporate and divisional R&D laboratories. Typically their jobs have a functional orientation. But increasingly companies have the position of **chief information officer (CIO),** often also called the chief technology officer (CTO). The CIO is a senior position at the corporate level with broad, integrative responsibilities. CIOs coordinate the technological efforts of the various business units; act as a voice for technology in the top management team; identify ways that technology can support the company's strategy; supervise new technology development; and assess the technological implications of major strategic initiatives such as acquisitions, new ventures, and strategic alliances. They also manage their organization's information technology (IT) group.[41]

In organizations that value the agility resulting from continuous learning, this position sometimes is a variation on the CTO known as a *chief innovation officer.* The chief innovation officer not only ensures that technology advances in line with the company's strategy, but also ensures that ideas and knowledge freely flow between R&D and other employees as well as between researchers and the company's management.[42]

Without the CIO's integrative role, different departments in an organization could easily adopt different technology tools and standards, leading to much higher equipment and maintenance expense and difficulties in connecting the different parts of the organization. Also, because organization technologists often have very specialized expertise, managers without such expertise may have difficulty supervising them effectively. A CIO can help managers ensure that the work technologists do is aligned with the strategic goals of the organization.

Chief technology officers also perform an important boundary role: they work directly with outside organizations. For example, they work with universities for funding research to stay abreast of technical developments and with regulatory agencies to ensure compliance with regulations, identify trends, and influence the regulatory process.

Other people play a variety of critical roles in developing new technology. Recall from Chapter 7 that it is the entrepreneur who, in an effort to exploit untried technologies, invents new products or finds new ways to produce old products. The entrepreneur opens up new possibilities that change the competitive structure of entire industries. For example, Steve Jobs started Apple Computer in his garage, helping to popularize the personal computer and years later the MP3 music player.

Key roles in acquiring and developing new technologies are the technical innovator, product champion, and executive champion.[43] The **technical innovator** develops the new technology or has the key skills needed to install

Sophie Vandebroek, chief technology officer and president of the innovation group of Xerox, took on this role with the goal of making Xerox's systems simpler, speedier, smaller, smarter, more secure, and socially responsible—what she calls the "six S's."

© Andrew Harrer/Bloomberg via Getty Images

and operate the technology. This person possesses the requisite technical skills, but he or she may not have the managerial skills needed to push the idea forward and secure acceptance within the organization. This is where the product champion gets involved. Introducing new technology into an organization requires someone to promote the idea. The **product champion**—often at the risk of his or her position and prestige—promotes the idea throughout the organization, searching for support and acceptance. The champion can be a high-level manager but often is not. If the champion lacks the power and financial resources to make the required changes independently, she or he must convince people who have such authority to support the innovation. In other words, product champions must get sponsorship.

Sponsorship comes from the **executive champion,** who has the status, authority, and financial resources to support the project and protect the product champion. Without this support and protection, the product champion, and thus the new technology, could not succeed. Resources needed to develop the innovation would be unavailable, and without protection, the champion would not be allowed to continue promoting the change.

---

technical innovator

A person who develops a new technology or has the key skills to install and operate the technology.

product champion

A person who promotes a new technology throughout the organization in an effort to obtain acceptance of and support for it.

executive champion

An executive who supports a new technology and protects the product champion of the innovation.

Organizing for Innovation

 LO 7 Successful innovation is a lot more than a great idea. A study by the Boston Consulting Group found that lack of good ideas is hardly ever the obstacle to profitable innovation. More often, ideas fail to generate financial returns because the organization isn't set up to innovate. The culture is risk averse, projects get bogged down, efforts aren't coordinated, and management can't figure out where to direct the company's money.[44] In contrast, as shown in Exhibit 17.8, innovation has a chance to flourish when positive values are in place, when the organization integrates internal and external knowledge, and when its people are encouraged to own and solve problems and to experiment continuously.

> More often, ideas fail to generate financial returns because the organization isn't set up to innovate.

In Chapter 9 we introduced the concept of learning organizations—companies that excel at solving problems, seeking and finding new approaches, and sharing new knowledge with all members of an organization. Such learning organizations are particularly well positioned to develop useful innovations. The innovations may involve a kind of ambidexterity, or doing two things at once. Some innovations are about exploiting existing capabilities—to improve production speed or product quality, for example. Or the innovation may involve exploring new knowledge—seeking to develop new products or services.[45] Both innovation processes are necessary. Innovative learning organizations use their existing strengths to improve their operations and thus improve their bottom lines. But they also learn to unleash people's creative energies and capabilities to develop new products and processes that will ensure their long-term competitiveness. In this section, we discuss some of the approaches managers use to organize for innovation.

Unleashing Creativity

3M has a strong orientation toward intrapreneurship and derives about one-third of its revenues from new products. 3M, Google, Apple, and IBM have well-established histories of producing

EXHIBIT 17.8
Requirements for
Innovation

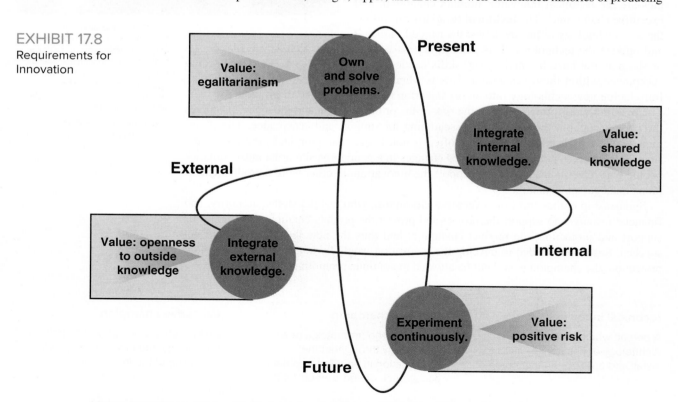

SOURCE: Dorothy Leonard Barton, "The Factory as Learning Laboratory," *Sloan Management Review* (1992), p. 34.

many successful new technologies and products. What sets these and other continuous innovators apart? The one thing these companies have in common is an organizational culture that encourages innovation.[46]

Consider the 3M legend from the early 1920s of inventor Francis G. Okie. Okie dreamed up the idea of using sandpaper instead of razor blades for shaving. The aim was to reduce the risk of nicks and avoid sharp instruments. The idea failed, but rather than being punished for the failure, Okie was encouraged to champion other ideas, which included 3M's first blockbuster success: waterproof sandpaper. A culture that permits failure is crucial for fostering the creative thinking and risk taking required for innovation.

As strange as it may seem, celebrating failure can be vital to the innovation process.[47] Failure is the essence of learning, growing, and succeeding. Innovative companies have many balls in the air at all times, with many people trying many new ideas. A majority of the ideas will fail, but it is only through this process that the few big hits will emerge that make a company an innovative star. Tom Kelley, co-founder of IDEO, says: "Creative confidence is the natural human ability to come up with breakthrough ideas combined with the courage to act on them."[48] This type of attitude from a manager can foster creative thinking throughout the ranks.

3M uses the simple set of rules listed in Exhibit 17.9 to help foster innovation. These rules can be—and are—copied by other companies. But 3M has an advantage in that it has followed these rules since its inception and has ingrained them in its culture. This culture is shared and passed on in part through stories. One such legend is about the 3M engineer who was fired because he refused to stop working on a project that his boss thought was wasting resources. Despite being fired, the engineer came to work as usual, finished the project, and demonstrated the value of his innovation. The engineer eventually was promoted to head a new division created to manufacture and market the innovation.

> Failure is the essence of learning, growing, and succeeding.

Bureaucracy Busting

Bureaucracy is an enemy of innovation. Although bureaucracy is useful to maintain orderliness and gain efficiencies, it also can work directly against innovation. Developing radically different technologies requires a more fluid and flexible (organic) structure that does not restrict thought and action. Although "fluid and flexible" can sometimes feel more like "chaotic and uncertain," companies take this approach because it is necessary

EXHIBIT 17.9
3M's Rules for an Innovative Culture

- **Set goals for innovation.** By corporate decree, 25 to 30 percent of annual sales must come from new products that are five years old or newer.
- **Commit to research and development.** 3M invests in R&D at almost double the rate of the average U.S. company. One R&D goal is to cut in half the time it takes to introduce new products.
- **Inspire intrapreneurship.** Champions are encouraged to run with new ideas, and they get a chance to manage their products as if they were running their own businesses. 3Mers are allowed to spend 15 percent of their time pursuing personal research interests unrelated to current company projects.
- **Facilitate, don't obstruct.** Divisions are kept small and are allowed to operate with a great deal of independence but have constant access to information and technical resources. Researchers with good ideas are awarded $50,000 Genesis grants to develop their brainstorms into new products.
- **Focus on the customer.** 3M's definition of quality is to demonstrate that the product can do what the customer—not some arbitrary standard—dictates.
- **Tolerate failure.** 3Mers know that if their ideas fail, they still will be encouraged to pursue other innovative ideas. Management knows that mistakes will be made and that destructive criticism kills initiative.

SOURCES: Company reports; R. Mitchell, "Masters of Innovation: How 3M Keeps Its New Products Coming," *BusinessWeek,* April 10, 1989, pp. 58–63; T. Katauskas, "Follow-Through: 3M's Formula for Success," *R&D,* November 1990; and T. J. Martin, "Ten Commandments for Managing Creative People," *Fortune,* January 16, 1995, pp. 135–36.

Bottom Line

Bureaucracy busting
encourages innovation.
*Name one way to bust
bureaucracy.*

in an environment of rapid change. Elmer's Products, which makes a variety of adhesives and presentation materials as well as the famous white glue, has established a policy of open innovation. A cross-functional team of seven employees is responsible for sharing ideas about innovation, and all employees are encouraged to submit ideas. About a dozen employees in another group are assigned to spend 25 to 50 percent of their time exploring ideas from sources outside the organization, including inventors, suppliers, other companies, and researchers at universities.[49]

To balance innovation with other business goals, companies often establish special temporary project structures that are isolated from the rest of the organization and allowed to operate under different rules. These units go by many names, including skunkworks (recall Chapter 7), greenhouses, and reserves. At General Motors, for example, chief talent officer Michael Arena launched InnovationXchange Lab. The lab's goal is to "connect employees and ideas across the business to amplify impact." The ultimate goal of these interactions is to create new innovations in response to external environmental pressures.[50]

To foster a culture that values innovation, software maker Intuit set up a program called Intuit's Lab. Adapting a policy that Google made famous, the company allows employees to spend 10 percent of their time on unstructured activities aimed at generating and developing new ideas. They can choose an idea they personally feel passionate about or can devote the time to learning about new technologies. Intuit also sponsors idea jams—days set aside for employees with an idea to assemble a team to develop the idea. Idea jams are one-day events that take place every three months. Employees also have access to workgroup software called Brainstorm, which helps them share ideas and recruit team members to work on the ideas during the idea jams and their unstructured time. Intuit's innovation catalysts are employees who coach teams and individuals across the company to ensure that ideas are practical and successful. Intuit provides cash awards for winning ideas, but the excitement of Innovation Lab and idea jams is what really motivates Intuit employees to contribute to innovations such as the mobile version of QuickBooks Online, GoPayment, and ViewMyPaycheck.[51]

Bureaucracy-busting managerial systems that encourage collaboration can facilitate innovation. At steel companies such as Chaparral and Nucor, for example, employees work in cross-functional teams to solve problems and create innovative solutions. These flat structures help create an environment that encourages creativity and cooperation. Teams focus on current issues and problems as well as future concerns and opportunities. In addition, teams collaborate with outside partners to bring knowledge into the organization so it can be integrated with existing ideas and information to create innovations. All the while, teams are supported by values of egalitarianism, information sharing, openness to outside ideas, and positive risk. The aim is to destroy the traditional boundaries between functions and departments to create collaborative, less bureaucratic learning laboratories.[52]

Design Thinking

design thinking

A human-centered approach
to problem solving and
solution finding that is based
on nonlinear iterations of
inspiration, ideation, and
implementation.

In recent years, organizations have increasingly turned to an innovative method of solving problems and finding creative solutions. **Design thinking** follows a human-centered approach to innovation that integrates the needs of customers, the potential of technology, and the requirements for business success.[53] Championed by the Institute of Design at Stanford University, design thinking relies on "close, almost anthropological observation of people to gain insight into problems that may not be articulated yet."[54] IDEO, a global design firm that uses design thinking when working with organizations, views the process as a "system of overlapping spaces rather than a sequence of orderly steps."[55] The company defines the three spaces in the following manner: (1) *inspiration* refers to the problem or solution that motivates the search for solutions; (2) *ideation* is the process of generating, developing and testing ideas, and (3) *implementation* is the path that leads from the project stage into customers' lives. The problem-solving process is not linear but rather moves in and out of these spaces in an iterative manner.

Traditionally, when a company wanted to redesign an existing or create a new product or service, it would rely on customer focus groups to provide feedback on projects that were already under development.[56] Design thinking differs in that it starts with developing a thorough understanding (through direct observation) of current and potential customers.

Design teams, consisting of individuals with diverse expertise (e.g., engineering, anthropology, design, marketing, and so forth), work together to identify "what people want and need in their lives and what they like or dislike about the way particular products are made, packaged, marketed, sold, and supported."[57] Experts like Jeanne Liedtka and Tim Ogilvie have developed practical applications that maximize organizational growth.[58]

Health care provider Kaiser Pemanente used design thinking to improve the process by which nursing shift changes were made at its hospitals. A core project team, consisting of a strategist (former nurse), a technology expert, a process designer, designers from IDEO, and others, observed

Courtesy of IDEO

how nurses at four hospitals typically spent 45 minutes of each shift debriefing nurses from the departing shift about the status of patients. Depending on the hospital, nurses used different methods to exchange and record patient information. The team found that some of the nurses, despite the significant time investment, missed or failed to relay important information about patients. Using the insights about how nurses share patient information when changing shifts, the core project team developed potential solutions through brainstorming and prototyping alternative ways for nurses to improve the quality of patient care. After evaluating the alternative solutions, the team decided on the following improvements: (1) the arriving and departing nurses would exchange information in front of their patients (instead of at the nurses' station), and (2) a new procedure and easy-to-use software would be developed to enable nurses to check notes from the previous shift's nurses and enter new notes. Upon measuring the results, Kaiser reported that the project resulted in a 50 percent reduction in the average time between a nurse's arrival and first contact with patients. The health care concern also reported an increase in nurses' job satisfaction. The shift change program was rolled out to all Kaiser health care facilities and a new innovation center (based on design thinking) was established to continuously improve the quality of patient care.[59]

Implementing Development Projects

A powerful tool for managing technology and innovations is the **development project**.[60] A development project is a focused organizational effort to create a new product or process via technological advances. For example, when MTV launched channels aimed at various Asian American markets, the company used development projects embedded in a culture that values innovation.

Development projects typically feature a special cross-functional team that works together on an overall concept or idea. Like most cross-functional teams, its success depends on how well individuals work together to pursue a common vision. And in the case of development projects, teams must interact with suppliers and customers frequently, making the complexity of their task that much greater. Because of their urgency and strategic importance, most development projects are conducted under intense time and budget pressures, thus presenting a real-time test of the company's ability to innovate.

Managers should recognize that development projects have multiple benefits. Not only are they useful for creating new products and processes, but they frequently cultivate skills and knowledge that can be used for future endeavors. In other words, the capabilities that companies derive from a development project frequently can be turned into a source of competitive advantage. For example, when Ford created a development project to design

development project

A focused organizational effort to create a new product or process via technological advances.

an air-conditioning compressor to outperform its Japanese rival, executives also discovered that they had laid the foundation for new processes that Ford could use in future projects. Their new capability in integrated design and manufacturing helped Ford reduce the costs and lead times for other product developments. Thus organizational learning had become an equally important criterion for evaluating the success of the project.

For development projects to achieve their fullest benefit, they should build on core capabilities (recall Chapters 4 and 9); have a guiding vision about what must be accomplished and why (Chapter 12); have a committed team (Chapters 12 and 14); instill a philosophy of continuous improvement (Chapter 9); and generate integrated, coordinated efforts across all units (Chapters 8 and 9).

Technology, Job Design, and Human Resources

Adopting a new technology typically requires changes in the way jobs are designed. Often the way the task is redefined fits people to the demands of the technology to maximize the technology's operation. But this often fails to maximize total productivity because it ignores the human part of the equation. The social relationships and human aspects of the task may suffer, lowering overall productivity.

sociotechnical systems

An *approach to job design that attempts to redesign tasks to optimize operation of a new technology while preserving employees' interpersonal relationships and other human aspects of the work.*

The **sociotechnical systems** approach to work redesign specifically addresses this problem. This approach redesigns tasks in a manner that jointly optimizes the social and technical efficiency of work. Beginning with studies on the introduction of new coal-mining technologies in 1949, the sociotechnical systems approach to work design focused on small, self-regulating work groups.[61] Later it was found that such work arrangements could operate effectively only in an environment in which bureaucracy was limited. Today's trends in bureaucracy bashing, lean and flat organizations, work teams, and an empowered workforce are logical extensions of the sociotechnical philosophy of work design. At the same time, the technologies of the information age—in which people at all organizational levels have access to vast amounts of information—make these leaner and less bureaucratic organizations possible.

Managers face several choices regarding how to apply a new technology. Technology can be used to limit the tasks and responsibilities of workers and "de-skill" the workforce, thus turning workers into servants of the technology. Alternatively, managers can select and train workers to master the technology, using it to achieve great accomplishments and improve the quality of their lives. Technology, when managed effectively, can empower workers as it improves the competitiveness of organizations.[62]

However, as managers make decisions about how to design jobs and manage employees, they also need to consider other human resource systems that complement the introduction of new technology. Exhibit 17.10, for example, shows how compensation systems

EXHIBIT 17.10

Compensation Practices in Traditional and Advanced Manufacturing Firms

Type of Compensation Practice	Traditional Factory	Integrated Manufacturing
Performance-contingent	Focus on individual incentives reflects division of labor and separation of stages and functions.	Extensive use of group incentives to encourage teamwork, cooperation, and joint problem solving.
Job-contingent	Use of hourly wage assumes that differences in employee contribution are captured in job classifications and that performance is determined largely by the production system.	Use of salary assumes that the employees' contributions transcend the job per se to affect output substantially. The distinctions between classes of employment are diminished.
Person-contingent	Seniority pay rewards experience as a surrogate for knowledge and skill in a stable environment and rewards loyalty to reduce uncertainty within the system.	Skill-based pay rewards continuous learning and the value added from increased flexibility in a dynamic environment.

SOURCE: S. A. Snell and J. W. Dean Jr., "Strategic Compensation for Integrated Manufacturing: The Moderating Effects of Jobs and Organizational Inertia," *Academy of Management Journal* 37 (1994), pp. 1109–40.

Management in Action

TESLA MOTORS AS INNOVATOR AND TECHNOLOGY PARTNER

Being a relatively tiny start-up in an industry of giants has posed risks for Tesla Motors because operating an auto company requires an enormous amount of money for product design and development, factories, and distribution networks. But in some ways, Tesla's situation as an upstart with a visionary founder has also been an advantage. The company can concentrate on electric vehicles without lines of already-popular cars stealing management's attention. And as a young 6,000-employee business, it doesn't have to cover labor and other expenses that became entrenched at Ford, General Motors, and Chrysler. It operates more like a high-tech firm, with employees lured to the company to do something extraordinary. Elon Musk holds weekly meetings to review progress on each model and critique designs.

The factory where Tesla builds the Model S has a history of innovation. General Motors built the plant and operated it until the 1980s, when U.S. managers began to realize that quality initiatives in Japan were leaving them behind. GM arranged with Toyota to operate the plant jointly. That venture ended, and the plant closed. When Tesla purchased it, Musk was able to hire experienced auto workers from the community.

According to Tesla's head of manufacturing, the time that elapsed from the Model S's initial design to production of the car was a little more than two years, in contrast to a norm of five or six years at a major auto maker. Because of Musk's determination to engineer the Model S from scratch, the company is more directly involved in making parts than is typical today. It makes the cars' battery packs and touch screen control panels, for example.

Success will inevitably bring growth. Recently, Tesla initiated construction of a massive electric battery factory outside Sparks, Nevada. In partnership with Panasonic, Musk expects battery production to begin by 2017. The factory is expected to produce batteries at lower costs due to innovative manufacturing and economies of scale. Also, Tesla will continue to pursue growth in Europe and Asia as well. The challenge will be to continue managing innovation as effectively in a bigger company.[63]

- How does Tesla Motors source and acquire new technologies? What are the advantages of this approach?
- How would you advise Tesla's managers to continue unleashing creativity as the company grows?

can be changed to facilitate the implementation of advanced manufacturing technology. In the contemporary setting, the use of group incentives, salary, and skill-based pay systems helps reinforce the collective effort (recall the use of cross-functional teams), professionalism, empowerment, and flexibility required for knowledge work. If a company's pay system is not aligned with the new technologies, it may not reward behavior that is needed to make the changes work. Worse, existing reward systems actually may reinforce old behaviors that run counter to what is needed for the new technology.

Taken as a whole, these ideas provide a set of guidelines for managing the strategic and organizational issues associated with technology and innovation. The issues are relevant whether a company is simply automating an activity or, as in the case of Tesla Motors, entering a new high-tech business (see "Management in Action: Onward"). In Chapter 18, we expand this discussion to focus on how organizations can reshape themselves to adapt to a dynamic marketplace. Managing change and organizational learning are central elements of what it takes to become a world-class organization.

KEY TERMS

chief information officer (CIO) p. 552
design thinking p. 556
development project p. 557
disruptive innovation p. 539

executive champion p. 553
innovation p. 534
make-or-buy decision p. 550
product champion p. 553
sociotechnical systems p. 558

technical innovator p. 553
technology p. 534
technology audit p. 543
technology life cycle p. 536

RETAINING WHAT YOU LEARNED

In Chapter 17, you learned that different forces, like scientific knowledge and capital resources, encourage development of new technologies. New technologies follow a predictable life cycle. Companies adopt technology at different times. Some desire to be first movers while others prefer to be followers. Technology can be managed for competitive advantage and used to support a firm's low-cost or differentiation strategy. Selecting an appropriate technology strategy depends on the degree to which the technology supports the organization's competitive requirements. A company assesses its technology needs by benchmarking, or comparing, the technologies it employs with those of both competitors and noncompetitors. New technologies can be acquired through acquisition and other means, or developed internally. People play many roles in managing technology such as chief information officer, entrepreneur, technical innovator, product champion, and executive champion. Innovative organizations establish cultures that value creativity and intrapreneurship, and have a structure that balances controlling existing processes with a flexibility that allows innovation. Successful development projects share characteristics like building on core capabilities, having a guiding vision of what needs to be achieved, and having a committed team.

LO 1   List the types of processes that spur development of new technologies.

- Forces that compel the emergence of a new technology include (1) a need for the technology, (2) the requisite scientific knowledge, (3) the technical convertibility of this knowledge, (4) the capital resources to fund development, and (5) the entrepreneurial insight and initiative to pull the components together.

LO 2   Describe how technologies proceed through a life cycle.

- New technologies follow a predictable life cycle. First, a workable idea about how to meet a market need is developed into a product innovation. Early progress can be slow as competitors experiment with product designs.
- Eventually a dominant design emerges as the market accepts the technology, and further refinements to the technology result from process innovations.
- As the technology begins to approach both the theoretical limits to its performance potential and market saturation, growth slows and the technology matures. At this point, the technology can remain stable or be replaced by a new technology.

LO 3   Discuss ways to manage technology for competitive advantage.

- Adopters of new technologies are categorized according to the timing of their adoption: innovators, early adopters, the early majority, the late majority, and laggards.

- Technology leadership has many first-mover advantages but also poses significant disadvantages. The same may be said for followership.
- Technology that helps improve efficiency will support a low-cost strategy, whereas technologies that help make products more distinctive or unique will support a differentiation strategy.
- Determining an appropriate technology strategy depends on the degree to which the technology supports the organization's competitive requirements and, if a technology leadership strategy is chosen, the company's ability, in terms of skills, resources, and commitment, to deal with the risks and uncertainties of leadership.

LO 4   Summarize how to assess technology needs.

- Assessing the technology needs of a company begins by benchmarking, or comparing, the technologies it employs with those of both competitors and noncompetitors. Benchmarking should be done on a global basis to understand practices used worldwide.
- Technology scanning helps identify emerging technologies and those still under development in an effort to project their eventual competitive impact.

LO 5   Identify alternative methods of pursuing technological innovation.

- New technologies can be acquired or developed. Options include internal development, purchase, contracted development, licensing, trading, research partnerships and joint ventures, and acquisition.
- The approach used depends on the existing availability of the technology; the skills, resources, and time available; and the importance of keeping the technology proprietary.

LO 6   Define key roles in managing technology.

- People play many roles in managing technology. For example, the chief information officer (CIO) is the person with broad, integrative responsibility for technological innovation.
- The entrepreneur is the person who recognizes the competitive potential of the technology and finds new ways to exploit opportunities.
- Technical innovators have the key skills needed to develop or install and operate the technology.
- Product champions are the person who promotes the new idea(s) to gain support throughout the organization.
- The executive champion is the person with the status and resources to support the project.

7 **Describe the elements of an innovative organization.**

- Organizing for innovation involves unleashing the creative energies of employees while directing their efforts toward meeting market needs in a timely manner.
- Companies can unleash creativity by establishing a culture that: values intrapreneurship; accepts and even celebrates failure as a sign of innovation; and reinforces innovation through goal setting, rewards, and stories of creative employees.
- The organization's structure should balance bureaucracy for controlling existing processes with a flexibility that allows innovation to take place. Development projects provide an opportunity for cross-functional teamwork aimed at innovation.

- Job design should take into account both social relationships and the technical efficiency of work so that jobs are within employees' ability but also empower them to work cooperatively and creatively.

 8 **List characteristics of successful development projects.**

- For development projects to achieve the fullest benefit, they should: (1) build on core capabilities; (2) have a guiding vision about what must be accomplished and why; (3) have a committed team; (4) instill a philosophy of continuous improvement; and (5) generate integrated, coordinated efforts across all teams and units.

DISCUSSION QUESTIONS

1. According to Francis Bacon, "A wise man will make more opportunities than he finds." What does this have to do with technology and innovation? What does it have to do with competitive advantage?

2. What examples of technological innovation can you identify? What forces led to the commercialization of the science behind those technologies? Did the capability exist before the market demand, or was the demand there before the technology was available?

3. Thomas Edison once said that most innovations are 10 percent inspiration and 90 percent perspiration. How does this match what you know about technology life cycles?

4. Why would a company choose to follow rather than lead technological innovations? Is the potential advantage of technological leadership greater when innovations are occurring rapidly, or is it better in this case to follow?

5. If you were in the grocery business, whom would you benchmark for technological innovations? Would the companies be inside or outside your industry? Why?

6. How would you see the executive champion, the chief information officer, and the product champion working together? Could the roles all be played by the same individual? Why or why not?

EXPERIENTIAL EXERCISES

17.1 TECHNOLOGY LIFE CYCLE

OBJECTIVES
To explore the different stages of the technology life cycle.

INSTRUCTIONS
Refer back to the technology life cycle in Exhibit 17.2. Review each product or technology listed below and indicate whether it is in the first, second, or third stage of the cycle.

STAGES
Stage 1: A new technology is created to address a need. Competitors experiment with operational designs and product characteristics. Progress is slow. The rate of product innovation is high.

Stage 2: As initial problems are resolved and a dominant design emerges, technology is refined through process innovations. Efficiencies and cost competitiveness are pursued.

Stage 3: The technology reaches the limit of its performance capabilities and usage. In this mature stage, development slows and production becomes increasingly costly.

Product or Technology	Stage 1	Stage 2	Stage 3
Apple Watch	_____	_____	_____
Twitter	_____	_____	_____
Microsoft Windows	_____	_____	_____
Google self-driving car	_____	_____	_____
McGraw-Hill Education's e-book	_____	_____	_____

17.2 INNOVATION FOR THE FUTURE

OBJECTIVES

To look ahead into the future.

INSTRUCTIONS

Choose a partner. Together, develop an innovative product or service that will be popular in the year 2025. As you develop your product or service, ask yourselves the following questions:

1. What trends lead you to believe that this product or service will be successful?

2. What current technologies, services, or products will your idea replace?

Present your idea to the class for discussion.

CONCLUDING CASE

WORLDWIDE GAMES

Players of video games often purchase their fun from Worldwide Games, which develops and markets game consoles, portable game devices, and software for playing games either on the company's hardware or on personal computers. Game enthusiasts are always on the lookout for game-playing experiences that are more intense, more lifelike, or more complex, so satisfying them drives constant innovation at Worldwide. The company has developed major and minor advances in screen resolution, processor speed, new kinds of controllers, creative story lines, and more. Its console division focuses on hardware technology, and its online division focuses on powerful new gaming software, often involving elaborate story lines played by subscribers around the world, using the Internet to collaborate or compete. Continuous innovation in both divisions essentially keeps Worldwide on a par with its major competitors, who also are constantly on the lookout for the best new idea.

In recent years, two related areas of technology have been essential for the growth of Worldwide and its competitors: social networking and the ability of broadband Internet connections to deliver fast audio and video streams for playing elaborate games online. Worldwide's console division has adopted this technology by inviting purchasers of its latest console to join its Players Network. Those who join the Players Network can use their console to make an Internet connection and play games with other members anywhere in the network. Each player uses his or her controller, console, and television display and sees all the participants' actions on the display. In addition, Worldwide's online division continues to push the limits of online games played with the processing power of the latest personal computers. For the most popular programs, gamers who pay a subscription fee create their own characters, or avatars, to act out the parts in the game. Although the personal data of the players are kept private, players can use the avatars' names to look up other players' track records and invite selected avatars to join their team.

Because a necessary component of both kinds of games—console based and computer based—is for players to register and pay a fee or join the Players Network, Worldwide collects not only money from customers but also information about them. That system came under real risk when hackers recently broke into first the Players Network database and then the registration records of Worldwide Online's subscribers.

As soon as the company detected an intrusion into the Players Network, it shut down the network. When the company's security employees realized they couldn't immediately prevent intrusions within a day or two, Worldwide announced that hackers had obtained the names and possibly the credit card numbers of its tens of millions of network members. Until the problem was fixed, they would be able to play games from disks loaded into their consoles but would not be able to use the network.

While the company was investigating the original security breach, it discovered that the Worldwide Online user database also had been hacked. The company immediately announced that breach, including the fact that some credit card accounts might have been accessed. It shut down that network as well until the security hole could be plugged.

Fixing the problem, which took about a month, included adding firewalls and encryption to the existing security measures. Afterward the company reopened both networks, apologized to consumers, and offered a month of free access to paid services. Returning customers had to download upgraded security software before they could resume play. The entire incident cost the company hundreds of millions of dollars for the investigation, upgrades, and lost sales.

As operations returned to normal, Worldwide tried to minimize the risk of future intrusions by putting an executive in charge of security. The company announced that it had hired a chief information security officer. This manager reports to the company's chief information officer, who reports to the chief transformation officer, who reports to the chief executive officer.

QUESTIONS

1. Is Worldwide Games a technology leader or a technology follower? What are the risks and benefits of staking out this position?

2. What opportunities might Worldwide be missing by not having its chief information officer report directly to the CEO?

3. What makes innovation important for Worldwide? Following the hacking incident, how might bureaucracy be expected to interfere with innovation? How should Worldwide engage in bureaucracy busting?

Operations Management in the New Economy

The business of a company—any company—is to transform certain inputs, by means of a process, into outputs. Bringing these outputs (the product) to market cost effectively will ensure the company's continued existence and well-being. The methods, systems, and mental framework by which a company transforms its inputs into outputs characterize its operations. A company maintains the health of its transformation process through management of these operations. Operations management is the analysis and implementation of this process.

Many factors impinge on a company's operations and managers. As company size increases, so do the number of variables. Effective management of the operation and its variables contributes in no small measure to the company's success, whether the company is small or large, diversified or devoted to core businesses, a network organization or a highly structured, centralized body. It holds true whether the company sells a tangible product (goods) or an intangible one (services) because in both cases the customer is buying the object of a desire or the satisfaction of a need.

EFFECTS OF CHANGE

We often read that operations management is in transition today. In actuality, it has always been in transition because the world is always changing. Changes may take the form of new products (imagine the first traders bringing spices to Europe in the early Middle Ages), new distribution channels (FedEx completely revamped our expectations about package delivery), alterations in the labor pool (women assumed many factory jobs during World War II when men were at war), or new technologies (gunpowder altered all the rules of war in 14th-century Europe).

Characteristic of the current age is the quickening rate at which change occurs, placing pressure on individuals to adapt quickly and rewarding those able to shift mental gears, personal habits, and priorities easily. Indeed, survival of the fittest applies not only to physical attributes but also to mental agility. Operations managers must be among the most fit to function effectively in today's world.

THE CONTEXT OF OPERATIONS MANAGEMENT

What does it mean to be an effective manager of an operation? It means responding to the needs of diverse parties within the company, ensuring smooth movement through all stages of the transformation process. We can even take the viewpoint that, within the process, the customer is the department receiving the result of the preceding stage. For example, in a printing company, the operator of the press is the customer of the prepress area. An effective manager works with this awareness, ensuring that each area supplies what the next one expects.

Operations management also means satisfying parties in the larger arena. For example, investors may want to know how well a new product line is faring in the market or whether a new manufacturing process is delivering as promised. The community may want assurances that wastes from the production process will not cause quality of life to suffer. The government may demand an accounting of any number of activities covered by regulations. Thus the manager of an operation does not exist in isolation but is part of an ongoing interaction among any number of parties.

In ages past, the world was home to many societies or cultures, which were mostly different one from another, but each was more homogeneous than is the case today. Buyers in a given community needed the same products. Everyone knew what those products were, and common agreement on quality prevailed. Also prevalent was a common understanding of the entitlements of various social levels. (What goods of what quality were the prerogative of the wealthy, for example.) Because items were individually made, customization was the norm; there was no other way to do business.

As the industrial age dawned in the 19th century, this situation changed. Suddenly the customer was no longer a few identifiable individuals but a growing mass of less well-defined persons, any of whom, with money, could have what was formerly the prerogative of the few. With industrialization came mass production, and one product for all buyers became the norm because there was no other cost-effective way to do business.

The modern-day corporation took shape against this background, and marketing was born. Now in the digital age we are witnessing a phenomenon that once would have sounded like an oxymoron: mass customization. What are the implications for today's managers?

When the product is static or has few variations, operations management quite justifiably focuses on the product (and its cost). This perspective has produced the orientation of traditional operations management. With the ability to manufacture many variations of the same product, with access to increasing amounts of information, the focus today has shifted to the customer's experience of the product: how he or she perceives to have been served by the vendor. The customer assesses whether the product contains the desired characteristics and quality at the best price. Management of an operation with this awareness probably will spell the success or failure of the company in today's environment.

But is today's customer truly different? Yes and no. Despite the fact that things change, things also stay the same. Human beings still engage in the same activities. They create community; they raise the next generation; they trade; they provide for themselves; and in the process, they learn, fight, and play. And today's managers still shuttle inputs through the transformation process into successful outputs. Most of the traditional notions about human activity still apply.

To explain any activity, however, one may use a variety of lenses (Galileo's lens was different from Ptolemy's, so he derived a different explanation of the universe). A manager may view the process from the standpoint of product specifications, cost limitations, customer satisfaction, or any number of viewpoints. The lens chosen will reflect a particular view of the world and its priorities and of the company's priorities.

Sometimes there are no right or wrong choices, only consequences. The lens that adequately explained a given phenomenon at one time may not serve today. What is reflected through the lens will form the guidelines for decisions, however, so the choice has far-reaching repercussions.

NEW PERSPECTIVES

From time to time, particular orientations or viewpoints burst onto the stage, altering perceptions and leaving changed priorities in their wake. Such is the case with W. Edwards Deming's total quality management, now an article of faith for many of today's managers. The Japanese readily embraced Deming's principles, taking an enviable and now imitated approach to customer satisfaction (see Chapter 9 of the text for Deming's 14 points). Western nations paid scant attention until they saw the results of offering quality in a customer-oriented operation.

For most of us, quality is what we see in the result (does the product meet manufacturing specifications?). In his lengthy essay *Zen and the Art of Motorcycle Maintenance,* Robert Pirsig associated achievement of quality with a state of mind: "Skilled mechanics and machinists of a certain sort . . . have patience, care and attentiveness to what they're doing, a kind of inner peace of mind that isn't contrived but results from a kind of harmony with the work."[1] More characteristic of the Eastern mind-set, this statement means that quality (good or bad) is not an attribute of the end product but, rather, is inherent in the way an individual interacts with the subject of his or her attention.

To achieve good quality requires knowing what is good and then having the mind-set suitable for achieving it. This attentiveness is related to the Japanese *kaizen,* a willingness and desire to improve constantly. Since the 1980s, Japanese business practices have been the object of study and implementation by Westerners, from specific procedures (such as *kanban,* the basis of just-in-time inventory management) to general philosophies (the *kaizen* that is part of Japanese general operations strategy). A manager anywhere today would be ill served by neglect of these concepts.

Likewise, companies that involve employees in the process are on the way to understanding that the people who interface with the product are crucial to its success. We will see how important this view is in a few pages.

CORPORATE ORGANIZATION

There are many ways to structure a company, and some of today's companies have taken their present form as a result of trends in the economy: mergers or acquisitions, diversification, alliances. With all, certain functions are still identifiable in most corporate organizations. The operation of that function is what commands the attention of its managers. Let us consider how some of these common functions support the operations management system.

Strategic Planning On the highest level, guiding the corporation from the broadest perspective is strategic, or long-range, planning. The firm's upper-level managers provide the corporation's direction, defining and refining its mission in the process. Management of this function entails answering questions such as these: What business are we in? What business should or will we be in? Who are our customers? How can or should we serve them? Do we want to focus on core businesses or diversify? Answers to these questions will help develop corporate goals, which, filtered through the company's management levels, give direction to its operation.

As stated earlier, the world is always changing. Good strategic planning seeks to anticipate change and then plan for it. Good planners also foster a feeling of confidence about what is likely to produce success. During the 1990s, when the rallying cry of much of corporate management was to stick to core businesses, GE chief Jack Welch built a successful conglomerate of widely diverse businesses, finding people with the mind-set to operate well within that structure and achieving effective coordination of all functions through its many divisions.

Marketing Of all the company's functions, marketing is closest to the customer. Its job is to identify customer needs (latent or manifest) and translate them back to the firm for its reaction. Its role in supporting the operations management system is therefore critical. Operations managers must then restate what marketing has communicated in terms that will bring about the needed response from the production mechanism. To support its efforts, marketing works with advertising to state the company's offerings in terms that are attractive to the buyer. Sales is part of the marketing function also; salespeople are those who take action to sell within an identified market. This is the front line, where information about customer needs and desires penetrates and gains the attention of the company.

A story told in sales circles is about the ABC Company (a shoe manufacturer), whose marketing head visited a remote area of the world to assess the market. He returned to report to his boss, "There's no market; they don't wear shoes." The marketing head of competitor XYZ Company made the same trip for the same purpose, reporting to his boss, "It's a terrific market! They've got no shoes!" Marketing's response to a circumstance can take a firm into new areas.

Research and Engineering Suppose the marketing function has identified a new need or potential market. Enter the design and engineering people, whose function is the development and refinement of the product and the processes that manufacture it. They design, develop, and test the product through all stages until it is ready for market launch. They interact with customers who participate in the testing of a new product prior to launching. They also interact with operations—the product attributes and the processes required to make them will become the responsibility of the operations management system. Even as a product is still on the drawing board, its design may change based on customer response, manufacturing procedures (i.e., what is feasible in the current setup), or prices of material or labor.

As researchers and developers, this part of the company is most in touch with what will be available in the future, and one of its functions is identification and implementation of solutions not currently in use. The result of the designers' work will affect purchasing (of parts, equipment, materials), inventory management (quantities of items to keep on hand), shop floor operation (equipment may need rearrangement), capacity requirements (maximum rate of production), and human resources (human skills needed and cost of acquisition).

Human Resources

This brings us to the next function: human resources. A company is its people. They form the culture, produce the product, and deliver it. The human resources function must seek, attract, and keep individuals having the skills, human qualities, and experience required by the operations management system. Effective management of human resources thus directly affects the entire production process. Any company wishing to build a plant in a geographically desirable area would be foolish not to take into account the human component: educational level, work ethic, habits, and expectations of the labor pool.

Some believe that there are no bad employees, only employees placed in wrong positions. Effective use of employees will provide operations managers with a valuable source of innovation and productivity gains because the employees are actually in contact with the product (and with the customer, in the case of a service business). They are the interface where quality is born. It cannot be stressed too heavily that one of the most valuable attributes of any employee is the ability to communicate: to articulate what's right about the work experience, what's wrong, and how to improve it. Dissatisfaction unexpressed is potential trouble; ideas not presented represent lost potential.

Purchasing

Just as human inputs matter, so do materials. Selecting inputs that will support the company's orientation and vision is the crucial role played by the purchasing function. Optimally, it is a source of expertise for the operations management system, providing information about the variety of materials and systems available for use by the production process. The performance of any operating division is ultimately dependent on goods and services supplied to it by purchasing. Will the materials produce the result intended by the design of the product? Will they allow themselves to be molded as intended by the production process? Will they support the level of quality promised?

Cost-effective supply of the right materials potentially represents enormous savings for the company. A purchasing manager was once heard to say, "The sales division would have to close $500,000 in new business to produce the money I just saved by changing suppliers."

Logistics

The logistics of moving inputs through transformation may or may not benefit from an overview of the entire process; the flow may take different names, depending on its location in the process. It may be called *inventory management* as inputs arrive, *scheduling* while in the transformation process, and *distribution* when outputs are en route to the customer. Smooth or poor coordination of the flow from supplier of materials to delivery to the customer has repercussions throughout the channel. If materials are not ready for a specific section of the production apparatus at the right time, equipment and machinery sit idle (a drain on profitability). Delays in delivery to customers mean delays in payment received, and that has an impact on the company's cash flow.

Finance

This brings us to the finance area. This function serves as an interface between the firm's managers and the financial community: banks, investment firms, and stockholders. These entities have a stake in the company's success or failure and at all times are poised to assist, advise, provide support, or withdraw it. Finance must explain the company's performance adequately to elicit the maximum amount of support from financial institutions. In so doing, it makes use of the accounting department. Not merely a mechanism for tracking costs, the accounting department provides information useful to managers in understanding the cost implications of their decisions. Such cost-monitoring information can help managers understand how their own costs compare with standard costs, for example. Accounting also can help derive the cost implications of introducing new equipment or technologies.

In another of its roles, the finance function must be knowledgeable about the firm's creditworthiness. Any decline in the company's ability to pay its bills will weaken its position vis-á-vis competitors. Finance also must monitor the creditworthiness of suppliers. If suppliers are not financially able to deliver what they promise, the operations management system will feel the impact immediately. The financial community watches the impact of all these decisions, basing its ratings (and therefore support) on the wisdom of the decision makers.

A Team Operation

The fineness with which one breaks down the preceding functions can vary, but it should be clear at this point that the operations management system is only one of those operating within the corporate context. In the best of all possible worlds, operations management works hand in glove with the other functions, alert to any harmful fragmentation or lack of communication. Communication is, of course, a two-way street, and just as operations people must be aware of the workings of the other functions, the latter must know what the operations management system perceives, needs, and expects.

Satisfying customer expectations is a corporate activity, the work of one body (from *corpus,* Latin for "body"), with the whole dependent on how well its parts work individually and how well they work together. Neglect of any one organ affects the body's ability to perform at optimum level.

PREPARING FOR THE FUTURE IN THE NEW ECONOMY

In addition to awareness of how the company is operating at present, every good manager will give thought to what could happen, what is likely to happen, and what is possible, both for the company as a whole and for his or her own sphere of influence. Stated another way, an effective manager has a sense of vision. This means being aware of changes or potential changes in customer demands and changes in the company's resources (technology, labor pool, financial support). A good manager must listen, being attentive to all facts, and then select the useful facts from among the many supplied. A manager must constantly ask, "What if . . .?"

With good vision and a healthy curiosity, a manager will more adequately handle factors impinging on the operations management system. The objective is to develop a sense of vision adequate to anticipate conceivable consequences. Let us consider some of today's challenges in what is often referred to as the **new economy.**

Globalization

A company's sphere of activity has always been what could be reached easily by current means of communication and transportation. What is reachable has constantly expanded. The entire world is today's operating arena, both for buying inputs and for selling outputs. This circumstance presents the operations management system with a new range of possibilities.

The possibility of outsourcing has always been present. That is, do we make a particular component of the product, or do we send it out for manufacture pursuant to our specifications? Today a manager may outsource locally or to any facility in the world offering the capability of supplying the need. It takes a lot of information, as well as sound judgment, to know which part of the process would benefit from being handled out of house.

The success of producing elsewhere depends in part on the characteristics of the elsewhere. In the 20th century, U.S. companies based in northern states sometimes would move certain manufacturing operations to the southern part of the country, taking advantage of lower labor costs. Although this required some adjustment in expectations, the adjustment is slight compared to manufacturing in Pacific Rim countries or Latin America, for example. The reason is simple: Each culture handles things in a particular way. A wise manager will not assume that a different culture will respond to expectations in the same manner as an American labor force would, and this circumstance may work to one's advantage or to one's detriment. Those who can anticipate potential problem areas are ahead of the game in the decision to manufacture offshore.

Then there is the globe as marketplace. To sell globally requires product design that accounts for differing tastes throughout the world's cultures. A small manufacturer of skin care products based on formulas from India began marketing her line in America some years ago. She reports that she had to make alterations to account for the fact that Americans would not use a product with an unusual smell, no matter how beneficial for the skin.[2] Nescafé markets its products all over the globe, but the instant coffee sold in Brazil does not taste like that sold in the United States—in each instance, the product must satisfy the taste of a different culture.[3]

The ease with which the operations management system can make these alterations has increased dramatically in the last few decades. Digital technology has made flexibility in manufacturing a much more attainable situation than was previously the case, offering enormous potential to vary the product.

Environment

Another challenge facing today's manager is the environment, meaning both the world and the milieu in which the company operates. In an earlier time, negative effects from a manufacturing process were absorbed unobtrusively by the surroundings. As population density increased and consumption skyrocketed, particularly in the Western nations, this ceased to be true. What occurs in one place on the planet has an impact on the rest of it. The manager's challenge is to care enough about the future without imperiling today's operations, and the decisions are not simple.

It is unfortunate that the issue of environmental responsibility traditionally has been cast in ethical terms. Although this stance is valid, and ultimately the reason for being good stewards of the planet, it does not help managers handle all the information required to make good decisions or quantify what is needed for decision making. In addition, consumers are often inconsistent, demanding recycled paper, for instance, and then choosing to buy whiter paper that is not recycled.

Certainly the past few decades have witnessed significant progress in the handling of the most blatantly offensive effects of manufacturing processes (waste streaming, emissions control). But making the right decision is not a clear-cut path. Consider the simple example of the supermarket checkout stand. "Would you like paper or plastic for your groceries?" The environmentally responsible buyer must choose between less than desirable alternatives. Paper (even if recycled) uses trees; plastic uses hydrocarbons and is not as easy to recycle. Decisions faced by operations managers are infinitely more complex.

Furthermore, if managers do not see to their societal responsibility, others will demand compliance. A corporation is not its own island in community waters because others are affected by its decisions: property owners, investors, the larger public, and tomorrow's adults. Surely we have learned by now that groups that do not police their own ranks effectively are sure targets for policing by others, whether governmental agencies or community organizations.

The alternatives for an operations manager are therefore to react or to take a leadership role, becoming knowledgeable about potential negative effects of the process managed by him or her and proposing ways to handle them. In the long term, if we are to manage our economy's activities for tomorrow rather than today, responsibility for the environment is not a choice.

Knowledge and Information

One of the features of the new economy is that in the transformation process, the major input is intellectual property: knowledge, research, information, and design. These inputs have supplanted (in value) the material inputs required to build physical units. When knowledge is the major raw material, launching the first unit of a product represents millions of dollars; the cost of the second and thereafter is minuscule.

The products themselves are of a different nature, and it often takes greater sophistication to use a new-economy product—thus, for example, people's reluctance to switch from a PC to a Mac or vice versa. As a result, customers are not as likely to be swayed by advertising as by their increasing knowledge of the product and its technology. Successful companies will be those that increase a customer's knowledge base in general and skill with their own products in particular.

As the information explosion continues to feed today's consumers and today's workforce, the knowledge acquired gives rise to expectations. As we will discuss later, today's consumers are far from being locked into only a few sources for their information. Rather, they swim in an ocean of facts, figures, perspectives, and opportunities.

Nor are today's employees like those of yesteryear. It is instead the case that, depending on his or her own personal needs or aspirations, an employee is drawn to (and will stay with) a specific job in a given company for two reasons: (1) the possibility of experiencing personal satisfaction or growth and (2) satisfaction in the human interaction prevalent at that company. The balance of these factors varies with the individual, but everyone draws from these two wells. Today's managers therefore must provide more than the means for an employee to put bread on the table. The company must offer ongoing professional development, opportunity for increased responsibility in the firm, and a satisfying place to work. Today's employees do not expect to be supervised, but rather coached along the path of success. Clearly the manager also must be knowledgeable and continue to grow, increasing in value as a mentor.

Technology The challenge of technology will occupy us for the rest of these pages. Technology has always existed and has always been neutral. That is, just as a knife serves to feed the family or to kill an adversary, new technologies can be used to help or harm. As with any challenge, managers can view technological innovation as something to react to, something to anticipate, something to plan for, or something from which to derive potential improvements and growth.

Technologies exist in various stages of development; that is, some are ready and available for use by the operations management system, some will be cost-effective in 5 or 10 years, and some are in embryo. Any forward-looking manager will be aware of all three. Technology companies (those that market the latest of a given technology, such as cellular phones) must monitor technology on two fronts. They must be aware of similar products on the market, constantly assessing the limits of their own products. They also must be aware of technologies potentially usable by their own operations, just as any nontechnology company would.

In its development, a technology tends to move to the hands of the user. Take the clock as an example. At one time in history, the only clock in the community was the one in the town square. Then wealthier people could purchase large timepieces known as grandfather clocks. By the middle of the 20th century, most adults owned a wristwatch, often a special gift received at graduation. Today children and adults have access to many timepieces, from those on their wrists to the many in the home, office, or car. We could trace a similar progression for other technologies, such as engines and, of course, computers (where the transition from mainframes to portable PCs occurred within a few decades of the last century).

The shift of a technology to the user is not always smooth. One of the potential stumbling blocks when a company embraces a technology is to discount the human factor involved in its use. We see this in small businesses constantly. The local copy shop brings in the latest copying and finishing equipment, offering everything from double-sided, spiral-bound reports graced with photos to personalized, artistic party invitations. The resulting product, however, is in part dependent on the skill and experience of the operator and the availability of sufficient personnel to work with customers.

Larger industrial equipment offers a similar scenario. At an earlier time in history, the operator of, for example, a multistory printing press would have 30 years to become familiar with the operation of that equipment before a new generation came on stream. In today's offices, employees barely become proficient at using the current popular software before a new or different version of it comes out. These improvements provide fertile ground for inefficiencies in the final analysis; technology can advance only at the rate at which human beings can use it effectively.

With this knowledge, any effective operations manager will have some type of formal technology management in place—some means of looking ahead, preparing for the effects of new technologies. When envisioning the potential of new technology (or technology in embryo), the best human characteristics to bring to the table are

1. Awareness (information plus perspective).
2. Imagination (the ability to create new scenarios from existing ones).

Awareness is the easiest to acquire. In fact, it can be bought from the many consultants standing ready to assist corporations in preparing for the future. One must cultivate powers of imagination within oneself.

THE INTERNET

That brings us to the current challenge for one's imaginative powers: the Internet. Opportunities and pitfalls abound on the web. What follows are some noteworthy experiences gained from successful and unsuccessful uses of the Internet. By the time this material sees print, much will have changed.

Several methods have emerged as options for exploiting an Internet operation. A regular **bricks and mortar** business can create its own in-house web group, or it can partner with a dot-com company that will operate the web end of its business for it. For example, when the three largest retailers in the country decided to jump on the **e-tailing** bandwagon in the late 1990s, their strategies differed. JCPenney and Sears formed their own in-house website divisions; Kmart, in contrast, contracted with a subsidiary, bluelight.com, to get its site up and running. Last, a business can elect to sell its products only on the Internet. Internet-only companies are referred to as **pure-play** operations. Amazon.com is an example.

Managers also have to figure out how to integrate web activities seamlessly into their operations. Poorly integrated systems can wreak havoc within an organization. For instance, the first Christmas Toys 'R' Us did business on the web, the company had to turn away customers because it couldn't fill the number of orders the site generated. To solve the problem, Toys 'R' Us formed an alliance with Amazon.com. Amazon handled the website and the online ordering process, and Toys 'R' Us managed inventory and shipping. Each company had expertise the other needed to sell toys online.

Alongside web sales, retailers are in various stages of deploying new technologies to offer the benefits of online shopping at the retail site. For example, a kiosk on the shopping floor can make information available electronically, providing shoppers the information they need to make a buying decision. Lamps Plus gives its customers access to high-resolution images they can zoom in on and manipulate to review fabric textures and sample different colors and products in a **360-degree view.** Pacific Sunwear lets its customers search for and display clothing for boys or girls by item, color, and price. Other sites, such as eBags and Amazon, offer online guides or customer reviews to help buyers make decisions.

These retailers, along with others such as Nordstrom, Eddie Bauer, and Macy's, are building on brand-name presence and a familiarity already created at the mall, in the dealership, and through catalog sales—an advantage not enjoyed by companies operating exclusively on the web.

Not long ago, the online auctioneer eBay and a few companies that built e-stores for other firms were the only ones operating in the black. However, pure-play companies can be successful. Approximately one-quarter of the 200 public Internet companies that survived the dot-bomb shakeout are profitable now under standard accounting rules. The biggest moneymakers are online travel, software, and

Amazon.com was slow to make a profit because of its initial start-up costs—for product and warehouses, for example. However, e-tailers offering travel products, software, and financial services have low overhead and can see a profit much faster.

© Simon Dawson/Bloomberg via Getty Images

financial services. Why? Because they sell pure information products—there are no products to store or ship. But even Amazon.com, which has long operated in the red, is finally showing a profit despite the fact that every time someone buys a book on Amazon, the company must turn around and purchase a copy from the publisher. Also, once pure-play companies recoup their initial start-up costs, they don't need to spend much more money as sales rise. No additional stores need to be built to reach consumers, for example.[4]

Nonetheless, technology tricks and novel business ideas are not enough. Customers still want speed, convenience, quality, and good service. In this regard, the web is no different from conventional stores and catalogs. Customers ultimately will cast their votes for the companies that provide the best product experience whether they see the product on the web or can touch it in stores.

COMPANYWIDE RESONANCE

Sales and marketing data collection is turned on its head by the Internet as companies record information about a user's habits during a website visit. For instance, if you buy a product on Amazon.com, during future visits, the site will make suggestions about similar products in which you might be interested. Many retailers are of the opinion that this type of **data mining** will make or break the operation in the future. That is, the ability to collect and use information from online customers will be crucial to successful marketing decisions.

Moreover, a company's web page can make it easy or hard for the customer to get the information leading to a purchase. As some have learned the hard way, it is not enough simply to place images that are successful in print on the web; each medium has its own characteristics.

The design of the company's website has a companywide impact. For example, if a customer on the web can verify that an item is available, the chances of closing the sale are increased. If a customer can find out the expected delivery date of the product and the means, the chances of a sale are increased even more. In this scenario, front- and back-end operations touch, and delivering the goods is still key to success.

Mountains of Data The purchasing function benefits from the web through sheer availability of information as well as ease of response to questions. Today a purchasing manager need not wait for a visit from a sales representative. In fact, under the impact of the web, businesses are seeing a realignment of the traditional relationships among producers, wholesalers, distributors, and retailers. In the business-to-business world, buyers previously faced a number of obstacles to getting the best deal: Suppliers were distant, research time was scarce, and intermediaries controlled most of the information. Enter Ariba, a web-based marketplace for industrial goods. Purchasing need only put out a contract on the web, and a flood of bids from suppliers may be the response. In a sense, web-based companies are becoming the new intermediaries, the conduit between producers and buyers.

Purchasing managers can go online to Ariba for industrial goods, National Transportation Exchange for trucking, Chemdex for biochemical supplies, and IMX Exchange for mortgage brokers to find loans, and this is only the start.

The Internet has also become the intermediary between employers and employees. Human resources departments can avail themselves of numerous web-based tools to find candidates. Not only are there gigantic job exchanges such as Monster.com, but intranets exist to keep job searches within companies. Job seekers and potential employers can access one another's information based on geographic preference, salary range, or skill sets.

Logistics, scheduling, and distribution tasks increasingly are plugged into web-based networks, benefiting from the ease of gathering weather data, traffic patterns, and late-breaking news. Tracking information about shipments can be downloaded from FedEx. Zip codes are available online from the U.S. postal service. These factors affect the company's ability to deliver the product on time and the availability of materials from suppliers, effects ultimately felt by the operations management system.

Changing Information Patterns To reduce printing costs and make documents widely available, companies are digitizing information. In some instances, they are posting it on the web. Different people residing in distant places can view the same information this way. Still, digitizing information is not without its obstacles. Not all people have the same hardware and software used for viewing and printing out information. Additionally, miscommunications can occur that otherwise might not if all employees were working under one roof.

Corporations must take these circumstances into account when deciding how to use the web because the decisions affect each of the company's functioning units. Posting certain kinds of information does not usually cause problems. For example, providing company address(es), phone numbers, hours of operation, and the like is more economically done on the web than by a live employee answering the

Companies can easily track their shipments by downloading the information directly from FedEx.

© AP Photo/Mark Humphrey

telephone. Many inquiries that in the print age were handled by mailing out an annual report, for example, may be handled more cost effectively on the web.

Supplying other types of information, however, might not be as free of repercussions as in the preceding examples. Depending on whether the company is a business-to-business or a business-to-consumer operation, buyers will want product information, forms and terms of payment, special sales, return policies, status of an order, shipping rates and turnaround, possibility of changing a current order, tracking information, or status of an order.

Providing and maintaining only one piece of this information—for example, change in an order—affects at least three departments: accounting, distribution, and marketing. Each department supplying the information must be aware of the consequences of making the information available and have a mechanism for handling changes. Coordination becomes an issue as well. For example, charges to a credit card account must not occur before the merchandise is shipped. Whether selling to another business or to consumers, online operation requires new networks. Companies forge ahead nonetheless in this burgeoning technology, realizing that the potential advantages are well worth the temporary discomforts.

INTELLECTUAL PROPERTY

We have mentioned that a characteristic of the new economy is the nature of the product: knowledge, design, and engineering, rather than hard manufacturing. Let us look at an environmental engineering firm and how the web affects its operation. The business of such a firm might include devising solutions to improve power plant operation. The activities of firms involved in the planning of any such industrial facility are subject to compliance with government regulations. Handling engineering projects, such as a new power plant, requires submission of an enormous amount of data to demonstrate that the firm has complied with and planned for all impacts on the community. A requirement might be, for example, that notification be given to every property owner within a certain radius of the plant. Downloading that information from title companies and then monitoring the notification process is only one of a multitude of tasks potentially manageable on the web.

The firm must provide the information to the various parties in certain forms, which gives rise to new information needs. For example, one way to verify that it has indeed shipped the requisite electric or print copies is by downloading tracking information from FedEx. It also can make its compliance documentation available in a read-only format on the web, allowing printing of sections by those who wish to do so.

In preparing to build a plant, all federal, state, and local regulations must be accounted for. The firm must provide information on how its power plant will affect traffic patterns, cultural resources, schools, water supply, flora and fauna, and air quality. It also must state its plans for handling hazardous materials generated during the construction and operation of the plant.

Managing the enormous body of information to respond in the ways illustrated would have been a near impossibility before computer management of data.

PITFALLS

What have been the experiences of those who have succeeded in e-commerce and those who have failed, and what can we learn from them? We already mentioned Toys 'R' Us and its inability to fill its orders on the web. In addition to losing business, it, along with other retailers such as Macys.com and Walmart, was subject to Federal Trade Commission investigation and fines regarding rules for order fulfillment. The FTC regulation states that if retailers cannot meet promised deadlines, they must notify customers, giving them the option of canceling the order. Could the management of these companies have foreseen the inability to fill orders and, if so, how?

Confidentiality of information is an issue. Responding to the public's concern, several states have passed laws to protect individuals from online snooping.[5] Amazon.com found itself under fire after it began charging different consumers different prices on the basis of information it had collected on them. Toys 'R' Us was hit with a class-action lawsuit claiming that it allowed market researchers to access consumer data from its website. The retailer responded that it had hired the firm to analyze customers' data to improve their shopping experience. Although breach of confidentiality predates the web, the enormity of any breach is compounded by the staggering amounts of digital data available for tapping. The Federal Trade Commission and Congress are attempting to pass laws and institute regulations to protect consumers.

Customer familiarity with the web is another issue. Despite what seems to be a flurry of online buying, media reports suggest that many customers are not buying online at all, or only infrequently, or only certain products. As with catalog shopping, the online industry will mature as consumers become more familiar with offerings and as web retailers improve in presentation and fulfillment.

Some customers are concerned about credit card data transmitted online and are therefore hesitant to shop. The misuse of credit card data is present, however, every time a clerk in a store records the data during a purchase. Although this is more a perception than a real problem, perception motivates people's actions, preventing some from making the leap into cybershopping.

Circumstances such as these are forcing the formation of new business models as companies grapple with all the variables, spurred on by the potential benefits.

NEW NEEDS AND DESIRES

Customers themselves are changing as it becomes possible to satisfy latent needs or desires. We have alluded to mass customization. Here are some specific examples of varying product features.

Setting up an assembly line or installing production equipment is part of the cost of manufacturing. Speaking of color choice in automobiles, Henry Ford once said, "They can have any color they want, as long as it's black." Alteration of a manufacturing process to vary a product feature was very costly. With the flexible manufacturing available in the digital age, manufacturers have the option of producing multiple flavors of bottled water, blue jeans tailored for different bodies, and a veritable artist's palette for automobile colors. Levi Strauss and Brooks now offer machine-customized garments, accommodating a vast array of body measurements. Barbie's friends can have hair and skin color, clothing, and even personalities picked by their young owners. Digital technology fuels the manufacturing capability; the web spurs demand.

The result is that customers' desire for customization and personalization has been moved to a new level. Shoppers previously settled for a product that was mostly, or approximately, what they wanted. They are now beginning to see that sometimes they can have a product endowed with precisely the features they want. The experience of product acquisition is therefore changing.

THE VALUE OF HUMAN ATTRIBUTES

What are the implications of all this change for traditional operations management? Changes are remembered as negative or positive, depending on how well one has survived them. There is no reason to believe that technological change is any more threatening than other kinds of change. Traditional human qualities still serve: vision, awareness, alertness, imagination, courage, steadfastness, persistence, flexibility, attentiveness, and goodwill.

Today's managers must be aware, noticing shifts in trends, habits and customs, possibilities, and ground rules. They must have or develop the vision to foresee the range of possibilities and then the imagination to create solutions. They must have the courage to strike out in new directions and be alert to adjustments required by the new direction. An effective manager will be flexible enough to make an adjustment and steadfast in the face of misunderstandings and mistakes. A manager will need to be persistent in following the chosen path, with attentiveness to all facets of the surroundings. Chances of success in any challenge are enhanced by goodwill.

Finally, he or she will need luck. Some say "it comes to you," and some say "you make your own." Most think that both are true.

KEY TERMS

bricks and mortar   A traditional organization operating from physical buildings and offices, p. 567

data mining   The collection and analysis of large amounts of customers' online information to inform different decisions within an organization, especially those related to marketing, p. 568

e-tailing   The process by which an organization sells some of its products or merchandise via the Internet, p. 567

new economy   A current perspective suggesting that the economic success of a region or company depends on its ability to thrive globally, operate in an environmentally responsible manner, and leverage knowledge workers and information for competitive advantage, p. 566

pure-play   Refers to an organization's decision to sell all of its products or services via the Internet, p. 568

360-degree view   Refers to a 3D image of a product that a customer can view on a computer, tablet, phone, or other electronic device, p. 568

DISCUSSION QUESTIONS

1. What is mass customization? How can products be mass-produced yet still be differentiated to appeal to individual market sectors? How has mass customization affected management's focus on the product?

2. Why was Deming's total quality management embraced by the Japanese long before Deming's philosophy became key to U.S. operations management? How does it relate to operations management?

3. How has the new economy changed operations management? What is the major input in the operations process as a result?

4. What must businesses consider in deciding to take advantage of new technology? How does new technology affect operations management decisions?

5. Why were many dot-com companies so short-lived at the end of the 20th century? Why would Amazon and Toys 'R' Us form an alliance? Which firm is likely to benefit more? Explain.

6. How can the Internet improve a firm's operations management?

7. What are the implications for operations management of customers being able to satisfy purchasing needs immediately by using the Internet? Have e-business functions fundamentally changed the way firms do business? Explain.

CHAPTER 18

Creating and Leading Change

> The world hates change, yet that is the only thing that has brought progress.
>
> —CHARLES KETTERING
>
> My interest is in the future because I am going to spend the rest of my life there.
>
> —CHARLES KETTERING

Management in Action

SHELL OIL'S MANAGERS FACE OFF WITH INVESTORS OVER CLIMATE CHANGE

At Shell's recent annual general meeting, investors fired a "hostile barrage of questions" at top management regarding the sustainability of its business strategy and commitment to the environment. Nearly 99 percent of attendees voted to support a motion for Shell to report on whether its activities were consistent with worldwide governments' goals to limit global warming. You'll recall from the "Social Enterprise" box in Chapter 1 that there is growing international support to limit the increase in global warming to 2 degrees Celsius.

Another important initiative was passed at the meeting. A group of 150 investors that control billions of dollars' worth of shares filed a resolution that included a "ban on corporate bonuses for activities that damage the climate and a requirement to invest in renewable energy."

Why are investors frustrated with Shell's top management? Part of it has to do with the company's unwillingness to deviate from its tried-and-true business strategy. As the more easily accessible oil and natural gas reserves have been exhausted, Shell has been taking greater risks by investing in controversial oil drilling projects in the Arctic Ocean and Nigerian Delta. Recently, the company acquired the BG Group that will give it access to productive reserves off the coast of Brazil. Some investors are wondering how much longer this strategy of extracting fossil fuels from environmentally sensitive regions can be sustained.

Another factor motivating Shell's investors to action is the political threat posed to the sustainability of the company by potential legislation aimed at limiting CO_2

© Christophe Morin/Bloomberg via Getty Images

emissions. In December 2015, governmental leaders met at the United Nations Climate Change Conference in Paris to establish goals for reducing greenhouse gas emissions to limit global warming to 2 degrees Celsius. Some of Shell's investors fear that such legislation may render the company's untapped oil reserves ("stranded assets") valueless. Some individuals are encouraging the company to manage this risk by accelerating investments in renewable energies like wind power.

During the annual general meeting, Ben van Beurden, chief executive officer of Shell, said the idea that oil companies' reserves may be overvalued due to pending climate legislation is "quite convincing and quite strong." However, he also said that it will take a long time for economies to shift away from carbon-based energy.[1]

Changes like the ones faced by, and required of, Shell Oil and other fossil fuel companies are not easy, do not happen automatically, and often require managers to overcome a host of obstacles. As you study this chapter, think about why the ability to change is both challenging and essential.

An ever-changing world is full of uncertainty and risk.[2] Now and in the foreseeable future, just a sampling of the many disruptive forces in play includes a fragile financial system, breakdowns in global trade, growing income inequality, environmental degradation, declining public health and education, and underperforming institutions.[3] These and other dynamic forces make it essential for organizations (and people) to cope, anticipate, adapt, and change.

Lest the preceding paragraph sound like gloom and doom, one useful perspective is to view problems as opportunities.[4] As but one example, manufacturing was presumed in recent years to be virtually dead in the United States, but global circumstances are changing, and visionary leaders and optimistic entrepreneurs are spearheading a manufacturing comeback.[5]

As you can imagine, currently and forevermore, some organizations and people deal with change more effectively than others. The challenge for organizations is not just to produce innovative new products but to balance a culture that is innovative and that builds a sustainable business. And for individuals, the ability to cope with change is related to their job performance, the rewards they receive,[6] their career success, and feelings they hold toward the organization.[7]

But coping with change isn't enough. Managers and their organizations need to create change and improve constantly to achieve world-class excellence and competitive advantage for the future. For Time Warner and its leaders, change in the media industry is something in the environment that they must respond to by making their own changes.

Becoming World Class

 LO 1

Managers today want, or *should* want, their organizations to become world class.[8] Being world class requires applying the best and latest knowledge and ideas and having the ability to operate at the highest standards of any place anywhere.[9] Thus becoming world class does not mean merely improving. It means becoming one of the very best in the world at what you do. To some people, striving for world-class excellence seems a lofty, impossible, unnecessary goal. But it is a goal that helps one survive and succeed in today's intensely competitive business world.

World-class companies create high-value products and earn superior profits over the long run. They demolish the obsolete methods, systems, and cultures of the past that impeded their progress and apply more effective organizational strategies, structures, processes, and management of human resources. And increasingly, companies are vehicles for accomplishing societal purposes. Business is an intrinsic part of society, and value can be measured not just in short-term profits but sustainable profits and contributions to society over time.[10] Great leaders, collaborating with others, build enduring institutions that can compete successfully on a global basis.[11]

Bottom Line

It's a worthy aspiration: becoming world class at every one of your competitive goals.
What does it mean to be world class at a goal such as quality or sustainability?

Sustainable, Great Futures

Two Stanford professors, James Collins and Jerry Porras, studied 18 corporations that had achieved and maintained greatness for half a century or more.[12] The companies included Sony, American Express, Motorola, Marriott, Johnson & Johnson, Disney, 3M, Hewlett-Packard, Citicorp, and Walmart. Over the years, these companies have been widely admired, been considered the premier institutions in their industries, and made a real impact on the world. Although every company goes through periodic downturns—and these firms are no exceptions over their long histories—these companies have consistently prevailed across the decades. They turn in extraordinary performance over the long run, rather than fleeting greatness.

The researchers sought to identify the essential characteristics of enduringly great companies. These great companies have strong core values in which they believe deeply, and they express and live the values consistently. They are driven by goals—not just incremental improvements or business-as-usual goals, but stretch goals (recall Chapter 13). They change continuously, driving for progress via adaptability, experimentation, trial and error, entrepreneurial thinking, and fast action. And they do not focus on beating the competition; they focus primarily on beating themselves. They continually ask, "How can we improve ourselves to do better tomorrow than we did today?"

But underneath the action and the changes, the core values and vision remain steadfast and uncompromised. Exhibit 18.1 displays the core values of several companies that were built to last. Note that the values are not all the same. In fact, no set of common values consistently predicted success. Instead the critical factor is that great companies *have* core values, *know* what they are and what they mean, and *live* by them—year after year.

The Tyranny of the *Or*

Many companies, and individuals, are plagued by the **tyranny of the *or*.** This refers to the belief that things must be either A or B and cannot be both. The authors of *Built to Last* provide many common examples: beliefs that you must choose either change or stability; be conservative or bold; have control and consistency or creative freedom; do well in the short term or invest for the future; plan methodically or be opportunistic; create shareholder wealth or do good for the world; be pragmatic or idealistic.[13] Such beliefs, that only one goal but not another can be attained, often are invalid and certainly are constraining—unnecessarily so.

tyranny of the *or*

The belief that things must be either A or B and cannot be both; that only one goal and not another can be attained.

EXHIBIT 18.1
Core Ideologies in Built-to-Last Companies

3M	Innovation—"Thou shalt not kill a new product idea."
	Absolute integrity.
	Respect for individual initiative and personal growth.
	Tolerance for honest mistakes.
	Product quality and reliability.
	"Our real business is solving problems."
Sony	To experience the sheer joy that comes from the advancement, application, and innovation of technology that benefits the general public.
	To elevate the Japanese culture and national status.
	Being pioneers—not following others, but doing the impossible.
	Respecting and encouraging each individual's ability and creativity.
Walmart	"We exist to provide value to our customers"—to make their lives better via lower prices and greater selection; all else is secondary.
	Swim upstream, buck conventional wisdom.
	Be in partnership with employees.
	Work with passion, commitment, and enthusiasm.
	Run lean.
	Pursue ever-higher goals.
Walt Disney	No cynicism allowed.
	Fanatical attention to consistency and detail.
	Continuous progress via creativity, dreams, and imagination.
	Fanatical control and preservation of Disney's "magic" image.
	"To bring happiness to millions" and to celebrate, nurture, and promulgate "wholesome American values."

SOURCE: From *Built to Last* by James C. Collins and Jerry I. Porras, Copyright © 1997 by James C. Collins and Jerry I. Porras. Reprinted by permission of the authors, HarperCollins Publishers, Inc. and Random House Group Limited.

The Genius of the *And*

**genius of the *and*;
organizational
ambidexterity**

Ability to achieve multiple
objectives simultaneously.

In contrast to the tyranny of the *or*, the **genius of the *and***—more academically, **organizational ambidexterity**—refers to being able to achieve multiple objectives at the same time.[14] It develops via the actions of many individuals throughout the organization. We discussed earlier in the book the importance of delivering multiple competitive values to customers, performing all the management functions, reconciling hard-nosed business logic with ethics, leading and empowering, and others. Authors Collins and Porras have their own list:[15]

- Purpose beyond profit *and* pragmatic pursuit of profit.
- Relatively fixed core values *and* vigorous change and movement.
- Conservatism with the core values *and* bold business moves.
- Clear vision and direction *and* experimentation.
- Stretch goals *and* incremental progress.
- Control based on values *and* operational freedom.
- Long-term thinking and investment *and* demand for short-term results.
- Visionary, futuristic thinking *and* daily, nuts-and-bolts execution.

You have learned about all of these concepts throughout this course and should not lose sight of any of them—either in your mind or in your actions. To achieve them requires the continuous and effective management of change.

Achieving Sustained Greatness

A study of 200 management techniques employed by 160 companies over 10 years identified the specific management practices that lead to sustained, superior performance.[16] The authors boiled their findings down to four key factors:

1. *Strategy*—focused on customers, continually fine-tuned based on marketplace changes, and clearly communicated to employees.
2. *Execution*—good people, with decision-making authority on the front lines, doing quality work and cutting costs.
3. *Culture*—one that motivates, empowers people to innovate, rewards people appropriately (psychologically as well as economically), entails strong values, challenges people, and provides a satisfying work environment.
4. *Structure*—making the organization easy to work in and easy to work with, characterized by cooperation and the exchange of information and knowledge throughout the organization.

Becoming world class doesn't apply only to the private sector.

You have been learning about these concepts throughout this course. Now, looking to the future, it is important to know that companies must continue to change and better themselves. Even companies that have had great performance and reputation over many years can founder.

Becoming world class doesn't apply only to the private sector. People worry about globalization's negative effects on local communities as plants shut down and people lose their jobs to overseas workers. But local communities do have options—not easy ones, but doable. A locality can strive to become a world-class center of *thinkers, makers,* or *traders.*[17] Thus Boston creates new ideas and technologies that often dominate world markets; Spartanburg–Greenville, South Carolina, is a world-class manufacturing region that is home to more than 80 international firms representing 18 countries; Silicon Valley, located in the San Jose, California, area is a hotbed for high-tech companies; and Miami, Florida, connects Latino and Anglo cultures the way Hong Kong and Singapore have historically bridged Chinese and British cultures. The keys to creating world-class local communities include visionary leadership, a climate friendly to business, a commitment to training workers, and collaboration among businesses and between business and local government.[18]

Organization Development

How do organizations become more ambidextrous and move in the other positive directions described throughout this book? This chapter discusses several general approaches that will create positive change. We begin here with an umbrella concept called organization development.

Probably the single most widely used approach to organizational change in the Western world, applied increasingly on a global scale,[19] is **organization development (OD).** OD is a systemwide application of behavioral science knowledge to develop, improve, and reinforce the strategies, structures, and processes that lead to organization effectiveness.[20] Throughout this course, you have acquired knowledge about behavioral science and the strategies, structures, and processes that help organizations become more effective. The systemwide component of the definition means that OD is not a narrow improvement in technology or operations but a broader approach to changing organizations, units, or people. The behavioral science component means that OD is not *directly* concerned with economic, financial, or technical aspects of the organization—although they may benefit through changes in the behavior of the people in the organization. The other key part of the definition—to develop, improve, and reinforce—refers to the actual process of changing for the better and for the long term.

Two features of organization development are important to note.[21] First, it aims to increase organizational effectiveness—improving the organization's ability to deal with customers, stockholders, governments, employees, and other stakeholders, which results in better-quality products, higher financial returns, and high quality of work life. Second, OD has an important underlying value orientation: It supports human potential, development, and participation in addition to performance and competitive advantage.

Many specific OD techniques fit under this philosophical umbrella (see Exhibit 18.2).[22] You learned about these topics throughout your management course. You also will learn more about the process of creating change in the rest of this chapter.

organization development (OD)

The systemwide application of behavioral science knowledge to develop, improve, and reinforce the strategies, structures, and processes that lead to organizational effectiveness.

The strategy of Cirque du Soleil is one of constant innovation: combining circus and theater and studying other industries such as car design, fashion, and restaurants to get ideas for new shows.

© Simon Fergusson/Getty Images

Intervention	Goals
Strategic	Helping organizations conduct mergers and acquisitions, change their strategies, and develop alliances.
Techno-structural	Relating to organization structure and design, employee involvement, and work design.
Human process	Improving conflict resolution, team building, communication, and leadership.
Human resource management	Attracting good people, setting goals, and appraising and rewarding performance.

EXHIBIT 18.2
Basic Types of OD Interventions

SOURCE: T. Cummings and C. Worley, *Organization Development and Change,* 8th ed. (Mason, OH: Thomson/South-Western, 2005).

Managing Change

 People are the key to successful change.[23] For an organization to be great, or even just to survive, people have to care about its fate and know how they can contribute. But typically leadership lies with only a few people at the top. Too few take on the burden of change; the number of people who care deeply, and who make innovative contributions, is too small. People throughout the organization need to take a greater interest and a more active role in helping the business as a whole. They have to identify with the entire organization, not just with their unit and close colleagues.

Shared leadership is crucial to the success of most change efforts—people must be not just supporters of change but also implementers.[24]

This shared responsibility for change is not unusual in start-ups and very small organizations. But too often it is lost with growth and over time. In large, traditional corporations, it is all too rare. Organizations need to rekindle individual creativity and responsibility permanently, instituting a true change in the behavior of people throughout the ranks. The essential task is to motivate people fully to keep changing in response to new business challenges.

Motivating People to Change

People must be motivated to change. But often they resist changing. Some people resist change more than others, but managers tend to underestimate the amount of resistance they will encounter.[25]

People at all levels of their organizations, from entry-level workers to top executives, resist change. For example, many banks and credit unions are switching from specialized roles in branches, such as tellers and personal bankers, to employing employees who are universal agents, able to process transactions, open accounts, and sell products. When they make this change, the main source of resistance is that the new jobs involve selling (identifying unmet customer needs and suggesting products and services). A typical branch employee is unaccustomed to selling and may even have a negative opinion of a salesperson's role, especially in a bank.[26]

At IBM, executives learned that lower-level managers were getting bogged down because they had to invest so much time and effort in obtaining approval from higher-ups. Former CEO Sam Palmisano announced that he would give first-level managers authority to spend $5,000 without prior approval—a daring move, considering that the authority applied to 30,000 managers. However, the managers felt uncomfortable with their new authority, and in the first year of the new program, they spent only $100,000 of the $150 million Palmisano had entrusted to them.[27] In other words, they were reluctant to change the way they worked, even though it stood to make their job easier.

Many people (and organizations) settle for mediocrity rather than aspire to excellence. They resist the idea of striving for excellence. When told by their managers, "We have to become world class," their reactions resemble the following statements:

- "Those world-class performance numbers are ridiculous! I don't believe them, they are impossible! Maybe in some industries, some companies . . . but ours is unique . . ."
- "Sure, maybe some companies achieve those numbers, but there's no hurry . . . We're doing all right. Sales were up 5 percent this year, costs were down 2 percent. And we've got to keep cutting corners . . ."
- "We can't afford to be world class like those big global companies; we don't have the money or staff . . ."
- "We don't need to expand internationally. One of our local competitors tried that a few years ago and lost its shirt."
- "It's not a level playing field . . . the others have unfair advantages . . ."

To deal with such reactions and successfully implement positive change, managers must understand why people often resist change. Many factors go into people's resistance to, ambivalence toward, and readiness for change.[28] Exhibit 18.3 shows some common

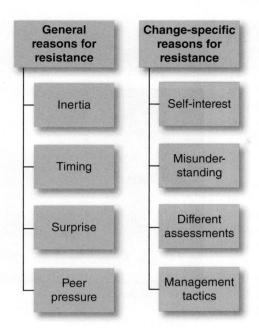

EXHIBIT 18.3
Reasons for Resistance
to Change

reasons for resistance. Some reasons are general and arise in most change efforts. Other reasons for resistance relate to the specific nature of a particular change.

General Reasons for Resistance   Several reasons for resistance arise regardless of the actual content of the change:[29]

- *Inertia.* Usually people don't want to disturb the status quo. The old ways of doing things are comfortable and easy, so people don't want to shake things up and try something new. For example, it is easier to keep living in the same apartment or house than to move to another.
- *Timing.* People often resist change because of poor timing. Maybe you would like to move to a different place to live, but do you want to move this week? Even if a place were available, you probably couldn't take the time. If managers or employees are unusually busy or under stress, or if relations between management and workers are strained, the timing is wrong for introducing new proposals. Where possible, managers should introduce change when people are receptive.
- *Surprise.* One key aspect of timing and receptivity is surprise. If the change is sudden, unexpected, or extreme, resistance may be the initial—almost reflexive—reaction. Suppose your school announced an increase in tuition, effective at the beginning of next term. Wouldn't you want more time to prepare? Managers or others initiating a change often forget that others haven't given the matter much thought; the change leaders need to allow time for others to prepare for the change.
- *Peer pressure.* Sometimes work teams resist new ideas. Even if individual members do not strongly oppose a change suggested by management, the team may band together in opposition. Peer pressure will cause individuals to resist even reasonable changes, especially if a group is highly cohesive and has antimanagement norms (recall Chapter 14). Of course peer pressure can be a positive force, too. Change leaders who invite—and listen to—ideas from team members may find that peer pressure becomes a driving force behind the change's success.

Change-Specific Reasons for Resistance   Other causes of resistance arise from the specific nature of a proposed change. Change-specific reasons for resistance include[30]

- *Self-interest.* Most people care less about the organization's best interest than they do about their own best interests. They will resist a change if they think it will cause

Multiple Generations at Work

Keep Aligning Your Skills with the Future of Work

A recent PricewaterhouseCoopers study about the changing nature of work stated: "Disruptive innovations are creating new industries and business models, and destroying old ones. New technologies, data analytics and social networks are having a huge impact on how people communicate, collaborate and work."

Given these changes, employees from every generation would be well advised to remain flexible with regard to job opportunities (see boundaryless organization in Chapter 15) and continually acquire skills and experiences that may be marketable in the future. Another suggestion is to try to work for organizations that fit with your personal values. This may not happen in your first or second job, but with persistence and networking, it is possible to find the organization that is right for you.

The same study predicted that three types of organizations will likely dominate the economy over the next 5 to 10 years. Individuals should use the following descriptions to judge whether there may be a good fit from an employment perspective:

1. *Large global corporations.* Driven by profit and growth, these "mega-corporations" will compete on economies of scale. Employees who are flexible and perform well under pressure will be rewarded with job security and generous pay and benefits.
2. *Social and environmental enterprises.* Motivated by a "powerful social conscience and green sense of

© Steve Debenport/Getty Images

responsibility," these organizations will pursue goals that benefit both business and society. Employees who show loyalty will appreciate working in an environment that's ethical and supports work–life balance.
3. *Small, agile companies.* Operating in a flexible, autonomous manner while minimizing fixed costs, these agile firms will seek a variety of specialized projects. Individuals who prefer to work as short-term contractors will enjoy flexible work arrangements and a variety of challenges.[31]

Of the three options above, where do you see yourself fitting? Best of luck to you.

them to lose something of value. What could people fear to lose? At worst, their jobs, if management is considering closing down a plant. A merger, reorganization, or technological change could create the same fear. Other possible fears include loss of the feeling of being competent in a familiar job, expectations that the job will become more difficult or time-consuming, and concerns about the organization's future (see "Multiple Generations at Work").

- *Misunderstanding.* Even when management proposes a change that will benefit everyone, people may resist because they don't fully understand it. People may not see how the change fits with the firm's strategy, or they simply may not see the change's advantage over current practices.[32] One company met resistance to the idea of introducing flexible working hours, a system in which workers have some say regarding the hours they work. This system can benefit employees, but a false rumor circulated among plant employees that people would have to work evenings, weekends, or whenever their supervisors wanted. As a result, the initiative was dropped.

- *Different assessments.* Employees receive different—and usually less—information than management receives. Such discrepancies cause people to develop different assessments of proposed changes. Some may be aware that the benefits outweigh the costs, whereas others may see only the costs and not the advantages.

This is a common problem when management announces a change, say, in work procedures, and doesn't explain to employees why the change is needed. Management expects advantages in terms of increased efficiency, but workers may see the change as another arbitrary, ill-informed management rule that causes headaches for those who must carry it out.

- *Management tactics.* Management may attempt to force the change and may fail to address concerns. Or it may fail to provide the necessary resources, knowledge, or leadership to help the change succeed. Sometimes a change receives so much exposure and glorification that employees resent it and resist. Managers who overpromise what they, or the change, can deliver may discover that the next time they want to introduce a change, they have lost credibility, so employees resist.

It is important to recognize that employees' assessments can be more accurate than management's; employees may know a change won't work even if management doesn't. In this case, resistance to change is beneficial for the organization. Thus, even though management typically considers resistance a challenge to be overcome, it may actually represent an important signal that a proposed change requires further, more open-minded scrutiny.[33]

A General Model for Managing Resistance

Motivating people to change often requires three basic stages, shown in Exhibit 18.4: unfreezing, moving to institute the change, and refreezing.[34]

Unfreezing In the **unfreezing** stage, management realizes that its current practices are no longer appropriate and the company must break out of (unfreeze) its present mold by doing things differently. People must come to recognize that some of the past ways of thinking, feeling, and doing things are obsolete.[35] A direct and sometimes effective way to do this is to communicate the negative consequences of the old ways by comparing the organization's performance with that of its competitors. As discussed in Chapter 15, management can share with employees data about costs, quality, and profits.[36] Sometimes an organization can open minds by easing employees into the transition gently and letting the more flexible employees deliver the message favoring change. When Washington State Employees Credit Union rewrote job descriptions to staff its branches with universal agents, it didn't force all the employees to change jobs. Rather, those who wanted to remain tellers or in other traditional roles could do so as long as they demonstrated a supportive attitude. In addition, the company selected and trained a group of branch employees to answer questions about the new universal-agent position.[37]

When managers communicate the need to change, they need to take care not to arouse people's defensiveness. Instead of unfreezing resistance, managers are likely to place employees on the defensive when they pin the blame for shortcomings directly and entirely on the workers.[38] Similarly, bombarding employees with facts aimed at inducing fear may only add to their resistance. When a problem seems huge, people often decide it is hopeless and don't face it. In these difficult situations, leaders more effectively unfreeze negative behavior with a message of hope and a commitment to collaborate so that they can accomplish successful change together.

unfreezing

Realizing that current practices are inappropriate and that new behavior is necessary.

EXHIBIT 18.4
Motivating People to Change

Unfreezing | Moving | Refreezing

Breaking from the old ways of doing things. | Instituting the change. | Reinforcing and supporting the new ways.

> The gap is between what is and what could be.

performance gap

The difference between actual performance and desired performance.

Bottom Line

A useful tactic for innovating toward a positive future is to imagine the difference between what *is* and what *could be*.

moving

Instituting the change.

force-field analysis

An approach to implementing the unfreezing/moving/refreezing model by identifying the forces that prevent people from changing and those that will drive people toward change.

An important contributor to unfreezing is the recognition of a performance gap, which can be a precipitator of major change. A **performance gap** is the difference between actual performance and the performance that should or could exist.[39] As an impetus for change, a performance gap can apply to the organization as a whole; it also can apply to departments, groups, and individuals.

A gap typically implies poor performance; for example, sales, profits, stock price, or other financial indicators are down. This situation attracts management's attention, and management introduces changes to try to correct things. But another, very important form of performance gap can exist. This type of gap can occur when performance is good but someone realizes that it could be better. Thus the gap is between what is and what could be. Important changes can and should be made even when performance is good.[40]

In the realm of change management, employees are particularly motivated by situations that combine the sense of urgency that comes from identifying a problem with the sense of excitement that comes from identifying an opportunity. Furthermore, managers communicating a performance gap should keep in mind that employees care about more than market share and revenues. Employees want to know how making a change can help them have a positive impact on their work group, their customers, their company, their community, and themselves. For example, a financial services company met resistance when it tried to persuade employees that a change would enhance the company's competitive position. Employees got on board only after the change leaders also started talking about how the change would help employees reduce errors, enable teams to avoid duplication of effort, make jobs more interesting, and help the organization fulfill its mission to deliver affordable housing.[41]

Lawrence Ellison, executive chairman and chief technology officer of Oracle, is well-versed in what it takes to convey a vision of change within his organization. Oracle has often acquired other companies, bringing tumultuous change for individual employees and managers within both organizations.

© David Paul Morris/Getty Images

Moving The next step, **moving** to institute the change, begins with establishing a vision of where the company is heading. You learned about vision in the leadership chapter. The vision can be realized through strategic, structural, cultural, and individual change. Strategic ideas are discussed throughout the book. Changes in structure may involve moving to the divisional, matrix, or some other appropriate form (discussed in Chapters 8 and 9). Cultural changes (Chapter 2) are institutionalized through effective leadership (Chapters 12 through 15). Individuals will change as new people join the company (Chapters 10 and 11) and as people throughout the organization adopt the leader's new vision for the future.

One technique that helps to manage the change process, **force-field analysis,** involves identifying the specific forces that prevent people from changing and the specific forces that will drive people toward change.[42] Managers operating under this concept investigate forces acting in opposite directions. Eliminating the restraining forces helps people unfreeze, and increasing the driving forces helps and motivates them to move forward.

The great social psychologist Kurt Lewin developed force-field analysis (and the unfreezing/moving/refreezing model). Lewin theorized that although driving forces may be more easily changed, shifting them may increase opposition (tension and/or conflict) within the organization and add restraining forces. Therefore, to create change, it is crucial to remove restraining forces.

Refreezing   Finally, **refreezing** means strengthening the new behaviors that support the change. Refreezing involves implementing control systems that support the change (Chapter 16), applying corrective action when necessary, and reinforcing behaviors and performance (Chapter 13) that support the agenda. Management should consistently support and reward evidence of movement in the right direction.[43]

In today's organizations, refreezing is not always the best third step if it creates new behaviors that are as rigid as the old ones. The ideal new culture is one of continuous change. Refreezing is appropriate when it permanently installs behaviors that focus on important business results and maintain essential core values. But refreezing should not create new rigidities that might become dysfunctional as the business environment continues to change.[44] The behaviors that should be refrozen are those that promote continued adaptability, flexibility, experimentation, assessment of results, and continuous improvement—in other words, lock in key values, capabilities, and strategic mission but not necessarily specific practices and procedures.

refreezing

Strengthening the new behaviors that support the change.

Specific Approaches to Enlist Cooperation

You can try to command people to change, but the key to long-term success is to use other approaches.[45] Developing true support is better than driving a program forward.[46] How, specifically, can managers motivate people to change?

Most managers underestimate the variety of ways they can influence people during a period of change.[47] Several effective approaches to managing resistance and enlisting cooperation are available, as described in Exhibit 18.5 and expanded here.

Education and Communication   Management should educate people about upcoming changes before they occur. It should communicate not only the nature of the

EXHIBIT 18.5   Methods for Managing Resistance to Change

Approach	Commonly Used in Situations	Advantage	Drawbacks
Education and communication	When there is a lack of information or inaccurate information and analysis.	Once persuaded, people will often help with the implementation of the change.	Can be very time-consuming if lots of people are involved.
Participation and involvement	When the initiators do not have all the information they need to design the change and when others have considerable power to resist.	People who participate will be committed to implementing change, and any relevant information they have will be integrated into the change plan.	Can be very time-consuming if participators design an inappropriate change.
Facilitation and support	When people are resisting because of adjustment problems.	No other approach works as well with adjustment problems.	Can be time-consuming and expensive and still fail.
Negotiation and rewards	When someone or some group will clearly lose out in a change and when that group has considerable power to resist.	Sometimes it is a relatively easy way to avoid major resistance.	Can be too expensive in many cases if it alerts others to negotiate for compliance.
Manipulation and cooptation	When other tactics will not work or are too expensive.	It can be a relatively quick and inexpensive solution to resistance problems.	Can lead to future problems if people feel manipulated.
Explicit and implicit coercion	When speed is essential, and the change initiators possess considerable power.	It is speedy and can overcome any kind of resistance.	Can be risky if it leaves people angry at the initiators.

SOURCE: Reprinted by permission of the *Harvard Business Review.* An exhibit from "Choosing Strategies for Change" by John P. Kotter and Leonard A. Schlesinger (March–April 1979). Copyright © 1979 by the Harvard Business School Publishing Corporation; all rights reserved.

change but its logic. This process can include one-on-one discussions, presentations to groups, and reports and memos. As we discussed in Chapter 15, effective communication includes feedback and listening. That provides an environment in which management can explain the rationale for the change—and perhaps improve it.

Participation and Involvement   The people who are affected by the change should be involved in the change's design and implementation. For major, organizationwide change, participation in the process can extend from the top to the very bottom of the organization.[48] When feasible, management should use the advice of people throughout the organization.

As you learned in Chapter 3, people who are involved in decisions understand them more fully and are more committed to them. People's understanding and commitment are important ingredients in the successful implementation of a change. Participation also provides an excellent opportunity for education and communication.

Facilitation and Support   Management should make the change as easy as possible for employees and support their efforts. Facilitation involves providing the training and other resources people need to carry out the change and perform their jobs under the new circumstances. This step often includes decentralizing authority and empowering people—that is, giving them the power to make the decisions and changes needed to improve their performance.

Offering support involves listening patiently to problems, being understanding if performance drops temporarily or the change is not perfected immediately, and generally being on the employees' side and showing consideration during a difficult period.

Negotiation and Rewards   When necessary and appropriate, management can offer concrete incentives for cooperation with the change. Perhaps job enrichment is acceptable only with a higher wage rate, or a work rule change is resisted until management agrees to a concession on some other rule (say, regarding taking breaks). Even among higher-level managers, one executive might agree to another's idea for a policy change only in return for support on some other issue of more personal importance. Rewards such as bonuses, wages and salaries, recognition, job assignments, and perks can be examined and perhaps restructured to reinforce the direction of the change.[49]

When people trust one another, change is easier. But change is further facilitated by demonstrating its benefits to people.[50] Describing benefits can take place in the context of negotiation or working together to find a mutually acceptable way to implement the change. A Colorado nonprofit agency called Envision did this when the state government slashed its funding, reducing the agency's budget by 7.5 percent. Envision provides a variety of services to adults and children with developmental disabilities and depends on employees' commitment to its mission. Executive director Mary Lu Walton set up a team of employees to figure out how to cut costs, and she encouraged them to focus on eliminating the tasks employees dislike. The team members restructured work, sparing seven of the ten jobs originally targeted for layoffs. Within a few months, Envision was a leaner organization with employees fully committed to the change.[51]

Manipulation and Cooptation   Sometimes managers use more subtle, covert tactics to implement change. One form of manipulation is cooptation, which involves giving a resisting individual a desirable role in the change process. The leader of a resisting group often is coopted. For example, management might invite a union leader to be a member of an executive committee or ask a key member of an outside organization to join the company's board of directors. As a person becomes involved in the change, he or she may become less resistant to the actions of the coopting group or organization.

Explicit and Implicit Coercion   Some managers apply punishment or the threat of punishment to those who resist change. With this approach, managers use force to make people comply with their wishes. For example, a manager might insist that subordinates cooperate with the change and threaten them with job loss, denial of a promotion, or an unattractive work assignment. Sometimes you just have to lay down the law.

Each approach to managing resistance has advantages and drawbacks and, like many of the other situational management approaches described in this book, each is useful in different situations. Look back at Exhibit 18.5, which summarizes the advantages, drawbacks, and appropriate circumstances for these approaches to managing resistance to change. As the exhibit implies, managers should not use just one or two general approaches, regardless of the circumstances. Effective change managers are familiar with the various approaches and know how to apply them according to the situation.

Throughout the process, change leaders need to build in stability. Recall from the companies that were built to last that they all have essential core characteristics of which they don't lose sight. In the midst of change, turmoil, and uncertainty, people need anchors onto which they can latch.[52] Making an organization's values and mission constant and visible can often serve this stabilizing function. In addition, strategic principles can be important anchors during change.[53] Maintaining the visibility of key people, continuing key assignments and projects, and making announcements about which organizational components will *not* change can also promote stability. Such anchors will reduce anxiety and help overcome resistance. As you read "Management in Action: Progress Report," consider how the leaders of Shell should rationalize their internal beliefs with those of the activist shareholders.

Harmonizing Multiple Changes

There are no silver bullets or single-shot methods of changing organizations successfully. Single shots rarely hit a challenging target. Usually many issues need simultaneous

Management in Action

SHELL BELIEVES DEMAND FOR FOSSIL FUELS WILL REMAIN STRONG

Powerful investors are attempting to unfreeze Shell's current business practices in favor of moving the company toward a more environmentally sustainable strategy. However, top managers at oil companies like Shell are continuing to operate under the assumption that demand for oil and natural gas will remain strong for several more decades.

In the foreseeable future, national populations and per capita income will continue to grow (especially in developing economies), fueling increased energy demand. By 2040, Shell estimates that fossil fuels will meet two-thirds of demand while renewable energies like wind power and solar will make up the remainder. This growth in demand will support a "profitable" price of oil and natural gas.

Shell remains skeptical that governments will take decisive action on the issue of global warming: "We do not see governments taking the steps now that are consistent with the 2-degree Celsius scenario." Some estimates suggest that governments would need to pass legislation that cuts greenhouse gases by 80 percent by the middle of the century. Such measures will likely cause short-term layoffs and economic disruption as the energy industry transforms itself to green energy production.

In its latest New Lens Scenarios report, Shell admits that even with advances in energy-efficient technologies and replacement of coal by natural gas, the build-up of greenhouse gases will likely cause atmospheric temperatures to increase more than 2 degrees Celsius. The report discusses how Shell plans to shift gradually to a greener, gas-focused energy company over the next several decades.

Ben van Beurden, Shell's CEO, defends his company's slow pace of change: "If there would be no further investment in oil production, the gap between supply and demand could be 70 million barrels per day by 2040." "Energy demand will continue to grow and that will have to be by and large met by fossil fuels," he added.[54]

- If you were the CEO of Shell, how would you respond to pressures from shareholders to become a more environmentally friendly company? What changes, if any, would you pursue in the short term? Long term?
- Do you agree with Shell's CEO that fossil fuels will be needed to meet energy demand for several more decades? Explain.

MANAGER'S BRIEF

PROGRESS REPORT

ONWARD

total organization change

Introducing and sustaining multiple policies, practices, and procedures across multiple units and levels.

attention, and any single, small change will be absorbed by the prevailing culture and disappear. **Total organization change** involves introducing and sustaining multiple policies, practices, and procedures across multiple units and levels.[55] Such change affects the thinking and behavior of everyone in the organization, can enhance the organization's culture and success, and can be sustained over time.

A survey at a Harvard Business School conference found that the average attendee's company had five major change efforts going on at once.[56] The problem is, these efforts usually are simultaneous but not coordinated. As a result, changes get muddled; people lose focus.[57] The people involved suffer from confusion, frustration, low morale, and low motivation.

> Many people complain about their companies' "flavor of the month" approach to change.

Because companies introduce new changes constantly, many people complain about their companies' "flavor of the month" approach to change. That is, employees often see many change efforts as just the company's jumping on the latest bandwagon or fad. The more these change fads come and go, the more cynical people become, and the more difficult it is to get them committed to making the change a success.[58]

So an important question is, Which change efforts are really worth undertaking? Here are some specific questions to ask before embarking on a change project:[59]

- What is the evidence that the approach really can produce positive results?
- Is the approach relevant to your company's strategies and priorities?
- Can you assess the costs and potential benefits?
- Does it really help people add value through their work?
- Does it help the company focus better on customers and the things they value?
- Can you go through the decision-making process described in Chapter 3, understand what you're facing, and feel that you are taking the right approach?

Management also needs to connect the dots—that is, integrate the various efforts into a coherent picture that people can see, understand, and get behind.[60] You connect the dots by understanding each change program and its goals, by identifying similarities among the programs and their differences, and by dropping programs that don't meet priority goals or demonstrate clear results. Most important, you do it by communicating to everyone concerned the common themes among the various programs: their common rationales, objectives, and methods. You show them how the various parts fit the strategic big picture and how the changes will make things better for the company and its people. You must communicate these benefits thoroughly, honestly, and frequently.[61]

Leading Change

Successful change requires managers to lead it actively. The essential activities of leading change are summarized in Exhibit 18.6.

The companies that lead change most effectively establish a sense of urgency.[62] To do so, managers must examine current realities and pressures in the marketplace and the competitive arena, identify both crises and opportunities, and be frank and honest about them. In this sense, urgency is a reality-based sense of determination, not just fear-based busyness. The immediacy of the need for change is an important component, in part because so many large companies grow complacent.

Exhibit 18.7 shows some common reasons for complacency. To stop complacency and create urgency, a manager can talk candidly about the organization's weaknesses compared with competitors, making a point to back up statements with data. Other tactics include setting stretch goals, putting employees in direct contact with unhappy customers and shareholders, distributing worrisome information to all employees instead of merely engaging in management happy talk, eliminating excessive perks, and highlighting to everyone the future opportunities that exist but that the organization so far has failed to pursue.

1. Establishing a sense of urgency

2. Creating the guiding coalition

3. Developing a vision and strategy

4. Communicating the change vision

5. Empowering broad-based action

6. Generating short-term wins

7. Consolidating gains and producing more change

8. Anchoring new approaches in the culture

EXHIBIT 18.6
Leading Change

SOURCE: Reprinted by permission of Harvard Business School Press. Exhibit from *Leading Change* by John P. Kotter, 1996. Copyright 1996 by the Harvard Business School Publishing Corporation; all rights reserved.

Ultimately, urgency is driven by compelling business reasons for change. Survival, competition, and winning in the marketplace are compelling; they provide a sense of direction and energy around change. Change becomes not a hobby, a luxury, or something nice to do, but a business necessity.[63]

To create a guiding coalition means putting together a group with enough power to lead the change. Change efforts fail when a sufficiently powerful coalition is not formed.[64] Major organization change requires leadership from top management, working as a team. But over time, the support must gradually expand outward and downward throughout the organization. Middle managers and supervisors are essential. Groups at all levels are

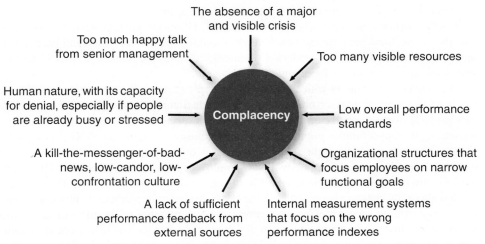

EXHIBIT 18.7
Sources of Complacency

The absence of a major and visible crisis

Too much happy talk from senior management

Too many visible resources

Human nature, with its capacity for denial, especially if people are already busy or stressed

Complacency

Low overall performance standards

A kill-the-messenger-of-bad-news, low-candor, low-confrontation culture

Organizational structures that focus employees on narrow functional goals

A lack of sufficient performance feedback from external sources

Internal measurement systems that focus on the wrong performance indexes

SOURCE: Reprinted by permission of Harvard Business School Press. Exhibit from *Leading Change* by John P. Kotter, 1996. Copyright 1996 by the Harvard Business School Publishing Corporation; all rights reserved.

the glue that can hold change efforts together, the medium for communicating about the changes, and the means for enacting new behaviors.[65]

Developing a vision and strategy, as discussed in earlier chapters, directs the change effort. This process involves determining the idealized, expected state of affairs after the change is implemented. Because confusion is common during major organizational change, the clearest possible image of the future state must be developed and conveyed to everyone.[66] This image, or vision, is a target or guideline that can clarify expectations, dispel rumors, and mobilize people's energies. The portrait of the future also should communicate how the transition will occur, why the change is being implemented, and how people will be affected by the change. The power of a compelling vision is one of the most important aspects of change and should not be underestimated or underused.

Communicating the change vision requires using every possible channel and opportunity to talk up and reinforce the vision and required new behaviors. It is said that aspiring change leaders undercommunicate the vision by a factor of 10, or even 100 or 1,000, seriously undermining the chances of success.[67] In delivering more messages, however, do not forget that communication is a two-way street. When consultant Steve Schumacher was hired to improve the performance of a division in which quality, productivity, and customer service had been declining, he started by setting up meetings in which employees described what they saw as the underlying problems. His message to them was simply that the company cared about their views and wouldn't make changes until they had been heard. Schumacher and his team then compiled a list of all the issues and shared it with every employee. Only then did he ask for volunteers to participate in planning solutions. The consulting team was flooded with volunteers. Not only were employees willing to change, but they were excited to be included in planning, and they hungered for a better understanding of where the company wanted to go and how they could contribute to that vision. Before long, as a result of this team effort, performance measures began to rise across the board.[68]

Empowering broad-based action means getting rid of obstacles to success, including systems and structures that constrain rather than facilitate. Encourage risk taking and experimentation and empower people by providing information, knowledge, authority, and rewards, as described in Chapter 13.

Generate short-term wins. Don't wait for the ultimate grand realization of the vision. You need results. As small victories accumulate, you make the transition from an isolated initiative to an integral part of the business.[69] Plan for and create small victories that indicate to everyone that progress is being made. Recognize and reward the people who made the wins possible, doing it visibly so that people notice and the positive message permeates the organization.

Make sure you consolidate gains and produce more change. With the well-earned credibility of previous successes, keep changing things in ways that support the vision. Hire, promote, and develop people who will further the vision. Reinvigorate the organization and your change efforts with new projects and change agents.

Finally, anchor new approaches in the culture.[70] Highlight positive results, communicate the connections between the new behaviors and the improved results, and keep developing new change agents and leaders. Continually increase the number of people joining you in taking responsibility for change.[71]

The conventional way in which organizations apply these eight steps of leading change has been to set up strategy or project teams to conduct annual strategy reviews or launch new projects over the course of months or years. However, this approach can be too slow for seizing the opportunities popping up in today's business environment. Therefore, John Kotter, who proposed the eight steps, now advises companies to become more agile in leading change by empowering networks of employees to accelerate change.[72] These networks bring together volunteers from all levels and functions of the organization who are excited about the change vision and have the skills needed to implement it. When someone in the organization sees a problem or opportunity, any member of the network can share the issue and invite others to join a team developing a solution. The teamwork is in addition to the employee's usual responsibilities, so the network requires highly committed people who experience the rewards of making a significant, visible contribution.

Shaping the Future

Most change is reactive. A better way to change is to be proactive. **Reactive change** means responding to pressure after a problem has arisen. It also implies being a follower. **Proactive change** means anticipating and preparing for an uncertain future. It implies being a leader and creating the future you want.

The road to the future includes drivers, passengers, and road kill. Put another way: on the road to the future, who will be the windshield, and who will be the bug?[73] Needless to say, it's best to be a driver.[74] How do you become a driver? By being proactive more than merely reactive, by really thinking about the future, and by *creating* futures.

reactive change

A response that occurs under pressure; problem-driven change.

proactive change

A response that is initiated before a performance gap has occurred.

Thinking about the Future

If you think only about the present or wallow in the uncertainties of the future, your future is just a roll of the dice. It is far better to exercise foresight, set an agenda for the future, and pursue it with everything you've got. So contemplate and envision the future.

Before the 20th century, people lived without antibiotics, automobiles, airplanes, tractors, and air conditioning. Imagine how this combination of inventions has revolutionized where and how well people live. And in just the past few decades, we have seen the invention and spread of personal computers, cell phones, and the mapping of the human genome. These innovations are still shaping how we learn, communicate, and treat disease.

> On the road to the future, who will be the windshield, and who will be the bug?

Will the 21st century bring transformations that are just as dramatic? Some people think the potential for innovation and growth is unprecedented in areas such as information technology, the biological sciences, agriculture, water supply, and clean energy technologies.[75] Futurists Fred Rogers and Richard Lalich predict smart machines and processes will transform how we live in the 21st century. They foresee advances in bioengineering that cure diseases, customized medicine that reduces health care costs, and genetic engineering of crops that increases food supplies.[76] Futurist Cynthia Wagner sees career opportunities stemming from researchers' growing knowledge of processes in the human brain. In the future, Wagner surmises, this knowledge will help bioengineers develop microelectrodes to translate paralyzed patients' brain signals into words and movements, and computer scientists will apply the knowledge to make advances in artificial intelligence.[77] Just as technologies change, so do additional trends rise and fall, recently including a (temporary, most likely) damper on globalization, rising distrust of business, a growing role of government, strains on natural resources, and changing patterns of global consumption.[78] Vast new markets exist, new kinds of companies are ready to be created, and new business models will emerge.[79] All offer prime opportunity to those who create the future.

Creating the Future

Companies can try different strategic postures to prepare to compete in an uncertain future. **Adapters** take the current industry structure and its future evolution as givens. They choose where to compete. This posture is taken by most companies by conducting standard strategic analysis and choosing how to compete within given environments. In contrast, **shapers** try to change the structure of their industries, creating a future competitive landscape of their own design.[80] For an example, see the nearby "Social Enterprise" box.

Companies are achieving success by reinventing industries. For example, Airbnb disrupted the travel industry by creating an online platform to connect travelers with private individuals who are willing to rent a room, condominium, or other accommodation. Other examples of industry disruptors include Uber (taxi industry) and PayPal (credit card industry).[81]

adapters

Companies that take the current industry structure and its evolution as givens, and choose where to compete.

shapers

Companies that try to change the structure of their industries, creating a future competitive landscape of their own design.

Social Enterprise

Using Co-creation to Build a Better Future

Co-creation is when diverse stakeholders come together to develop new practices. The stakeholders—social enterprises, for-profit companies, nonprofit entities educational instituations, or government agencies—leverage one another's strengths and resources in order to help solve social and environmental challenges. Stephanie Schmidt, managing director of Ashoka Europe, believes the social sector can learn from what companies do well: "It is scale, but also efficiency in terms of operations, product development, distribution, as well as innovation." At the same time, for-profit companies can learn how social enterprises are agile with strategies, operate on low budgets, and maintain extreme client-focus.

Here are two examples of how co-creation is making an impact on social and environmental problems:

BASF Agricultural Solutions (India) developed a digital platform to exchange information with farmers regarding the correct mix of seeds and chemicals to use when planting crops. The company trained farmers to "optimize their yield and to become better stewards of their land." Within one year, the co-creation effort resulted in farmers increasing their yields by 25 percent.

BASF has grown rapidly and become the market leader of argicultural products in India.

The City of Porto Alegre in southern Brazil co-creates by involving citizens in the allocations of about $200 million in public funds each year. Using live in-person and online broadcasts of town hall meetings, nearly 50,000 people participate in the budgeting process. Popular topics include the construction of schools and sewers in the most disadvantaged areas of the city. The World Bank has "credited Porto Alegre's participatory budgeting process with helping to reduce inequality in the city."

Co-creating is an exciting movement that holds real promise in bringing diverse stakeholders together to fight the world's most pressing problems—poverty, inequality, hunger, illiteracy, climate change, and diseases.[82]

Questions

- Can you think of additional examples in which diverse organizations have joined forces to address social or environmental problems?

- Do you believe this co-creation movement is sustainable or a passing fad? Explain.

Don't think taking risks and being fearless is only for companies; think of your own quest for personal advantage in the same way. Ultimately where you go, what you do, who you become are up to you.

© Punit Paranjpe/AFP/Getty Images

You need to create advantages. The challenge is not to maintain your position in the current competitive arena but to create new competitive arenas, transform your industry, and imagine a future that others don't see. Creating advantage is better than playing catch-up. At best, doing things to catch up buys time; it cannot get you out ahead of the pack or buy world-class excellence.[83] To create new markets or transform industries—these are perhaps the ultimate forms of proactive change.[84]

Exhibit 18.8 illustrates the vast opportunity to create new markets. Articulated needs are those that customers acknowledge and try to satisfy. Unarticulated needs are those that customers have not yet experienced. Served customers are those to whom your company is now selling, and unserved customers are untapped markets.

Business as usual concentrates on the lower-left quadrant. The leaders who recreate the game are constantly trying to create new opportunities in the other three quadrants.[85] For example, as a middle class emerges in populous and fast-developing nations such as India, China, and Brazil, some see problems in the strain this puts on the planet's resources. Others see unexploited opportunities to serve new customers with new kinds of products that are made more sustainably or enable consumers to live a more sustainable lifestyle.[86]

Other companies hope to meet unarticulated needs by developing and exploiting cutting-edge technology. The nanometer—one-billionth of a meter, 1/100,000 the width of a human hair, or about the size of 10 hydrogen atoms in a row—is the building block of a new industry, nanotechnology. The nanometer is so important because matter at this scale

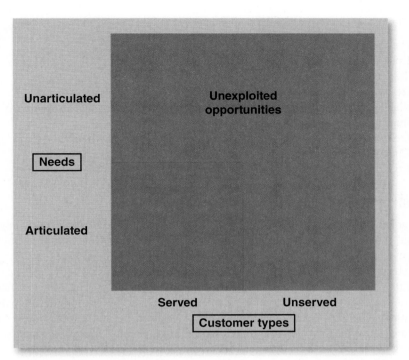

EXHIBIT 18.8
Vast Opportunity

often behaves differently—speeding electrons through circuits faster, conducting heat better, or offering qualities such as greater strength, durability, or reactivity.[87] Large and small companies are beginning to rush nano-based products into the marketplace. Current applications include nanotech silver (which has antimicrobial properties) in grooming products and odor-resistant socks, nanoscale features in semiconductors, and the use of nanoparticles as catalysts in making chemicals for use in coatings, paints, sunscreens, bumpers and catalytic converters for cars, and other products.[88] Applications under development include high-performance rechargeable batteries that can store hydrogen and other high-energy gases, nano-biochips that can detect cancer in a patient within minutes, and a nanotechnology material called graphene that can be used to produce a computer touchscreen one atom thick.[89]

Is nanotech—for that matter, are most industries of the future—being overhyped? By some estimates, products using nanotech materials have recently surpassed $1 trillion in global sales.[90] The expansion of this technology has been impressive, given that it is still under development. Sales of products applying nanotechnology have grown by more than 18 percent a year over the past few years.[91] However, there are concerns that the technology is untested and perhaps risky.[92] The particles are so small that they can pass through most manufactured filters as well as through cell walls, and their ability to react at the atomic level could cause unforeseen chemical and biological consequences. At the heart of the problem is a lack of experience with these materials, coupled with the fact that their properties are different from the same materials at a larger scale. Scientists have measured inhaled particles in the respiratory tract, for example, but have only begun to study whether cells' functions are impaired by contact with nanoparticles. Thus industry is challenged to apply this exciting new technology while protecting its workers and customers against the possibility of risks that aren't yet known.[93]

Who can meet such a challenge best? As you've read, technological change is a central part of the changing landscape, and competition often arises between newcomers and established companies.

All things considered, which should you and your firm do?

- Preserve old advantages or create new advantages?
- Lock in old markets or create new markets?
- Take the path of greatest familiarity or the path of greatest opportunity?
- Be only a benchmarker or a pathbreaker?
- Place priority on short-term financial returns or on making a real, long-term impact?
- Do only what seems doable or what is difficult and worthwhile?
- Change what is or create what isn't?
- Look to the past or live for the future?[94]

Shaping Your Own Future

If you are an organizational leader and your organization operates in traditional ways, your key goal should be to create a revolution, genetically reengineering your company before it becomes a dinosaur of the modern era.[95] What should be the goals of the revolution? You've been learning about them throughout this course.

But maybe you are not going to lead a revolution. Maybe you just want a successful career and a good life. You still must be able to choose and pursue long-term goals[96] and deal with an economic environment that is highly competitive and fast-moving.[97] Creating the future you want for yourself requires setting high personal standards. Don't settle for mediocrity; don't assume that good is necessarily good enough—for yourself or for your employer. Think about how not just to meet expectations but to exceed them; not merely to live with apparent constraints but break free of the unimportant, arbitrary, or imagined ones; and to seize opportunities instead of letting them pass by.[98]

> Look for positions that stretch you and for bosses who develop their protégés.

The most successful individuals take charge of their own development the way an entrepreneur takes charge of a business.[99] More specific advice from the leading authors on career management:[100] Consciously and actively manage your own career. Develop marketable skills and keep developing more. Make career choices based on personal growth, development, and learning opportunities. Look for positions that stretch you and for bosses who develop their protégés. Seek environments that provide training and the opportunity to experiment and innovate. And know yourself; assess your strengths and weaknesses, your true interests, and ethical standards. If you are not already thinking in these terms and taking commensurate action, you should start now.

Additionally, become indispensable to your organization. Be enthusiastic in your job and committed to doing great work, but don't be blindly loyal to one company. Be prepared to leave if necessary. View your job as an opportunity to prove what you can do and increase what you can do, not as a comfortable niche for the long term.[101] Go out on your own if it meets your skills and temperament.

This points out the need to maintain your options. More and more, contemporary careers can involve leaving behind a large organization and going entrepreneurial, becoming self-employed in the postcorporate world.[102] In such a career, independent individuals are free to make their own choices. They can flexibly and quickly respond to demands and opportunities. Developing start-up ventures, consulting, accepting temporary employment, doing project work for one organization and then another, working in professional partnerships, being a constant deal maker—these can be the elements of a successful career. Ideally, this self-employed model can help provide a balanced approach to working and to living life at home and with family because people have more control over their work activities and schedules.

This go-it-alone approach can sound ideal, but it also has downsides. Independence can be frightening, the future unpredictable. It can isolate road warriors who are always on the go, working from their cars and airports, and interfere with social and family life.[103]

Effective self-management is needed to keep career and family obligations in perspective and in control.

Coping with uncertainty and change is easier if you develop resilience. To become more resilient, practice thinking of the world as complex but full of opportunities; expect change, but see it as interesting and potentially rewarding, even if changing is difficult. Also, keep a sense of purpose, set priorities for your time, be flexible when facing uncertainty or a need to change, and take an active role in the face of change rather than waiting for change to happen to you.[104]

Learning and Leading

Continuous learning is a vital route to renewable competitive advantage.[105] People in your organization—and you, personally—should constantly explore, discover, and take action, as illustrated in Exhibit 18.9. With this approach, you can learn what is effective and what is not and adjust and improve accordingly. The philosophy of continuous learning helps your company achieve lower cost, higher quality, better service, superior innovation, greater sustainability, and greater speed—and helps you grow and develop on a personal level.

Commit to lifelong learning. Lifelong learning requires occasionally taking risks, moving outside your comfort zone, honestly assessing the reasons behind your successes and failures, asking for and listening to other people's information and opinions, and being open to new ideas.[106]

| **Commit to lifelong learning.**

EXHIBIT 18.9   Learning Cycle: Explore, Discover, Act

Explore
The first step is to explore current reality. The aim is to be as honest and open as possible about what is happening at present.

- Identify the problem/opportunity area.
- Check with the customers, suppliers, or other key stakeholders.
- Reveal hidden issues.
- Gather data.
- Look for root causes.
- Rethink the issue.

Act
Last but not least in the cycle is doing.

- Test solutions.
- Implement plan.
- Evaluate results.
- Celebrate success; recognize problems.

Discover
As people deepen their understanding of current reality, the issues and choices become clearer. They begin to see with new eyes.

- Identify possible solutions.
- Plan.
- Anticipate problems.

SOURCE: From *Leaning into the Future: Changing the Way People Change Organizations* by George Binney and Collin Williams; published by Nicholas Brealey Publishing Ltd., 1997. Reprinted by permission.

Level 5 Executive

Builds enduring greatness through a paradoxical blend of personal humility and professional will.

Level 4 Effective Leader

Catalyzes commitment to and vigorous pursuit of a clear and compelling vision, stimulating higher performance standards.

Level 3 Competent Manager

Organizes people and resources toward the effective and efficient pursuit of predetermined objectives.

Level 2 Contributing Team Member

Contributes individual capabilities to the achievement of group objectives and works effectively with others in a group setting.

Level 1 Highly Capable Individual

Makes productive contributions through talent, knowledge, skills and good work habits.

SOURCE: From *Good to Great.* Copyright © 2001 by Jim Collins. Reprinted from Jim Collins.

Through a career, a person can inhabit and grow through the hierarchy of stages illustrated in Exhibit 18.10 from Jim Collins's book *Good to Great.* The descriptions in the hierarchy suggest not only that you should do these things, but that you should do them well. Your first job may not include managerial responsibilities, but it will require you to be an individual contributor and probably to be part of a team. Level 3 is where managerial capabilities are required, whereas Level 4 distinguishes true leadership from competent management. Level 5 represents a leadership style that you read about briefly in Chapter 12, which combines strong will and determination with personal humility. The figure shows that Level 5 leadership represents a peak achievement, the ultimate contribution of a leader who can turn a good company into a great one.[107] You might ask yourself, What is my level now (or where will I be after graduation)? What do I aspire to? What have I learned to this point that can help me progress, and what do I need to learn to develop myself further?

A leader—and this could include you—should be able to create an environment in which "others are willing to learn and change so their organizations can adapt and innovate [and] inspire diverse others to embark on a collective journey of continual learning and leading."[108] Learning leaders exchange knowledge freely; commit to their own continuous learning as well as to others'; are committed to examining their own behaviors and defensiveness that may inhibit their learning; devote time to their colleagues, suspending their own beliefs while they listen thoughtfully; and develop a broad perspective, recognizing that organizations are an integrated system of relationships.[109]

Honored as one of the best management books of the year in Europe, *Learning into the Future* gets its title from a combination of the words *leading* and *learning*.[110] The two perspectives, on the surface, appear very different. But they are powerful and synergistic when pursued in complementary ways.

A successful future derives from adapting to the world *and* shaping the future; being responsive to others' perspectives *and* being clear about what you want to change; encouraging others to change *while* recognizing what you need to change about yourself; understanding current realities *and* passionately pursuing your vision; learning *and* leading.

Management in Action

WILL SHELL MOVE GRADUALLY TOWARD ENVIRONMENTALLY FRIENDLY POLICIES *AND* ACHIEVE ECONOMIC GROWTH?

Since its founding in 1907, Shell has adapted successfully to a myriad of external pressures. Today's challenges may be different. Many believe that current social, environmental, and political forces are combining in a way that will force disruptive change within Shell and the rest of the energy industry. Jeremy Leggett of the Carbon Tracker Initiative, a group that advises energy company investors, argues that "environmentally friendly policies and economic growth are not mutually exclusive."

The Carbon Tracker Initiative joins a chorus of other voices for change. Recently, the Norwegian sovereign wealth fund divested its shares in coal. Students at Edinburgh University convinced officials at the school to divest from three of the largest fossil fuel energy companies. Over 200 alumni (and parents) from Massachusetts Institute of Technology, Stanford University, Syracuse University, and other schools have diverted their post-graduation donations to a Multi-School Fossil Free Divestment Fund. The universities will receive the donations only if they divest their interests from fossil fuel companies. *The Guardian,* an international weekly newspaper, recently started a "Keep It in the Ground Campaign" that features 20 journalists who chronicle stories related to climate change. While recently discussing the environment, Pope Francis of the Catholic Church stated: "We are not faced with two separate crises, one environmental and the other social, but rather one complex crisis which is both social and environmental."

Are these forces from the macroenvironment (recall Chapter 2) sufficient to encourage Shell's top managers to move faster toward a more sustainable business strategy? It's unlikely. Shell CEO van Beurden concluded that Shell would be at the forefront of change but that it needed to find more oil in the short term to meet the demands of population growth and economic development in emerging markets. He commented further that in the second half of this century solar power would become dominant as a source of energy but the world would have to rely on oil and other traditional fuels in the meantime.

Time will tell if Shell's approach of delaying its shift toward greener energy was the correct one for investors and other stakeholders around the globe.[111]

— How much influence do external stakeholders like the ones mentioned above exert on Shell's top management?
— Do you think Shell should maintain its current pace of change or move faster toward greener energy technologies? Elaborate.

A Collaborative, Sustainable Future?

As you lead and learn into the future, we urge you to (1) bear in mind the long run, in addition to the immediate demands you must face, and (2) consider collaboration as a key to sustained success. At the outset of this chapter and throughout this book, you learned about many of today's big challenges. The good news is that new business models and new forms of collaboration are taking root, and others are waiting to be created.[112] Entrepreneurs with societal goals are driving new approaches to commerce. The private sector is tackling social and environmental issues, the public sector is enacting market-based approaches to delivering service, and nonprofits now pursue sustainable business models.

Business and tomorrow's leaders in every sector are vitally important for determining what the future will be. It would be naïve to think that, without more forward thinking and appropriate action, long-term considerations will overpower the many short-term pressures for immediate results. ("The Management in Action: Onward" spotlights this dilemma for oil companies like Shell.) And there still is the enduring controversy over the obligations of business. But a long-term focus and perspective, balanced with prudent financial considerations, is required to achieve sustainable financial success and the corporate purpose enduringly over time. It would be erroneous to assume that collaboration will replace competition. Competition has upsides and downsides, and although new competitors enter every field, former competitors sometimes become collaborators. Certainly at local levels and sometimes at regional and global levels, multisector clusters of businesses, schools, universities, nonprofits, and governments are collaborating in mutually beneficial and effective ways. People are learning to work more effectively together—not just within but across organizations and sector boundaries—to produce new models for action that revitalize business and change the world.[113]

KEY TERMS

adapters, p. 589

force-field analysis, p. 582

genius of the *and*, p. 576

moving, p. 582

organization development (OD), p. 577

organizational ambidexterity, p. 576

performance gap, p. 582

proactive change, p. 589

reactive change, p. 589

refreezing, p. 583

shapers, p. 589

total organization change, p. 586

tyranny of the *or*, p. 575

unfreezing, p. 581

RETAINING WHAT YOU LEARNED

In Chapter 18, you learned what it takes to achieve world-class excellence. Sustaining greatness requires having strong core values and striving for continuous improvement, among other things. It is critical to believe that multiple important goals can be achieved simultaneously and synergistically. Effective change management occurs when organizations move from their current state to a desired future state. Some general reasons that people resist change include inertia, poor timing, surprise, and self-interest. Motivating people to change requires a general process of unfreezing, moving, and refreezing. Specific techniques to motivate people to change include education and communication, participation and involvement, facilitation and support, negotiation and rewards, manipulation and cooptation, and coercion. Each approach has strengths, weaknesses, and appropriate uses, and multiple approaches can be used. Effective change requires active leadership, including creating a sense of urgency, forming a guiding coalition, developing a vision and strategy, and other actions. You can proactively forge the future by being a shaper more than an adapter, creating new competitive advantages, actively managing your career and your personal development, and becoming an active leader and a lifelong learner.

LO 1 Discuss what it takes to be world class.

- You should strive for world-class excellence, which means using the very best and latest knowledge and ideas to operate at the highest standards of any place anywhere.
- Sustainable greatness comes from, among other things, having strong core values, living those values constantly, striving for continuous improvement, experimenting, and always trying to do better tomorrow than today.
- It is essential not to fall prey to the tyranny of the *or*—that is, the belief that one important goal can be attained only at the expense of another. The genius of the *and* is that multiple important goals can be achieved simultaneously and synergistically.

LO 2 Describe how to manage and lead change effectively.

- Effective change management occurs when the organization moves from its current state to a desired future state without excessive cost to the organization or its people.
- People resist change for a variety of reasons, including inertia, poor timing, surprise, peer pressure, self-interest, misunderstanding, different information about (and assessments of) the change, and management's tactics.
- Motivating people to change requires a general process of unfreezing, moving, and refreezing, with the caveat that appropriate and not inappropriate behaviors be refrozen.
- More specific techniques to motivate people to change include education and communication, participation and involvement, facilitation and support, negotiation and rewards, manipulation and cooptation, and coercion. Each approach has strengths, weaknesses, and appropriate uses, and multiple approaches can be used. It is important to harmonize the multiple changes that are occurring throughout the organization.
- Effective change requires active leadership, including creating a sense of urgency, forming a guiding coalition, developing a vision and strategy, communicating the change vision, empowering broad-based action, generating short-term wins, consolidating gains and producing more change, and anchoring the new approaches in the culture.

LO 3 Describe strategies for creating a successful future.

- Preparing for an uncertain future requires a proactive approach.
- You can proactively forge the future by being a shaper more than an adapter, creating new competitive advantages, actively managing your career and your personal development, and becoming an active leader and a lifelong learner.

DISCUSSION QUESTIONS

1. Why do some people resist the goal of becoming world class? How can this resistance be overcome?

2. Generate specific examples of world-class business that you have seen as a consumer. Also, generate examples of poor business practice. Why and how do some companies inspire world-class practices while others do not?

3. How might blogging and other social forms of communication via social media affect the process of managing change? What are the professional and career implications of blogging for you?

4. Generate and discuss examples of problems and opportunities that have inspired change, both in businesses and in you personally.

5. Review the methods for dealing with resistance to change. Generate specific examples of each that you have seen and analyze why they worked or failed to work.

6. Choose some specific types of changes you would like to see happen in groups or organizations with which you are familiar. Imagine that you were to try to bring about these changes. What sources of resistance should you anticipate? How would you manage the resistance?

7. Develop a specific plan for becoming a continuous learner.

8. In your own words, what does the idea of creating the future mean to you? How can you put this concept to good use? Again, generate some specific ideas that you can really use.

9. In what ways do you think the manager's job will be different in 20 years from what it is today? How can you prepare for that future?

EXPERIENTIAL EXERCISES

18.1   OVERCOMING RESISTANCE TO CHANGE

OBJECTIVE

To learn how to overcome resistance to change.

INSTRUCTIONS

Refer back to Exhibit 18.5 on page 583 and the different ways to manage resistance to change. Next, think about the last time you tried to introduce a new idea or way of doing things at work, school, or some other organization. Describe the new idea and which approach(es) you used to overcome others' resistance to trying out the new idea.

RESISTANCE TO CHANGE WORKSHEET

Describe a new idea you tried to introduce at work, school, or some other organization:

_____

_____

_____

_____

Which (if any) of the following approaches to overcoming resistance to change did you use? (Please check all that apply)

_____Education and communication   _____Negotiation and rewards

_____Participation and involvement   _____Manipulation and cooptation

_____Facilitation and support   _____Explicit and coercion

What was the outcome? To what degree were you successful in overcoming the resistance to change? Explain.

_____

_____

_____

If you could go back in time, would you use a different approach to overcome the resistance to your new idea? Why or why not?

_____

_____

_____

18.2   NETWORKING SCENARIOS

1. Working on your own, develop a networking strategy for the following three scenarios. (10 min.)

2. Working with your partner or small group, collaborate on identifying the best strategy for dealing with each of the three scenarios. Each group should develop one best strategy for each scenario. (20 min.)

3. Each group reports, sharing its best strategies for each of the three scenarios (or at least one if not enough time is available). (2–3 min. per group per strategy)

4. The large group or class engages in discussion, using the questions at the end. (10 min.)

SCENARIOS

I. You are running for student government president. What steps would you take to make your candidacy a success?

1. _____

2. _____

3. _____

4. _____

5. _____

6. _____

II. You are in an internship and are interested in becoming a permanent full-time employee at the organization. What people would you approach and what steps could you take to obtain an offer?

1. _____

2. _____

3. _____

4. _____

5. _____

6. _____

III. You just moved to a new community, and your company's business growth relies heavily on referrals. How do you make contacts in a place where you don't know anyone? How can you build a client base?

1. _____

2. _____

3. _____

4. _____

5. _____

6. _____

QUESTIONS

1. What was difficult about this exercise?

2. What creative means were devised to build networks of contacts in these scenarios?

3. Which of these ideas would be easy to implement? Which would be difficult? What makes some strategies easier to do than others?

4. What personal qualities are needed actually to use these strategies?

5. How can someone who is shy about approaching new people use (some or all of) these strategies successfully?

6. What did you learn about yourself and others from this exercise?

SOURCE: Suzanne C. de Janasz, Karen O'Dowd, and Beth Z. Schneider, *Interpersonal Skills in Organizations*, McGraw-Hill/Irwin, 2002, p. 212. © 2002 The McGraw-Hill Companies. Reprinted with permission.

CONCLUDING CASE

EATWELL TECHNOLOGIES

Cristina Muñoz and P. R. (Pete) Prakash started EatWell Technologies as a result of conversations they held while they were graduate students in bioengineering. Both scientists were interested in how to develop crops offering superior nutrition in developing countries, and both believe that business innovation can and should drive social change. They focused their research on a genetically modified strain of rice that is drought tolerant and high in vitamin A and iron. Upon completing their studies, they wrote a business plan and formed EatWell Technologies to commercialize their new rice. Their aim was to sell first in Africa, where nutrition is an urgent problem and the potential for economic development presents huge opportunities for business. They selected Nigeria as their first target market.

Working through the government and with nongovernmental development organizations and local farmers, Cristina and Pete established a reputation for integrity and a desirable product. As farmers began purchasing their rice, the two owners hired research assistants, office staff, and sales representatives. They began to enjoy modest profits and started paying themselves a monthly salary—far from what they could earn as scientists in a large corporation but enough to live on. They began discussing what products to offer next. Cristina suggested they develop improved leafy greens to provide variety in local diets; Pete was inclined to add new strains of rice, their area of greatest knowledge.

The two entrepreneurs also realized that as their venture grew, it needed management expertise beyond their skills as scientists. They hired an experienced office manager, and the office staff appreciated her tactful guidance. They also interviewed Bill Jensen, a retired vice president of a community bank. Bill was impressed with the company's mission and thought an interesting retirement project would be to help EatWell become financially stronger. Pete, Cristina, and Bill reached an agreement by which Bill would become a third partner in exchange for investing $450,000. The partners met daily, and Bill helped the scientists track cash flow, choose suppliers, and meet experts who can help the business expand into new markets.

At one of their strategy meetings, Pete and Cristina agreed it is time to settle on the direction for product development: Will EatWell be a rice company, or should it diversify into green vegetables? Bill surprised them with a few PowerPoint slides about his idea. Bill pointed out that rice and leafy greens are commodities, and EatWell will never get much of a return from investing in commodities. Instead, he pointed out the value of the rice as a brand. Imagine where EatWell could go by incorporating the rice into other products, such as energy bars and breakfast cereal. They could go beyond farming into the cities and sell to Africa's rapidly growing middle class, who could pay a premium. They could even start paying themselves salaries in line with their expertise and the risks they took on by forming the company. Pete and Cristina were shocked. From their viewpoint, Bill had lost sight of the company's purpose.

DISCUSSION QUESTIONS

1. Review the first section of the chapter, about becoming world class. How can EatWell Technologies fulfill its social mission and be profitable?

2. In this case, where do you see resistance to change? How can leaders overcome the resistance? How should they?

3. Suppose you are coaching Pete and Cristina. What advice would you give them about shaping their future?

PART FIVE   SUPPORTING CASE

Technology Helps Dollar General Remain Competitive

More and more consumers determined to save money are winding up at deep-discount retailers popularly known as dollar stores. These relatively small stores—including Dollar General, Family Dollar, and Dollar Tree—offer food, clothing, and household items at deep discounts. Discounters such as Target and Walmart offer a wider selection, but more consumers are trading down to find the best possible prices.

Competing with Walmart on price is hardly an easy strategy. When Kathleen Guion took charge of store operations and store development for Dollar General, she got to work initiating a whole host of changes. Many of these were aimed at controlling costs and helping the stores run more efficiently, and many of the changes involved improving the technology used by store employees, bringing it more in line with industry standards.

Guion found that Dollar General used some truly low-tech approaches to activities involved in running the stores. When trucks pulled up with deliveries, for example, store employees pulled cartons out of the truck one by one and carried them into the store for stocking the shelves. And whenever items languished on shelves too long, the same employees would repack them in boxes and carry them into the back room for storage. Not only were these methods

slow, but employees hated lugging the boxes around. Calling her change program EZ Store, Guion simplified those jobs. She bought large wheeled bins called rolltainers, which employees use to move products from the trucks to back rooms to the sales floor. And when products don't sell as expected, the EZ Store plan calls for marking down the price low enough that the products do get sold. Not only does EZ Store make working for Dollar General more enjoyable by eliminating undesirable chores, but the greater efficiency gives employees more time to serve customers.

Under Guion's direction, Dollar General also upgraded its computer systems to deliver better information faster. The company introduced handheld scanners connected to an inventory management system so employees can quickly and accurately see which items need to be replenished and when. Computers linked to headquarters have been installed in the back rooms of all the stores. (Surprising as it may sound, until 2009, headquarters sent messages to stores via postal mail.) The company introduced computer-based training programs to improve employees' skills, as well as software for screening job candidates to identify which of them have qualities associated with success. And to reduce thefts in the stores, the company installed closed-circuit television systems.

Managers also have been given better technology. Dollar General bought district managers personal computers with software that monitors performance and flags exceptions to standards. It also gave them BlackBerry handheld devices so they can keep in touch with their people and keep up to date on store performance while they travel. The technology has enabled Dollar General to widen the district managers' span of control because fewer managers can keep up with more stores. More efficient management, in turn, has supported the company's program of rapidly opening new stores. (It now has more than 12,000 in 43 states).

These efficiency improvements are essential for remaining successful in the changing deep-discount retailing industry. Recently, Dollar General's competitor Dollar Tree surprised industry observers by announcing that it would be purchasing Family Dollar for nearly $9 billion. This new entity (it'll keep both brands) will be larger than Dollar General in both sales and number of stores. In response to the move, Dollar General CEO Richard Dreiling has postponed his retirement to help the retailer adjust to the new competitive landscape. The company plans to open 730 additional stores in the next 12 months. As Dollar General tries to maintain profitability, it will keep looking for ways to change how it does business, and technology will continue to play a role in the solutions. So far, it's a strategy that has fueled tremendous growth at Dollar General even as other retailers are struggling to maintain sales volume.

QUESTIONS

1. What types of control are important at Dollar General? Why are these important?

2. What technological innovations did Kathleen Guion introduce at Dollar General? How did these innovations support the company's strategy?

3. What challenges would you have expected Guion to face in introducing these changes? What principles of managing change would you have suggested she apply?

SOURCES: Based on company website, "Dollar General Opens 12,000th Store," May 30, 2015, http://www.dollargeneral.com; P. Ziobro, "Dollar Tree Wins the Battle for Family Dollar," *The Wall Street Journal* (online), January 22, 2015, http://www.wsj.com; M. Townsend, "Family Dollar Holders Accept $8.81 Billion Dollar Tree Bid," *Bloomberg Business* (online), January 22, 2015, http://www.bloomberg.com; "Operational Improvements Benefit Employees, Customers," *MMR*, May 17, 2010, Business & Company Resource Center, http://galenet.galegroup.com; J. Jannarone, "Will Dollar General Lead Retailers into Battle?" *The Wall Street Journal*, June 6, 2011, http://online.wsj.com; A. Zimmerman, "Dollar Stores Find Splurges Drying Up," *The Wall Street Journal*, July 11, 2011, http://online.wsj.com; C. Burritt, "Dollar Stores: More Brands, More Customers," *Bloomberg Businessweek*, July 29, 2010, http://www.businessweek.com; M. Jarzemsky, "Dollar General's Earnings Gain 15%," *The Wall Street Journal*, June 1, 2011, http://online.wsj.com; Dollar General, "About Us," http://dollargeneral.com; and Dollar General, "Dollar General Announces Kathleen Guion, Division President of Store Operations and Store Development, Will Transition to Retirement," news release, July 25, 2011, http://newscenter.dollargeneral.com.

CASE INCIDENTS

Robot Repercussion

Victor Principal, vice president of industrial relations for General Manufacturing, Inc., sat in his office reviewing the list of benefits the company expected to realize from increasing its use of industrial robots. In a few minutes, he would walk down to the labor management conference room for a meeting with Ralph McIntosh, president of the labor union local representing most of the company's industrial employees. The purpose of this meeting would be to exchange views and positions informally preliminary to the opening for formal contract negotiations later in the month, which would focus on the use of computer-integrated robotics systems and the resulting impact on employment, workers, and jobs.

Experts concluded that the impact of robot installation on employment would be profound, although the extent of the worker replacement was not clear. The inescapable conclusion was that robot usage had the capacity to increase manufacturing performance and decrease manufacturing employment.

Principal walked down to the conference room. Finding McIntosh already there, Principal stated the company's position regarding installation of industrial robots: "The company needs the cooperation of the union and our workers. We don't wish to be perceived as callously exchanging human workers for robots." Then Principal listed the major advantages associated with robots: (1) improved quality of product as a result of the accuracy of robots; (2) reduced operating costs because the per-hour operational cost of robots was about one-third of the per-hour cost of wages and benefits paid to an average employee; (3) reliability improvements because robots work tirelessly and don't require behavioral support; and (4) greater manufacturing flexibility because robots are readily reprogrammable for different jobs. Principal concluded that these advantages would make the company more competitive, which would allow it to grow and increase its workforce.

McIntosh's response was direct and strong: "We aren't Luddites racing around ruining machines. We know it's necessary to increase productivity and that robotic technology is here. But we can't give the company a blank check. We need safeguards and protection." McIntosh continued, "We intend to bargain for the following contract provisions:

1. Establishment of labor–management committees to negotiate in advance about the labor impact of robotics technology and, of equal importance, to have a voice in deciding how and whether it should be used.

2. Rights to advance notice about installation of new technology.

3. Retraining rights for workers displaced, to include retraining for new positions in the plant, the community, or other company plants.

4. Spreading the work among workers by use of a four-day workweek or other acceptable plan as an alternative to reducing the workforce."

McIntosh's final sentence summed up the union's position: "We in the union believe the company is giving our jobs to robots to reduce the labor force."

Their meeting ended amiably, but Principal and McIntosh each knew that much hard bargaining lay ahead. As Principal returned to his office, the two opposing positions were obvious. On his yellow tablet, Principal listed the requirements as he saw them: (1) A clearly stated overall policy was needed to guide negotiation decisions and actions; (2) it was critical to decide on a company position regarding each of the union's announced demands and concerns; and (3) a plan had to be developed.

As Principal considered these challenges, he idly contemplated a robot possessing artificial intelligence and vision capability that could help him in his work. Immediately a danger alarm sounded in his mind. A robot so constructed might be more than helpful and might take over this and other important aspects of his job. Slightly chagrined, Principal returned to his task. He needed help—but not from any smart robot.

SOURCE: J. Champion and J. James, *Critical Incidents in Management: Decision and Policy Issues,* 6th ed. McGraw-Hill/Irwin, 1989. © 1989 The McGraw-Hill Companies.

Implementing Strategic Change

James Fulmer, chief executive officer of Allied Industries, reviewed three notes he had exchanged with Frank Curtis, director of fiscal affairs, now president of a company owned by Allied. The two executives were going to meet in a few minutes to discuss problems that had recently surfaced. During the past decade, Allied had aggressively pursued a growth objective based on a conglomerate strategy of acquiring companies in distress. CEO Fulmer's policy was to appoint a new chief operating officer for each acquisition with instructions to facilitate a turnaround. Fulmer reviewed two of the notes he had written to Curtis.

Date: January 15
Memorandum
To: Frank Curtis, Director of Fiscal Affairs, Allied Industries
From: James Fulmer, Chairman, Allied Industries
Subject: Your Appointment as President, Lee Medical Supplies

You are aware that Allied Industries recently acquired Lee Medical Supplies. Mr. John Lee, founder and president of the company, has agreed to retire, and I am appointing you to replace him. Our acquisitions group will brief you on the company, but I want to warn you that Lee Medical Supplies has a history of mismanagement. As a distributor of medical items, the company's sales last year totaled approximately $300 million, with net earnings of only $12 million. Your job is to make company sales and profits compatible with Allied standards. You are reminded that it is my policy to call for an independent evaluation of company progress and your performance as president after 18 months.

Date: September 10
Memorandum
To: Frank Curtis, President, Lee Medical Supplies
From: James Fulmer, Chairman, Allied Industries
Subject: Serious Problems at Lee Medical Supplies

In accord with corporate policy, consultants recently conducted an evaluation of Lee Medical Supplies. In a relatively short period of time, you have increased sales and profits to meet Allied's standards, but I am alarmed at other aspects of your performance. I am told that during the past 18 months, three of your nine vice presidents have resigned and that you have terminated four others. An opinion survey conducted by the consultants indicates that a low state of morale exists and that your managerial appointees are regarded by their subordinates as hard-nosed perfectionists obsessed with quotas and profits. Employees report that ruthless competition now exists between divisions, regions, and districts. They also note that the collegial, family-oriented atmosphere fostered by Mr. Lee has been replaced by a dog-eat-dog situation characterized by negative management attitudes toward employee feelings and needs. After you have studied the enclosed report from the consultants, we will meet to discuss their findings. I am particularly concerned with their final conclusion that "a form of corporate cancer seems to be spreading throughout Lee Medical Supplies."

As Fulmer prepared to read the third note, written by Frank Curtis, he reflected on his interview with the consultants. Although Fulmer considered Curtis a financial expert and a turnaround specialist, his subordinates characterized Curtis as an autocrat better suited to be a marine boot camp commander.

Date: September 28
Memorandum
To: James Fulmer
From: Frank Curtis
Subject: The So-Called Serious Problems at Lee Medical Supplies

I have received your memorandum dated September 10, and reviewed the consultants' report. When you appointed me to my present position, I was instructed to take over an unprofitable company and make it profitable. I have done so in 18 months, although I inherited a family-owned business that by your own admission had been mismanaged for years. I found a group of managers and salespeople with an average company tenure of 22 years. Mr. Lee had centralized all personnel decisions so that only he could terminate an employee. He tolerated mediocre performance. All employees were paid on a straight salary basis, with seniority the sole criterion for advancement. Some emphasis was given to increasing sales each year, but none was given to reducing costs and increasing profits. Employees did indeed find the company a fun place to work, and the feeling of being a part of a family did permeate the company. Such attitudes were, however, accompanied by mediocrity, incompetence, and poor performance.

I found it necessary to implement immediate strategic changes in five areas: the organization's structure, employee rewards and incentives, management information systems, allocation of resources, and managerial leadership style. As a result, sales areas were reorganized into divisions, regions and districts. Managers who I felt were incompetent and/or lacking in commitment to my objectives and methods were replaced. Unproductive and mediocre employees were encouraged to find jobs elsewhere. Authority for staffing and compensation decisions was decentralized to units at the division, region, and district levels. Managers of those units were informed that along with their authority went responsibility for reducing costs and for increasing sales and profits. Each unit was established as a profit center. A new department was established and charged with reviewing performance of those units. Improved accounting and control systems were implemented. A program was developed to establish standards and monitor performance. Performance appraisals are now required for all employees. To encourage more aggressive action, bonuses and incentives are offered to managers of units showing increased profits. A commission plan based on measurable sales and profit performances has replaced straight salaries. Resources are allocated to units based on their performance.

My own leadership style has probably represented the most traumatic change for employees. Internal competition is a formally mandated policy throughout the company. It has been responsible for much of the progress achieved to date. Progress, however, is never made without costs, and I recognize that employees are not having as much fun as in the past. I was employed to achieve results and not to ensure that employees remain secure and happy in their work. Don't let a few crybabies unable to adjust to changes lead you to believe that problems take precedence over profits. Does it mean that I am not people oriented if I believe it is unlikely that a spirit of aggressiveness and competitiveness can coexist with an atmosphere of cooperativeness and family orientation? Do you feel that we are obligated to employees because of past practices? Frankly, I thought I had your support to do whatever was necessary to get this company turned around. In our meeting, tell me if you think my approaches have been wrong and, if so, tell me what I should have done differently.

Just as Fulmer finished reviewing the third memorandum, his secretary informed him that Curtis had arrived for their scheduled meeting. He realized he was undecided about how to communicate to Curtis his ideas and beliefs regarding how changes in an organization can best be implemented. One thing he did know: He didn't appreciate how Curtis had expressed his views in his memorandum, but he recognized that he probably should set aside emotions and respond to the questions Curtis posed.

SOURCE: J. Champion and J. James, *Critical Incidents in Management: Decision and Policy Issues,* 6th ed. McGraw-Hill/Irwin, 1989. © 1989 The McGraw-Hill Companies.

Chapter 1

1. Morten T. Hansen, Herminia Ibarra, and Urs Peyer, "The Best-Performing CEOs in the World," *Harvard Business Review,* November 2014, http://hbr.org; "Amazon.com," *Bloomberg Businessweek,* January 23, 2014, http://www.bloomberg.com; Adam Lashinsky, "Amazon's Jeff Bezos: The Ultimate Disrupter," *Fortune,* November 16, 2012, http://management.fortune.cnn.com; Adam Hartung, "Why Jeff Bezos Is Our Greatest Living CEO," *Forbes,* January 8, 2013, http://www.forbes.com.

2. Hansen, Ibarra, and Peyer, "The Best-Performing CEOs."

3. G. Bensinger, "Groupon Spooks Investors with Wider Loss," *The Wall Street Journal,* August 5, 2014, http://online.wsj.com.

4. S. Green, F. Hassan, J. Immelt, M. Marks, and D. Meiland, "In Search of Global Leaders," *Harvard Business Review,* August 2003, pp. 38–45.

5. "World's Most Admired Companies," *Fortune* (online), accessed January 17, 2015, http://fortune.com/worlds-most-admired-companies/.

6. "Global 500," *Fortune* (online), accessed January 17, 2015, http://fortune.com/global500/.

7. GE Works—2013 Annual Report, accessed January 17, 2015, http://www.ge.com/ar2013/pdf/GE_AR13.pdf.

8. See company website, http://www.com/investors.faqs.asp, accessed January 17, 2015.

9. PepsiCo's 2013 Annual Report, accessed January 17, 2015, http://www.pepsico.com/Assets/Download/PEP_Annual_Report_2013.pdf.

10. T. Bisoux, "Corporate Counter Culture," *BizEd,* November/December 2004, pp. 16–20, quoted on p. 19.

11. G. Huber, *The Necessary Nature of Future Firms* (Thousand Oaks, CA: Sage, 2004).

12. "The Expanding Role of Mobility in the Workforce," A Custom Technology Adoption Profile Commissioned by Cisco Systems, Forrester Research Inc., February 2012, http://www.cisco.com; Jay Greene and Cliff Edwards, "Desktops Are So Twentieth Century," *BusinessWeek,* December 8, 2006, http://www.businessweek.com.

13. F. Cairncross, *The Company of the Future* (Cambridge, MA: Harvard Business School Press, 2002).

14. Jessi Hempel, "Web 2.0: The Party's Over," *Fortune,* June 1, 2010, http://tech.fortune.cnn.com.

15. "Web 1.0 vs. Web 2.0 vs. Web 3.0 vs. Web 4.0 vs. Web 5.0; A Bird's Eye on the Evolution and Definition," Flatworldbusiness.com, accessed January 17, 2015.

16. Robert Austin, "Managing Knowledge Workers," *Science,* July 21, 2006, accessed at ScienceCareers.org, http://sciencecareers.sciencemag.org.

17. David Raths, "Hospital IT Departments Prescribe Portals for Physicians," *KMWorld,* February 2007, downloaded from Business & Company Resource Center, http://galenet.galegroup.com.

18. M. Hansen and B. von Oetinger, "Introducing T-Shaped Managers: Generation," *Harvard Business Review,* March 2001, pp. 106–16.

19. John Teresko, "Toyota's Real Secret," *Industry Week,* February 2007, downloaded from Business & Company Resource Center, http://galenet.galegroup.com.

20. P. Taylor, *The Next America* (New York: Public Affairs & Pew Research Center, 2014).

21. Shelly Banjo, "Firms Take Online Reviews to Heart," *The Wall Street Journal,* July 29, 2012, http://online.wsj.com.

22. S. Vozza, "How to Turn a Bad Review into a Great Opportunity," *Fast Company,* accessed January 17, 2015, http://www.fastcompany.com.

23. G. Satell, "A Look Back at Why Blockbuster Really Failed and Why It Didn't Have To," *Forbes,* September 5, 2014, http://www.forbes.com.

24. "Home and Abroad," *The Economist,* February 10, 2007, Business & Company Resource Center, http://galenet.galegroup.com; A. Wooldridge, "The World Turned Upside Down," *The Economist,* April 17, 2010, pp. 1–3.

25. Neal E. Boudette, "New U.S. Car Plants Signal Renewal for Manufacturing," *The Wall Street Journal,* January 26, 2012, http://online.wsj.com.

26. Fortune's Most Admired Companies (Innovation), http://fortune.com/worlds-mostadmired-companies/, accessed January 24, 2015.

27. Laura Landro, "Hospitals Take Consumers' Advice," *The Wall Street Journal,* February 7, 2007, http://online.wsj.com.

28. O. Port, "The Kings of Quality," *BusinessWeek,* August 30, 2004, p. 20.

29. Karla Ward, "Attracting Opposites," *Lexington Herald-Leader,* December 12, 2006; and Lisa McTigue Pierce, "How to Do It 'My Way,'" *Food & Drug Packaging,* January 2007, both downloaded from Business & Company Resource Center, http://galenet.galegroup.com.

30. D. A. Garvin, "Manufacturing Strategic Planning," *California Management Review,* Summer 1993, pp. 85–106.

31. Bureau of Labor Statistics, "Projections Overview," *Occupational Outlook Handbook,* March 29, 2012, http://www.bls.gov.

32. Sherri Begin, "The Art of Service," *Crain's Detroit Business,* February 12, 2007, downloaded from Business & Company Resource Center, http://galenet.galegroup.com.

33. Adam Lashinsky, "Chaos by Design," *Fortune,* October 2, 2006, http://money.cnn.com.

34. Teresko, "Toyota's Real Secret."

35. Ibid.

36. Gary McWilliams, "Wal-Mart's Radio-Tracked Inventory Hits Static," *The Wall Street Journal,* February 15, 2007, http://online.wsj.com.

37. Kris Maher, "Wal-Mart Seeks New Flexibility in Worker Shifts," *The Wall Street Journal,* January 3, 2007, http://online.wsj.com.

38. S. Cendrowski, "Singapore Airlines," *Fortune,* June 14, 2010, p. 22.

39. F. Gillette, "The Duke of Discomfort," *Bloomberg Businessweek,* September 6, 2010, pp. 58–61.

40. C. Kitching, "No More Mr. Meanie!" *Daily Mail,* October 30, 2014, http://www.dailymail.co.uk.

41. J. Pfeffer, "Building Sustainable Organizations: The Human Factor," *Academy of Management Perspectives* 24 (2010), pp. 34–45.

42. S. L. Hart, *Capitalism at the Crossroads,* 3rd ed. (Upper Saddle River, NJ: Wharton School Publishing, 2010).

43. P. Bisson, E. Stephenson, and S. P. Vigueire, "Global Forces: An Introduction," *McKinsey Quarterly,* June 2010, pp. 1–4.

44. Hansen, Ibarra, and Peyer, "The Best-Performing CEOs," p. 90.

45. B. Dumaine, "Searching for Profits in Patagonia," *Fortune,* March 21, 2011, pp. 97–105.

46. B. Doppelt, *Leading Change toward Sustainability* (Sheffield, UK: Greenleaf, 2010).

47. J. Smith, "The World's Most Sustainable Companies of 2014," *Forbes,* January 22, 2015, http://www.forbes.com.

48. R. Branson and P. Polman, "Fight Climate Change, Make Money," CNN (online), February 19, 2015, http://www.cnn.com; F. Harvey, "Richard Branson Leads Call to Free Global Economy from Carbon Emissions," *The Guardian,* February 5, 2015, http://www.theguardian.com; Organization website, B-Team, http://bteam.org, accessed February 23, 2015; Conference website, Conference of Parties, http://www.cop21.org, accessed February 23, 2015; B. Upbin, "Davos Dispatch: Richard Branson and The B Team Make Business Case for Human Rights," *Forbes* (online), January 22, 2014, http://www.forbes.com; IPCC, 2014: Summary for Policymakers. In: *Climate Change 2014: Mitigation of Climate Change.* Contribution of Working Group III to the Fifth Assessment Report of the Intergovernmental Panel on Climate Change [O., Edenhofer, R. Pichs-Madruga, Y. Sokona, E. Farahani, S. Kadner, K. Seyboth, A. Adler, I. Baum, S. Brunner, P. Eickemeier, B. Kriemann, J. Savolainen, S. Schlo ̈mer, C. von Stechow, T. Zwickel, and J.C. Minx (eds.)]. Cambridge University Press, Cambridge, United Kingdom and New York, NY, USA; and "OECD Environmental Outlook to 2050: The Consequences of Inaction," OECD, 2012, http://www.oecd.org, accessed February 26, 2015.

49. Vanessa Fuhrmans, "A Novel Plan Helps Hospital Wean Itself off Pricey Tests," *The Wall Street Journal,* January 12, 2007, http://online.wsj.com.

50. J. W. Cortada, *21st Century Business* (London: Financial Times/Prentice Hall, 2001).

51. D. Lepak, K. Smith, and M. S. Taylor, "Value Creation and Value Capture: A Multilevel Perspective," *Academy of Management Review* 23 (2007), pp. 180–94.

52. R. Webber, "General Management Past and Future," *Financial Times Mastering Management,* 1997.

53. Lashinsky, "Amazon's Jeff Bezos"; Debbie Hazel, "Retail's Power Players," Chain Store Age, January 2013, *Business Insights: Essentials,* http://bi.galegroup.com; Matt Warman, "Amazon: Don't Blame Us for the Revolution on the High Street," *Telegraph* (London), October 12, 2012, Business Insights: Essentials, http://bi.galegroup.com.

54. M. Menz, "Functional Top Management Team Members: A Review, Synthesis, and Research Agenda," *Journal of Management* 38 (2012) pp. 45–80.

55. D. Kreeger, "Is Your Organization Positioned to Meet the Challenge of Climate Change?" *World Climate Change Report,* October 22, 2009, pp. 1–7.

56. C. Ren and C. Guo, "Middle Managers' Strategic Role in the Corporate Entrepreneurial Process: Attention-Based Effects," *Journal of Management* 37 (2011) pp. 1586–1610.

57. A. Raes, M. Heijltjes, U. Glunk, et al., "The Interface of the Top Management Team and Middle Managers: A Process Model," *Academy of Management Review* 36 (2011), pp. 102–126.

58. Q. N. Huy, "In Praise of Middle Managers," *Harvard Business Review,* September 2001, pp. 72–79.

59. L. A. Hill, "New Manager Development for the 21st Century," *Academy of Management Executive,* August 2004, pp. 121–26.

60. C. Bartlett and S. Goshal, "The Myth of the Generic Manager: New Personal Competencies for New Management Roles," *California Management Review* 40, no. 1 (1997), pp. 92–116.

61. L. R. Sayles, "Doing Things Right: A New Imperative for Middle Managers," *Organizational Dynamics,* Spring 1993, pp. 5–14.

62. H. Mintzberg, *The Nature of Managerial Work* (New York: Harper & Row, 1973).

63. R. Katz, "Skills of an Effective Administrator," *Harvard Business Review* 52 (September–October), pp. 90–102.

64. Hill, "New Manager Development for the 21st Century."

65. H. Mintzberg, "The Manager's Job: Folklore and Fact," *Harvard Business Review* 53 (July–August 1975), pp. 49–61.

66. "Nontraditional Path: From Pre-Med Dropout to Next Aetna CEO," *DiversityInc.,* October 28, 2010, http://diversityinc.com; and Aetna, "Executive Biographies: Mark T. Bertolini," About Us: Corporate Profile, http://www.aetna.com, accessed February 25, 2011.

67. Hill, "New Manager Development for the 21st Century."

68. D. Goleman, R. Boyatzis, and A. McKee, *Primal Leadership: Realizing the Power of Emotional Intelligence* (Boston: Harvard Business School Press, 2002).

69. J. Antonakis, N. Ashkanasy, and M. Dasborough, "Does Leadership Need Emotional Intelligence?" *Leadership Quarterly* 20 (2009), pp. 247–261; E. A. Locke, "Why Emotional Intelligence Is an Invalid Concept," *Journal of Organizational Behavior* 26 (2005), pp. 425–431; F. Walter, M. Cole, and R. Humphrey, "Emotional Intelligence Sine Qua Non of Leadership or Folderol?" *Academy of Management Perspectives* (2011), pp. 45–49.

70. R. Boyatzis, "Get Motivated," *Harvard Business Review,* January 2004, p. 30.

71. W. George, "Find Your Voice," *Harvard Business Review,* January 2004, p. 35.

72. Stephen Xavier, "Control Yourself: What Role Does Emotional Intelligence Play in Executive Leadership?" *US Business Review,* March 2006, downloaded from Business & Company Resource Center, http://galenet.galegroup.com.

73. Ibid.

74. W. Kiechel III, "A Manager's Career in the New Economy," *Fortune,* April 4, 1994, pp. 68–72.

75. K. Inkson and M. B. Arther, "How to Be a Successful Career Capitalist," *Organizational Dynamics,* Summer 2001, pp. 48–60.

76. A. Ericsson, M. Prietula, and E. Cokely, "The Making of an Expert," *Harvard Business Review,* July–August, 2007, http://www.hbr.org; Geoffrey Colvin, "What It Takes to Be Great," *Fortune,* October 19, 2006, http://money.cnn.com.

77. L. M. Roberts, J. Dutton, G. Spreitzer, E. Heaphy, and R. Quinn, "Composing the Reflected Best-Self Portrait: Building Pathways for Becoming Extraordinary in Work Organizations," *Academy of Management Review* 30 (2005), pp. 712–36.

78. L. M. Roberts, "Changing Faces: Professional Image Construction in Diverse Organizational Settings," *Academy of Management Review* 30 (2005), pp. 685–711.

79. M. E. P. Seligman, *Authentic Happiness: Using the New Positive Psychology to Realize Your Potential for Lasting Fulfillment* (New York: Free Press, 2002).

80. E. W. Morrison, "Newcomers' Relationships: The Role of Social Network Ties during Socialization," *Academy of Management Journal* 45 (2002), pp. 1149–60.

81. R. Cotton, Y. Shen, and R. Llvne-Tarandach, "On Becoming Extraordinary: The Content and Structure of the Developmental Networks of Major League Baseball Hall of Famers," *Academy of Management Journal* 54 (2011), pp. 15–46.

82. P. Adler and S. Kwon, "Social Capital: Prospects for a New Concept," *Academy of Management Review* 27 (2002), pp. 17–40.

83. C. Conner, "New Research: 2014 LinkedIn User Trends (and 10 Top Surprises)," *Forbes,* May 4, 2014, http://www.forbes.com.

84. Jessi Hempel, "How LinkedIn Will Fire Up Your Career," *Fortune,* April 12, 2010, pp. 74–82; C. Galunic, G. Ertug, and M. Gargiulo, "The Positive Externalities of Social Capital: Benefiting from Senior Brokers," *Academy of Management Journal* 55 (2012), pp. 1213–31.

85. T. Peters, *Liberation Management* (New York: Alfred A. Knopf, 1992).

86. P. Drucker, "What Makes an Effective Executive?" *Harvard Business Review,* June 2004, pp. 58–63.

87. "Relentless.com: Amazon," *The Economist,* June 21, 2014, http://www.economist.com.

88. Lashinsky, "Amazon's Jeff Bezos"; Hazel, "Retail's Power Players"; Erika Andersen, "How the Best Leaders Are Kicking Everyone Else's . . . Results," *Forbes,* February 11, 2013, http://www.forbes.com.

Appendix A

1. C. George, *The History of Management Thought* (Englewood Cliffs, NJ: Prentice-Hall, 1972).

2. Ibid.

3. A. D. Chandler, *Scale and Scope: The Dynamic of Industrial Capitalism* (Cambridge, MA: Belknap Press of Harvard University Press, 1990).

4. Ibid.

5. J. Baughman, *The History of American Management* (Englewood Cliffs, NJ: Prentice Hall, 1969), chap. 1.

6. George, *The History of Management Thought,* chaps. 5–7; F. Taylor, *The Principles of Scientific Management* (New York: Harper & Row, 1911).

7. J. Case, "A Company of Business people," *Inc.,* April 1993, pp. 70–93.

8. J. Schlosser and E. Florian, "Fortune 500 Amazing Facts!" *Fortune,* April 2004, pp.

9. H. Fayol, *General and Industrial Management,* trans. C. Storrs (Marshfield, MA: Pitman Publishing, 1949).

10. George, *The History of Management Thought,* chap. 9; J. Massie, "Management Theory," in *Handbook of Organizations,* ed. J. March (Chicago: Rand McNally, 1965), pp. 387–422.

11. C. Barnard, *The Functions of the Executive* (Cambridge, MA: Harvard University Press, 1938).

12. George, *The History of Management Thought*; Massie, "Management Theory."

13. E. Mayo, *The Human Problems of Industrial Civilization* (New York: Macmillan, 1933): F. Roethlisberger and W. Dickson, *Management and the Worker* (Cambridge, MA: Harvard University Press, 1939).

14. A. Maslow, "A Theory of Human Motivation," *Psychological Review* 50 (July 1943), pp. 370–96.

15. A. Carey, "The Hawthorne Studies: A Radical Criticism," *American Sociological Review* 32, no.3 (1967), pp. 403–16.

16. M. Weber, *The Theory of Social and Economic Organizations,* trans. T. Parsons and A. Henderson (New York: Free Press, 1947).

17. George, *The History of Management Thought,* chap. 11.

18. D. McGregor, *The Human Side of Enterprise* (New York: McGraw-Hill, 1960).

19. C. Argyris, *Personality and Organization* (New York: Harper & Row, 1957).

20. R. Likert, *The Human Organization* (New York: McGraw-Hill, 1967).

21. L. von Bertalanffy, "The History and Status of General Systems Theory," *Academy of Management Journal* 15 (1972), pp. 407–26; D. Katz and R. Kahn, *The Social Psychology of Organizations,* 2nd ed. (New York: John Wiley & Sons, 1978).

22. J. Thompson, *Organizations in Action* (New York: McGraw-Hill, 1967); J. Galbraith, *Organization Design* (Reading, MA: Addison-Wesley, 1977); D. Miller and P. Friesen, *Organizations: A Quantum View* (Englewood Cliffs, NJ: Prentice-Hall, 1984).

23. R. E. Wright, "Teaching History in Business Schools: An Insider's View," *Academy of Management Learning & Education* 9 (2010), pp. 697–700.

24. S. Cummings and T. Bridgman, "The Relevant Past: Why the History of Management Should Be Critical for Our Future," *Academy of Learning & Education* 10 (2011), pp. 77–93.

Chapter 2

1. H. Tsukayama, "Facebook's Profit Doubles on Strong Mobile Ad Growth," *The Washington Post,* July 23, 2014, http://www.washingtonpost.com; Farhad Manjoo, "The Great Tech War of 2012," *Fast Company,* October 19, 2011, http://www.fastcompany.com; Facebook, "Key Facts," Facebook Newsroom, http://newsroom.fb.com; Christopher Williams, "Is Facebook Really a Mobile Company?" *Telegraph* (London), January 31, 2013, Business Insights: Essentials, http://bi.galegroup.com; "Facebook's Flotation," *The Economist,* May 21, 2012, http://www.economist.com; "Live and Unplugged," *The Economist,* November 21, 2012, http://www.economist.com.

2. J. Fuller and M. C. Jensen, "Just Say No to Wall Street," *Journal of Applied Corporate Finance* 14, no. 4 (Winter 2002), pp. 41–46.

3. "Project Loon," *MIT Technology Review* (online), http://www.technologyreview.com/featuredstory/534986/project-loon/, accessed February 19, 2015.

4. J. Mouawad, "Oil Innovations Pump New Life into Old Wells," *The New York Times,* March 5, 2007, http://www.nytimes.com.

5. Marc Levinson, "Job Creation in the Manufacturing Revival," Congressional Research Service Report for Congress R41898, June 20, 2012, available at http://www.fas.org/sqp/crs/misc/R41898.pdf.

6. U.S. Department of Health and Human Services (DHHS), "Small Employers: Top Five Things to Know," HealthCare.gov, http://www.healthcare.gov; Internal Revenue Service (IRS), "Small Business Health Care Tax Credit for Small Employers," http://www.irs.gov; DHHS,

"Large Employers: Insurance and Tax Information," *HealthCare.gov,* http://www.healthcare.gov; IRS, "Affordable Care Act Tax Provisions," http://www.irs.gov; DHHS, "About the Law: Provisions of the Affordable Care Act, by Year," *HealthCare.gov,* http://www.healthcare; gov; Jen Wieczner, "Why Your Boss Is Dumping Your Wife," *MarketWatch,* February 22, 2013, http://www.marketwatch.com.

7. Bureau of Labor Statistics, news release, "Employment Projections—2012–22," December 19, 2013, http://www.bls.gov.

8. Bureau of Labor Statistics, Table A4: "Employment Status of the Civilian Population 25 Years and Over by Educational Attainment," February 6, 2015, http://www.bls.gov/spotlight.

9. C. Paullin, "The Aging Workforce: Leveraging the Talents of Mature Employees," SHRM Foundation's Effective Practice Guidelines Series, September 2013, http://www.shrm.org; "Flex Strategies to Attract, Engage, & Retain Older Workers," Innovative Practices: Executive Case Report No. 5, The Sloan Center on Aging & Work at Boston College, http://www.bc.edu, accessed February 17, 2015; M. Hamilton, "Age 65 and Not Ready or Able to Go," *The Washington Post,* January 14, 2007, http://www.washingtonpost.com.

10. See, for example, J. Wright, "America's Skilled Trades Dilemma: Shortages Loom As Most-In-Demand Group of Workers Ages," *Forbes,* March 7, 2013, http://www.forbes.com; B. Arnoldy, "Too Prosperous, Massachusetts Is Losing Its Labor Force," *Christian Science Monitor,* January 9, 2007, http://www.csmonitor.com.

11. Bureau of Labor Statistics, news release, "Foreign-Born Workers: Labor Force Characteristics—2013," May 22, 2014, http://www.bls.gov.

12. Bureau of Labor Statistics, "Women in the Labor Force: A Databook," Report 1049, May 2014, http://www.bls.gov/cps/wlf-databook-2013.pdf.

13. Ibid.

14. Company press release, "Deloitte Named a Top 10 Organization for Working Mothers for Sixth Consecutive Year," http://www2.deloitte.com, accessed February 19, 2015.

15. M. Esterl, "PepsiCo Expands Distribution of Stevia-Sweetened Cola," *The Wall Street Journal,* January 26, 2015, http://www.wsj.com; Michael M. Grynbaum, "Health Panel Approves Restriction on Sale of Large Sugary Drinks," *The New York Times,* September 13, 2012, http://www.nytimes.com; Mike Esterl, "Is This the End of the Soft-Drink Era?" *The Wall Street Journal,* January 18, 2013, http://online.wsj.com; Angela Hanson, "Middle of the Road," *Convenience Store News,* October 1, 2012, Business Insights: Essentials, http://bi.galegroup.com; Stephanie Strom, "PepsiCo, Shifting Aim, Sees Promise in Yogurt," *The New York Times,* July 8, 2012, http://www.nytimes.

com; Alan Richman, "Refreshing Revival," *International Food Ingredients,* Autumn 2012, Business Insights: Essentials, http://bi.galegroup.com.

16. Company website, http://www.terracycle.com, accessed February 27, 2015; E. Young, "Waste Not, Want Not—Making Money from Rubbish," *BBC News* (online), February 1, 2015, http://www.bbc.com; "Fertilizer Company Grows Profits with Zero Waste," *Yahoo Finance* (online), June 10, 2014, http://finance.yahoo.com.

17. T. Webb, "BP to Cut Production Amid Impact of Deepwater Horizon Spill," *The Observer,* January 30, 2011, http://www.guardian.co.uk; "The Shores of Recovery," *The Economist,* April 23, 2011, Business & Company Resource Center, http://galenet.galegroup.com; C. Prentice, "Doing Business on the Gulf Coast, Post-Spill," *Bloomberg Businessweek,* April 19, 2011, http://www.businessweek.com; and Suzanne Goldenberg, "Justice Department Deal Reduces BP's Deepwater Horizon Fine by $3.4 Billion," *Guardian* (London), February 20, 2013, http://www.guardian.co.uk.

18. Esterl, "Is This the End of the Softdrink Era?"; "Cola Wars, Continued: Good for You, Not for Shareholders," *The Economist,* March 17, 2012, http://www.economist.com; Alan Rappeport, "Pepsi Calls for Ceasefire in Cola Wars," *Financial Times,* April 30, 2012, http://www.ft.com.

19. "Cola Wars, Continued"; Rappeport, "Pepsi Calls for Ceasefire."

20. Company press release, "PepsiCo and Theo Muller Group Open Muller Quaker Dairy Yogurt Manufacturing Facility," June 3, 2013, http://www.mullerquaker.com.

21. "Martha C. White, "Coke and Pepsi May Be Readying Another Cola War," *NBC News,* February 14, 2012, http://www.nbcnews.com.

22. D. J. Collis and C. A. Montgomery, *Corporate Strategy: Resources and Scope of the Firm* (New York: McGraw-Hill/Irwin, 1997).

23. G. Rich, "Novartis Joins Pfizer, Merck, AstraZeneca in Layoffs," *Investors Business Daily,* January 13, 2012, http://news.investors.com.

24. Strom, "PepsiCo, Shifting Aim"; Esterl, "Is This the End of the Soft-Drink Era?"

25. PepsiCo website, http://www.pepsico.com; Strom, "PepsiCo, Shifting Aim."

26. Danielle Kucera, "Inkling Builds a Better (and Pricier) E-Book," *Bloomberg Businessweek,* February 12, 2013, http://www.businessweek.com.

27. Richman, "Refreshing Revival."

28. Adapted from H. L. Lee and C. Billington, "The Evolution of Supply-Chain-Management Models and Practice at Hewlett-Packard," *Interfaces* 25, no. 5 (September–October 1995), pp. 42–63. See also Edward W. Davis and Robert E. Spekman, *The Extended Enterprise:*

Gaining Competitive Advantage through Collaborative Supply Chains (Upper Saddle River, NJ: Prentice Hall, 2004).

29. Company website, "Healthcare Supply Chain," http://www.ups.com, accessed February 19, 2015; M. Saenz and E. Revilla, "Creating More Resilient Supply Chains," *MIT Sloan Management Review,* Summer 2014, http://sloanreview. mit.edu.

30. Connie Bensen, "When Brand Advocates Become Employees: IdeaStorm PM Cy Jervis Shares Tips for Businesses," Dell Community: Social Business Connection, January 7, 2013, http:// en.community.dell.com.

31. B. McGrath, "7 Ways to Improve Your Social Media Engagement," *Social Media Examiner,* May 2, 2013, http://www. socialmediaexaminer.com.

32. Manjoo, "The Great Tech War of 2012"; Shayndi Raice, "Facebook Defends Ads as Quiet Period Ends," *The Wall Street Journal,* June 12, 2012, http://online. wsj.com; "Facebook: Search Me," *The Economist,* January 19, 2013, http://www. economist.com.

33. A. A. Buchko, "Conceptualization and Measurement of Environmental Uncertainty: An Assessment of the Miles and Snow Perceived Environmental Uncertainty Scale," *Academy of Management Journal* 37, no. 2 (April 1994), pp. 410–25.

34. A. F. Hagen, "Corporate Executives and Environmental Scanning Activities: An Empirical Investigation," *SAM Advanced Management Journal* 60, no. 2 (Spring 1995), pp. 41–47; R. L. Daft, "Chief Executive Scanning, Environmental Characteristics, and Company Performance: An Empirical Study," *Strategic Management Journal* 9, no. 2 (March/April 1988), pp. 123–39; and M. Yasai-Ardekani, "Designs for Environmental Scanning Systems: Tests of a Contingency Theory," *Management Science* 42, no. 2 (February 1996), pp. 187–204.

35. S. Ghoshal, "Building Effective Intelligence Systems for Competitive Advantage," *Sloan Management Review* 28, no. 1 (Fall 1986), pp. 49–58; and K. D. Cory, "Can Competitive Intelligence Lead to a Sustainable Competitive Advantage?" *Competitive Intelligence Review* 7, no. 3 (Fall 1996), pp. 45–55.

36. P. J. H. Schoemaker, "Multiple Scenario Development: Its Conceptual and Behavioral Foundation," *Strategic Management Journal* 14, no. 3 (March 1993), pp. 193–213.

37. R. R. Peterson, "An Analysis of Contemporary Forecasting in Small Business," *Journal of Business Forecasting Methods & Systems* 15, no. 2 (Summer 1996), pp. 10–12; and S. Makridakis. "Business Forecasting for Management: Strategic Business Forecasting," *International Journal of Forecasting* 12, no. 3 (September 1996), pp. 435–37.

38. R. A. D'Aveni, *Hypercompetition— Managing the Dynamics of Strategic Maneuvering* (New York: Free Press, 1994); and M. A. Cusumano, "Strategic Maneuvering and Mass-Market Dynamics: The Triumph of VHS over Beta," *Business History Review* 66, no. 1 (Spring 1992), pp. 51–94.

39. Model adapted from C. Zeithaml and V. Zeithaml, "Environmental Management: Revising the Marketing Perspective," *Journal of Marketing,* Spring 1984. Published by the American Marketing Association.

40. Strom, "PepsiCo, Shifting Aim."

41. P. Sikka, "Apple's App Store Earns 60% More Revenues Than Google Play," *Yahoo! Finance* (online), February 19, 2015, http://finance.yahoo.com; "iTunes App Store Now Has 1.2 Million Apps, Has Seen 75 Billion Downloads to Date," *Tech Crunch* (online) June 2, 2014, http:// techcrunch.com; L. Friedman, "The App Store Turns Five: A Look Back and Forward," *MacWorld,* July 8, 2013, http:// www.macworld.com.

42. A. Davis, "No Slowdown in Sight for 2014's M&A Frenzy," *Forbes* (online), June 24, 2014, http://www.forbes.com.

43. Company press release, "Sysco Reaches Agreement to Sell 11 US Foods Distribution Centers to Performance Food Group Contingent on Consummation of Sysco-US Foods Merger," February 2, 2015, http://investors.sysco.com, accessed February 20, 2015.

44. R. Miles and C. Snow, *Organizational Strategy, Structure, and Process* (New York: McGraw-Hill, 1978).

45. C. Zeithaml and V. Zeithaml, "Environmental Management: Revising the Marketing Perspective," *Journal of Marketing* 48 (Spring 1984), pp. 46–53.

46. Organization website (RED), http:// www.red.org/en/faq, accessed February 20, 2015.

47. K. Kennedy, M. Hoyer, and F. Schouten, "Some Top Medicare Beneficiaries Spend Heavily to Lobby," *USA Today* (online), April 29, 2014, http://www.usatoday.com.

48. W. P. Burgers, "Cooperative Strategy in High Technology Industries," *International Journal of Management* 13, no. 2 (June 1996), pp. 127–34; and J. E. McGee, "Cooperative Strategy and New Venture Performance: The Role of Business Strategy and Management Experience," *Strategic Management Journal* 16, no. 7 (October 1995), pp. 565–80.

49. A. Bluestein, L. Buchanan, M. Chafkin, J. Del Rey, A. Joyner, and R. McCarthy, "The Ultimate Business Tune-Up for Times Like These," *Inc.,* January 2009, http://www.inc.com.

50. Bureau of Labor Statistics, "Contingent and Alternative Employment Arrangements, February 2005," news release, July 27, 2005, http://www.bls. gov/cps/.

51. Tammy Erickson, "The Rise of the New Contract Worker," *Harvard Business Review,* September 7, 2012, http://blogs. hbr.org; Adecco, "2012 Job Market Perspectives," http://www.adeccousa.com; "Integrating Contingent Workers," *Baseline,* January 19, 2012, Business Insights: Essentials, http://bi.galegroup.com; and "Tech Talk," *Workforce Management,* August 1, 2012, Business Insights: Essentials, http://bi.galegroup.com.

52. M. B. Meznar, "Buffer or Bridge? Environmental and Organizational Determinants of Public Affairs Activities in American Firms," *Academy of Management Journal* 38, no. 4 (August 1995), pp. 975–96.

53. D. Lei, "Advanced Manufacturing Technology: Organizational Design and Strategic Flexibility," *Organization Studies* 17, no. 3 (1996), pp. 501–23; and J. W. Dean Jr. and S. A. Snell, "The Strategic Use of Integrated Manufacturing: An Empirical Examination," *Strategic Management Journal* 17, no. 6 (June 1996), pp. 459–80.

54. R. H. Kilmann, M. J. Saxton, and R. Serpa, *Gaining Control of the Corporate Culture* (San Francisco: Jossey-Bass, 1985); and K. S. Cameron and R. E. Quinn, *Diagnosing and Changing Organizational Culture: Based on the Competing Values Framework* (Englewood Cliffs, NJ: Addison-Wesley, 1998).

55. R. Fisman, "Even a Merger made in Heaven Can Get off to a Rocky Start," *Slate* (online), December 3, 2013, http:// www.slate.com.

56. C. Hymowitz, "In Deal-Making, Keep People in Mind," *The Wall Street Journal,* May 12, 2008, http://online.wsj.com.

57. Cameron and Quinn, *Diagnosing and Changing Organizational Culture.*

58. C. Groscurth, "Why Your Company Must Be Mission-Driven," *Gallup Business Journal,* March 6, 2014, http://www. gallup.com.

59. C. Gallo, "How Ritz-Carlton Maintains Its Mystique," *BusinessWeek,* February 13, 2007, http://www.businessweek.com.

60. R. Leifer and P. K. Mills, "An Information Processing Approach for Deciding upon Control Strategies and Reducing Control Loss in Emerging Organizations," *Journal of Management* 22, no. 1 (1996), pp. 113–37; S. A. Dellana and R. D. Hauser, "Toward Defining the Quality Culture," *Engineering Management Journal* 11, no. 2 (June 1999), pp. 11–15; and D. Cohen and L. Prusak, *In Good Company: How Social Capital Makes Organizations Work* (Cambridge, MA: Harvard Business School Press, 2001).

61. J. Koob, "Early Warnings on Culture Clash," *Mergers & Acquisitions,* July 1, 2006, Business & Company Resource Center, http://galenet.galegroup.com.

62. The Kennedy Group Ltd., "Culture vs. Climate," Kennedy Group Executive Strategies, http://thekennedygroup.com; R. L. Manning, "Development of the Psychological Climate Scale for Small Business," *Journal of New Business Ideas*

and Trends 8, no. 1 (2010), pp. 50–65; OCLC FirstSearch, http://newfirstsearch.org; and Grapevine Solutions, "Job Climate Surveys," http://www.grapevinesurvyes.com.

63. "Facebook's Focus at F8 Conference Shows Promise for Entrepreneurs," *Yahoo! Finance* (online), May 7, 2014, http://finance.yahoo.com; "Everything Facebook Announced at F8 2014 in One Handy List," *The Next Web* (online), April 30, 2014, http://thenextweb.com; S. Gibbs, "What Do Regular Facebook Users Need to Know About the F8 Conference?" *The Guardian,* May 1, 2014, http://www.theguardian.com.

64. Company website, https://www.facebook.com/business/a/online-sales/ad-targeting-details, accessed February 20, 2015.

Chapter 3

1. T. Reed, "Take a Look at American Airlines' New Boeing 787 Dreamliner," *Forbes* (online), January 25, 2015, http://www.forbes.com; I. Kottasova, "Are the Super Jumbo's Days Numbered?" *CNN Money* (online), December 11, 2014, http://money.cnn.com; Daniel Michaels, "Innovation Is Messy Business," *The Wall Street Journal,* January 24, 2013, http://online.wsj.com; Clive Irving, "How Boeings Dreamliner Was Grounded," *Daily Beast,* January 29, 2013, http://www.thedailybeast.com; and Jon Ostrower and Joann S. Lublin, "The Two Men behind the 787," *The Wall Street Journal,* January 24, 2013, http://online.wsj.com.

2. Ann Zimmerman, "The New Logistics of Christmas," *The Wall Street Journal,* December 13, 2012, http://online.wsj.com.

3. A. Ilyashov, "Michael Kors Taps Cathy Marie Robinson as SVP of Global Operations," *Fashion Week Daily* (online), May 12, 2014, http://fashionweekdaily.com.

4. M. Blenko, M. Mankins, and P. Rogers, "The Decision-Driven Organization," *Harvard Business Review,* June 2010, pp. 54–62.

5. M. Magasin and F. L. Gehlen, "Unwise Decisions and Unanticipated Consequences," *Sloan Management Review* 41 (1999), pp. 47–60.

6. M. McCall and R. Kaplan, *Whatever It Takes: Decision Makers at Work* (Englewood Cliffs, NJ: Prentice-Hall, 1985); and Luda Kopeikina, "The Elements of a Clear Decision," *MIT Sloan Management Review* 47 (Winter 2006), pp. 19–20.

7. B. Bass, *Organizational Decision Making* (Homewood, IL: Richard D. Irwin, 1983).

8. J. March, "Bounded Rationality, Ambiguity, and the Engineering of Choice," *Bell Journal of Economics* 9 (1978), pp. 587–608.

9. D. Messick and M. Bazerman, "Ethical Leadership and the Psychology of Decision Making," *Sloan Management Review* (Winter 1996), pp. 9–22.

10. I. Katz and B. Willis, "A CEO's Dilemma: When Is It Safe to Hire Again?" *Bloomberg Businessweek,* 2011. pp. 22–24.

11. Alex Taylor III, "The Greatest Business Decisions of All Time: Ford," *Fortune,* October 1, 2012, http://money.cnn.com/gallery/news/companies/2012/10/01/greatest-business-decisions.fortune/index.html.

12. Susumu Ogawa and Frank T. Piller, "Reducing the Risks of New Product Development," *MIT Sloan Management Review* 47 (Winter 2006), pp. 65–71.

13. McCall and Kaplan, *Whatever It Takes.*

14. Amy Barrett, "The Case for User Reviews," *Inc.*, September 1, 2010, http://www.inc.com.

15. Barrett, "The Case for User Reviews."

16. Q. Spitzer and R. Evans, *Heads, You Win! How the Best Companies Think* (New York: Simon & Schuster, 1997).

17. C. Gettys and S. Fisher, "Hypothesis Plausibility and Hypotheses Generation," *Organizational Behavior and Human Performance* 24 (1979), pp. 93–110.

18. E. R. Alexander, "The Design of Alternatives in Organizational Contexts: A Pilot Study," *Administrative Science Quarterly* 24 (1979), pp. 382–404.

19. Company website, https://www.pillpack.com; Company website, http://www.ideo.com/work/disrupting-the-drugstore.

20. A. R. Rao, M. E. Bergen, and S. Davis, "How to Fight a Price War," *Harvard Business Review,* March–April 2000, pp. 107–16.

21. Barrett, "The Case for User Reviews."

22. Ibid.

23. Rachel Emma Silverman, "Big Data Upends the Way Workers Are Paid," *The Wall Street Journal,* September 19, 2012, http://online.wsj.com.

24. Spitzer and Evans, *Heads, You Win!*

25. L. Bryan and D. Farrell, "Leading Through Uncertainty," *McKinsey Quarterly,* December 2008, http://www.mckinsey.com.

26. Barrett, "The Case for User Reviews."

27. McCall and Kaplan, *Whatever It Takes.*

28. E. Chhabra, "A Social Entrepreneur's Quandary: Nonprofit or For-Profit?" *The New York Times* (online), July 10, 2013, http://www.nytimes.com; E. Chhabra, "A Social Entrepreneur Transforms a Nonprofit into a Profit-Making Enterprise," *The New York Times* (online), July 10, 2013, http://www.nytimes.com; and N. Richardson, "Transformative Thinking for Sale," *Inc.* (online), May 28, 2013, http://www.inc.com.

29. Barrett, "The Case for User Reviews."

30. J. Pfeffer and R. Sutton, *The Knowing–Doing Gap* (Boston: Harvard Business School Press, 2000).

31. D. Siebold, "Making Meetings More Successful," *Journal of Business Communication* 16 (Summer 1979), pp. 3–20.

32. Barrett, "The Case for User Reviews."

33. I. Janis and L. Mann, *Decision Making* (New York: Free Press, 1977); and Bass, *Organizational Decision Making.*

34. Kopeikina, "The Elements of a Clear Decision."

35. Michaels, "Innovation Is Messy Business"; Ostrower and Lublin, "The Two Men behind the 787."

36. J. W. Dean Jr. and M. Sharfman, "Does Decision Process Matter? A Study of Strategic Decision-Making Effectiveness," *Academy of Management Journal* 39 (1996), pp. 368–96; and R. Nisbett and L. Ross, *Human Inference: Strategies and Shortcomings* (Englewood Cliffs, NJ: Prentice-Hall, 1980).

37. Messick and Bazerman, "Ethical Leadership."

38. T. Bateman and C. Zeithaml, "The Psychological Context of Strategic Decisions: A Model and Convergent Experimental Findings," *Strategic Management Journal* 10 (1989), pp. 59–74.

39. C. Isodore, "What You Need to Know About the Boeing Dreamliner," *CNN Money* (online), January 17, 2013, http://money.cnn.com.

40. Erin White, "Why Good Managers Make Bad Decisions," *The Wall Street Journal,* February 12, 2009, http://online.wsj.com.

41. D. Barton, "Capitalism for the Long Term," *Harvard Business Review,* March, 2011 pp. 84–91.

42. Messick and Bazerman, "Ethical Leadership."

43. N. Adler, *International Dimensions of Organizational Behavior* (Boston: Kent, 1990).

44. Joann S. Lublin, "Recall the Mistakes of Your Past Bosses, So You Can Do Better," *The Wall Street Journal,* January 2, 2007, http://online.wsj.com.

45. L. Perlow, G. Okhuysen, and N. Repenning, "The Speed Trap: Exploring the Relationship between Decision Making and Temporal Context," *Academy of Management Journal* 45 (2002), pp. 931–55.

46. K. M. Esenhardt, "Speed and Strategic Choice: How Managers Accelerate Decision Making," *California Management Review* 32 (Spring 1990), pp. 39–54.

47. Q. Spitzer and R. Evans, "New Problems in Problem Solving," *Across the Board,* April 1997, pp. 36–40.

48. G. W. Hill, "Group versus Individual Performance: Are N + 1 Heads Better than 1?" *Psychological Bulletin* 91 (1982), pp. 517–39.

49. N. R. F. Maier, "Assets and Liabilities in Group Problem Solving: The Need for an Integrative Function," *Psychological Review* 74 (1967), pp. 239–49.

50. Ibid.

51. B. Latane, K. Williams, and S. Harkins, "Many Hands Make Light the Work: The Causes and Consequences of Social Loafing," *Journal of Personality and Social Psychology* 37 (1979), pp. 822–32;

and J. George, "Extrinsic and Intrinsic Origins of Perceived Social Loafing in Organizations," *Academy of Management Journal* 35 (1992), pp. 191–206.

52. S. Murphy, S. Wayne, R. Liden, and B. Erdogan, "Understanding Social Loafing: The Role of Justice Perceptions and Exchange Relationships," *Human Relations* 56 (2003), pp. 61–84.

53. D. A. Garvin and M. A. Roberto, "What You Don't Know about Making Decisions," *Harvard Business Review,* September 2001, pp. 108–16.

54. Christopher Borrelli, "'Brave' Co-Director, Producer Take Up Arms to Promote Pixar's Latest," *Chicago Tribune,* June 21, 2012, http://www.chicagotribune.com.

55. A. Amason, "Distinguishing the Effects of Functional and Dysfunctional Conflict on Strategic Decision Making: Resolving a Paradox for Top Management Teams," *Academy of Management Journal* 39 (1996), pp. 123–48; and R. Dooley and G. Fyxell, "Attaining Decision Quality and Commitment from Dissent: The Moderating Effects of Loyalty and Competence in Strategic Decision-Making Teams," *Academy of Management Journal,* August 1999, pp. 389–402.

56. C. De Dreu and L. Weingart, "Task versus Relationship Conflict, Team Performance, and Team Member Satisfaction: A Meta-Analysis," *Journal of Applied Psychology* 88 (2003), pp. 741–49.

57. Cosier and Schwenk, "Agreement and Thinking Alike."

58. Ibid.

59. P. LaBerre, "The Creative Revolution," *Industry Week,* May 16, 1994, pp. 12–19.

60. G. Ruhe, "9 Cool College Start-ups," *Inc.* (online), http://www.inc.com, accessed March 1, 2015.

61. J. V. Anderson, "Weirder Than Fiction: The Reality and Myths of Creativity," *Academy of Management Executive* (November 1992), pp. 40–47; J. Krohe Jr., "Managing Creativity," *Across the Board,* September 1996, pp. 17–21; and R. I. Sutton, "The Weird Rules of Creativity," *Harvard Business Review,* September 2001, pp. 94–103.

62. K. DeStobbeleir, S. Ashford, and D. Buyens, "Self-Regulation of Creativity at Work: The Role of Feedback-Seeking Behavior in Creative Performance," *Academy of Management Journal* 54 (2011), pp. 811–31; and Y. Gong, S. Cheung, M. Wang, and J. Huang, "Unfolding the Proactive Process for Creativity: Integration of the Employee Proactivity, Information Exchange, and Psychological Safety Perspectives," *Journal of Management* 38 (2010), pp. 1611–33.

63. M. Bear, "Putting Creativity to Work: The Implementation of Creative Ideas in Organizations," *Academy of Management Journal* 55 (2012), pp. 1102–19; J. Perry-Smith and C. Shalley, "The Social Side of Creativity: A Static and Dynamic Social Network Perspective," *Academy of Management Review* 28 (2003),

pp. 89–106; and J. Perry-Smith, "Social yet Creative: The Role of Social Relationships in Facilitating Individual Creativity," *Academy of Management Journal* 49 (2006), pp. 85–101.

64. "Innovation from the Ground Up," *Industry Week,* March 7, 2007, http://www.industryweek.com (interview of Erika Andersen); T. M. Amabile, "A Model of Creativity and Innovation in Organizations," in *Research in Organizational Behavior,* ed. B. Straw and L. Cummings, vol. 10 (Greenwich, CT: JAI Press, 1988), pp. 123–68.

65. T. Amabile, C. Hadley, and S. Kramer, "Creativity under the Gun," *Harvard Business Review,* August 2002, pp. 52–61.

66. Rachel Emma Silverman, "Doodling for Dollars," *The Wall Street Journal,* April 24, 2012, http://online.wsj.com.

67. S. Farmer, P. Tierney, and K. Kung McIntyre, "Employee Creativity in Taiwan: An Application of Role Identity Theory," *Academy of Management Journal* 46 (2003), pp. 618–30.

68. "Innovation from the Ground Up."

69. K. Coyne and S. Coyne, "Seven Steps to Better Brainstorming," *McKinsey Quarterly,* March 2011, http://www.mckinsey.com.

70. L. Thompson, "Improving the Creativity of Organizational Work Groups," *Academy of Management Executive* 17 (2003), pp. 96–109.

71. "Accenture, Deloitte Name Crowdsourcing as a Key Trend For 2014," http://www.crowdsourcing.org, accessed March 2, 2015; Company website, http://www.weargustin.com, accessed March 2, 2015; K. Wagner, "5 Companies That Let Fans Lend a Hand," *Fortune* (online), June 24, 2013, http://fortune.com; J. Aquino, "The Pros and Cons of Crowdsourcing," *Customer Relationship Management* 17 (February 2013), pp. 31–34; and L. Faw, "Are Millennials Crowdsourcing Themselves Out of Jobs?" *Forbes* (online), October 22, 2012.

72. J. Walter, F. Fellermanns, and C. Lechner, "Decision Making within and between Organizations: Rationality, Politics, and Alliance Performance," *Journal of Management* 38 (2012), pp. 1582–1610.

73. T. Levitt, "Creativity Is Not Enough," *Harvard Business Review,* August 2002, pp. 137–44.

74. Dean and Sharfman, "Does Decision Process Matter?"

75. K. Eisenhardt, J. Kahwajy, and L. J. Bourgeois III, "How Management Teams Can Have a Good Fight," *Harvard Management Review,* July–August 1997, pp. 77–85.

76. C. M. Pearson and I. I. Mitroff, "From Crisis Prone to Crisis Prepared: A Framework for Crisis Management," *Academy of Management Executive,* February 1993, pp. 48–59.

77. Jordan Robertson and Eileen Sullivan, "U.S. Power Grid Hacked, Officials Say," *Chicago Tribune,* April 9, 2009, http://www.chicagotribune.com.

78. S. Moore, "Disaster's Future: The Prospects for Corporate Crisis Management and Communication," *Business Horizons,* January–February 2004, pp. 29–36.

79. G. Meyers with J. Holusha, *When It Hits the Fan: Managing the Nine Crises of Business* (Boston: Houghton Mifflin, 1986); and S. Bacharach and P. Bamberger, "9/11 and New York City Firefighters' Post Hoc Unit Support and Control Climates: A Context Theory of the Consequences of Involvement in Traumatic Work-Related Events," *Academy of Management Journal* 50 (2007), pp. 849–68.

80. McCall and Kaplan, *Whatever It Takes.*

81. J. Dutton, P. Frost, M. Worline, J. Lilius, and J. Kanov, "Leading in Times of Trauma," *Harvard Business Review,* January 2002, pp. 54–61.

82. Michaels, "Innovation Is Messy Business"; Andy Pasztor, "U.S. Sees Extended 787 Inquiry," *The Wall Street Journal,* January 24, 2013, http://online.wsj.com; Andy Pasztor, Yoree Koh, and Yoshio Takahashi, "Needed: Battery Expertise for 787 Probe," *The Wall Street Journal,* February 26, 2013, http://online.wsj.com; and "Is the Boeing Dreamliner Back in Business?" *MSN Money,* The Week, February 25, 2013, http://money.msn.com.

Chapter 4

1. T. Huddleston Jr., " 'Frozen' Heats Up Disney's Earnings," *Fortune* (online), February 3, 2015, http://www.fortune.com; Company website, "Company Interview," http://thewaltdisneycompany.com, accessed March 8, 2015; Walt Disney "At a Glance," *Forbes* (online), May 2014, http://www.forbes.com; Jennifer Reingold, "Bob Iger: Disney's Fun King," *Fortune,* May 9, 2012, http://management.fortune.cnn.com; "Fortune 500: 66, Walt Disney," *Fortune,* May 21, 2012, http://money.cnn.com; Walt Disney Company, "Company Overview," http://thewaltdisneycompany.com; and "Walt Disney Co., Burbank, CA," *ReferenceUSA,* http://referenceusa.com.

2. J. Bracker and J. Pearson, "Planning and Financial Performance of Small Mature Firms," *Strategic Management Journal* 7 (1986), pp. 503–22; and P. Waalewijn and P. Segaar, "Strategic Management: The Key to Profitability in Small Companies," *Long Range Planning* 26, no. 2 (April 1993), pp. 24–30.

3. W. Zhuoqioing, "Cafes Catch Cold from Starbucks Expansion Plan," *China Daily USA* (online), December 10, 2014, http://usa.chinadaily.com.

4. Company website, "Starbucks China Announces First-of-a-Kind Partner Development Program," December 17, 2014, http://www.starbucks.com.

5. D. Welch, "GM Doubles Profit in North America to Record on Truck Surge," *Bloomberg Business,* July 23, 2015, http://www.bloomberg.com; S. Terlep, "GM Caps Profitable Year," *The Wall Street Journal,* February 24, 2011, http://online.wsj.com; B. Cox, "For Big Three Automakers, an Unlikely Time for a Turnaround," *Fort Worth Star-Telegram,* April 15, 2011, http://www.star-telegram.com; and D. Barkholz, "Dealers: We Want More Cars!" *Automotive News,* August 23, 2010, Business & Company Resource Center, http://galenet.galegroup.com.

6. "Interview with Mark Cooper: Walmart Takes Collaborative Approach to Disaster Recovery," PricewaterhouseCoopers report, accessed March 8, 2015.

7. A. Murray, "JetBlue: Now Just Another Airline in a Lousy Business," *The Wall Street Journal,* February 21, 2007, http://online.wsj.com.

8. Company website, "Triple Bottom Line," http://www.novonordisk-us.com, accessed March 10, 2015.

9. Company website, "Novo Nordisk Publishes 2014 Integrated Annual Report Emphasizing Long-Term Thinking," http://www.novonordisk-us.com, accessed March 10, 2015.

10. A. Torsoli, "Novo Nordisk Fourth-Quarter Net Beats Estimates on Victoza," *Bloomberg Business* (online), January 30, 2015, http://www.bloomberg.com.

11. Jennifer J. Salopek, "Investing in Ideal Customer Service," *T+D,* October 2012, Business Insights: Essentials, http://bi.galegroup.com.

12. D. C. Hambrick and J. W. Fredrickson, "Are You Sure You Have a Strategy?" *Academy of Management Executive* 19, no. 4 (2005), pp. 51–62.

13. Brendan Byrnes, "Playing to Win: How Procter & Gamble Increased Its Market Cap by $100 Billion," *Motley Fool,* February 27, 2013, http://www.fool.com (interview with Roger Martin); unsigned review of *Playing to Win: How Strategy Really Works,* by A. G. Lafley and Roger Martin, *The Economist,* January 12, 2013, http://www.economist.com; and Dan Schawbel, "A. G. Lafley: Develop a Strategy to Win at Business," *Forbes,* February 5, 2013, http://www.forbes.com (interview with A. G. Lafley).

14. J. L. Bower and C. G. Gilbert, "How Managers' Everyday Decisions Create or Destroy Your Company's Strategy," *Harvard Business Review,* February 2007, pp. 72–79.

15. R. Kaplan and D. Norton, "Plotting Success with 'Strategy Maps,'" *Optimize,* February 2004, http://www.optimizemag.com; and R. S. Kaplan and D. P. Norton, "Having Trouble with Your Strategy? Then Map It," *Harvard Business Review,* September–October 2000.

16. B. Barnes, "Interactive Unit at Disney Cuts a Quarter of Its Staff," *The New York Times* (online), March 6, 2014; Walt Disney Company, "Company Overview"; Brooks Barnes, "Disney, Struggling to Find Its Digital Footing, Overhauls Disney.com," *The New York Times,* October 21, 2012, http://www.nytimes.com; Derrik J. Lang, "Disney Closing 'Epic Mickey' Video Game Developer," *Bloomberg Businessweek,* January 29, 2013, http://www.businessweek.com; and Associated Press, "Disney to Shutter Online Movie Store, Website," *Bloomberg Businessweek,* November 19, 2012, http://www.businessweek.com.

17. Bower and Gilbert, "Managers' Everyday Decisions"; and "Business: Fading Fads,"-*The Economist,* April 22, 2000, pp. 60–61.

18. S. W. Floyd and P. J. Lane, "Strategizing throughout the Organization: Management Role Conflict in Strategic Renewal," *Academy of Management Review* 25, no. 1 (January 2000), pp. 154–77.

19. Mission statements quoted from the organizations' websites: McDonald's, "Mission and Values," http://mcdonalds.com; Uber, "Mission," http://www.uber.com; and United Way, "Vision, Mission, Goals," http://www.unitedway.org.

20. Vision statements quoted from the organizations' websites: NASA Armstrong Flight Research Center, "Mission and Vision," http://www.nasa.org; City of Redmond, "City of Redmond Vision Statement," http://www.ci.redmond.wa.us; and MD Anderson Cancer Center, "Mission and Vision," http://www.mdanderson.org.

21. A. Martin, "The Happiest Meal: Hot Profits," *The New York Times,* January 11, 2009, http://www.nytimes.com.

22. A. A. Thompson and A. J. Strickland III, *Strategic Management: Concepts and Cases,* 8th ed. (New York: Richard D. Irwin, 1995), p. 23; R. Edward Freeman, J. S. Harrison, and A. C. Wicks, *Managing for Stakeholders* (New Haven, CT: Yale University Press, 2007).

23. Quoted from the company's website, "About Us," Ocean Renewable Power Company, http://www.orpc.co.

24. T. Haydon, "East Brunswick Landfill Garbage to Be Used as Power Source," *NJ.com* blog posting, November 13, 2011, http://blog.nj.com; and D. Porter, "One Man's Garbage Becomes Another's Power Plant," *Yahoo News,* October 28, 2008, http://news.yahoo.com.

25. A. Loten, "Running a Business in a Disaster Zone," *The Wall Street Journal,* December 30, 2010, http://online.wsj.com.

26. D. J. Collis and C. A. Montgomery, *Corporate Strategy: A Resource-Based Approach,* 2nd ed. (New York, McGraw-Hill/Irwin, 2005).

27. R. L. Priem, "A Consumer Perspective on Value Creation," *Academy of Management Review* 32, no. 1 (2007), pp. 219–35.

28. Jim Edwards, "Check Out the Insane Lengths Zappos Customer Service Reps Will Go To," *Business Insider,* January 9, 2012, http://articles.businessinsider.com; Zappos.com, "About," http://about.zappos.com; Mig Pascual, "Zappos: Five Out-of-the-Box Ideas for Keeping Employees Engaged," *U.S. News & World Report,* October 30, 2012, http://money.usnews.com.

29. A. Wilcox King, "Disentangling Interfirm and Intrafirm Causal Ambiguity: A Conceptual Model of Causal Ambiguity and Sustainable Competitive Advantage," *Academy of Management Review* 32, no. 1 (2007), pp. 156–78.

30. Accenture company report, "Achieving High Performance: The Value of Benchmarking," http://www.accenture.com, accessed March 8, 2015.

31. "Beware of Benchmarking Pitfalls Warns AXA Chief," *Europe Intelligence Wire,* May 13, 2010, Business & Company Resource Center, http://galenet.galegroup.com.

32. Company website, "Ernst & Young: Younger Managers Rise in the Ranks: Managing the Generational Mix and Preferred Workplace Perks," http://www.ey.com, accessed March 10, 2015; and V. Giang, "Here Are the Strengths and Weaknesses of Millennials, Gen X, and Boomers," *Business Insider* (online), September 9, 2013, http://www.businessinsider.com.

33. Company website, "About Next Day Flyers," http://www.nextdayflyers.com, accessed March 8, 2015; R. Myers, "That Sounds Like a Plan," *Inc.,* no. 36 (2014), pp. 90–92.

34. D. G. Sirmon, M. A. Hitt, and R. D. Ireland, "Managing Firm Resources in Dynamic Environments to Create Value: Looking inside the Black Box," *Academy of Management Review* 32, no. 1 (2007), pp. 273–92.

35. A. Bluestein, "The Success Gene," *Inc.,* April 2008, pp. 83–94.

36. P. Haspeslagh, "Portfolio Planning: Uses and Limits," *Harvard Business Review* 60, no. 1 (1982), pp. 58–67; R. Hamermesh, *Making Strategy Work* (New York: John Wiley & Sons, 1986); and R. A. Proctor, "Toward a New Model for Product Portfolio Analysis," *Management Decision* 28, no. 3 (1990), pp. 14–17.

37. Scott Malone, "GE to Return $18 Billion to Shareholders after Early NBC Deal," Reuters, February 13, 2013, http://www.reuters.com; Associated Press, "GE Energy and Other Firms Buy Wind Farms in France," *Bloomberg Businessweek,* January 2, 2013, http://www.businessweek.com; Julia Werdigier, "General Electric to Buy Avio for $4.3 Billion," *The New York Times,* December 21, 2012, http://dealbook.nytimes.com; General Electric, "Avio Acquisition Could Create Growth Opportunities beyond Aviation: Shipping and Oil and Gas Beckon," *GE Reports,* December 21, 2012, http://www.gereports.com; and General Electric, "Investor Relations," http://www.ge.com.

38. A. Davis, "No Slowdown in Sight for 2014's M&A Frenzy," *Forbes* (online), June 24, 2014, http://www.forbes.com.

39. M. Porter, *Competitive Advantage* (New York: Free Press, 1985), pp. 11–14.

40. K. Talley, "Wal-Mart Sees Shoppers' Pain," *The Wall Street Journal,* April 28, 2011, http://online.wsj.com.

41. R. Varadarajan, "Think Small," *The Wall Street Journal,* February 14, 2007, http://online.wsj.com.

42. F. F. Suarez and G. Lanzolla, "The Role of Environmental Dynamics in Building a First Mover Advantage Theory," *Academy of Management Review* 32, no. 2 (2007), pp. 377–92.

43. Robert Trigaux, "Now Public, Outback Parent Bloomin' Brands Sets Ambitious Expansion Plan," *Tampa Bay Times,* September 5, 2012, http://www.tampabay.com.

44. G. Norris, "GE Orders Two HondaJets for Supply Chain Flights," *Aviation Week* (online), October 21, 2014, http://aviationweek.com; and J. Scheck and P. Glader, "R&D Spending Holds Steady in Slump," *The Wall Street Journal,* April 6, 2009, http://online.wsj.com.

45. K. Carrig, S. Snell, and A. Onozuka, "In Search of Execution," University of Virginia, working paper, May 21, 2014.

46. R. A. Eisenstat, "Implementing Strategy: Developing a Partnership for Change," *Planning Review,* September–October 1993, pp. 33–36.

47. B. Tuttle, "America's Cheapest Airline Looks to Make Flights Even Cheaper," *Time* (online), October 29, 2014, http://time.com; and Jack Nicas, "Flying Spirit's 'Dollar Store in the Sky' to Profit," *The Wall Street Journal,* November 20, 2012, http://online.wsj.com.

48. Company website, "About Disney Interactive," http://www.disneyinteractive.com/about/, accessed March 9, 2015; T. Huddleston Jr., " 'Frozen' Heats Up Disney's Earnings," *Fortune* (online), March 7, 2015, http://fortune.com; Reingold, "Bob Iger"; Barnes, "Disney Struggling to Find Its Digital Footing"; Walt Disney Company, "Investor Relations," http://thewaltdisneycompany.com/investors; Daniel Rasmus, "Defining Your Company's Vision," *Fast Company,* February 28, 2012, http://www.fastcompany.com; Matthew Panzarino, "Disney and Netflix Just Pushed Streaming Video into Its Next Era," *Next Web,* December 4, 2012, http://thenextweb.com; Ethan Smith, "Disney CEO Turns Slump into a Springboard," *The Wall Street Journal,* November 8, 2010, http://online.wsj.com; Ethan Smith and Erica Orden, "Mickey, Darth Vader Join Forces in $4.05 Billion Deal," *The Wall Street Journal,* October 31, 2012, http://online.wsj.com; and Associated Press, "Disney Rolls Out More Live TV Apps with Comcast," *Bloomberg Businessweek,* June 14, 2012, http://www.businessweek.com.

Chapter 5

1. A. Barinka, "IBM's Rometty Takes 2014 Bonus Amid Struggles in Cloud Shift," *Bloomberg Business,* January 30, 2015, http://bloomberg.com; J. Bort, "IBM Reports Earnings: It's a Miss on Revenue but a Beat on Profits," *Business Insider,* January 20, 2015, http://www.businessinsider.com; Company website, "IBM Think Forum," October 8, 2014, http://www.ibm.com; Bill George, "How IBM's Sam Palmisano Redefined the Global Corporation," *HBR Blog Network: HBS Faculty,* January 18, 2012, http://blogs.hbr.org; IBM, "What Is a Smarter Planet?" http://www.ibm.com; Ann Bednarz, "IBM's Rometty Nets $16.2 Million in First Year as CEO," *Network World,* March 13, 2013, http://www.networkworld.com; Steve Lohr, "IBM's Rometty on the Data Challenge to the Culture of Management," *The New York Times,* March 7, 2013, http://bits.blogs.nytimes.com; and Steve Lohr, "The 2012 Patent Rankings: IBM on Top (Again), Google and Apple Surging," *The New York Times,* January 10, 2013, http://bits.blogs.nytimes.com.

2. V. Anand, B. Ashforth, and M. Joshi, "Business as Usual: The Acceptance and Perpetuation of Corruption in Organizations," *Academy of Management Executive* (May 2004), pp. 39–53; and B. Ashforth, D. Gioia, S. Robinson, and L. Trevino, "Re-viewing Organizational Corruption," *Academy of Management Review* 33 (July 2008), 670–84.

3. Edelman Berland, "2014 Edelman Trust Barometer: Executive Summary," http://www.edelman.com.

4. "Brazil Elite Profit from $3 Billion Petrobras Scandal as Laid-off Workers Pay the Price," *The Guardian* (online), March 20, 2015, http://www.theguardian.com.

5. M. Banaji, M. Bazerman, and D. Chugh, "How (Un)Ethical Are You?" *Harvard Business Review,* December 2003, pp. 56–64.

6. "Millennials in Adulthood," Pew Research Center Social Demographic Trends, March 7, 2014, http://www.pewsocialtrends.org/2014/03/07/millennials-in-adulthood/.

7. S. L. Grover, "The Truth, the Whole Truth, and Nothing but the Truth: The Causes and Management of Workplace Lying," *Academy of Management Executive* 19 (May 2005), pp. 148–57.

8. E. Spitznagel, " 'Operation Clean Turf' and the War on Fake Yelp Reviews," *Bloomberg Business* (online), September 25, 2013, http://www.bloomberg.com; and C. Anderson, "The Impact of Social Media on Lodging Performance," The Center for Hospitality Research, Cornell University, November 2012.

9. M. E. Guy, *Ethical Decision Making in Everyday Work Situations* (New York: Quorum Books, 1990).

10. O. C. Ferrell and J. Fraedrich, *Business Ethics: Ethical Decision Making and Cases,* 3rd ed. (Boston: Houghton Mifflin, 1997).

11. Ibid.

12. Guy, *Ethical Decision Making.*

13. Ferrell and Fraedrich, *Business Ethics.*

14. J. Hechinger and D. Armstrong, "Universities Resolve Kickback Allegations," *The Wall Street Journal,* April 3, 2007, http://online.wsj.com; J. Hechinger, "Probe into College–Lender Ties Widens," *The Wall Street Journal,* April 5, 2007, http://online.wsj.com; and Associated Press, "CIT Executives Placed on Leave Amid Student Loan Investigation," *The Wall Street Journal,* April 9, 2007, http://online.wsj.com.

15. Hechinger and Armstrong, "Universities Resolve Kickback Allegations"; and AP, "CIT Executives."

16. A. Spicer, T. Dunfee, and W. Biley, "Does National Context Matter in Ethical Decision Making? An Empirical Test of Integrative Social Contracts Theory," *Academy of Management Journal* 47 (2004), pp. 610–20; W. Bailey and A. Spicer, "When Does National Identity Matter? Convergence and Divergence in International Business Ethics," *Academy of Management Journal,* 2007, pp. 1462–80; and K. Martin, J. Cullen, J. Johnson, and K. Parboteeah, "Deciding to Bribe: A Cross-Level Analysis of Firm and Home Country Influences on Bribery Activity," *Academy of Management Journal,* 2007, pp. 1401–22.

17. L. Kohlberg and D. Candee, "The Relationship of Moral Judgment to Moral Action" in *Morality, Moral Behavior, and Moral Development,* ed. W. M. Kurtines and J. L. Gerwitz (New York: John Wiley & Sons, 1984).

18. L. K. Trevino, "Ethical Decision Making in Organizations: A Person–Situation Interactionist Model," *Academy of Management Review,* 1992, pp. 601–17.

19. S. Hannah, B. Avolio, and D. May, "Moral Maturation and Moral Conation: A Capacity Approach to Explaining Moral Thought and Action," *Academy of Management Review* 36 (2011), pp. 663–85.

20. A. Crane, "Modern Slavery as a Management Practice: Exploring the Conditions and Capabilities for Human Exploitation," *Academy of Management Review* 38 (2013), pp. 49–69.

21. J. Badarocco Jr. and A. Webb, "Business Ethics: A View from the Trenches," *California Management Review,* Winter 1995, pp. 8–28; and G. Laczniak, M. Berkowitz, R. Brookes, and J. Hale, "The Business of Ethics: Improving or Deteriorating?" *Business Horizons,* January–February 1995, pp. 39–47.

22. "Survey: Managers Rate High on Ethics, Professionalism," *Chief Learning Officer,* October 16, 2012, http://clomedia.com.

23. J. Kammeyer-Mueller, L. Simon, and B. Rich, "The Psychic Cost of Doing Wrong: Ethical Conflict, Divestiture Socialization, and Emotional Exhaustion," *Journal of Management* 38 (2012), pp. 784–808.

24. Anand, Ashforth, and Joshi, "Business as Usual."

25. S. Glover, "SOX Compliance Proves Beneficial to Organizations, Fuels Risk Consciousness," *National Underwriter*

Property & Casualty, November 15, 2010, pp. 34, 36; and P. Sweeney, "Will New Regulations Deter Corporate Fraud?" *Financial Executive,* January–February 2011, pp. 54–57.

26. R. E. Allinson, "A Call for Ethically Centered Management," *Academy of Management Executive,* February 1995, pp. 73–76.

27. R. T. De George, *Business Ethics,* 3rd ed. (New York: Macmillan, 1990).

28. B. W. Heineman Jr., "Avoiding Integrity Land Mines," *Harvard Business Review,* April 2007, pp. 100–8.

29. R. A. Cooke, "Danger Signs of Unethical Behavior: How to Determine If Your Firm Is at Ethical Risk," *Journal of Business Ethics,* April 1991, pp. 249–53.

30. L. K. Trevino and M. Brown, "Managing to Be Ethical: Debunking Five Business Ethics Myths," *Academy of Management Executive,* May 2004, pp. 69–81.

31. Ibid.

32. Heineman, "Avoiding Integrity Land Mines."

33. D. Messick and M. Bazerman, "Ethical Leadership and the Psychology of Decision Making," *Sloan Management Review,* Winter 1996, pp. 9–22.

34. C. Handy, *Beyond Uncertainty: The Changing Worlds of Organizations* (Boston: Harvard Business School Press, 1996).

35. J. Stevens, H. Steensma, D. Harrison, and P. Cochran, "Symbolic or Substantive Document? The Influence of Ethics Codes on Financial Executives' Decisions," *Strategic Management Journal* 26 (2005), pp. 181–95; and J. Weber, "Does It Take an Economic Village to Raise an Ethical Company?" *Academy of Management Executive* 19 (May 2005), pp. 158–59.

36. Ethics Resource Center website, http://www.ethics.org, accessed March 20, 2015.

37. R. J. Zablow, "Creating and Sustaining an Ethical Workplace: Ethics Resource Center (ERC)," "Code Construction and Content," *The Ethics Resource Center Toolkit,* http://www.ethics.org; and J. Brown, "Ten Writing Tips for Creating an Effective Code of Conduct," Ethics Resource Center, http://www.ethics.org.

38. G. R. Weaver, L. K. Trevino, and P. L. Cochran, "Corporate Ethics Programs as Control Systems: Influences of Executive Commitment and Environmental Factors," *Academy of Management Journal* 42 (1999), pp. 41–57.

39. L. S. Paine, "Managing for Organizational Integrity," *Harvard Business Review,* March–April 1994, pp. 106–17.

40. Government website, "ADA Amendments Act of 2008," http://www.eeoc.gov accessed March 20, 2015; F. Hall and E. Hall, "The ADA: Going beyond the Law," *Academy of Management Executive,* February 1994, pp. 7–13; and A. Farnham, "Brushing Up Your Vision Thing," *Fortune,* May 1, 1995, p. 129.

41. Trevino and Brown, "Managing to Be Ethical," p. 70.

42. Ibid.

43. Banaji, Bazerman, and Chugh, "How (Un) Ethical Are You?"

44. B. Gunia, L. Wang, L. Huang, J. Wang, and K. Murnighan, "Contemplation and Conversation: Subtle Influences on Moral Decision Making," *Academy of Management Journal* 55 (2012), pp. 13–33.

45. Anand, Ashforth, and Joshi, "Business as Usual"; and Remi Trudel and June Cotte, "Does Being Ethical Pay?" *The Wall Street Journal,* May 12, 2008, http://online.wsj.com.

46. T. Thomas, J. Schermerhorn Jr., and J. Dienhart, "Strategic Leadership of Ethical Behavior in Business," *Academy of Management Executive,* May 2004, pp. 56–66.

47. Trevino and Brown, "Managing to Be Ethical."

48. J. Bort, "IBM Reports Earnings: It's a Miss on Revenue but a Beat on Profits," *Business Insider,* January 20, 2015, http://www.businessinsider.com; George, "How IBM's Sam Palmisano Redefined the Global Corporation"; Leigh Nakanishi, "Technology's Achilles' Heel," Edelman Conversations: Global Practices, January 28, 2013, http://www.edelman.com; IBM, "IBM Policies," About IBM, http://www.ibm.com; IBM, "Our Values," IBM Employment, http://www-03.ibm.com; and Christopher M. Matthews, "Judge Limits Requirements to IBM, SEC Settlement," *The Wall Street Journal,* February 4, 2013, http://blogs.wsj.com.

49. B. Rokos and J. Katzanek, "325 Could Lose Jobs When Hemet Call Center Closes," *Press-Enterprise* (Riverside, CA), August 5, 2010, Business & Company Resource Center, http://galenet.galegroup.com; and B. Rokos, "Hilton Call Center Employees in Hemet Trained Overseas Workers before Losing Jobs," *Press-Enterprise* (Riverside, CA), August 13, 2010, Business & Company Resource Center, http://galenet.galegroup.com.

50. M.E. Schreiber and D.R. Marshall, "Reducing the Risk of Whistleblower Compaints," *Risk Management* 53, no. 11 (November 2006), OCLC FirstSearch, http://firstsearch.oclc.com; H. Wang and C. Qian, "Corporate Philanthropy and Corporate Financial Performance: The Roles of Stakeholder Response and Political Access," *Academy of Management Journal* 54 (2011), pp. 1159–81.

51. M. Hernandez, "Toward an Understanding of the Psychology of Stewardship," *Academy of Management Review* 37, 2012, pp. 172–93.

52. Company website, Kickboard for Teachers, http://www.kickboardforteachers, accessed March 21, 2015; J. Smith, "The Companies with the Best CSR Reputations," *Forbes* (online), October 2, 2013, http://www.forbes.com; R. Bies, J. Bartunek, T. Fort, and M. Zald, "Corporations as Social Change Agents: Individual, Interpersonal, Institutional, and Environmental Dynamics," *Academy of Management*

Review, 2007, pp. 788–93; and B. Liodice, "10 Companies with Social Responsibility at the Core," *AdvertisingAge,* April 19, 2010.

53. L. Preston and J. Post, eds., *Private Management and Public Policy* (Englewood Cliffs, NJ: Prentice-Hall, 1975).

54. Ferrell and Fraedrich, *Business Ethics.*

55. C. Flammer, "Corporate Social Responsibility and Shareholder Reaction: The Environmental Awareness of Investors," *Academy of Management Journal* 56 (2013), pp. 758–81; and H. Aguinis and A. Glavas, "What We Know and Don't Know about Corporate Social Responsibility: A Review and Research Agenda," *Journal of Management* (2012), pp. 932–68.

56. D. Matten and J. Moon, "'Implicit' and 'Explicit' CSR: A Conceptual Framework for a Comparative Understanding of Corporate Social Responsibility," *Academy of Management Review,* 2008, pp. 404–24.

57. A. Carroll, "Managing Ethically with Global Stakeholders: A Present and Future Challenge," *Academy of Management Executive,* May 2004, pp. 114–20.

58. L. Etter, "Smithfield to Phase Out Crates," *The Wall Street Journal,* January 25, 2007, http://online.wsj.com.

59. Godfrey, "The Relationship between Corporate Philanthropy and Shareholder Wealth"; and Wang and Qian, "Corporate Philanthropy and Corporate Financial Performance."

60. R. Giacalone, "A Transcendent Business Education for the 21st Century," *Academy of Management Learning & Education,* 2004, pp. 415–20.

61. M. Witzel, "Not for Wealth Alone: The Rise of Business Ethics," *Financial Times Mastering Management Review,* November 1999, pp. 14–19.

62. D. C. Korten, *When Corporations Ruled the World* (San Francisco: Berrett-Koehler, 1995).

63. Handy, *Beyond Uncertainty.*

64. D. Barton, "Capitalism for the Long Term," *Harvard Business Review,* March 2011, pp. 84–91.

65. D. Quinn and T. Jones, "An Agent Morality View of Business Policy," *Academy of Management Review* 20 (1995), pp. 22–42.

66. Coca-Cola Company, "About Water Stewardship," http://www.coca-colacompany.com; Coca-Cola Company, "Setting a New Goal for Water Efficiency," http://www.coca-colacompany.com; and Coca-Cola Company, "RAIN: The Replenish Africa Initiative," http://www.coca-colacompany.com.

67. B. McKay, "Why Coke Aims to Slake Global Thirst for Safe Water," *The Wall Street Journal,* March 15, 2007, http://online.wsj.com.

68. M. Delmas, D. Etzion, and N. Nairn-Birch, "Triangulating Environmental Performance: What Do Corporate Social

Responsibility Ratings Really Capture?" *Academy of Management Perspectives* 27 (2013), pp. 255–67; and N. Varchaver, "Chemical Reaction," *Fortune,* April 2, 2007, Business & Company Resource Center, http://galenet.galegroup.com.

69. D. Schuler and M. Cording, "A Corporate Social Performance–Corporate Financial Performance Behavioral Model for Consumers," *Academy of Management Review* 31 (2006), pp. 540–58.

70. M. Orlitzky, F. Schmidt, and S. Rynes, "Corporate Social and Financial Performance: A Meta-Analysis," *Organization Studies* 24 (2003), pp. 403–41; J. Peloza, "The Challenge of Measuring Financial Impacts from Investments in Corporate Social Performance," *Journal of Management* 35 (2009), pp. 1518–41.

71. D. Turban and D. Greening, "Corporate Social Performance and Organizational Attractiveness to Prospective Employees," *Academy of Management Journal* 40 (1997), pp. 658–72.

72. A. McWilliams and D. Siegel, "Corporate Social Responsibility: A Theory of the Firm Perspective," *Academy of Management Review* 26 (2001), pp. 117–27.

73. S. L. Hart and M. B. Milstein, "Global Sustainability and the Creative Destructions of Industries," *Sloan Management Review,* Fall 1999, pp. 23–33.

74. P. M. Senge and G. Carstedt, "Innovating Our Way to the Next Industrial Revolution," *Sloan Management Review,* Winter 2001, pp. 24–38.

75. C. K. Prahalad and M. R. Rangaswami, "Why Sustainability Is Now the Key Driver of Innovation," *Harvard Business Review,* September 2009, pp. 56–64.

76. Y. Chouinard, J. Ellison, and R. Ridgeway, "The Sustainable Economy," *Harvard Business Review,* October 2011, pp. 52–62.

77. RFX Blog, "RFX Global Companies Announce Caitlin Welby as President & CEO, Jim Morse as Chairman of the Board," January 20, 2015, http://www.rfxinc.com; C. Chafin, "Meet the 32-Year-Old, Yoga-Loving, Punk Rock, Tree Hugger CEO of a $100 Million Trucking Company," *Fast Company,* February 11, 2015, http://www.fastcompany.com.

78. C. Holliday, "Sustainable Growth, the DuPont Way," *Harvard Business Review,* September 2001, pp. 129–34; and P. Bansal and K. Roth, "Why Companies Go Green: A Model of Ecological Responsiveness," *Academy of Management Journal* 43 (2000), pp. 717–36.

79. D. Lubin and D. Esty, "The Sustainability Imperative," *Harvard Business Review,* May 2010, pp. 42–50; and R. Nidumolu, C. K. Prahalad, and M. R. Rangaswami, "Why Sustainability Is Now the Key Driver of Innovation," *Harvard Business Review* (September 2009), pp. 57–64.

80. P. Shrivastava, "Ecocentric Management for a Risk Society," *Academy of Management Review* 20 (1995), pp. 118–37.

81. Ibid.

82. Ibid.

83. "3M Deploys ChargePoint Electric Vehicle Charging Station at HQ," *Manufacturing Close-Up,* February 16, 2011, Business & Company Resource Center, http://galenet.galegroup.com.

84. M. Herbst, "Gore Rings a Green Alarm," *BusinessWeek,* March 22, 2007; E. Osnos, "In China's Toxic Air, Winds of Change," *Chicago Tribune,* March 13, 2007; and Xinhua News Agency, "Unclean Drinking Water Threatens Health of 320M Chinese: Report," *BBC Monitoring International Reports,* March 13, 2007, all downloaded from Business & Company Resource Center, http://galenet.galegroup.com.

85. K. Haanaes, D. Michael, J. Jurgens, and S. Rangan, "Making Sustainability Profitable," *Harvard Business Review,* March 2013, pp. 110–14.

86. Shrivastava, "Ecocentric Management."

87. M. Gunther, "Green Is Good," *Fortune,* March 22, 2007, http://money.cnn.com;

88. S. Waddock, "Leadership Integrity in a Fractured Knowledge World," *Academy of Management Learning & Education,* 2007, pp. 543–57.

89. R. Martin and A. Kemper, "Saving the Planet: A Tale of Two Strategies," *Harvard Business Review,* April 2012, pp. 48–56.

90. J. O'Toole, "Do Good, Do Well: The Business Enterprise Trust Awards," *California Management Review,* Spring 1991, pp. 9–24; and Shrivastava, "Ecocentric Management."

91. Patagonia, "The Footprint Chronicles," http://www.patagonia.com, accessed March 21, 2015.

92. B. Doppelt, *Leading Change toward Sustainability* (Sheffield, UK: Greenleaf, 2010).

93. Ibid.

94. M. Russo and P. Fouts, "A Resource-Based Perspective on Corporate Environmental Performance and Profitability," *Academy of Management Journal* 40 (1997), pp. 534–59; and R. D. Klassen and D. Clay Whybark, "The Impact of Environmental Technologies on Manufacturing Performance," *Academy of Management Journal* 42 (1999), pp. 599–615.

95. G. Unruh and R. Etternson, "Growing Green," *Harvard Business Review,* June 2010, pp. 94–100.

96. Ibid.

97. Ibid.

98. Ibid.

99. Siemens USA, "Energy Efficiency," http://www.usa.siemens.com; and Devan Schwartz, "Sky Lakes, Siemens Team Up for Energy Efficiency," *Herald and News* (Klamath Falls, OR), January 30, 2013, http://www.heraldandnews.com.

100. G. Colvin, "The King of Water," *Fortune,* July 5, 2010, pp. 52–59.

101. Marriott, "Reducing Our Footprint," http://www.marriott.com, accessed March 21, 2015.

102. J. Ball, "Green Goal of 'Carbon Neutrality' Hits Limit," *The Wall Street Journal,* December 30, 2008, http://online.wsj.com; and Google Inc., "Going Green at Google," Corporate Overview: Green Initiatives, Google Corporate home page, http://www.google.com/corporate/green/.

103. J. Rogers, "The CEO of Duke Energy on Learning to Work with Green Activists," *Harvard Business Review* (May 2011), pp. 51–54; and M. Tercek and J. Adams, *Nature's Fortune* (New York: Basic Books, 2013).

104. G. Pinchot and E. Pinchot, *The Intelligent Organization* (San Francisco: Berrett-Koehler, 1996); and S. L. Hart, *Capitalism as the Crossroads,* 3rd ed. (Upper Saddle River, NJ: Wharton School Publishing, 2010).

105. IBM, "Product Recycling Programs," http://www.ibm.com; A. MacArthur, "IBM's Smarter Cities Challenge Is Transforming Our World," *The New Global Citizen* (online), June 26, 2013, http://newglobalcitizen.com; IBM, "Responsibility at IBM," About IBM, http://www.ibm.com; IBM, "IBM Policies"; Jen Crozier, "Urban Challenges," *Citizen IBM Blog,* November 14, 2012, http://citizenibm.com; IBM, "EPA Recognizes IBM for Climate Change Leadership," news release, March 1, 2013, http://www.ibm.com; IBM, "Sustainability on a Smarter Planet," Smarter Planet: Sustainability, http://www.ibm.com; Nick Zieminski, "IBM's 'Building Whisperer' Sees Retrofit Boom," *Chicago Tribune,* May 8, 2012, http://articles.chicagotribune.com; Verne Kopytoff, "The Complex Business of Recycling E-Waste," *Bloomberg Businessweek,* January 8, 2013, http://www.businessweek.com; and IBM, "IBM's Energy Program Saves $43 Million and Avoids 175,000 Metric Tons of CO_2 Emissions," news release, July 2, 2012, http://www-03.ibm.com.

106. Tercek and Adams, *Nature's Fortune.*

107. Chouinard et al., "The Sustainable Economy."

108. Ibid.

109. Ibid.

110. B. McKibben, "Global Warming's Terrifying Math," *Rolling Stone* (2012), http://www.rollingstone.com/politics/news/global-warmings-terrifying-new-math-20120719; B. Smit and J. Wandel, "Adaptation, Adaptive Capacity and Vulnerability," *Global Environmental Change* 16 (2006), pp. 282–92; Tercek and Adams, *Nature's Fortune;* and E. Weber and P. Stern, "Public Understanding of Climate Change in the United States," *American Psychologist* 66 (2011), pp. 315–28.

111. S. L. Hart, "Beyond Greening: Strategies for a Sustainable World," *Harvard Business Review,* January–February 1997, pp. 66–76.

Appendix B

1. P. Hawken, A. Lovins, and L. Hunter Lovins, *Natural Capitalism* (Boston: Little Brown, 1999).
2. F. Rice, "Who Scores Best on the Environment?" *Fortune,* July 26, 1993, p. 114–22.
3. Stavins, "The Challenge of Going Green."
4. F. B. Cross, "The Weaning of the Green: Environmentalism Comes of Age in the 1990s," *Business Horizons,* September–October 1990, pp. 40–46.
5. Stavins, "The Challenge of Going Green."
6. J. Singh, "Making Business Sense of Environmental Compliance," *Sloan Management Review,* Spring 2000, pp. 91–100; L. Word, "A Green Museum: Preserving Collections in Sustainable Ways," National Endowment for the Arts, May 6, 2013, http://www.neh.gov.
7. J. Muller, "How GM Makes $1 Billion a Year by Recycling Waste," *Forbes* (online), February 21, 2013, http://www.forbes.com.
8. E. Smith and V. Cahan, "The Greening of Corporate America," *BusinessWeek,* April 23, 1990, pp. 96–103.
9. M. E. Porter, "America's Green Strategy," *Science,* April 1991, p. 168.
10. A. Kleiner, "What Does It Mean to Be Green?" *Harvard Business Review,* July–August 1991, pp. 38–47; and "Global Consumers Are Willing to Put Their Money Where Their Heart Is," Nielsen (online), June 17, 2014, http://www.nielsen.com.
11. D. C. Kinlaw, *Competitive and Green: Sustainable Performance in the Environmental Age* (Amsterdam: Pfeiffer & Co., 1993).
12. United States Environmental Protection Agency, "2013 TRI National Analysis: Introduction," http://www2.epa.gov, accessed March 21, 2015.
13. Rice, "Who Scores Best on the Environment?"; J. O'Toole, "Do Good, Do Well: The Business Enterprise Trust Awards," *California Management Review,* Spring 1991, pp. 9–24.
14. O'Toole, "Do Good, Do Well."
15. G. Hardin, "The Tragedy of the Commons," *Science* 162 (1968), pp. 1243–48.
16. D. Kirkpatrick, "Environmentalism: The New Crusade," *Fortune,* February 12, 1990, pp. 44–55.
17. Ibid.
18. R. Carson, *Silent Spring* (Boston: Houghton Mifflin, 1962); R. Paehlke, *Environmentalism and the Future of Progressive Politics* (New Haven, CT: Yale University Press, 1989), pp. 13–41, 76–143; R. Nash, ed., *The American Environment* (Reading, MA: Addison-Wesley, 1968); R. Revelle and H. Landsberg, eds., *America's Changing Environment* (Boston: Beacon Press, 1970); L. Caldwell, *Environment: A Challenge to Modern Society* (Garden City, NY: Anchor Books, 1971); and J. M. Petulla, Environmental Protection in the United States (San Francisco: San Francisco Study Center, 1987).
19. B. Commoner, *Science and Survival* (New York: Viking Press, 1963); and B. Commoner, *The Closing Circle: Nature, Man and Technology* (New York: Bantam Books, 1971).
20. R. Paehlke, *Environmentalism and the Future of Progressive Politics* (New Haven: Yale University Press, 1989).
21. P. Shrivastava, "Ecocentric Management for a Risk Society," *Academy of Management Review* 20 (1995), pp. 118–37.
22. Commoner, *The Closing Circle.*
23. Paehlke, *Environmentalism.*
24. Ibid.
25. Ibid.
26. P. Hawken, J. Ogilvy, and P. Schwartz, *Seven Tomorrows: Toward a Voluntary History* (New York: Bantam Books, 1982); and Paehlke, *Environmentalism.*
27. Porter, "America's Green Strategy."
28. "Green Teeth: The Government Amends its Environmental Law," *The Economist,* May 17, 2014.
29. S. Waddock and N. Smith, "Corporate Responsibility Audits: Doing Well by Doing Good," *Sloan Management Review,* Winter 2000, pp. 75–83.
30. C. Morrison, *Managing Environmental Affairs: Corporate Practices in the U.S., Canada, and Europe* (New York: Conference Board, 1991).
31. Ibid.
32. Kleiner, "What Does It Mean to Be Green?"
33. K. Fischer and J. Schot, *Environmental Strategies for Industry* (Washington, DC: Island Press, 1993).
34. J. Howard, J. Nash, and J. Ehrenfeld, "Standard or Smokescreen? Implementation of a Voluntary Environmental Code," *California Management Review,* Winter 2000, pp. 63–82.
35. Rice, "Who Scores Best on the Environment?"
36. C. Lockwood, "Building the Green Way," *Harvard Business Review,* June 2006, pp. 129–137.
37. G. Unruh, "The Biosphere Rules," *Harvard Business Review,* February 2008, pp. 111–17.
38. Rice, "Who Scores Best on the Environment?"
39. Ibid.
40. D. Kewalramani and R. Sobelsohn, "'Greenwashing': Deceptive Business Claims of Eco-Friendliness," *Forbes* (online), March 20, 2012, http://www.forbes.com; and W. S. Laufer, "Social Accountability and Corporate Greenwashing," *Journal of Business Ethics* 43 (2003), pp. 253–61.
41. S. Hart and M. Milstein, "Global Sustainability and the Creative Destruction of Industries," *Sloan Management Review,* Fall 1999, pp. 23–32; and H. Ellison, "Saving Nature While Earning Money," *International Herald Tribune,* June 23, 1997, p. 18.
42. J. Elkington and T. Burke, *The Green Capitalists* (London: Victor Gullanez, 1989); and M. Zetlin, "The Greening of Corporate America," *Management Review,* June 1990, pp. 10–17.
43. Smith and Cahan, "The Greening of Corporate America."
44. J. Carey, "Global Warming," *BusinessWeek,* August 16, 2004, pp. 60–69.
45. J. Stevens, "Assessing the Health Risks of Incinerating Garbage," *EURA Reporter,* October 1989, pp. 6–10.
46. Carey, "Global Warming."
47. A. Lovins, L. Hunter Lovins, and P. Hawken, "A Road Map for Natural Capitalism," *Harvard Business Review,* May–June 1999, pp. 145–58.
48. A. Kolk, "Green Reporting," *Harvard Business Review,* January–February 2000, pp. 15–16.
49. L. Blumberg and R. Gottlieb, "The Resurrection of Incineration" and "The Economic Factors," in *War on Waste,* ed. L. Blumberg and R. Gottlieb (Washington, DC: Island Press, 1989).
50. Carey, "Global Warming."
51. L. Blumberg and R. Gottlieb, "Recycling's Unrealized Promise," in Blumberg and Gottlieb, *War on Waste,* pp. 191–226.
52. Carey, "Global Warming."
53. Lovins, Lovins, and Hawken, "A Road Map for Natural Capitalism."
54. J. Elkington, "Towards the Sustainable Corporation: Win-Win-Win Business Strategies for Sustainable Development," *California Management Review,* Winter 1994, pp. 90–100.
55. Lovins, Lovins, and Hawken, "A Road Map for Natural Capitalism."
56. R. Nidumolu, C. K. Prahalad, and M. R. Rangaswami, "Why Sustainability Is Now the Key Driver of Innovation," *Harvard Business Review,* September 2009, pp. 57–64.
57. Carey, "Global Warming."
58. Dechant and Altman, "Environmental Leadership."
59. H. Ellison, "Joint Implementation Promotes Cooperation on World Climate," *International Herald Tribune,* June 23, 1997, p. 21.
60. Corbett and Van Wassenhove, "The Green Fee."
61. Polansky and Rosenberger, "Reevaluating Green Marketing."
62. Carey, "Global Warming."
63. D. Lubin and D. Esty, "The Sustainability Imperative," *Harvard Business Review* 42 (May 2010), pp. 42–50.
64. R. D. Klassen and D. Clay Whybark, "The Impact of Environmental Technologies on Manufacturing Performance," *Academy of Management Journal* 42 (1999), pp. 599–615.
65. D. Machalaba, "New Recyclables Market Emerges: Plastic Railroad Ties," *The Wall Street Journal,* October 19, 2004, p. B1.
66. Hart and Milstein, "Global Sustainability."
67. Ibid.

68. Ibid.
69. Lubin and Esty, "The Sustainability Imperative."
70. R. Martin and A. Kemper, "Saving the Planet: A Tale of Two Strategies," *Harvard Business Review,* April 2012, pp. 48–56.
71. Nidumolu et al., "Why Sustainability Is Now the Key Driver of Innovation."
72. Polansky and Rosenberger, "Reevaluating Green Marketing."
73. Hart and Milstein, "Global Sustainability."
74. A. Beard and R. Hornik, "It's Hard to Be Good," *Harvard Business Review,* November 2011, pp. 88–96.
75. Nidumolu et al., "Why Sustainability Is Now the Key Driver of Innovation."
76. Martin and Kemper, "Saving the Planet."
77. Hart and Milstein, "Global Sustainability."
78. M. Fong, "Soy Underwear? China Targets Eco-Friendly Clothes Market," *The Wall Street Journal,* December 17, 2004, pp. B1, B4.
79. Polansky and Rosenberger, "Reevaluating Green Marketing"; Nidumolu et al., "Why Sustainability Is Now the Key Driver of Innovation."
80. Nidumolu et al., "Why Sustainability Is Now the Key Driver of Innovation."
81. Polansky and Rosenberger, "Reevaluating Green Marketing."
82. Elkington, "Towards the Sustainable Corporation."
83. F. S. Rowland, "Chlorofluorocarbons and the Depletion of Stratospheric Ozone," *American Scientist,* January–February 1989, pp. 36–45.
84. Elkington, "Towards the Sustainable Corporation."
85. Y. Chouinard, J. Ellison, and R. Ridgeway, "The Sustainable Economy," *Harvard Business Review,* October 2011, pp. 52–62.
86. M. Lubber, "Sustainability: Ending the 'Tyranny of Short-Termism,'" April 1, 2011, www.ceres.org.
87. Ibid.
88. H. Ellison, "The Balance Sheet," *International Herald Tribune,* June 23, 1997, p.
89. P. B. Gray and D. Devlin, "Heroes of Small Business," *Fortune Small Business,* November 2000, pp. 50–64.

Chapter 6

1. J. Osawa, "For H-P, Fierce Competition from Lenovo Awaits in Servers," *The Wall Street Journal,* October 6, 2014, http://www.blogs.wsj.com; Gartner, "Worldwide Smartphone Sales to End Users by Vendor in 2013," press release, February 13, 2014, http://www.gartner.com; Loretta Chao, "As Rivals Outsource, Lenovo Keeps Production In-House," *The Wall Street Journal,* July 9, 2012, http://online.wsj.com; Saabira Chaudhuri, "Is the End of the PC Market Closer than We Think?" *The Wall Street Journal,* January 14, 2013, http://blogs.wsj.com; Bruce Einhorn, "Lenovo's Persistent PC Strategy in India," *Bloomberg*

Businessweek, November 6, 2012, http://www.businessweek.com; Joe McDonald, "Lenovo Profit Boosted by Smartphones, Tablets," *Bloomberg Businessweek,* January 30, 2013, http://www.businessweek.com; Paul Mozur, "Lenovo Profit Rose in Latest Quarter," *The Wall Street Journal,* January 30, 2013, http://online.wsj.com; Loretta Chao, "Chinese Tech Titans Eye Brazil," *The Wall Street Journal,* January 8, 2013, http://online.wsj.com; and Tom Orlik and Paul Mozur, "Lenovo Says Phones Are in the Black in China," *The Wall Street Journal,* January 23, 2013, http://online.wsj.com.
2. D. Wessel, "Big U.S. Firms Shift Hiring Abroad," *The Wall Street Journal,* April 19, 2011, http://online.wsj.com.
3. T. Smith, "First Look: Shanghai Disney Resort Images Revealed," *Disney Parks blog,* February 3, 2015, http://www.disneyparks.com; B. Fritz and J. Areddy, "Shanghai Disneyland Opening Pushed to First Half of 2016," *The Wall Street Journal* (online), February 2, 2015, http://www.wsj.com; E. Smith and J. T. Areddy, "Disney to Begin Shanghai Park," *The Wall Street Journal,* April 4, 2011, http://online.wsj.com.
4. M. S. Malone, "Living in a Bipolar Business World," *ABC News,* November 13, 2009, http://abcnews.go.com.
5. World Trade Organization, "World Trade Developments," *International Trade Statistics 2012,* p. 14, available at http://www.wto.org; World Trade Organization, "Trade Growth to Slow in 2012 after Strong Deceleration in 2011," news release, May 10, 2012, http://www.wto.org; and Mark Dorns, "Growing Appetite for American-Made Goods Overseas," Economics and Statistics Administration, March 22, 2011, http://www.esa.doc.gov.
6. United Nations Conference on Trade and Development (UNCTAD), "World Investment Report 2014," http://www.unctad.org, accessed March 21, 2015.
7. Ibid.
8. Bureau of the Census, *Statistical Abstract of the United States: 2011,* table 1290, p. 797, http://www.census.gov; and UN Conference on Trade and Development (UNCTAD), "Inward and Outward Foreign Direct Investment Flows," UnctadStat, http://unctadstat.unctad.org.
9. Reuters, "Deutsche Boerse Set for NYSE Deal as Nasdaq Bows Out," *LiveMint.com,* May 16, 2011, http://www.livemint.com; and F. Yan and A. Leung, "China's Geely Completes Volvo Buy," LiveMint.com, August 2, 2010, http://www.livemint.com.
10. C. Zappone, "China Poised for Global Shopping Spree," *CNNMoney,* March 30, 2007, http://money.cnn.com.
11. M. Martinez, "2014 Car Sales Best in U.S. Since '06," *Detroit News,* January 5, 2015, http://www.detroitnews.com; R. Rodriguez, "Peach Growers in Valley, China Fight for Market Share," *Fresno (Calif.) Bee,* January 31, 2011, http://www.fresnobee.com; and "AIADA:

Imports Increase Market Share," *Auto Remarketing,* December 7, 2010, http://www.autoremarketing.com.
12. B. Halvorson, "Buy American: Ten 2014 Vehicles That Wave the Stars and Stripes," *The Washington Post* (online), February 10, 2014, http://www.washingtonpost.com; and Edmunds, "Top 8 'Most American' Trucks for 2014," May 6, 2014, http://www.edmunds.com.
13. Joseph B. White, "What Is an American Car?" *The Wall Street Journal,* January 26, 2009, http://online.wsj.com.
14. New York Dehli, "Our Story," http://www.newyorkdelhi.com/our-story/, accessed March 21, 2015; and T. Nielsen, "Exporting: How Small Firms Started Trading Overseas," *The Guardian,* November 12, 2012.
15. G. Karol, "Pros and Cons of Doing Business with China," *Fox Small Business Center,* June 7, 2013, http://www.foxbusiness.com.
16. K. Peralta, "Outsourcing to China Cost U.S. 3.2 Million Jobs Since 2001," *U.S. News & World Report* (online), December 11, 2014, http://www.usnews.com.
17. D. Wessel and B. Davis, "Pain from Free Trade Spurs Second Thoughts," *The Wall Street Journal,* March 28, 2007, http://online.wsj.com.
18. "India's Outsourcing Business On the Turn," *The Economist* (online), January 19, 2013, http://www.economist.com.
19. J. Bryne, "IBM Now Employs More Workers in India Than U.S.," *The New York Post* (online), October 5, 2013, http://nypost.com.
20. Wessel, "Big U.S. Firms Shift Hiring Abroad."
21. Wessel and Davis, "Pain from Free Trade"; P. Levy, "Trade Truths for Turbulent Times: A Reply to Vladimir Masch," *BusinessWeek,* February 14, 2007, Business & Company Resource Center, http://galenet.galegroup.com; P. Restuccia, "Profs Claim the Threat of Outsourcing Is Overblown," *Boston Herald,* February 12, 2007, http://galenet.galegroup.com; and D. Blanchard, "Compete or Retreat," *Industry Week,* January 2007, http://galenet.galegroup.com.
22. M. Maynard, "A Lifeline Not Made in the U.S.A.," *The New York Times* (online), October 17, 2009, http://www.nytimes.com.
23. D. Whitford, "Where in the World Is Cheap Labor?" *Fortune,* March 22, 2011, http://money.cnn.com.
24. "Home or Abroad? Herd Instinct," *The Economist* (online), January 19, 2013, http://www.economist.com.
25. N. McLernon and J. Walters, "Insourcing Survey 2014," PricewaterhouseCoopers (online), March 2014, http://www.pwc.com; D. Anderson, J. Tweardy, M. Mancher, P. Lowes, J. Montrosse, and S. Chitre, "From Bangalore to Boston: The Trend of Bringing IT Back In-house," Deloitte (online), February 2013, http://www.deloitte.com.

26. C. Lombardi, "Survey: Software Companies Increasing Offshoring Work," *C/Net News,* January 12, 2007, http://news.com.com; "When Staying Put Trumps Offshoring," *McKinsey Quarterly,* December 7, 2004, online; and C. Koepfer, "A Look at Total Cost Can Change the View," *Production Machining,* January 2011, p. 6.

27. Koepfer, "A Look at Total Cost"; and Whitford, "Where in the World Is Cheap Labor?"

28. European Union, "About the EU," http://europa.eu; Central Intelligence Agency, "European Union," *The World Factbook,* http://www.cia.gov.

29. "Irish Welcome Portuguese to the Debt Club,'" *The Wall Street Journal,* April 7, 2011, http://blogs.wsj.com; S. Rastello and R. Christie, "IMF Will Work on Portugal Bailout Plan with European Union," *Bloomberg Businessweek,* April 8, 2011, http://www.businessweek.com; P. Kowsmann, "Portugal Reaches a Deal on Bailout," *The Wall Street Journal,* May 4, 2011, http://online.wsj.com; and M. Elliott, "Global Crises? Don't Panic," *Fortune,* April 21, 2011, http://money.cnn.com.

30. "Netflix Invades Europe: Why Expansion Beyond the U.S. Is So Critical?" *CNET,* September 19, 2014, http://www.cnet.com; and K. de Freytas-Tamura, "Data Storage Player Prepares to Compete Oveseas," *The New York Times* (online), March 31, 2013.

31. Liz Alderman, "Foreign Investment in Europe Starts Anew," *The New York Times,* March 4, 2012.

32. G. Smith, "E.U. Rejects Google's Latest Effort to Settle Antitrust Case," *Fortune* (online), September 9, 2014, http://www.fortune.com.

33. World Trade Organization, "World Trade Developments," p. 15.

34. Alex Frangos, "Behind China's Switch to High-End Exports," *The Wall Street Journal,* March 24, 2013, http://online.wsj.com; and Yajun Zhang, "China Begins to Lose Edge as World's Factory Floor," *The Wall Street Journal,* January 16, 2013, http://online.wsj.com.

35. "Three Snapshots of Chinese Innovation," *McKinsey Quarterly,* February 2012, http://www.mckinseyquarterly.com.

36. Bureau of Labor Statistics, Table 1: Manufacturing, Hourly Compensation Costs, U.S. Dollars, 2008–2012, "International Comparisons of Hourly Compensation Costs in Manufacturing Industries, by Country, 2008–2012," March 24, 2015, http://www.bls.gov/

37. G. Anand, "India Graduates Millions, but Too Few Are Fit to Hire," *The Wall Street Journal,* April 5, 2011, http://online.wsj.com.

38. S. McLain, "Uber Inks Marketing Deal with India's Times Internet," *The Wall Street Journal* (online), March 23, 2015, http://www.wsj.com.

39. A. van Agtmael, "Industrial Revolution 2.0," *Foreign Policy,* January–February 2007, Business & Company Company Resource Center, http://galenet.galegroup.com.

40. Office of the United States Trade Representative, "U.S.–APEC Trade Facts," http://www.ustr.gov, accessed March 24, 2015.

41. Agtmael, "Industrial Revolution 2.0"; and CEMEX website, http://www.cemex.com.

42. C. Simoes and I. Dantas, "Brazil's Economy: Growth May Have a Downside," *Bloomberg Businessweek,* June 10, 2010, http://www.businessweek.com; A. Ragir and D. Kopecki, "Brazil's Credit Boom Could End in Tears," *Bloomberg Businessweek,* January 6, 2011, http://www.businessweek.com; S. Nielsen, "Wind Power: Brazil's and Second Act," *Bloomberg Businessweek,* October 7, 2010, http://www.businessweek.com; and Polya Lesova and Michael Molinski, "Latin America's New Tigers Forge Ahead," *MarketWatch,* July 25, 2012, http://www.marketwatch.com.

43. "The Lure of Chilecon Valley," *The Economist* (online), October 15, 2012, http://www.economist.com.

44. Office of the United States Trade Representative, "Free Trade Agreements," http://www.ustr.gov.

45. U.S. Energy Information Administration, "How Dependent Are We on Foreign Oil?" *Energy in Brief,* July 13, 2012, http://www.eia.gov; and World Trade Organization, "World and Regional Export Profiles 2011," *International Trade Statistics* 2012, http://www.wto.org.

46. Hult Prize website, "2015 Hult Prize Online Challenge," http://www.hultprize.org, accessed March 26, 2015; D. Thorpe, "President Clinton Presents Hult Prize to Indian Social Entrepreneurs," *Forbes* (online), October 22, 2014, http://www.hultprize.org, accessed March 26, 2015; and D. Thorpe, "President Clinton Presents Hult Prize to Indian Social Entrepreneurs," *Forbes* (online), October 22, 2014, http://www.forbes.com.

47. M. Philips, "U.S. Oil Imports From Africa Are Down 90 Percent," *Bloomberg Business* (online), May 22, 2014, http://www.bloomberg.com; and K. Dhillon, "Why Are U.S. Oil Imports Falling?" *Time* (online), April 17, 2014, http://www.time.com.

48. F. Aquila, "Africa's Biggest Score: A Thriving Economy," *Bloomberg Businessweek,* June 28, 2010, http://www.businessweek.com; Sarah Frier, "For IBM, Africa Is Risky and Rife with Opportunity," *Bloomberg Businessweek,* February 21, 2013, http://www.businessweek.com.

49. H. Hong and Y. Doz, "L'Oréal Masters Multiculturalism," *Harvard Business Review,* June 2013, http://www.hbr.org.

50. Leslie Kwoh, "Cinnabon Finds Sweet Success in Russia, Mideast," *The Wall Street Journal,* December 25, 2012, http://online.wsj.com.

51. D. Cardwell, "U.S. Imposes Steep Tariffs on Chinese Solar Panels," *The New York Times* (online), December 16, 2014, http://www.nytimes.com.

52. Heineken International website, http://www.henekeninternational.com; and Heineken N.V. profile, Vintners.com, http://www.vintners.com.

53. S. Elliott, "Ford Tries a Global Campaign for Its Global Car," *The New York Times,* February 25, 2011, Business & Company Resource Center, http://galenet.galegroup.com.

54. "Ford Focus Tops Global Sales List," *The Economist Intelligence Unit,* April 10, 2014, http://www.eiu.com.

55. A.-W. Harzing, "An Empirical Analysis and Extension of the Bartlett and Ghoshal Typology of Multinational Companies," *Journal of International Business Studies* 31, no. 1 (2000), pp. 101–20; Sucheta Nadkarni, Pol Herrmann, and Pedro David Perez, "Domestic Mindsets and Early International Performance: The Moderating Effect of Global Industry Conditions," *Strategic Management Journal* 32, no. 5 (May 2011), pp. 510–31; S. M. Morris and S. A. Snell, "Intellectual Capital Configurations and Organizational Capability: An Empirical Examination of Human Resource Subunits in the Multinational Enterprise," *Journal of International Business Studies* 42, no. 6 (2011), pp. 805–27; and Elaine Ferndale, Jaap Paauwe, Shad S. Morris, Günther K. Stahl, Philip Stiles, Jonathan Trevor, and Patrick M. Wright, "Context-Bound Configurations of Corporate HR Functions in Multinational Corporations," *Human Resource Management* 49, no. 1 (January–February 2010), pp. 45–66.

56. J. Sandberg, "How Long Can India Keep Office Politics out of Outsourcing?" *The Wall Street Journal,* February 27, 2007, http://online.wsj.com.

57. Toshiro Wakayama, Junjiro Shintaku, and Tomofumi Amano, "What Panasonic Learned in China," *Harvard Business Review,* December 2012, pp. 109–113; and Daisuke Wakabayashi, "Panasonic to Pare Unprofitable Units," *The Wall Street Journal,* March 28, 2013, http://online.wsj.com.

58. J. Brown, "Jackpot!" *Bloomberg Businessweek* (online), May 8, 2014, http://www.bloomberg.com; J. Osawa, "Lenovo Completes Motorola Acquistion," *The Wall Street Journal* (online), October 30, 2014, http://www.wsj.com; L. Inge, "First U.S. Assembly Plant for China's Lenovo Opens in N.C.," National Public Radio, June 6, 2013, http://www.npr.org; Chao, "As Rivals Outsource"; Chao, "Chinese Tech Titans Eye Brazil"; Orlik and Mozur, "Lenovo Says Phones Are in the Black"; Juro Osawa, "Made in the USA by Apple and Lenovo," *The Wall Street Journal,* December 6, 2012, http://www.npr.org; Chao, "As Rivals Outsource"; Chao, "Chinese Tech Titans Eye Brazil"; Orlik and Mozur, "Lenovo Says Phones Are in the Black"; Juro Osawa, "Made in the USA by Apple and Lenovo," *The Wall Street Journal,* December 6, 2012, http://blogs.wsj.com; and Ian Sherr, "Lenovo Aims Higher in U.S.," *The Wall Street Journal,* January 10, 2013, http://online.wsj.com.

59. C. H. Moon, "The Choice of Entry Modes and Theories of Foreign Direct Investment," *Journal of Global Marketing* 11, no. 2 (1997), pp. 43–64; and I. Maignan and B. A. Lukas, "Entry Mode Decisions: The Role of Managers' Mental Models," *Journal of Global Marketing* 10, no. 4 (1997), pp. 7–22.

60. W. Mauldin, "U.S. Moves to Impose Tariffs on Chinese Tires," *The Wall Street Journal* (online), November 24, 2014, http://www.wsj.com.

61. 7-Eleven website, "7-Eleven Achieves Record Store Growth in 2012," http://www.7-eleven.com, accessed March 25, 2015.

62. M. Prewitt, "Breaking Down the Great Wall to Franchising in China," *Nation's Restaurant News,* March 12, 2007, Business & Company Resource Center, http://galenet.galegroup.com.

63. "Western Universities Expanding Joint Ventures in China," *ICEF Monitor* (online), September 30, 2014, http://monitor.icef.com.

64. S. Oster, N. Shirouzu, and P. Glader, "China Squeezes Foreigners for Share of Global Riches," *The Wall Street Journal,* December 28, 2010, http://online.wsj.com.

65. R. C. Beasley, "Reducing the Risk of Failure in the Formation of Commercial Partnerships," *Licensing Journal* 24, no. 4 (April 2004), p. 71; and Elie Chrysostome, Roli Nigam, and Chaire Stephen Jarilowski, "Revisiting Strategic Learning in International Joint Ventures: A Knowledge Creation Perspective," *International Journal of Management* 30, no. 1 (March 2013), pp. 88–98.

66. J. T. Areddy, "In China, Tire-Espionage Suit Treads Loudly," *The Wall Street Journal,* April 28, 2011, http://online.wsj.com; Bryan Vogel, "ITC Foreign-Based Misappropriation of Trade Secrets Actions," *InsideCounsel,* July 31, 2012, http://www.insidecounsel.com; and Julie Juan Li, Laura Poppo, and Kevin Zheng Zhou, "Relational Mechanisms, Formal Contracts, and Local Knowledge Acquisition by International Subsidiaries," *Strategic Management Journal* 31, no. 4 (April 2010), pp. 349–70.

67. K. Hille, "Western Faces Are Vital to China," *Financial Times,* December 9, 2010, Business & Company Resource Center, http://galenet.galegroup.com; and J. S. Lublin, "Finding Top Talent in China, India, Brazil," *The Wall Street Journal,* April 11, 2011, http://online.wsj.com.

68. R. Tung, "Selection and Training of Personnel for Overseas Assignments," *Columbia Journal of World Business* 15 (1981), pp. 68–78; and R. Tung, "Selection and Training Procedures of U.S., European, and Japanese Multinationals," *California Management Review* 25 (1981), pp. 57–71.

69. A. W. Andreason, "Expatriate Adjustment to Foreign Assignments," *International Journal of Commerce and Management* 13, no. 1 (Spring 2003), pp. 42–61.

70. P. Capell, "Know before You Go: Expats' Advice to Couples," *Career Journal Europe,* May 2, 2006, htp://www.careerjournaleurope.com; and Mila Lazarova, Mina Westman, and Margaret A. Shaffer, "Elucidating the Positive Side of the Work-Family Interface on International Assignments: A Model of Expatriate Work and Family Performance," *Academy of Management Review* 35, no. 1 (January 2010), pp. 93–117.

71. R. A. Swaak, "Expatriate Failures: Too Many, Too Much Cost, Too Little Planning," *Compensation & Benefits Review,* November/December 1995, pp. 50–52.

72. Capell, "Know before You Go."

73. G. M. Sprietzer, M. W. McCall, and J. D. Mahoney, "Early Identification of International Executive Potential," *Journal of Applied Psychology* 82, no. 1 (1997), pp. 6–29; R. Mortensen, "Beyond the Fence Line," *HRMagazine,* November 1997, pp. 100–9; "Expatriate Games," *Journal of Business Strategy,* July/August 1997, pp. 4–5; "Building a Global Workforce Starts with Recruitment," *Personnel Journal* (special supplement), March 1996, pp. 9–11; Ming Li, William H. Mobley, and Aidan Kelly, "When Do Global Leaders Learn Best to Develop Cultural Intelligence? An Investigation of the Moderating Role of Experiential Learning Style," *Academy of Management Learning & Education* 12, no. 1 (March 2013), pp. 32–50; and Nicola M. Pless, Thomas Maak, and Günther K. Stahl, "Developing Responsible Global Leaders through International Service-Learning Programs: The Ulysses Experience," *Academy of Management Learning & Education* 10, no. 2 (June 2011), pp. 237–60.

74. A. Paul, "How the Internet Shrinks the Distance between Us," *The Wall Street Journal,* March 16, 2007, http://online.wsj.com.

75. G. A. Fowler, "In China's Offices, Foreign Colleagues Might Get an Earful," *The Wall Street Journal,* February 13, 2007, http://online.wsj.com.

76. John Slocum, "Coming to America," *Human Resource Executive,* October 2, 2008, http://www.hrexecutive.com.

77. PricewaterhouseCoopers website, "Millennials Survey: Millennials at Work: Reshaping the Workplace," http://www.pwc.com, accessed March 26, 2015.

78. J. Brett, K. Behfar, and M. C. Kern, "Managing Multicultural Teams," *Harvard Business Review,* November 2006, pp. 84–91.

79. D. Stamps, "Welcome to America," *Training,* November 1996, pp. 23–30.

80. L. K. Trevino and K. A. Nelson, *Managing Business Ethics: Straight Talk about How to Do It Right* (New York: John Wiley & Sons, 1995).

81. Transparency International, "Leading Exporters Undermine Development with Dirty Business Overseas," news release, October 4, 2006, http://www.transparency.org.

82. J. G. Longnecker, J. A. McKinney, and C. W. Moore, "The Ethical Issues of International Bribery: A Study of Attitudes among U.S. Business Professionals," *Journal of Business Ethics* 7 (1988), pp. 341–46.

83. D. Searcey, "U.K. Law on Bribes Has Firms in a Sweat," *The Wall Street Journal,* December 28, 2010, http://online.wsj.com.

84. Ibid.; and J. Holzer and S. Raice, "IBM Settles Bribery Charges," *The Wall Street Journal,* March 19, 2011, http://online.wsj.com.

85. UPS, "The UPS Code of Business Conduct: Leading with Integrity," UPS Pressroom, http://www.pressroom.ups.com; and i-Sight, "International Code of Conduct: United Parcel Service," Best Practices, June 17, 2010, http://i-sight.com.

86. A. B. Desai and T. Rittenburg, "Global Ethics: An Integrative Framework for MNEs," *Journal of Business Ethics* 16 (1997), pp. 791–800; and P. Buller, J. Kohls, and K. Anderson, "A Model for Addressing Cross-Cultural Ethical Conflicts," *Business & Society* 36, no. 2 (June 1997), pp. 169–93.

87. E. Dou, "Lenovo's Smartphone Challenge: Battling Apple, Xiaomi in China with Motorola," *The Wall Street Journal* (online), February 3, 2015, http://www.wsj.com; J. Osawa, "Lenovo Takes on Apple, Samsung in Smartphones," *The Wall Street Journal* (online), August 14, 2014, http://www.wsj.com; Chao, "As Rivals Outsource"; Einhorn, "Lenovo's Persistent PC Strategy"; Chao, "Chinese Tech Titans Eye Brazil"; Sherr, "Lenovo Aims Higher in U.S."; and Bruce Einhorn, "In China's Smartphone Market, Lenovo Gets Busy," *Bloomberg Businessweek,* January 3, 2013, http://www.businessweek.com.

Chapter 7

1. Meghan Casserly, "Popchips: The Next $1 Billion Snack Food or Just Full of Hot Air?" *Forbes,* January 24, 2013, http://www.forbes.com; Nicole Hong, "New Kind of Chip Pops on the Scene," *The Wall Street Journal,* February 20, 2013, http://online.wsj.com; Laura Petrecca, "Popchips CEO Keith Belling Is Poptimist on Healthy Snacks," *USA Today,* April 12, 2010, http://usatoday30.usatoday.com; and Stacy Finz, "Popchips Doing Healthy Sales, Expanding to Britain," *San Francisco Chronicle,* March 1, 2012, http://www.sfgate.com.

2. S. Shane and S. Venkataraman, "The Promise of Entrepreneurship as a Field of Research," *Academy of Management Review* 25 (2000), pp. 217–26.

3. J. A. Timmons, *New Venture Creation* (Burr Ridge, IL: Richard D. Irwin, 1994).

4. Shane and Venkataraman, "The Promise of Entrepreneurship As a Field of Research."

5. M. A. Hitt, R. D. Ireland, D. Sirmon, and C. Trahms, "Strategic Entrepreneurship: Creating Value for Individuals, Organizations, and Society," *Academy of Management Perspectives* (May 2011), pp. 57–75.

6. W. Megginson, M. J. Byrd, S. R. Scott Jr., and L. Megginson, *Small Business Management: An Entrepreneur's Guide to Success,* 2nd ed. (Boston: Irwin McGraw-Hill, 1997).

7. J. Timmons and S. Spinelli, *New Venture Creation: Entrepreneurship for the 21st Century,* 6th ed. (New York: McGraw-Hill/Irwin, 2004), p. 3.

8. J. A. Timmons, *The Entrepreneurial Mind* (Andover, MA: Brick House, 1989).

9. J. Clifton, "American Entrepreneurship: Dead or Alive?" *Gallup Business Journal,* January 13, 2015, http://www.gallup.com; B. Casselman, "Risk-Averse Culture Infects U.S. Workers, Entrepreneurs," *The Wall Street Journal,* June 2, 2013, p. A1.

10. J. Hecht, "Are Small Businesses Really the Backbone of the Economy?" *Inc.* (online), December 17, 2014, http://www.inc.com.

11. D. J. Isenberg, "The Global Entrepreneur," *Harvard Business Review,* December 2008, pp. 107–11.

12. Timmons and Spinelli, *New Venture Creation.*

13. A. Loten, "Start-Ups Key to States' Economic Success," *Inc.,* February 7, 2007, http://www.inc.com.

14. Timmons and Spinelli, *New Venture Creation.*

15. Ibid.

16. D. Bricklin, "Natural-Born Entrepreneur," *Harvard Business Review,* September 2001, pp. 53–59, 58.

17. D. Williams, "The 4 Essential Traits of 'Intrapreneurs,'" *Forbes* (online), October 30, 2013, http://www.forbes.com; and Alexandra Levit, "'Insider' Entrepreneurs," *The Wall Street Journal,* April 6, 2009, http://online.wsj.com.

18. M. A. Hitt, R. D. Ireland, D. Sirmon, and C. Trahms, "Strategic Entrepreneurship: Creating Value for Individuals, Organizations, and Society," *Academy of Management Perspectives,* May 2011, pp. 57–75.

19. T. Hsieh, "Why I Sold Zappos," *Inc.* (online), June 1, 2010, http://www.inc.com.

20. R. Fairlie, "Kaufman Index of Entrepreneurial Activity," Ewing Marion Kauffman Foundation, April 2014, http://www.kaufmann.org; and C. Conner, "Who's Starting America's New Businesses? And Why?" *Forbes,* July 22, 2012.

21. inDinero, "About inDinero," http://www.indinero.com, accessed March 27, 2015; "Coolest College Start-Ups: Where Are They Now?" *Inc.,* March 2011, http://www.inc.com; E. Lee, "The Small-Business Numbers Cruncher," *San Francisco Chronicle,* January 3, 2011, Business & Company Resource Center, http://galenet.galegroup.com; M. Chafkin, "InDinero Fixes Money Management," *Inc.,* December 2010, http://www.inc.com; and A. Gardella, "Can a 20-Year-Old Help You Track Your Finances?" *The New York Times,* September 29, 2010, http://boss.blogs.nytimes.com.

22. M. Palmieri, "LM150 Lessons Learned: Embrace Your Mistakes," *Landscape Management* (online), June 12, 2014, http://www.landscapemanagement.net; and L. Kanter, "The Eco-Advantage," *Inc.,* November 2006, pp. 78–103 (NaturaLawn example on page 84).

23. H. Aldrich, *Ethnic Entrepreneurs: Immigrant Business in Industrial Societies* (Newbury Park, CA: Sage, 1990).

24. "Billionaire Immigrants," *Forbes* (online), http://www.forbes.com, accessed March 27, 2015; "Elon Musk," Biography (online), http://www.biography.com, accessed March 29, 2015.

25. J. Jennings and C. Brush, "Research on Woman Entrepreneurs: Challenges to (and from) the Broader Entrepreneurship Literature?" *Academy of Management Annals* 7 (2013), pp. 663–715; Timmons and Spinelli, *New Venture Creation.*

26. J. Collins and J. Porras, *Built to Last* (London: Century, 1996).

27. Ibid.

28. K. H. Vesper, *New Venture Mechanics* (Englewood Cliffs, NJ: Prentice Hall, 1993).

29. "Entrepreneur of 2012: Limor Fried," *Entrepreneur,* December 18, 2012, http://www.entrepreneur.com.

30. Vesper, *New Venture Mechanics.*

31. Johnson & Johnson, "Johnson & Johnson Announces Definitive Agreement to Collaborate with Google to Advance Surgical Robotics," press release, March 26, 2015, http://www.jnj.com.

32. D. Internicola, "New Fitness Centers Cater to Aging Baby Boomers," Reuters, January 7, 2013, http://www.reuters.com.

33. Timmons and Spinelli, *New Venture Creation.*

34. P. J. Sauer, "Serving Up Success," *Inc.,* January 2007, http://www.inc.com.

35. Panera, "Our History," http://www.panera.com, accessed March 29, 2015.

36. T. Bates, "A Comparison of Franchise and Independent Small Business Survival Rates," *Small Business Economics* 7 (1995), pp. 377–88.

37. K. Spors, "Franchised versus Nonfranchised Businesses," *The Wall Street Journal,* February 27, 2007, http://online.wsj.com.

38. Timmons and Spinelli, *New Venture Creation.*

39. "The Biggest Trends in Business for 2013," *Entrepreneur,* December 3, 2012, http://www.entrepreneur.com.

40. D. Fenn, "30 Under 30," *Inc.,* July 2, 2012.

41. Bigelow Aerospace, "The First Private Space Habitat Is Here," http://www.bigelowaerospace.com, accessed March 29, 2015; "Innovation: Inside the Space Station," *Inc.,* April 1, 2013, http://www.inc.com; and Andy Pasztor, "Nerve-Wracking Space Drama Swirls around Unmanned Cargo Capsule," *The Wall Street Journal,* March 1, 2013, http://online.wsj.com.

42. General Electric, "GE 2013 Global Impact: Investing in New Technologies and Business Models," http://www.ge.com, accessed March 29, 2015; *Entrepreneur,* "The Biggest Trends in Business for 2013"; April Joyner, "Thinking of Starting a Business? Check Out Consumer Health Technology," *Inc.,* April 8, 2013, http://www.inc.com; and General Electric, "GE and Startup Health Select 13 Consumer Health Companies for Entrepreneurship Program," news release, April 4, 2013, http://www.genewscenter.com.

43. J. J. Colao, "America's Most Promising Company Is Redefining Mobile: Meet 3Cinteractive," *Forbes,* January 23, 2013, http://www.forbes.com; Justine Griffin, "John Duffy, Small Business Leader, Palm Beach County," *South Florida Sun-Sentinel,* April 26, 2012, http://www.sun-sentinel.com; and 3Cinteractive, "About 3Cinteractive," http://www.3cinteractive.com/About/.

44. J. E. Lange, "Entrepreneurs and the Continuing Internet: The Expanding Frontier," in Timmons and Spinelli, *New Venture Creation,* pp. 183–220.

45. Ibid.

46. J. E. Vascellaro, "Selling Your Designs Online," *The Wall Street Journal,* April 5, 2007, http://online.wsj.com.

47. J. Short, T. Moss, and G. Lumpkin, "Research in Social Entrepreneurship: Past, Contributions and Future Opportunities," *Strategic Entrepreneurship Journal* 3 (2009), pp. 161–94; and S. Zahra and M. Wright, "Entrepreneur's Next Act," *Academy of Management Perspectives* (2011), pp. 67–83.

48. P. Dacin, M.T. Dacin, and M. Matear, "Social Entrepreneurship: Why We Don't Need a New Theory and How We Move Forward from Here," *Academy of Management Perspectives* 24 (2010), pp. 37–57.

49. T. Miller, M. Grimes, J. McMullen, and T. Vogus, "Venturing for Others with Heart and Head: How Compassion Encourages Social Entrepreneurship," *Academy of Management Review* 37 (2012), pp. 616–40.

50. J. Mair and I. Marti, "Social Entrepreneurship Research: A Source of Explanation, Prediction, and Delight," *Journal of World Business* 41 (2006), pp. 36–44.

51. D. Bornstein and S. Davis, *Social Entrepreneurship: What Everyone Needs to Know* (Oxford, UK: Oxford University Press, 2010).

52. Schwab Foundation for Social Entrepreneurship, "Social Entrepreneurs," http://www.schwabfound.org/entrepreneurs, accessed March 29, 2015.

53. Ibid.

54. Ibid.

55. M. Driver, "An Interview with Michael Porter: Social Entrepreneurship and the Transformation of Capitalism," *Academy of Management Learning & Education* 11 (2012), pp. 421–31.

56. M. Porter and M. Kramer, "Creating Shared Value," *Harvard Business Review* (January–February 2011), pp. 62–77.

57. H. Sabeti, "The For-Benefit Enterprise," *Harvard Business Review,* November 2011, pp. 98–194.

58. "Coca-Cola and Nely Galan Honor Latinas on International Women's Day and Beyond," *Yahoo Finance,* March 29, 2015, http://finance.yahoo.com; "Pioneer Studio Executive & Philanthropist," *Makers* (online), http://www.makers.com, accessed March 29, 2015; S. Cole, "Meet the Woman Inspiring Thousands of American Latina Entrepreneurs," *Fast Company* (online), March 16, 2015, http://www.fastcompany.com; D. Parnell, "Media Mogul Nely Galan, On Succeeding Through Diversity," *Forbes* (online), March 13, 2015, http://www.forbes.com; and "Inspiring Latina: Businesswoman and Entertainment Mogul Nely Galan," *Latina* (online), June 10, 2014, http://www.latina.com.

59. P. Omidyar, "eBay's Founder on Innovating the Business Model of Social Change," *Harvard Business Review,* September 2011, pp. 41–44.

60. Timmons, *New Venture Creation.*

61. M. Cardon, J. Wincent, J. Singh, and M. Drnovsek, "The Nature and Experience of Entrepreneurial Passion," *Academy of Management Review* 34 (2009), pp. 511–32.

62. J. R. Baum and E. A. Locke, "The Relationship of Entrepreneurial Traits, Skill, and Motivation to Subsequent Venture Growth," *Journal of Applied Psychology* 89 (2004), pp. 587–98.

63. M. Sonfield and R. Lussier, "The Entrepreneurial Strategy Matrix: A Model for New and Ongoing Ventures," *Business Horizons,* May–June 1997, pp. 73–77.

64. Lange, "Entrepreneurs and the Continuing Internet."

65. J. Rafflee and J. Feng, "Should I Quit My Day Job? A Hybrid Path to Entrepreneurship," *Academy of Management Journal* 57 (2014), pp. 936–63; and S. Venkataraman and M. Low, "On the Nature of Critical Relationships: A Test of the Liabilities and Size Hypothesis," in *Frontiers of Entrepreneurship Research* (Babson Park, MA: Babson College, 1991), p. 97.

66. Timmons and Spinelli, *New Venture Creation.*

67. Cari Tuna, "Tough Call: Deciding to Start a Business," *The Wall Street Journal,* January 8, 2009, http://online .wsj.com.

68. Freshly Picked, "Our Story," http://www.freshlypicked.com, accessed March 30, 2015; and C. Clifford, "From Pennies to Millions: What It Felt Like to Make Money for the First Time," *Entrepreneur,* March 25, 2015, http://www.entrepreneur.com.

69. L. Buchanan, "Create Jobs, Eliminate Waste, Preserve Value," *Inc.,* December 2006, pp. 94–106.

70. Houston Technology Center, http://www.houstontech.org, accessed March 30, 2015; and "12 Business Incubators Changing the World," *Forbes* (online), http://www.forbes.com, accessed March 30, 2015.

71. R. Price, "The Role of Service Providers in Establishing Networked Regional Business Accelerators in Utah," *International Journal of Technology Management* 27 (2004), pp. 465–74.

72. Norm Brodsky, "Street Smarts: Our Irrational Fear of Numbers," *Inc.,* January 2009, http://www.inc.com.

73. Jeremy Quittner, "Robin Chase: How I Survived a Huge Screw-Up," *Inc.,* February 28, 2013, http://www.inc.com.

74. D. McGinn, "Why Size Matters," *Inc.,* Fall 2004, pp. 32–36.

75. S. E. Needleman, "When It's Time to Take On Help," *The Wall Street Journal,* January 16, 2011, http://online.wsj.com.

76. Kanter, "The Eco-Advantage."

77. 37signals, "Two Big Announcements," https://37signals.com, accessed March 30, 2015; and J. Stillman, "Slow Business: The Case Against Fast Growth," *Inc.* (online), September 18, 2012, http://www.inc.com.

78. S. Finkelstein, "The Myth of Managerial Superiority in Internet Startups: An Autopsy," *Organizational Dynamics,* Fall 2001, pp. 172–85.

79. K. Hickey, "5 Lessons from Managing Our Startup's Rapid Growth," *Forbes* (online), April 9, 2013, http://www.forbes.com.

80. R. Weisman, "Bootstrappers Avoid Outside Money Ties," *Boston Globe,* February 5, 2007, Business & Company Resource Center, http://galenet.galegroup.com.

81. A. Cordeiro, "Sweet Returns," *The Wall Street Journal* (online), April 23, 2009, http://www.wsj.com.

82. G. Stalk and H. Foley "Avoid the Traps That Can Destroy Family Businesses," *Harvard Business Review,* (January–February, 2012) pp. 25–27.

83. P. F. Drucker, "How to Save the Family Business," *The Wall Street Journal,* August 19, 1994, p. A10.

84. D. Gamer, R. Owen, and R. Conway, *The Ernst & Young Guide to Raising Capital* (New York: John Wiley & Sons, 1991).

85. Ibid.

86. D. Buss, "Behind Big Fan Katy Perry, Should Popchips Leap into Super Bowl?" *Forbes* (online), November 30, 2014, http://www.forbes.com; K. Lukovitz, "Popchips' Next Stage Includes TV, Redesigned Site," *Marketing Daily* (online), September 25, 2014, http://www.mediapost.com; Popchips, "Paul Davis Joins Popchips as CEO Former Kettle CEO & Frito-Lay Executive Takes Over Leadership of Award Winning Brand," press release, January 2014, http://www.popchips.com; Casserly, "Popchips: The Next $1 Billion Snack Food?"; Hong, "New Kind of Chip"; Petrecca, "Popchips CEO Keith Belling"; Breeanna Hare, "Amidst Complaints, Popchips CEO Apologizes for Ashton Kutcher Ad," *CNN Wire,* May 3, 2012, Business Insights: Essentials, http://bi.galegroup .com; Bridget Goldschmidt,

"Pop Go the Snacks," *Progressive Grocer,* April 1, 2013, Business Insights: Essentials, http://bi.galegroup.com; and Hoover's, "Snack Foods Manufacturing Industry Profile," First Research Industry Profiles, http://www.firstresearch.com, last updated March 18, 2013.

87. Half Price Books, "What We Do to Be Green," http://www.hpb.com, accessed March 30, 2015; D. Eng, "Thriving in an Amazon World," *Fortune* (online), September 18, 2014, http://www.fortune.com; R. Hisrich and M. Peters, *Entrepreneurship: Starting, Developing, and Managing a New Enterprise* (Burr Ridge, IL: Irwin, 1994); and J. H. Ostdick, "Elevating the Bottom Line," *Success,* December 2010, pp. 59–64.

88. R. D. Hisrich and M. P. Peters, *Entrepreneurship: Starting, Developing, and Managing a New Enterprise* (Burr Ridge, IL: Irwin, 1994).

89. Ibid.

90. Small Business Administration, "Frequently Asked Questions about Small Business Finance," SBA Office of Advocacy, September 2011, http://www.sba.gov; and Ewing Marion Kauffman Foundation, "Six Myths about Venture Capital Offer Dose of Reality to Startups in *Harvard Business Review* Article," news release, April 16, 2013, http://www.kauffman.org.

91. Lending Club, "Business Loans," http://www.lendingclub.com, accessed March 31, 2015; Prosper, "Company Overview," http://www.prosper.com, accessed March 31, 2015; and I. Mount, "When Banks Won't Lend, There Are Alternatives, Though Often Expensive," *The New York Times* (online), August 1, 2012, http://www.nytimes.com.

92. S. Case, "Case: Hey, Washington, the JOBS Act You Passed Is Working," *The Wall Street Journal* (online), April 2, 2014, http://www.wsj.com; "JOBS Act, One Year Later: Hang Tight, Equity Crowdfunding Is Coming," *Entrepreneur,* April 5, 2013, http://www.entrepreneur.com; "Crowdfunding Industry on Fire: Trends to Watch," *Entrepreneur,* April 8, 2013, http://www.entrepreneur.com; Becky Yerak, "Is Promise Worth Peril?" *Chicago Tribune,* February 24, 2013, sec. 2, pp. 1, 3; and Sarah E. Needleman and Lora Kolodny, "Site Unseen: More 'Angels' Invest via Internet," *The Wall Street Journal,* January 23, 2013, http://online.wsj.com.

93. W. A. Sahlman, "How to Write a Great Business Plan," *Harvard Business Review,* July–August 1997, pp. 98–108.

94. Ibid.

95. M. Copeland, "Start Last, Finish First," *Business 2.0 Magazine* (online), February 2, 2006, http://www.money.cnn.com.

96. Sahlman, "How to Write a Great Business Plan."

97. M. Zimmerman and G. Zeitz, "Beyond Survival: Achieving New Venture Growth by Building Legitimacy," *Academy of Management Review* 27 (2002), pp. 414–21.

98. A. L. Stinchcombe, "Social Structure and Organizations," in J. G. March, ed., *Handbook of Organizations* (Chicago: Rand McNally, 1965), pp. 142–93.

99. Ibid.

100. L. Taylor, "Want Your Start-Up to Be Successful? Appearance Is Everything," *Inc.*, February 23, 2007, http://www. inc.com.

101. Ibid.

102. R. A. Baron and G. D. Markman, "Beyond Social Capital: How Social Skills Can Enhance Entrepreneurs' Success," *Academy of Management Executive,* February 2000, pp. 106–16.

103. J. Florin, M. Lubatkin, and W. Schulze, "A Social Capital Model of High-Growth Ventures," *Academy of Management Journal* 46 (2003), pp. 374–84.

104. J. Gangemi, "Young, Fearless, and Smart," *BusinessWeek,* October 30, 2006, http:// www.businessweek.com.

105. Attend.com, "Our Story," http://www. attend.com, accessed April 1, 2015; G. Skloot, "How Early-Stage Startups Can Attract Seasoned Executives," *Entrepreneur* (online), May 1, 2014, http:// www.entrepreneur.com; N. Fallow, "6 Ways to Keep Control of a Fast-Growing Startup," Fox Small Business Center, May 23, 2014, http://www.foxbusiness.com; and "Baby Boomers,Who Are More Successful as Entrepreneurs, Are Great Startup Assets," *Entrepreneur* (online), October 24, 2014, http://www.entrepreneur.com.

106. W. Harris, "Team Players," *Black Enterprise,* January 2007, Business & Company Resource Center, http://galenet. galegroup.com.

107. R. M. Kanter, *The Change Masters* (New York: Simon & Schuster, 1983).

108. W.L. Gore, "Consumer Products," http:// www.gore.com, accessed March 31, 2015; R. Kneece, "10 Inspiring Examples of Successful Intrapreneurship," *Wired* (online), September 17, 2014, http:// www.wired.com; and R. Safian, "Terri Kelli, the 'Un-CEO' of W.L. Gore, On How to Deal with Chaos: Grow Up," *Fast Company,* October 29, 2012, http://www. fastcompany.com.

109. R. M. Kanter, C. Ingols, E. Morgan, and T. K. Seggerman, "Driving Corporate Entrepreneurship," *Management Review* 76 (April 1987), pp. 14–16.

110. J. Argenti, *Corporate Collapse: The Causes and Symptoms* (New York: John Wiley & Sons, 1979).

111. Kanter et al., "Driving Corporate Entrepreneurship."

112. Y. Ling, Z. Simsek, M. Lubatkin, and J. Veiga, "Transformational Leadership's Role in Promoting Corporate Entrepreneurship: Examining the CEO–TMT Interface," *Academy of Management Journal,* 2008, pp. 557–76.

113. G. T. Lumpkin and G. G. Dess, "Clarifying the Entrepreneurial Orientation Construct and Linking It to Performance," *Academy of Management Review* 21 (1996), pp. 135–72; and G.G. Dess and G.T. Lumpkin, "The Role of Entrepreneurial Orientation

in Stimulating Effective Corporate Entrepreneurship," *The Academy of Management Executive* 19 (February 2005), pp. 147–56.

114. H. J. Sapienza, E. Autio, G. George, and S. A. Zahra, "A Capabilities Perspective on the Effects of Early Internationalization on Firm Survival and Growth," *Academy of Management Review* 31, no. (2006), pp. 914–33.

115. Casserly, "Popchips: The Next $1 Billion Snack Food?"; Hong, "New Kind of Chip"; and Petrecca, "Popchips CEO Keith Belling."

116. T. Bateman and J. M. Crant, "The Proactive Dimension of Organizational Behavior," *Journal of Organizational Behavior* (1993), pp. 103–18.

117. Lumpkin and Dess, "Clarifying the Entrepreneurial Orientation Construct."

118. C. Pinchot and E. Pinchot, *The Intelligent Organization* (San Francisco: Barrett-Koehler, 1996).

Chapter 8

1. "GM Has Record China Sales in 2013," *Auto News* (online), January 7, 2014, http://www.autonews.com; General Motors, *Annual Report 2013,* www. gm.com; Tim Higgins and Jeff Green, "GM Seen Planning Global Reorganization against 'Fiefdoms,'" *Bloomberg,* August 17, 2012, http://www.bloomberg.com; Qineqt, "General Motors Reorganization: Will the Glory Days Be Back?" *Seeking Alpha,* September 3, 2012, http:// seekingalpha.com; Paul A. Eisenstein, "Big Management Shake-Up on the Horizon at GM," *NBC News,* August 22, 2012, http://www.nbcnews.com; Ben Klayman, "Car Guy or Bean Counter?" Reuters, July 19, 2012, http://www.reuters. com; "Government in March Sold $621M Worth of GM Stock," *CBS News,* April 10, 2013, http://www.cbsnews.com; and Yuri Kageyama, "Toyota Top Selling Automaker Despite China Fall," *Detroit Free Press,* April 24, 2013, http://www. freep.com.

2. R. N. Ashkenas and S. C. Francis, "Integration Managers: Special Leaders for Special Times," *Harvard Business Review* 78, no. 6 (November–December 2000), pp. 108–16.

3. T. Malone, R. Laubacher, and T. Johns, "The Big Idea: The Age of Hyperspecialization," *Harvard Business Review* (online), July 1, 2011, http://www. hbr.org; A. West, "The Flute Factory: An Empirical Measurement of the Effect of the Division of Labor on Productivity and Production Cost," *American Economist* 43, no. 1 (Spring 1999), pp. 82–87.

4. P. Lawrence and J. Lorsch, *Organization and Environment* (Homewood, IL: Richard D. Irwin, 1969).

5. Ibid.; and B. L. Thompson, *The New Manager's Handbook* (New York: McGraw-Hill, 1994). See also S. Sharifi

and K. S. Pawar, "Product Design as a Means of Integrating Differentiation," *Technovation* 16, no. 5 (May 1996), pp. 255–64; and W. B. Stevenson and J. M. Bartunek, "Power, Interaction, Position, and the Generation of Cultural Agreement in Organizations," *Human Relations* 49, no. 1 (January 1996), pp. 75–104.

6. P. Puranam, H. Singh, and M. Zollo, "Organizing for Innovation: Managing the Coordination-Autonomy Dilemma in Technology Acquisitions," *Academy of Management Journal* 49, no. 2 (2006), pp. 263–80.

7. A. J. Ali, R. C. Camp, and M. Gibbs, "The Ten Commandments Perspective on Power and Authority in Organizations," *Journal of Business Ethics* 26, no. 4 (August 2000), pp. 351–61; and R. F. Pearse, "Understanding Organizational Power and Influence Systems," *Compensation & Benefits Management* 16, no. 4 (Autumn 2000), pp. 28–38.

8. J. Pfeffer, *Power: Why Some People Have It—and Others Don't* (New York: HarperCollins, 2010).

9. S. F. Shultz, Board Book: *Making Your Corporate Board a Strategic Force in Your Company's Success* (New York: AMACOM, 2000); and R. D. Ward, *Improving Corporate Boards: The Boardroom Insider Guidebook* (New York: John Wiley & Sons, 2000).

10. O. Faleye, R. Hoitash, and U. Hoitash, "The Trouble with Too Much Board Oversight," *MIT Sloan Management Review,* March 19, 2013, http://www. sloanreview.mit.edu; and T. Perkins, "The 'Compliance Board,'" *The Wall Street Journal,* March 2, 2007, http://online.wsj. com.

11. The Alternative Board, "About," http:// www.thealternativeboard.com, accessed April 4, 2015; and J. Aldridge, "The Alternative Board Expanding to Rapidly Growing Boerne Area," *San Antonio Biz Journal* (online), January 6, 2015, http:// www.bizjournals.com.

12. Margaret Heffernan, "You *Really* Need Outside Directors: Here's Why," *Inc.,* October 15, 2012, http://www.inc. com; Kingston Smith LLP, "Lessons Learned: Surviving the Recession," news release, February 20, 2009, http://www. kingstonsmithw1.co.uk; and Karl Stark and Bill Stewart, "Why You Need an Advisory Board," *Inc.,* January 24, 2012, http:// www.inc.com.

13. C. M. Daily and D. R. Dalton, "CEO and Board Chair Roles Held Jointly or Separately: Much Ado about Nothing?" *Academy of Management Executive* 11, no. 3 (August 1997), pp. 11–20.

14. T. Simons, L. H. Pelled, and K. A. Smith, "Making Use of Difference: Diversity, Debate, and Decision Comprehensiveness in Top Management Teams," *Academy of Management Journal* 42, no. 6 (December 1999), pp. 662–73; and C. Carl Pegels, Y. I Song, and B. Yang, "Management Heterogeneity, Competitive Interaction

Groups, and Firm Performance," *Strategic Management Journal* 21, no. 3 (September 2000), pp. 911–21.

15. S. Vickery, C. Droge, and R. Germain, "The Relationship between Product Customization and Organizational Structure," *Journal of Operations Management* 17, no. 4 (June 1999), pp. 377–91. See also N. Nohria, W. Joyce, and B. Roberson, "What Really Works," *Harvard Business Review* (July 2003).

16. Andrew R. McIlvaine, "Flat, Fast and . . . Risky?" *Human Resource Executive Online,* March 6, 2012, http://www.hreonline.com.

17. D. Van Fleet and A. Bedeian, "A History of the Span of Management," *Academy of Management Review* 2 (1977), pp. 356–72. Results of Corporate Executive Board survey reported in McIlvaine, "Flat, Fast and . . . Risky?"

18. "Span of Control vs. Span of Support," *Journal for Quality and Participation* 23, no. 4 (Fall 2000), p. 15; J. Gallo and P. R. Thompson, "Goals, Measures, and Beyond: In Search of Accountability in Federal HRM," *Public Personnel Management* 29, no. 2 (Summer 2000), pp. 237–48; and C. O. Longenecker and T. C. Stansfield, "Why Plant Managers Fail: Causes and Consequences," *Industrial Management* 42, no. 1 (January/February 2000), pp. 24–32.

19. S. Lloyd, "Managers Must Delegate Effectively to Develop Employees," Society for Human Resource Management (online), February 2, 2012, http://www.shrm.org; Z. X. Chen and S. Aryee, "Delegation and Employee Work Outcomes: An Examination of the Cultural Context of Mediating Processes in China," *Academy of Management Journal* 50, no. 1 (2007), pp. 226–38.

20. I. Kalb, "3 Ways Micromanagers Can Destroy a Company," *Business Insider* (online), July 7, 2014, http://www.businessinsider.com; S. Finkelstein, "In Praise of Micromanagement," *BBC* (online), October 3, 2013, http://www.bbc.com.

21. "How to Delegate More Effectively," *Community Banker,* February 2009, p. 14; B. Nefer, "Don't Be Delegation-Phobic," *Supervision,* December 2008, Business & Company Resource Center, http://galenet.galegroup.com; J. Mahoney, "Delegating Effectively," *Nursing Management* 28, no. 6 (June 1997), p. 62; and J. Lagges, "The Role of Delegation in Improving Productivity," *Personnel Journal,* November 1979, pp. 776–79.

22. G. Matthews, "Run Your Business or Build an Organization?" *Harvard Management Review,* March–April 1984, pp. 34–44.

23. N. Siggelkow and J. W. Rivkin, "When Exploration Backfires: Unintended Consequences of Multilevel Organizational Search," *Academy of Management Proceedings,* 2006, pp. BB1–BB6.

24. "Missing Its Targets," *Delaney Report,* November 26, 2012, Business Insights: Essentials, http://bi.galegroup.com.

25. J. R. Hollenbeck, A. P. J. Ellis, S. E. Humphrey, A. S. Garza, and D. R. Ilgen, "Asymmetry in Structural Adaptation: The Differential Impact of Centralizing versus Decentralizing Team Decision-Making Structures," *Organizational Behavior and Human Decision Processes* 114 (2011), pp. 64–74.

26. R. Forrester, "Empowerment: Rejuvenating a Potent Idea," *Academy of Management Executive* 14, no. 3 (August 2000), pp. 67–80; and M. L. Perry, C. L. Pearce, and H. P. Sims Jr., "Empowered Selling Teams: How Shared Leadership Can Contribute to Selling Team Outcomes," *Journal of Personal Selling & Sales Management* 19, no. 3 (Summer 1999), pp. 35–51.

27. K. Hara, "Nestlé's CEO Sees Decentralization as Key," *Nikkei Asian Review* (online), June 26, 2014, http://www.asia.nikkei.com; and A. Wittenberg-Cox, "How Nestlé Chile Reached Female Consumers," *Harvard Business Review* (online), July 30, 2012, http://www.hbr.org.

28. E. E. Lawler III, "New Roles for the Staff Function: Strategic Support and Services," in *Organizing for the Future,* J. Galbraith, E. E. Lawler III, & Associates (San Francisco: Jossey-Bass, 1993).

29. L. Barratt-Pugh and S. Bahn, "HR Strategy During Culture Change: Building Change Agency," *Journal of Management & Organization,* February 10, 2015, pp. 1–14; and A. Adams, "Changing Role of HR," *Human Resources,* June 2010, pp. 45–48.

30. Kiva, "About Us," http://www.kiva.org, accessed April 7, 2015.

31. Michael Bartlett, "Expanding Horizons," *Credit Union Journal,* November 26, 2012, Business Insights: Essentials, http://bi.galegroup.com.

32. G. S. Day, "Creating a Market-Driven Organization," *Sloan Management Review* 41, no. 1 (Fall 1999), pp. 11–22.

33. Johnson & Johnson, "Our Products," http://www.jnj.com, accessed April 5, 2015.

34. B. T. Lamont, V. Sambamurthy, K. M. Ellis, and P. G. Simmonds, "The Influence of Organizational Structure on the Information Received by Corporate Strategists of Multinational Enterprises," *Management International Review* 40, no. 3 (2000), pp. 231–252.

35. EMC, "Corporate Profile," http://www.emc.com, accessed April 5, 2015; and R. Enderle, "Customer Focus, Innovation Structure Prep EMC for Success," *CIO* (online), May 9, 2014, http://www.cio.com.

36. S. Ng and A. Prior, "Avon Executives Point to Signs of Sales Turnaround," *The Wall Street Journal* (online), July 31, 2014, http://www.wsj.com; and "A Look at Avon's Plan to Turn Around Its Ailing North American Division," *Forbes* (online), March 10, 2014, http://www.forbes.com.

37. "GM Ignition Switch Death Count Rises to 67," *CBS News* (online), March 16, 2015, http://www.cbsnews.com; "GM's Total Recall Cost: $4.1 Billion," *CNN Money* (online), February 4, 2015, http://money.cnn.com; General Motors, *Annual Report 2014;* Higgins and Green, "GM Seen Planning Global Reorganization"; "GM Names Mary Barra Chief Executive, Dan Akerson to Retire," *Los Angeles Times* (online), December 10, 2013, http://www.latimes.com; Eisenstein, "Big Management Shake-Up"; Klayman, "Car Guy or Bean Counter?"; Sharon Terlep, "GM's Chief Labors to Get Rebuilt Car Maker into Gear," *The Wall Street Journal,* June 11, 2012, http://online.wsj.com; and "Mary Barra: GM's Next CEO?" *Fortune,* December 17, 2012, http://management.fortune.cnn.com.

38. J. Galbraith, "Matrix Is the Ladder to Success," *Bloomberg Business* (online), http://www.businessweek.com, accessed April 5, 2015; W. Bernasco, P. C. de WeerdNederhof, H. Tillema, and H. Boer, "Balanced Matrix Structure and New Product Development Process at Texas Instruments Materials and Controls Division," *R&D Management* 29, no. 2 (April 1999), pp. 121–31; J. K. McCollum, "The Matrix Structure: Bane or Benefit to High Tech Organizations?" *Project Management Journal* 24, no. 2 (June 1993), pp. 23–26; R. C. Ford, "Cross-Functional Structures: A Review and Integration of Matrix," *Journal of Management* 18, no. 2 (June 1992), pp. 267–94; and H. Kolodny, "Managing in a Matrix," *Business Horizons,* March–April 1981, pp. 17–24.

39. D. Cackowski, M. K. Najdawi, and Q. B. Chung, "Object Analysis in Organizational Design: A Solution or Matrix Organizations," *Project Management Journal* 31, no. 3 (September 2000), pp. 44–51; J. Barker, "Conflict Approaches of Effective and Ineffective Project Managers: A Field Study in a Matrix Organization," *Journal of Management Studies* 25, no. 2 (March 1988), pp. 167–78; G. J. Chambers, "The Individual in a Matrix Organization," *Project Management Journal* 20, no. 4 (December 1989), pp. 37–42, 50; and S. Davis and P. Lawrence, "Problems of Matrix Organizations," *Harvard Business Review,* May–June 1978, pp. 131–42.

40. M. Staples, "Perspectives on Global Organizations," McKinsey & Company (2012), http://www.mckinsey.com; A. Ferner, "Being Local Worldwide: ABB and the Challenge of Global Management Relations," *Industrielles* 55, no. 3 (Summer 2000), pp. 527–29; and C. Bartlett and S. Ghoshal, "Matrix Management: Not a Structure, a Frame of Mind," *Harvard Business Review* 68 (July–August 1990), pp. 138–45.

41. J. Tata, S. Prasad, and R. Thorn, "The Influence of Organizational Structure on the Effectiveness of TQM Programs," *Journal of Managerial Issues* 11, no. 4 (Winter 1999), pp. 440–53; and Davis and Lawrence, "Problems of Matrix Organizations."

42. B. Hay and A. Gowdridge, "As the Traditional Workplace Breaks Down Will Leaders Adapt," *The Guardian* (online), January 21, 2015, http://www.theguardian.com; D. Schwabel, "10 Ways Millennials Are Creating the Future of Work," *Forbes* (online), December 16, 2013, http://www.forbes.com; Millennial Branding, "The Cost of Millennial Retention Strategy," August 6, 2013, http://www.millennialbranding.com; J. Menza, "Malcolm Gladwell: A Generational Tipping Point Is Coming," *CNBC* (online), January 31, 2013, http://www.cnbc.com; and J. Scorza, "Millennials Usher in New Social Paradigm," June 25, 2012, Society for Human Resource Management.org.

43. R. E. Miles and C. C. Snow, *Fit, Failure, and the Hall of Fame* (New York: Free Press, 1994); and G. Symon, "Information and Communication Technologies and Network Organization: A Critical Analysis," *Journal of Occupational and Organizational Psychology* 73, no. 4 (December 2000), pp. 389–95.

44. SendLove, "Send-Love—The Cool New Employee Recognition System," http://www.sendlove.com, accessed April 7, 2015; and D. Dahl, "A Radical Take on the Virtual Company," *Inc.*, March 1, 2011, http://www.inc.com.

45. Miles and Snow, *Fit, Failure, and the Hall of Fame.*

46. S. C. Kang, S. S. Morris, and S. A. Snell, "Relational Archetypes, Organizational Learning, and Value Creation: Extending the Human Resource Architecture," *Academy of Management Review* 32, no. 1 (2007), pp. 236–56.

47. J. G. March and H. A. Simon, *Organizations* (New York: John Wiley & Sons, 1958); and J. D. Thompson, *Organizations in Action* (New York: McGraw-Hill, 1967).

48. S. Rushton, "Rules Eat Up $250 Billion a Year in Profit and Productivity," news release, Deloitte (October 29, 2014), http://www2.deloitte.com; and P. S. Adler, "Building Better Bureaucracies," *Academy of Management Executive* 13, no. 4 (November 1999), pp. 36–49.

49. J. Galbraith, "Organization Design: An Information Processing View," *Interfaces* 4 (Fall 1974), pp. 28–36. See also S. A. Mohrman, "Integrating Roles and Structure in the Lateral Organization," in *Organizing for the Future*, ed. J. Galbraith, E. E. Lawler III, & Associates (San Francisco: Jossey-Bass, 1993); and B. B. Flynn and F. J. Flynn, "Information-Processing Alternatives for Coping with Manufacturing Environment Complexity," *Decision Sciences* 30, no. 4 (Fall 1999), pp. 1021–52.

50. Galbraith, "Organization Design"; and Mohrman, "Integrating Roles and Structure."

51. "Speaker Information: Michael Arena, Chief Talent Officer, General Motors Corporation," Talent Management Exchange, http://www.talentmanagementexchange.com, accessed May 8, 2015; R. Feloni, "GM CEO Mary Barra Explains How Shrinking the Dress Code to 2 Words Reflects her Mission for the Company," *Business Insider*s (online), March 27, 2015, http://www.businessinsider.com; G. Colvin, "Mary Barra's (Unexpected) Opportunity," *Fortune* (online), September 18, 2014, http://www.fortune.com; General Motors, *Annual Report 2013;* Higgins and Green, "GM Seen Planning Global Reorganization"; Qineqt, "General Motors Reorganization"; Eisenstein, "Big Management Shake-Up"; Klayman, "Car Guy or Bean Counter?"; Terlep, "GM's Chief Labors"; *Fortune,* "Mary Barra"; David Shepardson, "U.S. Sells Nearly 20 Percent of Remaining GM Shares," *Detroit News,* April 25, 2013, http://www.detroitnews.com; and *CBS News,* "Government in March Sold $621M."

Chapter 9

1. General Electric 2014 CEO Letter in the *2014 Annual Report,* http://www.ge.com/ar2014/ceo-letter/; A. Sorkin and M. de al Merced, "G.E. to Retreat from Finance in Post-Crisis Reorganization," *The New York Times* (online), April 10, 2015, http://www.nytimes.com; General Electric, "Fact Sheet," http://www.ge.com/company/fact-sheet; Geoff Colvin, "Grading Jeff Immelt," *Fortune,* February 10, 2011, http://management.fortune.cnn.com; Kate Linebaugh, "GE Feels Its Own Cuts," *The Wall Street Journal,* September 17, 2012, http://online.wsj.com; Michal Lev-Ram, "Why GE Is Betting on Software," *Fortune,* April 25, 2013, http://tech.fortune.cnn.com.

2. C. O'Reilly and M. Tushman, "Ambidexterity as a Dynamic Capability: Resolving the Innovator's Dilemma," Research Paper no. 1963, Stanford Graduate School of Business, March 2007, http://ssrn.com/abstract 5978493.

3. P. Sebastian, J. Fourne, J. Jansen, and T. Mom, "Strategic Agility in MNEs," *California Management Review* 56 (2014), pp. 13–38; P. M. Wright, L. Dyer, and M. G. Takla, "What's Next? Key Findings from the 1999 State-of-the-Art and Practice Study," *Human Resource Planning* 22, no. 4 (1999), pp. 12–20; and Donald Sull, "How to Thrive in Turbulent Markets," *Harvard Business Review,* February 2009, pp. 78–88.

4. T. Burns and G. Stalker, *The Management of Innovation* (London: Tavistock, 1961).

5. D. Krackhardt and J. R. Hanson, "Information Networks: The Company behind the Chart," *Harvard Business Review,* July–August 1993, pp. 104–11.

6. G. Hamel and C. K. Prahalad, "Competing for the Future," *Harvard Business Review,* July–August 1994, pp. 122–28.

7. K. Klein, "How to Keep Millennials from Getting Bored and Quitting," *Bloomberg Business* (online), August 22, 2014, http://www.bloomberg.com; R. Ray et al., "The State of Human Capital 2012," Research Report R-1501-12-RR, McKinsey & Company and The Conference Board, accessed April 13, 2015.

8. D. G. Sirmon, M. A. Hitt, and R. D. Ireland, "Managing Firm Resources in Dynamic Environments to Create Value: Looking inside the Black Box," *Academy of Management Review* 32, no. 1 (2007), pp. 273–92.

9. B. Rubin, "Starbucks to End Exclusivity Deal with Keurig," *The Wall Street Journal* (online), March 14, 2014, http://www.wsj.com.

10. Intel, "TAG Heuer, Google, and Intel Announce Swiss Smartwatch Collaboration," news release, March 19, 2015, http://www.intel.com.

11. G. Slowinski, E. Hummel, A. Gupta, and E. R. Gilmont, "Effective Practices for Sourcing Innovation," *Research-Technology Management,* January–February 2009, pp. 27–34.

12. R. C. Sampson, "R&D Alliances and Firm Performance: The Impact of Technological Diversity and Alliance Organization on Innovation," *Academy of Management Journal* 50, no. 2 (2007), pp. 364–86.

13. R. M. Kanter, "Collaborative Advantage: The Art of Alliances," *Harvard Business Review,* July–August 1999, pp. 96–108; J. B. Cullen, J. L. Johnson, and T. Sakano, "Success through Commitment and Trust: The Soft Side of Strategic Alliance Management," *Journal of World Business* 35, no. 3 (Fall 2000), pp. 223–40; and P. Kale, H. Singh, and H. Perlmutter, "Learning and Protection of Proprietary Assets in Strategic Alliances: Building Relational Capital," *Strategic Management Journal* 21, no. 3 (March 2000), pp. 217–37.

14. P. Senge, *The Fifth Discipline* (New York: Doubleday Currency, 1990).

15. D. A. Garvin, "Building a Learning Organization," *Harvard Business Review,* July–August 1993, pp. 78–91; D. A. Garvin, *Learning in Action: A Guide to Putting the Learning Organization to Work* (Boston: Harvard Business School Press, 2000); and V. J. Marsick and K. E. Watkins, *Facilitating Learning Organizations: Making Learning Count* (Aldershot, Hampshire: Gower, 1999).

16. Ibid.; and N. Anand, H. K. Gardner, and T. Morris, "Knowledge-Based Innovation: Emergence and Embedding of New Practice Areas in Management Consulting Firms," *Academy of Management Journal* 50, no. 2 (2007), pp. 406–28.

17. J. G. March, "Exploration and Exploitation in Organizational Learning," *Organization Science* 2, no. 1 (February 1991), pp. 71–87; and S.-C. Kang and S. A. Snell, "Intellectual Capital Architectures and Ambidextrous Learning: A Framework for Human Resource Management," *Journal of Management Studies* 46, no. 1 (2009), pp. 65–92.

18. M. Marchington and A. Kynighou, "The Dynamics of Employee Involvement and Participation During Turbulent

Times," *The International Journal of Human Resource Management* 23 (2012), 3336–54; R. J. Vandenberg, H. A. Richardson, and L. J. Eastman, "The Impact of High Involvement Work Process on Organizational Effectiveness: A Second-Order Latent Variable Approach," *Group & Organization Management* 24, no. 3 (September 1999), pp. 300–39; G. M. Spreitzer and A. K. Mishra, "Giving Up Control without Losing Control: Trust and Its Substitutes Effects on Managers Involving Employees in Decision Making," *Group & Organization Management* 24, no. 2 (June 1999), pp. 155–87; and S. Albers Mohrman, G. E. Ledford, and E. E. Lawler III, *Strategies for High Performance Organizations The CEO Report: Employee Involvement, TQM, and Reengineering Programs in Fortune 1000 Corporations* (San Francisco: Jossey-Bass, 1998).

19. D. Cooper, S. Dhiri, and J. Root, "Winning Operating Models, Bain & Company," September 14, 2012, http://www.bain.com; R. Pagnamenta, "Transformation That Could Rescue Unilever from the Slippery Slope," *The Times (London),* January 3, 2007; and "Unilever on Revival Track after Top Managers Culled," *Evening Standard (London),* May 3, 2007, Business & Company Resource Center, http://galenet.galegroup.com.

20. J. Smothers, M. Novicevic, M. Buckley, S. Carraher, L. Bynum, M. Hayek, and Alfred D. Chandler Jr., "Historical Impact and Historical Scope of His Works," *Journal of Management History* 16 (2010), pp. 521–26; Alfred Chandler, *The Economist,* May 17, 2007, http://www.economist.com; C. Farrell, and Alfred Chandler, "Big Business Big Loss," *Bloomberg Businessweek,* May 14, 2007, http://www.businessweek.com.

21. The American Customer Satisfaction Index, "ACSI: Retail Customer Satisfaction Drops Despite Improvements for Online Shopping," press release, February 18, 2015, http://www.theacsi.org; and Renee Dudley, "Walmart Faces the Cost of Cost-Cutting: Empty Shelves," *Bloomberg Businessweek,* March 28, 2013, http://www.businessweek.com.

22. Pagnamenta, "Transformation That Could Rescue Unilever."

23. L. L. Hellofs and R. Jacobson, "Market Share and Customers' Perceptions of Quality: When Can Firms Grow Their Way to Higher versus Lower Quality?" *Journal of Marketing* 63, no. 1 (January 1999), pp. 16–25.

24. E. Doerr, "Kobolds Spirit of America: Navy Seals, Made in America, and Pandemonium," *Forbes* (online), July 4, 2014, http://www.forbes.com; and J. Dean, "The Greatly Improbable, Highly Enjoyable, Increasingly Profitable Life of Michael Kobold, Inc.," May 2007, pp. 126–34.

25. Intuit, "Company Fast Facts," http://www.intuit.com, accessed April 11, 2015; V. Vara, "After GE," *The Wall Street Journal,* April 12, 2007, http://online.wsj.com.

26. D. DeRue, J. Hollenbeck, M. Johnson, D. Ilgen, and D. Jundt, "How Different Team Downsizing Approaches Influence Team-Level Adaptation and Performance," *Academy of Management Journal* 51 (2008), pp. 182–96; W. F. Cascio, "Downsizing: What Do We Know? What Have We Learned?" *Academy of Management Executive* 7 (February 1993), pp. 95–104; and S. J. Freeman, "The Gestalt of Organizational Downsizing: Downsizing Strategies as Package of Change," *Human Relations* 52, no. 12 (December 1999), pp. 1505–41.

27. Network for Good, "About Us," www.networkforgood.org, accessed April 12, 2015; Selco, "About Us," www.selco-india.com, accessed April 12, 2015; E. Howard, "10 Things We Learned About Scaling Global Social Enterprise," *The Guardian,* November 20, 2014, http://www.theguardian.com; R. Murphy and D. Sachs, "The Rise of Social Entrepreneurship Suggests a Possible Future for Global Capitalism," *Forbes* May 2, 2013, http://www.forbes.com.

28. M. Graser and D. McNary, "DreamWorks Animation Cutting 500 Jobs," *Variety* (online), January 22, 2015, http://www.variety.com; P. Bond, "Dreamworks Animation Planning Layoffs," *The Hollywood Reporter* (online), January 19, 2015, http://www.hollywoodreporter.com.

29. C. D. Zatzick and R. D. Iverson, "High-Involvement Management and Workforce Reduction: Competitive Advantage or Disadvantage?" *Academy of Management Journal* 49, no. 5 (2006), pp. 999–1015.

30. Cascio, "Strategies for Responsible Restructuring; Cascio, Downsizing"; and J. Ciancio, "Survivor's Syndrome," *Nursing Management* 31, no. 5 (May 2000), pp. 43–45.

31. General Electric, *2014 Annual Report*; General Electric, "Jeff Immelt: A Simpler, More Valuable GE," http://www.ge.com, accessed April 12, 2015; Lev-Ram, "Why GE Is Betting on Software," Kate Linebaugh, "The New GE Way: Go Deep, Not Wide," *The Wall Street Journal,* March 7, 2012, http://online.wsj.com; Beth Kowitt, "How a Top GE Exec Engineered Himself out of a Job," *Fortune,* August 3, 2012, http://management.fortune.cnn.com; Kate Linebaugh, "GE Shake-Up Will Audition New Leaders," *The Wall Street Journal,* July 20, 2012, http://online.wsj.com; Ashlee Vance, "GE Tries to Make Its Machines Cool and Connected," *Bloomberg Businessweek,* http://www.businessweek.com; and Peter Coy, "GE Builds a Better Battery," *Bloomberg Businessweek,* July 11, 2012, http://www.businessweek.com.

32. B. Kerschberg, "Five Steps to Master Big Data and Predictive Analytics in 2014," *Forbes* (online), January 3, 2014, http://www.forbes.com; "Predictive Analytics 101: Next-Generation Big Data Intelligence," Intel IT Center (online),

March 2013, http://www.intel.com; and "Predicting the Future, Part 1: What is Predictive Analytics?" IBM Developer Works (online), http://www.ibm.com, accessed May 27, 2015.

33. D. Carr, "Giving Viewers What They Want," *The New York Times* (online), February 24, 2013, http://www.nytimes.com; R. Baldwin, "Netflix Gambles on Big Data to Become the HBO of Streaming," *Wired* (online), November 29, 2012, http://www.wired.com.

34. S. Sluis, "Mobile Sales to Represent Half of E-Commerce by 2018," *Customer Relationship Management* 18 (2014), pp. 15–18; T. Wailgum, "CRM Definition and Solutions," *CIO,* March 6, 2007, http://www.cio.com; M. Burns, "CRM Survey 2011," *CA Magazine,* May 2011, http://www.camagazine.com; and M. Burns, "CRM Survey 2010," *CA Magazine,* April 2010, http://www.camagazine.com.

35. Salesforce, "Customer Success Stories," http://www.salesforce.com, accessed April 11, 2015; "Salesforce.com Offers Twitter Customer-Service App," *Information Week,* March 23, 2009, Business & Company Resource Center, http://galenet.galegroup.com.

36. K. Ishikawa, *What Is Total Quality Control? The Japanese Way,* trans. D. J. Lu (Englewood Cliffs, NJ: Prentice-Hall, 1985); and J. Seibert and J. Lingle, "Internal Customer Service: Has It Improved?" *Quality Progress* 40, no. 3 (March 2007), OCLC FirstSearch, http://firstsearch.oclc.org.

37. M. Porter, *Competitive Advantage: Creating and Sustaining Superior Performance* (New York: Free Press, 1985); and Internet Center for Management and Business Administration, "The Value Chain," Strategy pages, *NetMBA,* http://www.netmba.com.

38. B. Creech, *The Five Pillars of TQM: How to Make Total Quality Management Work for You* (New York: Plume Publishing, 1995); and J. R. Evans and W. M. Lindsay, *Management and Control of Quality* (Mason, OH: South-Western College Publishing, 1998).

39. National Institute of Standards and Technology, "Four U.S. Organizations Honored with the 2014 Baldrige National Quality Award," news release, November 12, 2014, http://www.nist.gov.

40. International Organization for Standardization, "ISO 9000 Quality Management," http://www.iso.org.

41. J. Champy, *Reengineering Management* (New York: HarperBusiness, 1995). See also M. Hammer and J. Champy, *Reengineering the Corporation* (New York: HarperCollins, 1992).

42. J. Woodward, *Industrial Organization: Theory and Practice* (London: Oxford University Press, 1965).

43. J. H. Gilmore and B. J. Pine, eds., *Markets of One: Creating Customer-Unique Value through Mass Customization* (Cambridge, MA: Harvard Business Review Press, 2000); and B. J. Pine, *Mass Customization:*

The New Frontier in Business Competition (Cambridge, MA: Harvard Business School Press, 1992).

44. M. Zhang, X. Zhao, and Y. Qi, "The Effects of Organizational Flatness, Coordination, and Product Modularity on Mass Customization Capability," *International Journal of Production Economics* 158 (2014), pp.145–55; F. Sahin, "Manufacturing Competitiveness: Different Systems to Achieve the Same Results," *Production and Inventory Management Journal* 41, no. 1 (First Quarter 2000), pp. 56–65.

45. S. Wadhwa and K. S. Rao, "Flexibility: An Emerging Meta-Competence for Managing High Technology," *International Journal of Technology Management* 19, no. 7–8 (2000), pp. 820–45.

46. A. Bozek and M. Wysocki, "Flexible Job Shop with Continuous Material Flow," *International Journal of Production Research* 53 (2015), pp. 1273–90; B. A. Peters and L. F. McGinnis, "Strategic Configuration of Flexible Assembly Systems: A Single Period Approximation," *IIE Transaction* 31, no. 4 (April 1999), pp. 379–90.

47. J. K. Liker and J. M. Morgan, "The Toyota Way in Services: The Case of Lean Product Development," *Academy of Management Perspectives* 20, no. 2 (May 2006), pp. 5–20; "Strategic Reconfiguration: Manufacturing's Key Role in Innovation," *Production and Inventory Management Journal* (Summer–Fall 2001), pp. 9–17; J. Jusko, "Lean Confusion," *Industry Week,* September 2010, pp. 32–34; and Sahin, "Manufacturing Competitiveness."

48. P. Guarraia, G. Carey, A. Corbett, and K. Neuhaus, "Lean Six Sigma for the Services Industry," Bain & Company May 20, 2008, http://www.bain.comm.

49. S. Silversthorne, "Can Lean Production Methods Work in Services?" *CBS News,* May 21, 2009, http://www.cbsnews.com; J. Hanna, "Bringing Lean Production to Service Industries," Harvard Business School Working Knowledge (online), October 22, 2007, http://www.hbs.edu.

50. Travis Hessman, "Leans High-Tech Makeover," *Industry Week,* November 14, 2012, http://www.industryweek.com.

51. W. Yang and K. Meyer, "Competitive Dynamics in an Emerging Economy: Competitive Pressures, Resources, and the Speed of Action," *Journal of Business Research* 68 (2015), pp. 1176–1185; C. H. Chung, "Balancing the Two Dimensions of Time for Time-Based Competition," *Journal of Managerial Issues* 11, no. 3 (Fall 1999), pp. 299–314; and D. R. Towill and P. McCullen, "The Impact of Agile Manufacturing on Supply Chain Dynamics," *International Journal of Logistics Management* 10, no. 1 (1999), pp. 83–96. See also G. Stalk and T. M. Hout, *Competing against Time: How Time-Based Competition Is Reshaping Global Markets* (New York: Free Press, 1990).

52. C. Swedberg, "Macy's Expands RFID and Beacon Deployments," *RFID Journal* (online), September 16, 2014, http://www.rfidjournal.com; M. O'Connor, "Can RFID Save Brick-and-Mortar Retailers After All?" *Fortune* (online), April 16, 2014, http://www.fortune.com.

53. M. Weistein, "Just-in-Time Technology Solutions," *Training* (online), September/October 2014, http://www.training.com.

54. Patrice Novotny, "Japan Manufacturers in Post-Tsunami Rethink," *Industry Week,* March 5, 2012, http://www.industryweek.com; Kelly Marchese, Siva Paramasivam, and Michael Held, "Bouncing Back: Supply Chain Risk Management Lessons from Post-Tsunami Japan," *Industry Week,* March 9, 2012, http://www.industryweek.com.

55. R. Miel and D. Sedgwick, "Just-in-Time Seats Die Out," *Automotive News,* August 4, 2010, Business & Company Resource Center, http://galenet.galegroup.com.

56. J. E. Ettlie, "Product Development Beyond Simultaneous Engineering," *Automative Manufacturing & Production* 112, no. 7 (July 2000), p. 18; U. Roy, J. M. Usher, and H. R. Parsaei, eds., *Simultaneous Engineering: Methodologies and Applications* (Newark, NJ: Gordon and Breach, 1999); and M. M. Helms and L. P. Ettkin, "Time-Based Competitiveness: A Strategic Perspective," *Competitiveness Review* 10, no. 2 (2000), pp. 1–14.

57. Richard J. Schonberger, "DFMA a Potent Lean Methodology," *Assembly,* April 2013, http://www.assemblymag.com.

58. R. Ashkenas, D. Ulrich, T. Jick, and S. Kerr, *The Boundaryless Organization: Breaking the Chains of Organizational Structure* (San Francisco: Jossey-Bass, 1995); R. W. Keidel, "Rethinking Organizational Design," *Academy of Management Executive,* November 1994, pp. 12–27; and R. Ashkenas, T. Jick, D. Ulrich, and C. Paul-Chowdhury, *The Boundaryless Organization Field Guide: Practical Tools for Building the New Organization* (San Francisco: Jossey-Bass, 1999).

59. General Electric, "What Is Six Sigma?," http://www.ge.com; "How GE Is Creating Software and Making Money Faster," *CIO Journal* (online), October 9, 2013, http://www.wsj.com; Guy Boulton, "GE Healthcare Systems CEO Sees Challenges, Opportunities," *Milwaukee Journal-Sentinel,* December 4, 2011, http://www.jsonline.com; General Electric, "What Is Six Sigma? The Roadmap to Customer Impact," n.d., http://www.ge.com/sixsigma/SixSigma.pdf; Ed Crooks, "Lean Cuts Fat off GEs Production Line," *Financial Times,* April 2, 2012, http://www.ft.com; Rachel King, "GE Becomes More Agile," *CIO Journal,* May 30, 2012, http://blogs.wsj.com; and General Electric, "GE Aviation Delivers Its First Production Wing Components for the Airbus A350 XWB," news release, March 7, 2013, http://www.businesswire.com.

Chapter 10

1. L. Gellman, "Everyone (Still) Wants to Work for Google," *The Wall Street Journal* (online), March 26, 2015, http://www.wsj.com; "100 Best Companies to Work for 2015," *Fortune,* accessed April 14, 2015; S. Phelps, "Cracking into Google: 15 Reasons Why More Than 2 Million People Apply Each Year," *Forbes* (online), August 5, 2014, http://www.forbes.com; J. D'Onfro and K. Smith, "Google Employees Reveal Their Favorite Perks about Working for the Company," *Business Insider* (online), July 1, 2014, http://www.businessinsider.com; R. Waters, "Google Tries New Angle on Hiring," *Financial Times,* February 7, 2011, Business & Company Resource Center, http://galenet.galegroup.com; M. Liedtke and B. Ortutay, "Google Wants to Be Cool Again," *Houston Chronicle,* January 22, 2011, Business & Company Resource Center, http://galenet.galegroup.com; Farhad Manjoo, "How Google Became Such a Great Place to Work," *Slate,* January 21, 2013, http://www.slate.com; and Meghan Casserly, "Here's What Happens to Google Employees When They Die," *Forbes,* August 8, 2012, http://www.forbes.com.

2. N. Gardner, D. McGranahan, and W. Wolf, "Question for Your HR Chief: Are We Using Our 'People Data' to Create Value?" *McKinsey Quarterly,* March 2011, https://www.mckinseyquarterly.com.

3. "HR's Impact on Shareholder Value," *Workforce Management,* December 11, 2006, Business & Company Resource Center, http://galenet.galegroup.com.

4. P. M. Wright and S. A. Snell, "Partner or Guardian? HR's Challenge in Balancing Value and Values," *Human Resource Management* 44, no. 2 (2005), pp. 177–82.

5. "Scaling Up: Catalyzing the Social Enterprise," A.T. Kearney (online), January 2015, http://www.atkearney.com; Greenling, "About Us," http://www.greenling.com, accessed April 18, 2015; M. Paisner, "Is Social Entrepreneurship Transforming Millennial Talent Acquisition," *Forbes* (online), April 17, 2015, http://www.forbes.com; N. Flores, "Austin's Social Entrepreneurs Redefine How to Drive Social Change," *Forefront Austin* (online), August 2011, http://www.forefrontaustin.com; and A. LaPlante, "MBA Graduates Want to Work for Caring and Ethical Employers," Graduate School of Stanford Business (online), January 1, 2004, http://www.gsb.stanford.edu.

6. E. Siedle, "The Greatest Retirement Crisis in American History," *Forbes* (online), March 20, 2013, http://www.forbes.com.

7. E. Snider, "Florida's Largest McDonald's Franchisee, Based in Tampa, Reacts to $1 Pay Bump for Corporate Employees," *Tampa Bay Business Journal* (online), April 8, 2015, http://www.bizjournals.com; R. Mullins, "They're Loving It," *Tampa Tribune,* March 20, 2011, Business &

Company Resource Center, http://galenet. galegroup.com; and J. R. Hagerty, "Help Wanted on Factory Floor," *The Wall Street Journal,* May 6, 2011, http://online.wsj.com.

8. "50 Fortune 500 Companies Offering Computer Science Internships," *Computer Science Degree Hub* (online), http://www. computersciencedegreehub.com, accessed April 14, 2015.

9. Kristina Peterson, "Bill to Boost Visas Cheers Tech Firms," *The Wall Street Journal,* January 29, 2013, http://online. wsj.com; Jessica Cook, "The Clock Is Ticking: Timing on Foreign Visas Is Essential," *Employee Benefit News,* April 15, 2013, p. 10; and Jonathan Rothwell and Neil G. Ruiz, "H-1B Visas and the STEM Shortage," Brookings Institution research paper, May 10, 2013, http://www. brookings.edu.

10. D. E. Hartley, *Job Analysis at the Speed of Reality* (Amherst, MA: HRD Press, 1999); F. P. Morgeson and M. A. Campion, "Accuracy in Job Analysis: Toward an Inference-Based Model," *Journal of Organizational Behavior* 21, no. 7 (November 2000), pp. 819–27; and J. S. Shippmann, R. A. Ash, L. Carr, and B. Hesketh, "The Practice of Competency Modeling," *Personnel Psychology* 53, no. 3 (Autumn 2000), pp. 703–40.

11. J. S. Schippmann, *Strategic Job Modeling: Working at the Core of Integrated Human Resources* (Mahwah, NJ: Lawrence Erlbaum Associates, 1999).

12. M. Applegate, "Difference Between the Internal & External Recruitment Strategies," *Houston Chronicle* (online), http://www.chron.com, accessed April 14, 2015; D. E. Terpstra, "The Search for Effective Methods," *HR Focus,* May 1996, pp. 16–17; H. G. Heneman III and R. A. Berkley, "Applicant Attraction Practices and Outcomes among Small Businesses," *Journal of Small Business Management* 37, no. 1 (January 1999), pp. 53–74; and J.-M. Hiltrop, "The Quest for the Best: Human Resource Practices to Attract and Retain Talent," *European Management Journal* 17, no. 4 (August 1999), pp. 422–30.

13. G. Crispin and M. Mehler, "10th Annual CareerXroads Source of Hire Report: by the Numbers," CareerXroads, March 2011, http://www.careerxroads.com; and J. Light, "Recruiters Rethink Online Playbook," *The Wall Street Journal,* January 18, 2011, http://online.wsj.com.

14. M. Feffer, "Expanding Employee Referrals into the Social Media World," *Society for Human Resource Management* 60 (April 4, 2015), http://www.shrm.org; N. Schwarz, "In Hiring, a Friend in Need Is a Prospect, Indeed," *The New York Times* (online), January 27, 2013, http://www.nytimes. com; and F. Hansen, "Employee Referral Programs, Selective Campus Recruitment Could Touch Off Bias Charges," *Workforce Management* 85 (June 26, 2006), pp. 59–60.

15. R. Myers, "Interviewing Techniques: Tips from the Pros," *Journal of Accountancy,*

August 2006, Business & Company Resource Center, http://galenet.galegroup. com; M. McDaniel, D. L. Whetzel, F. L. Schmidt, and S. D. Maurer, "The Validity of Employment Interviews: A Comprehensive Review and Meta-Analysis," *Journal of Applied Psychology* 79, no. 4 (August 1994), pp. 599–616; M. A. Campion, J. E. Campion, and P. J. Hudson Jr., "Structured Interviewing: A Note on Incremental Validity and Alternative Question Types," *Journal of Applied Psychology* 79, no. 6 (December 1994), pp. 998–1002; and R. A. Fear, *The Evaluation Interview* (New York: McGraw-Hill, 1984).

16. R. Myers, "Interviewing Techniques."

17. U.S. Merit Systems Protection Board, "The Federal Selection Interview: Unrealized Potential," February 2003, mspb.gov/ studies/interview.htm; Lauren Weber, "Now Hiring? Tips for Conducting Interviews," *The Wall Street Journal,* December 4, 2012, http://online.wsj.com; Frederick P. Morgeson, "The Science of Talent Selection," *Health Management Technology,* April 2012, EBSCOhost, http://web.ebscohost.com.

18. T. Lewin, "Dean at M.I.T. Resigns, Ending a 28-Year Lie," *The New York Times,* April 27, 2007, http://www.nytimes.com.

19. D. Jacobs, "The High Price of Career Lies," *Forbes* (online), May 14, 2012, http://www.forbes.com; and J. Pepitone, "Yahoo Confirms CEO Is Out after Resume Scandal," *CNN Money* (online), May 14, 2012, http://money.cnn.com.

20. D. Meinert, "Seeing behind the Mask," *HR Magazine,* February 2011, pp. 31–37.

21. Ibid., p. 37.

22. L. Weber and E. Dwoskin, "Are Workplace Personality Tests Fair?" *The Wall Street Journal* (online), September 29, 2014, http://www.wsj.com; Alton Lane, http:// www.altonlane.com, accessed May 12, 2015; T. Ackerman, "Does Psych Testing Result in Better Hires?" *Houston Chronicle,* June 21, 2010, Business & Company Resource Center, http://galenet. galegroup.com; Center for Advanced Human Resource Studies, "Should Personality Testing Be Part of the Hiring Process?" CAHRS ResearchLink, no. 12, November 2010, http://digitalcommons. ilr.cornell.edu; and E. Frauenheim, "Personality Tests Adapt to the Times," *Workforce Management,* February 1, 2010, Business & Company Resource Center, http://galenet.galegroup.com.

23. Weber and Dwoskin, "Are Workplace Personality Tests Fair?"

24. R. E. Ployhart, J. A. Weekley, and K. Baughman, "The Structure and Function of Human Capital Emergence: A Multilevel Examination of the Attraction-Selection-Attrition Model," *Academy of Management Journal* 49, no. 4 (2006), pp. 661–77.

25. R. Zeidner, "Putting Drug Screening to the Test," *HR Magazine,* November 2010, ProQuest, http://proquest.umi.com.

26. K. Steinmetz, "Report Predicts 18 States Will Legalize Pot by 2020," *Fortune* (online), January 26, 2015, http://www. fortune.com; and C. Rubin, "Medical Marijuana Laws Leave Employers Dazed and Confused," *Inc.,* February 12, 2010, http://www.inc.com.

27. Society for Industrial and Organizational Psychology, "How Many U.S. Companies Use Employment Tests?" http://www. siop.org, accessed April 14, 2015; P. M. Wright, M. K. Kacmar, G. C. McMahan, and K. Deleeuw, "P = f(MxA): Cognitive Ability as a Moderator of the Relationship between Personality and Job Performance," *Journal of Management* 21, no. 6 (1995), pp. 1129–2063; P. R. Sackett and D. J. Ostgaard, "Job-Specific Applicant Pools and National Norms for Cognitive Ability Tests: Implications for Range Restriction Corrections in Validation Research," *Journal of Applied Psychology* 79, no. 5 (October 1994), pp. 680–84; F. L. Schmidt and J. E. Hunter, "Tacit Knowledge, Practical Intelligence, General Mental Ability, and Job Knowledge," *Current Directions in Psychological Science* 2, no. 1 (1993), pp. 3–13; M. Roznowski, D. N. Dickter, L. L. Sawin, V. J. Shute, and S. Hong, "The Validity of Measures of Cognitive Processes and Generability for Learning and Performance on Highly Complex Computerized Tutors: Is the G Factor of Intelligence Even More General?" *Journal of Applied Psychology* 85, no. 6 (December 2000), pp. 940–55; and J. M. Cortina, N. B. Goldstein, S. C. Payne, H. K. Davison, and S. W. Gilliland, "The Incremental Validity of Interview Scores over and above Cognitive Ability and Conscientiousness Scores," *Personnel Psychology* 53, no. 2 (Summer 2000), pp. 325–51.

28. W. Arthur Jr., D. J. Woehr, and R. Maldegen, "Convergent and Discriminant Validity of Assessment Center Dimensions: A Conceptual and Empirical Reexamination of the Assessment Center Construct-Related Validity Paradox," *Journal of Management* 26, no. 4 (2000), pp. 813–35; and R. Randall, E. Ferguson, and F. Patterson, "Self-Assessment Accuracy and Assessment Center Decisions," *Journal of Occupational and Organizational Psychology* 73, no. 4 (December 2000), p. 443.

29. L. A. McFarland and A. M. Ryan, "Variance in Faking across Noncognitive Measures," *Journal of Applied Psychology* 85, no. 5 (October 2000), pp. 812–21; and D. E. Terpstra, R. B. Kethley, R. T. Foley, and W. Limpaphayom, "The Nature of Litigation Surrounding Five Screening Devices," *Public Personnel Management* 29, no. 1 (Spring 2000), pp. 43–54.

30. American Psychological Association, "The Truth about Lie Detectors (aka Polygraph Tests)," http://www.apa. org, accessed April 14, 2015; and D. S. Ones, C. Viswesvaran, and F. L. Schmidt, "Comprehensive Meta-analysis

of Integrity Test Validities: Findings and Implications for Personnel Selection and Theories of Job Performance," *Journal of Applied Psychology* 78 (August 1993), pp. 679–703.

31. S. Hananel, "Jobless People Need Not Apply?" *Houston Chronicle,* February 17, 2011, Business & Company Resource Center, http://galenet.galegroup.com.

32. J. McGregor, "The Biggest Mass Layoffs of the Past Two Decades," *The Washington Post* (online), January 28, 2015, http://www.washingtonpost.com.

33. S. Adams, "What to Do as Soon as You Get Laid Off," *Forbes* (online), February 18, 2015, http://www.forbes.com; R.-L. DeWitt, "The Structural Consequences of Downsizing," *Organization Science* 4, no. 1 (February 1993), pp. 30–40; and P. P. Shah, "Network Destruction: The Structural Implications of Downsizing," *Academy of Management Journal* 43, no. 1 (February 2000), pp. 101–12.

34. See *Adair v. United States,* 2078 U.S. 161 (1908); and D. A. Ballam, "Employment-at-Will: The Impending Death of a Doctrine," *American Business Law Journal* 37, no. 4 (Summer 2000), pp. 653–87.

35. L. Petersen, "Is It Less Risky to Terminate an Employee within the First 90 Days of Employment?" *HR Magazine* (online), September 2014, pp. 20–21, http://www.shrm.org; J. A. Segal, "A Warning about Warnings," *HR Magazine,* February 2009, pp. 67–70; International Public Management Association for Human Resources (IPMA-HR), "Progressive Discipline," IPMA-HR website, http://www.ipma-hr.org; U.S. Chamber of Commerce, "Progressive Discipline," http://business.uschamber.com; and D. Grote, "Positive Approach to Employee Discipline," *ManagerNewz,* March 12, 2007, http://archive.managernewz.com.

36. "How to Discipline and Fire Employees," *Entrepreneur* (online), http://www.entrepreneur.com, accessed April 14, 2015; J. W. Bucking, "Employee Terminations: Ten Must-Do Steps When Letting Someone Go," *Supervision,* May 2008, Business & Company Resource Center, http://galenet.galegroup.com; and M. Price, "Employee Termination Process Is Tough for Those on Both Sides," *Journal Record (Oklahoma City, OK),* October 23, 2008, Business & Company Resource Center, http://galenet.galegroup.com.

37. *Employer EEO Responsibilities* (Washington, DC: Equal Employment Opportunity Commission, U.S. Government Printing Office, 1996); N. J. Edman and M. D. Levin-Epstein, *Primer of Equal Employment Opportunity,* 6th ed. (Washington, DC: Bureau of National Affairs, 1994).

38. "Bank of America Fined $2 Million for Race Discrimination," *CNN Money* (online), September 24, 2013, http://money.cnn.com.

39. S. Pfeifer, "Jury Awards $185 Million to Ex-AutoZone Worker Demoted after Pregnancy," *Los Angeles Times* (online), November 18, 2014, http://www.latimes.com.

40. R. Gatewood and H. Field, *Human Resource Selection,* 3rd ed. (Chicago: Dryden Press, 1994), pp. 36–49; and R. A. Baysinger, "Disparate Treatment and Disparate Impact Theories of Discrimination: The Continuing Evolution of Title VII of the 1964 Civil Rights Act," in *Readings in Personnel and Human Resource Management,* ed. R. S. Schuler, S. A. Youngblood, and V. L. Huber (St. Paul, MN: West Publishing, 1987).

41. "ASTD 2013 State of the Industry: Continued Dedication to Workplace Learning," December 2013, http://www.td.org; "$164.2 Billion Spent on Training and Development by U.S. Companies," *TD* (online), December 12, 2013, http://www.td.org.

42. L. Miller, "ASTD 2013 State of the Industry Report: Workplace Learning Remains a Key Organizational Investment," *TD* (online), November 8, 2013, http://www.td.org.

43. Lorri Freifeld, "Verizon's #1 Calling," *Training,* January/February 2013, EBSCOhost, http://web.ebscohost.com.

44. Ibid.

45. University of Colorado Denver, "Study Shows Employees Learn Best from Video Games," news release, October 19, 2010, http://www.ucdenver.edu.

46. J. Gordon, "Building Brand Champions: How Training Helps Drive a Core Business Process at General Mills," *Training,* January–February 2007, *General Reference Center Gold,* http://find.galegroup.com.

47. K. Vasel, "The Skills Employers Wish College Grads Had," *Fox Business* (online), January 30, 2014, http://www.foxbusiness.com; "The Prepared U Project: An In-depth Look at Millennial Preparedness for Today's Workforce," Bentley University (online), January 29, 2014, http://www.bentley.edu.

48. T. Friedman, "How to Get a Job at Google," *The New York Times* (online), February 22, 2014, http://www.nytimes.com; J. Light, "Google Is No. 1 on List of Desired Employers," *The Wall Street Journal,* March 21, 2011, http://online.wsj.com; Waters, "Google Tries New Angle"; Digits, "Want to Work for Google? Here's How," *The Wall Street Journal,* June 8, 2011, http://online.wsj.com (video; interview with Joseph Walker); A. Fisher, "So You Want to Work at Google," *Fortune,* April 7, 2011, http://management.fortune.cnn.com; A. Bryant, "The Quest to Build a Better Boss," *The New York Times,* March 13, 2011, Business & Company Resource Center, http://galenet.galegroup.com; Manjoo, "How Google Became Such a Great Place to Work"; Joseph Walker, "School's in Session at Google," *The Wall Street Journal,* July 5, 2012, http://online.wsj.com.

49. For more information, see K. Wexley and G. Latham, *Increasing Productivity through Performance Appraisal* (Reading, MA: Addison-Wesley, 1994).

50. H. Bernardin, R. Konopaske, and C. Hagan, "A Comparison of Adverse Impact Levels Based on Top-down, Multisource, and Assessment Center Data: Promoting Diversity and Reducing Legal Challenges," *Human Resource Management* 51 (2012), pp. 313–41; and I. O'Boyle, "Traditional Performance Appraisal versus 360–Degree Feedback," *Training & Management Development Methods* 27 (2013), pp. 201–07.

51. F. Shipper, R. C. Hoffman, and D. M. Rotondo, "Does the 360 Feedback Process Create Actionable Knowledge Equally across Cultures?" *Academy of Management Learning & Education* 6, no. 1 (2007), pp. 33–50.

52. G. Toegel and J. Conger, "360 Degree Assessment: Time for Reinvention," *Academy of Management Learning and Education* 2, no. 3 (September 2003), p. 297; and L. K. Johnson, "Retooling 360s for Better Performance," *Harvard Business School Working Knowledge,* February 23, 2004, online.

53. M. Edwards and A. J. Ewen, "How to Manage Performance and Pay with 360-Degree Feedback," *Compensation and Benefits Review* 28, no. 3 (May/June 1996), pp. 41–46. See also S. Crabtree, "What Your Employees Need to Know," *Gallup Management Journal,* April 13, 2011, Business & Company Resource Center, http://galenet.galegroup.com; and R. S. Schuler, *Personnel and Human Resource Management* (St. Paul, MN: West Publishing, 1984).

54. Bureau of Labor Statistics, "Employer Costs for Employee Compensation—March 2015," news release, March 11, 2015, http://www.bls.gov.

55. Ibid.

56. L. Quast, "Job Seekers: 8 Tips to Negotiation Your Starting Salary," *Forbes* (online), March 31, 2014, http://www.forbes.com.

57. A. Colella, R. L. Paetzold, A. Zardkoohi, and M. J. Wesson, "Exposing Pay Secrecy," *Academy of Management Review* 32, no. 1 (2007), pp. 55–71; and Lauren Weber and Rachel Emma Silverman, "Workers Share Their Salary Secrets," *The Wall Street Journal,* April 16, 2013, http://online.wsj.com.

58. S. Gross and J. Bacher, "The New Variable Pay Programs: How Some Succeed, Why Some Don't," *Compensation and Benefits Review* 25, no. 1 (January–February 1993), p. 51; and G. Milkovich, J. Newman, and B. Gerhart, *Compensation,* 11th ed. (New York: McGraw-Hill/Irwin, 2013).

59. J. Dorfman, "Want a Job with Bonuses, 401(k) Match, Health Insurance, and More? Work for Walmart," *Forbes* (online), December 11, 2014, http://www.forbes.com; and K. Maher and K. Hudson, "Wal-Mart to Sweeten Bonus Plans for Staff," *The Wall Street Journal,* March 22, 2007, http://online.wsj.com.

60. J. Arthur and C. Huntley, "Ramping Up the Organizational Learning Curve: Assessing the Impact of Deliberate Learning on Organizational Performance under Gainsharing," *Academy of Management Journal* 48 (2005), pp. 1159–70; T. Welbourne and L. Gomez-Mejia, "Gainsharing: A Critical Review and a Future Research Agenda," *Journal of Management* 21, no. 3 (1995), pp. 559–609; L. P. Gomez-Mejia, T. M. Welbourne, and R. M. Wiseman, "The Role of Risk Sharing and Risk Taking under Gainsharing," *Academy of Management Review* 25, no. 3 (July 2000), pp. 492–507; D. Collins, *Gainsharing and Power: Lessons from Six Scanlon Plans* (Ithaca, NY: ILR Press, 1998); and P. K. Zingheim and J. R. Schuster, *Pay People Right!* (San Francisco: Jossey-Bass, 2000).

61. S. Brandt, "Minneapolis School Superintendent's Bonus Marked Down to $7,452," *Star Tribune* (online), November 13, 2013, http://www.startribune.com. See also D. W. Meyers, *Human Management: Principles and Practice* (Chicago: Commerce Clearing House, 1986); and J. P. Guthrie, "Alternative Pay Practices and Employee Turnover: An Organization Economics Perspective," *Group & Organization Management* 25, no. 4 (December 2000), pp. 419–39.

62. Lawrence Mishel and Natalie Sabadish, "CEO Pay and the Top 1%," Economic Policy Institute, May 2, 2012, http://www.epi.org; Stephen Miller, "Executive Pay: How Much Is Too Much?" *Society for Human Resource Management*, October 2, 2012, http://www.shrm.org; Nuno Fernandes, Miguel A. Ferreira, Pedro Matos, and Kevin J. Murphy, "Are U.S. CEOs Paid More? New International Evidence," *Review of Financial Studies* 26, no. 2 (2013), pp. 323–67.

63. S. Velasco, "CEO Pay Hits $10 Million, 257 Times Worker Pay: The Gap's Been Bigger," *Christian Science Monitor* (online), May 27, 2014, http://www.csmonitor.com; and M. J. Conyon, "Executive Compensation and Incentives," *Academy of Management Perspectives* 20, no. 1 (February 2006), pp. 25–44.

64. C. Forelle and J. Bandler, "The Perfect Payday," *The Wall Street Journal,* March 18, 2006, http://online.wsj.com.

65. Conyon, "Executive Compensation and Incentives."

66. J. D. Glater, "Stock Options Are Adjusted after Many Share Prices Fall," *The New York Times,* March 27, 2009, http://www.nytimes.com; Carol Bowie, "Post-Crisis Trends in U.S. Executive Pay," Harvard Law School Forum on Corporate Governance and Financial Regulation, February 27, 2012, https://blogs.law.harvard.edu; and Scott Thurm, " 'Pay for Performance' No Longer a Punchline," *The Wall Street Journal,* March 20, 2013, http://online.wsj.com.

67. A. Wayne and T. Black, "Obamacare Refutes Warning of Corporate America Cost Surge," *Bloomberg Business* (online), October 16, 2014.

68. C. O'Connor, "Target Joins Home Depot, Walmart, Others in Cutting Health Care for Part-Timers, Citing Obamacare," *Forbes* (online), January 22, 2014, http://www.forbes.com.

69. J. Hancock, "Small Businesses Drop Health Coverage and Shift Employees to Obamacare," *Kaiser Health News* (online), December 15, 2014, http://www.pbs.org.

70. Employee Benefit Research Institute, "Employer Spending on Health Insurance," in *EBRI Databook on Employee Benefits, updated May 2011,* http://www.ebri.org.

71. J. Marte, "Nearly a Quarter of Fortune 500 Companies Still Offer Pensions to New Hires," *The Washington Post* (online), September 5, 2014, http://www.washingtonpost.com.

72. E. C. Kearns and M. Gallagher, eds., *The Fair Labor Standards Act* (Washington, DC: BNA, 1999).

73. C. Fay and H. W. Risher, "Contractors, Comparable Worth and the New OFCCP: Deja Vu and More," *Compensation and Benefits Review* 32, no. 5 (September/October 2000), pp. 23–33; and G. Flynn, "Protect Yourself from an Equal-Pay Audit," *Workforce* 78, no. 6 (June 1999), pp. 144–46.

74. G. W. Bohlander, S. A. Snell, and A. W. Sherman Jr., *Managing Human Resources,* 12th ed. (Mason, OH: South-Western Publishing, 2001).

75. K. Maher, "Mine Probe Faults Massey," *The Wall Street Journal,* May 20, 2011, http://online.wsj.com.

76. Mine Safety and Health Administration, "MSHA Issues 2014 Preliminary Safety Data," news release, April 14, 2015, http://www.msha.gov; and Mine Safety and Health Administration, "Coal Fatalities for 1990 through 2010," Mining Fatality Statistics, http://www.msha.gov/stats/centurystats/coalstats.asp.

77. M. Flynn, "Safety and Health for Immigrant Workers," Centers for Disease Control and Prevention, December 4, 2014, http://www.blogs.cdc.gov.

78. L. Kahn, *Primer of Labor Relations,* 25th ed. (Washington, DC: Bureau of National Affairs Books, 1994); and A. Sloane and F. Witney, *Labor Relations* (Englewood Cliffs, NJ: Prentice-Hall, 1985).

79. S. Premack and J. E. Hunter; "Individual Unionization Decisions," *Psychological Bulletin* 103 (1988), pp. 223–34; L. Troy, *Beyond Unions and Collective Bargaining* (Armonk, NY: M. E. Sharpe, 1999); and J. A. McClendon, "Members and Nonmembers: Determinants of Dues-Paying Membership in a Bargaining Unit," *Relations Industrielles* 55, no. 2 (Spring 2000), pp. 332–47.

80. R. Sinclair and L. Tetrick, "Social Exchange and Union Commitment: A Comparison of Union Instrumentality and Union Support Perceptions," *Journal of Organizational Behavior* 16, no. 6 (November 1995), pp. 669–79. See also Premack and Hunter, "Individual Unionization Decisions."

81. D. Lewin and Richard B. Peterson, *The Modern Grievance Procedure in the United States* (Westport, CT: Quorum Books, 1998).

82. G. Bohlander and D. Blancero, "A Study of Reversal Determinants in Discipline and Discharge Arbitration Awards: The Impact of Just Cause Standards," *Labor Studies Journal* 21, no. 3 (Fall 1996), pp. 3–18.

83. Light, "Google Is No. 1"; Liedtke and Ortutay, "Google Wants to Be Cool Again"; Bryant, "The Quest to Build a Better Boss"; A. Efrati and P. W. Tam, "Google Battles to Keep Talent," *The Wall Street Journal,* November 11, 2010, http://online.wsj.com; M. Ahmed, "Why Sensible Uncle Is Being Consigned to the Back Seat," *Times (London),* January 22, 2011, Business & Company Resource Center, http://galenet.galegroup.com; C. C. Miller, "New Stage, New Skills," *The New York Times,* January 22, 2011, Business & Company Resource Center, http://galenet.galegroup.com; Manjoo, "How Google Became Such a Great Place to Work"; and Casserly, "Here's What Happens to Google Employees."

Chapter 11

1. M. Hembree, "Darrell Wallace, Jr. Driven to Chase Success, Not History," *USA Today* (online), February 21, 2015, http://www.usatoday.com; "Darrell Wallace, Jr. Wins Nascar Camping World Truck Series Finale . . . Now What?" *AutoWeek* (online), November 15, 2014; Louis Llovio, "Diversity Making Inroads in NASCAR," *Richmond (Va.) Times Dispatch,* April 22, 2013, http://www.timesdispatch.com; Bill Speros, "Class Set for NASCAR's Drive for Diversity," *ESPN.com,* January 16, 2013, http://espn.go.com; Richard E. Lapchick, "NASCAR's Chairman Puts Talk of Diversity into Action," *Sports Business Journal,* May 13–19, 2013, http://www.sportsbusinessdaily.com; Al Pearce, "NASCAR Continues Drive for Diversity with '13 Class," *Autoweek,* January 16, 2013, http://www.autoweek.com; and NASCAR, "Frequently Asked Questions," NASCAR Diversity, http://www.nascardiversity.com.

2. B. Eisenberg and M. Ruthsdotter, "Living the Legacy: The Women's Rights Movement 1848–1998," National Women's History Project, http://www.legacy98.org/move-hist.html.

3. Ibid.; R. Gladstone, "Women Run 30 Percent of All Businesses, but Only 5 Percent of the Biggest, Study Shows," *The New York Times* (online), January 12, 2015, http://www.nytimes.com; Bureau of Labor Statistics, "2014 Labor Force Statistics from the Current Population Survey," http://www.bls.gov/cps.

4. Shung J. Shin, Tae-Yeol Kim, Jeong-Yeon Lee, and Lin Bian, "Cognitive Team Diversity and Individual Team Member Creativity: A Cross-Level Interaction," *Academy of Management Journal* 55 (February 2012), pp. 197–212; David A. Harrison and Katherine J. Klein, "What's the Difference? Diversity Constructs as Separation, Variety, or Disparity in Organizations," *Academy of Management Review* 32 (October 2007), pp. 1199–1228; and Scott E. Page, "Making the Difference: Applying a Logic of Diversity," *Academy of Management Perspectives* 21 (November 2007), pp. 6–20.

5. "Why Diversity Matters?" Catalyst Information Center (online), July 2013, http://www.catalyst.org.

6. Bureau of Labor Statistics, "Table 1: Civilian Labor Force by Age, Sex, Race, and Ethnicity, 1992, 2002, 2012, and Projected 2022," news release, December 19, 2013, http://www.bls.gov.

7. M. Lopez, "In 2014, Latinos Will Surpass Whites as Largest Racial/Ethnic Group in California," Pew Research Center (online), January 24, 2014, http://www.pewre search.org.

8. Bureau of Labor Statistics, *Women in the Labor Force: A Databook,* Report 1049, May 2014, http://www.bls.gov/opub/reports/cps/womenlaborforce_2013.pdf.

9. N. Wu and A. Donovan, "NextGen Study: How Millennials View and Impact the Workplace," PricewaterhouseCoopers (online), accessed April 28, 2015; T. Meek, "Work/Life Balance: What It Means to Millennials," Coca-Cola website, October 1, 2014, http://www.coca-colacompany.com; R. Ashgar, "What Millennials Want in the Workplace (And Why You Should Start Giving It to Them)," *Forbes* (online), January 13, 2014, http://www.forbes.com; T. Haugen, "Workplaces of the Future: Creating an Elastic Workplace," *Resetting Horizons—Human Capital Trends 2013,* http://www.deloitte.com;

10. E. Patten, "On Equal Pay Day, Key Facts about the Gender Pay Gap," Pew Research Center (online), April 14, 2015, http://www.pewresearch.org;

11. B. Cronin, "Negotiating Tactics Play Role in Gender Pay Gap," *The Wall Street Journal* (online), April 1, 2013, http://www.wsj.com; Bureau of Labor Statistics (BLS), "Labor Force Characteristics by Race and Ethnicity, 2011," Report 1036, August 2012, http://www.bls.gov; AAUW, "The Simple Truth about the Gender Pay Gap," 2013, http://www.aauw.org; and Jessica Bennett, "How to Attack the Gender Wage Gap? Speak Up," *The New York Times,* December 15, 2012, http://www.nytimes.com.

12. Catalyst, "Still Too Few: Women of Color on Boards," http://www.catalyst.org, accessed April 21, 2015; C. Fairchild, "A New Pew Research Report Explores America's Perceptions about Women's Ability to Lead Companies," *Fortune*

(online), January 14, 2015, http://www.fortune.com; J. McGregor, "A Long Way to 50-50 on Corporate Boards," *The Washington Post* (online), May 30, 2014, http://www.washingtonpost.com;

13. P. Drexler, "The Tyranny of the Queen Bee," *The Wall Street Journal* (online), March 6, 2013, http://www.wsj.com; Robi Ludwig, "Bad Female Boss? She May Have Queen Bee Syndrome," *Today,* April 12, 2011, http://www.today.com; and Peggy Drexler, "The Tyranny of the Queen Bee," *The Wall Street Journal,* March 6, 2013, http://online.wsj.com.

14. U.S. Equal Employment Opportunity Commission, "Federal Jury Awards $105,000 in EEOC Sexual Harassment Case Against Racine IHOP," press release, November 23, 2009, http://www.eeoc.gov; B. Gregg, "Protect Young Employees from Harassment," *Diversity Inc.* (online), August 15, 2011, http://www.diveristyinc.com.

15. "National Restaurant Association Offers Training DVDs on Harassment Prevention, Social Media Use, and Customer Service," National Restaurant Association (online), press release, on April 22, 2014, http://www.restaurant.org; and S. Armour, "Companies Try to Educate Teen Workers about Harassment," *USA Today,* October 19, 2006, http://www.usatoday.com.

16. G. Bohlander, S. Snell, and A. Sherman, *Managing Human Resources,* 12th ed. (Mason, OH: South-Western Publishing, 2001); and W. Petrocelli and B. K. Repa, *Sexual Harassment on the Job: What It Is and How to Stop It* (Berkeley, CA: Nolo Press, 1998).

17. "Presidential Order Protects LGBT Workers at Federal Contractors," *Society for Human Resource Management* (online), July 21, 2014, http://www.shrm.org; D. Wilkie, "More Than Half of LGBT Workers Closeted," *Society for Human Resource Management* (online), May 15, 2014, http://www.shrm.org.

18. Bureau of Labor Statistics (BLS), "Table 1: Civilian Labor Force by Age, Sex, Race, and Ethnicity, 1992, 2002, 2012, and projected 2022," news release, December 19, 2013, http:// www.bls.gov; BLS, "Foreign-Born Workers: Labor Force Characteristics, 2012," news release, May 22, 2013, http://www.bls.gov; and Carol Morello and Ted Mellnik, "Census: Minority Babies Are Now Majority in United States," *The Washington Post,* May 17, 2012, http://articles.washingtonpost.com.

19. "The United States of Entrepreneurs," *The Economist,* March 14, 2009, http://www.economist.com.

20. BLS, "Labor Force Characteristics by Race and Ethnicity, 2013."

21. M. Bertrand and S. Mullainathan, "Are Emily and Greg More Employable Than Lakisha and Jamal?" NBER Working Paper No. 9873, July 2003, http://www.nber.org.

22. D. Pattison and H. Waldron, "Growth in New Disabled-Worker Entitlements, 1970–2008," *Social Security Administration Bulletin* (online), 73, no. 4 (2013), http://

www.ssa.gov; and M. P. McQueen, "Workplace Disabilities Are on the Rise," *The Wall Street Journal,* May 1, 2007, http://online.wsj.com.

23. Bureau of Labor Statistics, "Table 1: Employment Status of the Civilian Noninstitutional Population by Disability Status and Selected Characteristics, 2013 Annual Averages," http://www.bls.gov, accessed April 23, 2015.

24. U.S. Bureau of the Census, "Anniversary of Americans with Disabilities Act: July 26," Facts for Features CB11-FF.14, May 31, 2011, http://www.census.gov; and Bureau of Labor Statistics, "Persons with a Disability: Labor Force Characteristics—2009," news release, August 25, 2010, http://www.bls.gov/cps.

25. Equal Employment Opportunity Commission (EEOC), "Disability Discrimination," http://www.eeoc.gov; EEOC, "Notice Concerning the Americans with Disabilities Act (ADA) Amendments Act of 2008," http://www.eeoc.gov; and EEOC, "ADA Charge Data by Impairments/Bases: Resolutions, FY1997–FY2008," http://www.eeoc.gov.

26. Daniel de Vise, "Number of U.S. Adults with College Degrees Hits Historic High," *The Washington Post,* February 23, 2012, http://articles.washingtonpost.com; Bureau of the Census, "Kurt Bauman, Chief of the Education and Social Stratification Branch, Appeared on C-SPAN's 'Washington Journal' to Discuss Educational Attainment in the United States," newsroom, February 24, 2012, http://www.census.gov/newsroom/cspan/educ/; and BLS, "Foreign-Born Workers."

27. P. Taylor and the Pew Research Center, *The Next America* (New York: Public Affairs, 2014).

28. The Conference Board, "Growing Labor Shortages on the Horizon in Mature Economies," press release, on September 2, 2014, http://www.conference-board.org.

29. S. Vernon, "Will Boomers Really Be Able to Work Past 65?" *CBS News* (online), January 6, 2015, http://www.cbsnews.com.

30. P. Shergill, "Managing High-Performing but Demanding Gen Y," *HR Magazine* (online), August 22, 2014, http://www.hrmagazine.co.uk; N. A. Hira, "Attracting the Twenty-Something Worker," *Fortune,* May 15, 2007, http://money.cnn.com.

31. S. Gorman and N. Andrews, "The CIA Has Joined Facebook and Twitter," *The Wall Street Journal* (online), June 6, 2014, http://www.wsj.com; T. Hoffman, "Eight New Ways to Target Top Talent in '08," *Computerworld,* January 28, 2008, pp. 34, 36; and A. Kingsbury, "The CIA and NSA Want You to Be Their Friend on Facebook," *U.S. News & World Report Online,* February 5, 2009, Business & Company Resource Center, http://galenet.galegroup.com.

32. See, for example, R. Riccò and M. Guerci, "Diversity Challenge: An Integrated Process to Bridge the 'Implementation Gap,'" *Business Horizons* 57 (2014),

pp. 235–45; C. Francoeur, R. Labelle, and B. Sinclair-Desgangnè, "Gender Diversity in Corporate Governance and Top Management," *Journal of Business Ethics* 81, no. 1 (2008), pp. 83–95; A. McMillan-Capehart, J. R. Aaron, and B. N. Cline, "Investor Reactions to Diversity Reputation Signals," *Corporate Reputation Review* 13 (2010), pp. 184–97; P. Wang and J. L. Schwarz, "Stock Price Reactions to GLBT Nondiscrimination Policies," *Human Resource Management* 49, no. 2 (2010), pp. 195–216; R. C. Anderson, D. M. Reeb, A. Upadhyay, and W. Zhao, "The Economics of Director Heterogeneity," *Financial Management* 40, no. 1 (2011), pp. 5–38; M. Davidson, "Leveraging Difference for Organizational Excellence: Managing Diversity Differently," technical note UVA-OB-0767 (Charlottesville, VA: Darden Business Publishing, 2002); Eric Kearney, Diether Gebert, and Sven C. Voelpel, "When and How Diversity Benefits Teams: The Importance of Team Members' Need for Cognition," *Academy of Management Journal* 52 (June 2009), pp. 581–98.

33. A. Diaz-Uda, C. Medina, and B. Schill, "Diversity's New Frontier: Diversity ofThought and the Future of the Workforce," Deloitte University Press (online), July 23, 2013, http://www.dupress.com; N. Adler, *International Dimensions of Organizational Behavior*, 3rd ed. (Boston: PWS-Kent, 1997); and T. Cox and S. Blake, "Managing Cultural Diversity: Implications for Organizational Competitiveness," *Academy of Management Executives* 5 (August 1991), pp. 45–56.

34. Procter & Gamble, "Fulfilling Our Potential," corporate Purpose & People website, http://www.pg.com/en_US/company/purpose_people/diversity_inclusion.

35. See, for example, S. J. Tribble, "Cisco Accused of Bias in Hiring," *San Jose Mercury News,* May 10, 2007, http://www.mercurynews.com; G. Appleson, "Baby Boomers, Often Targeted in Layoffs, Fight Age Discrimination," *St. Louis Post-Dispatch,* April 29, 2007, Business & Company Resource Center, http://galenet.galegroup.com; "Class Action Suits in the Workplace Are on the Rise," *HR Focus,* April 2007, http://galenet.galegroup.com; M. Schoeff Jr., "Walgreen Suit Reflects EEOC's Latest Strategies," *Workforce Management,* March 26, 2007, http://galenet.galegroup.com; and Erika Hayes James and Lynn Perry Wooten, "Diversity Crises: How Firms Manage Discrimination Lawsuits," *Academy of Management Journal* 49 (December 2006), pp. 1103–18.

36. U.S. Equal Employment Opportunity Commission, http://www.eeoc.gov, accessed April 24, 2015.

37. B. Kreissl, "Managing a Multigenerational Workforce," *Canadian HR Reporter* 28 (2015), pp. 19–20; and R. R. Thomas Jr., "From Affirmative Action to Affirming Diversity," *Harvard Business Review,* March–April 1990.

38. K. Jesella, "Mom's Mad, and She's Organized," *The New York Times,* February 22, 2007, http://www.nytimes.com.

39. G. Avalos, "Study Looks at Diversity, Turnover," *Contra Costa Times (Walnut Creek, CA)*, October 13, 2006, Business & Company Resource Center, http://galenet.galegroup.com; Aparna Joshi and Hyuntak Roh, "The Role of Context in Work Team Diversity Research: A Meta-Analytic Review," *Academy of Management Journal* 52 (June 2009), pp. 559–627.

40. Adler, *International Dimensions of Organizational Behavior;* Cox and Blake, "Managing Cultural Diversity"; Brian Blume, Timothy Baldwin, and Katherine Ryan, "Communication Apprehension: A Barrier to Students' Leadership, Adaptability, and Multicultural Appreciation," *Academy of Management Learning and Education* 12, September 12, 2012, pp.158–72.

41. J. Nanley, A. Pugh, N. Romero, and A. Seals, "An Examination of Racial Discrimination in the Labor Market for Recent College Graduates: Estimates from the Field," Auburn University Department of Economics Working Paper Series no. 2014-06, http://www.http://cla.auburn.edu/econwp/.

42. J. D. Nordell, "Positions of Power: How Female Ambition Is Shaped," *Slate,* November 21, 2006, http://www.slate.com.

43. Adler, *International Dimensions of Organizational Behavior.*

44. Davidson, "Leveraging Difference for Organizational Excellence."

45. NASCAR, "New Names Fill 2015 NASCAR Drive For Diversity," press release on, January 26, 2015, http://www.nascar.com; NASCAR, "New Names Fill Drive For Diversity Roster," press release, January 26, 2015, http://www.nascar.com; Llovio, "Diversity Making Inroads in NASCAR"; Speros, "Class Set for NASCAR's Drive for Diversity"; Pearce, "NASCAR Continues Drive for Diversity"; NASCAR, "Frequently Asked Questions"; and Tom Bowles, "Drive for Diversity Drivers Talk Race and Gender in NASCAR," *SI.com (Sports Illustrated),* July 30, 2010, http://sportsillustrated.cnn.com.

46. K. A. Jehn, "Workplace Diversity, Conflict, and Productivity: Managing in the 21st Century," SEI Center for Advanced Studies in Management, Wharton School, University of Pennsylvania, Diversity, http://mktg-sun.wharton.upenn.edu/SEI/diversity.html; and Anne Nederveen Pieterse, Daan van Knippenberg, and Dirk van Dierendonck, "Cultural Diversity and Team Performance: The Role of Team Member Goal Orientation," *Academy of Management Journal* 56 (July 20, 2012), pp. 782–804.

47. A. J. Murrell, F. J. Crosby, and R. J. Ely, *Mentoring Dilemmas: Developmental Relationships within Multicultural Organizations* (Mahwah, NJ: Lawrence Erlbaum Associates, 1999). See a review of this book by M. L. Lengnick-Hall, "Mentoring Dilemmas: Developmental Relationships within Multicultural Organizations," *Personnel Psychology* 53, no. 1 (Spring 2000), pp. 224–27.

48. M.-J. Chen, "Becoming Ambicultural: A Personal Quest, and Aspiration for Organizations," *Academy of Management Review* 39 (2014), pp. 119–37; and P. Solman, "The Miracle of Profit-Sharing: Year 65 and Still No Layoffs," *PBS News Hour,* December 15, 2013, http://www.pbs.org.

49. A. Kalev, F. Dobbin, and E. Kelly, "Best Practices or Best Guesses? Assessing the Efficacy of Corporate Affirmative Action and Diversity Policies," *American Sociological Review* 71 (2006), pp. 589–617.

50. Change.org, "About," http://www.change.org, accessed April 29, 2015; C. Logorio Chafkin,"4 Smart Ways to Work on Your Diversity Problem," *Inc.* (online), November 7, 2014, http://www.inc.com; and A. Bluestein, "How Ben Rattray's Change.org Became a Viral Consumer Watchdog," *Fast Company* (online), September 2014, http://www.fastcompany.com.

51. Brett Berson, Jack Zenger, Kellan Elliott-McCrea, and Joseph Folkman, "Why Recruiting Women Requires Creativity," *Build,* February 25, 2013, http://thebuildnetwork.com.

52. R. Rosen, "Etsy CTO: Prioritizing Diversity in Our Hiring Fielded Better Women and Men," *The Atlantic* (online), February 7, 2013, http://www.theatlantic.com.

53. M. Crowley, "How SAS Became the World's Best Place to Work," *Fast Company* (online), January 22, 2013, http://www.fastcompany.com.

54. Society of Women Engineers, "Establishing a Flexible Career Arrangement Porgram," February 13, 2014, http://www.societyofwomenengineers.com; and M. D. Lee, S. M. MacDermid, and M. L. Buck, "Organizational Paradigms of Reduced-Load Work: Accommodation, Elaboration, and Transformation," *Academy of Management Journal* 43, no. 6 (December 2000), pp. 1211–34.

55. L. E. Overmyer Day, "The Pitfalls of Diversity Training," *Training and Development* 49, no. 12 (December 1995), pp. 24–29; S. Rynes and B. Rosen, "A Field Survey of Factors Affecting the Adoption and Perceived Success of Diversity Training," *Personnel Psychology* 48, no. 2 (Summer 1995), pp. 247–70; L. Ford, "Diversity: From Cartoons to Confrontations," *Training & Development* 54, no. 8 (August 2000), pp. 70–71; J. M. Ivancevich and J. A. Gilbert, "Diversity Management: Time for a New Approach," *Public Personnel Management* 29, no. 1 (Spring 2000), pp. 75–92; and Katerina Bezrukova, Karen A. Jehn, and Chester S. Spell, "Reviewing Diversity Training: Where We Have Been and Where We Should Go," *Academy of Management Learning and Education* 11 (June 2012), pp. 207–27.

56. "How to Increase Workplace Diversity," *The Wall Street Journal* (online), April 7, 2009, http://www.wsj.com; and M. Burkart, "The Role of Training in Advancing a Diversity Initiative," *Diversity Factor* 8, no. 1 (Fall 1999), pp. 2–5.

57. Korn Ferry, "Executive Survey Finds a Lack of Focus on Diversity and Inclusion Key Factors in Employee Turnover," press release on, March 2, 2015, http://www.kornferry.com.

58. D. M. Robinson and T. Reio Jr., "Benefits of Mentoring African-American Men," *Journal of Managerial Psychology* 27 (2012), pp. 406–21; "How Bad Is the Turnover Problem?" *HR Focus,* March 2007, Business & Company Resource Center, http://galenet.galegroup.com; B. Thomas, "Black Entrepreneurs Win, Corporations Lose," *BusinessWeek,* September 20, 2006, General Reference Center Gold, http://find.galegroup.com; and P. Shurn-Hannah, "Solving the Minority Retention Mystery," *The Human Resource Professional* 13, no. 3 (May/June 2000), pp. 22–27.

59. Ernst & Young, "Mentorship, Sponsorship Keys to Building a Strong and Committed Workforce," news release, April 12, 2011, http://www.ey.com/CA/en/.

60. K. Van Nuys, D. Globe, D. Ng-Mak, H. Cheung, J. Sullivan, and D. Goldman, "The Association Between Employee Obesity and Employer Costs: Evidence from a Panel of U.S. Employers," *American Journal of Health Promotion* 28 (May–June 2014), pp. 277–85.

61. R. Rodriguez, "Diversity Finds Its Place," *HR Magazine,* August 2006, Business & Company Resource Center, http://galenet.galegroup.com.

62. PepsiCo, "Diversity & Inclusion," http://www.pepsic.com, accessed April 27, 2015; PepsiCo, "Awards & Recognition," http://www.pepsico.com, accessed April 27, 2015.

63. Llovio, "Diversity Making Inroads in NASCAR"; Speros, "Class Set for NASCAR's Drive for Diversity"; Lapchick, "NASCAR's Chairman Puts Talk of Diversity into Action"; Joe Gibbs Racing, "Daniel Suarez," http://www.joegibbsracing.com, accessed April 27, 2015; NASCAR, "NASCAR Diversity Awards Celebrate Inclusion," press release on, February 21, 2014; Associated Press, "Jeremy Clements Looking for Redemption," SI.com *(Sports Illustrated),* March 15, 2013, http://sportsillustrated.cnn.com; Heather Tucker, "Jeremy Clements' Racial Remark Revealed," *USA Today,* March 1, 2013, http://www.usatoday.com; George Diaz, "Suspension for Racial Slur Reflects NASCAR's Commitment to Diversity," *Chicago Tribune,* March 6, 2013, http://articles.chicagotribune.com; and National Consortium for Academics and Sports, "Teamwork Leadership Institute," http://ncasports.org.

Chapter 12

1. Hewlett-Packard, "About HP," http://www.hp.com, accessed April 30, 2015; J. Hough, "Meg Whitman's Turnaround at HP," *Barrons* (online), April 5, 2015, http://www.barrons.com; "Split Shows Turnaround a Success: HP CEO Whitman," CNBC (October 6, 2014), http://www.cnbc.com; George Anders, "Meg Whitman Jolts HP as Its Reluctant Savior," *Forbes,* May 22, 2013, http://www.forbes.com; James Bandler and Doris Burke, "How HP Lost Its Way," *Fortune,* May 21, 2012, EBSCOhost, http://web.ebscohost.com; Ashlee Vance and Aaron Ricade La, "Mark Hurd, Leo Apotheker, Meg Whitman in Hewlett-Packard's Vertigo," *Bloomberg Businessweek,* January 14, 2013, EBSCOhost, http://web.ebscohost.com; Dean Takahashi, "Meg Whitman Says 'You Can Feel the Turnaround Taking Place at HP' (but Not at Dell)," *VentureBeat,* May 22, 2013, http://venturebeat.com; Kevin McLaughlin, "HP Is Losing Some Rock Star Big Engineers," *Business Insider,* May 20, 2013, http://www.businessinsider.com.

2. W. Bennis and B. Nanus, *Leaders* (New York: Harper & Row, 1985), p. 27.

3. J. Petrick, R. Schere, J. Brodzinski, J. Quinn, and M. Fall Ainina, "Global Leadership Skills and Reputational Capital: Intangible Resources for Sustainable Competitive Advantage," *Academy of Management Executive,* February 1999, pp. 58–69.

4. Bennis and Nanus, *Leaders.*

5. Ibid., p. 144.

6. E. E. Lawler III, *Treat People Right! How Organizations and Individuals Can Propel Each Other into a Virtual Spiral of Success* (San Francisco: Jossey-Bass,2003); G. Llopis, "The 6 Most Important Things Employees Need from Their Leaders to Realize High Potential," *Forbes* (online), September 30, 2013, http://www.forbes.com

7. Alejandra Cancino, "Deliberate Change of Pace Works for ITW Attorney," *Chicago Tribune,* May 6, 2013, sec. 2, pp. 1, 4.

8. L. Pollak, ""Millennials: Tomorrow's Leaders, Today," *The Hartford,* April 2014, http://www.thehartford.com; R. Asghar, "What Millennials Want in the Workplace (And Why You Should Start Giving It to Them)," *Forbes* (online), January 13, 2014, http://www.forbes.com; "The Deloitte Millennial Survey Executive Survey," Deloitte, January 2014, http://www2.deloitte.com; L. Stiller Rikleen, Esq., "Creating Tomorrow's Leaders: the Expanding Roles of Millennials in the Workplace," Boston College Center for Work & Family, http://www.bc.edu, accessed May 7, 2015;

9. J. Kouzes and B. Posner, *The Leadership Challenge* (San Francisco: Jossey-Bass, 1987).

10. "5 Influential CEOs Weigh in What Makes a Good Leader," *Entrepreneur* (online), February 25, 2013, http://www.entrepreneur.com.

11. Starbucks, "An Open Letter from Howard Schultz, CEO of Starbucks Coffee Company," Tuesday, September 17, 2013, http://www.starbucks.com.

12. A. Ruvio, Z. Rosenblatt, and R. Hertz-Lazarowitz, "Entrepreneurial Leadership Vision in Nonprofit vs. For-Profit Organizations," *Leadership Quarterly* 21 (2010), pp. 144–158; J. Baum, E. A. Locke, and S. Kirkpatrick, "A Longitudinal Study of the Relation of Vision and Vision Communication to Venture Growth in Entrepreneurial Firms," *Journal of Applied Psychology* 83 (1998), pp. 43–54.

13. E. C. Shapiro, *Fad Surfing in the Boardroom* (Reading, MA: Addison-Wesley, 1995).

14. Kouzes and Posner, *The Leadership Challenge* (1995).

15. Ibid.

16. W. Bennis and R. Townsend, *Reinventing Leadership* (New York: William Morrow, 1995).

17. Ibid.

18. D. Mattioli and K. Maher, "At 3M, Innovation Comes in Tweaks and Snips," *The Wall Street Journal,* March 1, 2010, http://online.wsj.com.

19. Kouzes and Posner, *The Leadership Challenge* (1987).

20. J. A. Conger, "The Dark Side of Leadership," *Organizational Dynamics* 19 (Autumn 1990), pp. 44–55.

21. J. Conger, "The Vision Thing: Explorations into Visionary Leadership," in *Cutting Edge Leadership 2000,* ed. B. Kellerman and L. Matusak (College Park, MD: James MacGregor Burns Academy of Leadership, 2000).

22. J. P. Kotter, "What Leaders Really Do," *Harvard Business Review* 68 (May–June 1990), pp. 103–11.

23. J. Jensen, "From Me to We," *Leadership Excellence* 31(2014), 65–66; M. E. Van Buren and T. Safferstone, "Collective Quick Wins," *Computerworld,* January 26, 2009, pp. 24–25.

24. G. Yukl, *Leadership in Organizations,* 3rd ed. (Englewood Cliffs, NJ: Prentice Hall, 1994).

25. R. House and R. Aditya, "The Social Scientific Study of Leadership: Quo Vadis?" *Journal of Management* 23 (1997), pp. 409–73.

26. K. Boal and P. Schultz, "Storytelling, Time, and Evolution: The Role of Strategic Leadership in Complex Adaptive Systems," *Leadership Quarterly* 18 (2007), pp. 411–28; R. D. Ireland and M. A. Hitt. "Achieving and Maintaining Strategic Competitiveness in the 21st Century: The Role of Strategic Leadership," *Academy of Management Executive,* February 1999, pp. 43–57.

27. P. Cappelli, H. Singh, J. V. Singh, and M. Useem, "Leadership Lessons from India," *Harvard Business Review,* March 2010, pp. 90–97.

28. J. Gardner, "The Heart of the Matter: Leader–Constituent Interaction," in

Leading & Leadership, ed. T. Fuller (Notre Dame, IN: University of Notre Dame Press, 2000), pp. 239–44, quote at p. 240.

29. R. E. Kelly, "In Praise of Followers," *Harvard Business Review* 66 (November–December 1988), pp. 142–48.

30. Bennis and Townsend, *Reinventing Leadership.*

31. Kelly, "In Praise of Followers."

32. J. R. P. French and B. Raven, "The Bases of Social Power," in *Studies in Social Power,* ed. D. Cartwright (Ann Arbor, MI: Institute for Social Research, 1959).

33. G. Yukl and C. Falbe, "Importance of Different Power Sources in Downward and Lateral Relations," *Journal of Applied Psychology* 76 (1991), pp. 416–23.

34. Ibid.

35. "S. Badal, "For Great Business Builders, Knowledge Is Power," *Gallup Business Journal* (online), September 30, 2014, http://www.gallup.com; L. Bryan, E. Matson, and L. Weiss, "Harnessing the Power of Informal Employee Networks," *The McKinsey Report* 4 (2007), pp. 44–55.

36. R. M. Stogdill, "Personal Factors Associated with Leadership: A Survey of the Literature," *Journal of Psychology* 25 (1948), pp. 35–71.

37. G. Moran, "Leadership: Nature or Nurture?" *Entrepreneur* (online), October 14, 2013, http://www.entrepreneur.com; S. Kirkpatrick and E. Locke, "Leadership: Do Traits Matter?" *The Executive* 5 (May 1991), pp. 48–60.

38. G. A. Yukl, *Leadership in Organizations,* 2nd ed. (Englewood Cliffs, NJ: Prentice-Hall, 1989).

39. T. Judge, J. Bono, R. Ilies, and M. Gerhardt, "Personality and Leadership: A Qualitative and Quantitative Review," *Journal of Applied Psychology* 87 (2002), pp. 765–80.

40. A. Grant, F. Gino, and D. Hofmann, "Reversing the Extroverted Leadership Advantage: The Role of Employee Proactivity," *Academy of Management Journal* 54 (2011), pp. 528–50.

41. R. Foti and N. M. A. Hauenstein, "Pattern and Variable Approaches in Leadership Emergence and Effectiveness," *Journal of Applied Psychology* 92 (2007), pp. 347–55.

42. J. P. Kotter, *The General Managers* (New York: Free Press, 1982).

43. T. Manning, "The Art of Successful Influence: Matching Influence Strategies and Styles to the Context," *Industrial and Commercial Training* 44 (2012), pp. 26–34; S. Zaccaro, R. Foti, and D. Kenny, "Self- Monitoring and Trait-Based Variance in Leadership: An Investigation of Leader Flexibility across Multiple Group Situations," *Journal of Applied Psychology* 76 (1991), pp. 308–15.

44. D. Goleman, "Leadership That Gets Results," *Harvard Business Review,* March–April 2000, pp. 78–90.

45. J. Misumi and M. Peterson, "The Performance-Maintenance (PM) Theory of Leadership: Review of a Japanese Research Program," *Administrative Science Quarterly* 30 (June 1985), pp. 198–223.

46. T. Judge, R. Piccolo, and R. Ilies, "The Forgotten Ones? The Validity of Consideration and Initiating Structure in Leadership Research," *Journal of Applied Psychology* 89 (2004), pp. 36–51.

47. G. Thomas, R. Martin, and R. Riggio, "Leading Groups: Leadership as a Group Process," *Group Processes & Intergroup Relations* 16 (2013), pp. 3–16.

48. Misumi and Peterson, "The Performance-Maintenance (PM) Theory."

49. Judge, Piccolo, and Ilies, "The Forgotten Ones?"

50. G. Graen and M. Uhl-Bien, "Relationship-Based Approach to Leadership: Development of Leader-Member Exchange (LMX) Theory of Leadership over 25 Years: Applying a Multi-Level Multi-domain Perspective," *Leadership Quarterly* 6, no. 2 (1995), pp. 219–47.

51. House and Aditya, "The Social Scientific Study of Leadership."

52. C. R. Gerstner and D. V. Day, "Meta-Analytic Review of Leader-Member Exchange Theory: Correlates and Construct Issues," *Journal of Applied Psychology* 82 (1997), pp. 827–44.

53. T. Rockstuhl, J. Dulebohn, S. Ang, and L. Shore, "Leader-member Exchange (LMX) and Culture: A Meta-analysis of Correlates of LMX Across 23 Countries," *Journal of Applied Psychology* 97 (2012), 1097–1130.

54. House and Aditya, "The Social Scientific Study of Leadership."

55. M. Mills and S. Culbertson, "High-Involvement Work Practices: Are They Really Worth It?" The *Academy of Management Perspectives* 23 (2009), pp. 93–95; J. Wagner III, "Participation's Effect on Performance and Satisfaction: A Reconsideration of Research," *Academy of Management Review,* April 1994, pp. 312–30.

56. R. White and R. Lippitt, *Autocracy and Democracy: An Experimental Inquiry* (New York: Harper & Brothers, 1960).

57. R. Charan, "Conquering a Culture of Indecision," *Harvard Business Review* 84 (2006), pp.108–117; J. Muczyk and R. Steel, "Leadership Style and the Turnaround Executive," *Business Horizons,* March–April 1999, pp. 39–46.

58. A. Tannenbaum and W. Schmidt, "How to Choose a Leadership Pattern," *Harvard Business Review* 36 (March–April 1958), pp. 95–101.

59. E. Fleishman and E. Harris, "Patterns of Leadership Behavior Related to Employee Grievances and Turnover," *Personnel Psychology* 15 (1962), pp. 43–56.

60. R. Likert, *The Human Organization: Its Management and Value* (New York: McGraw-Hill, 1967).

61. R. Blake and J. Mouton, *The Managerial Grid* (Houston: Gulf, 1964).

62. Misumi and Peterson, "The Performance-Maintenance (PM) Theory."

63. J. Wall, Bosses (Lexington, MA: Lexington Books, 1986), p. 103.

64. Tannenbaum and Schmidt, "How to Choose a Leadership Pattern."

65. To practice using the decision tree, please see V. H. Vroom, "Leadership and the Decision-Making Process," *Organizational Dynamics,* Spring 2000, pp. 82–93.

66. F. E. Fiedler, *A Theory of Leadership Effectiveness* (New York: McGraw-Hill, 1967).

67. P. Hersey and K. Blanchard, *The Management of Organizational Behavior* (Englewood Cliffs, NJ: Prentice Hall, 1984).

68. Yukl, *Leadership in Organizations.*

69. R. J. House, "A Path–Goal Theory of Leader Effectiveness," *Administrative Science Quarterly* 16 (1971), pp. 321–39.

70. J. Howell, D. Bowen, P. Dorfman, S. Kerr, and P. Podsakoff, "Substitutes for Leadership: Effective Alternatives to Ineffective Leadership," *Organizational Dynamics* 19 (Summer 1990), pp. 21–38.

71. R. G. Lord and W. Gradwohl Smith, "Leadership and the Changing Nature of Performance," in *The Changing Nature of Performance,* ed. D. R. Ilgen and E. D. Pulakos (San Francisco: Jossey-Bass, 1999).

72. Hough, "Meg Whitman's Turnaround at HP"; Anders, "Meg Whitman Jolts HP"; Bandler and Burke, "How HP Lost Its Way"; Vance and La, "Mark Hurd, Leo Apotheker, Meg Whitman"; "Split Shows Turnaround a Success: HP CEO Whitman."

73. S. Dionne, F. Yammarino, L. Atwater, and L. James, "Neutralizing Substitutes for Leadership Theory: Leadership Effects and Common-Source Bias," *Journal of Applied Psychology* 87 (2002), pp. 454–64.

74. B. M. Bass, *Leadership and Performance Beyond Expectations* (New York: Free Press, 1985).

75. T. Chamorro-Premuzic, "The Dark Side of Charisma," *Harvard Business Review* (online), November 16, 2012, http://www.hbr.org; Y. A. Nur, "Charisma and Managerial Leadership: The Gift That Never Was," *Business Horizons,* July–August 1998, pp. 19–26; and R. J. House, "A 1976 Theory of Charismatic Leadership," in *Leadership: The Cutting Edge,* ed. J. G. Hunt and L. L. Larson (Carbondale, IL: Southern Illinois University Press, 1977).

76. M. Brown and L. Trevino, "Socialized Charismatic Leadership, Values Congruence, and Deviance in Work Groups," *Journal of Applied Psychology* 91 (2006), pp. 954–62.

77. M. Potts and P. Behr, *The Leading Edge* (New York: McGraw-Hill, 1987).

78. J. Howell and B. Shamir, "The Role of Followers in the Charismatic Leadership Process: Relationships and Their Consequences," *Academy of Management Review* 30 (2005), pp. 96–112.

79. B. Galvin, P. Balkundi, and D. Waldman, "Spreading the Word: The Role of Surrogates in Charismatic Leadership

Processes," *Academy of Management Review* 35 (2010), pp. 477–494; B. Galvin, P. Balkundi, and D. Waldman, "Can Charisma Be Taught? Tests of Two Interventions," *Academy of Management Review* 35 (2010), pp. 477–94.

80. Galvin, Balkundi, and Waldman, "Can Charisma Be Taught? Tests of Two Interventions" J. Antonakis, M. Fenley, and S. Liechti, *Academy of Management Learning & Education* 10 (2011), pp. 374–96.

81. S. Yorges, H. Weiss, and O. Strickland, "The Effect of Leader Outcomes on Influence, Attributions, and Perceptions of Charisma," *Journal of Applied Psychology* 84 (1999), pp. 428–36.

82. G. Colony, "Apple = Sony," *Forrester Blogs,* April 25, 2012, http://blogs. forrester.com.

83. D. A. Waldman and F. J. Yammarino, "CEO Charismatic Leadership: Levels-of-Management and Levels-of-Analysis Effects," *Academy of Management Review* 24 (1999), pp. 266–85.

84. A. Erez, V. F. Misangyi, D. E. Johnson, M. A. LePine, and K. C. Halverson, "Stirring the Hearts of Followers: Charismatic Leadership as the Transferral of Affect," *Journal of Applied Psychology* 93 (2008), pp. 602–16.

85. A. Fanelli and V. Misangyi, "Bringing Out Charisma: CEO Charisma and External Stakeholders," *Academy of Management Review* 31 (2006), pp. 1049–61.

86. House and Aditya, "The Social Scientific Study of Leadership."

87. D. A. Waldman, G. G. Ramirez, R. J. House, and P. Puranam, "Does Leadership Matter? CEO Leadership Attributes and Profitability under Conditions of Perceived Environmental Uncertainty," *Academy of Management Journal* 44 (2001), pp. 134–43.

88. S. Boehm, D. Dwertmann, H. Bruch, and B. Shamir, "The Missing Link? Investigating Organizational Identity Strength and Transformational Leadership Climate as Mechanisms That Connect CEO Charisma with Firm Performance," *Leadership Quarterly* 26 (2015), 156–71; B. Agle, N. Nagarajan, J. Sonnenfeld, and D. Srinivasan, "Does CEO Charisma Matter? An Empirical Analysis of the Relationships among Organizational Performance, Environmental Uncertainty, and Top Management Team Perceptions of CEO Charisma," *Academy of Management Journal* 49 (2006), pp. 161–74.

89. J. M. Howell and K. E. Hall-Merenda, "The Ties That Bind: The Impact of Leader-Member Exchange, Transformational and Transactional Leadership, and Distance on Predicting Follower Performance," *Journal of Applied Psychology* 84 (1999), pp. 680–94; and B. M. Bass, "Leadership: Good, Better, Best," *Organizational Dynamics,* Winter 1985, pp. 26–40.

90. B. Thompson, "Take a Tip from Bezos: Customers Always Need a Seat at the Table," *Entrepreneur* (online), May 28, 2014, http://www.entrepreneur.com; Adam Lashinsky, "Amazon's Jeff Bezos: The Ultimate Disrupter," *Fortune,* November 16, 2012, http://management.fortune.cnn.com.

91. D. I. Jung and B. J. Avolio, "Effects of Leadership Style and Followers' Cultural Orientation on Performance in Group and Individual Task Conditions," *Academy of Management Journal* 42 (1999), pp. 208–18.

92. Bass, *Leadership.*

93. Bennis and Nanus, *Leaders.*

94. A. M. Grant, "Leading with Meaning: Beneficiary Contact, Prosocial Impact, and the Performance Effects of Transformational Leadership," *Academy of Management Journal* 55 (2012), pp. 458–76.

95. B. Bass, B. Avolio, and L. Goodheim, "Biography and the Assessment of Transformational Leadership at the World-Class Level," *Journal of Management* 13 (1987), pp. 7–20.

96. D. Williams, "Top 10 List: The Greatest Living Business Leaders Today," *Forbes* (online), July 24, 2012, http://www.forbes.com.

97. Y. Ling, Z. Simisek, M. Lubatkin, and J. F. Veiga, "The Impact of Transformational CEOs on the Performance of Small to Medium-Sized Firms: Does Organizational Context Matter?" *Journal of Applied Psychology* 93 (2008), pp. 923–34.

98. T. A. Judge and J. E. Bono, "Five-Factor Model of Personality and Transformational Leadership," *Journal of Applied Psychology* 85 (2000), pp. 751–65; and B. Bass, "Does the Transactional-Transformational Paradigm Transcend Organizational and National Boundaries?" *American Psychologist* 22 (1997), pp. 130–42.

99. C. Li, H. Zhao, and T. M. Begley, "Transformational Leadership Dimensions and Employee Creativity in China: A Cross-level Analysis," *Journal of Business Research* 68, no. 6 (2015), pp. 1149–56.

100. R. Piccolo and J. Colquitt, "Transformational Leadership and Job Behaviors: The Mediating Role of Core Job Characteristics," *Academy of Management Journal* 49 (2006), pp. 327–40.

101. A. Colbert, A. Kristof-Brown, B. Bradley, and M. Barrick, "CEO Transformational Leadership: The Role of Goal Importance Congruence in Top Management Teams," *Academy of Management Journal* 51 (2008), pp. 81–96.

102. T. Dvir, D. Eden, B. Avolio, and B. Shamir, "Impact of Transformational Leadership on Follower Development and Performance: A Field Experiment," *Academy of Management Journal* 45 (2002), pp. 735–44.

103. B. M. Bass, *Transformational Leadership: Industry, Military, and Educational Impact* (Mahwah, NJ: Lawrence Erlbaum Associates, 1998); T. Judge and R. Piccolo, "Transformational and Transactional Leadership: A Meta-analytic Test of Their Relative Validity," *Journal of Applied Psychology* 89 (2004), pp. 755–68.

104. G. Spreitzer and R. Quinn, "Empowering Middle Managers to Be Transformational Leaders," *Journal of Applied Behavioral Science* 32 (1996), pp. 237–61.

105. J. Collins, "Level 5 Leadership," *Harvard Business Review* 1 (2001), pp. 66–76; and J. Kline Harrison and M. William Clough, "Characteristics of 'State of the Art' Leaders: Productive Narcissism versus Emotional Intelligence and Level 5 Capabilities," *Social Science Journal* 43 (2006), pp. 287–92.

106. G. Satell, "Why Tim Cook's 'Level 5 Leadership' Might Not Be Enough to Secure Apple's Future," *Forbes* (online), June 4, 2013, http://www.forbes.com; D. Vera and M. Crossan, "Strategic Leadership and Organizational Learning," *Academy of Management Review* 29 (2004), pp. 222–40.

107. F. Luthans, *Organizational Behavior,* 10th ed. (New York: McGraw-Hill/Irwin, 2005); F. Luthans and B. Avolio, "Authentic Leadership Development," in *Positive Organizational Scholarship,* eds. K. Cameron, J. Dutton, and R. Quinn (San Francisco: Berrett-Koehler, 2003), pp. 241–58.

108. B. M. Bass, "Thoughts and Plans," in *Cutting Edge Leadership 2000,* ed. B. Kellerman and L. R. Matusak (College Park, MD: James MacGregor Burns Academy of Leadership, 2000), pp. 5–9.

109. N. Turner, J. Barling, O. Epitropaki, V. Butcher, and C. Milner, "Transformational Leadership and Moral Reasoning," *Journal of Applied Psychology* 87 (2002), pp. 304–11.

110. D. M. Mayer, M. Kuenzi, R. Greenbaum, M. Bardes, and R. Salvador, "How Low Does Ethical Leadership Flow? Test of a Trickle-Down Model," *Organizational Behavior and Human Decision Processes* 108 (2009), pp. 1–13.

111. Bass, "Thoughts and Plans"; J. Spangenburg, "The Effect of A Pseudotrans-formational Leader: Whitewater Rafting in a Hurricane," *International Journal of Management & Information Systems* (online) 16 (2012), p.325.

112. W. Bennis, "The End of Leadership: Exemplary Leadership Is Impossible without Full Inclusion, Initiatives, and Cooperation of Followers," *Organizational Dynamics,* Summer 1999, pp. 71–79.

113. Robert K. Greenleaf Center for Servant Leadership, "What Is Servant Leadership?" https://www.greenleaf.org; Larry W. Boone and Sanya Makhani, "Five Necessary Attitudes of a Servant Leader," *Review of Business* 83, no. 1 (Winter 2012), pp. 83–96.

114. R. Liden, S. Wayne, C. Liao, and J. Meuser, "Servant Leadership and Serving Culture: Influence on Individual and Unit Performance," *Academy of Management Journal* 57 (2014), pp. 1434-52; D. Parris

and J. Peachey, "A Systematic Literature Review of Servant Leadership Theory in Organizational Contexts," *Journal of Business Ethics* 113 (2013), pp. 377–93; D. Van Dierendonck, "Servant Leadership: A Review and Synthesis," *Journal of Management* 37 (2011), pp. 1228–61.

115. Emma Johnson, "How to Become a Servant Leader," *Success,* December 5, 2011, http://www.success.com.

116. M. Hogg, D. van Knippenberg, and D. E. Rasst III, "Intergroup Leadership in Organizations: Leading across Group and Organizational Boundaries," *Academy of Management Review* 37 (2012), pp. 232–55; T. Pittinsky (ed.), *Crossing the Divide: Intergroup Leadership in a World of Difference* (Cambridge, MA: Harvard Business Publishing, 2009); T. Pittinsky and S. Simon, "Intergroup Leadership," *Leadership Quarterly* 18 (2007), pp. 586–605.

117. D. Wang, D. Waldman, and Z. Zhang, "A Meta-analysis of Shared Leadership and Team Effectiveness," *Journal of Applied Psychology* 99 (2014), pp. 181–98; C. L. Pearce, "The Future of Leadership: Combining Vertical and Shared Leadership to Transform Knowledge Work," *Academy of Management Executive,* February 2004, pp. 47–57.

118. J. Carson, P. Tesluk, and J. Marrone, "Shared Leadership in Teams: An Investigation of Antecedent Conditions and Performance," *Academy of Management Journal* 50 (2007), pp. 1217–34.

119. R. Fisher and A. Sharp, *Getting It Done* (New York: HarperCollins, 1998); S. Kühl, T. Schnelle, and F. Tillmann, "Lateral Leadership: An Organizational Approach to Change," *Journal of Change Management* 5 (2005), pp. 177–89.

120. P. Schmitz, "Richard Murphy: A Powerful Example of Servant Leadership," *The Huffington Post* (online), April 10, 2013; D. Martin, "Richard L. Murphy, Who Aided Disadvantaged Youth, Dies at 68," *The New York Times* (online), February 15, 2013, http://www.nytimes.com.

121. S. Caldicott, "Why Ford's Alan Mulally Is an Innovation CEO for the Record Books," *Forbes* (online), June 25, 2014, http://www.forbes.com; J. Reed and B. Simon, "Adroit in Detroit," *Financial Times,* January 25, 2011, Business & Company Resource Center, http://galenet. galegroup.com; "Epiphany in Dearborn," Ford," *The Economist,* December 11, 2010, Business & Company Resource Center, http://galenet.galegroup.com; and J. LaReau, "Ford Slashes Debt, Spends on Operations," *Automotive News,* January 31, 2011, Business & Company Resource Center, http://galenet.galegroup.com.

122. P. Block, *The Empowered Manager* (San Francisco: Jossey-Bass, 1991).

123. Ibid.

124. Kouzes and Posner, *The Leadership Challenge* (1995).

125. L. W. Boone and M. S. Peborde, "Developing Leadership Skills in College and Early Career Positions," *Review of Business,* Spring 2008, Business & Company Resource Center, http://galenet. galegroup.com.

126. A. Gaines, "Straight to the Top," *American Executive,* August 2008, Business & Company Resource Center, http://galenet. galegroup.com; and S. J. Allen and N. S. Hartman, "Leadership Development: An Exploration of Sources of Learning," *SAM Advanced Management Journal,* Winter 2008, pp. 10–19, 62–63.

127. N. Amato, "Top 20 Companies for Leadership Development," *CGMA* (online), September 23, 2013, http://www .cgma.org.

128. M. McCall, *High Flyers* (Boston: Harvard Business School Press, 1998).

129. E. Van Velsor, C. D. McCauley, and R. Moxley, "Our View of Leadership Development," in *Center for Creative Leadership Handbook of Leadership Development,* ed. C. D. McCauley, R. Moxley, and E. Van Velsor (San Francisco: Jossey-Bass, 1998), pp. 1–25.

130. D. S. DeRue and N. Wellman, "Developing Leaders via Experience: The Role of Developmental Challenge, Learning Orientation, and Feedback Availability," *Journal of Applied Psychology* 94 (2009), pp. 859–75.

131. J. Clark, "HP Raises CEO Whitman's Pay 11% as Split-up Is Prepared," *Bloomberg Business,* February 2, 2015, http://www. bloomberg.com; Hough, "Meg Whitman's Turnaround at HP"; Anders, "Meg Whitman Jolts HP"; Bandler and Burke, "How HP Lost Its Way"; Vance and La, "Mark Hurd, Leo Apotheker, Meg Whitman"; Takahashi, "Meg Whitman Says 'You Can Feel the Turnaround'"; Bloomberg, "Biggest CEO Underachievers: Executives," Bloomberg Visual Data, http://www.bloomberg.com, last updated May 1, 2013; Henry Blodget, "Top CEOs Ranked by Their (Lousy) Stock Performance," *Yahoo Finance,* May 24, 2013, http://finance.yahoo.com.

Chapter 13

1. "SAS," Great Place to Work, http:// us.greatrated.com/sas, accessed May 8, 2015; SAS, "SAS Achieves Record Revenue in 2014—$3.09 Billion: Cloud Analytics and Data Visualization Offerings Influence 39th Consecutive Year of Growth," press release on, January 29, 2015, http://www. sas.com; Mark C. Crowley, "How SAS Became the World's Best Place to Work," *Fast Company,* January 22, 2013, http:// www.fastcompany.com; Omar Akhtar, "Best Companies: All-Stars," *Fortune,* January 24, 2013, http://money.cnn.com; "100 Best Companies to Work For 2013," *Fortune,* February 4, 2013, http://money. cnn.com; Great Place to Work, "World's Best Multinational Workplaces 2012," http://www.greatplacetowork.com; SAS, "SAS Ranks No. 1 in the World for Best Workplaces," news release, November 14, 2012, http://www.sas .com; SAS website, http://www.sas.com; Nicola Leske, "SAS Says Spurned IBM and Others for Independence," Reuters, June 21, 2012, http://in.reuters.com.

2. R. Kreitner and F. Luthans, "A Social Learning Approach to Behavioral Management: Radical Behaviorists 'Mellowing Out,'" *Organizational Dynamics,* Autumn 1984, pp. 47–65.

3. D. Katz and R. L. Kahn, *The Social Psychology of Organizations* (New York: John Wiley & Sons, 1966).

4. C. A. Bartlett and S. Ghoshal, "Building Competitive Advantage through People," *Sloan Management Review,* Winter 2002, pp. 34–41.

5. E. Locke, "Toward a Theory of Task Motivation and Incentives," *Organizational Behavior and Human Performance* 3 (1968), pp. 157–89.

6. Federal Bureau of Investigation, "Information Technology Strategic Plan: FY 2010-2015," http://www.fbi.gov, accessed May 8, 2015.

7. E. A. Locke, "Guest Editor's Introduction: Goal-Setting Theory and Its Applications to the World of Business," *Academy of Management Executive* 4 (November 2004), pp. 124–25.

8. G. P. Latham, "The Motivational Benefits of Goal-Setting," *Academy of Management Executive* 4 (November 2004), pp. 126–29.

9. E. A. Locke, "Linking Goals to Monetary Incentives," *Academy of Management Executive* 4 (November 2004), pp. 130–33.

10. E. E. Lawler III, *Treat People Right!* (San Francisco: Jossey-Bass, 2003).

11. Ibid.

12. J. Bono and T. Judge, "Self-Concordance at Work: Toward Understanding the Motivational Effects of Transformational Leaders," *Academy of Management Journal* 46 (2003), pp. 554–71.

13. C. Crossley, C. Cooper, and T. Wensing, "Making Things Happen through Challenging Goals: Leader Proactivity, Trust, and Business-Unit Performance," *Journal of Applied Psychology,* 2013, pp. 540–49.

14. A. Wilson, "Kansas Quick Lane Operation Is Well-Tuned," *Automotive News,* April 5, 2010, Business & Company Resource Center, http://galenet.galegroup.com.

15. K. N. Shaw, "Changing the Goal-Setting Process at Microsoft," *Academy of Management Executive* 4 (November 2004), pp. 139–43.

16. S. Kerr and S. Laundauer, "Using Stretch Goals to Promote Organizational Effectiveness and Personal Growth: General Electric and Goldman Sachs," *Academy of Management Executive* 4 (November 2004), pp. 134–38.

17. Ibid.

18. Latham, "Motivational Benefits of Goal-Setting."

19. T. Mitchell and W. Silver, "Individual and Group Goals When Workers Are Interdependent: Effects on Task Strategies and Performance," *Journal of Applied Psychology* 75 (1990), pp. 185–93.

20. A. Kleingeld, H. van Mierlo, and L. Arends, "The Effect of Goal Setting on Group Performance: A Meta-Analysis," *Journal of Applied Psychology* 96 (2011), pp. 1289–1304.

21. Latham, "Motivational Benefits of Goal-Setting."

22. D. H. Pink, *Drive: The Surprising Truth About What Motivates Us* (New York: Riverhead Books, 2009), pp. 98–99.

23. D. Welsh and L. Ordóñez, "The Dark Side of Consecutive High Performance Goals: Linking Goal Setting, Depletion, and Unethical Behavior," *Organizational Behavior and Human Decision Processes* 123 (2014), pp. 79–89.

24. M. Schweitzer, L. Ordonez, and B. Douma, "Goal Setting as a Motivator of Unethical Behavior," *Academy of Management Journal* 47 (2004), pp. 422–32.

25. C. Beaudoin, A. Cianci, and G. Tsakumis, "The Impact of CFOs' Incentives and Earnings Management Ethics on their Financial Reporting Decisions: The Mediating Role of Moral Disengagement," *Journal of Business Ethics* 128 (2015), pp. 505—518; M. A. Duran, "Norm-Based Behavior and Corporate Malpractice," *Journal of Economic Issues* 41, no. 1 (March 2007), Business & Company Resource Center, http://galenet.galegroup.com; and D. Durfee, "Management or Manipulation?" *CFO*, December 2006, http://galenet.galegroup.com.

26. G. Seijts and G. Latham, "Learning versus Performance Goals: When Should Each Be Used?" *Academy of Management Executive* 19 (February 2005), pp. 124–31; P. C. Early, T. Connolly, and G. Ekegren, "Goals, Strategy Development, and Task Performance: Some Limits on the Efficacy of Goal Setting," *Journal of Applied Psychology* 74 (1989), pp. 24–33; and C. E. Shalley, "Effects of Productivity Goals, Creativity Goals, and Personal Discretion on Individual Creativity," *Journal of Applied Psychology* 76 (1991), pp. 179–85.

27. R. C. Litchfield, "Brainstorming Reconsidered: A Goal-Based View," *Academy of Management Review* 33 (2008), pp. 649–68.

28. R. Fisher and A. Sharp, *Getting It Done* (New York: HarperCollins, 1998).

29. E. Thorndike, *Animal Intelligence* (New York: Macmillan, 1911).

30. A. D. Stajkovic and F. Luthans, "Differential Effects of Incentive Motivators on Work Performance," *Academy of Management Journal* 44 (2001), pp. 580–90.

31. B. Sims Jr., "Want Your Team to Perform Better? Try Positive Reinforcement," *Entrepreneur* (online), February 6, 2014, http://www.entrepreneur.com; J. Zaslow, "The Most-Praised Generation Goes to Work," *The Wall Street Journal*, April 20, 2007, http://online.wsj.com.

32. K. Butterfield, L. K. Trevino, and G. Ball, "Punishment from the Manager's Perspective: A Grounded Investigation and Inductive Model," *Academy of Management Review* 39 (1996), pp. 1479–1512.

33. S. Wiltermuth and F. Flynn, "Power, Moral Clarity, and Punishment in the Workplace," *Academy of Management Journal* 56 (August 2013) pp. 1002–1023.

34. Adam Madison, "Positive Results," *Rock Products*, September 1, 2008, Business & Company Resource Center, http://galenet.galegroup.com.

35. T. Judge and R. Piccolo, "Transformational and Transactional Leadership: A Meta-Analytic Test of Their Relative Ability," *Journal of Applied Psychology* 89 (2004), pp. 755–68.

36. S. Kerr, "On the Folly of Rewarding A While Hoping for B," *Academy of Management Journal* 18 (1975), pp. 769–83.

37. D. Levitin, "Why the Modern World Is Bad for Your Brain," *The Guardian* (online), January 18, 2015, http://www.theguardian.com; T. Bradberry, "Multitasking Damages Your Brain and Career, New Studies Suggest," *Forbes* (online), October 8, 2014, http://www.forbes.com; S. Lohr, "Science Finds Advantage in Focusing, Not Multitasking," *Chicago Tribune*, March 25, 2007, sec. 1, p. 10.

38. E. E. Lawler III, *Rewarding Excellence* (San Francisco: Jossey-Bass, 2000).

39. Colleen Leahey, "11 Top Perks from Best Companies," *Fortune*, January 18, 2013, http://money.cnn.com; "100 Best Companies to Work For: QuikTrip," *Fortune*, February 4, 2013, http://money.cnn.com.

40. J. H. Cho, "Lessons in Employee Appreciation," *Star-Ledger* (Newark, NJ), February 8, 2007, Business & Company Resource Center, http://galenet.galegroup.com.

41. J. Pfeffer and R. Sutton, *The Knowing–Doing Gap* (Boston: Harvard Business School Press, 2000).

42. J. S. Lublin, "Recall the Mistakes of Your Past Bosses, So You Can Do Better," *The Wall Street Journal*, January 2, 2007, http://online.wsj.com.

43. A. Vaccaro, "The Best Leaders Ask for More Feedback," *Inc.* (online), December 24, 2013, http://www.inc.com; S. Moss and J. Sanchez, "Are Your Employees Avoiding You? Managerial Strategies for Closing the Feedback Gap," *Academy of Management Executive* 18, no. 1 (February 2004), pp. 32–44.

44. Lawler, *Treat People Right!*

45. R. Cheramie, "An Examination of Feedback-seeking Behaviors, The Feedback Source and Career Success," *Career Development International* 18 (2013), pp. 712–31; S. B. Silverman, C. E. Pogson, and A. B. Cober, "When Employees at Work Don't Get It: A Model for Enhancing Individual Employee Change in Response to Performance Feedback," *Academy of Management Executive* 19, no. 2 (May 2005), pp. 135–47; and J. Jackman and M. Strober, "Fear of Feedback," *Harvard Business Review*, April 2003, pp. 101–7.

46. V. H. Vroom, *Work and Motivation* (New York: John Wiley & Sons, 1964).

47. R. E. Wood, P. W. B. Atkins, and J. E. H. Bright, "Bonuses, Goals, and Instrumentality Effects," *Journal of Applied Psychology* 84 (1999), pp. 703–20.

48. YouEarnedIt, "Company Spotlight," http://www.youearnedit.com, accessed May 11, 2015.

49. D. Ranil, "SAS's 2014 Revenue Rose to $3.09 Billion," *News Observer* (online), January 29, 2015, http://www.newsobserver.com; Crowley, "How SAS Became the World's Best Place to Work"; Buchanan, "How SAS Continues to Grow"; Steve Lohr, "The Nimble Dance of a Rich Legacy Software Company," *New York Times*, March 28, 2013, http://bits.blogs.nytimes.com; Kristin Burnham, "Five Tips for Social Business Adoption: How SAS Succeeded," *CIO*, May 21, 2012, http://www.cio.com.

50. A. H. Maslow, "A Theory of Human Motivation," *Psychological Review*, July 1943, pp. 370–96.

51. L. Mainicro and D. Gibson, "Managing Employee Trauma: Dealing with the Emotional Fallout from 9-11," *Academy of Management Executive*, August 2003, pp. 130–43.

52. M. Wahba and L. Birdwell, "Maslow Reconsidered: A Review of Research on the Need Hierarchy Theory," *Organizational Behavior and Human Performance* 15 (1976), pp. 212–40.

53. C. Seager, "Generation Y: Why Young Job Seekers Want More than Money," *The Guardian* (online), February 19, 2014, http://www.theguardian.com; M. Rafter, "Best Companies Offer Employees More Flexible Work Options," Great Place to Work, January 22 2014, http://www.usgreatrated.com; D. Schwabel, "Millennial Branding and Beyond.com Survey Reveals the Rising Cost of Hiring Workers from the Millennial Generation," August 6, 2013, http://www.millennialbranding.com.

54. W.L. Gore, "Associates' Standards of Ethical Conduct," http://www.gore.com, accessed May 11, 2015.

55. D. Rohde, "The Anti-Walmart: The Secret Sauce of Wegmans Is People," *The Atlantic* (online), March 23, 2012, http://www.theatlantic.com;

56. C. Alderfer, *Existence, Relatedness, and Growth: Human Needs in Organizational Settings* (Glencoe, IL: Free Press, 1972).

57. Wells Fargo, "Diane Schumaker-Krieg, Managing Director, Global Head of Research, Economics & Strategy," http://www.wellsfargo.com, accessed May 11, 2015; C. Hymowitz, "When the Paycheck Isn't Optional, Ambition Is Less Complicated," *The Wall Street Journal*, April 26, 2007, http://online.wsj.com.

58. C. Pinder, *Work Motivation* (Glenview, IL: Scott, Foresman, 1984).

59. D. McClelland, *The Achieving Society* (New York: Van Nostrand Reinhold, 1961).

60. D. McClelland and R. Boyatzis, "Leadership Motive Pattern and Long-Term Success in Management," *Journal of Applied Psychology* 67 (1982), pp. 737–43.

61. N. Adler, *International Dimensions of Organizational Behavior,* 2nd ed. (Boston: Kent, 1991); and G. Hofstede, *Cultures and Organizations* (London: McGraw-Hill, 1991).

62. "2014 Trends in Global Employee Engagement," *AON Hewitt* (online), http://www.aon.com, accessed May 11, 2015; N. R. Lockwood, "Leveraging Employee Engagement for Competitive Advantage: HR's Strategic Role," *HR Magazine,* March 2007, Business & Company Resource Center, http://galenet.galegroup.com.

63. E. E. Lawler III and D. Finegold, "Individualizing the Organization: Past, Present, and Future," *Organizational Dynamics,* Summer 2000, pp. 1–15.

64. Ibid.

65. T. M. Amabile, "A Model of Creativity and Innovation in Organizations," in *Research in Organizational Behavior,* ed. B. M. Staw and L. L. Cummings (Greenwich, CT: JAI Press, 1988), pp. 10, 123–67.

66. N. Madjar, E. Greenberg, and Z. Chen, "Factors for Radical Creativity, Incremental Creativity, and Routine, Noncreative Performance," *Journal of Applied Psychology* 96 (2011), pp. 730–43; C. M. Ford, "A Theory of Individual Creative Action in Multiple Social Domains," *Academy of Management Review* 21 (1996), pp. 1112–42.

67. G. Oldham and A. Cummings, "Employee Creativity: Personal and Contextual Factors at Work," *Academy of Management Journal* 39 (1996), pp. 607–34.

68. A. Fisher, "How Companies Kill Creativity," *Fortune* (online), October 17, 2013, http://www.fortune.com; T. Amabile, R. Conti, H. Coon, J. Lazenby, and M. Herron, "Assessing the Work Environment for Creativity," *Academy of Management Journal* 39 (1996), pp. 1154–84.

69. M. Campion and G. Sanborn, "Job Design," in *Handbook of Industrial Engineering,* ed. G. Salvendy (New York: John Wiley & Sons, 1991).

70. Team Rubicon, "Our Mission," http://www.teamrubiconusa.com, accessed May 16, 2015; *Team Rubicon Blog,* "Deploying Abroad," April 26, 2014, http://www.teamrubiconusa.com; Federal Emergency Management Agency, "Team Rubicon Volunteers Help Disaster Survivors in Vilonia, Arkansas," May 22, 2014, http://www.fema.gov.

71. Lawler and Finegold, "Individualizing the Organization."

72. "2013 List of 15 Top MBA Employers," *CNN Money,* http://www.money.cnn.com, accessed May 12, 2015.

73. M. Campion and D. McClelland, "Interdisciplinary Examination of the Costs and Benefits of Enlarged Jobs: A Job Design Quasi-Experiment," *Journal of Applied Psychology* 76 (1991), pp. 186–98.

74. F. Herzberg, *Work and the Nature of Men* (Cleveland: World, 1966).

75. J. R. Hackman, G. Oldham, R. Janson, and K. Purdy, "A New Strategy for Job Enrichment," *California Management Review* 16 (Fall 1975), pp. 57–71.

76. Pink, *Drive,* p. 119.

77. R. Rechheld, "Loyalty-Based Management" *Harvard Business Review,* March–April 1993, pp. 64–73.

78. "Motivation in Today's Workplace: The Link to Performance," *HR Magazine,* July 2010, pp. 1–9.

79. B. Trahant, "Recruiting and Engaging the Federal Workforce," *Public Manager,* Spring 2008, Business & Company Resource Center, http://galenet.galegroup.com.

80. J. Immelt, V. Govindarajan, C. Trimble, "How GE Is Disrupting Itself," *Harvard Business Review* 87 (October 2009), pp. 56–65.

81. Ashish Gambhir, "Use Online Feedback to Motivate, Engage Employees," *QSRweb.com,* April 16, 2012, http://www.qsrweb.com; Parasole website, http://www.parasole.com.

82. Campion and Sanborn, "Job Design."

83. S. Seibert, S. Silver, and W. A. Randolph, "Taking Empowerment to the Next Level: A Multiple-Level Model of Empowerment, Performance, and Satisfaction," *Academy of Management Journal* 47 (2004), pp. 332–49.

84. C. Argyris, "Empowerment: The Emperor's New Clothes," *Harvard Business Review,* May–June 1998, pp. 98–105.

85. R. Forrester, "Empowerment: Rejuvenating a Potent Idea," *Academy of Management Executive,* August 2000, pp. 67–80; N. Lorinkova, M. Pearsall, and H. P. Sims Jr., "Examining the Differential Longitudinal Performance of Directive versus Empowering Leadership in Teams," *Academy of Management Journal* 56 (2012), pp. 573–96; D. Liu, S. Zhang, L. Wang, and T. Lee, "The Effects of Autonomy and Empowerment on Employee Turnover: Test of a Multilevel Model in Teams," *Journal of Applied Psychology* 96 (2011), pp. 1305–16; M. T. Maynard, L. Gilson, and J. Mathieu, "Empowerment—Fad or Fab? A Multilevel Review of the Past Two Decades of Research," *Journal of Management* 38 (2012), pp. 1231–81; X. Zhang and K. Bartol, "Linking Empowering Leadership and Employee Creativity: The Influence of Psychological Empowerment, Intrinsic Motivation, and Creative Process Engagement," *Academy of Management Journal* 53 (2010), pp. 107–28.

86. R. C. Liden, S. J. Wayne, and R. T. Sparrowe, "An Examination of the Mediating Role of Psychological Empowerment on the Relations between the Job, Interpersonal Relationships, and Work Outcomes," *Journal of Applied Psychology* 85 (2000), pp. 407–16.

87. T. Peters and N. Austin, *A Passion for Excellence* (New York: Random House, 1985).

88. K. Thomas and B. Velthouse, "Cognitive Elements of Empowerment: An 'Interpretive' Model of Intrinsic Task Motivation," *Academy of Management Review* 15 (1990), pp. 666–81.

89. J. Kouzes and B. Posner, *The Leadership Challenge,* 2nd ed. (San Francisco: Jossey-Bass, 1995).

90. M. M. Butts, R. J. Vandenberg, D. M. DeJoy, B. S. Schaffer, and M. G. Wilson, "Individual Reactions to High Involvement Work Processes: Investigating the Role of Empowerment and Perceived Organizational Support," *Journal of Occupational Health Psychology* 14 (2009), pp. 122–36; Price Waterhouse Change Integration Team, Better Change (Burr Ridge, IL: Richard D. Irwin, 1995).

91. E. E. Lawler III, *The Ultimate Advantage: Creating the High Involvement Organization* (San Francisco: Jossey-Bass, 1992).

92. L. He, "Google's Secrets of Innovation: Empowering Its Employees," *Forbes* (online), March 29, 2013, http://www.forbes.com.

93. Kouzes and Posner, *The Leadership Challenge.*

94. W. A. Randolph and M. Sashkin, "Can Organizational Empowerment Work in Multinational Settings?" *Academy of Management Executive* 16 (2002), pp. 102–15.

95. J. Adams, "Inequality in Social Exchange," in *Advances in Experimental Social Psychology,* ed. L. Berkowitz (New York: Academic Press, 1965).

96. "A Closer Look: The Dodd-Frank Wall Street Reform and Consumer Protection Act," PricewaterhouseCoopers, http://www.pwc.com, accessed May 12, 2015; T. Jackson, "Dodd-Frank Will Only Deepen Corporate Pay Envy," *Financial Times,* March 21, 2011, Business & Company Resource Center, http://galenet.galegroup.com; M. E. Podmolik, "Kraft CEO Sees Bonus Cut as Goals Go Unmet," *Chicago Tribune,* April 1, 2011, sec. 1, pp. 21, 23; Emily Chasan, "Executive Pay Gets New Spin," *The Wall Street Journal,* September 25, 2012, http://online.wsj.com.

97. T. Weiss, "How to Prevent IT Sabotage Inside Your Company," *CIO* (online), August 19, 2011, http://www.cio.com; D. Skarlicki, R. Folger, and P. Tesluk, "Personality as a Moderator in the Relationships between Fairness and Retaliation," *Academy of Management Journal* 42 (1999), pp. 100–108.

98. J. Brockner, "Making Sense of Procedural Fairness: How High Procedural Fairness Can Reduce or Heighten the Influence of Outcome Favorability," *Academy of Management Review* 27 (2002), pp. 58–76; and D. De Cremer and D. van Knippenberg, "How Do Leaders Promote Cooperation? The Effects of Charisma and

Procedural Fairness," *Journal of Applied Psychology* 87 (2002), pp. 858–66.

99. M. Armstrong-Stassen, M. Freeman, S. Cameron, and D. Rajacic, "Nurse Managers' Role in Older Nurses' Intention to Stay," *Journal of Health Organization and Management,* 29 (2015), pp. 55–74.

100. Lawler, *Treat People Right!*

101. R. Shao, D. Rupp, D. Skarlicki, and K. Jones, "Employee Justice across Cultures: A Meta-Analytic Review," *Journal of Management* 39 (2013), pp. 263–301.

102. W. C. Kim and R. Mauborgne, "Fair Process: Managing in the Knowledge Economy," *Harvard Business Review,* July–August 1997, pp. 65–75.

103. T. Bateman and D. Organ, "Job Satisfaction and the Good Sold: The Relationship between Affect and Employee 'Citizenship,'" *Academy of Management Journal,* 1983, pp. 587–95.

104. A. de Castro, G. Gee, and D. Takeuchi, "Relationship between Job Dissatisfaction and Physical and Psychological Health among Filipino Immigrants," *American Association of Occupational Health Nurses Journal* 56 (2008), pp. 33–40; D. Henne and E. Locke, "Job Dissatisfaction: What Are the Consequences?" *International Journal of Psychology* 20 (1985), pp. 221–40.

105. J. Barling, E. K. Kelloway, and R. Iverson, "High-Quality Work, Job Satisfaction, and Occupational Injuries," *Journal of Applied Psychology* 88 (2003), pp. 276–83.

106. D. Bowen, S. Gilliland, and R. Folger, "HRM and Service Fairness: How Being Fair with Employees Spills Over to Customers," *Organizational Dynamics,* Winter 1999, pp. 7–23.

107. J. Harter, F. Schmidt, and T. Hayes, "Business-Unit-Level Relationship between Employee Satisfaction, Employee Engagement, and Business Outcomes: A Meta-Analysis," *Journal of Applied Psychology* 87 (2002), pp. 268–79.

108. S. Adams, "Most Americans Are Unhappy at Work," *Forbes* (online), June 20, 2014 http://www.forbes.com; The Conference Board, "U.S. Workers More Satisfied? Just Barely," press release, June 18, 2014, http://www.conference-board.org.

109. Heiner Evanschitzky, Christopher Groening, Vikas Mittal, and Maren Wunderlich, "How Employer and Employee Satisfaction Affect Customer Satisfaction: An Application to Franchise Services," *Journal of Service Research* 14, no. 2 (May 2011), pp. 136–48; and "Motivation in Today's Workplace," pp. 1–2, 4.

110. Erika Fry, "Low Key, High Quirk," *Fortune,* January 17, 2013, http://management.fortune.cnn.com; Plante Moran, "Careers at Plante Moran," http://www.plantemoran.com.

111. R. E. Walton, "Improving the Quality of Work Life," *Harvard Business Review,* May–June 1974, pp. 12, 16, 155.

112. E. E. Lawler III, "Strategies for Improving the Quality of Work Life," *American*

Psychologist 37 (1982), pp. 486–93; J. L. Suttle, "Improving Life at Work: Problems and Prospects," in *Improving Life at Work,* ed. J. R. Hackman and J. L. Suttle (Santa Monica, CA: Goodyear, 1977); B. Erdogan, T. Bauer, D. Truxillo, et al., "Whistle while You Work: A Review of the Life Satisfaction Literature," *Journal of Management* 38 (2012), pp. 1038–83.

113. P. B. Warr, "Well-Being and the Workplace," in D. Kahneman, E. Diener, and N. Schwarz, eds., *Well-Being: The Foundations of Hedonic Psychology* (New York: Russell Sage Foundation, 1999); and T. A. Wright and R. Cropanzano, "The Role of Psychological Well-Being in Job Performance: A Fresh Look at an Age-Old Quest," *Organizational Dynamics* 33 (2004), pp. 338–51.

114. T. Wright and D. Bonett, "Job Satisfaction and Psychological Well-being as Nonadditive Predictors of Workplace Turnover," *Journal of Management* 33 (2007), 141–60; J. K. Harter, F. L. Schmidt, and C. L. M. Keyes, "Well-Being in the Workplace and Its Relationship to Business Outcomes: A Review of the Gallup Studies," in C. L. M. Keyes and J. Haidt, eds., *Flourishing: The Positive Person and the Good Life* (Washington DC: American Psychological Association, 2003), pp. 205–24.

115. S. L. Robinson, "Trust and Breach of the Psychological Contract," *Administrative Science Quarterly* 41 (1996), pp. 574–99.

116. J. Robbins, M. Ford, and L. Tetrick, "Perceived Unfairness and Employee Health: A Meta-Analytic Integration," Journal of Applied Psychology 97 (2012), pp. 235–72; M. Dahl, "Organizational Change and Employee Stress," *Management Science* 57 (2011), pp. 240–56.

117. L. Grunberg, S. Moore, E. Greenberg, and P. Sikora, "The Changing Workplace and Its Effects A Longitudinal Examination of Employee Responses at a Large Company," *Journal of Applied Behavioral Science* 44 (2008), pp. 215–36; D. Rousseau, "Changing the Deal While Keeping the People," *Academy of Management Executive* 10 (1996), pp. 50–58.

118. E. Ridolfi, "Executive Commentary," *Academy of Management Executive* 10 (1996), pp. 59–60.

119. E. E. Lawler III, *From the Ground Up* (San Francisco: Jossey-Bass, 1996).

120. Ibid.

121. S. Ghoshal, C. Bartlett, and P. Moran, "Value Creation: The New Management Manifesto," *Financial Times Mastering Management Review,* November 1999, pp. 34–37.

122. R. Hoffman, B. Casnocha, and C. Yen, "Tours of Duty: The New Employer-Employee Contract," *Harvard Business Review,* June 2013, pp. 48–58.

123. Ram Charan, "Stop Whining, Start Thinking," *BusinessWeek,* August 14, 2008, http://www.businessweek.com.

124. Crowley, "How SAS Became the World's Best Place to Work"; Buchanan, "How SAS Continues to Grow"; Great Place to Work, "World's Best Multinational Workplaces 2014"; *Fortune,* "100 Best Places to Work For 2014"; Barber, "What Makes Workers Happy?"; Jenn Mann, "The Best Place to Work . . . in the World!" *SAS Voices,* November 14, 2012, http://blogs.sas .com; Roberta Matuson, "Why Most Recruitment Strategies Are Failing and What You Can Do to Fix This," *Forbes,* March 13, 2013, http://www.forbes.com.

Chapter 14

1. "Whole Foods Market Celebrates 18 Consecutive Years on Fortune's '100 Best Companies to Work For' List," press release on, March 5, 2015, http://www.media.wholefoodsmarket.com; K. Hope, "Are Executive Sleepovers the Best Way for Staff to Bond?" *BBC News* (online), April 8, 2014, http://www.bbc.com; John Mackey and Raj Sisodia, "Want to Hire Great People? Hire Consciously," *Fortune,* January 17, 2013, http://management.fortune.cnn.com; Andrea Davis, "Benefits Democracy: Whole Foods Takes Benefits to a Vote," *Employee Benefit News,* May 2012, p. 11; Jessica Rohman, "Whole Foods Market," *Great Place to Work blog,* March 6, 2013, http://www.greatplacetowork.com; Anne VanderMey, "World's Most Admired Companies 2013: Whole Foods Market," *Fortune,* March 18, 2013, http://money.cnn.com; "Groups Wield Power at Whole Foods," *Executive Leadership,* May 2013, Business Insights: Essentials, http://bi.galegroup.com; Whole Foods Market, "Careers," http://www.wholefoodsmarket.com/careers; "Fact Facts," http://media.wholefoodsmarket.com/fast-facts/.

2. J. Martin and K. Eisenhardt, "Rewiring: Cross-Business-Unit Collaborations in Multibusiness Organizations," *Academy of Management Journal* 53 (2010), pp. 265–301; E. C. Wenger and W. M. Snyder, "Communities of Practice: The Organizational Frontier," *Harvard Business Review,* January–February 2000, pp. 139–45.

3. "How Companies Use Teams to Drive Performance," Ernst & Young Insights (online), http://www.ey.com, accessed May 23, 2015; S. Cohen and D. Bailey, "What Makes Teams Work: Group Effectiveness Research from the Shop Floor to the Executive Suite," *Journal of Management* 23 (1997), pp. 239–90.

4. G. Chen, L. Donahue, and R. Klimoski, "Training Undergraduates to Work in Organizational Teams," *Academy of Management Learning and Education* 3 (2004), pp. 27–40.

5. Steve Minter, "Better Together," *Industry Week,* February 2012, Business Insights: Global, http://bi.galegroup.com.

6. E. Fleischauer, "Nucor Manager Says Teamwork Key to Success; Q1 Earnings Up," *Decatur (AL) Daily,* April 20, 2007, http://www.decaturdaily.com.

7. M. Mace, "Google Logic: Why Google Does the Things It Does the Way It Does," *The Guardian* (online), July 9, 2013, http://www.theguardian.com; A. Somech and A. Drach-Zahavy, "Translating Team Creativity to Innovation Implementation: The Role of Team Composition and Climate for Innovation," *Journal of Management* 39 (2013).

8. J. Jusko, "General Mills' Strategy Delivers," *IndustryWeek* (online), April 3, 2011, http://www.industryweek.com; P. Demetrakakes, "Packaging a Big Part of General Success," *Food and Beverage Packaging,* October 2008, Business & Company Resource Center, http://galenet.galegroup.com.

9. D. Nadler, J. R. Hackman, and E. E. Lawler III, *Managing Organizational Behavior* (Boston: Little, Brown, 1979).

10. A. C. Edmondson, "Teamwork on the Fly," *Harvard Business Review* April, 2012, pp. 72–80.

11. L. Gratton and T. Erickson, "Eight Ways to Build Collaborative Teams, *Harvard Business Review* (online), November 2007, http://www.hbr.com; M. Cianni and D. Wnuck, "Individual Growth and Team Enhancement: Moving toward a New Model of Career Development," *Academy of Management Executive* 11 (1997), pp. 105–15.

12. J. Hollenbeck, B. Beersma, and M. Schouten, "Beyond Team Types and Taxonomies: A Dimensional Scaling Conceptualization for Team Description," *Academy of Management Review* 37 (2012), pp. 82–106.

13. S. Cohen, "New Approaches to Teams and Teamwork," in J. Galbraith, E. E. Lawler III, and Associates, *Organizing for the Future* (San Francisco: Jossey-Bass, 1993).

14. Cohen and Bailey, "What Makes Teams Work."

15. "Task Force Launching to Examine Superstorm Sandy Problems," *Insurance Journal,* April 27, 2015, http://www.insurancejournal.com; "FEMA to Reopen 142,000 Claims by Hurricane Sandy Homeowners, NJ Senators Say," *NJ.com* March 11, 2015, http://www.nj.com.

16. L. Mullins, "Integration Crew for Maryland Bank," *American Banker,* February 13, 2007, General Reference Center Gold, http://find.galegroup.com; P. C. Earley and C. B. Gibson, *Multinational Work Teams* (Mahwah, NJ: Lawrence Erlbaum, 2002), p. 214.

17. K. Lagerstrom and M. Andersson, "Creating and Sharing Knowledge within a Transnational Team—The Development of a Global Business System," *Journal of World Business* 38 (2003), pp. 84–95; C. Snow, S. Snell, S. Davison, and D. Hambrick, "Use Transnational Teams to Globalize Your Company," *Organizational Dynamics,* Spring 1996, pp. 50–67.

18. B. Kirkman, B. Rosen, C. Gibson, P. Tesluk, and S. McPherson, "Five Challenges to Virtual Team Success: Lessons from Sabre, Inc.," *Academy of Management Executive* 16 (2002), pp. 67–80.

19. Edmondson, "Teamwork on the Fly."

20. J. Ferri-Reed, "Building Innovative Multi-Generation Teams," *The Journal of Quality and Participation* 37 (October 2014), pp. 20–22; R. Shehadi and D. Karam, "Five Essential Elements of the Digital Workplace," *Forbes* (online), March 31, 2014, http://www.forbes.com; T. Johns and L. Grafton, "The Third Wave of Virtual Work," *Harvard Business Review* (online), January 1, 2013, http://www.hbr.org.

21. V. Taras, D. Caprar, D. Rottig, R. Sarala, N. Zakaria, F. Zhao, et al. "A Global Classroom? Evaluating the Effectiveness of Global Virtual Collaboration as Teaching Tool in Management Education," *Academy of Management Learning & Education* 12 (2013), pp. 414–35.

22. R. Banker, J. Field, R. Schroeder, and K. Sinha, "Impact of Work Teams on Manufacturing Performance: A Longitudinal Field Study," *Academy of Management Journal* 39 (1996), pp. 867–90.

23. M. Muethel and M. Hoegl, "Shared Leadership Effectiveness in Independent Professional Teams," *European Management Journal* 31 (2013), pp. 423–32; J. Yeatts, M. Hipskind, and D. Barnes, "Lessons Learned from Self-Managed Work Teams," *Business Horizons,* July–August 1994, pp. 11–18.

24. B. Kirkman and D. Shapiro, "The Impact of Cultural Values on Job Satisfaction and Organizational Commitment in Self-Managing Work Teams: The Mediating Role of Employee Resistance," *Academy of Management Journal* 44 (2001), pp. 557–69.

25. C. Langfred, "The Downside of Self-Management: A Longitudinal Study of the Effects of Conflict on Trust, Autonomy, and Task Interdependence in Self-Managing Teams," *Academy of Management Journal,* 2007, pp. 885–900.

26. K. Peterson, "At Whole Foods, Paychecks Are Public," *CBS News Moneywatch* (online), March 5, 2014, http://www.cbsnews.com; Mackey and Sisodia, "Want to Hire Great People?"; Davis, "Benefits Democracy"; Rohman, "Whole Foods Market"; Whole Foods Market, "Careers"; *Executive Leadership,* "Groups Wield Power."

27. B. Kirkman and D. Shapiro, "The Impact of Cultural Values on Employee Resistance to Teams: Toward a Model of Globalized Self-Managing Work Team Effectiveness," *Academy of Management Review* 22 (1997), pp. 730–57.

28. M. Johnson, J. Hollenbeck, D. DeRue, C. Barnes, and D. Jundt, "Functional versus Dysfunctional Team Change: Problem Diagnosis and Structural Feedback for Self-Managed Teams," *Organizational Behavior and Human Decision Processes* 122 (2013), pp. 1–11; S. Sarker, S. Sarker, S. Kirkeby, and S. Chakraborty, "Path to 'Stardom' in Globally Distributed Hybrid Teams: An Examination of a Knowledge-centered Perspective Using Social Network Analysis," *Decision Sciences* 42 (2011), 339–70; B. Macy and H. Isumi, "Organizational Change, Design, and Work Innovation: A Meta-Analysis of 131 North American Field Studies—1961–1991," *Research in Organizational Change and Development* 7 (1993), pp. 235–313.

29. Jill Jusko, "2012 IW Best Plants Winner: Engaged Teams Keep Lockheed Martin Delivering on Time, Every Time," *Industry Week,* January 17, 2013, http:// www.industryweek.com.

30. Cohen and Bailey, "What Makes Teams Work."

31. J. Katzenbach and D. Smith, "The Discipline of Teams," *Harvard Business Review,* March–April 1993, pp. 111–20.

32. D. Mukherjee, S. Lahiri, D. Mukherjee, and T. Billing, "Leading Virtual Teams: How Do Social, Cognitive, and Behavioral Capabilities Matter?" *Management Decision* 50 (2012), pp. 273–290; S. Furst, M. Reeves, B. Rosen, and R. Blackburn, "Managing the Life Cycle of Virtual Teams," *Academy of Management Executive,* May 2004, pp. 6–20. Quotes in this paragraph are from pp. 11 and 12.

33. M. Marks, J. Mathieu, and S. Zaccaro, "A Temporally Based Framework and Taxonomy of Team Processes," *Academy of Management Review* 26 (2011), pp. 356–76; F. Morgeson, D. S. DeRue, and E. Karam, "Leadership in Teams: A Functional Approach to Understanding Leadership Structures and Processes," *Journal of Management* 36 (2010), pp. 5–39.

34. C. J. G. Gersick, "Time and Transition in Work Teams: Toward a New Model of Group Development," *Academy of Management Journal* 31 (1988), pp. 9–41.

35. J. R. Hackman, *Groups That Work (and Those That Don't)* (San Francisco: Jossey-Bass, 1990).

36. Ibid.; Edmondson, "Teamwork on the Fly."

37. I. Hoever, D. van Knippenberg, W. van Ginkel, and H. Barkema, "Fostering Team Creativity: Perspective Taking as Key to Unlocking Diversity's Potential," *Journal of Applied Psychology* 97 (2012), pp. 982–96.

38. R. Cross, "Looking before You Leap: Assessing the Jump to Teams in Knowledge-Based Work," *Business Horizons,* September–October 2000, pp. 29–36.

39. Geoff Colvin, "The Art of the Self-Managing Team," *Fortune,* December 5, 2012, http://management.fortune.cnn.com; Chana R. Schoenberger, "How to Get People to Work Together," *The Wall Street Journal,* September 7, 2012, http://blogs.wsj.com; John Baldoni, "The Secret to Team Collaboration:

Individuality," *Inc.,* January 18, 2012, http://www.inc.com.

40. N. Lorinkova, M. Pearsall, and H. P. Sims Jr., "Examining the Differential Longitudinal Performance of Directive versus Empowering Leadership in Teams," *Academy of Management Journal* 56 (2013), pp. 573–96; M. T. Maynard, L. Gilson, and J. Mathieu, "Empowerment— Fad or Fab? A Multilevel Review of the Past Two Decades of Research," *Journal of Management* 38 (2012), pp. 1231–81; S. Seibert, G. Wang, and S. Courtright, "Antecedents and Consequences of Psychological and Team Empowerment in Organizations: A Meta-Analytic Review," *Journal of Applied Psychology* 96 (2011), pp. 981–1003; G. Chen, P. N. Sharma, S. Edinger, D. Shapiro, and J.-L. Farh, "Motivating and Demotivating Forces in Teams: Cross-Level Influences of Empowering Leadership and Relationship Conflict," *Journal of Applied Psychology* 96 (2011), pp. 541–57.

41. A. Nahavandi and E. Aranda, "Restructuring Teams for the Reengineered Organization," *Academy of Management Executive,* November 1994, pp. 58–68.

42. B. Kirkman, B. Rosen, P. Tesluk, and C. Gibson, "The Impact of Team Empowerment on Virtual Team Performance: The Moderating Role of Face-to-Face Interaction," *Academy of Management Journal* 47 (2004), pp. 175–92.

43. J. R. Katzenbach and D. K. Smith, *The Wisdom of Teams* (Boston: Harvard Business School Press, 1993); and Maggie Starvish, "Why Leaders Need to Rethink Teamwork," *Forbes,* December 28, 2012, http://www.forbes.com.

44. Nadler et al., *Managing Organizational Behavior.*

45. Ibid.

46. Katzenbach and Smith, "The Discipline of Teams."

47. Ibid.

48. L. Gibson, J. Mathieu, C. Shalley, and T. Ruddy, "Creativity and Standardization: Complementary or Conflicting Drivers of Team Effectiveness?" *Academy of Management Journal* 48 (2005), pp. 521–31.

49. C. Meyer, "How the Right Measures Help Teams Excel," *Harvard Business Review,* May–June 1994, pp. 95–103.

50. J. R. Katzenbach and J. A. Santamaria, "Firing Up the Front Line," *Harvard Business Review,* May–June 1999, pp. 107–17.

51. D. Blumenthal, Z. Song, A. Jena, and T. Ferris, "Guidance for Structuring Team-Based Incentives in Health Care," *American Journal of Managed Care* 19 (2013), pp. 64–70; D. Knight, C. Durham, and E. Locke, "The Relationship of Team Goals, Incentives, and Efficacy to Strategic Risk, Tactical Implementation, and Performance," *Academy of Management Journal* 44 (2001), pp. 326–38; A. Kleingeld, H. van Mierlo, and L. Arends,

"The Effect of Goal Setting on Group Performance: A Meta-Analysis," *Journal of Applied Psychology* 96 (2011), pp. 1289–1304; C. Barnes, J. Hollenbeck, D. Jundt, D. S. De Rue, and S. Harmon, "Mixing Individual Incentives and Group Incentives: Best of Both Worlds or Social Dilemma?" *Journal of Management* 37 (2011), pp. 1611–35.

52. B. L. Kirkman and B. Rosen, "Powering Up Teams," *Organizational Dynamics* (Winter 2000), pp. 48–66.

53. E. E. Lawler III, *From the Ground Up* (San Francisco: Jossey-Bass, 1996).

54. M. Schippers, "Social Loafing Tendencies and Team Performance: The Compensating Effect of Agreeableness and Conscientiousness," *Academy of Management Learning & Education,* 13 (2014), pp. 62–81; A. Jassawalla, H. Sashittal, and A. Maishe, "Students' Perceptions of Social Loafing: Its Antecedents and Consequences in Undergraduate Business Classroom Teams," *Academy of Management Learning and Education,* 2009, pp. 42–54.

55. M. Erez, "Is Group Productivity Loss the Rule or the Exception? Effects of Culture and Group-Based Motivation," *Academy of Management Journal* 39 (1996), pp. 1513–37; A. Mas and E. Moretti, "Peers at Work" *The American Economic Review* 99 (2009), pp. 112–145.

56. Katzenbach and Smith, "The Discipline of Teams."

57. Y. Garbers and U. Konradt, "The Effect of Financial Incentives on Performance: A Quantitative Review of Individual and Team-Based Financial Incentives," *Journal of Occupational and Organizational Psychology* 87 (2014), pp. 102–37; and M. Johnson, J. Hollenbeck, S. Humphrey, D. Ilgen, D. Jundt, and C. Meyer, "Cutthroat Cooperation: Asymmetrical Adaptation to Changes in Team Reward Structures," *Academy of Management Journal,* 2006, pp. 103–19.

58. M. J. Pearsall, M. S. Christian, and A. P. J. Ellis, "Motivating Interdependent Teams: Individual Rewards, Shared Rewards, or Something Between?" *Journal of Applied Psychology* 95 (2010), pp. 183–91.

59. R. Wageman, "Interdependence and Group Effectiveness," *Administrative Science Quarterly* 40 (1995), pp. 145–80.

60. Mary K. Pratt, "Best Places Spotlight: NISC Supports Team Relationships," *Computerworld,* June 18, 2012, http://www.computerworld.com; "100 Best Places to Work in IT 2012: Employer Profile," *Computerworld,* June 18, 2012, http://www.computerworld.com; National Information Solutions Cooperative, "Careers: Benefits and Compensation," http://www.nisc.coop.

61. Lawler, *From the Ground Up.*

62. R. Rayasam, "Who's the Boss? In Some Companies, Its Nobody," *BBC* (online), January 7, 2015, http://www.bbc.com.

63. R. Preidt, "Work Teams Who Share Negative Emotions Better at Problem

Solving," *Bloomberg Businessweek,* November 23, 2010, http://www.businessweek.com.

64. "Intuit 2020 Report: Twenty Trends That Will Shape the Next Decade," http://www.intuit.com, accessed on May 26, 2015; E. Segran, "As Coworking Spaces Scale, Can They Keep Their Communal Vibe?" *The Atlantic* (online), February 27, 2015, http://www.theatlantic.com; C. Matthews, "Should We Worry about the Surge in Parttime Workers?" *Fortune* (online), July 22, 2014, http://www.fortune.com; A Vaccaro, "Number of Coworking Spaces Has Skyrocketed in the U.S.," *Inc.* (online), March 3, 2014, http://www.inc.com.

65. A. Grant, "Givers Take All: The Hidden Dimension of Corporate Culture,"*The McKinsey Quarterly* (2013), pp. 52–65; A. Srivastava, K. Bartol, and E. Locke, "Empowering Leadership in Management Teams: Effects on Knowledge Sharing, Efficacy, and Performance," *Academy of Management Journal,* 2006, pp. 1239–51.

66. L. A. DeChurch and J. R. Mesmer-Magnus, "The Cognitive Underpinnings of Effective Teamwork: A Meta-Analysis," *Journal of Applied Psychology* 95 (2010), pp. 32–53.

67. J. M. Levine, E. T. Higgins, and H. Choi, "Development of Strategic Norms in Groups," *Organizational Behavior and Human Decision Processes* 82 (2000), pp. 88–101.

68. M. Duffy, K. Scott, J. Shaw, B. Tepper, and K. Aquino, "A Social Context Model of Envy and Social Undermining," *Academy of Management Journal* 55 (2012), pp. 643–66; K. Jehn and E. Mannix, "The Dynamic Nature of Conflict: A Longitudinal Study of Intragroup Conflict and Group Performance," *Academy of Management Journal* 44 (2001), pp. 238–51.

69. J. O'Toole, *Vanguard Management: Redesigning the Corporate Future* (New York: Doubleday, 1985).

70. R. F. Bales, *Interaction Process Analysis: A Method for the Study of Small Groups* (Reading, MA: Addison-Wesley, 1950).

71. V. U. Druskat and J. Wheeler, "Managing from the Boundary: The Effective Leadership of Self-Managing Work Teams," *Academy of Management Journal* 46 (2003), pp. 435–57.

72. Katzenbach and Smith, *The Wisdom of Teams.*

73. V. Nicolaides, K. LaPort, T. Chen, A. Tomassetti, E. Weis, S. Zaccaro, and J. Cortina, "The Shared Leadership of Teams: A Meta-analysis of Proximal, Distal, and Moderating Relationships," *Leadership Quarterly* 25 (2014), 923–42; J. Carson, P. Tesluk, and J. Marrone, "Shared Leadership in Teams: An Investigation of Antecedent Conditions and Performance," *Academy of Management Journal,* 2007, pp. 1217–34.

74. S. E. Seashore, *Group Cohesiveness in the Industrial Work Group* (Ann Arbor: University of Michigan Press, 1954).

75. Banker et al., "Impact of Work Teams on Manufacturing Performance."

76. S. Wise, "Can a Team Have Too Much Cohesion? The Dark Side to Network Density," *European Management Journal* 32 (2014), pp. 703–11; B. Mullen and C. Cooper, "The Relation between Group Cohesiveness and Performance: An Integration," *Psychological Bulletin* 115 (1994), pp. 210–27.

77. R. Hasson, "How to Resolve Board Disputes More Effectively," *MIT Sloan Management Review 48* (2006), pp. 77–80; D. P. Forbes and F. J. Milliken, "Cognition and Corporate Governance: Understanding Boards of Directors as Strategic Decision-Making Groups," *Academy of Management Review* 24 (1999), pp. 489–505.

78. T. Simons, L. H. Pelled, and K. A. Smith, "Making Use of Difference: Diversity, Debate, and Decision Comprehensiveness in Top Management Teams," *Academy of Management Journal* 42 (1999), pp. 662–73.

79. Seashore, *Group Cohesiveness in the Industrial Work Group.*

80. B. Lott and A. Lott, "Group Cohesiveness as Interpersonal Attraction: A Review of Relationships with Antecedent and Consequent Variables," *Psychological Bulletin*, October 1965, pp. 259–309.

81. K. Dahlin, L. Weingart, and P. Hinds, "Team Diversity and Information Use," *Academy of Management Journal* 48 (2005), pp. 1107–23.

82. R. Gillett, "Productivity Hack of the Week: The Two Pizza Approach to Productive Teamwork," *Fast Company* (online), October 24, 2014, http://www.fastcompany.com.

83. B. L. Kirkman and B. Rosen, "Beyond Self-Management: Antecedents and Consequences of Team Empowerment," *Academy of Management Journal* 42 (1999), pp. 58–74.

84. Hackman, *Groups That Work.*

85. W. Bennis, *Organizing Genius* (Reading, MA: Addison-Wesley, 1997).

86. Cianni and Wnuck, "Individual Growth and Team Enhancement."

87. K. Jehn, "A Multimethod Examination of the Benefits and Detriments of Intragroup Conflict," *Administrative Science Quarterly* 40 (1995), pp. 245–82.

88. Wellins et al., *Inside Teams.*

89. J. A. Marrone, "Team Boundary Spanning: A Multilevel Review of Past Research and Proposals for the Future," *Journal of Management* 36 (2010), pp. 911–40.

90. D. G. Ancona, "Outward Bound: Strategies for Team Survival in an Organization," *Academy of Management Journal* 33 (1990), pp. 334–65.

91. Ibid.

92. W. De Vries, F. Walter, G. Van der Vegt, and P. Essens, "Antecedents of Individuals' Interteam Coordination: Broad Functional Experiences as a Mixed Blessing," *Academy of Management Journal* 57 (2013), pp. 1334–59; H. Bruns, "Working Alone Together: Coordination in Collaboration Across Domains of Expertise," *Academy of Management Journal* 56 (2013), pp. 62–83; M. Hogg, D. van Knippenberg, and D. Rast III, "Intergroup Leadership in Organizations: Leading Across Group and Organizational Boundaries," *Academy of Management Review* 37 (2012), pp. 232–55.

93. L. Sayles, *Leadership: What Effective Managers Really Do, and How They Do It* (New York: McGraw-Hill, 1979).

94. Ibid.

95. M. Holt, "Risks of Not Confronting Conflict in the Workplace," *Chron (Houston Chronicle),* http://www.smallbusiness.chron.com, accessed on May 25, 2015; M. Myatt, "5 Keys of Dealing with Workplace Conflict," *Forbes* (online), February 22, 2012, http://www.forbes.com; and P. Lencioni, "How to Foster Good Conflict," *The Wall Street Journal,* November 13, 2008, http://online.wsj.com.

96. A. Caron and T. Cummings, "A Theory of Subgroups in Work Teams," *Academy of Management Review* 37 (2012), pp. 441–70.

97. D. Staples and L. Zhao, "The Effects of Cultural Diversity in Virtual Teams versus Face-to-Face Teams," *Group Decision and Negotiation* 15 (2006), pp. 389–406; J. Chatman and F. Flynn, "The Influence of Demographic Heterogeneity on the Emergence and Consequences of Cooperative Norms in Work Teams," *Academy of Management Journal* 44 (2001), pp. 956–74; and R. T. Keller, "Cross-Functional Project Groups in Research and New Product Development: Diversity, Communications, Job Stress, and Outcomes," *Academy of Management Journal* 44 (2001), pp. 547–55.

98. J.-L. Farh, C. Lee, and C. Farh, "Task Conflict and Team Creativity: A Question of How Much and When," *Journal of Applied Psychology* 2010, pp. 1173–80; J. Shaw, J. Zhu, M. Duffy, K. Scott, H. A. Shih, and E. Susanto, "A Contingency Model of Conflict and Team Effectiveness," *Journal of Applied Psychology* 96 (2011), pp. 391–400; F. R. C. de Wit, L. Greer, and K. Jehn, "The Paradox of Intergroup Conflict: A Meta-Analysis," *Journal of Applied Psychology* 97 (2012), pp. 360–90; S. Thatcher and P. Patel, "Group Faultlines: A Review, Integration, and Guide for Research," *Journal of Management* 38 (2012), pp. 969–1009; "Fostering Team Creativity."

99. D. Tjosvold, *Working Together to Get Things Done* (Lexington, MA: Lexington Books, 1986).

100. T. Kim, C. Wang, M. Kondo, and T. Kim, "Conflict Management Styles: The Differences Among the Chinese, Japanese and Koreans," *International Journal of Conflict Management* 18 (2007), pp. 23–41; C. Tinsley and J. Brett, "Managing Workplace Conflict in the United States and Hong Kong," *Organizational Behavior and Human Decision Processes* 85 (2001), pp. 360–81.

101. K. W. Thomas, "Conflict and Conflict Management," in *Handbook of Industrial and Organizational Psychology,* ed. M. D. Dunnette (Chicago: Rand McNally, 1976).

102. D. Tynan, "IT Turf Wars," *InfoWorld. com,* February 14, 2011, Business & Company Resource Center, http://galenet.galegroup.com.

103. Ibid.

104. K. Conerly and A. Tripathi, "What Is Your Conflict Style? Understanding and Dealing with Your Conflict Style," *The Journal for Quality and Participation* 27 (2004), pp. 16–20; K. W. Thomas, "Toward Multidimensional Values in Teaching: The Example of Conflict Behaviors," *Academy of Management Review,* 1977, pp. 484–89.

105. R. Lau and A. Cobb, "Understanding the Connections Between Relationship Conflict and Performance: The Intervening Roles of Trust and Exchange," *Journal of Organizational Behavior* 31 (2010), pp. 898–917; C. O. Longenecker and M. Neubert, "Barriers and Gateways to Management Cooperation and Teamwork," *Business Horizons,* September–October 2000, pp. 37–44.

106. M. Johnson, J. Hollenbeck, S. Humphrey, D. Algen, D. Jundt, and C. Meyer, "Cutthroat Cooperation: Asymmetrical Adaptation to Changes in Team Reward Structures," *Academy of Management Journal* 49 (2006), pp. 103–119.

107. P. S. Nugent, "Managing Conflict: Third-Party Interventions for Managers," *Academy of Management Executive* 16 (2002), pp. 139–54.

108. M. Blum and J. A. Wall Jr., "HRM: Managing Conflicts in the Firm," *Business Horizons,* May–June 1997, pp. 84–87.

109. J. Leon-Perez, F. Medina, A. Arenas, and L. Munduate, "The Relationship Between Interpersonal Conflict and Workplace Bullying," *Journal of Managerial Psychology* 30 (2015), pp. 250–63; J. A. Wall Jr. and R. R. Callister, "Conflict and Its Management," *Journal of Management* 21 (1995), pp. 515–58.

110. J. Polzer, C. B. Crisp, S. Jarvenpaa, and J. Kim, "Extending the Faultline Model to Geographically Dispersed Teams: How Collocated Subgroups Can Impair Group Functioning," *Academy of Management Journal* 49 (2006), pp. 679–92.

111. F. Siebdrat, M. Hoegl, and H. Ernst, "How to Manage Virtual Teams," *MIT Sloan Management Review* 50 (2009), pp. 63–68; M. Montoya-Weiss, A. Massey, and M. Song, "Getting It Together: Temporal Coordination and Conflict Management in Global Virtual Teams," *Academy of Management Journal* 44 (2001), pp. 1251–62.

112. R. Standifer and J. A. Wall Jr., "Managing Conflict in B2B Commerce," *Business Horizons,* March–April 2003, pp. 65–70.

113. Mackey and Sisodia, "Want to Hire Great People?"; Rohman, "Whole Foods

Market"; Whole Foods Market, "Careers"; *Executive Leadership,* "Groups Wield Power"; Mike Sunnucks, "Language Dispute Puts Whole Foods in Workplace Spotlight,"*Phoenix Business Journal,* June 6, 2013, http:// www.bizjournals.com/ phoenix; Susanna Kim, "Whole Foods Says It Does Not Forbid Employees from Speaking Foreign Languages," *ABC News,* June 7, 2013, http://abcnews.go.com.

Chapter 15

1. "Telecommuting: What Marissa Mayer Got Right—and Wrong," *Time* (online), June 5, 2014, http://www.time.com; Rachel Emma Silverman, "At Yahoo, Working from Home Doesn't Work," *The Wall Street Journal,* February 25, 2013, http:// blogs.wsj.com; Amanda Enayati, "A Work-from-Home Mom Defends Yahoo's Mayer," *CNN.com,* February 27, 2013, http://www.cnn.com; Yuki Noguchi, "Experts Boil Telecommuting Decisions Down to Flexibility vs. Serendipity," *Morning Edition,* February 28, 2013, http://www.npr.org; Patricia Sellers, "Marissa Mayer: Ready to Rumble at Yahoo," *Fortune,* October 11, 2012, http://postcards.blogs.fortune.cnn.com; "Softening Yahoo's Image? Company Rolls Out Parental Leave, Other Benefits," *HR Focus,* June 2013, p. 7; Stephanie Mlot, "Marissa Mayer Addresses Yahoo Staff in First Memo," *PC Magazine,* July 2012, http://www.pcmag.com; "Mayer Brings Some Google to Yahoo, including Free Lunch," *PC Magazine,* July 2012, http://www.pcmag.com; Brad Stone, Brian Womack, and Emily Chang, "Reading the Mind of Marissa Mayer," *Bloomberg Businessweek,* July 23, 2012, http:// www.pcmag.com.

2. M. Venus, D. Stam, and D. van Knippenberg, "Leader Emotion as a Catalyst of Effective Leader Communication of Visions, Value-Laden Messages, and Goals," *Organizational Behavior and Human Decision Processes* 122 (2013), pp. 53–68; L. Penley, E. Alexander, I. E. Jernigan, and C. Henwood, "Communication Abilities of Managers: The Relationship to Performance," *Journal of Management* 17 (1991), pp. 57–76.

3. W. V. Haney, "A Comparative Study of Unilateral and Bilateral Communication," *Academy of Management Journal* 7 (1964), pp. 128–36.

4. J. R. Mesmer-Magnus and L. A. DeChurch, "Information Sharing and Team Performance: A Meta-Analysis," *Journal of Applied Psychology* 94 (2009), pp. 535–46.

5. Boris Groysberg and Michael Slind, "Leadership Is a Conversation," *Harvard Business Review,* June 2012, pp. 76–84.

6. I. Wickelgren, "Speaking Science: Why People Don't Hear What You Say," *Scientific American* (online), November 8, 2012, http://www.scientificamerican. com; M. McCormack, "The Illusion of Communication," *Financial Times*

Mastering Management Review, July 1999, pp. 8–9.

7. F. Flynn and S. Wiltermuth, "Who's with Me? False Consensus, Brokerage, and Ethical Decision Making in Organizations," *Academy of Management Journal* 53 (2010), pp. 1074–89; R. Cross and S. Brodt, "How Assumptions of Consensus Undermine Decision Making," *Sloan Management Review* 42 (2001), pp. 86–94.

8. S. Mohammed and E. Ringseis, "Cognitive Diversity and Consensus in Group Decision Making: The Role of Inputs, Processes, and Outcomes," *Organizational Behavior and Human Decision Processes* 85 (2001), pp. 310–35.

9. S. Parker and C. Axtell, "Seeing Another Viewpoint: Antecedents and Outcomes of Employee Perspective Taking," *Academy of Management Journal* 44 (2001), pp. 1085–100.

10. D. Tannen, "The Power of Talk: Who Gets Heard and Why," *Harvard Business Review,* September–October 1995, pp. 138–48.

11. Ibid.

12. Ibid.

13. Novo Nordisk website, "Our Triple Bottom Line," http://www.novonordisk.com, accessed June 8, 2015; J. Ochs, "Defining 'Social Enterprise,'" *Minnesota Business Magazine* (online), December 17, 2014, http://www.minnesotabusiness.com; J. Jervis, "Social Enterprises: Popular But Confusing, Says Study," *The Guardian* (online), January 8, 2013, http://www. theguardian.com; A. Field, "Salesforce. com's Thwarted Efforts to Trademark Social Enterprise Should Be a Wake Up Call," *Forbes* (online), September 11, 2012, http://www.forbes.com.

14. R. Merkin, V. Taras, and P. Steel, "State of the Art Themes in Cross-Cultural Communication Research: A Systematic and Meta-Analytic Review," *International Journal of Intercultural Relations* 38 (2014), pp. 1–23; C. Cramton and P. Hinds, "An Embedded Model of Cultural Adaptation in Global Teams," *Organization Science* 25 (2014), pp. 1056–81; L. K. Larkey, "Toward a Theory of Communicative Interactions in Culturally Diverse Workgroups," *Academy of Management Review,* April 1996, pp. 463–91.

15. L. A. Liu, C. H. Chua, and G. Stahl, "Quality of Communication Experience: Definition, Measurement, and Implications for Intercultural Negotiations," *Journal of Applied Psychology* 95 (2010), pp. 469–87.

16. C. Argyris, "Good Communication That Blocks Learning," *Harvard Business Review,* July–August 1994, pp. 77–85.

17. T. Donnelly, "How to Deliver Bad News to Employees," *Inc.* (online), January 14, 2011, http://www.inc.com; E. Krell, "The Unintended Word," *HR Magazine,* August 2006, General Reference Center Gold, http://find.galegroup.com.

18. C. Deutsch, "The Multimedia Benefits Kit," *The New York Times,* October 14, 1990, sec. 3, p. 25.

19. T. W. Comstock, *Communicating in Business and Industry* (Albany, NY: Delmar, 1985).

20. A. Cameron and J. Webster, "Multicommunicating: Juggling Multiple Conversations in the Workplace," *Information Systems Research* 24 (2013), pp. 352–71; N. L. Reinsch Jr., J. W. Turner, and C. H. Tinsley, "Multicommunicating: A Practice Whose Time Has Come?" *Academy of Management Review* 33 (2008), pp. 391–403.

21. E. Markowitz, "Don't Bet against Aaron Levie," *Inc.,* December 2014, pp. 30–34.

22. Michael Chui, James Manyika, Jacques Bughin, et al., "The Social Economy: Unlocking Value and Productivity through Social Technologies," McKinsey Global Institute, July 2012, http://www.mckinsey. com.

23. Microsoft Support, https://support.office. com, accessed on June 2, 2015; Hitachi Solutions Europe, Ltd., http://uk.hitachi-solutions.com, accessed on June 2, 2015.

24. Candor, http://www.usecandor.com, accessed on June 2, 2015; R. Greenfield, "Brainstorming Doesn't Work: Try This Technique Instead," *Fast Company* (online), July 29, 2014, http://www. fastcompany.com.

25. S. S. K. Lam and J. Schaubroeck, "Improving Group Decisions by Better Pooling Information: A Comparative Advantage of Group Decision Support Systems," *Journal of Applied Psychology* 85 (2000), pp. 565–73.

26. J. Goudreau, "How to Communicate in the New Multigenerational Office," *Forbes* (online), February 14, 2013, http:// www.forbes.com; M. Schmulen, "Memo to the Boss: Twitter's Not a Time Suck," *Fortune,* January 19, 2010, http://tech. fortune.cnn.com; D. Lindorff, "Facing Up to Facebook," *Treasury & Risk,* April 2011, Business & Company; J. Goudreau, "How to Communicate in the New Multigenerational Office," *Forbes* (online), February 14, 2013, http://www. forbes.com; M. Schmulen, "Memo to the Boss," Resource Center, http://galenet. galegroup.com; and S. Ali, "Why No One under 30 Answers Your Voicemail," *DiversityInc,* August 27, 2010, http:// www.diversityinc.com.

27. "Millennials Don't Care about Mobile Security, and Here's What to Do about It," *Wired,* September 2014, http://www. wired.com; E. Weise, "Bring Your Own Dilemmas: Dealing with BYOD and Security," *USA Today* (online), August 26, 2014, http://www.usatoday.com; T. Kaneshige, "12 Big BYOD Predictions for 2014," *CIO* (online), January 8, 2014, http://www.cio.com; "BYOD/BYOA: A Growing, Applicable Trend," *Comcast Business* (2014), http://www.inc.com; Gartner, "Gartner Predicts by 2017, Half of Employers Will Require Employees to Supply Their Own Device for Work Purposes," press release on, May 1, 2013, http://www.gartner.com.

28. S. Aral, "The Problem with Online Ratings," *MIT Sloan Management Review* 55 (2014), pp. 47–52; C. Naquin, T. Kurtzberg, and L. Belkin, "The Finer Points of Lying Online: E-Mail versus Pen and Paper," *Journal of Applied Psychology* 95 (2010), pp. 387–94.

29. C. Naquin and G. Paulson, "Online Bargaining and Interpersonal Trust," *Journal of Applied Psychology* 88 (2003), pp. 113–20.

30. N. Hill, K. Bartol, P. Tesluk, and G. Langa, "Organizational Context and Face-to-Face Interaction: Influences on the Development of Trust and Collaborative Behaviors in Computer-Mediated Groups," *Organizational Behavior and Human Decision Processes,* 108 (2009), pp. 187–201; B. Baltes, M. Dickson, M. Sherman, C. Bauer, and J. LaGanke, "Computer-Mediated Communication and Group Decision Making: A Meta-Analysis," *Organizational Behavior and Human Decision Processes* 87 (2002), pp. 156–79.

31. E. Martínez-Moreno, P. González-Navarro, A. Zornoza, and P. Ripoll, "Relationship, Task and Process Conflicts and Team Performance: The Moderating Role of Communication Media," *International Journal of Conflict Management* 20 (2009), pp. 251–68; R. Rice and D. Case, "Electronic Message Systems in the University: A Description of Use and Utility," *Journal of Communication* 33 (1983), pp. 131–52; and C. Steinfield, "Dimensions of Electronic Mail Use in an Organizational Setting," *Proceedings of the Academy of Management,* San Diego, 1985.

32. A. Farnham, "Kicked to Curb by Text: New, Awful Way to Be Fired," *ABC News* (online), July 16, 2013, http://www. abcnews.com; M. Gardner, "You've Got Mail: 'We're Letting You Go,' " *Christian Science Monitor,* September 18, 2006, http://www.csmonitor.com; and Linton Weeks, "Read the Blog: You're Fired," *National Public Radio,* December 8, 2008, http://www.npr.org.

33. J. Meister, "To Do: Update Company's Social Media Policy ASAP," *Forbes* (online), February 7, 2013, http://www. forbes.com.

34. K. Ferrazzi, "How to Avoid Virtual Communication," *Harvard Business Review* (online), April 12, 2013, http:// www.hbr.org; Reuters, "Is That Really What Your E-mail Meant to Say?" *Yahoo News,* February 14, 2007, http://www. hbr.org; Reuters, "Is That Really What Your E-mail Meant to Say?" *Yahoo News,* February 14, 2007, http://news.yahoo.com.

35. K. Byron, "Carrying Too Heavy a Load? The Communication and Miscommunication of Emotion by Email," *Academy of Management Review* 33 (2008), pp. 309–27.

36. Naquin, Kurtzberg, and Belkin, "The Finer Points of Lying Online."

37. T. Bradley, "Email vs. IM vs. SMS: Choosing the Right One," *PC World* (online), January 13, 2012, http://www.

pcworld.com; B. Glassberg, W. Kettinger, and J. Logan, "Electronic Communication: An Ounce of Policy Is Worth a Pound of Cure," *Business Horizons,* July–August 1996, pp. 74–80; Ali, "Why No One under 30 Answers Your Voicemail."

38. Ali, "Why No One under 30 Answers Your Voicemail."

39. A. Hopp, "Overwhelming Communication," *Training Journal* (online), April 23, 2014, http://www.trainingjournal.com; M. Totty, "Rethinking the Inbox," *The Wall Street Journal,* March 26, 2007, http://online.wsj. com; Reuters, "BlackBerrys, Laptops Blur Work/Home Balance: Poll," *Yahoo News,* April 5, 2007, http://news.yahoo.com; and M. Locher, "BlackBerry Addiction Starts at the Top," *PC World,* March 6, 2007, http:// www.pcworld.com.

40. Chui et al., "The Social Economy," p. 47.

41. Robby Macdonell, "Can We Talk for a Minute about Why Email Sucks So Much?" *RescueTime Blog,* February 16, 2013, http://blog.rescuetime.com.

42. Chui et al., "The Social Economy," p. 29.

43. C. Conner, "Why Every Organization Needs a Standard Response Time Policy," *Forbes* (online), August 16, 2013, http:// www.forbes.com.

44. S. Vozza, "Why Your Company Should Consider Banning Email," *Fast Company* (online), February 20, 2015, http://www. fastcompany.com; E. Horng, "No E-mail Fridays Transform Office," *ABC News,* March 10, 2007, http://abcnews.go.com.

45. K. Tausche, "JPMorgan Cuts the Cord on Voicemail," *CNBC* (online), May 2, 2015, http://www.cnbc.com.

46. D. Meinert, "Make Telecommuting Pay Off," *HR Magazine* 56 (online), June 11, 2011, http://www.shrm.org.

47. Ibid.

48. P. Economy, "5 Ways to Get the Most from Virtual Employees," *Inc.* (online), June 13, 2014, http://www.inc.com; T Mackintosh, "Is This the Year You Move to a Virtual Office?" *Accounting Technology,* May 2007, General Reference Center Gold, http://find.galegroup.com.

49. Company website, "Work with Us," http:// automattic.com/work-with-us/, accessed on May 3, 2015; Rachel Emma Silverman, "Step into the Office-less Company," *The Wall Street Journal,* September 4, 2012, http://online.wsj.com; Verne Kopytoff, "Why Some Company Offices Are Virtual," *Bloomberg Businessweek,* September 10, 2012, *EBSCOhost,* http:// web.ebscohost.com; Automattic, "Work with Us," http://automattic.com.

50. E. Hallowel, "The Human Moment at Work," *Harvard Business Review* (online), January–February 1999, http://www.hbr. org.

51. R. Lengel and R. Daft, "The Selection of Communication Media as an Executive Skill," *Academy of Management Executive* 2 (1988), pp. 225–32.

52. J. R. Carlson and R. W. Zmud, "Channel Expansion Theory and the Experiential Nature of Media Richness Perceptions,"

Academy of Management Journal 42 (1999), pp. 153–70.

53. L. Trevino, R. Daft, and R. Lengel, "Understanding Managers' Media Choices: A Symbolic Interactionist Perspective," in *Organizations and Communication Technology,* ed. J. Fulk and C. Steinfield (London: Sage, 1990).

54. J. Fulk and B. Boyd, "Emerging Theories of Communication in Organizations," *Journal of Management* 17 (1991), pp. 407–46.

55. A. Otani, "Richard Branson: Marissa Mayer's Yahoo Work Policy Is on the Wrong Side of History," *Bloomberg Business* (online), April 24, 2015, http://www. bloomberg.com; "Telecommuting: What Marissa Mayer Got Right——and Wrong"; Silverman, "At Yahoo, Working from Home Doesn't Work"; Kara Swisher, "'Physically Together': Here's the Internal Yahoo No-Work-from-Home Memo for Remote Workers and Maybe More," *All things D,* February 22, 2013, http://allthingsd.com; Enayati, "A Work-from-Home Mom"; Noguchi, "Experts Boil Telecommuting Decisions Down"; Mary C. Noonan and Jennifer L. Glass, "The Hard Truth about Telecommuting," *Monthly Labor Review,* June 2012, pp. 38–45; Claire Suddath, "Why Won't Yahoo! Let Employees Work from Home?" *Bloomberg Businessweek,* February 25, 2013, http://www.businessweek.com; Claire Suddath, "The Right Way for a CEO to Deliver Bad News," *Bloomberg Businessweek,* May 9, 2013, *EBSCOhost,* http://web.ebscohost.com.

56. L. Bossidy and R. Charan, *Confronting Reality: Doing What Matters to Get Things Right* (New York: Crown Business, 2004).

57. C. Beers, "Leading Through the Power of Persuasion," *Fast Company* (online), November 8, 2012, http:// www.fastcompany.com; M. McCall, M. Lombardo, and A. Morrison, *The Lessons of Experience: How Successful Executives Develop on the Job* (Lexington, MA: Lexington, 1988).

58. J. A. Conger, "The Necessary Art of Persuasion," *Harvard Business Review,* May–June 1998, pp. 84–95.

59. N. Morgan, "How to Become an Authentic Speaker," *Harvard Business Review,* November 2008, pp. 115–19.

60. N. Nohria and B. Harrington, *Six Principles of Successful Persuasion* (Boston: Harvard Business School Publishing Division, 1993).

61. Groysberg and Slind, "Leadership Is a Conversation," pp. 79–80.

62. H. K. Mintz, "Business Writing Styles for the 70's," *Business Horizons,* August 1972, cited in *Readings in Interpersonal and Organizational Communication,* ed. R. C. Huseman, C. M. Logue, and D. L. Freshley (Boston: Allyn & Bacon, 1977).

63. C. D. Decker, "Writing to Teach Thinking," *Across the Board,* March 1996, pp. 19–20.

64. M. Forbes, "Exorcising Demons from Important Business Letters," *Marketing Times,* March–April 1981, pp. 36–38.

65. R. Gillett, "Here's Why No One Gets Your Sarcastic Emails," *Fast Company* (online), May 30, 2014, http://www.fastcompany.com; T. Flood, "Top Ten Mistakes Managers Make with Email," *The Wall Street Journal,* February 3, 2010, http://online.wsj.com.

66. D. Jones, "Cisco CEO Sees Tech as Integral to Success," *USA Today,* March 19, 2007, p. 4B (interview with John Chambers).

67. G. Ferraro, "The Need for Linguistic Proficiency in Global Business," *Business Horizons,* May–June 1996, pp. 39–46; William W. Maddux, Peter H. Kim, Tetsushi Okumura, and Jeanne M. Brett, "Why 'I'm Sorry' Doesn't Always Translate," *Harvard Business Review,* June 2012, p. 26.

68. P. C. Early and E. Mosakowski, "Creating Hybrid Team Cultures: An Empirical Test of Transnational Team Functioning," *Academy of Management Journal* 43 (2000), pp. 26–49.

69. Ferraro, "The Need for Linguistic Proficiency."

70. C. Chu, *The Asian Mind Game* (New York: Rawson Associates, 1991).

71. Ferraro, "The Need for Linguistic Proficiency."

72. J. Smith, "10 Nonverbal Cues That Convey Confidence at Work," *Forbes* (online), March 11, 2013, http://www.forbes.com.

73. Comstock, *Communicating in Business and Industry.*

74. M. Korda, *Power: How to Get It, How to Use It* (New York: Random House, 1975).

75. A. Mehrabian, "Communication without Words," *Psychology Today,* September 1968, p. 52. Cited in M. B. McCaskey, "The Hidden Message Managers Send," *Harvard Business Review,* November–December 1979, pp. 135–48.

76. Ferraro, "The Need for Linguistic Proficiency."

77. Bernard T. Ferrari, "The Executive's Guide to Better Listening," *McKinsey Quarterly,* February 2012, https://www.mckinseyquarterly.com.

78. A. Athos and J. Gabarro, *Interpersonal Behavior* (Englewood Cliffs, NJ: Prentice-Hall, 1978).

79. M. K. Pratt, "Five Ways to Drive Your Best Workers out the Door," *Computerworld,* August 25, 2008, pp. 26–27, 30.

80. J. Kouzes and B. Posner, *The Leadership Challenge* (San Francisco: Jossey-Bass, 1995).

81. A. Vance, "Netflix, Reed Hastings Survive Missteps to Join Silicon Valley's Elite," *Bloomberg Business* (online), May 9, 2013, http://www.bloomberg.com.

82. G. Graham, J. Unruh, and P. Jennings, "The Impact of Nonverbal Communication in Organizations: A Survey of Perceptions," *Journal of Business Communications* 28 (1991), pp. 45–62.

83. Ibid.

84. E. Goodson, "Read a Plant—Fast," *Harvard Business Review*, May 2002, pp. 105–13; D. Upton and S. Macadam, "Why (and How) to Take a Plant Tour," *Harvard Business Review,* May–June 1997, pp. 97–106.

85. Goodson, "Read a Plant—Fast."

86. H. Seligson, "For American Workers in China, a Culture Clash," *The New York Times* (online), December 23, 2009, http://www.nytimes.com.

87. Chu, *The Asian Mind Game.*

88. A. Smidts, A. T. H. Pruyn, and C. B. M. van Riel, "The Impact of Employee Communication and Perceived External Prestige on Organizational Identification," *Academy of Management Journal* 49 (2001), pp. 1051–62.

89. X. Qin, R. Ren, Z. Zhang, and R. Johnson, "Fairness Heuristics and Substitutability Effects: Inferring the Fairness of Outcomes, Procedures, and Interpersonal Treatment When Employees Lack Clear Information," *Journal of Applied Psychology* 100 (2015), pp. 749–66; J. Koehler, K. Anatol, and R. Applebaum, *Organizational Communication: Behavioral Perspectives* (Orlando, FL: Holt, Rinehart & Winston, 1981).

90. J. Waldroop and T. Butler, "The Executive as Coach," *Harvard Business Review,* November–December 1996, pp. 111–17; S. Toye, "Coaching Comes of Age," *Training Journal* (2015), pp. 21–24.

91. D. T. Hall, K. L. Otazo, and G. P. Hollenbeck, "Behind Closed Doors: What Really Happens in Executive Coaching," *Organizational Dynamics,* Winter 1999, pp. 39–53; D. O'Neil, M. Hopkins, and D. Bilimoria, "A Framework for Developing Women Leaders: Applications to Executive Coaching," *The Journal of Applied Behavioral Science* 51 (2015), pp. 253–76.

92. D. Larcker, S. Miles, B. Tayan, and M. Gutman, "2013 Executive Coaching Survey," The Miles Group and Stanford University, August 2013, http://www.gsb.stanford.edu/faculty-research/publications/2013-executive-coachingsurvey.

93. T. Judge and J. Cowell, "The Brave New World of Coaching," *Business Horizons,* July–August 1997, pp. 71–77; E. E. Lawler III, *Treat People Right!* (San Francisco: Jossey-Bass, 2003); and L. A. Hill, "New Manager Development for the 21st Century," *Academy of Management Executive,* August 2004, pp. 121–26.

94. R. J. Bies, "The Delivery of Bad News in Organizations: A Framework for Analysis," *Journal of Management* 39 (2013), pp. 136–62.

95. J. Gutknecht and J. B. Keys, "Mergers, Acquisitions, and Takeovers: Maintaining Morale of Survivors and Protecting Employees," *Academy of Management Executive,* August 1993, pp. 26–36.

96. D. Schweiger and A. DeNisi, "Communication with Employees Following a Merger: A Longitudinal Field Experiment," *Academy of Management Journal* 34 (1991), pp. 110–35.

97. J. Case, "Opening the Books," *Harvard Business Review,* March–April 1997, pp. 118–27.

98. "How Total Transparency Saved My Company," *Inc.* (online), March 2014, http://www.inc.com.

99. S. Stevenson, "We Spent *What* on Paper Clips?" *Slate* (online), May 19, 2014, http://www.slate.com; "Hilcorp Hits #15 on Fortune's 100 Best Companies to Work For List," press release on, January 23, 2014, http://www.hilcorp.com; P. Patel, "Houston's Top Workplaces 2010: No. 1 Midsize Company, Hilcorp Energy Company," *Houston Chronicle,* November 7, 2010, Business & Company Resource Center, http://galenet.galegroup.com; and P. Patel, "Houston's Top Workplaces 2010 Q&A," *Houston Chronicle,* November 7, 2010, Business & Company Resource Center, http://galenet.galegroup.com.

100. W. V. Ruch, *Corporate Communications* (Westport, CT: Quorum, 1984).

101. L. Tost, F. Gino, and R. Larrick, "When Power Makes Others Speechless: The Negative Impact of Leader Power on Team Performance," *Academy of Management Journal* 56 (2013), pp. 1465–86.

102. J. Gardner, "The Heart of the Matter: Leader-Constituent Interaction," in *Leading & Leadership,* ed. T. Fuller (Notre Dame, IN: Notre Dame University Press, 2000), pp. 239–44.

103. R. Ashkenas, D. Ulrich, T. Jick, and S. Kerr, *The Boundaryless Organization* (San Francisco: Jossey-Bass, 1995).

104. Ruch, *Corporate Communications.*

105. H. Touryalai, "Marriott's Upgrade: New CEO Arne Sorenson Freshens Up the Brand for Millennials," *Forbes* (online), June 26, 2013, http://www.forbes.com.

106. A. Hutton, "Four Rules for Taking Your Message to Wall Street," *Harvard Business Review,* May 2001, pp. 125–32.

107. Koehler et al., *Organizational Communication.*

108. Rachel Emma Silverman, "The Science of Serendipity in the Workplace," *The Wall Street Journal,* April 30, 2013, http://online.wsj.com.

109. L. He, "Google's Secrets of Innovation: Empowering Its Employees," *Forbes* (online), March 29, 2013, http://www.forbes.com.

110. T. Harbert, "Teamwork for Techies," *Computerworld,* December 20, 2010, pp. 24–27.

111. N. B. Kurland and L. H. Pelled, "Passing the Word: Toward a Model of Gossip and Power in the Workplace," *Academy of Management Review* 25 (2000), pp. 428–38.

112. T. Grosser, V. Lopez-Kidwell, G. Labianca, and L. Ellwardt, "Hearing It through the Grapevine: Positive and Negative Workplace Gossip," *Organizational Dynamics* 41 (2012), 52–61; L. Abrams, R. Cross, E. Lesser, and D. Levin, "Nurturing Interpersonal Trust in Knowledge-Sharing Networks," *Academy*

of Management Executive 17 (November 2003), pp. 64–77.

113. R. L. Rosnow, "Rumor as Communication: A Contextual Approach," *Journal of Communication* 38 (1988), pp. 12–28.

114. L. Burke and J. M. Wise, "The Effective Care, Handling, and Pruning of the Office Grapevine," *Business Horizons,* May–June 2003, pp. 71–76.

115. K. Davis, "The Care and Cultivation of the Corporate Grapevine," *Dun's Review,* July 1973, pp. 44–47.

116. N. Difonzo, P. Bordia, and R. Rosnow, "Reining in Rumors," *Organizational Dynamics,* Summer 1994, pp. 47–62.

117. R. Ashkenas, D. Ulrich, T. Jick, and S. Kerr, *The Boundaryless Organization, Breaking the Chains of Organizational Structure* (San Francisco: Jossey-Bass, 1995).

118. R. M. Hodgetts, "A Conversation with Steve Kerr," *Organizational Dynamics,* Spring 1996, pp. 68–79.

119. "Marissa Mayer Docked $13 Million and Still Made $42 Million," CNN Money (online), April 30, 2014, http://money.cnn.com; B. Rigby and L. Maan, "Yahoo's Profit, Revenue Miss Street Forecasts as Costs Rise," Reuters (online), April 21, 2015, http://www.reuters.com; Swisher, "'Physically Together'"; Swisher, "Survey Says"; Enayati, "A Work-from-Home Mom"; Sellers, "Marissa Mayer"; Mlot, "Marissa Mayer Addresses Yahoo Staff"; "Yahoo! Telecommuting Ban May Be Unique, but Revisiting Arrangements Recommended," HR Focus, April 2013, pp. 1–3.

120. R. M. Fulmer, "The Evolving Paradigm of Leadership Development," *Organizational Dynamics,* Spring 1997, pp. 59–72; R. Gagnon, "GE Workout: Physical Fitness for Your Organization," *Huffington Post* (online), October 11, 2013, http://www.huffingtonpost.com.

121. General Electric, "GE Shares Skills, Intellectual Capital with CommonBond Communities," news release, December 4, 2006, http://www.genewscenter.com.

122. Ashkenas et al., *The Boundaryless Organization.*

Chapter 16

1. J. C. Collins and J. I. Porras, *Built to Last: Successful Habits of Visionary Companies* (New York: Harper Business, 1994).

2. Ramkumar Iyer and Nandita Bose, "Best Buy Profit Beats on Strong Demand for TVs, Smartphones," Reuters, May 21, 2015, http://www.reuters.com; E. Stych, "Best Buy Cutting 400 Jobs at Richfield Headquarters," *Minneapolis/St. Paul Business Journal* (online), February 26, 2013, http://www.bizjournals.com; Leslie A. Perlow and Erin L. Kelly, "Toward a Model of Work Redesign for Better Work and Better Life," *Work and Occupations* 41 (2014), pp. 111–34; Megan Lavey-Heaton, "Working from Home: How Yahoo, Best Buy and HP Are Making Moves," *The Guardian* (online), March 10, 2014, http://www.theguardian.com; Thomas Lee, "Best Buy Ends Flexible Work Program," *Minneapolis Star Tribune,* March 5, 2013, http://www.startribune.com; Lee Schafer, "Pitching In Is the New Rule at Best Buy," *Minneapolis Star Tribune,* February 16, 2013, http://www.startribune.com; Thomas Lee, David Shaffer, and Paul McEnroe, "Lost Empire: Can Best Buy Make a Comeback?" *Minneapolis Star Tribune,* March 25, 2013, http://www.startribune.com; Ann Zimmerman, "Can This Former Clerk Save Best Buy?" *The Wall Street Journal,* April 25, 2013; Joan E. Solsman, "Best Buy Increases Loyalty Rewards in Move to Spur Sales," *The Wall Street Journal,* April 3, 2013, http://online.wsj.com; Venessa Wong, "How Best Buy Has Changed Its Tune on Flexible Work," *Bloomberg Businessweek,* March 7, 2013, http://www.businessweek.com.

3. Steve Minter, "La-Z-Boy Never Rests on Continuous Improvement," *Industry Week,* January 2013, Business Insights: Essentials, http://bi.galegroup.com.

4. "BP Refinery Leaks Oil into Lake Michigan Near Chicago," *BBC News,* March 26, 2014, http://www.bbcnews.com; Tom Fowler, "BP Promotes a New Approach to Safety," *The Wall Street Journal,* February 13, 2013, http://blogs.wsj.com; Kjetil Malkenes Hovland, "Norway Orders BP Safety Review after Leak," *The Wall Street Journal,* April 29, 2013, http://online.wsj.com.

5. B. Plumer, "Here's All the Stuff That Supposedly Costs Us Billions in 'Lost Productivity,'" *The Washington Post* (online), July 6, 2013, http://www.washingtonpost.com.

6. W. G. Ouchi, "Markets, Bureaucracies, and Clans," *Administrative Science Quarterly* 25 (1980), pp. 129–41; R. Simons, A. Davila, and R. S. Kaplan, *Performance Measurement & Control Systems for Implementing Strategy* (Englewood Cliffs, NJ: Prentice Hall, 2000).

7. E. D. Pulakos, S. Arad, M. A. Donovan, and K. E. Plamondon, "Adaptability in the Workplace: Development of a Taxonomy of Adaptive Performance," *Journal of Applied Psychology* 85, no. 4 (August 2000), pp. 12–24; and K. A. Merchant and T. Sandino, "Four Options for Measuring Value Creation: Strategies for Managers to Avoid Potential Flaws in Accounting Measures of Performance," *Journal of Accountancy* 208, no. 2 (2009), pp. 34–38.

8. E. Gardner, "High-Quality Information," *Modern Healthcare,* March 5, 2007, General Reference Center Gold, http://find.galegroup.com; HealthPartners/Regions Hospital, "HealthPartners, Regions Partner to Prevent More than 380 Readmissions in 2012," news release, March 13, 2013, http://online.wsj.com.

9. "Why Measure What Matters?" *B Corporation* (online), May 22, 2015, http://www.bcorporation.net; Global Impact Investing Network, IRIS Metrics, https://iris.thegiin.org/metrics, accessed June 14, 2015; J. Anner, "Jessica Alba and the Impact of Social Enterprise," *Stanford Social Innovation Review* (online), September 26, 2014, http://www.ssireview.org; "When Measuring Social Impact, We Need to Move Beyond Counting," *Forbes* (online), July 15, 2013, http://www.forbes.com.

10. S. Ante and L. Weber, "Memo to Workers: The Boss Is Watching," *The Wall Street Journal* (online), October 22, 2013, http://www.wsj.com.

11. Julie Jargon, "McDonald's Tackles Repair of 'Broken' Service," *The Wall Street Journal,* April 10, 2013, http://online.wsj.com; Julie Jargon, "Your McDonald's Ordering Ritual Is About to Change," *The Wall Street Journal,* April 10, 2013, http://blogs.wsj.com; Martha C. White, "McDonald's Executive Says 'Service Is Broken,'" *NBC News,* April 12, 2013, http://www.nbcnews.com.

12. FedEx website, "Attributes Success to People-First Philosophy," http://www.fedex.com, accessed June 11, 2015.

13. Todd Henshaw, "Nano Tools for Leaders: After Action Reviews," *Wharton@Work,* April 2012, http://executiveeducation.wharton.upenn.edu; John Kello, "Upon Further Review: Benefits of Brief Post-Shift Huddles," *Industrial Safety & Hygiene News,* August 2012, p. 30; Stephen C. Harper, "Survival of the Swiftest," *Industrial Management,* January 2012, pp. 16–20.

14. B. Roberts, "Stay Ahead of the Technology Use Curve," *HR Magazine,* October 2008, Business & Company Resource Center, http://galenet.galegroup.com; and K. A. Carr, "Broaching Body Art," *Crain's Cleveland Business,* September 29, 2008, http://galenet.galegroup.com.

15. L. Howell, "Happy Valentine's Day! Please Sign This Love Contract Before You Go To Lunch . . ." *Austin HR,* February 17, 2014, http://www.austinhr.com; T. Hals, "Beware the Pitfalls of Office Romance," *Yahoo News,* February 13, 2007, http://news.yahoo.com; and M. Selvin, "'Love Contract'? It's Office Policy," *Los Angeles Times,* February 13, 2007, http://www.latimes.com.

16. Gary S. Kaplan, "Pursuing the Perfect Patient Experience," *Frontiers of Health Services Management,* Spring 2013, pp. 16–27. For an additional example in another type of organization, see David T. Goomas, Stuart M. Smith, and Timothy D. Ludwig, "Business Activity Monitoring: Real-Time Group Goals and Feedback Using an Overhead Scoreboard in a Distribution Center," *Journal of Organizational Behavior Management* 31 no. 3 (2011), pp. 196–209.

17. B. Miller, "Banish 'Annual' from Your Performance Review Vocabulary," *Entrepreneur* (online), October 10, 2014, http://www.entrepreneur.com; L. Barry, A. Erhardt-Lewis, S. Garr, and A. Liakopoulos, "Performance

Management Is Broken: Replace 'Rank and Yank' with Coaching and Development," Deloitte University Press, March 4, 2014, http://dupress.com/articles/hc-trends-2014-performance-management/; Deloitte, "Performance Management Is Broken," Global Human Capital Trends 2014: Engaging the 21st Century Workforce, http://www2.deloitte.com; J. Bersin, "Time to Scrap Performance Appraisal," *Forbes* (online), May 6, 2013, http://www.forbes.com.

18. M. Kownatzki, J. Walter, S. Floyd, and C. Lechner, "Corporate Control and the Speed of Strategic Business Unit Decision Making," *Academy of Management Journal* 56 (2013), pp. 1295–1324; V. U. Druskat, "Effects and Timing of Developmental Peer Appraisals in Self-Managing Work Groups," *Journal of Applied Psychology* 84, no. 1 (February 1999), p. 58; Baard Kuvaas, "The Interactive Role of Performance Appraisal Reactions and Regular Feedback," *Journal of Managerial Psychology* 26 no. 2 (2011), pp. 123–37.

19. PricewaterhouseCoopers, "2014 State of the Internal Audit Profession Study," March 2014, http://www.pwc.com; "Business Analytics: Numbers and Nuance," *CIO Insight*, January 12, 2011, Business & Company Resource Center, http://galenet.galegroup.com.

20. S. Waddock and N. Smith, "Corporate Responsibility Audits: Doing Well by Doing Good," *Sloan Management Review* 41, no. 2 (Winter 2000), pp. 75–83; L. L. Bergeson, "OSHA Gives Incentives for Voluntary Self-Audits," *Pollution Engineering* 32, no. 10 (October 2000), pp. 33–34; Scott M. Shafer and Sara B. Moeller, "The Effects of Six Sigma on Corporate Performance: An Empirical Investigation," *Journal of Operations Management* 30, no. 7–8 (November 1, 2012) pp. 521–32.

21. S. Aghili, "A Six Sigma Approach to Internal Audits," *Strategic Finance*, February 2009, Business & Company Resource Center, http://galenet. galegroup. com.

22. See, for example, Ryan Huang, "Six Sigma 'Killed' Innovation in 3M," *ZD Net* (online), March 14, 2013, http://www.zdnet.com; S. Chakravorty, "Where Process-Improvement Projects Go Wrong," *The Wall Street Journal* (online), January 25, 2010, http://www.wsj.com.

23. "Unlocking the Strategic Value of Internal Audit," Ernst & Young/Forbes Insight (2010), http://www.forbes.com; T. Rancour and M. McCracken, "Applying 6 Sigma Methods for Breakthrough Safety Performance," *Professional Safety* 45, no. 10 (October 2000), pp. 29–32; and G. Eckes, "Making Six Sigma Last," *Ivey Business Journal*, January–February 2002, p. 77.

24. J. L. Colbert, "The Impact of the New External Auditing Standards," *Internal Auditor* 5, no. 6 (December 2000), pp. 46–50.

25. Aghili, "A Six Sigma Approach"; Y. Giard and Y. Nadeau, "Improving the Processes," *CA Magazine,* December 2008, Business & Company Resource Center, http://galenet.galegroup.com; and G. Cheney, "Connecting the Dots to the Next Crisis," *Financial Executive,* April 2009, pp. 30–33.

26. J. D. Glater, "The Better the Audit Panel, the Higher the Stock Price," *The New York Times,* April 8, 2005, p. C4; and M. Alic and B. Rusjan, "Contribution of the ISO 9001 Internal Audit to Business Performance," *International Journal of Quality and Reliability Management* 27, no. 8 (2010), pp. 916–37.

27. Coca-Cola, "Hours of Work Improvement Guide," 2010, http://www.cocacola.com.

28. Jan Tullberg, "Triple Bottom Line—a Vaulting Ambition?" *Business Ethics: A European Review* 21 no. 3 (June 2012), pp. 310–24; Grant Davis, "The Triple Bottom Line Goal of Sustainable Businesses," *Entrepreneur,* April 24, 2013, http://www.entrepreneur.com; Rebecca Coons, "Corporate Social Responsibility: Pursuing the Triple Bottom Line," *IHS Chemical Week,* May 27–June 3, 2013, pp. 21–23.

29. Pam Schuneman, "Master the 'ABCs' of Activity-Based Costing," *Managed Care,* May 1997, http://www.managedcaremag.com; Ivana Drazic Lutilsky and Martina Dragija, "Activity Based Costing as a Means to Full Costing: Possibilities and Constraints for European Universities," *Management* 17 no. 1 (June 2012), pp. 33–57.

30. J. Farre-Mensa, "Managerial Myopia: Why Public Companies Underinvest in the Future," *Forbes* (online), February 3, 2013, http://www.forbes.com; K. Merchant, *Control in Business Organizations* (Boston: Pitman, 1985); and C. W. Chow, Y. Kato, and K. A. Merchant, "The Use of Organizational Controls and Their Effects on Data Manipulation and Management Myopia," *Accounting, Organizations, and Society* 21, nos. 2/3 (February/April 1996), pp. 175–92.

31. Lee, "Best Buy Ends Flexible Work Program"; Schafer, "Pitching In Is the New Rule"; Lee et al., "Lost Empire"; Larry Downes, "Why Best Buy Is Going out of Business . . . Gradually," *Forbes,* January 2, 2012; Zimmerman, "Can This Former Clerk Save Best Buy?"; Matthew Rocco, "Best Buy Cuts Headcount at HQ by 400," *Fox Business,* February 26, 2013, http://www.foxbusiness.com; Solsman, "Best Buy Increases Loyalty Rewards"; N. Halter, "Best Buy Plans to Trim $400 Million After Cutting $1 Billion, CEO Says," *Biz Journals* (online), March 3, 2015, http://www.bizjournals.com; N. Bose and S. Ramakrishnan, "Best Buy Announces First Buyback Since 2012, Profit Jumps," Reuters (online), March 3, 2015, http://www.reuters.com; E. Stych, "Best Buy Cutting 400 Jobs at Richfield Headquarters," *Biz Journals* (online),

February 26, 2013, http://www.bizjournals.com; Drew Fitzgerald, "Best Buy Posts Loss as Revenue Falls," *The Wall Street Journal,* May 21, 2013, http://online.wsj.com; Best Buy, "Best Buy Reports Better-than-Expected First Quarter Results," news release, May 21, 2013, http://phx.corporate-ir.net; Best Buy, "Best Buy Reports Fourth Quarter and Fiscal Year Results," news release, March 1, 2013, http://phx.corporate-ir.net.

32. E. E. Lawler III and J. Rhode, *Information and Control in Organizations* (Pacific Palisades, CA: Goodyear, 1976); A. Ferner, "The Underpinnings of 'Bureaucratic' Control Systems: HRM in European Multinationals," *Journal of Management Studies* 37, no. 4 (June 2000), pp. 521–39; and M. S. Fenwick, "Cultural and Bureaucratic Control in MNEs: The Role of Expatriate Performance Management," *Management International Review* 39 (1999), pp. 107–25.

33. Hindo, "At 3M, a Struggle between Efficiency and Creativity." See also Jason J. Dahling, Samantha L. Chau, and Alison O'Malley, "Correlates and Consequences of Feedback Orientation in Organizations," *Journal of Management* 38 no. 2 (2012), pp. 531–46.

34. S. Terlep, "GM's Latest Change Agent Tackles Designs, Red Tape," *The Wall Street Journal,* June 15, 2011, http://online.wsj.com.

35. J. Veiga and J. Yanouzas, *The Dynamics of Organization Theory,* 2nd ed. (St. Paul, MN: West, 1984).

36. K. Zezima, "Everything You Need to Know About the VA—and the Scandals Engulfing It," *The Washington Post* (online), May 30, 2014, http://www.washingtonpost.com.

37. Ibid.

38. Ibid.

39. C. Devine, "Bad VA Care May Have Killed More than 1,000 Veterans, Senator's Report Says," CNN (online), June 24, 2014, http://www.cnn.com.

40. M. Gelbart, "L&I Gets Ritz-Carlton Image Tips," *Philadelphia Inquirer,* March 10, 2009, http://www.philly.com.

41. D. Vater, Y. Cho, and P. Sidebottom, "The Digital Challenge to Retail Banks," Bain & Company, 2012, http://www.bain.com.

42. M. Hammer, "The Seven Deadly Sins of Performance Measurement and How to Avoid Them," *MIT Sloan Management Review* 48, no. 3 (Spring 2007), pp. 19–28.

43. Lawler and Rhode, *Information and Control in Organizations;* and J. A. Gowan Jr. and R. G. Mathieu, "Critical Factors in Information System Development for a Flexible Manufacturing System," *Computers in Industry* 28, no. 3 (June 1996), pp. 173–83.

44. Adrienne Selko, "Ethicon: Employee Engagement Results in Zero Product Recalls," *Industry Week,* January 17, 2013, http://www.industryweek.com.

45. R. S. Kaplan and D. P. Norton, *The Balanced Scorecard: Translating Strategy*

into Action (Boston: Harvard Business School Press, 1996); and Z. Hoque, "20 Years of Studies on the Balanced Scorecard: Trends, Accomplishments, Gaps and Opportunities for Future Research," *The British Accounting Review,* March 2014, pp. 33–59.

46. "National Marrow Donor Program (NMDP) Case Study," Balanced Scorecard Institute, http://www.theinstitutepress. com, accessed June 12, 2015; National Marrow Donor Program and Be The Match, "Key Messages, Facts & Figures," http://www.bethematch.org, accessed June 12, 2015.

47. R. Myers, "Going Away," *CFO,* May 2007, General Reference Center Gold, http://find. galegroup.com.

48. K. Moores and J. Mula, "The Salience of Market, Bureaucratic, and Clan Controls in the Management of Family Firm Transitions: Some Tentative Australian Evidence," *Family Business Review* 13, no. 2 (June 2000), pp. 91–106; and A. Walker and R. Newcombe, "The Positive Use of Power on a Major Construction Project," *Construction Management and Economics* 18, no. 1 (January/February 2000), pp. 37–44.

49. P. H. Fuchs, K. E. Mifflin, D. Miller, and J. O. Whitney, "Strategic Integration: Competing in the Age of Capabilities," *California Management Review* 42, no. 3 (Spring 2000), pp. 118–47; M. A. Lando, "Making Compliance Part of Your Organization's Culture," *Healthcare Executive* 15, no. 5 (September/October 1999), pp. 18–22; K. A. Frank and K. Fahrbach, "Organization Culture as a Complex System: Balance and Information in Models of Influence and Selection," *Organization Science* 10, no. 3 (May/June 1999), pp. 253–77; Serge A. Rijsdijk and Jan van den Ende, "Control Combinations in New Product Development Projects," *Journal of Product Innovation Management* 28 no. 6 (November 2011), pp. 868–80.

50. "100 Best Companies to Work For, 2009," *Fortune,* February 2, 2009, http://money. cnn.com.

51. Halter, "Best Buy Plans to Trim $400 Million After Cutting $1 Billion, CEO Says,"; Bose and Ramakrishnan, "Best Buy Announces First Buyback Since 2012, Profit Jumps,"; Stych, "Best Buy Cutting 400 Jobs at Richfield Headquarters"; Lee, "Best Buy Ends Flexible Work Program"; Schafer, "Pitching In Is the New Rule"; Lee et al., "Lost Empire"; Wong, "How Best Buy Has Changed Its Tune"; Thomas Lee, "Best Buy's CEO Hubert Joly Shines at His First Annual Meeting," *Minneapolis Star Tribune,* June 21, 2013, http://www. startribune.com; Hubert Joly, "Best Buy CEO on Leadership," *Minneapolis Star Tribune,* March 17, 2013, http://www. startribune.com; Jody Thompson, "ROWE Creators Set the Record Straight: Best Buy CEO Doesn't Understand ROWE," *Cali*

and Jody Blog (CultureRx), March 18, 2013, http://www.gorowe.com.

Chapter 17

1. J. Stoll and M. Ramsey, "Tesla First-Quarter Car Deliveries Rise Above 10,000," *The Wall Street Journal* (online), April 3, 2015, http://www.wsj.com; J. Lippert, "Will Tesla Ever Make Money?" *Bloomberg Business* (online), March 3, 2015, http://www.bloombergbusiness.com; Michael Levi, "How Tesla Pulled ahead of the Electric-Car Pack," *The Wall Street Journal,* June 20, 2013, http://online.wsj. com; Ashlee Vance, "Elon Musk, Man of Tomorrow," *Bloomberg Businessweek,* September 17, 2012, *EBSCOhost,* http:// web.ebscohost.com; Tesla Motors, "Model S Innovations: Technology," http://www. teslamotors.com; George Blankenship, "Inside Tesla," *Tesla Motors blog,* March 21, 2013, http://www.teslamotors.com; "General Electric Motors," *The Economist,* April 20, 2013, http://www.economist. com; Angus MacKenzie, "2013 Motor Trend Car of the Year: Tesla Model S," *Motor Trend,* January 2013, http://www. motortrend.com; Jason Cammisa, "Return to Power: The 2013 Tesla Model S," *Road & Track,* February 25, 2013, http://www. roadandtrack.com; Peter Valdes-Dapena, "Tesla: Consumer Reports' Best Car Ever Tested," *CNNMoney,* May 9, 2013, http:// money.cnn.com; and Mike Ramsey, "Tesla Motors Approaches Crossroad," *The Wall Street Journal,* February 10, 2013, http:// online.wsj.com.

2. B. Meyerson, "Top 10 Emerging Technologies of 2015," *Scientific American* (online), March 4, 2015, http:// www.scientificamerican.com; "Customer Service Robots to Roam the Aisles at Lowe's," *CBS News* (online), October 28, 2014, http://www.cbsnews.com.

3. R. A. Burgelman, M. A. Maidique, and S. C. Wheelwright, *Strategic Management of Technology and Innovation* (New York: McGraw-Hill, 2000); Panagiotis Ganotakis and James H. Love, "The Innovation Value Chain in New Technology-Based Firms," *Journal of Product Innovation Management* 29, no. 5 (September 2012), pp. 839–60.

4. D. C. L. Prestwood and P. A. Schumann Jr., "Revitalize Your Organization," *Executive Excellence* 15, no. 2 (February 1998), p. 16; C. Y. Baldwin and K. B. Clark, "Managing in an Age of Modularity," *Harvard Business Review* 75, no. 5 (September–October 1997), pp. 84–93; S. Gopalakrishnan, P. Bierly, and E. H. Kessler, "A Reexamination of Product and Process Innovations Using a Knowledge-Based View," *Journal of High Technology Management Research* 10, no. 1 (Spring 1999), pp. 147–66; J. Pullin, "Bombardier Commands Top Marks," *Professional Engineering* 13, no. 3 (July 5, 2000), pp. 40–46; M. Johnson, C. Christensen, and H. Kagermann, "Reinventing Your Business Model,"

Harvard Business Review (December 2008), pp. 50–59; C. M. Christensen, *The Innovator's Dilemma* (Boston: Harvard Business Publishing, 1997); and C. M. Christensen, S. D. Anthony, and E. A. Roth, *Seeing What's Next* (Boston: Harvard Business Publishing, 2004).

5. S. Biffi, "The Technological Transformation of Social Enterprise," *The Guardian* (online), January 29, 2015, http://www.theguardian.com; "Singularity University Announces Google Support for Increased Global Access and Diversity in Tech," *PR Newswire,* January 28, 2015, http://www.prnewswire. com; R. Norton-Taylor, "Dramatic Cut in Landmine Victims," *The Guardian* (online), December 3, 2012, http://www. theguardian.com; Bibak website, "What We Do," http://www.bibak.org, accessed June 18, 2015; International Campaign to Ban Landmines website, "Why Are Landmines Still a Problem?" http://www. icbl.org, accessed June 18, 2015.

6. M. Sawhney, R. C. Wolcott, and I. Arroniz, "The 12 Different Ways for Companies to Innovate," *MIT Sloan Management Review* 47, no. 3 (Spring 2006), pp. 75–81; Julian Birkinshaw, Gary Hamel, and Michael J. Mol, "Management Innovation," *Academy of Management Review* 33 (October 2008), pp. 825–45.

7. G. P. Pisano, *The Development Factory: Unlocking the Potential of Process Innovation* (Boston: Harvard Business School Press, 1996); and R. Leifer, C. M. McDermott, G. C. O'Connor, L. S. Peters, M. Rice, and R. W. Veryzer, *Radical Innovation: How Mature Companies Can Outsmart Upstarts* (Cambridge MA: Harvard Business School Press, 2000).

8. H. M. O'Neill, R. W. Pounder, and A. K. Buchholtz, "Patterns in the Diffusion of Strategies across Organizations: Insights from the Innovation, Diffusion Literature," *Academy of Management Review* 23, no. 1 (January 1998), pp. 98–114; E. M. Rogers, *Diffusion of Innovations* (New York: Free Press, 1995); and B. Guilhon, ed., *Technology and Markets for Knowledge: Knowledge Creation, Diffusion and Exchange within a Growing Economy,* Economics of Science, Technology and Innovation 22 (Dordrecht, Netherlands: Kluwer Academic Publishing, 2000).

9. S. Poser, "Trends in the Workplace: Gamification in the Enterprise," *Oracle Blogs,* May 18, 2015, http://blogs.oracle. com; J. Meister, "Future of Work: Using Gamification for Human Resources," *Forbes* (online), March 30, 2015, http:// www.forbes.com; A. Adkins, "Majority of U.S. Employees Not Engaged Despite Gains in 2014," Gallup (online), http:// www.gallup.com, January 28, 2015; Badgeville website, "Case Study: Deloitte," http://www.badgeville.com, accessed June 19, 2015; "Gamifying Business to Drive Employee Engagement and Performance," *Cognizant Reports,* September 2013, http:// www.cognizant.com.

10. M. E. Porter, *Competitive Strategy* (New York: Free Press, 1980).

11. Christensen, Anthony, and Roth, *Seeing What's Next;* Clayton Christensen, "Key Concepts: Disruptive Innovation," http://www.claytonchristensen.com; Innosight, "Expertise: Driving New Growth through Disruptive Innovation," http://www.innosight.com; Matthew Yglesias, "Stop 'Disrupting' Everything," *Slate,* May 1, 2013, http://www.slate.com.

12. S. A. Zahra, S. Nash, and D. J. Bickford, "Transforming Technological Pioneering in Competitive Advantage," *Academy of Management Executive* 9, no. 1 (1995), pp. 17–31; and M. Sadowski and A. Roth, "Technology Leadership Can Pay Off," *Research Technology Management* 42, no. 6 (November/December 1999), pp. 32–33.

13. L. Luk, "Apple Plans Force of Touch Technology for New iPhones," *The Wall Street Journal* (online), March 11, 2015, http://www.wsj.com.

14. J. Hodgson, "AstraZeneca Settles Suit, Protecting Crestor," *The Wall Street Journal* (online), March 25, 2013, http://www.wsj.com.

15. C. Trudell, Y. Hagiwara, and J. Ma, "Humans Replacing Robots Herald Toyota's Vision of Future," *Bloomberg Business* (online), April 7, 2014, http://www.bloomberg.com; M. Imai and G. Kaizen, *A Commonsense, Low-Cost Approach to Management* (New York: McGraw-Hill, 1997); and M. Imai and G. Kaizen, *The Key to Japan's Competitive Success* (New York: McGraw-Hill, 1986).

16. D. Lazarus, "An Insider's View of Generic-Drug Pricing," *Los Angeles Times* (online), March 25, 2013, http://www.latimes.com; M. Hiltzik, "How Big Pharma Distorts the Costs of Developing New Drugs," *Los Angeles Times,* April 3, 2011, http://articles.latimes.com; "Brand Drugs Soar as Generics Rise," *Journal of Nursing,* April 1, 2011, http://www.asrn.org; and J. J. Castellani, "The Role of Innovation in Addressing Global Health," remarks from the Undersecretary for Economic, Energy and Agricultural Affairs, U.S. Department of State, March 17, 2011, http://www.state.gov.

17. See Matthew Semadeni and Brian S. Anderson, "The Follower's Dilemma: Innovation and Imitation in the Professional Services Industry," *Academy of Management Journal* 53 (October 2010), pp. 1175–1193.

18. P. A. Geroski, "Models of Technology Diffusion," *Research Policy* 29, no. 4/5 (April 2000), pp. 603–25; and L. A. Thomas, "Adoption Order of New Technologies in Evolving Markets," *Journal of Economic Behavior & Organization* 38, no. 4 (April 1999), pp. 453–82.

19. A. Kellerman and S. Jones, "What It Will Take to Achieve the As-Yet-Unfulfilled Promises of Health Information Technology," *Health Affairs* 32 (January 2013), pp. 63–68; B. Japsen, "Despite Huge Investments in Electronic Health Records, Cost Savings Still Elusive," *Forbes* (online), January 7, 2013, http://www.forbes.com.

20. R. E. Oligney and M. I. Economides, "Technology as an Asset," *Hart's Petroleum Engineer International* 71, no. 9 (September 1998), p. 27; C. MacKechnie, "What Are the Types of Business Techology," *Chron* (online), http://smallbusiness.chron.com, accessed on June 15, 2014; and J. Manyika, M. Chul, J. Bughin, R. Dobbs, P. Bisson, and A. Marrs, "Disruptive Technologies: Advances That Will Transform Life, Business, and the Global Economy," *McKinsey & Company Report,* May 2013, http://www.mckinsey.com.

21. B. Meyerson, "Top 10 Emerging Technologies of 2015," *World Economic Forum,* March 4, 2015, https://agenda.weforum.org/2015/03/top-10-emerging-technologies-of-2015-2/

22. Ameet Sachdev, "Bewitched by Baxter: Robot Draws Admirers," *Chicago Tribune,* January 22, 2013, sec. 2, pp. 1–3.

23. M. O'Connor, "Can RFID Save Brick-and-Mortar Retailers After All?" *Fortune* (online), April 16, 2014, http://www.fortune.com; M. Bustillo, "Wal-Mart Radio Tags to Track Clothing," *The Wall Street Journal,* July 23, 2010, http://online.wsj.com; "RFID: Challenges and Opportunities," *MoreRFID,* June 30, 2011, http://www.morerfid.com; and D. Steinberg, "The $25 Billion Art Move," *The Wall Street Journal,* June 24, 2011, http://online.wsj.com.

24. E. Brown, "Performance of Facial Recognition Software Continues to Improve," National Institute of Standards and Technology's *Tech Beat* (online), June 3, 2014, http://www.nist.gov; "Not Dead Yet? Maybe Face Recognition Just Needs Repurposing," *Security Director's Report,* June 2011, pp. 2–5.

25. General Electric, "GE Cooling Technology, as Thin as a Credit Card, Enables Ultra-Thin Tablets, Laptops," news release, December 11, 2012, http://www.genewscenter.com.

26. Clint Boulton, "Printing Out Barbies and Ford Cylinders," *The Wall Street Journal,* June 5, 2013, http://online.wsj.com; Elizabeth Royte, "The Printed World," *Smithsonian,* May 2013, pp. 50–57.

27. McDonald's, "Types of Systems McDonald's Uses," January 22, 2012, http://mcdonaldmis.blogspot.com/2012/01/types-of-systems-mcdonalds-use.html; M. Kanellos, "For Fast-Food Help, Call in the Robots," *CNet News,* March 26, 2007, http://news.com.com.

28. "CBP, ICE HSI Report $1.2 Billion in Counterfeit Seizures in 2014," U.S. Customs and Border Protection, April 2, 2015, http://www.cbd.gov; J. Jusko, "Foiling Fakes," *Industry Week,* May 2007, General Reference Center Gold, http://find.galegroup.com.

29. Lynda Aiman-Smith and Stephen G. Green, "Implementing a New Manufacturing Technology: The Related Effects of Technology Characteristics and User Learning Activities," *Academy of Management Journal* 45 (April 2002), pp. 421–30; Deloitte, "2015 Global Life Sciences Outlook: Adapting in an Era of Transformation," http://www2.deloitte.com, accessed June 17, 2015.

30. "Fresh, but Far from Easy," *The Economist,* June 23, 2007, General Reference Center Gold, http://find.galegroup.com.

31. R. Reinhardt and S. Gurtner, "Differences Between Early Adopters of Disruptive and Sustaining Innovations," *Journal of Business Research* 68 (2015), pp. 137–45; R. Dewan, B. Jing, and A. Seidmann, "Adoption of Internet-Based Product Customization and Pricing Strategies," *Journal of Management Information Systems* 17, no. 2 (Fall 2000), pp. 9–28; P. A. Geroski, "Models of Technology Diffusion," *Research Policy* 29, no. 4/5 (April 2000), pp. 603–25; Rogers, *Diffusion of Innovations.*

32. Stoll and Ramsey, "Tesla First-Quarter Car Deliveries Rise Above 10,000"; Lippert, "Will Tesla Ever Make Money?"; Levi, "How Tesla Pulled Ahead"; Vance, "Elon Musk, Man of Tomorrow"; Blankenship, "Inside Tesla"; *The Economist,* "General Electric Motors"; MacKenzie, "2013 Motor Trend Car of the Year"; Cammisa, "Return to Power"; Valdes-Dapena, "Tesla: Consumer Reports' Best Car"; Ramsey, "Tesla Motors Approaches Crossroad"; Tesla Motors, "Supercharger," http://www.teslamotors.com; Ina Fried, "Musk: Mainstream Tesla Model 3–4 Years Out, Will Be 20 Percent Smaller than Model S," *All Things D,* May 29, 2013, http://allthingsd.com; Mike Ramsey and Tess Stynes, "Tesla Sees First-Ever Quarterly Profit," *The Wall Street Journal,* April 1, 2013, http://online.wsj.com; Mike Ramsey and Valerie Bauerlein, "Tesla Clashes with Car Dealers," *The Wall Street Journal,* June 18, 2013, http://online.wsj.com; Joseph B. White, "Tesla Has a Fresh $1 Billion—and Lots of Ways to Spend It," *The Wall Street Journal,* May 17, 2013, http://blogs.wsj.com.

33. E. Von Hippel, *The Sources of Innovation* (Oxford, UK: Oxford University Press, 1994); D. Leonard, *Wellsprings of Knowledge: Building and Sustaining the Sources of Innovation* (Cambridge, MA: Harvard Business School Press, 1998); and Melissa E. Graebner, Kathleen M. Eisenhardt, and Philip T. Roundy, "Success and Failure in Technology Acquisitions: Lessons for Buyers and Sellers," *Academy of Management Perspectives* 24, no. 3 (August 2010), pp. 73–92.

34. N. Clayton, "Israel at Center of Intel Empire," *The Wall Street Journal Tech Europe* (online), March 19, 2012, http://blogs.wsj.com; T. Krazit, "Intel R&D on

Slow Boat to China," *CNet News,* April 16, 2007, http://news.com.

35. "How the Unreal Engine Became a Real Gaming Powerhouse," *Popular Mechanics* (online), June 24, 2014, http://www. popularmechanics.com; "Online Gaming's Netscape Moment?" *The Economist,* June 9, 2007, http://find.galegroup.com.

36. B. Austen, "Bringing the Coffin Industry Back from the Dead," *The Atlantic* (online), December 2010, http://www. theatlantic.com.

37. Von Hippel, *The Sources of Innovation;* and Leonard, *Wellsprings of Knowledge.*

38. J. Hagedoorn, A. N. Link, and N. S. Vonortas, "Research Partnerships," *Research Policy* 29, no. 4/5 (April 2000), pp. 567–86; S.-S. Yi, "Entry, Licensing and Research Joint Ventures," *International Journal of Industrial Organization* 17, no. 1 (January 1999), pp. 1–24; Satish Nambisan and Mohanbir Sawhney, "Orchestration Processes in Network-Centric Innovation: Evidence from the Field," *Academy of Management Perspectives* 25 (August 2011), pp. 40–57; Ulrich Lichtenthaler, "Open Innovation: Past Research, Current Debates, and Future Directions," *Academy of Management Perspectives* 25 (February 2011), pp. 75–93; Esteve Almirall and Ramon Casadesus-Masanell, "Open versus Closed Innovation: A Model of Discovery and Divergence," *Academy of Management Review* 35 (January 2010), pp. 27–47; Corey C. Phelps, "A Longitudinal Study of the Influence of Alliance Network Structure and Composition on Firm Exploratory Innovation," *Academy of Management Journal* 53 (August 2010), pp. 890–913.

39. A. Ward and P. Waldmeir, "Chi-Med Draws on the Past for the Future," *Financial Times* (online), August 25, 2014, http://www.ft.com; Nestlé website, "New Partnership Gives Nestlé Health Science Access to One of the World's Leading Traditional Chinese Medicine Libraries," press release, November 28, 2012, http:// www.nestle.com.

40. Chris Dieterich, "Facebook, Google Lead Private Tech Acquisitions," *MarketWatch,* February 12, 2013, http://www.marketwatch. com; Sarah Perez, "Twitter Acquires Big Data Visualization Startup Luck Sort, Service to Shutter in Months Ahead," *TechCrunch,* May 13, 2013, http:// techcrunch.com; Keach Hagey, "Twitter Cozies Up to Television with New Ad Products," *The Wall Street Journal,* May 23, 2013, http://blogs.wsj.com.

41. P. Arandjelovic, L. Bulin, and N. Khan, "Why CIOs Should Be Business-Strategy Partners," *McKinsey Insights and Publications* (online), February 2015, http://www.mckinsey.com; T. Hoffman, "Change Agents," *ComputerWorld,* April 23, 2007, General Reference Center Gold, http://find.galegroup.com; Center for CIO Leadership, "Center for CIO Leadership Unveils 2008 Survey Results," news release, November 18, 2008, http:// www.marketwire.com; Center for CIO

Leadership, "CIO Leadership Survey Executive Summary," abstract, 2008, http://www.cioleadershipcenter.com; and G. H. Anthes, "The CIO/ CTO Balancing Act," *ComputerWorld* 34, no. 25 (June 19, 2000), pp. 50–51.

42. "Information Resources: The Evolution of R&D," *Research-Technology Management,* May–June 2011, pp. 65–66; and J. C. Spender and B. Strong, "Who Has Innovative Ideas? Employees," *The Wall Street Journal,* August 23, 2010, http:// online.wsj.com.

43. D. L. Day, "Raising Radicals: Different Processes for Championing Innovative Corporate Ventures," *Organization Science* 5, no. 2 (May 1994), pp. 148–72; C. Siporin, "Want Speedy FDA Approval? Hire a 'Product Champion,'" *Medical Marketing & Media,* October 1993, pp. 22–28; C. Siporin, "How You Can Capitalize on Phase 3B," *Medical Marketing & Media,* October 1994, pp. 72–72; and E. H. Kessler, "Tightening the Belt: Methods for Reducing Development Costs Associated with New Product Innovation," *Journal of Engineering and Technology Management* 17, no. 1 (March 2000), pp. 59–92.

44. J. P. Andrew, K. Haanæs, D. C. Michael, H. L. Sirkin, and A. Taylor, *Innovation 2009: Making Hard Decisions in the Downturn,* Boston Consulting Group Senior Management Survey, http://www. bcg.com.

45. J. G. March, "Exploration and Exploitation in Organizational Learning," *Organization Science* 2, no. 1 (1991), pp. 71–87; and S. C. Kang and S. A. Snell, "Intellectual Capital Architectures and Ambidextrous Learning: A Framework for Human Resource Management," *Journal of Management Studies* 46, no. 1 (2009), pp. 65–92.

46. Jeff DeGraff, "Why the 'Most Innovative Companies' Aren't," *Fortune,* March 13, 2013, http://management.fortune.com; Henry Chesbrough, "Why Bad Things Happen to Good Technology," *The Wall Street Journal,* June 19, 2012, http://online. wsj.com; Steven Levy, "Google's Larry Page on Why Moon Shots Matter," *Wired,* January 17, 2013, http://www.wired.com.

47. D. A. Fields, "How to Stop the Dumbing Down of Your Company," *Industry Week,* March 7, 2007, http://www.industryweek. com; L. K. Gundry, J. R. Kickul, and C. W. Prather, "Building the Creative Organization," *Organizational Dynamics* 22, no. 2 (Spring 1994), pp. 22–36; and T. Kuczmarski, "Inspiring and Implementing the Innovation Mind-Set," *Planning Review,* September–October 1994, pp. 37–48.

48. L. Buchanan, "Why Creativity Is like Karaoke," *Inc.* (online), October 2013, http://www.inc.com.

49. Steve Minter, "Priming the Supply Chain of Ideas," *Industry Week,* February 2013, Business Insights: Essentials, http:// bi.galegroup.com.

50. Talent Management Exchange, "Speaker Information," http://www. talentmanagementexchange.com, accessed June 18, 2015.

51. Intuit Labs, "How We Do It," http://www. intuitlabs.com/about/, accessed June 18, 2015; D. Tsuruoka, "Intuit Innovation Lab, 'Idea Jams' Aim to Spur Creativity," *Investor's Business Daily,* April 14, 2009, Business & Company Resource Center, http://galenet.galegroup.com.

52. Leonard, *Wellsprings of Knowledge;* D. Leonard-Barton, "The Factory as a Learning Laboratory," *Sloan Management Review,* Fall 1992, pp. 23–38; and A. K. Gupta and V. Govindarajan, "Knowledge Management's Social Dimension: Lessons from Nucor Steel," *Sloan Management Review* 42, no. 1 (Fall 2000), pp. 71–80.

53. T. Brown, "Design Thinking," *Harvard Business Review* 86, no. 6 (June 2008), pp. 84–92.

54. M. Korn and R. Silverman, "Business Education: Forget B-School, D-School Is Hot," *The Wall Street Journal* (online), June 7, 2012, http://www.wsj.com.

55. IDEO website, "About Ideo," http://www. ideo.com, accessed July 5, 2015.

56. Korn and Silverman, "Business Education."

57. Brown, "Design Thinking."

58. J. Liedtka and T. Ogilvie, *Designing for Growth: A Design Thinking Tool Kit for Managers* (New York: Columbia Business School Publishing, 2011).

59. Brown, "Design Thinking."

60. H. K. Bowen, K. B. Clark, C. A. Holloway, and S. C. Wheelwright, "Development Projects: The Engine of Renewal," *Harvard Business Review,* September–October 1994, pp. 110–20; C. Eden, T. Williams, and F. Ackermann, "Dismantling the Learning Curve: The Role of Disruptions on the Planning of Development Projects," *International Journal of Project Management* 16, no. 3 (June 1998), pp. 131–38; and M. V. Tatikonda and S. R. Rosenthal, "Technology Novelty, Project Complexity, and Product Development Project Execution Success: A Deeper Look at Task Uncertainty in Product Innovation," *IEEE Transactions on Engineering Management* 47, no. 1 (February 2000), pp. 74–87.

61. E. Trist, "The Evolution of Sociotechnical Systems as a Conceptual Framework and as an Action Research Program," in *Perspectives on Organizational Design and Behavior,* ed. A. Van de Ven and W. F. Joyce (New York: John Wiley & Sons, 1981), pp. 19–75; and A. Molina, "Insights into the Nature of Technology Diffusion and Implementation: The Perspective of Sociotechnical Alignment," *Technovation* 17, nos. 11/12 (November/December 1997), pp. 601–26.

62. Lynda Aiman-Smith and Stephen G. Green, "Implementing New Manufacturing Technology: The Related Effects of Technology Characteristics and User Learning Activities," *Academy of Management Journal* 45 (April 2002),

pp. 421–30; Terri L. Griffith, "Technology Features as Triggers for Sensemaking," *Academy of Management Review* 24 (July 1999), pp. 472–88.

63. Levi, "How Tesla Pulled Ahead"; Vance, "Elon Musk, Man of Tomorrow"; *The Economist,* "General Electric Motors"; White, "Tesla Has a Fresh $1 Billion"; Tesla, "Tesla's Gigafactory," http://www. teslamotors.com/gigafactory, accessed June 18, 2015; "Tesla Takes Big Bite of Apple's Staff with Over 150 Total Poaches," *Entrepreneur* (online), February 9, 2015, http://www.entrepreneur.com; Ben Rooney, "Tesla Shares Pop on $100 Million Toyota Deal," *CNNMoney,* July 20, 2011, http:// money.cnn.com; David Herron, "Tesla's Technology inside the Mercedes-Benz BClass Electric Drive," *Long Tail Pipe,* March 27, 2013, http://www.longtailpipe. com; Dana Hull, "Tesla Gears Up to Hire Manufacturing Workers," *Los Angeles Times,* January 17, 2012, http://articles. latimes.com.

Appendix D

1. R. M. Pirsig, *Zen and the Art of Motorcycle Maintenance* (New York: William Morrow and Company, 1974).
2. P. Raichur, *Absolute Beauty* (New York: HarperPerennial, 1986).
3. Nescafé: Nestlé (verified by T. Haywood via 1/16/01 e-mail that Nescafé and Nesquik flavors are modified for the market in which they are sold).
4. T. J. Mullaney and R. D. Hof, "Information Technology Annual Report," *BusinessWeek Online,* June 24, 2002.
5. J. Stinson, "Password protected: States pass anti-snooping laws," *USA Today* (online), July 8, 2014, http://www. usatoday.com; S. Sengupta, "No U.S. Action, So States Move on Privacy Law," *The New York Times* (online), October 30, 2013, http://www.nytimes.com.

Chapter 18

1. D. Joling, "Shell Heads for Alaska While Awaiting Final Drilling Permits Anchorage, Alaska," *ABC News* (online), June 26, 2015, http://www.abcnews.com; United Nations Conference on Climate Change website, "What Is a Cop?" http:// www.cop21.gouv.fr/en/cop21-cmp11/ what-cop, accessed June 25, 2015; "Shell Can't Afford to Wait Until 2050 to Adapt Its Business to Climate Change," *The Conversation* (online), May 26, 2015, http://www.theconversation.com; S. Farrell, "Climate Change Dominates Marathon Shell Annual General Meeting," *The Guardian* (online), May 19, 2015, http://www.theguardian.com; "The Elephant in the Atmosphere," *The Economist* (online), July 19, 2014, http:// www.economist.com.
2. V. Bruno and H. Shin, "Globalization of Corporate Risk Taking," *Journal of International Business Studies* 45 (2014),

pp. 800–20; M. Reeves and M. Deimler, "Adaptability: The New Competitive Advantage," *Harvard Business Review,* July–August 2011, pp. 135–41.
3. J. Bower, H. Leonard, and L. Paine, "Global Capitalism at Risk: What Are You Doing about It?" *Harvard Business Review,* September 2011, pp. 105–12.
4. Ibid.
5. J. R. Immelt, "The CEO of General Electric on Sparking an American Manufacturing Renewal," *Harvard Business Review,* March 2012, pp. 43–46.
6. T. A. Judge, C. J. Thoresen, V. Pucik, and T. M. Welbourne, "Managerial Coping with Organizational Change: A Dispositional Perspective," *Journal of Applied Psychology* 84 (1999), pp. 107–22.
7. M. Fugate, A. Kinicki, and G. Prussia, "Employee Coping with Organizational Change: An Examination of Alternative Theoretical Perspectives and Models," *Personnel Psychology* 61 (2008), pp. 1–36.
8. C. Giffi, A. Roth, and G. Seal, *Competing in World-Class Manufacturing: America's 21st Century Challenge* (Homewood, IL: Business One Irwin, 1990).
9. R. M. Kanter, *World Class: Thriving Locally in the Global Economy* (New York: Touchstone, 1995).
10. R. M. Kanter, "How Great Companies Think Differently," *Harvard Business Review,* November 2011, pp. 66–78.
11. Giffi, Roth, and Seal, *Competing in World-Class Manufacturing.*
12. J. Collins and J. Porras, *Built to Last* (London: Century, 1996).
13. Ibid.
14. C. Gibson and J. Birkinshaw, "The Antecedents, Consequences, and Mediating Role of Organizational Ambidexterity," *Academy of Management Journal* 47 (2004), pp. 209–26.
15. Collins and Porras, *Built to Last.*
16. N. Nohria, W. Joyce, and B. Roberson, "What Really Works," *Harvard Business Review,* July 2003, pp. 42–52.
17. R. M. Kanter, "Thriving Locally in the Global Economy," *Harvard Business Review,* August 2003, pp. 119–27.
18. Ibid.; R. M. Kanter, "How Great Companies Think Differently," *Harvard Business Review,* November 2011, pp. 66–78.
19. B. Burnes and B. Cooke, "The Past, Present and Future of Organization Development: Taking the Long View," *Human Relations* 65 (2012), pp. 1395–1429.
20. T. Cummings and C. Worley, *Organization Development and Change,* 8th ed. (Mason, OH: Thomson/South-Western, 2005).
21. Ibid.
22. Ibid.
23. J. Fairest, "Leading Employees Through Major Organizational Change," *Ivey Business Journal Online* 1 (July/August 2014); D. R. Conner, *Managing at the Speed of Change* (New York: Random House, 2006); and R. Teerlink, "Harley's

Leadership U-Turn," *Harvard Business Review,* July–August 2000, pp. 43–48.
24. E. E. Lawler III, *Treat People Right!* (San Francisco: Jossey-Bass, 2003).
25. P. Zigarmi and J. Hoekstra, "Leadership Strategies for Making Change Stick," *Perspectives* (Ken Blanchard Companies, 2008), http://www.kenblanchard.com; D. Erwin and Garman, "Resistance to Organizational Change: Linking Research and Practice," *Leadership & Organization Development Journal* 31 (2010), pp. 39–56.
26. Kevin Wack, "Reinventing the Branch Employee: A How-to Guide," *American Banker,* June 2013, Business Insights: Global, http://bi.galegroup.com.
27. Conner, *Managing at the Speed of Change;* and S. Oreg, "Resistance to Change: Developing an Individual Differences Measure," *Journal of Applied Psychology,* 2003, pp. 680–93.
28. S. Fuchs and R. Prouska, "Creating Positive Employee Change Evaluation: The Role of Different Levels of Organizational Support and Change Participation," *Journal of Change Management* 14 (2014), pp. 361–83; S. Oreg and N. Sverdlik, "Ambivalence toward Imposed Change: The Conflict between Dispositional Resistance to Change and the Orientation toward the Change Agent," *Journal of Applied Psychology* 96 (2011), pp. 337–49; A. Rafferty and S. L. Restubog, "The Impact of Change Process and Context on Change Reactions and Turnover during a Merger," *Journal of Management* 36 (2010), pp. 1309–38; A. Rafferty, N. Jimmieson, and A. Armenakis, "Change Readiness: A Multilevel Review," *Journal of Management* 39 (2013), pp. 110–35.
29. J. Stanislao and B. C. Stanislao, "Dealing with Resistance to Change," *Business Horizons,* July–August 1983, pp. 74–78; and J. D. Ford and L. W. Ford, "Decoding Resistance to Change," *Harvard Business Review,* April 2009, pp. 99–103.
30. J. P. Kotter and L. A. Schlesinger, "Choosing Strategies for Change," *Harvard Business Review,* March–April 1979, pp. 106–14; Ford and Ford, "Decoding Resistance to Change"; and Zigrami and Hoekstra, "Leadership Strategies."
31. M. Rendell, "The Future of Work: A Journey to 2022," PricewaterhouseCoopers (online), http://www.pwc.com/ humancapital, accessed June 25, 2015.
32. "HR Best Practices during Organizational Change," American Management Association (online), June 19, 2014, http:// www.amanet.org; D. Zell, "Overcoming Barriers to Work Innovations: Lessons Learned at Hewlett-Packard," *Organizational Dynamics,* Summer 2001, pp. 77–85.
33. E. B. Dent and S. Galloway Goldberg, "Challenging Resistance to Change," *Journal of Applied Behavioral Science,* March 1999, pp. 25–41; Ford and Ford, "Decoding Resistance to Change"; Zigarmi

and Hoekstra, "Leadership Strategies"; and J. Ford, L. Ford, and A. D'Amelio, "Resistance to Change: The Rest of the Story," *Academy of Management Review* 33 (2008), pp. 362–77.

34. G. Johnson, *Strategic Change and the Management Process* (New York: Basil Blackwell, 1987); and K. Lewin, "Frontiers in Group Dynamics," *Human Relations* 1 (1947), pp. 5–41.

35. E. H. Schein, "Organizational Culture: What It Is and How to Change It," in *Human Resource Management in International Firms,* ed. P. Evans, Y. Doz, and A. Laurent (New York: St. Martin's Press, 1990).

36. M. Beer, R. Eisenstat, and B. Spector, The Critical Path to *Corporate Renewal* (Cambridge, MA: Harvard Business School Press, 1990).

37. Wack, "Reinventing the Branch Employee."

38. E. E. Lawler III, "Transformation from Control to Involvement," in *Corporate Transformation,* ed. R. Kilmann and T. Covin (San Francisco: Jossey-Bass, 1988).

39. D. Hellriegel and J. W. Slocum Jr., *Management,* 4th ed. (Reading, MA: Addison-Wesley, 1986).

40. F. Vermeulen, P. Puranam, and R. Gulate, "Change for Change's Sake," *Harvard Business Review* 88 (June 2010), pp. 70–76.

41. C. Aiken and S. Keller, "The Irrational Side of Change Management," *McKinsey Quarterly,* April 2009, http://www.mckinseyquarterly.com.

42. Lewin, "Frontiers in Group Dynamics."

43. Schein, "Organizational Culture."

44. E. E. Lawler III, *From the Ground Up* (San Francisco: Jossey-Bass, 1995).

45. Q. Nguyen Huy, "Time, Temporal Capability, and Planned Change," *Academy of Management Review* 26 (2001), pp. 601–23.

46. J. Shin, M. Taylor, and M. Seo, "Resources for Change: The Relationships of Organizational Inducements and Psychological Resilience to Employees' Attitudes and Behaviors Toward Organizational Change," *Academy of Management Journal* 55 (2012), 727–48; B. Sugarman, "A Learning-Based Approach to Organizational Change: Some Results and Guidelines," *Organizational Dynamics,* Summer 2001, pp. 62–75.

47. Kotter and Schlesinger, "Choosing Strategies for Change."

48. R. H. Miles, "Beyond the Age of Dilbert: Accelerating Corporate Transformations by Rapidly Engaging all Employees," *Organizational Dynamics,* Spring 2001, pp. 313–21; D. Aguirre and M. Alpern, "10 Principles of Leading Change Management," Strategy1Business (online), June 26, 2014, http://www.strategy-business.com.

49. D. A. Nadler, "Managing Organizational Change: An Integrative Approach," *Journal of Applied Behavioral Science* 17 (1981), pp. 191–211; T. Laffoley, "Making Change Work," UNC Executive Development 2013, http://www.kenan-flagler.unc.edu.

50. D. Rousseau and S. A. Tijoriwala, "What's a Good Reason to Change? Motivated Reasoning and Social Accounts in Promoting Organizational Change," *Journal of Applied Psychology* 84 (1999), pp. 514–28.

51. Dori Meinert, "Wings of Change," *HR Magazine,* November 2012, Business Insights: Global, http://bi.galegroup.com.

52. C. F. Leana and B. Barry, "Stability and Change as Simultaneous Experiences in Organizational Life," *Academy of Management* Review 25 (2000), pp. 753–59; A. Muller and R. Kräussl, "The Value of Corporate Philanthropy During Times of Crisis: The Sensegiving Effect of Employee Involvement," *Journal of Business Ethics* 103 (2011), pp. 203–20.

53. O. Gadiesh and J. Gilbert, "Transforming Corner-Office Strategy into Frontline Action," *Harvard Business Review,* May 2001, pp. 72–79.

54. "The Elephant in the Atmosphere"; Shell website, "New Lens Scenarios: A Shift in Perspective for a World in Transition," http://www.shell.com, accessed June 25, 2015; The White House, "Fact Sheet: U.S. Reports Its 2025 Emissions Target to the UNFCCC," press release, March 31, 2015; L. Foderaro and M. Flegenheimer, "Building Toward a Goal of Reducing Emissions in New York City by 80 Percent," *The New York Times* (online), December 19, 2014, http://www.nytimes.com.

55. B. Schneider, A. Brief, and R. Guzzo, "Creating a Climate and Culture for Sustainable Organizational Change," *Organizational Dynamics,* Spring 1996, pp. 7–19.

56. The Price Waterhouse Change Integration Team, Better Change: *Best Practices for Transforming Your Organization* (Burr Ridge, IL: Irwin, 1995).

57. M. Beer and N. Nohria, "Cracking the Code of Change," *Harvard Business Review,* May–June 2000, pp. 133–41; A. Spaulding, L. Gamm, J. Kim, and T. Menser, "Multiproject Interdependencies in Health Systems Management: A Longitudinal Qualitative Study," *Health Care Management Review* 39 (2014), p. 31.

58. N. Nohria and J. Berkley, "Whatever Happened to the Take-Charge Manager?" *Harvard Business Review,* January–February 1994, pp. 128–37.

59. D. Miller, J. Hartwick, and I. Le Breton-Miller, "How to Detect a Management Fad—and Distinguish It from a Classic," *Business Horizons,* July–August 2004, pp. 7–16.

60. Price Waterhouse Change Integration Team, *Better Change.*

61. Ibid.

62. John P. Kotter, "Accelerate!" *Harvard Business Review,* November 2012, pp. 46–58; Kotter International, "Our Prinicples: Urgency," http://www.kotterinternational.com.

63. Lawler, *From the Ground Up.*

64. J. Kotter, *Leading Change* (Boston: Harvard Business School Press, 1996).

65. Schneider, Brief, and Guzzo, "Creating a Climate and Culture."

66. R. Beckhard and R. Harris, *Organizational Transitions* (Reading, MA: Addison-Wesley, 1977); A. Carton, C. Murphy, and J. Clark, "A (Blurry) Vision of the Future: How Leader Rhetoric about Ultimate Goals Influences Performance," *Academy of Management Journal* 57 (2014), pp. 1544–70.

67. Kotter, *Leading Change.*

68. S. Schumacher, "Waking Employees," *Rock Products,* September 1, 2010, Business & Company Resource Center, http://galenet.galegroup.com.

69. G. Hamel, "Waking Up IBM," *Harvard Business Review,* July–August 2000, pp. 137–46; and Deutschman, *Change or Die.*

70. Kotter, *Leading Change.*

71. D. Smith, *Taking Charge of Change* (Reading, MA: Addison-Wesley, 1996).

72. Kotter, "Accelerate!"

73. G. Hamel, "Killer Strategies That Make Shareholders Rich," *Fortune,* June 23, 1997, pp. 22–34.

74. G. Hamel and C. K. Prahalad, *Competing for the Future* (Boston: Harvard Business School Press, 1994).

75. Mckinley Conway, "Coming: The Biggest Boom Ever!" *The Futurist,* May–June 2010, Business & Company Resource Center, http://galenet.galegroup.com.

76. R. Docksai, "The Next Big Thing—or Things—in Innovation," *The Futurist* 48 (March/April 2014), pp. 56–57.

77. M. Cheung, "Phones to Replace the Wallet, a Smarter Internet, and More Futurist Predictions," *Computer Dealer News,* October 2010, p. 8; and C. G. Wagner, "70 Jobs for 2030," *The Futurist,* January–February 2011, pp. 30–33.

78. E. Beinhocker, I. Davis, and L. Mendenca, "The 10 Trends You Have to Watch," *Harvard Business Review* 87 (July/August 2009), pp. 5–60.

79. S. Zuboff and J. Maxim, *The Support Economy* (New York: Penguin, 2004); R. M. Kanter, "How Great Companies Think Differently," *Harvard Business Review,* November 2011, pp. 66–78.

80. H. Courtney, J. Kirkland, and P. Viguerie, "Strategy under Uncertainty," *Harvard Business Review,* November–December 1997, pp. 66–79.

81. Airbnb website, "About Us," http://www.airbnb.com, accessed June 23, 2015; B. Ritholtz, "The Future of New Business Is Disrupting Old Business," *The Washington Post* (online), January 29, 2015, http://www.washingtonpost.com; J. Boitnott, "5 San Francisco Companies Disrupting Entire Industries," *Inc.* (online), October 28, 2014, http://www.inc.com; B. Page, "5 Ways to Disrupt a Dying Industry," *Inc.* (online), February 3, 2015, http://www.inc.com.

82. F. Gouillart and T. Hallett, "Co-Creation in Government," *Stanford Social Innovation Review* (online), Spring 2015, http://www.ssireview.org; "Why Co-Creation Is the Future of All of Us," *Forbes* (online), February 3, 2014, http://www.forbes.com; Ashoka website, https://www.ashoka.org, accessed June 22, 2015;

83. Hamel and Prahalad, *Competing for the Future.*

84. Ibid.

85. Ibid.

86. A. Scott, "Sustainability: Building Better Practices," *Chemical Week,* October 11, 2010, pp. 24–27.

87. M. Courtney, "Small Is Beautiful," *Computing,* August 5, 2010, Business & Company Resource Center, http://galenet.galegroup.com; and G. E. King and L. Gibbs, "The Little Unknown," *Industrial Engineer,* July 2010, pp. 33–37.

88. King and Gibbs, "The Little Unknown"; P. Livingstone, "Billions of Pieces, Billions of Questions," *R&D Magazine,* October 2010, pp. 8–13; J. Katz, "Nanotechnology: Beyond the Hype," *Industry Week,* November 2010, pp. 22–26; and Occupational Safety & Health Administration, "Nanotechnology Applications," http://www.ohsa.gov, accessed June 23, 2015.

89. Courtney, "Small Is Beautiful"; Livingstone, "Billions of Pieces"; and Katz, "Nanotechnology."

90. National Science Foundation, "Market Report on Emerging Nanotechnology Now Available," Media Advisory 14-004 February 25, 2014, http://www.nsf.gov.

91. Global Information, "Global Market for Nanotechnology to Reach $3.3 Trillion by 2018," news release, *PR Newswire,* http://www.prnewswire.com; BCC Research, "Nanotechnology: A Realistic Market Assessment," report highlights, September 2012, http://www.bccresearch.com.

92. Julie Deardorff, "Scientists: Nanotech-Based Products Offer Great Potential but Unknown Risks," *Chicago Tribune,* July 10, 2012, http://articles.chicagotribune.com; Laura Walter, "Sizing Up Nanotechnology Safety," *EHS Today,* April 18, 2013, http://ehstoday.com; "Nanotechnology-Related Safety and Ethics Problem Emerging," *Science Daily,* April 28, 2012, http://www.sciencedaily.com.

93. Deardorff, "Scientists"; Walter, "Sizing Up Nanotechnology Safety"; "News in Nanotechnology," *EHS Today,* December 2012, p. 20.

94. Hamel and Prahalad, *Competing for the Future.*

95. J. Kotter, *The New Rules: How to Succeed in Today's Post-Corporate World* (New York: Free Press, 1995).

96. T. Bateman and B. Barry, "Masters of the Long Haul: Pursuing Long-Term Work Goals," *Journal of Organizational Behavior,* 2012.

97. Kotter, *The New Rules.*

98. T. Bateman and C. Porath, "Transcendent Behavior," in *Positive Organizational Scholarship,* ed. K. Cameron, J. Dutton, and R. Quinn (San Francisco: Barrett-Koehler, 2003).

99. L. A. Hill, "New Manager Development for the 21st Century," *Academy of Management Executive,* August 2004, pp. 121–26; and D. A. Ready, J. A. Conger, and L. A. Hill, "Are You a High Potential?" *Harvard Business Review* 88 (June 2010), pp. 78–84.

100. Lawler, *From the Ground Up;* and Kotter, *The New Rules.*

101. Lawler, *Treat People Right!*

102. M. Peiperl and Y. Baruck, "Back to Square Zero: The Post-Corporate Career," *Organizational Dynamics,* Spring 1997, pp. 7–22.

103. Ibid.

104. Conner, *Managing at the Speed of Change,* pp. 235–45.

105. J. W. Slocum Jr., M. McGill, and D. Lei, "The New Learning Strategy Anytime, Anything, Anywhere," *Organizational Dynamics,* Autumn 1994, pp. 33–37.

106. Kotter, *The New Rules.*

107. J. Collins, *From Good to Great* (New York: HarperBusiness, 2001).

108. Hill, "New Manager Development for the 21st Century," p. 125.

109. J. A. Raelin, "Don't Bother Putting Leadership into People," *Academy of Management Executive,* August 2004, pp. 131–35.

110. G. Binney, and C. Williams, *Leaning into the Future* (London: Nicholas Brealey, 1997).

111. "The Elephant in the Atmosphere"; Farrell, "Climate Change Dominates Marathon Annual General Meeting"; Company website, "Our History," Shell.com, accessed June 25, 2015; G. Naik, "Scientists Back Pope Francis on Global Warming," *The Wall Street Journal* (online), June 18, 2015, http://www.wsj.com; E. Howard and J. Parsons, "Keep It the Ground Climate Campaign," *The Guardian* (online), May 29, 2015, http://www.theguardian.com; C. Davenport and L. Goodstein, "Pope Francis Steps Up on Climate Change, to Conservatives' Alarm," *The New York Times* (online), April 27, 2015, http://www.nytimes.com; E. Howard, "The Biggest Story in the World: Inside *The Guardian*'s Climate Change Campaign," *The Guardian* (online), March 20, 2015, http://theguardian.com.

112. P. Omidyar, "How Great Companies Think Differently: eBay's Founder on Innovating the Business Model of Social Change," *Harvard Business Review,* September 2011, pp. 41–44; M. Porter and M. Kramer, "Creating Shared Value," *Harvard Business Review,* January–February 2011, pp. 62–77; H. Sabeti, "The For-Benefit Enterprise," *Harvard Business Review,* November 2011, pp. 99–104.

113. Ibid.

Autonomous work groups Groups that control decisions about and execution of a complete range of tasks, **447**

Autonomy, 428
Average employee, 329
Avio, 127

Avoidance A reaction to conflict that involves ignoring the problem by doing nothing at all or deemphasizing the disagreement, **459**

Avon Products, 261, 354, 367, 371
AXA Canada, 123

B

B Impact Assessment (BIA), 503
B-Lab, 503
B-Team, 12
Baby boomer retirements, 7
Baby boomers, 125, 232, 265
Baccarat, 503
Background checks, 315–316
Bad news/good news, 487
Bain, 312
Baking soda, 158

Balance sheet A report that shows the financial picture of a company at a given time and itemizes assets, liabilities, and stockholders' equity, **513**, 514

Balanced scorecard Control system combining four sets of performance measures: financial, customer, business process, and learning and growth, **521**, 522, 525

Baldridge Award, 292
Bank Boston, 152
Bank of America, 59, 152, 320, 367
Barnes & Noble, 52
Barrier Break, 221

Barriers to entry Conditions that prevent new companies from entering an industry, **51**

Barriers to strategy implementation, 131
BARS. *See* Behaviorally anchored rating scale (BARS)
Bartlett/Ghoshal typology of multinational companies, 188
Base technologies, 543
Basecamp, 225
BASF Agricultural Solutions, 590
Basic Needs, 219
Baskin-Robbin, 217
Batesville Casket Company, 551
Baxter robot, 545
Bayer, 169
BCG matrix, 126–127
Bechtel, 198, 262
Bed Bath & Beyond, 59
Bee Healthy (HEC Paris), 187
Behavioral appraisal, 326

Behavioral approach A leadership perspective that attempts to identify what good leaders do—that is, what behaviors they exhibit, **389**

Behavioral description interview, 315
Behaviorally anchored rating scale (BARS), 326
Being different worksheet, 375
Bell Labs, 550
Ben & Jerry's, 158

Benchmarking The process of comparing an organization's practices and technologies with those of other companies, **58, 123,** 544

Best Buy, 499, 516, 527
Best-case scenario, 57
Best Trust Bank, 495
BIA. *See* B Impact Assessment (BIA)
Bibak, 535
Big Bison Resorts, 439–440
Big data, 81, 289
Bigelow Aerospace, 218
Black lung disease, 335
Blake and Mouton's leadership grid, 392
Blockbuster, 8
Blogging, 142, 474
Bloomin' Brands, 129
Blue Cross/Blue Shield, 474
Bluefin Labs, 551
BMW, 4
Board of advisers, 251
Board of directors, 250–251
Bob's Red Mill baking soda, 158
Body language, 482
Boeing, 75, 86, 97, 262
Bonefish Grill, 129
Bonus, 331
Boomer retirements, 7

Bootlegging Informal work on projects, other than those officially assigned, of employees' own choosing and initiative, **233**

Borrow-use-return approach, 157
BOS/Origin, 171
Boston, Massachusetts, 576

Boundary-spanning Interacting with people in other groups, thus creating linkages between groups, **457**

Boundaryless organization Organization in which there are no barriers to information flow, 300, **489**–490

Bounded rationality A less-than-perfect form of rationality in which decision makers cannot be perfectly rational because decisions are complex and complete information is unavailable or cannot be fully processed, **94**

Box, 183, 474
BP Deepwater Horizon drilling rig explosion, 48–49, 170, 500
BPAmoco, 198
BrainScope, 218
Brainstorm, 556

Brainstorming A process in which group members generate as many ideas about a problem as they can; criticism is withheld until all ideas have been proposed, **92,** 93

Brand Champions, 323
Brand identification, 51
Brazil, 186
Breitt, Starr & Diamond LLC, 408
Bribery, 45, 203–204
Bribery Act (Britain), 203

Bricks and mortar A traditional organization operating from physical buildings and offices, **567**

Brigades, 49
Bring your own app (BYOA), 475
Bristol-Myers Squibb, 169
Broad-based action, 588

Broker A person who assembles and coordinates participants in a network, **266**

Brooks, 570
Brown Flynn, 417–418
Brown v. Board of Education, 349
Browning-Ferris, 170
Budget, 132
Budget period, 511
Budgetary controls, 510–511

Budgeting The process of investigating what is being done and comparing the results with the corresponding budget data to verify accomplishments or remedy differences; also called budgetary controlling, **510**

Buffering Creating supplies of excess resources in case of unpredictable needs, **61**

Building a dynamic organization, 14
Built to Last (Collins/Porras), 575
Built-to-last companies, 575

Bureaucracy A classical management approach emphasizing a structured, formal network of relationships among specialized positions in the organization, **34**–35, 61

Bureaucracy busting, 555–556

Bureaucratic control The use of rules, regulations, and authority to guide performance, **501**

Bureaucratic control systems, 501–522
Bureaucratic organizations, 61
Burger King, 294, 369
Burt's Bees, 152, 158

Business accelerators Organization that provides support and advice to help young businesses grow, **224**

Business ethics The moral principles and standards that guide behavior in the world of business, **143,** 145

Business incubators Protected environments for new, small businesses, **224**

Business model innovation, 534, 535

Business plan A formal planning step that focuses on the entire venture and describes all the elements involved in starting it, **228**, 229

Business strategy The major actions by which a business competes in a particular industry or market, **128**–129

Buy42.com, 221
BYOA. *See* Bring your own app (BYOA)

C

C-suite, 16
CafePress.com, 219

Cafeteria benefit program An employee benefit program in which employees choose from a menu of options to create a benefit package tailored to their needs, **334**

CAFTA-DR. *See* Central America-Dominican Republic-United States Free Trade Agreement (CAFTA-DR)
Cakes and Kids, 179
Calamities, 217
CalPERS, 172
Cameron Oil, 312
Campus recruiting, 313
Canada, 425
Candor, 474
Canon, 299
Capital budget, 511
Capterra, 79, 80, 82–84
Carbon-cutting and trading system, 170
Carbon footprint, **157**
Carbon Tracker Initiative, 595
Care at Hand, 218
Career advice from the experts, 21
Career development
    active contributor, 22–23
    career advice from the experts, 21
    connectedness, 23
    diverse workforce, 372
    emotional intelligence, 20
    qualities/actions of successful executives, 23–24
    self-reliance, 21
    specialist and generalist, 20–21
    survive and thrive, 22–23
CareerBuilder, 312
Carmike Cinema, 257

Carrying capacity The ability of a finite resource to sustain a population, **167**

Case incidents
    effective management, 103–104
    employee raiding, 103
    implementing strategic change, 601–602
    robot repercussion, 600–601
Cases
    Best Trust Bank, 495
    Big Bison Resorts, 439–440
    Breitt, Starr & Diamond LLC, 408
    DIY Stores, 304
    Dollar General, 599–600
    EatWell Technologies, 598–599
    Excel Pro Drilling Systems, 466
    Foxconn, 241–242
    Grizzly Bear Lodge, 531
    Invincibility Systems, 343–344

Ma Earth Skin Care, 164–165
    Magna Exteriors and Interiors, 496–497
    Net-Work Docs, 209
    Niche Hotel Group (NHG), 377–378
    ScrollCo, 241
    Soaring Eagle Skate Company, 101
    Stanley Lynch Investment Group, 274
    Tata Motors, 73
    USA Hospital Supply, 28–29
    Wish You Wood Toy Store, 136–137
    Worldwide Games, 562
    Zappos, 102, 378–379
Cash budget, 511
Cash cows, 127
Caspers Company, 312
Cassini Imaging Science, 454
Caterpillar, 357

Caux Principles Ethical principles established by international executives based in Caux, Switzerland, in collaboration with business leaders from Japan, Europe, and the United States, **143**

Caux Roundtable, 143
CEMEX, 186
Central America, 186
Central America-Dominican Republic-United States Free Trade Agreement (CAFTA-DR), 186
Central Intelligence Agency, 359
Centralization, 256

Centralized organization An organization in which high-level executives make most decisions and pass them down to lower levels for implementation, **255**

CEO. *See* Chief executive officer (CEO)
CEO pay, 146, 332–333, 431, 525
CERES Roadmap for Sustainability, 167

Certainty The state that exists when decision makers have accurate and comprehensive information, **77**

C.F. Martin & Company, 126
CFO. *See* Chief financial officer (CFO)
Change management
    anchoring new approaches in the culture, 588
    case incident, 601–602
    consolidating gains and producing more change, 588
    education and communication, 583–584
    empowering broad-based action, 588
    explicit and implicit coercion, 583, 584–585
    facilitation and support, 583, 584
    guiding coalition, 587–588
    harmonizing multiple changes, 585–586
    leading change, 586–588
    manipulation and cooptation, 583, 584
    motivating people to change, 578–583
    negotiation and rewards, 583, 584
    participation and involvement, 583, 584
    questions to ask, 586
    reactive/proactive change, 589
    resistance to change, 579–581
    sense of urgency, 586–587
    shared leadership, 578
    short-term wins, 588
    total organization change, 586
    unfreezing/moving/refreezing model, 581–583
    vision and strategy, 588

Change.org, 367
Change vision, 588
Chaparral, 556

Charismatic leader A person who is dominant, self-confident, convinced of the moral righteousness of his or her beliefs, and able to arouse a sense of excitement and adventure in followers, **398**

Charismatic leadership, 398–399
Checking references, 315
Chemdex, 569
Chemical industry, 169
Chemical Manufacturers Association, 170
Chevron, 198
Chi-Med, 551
Chicago Transit Authority, 170
Chick-fil-A, 413
Chief executive officer (CEO), 16, 251
Chief financial officer (CFO), 511

Chief information officer (CIO) Executive in charge of information technology strategy and development, 16, **552**, 553

Chief innovation officer, 552, 553
Chief operating officer (COO), 16
Chief technology officer (CTO), 552
Chile, 186
China, 184–185
    canned peaches, 177
    Duke Kunshan University (DKU), 195
    environmental problems, 157
    fake or pirated goods, 547
    foreign exchange reserves, 177
    groundwater pollution, 168
    Lenovo, 175, 192, 205
    market reforms, 177
    Panasonic, 191–192
    Shanghai Disney, 132, 176
    smog, 168
    trade with U.S., 184
    transformational leadership, 400
China National Petroleum, 5
Chrysler, 294
CIA, 64
Cianbro, 47
CIBA-GEIGY, 171
CIM. *See* Computer-integrated manufacturing (CIM)
Cinergy, 170
Cintas, 382
CIO. *See* Chief information officer (CIO)
Cirque du Soleil, 577
Cisco Systems, 170
Citicorp, 574
Citigroup, 318
Citrix Systems, 92
City of Boston, 367
City of Richmond, Washington, 118, 119
City of San Francisco, 171
Civil aspiration, 154
Civil Rights Act of 1964, 319, 349
Civil Rights Act of 1991, 320, 321

Clan control Control based on the norms, values, shared goals, and trust among group members, **501**, 525–526

Classical approaches to management, 30–35
Clínicas del Azúcar, 219
Clique, 270

Connect the dots, 586
Connectedness, 22

Conservation The environmental destruction that results as individuals and business consume finite resources (the commons) to serve their short-term interests without regard for the long-term consequences, **167**

Consideration, 390
Consolidated Natural Gas, 170
Constructive conflict, 90–91
Contemporary approaches to management, 35–36
Content theories, 421
Content validity, 318

Contingencies Factors that determine the appropriateness of managerial actions, **36**

Contingency perspective An approach to the study of management proposing that the managerial strategies, structures, and processes that result in high performance depend on the characteristics, or important contingencies, of the situation in which they are applied, **36**

Contingency plans Alternative courses of action that can be implemented based on how the future unfolds, **81, 110**

Contingent workers, 61
Continuous improvement, 9, 289, 291
Continuous learning, 593

Continuous process A process that is highly automated and has a continuous production flow, **294**

Continuous process technologies, 294
Contracted development of technology, 550
Contracting, 60

Control Any process that directs the activities of individuals toward the achievement of organizational goals, **500**. *See also* Managerial control

Control cycle, 501–505

Controlling The management function of monitoring performance and making needed changes, **15**

COO. *See* Chief operating officer (COO)
Cooperative action, 60

Cooperative strategies Strategies used by two or more organizations working together to manage the external environment, **60**

Cooptation, 60, 584

Coordination The procedures that link the various parts of an organization for the purpose of achieving the organization's overall mission, **249**

Coordination and communication, 268–269

Coordination by mutual adjustment Units interact with one another to make accommodations to achieve flexible coordination, **268**

Coordination by plan Interdependent units are required to meet deadlines and objectives that contribute to a common goal, **267**

Coordination by standardization, 267
CopyShark.net, 225

Core capability A unique skill and/or knowledge an organization possesses that gives it an edge over competitors, **122,** 280–281

Corning, 123, 308, 354
Corporate culture preference scale, 72
Corporate entrepreneurship, 233–235. *See also* Entrepreneurship
    building support for your idea, 233
    competitive aggressiveness, 235
    entrepreneurial orientation, 234
    innovativeness, 234
    intrapreneurial activity, 233–234
    management challenges, 234
    proactiveness, 235
    risk taking, 234
Corporate ethical standards, 147

Corporate governance The role of a corporation's executive staff and board of directors in ensuring that the firm's activities meet the goals of the firm's stakeholders, **252**

Corporate scandals, 140. *See also* Ethics

Corporate social responsibility (CSR) Obligation toward society assumed by business, **152**. *See also* Ethics

    economic responsibilities, 153
    ethical responsibilities, 153
    financial performance, 155
    legal responsibilities, 153
    philanthropic responsibilities, 154
    profit maximization perspective, 154
    social entrepreneurship, contrasted, 219
    social responsibility perspective, 154
    stewardship, 152
    transcendent education, 154
    triple bottom line, 153

Corporate strategy The set of businesses, markets, or industries in which an organization competes and the distribution of resources among those entities, **125–128**

Corrective action, 504–505
Cost budget, 511

Cost competitiveness Keeping costs low to achieve profits and be able to offer prices that are attractive to consumers, **10–11**

Cost-monitoring information, 565
Counterfeit goods, 547
Country club management, 392

Courage, 151–152, 402
Cradle-to-cradle production approach, 158
Creativity, 91–92, 361, 554–555
Creditworthiness, 565
Crestor, 541
Crisis, 95–97
Crisis management, 96
Criterion-related validity, 317–318
Critical incident technique, 326–327
CRM. *See* Customer relationship management (CRM)
Crowdfunder.com, 230
Crowdfunding, 230
Crowdsourcing, 93
CSR. *See* Corporate social responsibility (CSR)
CSX, 357
CTO. *See* Chief technology officer (CTO)
Cultural control, 501

Culture shock The disorientation and stress associated with being in a foreign environment, **200,** 201

CultureRx, 527

Current ratio A liquidity ratio that indicates the extent to which short-term assets can decline and still be adequate to pay short-term liabilities, **513**

Custom-made solutions New, creative solutions designed specifically for the problem, **79**

Customer, 54–55
Customer comments, 7
Customer division, 261
Customer feedback management software, 7
Customer relations, 289

Customer relationship management (CRM) A multifaceted process focusing on creating two-way exchanges with customers to foster intimate knowledge of their needs, wants, and buying patterns, **289–291**

Customer reviews, 84
Customer service, 54, 55
Cutting-edge technology, 590–591
CVS Caremark, 47
Cycle times, 298

D

Dabble time, 234
Danish Steell, 171

Data mining The collection and analysis of large amounts of customers' online information to inform different decisions within an organization, especially those related to marketing, **568**

Days Inn, 369
D4D (NASCAR), 347, 364, 373

Debt-equity ratio A leverage ratio that indicates the company's ability to meet its long-term financial obligations, **513**

Decentralization, 255–256

Decentralized organization An organization in which lower-level managers make important decisions, **255**

Deception, 142
Decision evaluation, 84
Decision making. *See* Managerial decision making
Decision making worksheet, 99–100
Decisional roles, 19
Decoding problems, 471
Deepwater Horizon drilling rig explosion, 48–49, 170, 500
Defects per million opportunities (DPMO), 508
Defender firms, 548

Defenders Companies that stay within a stable product domain as a strategic maneuver, **59**

Delegation The assignment of new or additional responsibilities to a subordinate, 225, **253–255**

Delivering strategic value, 14
Dell Inc., 54, 185, 294, 298, 312
Deloitte, 48, 372, 477, 538
Deloitte Consulting, 181
Demand forecasts, 310
Deming's 14 points of quality, 291

Democratic leadership A form of leadership in which the leader solicits input from subordinates, **391**

Demographic changes, 217

Demographics Measures of various characteristics of the people who make up groups or other social units, **46–48**

Department of Veterans Affairs, 517–518

Departmentalization Subdividing an organization into smaller subunits, 256, **257**

Design thinking A human-centered approach to problem solving and solution finding that is based on nonlinear iterations of inspiration, ideation, and implementation, **556–557**

Designer role, 266
Destructive conflict, 458
Detroit Institute of Arts, 9
Deutsche Asset Management, 172
Deutsche Boerse, 177

Development Helping managers and professional employees learn the broad skills needed for their present and future jobs, **322**

Development project A focused organizational effort to create a new product or process via technological advances, **557–558**

Devil's advocate A person who has the job of criticizing ideas to ensure that their downsides are fully explored, **91**

Dialectic A structured debate comparing two conflicting courses of action, **91**

Differentiation An aspect of the organization's internal environment created by job specialization and the division of labor, **248–249**

Differentiation strategy A strategy an organization uses to build competitive advantage by being unique in its industry or market segment along one or more dimensions, **128**

Digitizing information, 569
Dillon Reed, 424
Diovan, 51
Directive leadership, 390, 396
Disaster relief missions, 426

Discounting the future A bias weighting short-term costs and benefits more heavily than longer-term costs and benefits, **86, 87**

Diseconomies of scale, 285
Disney.com, 117, 132. *See also* Walt Disney Company
Disney Interactive Media, 117, 132
Disney Tsum Tsum, 132

Disruptive innovation A process by which a product, service, or business model takes root initially in simple applications at the bottom of a market and then moves "up market," eventually displacing established competitors, **539, 580**

Disseminator, 19
Distribution, 565
Disturbance handler, 19
Diverse workforce. *See* Managing diversity

Diversification A firm's investment in a different product, business, or geographic area, **58**

Diversified corporate strategy, 126
Diversity assumptions, 365
Diversity officer, 367

Diversity training Programs that focus on identifying and reducing hidden biases against people with differences and developing the skills needed to manage a diversified workforce, **324, 369, 371**

Divestiture A firm selling one or more businesses, **59**

Division of labor The assignment of different tasks to different people or groups, **248**

Divisional organization Departmentalization that groups units around products, customers, or geographic regions, **259**–262

DIY Stores, 304
Dodd-Frank Wall Street Reform and Consumer Protection Act, 431
Dogs, 127
Dollar Tree acquisition of Family Dollar, 600

Domain selection Entering a new market or industry with an existing expertise, **58**

Dow Chemical, 122, 159, 160, 169, 183, 198, 308
Dow Corning, 262
Dow Europe, 171
Dow Jones Industrial Average, 44
Dow Jones Sustainability Index, 170

Downsizing The planned elimination of positions or jobs, **285–287**

Downward communication Information that flows from higher to lower levels in the organization's hierarchy, **484–487**

DPMO. *See* Defects per million opportunities (DPMO)
Dreamliner, 75, 86, 97
DreamWorks Animation, 287
Drive, 388
Drug-Free Workplace Act, 316
Drug patents, 541
Drug testing, 316–317, 517
DSW, 361
Duke Kunshan University (DKU), 195
DuPont, 122, 155, 169, 171, 353

Dynamic network Temporary arrangements among partners that can be assembled and reassembled to adapt to the environment, **265**

Dynamic Organization (Parker), 33

E

E-gossip, 489
E-mail, 474, 475, 481
E-readers, 52

E-tailing The process by which an organization sells some of its products or merchandise via the Internet, **567**

E3 Initiative, 169
Early adopters, 537, 538–539, 547, 548
Early labor contract, 31
Early majority, 537, 539
Earnings management, 414
Eastman Chemical, 452
Eastman Kodak, 195
Eaton, 11
EatWell Technologies, 598–599
eBags, 568
eBay, 80, 219, 568

Ecocentric management Its goal is the creation of sustainable economic development and improvement of quality of life worldwide for all organizational stakeholders, **157**

Ecomagination, 156
EcoMall, 171
Economic crisis, 81
Economic dislocations, 217
Economic efficiencies, 52
Economic environment, 43–44
Economic Outlook, 57

Economic responsibilities To produce goods and services that society wants at a price that perpetuates the business and satisfies its obligations to investors, **153**

Economic strike, 337

Economies of scale Reductions in the average cost of a unit of production as the total volume produced increases, **30**

Economies of scope Economies in which materials and processes employed in one product can be used to make other related products, **284**

Eddie Bauer, 568
Edinburgh University, 595
Edmunds.com, 80
Edom Nutritional Solutions, 221
EEOC. *See* Equal Employment Opportunity Commission (EEOC)
Effective managers worksheet, 27
Effort-to-performance link, 419
Ego needs, 422

Egoism An ethical system defining acceptable behavior as that which maximizes consequences for the individual, 143, **144**

Electric car technology, 549
Electrolux, 171
Electronic and virtual conflict, 461
Electronic communication, 474–477
Electronic leaks, 476
Eli Lilly, 183
Elimination of waste, 298
Elmer's Products, 556
EMC, 261
Emerging technologies, 543
Emerson Electric, 519

Emotional intelligence The skills of understanding yourself, managing yourself, and dealing effectively with others, **20**

Empathy, 20, 154
Employee benefits, 333–335. *See* Human resources management (HRM)
Employee blogs, 142
Employee compensation, 330–335, 558
Employee discipline, 319
Employee drug testing, 316–317
Employee engagement, 538
Employee involvement, 298
Employee key behaviors, 413
Employee pay, 330–333
Employee raiding, 103
Employee Retirement Income Security Act (ERISA), 334–335
Employee termination, 318–319, 320
Employee training, 322–324

Employment-at-will The legal concept that an employee may be terminated for any reason, **318**–319

Employment discrimination, 359. *See also* Managing diversity
Employment interview, 314–315
Empowered organization, 526

Empowerment The process of sharing power with employees, thereby enhancing their confidence in their ability to perform their jobs and their belief that they are influential contributors to the organization, **61, 429,** 450, 454, 525

Encoding problems, 471
Encouraging creativity, 91–92
EndoChoice, 53
Energy industry, 595
Engagement level of employees, 538
Enron, 140

Entrepreneur Individual who establishes a new organization without the benefit of corporate sponsorship, 19, **214**

Entrepreneur magazine, 218

Entrepreneurial orientation The tendency of an organization to identify and capitalize successfully on opportunities to launch new ventures by entering new or established markets with new or existing goods or services, **234**

Entrepreneurial process, 212
Entrepreneurial strategy matrix, 221–222

Entrepreneurial venture A new business having growth and high profitability as primary objectives, **212**

Entrepreneurship The pursuit of lucrative opportunities by enterprising individuals, 210–244

advisory board, 232
business incubators/accelerators, 224
business plan, 228, 229
control systems, 226
corporate, 233–235
creating value, 212
defined, **212**
delegation, 225
economic environment, 223–224
entrepreneurial process, 212
entrepreneurial strategy matrix, 221–222
franchising, 217–218
going public (IPO), 226–227
idea, 216
information/resources, 243–244
Internet, 218–219
legitimacy, 231
management challenges, 224–227
misuse of funds, 225–226
myths, 212, 213
networking, 231
new business start-up worksheet, 240
next frontiers, 218

opportunity, 216–217
partners, 232–233
planning, 227–231
risk, 223
social, 219–220, 221
succession planning, 226
top management, 231
what does it take to succeed?, 215, 216, 220–221
Entry barriers, 51
Environmental analysis, 120
benchmarking, 58
competitor analysis, 120
environmental scanning, 56–57
forecasting, 57–58
human resources analysis, 120
industry and market analysis, 120
macroeconomic analysis, 120
political and regulatory analysis, 120
scenario development, 57
social analysis, 120
technological analysis, 120
Environmental cleanup services, 169
Environmental complexity, 56
Environmental dynamism, 56
Environmental issues. *See* Natural environment and sustainability
Environmental management partnerships, 169

Environmental movement An environmental philosophy that seeks to avoid waste, promote the rational and efficient use of natural resources, and maximize long-term yields, especially of renewable resources, **167**

Environmental Protection Agency (EPA), 46
Environmental response. *See* Responding to the environment

Environmental scanning Searching for and sorting through information about the environment, **56**–57

Environmental uncertainty, **56**
Environmentally focused stakeholder relationships, 169
Envision, 584
EPA. *See* Environmental Protection Agency (EPA)
Epic Games, 551
Equal employment laws, 319–321, 334
Equal Employment Opportunity Commission (EEOC), 46, 321, 354
Equal Pay Act, 321, 334
Equitable Life Assurance Society, 368

Equity theory A theory stating that people assess how fairly they have been treated according to two key factors: outcomes and inputs, **430**–432

ERG theory, 423–424
ERISA. *See* Employee Retirement Income Security Act (ERISA)
Ernst & Young, 354, 356, 357, 371–372
Ethel M. Chocolates, 170
Ethical behavior worksheet, 163

Ethical climate In an organization, the processes by which decisions are evaluated and made on the basis of right and wrong, **146**

Ethical decision making, 149–150

Ethical issue Situation, problem, or opportunity in which an individual must choose among several actions that must be evaluated as morally right or wrong, **143**

Ethical leader One who is both a moral person and a moral manager influencing others to behave ethically, **147**

Ethical leadership, 400

Ethical responsibilities Meeting other social expectations, not written as law, **153**

Ethical systems, 143–145
Ethicon, 260

Ethics The system of rules that governs the ordering of values, 140–152. *See also* Corporate social responsibility (CSR)

  aim, 142
  business, 143, 145
  Caux Principles, 143
  corporate ethical standards, 147–148
  corporate scandals, 140
  courage, 151–152
  current ethical issues, 146
  danger signs, 147, 148
  deceptive blogs, 142
  defined, **140**
  egoism, 143, 144
  ethical behavior worksheet, 163
  ethical climate, 146
  ethical decision making, 149–150
  ethical systems, 143–145
  ethics codes, 148, 149
  ethics programs, 148–149
  excuses, 150
  international context, 147, 203–204
  Kohlberg's model of moral development, 145
  lying/truth-telling, 141, 142
  relativism, 143, 144
  Sarbanes-Oxley Act. *See* Sarbanes-Oxley Act
  underlying values, 142–143
  universalism, 143–144
  utilitarianism, 143, 144
  virtue, **143,** 145
  whistleblowing, 152

Ethnocentrism The tendency to judge others by the standards of one's group or culture, which are seen as superior, **200**

Etsy, 368, 369
European Union (EU), 182–183
Evolution of management
  administrative management, 33
  bureaucracy, 34–35
  classical approaches, 30–35
  contemporary approaches, 35–36
  contingency perspective, 36
  early labor contract, 31
  early management concepts and influences, 30
  Fayol's 14 principles of management, 33
  first university programs, 30
  Hawthorne studies/Hawthorne effect, 33–34
  human relations, 33–34
  organizational behavior, 35

  quantitative management, 35
  scientific management, 31–32
  systematic management, 31
  systems theory, 35–36
  Theory X/Theory Y, 35
  timeline, 30
Excuses, 150

Executive champion An executive who supports a new technology and protects the product champion of the innovation, **553**

Executive Order 11246, 321
Executive Order 11375, 321
Executive pay, 146, 332–333, 431, 525
Executives of color, 357
Exelon, 480
Existence needs, 423, 424

Expatriates Parent-company nationals who are sent to work at a foreign subsidiary, **196,** 197

Expectancy Employees' perception of the likelihood that their efforts will enable them to attain their performance goals, **419**

Expectancy theory A theory proposing that people will behave based on their perceived likelihood that their effort will lead to a certain outcome and on how highly they value that outcome, **419**–420

Expert power, 388
Explicit and implicit coercion, 583, 584–585
Exploitation and exploration, 278. *See also* Organizational agility
Explore/discover/act cycle, 593
Exporting, 193–194

External audit An evaluation conducted by one organization, such as a CPA firm, on another, **509**

External environment All relevant forces outside a firm's boundaries, such as competitors, customers, the government, and the economy, **42**

External environment worksheet, 70–71
External locus of control, 396
External opportunities and threats, 119–121
External recruiting, 312–313

Extinction Withdrawing or failing to provide a reinforcing consequence, **416**

Extrinsic reward Reward given to a person by the boss, the company, or some other person, **425**

Extroversion, 388–389
Exxon Valdez oil spill, 170
ExxonMobil, 5, 45
Eye contact, 480, 482
EZ Store, 599

F
FAA. *See* Federal Aviation Administration (FAA)
Face recognition technology, 546
Facebook, 41, 55, 67, 214, 316, 353, 359, 474, 542
Facial expression, 482
Facilitation, 584
Fail-safing, 298
Failure, 555

Failure rate The number of expatriate managers of an overseas operation who come home early, **198**

Fair Labor Standards Act (FLSA), 319, 321, 334
Fairness, 430–432
Fake or pirated goods, 547
Fake reviews, 142
False performance data, 517
Falsifying records, 517–518
Family and Medical Leave Act, 321
Fayol's 14 principles of management, 33
FBI. *See* Federal Bureau of Investigation (FBI)
FCPA. *See* Foreign Corrupt Practices Act (FCPA)
FDA. *See* Food & Drug Administration (FDA)
FDI. *See* Foreign direct investment (FDI)
Federal Aviation Administration (FAA), 46
Federal Bureau of Investigation (FBI), 317, 413
Federal Express. *See* FedEx (Federal Express)
Federal Trade Commission, 218, 570
Federated Department Stores, 261
FedEx (Federal Express), 122, 171, 356, 454, 505, 569
Feedback
  appraisal by subordinates, 327
  creativity, 92
  decision evaluation, 84
  international management, 203
  job enrichment, 428
  performance appraisal, 328–329
  performance standards, 520
  reinforcing performance, 418
  teams, 444

Feedback control Control that focuses on the use of information about previous results to correct deviations from the acceptable standard, **505,** 506–507

Feedforward control The control process used before operations begin, including policies, procedures, and rules designed to ensure that planned activities are carried out properly, **505,** 506

Fictional blogs, 142

Fiedler's contingency model of leadership effectiveness A situational approach to leadership postulating that effectiveness depends on the personal style of the leader and the degree to which the situation gives the leader power, control, and influence over the situation, **394**–395

Figurehead, 19

Filtering The process of withholding, ignoring, or distorting information, **471,** 487

Final customer A customer who purchases products in their finished form, **54**

Finance and the environment, 172
Financial analysis, 121
Financial auditors, 458
Financial controls, 513–515
Financial ratios, 513, 515
Financial statements, 513–515
First-mover advantage, 540, 541
Five sources of power worksheet, 407
Flat organization, 252
FLEXcon, 444
Flexibility and agility. *See* Organizational agility

Flexible benefit programs Benefit programs in which employees are given credits to spend on benefits that fit their unique needs, **334**

Flexible factories Manufacturing plants that have short production runs, are organized around products, and use decentralized scheduling, **296**

Flexible processes Methods for adapting the technical core to changes in the environment, **62**

Flexible work arrangements, 47, 281, 352, 369
FLSA. *See* Fair Labor Standards Act (FLSA)
FMR, 353
Followership, 386
Food & Drug Administration (FDA), 46
Foolproofing, 298

Force-field analysis An approach to implementing the unfreezing/ moving/refreezing model by identifying the forces that prevent people from changing and those that will drive people toward change, **582**

Forces in the manager, 393
Forces in the situation, 393
Forces in the subordinate, 393
Ford Motor Company, 8, 59, 123, 152, 190, 195, 294, 317, 328, 360, 400, 508, 557–558

Forecasting Method for predicting how variables will change the future, **57–58**

Foreign Corrupt Practices Act (FCPA), 203, 204
Foreign direct investment (FDI), 176
Foreign-national employees, 201–203
Formal control system, 501–522

Formalization The presence of rules and regulations governing how people in the organization interact, **267**

Forming stage, 448–449
40K Plus Education, 221
Foundations of management, 1
Four "A's" model, 130
Four-stage model of dispute resolution, 460–461
401(k) plan, 334
Foxconn, 241–242
Fracking, 45

Framing effects A decision bias influenced by the way in which a problem or decision alternative is phrased or presented, **85**

Franchise Chat, 218

Franchising An entrepreneurial alliance between a franchisor (an innovator who has created at least one successful store and wants to grow) and a franchisee (a partner who manages a new store of the same type in a new location), 193, 194–195, **217–218**

Freshly Picked, 223
Friendship group, 270
Friendster, 542
Frivolity, 520

Frontline managers Lower-level managers who supervise the operational activities of the organization, **17**, 18

Frozen (film), 107
Frozen Free Fall, 132
Fuel cell technology, 546
Fuji Australia, 170
Full-cost accounting, 171
Functional areas, 129

Functional organization Departmentalization around specialized activities such as production, marketing, and human resources, **257–259**, 260

Functional strategies Strategies implemented by each functional area of the organization to support the organization's business strategy, **129**

Functions of the Executive, The (Barnard), 33
FundersClub, 230
Future directions (futurists), 589–595

G

GAAP. *See* Generally accepted accounting practices (GAAP)
Gainsharing plan, 331
Galan Entertainment, 220
Gambling, 85
Gamification, 538

Garbage can model Model of organizational decision making depicting a chaotic process and seemingly random decisions, **95**

Gatekeeper A team member who keeps abreast of current developments and provides the team with relevant information, **457**

Gay and lesbian employees, 354–355
GE. *See* General Electric (GE)
GE Healthcare, 428
Geely, 177
Gen Xers, 7, 125

Gen Y, 476
Gender issues, 351–355. *See also* Women
General Electric (GE), 5, 126, 127, 129, 146, 147, 156, 169, 176, 181, 218, 252, 277, 288, 292, 300, 308, 322, 489–490, 508, 512, 546
General Electric acquisition of Alstom, 127
General Electric Aviation, 369
General Mills, 354, 360, 444
General Mills acquisition of Pillsbury, 323
General Motors (GM), 8, 110, 166, 169, 184, 195, 247, 257, 261, 270, 284, 294, 353, 517
Generally accepted accounting practices (GAAP), 512
Generation Y, 359
Generational tipping point, 265
Generativity, 154

Genius of the *and* Ability to achieve multiple objectives simultaneously, **576**

Genpact, 524
Geographic division, 261
Glass ceiling, 353
Glassdoor, 312, 330
GlaxoSmithKline, 6
Global Fund, 60
Global Hyatt, 198
Global integration--local responsiveness worksheet, 207–208

Global model An organizational model consisting of a company's overseas subsidiaries and characterized by centralized decision making and tight control by the parent company over most aspects of worldwide operations; typically adopted by organizations that base their global competitive strategy on cost considerations, **190–191**

Global Research Technologies LLC, 169
Global reporting initiative (GRI), 158
Global-scale manufacturing facilities, 191
Globalization, 4–5. *See also* International management
GM. *See* General Motors (GM)
Go-it-alone approach, 592

Goal A target or end that management desires to reach, **109**

operational, 115
SMART, 109, 110, 414
strategic, 113, 119
stretch, 414
superordinate, 460
tactical, 115
team-based performance, 451

Goal displacement A decision-making group loses sight of its original goal and a new, less important goal emerges, **89**

Goal setting theory A motivation theory stating that people have conscious goals that energize them and direct their thoughts and behaviors toward a particular end, **413–415**

Going public (IPO), 226–227
Good news/bad news, 487

Good to Great (Collins), 594
Google, 10, 45, 55, 60, 152, 159, 183, 214, 217, 281, 283, 307, 312, 325, 339, 429, 444, 542, 548, 554
Google+, 54, 55
Google Universal Ticketing Systems (GUTS), 429–430
Gore & Associates, 102
Government initiatives and rule changes, 217
Governmental regulatory agencies, 46
Grameen Bank, 219
Grameen Foundation, 503
Grandfather clocks, 567

Grapevine Informal communication network, **489**

Graystone Industries, 477
Great Recession (2007–2009), 43
Greatest Business Decisions of All Time, The, 78
Greatest management principle in the world, 417
Green Mountain Coffee, 54, 152, 153
Green practices, 158
Greenhouse, 556
Greenhouse Challenge Plus (Australia), 11
Greenhouse gas (GHG) emissions, 11, 12
Greenling, 311
Grid training, 392
Grievance procedure, 337
Grizzly Bear Lodge, 531
Group. *See* Teamwork
Group culture, 65
Group Danone, 158
Group decision making, 88–93
    advantages/disadvantages, 88–89
    brainstorming, 92, 93
    constructive conflict, 90–91
    encouraging creativity, 91–92
    leadership style, 90
Group incentive plans, 331–332

Group maintenance behaviors Actions taken to ensure the satisfaction of group members, develop and maintain harmonious work relationships, and preserve the social stability of the group, **390**–391, 397

Groupon, 4, 474

Groupthink A phenomenon that occurs in decision making when group members avoid disagreement as they strive for consensus, **89,** 455

Growth need strength The degree to which individuals want personal and psychological development, **428**–429

Growth needs, 424
Guiding coalition, 587–588
Gustin, 93

H
H-1B visas, 312
H-E-B, 312
Hackman and Oldman model of job design, 427–429
Half Price Books, 226–227
Hard Rock Café, 111
Hard work, 21
Harlem Children's Zone, 402

Harley-Davidson, 544
Harpo, 357

Hawthorne effect People's reactions to being observed or studied resulting in superficial rather than meaningful changes in behavior, **34**

Hawthorne studies, 33
He works, she works worksheet, 377
Health care benefits, 47
Health care industry, 59
Health insurance, 333–334
HealthPartners, 502
Healthy-TX, 221
Healthymagination program, 218
Hefty, 171
Heineken, 190
Heinz, 190
Herman Miller, 169
Hermès International, 11

Hersey and Blanchard's situational theory A life-cycle theory of leadership postulating that a manager should consider an employee's psychological and job maturity before deciding whether task performance or maintenance behaviors are more important, **395**

Hershey Company, 149
Hertz, 507
Herzberg's two-factor theory, 427
Hewlett-Packard, 123, 170, 216, 353, 368, 381, 397, 404, 475, 512, 574
Hierarchical culture, 65
Hierarchical levels, 252

Hierarchy The authority levels of the organizational pyramid, **252**

High-bandwidth communication networks, 542

High-involvement organization A type of organization in which top management ensures that there is consensus about the direction in which the business is heading, **283**

Hilton International, 151, 190, 194
Historical overview. *See* Evolution of management
Hitachi Solutions Europe, 474
Hofstede's four dimensions, 200, 202
Holacracy, 102, 379
Holcim acquisition of Lafarge, 127
Home Depot, 333, 382, 509
Hon Hai, 185
Honda Motor Company, 8, 122, 129, 190, 328
Honeywell, 251, 372

Horizontal communication Information shared among people on the same hierarchical level, **488**

Horizontal structure, 256–266

Host-country nationals Natives of the country where an overseas subsidiary is located, **196**

Hostile work environment, 353, 354
Hourly wage, 558
Houston Technology Center (HTC), 224

HP. *See* Hewlett-Packard
HR planning process, 309–313
HRM. *See* Human resources management (HRM)
Huffington Post, 214
Hult Prize, 187

Human capital The knowledge, skills, and abilities of employees that have economic value, **309**

Human dignity, 143

Human relations A classical management approach that attempted to understand and explain how human psychological and social processes interact with the formal aspects of the work situation to influence performance, **33**–34

Human resources analysis, 120
Human resources assessment, 121

Human resources management (HRM) Formal systems for the management of people within an organization, 306–344

    average employee, 329
    collective bargaining, 336
    defined, **308**
    demand forecasts, 310
    disciplinary procedures, 319
    diverse workforce. *See* Managing diversity
    employee benefits, 333–335
    equal employment laws, 319–321, 334
    executive pay, 332–333
    grievance procedure, 337
    health and safety, 335
    job analysis, 312–313
    labor relations, 335–338
    labor supply forecasts, 310–311
    layoffs, 318
    legal interview worksheet, 342
    legal issues, 319–321
    pay decisions, 330–333
    pay raise worksheet, 343
    performance appraisal (PA), 325–329
    planning process, 309–313
    recruitment, 313–314
    reward systems, 329–335
    selection, 314–318
    sexual harassment, 353–354, 355
    stock options, 332–333
    strategic impact of human resources, 308
    termination, 318–319, 320
    training and development, 322–324
    underperforming employee, 329
    unionization, 336, 338
Huntsman Chemical, 413
Hurricane Katrina, 85
Hybrid analyzer firms, 548
Hydro Green Energy, 224
Hydrogen-powered fuel cell technology, 546

Hygiene factors Characteristics of the workplace, such as company policies, working conditions, pay, and supervision, that can make people dissatisfied, **427**

Hyperactive Bob, 547
Hyperactive Technologies, 547
Hyperloop, 215

I

IBM, 56, 122, 139, 151, 159, 169, 170, 180, 187, 204, 216, 262, 284, 318, 322, 326, 353, 354, 360, 403, 446, 474, 544, 554, 578
IBM Software Group, 477
Idea jams, 556
IdeaStorm, 54
IDEO, 79, 283, 308, 556
Illinois Tool Works (ITW), 382
Illiteracy, 484

Illusion of control People's belief that they can influence events even when they have no control over what will happen, **85**

IMing. *See* Instant messaging (IMing)
Immigration, 47
Impact value chain (IVC), 503
Impoverished management, 392
IMX Exchange, 569
Inanity, 519
InBev, 180
Incentive systems, 331
Income statement (profit and loss statement), 513, 515

Incremental model Model of organizational decision making in which major solutions arise through a series of smaller decisions, **94**

Independent action, 59–60

Independent strategies Strategies that an organization acting on its own uses to change some aspect of its current environment, **59**

India, 185
inDinero, 215
Inditex, 11
Individual incentive plans, 331
Individual pay decisions, 330
Individual retirement account, 334
Individualism/collectivism, 200, 202
Industrial pollution, 157
Industry and market analysis, 120
Industry disruptors, 589
Inertia, 579
Influencing the environment, 59–60
Informal authority, 250
Informal communication, 488–489
Informal influence tactics, 254
Information patterns, 569
Information processing capability, 269
Information processing demand, 268–269
Information technology, 95
Informational roles, 19

Informing A team strategy that entails making decisions with the team and then informing outsiders of its intentions, **457**

Infosys, 185

Initial public offering (IPO) Sale to the public, for the first time, of federally registered and underwritten shares of stock in the company, **226–227**

Initiating structure, 390, 391

Innovation The introduction of new goods and services; a change in method or technology; a positive, useful departure from previous ways of doing things, **8, 534**. *See also* Managing technology and innovation

Amazon, 24
competitive advantage, 309
corporate entrepreneurship, 234
diverse workforce, 361
Innovative products, 534
Innovators, 537, 538

Inpatriate A foreign national brought in to work at the parent company, **201**

Inputs Goods and services organizations take in and use to create products or services, **42**

Inshoring Moving work from other countries back to the headquarters country. Work may be done by a domestic provider or in-house, **181**

Inside directors, 250

Insourcing Producing in-house one or more of an organization's goods or services, **181**

Instagram, 214
Instant messaging (IMing), 474

Instrumentality The perceived likelihood that performance will be followed by a particular outcome, **419**

Integration The degree to which differentiated work units work together and coordinate their efforts, **248, 249–250**

Integrity, 389

Integrity-based ethics programs Company mechanisms designed to instill in people a personal responsibility for ethical behavior, **149**

Integrity tests, 317
Intel, 93, 122, 281, 547, 550
Intellectual property, 569
Intercontinental Hotels, 190

Intergroup leader A leader who leads collaborative performance between groups or organizations, **401**

Intermediary model Charging fees to bring buyers and sellers together, **219**

Intermediate customers A customer who purchases raw materials or wholesale products before selling them to final customers, **54**

Internal audit A periodic assessment of a company's own planning, organizing, leading, and controlling processes, **509**

Internal benchmarking, 123
Internal development of technology, 550
Internal environment, 62–68
    organization climate, 67–68
    organization culture, 63–67
Internal locus of control, 396
Internal recruiting, 312
Internal resource analysis, 121
Internal strengths and weaknesses, 121–123
International Franchise Association, 218
International Harvester, 391
International management, 174–209
    Africa, 187
    Asia, 183–185
    Bartlett/Ghoshal typology of multinational companies, 188
    bribery, 203–204
    China, 184–185. *See also* China
    consequences of increasingly integrated global economy, 175–177
    cultural issues, 198–203
    entry modes, 193
    ethics, 147, 203–204
    European Union (EU), 182–183
    expatriates, 196, 197
    exporting, 193–194
    failed global assignments, 199
    foreign direct investment (FDI), 176
    foreign-national employees, 201–203
    franchising, 193, 194–195
    global integration, 189
    global integration--local responsiveness worksheet, 207–208
    global manager, 198
    global model, 190–191
    Hofstede's four dimensions, 200, 202
    identifying international executive potential, 199
    India, 185
    inshoring, 181
    insourcing, 181
    international model, 189–190
    Japan, 183, 184. *See also* Japan
    joint venture, 193, 195
    licensing, 193, 194
    local responsiveness, 189
    medium-size and small firms, 179
    Middle East, 186–187
    multinational model, 190
    natural environment and sustainability, 168
    North and South America, 185–186
    offshoring, 180–181
    outsourcing, 180–181
    regional trade agreements, 185, 186
    top 10 global firms, 179
    transnational model, 191–193
    wholly owned subsidiary, 193, 195–196
    WTO, 182

International model An organizational model that is composed of a company's overseas subsidiaries and characterized by greater control by the parent company over the research function and local product and marketing strategies than is the case in the multinational model, **189–190**

International Monetary Fund, 182
International Organization for Standardization (ISO), 292
International Space Station, 218
Internships, 312

Interpersonal and communication skills People skills; the ability to lead, motivate, and communicate effectively with others, **19**

Interpersonal communication, 470–479
Interpersonal roles, 19
Interview
    job, 314–315
    termination, 319
Intolerance of ineffective humanity, 154
Intranet, 569
Intrapreneurial activity, 233–234

Intrapreneurs New venture creators working inside big companies, **214**

Intrapreneurship, 555

Intrinsic reward Reward a worker derives directly from performing the job itself, **425**

Intuit, 285, 556
Invalid data, 517
Inventory management, 565
Invincibility Systems, 343–344
Invisible hand, 144
iPad, 52, 539
IPO. *See* Initial public offering (IPO)
ISO. *See* International Organization for Standardization (ISO)

ISO 9001 A series of quality standards developed by a committee working under the International Organization for Standardization to improve total quality in all businesses for the benefit of producers and consumers, **292–293**

Ispat International, 6
Issue advertising, 59
IVC. *See* Impact value chain (IVC)

J

J. M. Huber Corporation, 505
Jack and Jake's, 221
Jamba Juice, 367
Japan
    apologies, 481
    clan control, 526
    homogeneous culture, 526
    kaizen, 289, 541, 564
    needs theories, 425
    silence, 482
    U.S. trading partner, 183, 184
    written memos, 391
Jargon, 481
J.B. Hunt, 156
JCPenney, 350, 357, 567
JetBlue, 110
JIT. *See* Just-in-time (JIT)
JLW Homes and Communities, 232

Job analysis A tool for determining what is done on a given job and what should be done on that job, **312–313**

Job-contingent compensation, 558
Job description, 312

Job enlargement Giving people additional tasks at the same time to alleviate boredom, **426–427**

Job enrichment Changing a task to make it inherently more rewarding, motivating, and satisfying, **427**, 428

Job exchange, 569
Job interview, 314–315

Job maturity The level of the employee's skills and technical knowledge relative to the task being performed, **395**

Job-posting system, 312

Job rotation Changing from one task to another to alleviate boredom, **426**

Job satisfaction, 433–434
Job sharing, 369
Job shop, 294
Job specification, 312
JOBS Act. *See* Jumpstart Our Business Startups Act (JOBS Act)
Johnson & Johnson, 59, 169, 217, 260, 308, 354, 357, 520, 574
Johnson & Johnson Tylenol poisonings, 95, 96
Johnson Controls, 299
Johnsonville Sausage Company, 102
Joint venture, 193, 195, 551
JPMorgan, 477
Jumpstart Our Business Startups Act (JOBS Act), 230

Just-in-time (JIT) A system that calls for subassemblies and components to be manufactured in very small lots and delivered to the next stage of the production process just as they are needed, **298–299**

JVC, 178

K

Kaiser Permanente, 357, 557
Kaizen, 289, 541, 564
Kanban, 564
Kawasaki Heavy Industries, 195
Kellogg Company, 59, 190, 204
Keurig Incorporated, 54
Key technologies, 543
Keychest, 132
Khan Academy, 472
Kickback, 144
Kickboard, 152
Kickstarter, 93, 230
Kindle e-reader, 52
Kiva, 257, 258
Kmart, 567

Knowledge management Practices aimed at discovering and harnessing an organization's intellectual resources, **6,** 269

Knowledge work, 525
Knowledge worker, 6
Kobold Watch, 285

Kohlberg's model of cognitive moral development Classification of people based on their level of moral judgment, **145**

Kollmorgen, 444

KPMG, 354
Kroger, 126, 360, 548
Kwell, 221
Kyosei, 143

L

Labor contract (1850s), 31
Labor force growth, 46
Labor force participation, 47–48
Labor laws, 335–336
Labor-Management Relations Act, 336
Labor-Management Reporting and Disclosure Act, 336

Labor relations The system of relations between workers and management, **335–338**

Labor supply forecasts, 310–311
Laggards, 537, 539

Laissez-faire A leadership philosophy characterized by an absence of managerial decision making, **391**

Lamps Plus, 568
Landmines, 535
Landrum-Griffin Act, 336

Large batch Technologies that produce goods and services in high volume, **294**

Large batch technologies, 294
Large global corporations, 580
Larger companies, 284
Larger industrial equipment, 567
Late majority, 537, 539

Lateral leadership Style in which colleagues at the same hierarchical level are invited to collaborate and facilitate joint problem solving, **401**

Lateral role relationships, 458
Latina entrepreneurs, 220

Law of effect A law formulated by Edward Thorndike in stating that behavior that is followed by positive consequences will likely be repeated, **414**

Laws and regulations, 45–46
Layoffs, 285–287, 318
Laz-Z-Boy, 500
Laziness, 519
Leader, 19
Leader behaviors, 389–393

Leader–member exchange (LMX) theory Highlights the importance of leader behaviors not just toward the group as a whole but toward individuals on a personal basis, **391**

Leader traits, 388–389
Leadership, 380–408
    authenticity, 400–401
    autocratic/democratic, 391
    charismatic, 398–399
    courage, 402
    developing leadership skills, 403–404
    different styles for different situations, 389

Fielder's contingency model, 394–395
five sources of power worksheet, 407
followers, 386
Hersey and Blanchard's situational theory, 395
key behaviors, 383
leader behaviors, 389–393
leader traits, 388–389
leadership grid, 392
level 5, 400
LMX theory, 391
management, distinguished, 385
Millennials, 383
opportunities for leaders, 401
path–goal theory, 395–397
personality characteristics, 388–389
power, 386–388
shared/lateral, 401
situational approach, 393
substitutes for leadership, 397–398
supervisory/strategic, 386
task-motivated/relationship-motivated, 395
transformational, 399–400
vision, 383–384, 385
Vroom model, 394
Leadership development, 403–404
Leadership grid, 392
Leadership motivation, 388–389
Leadership opportunities, 401
Leadership style, 90

Leading   The management function that involves the manager's efforts to stimulate high performance by employees, **14**–15

Leading and learning, 594

Lean manufacturing   An operation that strives to achieve the highest possible productivity and total quality, cost-effectively, by eliminating unnecessary steps in the production process and continually striving for improvement, 292, **296**–297

Lean six sigma, 292
Leaning into the Future (Binney/Williams), 593, 594
Learning and leaning, 594
Learning cycle (explore, discover, act), 593
Learning leader, 594

Learning organization   An organization skilled at creating, acquiring, and transferring knowledge, and at modifying its behavior to reflect new knowledge and insights, 282–**283**, 554

Least preferred co-worker (LPC), 395
Legal action, 59
Legal area and the environment, 170
Legal interview worksheet, 342

Legal responsibilities   To obey local, state, federal, and relevant international laws, **153**

Legitimacy   People's judgment of a company's acceptance, appropriateness, and desirability, generally stemming from company goals and methods that are consistent with societal values, **231**

Legitimate power, 387
Lehman Brothers, 85
Lending Club, 228
Lenovo, 175, 192, 205
Lesbian, gay, bisexual, or transgender (LGBT) employees, 354–355
Level 5 hierarchy, 594

Level 5 leadership   A combination of strong professional will (determination) and humility that builds enduring greatness, **400**

Leverage ratios, 513, 515
Leveraging difference, 363, 364
Levi Strauss, 198, 570
LGBT employees, 354–355

Liabilities   The amounts a corporation owes to various creditors, **513**

Liaison, 19
Liaison relationships, 458
Liaison roles, 269
Licensing, 193, 194, 551
Lie detector test, 317

Life-cycle analysis (LCA)   A process of analyzing all inputs and outputs, through the entire "cradle-to-grave" life of a product, to determine total environmental impact, **157**

Life-cycle theory of leadership, 395
Life Is Good, 60
Lifelong learning, 593
Lifestyle and taste changes, 217
Lincoln Electric, 366

Line departments   Units that deal directly with the organization's primary goods and services, **256**–257

LinkedIn, 22, 54, 313, 316, 359, 474
Lipitor, 51
Liquidity ratios, 513
Listening, 482–483
Listening feedback form, 494
Listening skills survey, 493–494
Living Goods, 286
L.L.Bean, 7
LMX theory. *See* Leader–member exchange (LMX) theory
Local content rules, 189
Lockheed Martin, 353, 447, 448
Locus of control, 396

Logistics   The movement of the right goods in the right amount to the right place at the right time, **297**–298, 565

L'Oréal, 158, 189
Louisiana-Pacific, 170
Louisville Gas and Electric, 170

Low-cost strategy   A strategy an organization uses to build competitive advantage by being efficient and offering a standard, no-frills product, **128**

Lower management, 252
Lowe's, 316
LPC. *See* Least preferred co-worker (LPC)
Lucasfilm, 132
Lucky Sort, 551
Lying/truth-telling, 141, 142

M

M&A. *See* Mergers and acquisitions (M&A)
Ma Earth Skin Care, 164–165
Maastricht Treaty, 182
Macroeconomic analysis, 120

Macroenvironment   The general environment; includes governments, economic conditions, and other fundamental factors that generally affect all organizations, **43**

demographics, 46–48
economy, 43–44
laws and regulations, 45–46
natural ecology, 48–49
social issues, 48
technology, 44–45
Macy's Group, 261, 298, 545, 568, 570
Magna Exteriors and Interiors, 496–497
Maintenance behaviors, 390–391, 397

Make-or-buy decision   The question an organization asks itself about whether to acquire new technology from an outside source or develop it itself, **550**

Malcolm Baldrige National Quality Award, 292

Management   The process of working with people and resources to accomplish organizational goals, **13**

case incident (effective management), 103–104
classical approaches, 30–35
contemporary approaches, 35–36
functions, 13–15
global expansion. See International management
historical overview. See Evolution of management
leadership, distinguished, 385

Management audit   An evaluation of the effectiveness and efficiency of various systems within an organization, **509**–510

Management by objectives (MBO)   A process in which objectives set by a subordinate and a supervisor must be reached within a given time period, **326**

Management bonus, 331
Management by wandering around (MBWA), 487
Management functions, 13–15
Management information system (MIS), 45
Management levels and skills, 15–20

Management myopia   Focusing on short-term earnings and profits at the expense of longer-term strategic obligations, **515**

Management process, 1
Management roles and activities, 18
Management skills, 18–20

Management teams   Teams that coordinate and provide direction to the subunits under their jurisdiction and integrate work among subunits, **445**

Manager
  decision making. *See* Managerial decision
    making
  decisional roles, 19
  frontline, 17
  informational roles, 19
  interpersonal roles, 19
  middle, 17
  top, 16
Managerial behaviors worksheet, 28
Managerial control, 498–531
  accounting audit, 512
  activity-based costing (ABC), 512
  balanced scorecard, 521, 522
  budgetary controls, 510–511
  bureaucratic control systems, 501–522
  clan control, 525–526
  concurrent control, 505, 506
  control cycle, 501–505
  corrective action, 504–505
  designing effective systems, 518–521
  dual responsibilities of control system, 132
  employee acceptance of control system,
    520–521
  empowered setting, 526
  entrepreneurship, 226
  feedback control, 505, 506–507
  feedforward control, 505, 506
  financial controls, 513–515
  management audits, 509–510
  market control, 523–525
  measuring performance, 502–504
  open communication, 521
  out-of-control company, 500
  performance standards, 502, 518–520
  planning, 500
  principle of exception, 504
  resistance to control, 518
  rigid bureaucratic behavior, 516–517
  six sigma, 508–509
  strategy map, 521, 522
  tactical behavior, 517–518
Managerial decision making, 74–104
  barriers to overcome, 85–87
  best decision?, 84–85
  characteristics of managerial decisions, 76–78
  conflict, 78
  decision making worksheet, 99–100
  discounting the future, 86, 87
  ethical decision making, 149–150
  evaluating alternatives, 80–81
  evaluating the decision, 84
  generating alternative solutions, 80–81
  group decision making, 88–93
  implementing the decision, 82–84
  lack of structure, 77
  making the choice, 82
  organizational decision making, 94–97
  planning steps, 109
  problem identification and diagnosis, 80, 81
  programmed/nonprogrammed decisions, 77
  psychological biases, 85–87
  ready-made/custom-made solutions, 80
  six-phase decision-making process, 79
  social realities, 87
  time pressures, 87
  uncertainty and risk, 77–78
Managerial performance test, 317
Managerial roles, 19
Managerial span of control, 252, 253
Managing culture, 66–67

Managing diversity Managing
a culturally diverse workforce by
recognizing the characteristics common

to specific groups of employees while
dealing with employees as individuals
and supporting, nurturing, and utilizing
their differences to the organization's
advantage, 346–379

  accommodating work and family needs, 369
  accountability, 372
  advantages of diverse workforce, 360–361
  affirmative action, 359
  age of workforce, 358–359
  alternative work arrangements, 369
  awareness building, 369–370
  being different worksheet, 375
  career development and promotion, 372
  challenges of diversity and inclusion,
    361–363
  communication problems, 362
  components of diversified workforce, 350
  defined, **348**
  diversity assumptions, 365
  diversity officer, 367
  diversity training, 369, 371
  educational levels, 358
  gender issues, 351–355
  he works, she works worksheet, 377
  historical overview, 348–349
  hostile work environment, 353, 354
  leveraging difference, 363, 364
  LGBT employees, 354–355
  mentoring, 371–372
  minorities and immigrants, 355–357
  mistrust and tension, 362
  multicultural organization, 365–366
  organizational assessment, 368
  race and ethnicity, 355–357
  recruitment, 368–369
  retaining employees, 370–372
  sexual harassment, 353–354, 355
  skill building, 370
  stereotyping, 362–363
  support groups, 371
  systems accommodation, 372
  top management, 367–368
  top ten companies for diversity, 357
Managing technology and innovation, 532–562
  adopter categories, 537–539
  assessing technology needs, 543–544
  bureaucracy busting, 555–556
  capability development, 547–548, 549
  conditions required for technological
    development, 536
  creativity, 554–555
  decision making, 545–549
  design thinking, 556–557
  development project, 557–558
  diffusion of technological innovations,
    537–539
  disruptive innovation, 539
  economic viability, 546–547, 549
  external technology trends, 544
  failure, 555
  human resource systems, 558–559
  job design, 558
  make-or-buy decision, 550
  managerial roles, 552–553
  market receptiveness, 545, 549
  organizational suitability, 548, 549
  requirements for innovation, 554
  shifting competitive impact from
    technology, 542
  speed with which innovation spreads, 539
  technological feasibility, 546, 549
  technology acquisition options, 550–552
  technology audit, 543

  technology followership, 542–543
  technology leadership, 540–542
  technology life cycle, 536–537
  types of innovation, 534, 535
Manipulation and cooptation, 583, 584
Manipulative game-playing, 414
Manufacturing waste, 171

Market control Control based on
the use of pricing mechanisms and
economic information to regulate
activities within organizations, **501,**
523–525

Marketing and the environment, 171
Marketing audit, 121
Marriott, 126, 159, 354, 574
Mary Kay Cosmetics, 425
Masculinity/femininity, 200
Mashable, 313

Maslow's need hierarchy A
conception of human needs organizing
needs into a hierarchy of five major
types, 34, **421**–423

Mass customization The
production of varied, individually
customized products at the low cost of
standardized, mass-produced products,
62, **295**–296

Mass Mutual Financial, 354
Massey Energy mine disaster, 335
Master budget, 511
Master Lock, 181
MasterCard, 357
Matrix diamond, 264

Matrix organization An organization
composed of dual reporting
relationships in which some employees
report to two superiors—a functional
manager and a divisional manager,
262–264, 269

Matsushita, 178
Mattel, 198

Maximizing A decision realizing the
best possible outcome, **82**

MBO. *See* Management by objectives (MBO)
MBWA. *See* Management by wandering around
    (MBWA)
McClelland's needs, 424
McCormick & Schmick's Seafood
    Restaurants, 361
McDonald's, 118, 119, 152, 153, 168, 170, 171,
    194, 294, 504
McKinsey, 92
McNeil Consumer Health Care, 357
Measuring performance, 502–504, 518–520
Mechanistic and organic worksheet, 302
Mechanistic approach to job design, 425

Mechanistic organization A form
of organization that seeks to maximize
internal efficiency, **278**

Media richness The degree to which
a communication channel conveys
information, **478**–479

Mediator A third party who intervenes to help others manage their conflict, **460**

Medical and hospital insurance, 333–334
Medieval times, 30
Mega-corporations, 580
Melting pot myth, 365
Mentoring, 371–372

Mentors Higher-level managers who help ensure that high-potential people are introduced to top management and socialized into the norms and values of the organization, **371**

Merck, 251, 357, 547

Merger One or more companies combining with another, **58**

Mergers and acquisitions (M&A), 58–59, 127, 158, 580
Merit pay, 332
Miami, Florida, 576
Microblogging, 474
Microsoft, 183, 214, 312, 356, 403, 541, 542, 548
Middle East, 186–187

Middle-level managers Managers located in the middle layers of the organizational hierarchy, reporting to top-level executives, **17**, 18

Middle management, 252
Middle-of-the-road management, 392
Millennial-friendly internal structure, 281
Millennial generation, 7, 125, 141, 201, 265, 352, 383. *See also* Multiple Generations at Work boxes
MillerCoors Brewing Company, 452
Mining, 335
Ministry of Supply, 225
Minorities and immigrants, 355–357. *See also* Managing diversity
MIS. *See* Management information system (MIS)

Mission An organization's basic purpose and scope of operations, **118**

Mission statement, 64–65, 118
Mississippi Health Services, 401
Mistakes, 418
Misunderstanding, 580
Mixed signals and misperception, 472–473
Mixx.com, 223
Model T, 32, 62
Modular corporation, 265
Module, 295
Mondelez International, 353
Monitor, 19

Monolithic organization An organization that has a low degree of structural integration—employing few women, minorities, or other groups that differ from the majority—and thus has a highly homogeneous employee population, **365**

Monsanto, 56, 171, 198
Monster. com, 312, 569

Moral philosophy Principles, rules, and values people use in deciding what is right or wrong, **143**

Motivating for performance, 410–440
  Alderfer's ERG theory, 423–424
  empowerment, 429–430
  equity theory, 430–432
  expectancy theory, 419–420
  extrinsic/intrinsic rewards, 425
  fairness, 430–432
  goal setting, 413–415
  Hackman and Oldham model of job design, 427–429
  Herzberg's two-factor theory, 427
  job rotation, enlargement, and enrichment, 426–427
  job satisfaction, 433–434
  Maslow's need hierarchy, 421–423
  McClelland's needs, 424
  need theories, 421–425
  performance-related beliefs, 419–420
  procedural justice, 432
  psychological contracts, 434
  quality of work life, 433
  reinforcing performance, 415–418
  rewards and punishments, 417–418
  teams, 451–452

Motivation Forces that energize, direct, and sustain a person's efforts, **412**

Motivators Factors that make a job more motivating, such as additional job responsibilities, opportunities for personal growth and recognition, and feelings of achievement, **427**

Motorola, 198, 292, 508, 574

Moving Instituting the change, **582**

MTV, 557
Müller Quaker Diary, 51
Multi-School Fossil Free Divestment Fund, 595

Multicultural organization An organization that values cultural diversity and seeks to utilize and encourage it, **366**

Multidomestic model, 190

Multinational model An organizational model that consists of the subsidiaries in each country in which a company does business, and provides a great deal of discretion to those subsidiaries to respond to local conditions, **190**

Multiple Generations at Work boxes
  align your skills with future of work, 580
  annual performance evaluation, 507
  Boomer retirements, 7
  business start-up, 232
  crowdsourcing, 93
  flexibility and work–life balance, 352
  gamification, 538
  leadership, 383
  Millennials and higher-order needs, 423
  Millennials and internal structure, 281
  Millennials and international work experience, 201
  Millennials and the lack of trust, 141
  older workers, 47
  online networks or traditional hierarchies?, 265
  personal smartphones/devices at work, 475
  soft skills and students' career prospects, 324
  strengths/weaknesses of each generation, 125

Multitasking, 417
Music industry, 537
Musicane, 231
Mutuality, 154
MyMPO, 231
MySpace, 542

N

NAFTA. *See* North American Free Trade Agreement (NAFTA)
NanoHealth (Indian School of Business), 187
Nanometer, 590
Nanoparticles, 591
NanoRidge Materials, 224
Nanotech silver, 591
Nanotechnology, 590–591
Narcissism, 519
NASA, 262
NASA Armstrong Flight Research Center, 118, 119
NASCAR, 347, 364, 373
NASDAQ Composite, 44
National Counterterrorism Center, 268
National Industries for the Blind (NIB), 358
National Information Solutions Cooperative (NISC), 452
National Labor Relations Act, 335
National Labor Relations Board (NLRB), 46, 335, 336
National Marrow Donor Program (NMDP), 521
National Public Radio, 488
National Restaurant Association, 354
National Retail Federation, 354
National Security Agency, 359
National Transportation Exchange, 569
National Venture Capital Association, 227
Natural disasters, 110
Natural ecology, 48–49
Natural environment and sustainability, 155–160, 166–172
  accounting (company actions), 171
  competitive advantage, 166
  conservation and environmentalism, 167
  cost-benefit analysis, 168
  cost effectiveness, 166
  cradle-to-cradle approach, 158
  ecocentric management, 157
  economics and the environment, 168
  environmental movement, 167
  finance (company actions), 172
  future directions, 158–160
  implementation, 169–172
  international perspectives, 168
  legal area (company actions), 170
  legal compliance, 166
  long-term thinking, 167
  managerial actions, 168–172
  marketing (company actions), 171
  operations (company actions), 170–171
  public affairs (company actions), 170
  public opinion, 166–167
  risk society, 156–157
  science and the environment, 167
  Silent Spring (Carson), 167–168
  strategic integration, 168–169
  strategy (company actions), 169–170
  sustainability performance indicators, 158
  systems thinking, 168–169
  take-make-waste production model, 155
  tragedy of the commons, 167
NaturaLawn of America, 215
Nature Conservancy, 160
NcNeil-PPC, 260
Need for achievement, 424

Need for affiliation, 424
Need for power, 424
Need theories, 421–425

Needs assessment An analysis identifying the jobs, people, and departments for which training is necessary, **322**

Negative reinforcement Removing or withholding an undesirable consequence, **416**

Negligent hiring, 315
Negotiator, 19
Nescafe, 566
Nestlé, 4, 159, 180
Nestlé Health Sciences, 551
Net working capital ratio, 513
Net zero greenhouse gas (GHG) emissions, 12
NetApp, 526
Netflix, 8, 122, 132, 183, 289
Network co-operator, 266
Network for Good, 286

Network organization A collection of independent, mostly single-function firms that collaborate on a good or service, **264–266**

New business start-up. *See* Entrepreneurship
New business start-up worksheet, 240

New economy A current perspective suggesting that the economic success of a region or company depends on its ability to thrive globally, operate in an environmentally responsible manner, and leverage knowledge workers and information for competitive advantage, **566**

New entrants, 51–52
New York City Board of Health, 48
New York Community Bancorp (NYCB), 112
New York Delhi, 179
Next Day Flyers, 124
NextSpace, 452
Niche Hotel Group (NHG), 377–378
Nike, 290
Nike+FuelBand, 538
Nikko Asset Management, 172
Nikon, 204
Nissan, 8
NLRB. *See* National Labor Relations Board (NLRB)
Noise, 470
Nokia, 262

Nonprogrammed decisions New, novel, complex decisions having no proven answers, **77**

Nonverbal communication interpretation worksheet, 493
Nonverbal skills, 482
Nook e-reader, 52
Nordstrom, 63, 128, 568
Norming stage, 449

Norms Shared beliefs about how people should think and behave, **452–453**

North American Free Trade Agreement (NAFTA) An economic pact that combined the economies of the United States, Canada, and Mexico into one of the world's largest trading blocs, 50, **186**

Not Mass Produced, 221
Novartis, 51, 204, 357
Novo Nordisk, 112, 169, 472
Nucor, 170, 444, 556
Nurturing role, 266

O

OB mod. *See* Organizational behavior modification (OB mod)
Obesity, 146
Observing, 484
Occupational Safety & Health Administration (OSHA), 46
Ocean Renewable Power Company (ORPC), 120–121
OD. *See* Organization development (OD)
OFCCP. *See* Office of Federal Contract Compliance Programs (OFCCP)
Office of Federal Contract Compliance Programs (OFCCP), 46, 321

Offshoring Moving work to other countries, **180–181**

Oil industry, 546
Older workers, 47
Omnica, 445
1-800-Flowers, 367
One-best-way myth, 365

One-way communication A process in which information flows in only one direction—from the sender to the receiver, with no feedback loop, **470**

Online job boards, 312
Online networks, 265
Online privacy, 146
Online snooping, 570
Only-one-way myth, 365

Open-book management Practice of sharing with employees at all levels of the organization vital information previously meant for management's eyes only, **486–487, 520**

Open system perspective of an organization, 36, 42

Open systems Organizations that are affected by, and that affect, their environment, **42**

Operational budget, 132
Operational goals, 115
Operational manager, 17

Operational planning The process of identifying the specific procedures and processes required at lower levels of the organization, **114**

Operations analysis, 121
Operations and the environment, 170–171
Operations management, 563–571

change, 563
company website, 568
corporate organization, 564–565
environment, 566
finance, 565
globalization, 566
human attributes, 570
human resources, 565
information patterns, 569
intellectual property, 569
Internet, 567–569
knowledge and information, 566–567
lens, 563–564
logistics, 565
marketing, 564
new needs and desires, 570
new perspectives, 564
pitfalls, 570
purchasing, 565, 568–569
pure-play companies, 568
research and engineering, 564–565
strategic planning, 564
teamwork, 565
technology, 567
what does it entail?, 563

Opportunity analysis A description of the good or service, an assessment of the opportunity, an assessment of the entrepreneur, specification of activities and resources needed to translate your idea into a viable business, and your source(s) of capital, **228**

Opposites, 366

Optimizing Achieving the best possible balance among several goals, **82**

Oral communication, 473
Oral reports, 502–503
Orbital Sciences Corporation, 218

Organic structure An organizational form that emphasizes flexibility, 61, **278**

Organization change. *See* Change management

Organization chart The reporting structure and division of labor in an organization, **248,** 249

Organization culture The set of important assumptions about the organization and its goals and practices that members of the company share, **63–67**

clan control, 526
competing values model of culture, 66
diagnosing culture, 64–66
managing culture, 66–67
strong/weak culture, 63–64
types of cultures, 65

Organization development (OD) The systemwide application of behavioral science knowledge to develop, improve, and reinforce the strategies, structures, and processes that lead to organizational effectiveness, **577**

Organization structure, 246–274

board of directors, 250–251
centralization/decentralization, 255–256
CEO, 251
delegation, 253–255
differentiation, 248–249
divisional organization, 259–262
formal/informal structures, 279
functional organization, 257–259, 260
hierarchical levels, 252
horizontal structure, 256–266
integration, 249–250
line/staff departments, 256–257
matrix organization, 262–264
network organization, 264–266
organization chart, 248, 249
organizational integration, 266–269
span of control, 252, 253
tall/flat organization, 252
top management team, 251
vertical structure, 250–256
Organizational agility, 276–304
boundaryless organization, 300
computer-integrated manufacturing
    (CIM), 296
concurrent engineering, 299
core capabilities, 280–281
customer relationship management (CRM),
    289–291
diverse workforce, 361
downsizing, 285–287
flexible factories, 296
flexible manufacturing, 295–297
formal/informal organizational structures, 279
high-involvement organization, 283
ISO 9001, 292–293
just-in-time (JIT), 298–299
lean manufacturing, 296–297
learning organization, 282–283
logistics, 297–298
mass customization, 295–296
mechanistic and organic worksheet, 302
organic structure, 278
organizational size, 284–287
quality initiatives, 291–293
reengineering, 293
responsive organization, 278–280
six sigma quality, 292
speed, 297–299
strategic alliance, 281–282
technology configurations, 294
total quality management (TQM), 291
value chain, 290

Organizational ambidexterity   Ability
to achieve multiple objectives
simultaneously, **576**

Organizational behavior   A
contemporary management approach
that studies and identifies management
activities that promote employee
effectiveness by examining the complex
and dynamic nature of individual, group,
and organizational processes, **35**

**Organizational behavior modification
(OB mod)**   The application of
reinforcement theory in organizational
settings, **415**

Organizational climate   The patterns
of attitudes and behavior that shape

people's experience of an organization,
67–68

Organizational communication, 484–490
Organizational control. *See* Managerial control
Organizational decision making, 94–97
Organizational flexibility, 361. *See also*
    Organizational agility
Organizational integration, 266–269
Organizational politics, 95
Organizational size, 284–287
Organizational structure. *See* Organization structure

Organizing   The management function
of assembling and coordinating human,
financial, physical, informational, and other
resources needed to achieve goals, **14**

Orientation training   Training
designed to introduce new employees
to the company and familiarize them
with policies, procedures, culture, and
the like, **323**

OSHA
    Occupational Safety & Health Act, 335
    Occupational Safety & Health Administration,
        46
Out-of-control company, 500
Outback Steakhouse, 129

Outcome   A consequence a person
receives for his or her performance, **419**

Outer space, 218

Outplacement   The process of helping
people who have been dismissed
from the company regain employment
elsewhere, **318**

Outputs   The products and services
organizations create, **42**

Outsourcing   Contracting with an
outside provider to produce one or more
of an organization's goods or services,
180–181

Overseas business (local language/customs), 481–482

P
PA. *See* Performance appraisal (PA)
Pacific Gas & Electric, 170
Pacific Sunwear, 568
Pacing technologies, 543
Packaging, 157
Panasonic, 191–193
Panera Bread, 217, 359
Paper-and-pencil honesty test, 317

Parading   A team strategy that entails
simultaneously emphasizing internal
team building and achieving external
visibility, **457**

Parallel teams   Teams that operate
separately from the regular work
structure and exist temporarily, **445**

Parasole restaurant group, 428

**Participation in decision
making**   Leader behaviors that
managers perform in involving their
employees in making decisions, **391**

Participative leadership, 396, 456
Participative management, 35, 283
Patagonia, 157, 312, 413
Patagonia Sur, 11

Path–goal theory   A theory that
concerns how leaders influence
subordinates' perceptions of their work
goals and the paths they follow toward
attainment of those goals, 395–397, **396**

Patient Protection and Affordable Care Act, 333.
    See also Affordable Care Act
Pay decisions, 330–333
Pay grade, 330
Pay level, 330
Pay raise worksheet, 343
Pay structure, 330, 331
PayPal, 215, 589
Pedigree dog food, 152
Peer advisory group, 251
Peer pressure, 579
Peer-to-peer loans, 228
Penske Truck Leasing Company, 524
People Operations (POPS), 325, 339
People skills, 19
People who are mentally and physically disabled,
    357–358
People with disabilities, 357–358
PepsiCo, 5, 48, 51–53, 58, 62, 93, 328, 353, 372

Perception   The process of receiving
and interpreting information, **471**

Perfect quality, 298

**Performance appraisal
(PA)**   Assessment of an employee's job
performance, **325**–329, 507

Performance-contingent compensation, 558
Performance data, 502
Performance Food Group, 59

Performance gap   The difference
between actual performance and
desired performance, **582**

Performance leadership behaviors, 390, 391
Performance norms, 455, 456
Performance-related beliefs, 419–420
Performance stage, 449
Performance standards, 502, 518–520
Performance tests, 317
Performance-to-outcome link, 419
Person-contingent compensation, 558
Personal goal setting worksheet, 438
Personal observation, 503
Personal safety alert (PSA), 506
Personal smartphones/devices at work, 475
Personality tests, 316
Personalized power, 424
Personnel management, 308. *See also* Human
    resources management (HRM)
Persuading, 454
Persuasive messages, 479–480
Persuasive sales people, 516
Peru, 186
Petroleo Brasileiro (Petrobras), 140
Pettiness, 519

PEURegen, 221
Pfizer, 51
P&G. *See* Procter & Gamble (P&G)
Pharmaceutical industry, 541, 547
Phased retirement, 47, 359
Philadelphia Department of Licenses and
Inspections, 518

Philanthropic responsibilities Additional behaviors and activities that society finds desirable and that the values of the business support, **154**

Philips N.V., 8, 178, 191, 289
Physical needs, 34
Physiological needs, 421, 422
PillPack, 80
Pinterest, 214
Pirated goods, 547
Pixar, 90, 308
Plan to Win (McDonald's), 119

Planning The management function of systematically making decisions about the goals and activities that an individual, a group, a work unit, or the overall organization will pursue, **13–14**

Planning and strategic management, 106–137
barriers to strategy implementation, 131
basic planning process, 108–113
benchmarking, 123
business strategy, 128–129
corporate strategy, 125–128
decision-making stages, 109
external opportunities and threats, 119–121
four "A's" model, 130
functional strategy, 129
hierarchy of goals and plans, 114
internal strengths and weaknesses, 121–123
mission, vision, and goals, 118–119
operational planning, 114
operations management, 564
questions to be answered, 113
resources and core capabilities, 122, 123
situational analysis, 108–109
SMART goals, 109, 110
strategic control, 131–132
strategic management process, 118
strategic planning, 113–114
strategy implementation, 129–131
strategy map, 115, 116
SWOT analysis, 124–125
tactical planning, 114

Plans The actions or means managers intend to use to achieve organizational goals, **109**

Plant Closing Bill, 321
Plante Moran, 433

Pluralistic organization An organization that has a relatively diverse employee population and makes an effort to involve employees from different gender, racial, or cultural backgrounds, **365**

"Plussing," 90
PMF Industries, 294
PNC Financial, 356
Podtector, 535
Political action, 59, 60
Political and regulatory analysis, 120

Polluter pays principle, 171
Pollution Prevention Pays, 170, 171
Pollution reduction program, 171
Polycast Technology, 369
Polygraph (lie detector test), 317
Popchips, 211, 227, 235
Population growth, 46
Porter's competitive environment model, 50
Portfolio, 126
Porto Alegre, Brazil, 590

Positive reinforcement Applying consequences that increase the likelihood that a person will repeat the behavior that led to it, **416**

Power The ability to influence others, **386–388**

Power distance, 200, 202
PPI. *See* Progress out of poverty index (PPI)
PPR Group, 171
Practical Computer Applications, 225
Pregnancy Discrimination Act, 334
Preliminary, concurrent, and feedback control worksheet, 531
Preliminary control, 506
Presentation and persuasion skills, 479–480
PricewaterhouseCoopers, 81, 160, 292, 354, 357
PricewaterhouseCoopers Hungary, 538

Principle of exception A managerial principle stating that control is enhanced by concentrating on the exceptions to or significant deviations from the expected result or standard, **504**

Proactive change A response that is initiated before a performance gap has occurred, **589**

Probing A team strategy that requires team members to interact frequently with outsiders, diagnose their needs, and experiment with solutions, **457**

Problem identification and diagnosis, 80, 81

Procedural justice Using fair process in decision making and making sure others know that the process was as fair as possible, **432**

Process engineering role, 266
Process innovation, 534, 535
Procter & Gamble (P&G), 34, 113, 167, 169, 190, 191, 196, 216, 262, 293, 322, 354, 357, 361
Procter & Gamble acquisition of Gillette, 64
Product approach to departmentalization, 260–261

Product champion A person who promotes a new technology throughout the organization in an effort to obtain acceptance of and support for it, **553**

Product innovation, 534, 535
Product manager, 269
Product Red, 60
Production budget, 511
Professional networking sites, 313

Profit and loss statement An itemized financial statement of the

income and expenses of a company's operations, **513, 515**

Profit maximization perspective, 154
Profit-sharing plan, 331–332
Profitability ratios, 515

Programmed decisions Decisions encountered and made before, having objectively correct answers, and solvable by using simple rules, policies, or numerical computations, **77**

Progress out of poverty index (PPI), 503
Progressive discipline, 521

Project and development teams Teams that work on long-term projects but disband once the work is completed, **445**

Project Loon (Google), 45
Project manager, 269
Prospector firms, 548

Prospectors Companies that continuously change the boundaries for their task environments by seeking new products and markets, diversifying and merging, or acquiring new enterprises, **59**

Prosper, 228
Provincialism, 519
Prudential Financial, 357

Pseudotransformational leaders Leaders who talk about positive change but allow their self-interest to take precedence over followers' needs, **401**

Psychological biases, 85–87

Psychological contract A set of perceptions of what employees owe their employers, and what their employers owe them, **434**

Psychological maturity An employee's self-confidence and self-respect, **395**

Public affairs and the environment, 170
Public policy exception (employment-at-will), 319
Public relations, 59
Puma, 171

Punishment Administering an aversive consequence, **416**

Purchasing, 565, 568–569
Purchasing company that owns technology, 551

Pure-play Refers to an organization's decision to sell all of its products or services via the Internet, **568**

Pyramid of global social responsibility, 153

Q

Quaker brand cereal, 51

Quality The excellence of your product (goods or services), **8–9**, 291–293

Quality of work life (QWL) programs Programs designed to create a workplace that enhances employee well-being, **433**

Quantitative management A contemporary management approach that emphasizes the application of quantitative analysis to managerial decisions and problems, **35**

Question marks, 127
Quick Lane Tire & Auto Center, 414
QuickenLoans, 285
Quid pro quo harassment, 353
QuikTrip, 417
Quotas, 189
QWL programs. *See* Quality of work life (QWL) programs

R

R. A. Jones & Co., 299
Race and ethnicity, 355–357. *See also* Managing diversity
Racial or ethnic slurs, 354
Radio frequency identification (RFID) tags, 298, 545
Rapid plant assessment, 484
Ratio analysis, 513, 515
Rational culture, 65
Razorfish, 484
RCA, 191

Reactive change A response that occurs under pressure; problem-driven change, **589**

Reading, 484

Ready-made solutions Ideas that have been seen or tried before, **79**

Real Medleys multigrain cereal, 51
Rechargeable batteries, 591

Recruitment The development of a pool of applicants for jobs in an organization, **313**–314, 368–369

Reengineering, 293
Reference checks, 315
Referent power, 387–388

Reflection Process by which a person states what he or she believes the other person is saying, **483**

Refreezing Strengthening the new behaviors that support the change, **583**

Refrigerated Food Express (RFX), 156
Regional approach to departmentalization, 261
Regional trade agreements, 185, 186
Regulators, 45, 46

Reinforcers Positive consequences that motivate behavior, **414**

Reinforcing performance, 415–418
Reinventing industries, 589
Relatedness needs, 423, 424
Relating, 454

Relationship-motivated leadership Leadership that places primary emphasis on maintaining good interpersonal relationships, **395**

Relationship-oriented behavior, 392

Relativism Philosophy that bases ethical behavior on the opinions and behaviors of relevant other people, 143, **144**

Reliability The consistency of test scores over time and across alternative measurements, **317**

Reliable PSD, 477
Repackaging, 157
Reply/Reply All, 476
Research partnership, 551
Reserves, 556
Resilience, 593
Resistance to change, 579–581
Resistance to change worksheet, 597
Resource allocator, 19

Resources Inputs to a system that can enhance performance, **122**

Responding to the environment
   adapting to the environment, 61–62
   cooperative action, 60
   independent action, 59–60
   influencing the environment, 59–60
   selecting a new environment, 58–59

Responsibility The assignment of a task that an employee is supposed to carry out, **253**

Responsible Care Initiative (chemical industry), 169
Responsive organization, 278–280
Restriction of Hazardous Substances Directive, 170
Results appraisal, 326
Results Only Work Environment (ROWE), 499, 527
Résumé, 313
Rethink Robotics, 545
Retirement benefits, 334

Return on investment (ROI) A ratio of profit to capital used, or a rate of return from capital, **515**

Return-on-investment calculations, 62
Reverse engineering, 244
Reverse logistics, 170
Reward power, 387
Reward systems, 329–335
Rewards and punishments, 417–418
RFID tags. *See* Radio frequency identification (RFID) tags
Rheedlen Center for Children and Families, 402

Right-to-work Legislation that allows employees to work without having to join a union, **337**

Right-to-work states, 337

Rightsizing A successful effort to achieve an appropriate size at which the company performs most effectively, **287**

Rigid bureaucratic behavior, 516–517

Risk The state that exists when the probability of success is less than 100 percent and losses may occur, **78**

Risk society, 156–157
Risk taking, 234
Ritz-Carlton Hotel, 65, 518–519
Robot repercussion, 600–601
Robotics technology, 534, 545
ROI. *See* Return on investment (ROI)

Roles Different sets of expectations for how different individuals should behave, **454**

Roman Empire, 30
Root Capital, 503
Royal Dutch Shell. *See* Shell
Rumors, 489
Russell Reynolds, 196
Ryanair, 11

S

Safety or security needs, 421, 422
Safeway, 126, 548
Salary, 558
Salary.command PayScale, 330
Sales budget, 511
Sales expense budget, 510
Sales Gravy, 313
Salesforce.com, 289
Same-sex harassment, 354
Samsung, 118, 119, 185
San Francisco Federal Credit Union (SFFCU), 259
SAP, 59

Sarbanes-Oxley Act An act passed into law by Congress in to establish strict accounting and reporting rules in order to make senior managers more accountable and to improve and maintain investor confidence, **145**

   company's financial performance, 525
   corporate governance, 252
   ethics codes, 148
   risk aversion, 146
   what it does, 145
   whistleblowing, 152
SAS, 280, 369, 411, 421, 435

Satisficing Choosing an option that is acceptable, although not necessarily the best or perfect, **82**, 89

Sautil, 286
SBA. *See* Small Business Administration (SBA)
Scale diseconomies, 285
Scale economies, 30
Scanning, 544

Scenario A narrative that describes a particular set of future conditions, **57**, **111**

Scenario development, 57

Team Rubicon, 426
triple bottom line, 112
waste elimination (Terracycle), 49
what is a social enterprise?, 472
will business school graduates work for social enterprises?, 311
zero CO$_2$ emissions, 12

Social entrepreneurship   Leveraging resources to address social problems, **219**–220, 221

Social facilitation effect   Working harder when in a group than when working alone, **451**

Social impact, 503
Social issues, 48

Social loafing   Working less hard and being less productive when in a group, **451**

Social media
    connecting to customers, 54
    ethical issues, 146
    job candidates, 316
    social capital, 22
    technology followership, 542
    training employees to use it properly, 475–476
    workplace communication, 474
Social needs, 422
Social realities, 87
Social responsibilities, 153. *See also* Corporate social responsibility (CSR)
Social Security, 333
Socialized power, 424

Sociotechnical systems   An approach to job design that attempts to redesign tasks to optimize operation of a new technology while preserving employees' interpersonal relationships and other human aspects of the work, **558**

Sodexo, 357
Soft drink industry, 48
Soft skills, 324
Solidarium, 221
Sony, 178, 185, 191, 216, 299, 574, 575
South Korea, 185
Southwest Airlines, 36, 59, 128, 309
SpaceX, 215, 218
Spam, 142

Span of control   The number of subordinates who report directly to an executive or supervisor, **252**, 253

Spartanburg–Greenville, South Carolina, 576

Specialization   A process in which different individuals and units perform different tasks, **248**

Spectrum Health, 8

Speed   Fast and timely execution, response, and delivery of results, **10,** 297–299

Speed trap, 87
Spirit Airlines, 131
Spokesperson, 19
Spotify, 214
Spreadshirt, 219

Sprint, 475
Sproxil, 219
St. David's Healthcare, 292
Stabilization relationships, 458

Staff departments   Units that support line departments, **257**

Stakeholders   Groups and individuals who affect and are affected by the achievement of the organization's mission, goals, and strategies, **119**

Standard   Expected performance for a given goal: a target that establishes a desired performance level, motivates performance, and serves as a benchmark against which actual performance is assessed, **502**

Standard and Poor's 500, 44

Standardization   Establishing common routines and procedures that apply uniformly to everyone, **267**

Stanley Lynch Investment Group, 274
Starbucks, 59, 109, 169, 282, 285, 359, 426
Starbucks Cards, 538
Stars, 127
Start-Up Chile, 186
Start-ups, 223. *See also* Entrepreneurship
Startup Health, 218
State Farm Insurance, 354, 428
Statement of profit and loss, 513, 515
Staying ahead of the competition, 13
Steinway, 129
Stereotyping, 362–363

Stewardship   Contributing to the long-term welfare of others, **152**

Stock indexes, 44
Stock market, 44
Stock options, 332–333, 417, 525

Stockholders' equity   The amount accruing to the corporation's owners, **513**

Stoneyfield's, 158
"Store within a store" business model, 516
Stories, 65
Storming stage, 449

Strategic alliance   A formal relationship created among independent organizations with the purpose of joint pursuit of mutual goals, **281**–282

Strategic budget, 132
Strategic control, 131–132

Strategic control system   A system designed to support managers in evaluating the organization's progress regarding its strategy and, when discrepancies exist, taking corrective action, **131**

Strategic decision making, 50

Strategic goals   Major targets or end results relating to the organization's

long-term survival, value, and growth, **113,** 119

Strategic leadership   Behavior that gives purpose and meaning to organizations, envisioning and creating a positive future, **386**

Strategic management   A process that involves managers from all parts of the organization in the formulation and implementation of strategic goals and strategies, **117**. *See also* Planning and strategic management

Strategic management process, 118
Strategic manager, 16

Strategic maneuvering   An organization's conscious efforts to change the boundaries of its task environment, **58**

Strategic planning   A set of procedures for making decisions about the organization's long-term goals and strategies, **113**

Strategic triangle, 299

Strategic vision   The long-term direction and strategic intent of a company, **118**

Strategy   A pattern of actions and resource allocations designed to achieve the organization's goals, **113**

Strategy and the environment, 169–170
Strategy implementation, 1, 129–131

Strategy map   A visual depiction that shows how an organization plans to convert its various assets into desired outcomes, 115, 116, **521,** 522

Stretch goals   Targets that are particularly demanding, sometimes even thought to be impossible, **414**

Strike, 337
Strong culture, 63, 65
Structured debates, 91

Structured interview   Selection technique that involves asking all applicants the same questions and comparing their responses to a standardized set of answers, **314**–315

Student Movement for Real Change (SMRC), 83
Student project group processes worksheet, 465
Student social entrepreneurs, 187

Subscription model   Charging fees for site visits, **219**

Substitute, 52

Substitutes for leadership Factors in the workplace that can exert the same influence on employees as leaders would provide, **397–398**

Subsystem, 36

Subunits Subdivisions of an organization, **252**

Subway, 217
Succession planning, 226
Sun Media, 214
Sun Microsystems, 356
Supercuts, 217

Superordinate goals Higher-level goals taking priority over specific individual or group goals, **460**

Superstorm Sandy, 95
Supervisor, 17

Supervisory leadership Behavior that provides guidance, support, and corrective feedback for day-to-day activities, **386**

Supplier, 53–54

Supply chain management The managing of the network of facilities and people that obtain materials from outside the organization, transform them into products, and distribute them to customers, **53**

Supporting case. *See* Cases
Supportive leadership, 390, 396
Surprise, 579

Survivor's syndrome Loss of productivity and morale in employees who remain after a downsizing, **287**

Sustainability The effort to minimize the use of resources, especially those that are polluting and nonrenewable, **11, 48, 153, 157.** *See also* Natural environment and sustainability

Sustainability 360 (Walmart), 171
Sustainability audit, 510
Sustainability performance indicators, 158

Sustainable growth Economic growth and development that meets present needs without harming the needs of future generations, **157**

Sustainable investing, 172
Sustained greatness, 576
Sweet Bites (University of Pennsylvania), 187

Switching costs Fixed costs buyers face when they change suppliers, **53**

SWOT analysis A comparison of strengths, weaknesses, opportunities, and threats that helps executives formulate strategy, **124–125**

Symbols, rites, and ceremonies, 65
Sysco–U.S. Foods proposed merger, 59

Systematic management A classical management approach that attempted to build into operations the specific procedures and processes that would ensure coordination of effort to achieve established goals and plans, **31**

Systems theory A theory stating that an organization is a managed system that changes inputs into outputs, **35–36**

T

"T-shaped" manager, 6
Tablet computers, 539, 542
Tactical behavior, 517–518
Tactical goals, 115
Tactical manager, 17

Tactical planning A set of procedures for translating broad strategic goals and plans into specific goals and plans that are relevant to a distinct portion of the organization, such as a functional area like marketing, **114**

Taft-Hartley Act, 336
TAG Heuer, 281
Taiwan, 185
Take-make-waste production model, 155
Talent Is Ageless (CVS Caremark), 47
Tall organization, 252
Target, 115, 312, 333, 360
Tariffs, 189
Task force, 269
Task identity, 428

Task-motivated leadership Leadership that places primary emphasis on completing a task, **395**

Task-oriented behavior, 392

Task performance behaviors Actions taken to ensure that the work group or organization reaches its goals, 390, 391, **397**

Task significance, 428

Task specialist role An individual who has more advanced job-related skills and abilities than other group members possess, **454**

Tata Consulting Services (TCS), 507
Tata Group, 180, 185
Tata Motors, 73
TBC. *See* Time-based competition (TBC)
TD Bank, 519

Team A small number of people with complementary skills who are committed to a common purpose, set of performance goals, and approach for which they hold themselves mutually accountable, 269, **448.** *See also* Teamwork

Team-based measurement systems, 451

Team-based performance goals, 451
Team-based rewards, 452
Team effectiveness, 450–451
Team leader, 17

Team maintenance role Individual who develops and maintains team harmony, **454**

Team management, 392
Team Rubicon, 426

Team training Training that provides employees with the skills and perspectives they need to collaborate with others, **323**

Teaming A strategy of teamwork on the fly, creating many temporary, changing teams, **445**

Teamwork, 442–466
cohesiveness, 454–455, 456
conflict, 458–462
contributions of teams, 444
lateral role relationships, 458
managing outward, 457
member contributions, 452
motivating teamwork, 451–452
norms, 453–454
operations management, 565
performance focus, 451
performance norms, 455, 456
phases of team development, 448–449
roles, 454
self-managed teams, 446–447
size of team, 456
social loafing, 451
team effectiveness, 450–451
teaming, 445
types of teams, 444–447
why groups fail, 450
Teamwork Leadership Institute (TLI), 373
Technical auditors, 458

Technical innovator A person who develops a new technology or has the key skills to install and operate the technology, **553**

Technical skill The ability to perform a specialized task involving a particular method or process, **18**

Technological advances, 44–45, 52
Technological analysis, 120
Technological barriers, 546
Technological change, 5–6
Technological discoveries, 217

Technology The systematic application of scientific knowledge to a new product, process, or service, **294, 534.** *See also* Managing technology and innovation

Technology acquisition options, 550–552

Technology audit Process of clarifying the key technologies on which an organization depends, **543**

Technology configurations, 294
Technology followership, 542–543

Technology leadership, 540–542

Technology life cycle   A predictable pattern followed by a technological innovation, from its inception and development to market saturation and replacement, **536–537**

Technology trading, 551
Teenaged workers, 354
Telecommunications, 45
Telecommunications industry, 59
Teleconferencing, 474
Telework, 146
Temporary workers, 61
Termination-at-will, 318

Termination interview   A discussion between a manager and an employee about the employee's dismissal, **319**

Terracycle, 49
Tesla Motors, 215, 533, 549, 559
Texas Instruments, 132
Texting, 474
TGIF (Google), 429
The Body Shop, 158
The Event Studio, 224
The Guardian, 595
Theory of Moral Sentiments, A (Smith), 154
Theory of Social and Economic Organizations, The (Weber), 34
Theory X, 35
Theory Y, 35
ThinkImpact, 83

Third-country nationals   Natives of a country other than the home country or the host country of an overseas subsidiary, **196**

37signals, 225
Threadless, 78
Three-dimensional (3D) printers, 546
3M, 157, 170, 171, 384, 403, 444, 509, 516–517, 541, 548, 554, 555, 574, 575

360-degree appraisal   Process of using multiple sources of appraisal to gain a comprehensive perspective on one's performance, **328**

360-degree view   Refers to a 3D image of a product that a customer can view on a computer, tablet, phone, or other electronic device, **568**

TIAA-CREF, 357
Timberland, 158

Time-based competition (TBC)   Strategies aimed at reducing the total time needed to deliver a good or service, **297**

Time Inc., 262
Time pressures, 87
Time Warner Cable (TWC), 256
Timepieces, 567
Title VII of Civil Rights Act, 319, 321, 353
TLI. *See* Teamwork Leadership Institute (TLI)
TOMS, 503
Tom's of Maine, 158
Tone of voice, 482

Top 10 global firms, 179

Top-level managers   Senior executives responsible for the overall management and effectiveness of the organization, **16,** 18

Top management, 252
Top management team, 16, 251

Total organization change   Introducing and sustaining multiple policies, practices, and procedures across multiple units and levels, **586**

Total quality, 9

Total quality management (TQM)   An integrative approach to management that supports the attainment of customer satisfaction through a wide variety of tools and techniques that result in high-quality goods and services, **291**

Toxic release inventory (TRI), 167
Toxic waste, 157
Toyota, 6, 8, 10, 158, 180, 183, 190, 196, 283, 296, 299
Toys "R" us, 76, 568, 570
TQM. *See* Total quality management (TQM)
Trader Joe's, 333

Traditional work groups   Groups that have no managerial responsibilities, **446**

Tragedy of the commons   An environmental philosophy postulating that the unintended negative effects of human economic activities on the environment are often greater than the benefits, and that nature should be preserved, **167**

Training   Teaching lower-level employees how to perform their present jobs, **322**

Training ABC, 370
Training and development, 322–324
Trait appraisal, 326

Trait approach   A leadership perspective that attempts to determine the personal characteristics that great leaders share, **388**

Trait scales, 326

Transaction fee model   Charging fees for goods and services, **219**

Transactional leaders   Leaders who manage through transactions, using their legitimate, reward, and coercive powers to give commands and exchange rewards for services rendered, **399**

Transactional leadership, 399

Transcendent education   An education with five higher goals that balance self-interest with responsibility to others, **154**

Transfer price   Price charged by one unit for a good or service provided to another unit within the organization, **523**

Transformational leader   A leader who motivates people to transcend their personal interests for the good of the group, **399**

Transformational leadership, 399–400

Transnational model   An organizational model characterized by centralizing certain functions in locations that best achieve cost economies; basing other functions in the company's national subsidiaries to facilitate greater local responsiveness; and fostering communication among subsidiaries to permit transfer of technological expertise and skills, **191–193, 445**

Trendsetter Barometer Business Outlook, 57

Triple bottom line   Economic, social, and environmental performance, 112, **153,** 510

TrueNorth chip, 544
Trust, 140, 141
Truth-telling, 141, 142
TRW, 262
TSG Consumer Partners, 235
Tsumu Tsumu, 117
Twitter, 474, 551

Two-factory theory   Herzberg's theory describing two factors affecting people's work motivation and satisfaction, **427**

Two-way communication   A process in which information flows in two directions—the receiver provides feedback, and the sender is receptive to the feedback, **470–471**

Tylenol poisonings, 95, 96
Typing test, 317

Tyranny of the *or*   The belief that things must be either A or B and cannot be both; that only one goal and not another can be attained, **575**

U

Uber, 118, 359, 589
Unattractive environment, 57

Uncertainty   The state that exists when decision makers have insufficient information, **77,** 399

Uncertainty avoidance, 200

Underperforming employee, 329
Unemployment insurance, 333
Unemployment rates, 43, 44

Unfreezing Realizing that current practices are inappropriate and that new behavior is necessary, **581**–582

Unfreezing/moving/refreezing model, 581–583
Unilever, 158, 171, 284, 285, 403
Union Carbide, 56
Union Carbide gas leak, 95, 96
Union Pacific Corporation, 170, 382

Union shop An organization with a union and a union security clause specifying that workers must join the union after a set period of time, **337**

Unionization, 336, 338
Unisys, 475
United Parcel Service (UPS), 53, 156, 204
United States
   achievement, esteem, self-actualization, 425
   bribery, 45
   business start-ups, 45
   contingent workers, 61
   diverse workforce, 349
   employee engagement, 538
   environmentalism, 166
   exports, 177
   federal government, 43
   generational tipping point, 265
   H-1B visas, 312
   health care costs, 543
   hierarchical layers, 252
   illiteracy, 484
   immigration, 47
   individualism, 200
   labor force growth, 46
   maintenance behaviors, 391
   mandated emissions standards, 168
   peer norms, 526
   racial and ethnic minorities, 348
   racial segregation, 349
   shortage of highly qualified workers, 311
   silence vs. conversation, 482
   supermarkets, 548
   tariffs, 189
   toxic waste sites, 157
   trading partners, 184
   wealth creation, 212
   women workers, 47
United Way, 118

Unity-of-command principle A structure in which each worker reports to one boss, who in turn reports to one boss, **263**

Universal values, 143

Universalism The ethical system stating that all people should uphold certain values that society needs to function, **143**–144

University system analysis worksheet, 36
Unstructured interview, 315
Upper Big Branch Mine explosion, 335
UPS. *See* United Parcel Service (UPS)

Upward communication Information that flows from lower to higher levels in the organization's hierarchy, **487**

U.S. Department of Veterans Affairs, 517–518
U.S. Postal Service, 569
US Coachways, 142
USA Hospital Supply, 28–29
USAA, 382
"Used-to-be," 434

Utilitarianism An ethical system stating that the greatest good for the greatest number should be the overriding concern of decision makers, 143, **144**

V

VA (Department of Veterans Affairs), 517–518

Valence The value an outcome holds for the person contemplating it, **420**

Valero Energy, 312

Validity The degree to which a selection test predicts or correlates with job performance, **317**–318

Value The monetary amount associated with how well a job, task, good, or service meets users' needs, **14**

Value-added manufacturing, 298

Value chain The sequence of activities that flow from raw materials to the delivery of a good or service, with additional value created at each step, **290**

Values, 142–143
Vanity, 519
Veil of ignorance, 150
Verizon, 312, 322–323

Vertical integration The acquisition or development of new businesses that produce parts or components of the organization's product, **126**

Vertical structure, 250–256
Viacom, 60
Viagra, 51
Video-sharing sites, 474
Videoconferencing, 474

Vigilance A process in which a decision maker carefully executes all stages of decision making, **84**

Vine, 551
Virginia Commonwealth University (VCU), 6
Virginia Mason Medical Center, 12, 506
Virtual corporation, 265

Virtual office A mobile office in which people can work anywhere, as long as they have the tools to communicate with customers and colleagues, **477**

Virtual teams Teams that are physically dispersed and communicate electronically more than face-to-face, **445**, 446, 450, 461

Virtue ethics Perspective that what is moral comes from what a mature person with "good" moral character would deem right, 143, **145**

Vision A mental image of a possible and desirable future state of the organization, **383**–384, 385

Vision failure, 385
Vision statement, 118
VMware, 475
Vocational Rehabilitation Act, 321
Voluntary action, 59

Vroom model A situational model that focuses on the participative dimension of leadership, **394**

W

Wage mix, 330
Wages, 330–333
Wagner Act, 335
Walgreen's, 361
Walmart, 5, 10, 59, 110, 115, 128, 153, 171, 214, 284, 298, 331, 333, 357, 545, 570, 574, 575
Walt Disney Company, 63, 107, 117, 132, 176, 216, 574, 575
WARN Act. *See* Worker Adjustment and Retraining Notification Act (WARN Act)
Warner Music, 59
Washington State Employees Credit Union, 581
Waste accounting, 171
Waste Management Inc., 170, 171
Water, 159, 172
Weak culture, 64
Wealth of Nations (Smith), 154
Web 2.0, 5
Web 3.0, 6, 7
Web job boards, 312
Wegmans Food Markets, 423
Welcyon, 217
Western Electric Company, 33
Western myopia, 86
Westpac Banking, 11
WeWork, 452
Weyerhaeuser, 56, 59, 86, 171
Wharton School, 30
What I Want from My Job worksheet, 439
"What if" plans, 110
WhatsApp, 542
Whirlpool, 198
Whistleblowing, 152
Whole Foods Market, 115, 152, 308, 413, 443, 447, 462
Whole Planet Foundation, 152
Wholly owned subsidiary, 193, 195–196
WHYCO Chromium Company, 169
Wiki, 474
Wild Flavors, 53
Wildcat strike, 337
Wipro, 185, 296
Wish You Wood Toy Store, 136–137
W.L. Gore, 122, 234, 312, 423, 444
Women
   educational attainment, 48
   excellent companies to work for, 354
   glass ceiling, 353
   labor force participation, 47
   sexual harassment, 353–354, 355
   struggle for acceptance in workforce, 348–349
   ten most powerful female executives, 353
Word choice, 481

Cheung, H., N-27
Cheung, M., N-46
Cheung, S., N-6
Chhabra, E., N-5
Chilakapati, Rakesh, 79, 80, 82, 84
Chitre, S., N-12
Cho, J. H., N-31
Cho, Y., N-41
Choi, H., N-35
Chouinard, Y., N-10, N-12
Chow, C. W., N-41
Christensen, Clayton, 539, N-42
Christian, M. S., N-35
Chrysostome, Elie, N-14
Chu, C., N-39
Chua, C. H., N-37
Chuanzhi, Liu, 175
Chugh, D., N-8, N-9
Chui, Michael, N-37, N-38
Chul, M., N-43
Chung, C. H., N-21
Chung, Q. B., N-18
Cianci, A., N-31
Cianni, M., N-34, N-36
Clark, Catherine, 503
Clark, J., N-30, N-46
Clark, K. B., N-42, N-44
Clayton, N., N-43
Clements, Jeremy, 373
Clifford, C., N-16
Clifton, J., N-14
Cline, B. N., N-25
Clinton, Bill, 187, 285
Clough, M. William, N-29
Cobb, A., N-36
Cober, A. B., N-31
Cochran, P., N-9
Cocuzza, Frank, 524
Cohen, D., N-4
Cohen, S., N-33, N-34
Cokely, E., N-2
Colao, J. J., N-15
Colbert, A., N-29
Colbert, J. L., N-41
Cole, M., N-2
Cole, S., N-15
Colella, A., N-23
Collins, D., N-23
Collins, J., 498, 574–576, 594, N-15, N-29, N-40, N-45, N-47
Collis, D. J., N-3, N-7
Colony, G., N-28
Colquitt, J., N-29
Coltrin, Sally A., 27, 28
Colvin, Geoff, N-2, N-10, N-19, N-34
Commoner, Barry, 168, N-11
Comstock, T. W., N-37, N-39
Conerly, K., N-36
Conger, J., 385, N-23, N-27, N-38, N-47
Conner, C., N-2, N-15, N-38
Conner, D. R., N-45, N-47
Connolly, T., N-31
Conti, R., N-32
Conway, Mckinley, N-46
Conway, R., N-16
Conyon, M. J., N-24
Cook, Jessica, N-21
Cook, Tim, 400
Cooke, B., N-45
Cooke, R. A., N-8
Coon, H., N-32
Coons, Rebecca, N-41
Cooper, C., 197, N-30, N-35
Cooper, D., N-19
Cooper Procter, William, 34
Coors, C., 263

Copeland, M., N-16
Corbett, A., N-21
Corbett, Charles J., N-11
Cordeiro, A., N-16
Cording, M., N-9
Cortada, J. W., N-1
Cortina, J., N-22, N-35
Cory, K. D., N-4
Cosier, Richard A., N-6
Cotton, R., N-2
Courtney, H., N-46
Courtney, M., N-46
Courtright, S., N-34
Covin, T., N-45
Cowell, J., N-39
Cox, T., N-26
Coy, Peter, N-20
Coyne, K., N-6
Coyne, S., N-6
Crabtree, S., N-23
Crall, Sharon, 369
Cramton, C., N-37
Crane, A., N-8
Crant, J. M., N-17
Creech, B., N-20
Crisp, C. B., N-36
Crispin, G., N-22
Cronin, B., N-25
Crooks, Ed, N-21
Cropanzano, R., N-33
Crosby, F. J., N-26
Cross, F. B., N-10
Cross, R., 258, N-34, N-37, N-39
Crossan, M., N-29
Crossley, C., N-30
Crowley, M., N-26, N-30, N-31, N-33
Crozier, Jen, N-10
Culbertson, S., N-28
Cullen, D., N-8, N-19
Culpan, T., 242
Cummings, A., N-32
Cummings, L., N-6, N-32
Cummings, S., N-3
Cummings, T., 577, N-36, N-45
Curiel, K., 357
Cusumano, M. A., N-4

D

Dacin, M. T., N-15
Dacin, P., N-15
Daft, R., N-4, N-38
Dahl, D., N-18
Dahlin, K., N-36
Dahling, J., N-41
Daily, C. M., N-17
Dalrymple, J., 242
Dalton, D. R., N-17
D'Amelio, A., N-45
Dantas, I., N-13
Dasborough, M., N-2
D'Aveni, R. A., N-4
Davenport, C., N-47
Davidson, M., 363, 364, N-25, N-26
Davila, A., N-40
Davis, A., N-4, N-7
Davis, Andrea, N-33, N-34
Davis, B., N-12
Davis, Edward W., N-3
Davis, Grant, N-41
Davis, I., N-46
Davis, Keith, 302, N-39
Davis, Paul, 227
Davis, S., N-5, N-15, N-18
Davison, H. K., N-22

Davison, S., N-34
Day, D. L., N-44
Day, D. V., N-28
Day, G. S., N-18
de al Merced, M., N-19
de Castro, A., N-32
De Cremer, D., N-32
De Dreu, C., N-6
de Freytas-Tamura, K., N-13
De George, R. T., N-8
de Janasz, Suzanne C., 26, 164, 437, 438, 598
de Vise, Daniel, N-25
De Vries, W., N-36
de WeerdNederhof, P. C., N-18
de Wit, F. R. C., N-36
Dean, J., 558, N-4, N-5, N-6, N-20
Deardorff, Julie, N-46, N-47
Dechant, Kathleen, N-11
DeChurch, L. A., N-35, N-37
Decker, C. D., N-38
Degnan, Julie, 179
DeGraff, Jeff, N-44
DeGroot, Christine, 351
Deimler, M., N-45
DeJoy, D. M., N-32
Del Rey, J., N-4
Delaney, Hollie, 378, 379
Deleeuw, K., N-22
Dellana, S. A., N-4
Delmas, M., N-9
Demetrakakes, P., N-33
Deming, W. Edwards, 9, 291, 564
DeNisi, A., N-39
Denning, S., 103
Dent, E. B., N-45
DeRue, D. S., N-20, N-30, N-34, N-35
Desai, A. B., N-14
Dess, G. G., N-17
DeStobbeleir, K., N-6
Deutsch, C., N-37
Devine, C., N-41
Devlin, D., N-12
Dewan, R., N-43
DeWitt, R.-L., N-22
Dhillon, K., N-13
Dhiri, S., N-19
Diaz, George, N-27
Diaz-Uda, A., N-25
Dickson, M., N-37
Dickter, D. N., N-22
Diener, E., N-33
Dienhart, J., N-9
Dieterich, Chris, N-44
Difonzo, N., N-39
Dinkins, David, 402
Dionne, S., N-28
Dobbin, F., N-26
Dobbs, R., N-43
Docksai, R., N-46
Doerr, E., N-20
Donahue, L., N-33
D'Onfro, J., N-21
Donnelly, J., Jr., 77
Donnelly, T., N-37
Donovan, A., N-25
Donovan, M. A., N-40
Dooley, R., N-6
Doppelt, B., N-1, N-10
Dorfman, J., N-23
Dorfman, P., N-28
Dorns, Mark, N-12
Dou, E., 242, N-14
Douma, B., N-30
Doz, Y, N-13
Doz, Y., N-45

Fugate, M., N-45
Fuhrmans, Vanessa, N-1
Fuld, Richard, 85
Fulk, J., N-38
Fuller, T., N-27, N-39
Fulmer, R. M., N-39
Furman, Matt, 527
Furst, S., N-34
Fyxell, G., N-6

G

Gabarro, J., N-39
Gadiesh, O., N-46
Gagnon, R., N-40
Gaines, A., N-30
Galan, Nely, 220
Galbraith, Jay R., N-3, N-18, N-19, N-34
Galbraith, John Kenneth, 532
Gallagher, M., N-24
Gallo, C., N-4
Gallo, J., N-17
Galunic, C., N-2
Galvin, B., N-28
Gambhir, Ashish, N-32
Gamble, James, 34
Gamer, D., N-16
Gamm, L., N-46
Gangemi, J., N-17
Ganotakis, Panagiotis, N-42
Gantt, Henry, 32
Garbers, Y., N-35
Gardella, A., N-15
Gardner, E., N-40
Gardner, H. K., N-19
Gardner, J., N-27, N-39
Gardner, M., N-38
Gardner, N., N-21
Gargiulo, M., N-2
Garlick, Saul, 83
Garman, A. N., N-45
Garr, S., N-40
Garvin, D. A., N-1, N-6, N-19
Garza, A. S., N-18
Gates, Bill, 214
Gatewood, R., N-23
Gebert, Diether, N-25
Gee, G., N-32
Gehlen, F. L., N-5
Gelbart, M., N-41
Gelles, D., 103
Gellman, L., N-21
George, Bill, N-8, N-9
George, C., N-2
George, G., N-17
George, J., N-6
George, William, 20, N-2
Gerhardt, M., N-28
Gerhart, B., N-23
Germain, R., N-17
Geroski, P. A., N-43
Gersick, C. J. G., N-34
Gerstner, C. R., N-28
Gerstner, Louis, 400
Gerwitz, J. L., N-8
Gettys, C., N-5
Ghoshal, S., 188, N-4, N-18, N-30, N-33
Ghosn, Carlos, 366
Giacalone, Robert, 154, N-9
Giang, V., N-7
Giard, Y., N-41
Gibbs, L., N-46
Gibbs, M., N-17
Gibbs, S., N-5
Gibson, C., N-34, N-35, N-45

Gibson, D., N-31
Gibson, J., 77
Gibson, L., N-35
Giffi, C., N-45
Gifford, Ryan, 364
Gilbert, C., 32, N-7
Gilbert, J., N-26, N-46
Gilbreth, Frank, 32
Gilbreth, Lillian, 32
Gillett, R., N-36, N-38
Gillette, F., N-1
Gilliland, S., N-22, N-33
Gilmont, E. R., N-19
Gilmore, J. H., N-20
Gilson, L., N-32, N-34
Gino, F., N-28, N-39
Gioia, D., N-8
Gjemre, Ken, 226
Glader, P., N-8, N-14
Gladstone, R., N-24
Gladwell, Malcolm, 265
Glass, Jennifer L., N-38
Glassberg, B., N-38
Glater, J. D., N-24, N-41
Glavas, A., N-9
Glickman, David, 423
Globe, D., N-27
Glover, S., N-8
Glueck, William F., 27, 28
Glunk, U., N-2
Glynn, G., N-24
Godfrey, P. C., N-9
Gold, M., 242
Goldberg, S. Galloway, N-45
Goldenberg, Suzanne, N-3
Goldman, D., N-27
Goldschmidt, Bridget, N-16
Goldstein, N. B., N-22
Goleman, D., N-2, N-28
Gomez-Mejia, L., N-23
Gong, Y., N-6
Gonzalez-Navarro, P., N-38
Goodheim, L., N-29
Goodnight, James, 5, 411, 421, 435
Goodson, E., N-39
Goodstein, L., N-47
Goomas, David T., N-40
Goos, Garson, 223
Gopalakrishnan, S., N-42
Gordon, J., N-23
Gorman, S., N-25
Goshal, S., N-2
Gottenbusch, Gary, 226
Gottlieb, R., N-11
Goudreau, J., N-37
Gouillart, F., N-46
Govindarajan, V., N-32, N-44
Gowan, J. A., Jr., N-41
Gowdridge, A., N-18
Gradwohl Smith, W., N-28
Graebner, Melissa E., N-43
Graen, G., N-28
Grafton, L., N-34
Graham, G., N-39
Grant, A., N-28, N-29, N-35
Graser, M., N-20
Gratton, L., N-34
Gray, P. B., N-12
Green, J., N-17, N-18
Green, Maria, 382
Green, Stephen G., N-43, N-44
Greenbaum, R., N-29
Greenberg, E., N-32, N-33
Greene, Jay, N-1
Greenfield, R., 379, N-37
Greening, D., N-10

Greenleaf, Robert, 401
Greer, L., N-36
Gregg, B., N-25
Griffith, Terri L., N-44
Grimes, M., N-15
Groening, Christopher, N-33
Groscurth, C., N-4
Gross, S., N-23
Grosser, T., N-39
Grote, D., N-23
Grove, Andy, 114
Grover, S. L., N-8
Groysberg, Boris, N-37, N-38
Grunberg, L., N-33
Grynbaum, Michael M., N-3
Guarraia, P., N-21
Guerci, M., N-25
Guilhon, B., N-42
Guion, Kathleen, 599
Gulate, R., N-45
Gundry, L. K., N-44
Gunia, B., N-9
Gunther, M., N-10
Guo, C., N-2
Gupta, A. K., N-19, N-44
Gurchiek, K., 379
Gurtner, S., N-43
Guthrie, J. P., N-23
Gutknecht, J., N-39
Gutman, M., N-39
Guy, M. E., N-8
Guzzo, R., N-46

H

Haanaes, K., N-10, N-44
Hackman, J. Richard, 428, N-32, N-33, N-34, N-36
Haden, Jeff, 320
Hadley, C., N-6
Hagan, C., N-23
Hagedoorn, J., N-43
Hagen, A. F., N-4
Hagerty, J. R., N-21
Hagey, Keach, N-44
Hagiwara, Y., N-42
Haidt, J., N-33
Hale, J., N-8
Hall, D. T., N-39
Hall, E., N-9
Hall, F., N-9
Hall-Merenda, K. E., N-29
Hallett, T., N-46
Hallowel, E., N-38
Hals, T., N-40
Halter, N., N-41, N-42
Halverson, K. C., N-28
Halvorson, B., N-12
Hambrick, D., N-7, N-34
Hamel, Gary, 280, 591, N-19, N-42, N-46, N-47
Hamermesh, R., N-7
Hamilton, Lynn, 480
Hamilton, M., N-3
Hammer, Michael, 519, N-41
Hananel, S., N-22
Hancock, J., N-24
Handmaker, David, 124
Handy, C., N-9
Haney, W. V., N-37
Hanna, J., N-21
Hannah, S., N-8
Hansen, F., N-22
Hansen, M., N-1